HISTORICAL

Dictionary

of the

GILDED AGE

HISTORICAL

Dictionary

of the

GILDED AGE

FOREWORD BY VINCENT P. DE SANTIS

EDITED BY

LEONARD SCHLUP   JAMES G. RYAN

M.E. Sharpe
Armonk, New York
London, England

Library of Congress Cataloging-in-Publication Data

Historical dictionary of the Gilded Age / edited by Leonard Schlup and
James G. Ryan.
    p. cm.
Includes bibliographical references and index.
ISBN 0-7656-0331-4 (cloth: alk. paper)
  1. United States—History—1865–1898–Dictionaries. I. Schlup, Leonard C., 1943–
II. Ryan, James G., 1950–

E661 .H59 2003
973.8′02—dc21

2002030924

Printed in the United States of America

The paper used in this publication meets the minimum requirements of
American National Standard for Information Sciences
Permanence of Paper for Printed Library Materials,
ANSI Z 39.48-1984.

MV (c)   10   9   8   7   6   5   4   3   2   1

Leonard Schlup dedicates this book to the memory of his grandparents:

Dora F. Boice Roberts (1873–1952)
Ada Breitenstine Schlup (1871–1947)
Daniel F. Schlup (1862–1951)
William H. Roberts (1868–1957)

James G. Ryan dedicates this book to his aunt, Anna W. Hughes, and his sister, Valerie Anne West, M.D.

Contents

CONTENTS

Foreword

The Gilded Age in American history originally meant the years of the Grant Presidency. In fact, it received its name from the title of an 1873 novel by Mark Twain and Charles Dudley Warner that satirized the excesses of that maligned era in our history. In time, though, the Gilded Age was expanded to include the period from the end of Reconstruction to the end of the nineteenth-century. Also it went from being a transitional era between Reconstruction and the Progressive Movement to one of the beginnings of modern America.

During the Gilded Age the United States became the leading industrial nation in the world, built a powerful Navy, defeated a reputed world power, Spain, and acquired an overseas empire. It was also transformed by a number of far reaching developments—the rise of industrial capitalism that controlled nationwide industries, the passing of the physical frontier with the settlement of the last American West, the eclipsing of countryside and farm by city and factory, the significant changes in communication and transportation through the telephone and the transcontinental railroads, the important innovations in agriculture, the new blood added to American life by a huge influx of immigrants, the rise of large-scale labor unions, and the emergence of the United States as a world power. Everything in these years seemed to be in motion. It was as Howard Mumford Jones tells us, the Age of Energy.

But to Twain and Warner and to many other contemporaries of the Gilded Age such as E. L. Godkin of the *Nation* and Henry Adams and James Bryce, the Gilded Age was basically acquisitive and corrupt, with little cultural depth. The period politicos to them were mercenary and neglectful of the public welfare. And the business leaders exploited the country's resources and accumulated huge fortunes from government aid and favors.

Seldom has any period in American history been maligned as much as the Gilded Age. Leading contemporaries such as Godkin and Adams severely criticized the public and political life of the Gilded Age and the coarseness and immorality of its new urban and industrial society. Historians and other writers until recently competed with one another to find suitable disparaging phrases to censure the political and economic life of the Gilded Age. They condemned the era's political leaders for evading the "real issues" and for being merely a group of spoilsmen. They labeled most of the businessmen as Robber Barons exploiting the nation's resources and its workers. For many years the Gilded Age was portrayed and reproached for being barren, sterile, corrupt, negative, and monotonous, as writers sought even more ways to defame it. Seldom did anyone mention the creative and solid achievements of the period that has had a lasting effect upon American life. So for a long time the Gilded Age labored under a heavy cross of reproof.

In recent years, however, historians and other writers have taken a closer look at the Gilded Age and have uncovered its cultural, literary, and technological attainments long overshadowed by the attention given to its political and economic life. They discovered it was not as sterile and barren as so many of its critics had said, but that it was on of the most intellectually fertile eras in American history. They also presented a more-balanced picture of Gilded Age businessmen, by stressing the important contributions they made to the economic development of the country, the new technology they introduced in industry, and the social good they sometimes did with their wealth.

Likewise modern historians, in an effort to counterbalance the traditional censure of Gilded Age politics, have tried to show the importance of politics to Americans of that time. They have pointed out that contrary to the conventional view, political questions were significant and that basic issues divided the major parties. They now contend that probably no other generation than the Gilded Age has been so knowledgeable about its political matters, and that voters were more mobilized or more involved in governing the country.

One of the new and widely used college textbooks in American history, where many Americans learn their American history, supports the new view about Gilded Age business and politics. "In the decades after the Civil War, American industry transformed itself into a new wonder of the world," the authors write. As for the basic structure of government, it "changed dramatically in the last quarter of the nineteenth century," and gradually the Republicans and Democrats adapted "to the demands of governmental expansion."[1]

Whatever its flaws and shortcomings, and whatever our views about it may be, the America of the Gilded Age believed in itself and believed it was grappling with "real" issues and "real" problems. And, unlike the America of today, the Gilded Age for nearly all of its years was virtually free of involvement in international affairs and devoted itself to its own self-interest.

The Gilded Age was one of the most remarkable generations in American history. It was a time of exciting and important scientific technological inventions and improvements such as the electric light, the telephone, and the typewriter. It was also a significant and fertile period in intellectual and cultural matters, with the birth of new social sciences such as anthropology and sociology, the organization of the American Library Association, the establishment of graduate degree programs in leading American universities, and the formation of professional organizations such as the American Historical Association. These were singular and stimulating years in many ways, and they belie the impression that the Gilded Age was largely a era of false glitter, jobbery, dullness, self seeking, and so on.

There was such a rapid and vast industrial growth during the Gilded Age that the United States became the world's leading industrial power. Since the United States was also the largest producer of food and raw materials, it became potentially the richest and most powerful nation in the world. In addition there was nearly a doubling of the population from 40 million in 1870 to 76 million in 1900.

Accompanying this enormous industrial expansion were major advances in science, especially chemistry and physics that provided the principles for the new technology. Inventions spurring industrial growth were made in transportation, communications, electrical power, the production of steel, and the use of oil. The telegraph was in use before the Civil War, and in the Gilded Age came the submarine cable, the telephone, the stock ticker, the typewriter, and Marconi's wireless telegraphy from which came the radio, radar, and television. Of major importance was the use of electricity and the workable electric railway and a practical dynamo and electric motor.

Equally revolutionary was the development of ways to mass-produce steel through the open-hearth or Bessemer process, an invention of the 1850s. What had previously been a rare metal could now be mass-produced and was one of the key reasons for the America Industrial Revolution of the Gilded Age. At the same time the oil industry went from a few gallons before the Civil War—when oil was used as a medicinal potion for ailments ranging from whooping cough to acne-to about 50 million barrels annually by the 1890s, when it became an illumination oil.

These inventions and developments increased productivity considerably. They also offered opportunities for great wealth to entrepreneurs with drive and initiative to compete in a free-enterprise system that accepted graft, corruption, and the worship of material things. Many took the chance, and a number of them, such as Andrew Carnegie and John D. Rockefeller, acquired huge fortunes. These Captains of Industry, as they called themselves, or Robber Barons, as their critics labeled them, were at the top of the social and economic structure in the Gilded Age. By 1900, it was estimated that one-tenth of the population owned nine-tenths of the wealth of the country.

Though social critics assailed the new rich for their coarse taste and lack of business ethics, ordinary Americans saw the rich as respected members of society, pillars of the churches, and philanthropists who occupied positions of prestige and power both in the country and abroad. Thus, large numbers of Americans admired the successful businessmen and hoped to duplicate their success.

In contrast with the visible wealth and comforts of the new entrepreneurs were the wretched living conditions of the workers brought in large numbers by the lure of jobs. Tenements were built to crowd as many people as possible into the smallest accessible space. Jacob Riis, the reformer, estimated in 1890, that about 330,00 persons were living in one square mile on the Lower East Side of New York City.

Whether the worker received a fair share of the economic growth of the Gilded Age remains a debatable matter. With half of the period in a recession or depression, it is uncertain how many workers shared the benefits. Between 1870 and 1890 both money and real wages increased, the former by more that 10 percent and the latter from 10 to 25 percent.

Skilled and white-collar workers received the highest wages. Adult males received about 75 percent more for similar work than women, and two to three times as much as children.

According to the folklore of the times, opportunity for advancement knew no limit. There is not much evidence, however, to support such optimism. On the contrary, the available evidence indicates that only an immeasurable minority of unskilled workers achieved the rags-to-riches rise that so many Americans in the Gilded Age assumed to be so common.

American not only became industrialized in the Gilded Age but also urbanized. From 1860 to 1900, the percentage of Americans living in cites doubled from 19.8 to 39.7. Even more so was the concentration of Americans in large metropolitan areas such as New York City, Chicago, and Philadelphia, which together then had millions of inhabitants.

Hordes of European immigrants poured into the cities to meet some of the demands in non-agricultural employment that rose 300 percent. By the 1890s for example, New York City had as many Italians as Naples, as many Germans as Hamburg, and twice as many Irish as Dublin. By 1910, it was estimated that one-third of the inhabitants of the nation's largest cities were foreign-born.

In addition to the size of this large movement of people were its origins. Previously, nearly all immigrants had come from northern and western Europe. Now the tide flowed from southern and eastern Europe-Italy, Austria-Hungary, Poland, and Russia. In the 1860s these groups made up only about 1.4 percent of all immigrants. This rose to 7.3 percent in the seventies, to 18.3 percent in the eighties, to 51 percent in the nineties, and 70 percent in the first decade or so in the twentieth century.

Most of the "old" immigrants had been able to read and write, most were Protestants, and most settled on farms. In contrast, most newer immigrants were illiterate, were Roman Catholic, Greek Orthodox, or Jewish, and most of them turned to industry and settled in the cities. Their coming created many problems in the urban areas, where large numbers of people arrived on top of one another. There were too many to be housed, too many for water or sewage or transportation facilities, and too many for the police and fire departments to look after.

A strong influence on Gilded Age Americans was Charles Darwin's theory of evolution and the idea of the "survival of the fittest" as Herbert Spencer applied it to social and economic life. It was invaluable to the new industrial order, as it seemed to justify the acquisition of wealth and power and gave a credible explanation of why some became wealthy while others stayed poor. The new doctrine thus opposed poor relief and public education, and justified poverty and slums. Any governmental attempt to change the situation would be interfering with the natural law and impeding progress.

Much of the reasoning of Social Darwinism was found in the other dominant theory of the time—laissez faire. Beyond what was necessary to maintain law and order and to protect life and property, the government was not to interfere in the conduct of business or in personal matters. During most of the late nineteenth century these views prevailed in America and were upheld by prominent educators, editors, clergymen, and economists.

In the 1880s a number of sociologists and economists revolted against the fatalism and lack of social responsibility of Social Darwinism. These "reform Darwinists," such as Edward A. Ross and Lester Ward, maintained that societies could direct their own destinies and improve their economic system. Some even advocated social planning and state management.

Economists also challenged the laissez-faire doctrine. In 1885, some of them organized the American Economic Association, which boldly declared that the state was "an agency whose positive assistance is one of the indispensable conditions of human progress." A number of leading academic economists such as Richard T. Ely, Simon Nelson Patten, and John R. Commons, began to dissent from the classical belief in absolute economic laws valid for all societies, and to insist that society, constantly changing, had to be examined in terms of process and

growth. They rejected Spenser's fatalism that progress resulted from the struggle for existence and the consequent removal of the unfit.

Contrary to those who have contended that Gilded Age cultural life was sterile, its intellectual and artistic developments were impressive. Two new social sciences appeared, with Lewis Henry Morgan founding anthropology and Lester Ward sociology. The era also witnessed a major change in higher education through the elective system sponsored at Harvard University by President Charles W. Eliot.

Two of the most important poets in American literature lived and wrote during the Gilded Age. One of them was Emily Dickinson who was practically unknown to her contemporaries, because only a few of her poems were published during her lifetime, and also because she was a recluse much of her life in Amherst, Massachusetts. In striking contrast was Walt Whitman, whose revolutionary poetry was widely published and read. Though a number of critics objected to his departures from the conventions of versification and to his frankness about sex, he became for many others the very choice of America—enthusiastic, optimistic, energetic, and free.

Thus the Gilded Age lived in its own right. In its own right it was much more than a transitional period between Reconstruction and Progressivism. It was a most significant age of energy in all kinds of ways. It was also an era that witnessed the emerging and shaping of modern America. Gilded Age Americans took pride in a long list of accomplishments. They very much believed in what they had done and in themselves, something that Americans might no longer do.

Note

1. John Mack Faragher, Mari Jo Buhle, Daniel Czitrom, and Susan H. Armitage, *Out of Many: A History of the American People*, third ed., Prentice Hall, 2001, pp. 550, 581, 583.

—Vincent P. De Santis

Introduction

Certain periods in American history have unique qualities and characteristics. During the Gilded Age, from 1868 through 1901, events and people transformed the United States from an agricultural, rural, and relatively homogeneous society into a republic marked by industrialization, urbanization, and greater diversity. Domestic developments and foreign policy initiatives reshaped the nation's political landscape, turning an epoch of equilibrium and legislative ascendancy into a distinct time of political realignment, presidential prerogative, and international stature.

This complex era of contradictions acquired its name from Mark Twain's novel *The Gilded Age: A Tale of Today*, published in 1873 with New England editor Charles Dudley Warner.[1] Twain and Warner depicted the acquisition of wealth as unbridled American materialism, and satirized a luxuriant and opulent society. They deliberately chose the word "gilded," referring to a bright, sparkling surface glitter that made the commonplace appear valuable and attractive. For too long, historians such as Matthew Josephson echoed Twain and Warner, and dismissed the Gilded Age as a complacent and lackluster period. Such approaches made it seem less impressive than the Civil War's emotional fervor or the Progressive Era's reform impulse.[2]

Fortunately, revisionist historians no longer accept such a simplistic evaluation. In fact, since the 1960s, the Gilded Age's reputation has undergone a dramatic metamorphosis. Hundreds of books, articles, essays, dissertations, and professional convention papers have reinterpreted the post-Civil War period as an important time, one when the conflict between traditions and innovations helped shape modern America.

A historical dictionary of the Gilded Age has long been needed. This single-volume work serves as a convenient ready-reference source for historians, librarians, and others. It fills a gap in the scholarship and completes, in an accessible format, a sequence of timely publications that covers American history from the Civil War through the 1920s. Similar essential contributions were compiled previously by Mark M. Boatner in *The Civil War Dictionary*, by Hans L. Trefousse in the *Historical Dictionary of Reconstruction*, by John D. Buenker and Edward R. Kantowicz in the *Historical Dictionary of the Progressive Era*, and by James S. Olson in the *Historical Dictionary of the 1920s*. Along with these useful books, published in the late 1980s and early 1990s, researchers now have for their benefit an uninterrupted series of historical dictionaries encompassing the years from 1861 through 1929.

The *Historical Dictionary of the Gilded Age* offers selective coverage. It excludes certain common subjects to allow space to incorporate more meaningful topics, including those concerning members of historically neglected minority groups. Compiling the volume has been a formidable task requiring much subjective judgment. We do not pretend to offer an all-inclusive, lengthy encyclopedia. Biographical sketches of many absent individuals appear in *American National Biography*, *Dictionary of American Biography*, *National Cyclopedia of American Biography*, *Biographical Directory of the American Congress*, volumes of *Who Was Who in America*, obituaries in regional newspapers and the *New York Times*, and specialized reference books on prominent personalities in fields such as art, music, religion, education, and literature.

Several features characterize the *Historical Dictionary of the Gilded Age*. First, the alphabetical order of hundreds of entries is in keeping with a dictionary contour and quick-reference style, providing factual information with which to assess the item's historical significance to Gilded Age America. At the end of each entry, in parentheses, some brief bibliographical citations direct readers wishing to pursue additional research on the topic. Second, a section presents concise biographical information on each contributor. Third, the book lists a chronology of selected events for each year from 1868 to 1901. Fourth, there is a short bibliography of general books, rather than specialized studies, pertaining to the Gilded Age to assist people in learning more about the period. Fifth, an index supplies a user-friendly guide for locating and cross-referencing topics and individuals. Finally, Professor Vincent P. De Santis, a renowned scholar of Gilded Age history, has written a foreword.

Many historians who lacked the time to contribute essays nevertheless heartily endorsed this project as a valuable work meriting recognition, and expressed a desire to utilize the book in their future endeavors. Gratitude and appreciation are extended to our many contributors across the country; including Christopher Cumo in Ohio, Harvey G. Hudspeth of Mississippi, Douglas Steeples in Georgia, and Philip H. Young of Indiana, who completed numerous essays. The interest of all participants in this project, and their determination to achieve its successful completion, inspired many.

The editors' intention has been to invite persons both within and outside academe to participate. We are acutely aware that since the 1970s, the historical profession has produced a surplus of advanced degrees in American history, even as the percentage of historians with full-time jobs in the field has contracted dramatically. Graduate education may inculcate a sense of perspective, but unemployment offers little fulfillment. Accordingly, we have sought to provide the many adjuncts, unemployed historians, historians forced by the oversupply to work in other fields, historians who have to depend on their spouses for financial support, students, librarians, journalists, administrators, archivists, musicians, retirees, museum curators, community college instructors, high school teachers, members of minority groups (women, African-Americans, Hispanic Americans, Asian Americans, Native Americans, and gay and lesbian members of our society), ministers, lawyers, physicians, recreational directors, nutrition experts, scientists, morticians, historical society workers, journal editors, and a former presidential candidate, among others, with an opportunity to produce. We have no power to redress the frustration of potential scholars, but we believe our modest, ecumenical approach has turned out to be the *Historical Dictionary of the Gilded Age*'s most salient feature. Seasoned scholars and recognized experts on a subject, newly minted Ph.D.s seeking a first publication, and other enthusiasts who answered our advertised invitations have joined in offering essays.

We believe this volume will become a standard reference book on the Gilded Age, and we urge other scholars to reach out to the academically dispossessed. The editors thank Peter Coveney, a former executive editor at M.E. Sharpe, for his instantaneous endorsement of this project and his steadfast willingness to facilitate in every way this newest addition to the growing M.E. Sharpe collection. Similarly, Peter LaBella and Andrew Gyory enthusiastically and patiently guided the project during its latter stages. Esther L. Clark displayed remarkable forbearance in fielding questions from many sources and directions. Over the years, the project has seen a legion of compensated typists come and go. Beth Cumberlidge, Lupe Aaron, Gail Davis, and Laura Kondratick deserve special mention for the volume and quality of their work. James G. Ryan expresses appreciation to his interim department head at Texas A&M University at Galveston, Dr. William Seitz, and the entire administration, for authorizing a reduced teaching load. It greatly facilitated this project's completion.

Notes

1. Mark Twain and Charles Dudley Warner, *The Gilded Age: A Tale of Today* (Hartford, Conn.: American Publishing Co., 1873).
2. Matthew Josephson, *The Politicos, 1865–1896* (New York: Harcourt Brace, 1938).

HISTORICAL

Dictionary

of the

GILDED AGE

ABBOTT, LYMAN (18 December 1835–22 October 1922), clergyman. Abbott was born in Roxbury, Massachusetts, and graduated from New York University in 1853. He passed the bar examination three years

later, and settled in Brooklyn, New York, where he came under the influence of Henry Ward Beecher, a preeminent preacher. Abbott abandoned his law practice in 1859, to study theology in Farmington, Maine. The next year he accepted the pastorate of the Congregational church in Terre Haute, Indiana, then returned to New York after the Civil War. He became editor of *The Illustrated Christian Weekly* (1870) and of *Christian Union* (1876), in 1893 changing the name of the latter, a widely circulating paper, to *Outlook*. In 1888, he began serving as pastor of the Plymouth Congregational Church in Brooklyn. A national figure in the Gilded Age and the early twentieth century, Abbott advocated Protestant progressivism and social reform. He abhorred isolationism, endorsing America's role in the Spanish-American War. His most significant book, *The Evolution of Christianity*, appeared in 1892. Abbott died in New York City.

Further Reading: Lyman Abbott, *Reminiscences*, 1915; Ira V. Brown, *Lyman Abbott, Christian Evolutionist: A Study in Religious Liberalism*, 1953; *New York Times*, 23 October 1922.

Leonard Schlup

ADAMS, CHARLES FRANCIS (27 May 1835–20 March 1915), historian and railroad official. Adams was born in Boston, Massachusetts, the son of a diplomat, grandson of one president, and great-grandson of another. He graduated from Harvard in 1856, served in the Civil War, and became intrigued with railroads. He chaired the Massachusetts Board of Railroad Commissioners from 1872 to 1879. An advocate of moderate railroad regulation, Adams headed the Union Pacific from 1884 to 1890. In addition, he was an active civic leader, promoting town meetings and encouraging reforms in education that emphasized reading, writing, arithmetic, and individual instruction. School districts throughout the nation copied the "Quincy System," a product of his participation of the government of Quincy, Massachusetts. President of the Massachusetts Historical Society from 1895 until his death, Adams wrote biographies of Richard Henry Dana and of his own father, the elder Charles Francis Adams. Unlike some members of his famous family, Adams projected optimism. A "Mugwump" who endorsed civil service reform and free trade, he opposed the annexation of the Philippine Islands to the United States in 1899. He was an honest person, consumed with conviction, who preached improvement of government and society. Adams died in Washington, D.C.

Further Reading: Charles Francis Adams, *Charles Francis Adams, 1835–1915: An Autobiography*, 1916; Edward Chase Kirkland, *Charles Francis Adams, Jr., 1835–1915: The Patrician at Bay*, 1965.

Leonard Schlup

ADAMS, CHARLES KENDALL (24 January 1835–26 July 1902), historian and educator. Born in Derby, Vermont, Adams spent his boyhood working on his family's Iowa farm. As a student at the University of Michigan, he endured financial difficulties times, but through his diligence and the influence of Professor Andrew D. White, he gained a full professorship at his alma mater, where he introduced the seminar method of instructing advanced students. A popular and successful lecturer, Adams succeeded White as president of Cornell University (1885–1892). There he established a law school, erected a library, and appointed eminent professors. As president of the University of Wisconsin at Madison, Adams obtained needed appropriations from the state legislature for new buildings, including the important library. Among his publications were *Democracy and Monarchy in France* (1874) and *Manual of Historical Literature* (1882). After his health declined in 1900, he recuperated in Germany and Italy before returning to Wisconsin in 1901, only to collapse on campus. He resigned the presidency in October 1901. Adams retired to California, where died at Redlands.

Further Reading: Charles Forster Smith, *Charles Kendall Adams: A Life Sketch*, 1924.

Leonard Schlup

ADAMS, HENRY BROOKS (16 February 1838–27 March 1918), historian and writer. Adams was born to a famous political family in Boston, Massachusetts. He graduated from Harvard College in 1858, toured Europe, then served as private secretary to his father, President Abraham Lincoln's minister to Great Britain. In London, Adams became acquainted with prominent political, economic, and literary figures. His personal pessimism prohibited Adams from believing in the uplifting progression of human society. Indeed, he asserted that presidential history from George Washington to Ulysses S. Grant refuted Charles Darwin's theory of evolution. Upon Adams's return to the United States in 1868, he resided in Washington, D.C., where he contributed articles to *The North American Review* and *The Nation*, directing his most vitriolic criticism at the corruption in the Grant administration. From 1870 to 1877 Adams taught history at Harvard. Thereafter he returned to the capital, but took numerous trips to Europe, including annual stays in Paris. From 1889 to 1891 he published his monumental nine-volume *History of the United States During the Administrations of Thomas Jefferson and James Madison*. Adams also contributed other scholarly books, including biographies of Albert Gallatin and John Randolph. Adams's home on Lafayette Square, across from the White House afforded him the opportunity to entertain people of intelligence and leadership, including the diplomat John Hay and the naturalist Clarence King. Adams gained further recognition with the private issuance in 1904–1906, and the publication in 1918, of *The Education of Henry Adams*. Opposed to American annexation of the Philippine Islands in 1899 and fearful of revolution in Russia in the early twentieth century, Adams continued to convey his thoughts. The outbreak

of World War I in 1914 confirmed his apprehensions. Adams died in Washington.

Further Reading: Ernest Samuels, *Henry Adams*, 1989; Edward Chalfant, *Better in Darkness, 1862–1891*, 1994; Brooks D. Simpson, *The Political Education of Henry Adams*, 1996.

Leonard Schlup

ADAMS, HERBERT BAXTER (16 April 1850–30 July 1901), historian. Born in Shutesbury, Massachusetts, Adams was graduated from Amherst College and then studied in Heidelberg, Germany. A key figure in Gilded Age intellectual life, Adams became prominent in 1876 as professor of history at Johns Hopkins University, the first U.S. university to offer a graduate program in history. Germanic thought and institutions influenced Adams profoundly. He believed a scientific approach could reveal undisputable truth, and that history was past politics. Director of the one of the first historical seminars, he taught such later scholars as Woodrow Wilson, John S. Bassett, and Frederick Jackson Turner. Adams also helped to found the American Historical Association in 1884, and directed it away from amateurs toward a firm grounding in the Germanic scientific method.

His publications include *The Study of History in American Colleges and Universities* (1887), *Thomas Jefferson and the University of Virginia* (1888), and *Public Libraries and Popular Education* (1900). Unfortunately, Adams accepted, and filled his writings with, the now discredited "germ" theory of democracy. This notion held that Teutonic tribes initiated representative government and passed it on to Anglo-Saxons; they in turn brought the concept to the New World, where it later bloomed into a democratic United States. Such nativism complemented varied forms of Darwinian naturalism that existed across the Gilded Age's ideological landscape. Ironically, fate saved Adams from being remembered merely for his teaching and organizational skills. Frederick Jackson Turner's famous essay, "The Significance of the Frontier in American History," was a brilliant refutation of the germ theory, and so the professor is forever linked to his student's monumental statement of American exceptionalism.

Further Reading: John Higham, "Herbert Baxter Adams and the Study of Local History," *American Historical Review* 89 [1984]: 1225–1239; W. Stull Holt, *Historical Scholarship in the United States, 1876–1901 as Revealed in the Correspondence of Herbert B. Adams*, 1938; Johns Hopkins University, *Herbert B. Adams: Tributes of Friends, with a Bibliography of the Department of History, Politics and Economics of the Johns Hopkins University, 1876–1901*, 1902.

Donald K. Pickens

ADDAMS, JANE (6 September 1860–21 May 1935), social worker, peace activist, and humanitarian. Addams devoted her life to alleviating the social ills produced by industrialization and international conflict. Born in Cedarville, Illinois, she was graduated from Rockford (Illinois) Female Seminary and pursued medical studies for a year at the Woman's Medical College of Pennsylvania. On visits to Europe in the 1880s, she viewed the cities' poor and Toynbee Hall, a settlement house in London. Addams returned to the United States and in 1889, in Chicago, established Hull-House in an immigrant neighborhood, in an effort to eliminate barriers between the classes. It offered a variety of programs from day nurseries to college courses for all races and nationalities, and served as a boardinghouse for working women. A music school and theater encouraged artistic expression. Hull-House, whose visitors included Theodore Roosevelt, became one of Chicago's major tourist attractions.

Addams was involved in politics, and also promoted international peace. She lectured and wrote several books and articles on subjects ranging from child labor to employment insurance. Her first book, *Democracy and Social Ethics* (1902), defines social ethics needed in a modern industrial society. Her first autobiography, *Twenty Years at Hull-House* (1910), brought high acclaim. Having served as an officer of numerous women's organizations, she received the Nobel Peace Prize in 1931. She also helped to found the American Civil Liberties Union. She died at Hull-House. Many Americans consider Jane Addams one of the greatest women in U.S. history.

Further Reading: Jean Bethke Elshtain, *Jane Addams and The Dream of American Democracy: A Life*, 2002; Cornelia

Lynde Meigs, *Jane Addams, Pioneer for Social Justice: A Biography*, 1970; *Jane Addams, Twenty Years at Hull-House with Autobiographical Notes*, 1990.

Jane F. Lancaster

ADDICKS, JOHN EDWARD O'SULLIVAN (21 November 1841–7 August 1919), business and political speculator. Born in Philadelphia, Pennsylvania, Addicks dabbled in various interests, including the flour business, real estate, and dry goods, prior to building and promoting gasworks in various cities. He organized the Chicago Gas Trust and the Bay State Gas Company, which caused him to be known as "Gas Addicks" and the "Napoleon of Gas." In 1892 he emerged as president of the Brooklyn Gas Company. In 1888, after becoming wealthy and pursuing interests in local politics, Addicks decided that he wanted to be a U.S. senator from Delaware. He made his official announcement in 1889, established residency in a private home, and spent some three million dollars over the next seventeen years to win supporters, build up the Union faction within the Republican Party, and attempt to obtain a majority vote of the Delaware legislators for election to the national upper chamber. Several times he either nearly succeeded, won a plurality, or prevented an election, thereby resulting in a few Congresses in which Delaware was represented by only one senator or unrepresented entirely, as in the Fifty-seventh Congress. His spectacular campaigns attracted national attention. Ultimately, Addicks failed in his political endeavor, experienced financial disasters, and died in poverty in New York City.

Further Reading: *New York Times*, 8 August 1919; *New York Herald*, 8 August 1919.

Leonard Schlup

ADDYSTON PIPE AND STEEL COMPANY v. UNITED STATES (175 U.S. 211). This case tested whether the United States, under the Sherman Antitrust Act of 1890, could initiate action against price-fixing schemes by groups of firms. In *Addyston Pipe*, six manufacturers of cast-iron pipe conspired to win contracts at higher prices by collaborating to submit bids which would guarantee that one of the six would win each contract. The winner then paid a bonus to the other companies, which had submitted inflated bids. The companies defended the practice as their best effort to stay in business amid stiff competition. Writing for a unanimous court in December 1899, Justice Rufus W. Peckham ruled that Congress had the power to regulate price-fixing schemes, because a cartel like Addyston Pipe represented the formation of a private government trying to regulate interstate transactions. Previous court opinion had held that regulation violated the constitutional protection of the liberty to engage in private contracts. Contracts that directly restrained interstate trade were a form of regulation of commerce, and therefore a usurpation of congressional power. Congressional power to regulate trusts through the Sherman Act and subsequent legislation now had the protection of a unanimous court decision.

Further Reading: Owen M. Fiss, *History of the Supreme Court of the United States*, vol. 8: *Troubled Beginnings of the Modern State, 1888–1910*, 1993, pp. 125–159; Louis Fisher, *American Constitutional Law*, 3rd ed., 1999, pp. 359–360.

Thomas C. Sutton

AFRICAN AMERICANS. African Americans gained citizenship in 1868, but were vilified in nearly every sector of the nation. Southern whites were smarting from their humiliating defeat and the social impact of the Civil War, and northern whites generally refused to accept African Americans as equals.

Only 10 percent of the black population of 4,880,009 lived in the North, where they secured jobs as laborers at an unprecedented rate despite concerted efforts to prevent them from competing with whites. African-American men were denied employment because whites threatened to strike. Many had to settle for jobs as waiters, porters, or bartenders, and African-American women were forced to take in washing or work as domestics. They were often the victims of frustrated white immigrants, who themselves bore the brunt of bigotry and discrimination from the general population. African Americans were 85 to 90 percent Baptist or Methodist; in urban areas they huddled together in small ghettos for protection; and in 1900 their mortality rates were 47 percent higher than those of whites.

In the South, African Americans began to function as full-fledged citizens with assistance from white northern "carpetbaggers." With Republican Party affiliations, they were elected as legislators in every southern state and as lieutenant governor and secretary of state in South Carolina, and eighteen served in the U.S. Congress. Many African Americans held important local positions in their community; some became tradesmen and entrepreneurs, but most struggled to make the transition from slavery to freedom. However, these advancements were enforced by federal troops and not supported by a firm economic base. White southerners still owned the land and controlled virtually all commerce. When federal troops left in 1877, white southerners began a systematic process of whipping African Americans into submission with special laws passed to prevent them from voting. Also, the Ku Klux Klan began a reign of widespread terror. By the 1890s, African-American lawmakers were voted out of office, debarred from office, or killed in broad daylight.

Some African Americans tried to escape white oppression by migrating to the West; however, "black laws" followed them as their white neighbors tenaciously held to the folkways, mores, and legislation of northern and southern states. As each territory sought statehood, the single most pressing issue was the status of African Americans. Nevertheless, a large African-American migration from the South began in 1879, as blacks filled a labor shortage in frontier areas. They secured jobs as ranch hands and domestic servants, and African-American cowboys became commonplace on the Texas plains, helping to open the Chisholm Trail that linked the cattle industry to the northern consumption of beef. African Americans played prominent roles in western expansion, especially the "Buffalo Soldiers," who campaigned for twenty-four years against Native Americans, outlaws, and Mexican revolutionaries. The Buffalo Soldiers also built frontier posts and laid foundations for several towns and cities. Although they helped to pacify the western frontier, the white population generally despised them, and prejudice and discrimination often robbed them of simple justice. Buffalo Soldiers represented 20 percent of the U.S. Calvary in the West. They fought heroically in several Indian wars, and along with other African Americans led by white officers, they served gallantly in the Spanish-American War of 1898.

Lacking representation as well as protection from local, state, and federal authorities, African Americans looked to national black leaders to plead their causes. The most prominent was Booker T. Washington, who had earned an enviable reputation in education as black literacy rose from 21 percent in 1865 to 50 percent in 1895. Washington essayed a program of appeasement and submission to white oppression, and urged African Americans to subordinate their political, social, and civil strivings to economic development. In contrast, W. E. B. Du Bois began to emerge as spokesman for equal treatment, but was largely ignored and scorned as a radical supported by a small army of African-American intellectuals. Black leaders were unable to stem the tide of oppression that forced African Americans into a caste system based on allegedly innate biological inferiority. Moreover, vicious efforts to hold them down were legalized.

African Americans became the scapegoat for the economic depression of the 1890s. This set the stage for the U.S. Supreme Court's 1896 *Plessy* v. *Ferguson* decision, which legalized segregation and set back black-white relations dramatically. African Americans were disenfranchised, stripped of opportunities for economic improvement, and relegated to ghettos where their housing, education, and social services were far inferior to those of whites. This subjugation was vigorously enforced in both the North and the South by horrific lynchings, which occurred on an average of one every two days. As the Progressive movement for social justice began, conditions for whites improved. They declined for African Americans, however. Thus, in their first three decades of citizenship, African Americans became the pivotal issue for a new socio-political order that victimized them with violence, deprivations, and

subjugation that would continue well in the twentieth century.

Further Reading: John Hope Franklin, *From Slavery to Freedom: A History of African Americans* (8th ed.), 2000; Molefi Kete Asante, *African American History: A Journey of Liberation*; 1995. James Oliver Horton, ed., and Lois E. Horton, ed., *A History of the African American People: The History, Traditions and Culture of African Americans*, 1995.

Berman E. Johnson

AGRICULTURAL WHEEL. The origins of the Agricultural Wheel can be traced to a meeting of seven farmers in Prairie County, Arkansas, in 1882. Drawn together by concerns over depressed farm prices and mounting debt, six of the seven founders were landowners, and all were Democrats who agreed on the need for self-protection through cooperative effort. They chose the name of the organization to reflect their belief that agriculture was the great wheel that drove all other economic endeavors.

Worried farmers quickly allied themselves with the Prairie County Wheelers, and in April 1883 Arkansas granted the organization a state charter. Two years later the Arkansas State Wheel met at Litchfield, Arkansas, and united with another agricultural reform group, the Brothers of Freedom, to establish the National Agricultural Wheel. Isaac McCracken, the founder of the Brothers of Freedom, became the first and only president of the national Wheel. Spreading rapidly into surrounding states, the Wheel held its first national convention in 1886 at McKenzie, Tennessee. By 1887 it claimed 500,000 members in seven states.

Like other agrarian reform movements, the Wheel championed a radical program that included currency expansion through the free coinage of silver; an end to national banks; regulation or nationalization of railroads, telephones, and telegraph; restriction of the sale of public lands to American citizens; an income tax; and the popular election of U.S. senators. Individually, farmers were encouraged to join local cooperatives to purchase seed, fertilizers, and farm equipment, and sell their farm products in bulk. The Wheel advocated safety-first agriculture to end the debt cycle and denounced the one-crop (cotton) mentality of southern farmers. The efforts of the Agricultural Wheel officially ended in 1889 when it merged with the Southern Farmers' Alliance to form the Farmers' and Laborers' Union.

Further Reading: W. Scott Morgan, *History of the Wheel and Alliance and the Impending Revolution*, 1889; Connie L. Lester, "Grassroots Reform in the Age of New South Agriculture and Bourbon Democracy: The Agricultural Wheel, the Farmers' Alliance, and the People's Party in Tennessee, 1884–1892," Ph.D. diss., University of Tennessee at Knoxville, 1998.

Connie L. Lester

AGRICULTURE. As has been true throughout American history, the South was more agrarian than the North during the Gilded Age. Slavery's demise left intact the plantations in Louisiana and in coastal South Carolina and Georgia, where profits from sugar and rice, respectively, permitted landowners to pay enough to attract laborers. Overseers organized workers into gangs and disciplined them by withholding pay and levying fines. Especially onerous were the Black Codes, which bound freedmen to their employers.

Elsewhere, landowners subdivided a plantation, assigning some plots to sharecroppers, renting others to tenants, and farming the remainder with help from family and hired laborers. By 1880 tenancy had emerged as the dominant arrangement between landowner and laborer in the South: tenants farmed 40 percent of the land; wage laborers, but 9 percent. Landowners required tenants to plant cotton, to the detriment of food production. In the lower South, corn production fell from twenty-nine to seventeen bushels per person between 1870 and 1880. Between 1870 and 1890 the ratio of cotton to corn output doubled. Consequently the South went from being a net food exporter to a net importer during these years.

Much of the food that the South imported came from the North, especially from the Midwest and West. Between 1870 and 1900 the number of farms in the Midwest tripled, and west of the Mississippi River the number leaped sevenfold. This expansion fueled an annual increase in farm output of 2.5 percent between 1869 and 1899, with corn production growing 3.1 percent per year and wheat production rising 2.2 percent. Little of this growth, however, was intensive. In Ohio, for example, corn yields per acre stagnated between 1870 and 1900.

By 1901, Northern agriculture comprised three regions. Between western Ohio and central Kansas and Nebraska, farmers raised corn and hogs. In western Minnesota, the Dakotas, and western Kansas and Nebraska, farmers grew wheat. In Montana, Wyoming, and Colorado stretched the grasslands that fattened cattle.

South or North, the Gilded Age farmer competed in a global market. Between 1870 and 1890 corn fell from seventy to forty cents per bushel, wheat dropped from a dollar to seventy cents per bushel, and cotton prices declined by nearly one-third. This income reduction, along with fluctuating railroad rates, spiraling interest rates, and rising land prices, led farmers to seek economic and political reforms through the Grange, the Greenback Labor movement, the Farmers' Alliance, and the People's Party. All advocated railroad regulation, the free coinage of silver, female suffrage, a graduated income tax, a secret ballot, direct election of U.S. senators, and the eight-hour day. Advocacy of such reforms laid a foundation for the Progressive Era.

Further Reading: Willard W. Cochrane, *The Development of American Agriculture*, 1979; Fred A. Shannon, *The Farmer's Last Frontier*, 1945.

Christopher Cumo

AGUINALDO, EMILIO (23 March 1869–6 February 1964), Philippine nationalist military and political leader. Born near Cavite on Luzon and educated at the University of Santo Tomás in Manila, Aguinaldo was mayor of Cavite Viejo and led a local faction of the Katipunan, a revolutionary group, in the 1896 Filipino insurrection against Spanish rule. During the Spanish-American War, he aided the American forces in his homeland, but then broke with the Americans on the independence issue. A provisional congress proclaimed him president of the Republic of the Philippines in 1899. Aguinaldo fought a costly war against American forces until his capture on 23 March 1901. To suppress the Filipino uprising, the United States dispatched 70,000 troops. Organized resistance ended by late 1899, but guerrilla warfare continued until mid-1902. The Anti-Imperialist League condemned President William McKinley's Philippines policy. Aguinaldo was granted a pension by the American government after taking an oath of allegiance to the United States. He then retired to private life. During World War II, the elderly Aguinaldo was forced to participate in anti-American propaganda by the Japanese government. Following the liberation of the Philippines, he was taken into custody by American troops and held on suspicion of collaboration with the enemy, but was subsequently exonerated. He died in Manila.

Further Reading: John M. Gates, *Schoolbooks and Krags*, 1973; Stuart C. Miller, *"Benevolent Assimilation": The American Conquest of the Philippines*, 1982.

Alexander M. Bielakowski

AKRON RIOT OF 1900. The outgrowth of a mob action against an African-American resident, the Akron Riot of 1900 began on 20 August 1900 with the arrest of Louis Peck, a forty-year-old black bartender. Peck was charged with molesting a six-year-old white girl earlier in the day, and by late afternoon an angry crowd had gathered downtown at an intersection dubbed Hall's Corners (the intersection of Market and Howard Streets). A few blocks south, where Peck was jailed in the Akron City Building, the sheriff decided to transfer the prisoner to Cleveland.

As afternoon turned to evening, the crowd continued to grow, moving south to mill around the Bowery, Howard, and the Main Street intersection, on which the City Building fronted. A delegation from the crowd demanded that police turn over Peck, and was angered further by the chief's insistence that Peck was no longer in the building. The delegation, allowed to search the jail, did not find Peck there, but suspected the police were merely shifting the prisoner from room to room to avoid detection.

As darkness fell, the mob grew still louder and more menacing, causing some police to panic and fire warning shots above the crowd. Unfortunately, two children who were uphill to the east of the building were struck and killed by the police bullets. Shortly thereafter the police fled, and the crowd burned the City Building and nearby Columbia Hall. Arriving

firemen were attacked and withdrew, allowing both structures to burn to the ground.

The next day, amid national press attention, the Ohio National Guard took up positions around the ruins as hundreds came to view the scene. A grand jury was convened and handed down indictments that led to the convictions of several crowd members. Some minors who participated in the violence were sent to reform school.

Peck was brought back to Akron, where he stood trial on the molestation charges. He was convicted in a twenty-minute trial with no legal representation, and sent to the Ohio Penitentiary. He served thirteen years before several Akron lawyers were able to gain his unconditional pardon from the governor.

Further Reading: Karl H. Grismer, *Akron and Summit County*, 1952; C. R. Quine, *The Great Akron Riot* [pamphlet], 1951.

Stephen Paschen

***ALABAMA* CLAIMS.** During the American Civil War, the British allowed English shipyards to build warships for the Confederacy. The vessels acted as commerce raiders that caused significant direct and indirect damage to the Union. Not only did the raiders (among them the *Alabama*) destroy some 250 Union merchantmen, but they also drove up insurance rates, forced American merchants to reflag their ships, and perhaps prolonged the war. The American government argued that the British government violated neutrality laws by selling war matériel to a belligerent, and demanded that the British pay for the damages caused by the Confederate warships. These demands for reparations became known as the "*Alabama* claims."

Although the United States had challenged British violations of neutrality from the early days of the Civil War, the *Alabama* claims would reach center stage in Anglo-American relations in 1869. American claims encompassed three major demands: compensation for direct damages caused by the warships, an indemnity for indirect damages, and an apology by the British government. In 1869, Great Britain agreed to pay for direct damages, but the U.S. Senate rejected the agreement, for it did not include an apology or an indemnity for indirect damages, immoderately valued by Senator Charles Sumner at over $2 billion. Negotiations over the claims began again in 1871 as part of the Treaty of Washington, a general arbitration agreement that addressed several outstanding bilateral issues.

The arbiters found against the British and ordered payment of $15.5 million in direct damages but no indirect damages. The general agreement also included a British expression of regret for the *Alabama* matter, settlement of a fisheries dispute, and an agreement over disputed territory in the Pacific Northwest. More significantly, the settlement repaired Anglo-American relations and established a precedent for the arbitration of international disputes.

Further Reading: Adrian Cook, *The Alabama Claims, American Politics, and Anglo-American Relations, 1865–1872*, 1975.

John D. Coats

ALASKA COMMERCIAL COMPANY. After the United States purchased Alaska from Russia in 1867, many business figures rushed north to buy imperial real property and that of the Russian-American Company. In October 1868, rival investor groups from San Francisco and New London, Connecticut, realized that profits depended on monopolizing the supplying of Alaskan trading stations and of fur seal harvesting in the Pribilof Islands. They formed the Alaska Commercial Company and gained a twenty-year U.S. government lease on 13 August 1870. Not surprisingly, investors were quickly realizing annual profits exceeding 50 percent of the stock's par value. Controversy ensued, and Congress investigated the company at least four times. Although no overt misdeeds were found, upon the lease's expiration in 1890 Congress awarded the franchise to the Northern Commercial Company, a San Francisco competitor.

The Alaska Commercial Company never fully recovered, despite diversification, but limped along for another fifty years. After reorganizations in 1942 and the 1970s, it sold remaining assets to the Community Education Development Corporation, a Native-owned entity.

Further Reading: Samuel P. Johnston, *Alaska Commercial Company, 1868–1940*; Frank H. Sloss, "Who Owned the Alaska Commercial Company?" *Pacific Northwest Quarterly*, 8 (1977): 120–130; Nelson H. H. Graburn, Molly Lee, and Jean-Loup Rosselot, *Catalogue Raisonné of the Alaska Commercial Company Collection, Phoebe Apperson Hearst Museum of Anthropology*, 1996.

Claus-M. Naske

ALCORN, JAMES LUSK (4 November 1816–19 December 1894), Mississippi governor and U.S. senator. Born in Galconda, Illinois, Alcorn attended public schools in Kentucky, then graduated from Cumberland College. He was admitted to the Mississippi bar, and won election to that state's house of representatives in 1846. After serving in the state senate, he unsuccessfully challenged Democrat L.Q.C. Lamar for Congress. Elected as a pro-Union delegate to the 1861 Mississippi constitutional convention, Alcorn nevertheless signed the Ordinance of Secession. In the war that followed, he was a brigadier general of state troops. Returned to the legislature in 1863, Alcorn was elected to the U.S. Senate under President Andrew Johnson's lenient Reconstruction policies. Denied the seat, he returned to his plantation and law study. He joined the Republican Party, and by 1868 had emerged as one of most prominent southern Unionists. Elected Mississippi's first Republican governor in 1869, he resigned in 1871 to accept a U.S. Senate seat. Alcorn lost a gubernatorial bid 1873, and left the Senate four years later, shortly after Mississippi's conservative white Democratic "Redemption." He emerged from retirement briefly as a delegate to the state's 1890 constitutional convention.

Further Reading: John Skates, *Mississippi: A Bicentennial History*, 1977; Lillian Pereyra, *James Lusk Alcorn: Persistent Whig*, 1966.

Harvey Gresham Hudspeth

ALCOTT, LOUISA MAY (29 November 1832–6 March 1888), author and humanitarian. The daughter of progressive parents, Alcott was born in Germantown, Pennsylvania, and grew up in Concord, Massachusetts, surrounded by notable authors and intellectuals, including Nathaniel Hawthorne, Margaret Fuller, Ralph Waldo Emerson, and Henry David Thoreau. She began writing for small papers in the late 1850s, and her first story in the *Atlantic Monthly* appeared in 1859. When the Civil War broke out, she became a nurse, and was treated with the mercury compound calomel to prevent infectious diseases. The mercury poisoned her and began a process of nerve and muscle deterioration that eventually led to her death. Alcott published a memoir of her work as a nurse, *Hospital Sketches*, in 1863.

To support her family and herself, she also wrote serial gothic romances under the pseudonym A. M. Barnard. In 1864 she published her first novel, a romance called *Moods*, and in 1868 she began writing the now-classic and largely autobiographical novel *Little Women*. The profit Alcott received from the two-volume publication enabled her to pay all her family's debts. When her brother-in-law died in 1871, Alcott wrote *Little Men*, as a tribute to him and to ensure that her sister and nephews would not suffer financially. Despite physical deterioration, she worked on, penning one more adult novel, *Work*, in 1873 and several more serial and juvenile pieces. The resulting income enabled Alcott to provide for her ailing parents.

As a self-proclaimed "spinster" during the Gilded Age, Alcott bore the burden of her parents' care bravely, despite her own poor health. Her father's death on 4 March 1888 marked the end of Alcott's obligation, and she died two days later.

Further Reading: Martha Saxton, *Louisa May: A Modern Biography of Louisa May Alcott*, 1977.

Jessica Matthews

ALDRICH, NELSON WILMARTH (6 November 1841–16 July 1915), U.S. senator. Born in Foster, Rhode Island, to a family of modest means, Aldrich began working at age seventeen in Providence for a wholesale grocer. Diligence and ability brought rapid promotions, and he eventually became a millionaire financier. Aldrich entered local politics in 1869, rising to the Forty-sixth Congress in 1878. In 1881, Senator Ambrose Burnside died and Aldrich was elected to replace him. He became a dominant figure in Rhode Island politics and enjoyed a secure seat for thirty years.

An ardent protectionist, Aldrich was recognized as a genius in parliamentary procedure. He and fellow Republicans William B. Allison of Iowa, Orville H. Platt of Connecticut, and John C. Spooner of Wisconsin dominated the Senate from 1897 until 1903, as supporters of presidents William McKinley and Theodore Roosevelt. In 1906, Aldrich challenged Roosevelt's leadership over the Hepburn Bill, which would have given the Interstate Commerce Commission power to set railroad rates.

Aldrich developed an interest in economics and finance, and visited Europe's central banks. Under challenge from western senators, he did not seek reelection in 1908. His interest in banking continued, but many of his ideas were not adopted because the Democrats had captured the White House and Congress in 1912. He died suddenly at the age of seventy-four.

Further reading: Nathaniel W. Stephenson, *Nelson W. Aldrich, A Leader in American Politics*, 1971.

William C. Binning

ALGER, HORATIO, JR. (13 January 1832–18 July 1899), writer of stories for boys. Born in Revere, Massachusetts, Alger attended Harvard and published his first work in 1849, while still a student. After a brief stint as a minister, he moved to New York and began his writing career in 1866. He wandered the streets, gathering material that would result in the publication of eighteen juvenile novels between 1867 and 1873. Most famous was his Ragged Dick series, in which themes of persistence, luck, and an adult patron first appeared. They formed the basic plotline of all his subsequent work. These novels represented the dominant theme of an emerging America as the land of opportunity with the promise of fulfilling the dream of upward mobility and financial success. Alger died in Natick, Massachusetts. His popularity declined after the Gilded Age, but he enjoyed a revival in the booming 1920s, counting such famous people as Herbert Hoover among his readers. Today Alger's name is synonymous with the rags-to-riches success story.

Further Reading: Carol Nackenoff, *The Fictional Republic: Horatio Alger and American Political Discourse*, 1994.

C. Edward Balog

ALGER, RUSSELL ALEXANDER (27 February 1836–24 January 1907), governor, senator, secretary of war. Born to a poor family in a log cabin in Ohio, Alger was orphaned at age eleven and worked as a farmhand and teacher to support his to younger siblings. He attended public school and an academy, and completed law training in 1857. In the Civil War, Alger served as captain of a Michigan volunteer company and later commanded Michigan's Fifth Cavalry Regiment. He reached brevet major general before leaving the army in 1864. Alger settled in Detroit after the war and earned a fortune in the lumber industry during the 1870s. A Republican, he was elected governor of Michigan in 1884 and served one term. President William McKinley appointed him secretary of war in March 1897. During the Spanish-American War, Alger shouldered much of the blame for preexisting army problems with organization, supply, and administration. McKinley requested his resignation in 1899. Alger died eight years later while serving as a U.S. senator from Michigan.

Further Reading: Graham Cosmas, *An Army for Empire*, 1994; *New York Times*, 25 January 1907.

Michael W. Vogt

ALLEN, CHARLES HERBERT (15 April 1848–20 April 1934), businessman, congressman, assistant secretary of the navy, and diplomat. Born in Lowell, Massachusetts, Allen graduated from Amherst College in 1869. As a young man he manufactured wooden boxes with his father, a merchant. Allen won a seat on the Lowell board of education and held other local offices. He also served in the state legislature and, from 1885 to 1889, in the U.S. House of Representatives. In 1890 Allen ran unsuccessfully for governor of Massachusetts as a Republican. He was state prison commissioner in 1897 and 1898. When Assistant Secretary of the Navy Theodore Roosevelt resigned to participate in the Spanish-American War, President William McKinley selected Allen, an expansionist, as his successor. Allen held this appointment until 1900. The Foraker Act brought civil rule to conquered Puerto Rico, and McKinley installed Allen as the island's governor. Allen traveled widely and detailed political, economic, and social conditions for Washington, perceiving Puerto Rico as a coveted prize in the age of imperialism. He resigned in September 1901 and returned to Lowell where from 1902 to 1907 he served as president of the Appleton National Bank, and he died in Lowell.

Further Reading: *New York Times*, 21 April 1934; Charles H. Allen, "How Civil Government Was Established in Porto Rico," *The North American Review* 174 [1902]:159–174; Leonard Schlup, "Governor Charles H. Allen and His Role in Puerto Rico," *Lamar Journal of the Humanities* 21 [1995]: 5–20.

Leonard Schlup

ALLEN, WILLIAM VINCENT (28 January 1847–12 January 1924), Populist senator. Allen was born in Midway, Ohio, but reared in Iowa. He served in the Union Army, attended Upper Iowa University, and read law. He was admitted to the Iowa bar in 1869 and moved to Madison, Nebraska, in 1884. Originally a Republican, Allen was elected district judge on the Populist ticket in 1891. Populists and Democrats combined to elect him to the U.S. Senate in 1893. There Allen advocated banking and monetary reform, aid to the destitute, and anti-imperialism. He led opposition to repeal of the Sherman Silver Purchase Act in 1893, at one point setting the contemporary record for the length of a filibuster (fifteen hours). Many viewed Allen as a relatively conservative Populist. He publicly identified the Southern Farmers Alliance's subtreasury plan as the Populist program's "weak point," thereby angering radicals. He did, however, endorse greenbacks and government ownership of railroads. As chairman of the Populists' 1896 national convention, he used his position to further nomination of fellow Nebraskan William Jennings Bryan, a Democrat.

Allen lost his Senate seat in 1899 but won a district judgeship. When his successor-elect to the Senate died, Democratic governor William A. Poynter attempted to further fusion with Populists by appointing Allen to fill the position, which he held until 1901. Allen broke with fusion when the pro-gold standard eastern wing of the Democratic Party gained control in 1904. Thomas E. Watson of Georgia narrowly defeated him for the Populist presidential nomination the same year. Allen was elected district judge in a nonpartisan race in 1916, and served in this position until his death in Madison.

Further Reading: Gene Clanton, *Congressional Populism*, 1998; Addison E. Sheldon, "Nebraskans I Have Known— William Vincent Allen," *Nebraska History* [1938]. 191–206; Albert Watkins and J.S. Morgan, *History of Nebraska*, 1913.

Worth Robert Miller

ALLISON, WILLIAM BOYD (2 March 1829–4 August 1908), senator. Allison was born in Perry Township, Ohio, and attended Wooster Academy and Western Reserve University in Cleveland, but did not earn a college degree. Instead he read law, was admitted to the bar at age twenty, and moved to Dubuque, Iowa, where in 1872 he was elected, as a Republican, to the U.S. Senate.

Although representing an agricultural state, he voted against the farm program of inflation and low tariffs. He helped draft the Bland-Allison Act of 1878, which was a victory for the opponents of inflation; though it required the Treasury to buy silver, as farmers hoped, the Treasury bought only $308 million of it between 1878 and 1890, too little to expand the money supply faster than the growth of goods and services. An even more resounding defeat for farmers came in 1900 when Allison voted for the Gold Standard Act, which dropped silver as legal tender and thereby guaranteed an inelastic currency. Three years earlier Allison had abandoned farmers and joined protectionists in voting for the Dingley Tariff, which raised duties to the highest levels to that date.

He did not join the Progressives. After thirty-five years in the Senate, he returned to Dubuque, where he died.

Further Reading: Leland L. Sage, *William Boyd Allison: A Study in Practical Politics*, 1956.

Christopher Cumo

ALTGELD, JOHN PETER (30 December 1847–12 March 1902), governor. After emigrating as a child from Nieder Selters, Nassau, in southern Germany, Altgeld grew up in Ohio with little formal education. Still in his teens, he served with the Sixty-fourth Ohio Infantry

in the Civil War. He left home for the West in 1869, working in railroad construction in Kansas and Arkansas and as a farmhand in Missouri. Having settled in Andrew County, Missouri, he read law and set up practice in Savannah, Missouri, in 1871. Elected county prosecutor in 1874, he resigned after a year for more promising opportunities in Chicago. There he launched a law practice that, with successful real estate and street railway investments, brought Altgeld considerable wealth. Most of it was lost in the panic of 1893. He entered politics in 1884, when he ran a strong losing race for Congress as a Democrat, winning 45 percent of the vote in a heavily Republican district. In the same year he wrote *Our Penal Machinery and Its Victims*, which argued that prison was more likely to make habitual criminals than to reform its inmates. He urged speedier trials and an end to compensation for prosecutors for each criminal convicted. This was typical of his lifelong support for society's underdogs.

With labor support, Altgeld was elected to the Cook County Superior Court as a Democrat in 1886; he became its chief justice in 1890 and served until 1891. He continued to support labor causes such as the eight-hour day, and in 1892 the Democrats nominated him for governor. Large Democratic numbers in Chicago swept him into office. Almost immediately, Altgeld was pressed by his friend Clarence Darrow and others to offer clemency to the three prisoners still held for the Haymarket Riot of 1886. He had earlier refused to be active on their behalf, but after a careful review of the trial record, pardoned the three in June 1893, citing numerous trial irregularities. Intense public and editorial criticism from across the nation quickly assaulted Altgeld.

In July 1894, Altgeld denounced President Grover Cleveland's sending of federal troops to Illinois during the Pullman strike as an unconstitutional violation of local self-government. He won passage of an eight-hour working day for women (later voided by the Illinois Supreme Court), but failed to secure enactment of his proposals for labor arbitration, court reform, and penal reform. He did succeed in obtaining larger appropriations for the University of Illinois and for expanding state parks, and he ordered competitive bidding for state contracts and appointed women to high state offices. Among these was Florence Kelley of Hull-House, selected as factory inspector. In an election marked by much fraudulent voting, Altgeld lost the governorship in 1896. His last hurrah was an unsuccessful race for mayor of Chicago in 1899. When Altgeld died, Darrow said the poor, the weak, and the defenseless had lost their truest friend.

Further Reading: Harry Barnard, *Eagle Forgotten: The Life of John Peter Altgeld,* 1932; Ray Ginger, *Altgeld's America,* 1958.

Mario R. DiNunzio

AMERICA IN 1900. On New Year's Day in 1900, snow fell over much of the northern and eastern United States. Americans, for the second time as a nation, crossed into a new century, remembering the progress of the past while anticipating a promising future. Few could have anticipated that the next hundred years would become the American century. Seventy-six million people lived in forty-five states in a country still young in history and spirit. Times seemed prosperous, but vast disparity separated the wealthy from poor groups, and sexism and racism permeated society. Headline events may be illustrative. Yale had won the national college football championship. Illiteracy in the United States reached a new low of 10.7 percent of the population. The Boxer Rebellion occurred in China when a coterie of nationalists sought to remove foreigners from that country and troops from various countries quelled the uprising. The center of the U.S. population was six miles southeast of Columbus, Indiana. Congress passed the Gold Standard Act, establishing the gold standard. Among books published in 1900 were *Sister Carrie,* by Theodore Dreiser, and *The Wonderful Wizard of Oz*, by L. Frank Baum. There were eight thousand registered automobiles in the country and ten miles of paved roads. A hurricane killed six thousand people in Galveston, Texas. The most popular song of the year was "Good-bye, Dolly Gray." William McKinley won reelection as president. The Eastman Kodak Company introduced the Brownie box camera. Over a million and a quarter telephones were operating in the United States. Symphony Hall opened in Boston. Booker T. Washington organized the National Negro Business League. New York was the largest city, with nearly three and a half million inhabitants. Congress approved the Foraker Act to establish civil rule for Puerto Rico. Army surgeon Walter Reed discovered that mosquito bites transmitted yellow fever. W.E.B. Du Bois addressed representatives to the Pan-American Conference, warning that the color question would surface as the greatest danger facing the country in the century. In Missouri a young man wrote an essay on courage in which he observed: "The virtue I call courage is not in always facing the foe but in taking care of those at home." The author, Harry S Truman, assumed the American presidency in 1945, and his domestic and foreign policies dramatically shaped the second half of the twentieth century. Many of the critical issues in 1900 remained prominent in the year 2000.

Further Reading: Noel Jacob Kent, *America in 1900,* 2000; Judy Crichton, *America 1900: The Turning Point,* 1998.

Leonard Schlup

AMERICAN BAR ASSOCIATION. Until the late nineteenth century, lawyers were a largely unorganized group. With the advent of industrial society, and its need for "professionals" in middle and top management positions, the drive to organize the bar grew steadily. Local and state bar associations were formed in the early 1870s; New York was the first in 1870, and Iowa followed suit in 1874. The American Bar Association (ABA) was formed in 1878.

The initial purposes included a desire to cultivate more civilized relations among members and to weed out the more corrupt and disreputable among the profession. The ABA (like most local and state associations) was, prior to the Progressive Era, little more than a gathering of affluent lawyers enjoying the elegance of Saratoga, New York, where it was founded. By the early twentieth century, however, the ABA sponsored a drive for uniform state laws covering everything from marriage and divorce to contract relations.

Further Reading: Lawrence M. Friedman, *A History of American Law*, 2nd. ed., 1985; Burton J. Bledstein, *The Culture of Professionalism*, 1976.

Sam S. Kepfield

"AMERICAN BOY." In May 1900, Theodore Roosevelt's article "The American Boy" appeared in *St. Nicholas*, a monthly magazine suggested to Scribner's in 1872 by Dr. Josiah G. Holland and edited by Mary Mapes Dodge. Along with *Our Young Folks, Wide Awake,* and *Youth's Companion, St. Nicholas* surfaced in the late nineteenth century as a popular illustrated magazine for children ages five to eighteen that featured stories by prominent people as well as writers of children's stories. Roosevelt contributed a piece on boyhood in Gilded Age America in which he freely offered his advice and outlined his conception of Victorian boyhood and manhood. Urging boys to work hard at their studies for the sake of knowledge as well as character development, he equated shiftlessness and indifference in studying with an inability to succeed in life. He expected American boys to become good men of whom America could be proud. Noting with pleasure the interest in athletics, Roosevelt commented that sons of rich parents especially should engage in manly exercises because they lacked the rugged outdoor environment characteristic of hardworking farm boys. He endorsed both physical and moral courage, and denounced cowardice as contemptible. Roosevelt advised boys to hit the line hard; to be virtuous, honest, clean, truthful, gentle, brave, and tender; and not to preach about their good conduct.

Further Reading: Theodore Roosevelt, *The Strenuous Life*, 1900.

Leonard Schlup

AMERICAN ECONOMIC ASSOCIATION.

Organized in 1885 at Saratoga, New York, the American Economic Association (AEA) grew out of the disillusionment of a number of young economists with the premises behind the laissez-faire philosophy. The AEA was the first economic group to contend that the state must contribute actively and positively to the progress of the people. It argued that class warfare could spread across the nation unless efforts were made to prevent additional degradation of workers. The purpose of the American Economic Association was to encourage research, publication, and discussion about economics. The 186 founding members included Woodrow Wilson, Henry Adams, and Richard T. Ely, who was then professor of political economy at Johns Hopkins University. Currently the AEA maintains its business office and headquarters in Nashville, Tennessee.

Further Reading: Edward C. Kirkland, *American Economic History Since 1860*, 1960; Louis P. Cain and Jonathan R. T. Hughes, *American Economic History*, 1997; Richard T. Ely Papers, State Historical Society of Wisconsin, Madison.

Leonard Schlup

AMERICAN FEDERATION OF LABOR.

Formed in Columbus, Ohio, in 1886, when dissident Knights of Labor united with the Federation of Organized Trade and Labor Unions, the American Federation of Labor (AFL) was a confederation of the nation's largest independent trade unions. Its primary purpose was to lobby the national legislature, coordinate the activities of member unions, resolve conflicts over jurisdiction, and promote trade unionism generally. Constituent unions retained the power to negotiate contracts, call strikes, organize workers, and establish work rules.

With the exception of 1895, Samuel Gompers served as the AFL's president from its inception until his death in 1924. Under his guidance, the AFL pursued "pure-and-simple" unionism, the belief that conflict between workers and employers was primarily economic rather than political. Thus, to improve the lives of workers, the AFL stressed the use of economic tools, including strikes, boycotts, union labels, and collective bargaining. Since unskilled and semiskilled workers, including African Americans, women, and newly arrived immigrants had little economic power, the AFL dismissed them as unorganizable. Politics played a secondary role in the AFL's strategy. Gompers warned that it divided workers and subjected labor to the whims of more powerful business interests. While "pure and simple" unionists usually controlled the AFL during the Gilded Age, a coalition of Socialists and Populists hoping to transform the AFL into a producer-based political party succeeded in ousting Gompers from the presidency in 1895. He returned the following year, however, and consolidated power. Under his stewardship the AFL replaced the Knights of Labor as the nation's most powerful labor organization. Membership grew steadily from fewer than 150,000 members in 1886 to just under 600,000 at the turn of the century. By 1904 over 1.6 million workers belonged to AFL unions.

Further Reading: Philip Taft, *The AFL in the Time of Gompers*, 1957; Julie Greene, *Pure and Simple Politics: The American Federation of Labor and Political Activism, 1881–1917*, 1998.

Michael Pierce

AMERICAN HISTORICAL ASSOCIATION.

The formation of the American Historical Association on 9 September 1884 was part of a broader movement of professionalization among learned callings during the last third of the nineteenth century. During a meeting of the American Social Science Association at the United States Hotel in Saratoga Springs, New York, twenty-five historians withdrew for a separate organizational session. Present were several who had led in introducing the seminar and German ideals of the scientific study of history to the United States, including the Harvard librarian Justin Winsor, Herbert Baxter Adams, and John Franklin Jameson. Efforts to secure national visibility resulted in conferral of a congressional charter in 1889. With the establishment of the *American Historical Review* in 1895, professional historians with graduate degrees had fully supplanted the gentleman amateurs who had earlier dominated American historical writing.

Further Reading: David D. Van Tassell, "From Learned Society to Professional Organization: The American Historical Association, 1884–1900," *American Historical Review* 89 [1984]: 929–956; Morey D. Rothberg, " 'To Set a Standard of Workmanship and Compel Men to Conform to It': John Franklin Jameson as Editor of the *American Historical Review*," *American Historical Review* 89 [1984]: 957–975.

Douglas Steeples

AMERICAN HUMANE ASSOCIATION.

On 3 March 1873, Congress enacted a law pro-

hibiting livestock shippers and dealers from transporting animals for more than twenty-eight hours without food, water, or rest. After this first federal humane law's enactment, John G. Shortall, president of the Illinois Humane Society, continued to agitate for a national convention of local humane societies to protest overcrowded railroad cars, expose their unsanitary conditions, and educate people in proper attitudes and actions toward living things. He believed such legislation would preserve and strengthen America's national heritage and moral values. Shortall's endeavor succeeded on 9 October 1899, when representatives of twenty-seven local humane societies met in Cleveland, Ohio, to expand agitation. The delegates elected Edwin Lee Brown of Illinois as chairman and passed a resolution condemning the inhumane manner of transporting livestock by rail. Leaders included Abraham Firth of Massachusetts; Joseph L. Smith of Ohio; Caroline Earle White, founder of the Women's Pennsylvania Society for the Prevention of Cruelty to Animals; and Henry Bergh of New York, known as America's first humanitarian, who served as president of the American Society for the Prevention of Cruelty to Animals from 1866 to 1888. Among other leaders were Elbridge T. Gerry of New York, William O. Stillman of New York, and the actress Minnie Maddern Fiske. In 1901 Zadock Street traveled the nation to inspect stockyards, slaughterhouses, and railroad cars. Ultimately, issues surrounding child protection interlinked with AHA concerns. In 1883, the AHA promoted passage of national legislation dealing with cruelty to and violence against children.

Animal welfare, a Gilded Age reform movement, provided a rich legacy of leadership and accomplishment in the protection of children and animals.

Further Reading: American Humane Association Archives, Englewood, Colo.; *First Annual Meeting of the International Humane Society*, 1877; American Humane Association, *Timeline of Historic Events, 1877–2000*, 2000; Etta Angell Wheeler, *The Story of Mary Ellen, Which Started the Child Saving Crusade Throughout the World*, 1874.

Leonard Schlup

AMERICAN LIBRARY ASSOCIATION. Several late nineteenth-century forces fostered a professional library association's development. Reconstruction's end, urbanization, and improved transportation made the nation more cosmopolitan. Other professional associations existed, including the American Medical Association (1847) and the National Education Association (1857). More libraries had appeared, due in no small part to Andrew Carnegie's $4 million donation. An attempt to form a professional association of librarians had failed before the Civil War. By 1876, however, librarians were again interested in the idea. An October convention officially established the ALA. Leading early figures included Justin Winsor, Richard Bowker, Melvil Dewey, and William Poole. The *American Library Journal* published its first issue on 30 September 1876, and had become the association's official publication by 28 February 1877. In September 1877 the title was changed to *Library Journal*. Despite early financial problems and some reorganization, the association continues to the present.
Further Reading: Dennis Thomison, *A History of the American Library Association 1876–1972*, 1978.

Mark E. Ellis

AMERICAN PROTECTIVE ASSOCIATION. Founded in 1887 at Clinton, Iowa, by Henry F. Bowers, the American Protective Association (APA) was a clandestine anti-Catholic organization active principally in the Midwest between 1893 and 1896. It had approximately 70,000 members by 1892, but membership surged upward after 1893, due to the replacement of Bowers by the practical and politically astute William J. Traynor and to APA propaganda ascribing the panic of 1893 to papal plots. Increasing Irish political power in Boston and New York, the prolonged school controversy in the early 1890s, the rapid expansion of parochial schools, the arrival of large numbers of Catholic immigrants, and rumors that Catholics intended to slaughter Protestants aggravated anti-Catholic sentiment.

By 1896 the APA claimed a membership of 2.5 million, making it one of the largest and most powerful anti-immigrant and anti-Catholic organizations of the late nineteenth century. Members took an oath not to employ Catholics in any capacity or to vote for Catholics seeking public office. They further pledged to work to retard the power of the pope in the United States and promote the interest of all Protestants. The APA published a magazine and several weekly newspapers. It elected William S. Linton, a Michigan businessman and Republican political figure, to the U.S. House of Representatives in 1894, and influenced local elections in other areas. The APA—denounced by the prominent Congregational clergyman Washington Gladden, torn by internal dissension, wrecked by Traynor's refusal to endorse William McKinley for president in 1896, and handicapped by Traynor's unsuccessful attempt to create a minor political party—experienced a decline in members and influence by the century's end. It remained in existence, though weakened, until 1911.
Further Reading: Donald L. Kinzer, *Episode in Anti-Catholicism: The American Protective Association*, 1964; Frederic R. Coudert, "The American Protective Association," *Forum* 17 [1894]: 513–523; Les Wallace, *The Rhetoric of Anti-Catholicism: The American Protective Association, 1887–1911*, 1990.

Leonard Schlup

AMERICAN RAILWAY UNION. On 20 June 1893, at the beginning of a depression, fifty railroad workers formed the American Railway Union (ARU) in Chicago. Prior to that time, various brotherhoods, such as the Engineers, had constituted the trade unions on the railroads. Eugene V. Debs, prominent in the Brotherhood of Locomotive Firemen since 1880, was disgusted with internal warfare among the brotherhoods. He wanted a single organization to represent all crafts of railroad employees and to protect them from corporate exploitation. As one of the founders of the ARU, Debs became president; George W. Howard was vice president; and Sylvester Keliher filled the office of secretary. Before its first convention in June 1894, the ARU had enrolled between 125,000 and 140,000 men in one great brotherhood. In that same year the ARU won the first strike by any union against a major railroad. According to its constitution, the ARU would include "all railway employees born of white parents." It sought to protect members in all matters relating to wages and working conditions. Pledged to conservative methods, it was one of America's first industrial unions. It quickly met overwhelming resistance from corporations and the U.S. government.

Further Reading: Philip Taft, *Organized Labor in American History*, 1964.

Leonard Schlup

AMERICAN SOCIETY FOR THE PREVENTION OF CRUELTY TO ANIMALS. Founded in New York City in 1866 by Henry Bergh, the American Society for the Prevention of Cruelty to Animals (ASPCA) is the oldest humane organization in the United States. Its purpose has been to promote humane principles, prevent cruelty, and alleviate pain and suffering of animals through a nationwide program of information dissemination, recognition of situations, and advocacy programs. In 1866 the society's endeavors prompted New York legislators to enact the nation's first effective anti-cruelty law. In 1867 the society operated the first ambulance for injured horses, two years before New York's Bellevue Hospital started using ambulance service for humans. Seven years later, Bergh assisted in organizing the Society for the Prevention of Cruelty to Children. The next year he invented a canvas sling to rescue horses mired in mud or water. In 1894 the chapter in New York City assumed the Herculean task of caring for the city's stray and unwanted animal population. As a result of its notable achievements and rapid growth during the Gilded Age, the ASPCA remains a significant humane organization in twenty-first century America.

Further Reading: Gerald Carson, *Men, Beasts, and Gods: A History of Cruelty and Kindness to Animals*, 1972.

Leonard Schlup

AMERICAN TELEPHONE AND TELEGRAPH COMPANY. Formed in 1877 by the inventor Alexander Graham Bell and two financial backers, the company that became American Telephone and Telegraph (AT&T) introduced the telephone and established it as the first widespread means of interactive communication at a distance, thereby transforming American business and social life. It operated as a patent monopoly until Bell's two telephone patents expired in 1893 and 1894. During this era, the company, with its affiliates and subsidiaries, concentrated on serving the most lucrative markets, primarily cities in the North and Midwest. After 1894, the company faced intense competition from thousands of independent companies throughout the country. With competition, the number of telephones boomed, from 285,000 in 1894 to 1,801,000 in 1901. AT&T itself was formed in 1885 as a subsidiary of the parent American Bell Telephone Company to create and operate the nation's original long-distance network. Building out from New York, AT&T reached its initial goal of connecting New York and Chicago in 1892. By 1901, AT&T's domain reached the Great Plains; a separate network served the west coast. On 31 December 1899, AT&T acquired the assets of American Bell and became the parent company of the Bell System. In 1913 the federal government sanctioned AT&T as the national telephone monopoly, a position it maintained until 1984.

Further Reading: John Brooks, *Telephone: The First Hundred Years*, 1976; Robert Garnet, *The Telephone Enterprise*, 1985.

Sheldon Hochheiser

AMERICAN WOMAN SUFFRAGE ASSOCIATION. The American Woman Suffrage Association (AWSA) was founded in 1869. The organization, created by Lucy Stone and Henry Blackwell to work for state-by-state franchise amendments, came as a result of a dispute about whether state or federal approaches to woman suffrage should be taken. As a result of the differing strategies, a growing tension between the AWSA and the National Woman Suffrage Association (NWSA) organizations developed until the two combined in 1890 to work toward both approaches simultaneously. Blackwell even assured southern legislators that they could support woman suffrage because it would numerically strengthen white supremacy.

Further Reading: Marjorie Spruill Wheeler, *New Women of the New South: The Leaders of the Woman Suffrage Movement in the Southern States*, 1993.

Ann Mauger Colbert

AMES, OAKES. (10 January 1804–8 May 1873), capitalist, manufacturer, politician. Born in North Easton, Massachusetts, Ames took over and expanded his father's shovel-making business. By 1850 he had become a Free Soiler and a director of the Emigrant Aid Society. Highly regarded for his business expertise, Ames was elected to Congress in 1862, serving until 1873. He and his brother became involved in the Crédit Mobilier scandal to construct the Union Pacific Railroad. One of his improper acts involved selling discounted shares to his fellow members of Congress. The *New York Sun* called him "the King of Frauds," but Ames contended his motives were purely patriotic. Most investigative boards concluded he had not contemplated bribery, but merely followed the business tactics of his times. Ames received a large reception when he returned home to constituents. In ill health and suffering financial reverses, he was stricken by pneumonia and died in North Easton.

Further Reading: J. A. Garfield, *Review of the Transactions of the Credit Mobilier*, 1873; J. B. Crawford, *The Credit Mobilier of America*, 2 vols., 1880–1881; *New York Times*, 11 May 1873.

Nicholas C. Polos

ANGELL, JAMES BURRILL (7 January 1829–1 April 1916), journalist, educator, and diplomat. Born in Scituate, Rhode Island, Angell was educated in local schools and graduated from Brown University in 1849. In 1866 he became president of the University of Vermont, where he served for five years. In 1871 he left to serve as president of the University of Michigan, remaining until 1909. There he helped expand the curriculum, broaden the range of elective studies, and allow enrollment of African Americans (1868) and women (1870). He also established the nation's first medical school requirements (1874), the first American chair in the science and art of teaching (1879), and the first instruction in forestry (1882). Angell also wrote *Progress in International Law* (1875), edited other books, and penned essays and articles.

In addition, Angell served as a diplomat on several occasions. As U.S. minister to China in 1880–1881, he helped negotiate immigration and commercial treaties, both of which led to the Chinese Exclusion Act of 1882. In 1887, President Grover Cleveland asked Angell to serve with Secretary of State Thomas F. Bayard and William L. Putnam of Maine on the Anglo-American Northeastern Fisheries Commission to negotiate a North Atlantic fishing rights agreement. Although the Senate rejected it, a modus vivendi using its terms was reached with Canada. Finally, as minister to Turkey in 1897–1898, Angell helped preserve Turkish neutrality in the Spanish-American War. Angell died at his Ann Arbor, Michigan, residence.

Further Reading: James Burrill Angell, *Reminiscences*, 1912; Wilfrid B. Shaw, ed., *From Vermont to Michigan: The Correspondence of James Burrill Angell, 1869–1871*, 1936; Shirley Wheeler Smith, *James Burrill Angell: An American Influence*, 1954.

Philip T. Heyn

ANSON, ADRIAN CONSTANTINE "CAP" (11 April 1852–14 April 1922), professional baseball player and manager. The first white child born in Marshalltown, Iowa, Anson, one of the greatest early professional baseball players, was elected to the Baseball Hall of Fame in 1939. Nicknamed "Cap," short for "captain," he played in the National Association from its inception in 1871 and in the National League after its formation in 1876. He had an exceptionally long twenty-seven-season career. Employing a split grip, he compiled a remarkable .333 lifetime batting average, hitting over .300 twenty-five times. He also won two batting crowns and eight RBI titles. Originally a third baseman, Anson later switched to first base; he was a notoriously bad fielder at both positions, making a record fifty-eight errors during the 1878 season. In 1879, he was named player-manager of the Chicago White Stockings, and led them to four pennants in six years. He is best known for devising the platoon system, and historians credit him with establishing the practice of spring training. He also was instrumental in the "gentleman's agreement" that barred African Americans from major league baseball until 1947. Fired by the White Stockings in 1897, Anson attempted unsuccessfully to organize a rival professional league, the American Association. He spent his remaining years performing in vaudeville shows and also served a term as a city clerk in Chicago, where he died.

Further Reading: Jerry E. Clark, *Anson to Zuber: Iowa Boys in the Major Leagues*, 1992.

Steve Bullock

ANTHONY, HENRY BOWEN (1 April 1815–2 September 1884), journalist, governor, and U.S. senator. Born in Coventry, Rhode Island, Anthony graduated from Brown University in 1833, edited and later owned the *Providence Journal* at the time of the Dorr Rebellion in 1842, and served as governor of Rhode Island from 1849 to 1851. From 1859 until his death in Providence, Rhode Island, Anthony held a seat in the U.S. Senate. A Republican, he was president pro tempore in the Forty-first, Forty-second, and Forty-third Congresses. He spent twenty-two years on the Public Printing Committee, and served on several others. Anthony strongly supported protective tariffs and a sound currency. With personal charm, gentlemanly conduct, and intellectual abilities, he acquired a reputation as a congenial colleague in the upper chamber and by the late 1870s and early 1880s had become known as the "Father of the Senate."

Further Reading: *Providence Journal*, 3 September 1884.

Leonard Schlup

ANTHONY, SUSAN BROWNELL (15 February 1820–13 March 1906), women's rights/suffrage leader. Born near Adams, Massachusetts, Anthony became more radical and active after the Fourteenth Amendment's ratification in 1868. The measure gave all persons born or naturalized in the United States citizenship rights. Although it targeted former slaves, Anthony interpreted its wording literally. In November 1872, she tested her own native citizenship by voting with fifteen other women in Rochester, New York. The action brought arrest, incarceration, and a hundred-dollar fine she never paid.

Anthony's women's rights campaigns led her to publish an unsuccessful newspaper, *The Revolution*. She had greater success with the first three volumes of *The History of Woman Suffrage*, a collection of contemporary documents that she feared might be lost. The fourth volume appeared in 1902, and the fifth and sixth after her death. She died in Rochester, New York.

By the end of the nineteenth century, most women had not achieved voting rights. Many of the other reforms Anthony had championed were beginning to display promise, however. Indeed, women were beginning to succeed in many professional fields. Such second- and third-generation "advanced" women displayed their appreciation by referring to her as "Aunt Susan." Although she never voted legally, her motto, "failure is impossible," displayed her faith in her cause.

Further Reading: Kathleen Barry, *Susan B. Anthony: A Biography*, 1988; Alma Lutz, "Susan Brownell Anthony," in *Notable American Women*, ed. Edward T. and Janet James, 1971.

Ann Mauger Colbert

ANTI-CHINESE RIOT OF 1871. During the nineteenth century, Chinese immigrants settled the West, where corporations welcomed their reluctance to unionize. In California, white racism combined with fear the Chinese would depress wages in mining, agriculture, and food services, and on the railroads. Labor leaders and racial purists had little trouble whipping up popular agitation over the odors, gambling, and prostitution in Chinese camps. During the Civil War, California governor Leland Stanford led a crusade to ban Chinese immigration, but his proposal did not go far enough for xenophobes.

Tensions peaked in 1871, when rival Chinese gangs in Los Angeles clashed. Police attempted to stop the fight, but the gangs shot at them, wounding several and killing one civilian. News of the shootings galvanized whites to attack the Chinese district. In a daylong orgy of violence, whites shot or lynched eight Chinese and burned their homes and shops. Violence did not end here. The depression of 1873 led whites to renew their attacks on the Chinese, which continued throughout the decade.

Further Reading: Betty Lee Sung, *The Story of the Chinese in America*, 1967.

Christopher Cumo

ANTI-IMPERIALISM. The American anti-imperialist movement was well-educated and bipartisan, and centered in New England. Its members included writers, intellectuals, businessmen, politicians, labor leaders, and authors. Among the more famous were Carl Schurz, Andrew Carnegie, Grover Cleveland, William Jennings Bryan, Thomas B. Reed, Benjamin Harrison, Mark Twain, Samuel Gompers, and Jane Addams.

The incongruity between imperialism and traditional American values formed the core position of the anti-imperialists. They saw the appropriation of other lands and peoples as the antithesis of the nation's democratic mission. They considered territorial acquisition illegal, unprecedented, and without constitutional authority. In addition, they feared the requisite growth of military force needed to take, protect, and defend overseas possessions.

The anti-imperialists viewed continental expansion differently. National growth, they argued, had necessitated prior land acquisitions. Moreover, the areas had been sparsely populated, were eventually settled by American citizens, and were admitted to the union as territories and states. Hawaii's annexation in July 1898, and that of Guam, Puerto Rico, and the Philippines after the Spanish-American War, precipitated the founding of the Anti-Imperialist League in Boston, Massachusetts, in November 1898. Other leagues and associations were organized, and eventually their membership swelled to 700,000. The league members lectured, wrote, published newspapers and leaflets, and spread their message across the United States. They were, however, as racist in their arguments as their opponents. Anti-imperialists feared the importation of cheap, foreign laborers and the possibility of their becoming U.S. citizens.

Events in the Philippines, especially the bloody, three-year war fought against the Insurrectos, vindicated the anti-imperialist position. The increase in troop numbers and the loss of life on both sides was exactly what some anti-imperialists had prophesied. The League was, however, despite its protests, unable to deter American entry into World War I in 1917. The League disbanded on 27 November 1920.

Further Reading: E. Berkley Tompkins, *Anti-Imperialism in the United States*, 1970; Robert L. Beisner, *Twelve Against Empire: The Anti-Imperialists, 1898–1900*, 1968; Christopher Lasch, *The World of Nations*, 1973.

Michael W. Vogt

ANTI-IMPERIALIST LEAGUE. Founded in Boston, Massachusetts, in November 1898 to protest the treaty ending the Spanish-American War, the League united a diverse group of Americans who opposed the acquisition of colonies. Boasting a membership that included Andrew Carnegie, William Jennings Bryan, Samuel Gompers, and Mark Twain, the League especially protested the acquisition of the Philippines. The group's arguments reflected its diversity: democracies should not subjugate other peoples; non-Anglo peoples would corrupt America; and formal colonies were unconstitutional and costly. Anti-imperialists in the U.S. Senate narrowly failed to block ratification of the Treaty of Paris (1899) and the annexation of the Philippines. Yet the action ultimately soured American opinion on formal colonization after the United States spent three years fighting Filipino nationalists in a war that took the lives of more than 5,000 American soldiers and 200,000 Filipinos.

Further Reading: Robert Beisner, *Twelve Against Empire: The Anti-Imperialists, 1898–1900*, 1968; E. Berkeley Tompkins, *Anti-Imperialism in the United States*, 1970.

John D. Coats

ANTI-ITALIAN RIOT of 1891. During the nineteenth century a scarcity of work in Italy led Italians to come to the United States in large numbers for the first time. They did not assimilate easily into American culture, however. The Protestant majority suspected them of being loyal to the pope. Americans who drank beer or whiskey mocked Italians for drinking wine. Public education advocates disliked their support of parochial schools.

Italians could turn to the Mafia for protection from nativists, but it displayed little regard for law. When the New Orleans police chief, who had investigated the Mafia, was murdered in 1890, police arrested nineteen Italians. Despite evidence of guilt, their trial ended in acquittal. In response, attorney William Parkerson urged a crowd of 6,000 that gathered after the trial to use vigilantism where justice had failed. Fifty stormed the jail and killed eleven of the nineteen who had been kept there for safety. Three of the dead were Italian citizens. In protest, their government recalled the Italian ambassador. To make amends, the United States paid Italy 125,000 lire, but the violence did not end. Nativists in Louisiana murdered three more Italians in 1896 and another five in 1899.

Further Reading: Philip M. Rose, *The Italians in America*, 1922.

Christopher Cumo

ANTI-MONOPOLY PARTY.

ANTI-MONOPOLY PARTY. Established in Chicago in 1884 by the Anti-Monopoly Organization of the United States, this third party reflected the growing number of local minor parties formed in reaction to Gilded Age conditions. At the national convention held in the Hershey Music Hall in Chicago on 14 May 1884, to which seventeen states sent representatives, delegates approved a platform urging the national government to regulate interstate commerce and curtail monopoly power. They wanted corporations to be placed under legal regulations, and favored greater cooperation between labor and capital as well as arbitration to resolve disputes. Anti-Monopolists advocated an interstate commerce law, the direct election of federal senators, reduced public expenditures, the establishment of bureaus of labor statistics, a graduated income tax, elimination of grants of public lands to corporations, and terminating foreign contract labor.

Delegates nominated the wealthy Benjamin F. Butler of Massachusetts as the party's presidential standard-bearer. A vociferous Radical Republican and unrelenting critic of President Andrew Johnson, Butler had served in the House of Representatives from 1867 to 1875, and again as a Greenbacker from 1877 to 1879. In 1882, after numerous earlier attempts, he succeeded in winning the governorship of Massachusetts. Butler's vice presidential running mate in 1884 was Absolom Madden West of Mississippi, a former Confederate and a railroad president, who embraced the Greenback-Labor movement. The Butler-West ticket polled 175,370 votes (less than 2 percent of the popular vote), losing the contest to the New York Democrat Grover Cleveland. Most Anti-Monopolists later joined the Populist Party.

Further Reading: Earl R. Kruschke, *Encyclopedia of Third Parties in the United States*, 1991.

Leonard Schlup

ANTI-SALOON LEAGUE.

ANTI-SALOON LEAGUE. The Anti-Saloon League (ASL), the first modern political pressure group, transformed the temperance movement. In the 1890s, despite two generations of prohibition agitation, the temperance movement lay in the doldrums. The existing political structure stymied prohibition progress and the liquor industry, through the urban saloon, was becoming more established in American life. In 1893, Howard Hyde Russell, unhappy that the partisan approach of the Prohibition Party and the Woman's Christian Temperance Union (WCTU) had not brought dry progress, organized the Ohio Anti-Saloon League. Two years later the League federated itself into a national organization.

The League differed dramatically from the Prohibition Party and WCTU in organization, political style, and approach. Whereas the former were democratic and open, the League was bureaucratic and secretive; whereas they favored voluntarism, it rapidly professionalized. They were uncompromising and visionary, but the ASL was opportunistic and pragmatic. They sought total national prohibition, while the ASL welcomed lesser anti-liquor measures. Most important, whereas the Prohibition Party and WCTU challenged the political order, the ASL worked within its existing structure. Under Russell's leadership (1895–1903), the League perfected its omni-partisan and limited-means approach. Styling itself "the church in action against the saloon," the ASL organized Protestants (especially Methodists, Baptists, Presbyterians, and Congregationalists) into a political voting bloc. It then used that voting bloc to favor legislators and officials, regardless of party affiliation, who would support League plans. It also threatened and punished politicians who opposed ASL programs. Invariably, the League worked almost exclusively within the two major political parties. In this period its measures consisted of enforcement of existing regulations on the liquor trade and the adoption of local option prohibition. Before the turn of the twentieth century, the League approach began to work, and it grew while the Prohibition Party shrank. Significantly, in 1897 the WCTU began cooperation with the ASL. Thus, by the end of the first decade of the twentieth century, the ASL dominated the temperance movement and was well positioned to engineer national prohibition's creation.

Further Reading: K. Austin Kerr, *Organized for Prohibition: A New History of the Anti-Saloon League*, 1985; Peter Odegard, *Pressure Politics: The Story of the Anti-Saloon League*, 1928; Thomas R. Pegram, *Battling Demon Rum: The Struggle for a Dry America, 1800–1933*, 1998.

Richard F. Hamm

ARBOR DAY. The idea for Arbor Day is credited to J. Sterling Morton, a newspaper editor, farmer, and secretary of agriculture in the second administration of Grover Cleveland. On 4 January 1872, Morton, in an address before the Nebraska State Horticultural Society, suggested setting aside a day to plant trees, hedges, and orchards. The state agricultural board agreed, and that same day designated 10 April as Arbor Day. Two years later the board passed a resolution memorializing the governor, annually, to require the public to plant forest, fruit, and ornamental trees.

Other states followed Nebraska's lead. Kansas and Tennessee adopted Arbor Day in 1875; North Dakota and Ohio did so in 1882. In 1885 Nebraska made Arbor Day a legal holiday. By 1888 some thirty states and territories celebrated Arbor Day. The idea also found favor abroad. In 1896 Spain adopted it, and Italy did so in 1902.

Celebrations became especially popular in the public schools. Indeed, ceremonies surrounding tree planting stimulated a new conservationist sensibility among America's children and aroused the nation's interest in the deforestation problem.

Further Reading: Leigh Eric Schneider, "From Arbor Day to the Environmental Sabbath: Nature, Liturgy, and American Protestantism," *Harvard Theological Review* 84 [1991]: 299–323; Richard C. Davies, ed., *Encyclopedia of American Forest and Conservation* [1983], 21–23; James C. Olsen, "A Pioneer Expression of Concern for Environment," *Nebraska History* 53 [1972]: 6–13.

Richard Harmond

ARCHITECTURE. During the Gilded Age, American architecture achieved international significance. It began with the Romanesque revival of Henry Hobson Richardson; included the work of Richard Morris Hunt, Frank Furness, Daniel Burnham, John Wellborn Root, and Louis Sullivan; and culminated with the early work of Frank Lloyd Wright and the Classical Revival of C. F. McKim, W. R. Mead, and Stanford White. The era also saw the of establishment of schools of architecture within the United States, the first being at the Massachusetts Institute of Technology in 1868. Architects were influenced by and educated at the Ecole des Beaux-Arts in Paris, and became known to the general public.

Structural experimentation resulting in the skyscraper became America's single greatest contribution to international architecture. Previously, building height was limited due to vertical transportation and building strength. Perfection of the elevator in the 1860s and mass production of steel made possible the increasing of building height within the crowded cities, especially New York and Chicago.

By the 1890s, in order to expedite building construction, architects adapted factory production. Houses of 1870–1880 were characterized by a juxtaposed arrangement of large halls, tight kitchens, and small bedrooms, resulting in eccentric exteriors. Many historical styles, including Renaissance, Second Empire, Queen Anne, Eastlake, Romanesque, Italiante, shingle style, Mission, Tudor, Norman, Georgian, and Classical Revival dominated the age. After the 1880s, American houses became monumental, ornate, and grand, reflecting immense wealth and extravagant fortunes.

The era also featured an explosion in the development of memorials, parks, and statues in the Victorian style, and the growth of company towns adjacent to mills in New England, and railroad and mines in the West. The railroad town was based on the ideas of George Pullman (Pullman, Illinois, 1880). City streets were made of macadam, cobblestone, and granite. From 1885 on, asphalt became the modern street surface.

Further Reading: David P. Handlin, *American Architecture*, 1989; J. C. Palmes, *Sir Banister Fletcher's A History of Architecture*, 1975; Spiro Kostof, *America by Design*, 1987.

Ralph G. Giordano

ARCHULETA, DIEGO (27 March 1814–21 March 1884), political and military leader in New Mexico. Born in Alcalde, New Mexico, Archuleta held governmental positions for both Mexico and the United States. During the Civil War, he served the Union cause as a brigadier general in the New Mexico militia. In the 1850s, after New Mexico had become a U.S. territory, Archuleta championed local interests in the fourth, fifth and sixth legislative assemblies. He was elected to the Council (Senate) in 1863, and was reelected six times. A defender of his people's culture, institutions and territory, he died in office.

Further Reading: Maurilio E. Vigil, *Los Patrones: Profiles of Hispanic Political Leaders in New Mexico History*, 1980; David J. Weber, *Foreigners in Their Native Land: Historical Roots of the Mexican Americans*, 1973.

Santos C. Vega

ARMOUR, PHILIP DANFORTH. (16 May 1832–6 January 1901), meatpacker and grain dealer. Born in Stockbridge, New York, Armour attended public school there and Cazenovia Academy, mined gold in California, and opened a grocery business in Milwaukee, Wisconsin. He amassed a fortune by anticipating the collapse of pork prices with the Confederacy's imminent fall. He founded Armour & Company in Chicago in 1867, and soon made it one of the world's largest meatpacking enterprises. Armour concentrated slaughtering in Chicago, canned the meat on a large scale and transported fresh meat for export in refrigerated railroad cars. As a result, he helped transform the industry, and with Gustavus Swift, Nelson Morris, and G. D. Hammond, created a handful of giant meatpacking companies effectively able to deal with railroads, meat producers, labor, consumers, and competition. One of the nation's wealthiest men, he was distinguished for philanthropy. The Armour Institute of Technology, established at Chicago in 1892, later became the Illinois Institute of Technology.

Armour was successfully involved in a number of highly publicized contests for competitive advantage on Chicago commodity exchanges. In the Panic of 1893 he personally provided the financial credit needed to rescue the city's banks and municipal government, as well as the Chicago Exposition. Though eventually exonerated, Armour was reputedly dismayed by the 1898–1899 federal investigation of the quality of meat provided to the armed forces during the Spanish-American War. He died in Chicago a year and a half later.

Further Reading: Harper Leech and John Charles Carroll, *Armour and His Times*, 1938; Philip D. Armour, "The Packing Industry," in *One Hundred Years of American Commerce*, ed. Chauncey M. Depew, 1895; *New York Times*, 7 January 1901.

Charles W. Macune, Jr.

ART. The industrialism that transformed American life during the Gilded Age promoted developments in the fine arts. The period began with strong interest in the romantic tradition of the Hudson River School and significant work in portraiture, genre, and folk subjects. It closed with extensions of these traditions and subjects, as well as strong attachments to western European art. The American art scene thus retained a sense of the nation's special attributes and attitudes, while artists became increasingly cosmopolitan in their approaches and subjects.

A new generation of well-trained artists, and enhanced support from the expanding middle class, as well as from government in decorating public buildings, sustained these developments. The National Academy of Design in New York City was principal guardian of the inherited traditions of both Europe and the United States. Every significant city, however, boasted artistic organizations. Artists could teach and study at prestigious schools such as the Art Students League in New York, the Pennsylvania Academy of Fine Arts in Philadelphia, or similar facilities elsewhere. A new generation, determined to be in the international mainstream, studied in Munich, London, Paris, or some other art center. They learned technique and encountered societies that valued the arts as enterprises and as counterweights to materialism.

The number of artists and the quantity of their production increased dramatically in painting, sculpture, design, and allied arts. Sales never equaled production, but exhibitions and competitions appeared almost everywhere. Many artists worked in enterprises that industrialism had created or enhanced, such as illustrating books and magazines, designing home furnishings, and decorating buildings. Quality criticism in the public press, magazines aimed at the influential middle class, and specialty art journals explained art to a widening audience. The general focus was on the cultural roles of the arts as well as on skill.

The nation's increasing wealth and growing knowledge of the arts supported major museums. No city considered itself important or in the mainstream unless it had art collections. These institutions were dedicated to displaying cross sections of different kinds of art, to accumulating special holdings, and to educating the public about the arts' roles in civic and personal life. Collectors began to endow museums and teaching institutions with both funds and the fruits of their interests. These individuals were generally cosmopolitan, with collections of antiquities, coins and medals, sculpture, books and manuscripts, and Asian art, as well as both old masters and contemporary European and American painting.

The nation greatly benefited from the determination of many groups and individuals to make American art, museums, and art educational facilities the equal of any other nation's, and a force in world aesthetics.

Further Reading: H. Wayne Morgan, *New Muses: Art in American Culture, 1865–1920*, 1978; Brooklyn Museum, *The American Renaissance, 1876–1917*, 1979.

H. Wayne Morgan

ARTHUR, CHESTER ALAN (5 October 1829–17 November 1886), vice president and president. Born in Fairfield, Vermont, Arthur graduated from Union College in 1848. After teaching in secondary schools in Vermont and New York State, he practiced law in New York City. During the Civil War he held the ranks of engineer in chief, inspector general, and quartermaster general of the New York State militia. From 1863 to 1871, he rose steadily in state Republican ranks, becoming a leading protégé of Senator Roscoe Conkling, who headed the Stalwart wing of the party. In 1871 President Ulysses S. Grant appointed him collector of the New York Customhouse, the greatest source of patronage in the entire nation. Seven years later, however, President Rutherford B. Hayes

suspended him, charging that operations at the Customhouse were corrupt and inefficient. Personally his life was marred with tragedy; when he was thirty-four, a son died; when he was fifty, his wife.

In 1880 the Republican Party nominated Arthur to be the running mate of James A. Garfield of Ohio, doing so in order to appease the Stalwarts. Arthur, who coordinated scores of rallies, might well have been the first "advance man" in American history. He also launched a secret fund aimed at securing a Republican victory in Indiana, a "swing" state. Once elected vice president, Arthur supported Conkling, then involved in a major patronage dispute with Garfield. When, on 19 September 1881, Garfield succumbed to an assassin's bullet, Arthur became president.

Thereafter, Arthur broke with the Stalwarts. Certain of his appointments were deemed strong. The highly respected Frederick T. Frelinghuysen, for instance, became secretary of state. Other appointments, such as William E. Chandler as secretary of the navy, were judged by reformers as continuations of the spoils system. In the star route frauds, a Post Office Department scandal, the defendants were found innocent, a verdict that greatly embarrassed Arthur. In his first State of the Union Address, he called for civil service reform, though only after the Democrats captured the House of Representatives in 1882 was the cause taken seriously. On 18 January 1883, Arthur signed the Pendleton Act, which provided for a five-member Civil Service Examination Board and competitive examinations for selected federal employees.

In 1882, Arthur signed the Chinese Exclusion Act, banning the entry of Chinese laborers into the United States for ten years. He appointed a tariff commission in the hope of depoliticizing a highly partisan issue, although the resulting tariff of 1883 embodied little reform. He promoted modernization of the U.S. Navy, presiding over the construction of the nation's first steel-plated cruisers and the creation of the Naval War College at Newport, Rhode Island. Foreign policy failures included the inability to mediate a conflict between Peru and Chile, to block German and French bans on American pork, to secure a treaty with Nicaragua giving the United States co-ownership of a canal there, and to institute reciprocal trade with Mexico, Cuba, Puerto Rico, and Santo Domingo.

As president Arthur always conducted himself regally, focusing on the ceremonial and the symbolic. He seldom worked an entire day; much of his apparent lethargy was caused by Bright's disease, a fatal kidney ailment. In 1884 he made a nominal bid for a second term, realizing that reluctance would raise suspicions about his health, competency, and courage. After leaving the White House, he moved to New York City, formally serving as counsel to his old law firm while in reality becoming an invalid. He died in New York City.

Further Reading: David M. Pletcher, *The Awkward Years: American Foreign Policy Under Garfield and Arthur*, 1962; Thomas C. Reeves, *Gentleman Boss: The Life of Chester Alan Arthur*, 1975; Justus D. Doenecke, *The Presidencies of James A. Garfield and Chester A. Arthur*, 1981.

Justus D. Doenecke

ARTHUR, ELLEN LEWIS HERNDON (30 August 1837–12 January 1880), wife of President Chester A. Arthur. Born in Culpepper County, Virginia, Ellen Herndon married Chester A. Arthur, an ambitious New York politician, on 25 October 1859. They had three children (their first son died in infancy). Chester enjoyed political and financial success. Ellen supported her husband's career, although she often felt lonely when politics forced them apart. She enjoyed the finest fashions from London, was active in charities, and was a capable hostess. A gifted vocalist, Ellen performed in public. The Arthurs stood on opposite sides of the Civil War. While Chester served as quartermaster general of the New York State militia, Ellen supported the South and had relatives who owned slaves. Arthur jokingly called Ellen his "little rebel wife." This was one of many contentious issues in their marriage, and their differences caused them to consider separating. In January 1880, while her husband was in Albany, New York, Ellen attended a concert in New York City. She caught pneumonia and died a few days later, at age forty-two. Roughly eighteen months later, President James Garfield was assassinated, and Vice President Chester

Arthur entered the White House. His sister Mary Arthur McElroy served as social hostess. He grieved the loss of Ellen, having flowers placed daily next to her portrait and donating a stained glass window to St. John's Episcopal Church in Washington, D.C., in her memory.

Further Reading: Thomas C. Reeves, *Gentleman Boss: The Life of Chester Alan Arthur*, 1975; Robert P. Watson, *First Ladies of the United States*, 2000.

Robert P. Watson

ASPINWALL, WILLIAM HENRY (16 December 1807–18 January 1875), merchant. Born in New York City, Aspinwall was educated at Bancel's Boarding College, where he gained fluency in French and Spanish that he later used in business. He headed Howland and Aspinwall, an international import-export firm, and established the Pacific Mail Steamship Company, which contracted to carry U.S. mail to San Francisco via the Isthmus of Panama. Growing out of this venture was the Panama Railroad. Until the Union Pacific was completed in 1869, Panama was the quickest route between the east and west coasts of the United States. Aspinwall reaped enormous financial rewards, retiring as one of the nation's richest men. He quietly enjoyed his wealth and came to be called the "merchant prince." He represented the rising mercantile aristocracy that established lavish country seats, supported civic and philanthropic interests, and fostered cultural appreciation. In his leisure time Aspinwall traveled and developed a keen interest in fine art. He displayed his prized collection of the great masters to the public in an annex of his townhouse. Later he helped establish the Metropolitan Museum of Art and became a trustee of the Lenox Library, which merged into the New York Public Library. Aspinwall died in New York City.

Further Reading: Duncan S. Somerville, *The Aspinwall Empire*, 1983; John Haskell Kemble, *The Panama Route 1848–1869*, 1943; "The Aspinwall Gallery," *Harper's Weekly*, 26 February 1859.

Janet Butler Munch

ASTOR, JOHN JACOB IV (13 July 1864–15 April 1912), army officer and hotel magnate. Astor was born in Rhinebeck, New York, heir to the family fortune established by his great-grandfather, the fur trader John Jacob Astor. Astor attended St. Paul's School in Concord, New Hampshire, and graduated from Harvard in 1888. A mechanical inventor, he won the first prize at the World Columbian Exhibition in Chicago in 1893 for his pneumatic road improver, which removed dirt from roads, and in 1894 he established himself as an author with his science fiction novel *Journey in Other Worlds*. In 1897 Astor established the Waldorf-Astoria hotel in New York City with his cousin William Waldorf, and furthered his hotel interests when he built the St. Regis Hotel (1904) and the Knickerbocker Hotel (1906). He began a military career in 1895 with peacetime service as a member of New York Governor Levi P. Morton's military staff. In 1898 Astor fought in the Spanish-American War as a lieutenant colonel and was promoted to colonel at the close of the war. He was the wealthiest passenger to die in the sinking of the *Titanic* in 1912.

Further Reading: Lucy Kavaler, *The Astors: A Family Chronicle of Pomp and Power*, 1966.

Lisa De Palo

ATKINSON, WILLIAM YATES (11 November 1854–8 August 1899), governor of Georgia. Born in Oakland, Georgia, Atkinson grew up in a large farm family. He attended public schools before entering the University of Georgia. After graduation, he studied law and was admitted to the bar.

Appointed county solicitor by Governor Alfred H. Colquitt, Atkinson was subsequently elected to the Georgia state legislature in 1886. He served there for eight years. Atkinson championed educational reform and bills making the office of commissioner of agriculture elective, placing the telegraph and express companies under the regulative control of the railroad commission, limiting the pay of oil inspectors to $1,500 a year, and creating the state college for women at Milledgeville. Soon he emerged as a major figure in the state Democratic Party, and led it to victory over the combined efforts of the Populist and Republican parties in 1892. Defeating former Confederate general Clement A. Evans in the 1894 contest for governor, he became Georgia's chief executive at age forty. This was reportedly the first time in state his-

tory that a civilian had beaten a Confederate veteran. After an uneventful second term, Atkinson retired from public office in 1899. Resuming his law practice, he died just a few months later in Newnan, Georgia, at age forty-four.

Further Reading: William F. Northen, ed., *Men of Mark in Georgia*, 1908/1974; *Atlanta Constitution*, 9 August 1899.

Harvey Gresham Hudspeth

ATLANTA COMPROMISE. This was a concept and vision for the American South set out in a famous speech by Booker T. Washington at the Cotton States and International Exposition, held at Atlanta, Georgia, in 1895. After "Jim Crow" laws racially segregated public facilities in the American South, Washington, a leading African American and an ally of white southerners, pledged support to the "New South." He argued that African Americans should focus on economic uplift through industrial and vocational education, thereby helping the South rise to industrial and agricultural maturity. By so doing, Washington downplayed the need for civil and political rights for African Americans—the heart of the Reconstruction struggle and the program of Washington's key African-American opponent, W. E. B. Du Bois, who coined the term "Atlanta Compromise."

Further Reading: Booker T. Washington, *Up from Slavery*, 1901; C. Vann Woodward, *The Strange Career of Jim Crow*, 1955; *Origins of the New South, 1877–1913*, 1951.

Kevin Mattson

AUSTRALIAN BALLOT. After the presidential election of 1884, in which Grover Cleveland defeated James G. Blaine, concern for the integrity of the electoral process increased dramatically. The degree to which political parties controlled voting and elections drew special attention. At least one reaction was that by 1888, every state had adopted the Australian ballot. This marked perhaps the single most significant political change during the Gilded Age. Previously, votes were cast either by voice or through ballots printed and distributed in advance by the political parties. Designed to make one's choice apparent to observers, such as a local politician or an employer, the ballots used color coding or some other readily observable device. The situation encouraged voter fraud and coercion.

Use of the Australian ballot, so named because it was first implemented in Australia in the 1850s, meant that voting now would take place in private, and ballots would be cast in secret. Furthermore, those ballots would be printed and provided to voters in a nonpartisan manner by the government. Each ballot now included all candidates for office, not merely those of one party. For the first time voters could readily engage in split-ticket voting. The significance of this change is evidenced by the substantial increase in split-ticket voting after 1888.

Further Reading: Eldon Cobb Evans, *A History of the Australian Ballot System in the United States*, 1917; L. E. Fredman, *The Australian Ballot: The Story of an American Reform*, 1968.

Donald E. Greco

BABCOCK, ORVILLE ELIAS

(25 December 1835–2 June 1884), army general, engineer, and presidential private secretary. Born in Franklin, Vermont, Babcock was graduated from West Point in 1861. During the Civil War, he served as aide de camp to Ulysses S. Grant, and eventually rose to brigadier general. President Grant made Babcock his private secretary and, simultaneously, superintending engineer of buildings and grounds in Washington, D.C. Controversy marked Babcock's tenure in office. His 1869 inspection tour of the Dominican Republic, in response to local lobbyists, embarrassed the administration when Babcock exceeded orders and returned with an annexation treaty. A congressional investigation into the administration of Alexander R. Shepherd, governor of the District of Columbia, implicated Babcock in planting stolen documents on one of Shepherd's enemies. In 1875, Babcock was accused of complicity with the Whiskey Ring, which defrauded the Internal Revenue Service of excise taxes. He was acquitted of all charges, but a shadow of public doubt clouded Grant's administration, and the president reluctantly removed Babcock from his inner circle. Babcock's final position was chief inspector of lighthouses for the fifth and sixth districts. He drowned while inspecting a proposed lighthouse site in Mosquito Inlet, Florida.

Further Reading: William S. Mc Feely, *Grant: A Biography*, 1981; Mary E. Seematter, "The St. Louis Whiskey Ring," *Gateway Heritage* 8 (1988): 32–42; Orville E. Babcock Papers, Newberry Library, Chicago.

Janet Butler Munch

BACON, AUGUSTUS OCTAVIUS

(20 October 1839–14 February 1914), U.S. senator. Bacon was born in Bryan County, Georgia, graduated in 1859 from the University of Georgia, and practiced law in Atlanta. After serving in the Confederate Army, he settled in Macon, Georgia, and entered politics. From 1871 to 1886 he served in the Georgia House of Representatives, holding the post of speaker for eight years. Bacon failed narrowly in a gubernatorial bid in 1883. Between 1895 and 1914, Bacon was the first Georgian to serve three consecutive full terms in the U.S. Senate and the first elected directly by the people. An anti-imperialist, Bacon strongly opposed acquisition of the Philippines in 1899. He introduced a resolution, defeated by the vice president's tie-breaking vote, declaring the purpose of the United States was not permanently to retain the islands but to give the Filipinos their independence. The discussion on this resolution between Bacon and Senator John Coit Spooner, a Republican representing Wisconsin, constituted one of the great deliberative arguments in Senate history. An active participant in tariff cogitations, issues of foreign affairs, and matters of constitutional concern, Bacon emerged as an influential Gilded Age Southern Democrat. He died in Washington and bequeathed his home, "Baconsfield," to the city of Macon.

Further Reading: Lola Carr Steelman, "The Public Career of Augustus Octavius Bacon," Ph.D. diss., University of North Carolina at Chapel Hill, 1950; *New York Times*, 15 February 1914.

Leonard Schlup

BALTIMORE PLAN.

The currency question was one of the most contentious issues of the age. Bimetallists, monometallists, international bimetallic advocates, and others pleaded for their particular causes. Republicans and Democrats had their silver factions; the latter party split openly in 1896 between hard money adherents and supporters of silver. William Jennings Bryan's followers favored the free and unlimited coinage of silver at a ration of sixteen to one with gold, a philosophy repugnant to President Grover Cleveland. Another currency proposition was formulated in 1894 by a group of Baltimore bankers acting as an association. The Baltimore Plan proposed to amend the National Banking Act of 1863 so that it no longer required government bonds as security for circulation but instead provided a safety fund. The plan would allow banks to issue circulation to 50 percent of their paid-up, unimpaired capital. Notes of failed banks would be redeemed by the government. A guarantee equal to 5 percent of the outstanding circulation would be accumulated and maintained by gradual taxation upon such circulation. From this safety fund, the government could redeem notes of failed banks.

The Baltimore Plan had nothing to do with the money of ultimate redemption, whether gold, silver, or greenbacks. It simply provided a banknote currency redeemable in lawful money. Free silverites severely criticized this proposal because it did not utilize silver. Because the Constitution empowered Congress with the authority to coin money and regulate its value, proponents of the Baltimore Plan believed that elasticity embodied in the safety fund principle would produce an expansion of commercial interests. They also contended that national relief from the vexatious and injurious currency agitation would result from the adoption of a system that would relieve banks from unreasonable restrictions. Among those who endorsed the Baltimore Plan was Alonzo Barton Hepburn, president of the Third National Bank of New York and former U.S. bank examiner for New York and comptroller of the currency.

Further Reading: Alonzo B. Hepburn, "The 'Baltimore Plan' of Currency Reform," *The Forum* 18 (1894): 385–395.

Leonard Schlup

BANCROFT, GEORGE (3 October 1800–17 January 1891), author, historian, and diplomat. Bancroft was born in Worcester, Massachusetts, graduated from Harvard College in 1817, and studied for the ministry in Europe. He received a doctorate from the Georgia Augusta University in Göttingen, Germany, in 1820. He returned to the United States in 1822. Bancroft taught, wrote articles for the *North American Review*, and began publishing his monumental *History of the United States*. He aligned himself with the Democratic Party and ultimately moved to Boston. Bancroft served as President

James K. Polk's secretary of the navy and later was ambassador to Great Britain (1846–1849). He voted for President Abraham Lincoln in the election of 1864 and supported the reconstruction policies of President Andrew Johnson, under whom he served as U.S. minister to Prussia from 1867 to 1874. There he defended the programs of Chancellor Otto von Bismarck. Upon returning to the United States, Bancroft settled in Washington, D.C. In 1885, he was elected president of the American Historical Association, in recognition of his commitment to history and his substantial scholarship. He died in Washington, D.C.

Further Reading: Robert H. Canary, *George Bancroft*, 1974; Lillian Handlin, *George Bancroft, the Intellectual as Democrat*, 1984.

Leonard Schlup

BANDELIER, ADOLPH FRANCIS ALPHONSE (6 August 1840–18 March 1914), explorer, anthropologist, and historian. Born in Bern, Switzerland, Bandelier immigrated to Illinois in 1848. Seven years later, he began his study of geology at the University of Bern. In 1880, the Archaeological Institute of America commissioned Bandelier to conduct research expeditions in the territories of New Mexico and Arizona. He stayed there until 1889. His explorations, generally accomplished on foot, covered a vast range of territory. While living for a time with the Pueblos, Bandelier studied their life and customs. He revealed the results of his work in various publications in the 1890s. Bandelier died in Seville, Spain. Two years after his death, the Pueblo ruins in the canyon of Rito de los Frijoles near Los Alamos, New Mexico, were established as the Bandelier National Monument in his honor.

Further Reading: F. W. Hodge, "Adolph Francis Alphonse Bandelier," *American Anthropologist* 16 (1914): 349–358.

Leonard Schlup

BANKING. The National Banking Act of 1863 governed banking in the United States during the Gilded Age. It created a system of free banking by independent units subject to only a few general legal requirements. Institutions chartered as national banks had to be capitalized at $50,000 or more. They were allowed to deposit with the comptroller of the currency federal bonds, in return for national banknotes equal to 90 percent of their value. This arrangement assured a federal bond market and established the first uniform national currency. Encouraged by a 10 percent annual tax on their note issues, state banks sought national charters. No branch banks were permitted.

Under this system, banking lacked coherence. Reserves were scattered in designated reserve cities, and sometimes pyramided. The new currency system was inelastic and unresponsive to business needs. Circulation contracted during trade expansions, for when interest rates rose in reply to increased demand for currency, prices of fixed-return bonds fell to keep rates competitive. Banks then returned their notes to the comptroller, withdrew their bonds, and sold them to avert further losses in a falling market. Such sales forced prices even lower and interest rates even higher. The reverse occurred when trade contracted. Tight credit during harvest season was usual. The bank-note supply was critical only in rural areas; elsewhere 90 percent of trade was conducted with checks. When loss of confidence in banks coincided with currency shortages, however, runs and bank failures could occur, precipitating recession.

Further Reading: Milton Friedman and Anna Jacobson Schwartz, *A Monetary History of the United States, 1867–1960*, 1960; Alexander Dana Noyes, *Forty Years of American Finance*, 1906; Fritz Redlich, *The Molding of American Banking: Men and Ideas*, 1951.

Douglas Steeples

BANNOCK WAR OF 1878. Increasingly constricted on the Fort Hall reservation in Idaho, some Bannocks, traditionally a migratory people, turned to violence in May 1878 when whites invaded their lands in the Camas Prairie. Led by the enterprising chief Buffalo Horn, they were joined by Cayuses, Umatillas, Wallawallas, and, most important, Paiutes from the Malheur reservation under chiefs Egan and Oytes. At its peak, the Indian force numbered close to a thousand.

The Native Americans were divided, however, with such important figures as Winnemucca and his daughter Sarah arguing for peace. Moreover, the coalition suffered a crippling blow when Buffalo Horn died in a skirmish on 8 June. Then on 23 June the First Cavalry defeated the Indians at Harvey Lake. Over the next two months, Egan was killed and Oytes was captured. Dispirited, the remnants of the group scattered. A few Bannocks heading for Canada attacked Dr. F. V. Hayden's survey team in far northeastern Idaho; escaping Paiutes raided Chinese miners on the Salmon River. Pursued by Crows and U.S. cavalry, the last Bannock-Paiute fugitives decided to surrender on 12 September at Dry Fork, in Wyoming.

In all, the war had cost the lives of nine soldiers, twenty-four white civilians, and, by one count, seventy-eight Indians. In a poignant assessment, General George Crook noted that some Bannocks, faced with starvation, understandably chose death on the warpath instead.

Further Reading: George F. Brimlow, *The Bannock Indian War of 1878*, 1938; Frederick A. Mark, "The Bannock Indian War of 1878," in *Great Western Indian Fights*, edited by B. W. Allred et al., 1960; Robert H. Ruby and John A. Brown, *Indians of the Pacific Northwest: A History*, 1981.

Malcolm Muir, Jr.

BARBER, OHIO COLUMBUS (20 April 1841–4 February 1920), businessman and inventor. Born in Middlebury, Ohio (later annexed by Akron), Barber was educated in local schools and entered his father's match manufacturing business at age sixteen. The younger Barber's gift for sales and business acumen transformed the company from a small storefront operation to a nationally important manufacturing concern. It was incorporated as the Barber Match Company in 1868, and by 1881 it had become the Diamond Match Company, absorbing twenty-eight rivals. Within a decade, however, a tax dispute with the city of Akron spurred Barber to plan his own nearby community, named Barberton, around a deep natural lake. Diamond's manufacturing operations were moved to the new community, and the firm became the largest employer. Barber invested in and directed several banks and at least seven other corporations, and served as the Akron Chamber of Commerce's first president.

Further Reading: Karl H. Grismer, *Akron and Summit County*, 1952; Samuel A. Lane, *Fifty Years and Over of*

Akron and Summit County, 1892; Scott Dix Kenfield, *Akron and Summit County, Ohio, 1825–1928*, 1928.

Stephen Paschen

BARBONCITO (1820–16 March 1871), Navajo tribal leader. Born at Canyon de Chelly in what is now Arizona, Barboncito, known as "the Orator," was a military and religious figure. A major chief during the 1863–1866 Navajo War, he was taken prisoner, in September 1864, at his birthplace by troops under Colonel Christopher "Kit" Carson. Forced to resettle at Bosque Redondo in eastern New Mexico, following a trek known as the "Long Walk" (350 miles), Barboncito and his people endured unbearable living conditions. In June 1865, he escaped with approximately five hundred followers. Later he journeyed to the nation's capital, where he met President Andrew Johnson and expressed Native American concerns. On 1 June 1868 Barboncito was one of the Navajo leaders who negotiated a treaty with the United States that permitted the Navajos to return to their homeland and established the Navajo reservation in New Mexico and Arizona. At the time, General William Tecumseh Sherman appointed Barboncito principal chief of the Navajo tribe. Barboncito eloquently articulated his stand when he told the federal government: "I hope to God you will not ask me to go to any other country than my own. We do not want to go to the right or left, but straight back to our country." He died at Canyon de Chelly.
Further Reading: Peter Iverson, *The Navajos*, 1990; Dana Coolidge and Mary Roberts Coolidge, *The Navajo Indians*, 1930; Raymond Friday Locke, *The Book of the Navajo*, 1992.

Leonard Schlup

BARELA, CASIMIRO (4 March 1847–December 1920), businessman, state senator. Barela was born at Embudo, New Mexico. In 1867, his family moved to southern Colorado, where he engaged in livestock raising and in merchandising. Later, he held extensive properties in New Mexico and owned a large cattle operation in Colorado. In 1869 Barela was elected justice of the peace. Thereafter he served as county assessor, territorial legislator, and sheriff of Las Animas County. In 1875, he was a delegate to the state constitutional convention.

Barela championed the causes of his Hispanic constituents and won election to the first Colorado state senate in 1876. He served in that post without a break for forty years and became known as the perpetual senator of Colorado.
Further Reading: Charles S. Vigil, *This Side Down, Up: The Saga of Casimino Barela*, 1977; Timothy O'Connor, *Proceedings of the Constitutional Convention, Colorado, 1875–1876*, 1907.

Santos C. Vega

BARKER, WHARTON (1 May 1846–8 April 1921), financier, writer, and Populist leader. Born in Philadelphia, Pennsylvania, Barker attended public schools there and, in 1866, was graduated from the University of Pennsylvania. For years he was a member of the banking firm of Barker Bothers and Company. In the late 1870s, he spent time in Russia and the Orient, promoting development of coal and iron mines. In 1880, interested in domestic political, social, and economic questions, Barker began publishing *The American*, a weekly periodical. A nominal Republican, he opposed a third presidential term for Ulysses S. Grant, early advocated James A. Garfield's nomination in 1880, and eight years later favored selection of Benjamin Harrison as the GOP standard-bearer. Urging that the federal government issue "absolute" money, Barker supported bimetallism as a temporary solution to a complex financial problem. In 1896 he endorsed William Jennings Bryan for the presidency over William McKinley. Shortly thereafter he affiliated with the Populists, accepting most of their beliefs. In May 1900, at Cincinnati, Ohio, Barker emerged as the presidential nominee of the middle-of-the-road (anti-fusionist) faction of the Populist Party with Ignatius Donnelly of Minnesota as his running mate. They received 50,373 votes nationwide, carrying no states. Barker removed himself from politics after his defeat, but continued writing voluminously on social issues. He died in Philadelphia.
Further Reading: *New York Times*, 9 April 1921; *New York Tribune*, 9 April 1921.

Leonard Schlup

BARNUM, PHINEAS TAYLOR (5 July 1810–9 November 1891), author, circus owner, and showman. Barnum was born in Bethel,

Connecticut, and established himself as a premier showman in 1835 by exhibiting Joice Heth, purportedly George Washington's 160-year-old nurse. In 1842 he established the American Museum in New York. Through a blend of Yankee ingenuity, the Puritan work ethic, and highly developed self-promotion, he took it on the road by 1851. It quickly became the most popular show in the United States.

In 1871 Barnum, with Dan Costello and William C. Coup, launched Barnum's Great Traveling Museum, Menagerie, Caravan, Hippodrome and Circus. The show opened in Brooklyn, New York, under three acres of canvas and grossed $400,000 the first season. The next year Barnum purchased James Cooke's Hippotheatron, in Lent's Iron Building at Broadway and Fourteenth Street in the borough of Manhattan, then America's only permanent circus. By 1873 Barnum had the first three-ring circus, simply a hippodrome track around the other two rings. In 1881 his show added a third, separate ring. Combined briefly with Adam Forepaugh's circus in 1885, Barnum's circus boasted four rings, two stages, and an outer track around the lot.

In 1882 Barnum bought Jumbo, an African elephant, for $10,000, spent another $20,000 transporting him from London to America, and earned his money back in two weeks. Within six weeks, people had paid $336,000 to see the animal. A train killed Jumbo in 1885 at St. Thomas, Ontario. Jumbo's skeleton ended up in the Museum of Natural History, and his hide was stuffed for display at Tufts University in Medford, Massachusetts. In 1884 Barnum purchased Joung Taloung, a "sacred," "white" (actually mottled gray) Burmese elephant, an action that precipitated a propaganda battle in which Forepaugh whitewashed an elephant. The entire event contributed the phase "white elephant" to the American idiom.

In 1889 Al Bailey took the Barnum and Bailey Circus to England. At this Greatest Show on Earth tour, Barnum appeared twice daily. He became synonymous with his museum in his lifetime, and he continues to be synonymous with his American circus posthumously. Bailey sold half of his Forepaugh Circus interests in 1905 to Ringling Brothers. At Bailey's death in 1907, the Ringlings purchased all of Barnum and Bailey and took full control of the Forepaugh-Sells Circus. By 1898 the Ringling Brothers' Barnum and Bailey Circus tent accommodated fourteen thousand spectators at each performance. The single most read book (besides the Bible) in nineteenth-century America remains Barnum's autobiography, *Struggles and Triumphs* (1879). Barnum died in Bridgeport, Connecticut.

Further Reading: Howard Lovton, *The Golden Age of Circus*, 1997; P. T. Barnum, *Struggles and Triumphs*, or *Forty Years Recollection of PT Barnum*, 1981; Larry D. Griffin, "Barnumized Objects: P. T. Barnum, the American Museum and the Creation of Cultural Contexts," *Journal of Unconventional History*, 9, 2; 1998, 52–70.

Larry D. Griffin

BARTON, CLARA (25 December 1821–12 April 1912), "Angel of the Battlefield." Barton, born in Oxford, Massachusetts, is best known for her work on behalf of Union soldiers during the Civil War and her role as founder of the American Red Cross. After the war, Abraham Lincoln appointed Barton to help wives and families of missing soldiers find their loved ones. The work was exhausting and depressing, and on the advice of friends and relatives, Barton took an extended holiday in Europe. While there, however, she could not resist joining the International Red Cross during the Franco-Prussian War, and worked with that organization from 1870 to 1871. Upon returning to the United States in 1873, she sought to begin a branch of the Red Cross in the United States. This could be accomplished only upon U.S. acceptance of the Geneva Convention. For the next several years, Barton divided her energies between lobbying for the ratification of the convention, the women's suffrage movement, and publicizing the need for an American Red Cross. Once Congress accepted the convention in 1882, Barton threw herself wholeheartedly into making the Red Cross a success, serving a lengthy term as the organization's first president (1882–1904) and almost single-handedly funding its growth. This work was interrupted by a brief period as superintendent of the Massachusetts Reformatory for Women. The Red Cross, however remained Barton's true passion, and she pursued it adamantly until her death at Glen Echo, Maryland.

Further Reading: Elizabeth Brown Pryor, *Clara Barton: Professional Angel*, 1987.

Jessica Matthews

BASSETT, EBENEZER DON CARLOS (16 October 1833–1908), educator and diplomat. Bassett was born in Litchfield, Connecticut, of mixed black and white heritage. He attended Wesleyan Academy at Wilbraham, Massachusetts, was graduated with honors from Connecticut State Normal School, and attended Yale College. He then served as a principal and teacher at a black school for Quakers in Philadelphia. In 1869, President Ulysses S. Grant appointed Bassett U.S. minister to Haiti and the Dominican Republic, making him the first African-American diplomat. Bassett resigned in 1877 and returned to New Haven. From 1879 to 1888, he served as consul-general to Haiti in New York. When Frederick Douglass was appointed American minister to Haiti and the Dominican Republic in 1889, Bassett served as his interpreter and adviser. Bassett wrote a handbook on Haiti for the Pan American Union in 1902. He returned to Philadelphia, where he died of heart failure.

Further Reading: Lerone Bennett, *Before the Mayflower: A History of Black America*, 1988; Charles Wynes, "Ebenezer Don Carlos Bassett, America's First Black Diplomat," Pennsylvania History 51 (1984): 232–240; William S. McFeely, *Frederick Douglass*, 1991.

Abel A. Bartley

BATE, WILLIAM BRIMAGE (7 October 1826–9 March 1905), Tennessee governor and U.S. senator. Born in Castalian Springs, Tennessee, Bate received a rudimentary education in a log schoolhouse. After service in the Mexican War, he established a Democratic weekly newspaper and entered politics. Bate studied law at Cumberland University, was elected to the state house of representatives in 1848, and was chosen Nashville's district attorney in 1854. After declining nomination for Congress in 1859, he served as a Breckinridge elector in the 1860 presidential election. A Confederate regimental colonel, Bate was severely wounded at the battle of Shiloh. He refused to allow his leg to be amputated, and fought the rest of the war on crutches. Subsequently known as "Old Shiloh," he rose to major general.

Bate returned to law and politics in Nashville in 1865, was defeated in two U.S. Senate bids, then was elected governor in 1882. His most notable achievement was presiding over the final settlement of his state's post-Reconstruction debt controversy. Reelected to two two-year terms, Bate subsequently reached the Senate on his third try in 1886. Forming a close working relationship with a fellow Bourbon Democrat, Isham Harris, Bate won reelection three times and died in office in Washington, D.C.

Further Reading: *New York Times*, 10 March 1905; Leonard Schlup, "Imperialist Dissenter: William B. Bate and the Battle Against Territorial Acquisitions, 1898–1900," *Southern Studies* 6 (1995): 61–84.

Harvey Gresham Hudspeth

BATES, KATHARINE LEE (12 August 1859–28 March 1929), poet and professor. Bates was born in Falmouth, Massachusetts. She and her widowed mother moved to Wellesley, Massachusetts, in 1871. Bates earned undergraduate and graduate degrees from Wellesley College, and ultimately became full professor and head of its English department. For over forty years, Bates published poetry books, including *The College Beautiful and Other Poems* (1887). She also recorded her European travels and composed verses, stories, and plays for children. With her life partner/companion, Professor Katharine Coman, Bates enjoyed academe and affiliated with various women's groups. *Yellow Clover: A Book of Remembrance* (1922), arguably Bates's strongest collections of poems, represented a splendid memorial to the love and comradeship between Coman and Bates. In 1893, Bates joined a group of instructors determined to reach to the summit of Pike's Peak. They hired a prairie wagon pulled by horses, but near the top they rode mules. Tired from the excursion, Bates experienced reinvigoration when she saw a particularly beautiful view from a fourteen thousand-foot summit. Electrified and inspired by the scenery, she began putting her thoughts to paper.

The resulting poem, "America the Beautiful," first appeared in print on 4 July 1895 in

The Congregationalist, a weekly journal. Within a few months Silas G. Pratt set the words to the tune of the hymn "Materna." The music by S. A. Ward later became the most widely accepted version. Over the years Bates rewrote certain sections to simplify the text. Amazed by its immediate and permanent success, she declared Americans to be idealists at heart, with fundamental faith in human brotherhood. Bates's work ultimately emerged as the country's unofficial second national anthem. She retired in 1925 to her home in Wellesley, where she died. The only payment she ever received for "America the Beautiful" was a small check from *The Congregationalist*.

Further Reading: Dorothy Burgess, *Dream and Deed: The Story of Katharine Lee Bates*, 1952; Lynn Sherr, *America the Beautiful: The Stirring True Story Behind Our Nation's Favorite Song*, 2001; Katharine Lee Bates Papers, Wellesley College Archives.

Leonard Schlup

BAUM, LYMAN FRANK (15 May 1856–6 May 1919), writer. Born in Chittenango, New York, Baum suffered from heart disease as a youth, and was educated by private tutors. While still a teen, he published amateur newspapers and managed theaters. For four years, beginning in 1878, Baum acted, and in 1882 he produced his first play, the musical *Maid of Arran*. That year he married Maud Gage, who eventually bore him four sons. In 1888 they moved to Aberdeen, Dakota Territory, where Baum operated a store, worked as a journalist, and witnessed agrarian unrest that culminated in the founding of the People's Party.

During the 1890s Baum wrote for the *Chicago Evening Post*, published a trade magazine, and began churning out children's books. He achieved modest success with *Mother Goose in Prose* (1897). In 1899 he teamed with the illustrator William W. Denslow on *Father Goose, His Book*, which became a children's classic. Next Baum and Denslow created *The Wonderful Wizard of Oz* (1900), which won Baum enduring fame. In all, he wrote fourteen Oz stories. He collaborated on a musical version of *The Wizard*, which ran on Broadway from 1902 to 1911. He published several adult novels, but the success of his Oz sequels led him to concentrate on children's literature.

Baum moved to Hollywood, California, in 1910, went bankrupt, then recovered through the money brought in by Oz sequels and other children's books written under noms de plume. In 1914, he formed the Oz Film Manufacturing Company, but movie audiences had little taste for children's tales and the venture foundered. He died in Hollywood. Two posthumously published Oz books followed, and for a time the franchise was kept alive by other writers. In all, Baum wrote more than ninety books, thirty plays, a dozen poems, ten film scripts, and scores of stories and articles.

Some scholars see *The Wonderful Wizard of Oz* as a Populist Party fable. Most contemporary audiences know Baum mainly from the 1939 MGM feature film, which departs from the book significantly. Baum and his heirs insisted that Oz was simply a children's story, but Populist themes nonetheless resonate through the text.

Further Reading: *Chicago Tribune*, 18 May 1919; Michael O. Riley, *Oz and Beyond: The Fantasy World of L. Frank Baum*, 1997; Vicki Baum, *It Was All Quite Different: The Memoirs of Vicki Baum*, 1964.

Robert E. Weir

BAYARD, THOMAS FRANCIS (29 October 1828–28 September 1898), U.S. senator and diplomat. Born in Wilmington, Delaware, Bayard attended private schools, avoided college, but read law and was admitted to the Delaware bar in 1851. In 1869 he entered the Senate, and soon emerged as a leader of the Democratic minority. In 1885 he left the Senate to become President Grover Cleveland's secretary of state. His major diplomatic efforts—to protect the Bering Sea fur seals, achieve a compromise territorial settlement in Samoa, and guard American fishing rights in Canadian waters—failed. The Republican-controlled Senate rejected his 1888 agreement on Canadian fishing. With Cleveland's return to the White House in 1893, Bayard received the appointment to Britain, where for the first time an American diplomat held the title of ambassador rather than minister. In London, Bayard assumed a moderate position on issues in dispute, only to be censured by the U.S. House of Representatives. He returned home in 1897 and retired. He died in Dedham, Massachusetts.

Further Reading: Charles Callan Tansill, *The Foreign Policy of Thomas F. Bayard, 1885–1897,* 1940.

Norman A. Graebner

BAYARD-CHAMBERLAIN TREATY. The rights of U.S. and Canadian fishermen to troll each other's waters stirred intermittent tensions from the War of 1812 on. A "fish war" in the mid-1880s led to the appointment of a six-man commission. President Grover Cleveland's secretary of state, Thomas Francis Bayard, headed the American team. Joseph Chamberlain, former Liberal cabinet minister who had broken with William Ewart Gladstone on the subject of Irish home rule, was sent to Washington by Lord Salisbury, the Conservative prime minister, to head the British-Canadian team. Three months of negotiation resulted in a reciprocal fishing-rights treaty in February 1888. That August, however, the Republicans defeated it on a party line vote, hoping to gain Irish-American votes in that year's presidential election. However, a separate protocol secured for American fishermen (on payment of a small fee) most of the treaty's privileges. Meanwhile, the mission to the United States by the twice-widowed, fifty-two-year-old Chamberlain, led to his marriage to twenty-four-year-old Mary Endicott, the daughter of Cleveland's secretary of war. He assured her that she was the real treaty and that the other did not matter.

Further Reading: J. L. Garvin, *The Life of Joseph Chamberlain,* vol. 2, 1933; W. Stull Holt, *Treaties Defeated by the Senate,* 1933.

Walter L. Arnstein

BEAN, ROY (1825?–16 March 1903), justice of the peace, businessman, frontier trader. Born to an impoverished backwoods family in Mason County, Kentucky, Roy Bean traveled to the southwestern frontier in 1847. He lived a transient life as a young man and reportedly killed two men in duels. During the Civil War, Bean served with the Confederate Army, and later profited as a blockade runner. He lived comfortably with his wife for sixteen years in San Antonio, Texas, then in 1882 moved to West

Texas and founded the settlement of Langtry. Despite a lack of formal education in law or law enforcement, Bean gained appointment as justice of the peace. He earned a reputation for his unorthodox court rulings, which included fining a dead man $40.00. Judge Bean spent his remaining years dispensing his own brand of frontier justice in a wood frame saloon, earning a living through liquor sales and fines. He died in Langtry.

Further Reading: C. L. Sonnichsen, *The Story of Roy Bean: Law West of the Pecos,* 1943; Jay Monaghan, ed., *The Book of the American West,* 1968.

Michael W. Vogt

BECK, JAMES BURNIE (13 February 1822–3 May 1890), U.S. representative and senator. A native of Dumfriesshire, Scotland, Beck immigrated to the United States in 1838, studied law, and was graduated from Transylvania University in Kentucky. There he formed a partnership with John C. Breckinridge, later vice president and Confederate secretary of war. In 1866 Beck was elected to the U.S. House of Representatives, where he served from 1867 to 1875. He served on the Committee on Reconstruction, quickly emerging as a leading Democratic spokesman on southern issues in floor debates with Thaddeus Stevens and other Radical Republicans. A former slaveholder, Beck initially advocated compensated emancipation. He opposed President Andrew Johnson's impeachment, expanded civil rights for blacks, and passage of the Fifteenth Amendment. After touring the South with other legislators to investigate violence against and harassment of ex-slaves, Beck cited states' rights in refusing to support bills aimed at the Ku Klux Klan and other terrorist groups. In 1876 the Kentucky legislature named Beck to the U.S. Senate; he was reelected in 1882 and 1888. On the Finance and Appropriations committees, he devoted particular attention to tariff legislation. He believed ardently in free trade and tariffs for revenue only. Beck died in Washington, D.C.

Further Reading: T. Ross Moore, "The Congressional Career of James B. Beck, 1867–1875," M.A. thesis, University of Kentucky, 1950; *Louisville Courier-Journal,* 4 May 1890; *New York Times,* 4 May 1890.

Thomas H. Appleton Jr.

BEER, WILLIAM (1 May 1849–1 February 1927), librarian and mining engineer. Beer was born in Plymouth, England. After attending a college preparatory school and studying mining in Paris, he was named director of the Cottonian Library in Plymouth at age twenty. By 1884, he had emigrated to the United States and worked for several mining companies. In May 1989 he again displayed interest in libraries when he attended his first conference of the American Library Association. In July 1890 he was appointed librarian of the public library of Topeka, Kansas. A year later he joined the Howard Memorial Library in New Orleans. He strove continually to develop the collection and used his vacations for book-buying trips to England and the Continent. In 1896 he was appointed librarian of the Fisk Free and Public Library, also in New Orleans; he held both positions until he resigned from the Fisk in 1906. Beer continued his work at the Howard, where he became the region's representative to the American Library Association, and he presented numerous papers. His untiring efforts to develop libraries in New Orleans occurred while southern libraries often lagged behind those in other areas of the United States.

Further Reading: Joe W. Kraus, "William Beer and the New Orleans Libraries, 1891–1927," *ACRL Monographs*, no. 1, 1952.

Mark E. Ellis

BELKNAP, WILLIAM WORTH (22 September 1829–13 October 1890), secretary of war. Belknap was born in Newburgh, New York, attended Princeton College and the Georgetown School of Law, and was admitted to the Iowa bar in 1851. During the Civil War, he rose to brigadier general, and was appointed as President Ulysses S. Grant's secretary of war in 1869. A congressional investigation revealed that Belknap had accepted bribes from John S. Evans, an Indian trader at Fort Sill, Oklahoma Territory, who was seeking to retain his position. Belknap resigned on 2 March 1876, after the House impeached him. He holds the distinction of being the only U.S. cabinet member impeached for actions while in office. That Belknap was a member of the Grant administration, and the affair's place in the litany of

misdeeds linked to Grant and the Republicans, led many to call this the "Indian-Ring" scandal. The charges (never directly disputed) claimed that Belknap had accepted over $24,000 in bribes from 1870 through 1876. Despite his resignation, impeachment proceedings moved to the Senate for trial. The verdict was thirty-five votes to convict and twenty-five to acquit. Of the latter, twenty-two indicated that Belknap's resignation placed him outside the Senate's jurisdiction. Following his resignation, Belknap lived in Philadelphia, and later returned to Washington, D.C., to resume his private law practice. He died there.

Further Reading: *Washington Post*, 14 October 1890.

Jerome D. Bowers II

BELL, ALEXANDER GRAHAM (3 March 1847–2 August 1922), inventor and educator. Born in Edinburgh, Scotland, Bell was later known as the "teacher of the deaf." He became professor of vocal physiology in 1873 at Boston University, and two years later hired Thomas A. Watson as his associate. In 1876, Bell completed his application and received patent number 174,465 on 7 March 1876. The first sentence transmitted by a telephone, "Mr. Watson, come here, I want to see you," came three days later. Bell enjoyed publicizing his inventions on lecture tours. In 1882, the year in which he became a U.S. citizen, Bell moved to Washington, D.C. Four years later he purchased a summer home near Baddeck, Nova Scotia. In 1881 Bell invented a device to try to locate the assassin's bullet in the body of President James A. Garfield; the effort proved futile. Bell died at his Baddeck home.

Further Reading: Robert V. Bruce, *Bell: Alexander Graham Bell and the Conquest of Solitude*, 1973; Alexander Graham Bell Papers, Manuscripts Division, Library of Congress.

Leonard Schlup

BELLAMY, EDWARD (26 March 1850–22 May 1898), author and social reformer. Bellamy was born in Chicopee Falls, Massachusetts. Although he published four other novels and several essays, his fame rests on his very popular *Looking Backward, 2000–1887* (1888). A trenchant critique of Gilded Age economics, it rejected both unrestrained capitalism and Marxism to promote a philosophy he called Nationalism. By the late 1880s Nationalist Clubs around the country were promoting Bellamy's utopian dream as outlined in his novel. The book portrays a society that has reached consensus regarding social structure and has achieved a state free of exploitation. It is therefore able to provide adequately for all citizens in the "industrial army." Darwin's influence is apparent throughout. Bellamy's novel and the movement it spawned represent the search for order and stability in the churning society of industrializing America. By the time Bellamy died at Chicopee Falls, the Nationalist movement had run its course, but the novel remains popular among those attracted to utopian schemes and fin de siècle projections.

Further Reading: Arthur E. Morgan, *Edward Bellamy*, 1944; John L. Thomas, *Alternative America: Henry George, Edward Bellamy, Henry Demarest Lloyd and the Adversary Tradition*, 1983.

C. Edward Balog

BELLAMY, FRANCIS (18 May 1855–21 August 1931), clergyman and editor. Born in Mount Morris, New York, Bellamy graduated from the University of Rochester in 1876 and Rochester Theological Seminary in 1879. He held Baptist pastorates in Little Falls, New York, and Boston, Massachusetts, until 1891. Bellamy left the ministry because of the liberality of his views. From 1891 until 1903, he was an editor and writer for *Youth's Companion* and other publications, including *Ladies' Home Journal*, and freelanced widely. Between 1898 and 1901, Bellamy was an editor with Silver Burdett in New York City and a feature writer for the *New York Sun*. While holding a position with the National Education Association, Bellamy helped plan public schools' celebration of Columbus Day in 1892. He structured the quadricentennial observance around a flag-raising ceremony and salute. For this occasion he composed the first pledge of allegiance, inspired by intensive study of U.S. history from the Declaration of Independence through the Civil War. The "Pledge of Allegiance" appeared in the 8 September 1892 issue of *Youth's Companion*, a leading family mag-

azine. From time to time, additional words enlarged and somewhat changed Bellamy's simple version. Congress officially sanctioned the pledge of allegiance in 1945. Bellamy died in Tampa, Florida.

Further Reading: Margarette S. Miller, *Twenty-three Words: A Biography of Francis Bellamy, Author of the Pledge of Allegiance*, 1976; John Baer, *The Pledge of Allegiance: A Centennial History, 1892–1992*, 1992.

Leonard Schlup

BELMONT, AUGUST (8 December 1813–24 November 1890), financier. Born in Alzey, in the Rhenish Palatinate region of Germany, Belmont began his career at age fifteen, sweeping floors in the Rothschild Brothers' Frankfurt branch. He quickly earned promotions. At the onset of the Panic of 1837 in the United States, he arrived in New York, where he remained an associate of the House of Rothschild for the rest of his life. However, he soon established August Belmont & Company, specializing in foreign exchange, commercial and private loans, and related matters, which resulted in his becoming one of the nation's leading bankers.

Belmont also became a major political figure. He served as Austrian consul general to the United States, as U.S. chargé d'affaires at The Hague, and as Democratic National Committee chairman from 1860 to 1872. Though opposed to Abraham Lincoln's election, Belmont remained a staunch Unionist during the Civil War, using his contacts with the Rothschilds and others to help prevent Britain and other nations from recognizing or financially supporting the Confederacy. Despite formal retirement from politics after 1872, he remained one of the Democratic Party's influential elder statesmen throughout the Gilded Age. In New York, he played a pivotal role in transforming the New York Academy of Music into a quality opera company. Belmont died in New York City.

Further Reading: David Black, *The King of Fifth Avenue: The Fortunes of August Belmont*, 1981; Irving Katz, *August Belmont: A Political Biography*, 1968.

W. Thomas White

BENEDICT, ELIAS CORNELIUS (24 January 1834–23 November 1920), banker and stockbroker. Born in Somers, New York, Benedict was a sound money Democrat who originated the Gold Exchange Bank, an outgrowth of post-Civil War speculation. He was one of President Grover Cleveland's hunting and yachting companions. It was on Benedict's yacht, *Oneida*, anchored in New York's East Harbor, that Cleveland underwent secret surgery, in July 1893, to remove a malignant growth in his mouth. Benedict conspired with a few of the president's other close friends to keep the operation from the public. Benedict died at his residence "Indian Harbor," in Greenwich, Connecticut.

Further Reading: *New York Times*, 25 November 1920.

Leonard Schlup

BERING SEA CONTROVERSY. The 1867 purchase of Alaska brought the United States two islands that served as breeding grounds for about 80 percent of northern fur seals. To regulate harvesting, the government granted exclusive rights to kill the animal on land to a private American company.

In 1880 Canadians began hunting seals on the water. The United States objected, declaring possession of the breeding grounds brought ownership of the animals. In 1886 and again in 1889, America dispatched revenue cutters to the Bering Sea to protect the herd. Tensions mounted as officials boarded Canadian vessels and seized the gains of their hunting. In 1891, the British sent Royal Navy ships to the region. The controversy threatened war, but both powers sensibly agreed to to international arbitration.

In 1893 the Paris Tribunal ruled the United States could not claim seals outside its territorial waters. The body ordered compensation for Canadian sealers while extending the territorial waters to a sixty-mile radius. This solution failed to arrest the rapid decline of the seal population. By 1910 the herd, once over 2.5 million strong, numbered only 130,000. The next year a treaty signed by the United States, Great Britain, Japan, and Russia ended the practice of pelagic sealing.

Further Reading: Briton Cooper Busch, *The War Against the Seals: A History of the North American Seal Fishery*, 1987; Charles S. Campbell, Jr., "The Anglo-American Cri-

sis in the Bering Sea, 1890–1891," *Mississippi Valley Historical Review* 48 (1961): 393–414.

Gregory Dehler

BERKMAN, ALEXANDER (21 November 1870–28 June 1936), anarchist and author. Berkman was born in Vilnius, Lithuania (then part of Russia), and turned to radical ideas as a student in St. Petersburg. He was expelled from school for writing an atheistic essay, and immigrated to New York City in 1887. There he became a vocal anarchist. In 1892, Berkman attempted to assassinate Henry Clay Frick, chairman of the Carnegie Steel Company, in Pittsburgh. The deed was a political protest in support of the striking steelworkers in Homestead, Pennsylvania, who were members of the Amalgamated Association of Iron and Steel Workers. Frick, Andrew Carnegie's partner, had employed the Pinkerton guards who shot eleven strikers and defeated the largest and best-organized union in the United States. Berkman told his lifelong partner, Emma Goldman, that he wanted to kill Frick as an *attentat*, a political act of violence to arouse the people against their oppressors. Frick, however, survived the gun and knife attack in his office. Berkman spent fourteen years in the Western Penitentiary of Pennsylvania, much of the time in solitary confinement and under harsh conditions. He was abandoned by the American labor movement and most radical colleagues.

Released in 1906, Berkman recovered his health and political energy after he wrote *Prison Memoirs of an Anarchist*, published in 1912 by Goldman. The book, written in a simple, direct, and even sentimental style, became a radical classic; it is the autobiography of a passionate ideologue. Disillusioned by the conservative nature of the American left and the Soviet government, Berkman committed suicide in Nice, France.

Further Reading: *New York Times*, 2 July 1936; Emma Goldman, *Living My Life*, 2 vols., 1931; Gene Fellner, ed., *Life of an Anarchist: The Alexander Berkman Reader*, 1992.

Peter C. Holloran

BERLIN CONFERENCE ON SAMOA (1889). In late 1888 and early 1889, Germany intervened in a Samoan civil war. By January

1889, German marines had ousted King Malietoa and installed Tamasese, who was more favorable to them. The United States responded by sending three warships, and Congress allocated money for a naval station in Pago Pago to protect American property and citizens. These events convinced the three powers involved in Samoa—Germany, Great Britain, and the United States—to plan a conference of nine sessions from April to May. Secretary of State James G. Blaine dispatched John A. Kasson, William Walter Phelps, and George H. Bates as U.S. representatives.

The United States opposed a tripartite sharing scheme because it wanted Samoa to remain independent with equal status among the three powers. The Final Act, signed on 14 June 1889, contained important measures: new taxes and duties to pay for the Samoan government; the de jure recognition of lands taken by Western powers before August 1879; renewal of the municipal council to run the city of Apia; and the president of the council to be in charge of Samoan finances. In addition, Malietoa would return to the throne, and his successor would be elected. Finally, a Supreme Court, headed by a chief justice nominated by the king of Sweden and Norway, would function as a final court of appeal on land disputes and election results. Although the conference prevented further bloodshed, it provided only a temporary fix for Samoa's instability, and the United States later became further entangled in its affairs. Samoans had to tolerate an unpopular king who had little control over the purse strings, taxes, and dubious land sales. The clash between Samoan chiefs and occupying white forces was left unresolved.

Further Reading: Paul M. Kennedy, *The Samoan Tangle*, 1974; Charles Tansill, *The Foreign Policy of Thomas F. Bayard*, 1940; Alice F. Tyler, *The Foreign Policy of James G. Blaine*, 1927.

Bryan Craig

BERRY, JAMES HENDERSON (15 March 1841–30 January 1913), governor of Arkansas and U.S. senator. Born in Jackson County, Alabama, Berry attended public schools, enlisted in the Confederate Army in 1861, lost a leg at the battle of Corinth (1862), and was taken prisoner by Union forces. Paroled in 1863, he turned to teaching in Texas. After moving to Arkansas at war's end, Berry was admitted to the bar in 1866. He won election as a Democrat to the state house of representatives and briefly served as speaker. Having served as a circuit court judge from 1878 to 1882, he was elected governor in 1882.

Berry supported a constitutional amendment that repudiated most of the Reconstruction era state debt. He also helped create a railroad commission with taxing power. Accompanying legislation, however, effectively limited the revenue generated. Unsuccessful in his efforts to abolish the state's convict lease system, in 1884 Berry sought a U.S. Senate seat instead of reelection as governor. He lost a narrow three-way contest, but in early 1885 was elected to fill a vacancy created by the appointment of Augustus Hill Garland, Arkansas's other senator, as U.S. attorney general. Berry, a Bourbon conservative, remained in the Senate until losing a bid for a fifth term in 1906. He spent his final years in retirement and died in Bentonville, Arkansas.

Further Reading: Timothy P. Donovan, ed., *The Governors of Arkansas*, 1995.

Harvey Gresham Hudspeth

BESSEY, CHARLES EDWIN (21 May 1845–25 February 1915), botanist. Born in Wayne County, Ohio, Bessey earned an undergraduate degree from Michigan Agricultural College (now Michigan State University) in 1869. The following year he became the first instructor in botany and horticulture at Iowa State College of Agriculture (now Iowa State University) in Ames. He spent a few months in the early 1870s at the Harvard College Botanical Garden, where he met fellow botanist Asa Gray. In 1875 Bessey joined others in founding the Iowa Academy of Sciences, serving as its first president. His *The Essentials of Botany* appeared in 1884, and became the most widely used text for classes in the subject throughout the country. In 1884 Bessey accepted a professorial appointment at the University of Nebraska. He was dean of its Industrial College (1884–1888, 1895–1909) and acting chancellor (1888–1891). Bessy, urging establishment of state agricultural experiment stations, served as director of Nebraska's station for two years in the late 1880s. He also was botanical editor of *American Naturalist* from 1880 to 1897, espoused the "new botany" philosophy, and promoted the idea of a more significant place for botany in the American Association for the Advancement of Science. He died in Lincoln, Nebraska.

Further Reading: Richard A. Overfield, *Science with Practice: Charles E. Bessey and the Maturing of American Botany*, 1993; Charles E. Bessey Papers, University of Nebraska Archives and Nebraska State Historical Society Library, Lincoln.

Leonard Schlup

BEST-SELLING NOVELS. With literacy high and the middle class growing apace, reading was an enormously popular leisure activity during America's Gilded Age. Best-selling novels of this period fall into three categories: religious inquiry; stirring adventure blending into opulent romance; and miscellaneous "hits."

The first category covers novels such as *Gates Ajar* (1868), *Barriers Burned Away* (1872), *Ben Hur* (1880), *Robert Elsmere* (1888), *In His Steps* (1896), and perhaps *The Damnation of Theron Ware* (1896). All were tremendously popular investigations of the role Christian faith should play in daily life and/or interpretations of the Bible's directives. One can see growing interest in the "social gospel" by comparing the message advanced in *St. Elmo* (1868) and in the much later *If Christ Came to Chicago* (1894). The latter is as focused on reform as *Looking Backward* (1888), the single most popular utopian novel of the nineteenth century.

Adventurous escapades and splendid settings were liked even better, whether in "dime novels" or more respectable forms. Splendidly successful British authors included Robert Louis Stevenson, Arthur Conan Doyle, Ian Maclaren, and Rudyard Kipling. Their work sometimes had the air of the Ruritania books that described a Mitteleuropa awash in identical princes, diplomatic pomp, and complex intrigue. Exotica by Marie Corelli and *The Prisoner of Zenda* (1894) developed this appetite, after which *Trilby* (1894) brought a sanitized Bohemia to parlor fiction. Meanwhile, in the nursery, the earnest tones of *Little Women* and *Ragged Dick* (both 1868) dominated children's fare. No doubt many were read "Uncle Remus" stories (1881 et al.) as well.

Difficult-to-classify best-sellers such as *Coin's Financial School* (1894) and *Quo Vadis?* (1896) set oddly alongside the rosy optimism in *Mrs. Wiggs of the Cabbage Patch* (1901). One detective novel was a huge success: *The Leavenworth Case* (1878). A brief, intense taste for stories of colonial days is seen in the success of *The Choir Invisible* (1897) and *Hugh Wynne* (1898). Humorous best-sellers included many works by Mark Twain, the homespun *David Harum* (1898), and *D'ri and I* (1901).

Further Reading: James D. Hart, *The Popular Book: A History of America's Literary Taste*, 1950.

Barbara Ryan

BEVERIDGE, ALBERT JEREMIAH (6 October 1862–27 April 1927), U.S. senator and biographer. Born in Highland County, Ohio, Beveridge graduated from Asbury College (now DePauw University) in 1885, gained admittance to the bar in 1887, and practiced law in Indianapolis until 1899. Winning election as a Republican to the U.S. Senate in 1898, he held presidential aspirations that were well known during his first term. An imperialist in the aftermath of the Spanish-American War, Beveridge favored American access to overseas markets and investments in order to perpetuate prosperity at home. He championed the acquisition of the Philippine Islands and urged the retention of Cuba. Later he opposed statehood for New Mexico and Arizona for racial and political reasons. Aligned with Theodore Roosevelt, Beveridge belonged to the Progressive faction of the GOP. Eventually he grew more conservative. He lost his Senate seat in the Democratic stampede of 1910. His biographies of Chief Justice John Marshall and President Abraham Lincoln gave him a solid reputation as an author and historian. Beveridge died in Indianapolis.

Further Reading: John Braeman, *Albert J. Beveridge: American Nationalist*, 1971; Albert J. Beveridge Papers, Manuscripts Division, Library of Congress.

Leonard Schlup

BIG BUSINESS. Giant enterprise put the gilding on the Gilded Age. In *The Visible Hand: The Managerial Revolution in American Business* (1977), Alfred D. Chandler, Jr., reports little evidence of big business before 1840. Glenn Porter's *Rise of Big Business, 1860–1910* (1973) and David O. Whitten's *Emergence of Giant Enterprise, 1860–1914: American Commercial Enterprise and Extractive Industries* (1983) reinforce Chandler in detailing big business development after the Civil War. Big business was purposefully designed to maximize the economies of scale and scope associated with mass production, wholesale distribution, and retailing. Chandler emphasizes the internalization of market operations within the single enterprise as key to the managerial revolution. Giant enterprises functioned as economies within the larger national economy. Each division had its place on the firm's organizational chart, one defined by function and its relationship to every other division.

Most specialists agree modern big business was founded by railroads as they evolved from local to international operations. Efficient structure was essential to economies of scale; use of small business techniques in a giant enterprise brought operational and financial disaster. Chandler credits Pennsylvania Railroad executives with the creation of a viable structure emulated widely during the Gilded Age.

Further Reading: Edward C. Kirkland, *Industry Comes of Age: Business, Labor, and Public Policy, 1860–1897*, 1961.

David O. Whitten

BIGELOW, JOHN (25 November 1817–19 December 1911), writer, diplomat, and intellectual. Born in Bristol (Malden-on-Hudson), New York, Bigelow graduated from Union College in 1835, wrote essays for literary magazines, and teamed with William Cullen Bryant on the *New York Evening Post* (1848–1861). An abolitionist who broke with the Democratic Party over free soil, Bigelow, a convert to Swedenborgism, favored John C. Frémont for the presidency in 1856. He was appointed consul general at Paris, in 1861, and minister to France in 1865. There he warned Napoleon III against military intervention in Mexico. After resigning in 1866, Bigelow pursued a writing career that produced a biography of Benjamin Franklin in 1874 and a ten-volume *Complete Works of Benjamin Franklin* (1887–1888). Bigelow, a member of New York City's elite Century Club, endorsed postwar Republican policies but abhorred the scandals of President Ulysses S. Grant's administration. Switching his political allegiance to the Democratic Party, Bigelow won election as New York's secretary of state. He fervently supported his longtime close friend, Governor Samuel J. Tilden, for president in 1876, defended his record, and published a biography of him in 1895. Bigelow died in New York City.

Further Reading: Margaret Clapp, *Forgotten First Citizen: John Bigelow*, 1947; John Bigelow, *Retrospections of an Active Life*, 3 vols., 1909; *New York Times*, 20 December 1911.

Leonard Schlup

BILLINGS, JOHN SHAW (12 April 1838–11 March 1913), medical pioneer, bibliographer, and librarian. Born in Allensville, Indiana, Billings graduated from Miami University of Ohio (1857) and the Medical College of Ohio (1860). During the Civil War, he rose to lieutenant colonel in the Medical Corps while performing surgery in makeshift field hospitals. In 1864, he transferred to the Surgeon-General's Office, where he stayed for thirty-one years. He began developing a national library of medicine even before he was assigned this task in 1883. A prolific writer, Billings promoted public hygiene, hospital design, and organization of medical literature. His *National Medical Library Index-Catalogue* was an exhaustive index to all historical and current medical literature; with his monthly updates beginning in 1897, it evolved into the *Index-Medicus*. In 1896, Billings moved to New York City to direct the creation of the New York Public Library—his crowning achievement. There, until 1913, he standardized and reclassified all holdings, and aided the construction of a grand new central building and the formation of an extensive branch library system.

Further Reading: Harry Miller Lydenberg, *John Shaw Billings, Creator of the National Medical Library and Its Catalogue*, 1924; Janet Foote, "John Shaw Billings: A Nineteenth Century Information-Age Pioneer," *Bookman's Weekly* 93 (1994): 2620–2630; Carleton B. Chapman,

"John Shaw Billings, 1838–1913: Nineteenth Century Giant," *Bulletin of the New York Academy of Medicine* 63 (1987): 386–409.

Philip H. Young

BIMETALLIC MONETARY COMMISSION OF 1897. Elected in part on a platform pledge to seek an international agreement to coin both gold and silver at fixed weight/value ratios, President William McKinley appointed this body on 12 April 1897. At its head was Colorado's junior senator, Edward Oliver Wolcott, already in Europe in anticipation of the assignment. Joining him were former Vice President Adlai Ewing Stevenson and Massachusetts banker Charles J. Paine, also bimetallists. By July it was clear that French unhappiness with proposals to raise American customs duties was a major obstacle to success, and that neither France nor Britain would agree unless the other assented. When Britain refused to reopen India's mints to coin silver, the mission ended in October. Afterward, McKinley reluctantly concluded that there was no alternative to a single gold standard, a position that all save the staunchest silverites accepted. The commission's failure effectively ended agitation for the unlimited coinage of silver that had marked American politics throughout the depression of the 1890s.

Further Reading: H. Wayne Morgan, *William McKinley and His America*, 1963; Lewis L. Gould, *The Presidency of William McKinley*, 1980.

Douglas Steeples

BIMETALLISM. Alexander Hamilton, the first secretary of the Treasury, proposed a bimetallic currency like that of Great Britain. He hoped the use of two metals as legal tender would create a money supply large enough to accommodate a growing American economy. The Treasury would coin gold and silver, and Congress would set the value of each. The Coinage Act of 1792 defined gold as fifteen times more precious than silver. In reality, however, only the metal that Congress overvalued tended to circulate, because investors exchanged the undervalued metal overseas. The official ratio drove gold from circulation. In 1834 Congress attempted to reintroduce gold by elevating its value to sixteen times that of

silver. Gold strikes in California in the late 1840s increased the supply and left silver undervalued; between 1860 and 1869 the amount of silver in circulation declined from $21 million to less than $6 million. The dearth of silver led Congress in 1873 to direct the Treasury to stop minting the silver dollar, resulting in debates for the next two decades over a gold conspiracy and the restoration of silver. In 1900 Congress dropped silver as legal tender and thereby ended more than a century of bimetallism.

Further Reading: Milton Friedman and Anna Schwartz, *A Monetary History of the United States, 1867–1960*, 1963; Paul Studenski and Herman Krooss, *A Financial History of the United States*, 1952; James L. Laughlin, *The History of Bimetallism in the United States*, 1990.

Christopher Cumo

BINGHAM, JOHN ARMOR (21 January 1815–19 March 1900), representative and diplomat. Born in Mercer, Pennsylvania, but living most of his life in Cadiz, Ohio, Bingham became an attorney known for his campaign eloquence. An active Whig and early Republican, he was elected to Congress for four terms (1855–1863) before serving as special judge advocate in the trial of the conspirators in the assassination of President Abraham Lincoln, on the Joint Committee of Fifteen on Reconstruction, and as chairman of the Board of Managers in President Andrew Johnson's impeachment trial. Bingham, in fact, made the closing argument in that case. He also drafted key provisions of the Fourteenth Amendment. Returned to Congress (1865–1873), he bought and sold Crédit Mobilier stock, opposed civil service reform, and supported the "salary grab" bill (see Salary Grab Act entry). Defeated in 1872, he was appointed by President Ulysses S. Grant as minister to Japan. His vigorous defense of Japanese rights and his opposition to the British-led "cooperative" policy were notable features of a diplomacy whose twelve-year tenure benefited by having as president fellow Ohio Republicans Rutherford B. Hayes and James A. Garfield. Retiring in 1885, when Democrat Grover Cleveland captured the presidency, Bingham returned to Cadiz, where he died.

Further Reading: Erving E. Beauregard, *Bingham of the Hills: Politician and Diplomat Extraordinary*, 1989; Philip

N. Dare, "John A. Bingham and Treaty Revision with Japan: 1873–1885," Ph.D. diss., University of Kentucky, 1975.

Jack Hammersmith

BIRTH CONTROL. Throughout the Gilded Age, the birthrate of white, native-born Americans declined steadily. Historians are still uncertain whether birth control or abstinence played a larger role in this trend. Many marriage manuals written during the period mentioned the need to establish companionate relationships and limit family size. Although they recommended abstinence, they also frequently mentioned various birth control methods. The Comstock laws of 1873 made abortion, as well as the manufacture, distribution, and sale of birth control devices, a federal crime. By 1885, twenty-four states had similar laws on the books. The fear that sex would become divorced from procreation and love, resulting in the destruction of marriage and furthering decay in an already weakened family structure, were the main motives behind making birth control illegal. The middle class associated birth control with prostitution. Feminists opposed birth control because they believed it made it easier for husbands to force themselves on their wives. Younger and more radical feminists reversed this position as the new century dawned, promoting contraception as a way of giving women more control over family planning and allowing them greater social freedom. Those who favored contraception included homeopathic practitioners, free-love advocates, and working-class women who did not trust their husbands to manage the family's birth control needs or feed the extra mouths.

Because of their class sympathies, doctors tended to advise against birth control. Rising abortion rates caused many in the medical profession to support the Comstock laws and their vigorous enforcement. The illegality of birth control and the zeal of vice crusaders drove most of the market underground. Manufacturers and distributors tended to be small, local, and foreign-born rather than large national businesses. Some items, however, such as condoms, could be produced only by concerns possessing heavy machinery. Juries were often sympathetic to the accused, but conviction could lead to hard labor.

Natural methods of birth control included coitus interruptus, which is suspected of being the most popular form of birth control, and the rhythm method. Synthetic materials included the condom, which was inexpensive and widely available, and petroleum jelly, which was ineffective. Women could also opt for pessaries (diaphragms and sponges) or douches, or use syringes to inject spermicidal substances into the uterus after intercourse. In addition, a wide array of abortifacients were available from pharmacists and doctors. Many doctors who performed abortions also ran mail-order businesses selling birth control devices and abortion-inducing medicines.

Further Reading: Janet Farrell Brodie, *Contraception and Abortion in Nineteenth Century America*, 1994; James Reed, *From Private Vice to Public Virtue: The Birth Control Movement and American Society Since 1830*, 1978; Andrea Tone, "Black Market Birth Control: Contraceptive Entrepreneurship in the Gilded Age," *Journal of American History* 87 (2000): 435–459).

Gregory Dehler

BJERREGAARD, CARL HENRIK ANDREAS (24 May 1845–28 January 1922), librarian and philosopher. Born in Fredericia, Denmark, Bjerregaard graduated from the University of Copenhagen in 1863, entered the Danish military, and was curator of the natural history museum and professor of botany at Fredericia College. He immigrated to New York City in 1873. Six years later, he joined the staff of the Astor Library (New York Public Library), where he remained until his death. Bjerregaard secured an appointment as librarian in 1881; in 1889 he assumed the position of chief of the reading room. A noted speaker and author on the theosophical movement and Eastern philosophies, he published seven books between 1896 and 1913. Bjerregaard understood mysticism to mean "a life directed towards the transcendental; a life not only free from illusions, but a life which has made its devotees living channels of themselves and filled them with the Universal."

Further Reading: *New York Times*, 29 January 1922.

Leonard Schlup

BLACK AMERICAN NATIONALISM.

Black nationalism represents the manifestation of racial solidarity by blacks, shaped and driven by the desire to achieve meaningful freedom, equality and justice. Racial pride and solidarity are the foundations on which black nationalist movements have developed.

The Compromise of 1877 ushered in the era of legalized discrimination, also known as Jim Crow. During the 1890s new constitutions in southern states began a slow but steady process of abridging African-American rights and, inadvertently, provoking nationalist reactions. Most blacks cherished integration, encouraged by the apparent success of Frederick Douglass and others. Yet some, like T. Thomas Fortune, though equally optimistic, began gravitating toward separatism. Fortune's "Race first, then party," slogan captured the dilemma facing blacks. Although essentially American in aspirations, many black nationalists advocated strategies that emphasized racial consciousness and identity.

Impelled by alienation, some black leaders embraced a variant of separatist nationalism called internal statism: the establishment of independent black settlements within the nation. Proponents moved in a series of "exoduses" to create all-black settlements in Oklahoma, Ohio, and Kansas. The dominant black nationalism of the Gilded Age, however, sought a new and independent black nationality abroad. This choice became attractive in the early 1880s with the formation of the Liberian Exodus Company in South Carolina. Organizers solicited the assistance of the American Colonization Society in repatriating blacks to Liberia. Convinced that blacks would never be accepted in America, these emigrationists sought a new nationality in Africa where, unencumbered by racism, they could realize their potentials as human beings. Emigrationism reached its apogee in the 1880s and 1890s, led by Alexander Crummell (1819–1898) and Henry McNeal Turner (1834–1915). They based their nationalism on the perception of black Americans as civilized beings whose ultimate salvation lay in the fulfillment of a historical responsibility of helping to uplift their kindred in Africa to a level that would enable both groups to effectively resist and overcome European domination. Both men pointed to the seemingly inexhaustible resources of Africa as precisely the foundation needed for radically transforming the black experience.

Crummell espoused a Pan-African Christian brotherhood of black Americans and continental Africans, designed to advance mutual interests and elevation. He published and lectured extensively on emigration, and implored blacks to embrace African nationality. He settled briefly in Liberia. Turner denounced and renounced American society and values. He mounted a spirited campaign for emigration, exhorting black Americans and Africans to unite against the threat of Eurocentric nationalism and domination. His ideas struck a responsive chord among impoverished rural blacks, and in the early 1890s, Turner helped organize several resettlement trips to Liberia.

Emigration remained a minority movement, however, and by the early twentieth century was overshadowed by the persuasive force of a new integrationist ideology that promised change through reconciliation and cooperation with whites—the accommodationist philosophy of Booker T. Washington.

Further Reading: Wilson J. Moses, *The Golden Age of Black Nationalism*, 1978.

Tunde Adeleke

BLACK ELK

BLACK ELK (December 1863–17 August 1950), Lakota holy man. (Nicholas) Black Elk was born in what is now Wyoming as a member of the Oglala tribe that included Red Cloud, Crazy Horse, and other prominent leaders. He is best remembered for the text in *Black Elk Speaks*, an artistic biography published by Nebraska poet John Neihardt in 1932.

Black Elk's early years were disrupted by flight and fear. After the Great Sioux War of 1876, many in his society fled to Canada with Sitting Bull, then filtered back to the Pine Ridge reservation in southwestern Dakota Territory. During the years of turmoil, Black Elk had a vision that haunted him for the remainder of his life. It concerned spirits from the west, which always signified great importance and responsibility. He never overcame his inability to interpret the message for his people. Nevertheless, he accepted conversion to Roman Catholicism and gradually retired his Native American sacred objects. Conversations with Neihardt revealed he never had abandoned traditional beliefs, however.

From 1886 to 1889 Black Elk traveled through the eastern states and western Europe as a performer in William (Buffalo Bill) Cody's Wild West Show. In 1889 he returned to witness the reduction of Lakota land claims to reservations created by the Sioux Agreement of 1889. He witnessed the Ghost Dance as an expression of hope for Native American triumph, then, after its suppression, in 1904 accepted baptism by Jesuits, who gave him the name Nicholas. By 1907, he began to visit Lakota communities as a Christian missionary.

Neihardt drew a profile of a man tortured by unfulfilled promise, unrequited spirituality, and covert traditionalism. Yet Black Elk's published biography portrayed a leader in cross-cultural understanding during an era when federal officials and missionaries worked to suppress the traditional cultures of tribal members by their acculturation into the ways of the whites. As an elder, Black Elk traveled with Neihardt into the Black Hills, where he appealed to the Great Spirit (Wakantanka Tunkasila) on behalf of his people. At his death, little could he have suspected the magnitude of his influence on Native Americans in their stand against the forces of cultural imperialism. Little could he have understood the future impact of his philosophy on non-Indian readers.

Further Reading: Raymond Demallie, ed., *The Sixth Grandfather: Black Elk's Teachings Given to John Neihardt*, 1984; Julian Rice, *Black Elk's Story: Distinguishing Its Lakota Purpose*, 1991; Michael Steltenkamp, *Black Elk: Holy Man of the Oglala*, 1993.

Carol Goss Hoover

BLACK FRIDAY (24 September 1869). This was a panic caused when financiers Jay Gould and James Fisk attempted to corner the gold market. On 18 March 1869 Congress provided for gold specie repayment of the Civil War debt. On 20 September, Fisk and Gould began purchasing the precious metal on the open market; within four days they controlled enough to increase its price from $132 to $163 per ounce. They convinced other investors to join them by

claiming the federal government was purposely hoarding gold.

The commodity's rapid price inflation halted only when President Ulysses S. Grant, through Treasury Secretary George S. Boutwell, released $4 million in federal gold reserves. This action, instead of merely countering Fisk and Gould, caused the price of gold to fall, and the trading frenzy ceased. Fisk and Gould claimed to have made over $11 million, whereas many other small and large investors declared themselves ruined. Actually, Gould got most of this amount by deserting the market without telling his partner.

The panic's overall financial effects were largely limited to those few who speculated in gold specie and were bilked by Fisk and Gould. Political fallout for Grant, however, reached more widely. It permanently tainted his administration with scandal by implicating him in the price-raising scheme and subsequent sell-off, and also revealed his inability to deal with financial matters.

Further Reading: William S. McFeely, *Grant: A Biography*, 1981; Mark W. Summers, *The Era of Good Stealings*, 1993.

Jerome D. Bowers II

BLACK HILLS GOLD RUSH. The Black Hills gold rush was more spectacular than others across the West mainly because of its consequences: the opening of the largest mineral bonanza in North America, and the most pronounced and protracted controversy in the history of Indian-white relations. Lakota Sioux had been aware of gold deposits long before one non-Indian discovered them in 1834 and another attempted to mine them, until evicted by tribal soldiers in 1854. The Grattan Incident of that year, followed by the Fetterman Massacre of federal troops in 1866, exposed the danger of a continued search, and terms of the 1868 Fort Laramie Treaty clearly forbade it. Nevertheless, by 1872, prospectors returned as a result of depletion of placer deposits elsewhere. Successive exploratory expeditions, led by Colonel George Custer (1874) and Colonel Richard Irving Dodge with Walter P. Jenney (1875), confirmed previous reports about a possible bonanza in gold.

Lakotas called for the removal of prospectors. On 3 November 1875, General Philip Sheridan accompanied the U.S. secretaries of war and interior to a meeting with President Ulysses S. Grant, and came away with the impression that the government would "wink at" subsequent intrusions. "Quietly cause the troops in your Department to assume such attitude as will meet the views of the President in this respect," Sheridan wrote to General Alfred Terry.

A consequence was the Great Sioux War of 1876, which included the deaths of George Custer and his Seventh Cavalry, followed by the illegal seizure of the Black Hills and surrounding area by Congress with the Sioux Agreement of 28 February 1877. Other results were development of the rich Homestake Mine and the division of Dakota Territory in a way that produced the state of South Dakota containing the Black Hills, in 1889. Another consequence was the initiation of a formal petition by Sioux in 1887 that produced the Black Hills Claim against the United States. Approximately a century later, Congress agreed with the U.S. Court of Claims and U.S. Supreme Court that the 1877 agreement had been a "ripe" instance "of dishonorable dealing" in violation of the 1868 Fort Laramie Treaty. Signatory tribes refused to accept a financial award without the return of remaining federal land in the Black Hills and surrounding area. At the end of the twentieth century, a claims fund was daily growing from interest on more than half a billion dollars because Congress had declined to return the public land to its original owners.

Local residents regard the gold rush as a key to the development of western South Dakota by non-Indians. Federal officials, tribal members, and many national observers view it as a root cause of a major controversy in Indian-white relations that continues today.

Further Reading: Joseph H. Cash, *Working the Homestake*, 1973; Herbert T. Hoover, "The Sioux Agreement of 1889 and Its Aftermath," *South Dakota History* 19 (1989): 56–94; Frank Pommersheim, "The Black Hills Case: On the Cusp of History," *Wicazo Sa Review* 4 (1988): 18–25.

Herbert T. Hoover

BLACK, GREENE VARDIMAN (3 August 1836–31 August 1915), dentist. Black was born in a rural area near Winchester, Illinois, and began to practice dentistry in 1857. After serving in the Civil War, he opened an office in Jacksonville, Illinois. During the next three decades his reputation skyrocketed. A lecturer at the Missouri Dental College in the 1870s and professor of dental pathology at the Chicago College of Dental Surgery in the 1880s, Black introduced the teaching of dental techniques in 1887. In the 1890s he served as professor of dental pathology at the University of Iowa and at the Northwestern University Dental School. In 1897 he rose to dean of the school of dentistry and professor of operative dentistry at Northwestern. Black published numerous articles in dental journals, wrote monographs and textbooks, pioneered in offering new methods and practices regarding teeth, cavities, and fillings, engaged in experimental work, and traveled the nation. He also invented a cord dental engine. Black preferred not to commercialize his achievements, but the Black method stood the test of time. Before his death in Chicago, he had become a prominent Gilded Age dentist, receiving honorary degrees and serving in 1901 as president of the National Dental Association.

Further Reading: Greene Vardiman Black, *Dental Anatomy*, 1891; Malvin E. Ring, *Dentistry: An Illustrated History*, 1985.

Marvin D. Cohen

BLACK, JAMES (23 September 1823–16 December 1893), lawyer and prohibitionist. Black was born in Lewisburg, Pennsylvania, and and attended Lewisburg Academy before studying law. Admitted to the bar in 1846, he opened an office in Lancaster County. As a teenager Black had been forced to drink alcohol with other boys. On recovering from the effects, he had vowed to abstain forever. Black helped organize temperance societies, and successfully campaigned in 1855 for the election of two Prohibition Party members to the state legislature. Following the Civil War, Black, like Neal Dow of Maine, worked fervently for temperance reform. At the National Temperance Convention in 1865, he presented a plan to alert Americans to the consequences of overindulgence through a national publishing house. In 1867 he established and chaired the first state prohibition convention in Pennsylvania. Five years later, Black secured the presidential nomination of the Prohibition Party, with John Russell of Michigan as his running mate. He polled 5,608 votes nationally. From that time until his death in Lancaster, Black continued to build his personal library of material on temperance, lectured widely, and voiced his opinion on matters pertaining to the platforms of the Prohibitionists, a minor political party in Gilded Age America.

Further Reading: *Daily New Era* (Lancaster), 16 December 1893; James Black, *History of the Prohibition Party*, 1885.

Leonard Schlup

BLACK, JEREMIAH SULLIVAN (10 January 1810–19 August 1883), U.S. attorney general and secretary of state. Born near Stony Creek, Pennsylvania, Black passed the bar examination in 1830 and secured election to the Pennsylvania Supreme Court twenty-one years later. President James Buchanan, a fellow Pennsylvania Democrat, appointed him U.S. attorney general in 1857. In that post Black argued that secession was unconstitutional but that the federal government lacked power to force a state to return to the Union. He later served for two months as Buchanan's last secretary of state. Resuming his law practice during the Civil War, Black opposed Radical Reconstruction, campaigned for presidential candidate Horatio Seymour in 1868, and helped write Pennsylvania's new state constitution in 1873. Black also penned highly partisan articles, supported Christianity against Robert G. Ingersoll's agnostic proclamations, described Samuel J. Tilden's presidential defeat in 1876 as a great fraud, and defended his conservative interpretation of the Constitution. He died in York, Pennsylvania.

Further Reading: William N. Brigance, *Jeremiah Sullivan Black: A Defender of the Constitution and the Ten Commandments*, 1934; *New York Times*, 20 August 1883; Jeremiah S. Black Papers, Manuscripts Division, Library of Congress.

Leonard Schlup

BLACK, JOHN CHARLES (27 January 1839–17 August 1915), lawyer and government official. Black was born in Lexington, Mississippi, and as a youth lived in Kentucky, Pennsylvania, Indiana, and Illinois. After serving in the Union Army during the Civil War, he graduated from Wabash College in Indiana. He studied law, passed the Illinois bar exam in 1867, and practiced in Danville and Chicago. Unsuccessfully, Black sought a congressional seat in 1866, 1880, and 1884, the lieutenant governorship of Illinois in 1872, and a U.S. Senate seat in 1878. In 1885, President Grover Cleveland selected Black, a Democrat, to be commissioner of pensions. Black ran the office economically and reduced the expenses. After leaving the commissionership in 1889, he practiced law in Chicago. Three years later he won election as congressman-at-large from Illinois, and held the seat from 1893 (the year in which he received the Congressional Medal of Honor for bravery during the Civil War) to 1895. He then resigned to accept appointment as U.S. attorney for the northern district of Illinois, a post he held until 1897. Between 1903 and 1913, Black was a member of the U.S. Civil Service Commission, including service as its president. He died in Chicago.

Further Reading: *Chicago Tribune*, 18 August 1915; John Charles Black Papers, Illinois State Historical Library, Springfield.

Leonard Schlup

BLACK WOMEN SUFFRAGISTS. Historians of the women's suffrage movement long assumed African-American women were uninterested in suffrage and characterized black men as actively hostile to the movement. Such misconceptions were based on the writings of nineteenth-century white women suffragists, who often deliberately omitted voices and actions of African Americans from their official accounts. In truth, African-American women were active in the movement from its earliest years, although throughout the century they were forced to fight sexism and racism simultaneously.

In the 1860s abolitionist leaders such as Sojourner Truth, Harriet Purvis, and Sarah Remond held positions in the short-lived American Equal Rights Association (AERA). Remond lectured on women's rights throughout New York State, and Purvis helped form the interracial Philadelphia Suffrage Association. The AERA splintered in 1870 over the Fourteenth Amendment, which failed to provide voting rights for women and introduced the word "male" into the Constitution. Although African-American women were active in both national associations that emerged after the split, more chose to affiliate with the American Woman Suffrage Association, which supported the Fourteenth Amendment and had deeper roots in abolitionist circles. By contrast, after 1870 the rival National Woman Suffrage Association adopted an increasingly anti-black and anti-immigrant rhetoric in order to win white male support for a restricted suffrage based on literacy qualifications.

Despite this racist strategy, African-American reformers, both male and female, continued to campaign actively for women's suffrage. In 1880 Mary Ann Shadd Carey, a former abolitionist, journalist, and lawyer, organized the first separate African-American suffrage group, the Colored Women's Progressive Franchise Association, in Washington, D.C. During this decade African-American women formed thousands of local clubs to address social and political problems. Abolitionist and poet Frances Ellen Watkins Harper, the first black member of the Woman's Christian Temperance Union's executive board, traveled widely in the 1880s and 1890s, lecturing and writing on temperance and women's suffrage. In 1895 members of the New York and Pennsylvania African-American Woman's Loyal Union collected over ten thousand signatures on a suffrage petition. The National Association of Colored Women, founded in 1896, included women's suffrage as a major department, as did the far larger Baptist Woman's Convention. By 1900 state suffrage societies of African-American women existed in over a dozen states. Prominent African Americans such as the journalist Ida B. Wells-Barnett and the abolitionist Frederick Douglass, who had unfailingly supported woman's suffrage since the 1848 Seneca Falls Women's Rights Convention, along with hundreds of others, were vocal advocates of women's suffrage during the Gilded Age.

Further Reading: Ann D. Gordon, ed., *African American Women and the Vote, 1837–1965*, 1997; Rosalyn Terborg-Penn, *African American Women in the Struggle for the Vote, 1850–1920*, 1998.

L. Mara Dodge

BLACKBURN, JOSEPH CLAY STILES (1 October 1838–12 September 1918), U.S. senator. Born near Spring Station, Kentucky, Blackburn was graduated from Centre College in Danville, Kentucky, in 1857. He practiced law in Chicago from 1858 until 1860, when he returned to his home state. He served the Confederacy during the Civil War, then moved to Versailles, Kentucky, in 1868. Blackburn held a seat in the state legislature, then won election as a Democrat to the U.S. House of Representatives, taking office in 1875. There his investigations helped disclose scandals of the Grant administration. Blackburn was elected to the Senate in 1884, and served two terms before being defeated as a free coinage public figure in the Republican landslide of 1896. Reelected to the Senate in 1900, Blackburn remained there until his unsuccessful reelection bid in 1906. On 1 April 1907, President Theodore Roosevelt appointed Blackburn governor of the Canal Zone, where he remained until November 1909. Blackburn died in Washington, D.C.

Further Reading: Leonard Schlup, "Joseph Blackburn of Kentucky and the Panama Question," *The Filson Club History Quarterly* 51 (1977): 350–362; *Louisville Evening Post*, 12 September 1918.

Leonard Schlup

BLACKWELL, ALICE STONE (14 September 1857–16 May 1950), social reformer and advocate of women's rights. The daughter of Henry Browne Blackwell, a hardware merchant, and Lucy Stone, a woman's suffrage champion, Blackwell was born in Orange, New Jersey; moved to Dorchester, Massachusetts, with her family in 1869; and graduated Phi Beta Kappa in 1881 from Boston University. Her aunt, Elizabeth Blackwell, was the first American woman to earn a degree in medicine. Alice

Blackwell's full life consisted of being editor of *Woman's Journal*, a periodical published by her parents, and, from 1887 to 1905, the editor of *Woman's Column*, a weekly circulating broadside. In 1890, she assisted in establishing the National American Woman Suffrage Association, which she served as recording secretary for the next two decades. Active in humanitarian and social crusades during the Gilded Age, Blackwell belonged to the Women's Trade Union League, the Woman's Christian Temperance Union, and the National Association for the Advancement of Colored People. She contended that women would bring a moral dimension to politics and promoted female voting rights by founding the Massachusetts League of Women Voters. In 1896, she translated and published a collection of Armenian poems. Blackwell's legacy continued long after her death in Cambridge, Massachusetts.

Further Reading: Marlene Deahl Merrill, ed., *Growing Up in Boston's Gilded Age: The Journal of Alice Stone Blackwell, 1872–1874*, 1990; *New York Times*, 16 May 1950; *Boston Globe*, 16 May 1950.

Leonard Schlup

BLACKWELL, ANTOINETTE LOUISA BROWN (20 May 1825–5 November 1921), author, minister, and social reform advocate. The first female ordained minister in the United States, Brown, who married Samuel Charles Blackwell in 1856, was born in Henrietta, New York. She was graduated in 1847 from Oberlin College, taught school, and moved to New York City. There she undertook charitable work in poverty-stricken areas. Blackwell opposed slavery, favored temperance, and supported women's rights. She attended the first National Woman's Rights Convention, and in 1852 accepted a ministerial post with the Congregational church of South Butler, New York. Joining Lucy Stone in founding the American Woman Suffrage Association, Blackwell endorsed the Fifteenth Amendment. In 1873, she helped establish the Association for the Advancement of Women, an organization designed to promote the general amelioration of women's conditions. Eighteen years later, living in New Jersey and holding a Unitarian pulpit, Blackwell won election as president of the New Jersey Woman Suffrage Association. Influenced by the evolutionary theories of Herbert Spencer and Charles Darwin, Blackwell published several books, including *Studies in General Science* (1869), *The Sexes Throughout Nature* (1875), *The Physical Basis of Immorality* (1876), and *The Philosophy of Individuality* (1893). She died in Elizabeth, New Jersey.

Further Reading: Elizabeth Cazden, *Antoinette Brown Blackwell: A Biography*; Blackwell Family Papers, Manuscripts Division, Library of Congress.

Leonard Schlup

BLAINE, JAMES GILLESPIE (31 January 1830–27 January 1893), speaker of the House of Representatives and secretary of state. Born in West Brownsville, Pennsylvania, Blaine attended local schools and was graduated from Washington College in 1847. After teaching briefly, he settled at Augusta, Maine, where he became a newspaper editor. A Whig and later a Republican, he served in the Maine House of Representatives from 1859 to 1862, the last two years as speaker. In 1862 he won election to the federal Congress. An able debater and skillful tactician, he rose in 1869 to the House speakership, a post he held for three terms. There he earned high marks for fairness and his grasp of procedure. In 1876 he was appointed, and then elected, to the Senate. During Reconstruction, Blaine sided more often with moderate Republicans, although he did embrace black suffrage, the key element of the Radical program. A popular campaign orator, during nearly every election season he traveled through several states, making speeches for Republican candidates and winning a broad personal following. He was considered a possible presidential nominee at five Republican conventions (1876–1892). His chances in 1876 fell victim in part to allegations of corrupt railroad dealings, charges that dogged his entire subsequent career.

In the late 1870s and 1880s Blaine led the "Half-Breed" Republican faction, a group that sought to move away from sectional issues and focus instead on the nation's economic development. He favored a stable, specie-based currency; government subsidies for some businesses; and, most important, a protective tariff. Denied the presidential nomination in 1880, he campaigned vigorously for James A. Garfield, who appointed him secretary of state. During his nine-month stint in the State Department, he promoted wider hemispheric trade (1881).

The Republicans nominated Blaine for president in 1884. Mudslinging marred the bitter contest with Grover Cleveland, but Blaine sought to raise the level of the campaign by an extended speaking tour emphasizing the tariff and other issues. He narrowly lost the pivotal state of New York, and the election. In 1888 he refused to seek the nomination, disappointing many supporters. He campaigned for Benjamin Harrison, who won, and reappointed him to head the State Department. Resuming his energetic hemispheric policy, Blaine hosted the first Pan-American Conference in Washington, sought bases for the growing American navy, and championed reciprocity agreements to expand trade, particularly in Latin America. Disagreements with Harrison led to his resignation just before the 1892 Republican Convention, at which Harrison easily defeated him for the nomination. Blaine died several months later in Washington, D.C.

Further Reading: James G. Blaine Family Papers, Library of Congress, Washington; David Saville Muzzey, *James G. Blaine: A Political Idol of Other Days*, 1934; Charles W. Calhoun, "James G. Blaine and Republican Party Thought," in Ballard Campbell, ed., *The Human Tradition in the Gilded Age and Progressive Era*, 1999.

Charles W. Calhoun

BLAIR EDUCATION BILL. The crusade for southern education following the Civil War fueled a simmering debate over the federal role in support of state and local school expenditures. Stung by defeats of other proposed pieces of federal aid legislation in the 1870s, New Hampshire Senator Henry W. Blair introduced a bill in 1882 to provide $120 million, through land grants, to aid establishment and temporary support of common schools throughout the nation. The bill provided for appropriation of funds over a ten-year period, the amount to be determined by the number of illiterates in each state over the age of ten in proportion to the number of illiterates in the United States. To be eligible for such aid, states would need to maintain a common, nonsectarian school system for all children; supply statistics and other survey information to the secretary of the interior; provide a basic academic curriculum; and guarantee that no monies would be spent on school construction or rentals. It was expected that the grants, to be administered by state and local officials, would be matched by the states.

Blair modified his original proposal to $77 million over eight years; it was reintroduced and passed there in the Senate in 1884, 1886, and 1888, but never taken up by the House. A fifth attempt to pass the Blair bill failed in the Senate in 1890. Support for the bill came from the Southern Alliance of farmers, the Knights of Labor, and, by 1886, the American Federation of Labor. Although it received widespread backing from both Republican and Democratic senators, several business groups, and such education organizations as the National Education Association and the National Education Assembly, the measure was ultimately defeated by strong opposition from southern Congressmen and numerous religious leaders. While supporters generally viewed at the legislation as an extension of reconstruction efforts in the South, they also argued that its benefits were designed to meet the educational needs of the entire nation. Opponents feared that the provision of federal aid, though restricted to eight years, would create continued pressures for support and unwise restrictions on local educational initiatives and biases.

Further Reading: Gordon C. Lee, *The Struggle for Federal Aid. First Phase: A History* of the Attempts to Obtain Federal Aid for the Common Schools, 1949; Daniel Wallace Crofts, "The Blair Bill and the Elections Bill: The Congressional Aftermath to Reconstruction," Ph.D. diss., Yale University, 1968.

Kim P. Sebaly

BLAND, RICHARD PARKS (19 August 1835–15 June 1899), congressman. Bland was born near Hartford, Kentucky, and lived in California, Colorado, and the Utah Territory, where he taught school, was a prospector, and studied law. He moved to Missouri in 1865. Having learned much about silver as a metal and as a standard of value, Bland sympathized with frustrated farmers and debtors who suffered during periods of postwar economic decline. A Democrat, in 1872 he won election to the U.S. House of Representatives, and was reelected until 1894, then served again from 1897 to 1899. Chair of the Committee on Mines and Mining at various times, Bland supported expanded silver production and unlimited silver coinage. He cosponsored the Bland-Allison Act of 1878, which required the federal government to encourage bimetallism and assist silver producers by making monthly purchases of silver bullion; this was a compromise bill passed over President Rutherford B. Hayes's veto.

For the next two decades Bland led the struggle in the House for the restoration of bimetallism, attending monetary conferences and writing articles. In 1893 he vigorously fought against repealing the Sherman Silver Purchase Act of 1890, warning President Grover Cleveland that free coinage Democrats would place principle above party loyalty. Bland was a leading candidate among soft money Democrats and Silver Republicans for the 1896 presidential nomination, but yielded to William Jennings Bryan after three ballots at the national convention. During William McKinley's presidency, Bland denounced the annexation of Hawaii in 1898 in a House address, employing a wide array of constitutional and political objections that some anti-imperialists used two years later in attacking the acquisition of the Philippine Islands. Nicknamed "Silver Dick," Bland was the dean of silver advocates in Congress. He died in Lebanon, Missouri.

Further Reading: William Vincent Byars, ed., *"An American Commoner": The Life and Times of Richard Parks Bland,* 1900; Harold Alanson Haswell, Jr., "The Public Life of Congressman Richard Parks Bland," Ph.D. diss., University of Missouri at Columbia, 1951; *St. Louis Globe-Democrat,* 16 June 1899.

Leonard Schlup

BLAND-ALLISON ACT OF 1878. After the discovery of new silver lodes in the American West in the 1870s, miners and other advocates of cheap money called for the federal government's unlimited coinage of silver, a metal that had been demonetized in 1873 when its commodity value exceeded its coined value. Silver forces found an eloquent spokesman in Congressman Richard P. Bland of Missouri. On 5 November 1877, Bland introduced a measure

calling for the unlimited coinage of a legal tender silver dollar of 412.5 grains. Bland's bill provided that the new dollar would circulate freely with gold at the ratio of sixteen to one, and could be used for payment of all legal debts. The bill passed the House of Representatives 163 to 34. Bland's bill moved on to the Senate Finance Committee, chaired by Iowa's William B. Allison. That body replaced the unlimited coinage provision with an amendment limiting silver dollar mintage to between two million and four million per month. After sharp debate, the measure passed the Senate on 16 February 1878. Senator Allison was so instrumental in reshaping Bland's original bill that it became known as the Bland-Allison Act.

The bill was now President Rutherford B. Hayes's to decide. Hayes had kept silent during the congressional silver debate, but believed the measure had been pushed by self-serving western silverites who wanted to dump their newfound ores on the government. To Hayes, remonetization was an illusory and potentially disastrous shortcut to temporary prosperity. In the long term, cheap money would alienate the nation's creditors and undermine the economy. On those grounds, Hayes vetoed the Bland-Allison Act on 28 February 1878. Congress reacted swiftly. Not even allowing the president's message the courtesy of a printing, both houses overrode the veto. Hayes's fears had been ill-founded, for the nation's economy improved in the next several months and there was no great impairment of credit, although the silver issue continued to be a prominent political topic well into the 1890s.

Further Reading: Irwin Unger, *The Greenback Era: A Social and Political History of American Finance, 1865–1879,* 1964.

Frank P. Vazzano

BLATCHFORD, SAMUEL (9 March 1820–7 July 1893), Supreme Court justice. Blatchford was born in New York City and graduated from Columbia College. He became an admiralty law specialist and published voluminously in that field. In 1867, Blatchford was named judge for the Southern District of New York. In 1872, he was elevated to the Second Circuit Court of Appeals, and ten years later President Chester A.

Arthur appointed him to the Supreme Court. There Blatchford authored 435 opinions that were uncontroversial and avoided the day's great issues. An exception was his stand with the majority in *Chicago, Milwaukee and Saint Paul Railway Company* v. *Minnesota* (134 U.S. 418 [1890]). The case concerned Minnesota Railroad and Warehouse Commission rate schedules, which were not subject to judicial review. Blatchford wrote that the commission's actions violated the Fifth and Fourteenth amendments. Although he did not expressly overturn *Munn* v. *Illinois* (94 U.S. 113 [1877]), he came under sharp criticism. Two years later, however, he wrote the opinion in *Budd* v. *New York*, (143 U.S. 517 [1892]), which upheld grain elevator charges along the Erie Canal. In reaffirming *Munn*, and seeming to contradict his opinion in the *Chicago* case, Blatchford held that rates fixed directly by the legislature, rather than set by a commission, lay within the state's police power. He died in Newport, Rhode Island.

Further Reading: Arnold Paul, "Samuel Blatchford," in *The Justices of the United States Supreme Court, 1789–1969: Their Lives and Major Opinions*, ed. Leon Friedman and Fred L. Israel, 1969; *New York Times*, 8 July 1893.

Sam S. Kepfield

BLISS, AARON THOMAS (22 May 1837–16 September 1906), governor. Born in Peterboro, New York, Bliss attended local schools, engaged in mercantile pursuits, and fought in the Civil War. He moved to Saginaw, Michigan, in 1865 and headed a successful lumber firm there. He served as a Republican in the Michigan senate in 1882 and in the U.S. House of Representatives from 1889 to 1891. Bliss lost a bid for reelection in 1890, but was chosen governor of Michigan in 1900, an office he held from 1901 to 1905. A Progressive, he advanced the state's educational institutions and favored equal taxation of railway properties. Bliss died in Milwaukee, Wisconsin.

Further Reading: *New York Times*, 17 September 1906.

Leonard Schlup

BLIZZARD OF 1888. On Sunday, 11 March 1888, a blizzard of nearly unprecedented proportions paralyzed the United States from Maine to Maryland along the Atlantic coast, and the interior area from Buffalo, New York, to Pittsburgh, Pennsylvania. The storm brought havoc to ten states and one-fourth of the nation's population. Coming unexpectedly at the end of one of the mildest winters in seventeen years, when shrubs and flowers were already starting to bud, the great white hurricane proved devastating. A cloudy, rainy day suddenly changed; the sky turned black; and hail, sleet and snow pelted the ground. Ships at sea along the coast signaled distress calls; they included the steam ferry *Hartford*, which wrecked off the Long Island shore. Trains crashed and left their wreckage half-buried in deep snow. The blizzard crippled railroads everywhere in the affected region; struck New Haven, Connecticut, with great severity; and buried Pittsfield, Massachusetts, in feet of snow. Particularly ravaged was New York City, where winds blowing Arctic cold air plummeted temperatures, grinding the metropolis to a halt. Uprooted trees, torn signs, loose debris, and overturned vans dotted the landscape. The ferocious weather cut off the nation's capital from the rest of the country and stranded government officials. This catastrophe moved a national legislator to remark that people could not control the elements or prevent another blizzard, but they could protect communications by placing overhead wires underground in the urban areas to shield them from the caprices of nature. The *New York World* estimated that on 12 and 13 March the city's businesses lost between $2 and $3 million. Astounding stories about the blizzard of 1888, with its toll in lives and property, lingered for years.

Further Reading: Irving Werstein, *The Blizzard of '88*, 1960; Mary Cable, *The Blizzard of '88*, 1988.

Leonard Schlup

BLOUNT, JAMES HENDERSON (12 September 1837–8 March 1903), congressman and diplomatic envoy. Born near Clinton, Georgia, Blount graduated from the University of Georgia in 1858. He opened a law office the next year, fought in the Confederate Army, moved to Macon in 1872, and served, as a Democrat, in the U.S. House of Representatives from 1873 to 1893. There he denounced both the Civil

Rights Act of 1875 and the Tariff of 1890, favored the Bland-Allison Act of 1878, accepted the Sherman Antitrust Act of 1890, supported national prohibition, and saw little value in civil service reform. A bimetallist and anti-imperialist who displayed antagonism toward a large navy and an isthmian canal, Blount on 20 March 1893 accepted President Grover Cleveland's appointment as special commissioner to Hawaii to investigate the overthrow of the Hawaiian monarchy two month earlier. His task included ascertaining whether a majority of Hawaiians wanted annexation. Near the end of July, Blount submitted a lengthy, controversial report to the president, concluding that the islanders would reject annexation and that the former U.S. minister to Hawaii, John L. Stevens, and others had assisted in toppling Queen Liliuokalani from power. The episode had occurred during the final weeks of Benjamin Harrison's presidency. Largely because of this straightforward account, Cleveland refused to resubmit the Hawaiian annexation treaty to the Senate. Blount returned to Georgia, and resumed his life as a planter and lawyer. He died in Macon.

Further Reading: Tennant S. McWilliams, "James H. Blount, the South, and Hawaiian Annexation," *Pacific Historical Review* 57 (1988): 25–46; Thomas J. Osborne, *"Empire Can Wait": American Opposition to Hawaiian Annexation, 1893–1898*, 1981; *New York Times*, 9 March 1903.

Leonard Schlup

BLOXHAM, WILLIAM DUNNINGTON (9 July 1835–15 March 1911), governor. Bloxam was born in Tallahassee, Florida, graduated from the College of William and Mary in Virginia in 1856, and won election to the Florida House of Representatives. He served in the Confederate Army until poor health caused him to be sent home. In the postwar era, he joined conservatives in opposing Reconstruction governments in the South. Bloxham won the Florida lieutenant governorship in 1870. Following redemption, he was appointed secretary of the state in 1876 and was elected governor in 1880. His administration (1881–1885) was noteworthy for elimination of the state debt and reduction in taxation. When his term as chief executive expired, Bloxham declined President

Grover Cleveland's offer to enter the diplomatic service as minister to Bolivia, but he accepted appointment as U.S. surveyor general of Florida. He served until his appointment as state comptroller in 1889. Elected in 1892 to that position, he recommended reforms dealing mainly with finances and assessments. From 1897 to 1901, Bloxham again was governor of Florida, which was the site of army encampments and embarkations during the Spanish-American War of 1898. He died in Tallahassee.

Further Reading: Edward C. Williamson, *Florida Politics in the Gilded Age, 1877–1893*, 1976; *Atlanta Journal*, 16 March 1911; W. W. Davis, *The Civil War and Reconstruction in Florida*, 1913.

Leonard Schlup

BOAS, FRANZ (9 July 1858–21 December 1942), anthropologist. Born in Minden, Westphalia, Germany, Boas earned a doctorate in physics from the University of Kiel in 1881. Two years later, he studied American Eskimos in the Northwest Territories. In 1887 he accepted the position of assistant editor of *Science* magazine in New York and became a U.S. citizen four years later. Boas started his forty-year career as professor of anthropology at Columbia University in 1899. A cultural relativist, he rejected racial theories of intelligence and compared U.S. discrimination against African Americans to European bias against Jews. His essay "The Decorative Art of the Indians of the North Pacific Coast," published in *Bulletin of the American Museum of Natural History* (1897), became a classic work in the field. A pioneer of modern folklore research and the father of modern anthropology, Boas died in New York City, a nationally recognized anthropologist, educator, and scholarly writer.

Further Reading: Marshall Hyatt, *Franz Boas: Social Activist*, 1990; *New York Times*, 22 December 1942.

Leonard Schlup

BOIES, HORACE (7 December 1827–4 April 1923), governor. Boies was born in Erie County, New York, and attended public schools there. At age twenty-one he began studying law informally, and passed the bar exam in 1849. In 1867 he took his practice to Waterloo, Iowa. Previously a Whig and a Republican, Boies switched to the Democrats in 1884 when the

GOP supported a prohibition amendment to the state constitution. Himself abstinent, Boies argued that those who were financially harmed by the measure should be compensated. In 1888, his anti-prohibition stance brought him election as the first Democratic governor since 1856. During his administration he battled for, but did not succeed in passing, a state liquor license law. However, the liquor issue won him a second term in 1891.

Boies's political following during the early 1890s extended beyond Iowa to the South and the West. He spoke frequently on the tariff issue and gained sufficient support nationally to become a presidential candidate in 1892. Grover Cleveland, after winning the presidency, offered to name Boies secretary of agriculture. Boies declined the offer. Boies lost the governorship in 1893. After the defeat, he remained active and led the Iowa Democratic Party away from the silver issue, which constituted much of the national political debate during the 1890s. After losing a congressional race in 1902, Boies retired to his farms in Iowa, Nebraska, and Canada.

Further Reading: Jean B. Kern, "The Political Career of Horace Boies," *Iowa Journal of History* 47 (1949): 215–246; *Waterloo Iowa Tribune*, 6 April 1923.

Michael W. Vogt

BOLTON, HENRY CARRINGTON (28 January 1843–19 November 1903), chemist. Born in New York City, Bolton graduated from Columbia College in 1862, studied chemistry in Europe, and received a doctorate from the University of Göttingen. In 1868, he opened a private research laboratory in New York City. Five years later, he published a work on the fluorescent and absorption spectra of uranium salts. Bolton was a founder of the American Chemical Society in 1876. From 1875 to 1877, he taught chemistry at the Woman's Medical College of the New York Infirmary. In 1877, he began teaching at Trinity College in Hartford, Connecticut, where he built a new chemical laboratory, acquired a large mineral collection, and published some three hundred monographs, journal articles, and addresses. His *Catalogue of Scientific and Technical Periodicals, 1665–1882* appeared in 1885. Eight years later, he published *A Select Bibliography of Chemistry, 1492–1892*. Bolton's encyclopedic knowledge encompassed interests including genealogy, medicine, Hawaii, glaciers, and history. He lectured on the history of chemistry at George Washington University. Colleagues speculated that he belonged to more scientific societies than any other American during the Gilded Age. Bolton died in Washington, D.C.

Further Reading: New York *Times*, 20 November 1903; C. A. Browne, "Henry C. Bolton," *Journal of Chemical Education* 17 (1940): 457–461, Henry C. Bolton Papers, Manuscripts Division, Library of Congress.

Leonard Schlup

BONNEY, WILLIAM H. (BILLY THE KID) (1859?–14 July 1881), frontier desperado. Born Henry McCarty, the son of Irish immigrants in New York City, he spent his formative years moving about the trans-Mississippi West with his widowed mother, Catherine. In 1873 she remarried William Antrim, a part-time carpenter and bartender, and the family settled in Silver City, New Mexico. Following her death from tuberculosis in 1874, Billy adopted his stepfather's name, becoming known first as Henry Antrim and later as "Kid Antrim." His first encounter with the law came at age fifteen, when he was jailed for stealing clothes from two Chinese merchants. He escaped to the small settlement of Bonito, near Camp Grant in the Arizona Territory.

There he shot to death a local bully, a blacksmith named Frank P. "Windy" Cahill, on 17 August 1877. The Kid fled to the small town of Mesilla in New Mexico's Pecos Valley, where he assumed the alias William H. Bonney. He found employment as a cattle guard on the ranch of John Tunstall, who, with John Chisum and Alexander McSween, constituted one of the factions in the Lincoln County War of 1878 and 1879. (Tunstall was subsequently murdered by the opposing Murphy-Dolan forces.) The Kid joined a posse hunting Tunstall's killers. The group captured the culprits, but before the prisoners could be jailed in Lincoln, New Mexico, Billy killed the two men. Three weeks later, on Lincoln's main street, the Kid and several others murdered Sheriff James A. Brady and his deputy when they tried to arrest him. Now wanted for the murder of two peace officers, Billy offered his allegiance to Tunstall's ally, McSween, and participated in the final battle of the war, a five-day siege and gunfight in which McSween was killed and his house torched. Billy escaped the inferno and started rustling stock from Texas ranchers and Mescalero reservation Apaches.

In return for testifying against Murphy-Dolan faction members, the Kid was promised amnesty by Governor Lew Wallace. Unable to tolerate protective custody, Billy walked away from his makeshift jail and fled to Fort Sumner. Following a December 1880 gun battle with lawmen at Stinking Springs, New Mexico, Billy was again captured and jailed. On 28 April 1881, while awaiting trial in the Lincoln County Courthouse, he overpowered guards and escaped. He was finally surrounded by Sheriff Pat Garrett at Pete Maxwell's ranch in Fort Sumner. On the night of 14 July 1881, Garrett shot Billy in Maxwell's darkened bedroom, the Kid having given himself away with the whispered query *"Quien es? Quien es?"* (Who is it?)

Further Reading: Frederick Nolan, *The Lincoln County War: A Documentary History*, 1992; Robert M. Utley, *Billy the Kid: A Short and Violent Life*, 1989; Jon Tusca, *Billy the Kid: His Life and Legend*, 1994.

Maurice Law Costello

BOOTH, EDWIN THOMAS (13 November 1833–7 June 1893), actor and theatrical manager. Born in in Bel Air, Maryland, Booth received sporadic formal education, much of his youth being spent on tour with his father, Junius Brutus Booth, an accomplished actor. The younger Booth began acting in 1847, established his fame on the New York stage in 1864–1865 with one hundred consecutive performances as Hamlet, and spent the remainder of his career building a reputation as the foremost American actor of the Gilded Age. Excelling in Shakespearean roles, notably as Iago in *Othello*, Shylock in *The Merchant of Venice*, and *Hamlet*, Booth was a key figure in the transition from the declamatory style of acting exemplified by his predecessor and namesake, Edwin Forrest, to the "natural" school that marked the beginning of realism on the American stage. The slightly built Booth's style has been characterized as effeminate and graceful, and his speech as eloquent, with exceptional range. His success has been attributed to the great care and time he spent studying each of his roles. After acquiring managerial experience, he opened Booth's Theatre in New York in February 1869. On the cutting edge of technology, it featured a level stage (the raked stage had been the convention), hydraulic elevators for moving scenery, trapdoors, and substantial working space both below and above the stage itself. He is credited with introducing the practice of "free plantation" in scenery, anchoring scenic pieces to movable stage braces rather than to fixed grooves on the stage floor.

Although Booth was admired for his talent and personality, his career was marked by misfortune. He retired briefly in 1865 after his brother, John Wilkes Booth, assassinated President Lincoln, and was forced to relinquish control of Booth's Theatre in 1873 due to bankruptcy. In order to ease his financial burden, Booth spent most of his remaining career publishing editions of Shakespeare and touring in Europe and America, despite an attempt on his life during an 1879 performance in Chicago. Booth died in New York City.

Further Reading: L. Terry Oggel, *Edwin Booth: A Bio-Bibliography*, 1992; Eleanor Ruggles, *Prince of Players: Edwin Booth*, 1953.

James Harley

BORDEN, LISBETH ANDREW (9 June 1860–2 June 1927), accused murderess. Lizzie Borden was born in Fall River, Massachusetts, to Andrew J. and Sarah Morse Borden. After Sarah died, Andrew's marriage to Abby Durfee Gray caused tensions. It was widely believed that Lizzie killed Andrew and Abby with an axe on 4 August 1892 over real estate and inheritance. When authorities arrived, they found Lizzie's calm demeanor and self-possession suspicious, and at an inquest on 9 August, her testimony was filled with inconsistencies. Two days later she was arrested. Despite public shock and outcry over a woman's being imprisoned for murder, the ensuing investigation moved slowly. Her trial began on 5 June 1893, and fifteen days later she was acquitted for two reasons. First, the prosecution possessed neither a murder weapon nor a bloodstained garment that could link Lizzie directly to the killings; second, the court excluded Borden's incriminating inquest testimony because she had not been formally arrested at the time of questioning. Although public support was strong before the trial, it quickly waned after her acquittal. A woman linked to a murder scandal did not fare well in Gilded Age America. Lizzie spent her remaining years an outcast in Fall River, where she died of pneumonia at age sixty-six.

Further Reading: Victoria Lincoln, *A Private Disgrace*, 1967; Joyce G. Williams, J. Eric Smithburn, and M. Jeanne Peterson, eds., *Lizzie Borden: A Case Book of Family and Crime in the 1890s*, 1980; Arnold R. Brown, *Lizzie Borden: The Legend, the Truth, the Final Chapter*, 1991.

Jessica Matthews

BOUDINOT, ELIAS CORNELIUS (1 August 1835–27 September 1890), Cherokee lawyer, businessman, and assimilationist. Born in New Echota, Georgia, in the year his father signed the Cherokee treaty, Boudinot studied law in Arkansas and gained admittance to the bar in 1856. He then turned to journalism, editing newspapers in Fayetteville and Little Rock. A Democrat, Boudinot served in the Confederate Army. In 1866 he represented the Southern Cherokee in negotiations that culminated in a tribal treaty with the federal government. With his uncle, Stand Watie, Boudinot created the Watie and Boudinot Tobacco Company, which U.S. marshals seized in 1869 for nonpayment of taxes, even though Article 10 of the 1866 treaty promised immunity from agricultural taxes. In the 1871 *Cherokee Tobacco* case, the U.S. Supreme Court ruled that a congressional act could supersede or abrogate a treaty previously entered into, and that Boudinot's enterprise could be held accountable for unpaid excise taxes. Boudinot advocated dividing Native American lands into individual allotments. He lectured, farmed, and practiced law in Indian Territory until his death at Fort Smith, Arkansas.

Further Reading: Lois E. Forde, "Elias Cornelius Boudinot," Ph.D. diss., Columbia University, 1951; Robert K. Heimann, "The Cherokee Tobacco Case," *Chronicles of Oklahoma* 41 (1963): 299–322; Thomas Burnell Colbert, "Visionary or Rogue?: The Life and Legacy of Elias Cornelius Boudinot," *Chronicles of Oklahoma* 65 (1987): 268–281.

Leonard Schlup

BOUQUILLON, THOMAS JOSEPH (16 May 1840–5 November 1902), Catholic priest, educator, and moral theologian. Born in Warneton, Belgium, Bouquillon graduated from the Gregorian University in Rome, and was ordained in 1865. Two years later he earned a doctorate in moral theology, which was essentially a practical science concerned with character and behavior. Moral theology included everything relating to man's free actions and the last, or supreme, end to be attained through them. Observing the antimodernist ideas of Pope Pius IX and the scholastic revival under Pope Leo XIII, Bouquillon was influenced primarily by Thomas Aquinas's philosophy as expressed in the *Summa Theologica*. While teaching moral theology in Belgium and France, he published *Institutiones Theologia Moralis Fundamentalis* (1873), a textbook that appeared in several revised editions and was widely used in educating Roman Catholic priests in Europe and the United States. In 1885 he entered a Benedictine monastery, where he researched and wrote on Christian social ethics.

Four years later Bouquillon accepted Bishop John J. Keane's invitation to join the theology faculty of the newly established Catholic University of America in Washington, D.C. There he enlarged the theological library's collection, published articles, and advocated use of the social sciences. He taught for the remainder of his life, fostering an awareness of social Catholicism. When Archbishop John Ireland of Saint Paul, Minnesota, acknowledged in 1890 the necessity for public education and the state's duty to provide it for students, Bouquillon defended Ireland's position, and gave his written endorsement in 1891 in the pamphlet *Education: To Whom Does It Belong?* One of the more liberal members of Catholic University of America faculty, Bouquillon readily and openly entertained new ideas, and supported the Americanization of immigrant Catholic churches. In 1902 he retired from teaching and moved to Brussels, where he died.

Further Reading: *Catholic University Bulletin,* 9 January 1903, 152–63; C. J. Nuesse, "Thomas Joseph Bouquillon (1840–1902), Moral Theologian and Precursor of the Social Sciences in the Catholic University of America," *Catholic Historical Review* 72 (1986): 601–619.

Leonard Schlup

BOURBONISM. The derisive term Bourbonism refers to actions taken by conservative Southern Democrats from the late 1870s to about 1900. Bourbon evoked images of the French royal family restored to the throne in 1814, having learned nothing and having forgotten nothing from the French Revolution. American Bourbons, sometimes known as Redeemers, allegedly responded in similar fashion to the Civil War.

In wresting control of state governments from Republicans, Bourbon Democrats claimed to be restoring home rule and purging Northern corruption. Once in power, they downsized bureaucracies in the name of good government. They also trimmed or abolished school systems, initiated convict leasing, slashed taxes, and repudiated millions of dollars of Reconstruction-era debt. Staunchly committed to agricultural interests, they favored the sort of industrial development—railroads and textile mills—that resembled the plantation South rather than replacing it. Bourbon legislatures passed laws favoring landowners over tenants and sharecroppers. In effect, home rule meant white rule, secured through race baiting, terrorism, and ultimately disfranchisement of African Americans and white Republicans. Bourbonism's enduring legacy, therefore, is the creation of a Solid South built on one-party politics, white supremacy, and stunted industrial development.

Further Reading: C. Vann Woodward, *Origins of the New South, 1879–1913*, 1951; Michael Perman, *The Road to Redemption: Southern Politics, 1869–1879*, 1984; Mark Wahlgren Summers, *The Era of Good Stealings*, 1993.

Keith Harper

BOURKE, JOHN GREGORY (23 June 1846–8 June 1896), colonel, author, and ethnologist. Born in Philadelphia, Pennsylvania, Bourke enlisted in the Union Army at age sixteen, received a Medal of Honor, and graduated from the U.S. Military Academy in 1869. He joined General George Crook's staff when the latter assumed command of the Department of Arizona. Bourke spent the remainder of his life serving with the Third Cavalry. Interested in Native American customs and traditions, he undertook intensive research and study of Native American lives. He proved to be an astute and scientific observer. Bourke published books and articles on Native Americans with whom he came into contact, including *The Medicine Men of the Apache*, *The Snake Dance of the Moquis*, *On the Border with Crook*, and ten papers in the *American Anthropologist*. Bourke's remarkably full diaries ran to 124 volumes. His writings became classics, relevant for all times. After rendering assistance against Mexican marauders in 1891, Bourke was assigned to Fort Ethan Allen, Vermont, where he died.

Further Reading: Peter Cozzens, ed., *Eyewitnesses to the Indian Wars, 1865–1890*, 2001; F. W. Hodge, "John Gregory Bourke," *American Anthropologist* 9 (1906): 245–248; John G. Bourke Diaries, U.S. Military Academy Library, West Point, New York.

Leonard Schlup

BOUTWELL, GEORGE SEWALL (28 January 1818–27 February 1905), governor, representative, and senator. Born in Brookline, Massachusetts, Boutwell established careers in law, business and politics. During the Civil War, he was a Republican congressman who worked vigorously for emancipation, black suffrage, and the prosecution of the Union war effort. Boutwell played a prominent role in the House of Representatives during Andrew Johnson's presidency, strongly advocating Johnson's impeachment and helping draft and support the Fourteenth and Fifteenth amendments. In 1869 he was named secretary of the Treasury by President Ulysses S. Grant; his primary achievement was reducing the national debt by more than $350 million. The James Fisk-Jay Gould scheme to corner the gold market (1869) marred his tenure, and Boutwell resigned. He served as a senator from Massachusetts from 1873 to 1877. Under President Rutherford B. Hayes, he codified the U.S. statutes and was U.S. counsel before the French and American Claims Commission. In his later years, Boutwell returned to private practice, focusing on international law. He served as president of the Anti-Imperialist League from 1898 until his death in Groton, Massachusetts. A lifelong supporter of the underdog, Boutwell advocated Philippine independence and civil rights for African Americans.

Further Reading: Thomas H. Brown, *George Sewall Boutwell: Human Rights Advocate*, 1989; New York *Times*, 28 February 1905.

Ed Bradley

BOWKER, RICHARD ROGERS (4 September 1848–12 November 1933), literary and liberal leader. Born in Salem, Massachusetts, Bowker was graduated from the Free Academy (later the College of the City of New York) in 1868. As literary editor of the *New York Evening Mail* and later of the *New York Tribune*, he reviewed books and wrote columns that brought him international recognition. His work at *Publishers' Weekly*, beginning in 1872, underscored a lifelong association with the book trade. Bowker collaborated with Frederick Leypoldt and Melvil Dewey to found the American Library Association and launch *Library Journal*, which he edited for fifty years. He wrote two books on international copyright.

Bowker supported social engineering through democratic liberalism. His fight for free trade, international copyright, and social improvement culminated in the independent Republican or "Mugwump" movement, whose high point was the widespread support received in the presidential campaign of 1884. From 1890 to 1899 Bowker was first vice president of the Edison Electric Illuminating Company. Thereafter, he continued his liberal political activities during New York's civic renaissance, supporting general education, especially at his alma mater. World War I and events of the 1920s discouraged Bowker, although he continued to work for education and the library movement until his death in Stockbridge, Massachusetts.

Further Reading: E. McClung Fleming, *R. R. Bowker, Militant Liberal*, 1952; Milton James Ferguson, "Richard Rogers Bowker," in *Pioneering Leaders in Librarianship*, 1953.

Philip H. Young

BOXER REBELLION. This was a Chinese nationalist uprising against foreigners, Christians, and the Qing (Ch'ing) government in 1900. In 1898 a secret society of Chinese, Yihetuan, (the Boxers United in Righteousness), began to emerge in northwest Shandong. Mostly poor peasants and laborers made desperate by many natural disasters, they were joined by several female groups. In 1899, the Boxers attacked Christian missionaries and converts in China's northeastern provinces.

They considered the introduction of foreign goods disruptive to the traditional Chinese economy, and foreign constructions as harmful to the natural harmony. This sentiment was shared by many Chinese, including some Qing government officials. Since defeats in the Opium Wars (1839–1842, 1856–1860), China had been forced to sign humiliating treaties with Western powers and Japan, and had made territorial concessions to foreign countries. Many Chinese began to fear their country would be carved up like a melon.

In the spring of 1900, Boxers occupied the Chinese capital, Beijing (Peking), and laid siege to foreign legations there and in Tianjin. The Boxers defeated an army of two thousand sent by Western powers to protect their citizens. On 21 June the dowager empress declared war against foreign powers. On 14 July, an international expedition numbering nearly twenty thousand and under a joint command structure of eight Western nations, including the United States, occupied Tianjin. It took Beijing on 14 August, and forced the imperial government to sign the Boxer Protocol on 7 September 1901. It forced China to pay an enormous indemnity, allow armed foreign guards to protect the legation quarter in perpetuity, and execute leading Boxer supporters.

Fearing the incident might lead to China's partition, the United States declared its determination to preserve China's safety, peace, and administrative entity. Russia nevertheless expanded its sphere of influence in Manchuria during the rebellion. The Boxers' defeat discredited the ruling Qing Dynasty and accelerated political development toward revolution.

Further Reading: Joseph Esherick, *The Origins of the Boxer Uprising*, 1987; Jonathan D. Spence, *The Search for Modern China*, 1990.

Xiaojian Zhao

BRADLEY, JOSEPH PHILO (14 March 1813–22 January 1892), attorney and Supreme Court justice. Bradley was born in Berne, New York. He was graduated from Rutgers University in 1836 and admitted to the New Jersey bar in 1839. Appointed to the Supreme Court by President Ulysses S. Grant in 1870, he served until his death in Washington, D.C. Bradley was the final member added to the electoral commission appointed to decide the disputed 1876 presidential election, and he cast the deciding vote in favor of Rutherford B. Hayes. As an associate justice he is best known for his majority opinion in the *Civil Rights Cases* (1883), which overturned the 1875 Civil Rights Act's prohibitions against private discrimination in public accommodations. Despite his background as an advocate for rail interests, Bradley sympathized with attempts to expand the commerce clause of the Constitution to allow greater regulation of private enterprise. In *Munn* v. *Illinois* (1877), he joined the majority in upholding the Illinois regulation of the rail industry, recognizing a state's power to act in the public interest and giving rise to the "public interest doctrine."

Further Reading: Joseph P. Bradley, *Miscellaneous Writings of the Late Hon. Joseph P. Bradley . . . with a Sketch of His Life by Charles Bradley; and a Review of His "Judicial Record" by William Draper Lewis; and an Account of His "Dissenting Opinions" by A. Q. Keasbey . . .* , 1986.

R. Volney Riser

BRADLEY, MILTON (8 November 1836–30 May 1911), businessman and manufacturer of games. Bradley was born in Vienna, Maine, and completed high school in Lowell, Massachusetts, in 1854. He held a variety of jobs, including draftsman and lithographer, prior to beginning his career in manufacturing games and educational materials, such as games for soldiers, the Zoetrope, and the Myrioptican. With the advent of more leisure time and diversions in Gilded Age America, his games found popularity. Bradley also became interested in the kindergarten movement, and in 1869 published Edward Wiebe's book *Paradise of Childhood*, the first study dealing with kindergarten teaching published in English. Bradley manufactured kindergarten items and printed two magazines to promote his educational materials, as well as three works in the 1890s on teaching colors to children. A person of perseverance, he earned a solid reputation in the late nineteenth century for his advocacy of kindergarten and the creation of games to give Americans more enjoyment.

Further Reading: James J. Shea, Jr., *The Milton Bradley Story*, 1973; James J. Shea, Jr., and Charles Mercer, *It's All in the Game*, 1960.

Leonard Schlup

BRADLEY, WILLIAM O'CONNELL (18 March 1847–23 May 1914), governor and senator. Born in Garrard County, Kentucky, Bradley at age fifteen served as a recruiting officer before briefly entering the Union Army as a private. The precocious young man was admitted to the bar at eighteen by special act of the Kentucky General Assembly. Bradley was elected Garrard County attorney in 1870. A longtime standard-bearer for the minority Republican Party, he was its candidate for Congress in 1872 and 1876, and was nominated five times for U.S. senator. He attended most Republican National Conventions between 1880 and 1908. A legendary orator, Bradley seconded the nomination of President Theodore Roosevelt in 1904. He received 106 votes for vice president at the 1888 Republican National Convention and was a favorite son presidential candidate in 1896. Known as the outstanding southern Republican, he served twelve years on the National Committee. President Benjamin Harrison appointed him minister to Korea in 1889, but he declined to serve. After losing the Kentucky gubernatorial election of 1887, Bradley won in 1895, becoming the first Republican to hold the office. He was elected to the U.S. Senate in 1908, and served there until his death in Washington, D.C.

Further Reading: M. H. Thatcher, *Stories and Speeches of William O. Bradley*, 1916; *William O'Connell Bradley: Memorial Addresses Delivered in the Senate of the United States*, 1916; *Louisville Courier-Journal*, 24–25 May 1914.

Thomas E. Stephens

BRADWELL, MYRA COLBY (12 February 1831–14 February 1894), lawyer. Colby was born in Manchester, Vermont, and married James B. Bradwell of Illinois in 1852. Together they taught school briefly in Memphis, Tennessee, before moving to Chicago in 1854. There Bradwell's husband was admitted to the Illinois bar. Myra Bradwell was active in social and community activities, and studied law under her husband. In 1868 she began editing and publishing the *Chicago Legal News*, a successful weekly. In her columns, she advocated regulation of railroads and monopolies, the establishment of bar associations, and additional, improved courtrooms and procedures. Hardly any aspect of law escaped her notice. She helped organize the American Woman Suffrage Association and served on the executive committee of the Illinois Woman Suffrage Association. Although she had passed the required examinations and applied for admission to the Illinois bar in 1869, the state supreme court denied her petition because she was a woman, apparently ignoring the fact that Bradwell had been an honorary member of the bar since 1872 and had served four terms as its vice president. In 1890, the Illinois Supreme Court finally allowed her to practice law; two years later she appeared before the United States Supreme Court. In 1893, her body wracked by cancer, she toured the World's Columbian Exposition at Chicago in a wheelchair, having been an early advocate and lobbyist in Congress for that city as the fair's location. Arguably the nation's preeminent female lawyer during the Gilded Age, Bradwell died in Chicago.

Further Reading: *Chicago Legal News*, 17 February, 24 February, 12 May 1894.

Leonard Schlup

BRADY, JAMES BUCHANAN (12 August 1856–13 April 1917), financier and philanthropist. Born in New York City, Brady worked for the New York Central Railroad; Manning, Maxwell and Moore Manufacturing Company; and the Fox Pressed Steel Car Company. He amassed a considerable fortune as a shrewd salesman of railroad equipment. His collection of costly diamond jewelry, gaudy clothes, eccentric behavior, massive girth, gargantuan appetite, and gustatorial exploits attracted wide attention and earned him the sobriquet "Diamond Jim" Brady. Known to eat six or seven giant lobsters, dozens of oysters, clams, and crabs, two ducks, steak, and many desserts at a single setting, Brady would mash a pound of caviar into his baked potatoes. His gigantic meals prompted a New York restaurateur to comment that Brady was the best twenty-five

customers he had. Kidney surgery revealed that Brady's stomach was six times larger than normal. The flamboyant Brady introduced New York to the electric automobile. A regular figure on Broadway, he enjoyed a lengthy relationship with the actress Lillian Russell, to whom he offered a million dollars as part of a marriage proposal. She declined the package. Brady donated the money to establish the James Buchanan Brady Urological Institute of Johns Hopkins Hospital in Baltimore, Maryland. He died in Atlantic City, New Jersey.

Further Reading: H. Paul Jeffers, *Diamond Jim Brady: Prince of the Gilded Age*, 2001.

Leonard Schlup

BRADY, JOHN GREEN (25 May 1847–17 December 1918), missionary, businessman, and governor of Alaska. A New York City "street urchin" until rescued by Charles Loring Brace's Children's Aid Society, Brady acquired his middle name when Judge Green of Tipton, Indiana, took him in charge. Brady attended Yale, and was graduated from Union Theological Seminary in New York City in 1877. When his aspiration to found a school for abandoned boys in Texas failed, he carried his ministry north to Alaska's capital, Sitka. Disillusioned at the pace of these labors and awakened to local commercial prospects, he entered business and government after helping establish a manual arts school for native boys and girls at Sitka. Congress approved the Alaska Organic Act in 1884, and Brady won appointment as one of Alaska's first commissioners (justices of the peace). His merchandising-lumbering activities at Sitka and at the boom town of Juneau prospered, and Brady struggled to fortify native abilities to withstand the onrushing culture shock of Americanization.

From 1897 to 1906 Brady served as Alaska's territorial governor. Although tireless in publicizing Alaska's diverse potential, he advocated a go-slow policy when it came to home rule, rightly fearing that the transient miners lacked the permanence of Midwestern settlers. Canada's 1898 Klondike gold rush stimulated commerce in southeastern Alaska; similar frenzies across Alaska followed. Governor Brady succumbed to speculator contagion. Mesmerized by the charlatan Harry Reynolds, Brady identified himself with what became the fraudulent Reynolds-Alaska Development Company. After submitting his resignation to President Theodore Roosevelt in 1906, the ex-governor sought to redeem his reputation through activities stretching from China to New York City. His Sitka burial ceremony was handled by local natives.

Further Reading: Ted C. Hinckley, *Alaskan John G. Brady* 1982; and *The Canoe Rocks*, 1996.

Ted C. Hinckley

BRADY, MATHEW B. (1823–15 January 1896), war and portrait photographer. The events of Brady's early years are uncertain. He claimed to have been born in Warren County, New York, but at least one biographer has named his birthplace as Ireland. Somehow, young Brady met the portrait artist William Page and learned how to compose visually. In 1839 he saw a letter from Samuel F. B. Morse in the *New York Observer* describing Louis Daguerre's new photographic process, and was immediately fascinated by photography's possibilities. Brady became one of Morse's earliest students at the first photography school in America. After several years' study and work, Brady opened his gallery on Broadway in New York City around 1845. A perfectionist in his art, he sought to photograph the best-known persons of his day, including Edgar Allan Poe, Andrew Jackson, President James Polk, Horace Greeley, James Fenimore Cooper, Jenny Lind, and Abraham Lincoln. His collection of their images made him reasonably wealthy and much in demand as a photographer.

With permission from Lincoln but no government remuneration, Brady and his assistants photographed the Civil War, providing the first war scenes that most Americans had ever witnessed. His equipment was too cumbersome to capture actual fighting, but his postbattle scenes were so dramatic that they sold thousands of copies. Brady and his associates were not above moving corpses and making other rearrangements to heighten effect. The war depleted Brady's financial reserves, and he tried to rebuild his business in Washington, D.C., by pho-

tographing the famous. His subjects included Clara Barton, Frederick Douglass, President Andrew Johnson, and Robert E. Lee and other Southern generals. Brady was forced into bankruptcy, however. The U.S. government repeatedly refused to purchase his collection of war images at a fair price, finally obtaining them in 1874 for less than $3000. He continued to take portraits in his final years, working out of the Pennsylvania Railroad ticket office near the Treasury Department. He died in Washington, D.C., in the "alms ward" of a hospital just two weeks before the first major exhibition of his war photography. He was buried in Arlington National Cemetery with many of the generals and soldiers he had preserved for posterity.

Further Reading: James D. Horan, *Mathew Brady: Historian with a Camera*, 1955; George Hobart, *Mathew Brady*, 1984.

Richard Digby-Junger

BRAGG, EDWARD STUYVESANT (20 February 1827–20 June 1912), congressman and diplomat. Bragg was born in Unadilla, New York, and moved to Wisconsin in his early twenties to practice law. After distinguished Union Army service during the Civil War, Bragg, a Democrat, was elected to the Wisconsin Senate as a Democrat in 1867 and to the U.S. House of Representatives in 1877. Bragg served four terms altogether, chairing the Military Affairs Committee during the Forty-ninth Congress. President Grover Cleveland in 1888 appointed him envoy extraordinary and minister plenipotentiary to Mexico; Bragg remained there until 1889. An advocate of sound money and an uncompromising opponent of William Jennings Bryan, Bragg at first endorsed the National "Gold" Democratic ticket headed by John M. Palmer in 1896 but in the end supported Republican William McKinley for the presidency. President Theodore Roosevelt selected Bragg to fill the post of consul general to Cuba in 1902, and a year later, consul general to Hong Kong. After resigning in 1906, Bragg returned to Wisconsin, where he died at Fond du Lac.

Further Reading: *New York Times*, 21 June 1912; J.G. Hardgrove, "General Edward S. Bragg's Reminiscences," *Wisconsin Magazine of History* 33 (1950): 281–309; Edward S. Bragg Papers, State Historical Society of Wisconsin, Madison.

Leonard Schlup

BRECKINRIDGE, WILLIAM CAMPBELL PRESTON (28 August 1837–19 November 1904), congressman and journalist. Born in Baltimore, Maryland, Breckinridge attended school in Pennsylvania and Kentucky, and in 1855 was graduated from Centre College in Danville, Kentucky. He was descended from a distinguished family that included a grandfather who was a U.S. senator and attorney general, and a cousin who was vice president. Although his father and two brothers were Unionists during the Civil War, Breckinridge served as a colonel in the Confederacy's Ninth Kentucky Cavalry (1862–1865). From 1866 to 1868 he was editor of the *Lexington Observer and Reporter*. He became a lawyer and a spokesman for the New South and New Departure Democrats. Known as the "Silver-Tongued Orator," he initially failed to win political office because of his progressive racial views. In 1884 he was elected to Congress and served until 1895, when he lost a reelection bid following a sex scandal. He resumed his legal practice and became the chief editorial writer for his son's newspaper, the *Lexington Morning Herald* (1897–1904). He helped lead the Gold Democrats, opposed Democratic nominee William Goebel in the 1899 gubernatorial election, but maintained his progressive stance on racial and education issues. He died in Lexington, and was buried there.

Further Reading: James C. Klotter, *The Breckinridges of Kentucky, 1760–1981*, 1986.

Melba Porter Hay

BREWER, DAVID JOSIAH (20 June 1837–28 March 1910), associate justice of the U.S. Supreme Court. Brewer was born in Smyrna, Turkey, the nephew of Supreme Court Justice Stephen J. Field. He was graduated from Yale University in 1856, read law under his uncle David Dudley Field, and completed his studies at Albany Law School in 1858. He then moved to Leavenworth, Kansas Territory, to practice law; there he entered Republican politics and held elected judicial positions. He sat on the Kansas Supreme Court from 1870 to 1884. In

the latter year President Chester A. Arthur appointed Brewer to the Eighth Circuit Court, and in 1890 President Benjamin Harrison nominated him to the U.S. Supreme Court. Brewer served for twenty years. Generally his opinions protected business interests. He joined with others in 1895 to invalidate a federal income tax. The vacillation of his opinions between conservative and moderate reflected the paradoxical nature of change in his day. He was a recognized orator who supported woman's suffrage, headed the commission to investigate a boundary dispute involving Venezuela and Great Britain (1895–1897), and advocated international tribunals to adjudicate similar problems. Brewer also criticized imperialist expansion. In many ways he epitomized the Supreme Court during the Gilded Age, and left his legacy on the bench. He died in Washington, D.C.

Further Reading: David J. Brewer Papers, Yale University Library, New Haven, Connecticut; *New York Times*, 29 March 1910; Michael J. Brodhead, *David J. Brewer: The Life of a Supreme Court Justice, 1837–1910*, 1994.

Leonard Schlup

BREWSTER, BENJAMIN HARRIS (13 October 1816–4 April 1888), attorney general of the United States. Born in Salem County, New Jersey, Brewster was severely burned and scarred about his face in infancy. He graduated from Princeton College in 1834 and became a well-known Philadelphia lawyer, noted for his exceptional legal abilities as well as his peculiarities in dress and manners. Brewster switched political allegiance from the Democrats to the Republicans and associated in Pennsylvania politics with Simon Cameron. He was Pennsylvania's attorney general in 1867 and 1868. In 1881 he gained national attention when he held the position of special counsel for the government in the *Star Route* prosecutions. Shortly after the death of President James A. Garfield, Attorney General Wayne MacVeagh resigned his cabinet portfolio, and President Chester A. Arthur elevated Brewster to fill that vacancy, where he remained until retirement in 1885. Brewster's propensity for social entertainment helped to give the Arthur administration its reputation for social activity. Brewster died in Philadelphia.

Further Reading: Eugene C. Savidge, *Life of Benjamin Brewster, with Discourses and Addresses*, 1891; *New York Times*, 5 April 1888.

Leonard Schlup

BRICE, CALVIN STEWART (17 September 1845–15 December 1898), railroad builder and senator. Born in Denmark, Ohio, Brice first gained recognition in the 1870s and 1880s as a corporate lawyer and financier of a dozen railways. The New York, Chicago and St. Louis Railway (the Nickel Plate) was his greatest project. An influential Democrat, he served as a delegate-at-large to the national convention in 1888, and as a Democratic National Committee member and chair of the National Campaign Committee that year. In 1891 he began a single term in the U.S. Senate, where he was a member of the Steering and Appropriations committees. A conservative Democrat, he retired after the advent of William Jennings Bryan, free silver politics, and populism. He died in New York City.

Further Reading: *Lima [Ohio] Times-Democrat*, 16, 19, 20 December 1898; *New York Times*, 16 December 1898.

Norman E. Fry

BRIGGS, CHARLES AUGUSTUS (15 January 1841–8 June 1913), biblical scholar, theologian. Briggs was born in New York City, graduated from the University of Virginia, and studied at Union Theological Seminary in New York City from 1861 to 1863. He later did graduate work in Old Testament studies and theology at the University of Berlin, and returned to the United States in 1869. He served as pastor of the First Presbyterian Church in Roselle, New Jersey, until 1874. In that year Union Theological Seminary appointed him professor of Hebrew, and he spent the remainder of his teaching career there.

Briggs's ministry was closely linked to a publishing career. In 1881, he became coeditor of *The Presbyterian Review*, a journal of thought, which eventually brought his views into severe conflict with other Presbyterians and even his coeditor, Archibald Alexander Charles Hodge. Briggs advocated Protestant liberalism, and emphasized scientific rigor, historical research, archaeological evidence, and doctrinal skepticism in pursuit of biblical truths. He also accepted Darwin's theory of the survival of the fittest. In 1889, he delivered a sermon in which he declared orthodoxy a matter of opinion that varied according to the times in which one lived.

In 1891, Briggs delivered an inaugural address, "The Authority of Holy Scripture," to mark his appointment as chair of the department of biblical theology at Union. In it, he rejected the doctrine that God provided verbal inspiration for the precise text and wording of the Bible. As a result, the Presbyterian General Assembly refused to approve his appointment. This led to his heresy trial in 1892, one among a larger wave of accusations and trials throughout the century's final two decades. Though Briggs was acquitted, the General Assembly nevertheless suspended him from the ministry in 1893. Union Theological expressed support for Briggs by withdrawing from the Presbyterian General Assembly and maintaining Briggs in the post for life.

These events and ideas triggered a powerful conservative backlash among Presbyterians and eventually led to Briggs's decision to leave the church in 1898. He was subsequently ordained as an Episcopal priest. In his final years he shifted his thinking and writing to the subject of ecumenism among all Christians worldwide. His trial was the most famous and closely followed of all Presbyterian actions in the late nineteenth century, and closely foreshadowed deeper divisions that would appear early in the twentieth century. He died in New York City.

Further Reading: Sydney Ahlstrom, *Theology in America*, 1983; William R. Hutchinson, *American Protestant Thought in the Liberal Era*, 1985; Jon H. Roberts, *Darwinism and the Divine in America: Protestant Intellectuals and Organic Evolution, 1859–1900*, 1988.

Jerome D. Bowers II

BRIGHAM, JOSEPH HENRY (12 December 1838–30 June 1904), farm leader. Brigham was born in Lodi, Ohio, where he attended a one-room schoolhouse until his family moved to Delta, Ohio, in 1853. Although he identified himself as a farmer, husband, and father of seven children, his public life left little time for farm and family. In 1873 Brigham joined the

Ohio Grange, where he established a reputation as a forceful speaker. His oratorical skills and Civil War record as a Union colonel helped him to be elected master in 1878. In that office, he advocated cooperative marketing, railroad regulation, and agricultural science. A state senator in 1882, he helped draft and enact the bill creating the Ohio Agricultural Experiment Station. Subsequently, he served as treasurer of the station's governing board and a trustee of Ohio State University. Brigham championed the Hatch Act (1887), which granted $15,000 annually to each state to create or maintain an experiment station.

Brigham's role in promoting the Hatch Act led Grange masters throughout the United States to elect Brigham master of the National Grange in 1888. He held the position until 1897, when President William McKinley appointed him assistant secretary of agriculture. In both positions he sought additional funds for the experiment stations, which Congress finally granted in 1906. His wife's death in 1903 led him to retire to Delta, where he died.

Further Reading: John F. Dowler, *Centennial History: Ohio State Grange 1873–1973*, 1973; *Experiment Station Record* 16 (September 1904): 1–3.

Christopher Cumo

BRINKERHOFF, ROELIFF (28 June 1828–4 June 1911), Liberal Republican and philanthropist. Born in Cayuga County, New York, Brinkerhoff had made his fortune in law by the time of the Civil War. He served as quartermaster for various armies in several departments. A close friend of Secretary of War Edwin Stanton, he witnessed Abraham Lincoln's assassination. After the war Brinkerhoff entered politics. Unhappy with the Republican Party's stance on protective tariffs, he soon became identified as a leader of the Liberal Republican movement. In 1872, Brinkerhoff supported revision of Republican economic policies, especially those related to the tariff. Elected chairman of Ohio's Republican Executive Committee, he lost heart when his faction of the party went down to defeat in the mid-1870s. He rejoined the Democrats near the decade's end, and thereafter devoted his energies to philanthropy. In 1878 he was appointed to the Ohio State Board of Charities, and in 1880 became president of the National Conference of Charities and Corrections. Devoted to prison reform, Brinkerhoff belonged to the National Prison Association throughout the 1880s and succeeded former President Rutherford B. Hayes as its head in 1893. At the time of his death in Mansfield, Ohio, Brinkerhoff had achieved international status as a philanthropic reformer.

Further Reading: Roeliff Brinkerhoff, *Recollections of a Lifetime*, 1900; Irene C. Hanson, *The Contribution to Social Work Made by Roeliff Brinkerhoff (1828–1911)*, 1938; *Mansfield [Ohio] Shield*, 5 June 1911.

Christian B. Keller

BRISBANE, ARTHUR (12 December 1864–25 December 1936), journalist and editor. Born in Buffalo, New York, Brisbane as a youth learned about Fourierism, the philosophy of the French socialist reformer François Marie Charles Fourier, who preached the reorganization of society into small, self-sufficient, cooperative, utopian agricultural communities. In 1885, Brisbane was the European correspondent for the *New York Sun*, owned by Charles Dana. Two years later he assumed control of that newspaper's evening edition. Brisbane, who enthusiastically promoted lurid crime news and phrenology, joined the staff of Joseph Pulitzer's *World* in 1890, and in 1897, the Hearst organization. Brisbane's headlines and stories before and during the Spanish-American War of 1898 made him one of the yellow journalists noted for their sensationalism. In 1900, Brisbane launched the *Chicago American*. He died in New York City.

Further Reading: Arthur Brisbane Papers, George Arents Research Library, Syracuse University; Oliver Carlson, *Brisbane: A Candid Biography*, 1938; Joyce Milton, *The Yellow Kids*, 1989.

Leonard Schlup

BRISTOW, BENJAMIN HELM (20 June 1832–22 June 1896), politician and cabinet member. Born at Elkton, Kentucky, Bristow was graduated from Jefferson College in Pennsylvania, studied law under his father, fought in the Union Army, and participated in the capture of the Confederate raider John Hunt Morgan. An unconditional Unionist, Bristow won election to the Kentucky senate, where he worked to build the Republican Party. As U.S. attorney for Kentucky, he defended the Civil Rights Act of 1866. Later, as solicitor general of the United States (1870–1872), he argued many Reconstruction issues in court. President Ulysses S. Grant nominated him as attorney general, but pressure from machine politicians forced withdrawal of his name. Bristow helped found the American Bar Association and served as its second president. His great ambition was to be a Supreme Court justice, but when his law partner, John Marshall Harlan, received the nomination in 1877, his chances evaporated.

As secretary of the Treasury from 1874 to 1876, Bristow exposed several frauds, most notably the Whiskey Ring. When the evidence pointed to Grant's friends, the president intervened. Bristow resigned in protest. His reform spirit made him a contender for the 1876 Republican presidential nomination, but party bosses blocked that effort. Thereafter he resumed his legal career. He died in New York City.

Further Reading: Ross A. Webb, *Benjamin Helm Bristow: Border State Politician*, 1967.

Damon Eubank

BROOKLYN BRIDGE. Construction of the Brooklyn Bridge across the East River between the boroughs of Brooklyn and Manhattan in New York City began in 1869; when completed in 1883, it was, at 1595 feet, more than half again as long as any earlier bridge. It was designed and engineered by John Augustus Roebling (1806–1869), inventor and promoter of the twisted wire cable that made such a span possible; the Brooklyn Bridge uses parallel, galvanized drawn-steel wires that were spun in place to create an ultimate strength of 71.5 tons per square inch. Roebling died of an injury sustained during the final survey of the site in 1869, and his daring plan was accomplished by his son, Washington Augustus Roebling (1837–1926). He had to direct the bridge's construction from a nearby house after he contracted caisson disease (the bends), following a descent into one of the underwater chambers in 1872. The soaring Gothic openings in the bridge's towers are a concession to the European his-

torical references that characterize Gilded Age architectural ideals. This monumental achievement became a world-famous symbol of American technology and engineering.

Further Reading: John Augustus Roebling, *Long and Short Span Railway Bridges*, 1869; Alan Trachtenberg, *Brooklyn Bridge: Fact and Symbol*, 1979; Brooklyn Museum, *The Great East River Bridge, 1883–1983*, 1983.

David G. Wilkins

BROOKS, PHILLIPS (13 December 1835–23 January 1893), Episcopal bishop of Massachusetts. Born in Boston, Brooks was graduated form Harvard College in 1855 and from the Virginia Theological Seminary in 1859. Ten years later, he was elected rector of Trinity Church in Boston. An outspoken supporter of the Union who denounced slavery and favored black enfranchisement, Brooks attracted attention for his thought-provoking sermons, poems, and essays; his European travels; and his religious ideas. In 1868 he wrote the Christmas carol "O Little Town of Bethlehem." He preached rapidly without extravagant language, in a high-pitched voice that could be heard easily. Defining the sermon as an instrument to proclaim truth through personality, Brooks on occasion participated in interdenominational services. His keen intellect, inquiring mind, perceptive reflections, and voracious appetite for reading led him to study numerous theological treatises. He argued that human capabilities were considerable and that in Christ, God and man had met. Brooks in 1891 accepted the bishopric of Massachusetts. Fifteen months later, he died in Boston, leaving a legacy that sought to encourage orthodox Trinitarianism, awaken faith in Jesus Christ, and raise the hopes of each individual. The combination linked him to both liberal and conservative Christians in his day and throughout the next century.

Further Reading: Raymond W. Albright, *Focus on Infinity: A Life of Phillips Brooks*, 1961; Phillips Brooks Papers, Houston Library, Harvard University.

Leonard Schlup

BROWN, BENJAMIN GRATZ (28 May 1826–13 December 1885), senator and governor. Born in Lexington, Kentucky, Brown graduated from Yale University in 1847 and received a law degree before moving to St. Louis in 1849. There he edited the *Missouri Democrat*, promoting emancipation and the views of Senator Thomas Hart Benton. From 1852 to 1859, Brown served in the state legislature. An antislavery Democrat, he lost his bid for reelection after leaving his party in 1858. In 1863, Brown filled Missouri's vacant Senate seat, identifying with the Radical Republicans during his four years in the upper house. In order to hasten emancipation, he organized the Louisville "Freedom Convention" in 1864. Two years later, Brown inspired the Liberal Republican movement, demanding immediate suffrage for freed slaves and amnesty for ex-Confederates, themes he reiterated during his successful 1870 gubernatorial campaign. Though accused of mismanagement as Missouri's governor, he ran for vice president in 1872, paired with Horace Greeley on the Liberal Republican ticket. Brown died in St. Louis.

Further Reading: Norma L. Peterson, *Freedom and Franchise: The Political Career of B. Gratz Brown*, 1968; William E. Parrish, *Missouri Under Radical Rule: 1865–1870*, 1965.

Jane M. Armstrong

BROWN, HALLIE QUINN (10 March 1849–16 September 1949), African-American educator, speaker, and author. Born in Pittsburgh, Pennsylvania, the daughter of former slaves, Brown graduated in 1873 from Wilberforce College in Ohio. Shortly thereafter she commenced work as a lecturer for the Lyceum and also taught in elementary schools in South Carolina and Mississippi. She published *Bits and Odds: A Choice Selection of Recitations* in 1880. Two years later Brown joined the Wilberforce Concert Company, a group of singers who toured the nation. Dean of Allen University in Columbia, South Carolina, from 1885 to 1887 and a public schoolteacher in Dayton, Ohio, from 1887 to 1891, Brown taught under Frederick Douglass at Tuskegee Institute in Alabama prior to returning to Wilberforce University, where she served as professor of elocution and a trustee. In addition, she spent several years in Europe helping to raise funds for Wilberforce. In 1893 Brown attended the World's Columbian Exposition in Chicago and

in Ohio formed the Colored Women's League. Active in the Women's Christian Temperance Union in the 1890s and in the African Methodist Episcopal Church, Brown contributed to several causes in the twentieth century, earning the distinction of becoming the first woman to speak from the front porch of Senator Warren G. Harding's home in Marion, Ohio, during the presidential campaign of 1920. She died in her one hundredth year at her home in Wilberforce.

Further Reading: Ann Jennette S. McFarlin, "Hallie Quinn Brown: Black Woman Elocutionist," *Southern Speech Communication Journal* 46 (1980): 72–82; Erlene Stetson, "Black Feminism in Indiana, 1893–1933," *Phylon* 64 (1983): 292–98.

Leonard Schlup

BROWN, HENRY BILLINGS (2 March 1836–4 September 1913), U.S. Supreme Court justice. Born in South Lee, Massachusetts, Brown was graduated from Yale University in 1856, was admitted to the Michigan bar, and subsequently was appointed federal deputy marshal. After an unsuccessful congressional bid as a Republican, Brown was appointed district court judge for eastern Michigan by President Ulysses Grant in 1875. President Benjamin Harrison elevated him to the Supreme Court fifteen years later. Although placed on the Court for his admiralty law expertise, Brown became known for larger issues. Authoring the Court's *Insular Cases* decision, in 1901 he provided the legal justification for acquisition of the Philippines and Puerto Rico. He was the only northern justice to vote to uphold the income tax's legality in *Pollock* v. *Farmers Loan and Trust Company* (1895). He wrote the majority opinion in the *Plessy* v. *Ferguson* decision (1896). By upholding a Louisiana statute requiring "separate, but equal" public transportation facilities, Brown introduced the "Jim Crow" concept into constitutional law.

Brown's effectiveness was severely reduced in 1900 when he lost the sight in his right eye. Thereafter he was unable to perform his duties without assistance. He retired in 1906, and died in Bronxville, New York, after a lengthy illness.

Further Reading: *New York Times*, 5 September 1913; Robert J. Glennon, Jr., "Justice Henry Billings Brown: Values in Tension," *University of Colorado Law Review* 44 (1973): 553–604.

Harvey Gresham Hudspeth

BROWN, MARGARET (18 July 1867–26 October 1932), socialite. Born in Hannibal, Missouri, Margaret "Maggie" Tobin traveled to the mining town of Leadville, Colorado, where she worked in a dry goods store. In 1886, she married James Joseph Brown, superintendent of a mining company. Unlike her husband, Brown acquired a taste for high living, expensive clothes, and Eastern society, entertaining lavishly at her Seventh Street home. Discovery of a rich gold mine in 1893 made the Browns wealthy. The following year they moved to Denver, where they purchased a $30,000 mansion. Brown was listed in the social directory, and her name appeared regularly on Denver's society pages. The press emphasized her fashionable wardrobe, ornate jewelry, hairstyles, parties, and outspoken personality. She gave generously to charities. Brown supported an equal rights amendment for women. Her indomitable spirit helped sustain hope among passengers in her lifeboat after the sinking of the *Titanic* in 1912. Following that catastrophe, Brown turned crusader and formed a committee of wealthy survivors to raise money for destitute victims of the disaster. Popularized in the twentieth century as "Molly" Brown, she epitomized the sumptuous lifestyle of Gilded Age high society in Colorado. Brown died alone and almost penniless in New York City.

Further Reading: Kristen Iversen, *Molly Brown: Unraveling the Myth*, 1999.

Leonard Schlup

BRUCE, BLANCHE KELSO (1 March 1841–17 March 1898), U.S. senator and African-American political leader. The first African American to serve a full term in the U.S. Senate and the nation's second African-American senator, Bruce was born a slave in Farmville, Virginia. He escaped during the Civil War; settled in Hannibal, Missouri; studied at Oberlin College in Ohio; and ultimately became a successful planter in Mississippi during Reconstruction. In 1874 the Mississippi legislature elected Bruce to the U.S. Senate, where

he remained until he retired in 1881. During his term, he advocated federal action to protect African Americans' voting rights in the South, supported citizenship for Native Americans, opposed legislation to exclude Chinese immigrants, chaired the Freedmen's Bank Committee, favored assimilation of blacks and whites into American society, promoted education for blacks, and opposed schemes to persuade African Americans to emigrate to other countries. He refused the post of ambassador to Brazil in 1881 because the nation permitted slavery. Later that year President James A. Garfield appointed Bruce register of the Treasury, in which capacity he served from 1881 to 1885. Under President Benjamin Harrison he was recorder of deeds for the District of Columbia. He again was register of the Treasury during William McKinley's administration. A popular Republican speaker, Bruce died in Washington, D.C.

Further Reading: Kenneth Eugene Mann, "Blanche Kelso Bruce: United States Senator Without a Constituency," *Journal of Mississippi History* 38 (1976): 183–198; Blanche K. Bruce Papers, Rutherford B. Hayes Presidential Center Library, Fremont, Ohio; Blanche K. Bruce Papers, Howard University Library, Washington D.C.

Leonard Schlup

BRYAN, WILLIAM JENNINGS (19 March 1860–26 July 1925), congressman, Democratic Party leader, and presidential candidate. Born in Salem, Illinois, Bryan was graduated from Illinois College in 1881 and from Union Law School, Chicago, in 1883. In 1887 he moved to Lincoln, Nebraska. Three years later, he was elected to the House of Representatives, partly due to his effectiveness as a campaigner and partly to the disruption of state politics created by the emergence of the People's Party that year. Bryan won reelection in 1892. As a congressman, he gained national attention for some of his speeches, especially one favoring an income tax. He also led opposition to repeal of the Sherman Silver Purchase Act in 1893.

In Nebraska, Bryan favored cooperation with the Populists, and he was a key figure in the election of the Populist William V. Allen to the U.S. Senate in 1892. In 1894, he led Nebraska Democrats to support Populists for state offices; the fusion candidate for governor, Silas Holcomb, was successful. Bryan did not seek a third term in Congress in 1894. During much of 1895 and early 1896, he traveled the country as an *Omaha World-Herald* journalist and tireless advocate for the free and unlimited coinage of silver. He understood the impact of currency deflation on debtors, especially debtor farmers, and he effectively presented the case for a stable, silver-based currency in metaphors appealing to rural audiences. By the opening of the 1896 Democratic National Convention, a majority of the delegates favored silver. As a Platform Committee member, Bryan spoke to the gathering on the silver debate. His "Cross of Gold" speech has become the standard example for capturing a convention through oratory. Though not a declared candidate when he began to speak, he won the presidential nomination on the fifth ballot. The Populists and the Silver Republicans also nominated him. In a hard-fought campaign against William McKinley, the Republican nominee, Bryan lost.

When the United States declared war on Spain in 1898, Governor Holcomb named Bryan as colonel of the Third Nebraska Volunteer Regiment, which spent the entire war in a Florida camp. In 1900, Bryan again sought the presidency, basing his campaign on opposition to imperialism and monopolies and on support for silver coinage. He faced no opposition for the Democratic and Silver Republican presidential nominations, but the Populists divided, with one faction supporting Bryan and the other running its own candidate. McKinley won by a larger margin than in 1896.

Bryan remained the Democratic Party's most significant leader for another decade, speaking frequently throughout the country and editing a weekly newspaper, *The Commoner*. As party head, Bryan led many Democrats to reject the commitment to minimal government characteristic of most of their party's leaders from Andrew Jackson to Grover Cleveland. Instead, Bryan and his allies fused the antimonopolism of Jackson to a commitment to governmental intervention on behalf of "the people" and against powerful economic interests, an approach similar to that of Bryan's Populist allies. He repeatedly wrote into Democratic platforms his opposition to monopoly; at various times, he proposed antitrust actions, licensing to bar

from interstate commerce any corporation with more than a 50 percent market share, and government ownership as solutions to the problems of monopoly in various circumstances. He sought the presidency, again unsuccessfully, in 1908. In 1912, he supported Woodrow Wilson at a key moment in the Democratic National Convention. As president, Wilson appointed Bryan secretary of state. During Bryan's final decade, he promoted woman suffrage and prohibition, and prominently opposed the teaching of evolution, which, he believed, undermined the religious faith that he considered the basis of a moral society. He died in Dayton, Tennessee.

Further Reading: William Jennings Bryan Papers, Library of Congress; Paolo E. Coletta, *William Jennings Bryan*, 3 vols., 1964–1969; Robert W. Cherny, *A Righteous Cause: The Life of William Jennings Bryan*, 1985.

Robert W. Cherny

BRYCE, JAMES (10 May 1838–22 January 1922), scholar. Bryce was born in Belfast, Ireland, and was graduated from Trinity College, Oxford, to which he returned in 1870 as Regius Professor of civil law. That year he visited Boston, New York City, and Washington, D.C., with a friend, Albert Venn Dicey. The tour convinced Bryce that the United States was closer to democracy than any European nation, a conviction strengthened by a second visit, from 1881 to 1883. In January 1886 Bryce and Lord John Acton founded the *English Historical Review*, which remains an influential journal. Two years later Bryce published *The American Commonwealth*, in which he asserted that political power lay with "the will of the people." His confidence in American political institutions was not unlimited, however; he disliked both the spoils system and machine politics. Critics hailed *The American Commonwealth* as a companion to Alexis de Tocqueville's *Democracy in America*, though Woodrow Wilson, then a Princeton University professor, found it superficial in tracing the development of political institutions.

Bryce's faith in democracy did not extend to colonies. An imperialist, he believed Europe and the United States had a duty to gain colonies in order to spread Christianity and capitalism, a view he promoted in *Impressions of South Africa* (1897). Bryce died in Sidmouth, England.

Further Reading: Louis Auchincloss, "Lord Bryce," *American Heritage* 32 (1981): 98–104.

Christopher Cumo

BUCHANAN, JOHN PRICE (24 October 1847–14 May 1930), Farmers' Alliance leader and state governor. A native of Williamson County, Tennessee, and a Confederate veteran, Buchanan served in the Tennessee legislature as a Democrat from 1887 to 1891. There he led the state's small farmer ("Wool Hat") faction, which had previously followed Andrew Johnson. In 1888, he became head of the state's Farmers' Alliance. One year later it merged with the Agricultural Wheel to form the Tennessee Farmers and Laborers Union, again headed by Buchanan. Backed by Southern Alliance vice president John H. McDowell, Buchanan was elected governor in 1890. Alliance candidates also took control of the assembly. Buchanan and his "Farmers' Legislature" became bogged down in the Coal Miners War, a series of East Tennessee uprisings by opponents of the convict labor system. Although Buchanan called out state troops, he failed to restore order completely. When a special legislative session refused to end the leasing system, Buchanan lost public support. In 1892, he declined his party's renomination, but ran as an independent. Though he received McDowell's unofficial support and that of the newly formed Populist Party, rumors of a Populist/Republican bargain hampered his campaign. Supposedly the Populists would help the GOP secure the governorship in return for Republican support for McDowell for U.S. senator. After his defeat, Buchanan retired and never again sought elective office.

Further Reading: Robert E. Corlew, *Tennessee: A Short History*, 1981.

Harvey Gresham Hudspeth

BUCHTEL, JOHN RICHARD (18 January 1822–23 May 1892), industrialist and philanthropist. Born to a poor family in Green Township, Ohio, Buchtel received no formal education. He bought farms, and opened coal and iron mines. In 1865 he became president of the Akron branch of Aultman, Miller, and Company, which made mowers and reapers. Buchtel helped organize and finance various local companies; his timely loan to Dr. Benjamin F. Goodrich helped him start a rubber factory in Akron. Buchtel contributed liberally to the construction of churches in his region and donated to the Akron Library Association. He belonged to the Universalist Church, which established a coeducational, nonsectarian college in Akron in 1870. Named Buchtel College to honor its chief benefactor, whose gifts totaled more than a half-million dollars, the institution became the University of Akron forty-three years later. Buchtel, stricken with paralysis in 1887, suffered severe business reverses and gave away nearly all his wealth; he was almost destitute by the time of his death in Akron.

Further Reading: Karl H. Grismer, *Akron and Summit County*, 1952; Bierce Library and Archives, University of Akron.

Leonard Schlup

BUCKNER, SIMON BOLIVAR (1 April 1823–8 January 1914), state governor and vice presidential candidate. Born near Munfordville, Kentucky, Buckner, a West Point graduate and Mexican War veteran, rose to lieutenant general in the Confederate Army. He is most remembered as the man who surrendered Fort Donelson to Ulysses Grant, who thereby earned the sobriquet "unconditional surrender." Buckner won the 1887 Kentucky gubernatorial race as handpicked Bourbon candidate of the *Louisville Courier-Journal* and the Louisville and Nashville Railroad. In office, however, he quickly distinguished himself for honesty, integrity, and independence by vetoing more private interest bills than his ten predecessors combined. An unlikely progressive, Buckner wanted a general incorporation law, stricter regulation of trusts and turnpike companies, and conservation of forests, but these and other advanced ideas were defeated. He did succeed in pushing through a state board of tax equalization, a parole system for convicts, and codification of school laws. Buckner also provided a calm and steady hand when the state was rocked by the news in March 1888 that Treasurer James Tate had embezzled nearly $250,000. Unlike other governors, Buckner applied his pardoning power judiciously. He faced the additional burden of suppressing mountain blood feuds. At the 1890–1891 Constitutional Convention, Buckner helped streamline the legislature, but unsuccessfully sought to eliminate all property tax exemptions.

Buckner failed to win a U.S. Senate seat in 1895 and left the Democratic Party the next year when William Jennings Bryan captured it for free silver. In protest, Buckner became John M. Palmer's running mate on the Gold Democrat ticket. He retired following this defeat, and he died at his estate, Glen Lily, near Munfordville.

Further Reading: Arndt M. Stickles, *Simon Bolivar Buckner: Borderland Knight*, 1940; Lowell H. Harrison, "Simon Bolivar Buckner," in *Lowell H. Harrison, ed., Kentucky's Governors, 1792–1985*, 1985, pp. 100–103.

Edward Scott Blakeman

BUFFALO SOLDIERS. In 1866 Congress enacted legislation to increase the nation's peacetime military establishment. The act included a provision for voluntary enlistment of African Americans to patrol regions with Native American populations in Kansas, Oklahoma, Texas, New Mexico, and other areas. Approximately twelve thousand black men formed army regiments consisting of the Twenty-fourth and Twenty-fifth Infantry and the Ninth and Tenth Cavalry divisions. The Plains Indians referred to the African-American troops as "buffalo soldiers" because of the resemblance of hair texture. Constituting nearly 20 percent of army soldiers stationed in the West, these African Americans engaged in combat with Crazy Horse and Geronimo; in fact, it was almost exclusively buffalo soldiers who fought Apaches. One of the last engagements occurred in 1890 at the Battle of Wounded Knee. Military successes of buffalo soldiers contributed to the conquest of the American West. Ironically, African-American soldiers participated in war against a native race that had long been subjugated by whites. Emanuel Stance, first sergeant of Company F, Ninth Cavalry, was one

of eighteen African Americans to receive the Medal of Honor for service in the Native American campaigns during the years following the Civil War. Moreover, three African Americans graduated from the U.S. Military Academy at West Point in the postbellum period: Henry Ossian Flipper (1887), John H. Alexander (1887), and Charles A. Young (1889).

Further Reading: William H. Leckie, *The Buffalo Soldiers: A Narrative of the Negro Cavalry in the West*, 1967; Charles L. Kenner, *Buffalo Soldiers and Officers of the Ninth Cavalry, 1867–1898: Black and White Together*, 1999; Frank N. Schubert, *Black Valor: Buffalo Soldiers and the Medal of Honor, 1870–1898*, 1997.

Leonard Schlup

BURBANK, LUTHER (7 March 1849–11 April 1926), horticulturist. Born in Lancaster, Massachusetts, he attended public schools and Lancaster Academy. Showing an early aptitude for science and mechanics, at age twenty-two he hybridized the Burbank potato. After moving to Santa Rosa, California, in 1875, Burbank began experiments to produce new forms of plant life through cross-fertilization and natural selection. His masterful, exacting technique, although based largely on intuition, enabled him to introduce between eight hundred and a thousand new plants. Among the most famous are the russet potato and the Shasta daisy. Burbank remained controversial in the scientific community, whose members divided over whether he was a self-taught genius or a self-promoting commercial breeder. Negative press that he received for various unsuccessful moneymaking schemes and his proclamation of himself as a psychic and an infidel did not diminish his wide popular acclaim as the "plant wizard." Burbank the plant man stood alongside Thomas A. Edison the inventor and Henry Ford the carmaker as a personification of Gilded Age ingenuity. He died in Santa Rosa. His authority was posthumously cited in Congress in 1930, when it passed a patent protection bill for originators of new or distinctively different trees and plants.

Further Reading: Peter Dreyer, *A Gardener Touched with Genius: The Life of Luther Burbank*, 1975; Ken Kraft and Pat Kraft, *Luther Burbank: The Wizard and the Man*, 1967.

James Summerville

BURCHARD, SAMUEL DICKINSON (6 September 1812–25 September 1891), Presbyterian minister. Burchard was born in Steuben, New York, and attended the local public schools and Centre College in Kentucky. He received his religious training at the Transylvania Presbytery and for forty years was pastor of the Houston Street Presbyterian Church, in New York City, where he denounced slavery and alcohol. In 1879 he became pastor of the Murray Hill Presbyterian Church, also in New York. After 1866 he served as chancellor of Ingham University, and later as president of Rutgers Female Academy.

A Republican, Burchard may have cost candidate James G. Blaine the presidency in October 1884, by calling the Democrats a party of "rum, Romanism, and rebellion." The insult undid Blaine's attempt to gain Irish votes, and he lost the election by fewer than thirty thousand votes. Afterward Republicans and Democrats ridiculed Burchard, who refused to apologize or retract his words. The only defense he offered—that God had used him for a higher purpose—satisfied no one. Burchard died in Saratoga, New York.

Further Reading: Leonard D. White, *The Republican Era, 1869–1901*, 1958; Allen Nevins, *Grover Cleveland: A Study in Courage*, 1933; *New York Times*, 26 September 1891.

Christopher Cumo

BURGESS, JOHN WILLIAM (26 August 1844–13 January 1931), political theorist and university dean. Born in Giles County, Tennessee, Burgess attended Cumberland University before serving as scout and quartermaster during the Civil War (1862–1864). After receiving his A.B. degree from Amherst College in 1867, he studied law in Springfield, Massachusetts, then moved west to begin a teaching career at Knox College in Illinois. From 1871 to 1873 he studied history and political philosophy at the German universities of Göttingen, Leipzig, and Berlin. After three years as professor at Amherst, he joined Columbia University in 1876. He led the establishment of its school of political science in 1880, the first of its kind in the United States. In 1886, Burgess and his colleagues began publishing the *Political Science*

Quarterly and launched the Academy of Political Science. His work culminated in the publication of *Political Science and Comparative Constitutional Law* (1890–1891), which outlined the nation-state's significance in protecting individual liberties. Burgess served as dean of Columbia's graduate school from 1909 until his retirement in 1912. He died in Brookline, Massachusetts.

Further Reading: Thomas Bender, *New York Intellect*, 1987; John W. Burgess, *Reminiscences of an American Scholar: The Beginnings of Columbia University*, 1934; R. Gordon Hoxie, "John W. Burgess: American Scholar," Ph.D. diss., Columbia University, 1950.

Kim P. Sebaly

BURK, MARTHA JANE CANNARY ("CALAMITY JANE") (1852?–2 August 1903), western heroine. Born in Princeton, Missouri, Martha Jane Cannary spent her early childhood in the northern interior West. In 1865 her parents finally settled in Virginia City, Montana, a gold rush town in the heart of Sioux-Cheyenne country. Orphaned at age thirteen, she matured into a tall, comely, self-reliant frontier woman who learned to ride and shoot and drive teams. She habitually wore men's clothing, striding about the gold camps carrying a rifle and brace of revolvers. There is positive evidence that in 1876 she acompanied General George Crook's punitive expedition against the Sioux and Cheyenne in the Black Hills. During the campaign, Calamity served as a bona fide teamster and, possibly, moonlighted as a camp follower. Her nickname derives from the diary of a trooper in General Crook's regiment who wrote: "Calamity is hear [*sic*] going up with the troops."

Sometime in June 1876, Calamity arrived in Deadwood, South Dakota, with a party of flamboyant, buckskin-clad plainsmen that included Wild Bill Hickok. Two months later he was murdered at the Number Ten Saloon while playing poker. Calamity's brief association with Wild Bill has fostered the myth that the two were secretly married and had a child. By 1877 Calamity had become a legend in her own right, regularly featured as the "dashing female partner" of Deadwood Dick in Edward L. Wheeler's dime novels. She remained in the

Black Hills gold camps until 1880, living with a succession of "husbands." Between 1880 and 1895 she led a vagabond existence, working as a teamster hauling supplies to the mining camps of Montana, Dakota Territory, Wyoming, and Colorado, raising a commotion wherever she happened to alight.

By 1895 Calamity had become the companion of Clinton Burk(e), a native Texan and fellow teamster. Thereafter, she called herself Mrs. Martha E. Burk(e). The following year Calamity joined the "dime museum" (carnival) of Kohl and Middleton, appearing on stage dressed in buckskin trousers and jacket and billed as "the famous woman scout of the Wild West." To bolster the company's press releases, Calamity wrote a brief autobiography that she sold on tour for a few pennies. Her tenure in show business ended abruptly in 1901, at the Pan-American Exposition in Buffalo, New York, where, after knocking out a policeman during a drunken brawl, she was arrested. Buffalo Bill Cody bought her ticket back to Deadwood, South Dakota, where she died penniless. At her request, she was buried next to the grave of Wild Bill Hickok in Mt. Moriah Cemetery, Deadwood.

Further Reading: Roberta Beed Sollid, *Calamity Jane*, rev. ed., 1995; Nolie Mumey, *Calamity Jane, 1852–1903: A History of Her Life and Adventures in the West*, 1950; Doris Faber, *Calamity Jane, Her Life and Legend*, 1992.

Maurice Law Costello

BURLINGAME TREATY OF 1868. This was a mutual agreement between the United States and China and an amendment to the 1858 Treaty of Tianjin. Anson Burlingame was U.S. minister to the Qing (Ch'ing) government. A former Massachusetts congressman with a genial sympathy for China, he won the confidence of the Qing rulers. In 1867, China asked him to help normalize diplomatic relations with the Western world. Representing the Chinese government, he signed the Burlingame Treaty with the U.S. government in July 1868. The pact secured greater privileges for American citizens in China. It also contained two important provisions that protected Chinese immigrants in America. In one article both countries recognized the inalienable human right to change homeland and allegiance, as well as the mutual advantage of free migration. Another article granted Chinese subjects visiting or residing in the United States the same privileges, immunities, and exemptions enjoyed by the citizens or subjects of the most favored nation.

The Burlingame Treaty became a major obstacle for the anti-Chinese forces in the United States. In 1880 the United States negotiated a new treaty with China, under which the United States gained the unilateral right to limit Chinese immigration, thereby opening the way for federal exclusion laws.

Further Reading: Walter LaFeber, *The New Empire: An Interpretation of American Expansion, 1860–1898*, 1963; Charles J. McClain, *In Search of Equality: The Chinese Struggle Against Discrimination in Nineteenth-Century America*, 1994.

Xiaojian Zhao

BURNHAM, DANIEL HUDSON (4 September 1846–1 June 1912), architect and urban planner. Born in Henderson, New York, but ultimately established in Chicago, Burnham studied with Tilly Brown Hayward and William Le Baron Jenney. In 1873 he formed a partnership with John Wellborn Root. At first their firm designed residences, such as the Gothic Revival–style home of the magnate John B. Sherman. During the 1880s Burnham and Root built some of Chicago's early skyscrapers, including the Montauk Block, the Rookery, and the Rand-McNally Building. The Masonic Temple, at twenty-two stories, was the world's tallest building in 1892. In 1890 Burnham and Root became consulting architects to the World's Columbian Exposition, held in 1893 to commemorate the European arrival in the Americas. They worked with landscape architects Frederick Law Olmsted and Henry Sargent Codman, and some of America's most established firms designed the pavilions. The grand vistas of the plan and the classical emphasis in the architecture re-created the splendor of imperial Rome in the American Midwest and revealed the extent to which the Gilded Age style was indebted to European models and inspiration. After Root's untimely death, Burnham continued as project director. This complex inspired monumental city planning and the "city beautiful" movement in urban America. Burnham's own plans, especially for Washington, D.C., were significant in their integration of parks within city centers.

After 1893, Burnham's firm designed elegant, classically detailed office buildings and department stores, including Marshall Field's in Chicago. Burnham died in Heidelberg, Germany, but the impact of his monumental classicism and grand urban schemes continued.

Further Reading: Carl Condit, *The Chicago School of Architecture: A History of Commercial and Public Building in the Chicago Area, 1875–1925*, 1964; Thomas Hines, *Burnham of Chicago*, 1974; Charles Moore, *Daniel H. Burnham: Architect, Planner of Cities*, 1921.

Ann Thomas Wilkins

BURNHAM, FREDERICK RUSSELL (11 May 1861–1 September 1947), explorer, miner, and scout. Born in Tivoli, Minnesota, Burnham moved with his family to Los Angeles, California, in 1871. He struck gold while a civilian scout in Arizona Territory, on 25 December 1883. Ten years later, he and his wife journeyed to Africa, which captured their imagination and fascinated them. During one expedition, Burnham and two companions were the first white persons to set foot in Bulawayo (in what is now Zimbabwe). Burnham also developed mining interests in Rhodesia; he participated in the Alaskan gold rush near the end of the century; and he served as chief of scouts for the British army during the Boer War. For his many services, Burnham was raised to the rank of major in the British army and received honors from Queen Victoria. His restless and exciting life in many ways personified the frontier spirit prevalent in Gilded Age America. He died in Santa Barbara, California.

Further Reading: Frederick R. Burnham Papers, Sterling Library, Yale University; Frederick R. Burnham, *Scouting on Two Continents*, 1926; Richard Bradford and Mary E. Bradford, eds., *An American Family on the African Frontier: The Burnham Family Letters, 1893–1896*, 1994.

Leonard Schlup

BURPEE, WASHINGTON ATLEE (5 April 1858–25 November 1915), seedsman, entrepreneur. Born in Sheffield, New Brunswick, Canada, and schooled in Philadelphia, Burpee dropped out of the University of Pennsylvania

in 1876. With a partner, he opened a seed, pigeon, and poultry store in Philadelphia. Shortly thereafter, he formed W. Atlee Burpee & Company. Pioneering modern industrial research and mass distribution techniques in the mail-order seed business, Burpee rapidly prospered. His firm early utilized field trials for crops. In 1888, it purchased a large farm at Doylestown, Pennsylvania, for its research center. Later it added facilities at Sunnybrook, New Jersey, and Lompoc, California. It introduced the original large bush lima beans in 1890, other varieties of limas afterward, and iceberg lettuce before 1900. It also led in improving cabbages, sweet corn, and squashes, and in offering new varieties of tomatoes, celery, onions, culinary peas, and many types of flowers. Burpee's firm employed three hundred workers, who processed ten thousand orders daily. Burpee was a director of Philadelphia's Market Street National Bank and the Northern Trust Company, and a member or officer of numerous horticultural groups.

Further Reading: *National Cyclopedia of American Biography*, 16 (1937), 286; Burpee Company, *Forty Years of Burpee Service*, 1916; Joseph J. Fucini and Susan Franklin, *Entrepreneurs: The Men and Women Behind Famous Brand Names and How They Made It*, 1985.

Douglas Steeples

BURRILL, THOMAS JONATHAN (25 April 1839–14 April 1916), botanist, educator, and naturalist. Burrill was born on a farm near Pittsfield, Massachusetts; graduated from the Illinois State Normal School (now Illinois State University) in 1865; and three years later became assistant professor of natural history at the University of Illinois at Urbana-Champaign. For nearly a half century, he played an important role in the Illinois Horticultural Society and in the School of Agriculture at the university. Burrill also served as vice president of the university, and as acting president and president of the Society of American Bacteriologists. His pathological investigations, scientific labors, and publications earned him a respected reputation throughout the Midwest and elsewhere during the Gilded Age.

Further Reading: *New York Times*, 16 April 1916; *Chicago Daily Tribune*, 15 April 1916.

Leonard Schlup

BUTLER, BENJAMIN FRANKLIN (5 November 1818–11 January 1893), Civil War general, congressman, and governor of Massachusetts. Born in Deerfield, New Hampshire, Butler was reared in Lowell, Massachusetts, and educated at Waterville College (now Colby College) in Maine. Establishing a flourishing law practice in Lowell and Boston, he served several terms in the state legislature as a Democrat, and in 1860 ran for governor on the Breckinridge ticket. In 1861 he rallied to the Union and was the commanding general of troops that secured Washington and Baltimore. At Fortress Monroe, he called runaway slaves used by the Confederate Army contraband, and soon joined the Radical Republicans. Having accompanied Admiral David G. Farragut in the capture of New Orleans (1862), he administered the city with an iron hand. Though frequently accused of corruption, nothing could ever be proven against him. In 1864, after failing effectively to menace Richmond as commander of the Army of the James and to capture Fort Fisher, he was sent home.

In 1866 Butler was elected to Congress, where he played an important part in the impeachment of Andrew Johnson. In 1869 he became chairman of the House Committee on Reconstruction, and was instrumental in the imposition of additional conditions on the still unreconstructed states, as well as the passage of the 1871 Ku Klux Klan Act and the 1875 Civil Rights Act. Defeated for reelection in 1874, he was returned to Congress two years later, from a different district. In the meantime he had been seeking the governorship of Massachusetts. But, anathema to the Boston Brahmins because of his dubious reputation and soft-money views, he failed in 1871 and 1873. As an independent Democrat and Greenbacker in 1878 and 1879, he was unsuccessful again; only after rejoining the Democrats did he finally secure the office in 1882. As governor, he appointed the first Irish judge and the first African American to a judicial position. Although he was unable to win reelection in 1883, in 1884 he sought the presidency as an independent candidate of the People's Party. He died at Lowell, Massachusetts, after completing his flamboyant memoirs, *Butler's Book.*

Further Reading: Hans L. Trefousse, *Ben Butler: The South Called Him Beast*, 1957, 1974; Richard S. West, Jr., *Lincoln's Scapegoat General: A Life of Benjamin Butler, 1818–1893*, 1965; Howard P. Nash, Jr., *Stormy Petrel: The Life and Times of General Benjamin F. Butler, 1818–1893*, 1969.

Hans L. Trefousse

BUTLER, MARION (20 May 1863–3 June 1938), senator and Populist leader. Born and reared in Sampson County, North Carolina, Butler was graduated from the University of North Carolina in 1885 and became a high school principal. Later he edited a county newspaper, the *Clinton Caucasian*. In 1890 he was elected to the North Carolina senate and as head of the Farmers' Alliance. In 1892 he was chosen to chair the Populist Party's state executive committee. Butler led the Populists into cooperation with the Republican Party, called "fusion," which brought the combined party electoral victories in 1894 and 1896. The fusionist legislature elected Butler, as a Populist, to the U.S. Senate, where he concentrated on currency issues, postal savings banks, and the expansion of rural free delivery. Butler chaired the Populist Party's national executive committee between 1896 and 1903 and became a Progressive Republican in 1904.

Butler opened a law office in Washington, D.C., during the summer of 1899; he lobbied and pursued private claims, especially those of Native American tribes, against the federal government. He combined support of the radical issues he had taken up in the 1890s with New South ideas of regional development and white supremacy. Her died in Takoma Park, Maryland.

Further Reading: James Logan Hunt, "Marion Butler and the Populist Ideal, 1863–1938," Ph.D. diss., University of Wisconsin at Madison, 1990; Marion Butler Papers, Southern Historical Collection, University of North Carolina, Chapel Hill.

Bruce Palmer

BUTLER, NICHOLAS MURRAY (2 April 1862–7 December 1947), university president and internationalist. Born in Elizabeth, New Jersey, Butler attended Columbia University, where he completed his Ph.D. in philosophy in 1884. Hired to teach at his alma mater, Butler rose through the faculty ranks and became its president in 1902. He was active in numerous areas. In 1887, he led the Industrial Education Association. In 1894–1895, while piloting the National Education Association, he helped create both the Committee of Ten and the Committee on College Entrance Requirements, precedent-setters in developing national standards and definitions by professional organizations. In 1900, Butler was appointed secretary of the College Entrance Examination Board.

A fixture at the Republican National Convention and an internationalist, Butler supported limited government by the trained and enlightened elite. He published his speeches in 1913 as *The International Mind*. Butler served as president of the Carnegie Endowment for International Peace; in 1931, he shared the Nobel Peace Prize with Jane Addams. He retired on October 1, 1945, and died in New York City later that year.

Further Reading: Nicholas M. Butler, *Across the Busy Years*, 2 vols., 1939; Albert Marrin, *Nicholas Murrav Butler*, 1976; Richard Whittemore, *Nicholas Murray Butler and Public Education*, 1970.

Charles F. Howlett

BUTTERWORTH, BENJAMIN (22 October 1837–16 January 1898), lawyer and congressman. Butterworth was born in Hamilton Township, Ohio, attended Ohio University, and was graduated from the Cincinnati Law School in 1861. A Quaker who fought as a major in the Civil War, he settled in Cincinnati in 1875. There he won election as a Republican to the U.S. House of Representatives in 1878 and 1880, then lost a reelection bid in 1882. In 1883 President Chester A. Arthur appointed Butterworth commissioner of patents. He helped lead Arthur's unsuccessful attempt to obtain the Republican presidential nomination in 1884, the year Buterworth reclaimed his House seat. He served from 1885 to 1891, supporting the eight-hour law, commercial trade with Canada, adequate pensions for veterans, the federal elections bill of 1890, Secretary of State James G. Blaine's reciprocity doctrine, and tariff revision without endangering protectionism. He championed Benjamin Harrison's presidential candidacy in 1888 and 1892, advising the nominee on various issues by mail. In 1897 President William McKinley made Butterworth patent commissioner again. He was a star stump speaker and party stalwart who on occasion demonstrated independent streaks and sympathy for labor. He died in Thomasville, Georgia.

Further Reading: Leonard Schlup, "Rejuvenated Republican: Benjamin Butterworth of Ohio and His Letter to Benjamin Harrison in 1888," *Research Journal of Philosophy and Social Sciences* (1996): 29–36; *Cincinnati Times-Star*, 17 January 1898; *New York Times*, 17 January 1898.

Leonard Schlup

CABLE, GEORGE WASH-INGTON (12 October 1844–31 January 1925), American writer. Born in New Orleans, Cable became a master of the short story, a popular literary form following the Civil War, and helped establish the Southern theme in American literature in the 1880s. His career began with a weekly column in the *New Orleans Picayune*. After 1869, he wrote unusual romances gleaned from local life. *Scribner's Monthly* and *Century* magazines published his stories, which earned him national fame. In *Old Creole Days* (1879) and in other works such as *The Grandissimes* (1880) and *The Creoles of Louisiana* (1884), he wrote about Louisiana's French-speaking people.

Accused of portraying Creoles as mixed bloods and of promoting equal treatment for African Americans in *The Silent South* (1885), Cable moved to Massachusetts, where he helped found the People's Institute at Northampton, did humanitarian work for African Americans, and produced several volumes of romantic writings. He died at his winter home in St. Petersburg, Florida, and was buried at Northampton.

Further Reading: Lucy Leffingwell Cable Bikle, *George W. Cable: His Life and Letters*, 1967; Louis D. Rubin, Jr., *George W. Cable: The Life and Times of a Southern Heretic*, 1969; *New York Times*, 1 February 1925.

Jane F. Lancaster

CAFFERY, DONELSON (10 September 1835–30 December 1906), senator. Born in St. Mary's Parish, Louisiana, Caffery attended private schools and St. Mary's College in Baltimore, Maryland, and studied law at Louisiana University in New Orleans. He practiced law and engaged in sugar planting before and after serving in the Confederate Army. As Reconstruction ended, Caffery was tried and acquitted of anti-Union activities.

A lifelong fiscal and monetary conservative, Caffery fought the repudiation of the Reconstruction-era state debt when he was a member of Louisiana's constitutional convention in 1879. Shortly after winning a state senate seat in 1892, he was appointed to complete the term of deceased U.S. Senator Randall L. Gibson. Reelected in 1894, Caffery supported the gold standard and Grover Cleveland's anti-imperialist policies, and bitterly opposed William Jennings Bryan and the Democratic Party's 1896 free-silver platform. Caffery led the movement to form the National Democratic Party, which nominated John M. Palmer. Caffery declined that party's nomination in 1900, and retired from the Senate in 1901. He returned to the law and sugar cultivation, and died at New Orleans.

Further Reading: Lucile Roy Caffery, *The Political Career of Senator Donelson Caffery*, 1944; Alcee Fortier, *Louisiana*, vol. 1, 1914; *New Orleans Times Democrat*, 31 December 1906.

Hutch Johnson

CAHENSLYISM. This was a controversy that erupted among American Catholics in the 1890s. Peter Paul Cahensly (1838–1923) was a member of the German parliament and a lay leader of St. Raphael's Society, organized for the protection of Catholic emigrants. In 1890 he petitioned Pope Leo XIII for separate churches for each nationality, appointment of bishops and priests of the same ancestral heritage as the local faithful and speaking the same language as the majority of members of a diocese, parochial schools where instruction was in the children's native language, and representation of immigrant ethnic groups in the American hierarchy. Essentially Cahensly's plan would have divided the foreign-born Catholic population of the United States by European nationalities for ecclesiastical purposes. The proposal met fierce opposition from the American party in the church as well as from journalists. Although the pope never acted upon Cahensly's memorandum, it continued as a partisan factor enveloping the Americanism controversy within the Roman Catholic Church in the United States at the end of the nineteenth century.

Further Reading: John J. Meng, "Cahenslyism: The First Stage, 1883–1891," *Catholic Historical Review* 31 (1946): 380–413; and "Cahenslyism: The Second Chapter, 1891–1910," *Catholic Historical Review* 32 (1947): 302–340.

Leonard Schlup

CALDWELL, ALEXANDER (1 March 1830–19 May 1917), U.S. senator and railroad builder. Born at Drake's Ferry, Pennsylvania, Caldwell received a public school education, fought in the Mexican War, and ran a cartage business. He helped build the Missouri Pacific and Kansas Central railroads, speculated in town development and manufacturing, and operated several farms, thereby becoming one of Kansas's wealthier citizens.

In 1871 Caldwell won the U.S. Senate seat formerly held by Edmund Ross. After investigating bribery charges, a Senate committee recommended that his election be declared invalid, forcing Caldwell to resign in March 1873. He was the second U.S. senator from Kansas to leave office under a cloud of suspicion that year. Caldwell secured land on which Fort Hays State University was erected and made improvements to Fort Leavenworth. He supported monetary inflation, anti-Ku Klux Klan legislation, the Amnesty Act of 1872, and the "Salary Grab Act." After resigning, he reentered business and eschewed politics. He died in Kansas City, Kansas.

Further Reading: Robert S. La Forte, "Gilded Age Senator: The Election, Investigation, and Resignation of Alexander Caldwell, 1871–1873," *Kansas History* 21 (1998/1999): 234–255; Mark Plummer, *Samuel J. Crawford of Kansas*, 1971; Kyle Sinsi, "Politics on the Plains: Thomas Carney and the Pursuit of Office During the Gilded Age," *Heritage of the Plains* 25 (1992): 25–38.

Robert S. La Forte

CALL, WILKINSON (9 January 1834–24 August 1910), U.S. senator. Born in Russellville, Kentucky, Call attended common schools, studied law in Florida, and was admitted to the bar there. A Confederate Army volunteer, he rose to adjutant general of Florida troops. Elected to the U.S. Senate in December 1865, Call, like most other Confederate leaders, was denied his seat by the Radical Republican majority. The post-Reconstruction Florida legislature reelected him in 1879, and he won two subsequent terms.

Heavily influenced by Florida's agrarian protest movement of the early 1890s, Call and Napoleon Bonaparte Broward emerged as leaders of the liberal Democratic faction that championed the National Farmers' Alliance pro-Populist platform. Call, campaigning actively for William Jennings Bryan in 1896, incurred the enmity of Florida's powerful conservative interests. In March 1897, Governor William D. Bloxham named a conservative, John A. Henderson, to serve until the legislature could elect a successor for Call. The Senate, charging that Bloxham had overstepped his authority, refused to seat Henderson, and thus left the matter for the Florida legislature to decide. After several inconclusive ballots, Call withdrew in favor of fellow liberal Stephen R. Mallory, Jr. Retiring from public life, Call resided in Washington, D.C., until his death.

Further Reading: *New York Times*, 25 August 1910; Samuel Proctor, *Napoleon Bonaparte Broward*, 1950.

Harvey Gresham Hudspeth

CAMERON, JAMES DONALD (14 May 1833–30 August 1918), secretary of war, senator, Republican National Committee chair. Cameron was born in Middletown, Pennsylvania, the son of the powerful Pennsylvania politician, and later President Lincoln's secretary of war, Simon Cameron. The younger Cameron was graduated from Princeton University and worked in his family's businesses (banking and the Northen Central Railroad).

In 1866 Cameron helped orchestrate his father's defeat of Pennsylvania Governor Andrew Curtin for the U.S. Senate. Cameron's role in the Republican political machine, especially his influence in winning the presidential election of 1876, led to his appointment and short-lived service as secretary of war under President Ulysses S. Grant (1876–1877). In this post he helped Rutherford B. Hayes win electoral votes in Florida and Louisiana by placing federal troops under control of state Republican politicians. Many influential Republicans felt Cameron should be reappointed. Hayes, however, wanted to distance himself from the Grant-era corruption, and refused to reappoint Cameron. In disgust, Cameron's father resigned his Senate seat in 1877, and the Pennsylvania legislature placed the son there. He served until 1897.

For one year (1879–1880) Cameron also chaired the Republican National Committee. Like his father, he was a behind-the-scenes politician. He helped lead the unsuccessful 1880 movement to nominate Grant for a third term. In 1897 Cameron returned to his family farm, "Donegal," in Lancaster County, Pennsylvania, where he died.

Further Reading: Robert Harrison, "Blaine and the Camerons: A Study in the Limits of Machine Power," *Pennsylvania History* 49 (1982): 157–175; Frank B. Evans, *Pennsylvania Politics, 1872–1877: A Study in Political Leadership,* 1966.

Jerome D. Bowers II

CAMP, WALTER CHAUNCEY (7 April 1859–14 March 1925), college athlete, coach, and administrator. Born in New Britain, Connecticut, Camp was the originator of American football. In 1876, as a rugby player for Yale University, he devised rules and regulations that became the basis for football in the United States. Camp's contributions to the game include its most fundamental aspects: the play from scrimmage; eleven men on each side; and set plays for the offensive unit. He played on the Yale football teams from 1877 to 1882 and led them to twenty-five wins against only one defeat. He also was head football coach for Yale from 1876 until 1910, and was instrumental in establishing the National Collegiate Athletic Association. Camp also chaired the American Football Rules Committee, which determined various changes during his lifetime. In 1898 he established an annual list of All-American football players, recognizing outstanding collegiate players throughout the nation. Camp spent his later years in New York City, where he died. Even today, All-America teams are named in his honor.

Further Reading: John S. Martin, "Walter Camp and His Gridiron Game," *American Heritage* 12 (1961): 50–55. 77–81.

Steve Bullock

CANNON, FRANK JENNE (25 January 1859–25 July 1933), editor and senator. Born in Salt Lake City, Utah, Cannon graduated from the University of Utah in 1878, worked as a newspaper reporter in San Francisco, and moved to Ogden, Utah, in 1882. There he held various local political offices. He became editor of the *Ogden Herald* in 1887 and established the *Ogden Standard* the following year. When the territory became a state, Cannon, a Republican, won election to the federal House of Representatives, where he served from 1895 until 1896. He then was a member of the U.S. Senate from 1896 to 1899. A strong advocate of the free and unlimited coinage of silver, Cannon joined the Silver Republicans who walked out of the Republican National Convention in 1896 to protest the party platform's commitment to sound money. At first Cannon favored Senator Henry M. Teller of Colorado for the Silver Republican presidential nomination, but he subsequently endorsed William Jennings Bryan, the Democratic and Populist standard-bearer, who lost the election to William McKinley. Cannon was unsuccessful in a bid to secure re-election to the Senate in 1898. He affiliated with the Democratic Party in 1900, again supporting Bryan. Cannon was Democratic state chairman from 1902 until 1904. Thereafter, he concentrated on newspaper work and mining. He died in Denver, Colorado, where he had moved in 1909.

Further Reading: Leonard Schlup, "Utah Maverick: Frank J. Cannon and the Politics of Conscience in 1896," *Utah Historical Quarterly* 62 (1994): 335–348.

Leonard Schlup

CAREY ACT. The depression of the 1890s hit western states particularly hard. In an attempt to encourage land settlement, particularly in his own state, Wyoming Senator Joseph M. Carey pushed legislation to promote reclaiming arid lands for agriculture. The Carey Desert Land Act (1894) promised arid states up to one million acres from the public domain if they irrigated and settled the land. The states were required to accept the legislation, supervise construction of irrigation projects, set land and water prices, and deliver the reclaimed land to settlers in 160-acre tracts. Farmers received cheap land (fifty cents an acre), but paid a per-acre charge for water rights and construction costs.

Wyoming, Colorado, Idaho, and Utah accepted the legislation, but the act failed to promote irrigation development. The private companies in charge of project construction ran out of money long before they could sell the land to settlers, and often built shoddy, inadequate irrigation works. Most of the projects were far removed from markets and railheads, and the farmers lacked the capital to be able to wait until their farms returned a profit. By 1898 western sentiment for federal reclamation made Carey Act projects less attractive.

Further Reading: Donald J. Pisani, *To Reclaim a Divided West*, 1992; Paul W. Gates, *History of Public Land Law Development*, 1968.

Brad F. Raley

CAREY, JOSEPH MAULL (19 January 1845–5 February 1924), governor and senator. Born in Milton, Delaware, Carey received a law degree from the University of Pennsylvania and gained admittance to the Pennsylvania bar in 1867. Two years later, President Ulysses S. Grant appointed him U.S. attorney for Wyoming Territory. There, from 1872 to 1876, he was associate justice of the supreme court. A powerful cattle baron, Carey helped form what became known as the American National Livestock Association and the Wyoming Stock Growers Association. From 1885 to 1890, Carey, a Republican who had been mayor of Cheyenne from 1881 to 1885, was the territorial delegate to Congress. Called the "Father of Wyoming Statehood," he became the first U.S. senator when it entered the Union 1890. He wrote the Carey Arid Land Act of 1894, which authorized the president to grant to states having public land a maximum of one million acres for reclamation, settlement, irrigation, and cultivation. Defeated for reelection in 1895, and removed from the Republican National Committee, Carey returned to his Cheyenne law practice and ranching business. He feuded with Francis E. Warren, head of the powerful Republican machine. In 1910 Carey achieved rehabilitation when he won the governorship as a Democrat, serving from 1911 to 1915. Carey died in Cheyenne.

Further Reading: Lewis L. Gould, "Joseph M. Carey and Wyoming Statehood," *Annals of Wyoming* 37 (1965): 157–169; George W. Paulson, "The Congressional Career of Joseph Maull Carey," *Annals of Wyoming* 35 (1963): 21–81; Cheyenne *Leader*, 8 February 1924.

Leonard Schlup

CARLISLE, JOHN GRIFFIN (5 September 1835–31 July 1910), Speaker of the House, senator, and secretary of the Treasury. Born in what is now Kenton County, Kentucky, Carlisle was admitted to the Kentucky bar in 1858. After serving as state senator and lieutenant governor, Carlisle, a Democrat, was elected in 1876 to the U.S. House of Representatives. An expert in parliamentary procedure, he was named Speaker of the House in 1883 and twice reelected. He was mentioned prominently as a possible nominee for the presidency, but his southern heritage proved to be an insurmountable drawback. In 1888, he declined President Grover Cleveland's offer of appointment as chief justice of the United States. When Senator James B. Beck died suddenly in May 1890, the Kentucky legislature chose Carlisle to complete his term.

Carlisle resigned from the Senate in February 1893, to become secretary of the Treasury in the second Cleveland administration. During the depression that began in 1893, Cleveland and Carlisle secured the repeal of the Sherman Silver Purchase Act of 1890, advocated a tariff for revenue only, and allied themselves with the Democratic Party's gold wing at great political cost. In 1896, Carlisle campaigned in Kentucky on behalf of John M. Palmer and the Gold Democrats. The following year he retired to New York City, where he established a law practice. He strongly opposed the acquisition of the Philippines, but otherwise avoided the political arena. He died in New York City.

Further Reading: James A. Barnes, *John G. Carlisle, Financial Statesman*, 1931; *New York Times*, 1 and 2 August 1910; *Louisville Courier-Journal*, 1 August 1910.

Thomas H. Appleton, Jr.

CARNEGIE, ANDREW (25 October 1835–11 August 1919), steel magnate and philanthropist. Born in Dunfermline, Scotland, Carnegie, who lacked a formal education, began working for the Pennsylvania Railroad at an early age. By 1859, he headed its western division. During the Civil War, the Union War Department placed him in charge of military transportation and telegraph communications.

After 1865, embodying Horatio Alger's "rags to riches" theme, Carnegie managed and invested in telegraph, oil, iron, bridge, and railroad concerns. He also sold bonds in Europe. The embodiment of thrift and cautious expenditure, he rode the growing steel industry to fame and fortune. His business acumen was based on his ability to fully utilize the practice of vertical integration. By the 1890s, his steel company had no rival. Carnegie Steel operated its own coal and iron mines, shipping and railroad lines, and steel mills. Efficient management and low labor costs marked his corporate leadership style. Success enabled him to spend half of each year in Scotland, whence he ran his company through voluminous directives to subordinates in Pittsburgh. In 1901, he sold his business to a new corporation, United States Steel.

In a famous essay, "Gospel of Wealth," published in the late 1880s, Carnegie detailed his anti-labor, pro-philanthrophic views. A staunch social Darwinist, he displayed his contempt for unions during the bitter Homestead steel strike (1892). Carnegie's destruction of the Amalgamated Association of Iron and Steel Workers, through the use of force and Pinkerton detectives, led to a public outcry against his tactics. More than other Gilded Age entrepreneurs, Carnegie is associated with the "public be damned" attitude.

By contrast, Carnegie's philanthropic endeavors included nearly $350 million in donations that established of thousands of libraries and the Carnegie Institute in Pittsburgh. The Carnegie Corporation installed church organs and oversaw numerous higher education projects. Carnegie's preoccupation with higher learning was an attempt to ingratiate himself with the scholarly world and compensate for his own lack of formal education—and, possibly, to deflect attention from his insensitivity toward working-class Americans. He also spent lavishly on the arbitration movement, creating the Carnegie Endowment for International Peace, a scholarly think tank still in existence. He died in Shadowbrook, Massachusetts.

Further Reading: Louis M. Hacker, *The World of Andrew Carnegie, 1865–1901*, 1968; Burton J. Hendrick, *The Life of Andrew Carnegie*, 2 vols., 1932; Joseph Frazier Wall, *Andrew Carnegie*, 1970.

Charles F. Howlett

CARPENTER, MATTHEW HALE (22 December 1824–24 February 1881), senator and lawyer. Born Decatur Merritt Hammond Carpenter in Moretown, Vermont, Carpenter received a private legal education. In 1848, he moved to Wisconsin, where he became a prominent lawyer and antislavery Democrat in Beloit and Milwaukee. After supporting Abraham Lincoln's administration, he joined the Republican Party in 1866 and appeared before the Supreme Court in cases concerning southern Reconstruction. His arguments established constitutional precedents for restoring rebel states to the Union.

Elected to the Senate in 1869, Carpenter served as the institution's president pro tempore for one Congress. In 1873, he promoted a congressional salary raise and other politically unpopular causes. Vilified in the press, he lost the 1875 election. The following year, Carpenter successfully defended former Secretary of War William W. Belknap during his Senate impeachment trial. In poor health, Carpenter returned to the Senate in 1879, but died in Washington, D.C., before completing his term.

Further Reading: Edwin B. Thompson, *Matthew Hale Carpenter, Webster of the West*, 1954; Frank A. Flower, *Life of Matthew Hale Carpenter*, 1883; Herman J. Deutsch, "Carpenter and the Senatorial Election of 1875 in Wisconsin," *Wisconsin Magazine of History* 16 (1932): 26–46.

Jane M. Armstrong

CARR, ELIAS (25 February 1839–22 July 1900), governor and agrarian activist. Born on his family's plantation near Tarboro, North Carolina, Carr was educated at the Oaks School and the universities of North Carolina and Virginia. For thirty years, he successfully oversaw cultivation of his inherited lands, increasing their yield through crop rotation and use of modern fertilizers. His prosperity, when neighbors were suffering economically, led him to identify with the agrarian movement of the 1880s. Distressed by local conditions, Carr attended the Farmers Convention in St. Paul, Minnesota, in 1886. He was elected president of the North Carolina Farmers' Alliance in 1891. In this capacity, he advocated rural school construction and state railroad regulation. Yet Carr rejected extreme measures and the formation of a third, agrarian-based party, thereby becoming identified as a moderate.

The reputation served him well when the Democrats nominated him as a compromise candidate for governor of North Carolina in 1892. His term as governor (1893–1897) was marked by state party unity but opposition to the Cleveland administration. He worked assiduously to improve the road and prison systems. He died at his family home, and was mourned as one of the state's least selfish and most respected governors.

Further Reading: Lala Carr Steelman, "The Role of Elias Carr in the North Carolina Farmers' Alliance," *North Carolina Historical Review* 57 (1980): 133–158; *Raleigh Morning Post*, 30 August 1900.

Christian B. Keller

CARTER, JAMES COOLIDGE (14 October 1827–14 February 1905), lawyer. Carter was born in Lancaster, Massachusetts, graduated from Harvard College in 1850, and was admitted to the New York bar in 1853. He spent the next half-century with the New York City firm of Davies and Scudder. Carter gained a national reputation for his powerful voice, masterful vocabulary, and belief that nothing was finally decided correctly. Participation in the Tweed Ring cases and association with Governor Samuel J. Tilden stimulated his interest in municipal reform. A founder of the National Municipal League and its president for nine years, Carter was counsel in many significant cases in New York State. During the 1880s, he led a spirited fight against David Dudley Field's codification of the civil code of substantive law that had been adopted by the legislature but vetoed by the governor. As a member of the New York City Bar Association Committee, in 1883 Carter prepared a paper titled "The Proposed Codification of Our Common Law," which was widely distributed; his debate with Field lasted until the code's final defeat. Perhaps Carter's most notable effort was his brilliant, but unsuccessful, support of the constitutionality of the income tax before the U.S. Supreme Court in 1895. He was counsel for the United States at the Bering Sea Fur Seal Arbitration Tribunal at Paris in 1893, and president of the American Bar Association in 1894 and 1895. Carter died in New York City.

Further Reading: *New York Times*, 15 February 1905.

Leonard Schlup

CARTER, THOMAS HENRY (30 October 1854–17 September 1911), U.S. senator. Born near Portsmouth, Ohio, Carter studied law in Iowa before forming a law partnership in Helena, Montana (1882). His political career began in 1888 when he secured the Republican nomination as Montana's territorial delegate to Congress and won a surprising victory over William A. Clark, a mining baron. When Montana gained statehood in 1889, Carter took the lone congressional seat. In the House of Representatives he advocated liberal homestead legislation and endorsed the free and unlimited coinage of silver. Carter was defeated for reelection in 1890, but President Benjamin Harrison named him to serve as commissioner of the General Land Office. There Carter worked to satisfy the complaints of western farmers, miners, and timber men. In 1892 Harrison asked Carter to coordinate his renomination at the Republican National Convention, and Carter chaired the Republican National Committee.

Following Harrison's defeat, Carter returned to Montana but was soon elected to the U.S. Senate. He served from 1895 to 1901 and from 1905 to 1911. Carter drafted the Forest Management Act of 1897 and was instrumental in establishing Glacier National Park. Although he opposed high protective tariffs, he supported the Dingley Tariff of 1897 after amendments had been added to protect western raw materials. Carter refused to join the Silver Republicans in 1896, but he fought for international bimetallism and allied himself with copper and large capitalistic and business interests in his state. He also favored civil service reform, postal savings banks, and the secret ballot, but disapproved of direct election of senators and primary elections. Carter died in Washington, D.C.

Further Reading: Leonard Schlup, "Gilded Age Republican: Thomas H. Carter of Montana and the Presidential Campaign of 1892," *Midwest Review* 15 (1993): 51–70; *Helena Daily Independent*, 18 September 1911; Thomas H. Carter Papers, Manuscripts Division, Library of Congress.

Leonard Schlup

CARVER, GEORGE WASHINGTON (ca. 1864/1865–5 January 1943), agricultural researcher and educator. Born in Diamond Grove, Missouri, to a slave owned by Moses Carver, George Carver was orphaned as an infant and, along with his brother, was raised by the Carvers. People in the community recognized Carver as being very bright and talented, especially in regard to plants. Unable to get an adequate education in Diamond Grove, he left at an early age and traveled around the Midwest, seeking an education and doing odd jobs. After unsuccessfully seeking to enroll in Highland College, Carver entered Simpson College in Iowa (1890) as an art major. One teacher suggested he might want to utilize his botanical skills, since it was very difficult for a black man to make a living as an artist. Carver therefore enrolled the next year at Iowa State College, to study horticulture. Iowa State was a recognized leader in agriculture, and the distinguished faculty was impressed by Carver's skills, especially in hybridization and mycology. They encouraged him to do postgraduate work, and he received his masters' degree in 1896.

Although he was asked to continue to teach freshman classes at his alma mater, Carver decided instead to accept the offer of Booker T. Washington to establish and lead a school of agriculture at Tuskegee Normal and Industrial Institute in Alabama. The Gilded Age witnessed a boom in scientific agriculture partly as a result of the Morrill and Hatch acts, and Carver was in the mainstream of the emerging research while at Iowa State. However, after he arrived in Macon County, Alabama, he discovered that many of the tenets of scientific agriculture could be applied only with great difficulty in the Deep South. He found former slaves who were trapped in a vicious cycle of poverty and debt. Becoming sharecroppers, most black, landless farmers had neither the freedom nor the resources to practice much of the emerging technology. In addition, the funds for research at Tuskegee were quite limited. Although Tuskegee received state funding to establish an agricultural experiment station, the $1500 appropriation was the only source of research funds, and that amount was often tapped for other purposes.

By necessity as well as inclination, Carver's focus came to be on methods that required little expense. During his first twenty years at Tuskegee, he sought ways to lessen sharecroppers' needs for commercial goods, hoping to allow them to break the bonds of debt that held many in virtual peonage. He taught them how to enrich their land without commercial fertilizer, how to paint their houses with paint made from native clays, how to meet their need for protein with peanut products, how to can and preserve food to last through the year, and generally how to use available resources to replace store-bought goods. He spread the message through farmers' institutes, fairs, and even a wagon outfitted as a portable school.

To encourage farmers to diversify, Carver created exhibits of the many products one could create from such crops as peanuts, cowpeas, and sweet potatoes. These exhibits and Carver's testimony before U.S. House of Representatives tariff hearings on a peanut tariff won him fame as an inventor and a chemist. Later in life he attempted to commercialize his products; however, their being simple products of readily available resources made commercial success unlikely. His fame increased as his useful work declined, but Carver remained an apostle for interracial understanding and an inspiration to young African Americans. Although he never earned more than $1200 a year, by practicing his message of thrift he was able to accumulate enough money to establish a museum and a research foundation at Tuskegee before his death there.

Further Reading: Linda O. McMurry, *George Washington Carver: Scientist and Symbol*, 1981; Gary R. Kremer, *George Washington Carver in His Own Words*, 1987.

Linda O. McMurry

CASSATT, MARY (22 May 1844–14 June 1926), artist. Born in Allegheny City, Pennsylvania, Cassatt studied art at the Pennsylvania Academy of the Fine Arts in Philadelphia in 1860, and in Paris after the Civil War. Undaunted by existing gender restrictions, she arranged private lessons with renowned French artists, including Jean-Léon Gérôme and Thomas Couture. An admirer of Spanish art, Cassatt was popular in Europe; from 1868 to 1874, her paintings were repeatedly accepted for the prestigious annual Paris Salon. She settled in Paris in 1874 and, inspired by the Impressionist work of Edgar Degas, began depicting the life of upper-class women. Although she never married nor had children of her own, Cassatt produced paintings that eloquently capture mother-child interactions. In May 1877, Degas invited Cassatt to exhibit with the Impressionists at their next independent show. She was the only American ever to do so. With two pastels and four paintings, including *Portrait of a Little Girl* (1878), Cassatt made her debut with the Impressionists at their fourth group exhibition in 1879. She exhibited with them until their last group show in 1886.

In 1890, shortly after seeing a display of Japanese prints in Paris, Cassatt produced a suite of color drypoints and aquatints that echo the bold, decorative forms and linear patterning of Japanese woodcuts. At the height of her career, she also undertook a mural project, *Modern Woman* (1893), commissioned for the Women's Building at the World's Columbian Exposition in Chicago. That same year Cassatt's first retrospective exhibition was held at the Paris galleries of Durand-Ruel. Soon thereafter, Cassatt purchased Beaufresne, a château at Mesnil-Théribus, about fifty miles northwest of Paris, which was her home for the rest of her life.

During the latter part of her career, Cassatt served as an indispensable adviser to the American collectors Henry O. and Louisine Havemeyer. In 1904 she was named a Chevalier of the Légion d'Honneur. She continued to paint until cataracts weakened her eyesight significantly. She died at Beaufresne.

Further Reading: Adelyn Dohme Breeskin, *Mary Cassatt: A Catalogue Raisonné of the Oils, Pastels, Watercolors,* and *Drawings,* 1970; Nancy Mowll Mathews, *Mary Cassatt: A Life,* 1994; Judith Barter, Erica E. Hirshler, George T. M. Shackleford, Kevin Sharp, Harriet K. Stratis, and Andrew J. Walker, *Mary Cassatt: Modern Woman,* 1998.

Lacey Jordan

CASSIDY, BUTCH (13 April 1866–1909 or 1937), frontier desperado. Cassidy was born Robert Leroy Parker in Beaver, Utah. In 1878 his family moved to Circleville, Utah, where he learned the criminal basics from ex-outlaw Mike Cassidy, whose surname he later assumed.

Butch Cassidy's career began with rustling, but by 1889 he had switched to bank and train robbery. Shortly after hitting a Telluride, Colorado, bank for $10,500, Cassidy joined Ellsworth "Elza" Lay, Harry Longabaugh (the Sundance Kid), the psychopathic killer Harvey Logan (Kid Curry), Ben Kilpatrick, and Will Carver. They formed the "Wild Bunch." Arguably the best-organized gang in the West, they staged robberies in remote areas where pursuit was slow. Working in Montana, Nevada, and Wyoming, members operated with horse relays kept a hard ride from crime scenes, and maintained hideouts in Colorado and Utah. By 1900 they disbanded, having attracted Pinkerton agents. Cassidy and Sundance, with the latter's inamorata, Etta Place, fled to Argentina in 1901 or 1902. Exploits continued there and in Bolivia and Chile. In 1909 Butch and Sundance were reported killed in San Vicente, Bolivia. However, Cassidy's sister, Lulu Betenson, claims in *Butch Cassidy, My Brother* (1976), that he came home in 1925 and died in Washington State in 1937. In *The Rise and Fall of the Sundance Kid* (1983), Edward M. Kirby asserts that Sundance, alias Hiram BeBee, died a prisoner in 1955 and is buried near Salt Lake City.

Further Reading: James D. Horan, *The Wild Bunch,* 1958.

Jack Burrows

CATCHINGS, THOMAS CLENDINEN (11 January 1847–24 December 1927), congressman. A sound money Democrat, Catchings was born near Brownsville, Mississippi. He attended the University of Mississippi, joined the Confederate Army in 1861, practiced law in

Vicksburg during the postwar era, and won election as attorney general of Mississippi in 1877 and 1881. Catchings served in the U.S. House of Representatives from 1885 to 1901. His committee assignments included those on levees and improvements of the Mississippi River, railways and canals, and rivers and harbors. He favored tariff reductions. In the 1890s currency imbroglio, Catchings supported President Grover Cleveland and rejected free silver. He died in Vicksburg, Mississippi.

Further Reading: Leonard Schlup, "Bourbon Democrat: Thomas C. Catchings and the Republican of Silver Monometallism," *Journal of Mississippi History* 57 (1995): 207–223.

Leonard Schlup

CATHOLICISM. American Catholicism underwent a major transformation during the Gilded Age. Once a denomination of Irish laborers and German farmers, American Catholicism became multinational as eastern and southern Europeans flocked to the United States to a seek a new life. Their Catholicism, unchanged for centuries, provided spiritual strength in a strange new land. It is no surprise, therefore, that these new immigrants worked to sustain their Old World religion. Most Americans were uneasy at the arrival of millions of immigrant Catholics. They were dismayed at their poverty, illiteracy, and criminality, and concerned about their religion. Many patriotic Americans wanted to know what could be done to limit the influence of these new immigrants and their "foreign" religion on the American way of life.

In an effort to bring order to the growth in American Catholicism, the American bishops gathered in a national council at Baltimore in 1884. The council codified canon law in the administration of American dioceses, proposed a national Catholic university, commissioned the compilation of a national catechism, and mandated establishment of schools in each parish. The bishops also wrestled with the question of labor unions and secret societies. Many of the more liberal bishops were favorably disposed toward these organizations, noting that unions did much to protect workers. The conservatives, however, were deeply suspicious of such organizations, and moved to have them condemned. The end result was a condemnation of secret societies, but no recommendation on labor unions. In fact, by the end of the Gilded Age, the Church had gained the reputation as a defender of the workingman.

With the coming of the twentieth century, Catholic leaders prepared to take a more active role in American society as well as international Church affairs. The Gilded Age had laid the foundation for that new role.

Further Reading: James Hennesey, *American Catholics*, 1981; Jay P. Dolan, *American Catholic Experience*, 1984; Timothy Walch, *Catholicism in America*, 1989.

Timothy Walch

CATT, CARRIE CHAPMAN (9 February 1859–9 March 1947), suffragist and peace advocate. Born Carrie Clinton Lane in Ripon, Wisconsin, she was graduated from Iowa State Agricultural College (now Iowa State University) in 1880. She taught high school in Mason City, Iowa, and later served as principal and superintendent. Catt married Leo Chapman, owner and editor of the *Mason City Republican*, in 1885 and George Catt, an engineer, in 1890. Two years later the Catts moved to New York. There Carrie Catt headed the business committee of the National American Woman Suffrage Association in the 1890s, and was its president from 1900 until 1904. At the World's Columbian Exposition at Chicago in 1893, Catt met women from over twenty-seven nations. In 1902, she founded the International Woman Suffrage Alliance in Washington, D.C. After the ratification of the Nineteenth Amendment, in 1920, Catt devoted her attention to world peace and human rights. She died in New Rochelle, New York.

Further Reading: Robert B. Fowler, *Carrie Catt, Feminist Politician*, 1986; Jacqueline Van Voris, *Carrie Chapman Catt: A Public Life*, 1996; Carrie Chapman Catt Papers, Manuscripts Division, Library of Congress.

Leonard Schlup

CENTENNIAL EXPOSITION OF 1876. Held on 236 acres in Philadelphia's Fairmount Park from 10 May to 10 November 1876, America's first world's fair celebrated the hundredth anniversary of the Declaration of Independence. Though formally commemorating a historical event, the exhibition's true focus was the entry of the United States into the modern industrial world. The Centennial Exposition drew more than eight million visitors who paid the expensive 50-cent admission to see thirty-one thousand carefully classified exhibits of science, commerce, technology, art, and agriculture from around the globe. The fair's centerpiece was the massive Corliss Engine (the world's largest steam engine) that powered all the devices in Machinery Hall through seventy-five miles of belts and shafts. Visitors could also see innovations ranging from Alexander Graham Bell's telephone to the Remington typewriter that foreshadowed the marvels of modern America.

Further Reading: Thomas J. Schlereth, *Artifacts and the American Past*, 1980; Robert W. Rydell, *All the World's a Fair: Visions of Empire at American International Expositions, 1876–1916*, 1984; Centennial collections at the Free Library of Philadelphia and the Philadelphia City Archives.

John H. Hepp IV

CHADWICK, HENRY (5 October 1824–20 April 1908), baseball writer. Born in Exeter, England, Chadwick is best known as the first and most proficient early professional baseball writer. After immigrating to the United States in 1837, Chadwick became a prolific chronicler of the game. He wrote numerous books, essays, articles, and pamphlets, spending more than sixty years championing the American pastime. An outspoken opponent of the raucus behavior, drinking, and and gambling associated with early professional baseball, he wrote the first hardcover book devoted exclusively to the sport, *The Game of Base Ball*, in 1868. Chadwick invented the box score, which remains in use today. He also compiled the first known baseball rule book. In 1894 the National League made him an honorary member. After a long career, Chadwick died in Brooklyn, New York. He was elected to the Baseball Hall of Fame in 1938.

Further Reading: David Q. Voigt, *American Baseball*, 1983.

Steve Bullock

CHANDLER, WILLIAM EATON (28 December 1835–30 November 1917), secretary of the navy and senator. Born in Concord, New Hampshire, Chandler was graduated from Harvard Law School in 1854. After working as a court reporter and a newspaper publisher, he served in the New Hampshire assembly from 1863 to 1867, and was chosen speaker. Abraham Lincoln appointed him naval solicitor and judge advocate. From 1865 to 1867 he was assistant secretary of the Treasury. Returning to his native state, he controlled the Republican Party apparatus and sided with the Half-Breed faction. During the political crisis of 1876, he helped devise the scheme that ensured Rutherford B. Hayes's presidential victory. At the 1880 Republican Party convention he served as James G. Blaine's floor leader.

President James A. Garfield nominated Chandler as solicitor general in 1881. The Senate rejected him, the southerners finding him too pro-black and certain conservative Republicans seeing him as unqualified. When, however, President Chester A. Arthur nominated him for secretary of the navy, a year later, the Senate confirmed him. In office (1882–1885), he was a strong reformer, reducing the officer corps, creating a much-needed Naval War College at Newport, Rhode Island, and overseeing construction of three armor-plated cruisers and one dispatch boat. At the same time, he directed Arthur's southern strategy, designed to strengthen the Republican Party by cooperating with Democratic defectors.

In 1887 Chandler was appointed to the Senate to fill Austin F. Pike's unexpired term, and two years later he was elected to a term of his own. After Chandler's defeat in 1901, President William McKinley appointed him chairman of the Spanish Treaty Claims Commission. He died in Concord.

Further Reading: Leon Burr Richardson, *William E. Chandler, Republican*, 1940.

Justus D. Doenecke

CHASE, SALMON PORTLAND (13 January 1808–7 May 1873), secretary of the Treasury and chief justice of the U.S. Supreme Court. Born in Cornish, New Hampshire, Chase was graduated from Dartmouth College in 1826, read law under William Wirt, was admitted to the bar in 1829, and settled in Cincinnati. He became recognized for his defense of antislavery laws in court. In 1849, he was elected to the U.S. Senate by a coalition of Free Soilers and Democrats. He became dismayed with the pro-slavery Democratic Party interests, joined the emerging Republican Party in 1855, and was elected governor of Ohio in that year.

Serving as Lincoln's secretary of the Treasury from 1861 to 1864, Chase had to raise money to finance the Civil War. He considered Lincoln weak, and spearheaded anti-Lincoln sentiment in the cabinet. An effort to draft Chase to challenge Lincoln for the Republican nomination in 1864 failed. After Chief Justice Roger B. Taney died on 12 October 1864, Lincoln nominated Chase for that position. Chase was a proponent of African-American suffrage after the war. His court generally refused to rule on the constitutionality of the Reconstruction Acts. Chase presided over President Andrew Johnson's impeachment trial. In 1868 he was the focus of an unsuccessful draft for the Democratic presidential nomination. He died in New York City.

Further Reading: John Nevin, *Salmon P. Chase*, 1995.

William C. Binning

CHAUTAUQUA. Begun in 1874 as a two-week summer training course for Sunday school teachers, Chautauqua soon became the leading institution for nonsectarian adult education in the United States. Lewis Miller, an Ohio inventor and manufacturer of farm machinery, and John H. Vincent, a Methodist minister and Sunday school reformer, organized instruction in Sunday school management, teaching, and Bible study on the shores of Lake Chautauqua in western New York. In 1878 they expanded the popular summer program into the year-round, nonsectarian Chautauqua Literary and Scientific Circle, which offered guided correspondence courses and formal examinations for individuals in home reading and study groups across the nation. Schools of languages and theology and the Teachers' Retreat were established at the rapidly expanding Chautauqua assembly to form the Chautauqua University, chartered in 1883 by the State of New York. The College of Liberal Arts was established in 1885 with William Rainey Harper as principal to supervise instruction in the university's eleven general academic departments, ten schools of sacred literature, and normal school programs.

By 1892, over one hundred thousand students were taking residential, correspondence, and extension courses under the Chautauqua movement's formal organization. National leaders flocked to Chautauqua to lecture and to listen. Frances Willard, who delivered a temperance speech in 1876, was the first woman to address the assembly. Charles W. Eliot outlined his recommendations for educational reform before Chautauqua audiences. Miller's son-in-law, Thomas A. Edison, was a regular visitor. President James A. Garfield, Susan B. Anthony, and Jacob Riis lectured at Chautauqua in 1892. Ida Tarbell honed her reporting skills while serving as a reporter and editor for the community's monthly magazine, *The Chautauquan* (1880–1900).

The residential Chautauqua inspired Chautauqua-like assemblies through the country. Nearly 150 independent Chautauquas with permanent dwellings and lectures halls emerged by 1901 in small communities and lakeside resorts, a few of them receiving organizational assistance from Miller and Vincent. Circuit Chautauquas, connected by railroads, were held under tents and in open-air amphitheaters.

Further Reading: Theodore Morrison, *Chautauqua: A Center for Education, Religion and the Arts in America*, 1974; Arthur E. Bestor, Jr., *Chautauqua Publications: An Historical and Bibliographical Guide*, 1934; Richard K. Bonnell, "The Chautauqua University: Pioneer University Without Walls, 1883–1898," Ph.D. diss., Kent State University, 1988.

Kim P. Sebaly

CHAVEZ, J. FRANCISCO (27 June 1833–1904), soldier, lawyer, statesman. Chavez was born in Las Padillas, Nuevo Mexico, Mexico, in what today is Bernalillo County, New Mexico. He attended St. Louis University, then rose to major in the First New Mexico Infantry, fighting Confederate forces during the Civil War. With the return of peace, Chavez studied law, was admitted to the bar, and became known as a bilingual criminal lawyer. He was elected Republican territorial delegate to the U.S. Congress, serving from 1865 to 1867 and from 1869 to 1871. He was district attorney for the Second Judicial District, including Valencia and Bernalillo counties, from 1875 until 1877. Elected to the New Mexico Territorial Legislative Council (Senate) in 1875, he served for nearly thirty years. He died in Albuquerque. During his tenure, his colleagues chose him to preside over the chamber eight times. He was also president of the territory's constitutional convention of 1879.

Further Reading: Maurilio E. Vigil, *Los Patrones: Profiles of Hispanic Political Leaders in New Mexico*, 1980.

Santos C. Vega

CHEATHAM, HENRY PLUMMER (27 December 1857–29 November 1935),

congressman and public official. Born a slave near Henderson, North Carolina, Cheatham worked as a domestic servant, thereby gaining access to cultural and academic advantages. In 1882 he was graduated from Shaw University in Raleigh, North Carolina, and secured an appointment as principal of the Plymouth Normal School in Plymouth, North Carolina. Cheatham resigned three years later to return to his native Vance County as recorder of deeds. Running in 1888 as the Republican candidate from the Second Congressional District, Cheatham won by gaining a large African-American vote; he was the only African American to serve in the Fifty-first Congress. Reelected in 1890, he sponsored bills to reimburse investors in the Freedman's Bank, and for federal aid to education. He lost a second reelection bid. In 1897, President William McKinley appointed Cheatham recorder of deeds for the District of Columbia, in which capacity he served until 1901. He became superintendent of an African-American orphanage in Oxford, North Carolina, in 1907, a position he held until his death there.

Further Reading: Eric Anderson, *Race and Politics in North Carolina, 1872–1901: The Black Second*, 1981; Maurine Christopher, *America's Black Congressmen*, 1971; Frenise A. Logan, *The Negro in North Carolina, 1876–1894*, 1964.

Abel A. Bartley

CHESNUTT, CHARLES (20 June 1858–15 November 1932),

fiction writer. Born free in Cleveland, Ohio, Chesnutt became the Gilded Age's premier African-American storyteller. A boyhood in North Carolina lay behind *The Con-jure Woman* (1899), a collection of short stories narrated by a freedman named "Uncle Julius," whose "broken" English partly obscures his shrewdness and wit. Praise from the critic William Dean Howells led Chesnutt to publish another collection, *The Wife of His Youth and Other Stories of the Color Line* (1899). Acknowledgment of miscegenation in this work offended many whites.

Demonstrating talent beyond dialect story limits, Chesnutt wrote a biography of Frederick Douglass and *The House Behind the Cedars* (1900), an anti-romance about mixed-race siblings who pass for white. A year later, he offered a fictionalized treatment of the Wilmington, North Carolina, race riot, *The Marrow of Tradition*. It was followed by *The Colonel's Dream* (1905), the story of a southern white idealist. Poor reception of the latter discouraged Chesnutt from making literature his full-time career.

Initially enthusiastic about Booker T. Washington, Chesnutt came to support W. E. B. Du Bois's Niagara Movement. He protested the racism of D. W. Griffith's popular film, *Birth of a Nation*. He died in Cleveland.

Further Reading: Helen M. Chesnutt, *Charles Waddell Chesnutt: Pioneer of the Color Line*, 1952; Noel Heermance, *Charles W. Chesnutt: America's First Great Black Novelist*, 1974; William L. Andrews, *The Literary Career of Charles Waddell Chesnutt*, 1980.

Barbara Ryan

CHICAGO FIRE OF 1871.

The summer of 1871 was especially dry in Chicago. By autumn, the city had experienced over two dozen fires. Because of the severity of fires in the previous decades, the city had replaced its volunteer fire departments with professionals. Yet in 1871 the city employed only 185 firefighters to protect a city of more than 330,000 people. Thus, when a fire began on the evening of 8 October 1871, it quickly grew into an unstoppable conflagration that burned for over a day, taking much of the city with it. The size and scale of the "Great Fire" soon became legendary.

It began in the vicinity of Patrick and Catherine O'Leary's dairy barn in southern Chicago. Legend offers that the blaze started when one of Mrs. O'Leary's cows kicked over a lit lantern. The tale, however, was a journalistic fiction. The actual origins of the fire remain unknown, and the story of Mrs. O'Leary represents the nativist panic many felt toward the new inhabitants of the booming industrial city. With a strong southwest wind pushing it, the fire spread quickly through the predominantly wooden city. It leaped across the south branch of the Chicago River and struck the city's financial and commercial heart. Nearly every building in downtown Chicago fell victim to the spreading flames. One of the few spared was the limestone water tower, which still stands as a monument to the fire. The wooden roof of the adjoining pumping station caved in, however, cutting off the flow of water to the city and further hampering attempts to fight the flames.

Not until the morning of 10 October did the flames die out. By then, the "Burned District" measured over four miles long and averaged a width of three-fourths of a mile. In all, more than two thousand acres had burned. Damage reports estimated that the fire had killed nearly three hundred persons and destroyed over eighteen thousand buildings at an estimated cost of $200 million.

Further Reading: Carl Smith, *Urban Disorder and the Shape of Belief: The Great Chicago Fire, the Haymarket Bomb, and the Model Town of Pullman*, 1995; Karen Sawislak, *Smoldering City: Chicagoans and the Great Fire, 1871–1874*, 1995; Ross Miller, *American Apocalypse: The Great Fire and the Myth of Chicago*, 1990.

S. Paul O'Hara

CHICAGO PLATFORM OF 1896. Democrats approached their 1896 national convention in Chicago profoundly divided. Incumbent president Grover Cleveland had endured a severe national depression, and had utterly estranged the party's agrarian wing. His opposition to "free silver" inflation, reliance on gold borrowed from eastern bankers, and use of troops to quell the 1894 Pullman strike came when western and southern Democrats were much influenced by the economic theories of the Farmers' Alliance and the People's Party.

Westerners and southerners dominated the convention and nominated pro-silver orator William Jennings Bryan of Nebraska. His platform advocated currency inflation through the free coinage of silver, ignoring the Populists' fiat money preferences and Subtreasury proposal. It sought a national income tax amendment (in response to the Supreme Court's *Pollock* v. *Farmers Loan and Trust Company* decision of 1895) and stricter railroad regulation. The document, seemingly aimed as much at Cleveland as the Republicans, denounced his financial and labor policies. Bryan and his platform were just populistic enough to tempt the People's Party into a disastrous fusion. A number of Gold Democrats supported the breakaway candidacy of John M. Palmer of Illinois. In the end, the Chicago Platform is known chiefly as the document that helped launch Bryan's first presidential race.

Further Reading: John D. Hicks, *The Populist Revolt*, 1931; Lawrence Goodwyn, *Democratic Promise: The Populist Moment in America*, 1976; William Jennings Bryan, *The First Battle: A Story of the Campaign of 1896*, 1896.

Paul M. Pruitt, Jr.

CHINESE EXCLUSION ACT OF 1882. This act was the first federal immigration legislation that singled out a group of people on racial grounds. During the 1870s the anti-Chinese forces, especially those from California, were determined to curtail Chinese immigration through federal legislation. In 1875 the Page Law was enacted to forbid the entry of Chinese, Japanese, and Mongolian contract laborers, prostitutes, and felons. The law reduced the influx of Chinese women but not men. The next year Congress authorized a joint special committee to investigate Chinese immigration. In 1879 the Fifteen Passenger Bill passed both houses of Congress, but President Rutherford Hayes vetoed it on grounds that it violated obligations under the Burlingame Treaty. Congress in 1882 passed the Miller Bill, suspending the immigration of Chinese laborers for twenty years. President Chester Arthur considered the time period too long, and vetoed it.

Anti-Chinese advocates in Congress revised the Miller Bill to accommodate the president's objection. On 6 May 1882, he signed the revised bill, known as the Chinese Exclusion Act. It suspended the immigration of Chinese laborers for ten years, except for those who already had immigrated or might arrive within ninety days after the law was enacted. It also officially denied Chinese immigrants citizenship rights. After 1882, the United States was no longer a country of free immigration.

The Chinese Exclusion Act was amended several times. The 1888 Scott Act rejected admission to any Chinese who had not returned to the United States before the law's passage, and canceled certificates that had promised their reentry. The 1892 Geary Act extended the exclusion for another ten years and required all Chinese laborers to carry certificates of residence. A 1902 amendment extended exclusion for another ten years. In 1904 the exclusion was made permanent. The Chinese exclusion acts were not repealed until 1943.

Further Reading: Roger Daniels, *Asian America: Chinese and Japanese in the United States Since 1850*, 1988; Charles J. McClain, *In Search of Equality: The Chinese Struggle Against Discrimination in Nineteenth-Century America*, 1994; Andrew Gyory, *Closing the Gate: Race, Politics, and the Chinese Exclusion Act*, 1998.

Xiaojian Zhao

CHOATE, JOSEPH HODGES (24 January 1832–14 May 1917), trial lawyer and diplomat. Choate was born in Salem, Massachusetts, and graduated from Harvard College (1852) and its law school (1854). Rapidly he became one of the nation's most prominent attorneys, known for his formidable intellect and oratorical skills. Counsel for such corporations as Standard Oil, American Sugar Refining, and American Tobacco, Choate also defended the estates of such notables as Cornelius Vanderbilt, Samuel J. Tilden, and Alexander T. Stewart, and the endowment of Leland Stanford. He emerged as lead counsel in *Pollock* v. *Farmer's Loan and Trust Co.* (1895), in which he argued the unconstitutionality of the 1894 income tax law before the U.S. Supreme Court. The Court not only struck down the 1894 law but also reversed an earlier decision, in *Springer* v. *United States* (1881), that had upheld income tax collection.

Choate, though influential in New York Republican politics, never held elected office. He nominated Theodore Roosevelt for the state assembly. Choate's efforts against corruption led to the ouster of Tammany's infamous William "Boss" Tweed. President William McKinley

appointed Choate ambassador to Great Britain in 1899, and he served with distinction for six years. During his tenure, Choate helped secure British agreement to the Hay-Pauncefote Treaty of 1901, which sped the Panama Canal's construction. He also smoothed the way for British, French, and Russian acceptance of Secretary of State John Hay's "Open Door" policy for China's markets. Choate died in New York City.

Further Reading: Theron George Strong, *Choate: New-Englander, New Yorker, Lawyer, Ambassador*, 1917; William V. Rowe, "Joseph H. Choate and the Right Training for the Bar," *Case and Comment* 24 (September 1917): 264–276; D. M. Marshman, Jr., "The Four Ages of Joseph Choate," *American Heritage* 26 (1975): 32–40, 96–97.

Janet Butler Munch

CHOPIN, KATE O'FLAHERTY (8 February 1850–22 August 1904), author. Born in St. Louis, Missouri, O'Flaherty married Aurelian Roselius Oscar Chopin in 1870; they moved first to New Orleans and later to northwestern Louisiana. After her husband's death in 1882, Chopin returned to St. Louis. Despite setbacks in her personal and professional life, she persevered with her writing to supplement the family's income. Chopin finished her first novel, *At Fault*, in 1890. Four years later Houghton, Mifflin published her collection of short stories, *Bayou Folk*. Her fiction reflected her Louisiana experience as well as the influence of the French writer Guy de Maupassant. Chopin's most significant work, *The Awakening*, appeared in 1899. A pioneer of feminist awareness and realism, Chopin left her mark on Gilded Age literature. She died in St. Louis.

Further Reading: Emily Toth, *Kate Chopin*, 1988.

Leonard Schlup

CHURCH, LOUIS KOSSUTH (11 December 1846–25 November 1897), territorial governor. Born in Brooklyn, New York, Church studied law at Columbia University, practiced in New York City in the 1870s, and was a Democratic member of the New York State Assembly from 1882 to 1885. There he worked with Theodore Roosevelt to achieve municipal and educational reforms. In 1885, President Grover Cleveland appointed Church associate chief justice for the fifth judicial district of the supreme court of the Dakota Territory. Two years later Cleveland named him territorial governor. Church served from February 1887 until March 1889. Disagreements over patronage, personal animosities, and intraparty factionalism marked Church's tumultuous tenure. His letters to Cleveland reveal the extent to which partisanship and bitter rivalries plagued that era of Dakota history. Nevertheless, Church managed to score some successes. Upon leaving office, he moved to Washington State, maintained a general law practice, was president of the Everett chamber of commerce, chaired the Democratic state convention in 1892, and was active in his church and local community affairs. He died in Juneau, Alaska.

Further Reading: Leonard Schlup, "The Private Letters of Governor Louis K. Church to President Grover Cleveland, 1887–1889," *South Dakota History* 26 (1996): 227–54.

Leonard Schlup

CHURCH, ROBERT REED (18 June 1839– 29 August 1912), African-American landowner and capitalist. Born in either Memphis, Tennessee, or Holly Springs, Mississippi, the son of a house servant and her white master, Church participated in the 1866 Memphis race riot, operated a saloon, unsuccessfully sought election to city government in the 1880s, and purchased valuable land at low prices during the yellow fever epidemics of 1878 and 1879. With his savings invested in real estate, Church became a prosperous Memphis landowner. He was one of the wealthiest African Americans of the Gilded Age, representing the black capitalism advocated by Booker T. Washington. Church constructed a park for African Americans, financed a black bank, and served as a delegate to the Republican National Convention of 1900. He died in Memphis.

Further Reading: *Memphis Commercial Appeal*, 30 August 1912; Annette E. Church and Roberta Church, *The Robert R. Churches of Memphis*, 1974.

Leonard Schlup

CINCINNATI RIOT OF 1884. In 1884 William Berner, who had confessed to murder in Cincinnati, received twenty years' imprisonment rather than death. After the sentencing, some ten thousand protesters gathered at the courthouse to denounce the leniency of the pun-

ishment. From there they marched on the jail, intent on killing Berner. Civic leaders at first approved of the vigilantism and became alarmed only when the mob failed to find Berner, who had been moved to the state penitentiary for his protection, and set the jail on fire. Town elders now suspected the mob of including socialists and anarchists, whom they branded "the dangerous classes." The next night the mob set fire to the courthouse, and the militia that was to protect it fired on rioters with Gatling guns. The riot continued a third night, and in the end more than fifty people died.

Further Reading: Leonard Woolsey Bacon, *Lessons from the Riot in Cincinnati*, 1884; Richard Hofstadter and Michael Wallace, eds., *American Violence: A Documentary History*, 1970.

Christopher Cumo

CIRCUMCISION. The medical history of circumcision in the United States began in New York City on 9 February 1870. James Marion Sims, an eminent gynecologist, summoned Dr. Lewis A. Sayre, an innovative orthopedic surgeon and teacher, for consultation on the perplexing case of a five-year-old Wisconsin boy who experienced problems in walking and standing. The boy had an irritated and imprisoned penis, and Sayre therefore performed a circumcision at Bellevue Hospital. The surgery, viewed by medical students, restored the child's health and appetite, and he was able to walk properly within a short time. Shortly thereafter Sayre operated on the foreskin of a teenage boy, who almost immediately recovered from a partial paralysis. Sayre, elected president of the American Medical Association in 1880, later published his findings in the *Transactions of the American Medical Association*. Because of Sayre's professional standing, the medical world took him seriously in an era of surgical experimentation on the genitalia of both sexes as a means to alleviate psychological symptoms. Sayre operated on a number of male children confined to the Manhattan State Hospital's Idiot Asylum on Randall's Island, but no patient recovered enough to be discharged.

Sayre's critics included Drs. J. M. McGee and Langdon C. Gray, who argued for circumcision not to relieve irritation but as a preventive, hygienic measure. Gilded Age Americans identified personal cleanliness with good morals, sound health, and upright character. In an age obsessed with social and racial hierarchies, people were ranked from clean to dirty. Some medical experts claimed the penis was a source of contamination, and asserted that circumcision purified the male sex organ and prevented it from becoming a time bomb ready to explode in a burst of disease and filth. Another factor responsible for the growth of circumcision in the United States was the masturbation hysteria that swept the age. Reduction of genitalia by removing a significant segment of the male's sexual equipment became a deliberate surgical intervention to debilitate and desensitize the penis in an attempt to prevent child sexual "self-abuse," a concern eliciting squeamishness in Victorian America, a culture nervous about sex. Those who feared masturbation could cause epilepsy, alcoholism, headaches, criminality, tuberculosis, malnutrition, insanity, and death considered circumcision a convenient remedy.

Dr. John Harvey Kellogg, the breakfast cereal tycoon, preached that boys masturbate because the foreskin, an erotically sensitive area, rubs on the head of the penis. He reasoned that male children circumcised at birth would remember the pain and would be less likely to engage in self-manipulation later. Dr. John Ashurst, professor of clinical surgery at the University of Pennsylvania, and Dr. Peter Charles Remondino, a physician and public health official, stridently championed universal circumcision at a time when the number of hospitals in America skyrocketed from fewer than two hundred in the early 1870s to four thousand by 1910. The percentage of males circumcised in the United States increased from 0.001 percent in 1860 to 10 percent in 1887, 15 percent in 1895, and 25 percent by 1900. In addition to producing attractive physical results, circumcision became a mark of social distinction, gaining a place in the fin-de-siècle social order. Outside Judaism, circumcision surfaced as the province of doctors and parents with sufficient income to pay for the elective procedure. By the turn of the century and throughout the next, it was a panacea as well as a ritual mutilative surgery firmly enshrined in standard American

medical practice. More recently a growing number of physicians and parents have questioned the need for this routine measure. Pro-choice men and advocates of male rights, vigilant against surgical mistakes and cognizant of human dignity, maintain that nature knows more about designing the penis than twenty-first century doctors.

Further Reading: David L. Gollaher, "From Ritual to Science: The Medical Transformation of Circumcision in America," *Journal of Social History* 28 (1994): 5–36; Peter C. Remondino, *History of Circumcision from the Earliest Times to the Present*, 1891.

Leonard Schlup

CITIES. In 1900, nineteen American cities had populations of two hundred thousand or more; the Gilded Age was a time of great cities. The three largest, containing over a million people each, were New York (3,437,202), Chicago (1,698,575), and Philadelphia (1,293,697). In 1860, New York, long the nation's major commercial city, became the leading manufacturing center. Its population in 1890, without Brooklyn, was 2,507,414. Local geography helped make New York more densely populated than any other city in the United States. The wealthy found the city ideal for their way of life. Upper Fifth Avenue became known for its grand homes after the mansions of William K. Vanderbilt and John Jacob Astor were built in the 1880s. These exclusive residences were constructed beside one another without the usual grassy grounds found in other major cities.

By the late 1860s tenements were built expressly for the poor, which made the extremes of wealth and poverty starkly visible. The "dumbbell" tenement, introduced in 1879, became the standard structure in the next two decades. The Tenth Ward, on the Lower East Side, which attracted Russian and Polish Jews (New York had the largest Jewish population), was the most crowded area in the country. In 1870 New York became the first American city to build an apartment house for multiple dwelling. In 1898 the Unification Act combined the city of New York and the city of Brooklyn with Bronx County (a portion of Westchester County), Queens County (a portion of Long Island), and Richmond County (Staten Island) into one city. Manhattan and Brooklyn were as magnets for European immigrants. Characteristic of New York was its combination of individuality and heterogeneity. Also distinctive in the post–Civil War era were its expanding advertising and publishing industries and new cultural institutions such as the Metropolitan Museum of Art (1879).

Chicago, whose population in 1840 was a mere 4,470, became newsworthy in the postbellum period for its population growth. It also became the largest railroad center, and consequently the commercial metropolis, of the Northwest, notably important for its grain and lumber trade and for its pork and beef. The business community, exemplifying the bold nature that capitalism assumed after the war, initiated the concept of the organized industrial district (building factories near workers' residences). During the 1880s Chicago initiated the building of wrought-iron and steel-skeleton skyscrapers. The city felt the full force of the European migration to the United States, and included the largest Swedish settlement in the country and a large number of Germans (161,039 in 1890). By 1900 Italian inhabitants were ethnically concentrated in some sixteen distinct settlements: called "Little Italies." Chicago was more prone than any other city to promote suburbs.

Philadelphia, coextensive with the county of Philadelphia, was the largest city in the United States. Its spacious territory enabled people to build on the ground rather than upward. Noted for its small homes, the city offered many houses for workers, including the poor. In 1870 Philadelphia was the first in the country in the number of manufacturing establishments; notable were iron and locomotive works and boot and shoe factories. In 1890, Irish (110,935) and Germans (74,974) predominated among its foreign-born.

St. Louis, roughly midway between the Mississippi River's source and its mouth, and long Chicago's rival, was the second greatest railroad center. In 1881 it became the largest market for wheat, flour, and cotton in the world. St. Louis was an important manufacturing city, behind only New York and Philadelphia. Boston was the leading city in the United States for

educational institutions and libraries. In 1890 it ranked third in the number of Irish-born (71,441), 16 percent of the population. Baltimore, in the years following the Civil War, led all southern cities in commerce and manufacturing. Its businesses included iron and locomotive works and nail factories. After 1870, its manufacture of boys' and men's clothing expanded rapidly, virtually dominating the southern market by 1895. Important also for its canning industry, it became the leading center for oyster packing by 1900.

Further Reading: Willard Glazier, *Peculiarities of American Cities*, 1886; Donald J. Bogue, *The Population of the United States: Historical Trends and Future Projections*, 1985; J. K. Paulding, "A Plea for New York," *Atlantic Monthly* 87 (1901): 172–179.

Bernard Hirschhorn

CIVIC ORGANIZATIONS. Primarily through business and professional efforts, a movement to reform American urban governments developed between 1870 and 1900. Organizations sought to extend civil service to the municipal level and to revamp nomination and election machinery to secure honest, efficient, and economical administration of government. They also supported municipal charters that included home rule, separation of local elections from state and national elections, and nonpartisan government.

Municipal reform organizations varied. There were those which publicized political information for voters, such as the Municipal Voters League of Chicago, the Citizens' Association of Boston, and the Municipal League of Philadelphia. Others endorsed a slate of candidates taken from the parties' nominees, including the Library Hall Association of Cambridge, Massachusetts. There were also municipal political parties and city clubs. Public health issues concerned such organizations as the Philadelphia branch of the National Woman's Health Protective Association and the Ladies' Health Protective Association of New York.

In 1893 the Municipal League of Philadelphia—the city's premier civic organization—encouraged by the influential City Club of New York, summoned a national conference on good city government. It convened at Philadelphia in January 1884; in May 1894 the National Municipal League was organized, and its first annual conference was held at Minneapolis that December. In 1900 the National Municipal League published its "Municipal Program," committing itself to a strong mayor and a strengthened council. Without question, civic organizations became nongovernmental associations in the realm of city government.

Further Reading: Frank Mann Stewart, *A Half Century of Municipal Reform: The History of the National Municipal League*, 1950; William Howe Tolman, *Municipal Reform Movements*, 1895.

Bernard Hirschhorn

CIVIL RIGHTS CASES (109 U.S. 3). The *Civil Rights Cases*, heard by the U.S. Supreme Court in 1883, tested the constitutionality of the Civil Rights Act of 1875, which prohibited racial discrimination in public places such as theaters and inns. The Court struck down the law as unconstitutional, thus inviting further segregation.

A number of cases in which a person of color had been denied access to a privately owned establishment came before the courts in the late 1870s. By 1883, five of them, from various parts of the country, reached the High Court. Solicitor General Samuel F. Phillips argued the cases collectively. He asserted that the establishments, while privately owned, were subject to state regulation, and thus obligated under the law to offer equal access to all races. He argued that racial discrimination violated the Thirteenth Amendment, by subjecting blacks to a form of servitude, and the Fourteenth Amendment, because it denied equal rights to some citizens on the basis of their color. The court disagreed.

On 15 October 1883, Justice Joseph Bradley delivered the majority opinion. The court ruled that Congress could not legislate integration or force private entrepreneurs to serve a black clientele, and that discrimination was not a form of slavery. These cases did not violate the Fourteenth Amendment, which applied only to state action, and not that of individuals within the state. The lone dissenter, Justice John Marshall

Harlan, argued that the majority position followed the letter of the law but not its intent. Congress, he insisted did have the power to protect people against the deprivation of their civil rights in public places, even those which were privately owned. The ruling interpreted the Constitution narrowly, and led to subsequent denials of other basic rights.

Further Reading: Richard Bardolph, *The Civil Rights Record: Black Americans and the Law, 1848–1970*, 1970; Derrick A. Bell, ed., *Civil Rights: Leading Cases*, 1980; John R. Howard, *The Shifting Wind: The Supreme Court and Civil Rights from Reconstruction to Brown*, 1999.

Kevin B. Witherspoon

CIVIL SERVICE REFORM. The spoils system, machine politics, and political assessments filled government offices with incompetents and brought cries for good government. Under President Ulysses S. Grant, the first Civil Service Commission (1871) was empowered to oversee competency examinations of potential civil servants. Later, Rutherford B. Hayes reformed the bastion of Stalwart (spoilsmen) power, the New York Customhouse. These limited improvements spawned organizations seeking more substantial change, such as the New York Civil Service Reform Association, led by George William Curtis.

Although most reformers were Republicans, in December 1880, Democratic Senator George H. Pendleton of Ohio introduced two bills to overhaul the civil service and end political assessments. Little movement occurred in Congress until a self-proclaimed Stalwart assassinated President James A. Garfield in 1881. Only a discouraging midterm election, however, encouraged enough Republicans to support the reform bill. Republicans saw it as a means to preserve their own in office should they lose the White House in 1884. Democrats supporting the reform, did so on the basis of Pendleton's argument that it would restore Jacksonian ideals by opening government positions to the common man. The Pendleton Act (1883) empowered a three-man Civil Service Commission to inaugurate a merit system based on competitive examinations. The act outlawed political assessments and allowed future presidents to add to the 10 percent of government positions covered initially by the law. They did so, ironically enough, often to protect their own appointees. Ultimately Pendleton lost his Senate seat because Ohio Democrats believed the law would cause Democrats to forfeit political spoils once the party gained the presidency.

Further Reading: Ari Hoogenboom, *Outlawing the Spoils: A History of the Civil Service Reform Movement, 1865–1883,* 1961; Paul P. Van Riper, *History of the United States Civil Service,* 1958; Thomas S. Mach, " 'Gentleman George' Hunt Pendleton: Study in Political Continuity," Ph.D. diss., University of Akron, 1996.

Thomas S. Mach

CLARK, EDWARD (15 August 1822–6 January 1902), architect. Born and educated in Philadelphia, Pennsylvania, Clark learned mechanical and freehand drawing from his father and became superintendent of construction on the Patent Office and Post Office additions in Washington, D.C. When the architect of the U.S. Capitol, Thomas Ustick Walter, for whom Clark had worked as chief assistant, tendered his resignation in 1865, President Andrew Johnson appointed Clark to the post. Clark introduced technological improvements to the building: electricity, steam heat, and elevators. He enlarged the grounds and commissioned Frederick Law Olmsted to landscape the grounds. In addition, Clark oversaw the reconstruction of the west central interior, and is credited with having designed the marble terraces on the north, south, and west fronts. Clark served as architect of the Capitol until his death in Washington, D.C. In addition, Congress chose him as one of the commissioners charged with completing the Washington Monument. Clark also was a member of and contributed to several scientific, artistic, and architectural societies.

Further Reading: Henry F. Withey and Elsie R. Withey, *Biographical Dictionary of American Architects,* 1956; William C. Allen, *The United States Capitol: A Brief Architectural History,* 2000; Donald R. Kennon, ed., *The United States Capitol: Designing and Decorating a National Icon,* 2000.

Leonard Schlup

CLARK, WILLIAM ANDREWS (8 January 1839–2 March 1925), U.S. senator and mining entrepreneur. Born near Connellsville, Pennsylvania, Clark studied law at Iowa Wesleyan University before moving to Montana in 1863. The next year he was president of the state constitutional convention. Elected as a Democrat to the U.S. Senate, he served from 4 December 1899 until 15 May 1900, when he resigned before the chamber passed a resolution declaring his election void because of fraud. Again elected to the Senate, he held a seat for one full term (1901–1907). His major interests involved business more than politics. A banker, mine operator, and railroad magnate, Clark in 1912 founded Clarkdale, a company mining town in Arizona. Using the most modern construction materials, he planned and developed the town, which he owned, as a monument to himself. Clark also owned the United Verde Copper Company on Cleopatra Hill in nearby Jerome. He created his separate railroad line, the United Verde and Pacific, which subsequently made his company the richest privately owned copper firm in the world. Clark died in New York City.

Further Reading: Forrest L. Foot, "The Senatorial Aspirations of William A. Clark, 1898–1901: A Study in Montana Politics," Ph.D. diss., University of California at Berkeley, 1941; William Mangam, *The Clarks: An American Phenomenon,* 1941.

Leonard Schlup

CLARKSON, JAMES SULLIVAN (17 May 1842–31 May 1918), railroad promoter, businessman, editor, and postmaster. Clarkson was born in Brookville, Indiana. Before the Civil War he was an abolitionist who participated in the Underground Railroad. From 1868 to 1889 he was editor in chief of the *Iowa State Register* in Des Moines. He chaired the Iowa Republican State Committee from 1869 to 1871. After declining President Ulysses S. Grant's invitation to represent the United States in Switzerland, Clarkson served as Des Moines postmaster from 1871 to 1877. During part of Benjamin Harrison's presidency (1889–1890), he was first assistant postmaster general, and in 1892 he promoted Harrison's renomination and reelection. Clarkson was a member of the Republican League from 1891 to 1892, and surveyor of customs in New York City from 1902 to 1910.

He organized and became president of the companies that built two railways into Des Moines. Clarkson died in Tarrytown, New York.

Further Reading: *New York Times*, 1 June 1918; Homer E. Socolofsky and Allan B. Spetter, *The Presidency of Benjamin Harrison*, 1987.

Leonard Schlup

CLEMENS, SAMUEL LANGHORNE (MARK TWAIN) (30 November 1835–21 April 1910), novelist and essayist. Born in Florida, Missouri, Clemens grew up in to Hannibal, Missouri. He attended public schools until age twelve, when his father's death forced him to become a printer's apprentice. This work stimulated his interest in writing, and he became a journalist at a newspaper that his brother Orion edited.

In 1862 Clemens began to use the pseudonym Mark Twain while a reporter in Virginia City, Nevada, and under this name he built an outstanding reputation as a novelist and essayist, one of the greatest of the era. His *Gilded Age* (1873), written with Charles Dudley Warner, named the era stretching from the ratification of the Fourteenth Amendment (1870) to the beginning of Theodore Roosevelt's presidency (1901). Three years later his *Adventures of Tom Sawyer* focused on his childhood exploits in Hannibal and confirmed him as a novelist of the American Midwest. He set *A Tramp Abroad* (1880) and *The Prince and the Pauper* (1882) in Europe, then returned in 1883 to the Midwest with *Life on the Mississippi*. That river was his setting for *The Adventures of Huckleberry Finn* (1884), which the public library in Concord, Massachusetts, banned in 1885 for admitting that racism was dividing the United States and for its crude language and casual morals. In 1894 he again warned readers against racism in *The Tragedy of Pudd'nhead Wilson*.

Clemens opened a publishing company in 1881, but it lost $200,000 before closing in 1894. The next year he began a successful lecture tour that took him to India, South Africa, and Australia, raising money to pay his debts. He died in Redding, Connecticut, leaving unfinished several manuscripts, including his autobiography.

Further Reading: Justin Kaplan, *Mr. Clemens and Mark Twain*, 1966; Jahn Lauber, *The Making of Mark Twain: A Biography*; 1985; Andrew J. Hoffman, *Inventing Mark Twain: The Lives of Samuel Langhorne Clemens*, 1997.

Christopher Cumo

CLENDENIN, HENRY WILSON (1 August 1837–18 July 1927), editor and publisher. Clendenin was born in Schellsburg, Pennsylvania, studied at various public and private schools, and mastered several languages. He held newspaper positions in Indiana, Iowa, Pennsylvania, and Illinois before and after serving in the Union Army during the Civil War. In 1882 Clendenin and William Rees purchased the *Illinois State* Register, a daily morning newspaper that had been operating at a financial loss. They built it into a political influence throughout the state and nation, with Clendenin as president and editor in chief. Clendenin was vice chairman of the Illinois Democratic Central Committee from 1884 to 1885; supported Grover Cleveland for president in 1884, 1888, and 1892; and worked on behalf of vice presidential candidate Adlai E. Stevenson during the 1892 contest. He was postmaster of Springfield, Illinois, from 1886 to 1890, and attended the turbulent Democratic National Convention at Chicago in 1896, hoping to bring about Stevenson's nomination for president. Clendenin affiliated with numerous organizations, including the Young Men's Christian Association, the Lincoln Public Library in Springfield, and the Illinois Historical Society, and from 1879 to 1887 he was secretary of the Northwestern Associated Press. He died in Springfield.

Further Reading: *Illinois State Register*, 19 July 1927.

Leonard Schlup

CLEVELAND, FRANCES FOLSOM (21 July 1864–29 October 1947), wife of President Grover Cleveland. Folsom was born in Buffalo, New York, to Oscar Folsom (Cleveland's law partner) and Emma Harmon. In July 1874, her father was killed and Cleveland became her guardian. Frankie, as she was often called, was graduated from Wells College in 1884 and toured Europe with her mother. At this time she became secretly engaged to Cleveland. On 2 June 1886 she married the president at the White House, becoming, at age twenty-one, the youngest First Lady in history. The Clevelands had five children: Ruth (1891; the inspiration for the Baby Ruth candy bar), Esther (1893), Marion (1895), Richard Folsom (1897), and Francis Grover (1903). They spent two nonconsecutive terms in the White House.

During her time in the public eye, more attention was paid to Cleveland's appearance than to her activities. She was extremely popular, setting a tone of elegance and grace. Because she was so admired and emulated, her name began to be used for advertising purposes without her consent. Family-centered, Mrs. Cleveland did not involve herself deeply in her husband's duties. In 1887 she participated in a monthlong trip across the United States. During the election of 1888, rumors of spousal abuse by President Cleveland spurred her to respond to the charges through a letter to a woman in Massachusetts. The First Lady held receptions for women two days a week, one of them on Saturday so that working women might attend.

Deeply interested in educational causes, Cleveland established a White House kindergarten for her children, and those of friends and members of diplomatic missions. She became one of the first female trustees of Wells College in 1887. Grover Cleveland died in 1908, and Frances Cleveland became the first widow of a president to remarry, wedding Thomas Jax Preston, Jr., in 1913. During World War 1, she headed the National Security League's Speakers' Bureau. Later in life, she learned braille and translated books for blind readers. She died at a son's home in Baltimore, Maryland, and was buried next to President Cleveland.

Further Reading: "Mrs. Preston Dies, Wed to Cleveland," *New York Times*, 30 October 1947; "Frances (Clara) Folsom Cleveland," in Lewis L. Gould, ed., *American First Ladies: Their Lives and Their Legacy*, 1996; Betty Boyd Caroli, *First Ladies*, 1987.

Terri Pederson Summey

CLEVELAND, GROVER (18 March 1837– 24 June 1908), mayor, governor, president. Born in Caldwell, New Jersey, Cleveland was admitted to the Buffalo, New York, bar in 1859 and joined a law firm immediately thereafter. During the Civil War, he became an assistant district attorney of Erie County. In 1870, as a Democrat, he was elected sheriff, and served for three years. As mayor of Buffalo from 1880 to 1882, he crusaded against corruption, then won the gubnatorial election. In 1884, he defeated Republican James G. Blaine to become president of the United States, surviving the exposé that earlier in life he had fathered an illegitimate child.

Cleveland opposed mandatory silver coinage and supported the modernization of the navy, civil service reform, and a presidential succession act. He signed the latter in 1886, and successfully battled the Senate over his appointment and removal authority under the Tenure of Office Act. He vetoed an unprecedented number of relief and pension bills, insisting on his authority as president to ensure honesty and legality. Of particular significance for the future, he signed the Interstate Commerce Act and the Dawes General Allotment Act in 1887, but vetoed the Dependent Pension Bill. When he tried to return captured Confederate battle flags to southern states in 1887, he created a firestorm of protest and had to back down.

Cleveland ran for reelection in 1888, receiving nearly 100,000 more votes than his Republican opponent, Benjamin Harrison, but losing in the electoral college. When he ran once more against Harrison in 1892, he failed to gain a popular majority, but this time won the electoral count. Cleveland became the only president in American history to serve nonconsecutive terms. Shortly after his second inauguration, a stock market crash set off the Panic of 1893, which consumed his entire second term. He refused to take firm action against the economic crisis, reflecting the Gilded Age's conventional wisdom that businessmen, not politicians, had responsibility for the nation's economy. He did, however, obtain loans for the government from the banker J. P. Morgan and used army troops against Pullman strikers in Chicago. He also continued to veto pension bills and signed a repeal of the Sherman Silver Purchase Act. In foreign policy, he opposed annexation of Hawaii and recognized the islands as an independent republic. His secretary of state, Richard Olney, reinterpreted the Monroe Doctrine, insisting that it gave the United States the right to arbitrate a boundary dispute between Great Britain and Venezuela (Olney Corollary).

Cleveland spent his post–White House years as a professor at Princeton University, an author of magazine articles, and an insurance company executive. He died in Princeton, New Jersey.

Further Reading: Allan Nevins, *Grover Cleveland: A Study in Courage*, 1932; Richard E. Welch, Jr., *The Presidencies of Grover Cleveland*, 1988; John F. Marszalek, ed., *Grover Cleveland: A Bibliography*, 1988.

John F. Marszalek

CLEVELAND'S ELECTORAL STRATEGY IN 1892.

With other Democratic Party leaders, Grover Cleveland worried that the burgeoning Populist movement in certain southern states, the solid area of the Democratic presidential coalition, could siphon off sufficient support to reelect President Benjamin Harrison in 1892. Cleveland and his advisers crafted a strategy to reduce the Populist threat and to compromise with discontented farmers upset at falling crop prices and increasing debts. Cleveland dispatched his running mate, Adlai E. Stevenson, to Virginia, Maryland, West Virginia, North Carolina, Kentucky, Tennessee, Georgia, and Alabama to delineate a conservative counterattack. Their plan consisted of five parts. First, southern Democrats who refrained from voting for the Populists would be rewarded by efforts to defeat the Republican-sponsored federal elections law, designed to protect African-American voters. Second, a Cleveland administration would continue to direct economic benefits to the South. Third, Democrats would demonstrate their appreciation for southern support through patronage. Fourth, the party's highest officials would resume endeavors to reinstate the South's former place in the Union. Fifth, Democrats would reduce tariffs and practice frugality in government. Together these proposals constituted a significant challenge to the Populist danger, and with this program Democrats bargained to hold a wavering South. The program for economic and political revitalization compensated for the more radical Populist ideas. The strategy worked; Cleveland and Stevenson carried the South in 1892 and won the election.

Further Reading: Leonard Schlup, "Conservative Counterattack: Adlai E. Stevenson and the Compromise of 1892 with Democrats in Tennessee and the South," *Tennessee Historical Quarterly* 53 (1994): 114–129; Leonard Schlup, "Adlia E. Stevenson and the 1892 Campaign in North Carolina: A Bourbon Response to Southern Populism," *Southern Studies* 2 (1991): 131–149; Leonard Schlup, "Adlai E. Stevenson and Southern Politics in 1892," *Mississippi Quarterly* 47 (1993–1994): 58–78.

Leonard Schlup

CLEVELAND'S SURGERY.

Two operations on President Grover Cleveland (1 July and 17 July 1893) for epithelial cancer of the mouth were a closely guarded secret kept from the public and even Vice President Adlai E. Stevenson. In fact, details of the surgeries, performed aboard a yacht anchored in New York's East River, were not divulged until 1917 by Dr. William Williams Keen. A sound money Democrat, Cleveland feared that news of his precarious physical condition would precipitate a Wall Street crisis. He remained silent to maintain stability in an economy staggered by the Panic of 1893. Those present on the yacht included his wife, Frances; the owner, his close friend Commodore Elias C. Benedict; the crew; and physicians Joseph Decatur Bryant and William W. Keen. Secretary of War Daniel S. Lamont was the only government official there and the only cabinet member cognizant of the surgeries.

Cleveland, a habitual cigar smoker and consumer of beer, was corpulent. Physicians feared he might suffer a stroke on the operating table, die from hemorrhage, or develop a postoperative infection. After they successfully removed his entire left upper jaw and part of the palate, they inserted an artificial device of vulcanized rubber. The Clevelands sailed to their summer home at Buzzards Bay, Massachusetts, and planned a summer's recovery. Lamont shrewdly repudiated circumstantial news accounts by notifying the press that Cleveland had experienced an attack of rheumatism in his foot and knee. The first lady perpetuated the masquerade in private letters. Visitors heard the chief executive complaining that the doctors had nearly killed him. At first his facial appearance was changed, but there was no external scar.

In the meantime, Stevenson was a near-president without ever knowing. Cleveland, by denying Stevenson important information and not providing necessary briefings to assure an orderly continuation of governmental activity, adopted principles inconsistent with the national interest. In 1975 Dr. Gonzalo E. Aponte led an investigation of the personal notes of Cleveland's doctors and tissue samples of the upper jaw preserved in the Muetter Museum at the College of Physicians in Philadelphia. It was concluded that the lesion was a verrucose carcinoma, a slowly growing, low-grade tumor, and that he did not need a hurried operation in a frantic atmosphere.

Further Reading: Leonard Schlup, "Presidential Disability: The Case of Cleveland and Stevenson," *Presidential Studies Quarterly* 9 (1979): 303–310; William W. Keen, "The Surgical Operations on President Cleveland in 1893," *Saturday Evening Post* 190 (1917): 24–25, 53, 55; John J. Brooks, Horatio T. Enterline, and Gonzalo E. Aponte, "The Final Diagnosis of President Cleveland's Lesion," *Transactions and Studies of the College of Physicians of Philadelphia* 2 (1980): 1–25.

Leonard Schlup

COCHRANE, ELIZABETH (NELLIE BLY)

(5 May 1864–27 January 1922), journalist. Born Elizabeth Cochran in Cochran's Mills, Pennsylvania, near Pittsburgh, she was educated at home except for a brief period in 1879 when she attended a normal school in Indiana, Pennsylvania, and added an "e" to her name. She moved to Pittsburgh at age sixteen, and became one of the few women newspaper reporters of the era when she took a job on the *Pittsburgh Dispatch* in 1885. She took her pen name, "Nellie Bly," from a popular song. She established a reputation as an investigative reporter who exposed poor conditions in factories. In 1886–1887 the *Dispatch* sent her to Mexico, where she reported on social ills. After her return she moved to New York and became a national celebrity as a stunt reporter (1887–1895) for the *New York World*. She repeatedly posed as a victim to gain material for exposés, including reports on brutality in a mental asy-

lum to which she had been committed after feigning insanity. Her most famous exploit lacked the social content of her investigations. It was a seventy-two-day trip around the world, from 14 November 1889 to 25 January 1890, to beat the fictional eighty-day record of Jules Verne's hero, Phineas Fogg. In 1895 she left journalism to marry. She returned in 1919, on the *New York Journal*, but did not regain her former status. She died in New York City.

Further Reading: Brooke Kroeger, *Nellie Bly*, 1994.

Maurine H. Beasley

COCKRAN, WILLIAM BOURKE (28 February 1854–1 March 1923), lawyer, congressman, and political leader. Born in County Sligo, Ireland, and educated in Ireland and France, Cockran moved to the United States in 1871. He studied law, won admittance to the bar in 1876, and practiced in New York City. Cockran quickly became active in local Democratic politics. A Tammany delegate to the 1884 Democratic National Convention, he delivered a forceful speech attacking the presidential nomination of New York Governor Grover Cleveland, and at the 1892 convention, he nominated Senator David B. Hill. Cockran served in the U.S. House of Representatives (1887–1889, 1891–1895, 1905–1909, and 1921–1923) until his death in Washington, D.C. He supported organized labor and fought immigration restriction. Cockran vehemently opposed William Jennings Bryan's free silver presidential candidacy in 1896, campaigning instead for Republican William McKinley. Disappointed by American acquisition of overseas possessions, he returned to the Democrats in 1900 and supported Bryan for president on an anti-imperialist platform. Whether Cockran was condemning prohibition, free silver, imperialism, or anyone with whom he disagreed, he played a vital role in Gilded Age politics.

Further Reading: Florence Teicher Bloom, "The Political Career of William Bourke Cockran," Ph.D. diss., City University of New York, 1970; James McGurrin, *Bourke Cockran: A Free Lance in American Politics*, 1948; William Bourke Cockran Papers, New York Public Library, New York City.

Leonard Schlup

COCKRELL, FRANCIS MARION (1 October 1834–13 December 1915), U.S. senator. Cockrell was born in Warrensburg, Missouri, graduated from Chapel Hill College in 1853, practiced law in Warrensburg, and served in the Confederate Army during the Civil War. Known for his commanding appearance, honesty, ability, personal mannerisms, and corncob pipe, Cockrell was a successful lawyer who easily made friends. He was elected to the U.S. Senate as successor to Carl Schurz. Cockrell, a Democrat who followed his party's doctrines, served there from 1875 to 1905. At the Democratic National Convention of 1904, in St. Louis, William Jennings Bryan, a former presidential contender, placed Cockrell's name in nomination for the presidency. He lost the nomination to Judge Alton B. Parker of New York, and suffered defeat in Missouri that year when a Republican legislature selected William Warner to succeed him in the Senate. President Theodore Roosevelt appointed Cockrell to the Interstate Commerce Commission, in which capacity he served from 1905 to 1910. He died Washington, D.C.

Further Reading: *Warrensburg Standard-Herald*, 17 December 1915; Francis Cockrell, *The Senator from Missouri: The Life and Times of Francis Marion Cockrell*, 1962; Hugh P. Williamson, "Correspondence of Senator Francis Marion Cockrell: December 23, 1888," *Bulletin of the Missouri Historical Society* 28 (1969): 296–305.

Leonard Schlup

CODY, WILLIAM FREDERICK (BUFFALO BILL) (26 February 1846–10 January 1917), frontiersman and showman. Born in Le Claire, Iowa, Cody grew up in Kansas, rode for the Pony Express, and fought for the north in the Civil War. In 1867, as a buffalo hunter for the Union Pacific Railroad, he earned his famous nickname. From 1868 until 1872 he was chief scout for the U.S. Fifth Cavalry. Edward Z. Judson, whose pen name was Ned Buntline, made Cody a dime novel hero in 1869 and in 1872 launched Cody's eleven-year career as a part-time stage actor. These events, plus his killing of Yellow Hand in an 1876 fight with the Cheyennes, spread Cody's fame and led to publication of his autobiography when he was thirty-three.

Capitalizing on nostalgia for the rapidly disappearing frontier, Cody organized a traveling show, Buffalo Bill's Wild West, in 1883. By the decade's end, owing to a series of European tours, Cody had achieved international fame. The show was a featured attraction of the World's Columbian Exposition at Chicago in 1893. For thirty years, Buffalo Bill's Wild West popularized America's frontier past and showcased such personalities as Phoebe Ann Moses (Annie Oakley); William Levi (Buck) Taylor, the original cowboy hero; and, briefly, the Sioux leader Sitting Bull. Its success spawned a host of imitators, some of which endured until the depression of the 1930s forced their closure. Buffalo Bill's Wild West ended its run in 1913. Cody died in Denver, Colorado.

Further Reading: Don Russell, *The Lives and Legends of Buffalo Bill*, 1960; Nellie Snyder Yost, *Buffalo Bill*, 1979; Sarah J. Blackstone, *Buckskins, Bullets and Business*, 1986.

William W. Savage, Jr.

COEUR D'ALENE. Northern Idaho's silver and gold mines were discovered in 1882 but did not experience a rush until 1885. Warner, Idaho, reportedly had a population of almost four thousand within two months, and other camps quickly appeared. Spokane, Washington, served as the gateway.

Corporations soon gained control of the entire district. Miners countered by forming a union in the fall of 1890; in 1893 it allied with the Western Federation of Miners (WFM). The union, meanwhile, struck during the winter of 1890–1891 for wages of $3.50 a day. Their victory was followed by a lockout in January 1892 and a long, bitter strike. In July, a violent battle ensued; buildings were dynamited, five men were killed, and captured nonunion miners were driven from the district. The National Guard intervened, but not until November did peace return and the mines reopen at the old wage rate. Neither side was satisfied.

In April 1899, violence erupted again over wages and nonunion workers. Federal troops arrived to restore order. The union was broken, men were arrested, trials were held. Workers protested these actions throughout the nation. In 1901, the troops left. Coeur d'Alene remained in the limelight through a sensational 1907 trial of several WFM officials accused of ordering the killing of Idaho's former governor, Frank Steunenberg, in 1905.

Further Reading: William Greever, *The Bonanza West*, 1963; Richard E. Lingenfelter, *The Hardrock Miners*, 1974; John Fahey, *Hecla: A Century of Western Mining*, 1990.

Duane A. Smith

COFFEEN, HENRY ASA (14 February 1841–9 December 1912), congressman. Born near Gallipolis, Gallia County, Ohio, Coffeen taught at Hiram College in his native state before moving to Sheridan, Wyoming, in 1884. There, as a member of the constitutional convention, he helped frame the new state's basic document in 1889. Elected as a Democrat to the Fifty-third Congress, he served from 1893 to 1895. During his term, Coffeen conferred with President Grover Cleveland on patronage matters and building the Democratic Party in Wyoming, favored a graduated income tax, advocated the free coinage of silver, supported tariff reform, and articulated his stand against "the organized greed and cunning avarice of the money power." Coffeen was unsuccessful in his bid for reelection in the Republican landslide of 1894, and returned to private life. A prominent rancher, writer, miner, journalist, and businessman who had belonged to the Knights of Labor, Coffeen was a principal Gilded Age political figure who fought for western interests.

Further Reading: Leonard Schlup, "I Am Not a Cuckoo Democrat! The Congressional Career of Henry A. Coffeen," *Wyoming Annals* 66 (1994): 30–47.

Leonard Schlup

COINAGE ACT OF 1873. The United States had accepted both gold and silver as legal tender since 1792, but between 1860 and 1869 the amount of silver in circulation dropped from $21 million to less than $6 million because it was undervalued in the United States and therefore was exchanged for gold overseas. With so little silver in circulation, the comptroller of the currency recommended in 1870 that Congress direct the Treasury to stop coining the silver dollar, a proposal that would virtually eliminate silver from circulation because the silver dollar was the major silver coin being minted. Congress adopted this proposal in the Coinage Act of 1873 (known as the Crime of '73), without immediate controversy.

Thereafter silver prices fell as European countries followed Great Britain's lead in selling off silver as a prelude to adopting the gold standard. Silver discoveries in the American West further increased the amount of silver available for cheap purchase. No one could buy silver at discount and sell it dear to the Treasury, however, because the Treasury was no longer coining the silver dollar. Americans who had silver and those who wanted inflation denounced the Coinage Act of 1873 and agitated for unlimited coinage of silver. Despite their efforts, in 1900 Congress passed the Gold Standard Act, dropping silver as legal tender.

Further Reading: Allen Weinstein, "Was There a 'Crime of 1873'?: The Case of the Demonetized Dollar," *Journal of American History* 54 (1967): 307–26; Milton Friedman and Anna Schwartz, *A Monetary History of the United States, 1867–1960*, 1963; Paul Studenski and Herman Krooss, *A Financial History of the United States*, 1952.

Christopher Cumo

COKE, RICHARD (13 March 1829–14 May 1897), Texas governor and senator. Born near Williamsburg, Virginia, Coke studied civil law at the College of William and Mary, and moved to Waco, Texas, in 1850. He supported the Confederacy at the Texas secession convention and served as a Confederate infantry captain throughout the Civil War. Governor Andrew Jackson Hamilton appointed Coke Ninth District Court judge in 1865; in 1866 he won election to the state supreme court, but General Philip H. Sheridan removed him. Coke became Redeemer governor when he defeated Radical Republican Governor Edmund J. Davis in 1874.

During Coke's administration Texas adopted a new constitution that reflected the state's predominantly agrarian population. Amended several hundred times, it remains in place today, despite the state's modern urban status. Coke also presided over establishment of Texas Agricultural and Mechanical College (now a university). He was elected to the U.S. Senate in 1876, and reelected in 1883 and 1889. He died in Waco.

Further Reading: Kenneth Hendrickson, *The Chief Executives of Texas*, 1996; John W. Payne, Jr., "Richard Coke," *The New Handbook of Texas*, vol. 2, (1996): 193; Archie

P. McDonald, *"On This Day of New Beginnings": Inaugural Addresses of Texas Governors*, 1979.

Archie P. McDonald

COLCORD, ROSWELL KEYES (25 April 1839–30 October 1939), governor. Born in Searsport, Maine, Colcord was educated in public schools, and worked as a ship's carpenter. He moved to California in 1856, and to Nevada in 1860. Manager and owner of mines and mills in Nevada while pursuing his interest in government, Colcord advocated the free coinage of silver, an expensive liquor license, immigration restriction, a rigid barrier separating religion from politics and public schools, and a tariff for revenue (but with incidental protectionist duties). In 1890 he received the Republican gubernatorial nomination and won election as the state's sixth governor, serving from 1891 to 1895. Three years later, he became superintendent of the U.S. mint in Carson City. Various nonpolitical activities and a lengthy retirement dominated his final years. He died in Carson City.
Further Reading: New York *Times*, 31 October 1939.

Leonard Schlup

COLFAX, SCHUYLER (23 March 1823–13 January 1885), vice president, politician. Born in New York City, Colfax traveled westward with his family at age thirteen to Carlisle, Indiana. He worked as an auditor and correspondent, and studied law before entering Whig politics. Colfax was elected to the House of Representatives in 1855, and served continuously from 1863 to 1869 as Speaker of the House. His record and support of African-American rights brought him the Republican vice presidential nomination in 1868. While vice president he was implicated in the Crédit Moblier scandal, and admitted to receiving a questionable campaign contribution. Although he was never censured, his political career ended. He spent his remaining years lecturing, and died suddenly, at age sixty-one, in Mankato, Minnesota.
Further Reading: O. J. Hollister, *Life of Schuyler Colfax*, 1886; Sean Dennis Cashman, *America in the Gilded Age*, 1988.

Michael W. Vogt

COLGATE, JAMES BOORMAN (4 March 1818–7 February 1904), businessman and philanthropist. Born in New York City, Colgate acquired money and influence through several business operations, including James B. Colgate and Company. A founder and president of the New York Gold Exchange, and later director of the Bank of the State of New York, he supported the remonetization of silver in the 1890s, despite the negative sentiments of most of his business associates, who feared an inflationary spiral. Colgate gave generously to educational and religious institutions as well as the arts.
Further Reading: *New York Herald*, 8 February 1904; *New York Tribune*, 8 February 1904.

Leonard Schlup

COLLECTOR v. DAY (11 Wallace 113). Between 1864 and 1867, Congress passed the Revenue Acts, levying a general income tax, in part to finance Civil War and Reconstruction costs. J. M. Day, a Massachusetts probate judge, paid under protest, contending salaries of state officers should not be subject to federal taxes. Day filed suit against a Mr. Buffington, the U.S. internal revenue collector for the district of Massachusetts. The circuit court found for Day. Buffington challenged on procedural grounds. In April 1871 the Supreme Court ruled 8–0 for Day, with Justice Samuel Nelson writing that public salaries of state officers are protected from federal taxation. Citing the *Dobbins* case, where the Court ruled states could not tax federal employees, Nelson held that the same protection extended to state officers in regard to federal tax. The ruling treated state and the federal governments as equals; restrictions on taxation must be reciprocal. *Collector* v. *Day* is at times interpreted as Supreme Court invalidation of acts of Congress, but is more properly viewed as the result of typical constitutional mechanisms. Congress passes general laws; in specific instances they can be challenged either at the executive level, concerning implementation, or through the courts. In this case, the Revenue Acts were not ruled invalid. Rather, their application to a specific class was restricted.

Further Reading: Charles Fairman, *History of the Supreme Court of the United States*, vol. 6, *Reconstruction and Reunion 1864–1888*, 1971, pp. 1419–1421, 1435–1437.

Thomas C. Sutton

COLLEGE SETTLEMENTS ASSOCIATION.

Founded in 1890 by recent graduates of elite women's colleges including Bryn Mawr, Radcliffe, Smith, and Vassar, the association addressed the concerns of many Americans regarding the conditions faced by a growing immigrant population. Within a few years of its founding, it sponsored settlement houses in Baltimore, Boston, New York, and Philadelphia. These houses, usually staffed by the students and recent graduates of the sponsoring colleges, offered neighborhood immigrant residents a variety of programs including child care, children's activities, and classes in English and hygiene. The settlement houses also supported trade union activity, and worked for passage of legislation to relieve the poor living and working conditions faced by most urban immigrants, while simultaneously providing opportunities for the employment of middle- and upper-class white women.

Further Reading: John P. Rousmaniere, "Cultural Hybrid in the Slums: The College Woman and the Settlement House, 1889–1894," *American Quarterly* 22 (1970): 45–66; College Settlement Association Records, Sophia Smith Collection, Smith College.

Kathleen Banks Nutter

COLLEGES AND UNIVERSITIES.

In many ways, higher education in America took on its modern form during the Gilded Age. After the Civil War, the American version of the university was created, state universities rose in prominence, professional programs expanded, and opportunities for women increased dramatically. Between 1870 and 1900, both college enrollment and faculty positions increased fivefold as existing institutions expanded and new ones were founded. Perhaps the most significant innovation was the adoption of the German model of the university, in which research and graduate and professional training took center stage, replacing the largely classical schooling of the antebellum colleges. Johns Hopkins and the University of Chicago were founded on this new model, and many established institutions, such as Harvard, Princeton, and Yale, adopted it. The large, multipurpose university became commonplace throughout the country by century's end. Building in part upon federal support contained in the Morrill Acts of 1862 and 1890, state universities increased in size, number, and scope during the Gilded Age. Cornell was the archetype of this new state institution.

By 1900, four of the eight American universities with enrollments over twenty-five hundred were state universities. Graduate and professional programs expanded at both private and state universities as formal education and state licensing examinations replaced the antebellum practice of some education coupled with on-the-job training for most professions. Law, medical, and engineering programs increased in both number and rigor throughout the Gilded Age. Finally, women made great strides in higher education following the Civil War as their educational opportunities increased. Many of the new state universities admitted female students, while other institutions, such as Columbia, Harvard, and the University of Pennsylvania, established parallel or related colleges for female undergraduates. Women's colleges increased from a mere handful in 1860 to over one hundred in 1901. Elite women's institutions multiplied rapidly: Vassar opened in the 1860s, Smith and Wellesley in the 1870s, and Bryn Mawr in the 1880s. Despite such changes, higher education remained restricted largely to white, middle class and above, Protestants during the Gilded Age. African Americans faced the most limitations, including separate, inferior facilities in many states.

Further Reading: Burton J. Bledstein, *The Culture of Professionalism: The Middle Class and the Development of Higher Education in America*, 1976; Barbara Miller Solomon, *In the Company of Educated Women: A History of Women and Higher Education in America*, 1985; most colleges and universities of the period maintain archives.

John H. Hepp IV

COLMAN, NORMAN JAY

(16 May 1827–2 November 1911), agriculturalist. Colman was born near Richfield Springs, New York, where he attended public school, and was graduated from Louisville Law University. He practiced law in Indiana and in St. Louis,

Missouri, though his interests lay in politics and agriculture.

In 1865 Colman was elected to the Missouri legislature as a Democrat and started an agricultural newspaper *Coleman's Rural World*. In addition he founded the Missouri Horticultural Society and was president of the Missouri Livestock Breeders Association, the state fair, and the Board of Agriculture. As a trustee of the University of Missouri for fifteen years, Colman reaffirmed its primary purpose of agricultural education and experimentation. He helped establish Farmers' Institutes in Missouri and often spoke at them.

In 1885, President Grover Cleveland appointed Colman commissioner of agriculture. Colman joined the National Grange, the land-grant colleges, and the experiment stations in convincing Congress to pass the Hatch Act, which would fund the stations (1887). In addition he led the campaign to elevate the Department of Agriculture to cabinet status, which Congress did in 1889, making Colman the only man to have been both commissioner and secretary of agriculture. That year Colman returned to his livestock farm near St. Louis, Missouri, where he died.

Further Reading: Alfred C. True, *A History of Agricultural Experimentation and Research in the United States, 1607–1925*, 1937.

Christopher Cumo

COLQUITT, ALFRED HOLT (20 April 1824–26 March 1894), governor and senator. Born in Monroe, Georgia, Colquitt graduated from Princeton University in 1844, gained admittance to the bar in 1846, and served in the Mexican War and the Confederate Army. He held a seat in the U.S. House of Representatives from 1853 to 1855, belonged to the Democratic Party, and owned one of the largest plantations in Georgia during the post-Civil War era. Easily elected governor of Georgia in 1876, Colquitt advocated sectional reconciliation, tax reduction, industrialization, and limited government. A Bourbon Democrat, he won a second term in 1880. Elected to the U.S. Senate in 1883, Colquitt retained his seat until his death in Washington, D.C. Colquitt's senatorial tenure was marked by his vehement opposition to protective tariffs.

Further Reading: Lewis Wynne, "The Bourbon Triumvirate (Alfred H. Colquitt, John B. Gordon, Joseph E. Brown): A Reconsideration," *Atlanta Historical Journal* 24 (1980): 39–56.

Leonard Schlup

COMIC STRIPS. The American comic strip originated at the close of the nineteenth century. It drew on traditions of European caricature, satirical art, graphic stories, the illustrated book, and cartoon comic periodicals published at home and abroad. Richard Felton Outcault initiated its development by contributing large panels set in "Hogan's Alley" to Joseph Pulitzer's *New York World* newspaper in 1895. By 1896 he had developed it into a sequential narrative with word-filled balloons featuring an urchin known as the Yellow Kid.

In 1897, German-born Rudolph Dirks created "The Katzenjammer Kids" for Hearst's *New York Journal*. Appearing regularly, it contained mature comic strip features: panels with continuing characters and balloon dialogue, and a narrative depending on a blend of words and pictures for its humor. The strip, which for over a hundred years, was soon joined by Frederick Burr Opper's "Happy Hooligan," Outcault's "Buster Brown," Winsor McCay's "Little Nemo in Slumberland," Henry Conroy "Bud" Fisher's "Mutt and Jeff," and George Herriman's "Krazy Kat" early in the new century, with hundreds more to follow. So popular did this new entertainment form prove that the survival of a newspaper would often depend on the comic strips it carried. The early examples provide Gilded Age historians with rich cultural and social material.

Further Reading: Bill Blackbeard, *R. F. Outcault's The Yellow Kid*, 1995; David Kunzle, *The History of the Comic Strip: The Nineteenth Century*, 1990; M. Thomas Inge, *Comics as Culture*, 1990.

M. Thomas Inge

COMISKEY, CHARLES ALBERT (15 August 1859–26 October 1931), professional baseball player and team owner. Born in Chicago, Illinois, Comiskey attended St. Mary's College in Kansas, where he played baseball. In 1879, he signed a professional contract with the Dubuque Rabbits of the Northwestern League. After the league collapsed, Comiskey became player-manager of the St. Louis Browns of the American Association. He guided them to four consecutive league titles from 1885 to 1888. In 1890, Comiskey bolted to play for the Chicago "brotherhood" team in the short-lived Players League. He returned briefly to the Browns until the American Association folded in 1891. From 1892 to 1895, Comiskey was player-manager of the Cincinnati Reds in the National League. Then he joined sportswriter Ban Johnson in forming the Western League. Comiskey purchased the Sioux City, Iowa, franchise, then moved it to St. Paul, Minnesota. The Western League became the American League in 1899, and Comiskey transferred his team from St. Paul to Chicago, where it became known as the White Stockings. Having spent lavishly to recruit established stars, Comiskey's White Stockings defeated the Chicago Cubs in the 1906 World Series. In 1910, Comiskey built the concrete and steel Comiskey Park on Chicago's South Side. He died in Eagle River, Wisconsin, leaving the team to his son.

Further Reading: Gustav Axelson, *Commy: The Life Story of Charles A. Comiskey*, 1919; Richard C. Lindberg, *Stealing First: The White Sox from Comiskey to Reinsdorf*, 1994; *New York Times*, 26 October 1931.

Ron Briley

COMPROMISE OF 1877. After the Republican-dominated Electoral Commission of 1877 declared Florida's and Louisiana's disputed votes for Rutherford B. Hayes in an 8–7 party-line vote, Democrats knew the commissioners would vote identically on the two remaining states in question, South Carolina and Oregon. Convinced that the Republicans were "stealing" the election, congressional Democrats threatened to prevent Hayes's inauguration by filibustering so that the election returns could not be officially counted. The resultant presidential interregnum could prove disastrous, especially since rumors of outright revolution already ran rampant in Washington. Word circulated that General William T. Sherman already had three thousand troops prepared to quell any violence in the nation's capital.

Against this potentially disastous backdrop,

worried politicos on both sides, in a series of late February meetings at Washington D.C.'s Wormley House Hotel, frantically sought compromise. With Hayes's sanction, some supporters, notably fellow Ohioans James A. Garfield, John Sherman, and Stanley Matthews, met with moderate southern leaders, including Kentucky's John Young Brown and Georgia's John B. Gordon. The bargainers were bold and explicit; Hayes's men asked what concessions they would have to make to ensure his inauguration. The reply was equally frank: withdrawal of federal troops from the final two "reconstructed" states, Louisiana and South Carolina (thereby dispatching their moribund Republican governments); appointment of a southerner to Hayes's cabinet; and internal improvements for the war-torn South. In return, Democrats were to acquiesce in Hayes's tainted election and support a Republican sympathetic to the South for Speaker of the House. Hayes accepted the conditions. Indeed, he was already committed to a conciliatory southern policy.

Critics do not believe that the Compromise of 1877 was much of a compromise at all because some of its provisions were never implemented. Whatever the true particulars of the Wormley House bargain, Hayes gained the presidency, removed the troops, and appointed David M. Key of Tennessee postmaster general. He cooled, however, on federal subsidies for internal improvements in the South after the majority party Democrats refused to support James A. Garfield for the House speakership in October 1877.

Further Reading: C. Vann Woodward, *Reunion and Reaction: The Compromise of 1877 and the End of Reconstruction*, 1951; Allan Peskin, "Was There a Compromise of 1877?" *Journal of American History* 60 (1973): 63–75.

Frank P. Vazzano

COMSTOCK ACT OF 1873. Congress passed the Comstock Act to combat obscene literature and sex devices. Named for Anthony Comstock, a zealous crusader against vice and obscenity, the measure criminalized publication, distribution, and possession of information about, or devices or medications for, unlawful abortion or contraception. Convicted violators could receive up to five years' imprisonment with hard labor and a fine reaching $2000. The Comstock Act also prohibited distribution of pornographic materials through the U.S. mail and importation of forbidden items from abroad. Founder of the New York Society for the Suppression of Vice, Comstock secured an appointment as special agent of the U.S. Post Office Department, with broad responsibilities for prosecuting violators of the 1873 law. He held this position for the remainder of his life, boasting of the number of "libertines" he had driven to suicide.

Scores were convicted for mailing pamphlets on birth control. Censors condemned scientific books; pharmacists faced arrest for revealing details about contraception; and hundreds of people endured imprisonment. Insisting for religious reasons that abstinence and the rhythm method were the only moral means of birth control, Comstock bragged that he had convicted enough people to fill a train of sixty-one passenger cars. In the first six months of policing the postal service, Comstock seized 194,000 obscene pictures and photos, 134,000 pounds of obscene books, 14,200 stereopticon slides, 60,300 rubber items, 5,500 sets of obscene playing cards, and 31,500 boxes of aphrodisiacs.

In 1890 Comstock apprehended Julius Schmidt, a German immigrant, for selling contraceptives. After Schmidt paid the fine, he entered the rubber trade, selling Sheik and Ramses brand condoms. Comstock's activities undoubtedly made contraception known to some Americans who had never heard of it. Its banning persuaded some fiercely independent individuals to adopt the practice. Indeed, birth control quickly blossomed into a gigantic bootleg industry, being as popular among Victorian Americans as liquor was during prohibition in the 1920s, and offering more products and options for both men and women than existed a century later. Although some items were ineffective or dangerous, others proved highly successful. With husbands and wives each using one or more methods of contraception, the birthrate in the United States fell by more than half between 1880 and 1940. Comstockery began crumbling in the twentieth century, but ves-

tiges of the Gilded Age law persisted into the 1990s.

Further Reading: Nicola Beisel, *Imperiled Innocents: Anthony Comstock and Family Reproduction in Victorian America*, c. 1997; DeRobine M. Bennett, *Anthony Comstock: His Career of Cruelty and Crime*, 1971; Andrea Tone, *Devices and Desires: A History of Contraceptives in America*, 2002.

Leonard Schlup

COMSTOCK, ANTHONY (7 March 1844–21 September 1915), vice crusader. Born in New Canaan, Connecticut, Comstock was reared in rural New England, where the Congregational Church impressed on him the need for strict community supervision of private morals. During the Civil War, he joined the Union Army and was sent to Florida. There, as a Christian Commission member, he spent more time battling vice than rebels, though his comrades seldom appreciated his calls for temperance and moral purity. After the war, Comstock entered the dry goods business in New York City, where he became deeply concerned for the moral well-being of his fellow clerks. In 1868, after New York State passed a law banning the sale of pornography, Comstock began his career as a vice crusader by persuading police to arrest two booksellers. In 1872, he joined the Young Men's Christian Association. The following year wealthy patrons provided Comstock with a professional salary, to allow him to crusade on a full-time basis. Shortly thereafter, he successfully lobbied Congress to pass a sweeping federal law banning pornography, abortion, and the discussion, manufacture, sale, and distribution of birth control devices. The statute became known as the Comstock Law; by 1885 twenty-four states had adopted similar legislation. The federal government soon granted Comstock broad powers of arrest when he was appointed postal inspector, although he did not accept a salary until 1906.

For the rest of his life Comstock relentlessly battled vice, as he defined it. He and his fellow crusaders of the New York Society for the Suppression of Vice, an organization he formed to fight vice, arrested dealers in pornography and those selling birth control items. They raided pool halls, racetracks, and lotteries, and on occasion shut down art galleries. Comstock devoted relatively little energy to combating prostitution and alcohol consumption. His raids could be dangerous, and he sustained numerous serious injuries. His methods were controversial: he singled out immigrants and used entrapment. Never one to shy away from the spotlight, Comstock used public criminal trials to gain publicity for his cause. Toward the end of his career, he claimed to have gained the convictions of over thirty-six hundred people and destroyed in excess of 160 tons of illicit material. He died in Summit, New Jersey, his name synonymous with vice control and Victorian morality.

Further Reading: Nicola Beisel, *Imperiled Innocents: Anthony Comstock and Family Reproduction in Victorian America*, c. 1997; Helen Lefkowitz Horowitz, "Victoria Woodhull, Anthony Comstock, and Conflict over Sex in the United States in the 1870s," *Journal of American History* 87 (2000): 403–434; Robert Christian Johnson, "Anthony Comstock: Reform, Vice, and the American Way," Ph.D. diss., University of Wisconsin, 1973.

Gregory Dehler

COMSTOCK LODE. A vein of precious metals running for two and one-half miles along Mount Davidson, Nevada, the Comstock Lode was discovered in January 1859. It was the first major silver/gold quartz ledge developed in the United States. A challenge that spurred development of new mining and reduction techniques, the Comstock became a training ground for mining engineers and a proving ground for techniques and equipment. It also cradled miners' unionism. The first boom lasted from 1860 to 1864, providing wealth that helped the North win the Civil War and bringing Nevada statehood. It also gave birth to Virginia City, the most famous mining town of the Gilded Age. Americans had never seen such flamboyance. Virginia City became an important political, financial, and social hub for the entire region. Comstock wealth made San Francisco a major city, and encouraged prospectors to scurry all over Nevada looking for similar strikes. Six years of decline followed but exploration continued, finally yielding additional discoveries that produced the Comstock's greatest boom, the "Big Bonanza," from 1870 to 1878. Thereafter production declined, and miners and others drifted away, but the Comstock's $300

million production over twenty years left it a "yardstick" to be measured against.

Further Reading: Ronald M. James and C. Elizabeth Raymond, *Comstock Women*, 1998, Dan DeQuille, *History of the Big Bonanza*, 1876; Grant Smith, *History of the Comstock Lode*, 1943.

Duane A. Smith

CONGRESS. The response of Congress throughout much of the Gilded Age was to ensure a maximum of laissez-faire and a minimum of interference in the country's business life. Pork barrel politics ran rampant; lobbyists stretched the boundaries of propriety; and government ethics reached a low ebb as news of the Whiskey Ring, the Crédit Mobilier, and other scandals shocked the nation. Much of legislators' time went to gratifying individual and business constituents, such as veterans wanting help obtaining pensions, and distillers and merchants seeking tax relief or special Treasury consideration; general legislation was crushed beneath a mountain of parochial favors. Such tight control over patronage, as well as over the executive branch's pocketbook, kept Congress supreme.

But despite the folly, corruption, and backbiting personality clashes that marred its record and public image, Congress was exceedingly busy during the Gilded Age. Though currency issues stood in the forefront of congressional discussions, there remained much unfinished business dealing with Reconstruction. At the end of the Fortieth Congress, the Fifteenth Amendment to the Constitution was passed, granting voting rights to all males, regardless of color. In 1870, Congress created the Department of Justice, and in 1871, established the Civil Service Commission. The next year Yellowstone National Park was designated as the first national park; thus vast territories with timber, mineral, and water resources were set aside for the common good rather than private commercial advantage. Also enacted in 1872 was the General Mining Act.

The Gilded Age witnessed development of the modern Congress: an institution increasingly directed by the seniority system and strong committee chairs. Congress itself changed most by changing less, that is, by lengthening its members' tenure. The average number of first-term members in the Forty-sixth to Fifty-sixth Congresses was 42.6 percent; in the Fifty-seventh to Seventy-second Congresses, 22.9 percent. Such security for office-holders gave a distinctive character to Congress: lifelong careers with experience and clubbiness counted more than ever before.

In the House the transformation in procedure required a speaker with enough power to direct the chamber's business efficiently. Until the Civil War most speakers held office briefly and with little effect; they were essentially parliamentarians. The election of Republican Thomas B. Reed of Maine in 1889 changed the office and ushered in the landmark era of "Reed Rules" (1890). Reed cracked down on dilatory motions and abuses of parliamentary procedure meant to stall business. Gradually his Rules Committee converted the speaker's actions into official regulations. As speaker, Reed obtained the power to count quorums and limit the ability of the Democratic minority to block legislation.

The Senate underwent a similar evolution. In the 1880s Woodrow Wilson analogized the body to a small, select, and leisurely House of Representatives. By 1901, however, the upper body had forceful leadership and more clearly defined party structures, as the Republican Steering Committee controlled the all-important committee assignments and took over the scheduling of legislative business.

Further Reading: Margaret Susan Thompson, *The "Spider Web": Congress and Lobbying in the Age of Grant*, 1985; Alvin M. Josephy, Jr., *The American Heritage History of the Congress of the United States*, 1975.

Colton C. Campbell

CONGRESSIONAL POPULISM. From 1891 to 1903, beginning with the Fifty-second and ending with the Fifty-seventh Congress, one of the nation's more influential and colorful third-party movements claimed seats in the national legislature. Officially designated the People's Party of America, the phenomenon soon came to be identified by friends and foes alike as the Populist Party, with adherents known as Populists and proponents of Populism.

Although the movement was decidedly re-gional and agrarian, with its principal following in western and southern states, its program was national in scope and fundamentally economic in nature. The Populists' objective, as they saw it, was to restore to the people rights and powers usurped by corporations and privileged individuals during the nation's post–Civil War industrial transformation. To accomplish that end, the party's congressmen boldly and unequivocally championed a role for the national government that was, for all practical purposes, nearly four decades ahead of its time. They were especially prescient in addressing issues growing out of the great depression that commenced with the Panic of 1893. They displayed similar vision in contemplating the many potential and serious consequences they believed would flow inevitably from the nation's venture into imperialism in 1898.

In the Senate, Populism's most outstanding leaders included William V. Allen of Nebraska, William Peffer of Kansas, James Kyle of South Dakota, North Carolina's Marion Butler, and George Turner from Washington State. In the House, the list of notables included Kansans Jeremiah Simpson and William Baker, Georgia's Thomas E. Watson, Colorado's John Bell, and Omer Kem and William Neville from Nebraska.

Clearly these leaders, and colleagues of lesser personal renown but equal sincerity, made a valiant though still underappreciated attempt to reinvigorate the nation's commitment to universal human rights at a time when events and popular trends strongly dictated otherwise. In the end, the party played a significant educational role at a crucial turning point in the nation's history—a role that was nowhere more vital than on the floors of Congress. As a result of the Populist revolt, and William Jennings Bryan's subsequent emergence as the leading figure within the Democratic Party, the level of American political discourse was altered so as to enable the nation to move toward long-overdue adjustments dictated by the new society that had emerged from the industrial revolution.

Further Reading: Lawrence Goodwyn, *Democratic Promise*, 1976; Gene Clanton, *Populism: The Humane Prefer-*

ence in America, 1890–1900 (1991), and *Congressional Populism and the Crisis of the 1890s,* 1998.

Gene Clanton

CONKLING, ROSCOE (30 October 1829–18 April 1888), senator. Born in Albany, New York, Conkling attended Auburn Academy before joining the Utica bar in 1850. Whig district attorney of Oneida County and later mayor of Utica, he served as a Republican in the U.S. House of Representatives during the early 1860s. Elected to the Senate in 1867, he gained the reputation of being a staunch Radical, an archpartisan, and the leader of a powerful state machine. He was so concerned with wielding political power that in 1873 he declined the post of chief justice of the Supreme Court. In 1876 he aspired to the presidency, but personal arrogance and dubious political ties made the candidacy short-lived. A year later he helped design the Electoral Commission Act of 1877, which resolved the Hayes-Tilden election controversy. By 1880, he headed his party's Stalwart wing, a faction noted for its hostility toward the South, allegiance to Ulysses S. Grant, and powerful figures such as Pennsylvania's James Donald Cameron and Illinois's John A. Logan. Bitterly disappointed by Garfield's presidential nomination, Conkling nonetheless campaigned, hoping to obtain choice patronage slots for Stalwarts. When Garfield appointed a prominent member of the rival Half-Breed faction as collector of the port of New York, Conkling resigned his Senate seat in protest. After the New York State legislature refused to send him back to the Senate, he spent the rest of his life engaged in a lucrative legal practice in New York City. He died there.

Further Reading: Donald Burr Chidsey, *The Gentleman from New York: A Life of Roscoe Conkling,* 1935; David M. Jordan, *Roscoe Conkling of New York: Voice in the Senate,* 1971; Sara Lee Burlingame, "The Making of a Spoilsman: The Life and Career of Roscoe Conkling from 1827 to 1873," Ph.D. diss., Johns Hopkins University, 1974.

Justus D. Doenecke

CONSERVATION OF NATURAL RESOURCES. The initial attempts to conserve the United States' natural resources occurred between 1868 and 1901. Previously the public had assumed the nation possessed an unlimited supply of timber, water, and wildlife. During the post-Civil War economic boom, some noticed with alarm the destruction of forests around the Great Lakes for railroads, fuel, and housing. By 1877, Interior Secretary Carl Schurz predicted only a twenty-year supply of timber at the current rate of depletion. Between 1870 and 1883 overhunting reduced the Plains buffalo from over six million to a few hundred. The passenger pigeon population declined from hundreds of millions to extinction by 1914.

In response, private and governmental organizations began promoting conservation and the idea of limited resources. In 1872 Congress created Yellowstone as the first national park, preserving some of America's most beautiful scenery and providing a no-hunting zone for endangered species. In 1879 the Agriculture Department created a Forestry Division. The American Forestry Association (1875) promoted Arbor Day and forest reserves. The Boone and Crockett Club (1887) sought to protect species endangered by commercial hunting. The Audubon Society (1886) opposed the common practice of using bird plumage for women's hats and tried to protect habitats. The Sierra Club was formed (1892) to protect Yosemite from developers and timber companies.

While some conservationists wanted a pristine wilderness, others sought renewable resources. During the 1890s the National Irrigation Association sought to develop arid lands. In 1898 Gifford Pinchot transformed the Forestry Division policy from saving trees to harvesting them efficiently. In 1901 the National Rivers and Harbors Congress pushed to develop commercial waterways. Most important conservation legislation came in the twentieth century, but impetus for it originated in the Gilded Age. The cause needed a strong leader, such as Theodore Roosevelt, to turn it into national issue.

Further Reading: Samuel P. Hays, *Conservation and the Gospel of Efficiency: The Progressive Conservation Movement, 1890–1920,* 1959; John F. Reiger, *Sportsmen and the Origins of Conservation,* 1975; Alfred Runte, *National Parks: The American Experience,* 1979.

Brad F. Raley

COOPER, ANNA JULIA HAYWOOD (10 August 1858–27 February 1964), educator. Born in Raleigh, North Carolina, the daughter of a slave, Haywood in 1877 married George A. C. Cooper, a teacher of Greek at St. Augustine's Normal School and Collegiate Institute in Raleigh. She earned an undergraduate degree from Oberlin College in 1884 and a master's degree there in 1887. She was principal of the M Street High School in Washington, D.C., from 1902 to 1906, and in 1929 became president of Frelinghuysen University there. She was an advocate of human rights, a lecturer, a feminist, and an author. During the 1890s, a significant period in the fostering of African-American political and intellectual thought, Cooper started groups and clubs devoted to learning and culture for African-American women, and demanded respect for the views of people of her race. Cooper was the only woman elected to membership in the American Negro Academy, an organization founded in 1897 by Alexander Crummell. At the Pan-American Conference in London in 1900, Cooper presented an address titled "The Negro Problem in America." She received a Ph.D. from the Sorbonne at the age of sixty-six, becoming the fourth African-American woman to earn a doctorate. Cooper died at her Washington, D.C., home.

Further Reading: Anna Julia Haywood Cooper, *A Voice from the South by a Black Woman of the South*, 1892; Leona C. Gabel, *From Slavery to the Sorbonne and Beyond: The Life and Writings of Anna J. Cooper*, 1982.

Leonard Schlup

COOPER, PETER (12 February 1791–4 April 1883), inventor, entrepreneur, and philanthropist. Cooper, born in New York City, was self-educated and apprenticed to a coachmaker. He amassed a fortune through ownership of several businesses and numerous patents. Successful operation of the nation's premier glue factory from 1821, iron works from 1829, and presidency of the New York, Newfoundland and London Telegraph Company from 1854 to 1872 made Cooper a widely heralded industrial innovator. For his many achievements in iron and steel production and fabrication, including the first successful steam locomotive in the United States (1830), Cooper was awarded the Bessemer Gold Medal of the Iron and Steel Institute of Great Britain in 1879. Further investments in real estate provided the wealth Cooper needed to establish Cooper Union in 1859, the nation's first comprehensive urban adult education center. As president of the Citizens Association of New York City from 1865 to 1871, he led the struggle against William Tweed's control of Tammany Hall. Throughout his adult life, Cooper championed reforms in sanitation and public health, housing, and education. For his support of the movement to make Civil War bonds issued as greenbacks permanent legal tender, Cooper was nominated for president by the Greenback Party in 1876. He died in New York City.

Further Reading: Edward C. Mack, *Peter Cooper: Citizen of New York*, 1949; Allan Nevins, *Abram S. Hewitt with Some Account of Peter Cooper*, 1935.

Kim P. Sebaly

COORS, ADOLPH (1847–5 June 1929), brewer. Born in the Prussian town of Barmen, Coors began his career at age fourteen as an apprentice in the business office of the Wenker Brewery in Dortmund. Orphaned the following year, he remained at the brewery until age twenty-one, when he immigrated to Baltimore, Maryland, as a stowaway. He drifted to Naperville, Illinois, in 1869, and worked in a brewery there for four years. Coors moved to Denver, Colorado, in 1872 and purchased an interest in a bottling company. A year later, he and a partner founded Schueler and Coors to brew their own beer. By 1880 he was able to purchase Schueler's share, and began operating the Adolph Coors Company. A wealthy man with varied financial interests by the time statewide prohibition took effect 1916, Coors did not live to see repeal. Instead he jumped to his death from the sixth floor of a hotel in Virginia Beach, Virginia.

Further Reading: Dan Baum, *Citizen Coors: An American Dynasty*, 2000.

James D. Ivy

COPPIN, FRANCES MARION JACKSON (1837–21 January 1913), educator and civic leader. Born a slave in Washington, D.C., Jackson won emancipation at age twelve when an aunt, Sarah Orr Clark, purchased her niece's freedom for $125. Jackson moved to Massachusetts and Rhode Island, where she worked as a domestic servant to pay for private tutorial lessons. In 1865 she earned a degree from Oberlin College in Ohio, where she was her class poet. She also taught music. In 1869 she became the first African-American woman to head an institution of higher education when she became principal of the Institute for Colored Youth (later Cheyney University) near Philadelphia, Pennsylvania. There she made many improvements, including the abolition of corporal punishment, teaching of personal integrity and respect for others, and the opening in 1889 of an industrial department to train black men and women in technical skills and trades. In 1878 she started writing columns for the *Christian Recorder*, a newspaper of the African Methodist Episcopal Church, of which she was a member. She married Levi Jenkins Coppin, a minister, in 1881. Fanny Coppin, as she was known, was active in the crusade for woman suffrage and other reforms, and was elected vice president of the National Association of Colored Women in 1897. She retired from university administration in 1902, traveled widely, and served as a missionary to South Africa. Coppin died in Philadelphia. Coppin State College in Baltimore, Maryland, was named in her honor.

Further Reading: Frances Jackson Coppin, *Reminiscences of School Life, and Hints on Teaching*, 1913; *Philadelphia Tribune*, 1 February 1913; Linda M. Perkins, *Fanny Jackson Coppin and the Institute for Colored Youth, 1865–1902*, 1987.

Leonard Schlup

CORBETT, JAMES JOHN (1 September 1866–18 February 1933), professional boxer. Nicknamed "Gentleman Jim" for his tidy appearance, Corbett was born in San Francisco. Attracted to boxing primarily to supplement his relatively low pay as a bank clerk, he began his professional career in 1889. In the years before he gained fame, the Olympic Club in San Francisco employed him to teach the art of pugilism. Corbett brought a sense of respectability to the ring because of his appearance and, for

a boxer, extensive education. In 1892 he won several impressive professional victories, earning a title bout with the current heavyweight champion, John L. Sullivan, in New Orleans. The younger, quicker Corbett utilized a punishing jab, which he had devised, to win one of the most important fights in boxing history. The bout was the first heavyweight championship fight to feature the Queensbury Rules, requiring the use of gloves. Corbett lost his title to Robert Fitzsimmons in 1897 and spent his later years as an actor and entertainer. He died a fairly wealthy man in Bayside, New York.

Further Reading: Henry Cooper, *The Great Heavyweights*, 1978; Elliott J. Gorn, *The Manly Art: Bare-Knuckle Prize Fighting in America*, 1986.

Steve Bullock

CORLISS, GEORGE HENRY (2 June 1817–21 February 1888), manufacturer and inventor. Born in Easton, New York, Corliss studied at Castleton Academy, opened a store in Greenwich, Connecticut, and later moved to Providence, Rhode Island, to work for Fairbanks, Bancroft, and Company. Ultimately he received patents for his improvements in steam engines and organized a company in Providence, Corliss, Nightingale, and Company, which constructed the first steam engine incorporating his improvements. As president of Corliss Engine Company, he directed business activities and worked on design improvements. A Republican presidential elector in 1876, he had served in Rhode Island's General Assembly from 1868 to 1870. He died in Providence.

Further Reading: Robert H. Thurston, *History of the Growth of the Steam Engine*, 1902.

Leonard Schlup

COTTON STATES AND INTERNATIONAL EXPOSITION OF 1895. Opened on 18 September 1895, the Atlanta Exposition was one in a long series of regional fairs designed to showcase post-Reconstruction southern progress to the outside world. Strongly backed by former Radical Republican Governor Rufus Bullock, it operated on a $200,000 appropriation allocated by Congress with the enthusiastic support of Speaker of the House Charles F. Crisp, a Georgia Democrat. Lasting fifty-four days, the exposition attracted 1.2 million visitors. Its success, however, was hampered by Atlanta's population of only one hundred thousand, 40 percent of which was black. Additionally, the nation at the time was in a depression brought on by the Panic of 1893. To make matters worse, critics complained that the fair was at best a pale imitation of Chicago's World's Columbian Exposition of 1893.

Attempting to fulfill African-American Congressman George Washington Murray's hope that it would show America to be truly cosmopolitan rather than merely a "white man's country," the exposition included a "Negro Building" that reportedly demonstrated black progress. The exposition gained a lasting place in history as the site of Booker T. Washington's controversial "Atlanta Compromise" address. Having helped procure the congressional appropriation of funds, Washington, as president of the Tuskegee Normal and Industrial Institute, was given the rare and unusual honor (as an African American) of addressing the mixed-race audience during the exposition's opening ceremonies. Taking full advantage of his opportunity, he delivered a speech that expressed both his philosophy of life and his vision for black America on the eve of the twentieth century. Known as the "Tuskegee Idea," Washington's address urged black accommodation in response to white racial restrictions. Advocating economic endeavors over efforts at political equality, the address has been both denounced as an act of "race treason" and praised as an act of pragmatic realism. Whichever the case, the "Atlanta Compromise" helped mark the standard of American race relations for the next twenty years.

Further Reading: Louis Harlan, *Booker T. Washington: The Making of a Black Leader, 1856–1901*, 1972; Tunde Adelike, ed., *Booker T. Washington: Interpretative Essays*, 1998.

Harvey Gresham Hudspeth

COUNTERCULTURE. Although gentility, sentimentality, and Christian domesticity marked Gilded Age culture, a widespread aesthetic art movement challenged the era's norms. Oscar Wilde, the "Apostle of Aestheticism,"

symbolized this countercultural strain during his 1882 American tour. He argued that art and beauty, not moralism or prescribed conventions, should define culture. Thus Americans found in aestheticism, this mingling of art and everyday life, a bohemian excursion from Victorian models and constraints. The view of the human interior as a theatrical exotic site, use of opiates among genteel women, and androgynous gender role experimentation characterized popular aestheticism in the 1870s and 1880s. Women used it to gain professional stature, cultural agency, and independence through such endeavors as textile design, china painting, and pottery making. Aestheticism offered, as well, a means for women to experiment with the occult, the fantastic, and the borderline. For instance, artistic dress, an uncorseted Pre-Ralphaelite model advanced by Wilde, appalled Victorian moralists, who jailed women wearing these gowns. For men, aestheticism offered new choices—as a decorator/artist or even as an "invert" or homosexual. The two decades of aesthetic experimentation ended with the return of "virility" in the 1890s and with America's plunge into imperialist ventures.

Further Reading: Roger B. Stein, *John Ruskin and Aesthetic Thought in America*, 1967; Doreen Bolger Burke, ed., *In Pursuit of Beauty*, 1986; Douglass Shand-Tucci, *Boston Bohemia*, 1995.

Mary Warner Blanchard

COUSINS, ROBERT GORDON (31 January 1859–20 June 1933), congressman. Born in Tipton, Iowa, Cousins attended local public schools and was graduated in 1881 from Cornell College in Mount Vernon. The next year he passed the bar and established a practice in his hometown; in 1885 he was elected to the state legislature. A prosecutor from 1888 to 1890, Cousins, a Republican, was elected to the first of eight congressional terms in 1892. He rose to chair the House Foreign Affairs Committee. He supported the American invasion of Cuba and annexation of Hawaii and Wake Island in 1898, the establishment of an American-appointed government in Puerto Rico in 1900, and the naming of William Howard Taft as governor of the Philippines in 1901. After

Cousins retired from Congress, he became a popular lecturer. He died in Iowa City.

Further Reading: Jacob A. Swisher, *Robert Gordon Cousins*, 1938.

Christopher Cumo

COWBOYS. Though ennobled in American culture by easterners such as Theodore Roosevelt, Frederic Remington, and Owen Wister, the cowboy was in fact a hired hand (an unskilled laborer in the context of the times) employed by cattlemen for the purpose maintaining and transporting livestock. Most cowboys worked the ranges of the trans-Mississippi West between 1865 and 1890, although actual figures are unavailable owing to the nature of the ranching business. Cattle were counted because they were worth money, but cowboys were not because they were often easily replaced transients. The work—hard, dirty, and characterized by long hours and low pay—was, for most, temporary employment. Generally held in low esteem by their employers and reviled by western newspaper editors, cowboys nevertheless enjoyed a temporal and spatial context suggesting dramatic potential to showmen, writers, and artists. William F. Cody presented William Levi "Buck" Taylor to Buffalo Bill's Wild West Show audiences in 1884 as "King of the Cowboys," and in 1888 Theodore Roosevelt published *Ranch Life and the Hunting-Trail*, lionizing characters he had known in North Dakota. Publication of Owen Wister's novel *The Virginian* (1902) established the "cowboy without cows" as the normative figure in twentieth-century popular entertainment, emphasizing heroic potential over the reality of manual labor.

Further Reading: William W. Savage, Jr., *The Cowboy Hero*, 1979, and *Cowboy Life*, 1975; Richard W. Slatta, *Cowboys of the Americas*, 1990.

William W. Savage, Jr.

COXEY, JACOB SECHLER (16 April 1854–18 May 1951), businessman and politician. Born near Harrisburg, Pennsylvania, Coxey received eight years of schooling before joining his father in a local iron mill. After working his way up to stationary engineer, Coxey quit to join an uncle in a successful scrap metal venture. In 1881 Coxey moved to Massillon, Ohio, and bought a quarry that became the centerpiece of a profitable silica business. As he prospered, he turned increasingly to politics, and ran for the Ohio senate as a Greenbacker in 1885. In 1891 he joined the newly formed People's Party and proposed that the U.S. Congress fund a national road-building program by issuing greenbacks to states and municipalities. The plan would put the unemployed to work building internal improvements, and stimulate economic development by increasing the currency supply.

When the Panic of 1893 threw 3 million Americans out of work, Coxey became even more convinced of the need for his plan in the face of Congress's perceived indifference. To publicize the program and the plight of the unemployed, Coxey, with fellow Greenbacker Carl Browne, called for a mass meeting in Massillon and a march to the nation's capital. Terming the project a "petition in boots" and the "army" the "Commonweal of Christ," Coxey began his march in March 1894 with a little more than a hundred marchers and a dozen journalists. As they moved across Pennsylvania and Maryland, hundreds more joined. That spring a dozen other "armies" began similar treks to the nation's capital from various quarters. The idea of thousands of unemployed men descending on Washington frightened many leaders. When Coxey arrived at the Capitol, he was met by a crowd of twenty thousand and was promptly arrested for displaying a banner. A local judge jailed him for twenty days.

Upon release, Coxey returned to Massillon to run for Congress as a Populist in the fall of 1894. Receiving about 25 percent of the vote, he assumed state leadership of the party and was considered one of the favorites for the 1896 presidential nomination. In 1895 he ran for governor of Ohio, but received just 6 percent of the vote. Although Coxey reluctantly campaigned for William Jennings Bryan in 1896, he opposed fusion. When he ran for governor again as a Populist in 1897, he garnered a mere 2 percent of the vote. Coxey sank from the political scene after 1897 but resurfaced during the 1930s, when he was elected mayor of Massillon and sought the presidency on the Farmer-Labor ticket.

Further Reading: Carlos Schwantes, *Coxey's Army: An American Odyssey*, 1985; Jacob Coxey Papers, Ohio Historical Society, Columbus.

Michael Pierce

CRANDALL, FRANCIS ASBURY (28 November 1837–9 July 1915), editor and librarian. Born in Carbondale, Pennsylvania, Crandall was editor and publisher of newspapers in Iowa, New York, Pennsylvania, Rhode Island, and Missouri during the 1860s, 1870s, and 1880s. He was managing editor of the *Buffalo Evening Times* in 1895 when he became the first U.S. superintendent of documents. His position lasted until 1897. From 1897 to 1906, Crandall served as librarian of public documents with the Government Printing Office in Washington, D.C., where he died.

Further Reading: *New York Times*, 10 July 1915.

Leonard Schlup

CRANE, STEPHEN (1 November 1871–5 June 1900), author. Crane was born in Newark, New Jersey. His lifetime coincides almost exactly with the Gilded Age. Born after the Civil War and dead by the turn of the century, he is widely considered a particularly accurate mirror of his times. He published his first story in 1891, while a student at Syracuse University, and left college that same year to begin writing for newspapers. Unable to find a publisher, he financed his first novel, *Maggie, A Girl of the Streets* (1893). This portrayal of the brutality and misery of New York slum life shocked many readers, but it established Crane as a modern writer influenced by the naturalism of the age. In 1895 he toured the West and Mexico as a roving correspondent, and in that same year his *Red Badge of Courage* was accepted for publication. A best-seller, this short novel made Crane a literary celebrity. The book's pioneering use of color to describe overwhelming natural forces, and Crane's departure from the literal realism of *Maggie* to depict the constant impact of the external on the characters, make it difficult to overstate Crane's significance to literary naturalism. His short story "The Open Boat" (1898), which portrays the helplessness of shipwreck survivors as they are controlled by the forces of the sea in their effort to reach shore, is one of the best brief examples of naturalistic writing. Crane died in Badenweiler, Germany.

Further Reading: Linda Davis, *Badge of Courage: The Life of Stephen Crane*, 1998; Edwin Harrison Cady, *Stephen Crane*, 1980.

C. Edward Balog

CRAZY HORSE (TASUNKE WITKO) (ca. 1842/1844–5 September 1877), Oglala Sioux chief. In his youth, this future leader of the Sioux Confederacy, born near Bear Butte (now in South Dakota), was known as Curly and also as the "Strange One" because he liked solitude and showed little interest in the traditional dancing, singing, and wearing of feathers and paint. At age seventeen, his bravery in battle earned him his father's name, Crazy Horse.

Crazy Horse opposed the reservation policy of the U.S. government because of the hardships that it inflicted upon many Native Americans. He observed soldiers and other whites who scattered Indian villages, destroyed goods and lodges, and mined gold in the Black Hills. Consequently, he participated in the Fetterman Massacre, an attack near Fort Phil Kearny, in 1866, and the battle of the Rosebud (1876). He also led warriors in the battle of the Little Big Horn (1876), that annihilated General George A. Custer and his forces.

When told in 1877 that he could have a reservation in the Powder River country, Crazy Horse surrendered. He was fatally injured at Fort Robinson, Nebraska, as he resisted incarceration. His parents buried his bones near Wounded Knee Creek. A sculpture of Crazy Horse is being carved on a mountain in the Black Hills.

Further Reading: Mari Sandoz, *Crazy Horse: The Strange Man of the Oglalas*, 1942; Dee Brown, *Bury My Heart at Wounded Knee: An Indian History of the American West*, 1970; Robert A. Clark, ed., *The Killing of Chief Crazy Horse*, 1988.

Jane F. Lancaster

CRÉDIT MOBILIER. This was the first of several scandals plaguing the presidency of Ulysses S. Grant. On 4 September 1872, as he ran for reelection, the *New York Times* exposed massive fraud. Crédit Mobilier, a French-owned firm, had been hired to build the Union Pacific portion of the transcontinental railroad. Board members stole millions of federal subsidy dollars by creating fictitious subcontracting outfits, and inflating material and labor costs. To conceal their actions and impede potential investigations, they transferred company stock to congressmen. Legislators not linked to the company, however, created a select investigation committee, which implicated newly elected Vice President Schuyler Colfax, Massachusetts Representative Oakes Ames, Speaker of the House James G. Blaine of Maine, and thirteen other leading politicians. Although the committee exonerated them all, it revealed that of the $73 million given to Crédit Mobilier, only $50 million went into building the railroad. News that the remainder had gone into individual bank accounts led to widespread distrust of government. Grant, though tarnished, overcame the scandal through political maneuvers and the unpopularity of his election opponent, Horace Greely. The Union Pacific, however, heavily burdened with debt, found itself under the control of the popular regulatory reformer Charles Francis Adams by 1884.

Further Reading: Mark W. Summers, *The Era of Good Stealings*, 1993; William S. McFeely, *Grant: A Biography*, 1981.

Jerome D. Bowers II

CRIME. Although many believed crime rose as Gilded Age America rapidly urbanized and industrialized, statistics demonstrate the opposite. As in all the developed world, American murder rates fell by about one-third from the end of the Civil War to 1900. Arrests for other felonies and misdemeanors likewise declined. Industrial societies demand education, sobriety, and order, and enforce them through professional, urban police forces.

Four forms of crime characterized this period, each linked to, but not exclusively experienced in, particular geographic regions: lynching; frontier disorder; organized crime; and labor-management violence. As the South imposed a strict white supremacy code in the 1890s, the region saw the peak of lynchings and other forms of intimidation directed against Af-

rican Americans. Vigilante "justice" prevailed in the West, where a mobile, young, predominantly male, and often armed population outpaced legal and policing systems. Western towns, although never as bloody as the frontier myth suggests, were plagued by bandits, occasional shoot-outs, and widespread disorderly behavior. In the urban North, crime became more professional, particularly gambling and prostitution. In industrial parts of the North, the labor/capital struggle regularly flared into violent confrontations. From the railroad strike of 1877 to the Pullman strike of 1894, class conflict was the most visible sign of disorder.

Further Reading: Lawrence Friedman, *Crime and Punishment in American History*, 1993; Roger Lane, *Murder in America: A History*, 1997.

Michael Ayers Trotti

CRISP, CHARLES FREDERICK (29 January 1845–23 October 1896), speaker of the House of Representatives. Born in Sheffield, England, Crisp emigrated to the United States with his parents, settling in Georgia in 1845. He attended Savannah and Macon public schools, served in the Confederate Army, and gained admission to the bar in 1866. Subsequently, he won a seat in the state legislature, and held various local judgeships. Elected as a Democrat to the federal House of Representatives, Crisp served there from 1883 until his death in Atlanta, Georgia. He chaired the Rules Committee in the Fifty-second and Fifty-third Congresses and was speaker at the same time (1891–1895). He supported tariff reform, the Interstate Commerce Act of 1887, the Sherman Silver Purchase Act of 1890, and free silver. During the early summer of 1896, Crisp debated fellow Georgian Hoke Smith, secretary of the interior, in four Georgia towns on the vexatious currency issue. Smith advocated sound money while Crisp stood for sixteen to one. Crisp won the Democratic nomination in 1896 for a seat in the U.S. Senate, and a silver legislature unquestionably would have elected him, had he survived.

Further Reading: Leonard Schlup, "Mr. Speaker: Charles F. Crisp and American Politics, 1891–1896," *Journal of Southwest Georgia History* 10 (1995); 1–22; Preston St.

Clare Malone, "The Political Career of Charles Frederick Crisp," Ph.D. diss., University of Georgia, 1962.

Leonard Schlup

CRITTENDEN, THOMAS THEODORE (1 January 1832–29 May 1909),

representative and governor. Born in Shelby County, Kentucky, and educated at Centre College, Crittenden studied law under his uncle, Senator John J. Crittenden. He was admitted to the bar and moved to Missouri to open his practice in 1857. He rose to brigadier general in the Union Army during the Civil War. His humiliating surrender of the garrison at Murfreesboro in July 1862 effectively ended his military career.

Crittenden returned to law after the war. He won election to the U.S. House of Representatives in 1872 as a conservative Democrat. He narrowly lost renomination in 1874. In 1876 he won the seat back, and four years later he was elected governor. His most significant achievement was winning a suit against the Hannibal & St. Joseph Railroad for money owed the state. His efforts to break up the James gang also made his term memorable. After a single term, Crittenden returned once more to his law practice in 1885. During the second Cleveland administration he served as consul general in Mexico. He died in Kansas City, Missouri.

Further Reading: H. H. Crittenden, *The Crittenden Memoirs*, 1936.

Damon Eubank

CRITTENTON, CHARLES NELSON (20 February 1833–16 November 1909),

businessman and founder of the National Florence Crittenton Mission. Crittenton was born on a farm near Henderson, New York. In 1861, he started what ultimately became a wholesale drug distribution business in New York City, from which he accumulated a fortune. He suffered a grievous and devastating loss in 1882, the death from scarlet fever of his beloved four-year-old daughter Florence. Shortly thereafter, in a search for direction, Crittenton, an Episcopalian, assumed active roles in evangelistic and missionary endeavors, especially the redemption of women. With able supporters, such as Smith Allen, he founded an organization to help women of the streets to repent and live better lives. A rescue home, named after his daughter and located amid saloons and streetwalkers, opened at 27 Bleecker Street in Greenwich Village on 19 April 1883. It sought to restore "fallen women" to American society.

Joining with temperance reformer Frances Willard and others, Crittenton founded similar institutions elsewhere. By 1895 they formed a national network, linked under a corporation charter, known as the National Florence Crittenton Mission; he served as president until his death. Dr. Kate Waller Barrett, an obstetrician from Atlanta, Georgia, was Crittenton's most important collaborator. By 1897, forty-six Florence Crittenton homes operated under the premise that the facilities should do everything possible, in a Christian and parental atmosphere, to keep mother and child together.

On 9 April 1898, President William McKinley signed a special congressional act chartering the Mission, and making it the first charitable entity to receive such high approbation. Crittenton's philanthropic ventures pioneered rescue efforts to aid prostitutes, unmarried mothers, and their children. His politicized organization developed into one of the most significant social welfare movements of its time. Crittenton died in San Francisco, California. His autobiography, *The Brother of Girls*, appeared in 1910.

Further Reading: *San Francisco Chronicle*, 17 November 1909; *New York Times*, 17 November 1909; Katherine G. Aiken, *Harnessing the Power of Motherhood: The National Florence Crittenton Mission, 1883–1925*, 1998.

Leonard Schlup

CROLY, JANE CUNNINGHAM (19 December 1829–23 December 1901),

journalist, writer, and women's club activist. Born in Market Harborough, Leicestershire, England, Cunningham immigrated to New York in 1841. She began her journalism career in the 1850s, writing a column for women in the *New York Herald*. Using the pen name Jennie June, she soon emerged as a syndicated columnist. In 1856 she married David Goodman Croly, a *Herald* staff writer. Their son, Herbert Croly, became the first editor of the *New Republic*. From 1862 to 1872, Jane Croly managed the woman's department of the *New York World*. Editor of women's periodicals and author of several books and collections of her columns, Croly advocated better educational and professional opportunities for females. She established the New York Women's Press Club in 1889, served as its president for many years, taught journalism to women, and helped to found the Association for the Advancement of Women and the General Federation of Women's Clubs. In 1898 she published *History of the Women's Club Movement in America*. Croly died in New York City.

Further Reading: Jane C. Croly, *Memories of Jane Cunningham Croly—"Jennie June,"* 1904; Henry Ladd Smith, "The Beauteous Jennie June: Pioneer Woman Journalist," *Journalism Quarterly* 40 (1963): 169–174; *New York Times*, 24 December 1901.

Leonard Schlup

CROOK, GEORGE (8 September 1828–21 March 1890), military officer. Born near Taylorsville, Ohio, Crook graduated from the U.S. Military Academy in 1852. While serving in California and Oregon, he came to understand and appreciate that Native Americans were fighting to preserve their lands and way of life. A prominent Union officer during the Civil War, Crook joined military officials in attempting to subdue Native Americans in the West after the Civil War. In 1875, Brigadier General Crook received orders to command the Military Department of the Platte in Omaha, Nebraska. Eight years later, with approximately two hundred western Apache scouts and fifty soldiers and officers, he marched through Arizona into Mexico to search for raiding Chiricahuas Apaches and negotiated their peaceful return to Arizona reservations. Crook encountered criticism for his benevolent treatment of Native Americans, a people for whom he advocated civil rights and the franchise. Crook died in Chicago.

Further Reading: Martin Schmitt, ed., *General George Crook: His Autobiography*, 1986; Joseph C. Porter, *Paper Medicine Man: John Gregory Bourke and His American West*, 1986.

Leonard Schlup

"CROSS OF GOLD" SPEECH OF 1896. Although the United States once accepted both gold and silver as legal tender, Congress demonetized the latter in 1873. The move outraged farmers, who favored unlimited coinage of silver as a way of inflating the money supply and thereby increasing food prices. In 1878 and 1890 Congress made gestures toward increasing silver circulation, but in 1893 it ended silver redemption of Treasury notes.

This polarized the nation. In the election of 1896, Republicans nominated William McKinley for president on a gold standard platform. Democrats repudiated their own pro-gold incumbent, Grover Cleveland. Instead they chose William Jennings Bryan, a Nebraska lawyer favoring unlimited silver coinage, in a bid to attract farmers who supported the People's Party. Bryan's acceptance oration, known as the "Cross of Gold" Speech, electrified inflationists by promising the Democratic Party would not allow capitalism to crucify workers on a cross of gold. In its support for inflation, the speech repudiated the party's gold-standard wing. The Democrats' division over the silver issue guaranteed Bryan's defeat, the speech notwithstanding. With McKinley in the Oval Office, Congress adopted the gold standard in 1900.

Further Reading: Stanley Jones, *The Presidential Election of 1896*, 1964; William Jennings Bryan, *The First Battle: A Story of the Campaign of 1896*, 1896; Paul W. Glad, *The Trumpet Soundeth: William Jennings Bryan and His Democracy, 1896–1912*, 1960.

Christopher Cumo

CRUMMELL, ALEXANDER (3 March 1819–10 September 1898), clergyman and Pan-Africanist. Born in New York City, Crummell became an Episcopal priest in 1844, assumed a role in the antislavery movement, studied in England, and lectured in the United States and abroad. His speeches in Liberia, support of Liberia College, and professorship of English and moral philosophy at Liberia College provided him with academic credentials before his return to the United States in 1872. Seven years later Crummell established the congregation of Saint Luke's in the nation's capital, where he remained as rector until his retirement in 1894. In 1882 he published *The Greatness of Christ and Other Sermons*. An advocate of a strong central government in the Federalist tradition of Alexander Hamilton, a racial chauvinist, and a person known for his prickly disposition and contentious temperament, Crummell contended that African Americans could offer a conservative balance to the radicalism of various immigrant groups in the United States. In 1897 he founded the American Negro Academy. Crummell promoted stable families and the development of individual character. He died in Red Bank, New Jersey.

Further Reading: Gregory U. Rigsby, *Alexander Crummell: Pioneer in Nineteenth-Century Pan-African Thought*, 1987; Wilson J. Moses, *Alexander Crummell: A Study of Civilization and Discontent*, 1989.

Leonard Schlup

CULBERSON, CHARLES ALLEN (19 June 1855–19 March 1925), governor and senator. Culberson was born in Dadeville, Alabama; his family took him to Upshur County, Texas, in 1856. He attended local schools and was graduated from Virginia Military Institute and the University of Virginia law school. He practiced in Daingerfield and later in Dallas, Texas. Culberson was elected state attorney general in 1890, succeeding James S. Hogg. Culberson's most significant case was the defense of the state's new railroad regulatory commission. He was elected governor in 1894 and reelected two years later, and was the second of five Progressive governors who gained office with the assistance of Edward M. House, who later played a significant role in the administration of President Woodrow Wilson. At House's urging, in 1899 the legislature selected Culberson to succeed Roger Q. Mills as U.S. senator from Texas, and kept him in the Senate for twenty-four years. He served as Judiciary Committee chairman and minority leader despite ill health and alcohol dependency. Culberson lost his first election in 1922 because of illness and his opposition to the Ku Klux Klan, and died in Washington, D.C., three years later.

Further Reading: Kenneth E. Hendrickson, *The Chief Executives of Texas*, 1995; William Madden, *Charles Allen Culberson*, 1929; Robert L. Wagner, "Charles Allen Culberson," *The New Handbook of Texas* 2 (1996): 435–436.

Archie P. McDonald

CULBERSON, DAVID BROWNING (29 September 1830–7 May 1900), state legislator and congressman. Culberson was born in Troup County, Georgia. He attended Brownwood Institute in LaGrange, Georgia, and studied law under Alabama's chief justice, William B. Chilton, at Tuskegee. He practiced in Dadeville, Alabama, before moving to Upshur County, Texas, in 1856, then to the town of Jefferson in 1861. One of his sons, Charles Allen Culberson, served as 1860 governor of Texas from 1895 to 1899.

Culberson represented Upshur County in the state legislature (1859–1861). He resigned because he opposed secession, but served as an infantry lieutenant colonel during the Civil War. He returned to Jefferson in 1865 to practice law, and was a member of Abe Rothschild's defense team during the "Diamond Bessie" murder trial in 1878. Culberson served as a presidential elector in 1868 and was elected a state senator in 1873. He resigned this post to move to the U.S. House of Representatives in 1875, and remained a congressman until 1897. He supported prohibition, states' rights, and antitrust legislation. He died in Jefferson.

Further Reading: Anne W. Hooker, "David Browning Culberson," *The New Handbook of Texas* 2 (1996): 436; Alwyn Barr, *Reconstruction to Reform: Texas Politics, 1876–1900*, 1971; Leonard Schlup, "Political Patriarch: David B. Culberson and the Politics of Railroad Building, Tariff Reform, and Silver Coinage in Post-Civil-War America," *East Texas Historical Journal* 34 (1966): 30–39.

Archie P. McDonald

CULINARY ARTS. Most Gilded Age Americans ate regional or ethnic cuisines based on tradition and available food supplies. New Englanders tended to eat boiled meats, root vegetables, salads, and foods from the ocean; southerners continued their "hog-and-hominy" diets, supplemented with rice, greens, and fish; westerners consumed game, beef, pork, dairy, and wheat products; and ethnic enclaves dined on traditional fare as local supplies allowed. Eating habits changed slightly as transportation and preservation technology allowed consumers to purchase victuals from outside their locality without regard to season. However, the nouveaux riches contributed to U.S. culinary arts by introducing French cuisine and public dining as status symbols. Every major city, boomtown, and seaside resort boasted that it had an eatery as high class as Delmonico's restaurant in New York or the Palmer House Hotel in Chicago. Fred Harvey's railroad depot restaurants helped spread French-inspired foods and culinary techniques through the hinterlands. In 1895 Delmonico's longtime chef, Charles Ranhofer, published his massive professional cookbook, *The Epicurean,* which provided scores of menus and hundreds of recipes combining American foods such as canvasback duck, turkey, and oysters with French culinary artistry. Rather than establish a model for the future American dietary, *The Epicurean* summarized the era's fascination with French cuisine.

Further Reading: Richard O. Cummings, *The American and His Food,* 1941; Waverly Root and Richard deRochemont, *Eating in America: A History,* 1976.

Martin T. Olliff

CULLOM, SHELBY MOORE (22 November 1829–28 January 1914), governor, congressman, and senator. Cullom, born in Kentucky, left his family's Illinois farm in 1850 to study law in Springfield. He entered politics a Free Soiler in 1856, but soon joined the new Republican Party. He served in numerous elective offices: several terms in the state legislature, where he was speaker of the House during the sessions of 1861 and 1873; in the U.S. House of Representatives from 1865 to 1871; as governor from 1876 to 1883; and five terms in the U.S. Senate from 1883 to 1913. He supported railroad regulation at both the state and federal levels. He worked to establish the Interstate Commerce Commission in 1887 and chaired the Senate Committee on Interstate Commerce. He headed the Hawaiian Commission, which drafted legislation providing for territorial government. In 1898, he supported the war against Spain and the acquisition of the Philippines, though he later doubted the wisdom of taking the islands. Cullom considered running for the presidency in 1888 and 1896, but drew little support. In 1901 he became chairman of the Senate Foreign Relations Committee. A loyal Republican, he nevertheless disagreed with party regulars on some issues; he favored lower tariffs and antitrust legislation. He played an important role in support of the Hepburn Act

of 1906. Losing a primary election in 1912 ended his Senate career.

Further Reading: Shelby Cullom, *Fifty Years of Public Service,* 1911; James W. Neilson, *Shelby M. Cullom: Prairie State Republican,* 1961.

Mario R. DiNunzio

CULTURAL CHANGE. In the Gilded Age, American culture turned in two distinct directions. First, it became more elaborate and varied. The era brought the bicycle, the phonograph, Eastman's Kodak camera, burlesque, vaudeville, professional baseball, the automobile, and the motion picture. Amid this cultural abundance, "high" culture—opera, fine art museums, Shakespeare, classical music—became more distinct from the pastimes of the common folk. One trend, then, was toward both the growth and the differentiation of cultural offerings and their audiences. Complicating this tendency toward cultural elaboration, America's vigorous popular culture became increasingly oriented toward working- and middle-class men and women, mixing them more than ever into a common mass culture. Newspapers emerged as a mass medium, and vaudeville and variety shows attracted a wide range of the urban population. In the 1890s, cities developed amusement parks, such as Coney Island, that championed this new ideal of active, physical fun for mixed groups.

Both trends found expression in the World's Columbian Exposition at Chicago (1893). Juxtaposed against its beautiful "White City," which embodied the ideals of high culture with its grand neoclassical architecture, was the more popular midway, filled with rides, food, and active fun enjoyed by a heterogeneous crowd.

Further Reading: Lawrence Levine, *Highbrow/Lowbrow,* 1988; John F. Kasson, *Amusing the Million,* 1978.

Michael Ayers Trotti

CUNNINGHAM* v. *NEAGLE, 135 U.S. 1 (1890). When David S. Terry assaulted Supreme Court Justice Stephen J. Field, David Neagle, the U.S. marshal assigned to protect Field, shot and killed Terry. After Neagle was taken into state custody, he petitioned a federal court for a writ of habeas corpus, which was granted. Sheriff Cunningham appealed. No federal statute authorized the federal government to protect judicial officers. The case raised the issue of whether a federal statute, allowing for the writ of habeas corpus for prisoners held upon acts done "in pursuance of a law of the United States," applied absent a statute.

Supreme Court Justice Samuel F. Miller, in a 6–2 opinion (Justice Field recused himself), held that Neagle, in the performance of his duties, was acting pursuant to federal law, and therefore was entitled to be discharged from state custody, even absent a federal statute. Justice Miller thought the constitutional supremacy of the federal government over the states required an expansive interpretation of "law." That concept included any duty reasonably implicit in the Constitution. The president's duty to take care that the laws be executed faithfully empowered him to provide protection for Justice Field. The case stands for broad interpretation of federal law and presidential power.

Further Reading: James W. Ely, Jr., *The Chief Justiceship of Melville W. Fuller, 1888–1910*, 1995; Peter M. Shane and Harold H. Bruff, *Separation of Powers Law*, 1996; Bernard Schwartz, *A History of the Supreme Court*, 1993.

Joel K. Goldstein

CURRENCY ISSUE. Between 1873 and 1896 a struggle between monetary conservatives and inflationists dominated American politics. Depressions in the 1870s, 1880s, and 1890s, with persistent price deflation, drove the conflict. Conservatives believed the only sound basis for a monetary system was a fixed gold standard of value, or a gold and silver standard at a fixed ratio reflecting their values as determined through international agreement. Inflationists at first emphasized fiat paper currency. The Coinage Act of 1873, ending the coinage of silver dollars, opened the conflict. Passage in 1875 of the Specie Resumption Act, requiring the Treasury to begin payments in gold alone on 1 January 1879 and reducing the volume of federal currency issues (the Civil War "greenbacks") by 20 percent, intensified it. Growing western influence shifted attention increasingly away from paper currency toward bimetallism, and then the free coinage of silver, as the favored inflationary program after the late 1870s. The

issue lost urgency after William McKinley's presidential triumph in 1896, the Alaska gold rush, and the return of prosperity during the following years.

Further Reading: Milton Friedman and Anna Jacobson Schwartz, *A Monetary History of the United States, 1867–1960*, 1963; Irwin Unger, *The Greenback Era: A Social and Political History of American Finance, 1865–1879*, 1964; Douglas Steeples and David O. Whitten, *Democracy in Desperation: The Depression of 1893*, 1998.

Douglas Steeples

CURRIER & IVES, celebrated lithographers who produced highly popular, hand-colored prints of American life. Nathaniel Currier (27 March 1813–20 November 1888), born in Roxbury, Massachusetts, attended public schools until 1828, when he was apprenticed at a pioneering Boston lithographic firm. At age twenty-two, he founded his own New York City business, and succeeded by rapidly producing dramatic re-creations of newsworthy events, especially disasters. In 1852, he hired James Merritt Ives (5 March 1824–3 January 1895) as a bookkeeper, and they formed a partnership in 1857. Ives, born in New York City, proved an able artist and businessman despite having scant formal education. Together they produced more than seven thousand lithographs, appealing to virtually every popular taste and interest. Their work depicted landscapes and cityscapes, sentimental domestic scenes, political cartoons, scenes from American history, and illustrations of recreational and sporting events. They hand-colored almost every print, and many noteworthy artists worked for them, including Louis Maurer, Thomas Worth, Arthur F. Tait, and George Henry Durrie. The Manhattan-based firm marketed its merchandise through direct sales and mail order, as well as via pushcart peddlers and an international network of dealers. Currier retired in 1880, and died in New York City in 1888. Ives died in New York City seven years later.

The perfection of chromolithography in the 1860s, however, and rapid improvements in steam-powered printing negated Currier and Ives's expertise. By the end of the Gilded Age, a proliferation of stereographs, photographs, and engravings in periodicals provided Americans access to affordable decorative art and illustration, and undermined the uniqueness of the firm's works. The retail shop closed in 1896, and the firm's last known dated prints were issued in 1898, covering Spanish-American War events. The business closed in 1907. Since then, their prints have become prized collector's items, and comprise a rich and irreplaceable panorama of American life in the Gilded Age.

Further Reading: Bryan F. Le Beau, *Currier & Ives: America Imagined*, 2001; Walton Rawls, *The Great Book of Currier & Ives' America*, 1979; C. Carter Smith and Cathy Coshion, eds., *Currier & Ives: A Catalogue Raisonné*, 1984.

Jon Sterngass

CURRY, JABEZ LAMAR MONROE. (5 June 1825–12 February 1903), educator, politician, and diplomat. Born in Lincoln County, Georgia, Curry graduated from Franklin College (now University of Georgia) in 1843 and from Harvard Law School two years later. A state legislator and antebellum federal representative, Curry served in the Confederate Congress. After the Civil War, he became president of Howard College in Marion, Alabama. He prepared for ordination as a Baptist minister, advocated strong graded public school systems, and emphasized education to help the devastated South recover from the military conflict. In 1868 Curry became professor of history and English literature at Richmond College, and in 1881 he was named general agent of the Peabody Fund for Education in the South, a post he held for over two decades.

An amiable, aristocratic southern gentleman, Curry was the most influential southern educational reformer during the postbellum period. He strongly endorsed free public education for everyone. Curry lobbied for the Blair Bill, favored federal aid to education, opposed Populism, maintained conservative economic views, denounced lynching, supported industrial education, believed in laissez-faire concepts of limited government, defended segregation of the races in schools, and contended black enfranchisement had been politically and socially improper.

In 1885 President Grover Cleveland appointed Curry minister to Spain, where he remained until 1889. Curry's publications included *Constitutional Government in Spain* (1889) and *Civil History of the Government of the United States* (1901). He died in Asheville, North Carolina.

Further Reading: Jessie Pearl Rice, *J. L. M. Curry: Southerner, Statesman, and Educator*, 1949; Jabez L. M. Curry Papers, Manuscripts Division, Library of Congress.

Leonard Schlup

CURTIS, GEORGE WILLIAM. (24 February 1824–31 August 1892), journalist, editor, reformer. Curtis was born in Providence, Rhode Island, attended school in Massachusetts, and later received private tutoring in New York. His journalistic talents became evident in the 1840s while he was on a four-year European tour.

Curtis edited *Harper's Weekly*, the northern counterpart to the *Southern Review*, from 1863 to 1892, and was active politically. Although he abhorred slavery, after the Civil War he sought national harmony and believed African Americans should no longer be a political issue. During the Gilded Age, Curtis was a "Mugwump," a highly intelligent and socially prominent Republican, who supported reform in politics, civil service, industry, and trade. As head of the Civil Service Commission, he worked for its reform. Nonetheless, by 1884, he and other "Mugwumps" supported Grover Cleveland for president rather than the Republican candidate, James G. Blaine.

Curtis devoted several decades to public and charitable movements on Staten Island, in New York City. He was a skilled orator, but his writings are considered his most valuable societal contribution. He died on Staten Island.

Further Reading: Edward Cary, *George William Curtis*, 1894; G. T. Blodgett, *The Gentle Reformers*, 1966; *New York Times*, 1 September 1892.

Jane F. Lancaster

CUSTER, GEORGE ARMSTRONG. (5 December 1839–25 June 1876), U.S. Army officer. Custer was born in New Rumley, Ohio, earned a teaching certificate in 1856 at Hopedale, then attended West Point, where he excelled in all but academics. He graduated last in the class of 1861, which had been depleted by desertions to the Confederacy.

That year Custer landed an Army of the Potomac staff position. In June 1863, he received command of the Michigan Cavalry Brigade and a brevet brigadiership. At Gettysburg he routed Jeb Stuart. A daring victory at Winchester in September 1864 earned Custer his own division, which promptly defeated the Confederates at Toms Brook in October, bringing a second star. Custer also played a prominent role at Appomattox in April 1865.

After brief duty in Texas, Custer in 1866 accepted the lieutenant colonelcy of the Seventh Cavalry Regiment, newly formed at Fort Riley, Kansas, to patrol Indian country. In 1867, a court martial suspended him for one year for using government property during an unauthorized leave, abandoning wounded men, and shooting deserters without trial. Upon returning in 1868, he led an attack on Black Kettle's village on the Washita River in Oklahoma, his first major Indian battle. Numerous noncombatants were killed.

By 1873 the "Indian problem" had shifted north. The Seventh relocated to Fort Abraham Lincoln, Dakota Territory, from which Custer launched the 1874 Black Hills expedition. Called to Washington late in 1875, he testified against corrupt officials, including President Grant's brother. An infuriated Grant stripped Custer of his command, but General Philip Sheridan intervened, enabling Custer to lead his regiment in the 1876 campaign to force the Sioux onto their reservation. On 25 June, while attempting to corral the Indians (including Northern Cheyenne), he and a third of his regiment were killed on the Little Big Horn River, Montana Territory.

Further Reading: Robert M. Utley, *Cavalier in Buckskin: George Armstrong Custer and the Western Military Frontier*, 1988; Gregory J. W. Urwin, *Custer Victorious: The Civil War Battles of General George Armstrong Custer*, 1983; Jay Monaghan, *Custer: The Life of General George Armstrong Custer*, 1959.

Richard A. Fox

CUTCHEON, BYRON M. (11 May 1836–12 April 1908), congressman. Born in Pembroke, New Hampshire, Cutcheon graduated from the University of Michigan in 1861, taught school, and fought in the Civil War. For his exploits in the latter, he received the Congressional Medal of Honor in 1891. From 1877 to 1883, Cutcheon was a lawyer, prosecuting attorney, and postmaster of Manistee, Michigan. He won election as a Republican to the U.S. House of Representatives, where he served from 1883 to 1891. Cutcheon chaired the Committee on Military Affairs in the Fifty-first Congress. Defeated for reelection in the Democratic victories of 1890, he resumed his law practice in Grand Rapids, Michigan, and also worked as an editorial writer for the *Detroit Daily Tribune* and *Detroit Journal* from 1895 to 1897. Cutcheon died in Ypsilanti, Michigan.

Further Reading: *New York Times*, 13 April 1908.

Leonard Schlup

CUTTER, CHARLES AMMI (14 March 1837–6 September 1903), librarian. Born in the Charlestown district of Boston, Massachusetts, Cutter studied at Harvard College and, from 1856 to 1859, Harvard Divinity School, where he decided to become a librarian. After being graduated, he assisted the bibliographer Ezra Abbot in completely recataloging the Harvard College library (1860–1868), then one of the largest in the United States. They produced the nation's first public card catalog. In 1868 Cutter joined the Boston Athenaeum, a large public library, whose card catalog he made a model that others emulated. His contributions to the *Report on Public Libraries* in 1875 included "Rules for a Printed Dictionary Catalogue," which went through four subsequent editions and is still a standard resource. In 1893 Cutter joined the Forbes Library of Northampton, Massachusetts, where he systematized the acquiring and classifying of a book collection for general public use.

Cutter foresaw centralized cataloging of books and printing of catalog cards, which became the standard Library of Congress practice. He was active in the newly formed American Library Association and in state library clubs, and he was closely involved with *Library Journal*, the publication of the new library movement following 1876. Cutter is especially remembered for his tabular system for abbreviating names of authors, the "Cutter letter and number" to refine the call number. He died in Walpole, New Hampshire.

Further Reading: William Parker Cutter, *Charles Ammi Cutter*, 1931; Francis L. Miksa, ed., *Charles Ammi Cutter, Library Systematizer*, 1997.

Philip H. Young

CZOLGOSZ, LEON (1873?–29 October 1901), assassin of President William McKinley. Plagued by a troubled personality, Czolgosz, a native of Detroit, was ill-tempered, withdrawn, a loner. He was the fourth child of Polish immigrants; his mother died when he was twelve; and the family remained poor throughout his life. As a young man he left the family farm to work in a wire mill in Cleveland, Ohio. He believed the government was the enemy of the working class, a view probably reinforced by the radical publications and meetings to which he was attracted. He was drawn to anarchist groups in Cleveland and Chicago, but was regarded with suspicion by their organizers because of his strange personality. In July 1901, he moved to Buffalo, New York, and learned that President McKinley would visit the Pan-American Exposition there. On 6 September, Czolgosz concealed a revolver in his bandaged right hand and blended into a receiving line greeting the president in the Temple of Music. As McKinley extended his hand to him, Czolgosz fired two shots into the president's abdomen. Fatally wounded, McKinley died on 14 September. Czolgosz was quickly tried, found guilty, and electrocuted less than two months after the assassination.

Further Reading: A. Wesley Johns, *The Man Who Shot McKinley*, 1970; H. Wayne Morgan, *William McKinley and His America*, 1963.

Mario R. DiNunzio

DALTON GANG. This western outlaw band terrorized parts of Kansas and Oklahoma for seventeen months in 1891–1892. Led by Robert R. "Bob" Dalton, the gang included his brothers Gratton and Emmett, along with,

at various times, George "Bitter Creek" Newcomb, Charley Pierce, Charley "Black Face" Bryant, William Power (a.k.a. Tom Evans or Bill Powers), Dick Broadwell, Bill McElhanie, and William "Bill" Doolin. The Dalton brothers were born in Cass County, Missouri, on the Missouri-Kansas frontier, the same violent region that spawned the James-Younger gang. Indeed, the Daltons were first cousins of the Younger brothers, who in turn were kin to Frank and Jesse James.

Between May 1891 and July 1892, the Dalton gang staged four successful train robberies in what is now Oklahoma. Enduring fame, however, eluded the outlaws until their disastrous raid on Coffeyville, Kansas. Allegedly in a bid to surpass the exploits of the James gang, Bob Dalton concocted a reckless plan to rob two banks simultaneously. On 5 October 1892, the three Daltons, accompanied by Broadwell and Power, rode into an unsuspecting but heavily armed Coffeyville. Their dual heist quickly dissolved into a gun battle, and only Emmett Dalton survived the ensuing slaughter, which also claimed the lives of four townsmen. Badly wounded, Emmett was subsequently convicted of second degree murder and sentenced to life in prison. Pardoned in 1907, he quietly spent his final years in Los Angeles, California, where he died.

Meanwhile, Bill Doolin had teamed up with Bill Dalton, a brother of his erstwhile companions, and formed a new gang, which included Newcomb, Pierce, McElhanie, and eleven others. Doolin's gang rode for nearly three years before splitting up in April 1895. On 25 August 1896, Doolin was ambushed and killed by a posse near Lawton, Oklahoma.

Further Reading: Robert Barr Smith, *Daltons! The Raid on Coffeyville, Kansas*, 1996; Nancy B. Samuelson, *The Dalton Gang Story: Lawmen to Outlaws*, 1992; Col. Bailey C. Hanes, *Bill Doolin, Outlaw O.T.*, 1968.

Michael Magliari

DALY, JOHN AUGUSTIN (20 July 1838–7 June 1899), theatrical manager and dramatist. Born in Plymouth, North Carolina, Daly was educated privately in Norfolk, Virginia, and in New York City public schools. He began his theater career as a journalist in 1860, and over the next decade served as chief drama critic for five metropolitan newspapers, including the *New York Times*. As a dramatist, Daly first garnered recognition for *Leah the Forsaken* (1862), then achieved lasting acclaim with *Under the Gaslight* (1867). Reflecting the new fascination of the day, it was the first melodrama to incorporate the rail locomotive as a central plot device. Daly also won fame over the next thirty years for adaptations of French, German, and Shakespearean plays, as well as dramatizations of popular novels. His chief significance, however, lies in managerial innovation. Controlling his own theater after 1869, he abandoned the "actor-manager" convention, thereby serving as one of the first modern directors. Criticized for the control he demanded over actors' performances, Daly nonetheless advanced "natural" acting through his direction, and rejected the "star system" for ensemble playing. Daly's innovations enabled his group to become the first American company to tour Europe, which it did nine times between 1884 and 1897. Daly died on tour in Paris.

Further Reading: Joseph Francis Daly, *The Life of Augustin Daly*, 1917; Marvin Felheim, *The Theater of Augustin Daly: An Account of the Late Nineteenth Century American Stage*, 1956.

James Harley

DANA, JOHN COTTON (19 August 1856–21 July 1929), librarian and museologist. Born in Woodstock, Vermont, Dana was graduated from Dartmouth College in 1878, studied law, and worked as a civil engineer. His concern for social welfare led him down other avenues, however. In 1889 he became director of the

Denver Public Library, which he built from its beginnings to national renown. In 1896 he served as president of the American Library Association. In 1902 Dana became head of the Free Public Library of Newark, New Jersey, where he implemented his views about librarianship, focusing on service. He felt that a book's worth was in its use and that a library should not be a cold collection of rare books. Perhaps his greatest achievement was promoting open shelves for the public. Dana strongly believed libraries should focus on education, and he instituted new ideas toward that end, such as providing popular fiction, a children's department, photo and pamphlet collections, and significant exhibits. He created the first branch library dedicated to business, and was an avid supporter of developing high school libraries. In 1909 his efforts to launch the Special Libraries Association came to fruition, and he served as its first head.

Dana's support of important exhibits led to the library's acquisition of objects that, under his direction, in 1909 formed the collection of the Newark Museum of Art, Science and Industry. Dana loved American art and collected prints, posters, and all types of ephemera. He viewed museums much as he viewed libraries: as vehicles for local crafts and art, and public enlightenment, and as instruments of international goodwill. He made the museum an interactive learning place rather than a gallery of dead objects. Dana died in New York City. His legacy is kept alive in the library profession by an annual John Cotton Dana Award given to a library that has executed the best public relations campaign and activities.

Further Reading: [Newark Public Library], *John Cotton Dana, 1856–1929*, 1930; Chalmers Hadley, *John Cotton Dana: A Sketch*, 1943; Carl A. Hanson, "Access and Utility: John Cotton Dana and the Antecedents of Information Science, 1889–1929," *Libraries and Culture* 29 (1994): 186–204.

Philip H. Young

DANA, WILLIAM BUCK (26 August 1829–10 October 1910), publisher and entrepreneur. Born in Utica, New York, and schooled at the Mount Vernon (New York) Academy, Dana was graduated from Yale in 1851. After practicing law for a decade, he purchased the lead-

ing business monthly, *Hunt's Merchants' Magazine*.

On 1 July 1865, Dana used telegraphic communication to begin publishing the first business weekly, the *Commercial and Financial Chronicle*. Unrivaled in timeliness, comprehensiveness, and accuracy, it became the country's foremost business publication. It added supplements on banking in 1868, government and railroad securities in 1875, electric railroads in 1895, and other investment channels thereafter. Subscribers numbered forty-five hundred by 1870, and thrice that many twenty years later. The paper steadfastly championed sound money, favoring first international bimetallism and later the gold standard. It criticized government regulation of railroads and trusts as socialistic.

Dana developed and owned the Palisade Mountain House, a resort hotel atop the Hudson River palisades, from 1871 to 1883. Active in the affairs of the *Chronicle* until his death, he wrote two books: *Cotton from Seed to Loom* (1878) and *A Day for Rest and Worship* (1911). He died in New York City.

Further Reading: Douglas Steeples, "William Dana: Man of Enterprise," *Essays in Economic and Business History* 12 (1994): 164–174, and "Young Will Dana: The Education of an Entrepreneur," *ibid.* 11 (1993): 326–343.

Douglas Steeples

DANIEL, JOHN WARWICK (5 September 1842–29 June 1910), senator. Born in Lynchburg, Virginia, Daniel attended private schools and Lynchburg College before enlisting in the Confederate Army. Injuries sustained in the Battle of the Wilderness (May 1864) left him on crutches for life. After studying law at the University of Virginia (1865–1866), he joined his father's practice. He entered politics as a Democrat, with election to the House of Delegates, where he served from 1869 to 1872. A six-year state senate term followed. He ran unsuccessfully for the governorship in 1881, but three years later won a seat in the U.S. House of Representatives and, in 1885, a seat in the U.S. Senate. Daniel held the latter for life.

An eloquent orator serving Virginia's Cult of the Lost Cause, Daniel sponsored no important legislation. A respected public servant nonetheless, he opposed President Grover Cleveland's demand for repeal of the Sherman Silver Purchase Act. In 1896 he vigorously supported William Jennings Bryan for the presidency. At the Virginia constitutional convention of 1901–1902, Daniel served as chair of the committee that drafted articles disenfranchising African Americans and poor whites. He died in Lynchburg.

Further Reading: William M. Thornton, *John Warwick Daniel*, 1915; Richard B. Doss, "John Warwick Daniel: A Study in Virginia Democracy," Ph.D. diss., University of Virginia, 1955; John Warwick Daniel Papers, University of Virginia Library, Charlottesville.

James R. Sweeney

DAVIS, BANCROFT (29 December 1822–27 December 1907), diplomat and court reporter. Born John Chandler Bancroft Davis in Worcester, Massachusetts, he graduated from Harvard College in 1847, practiced law in New York City, and worked as American correspondent for the London *Times* from 1854 to 1861. In 1869, President Ulysses S. Grant appointed him first assistant secretary of state under Secretary of State Hamilton Fish. Davis served as American secretary on the joint commission to resolve the *Alabama* claims, and prepared a five-hundred-page document presenting the American case, helped draft the Treaty of Washington of 1871. Three years later President Grant named him minister to Germany, where Davis succeeded his uncle, the historian George Bancroft. In 1878, President Rutherford B. Hayes selected Davis for the U.S. Court of Claims, and in 1881, President Chester A. Arthur invited him to return to the State Department to assist Secretary of State Frederick T. Frelinghuysen. In 1883 Davis became reporter of the U.S. Supreme Court, an appointment he held for the next nineteen years. He edited and annotated volumes 108 through 186 of the *U.S. Reports*. In 1893 Davis published *Mr. Fish and the Alabama Claims*. Davis died in Washington, D.C.

Further Reading: *New York Tribune*, 28 December 1907; *Washington Post*, 28 December 1907; Bancroft Davis Papers, Manuscripts Division, Library of Congress.

Leonard Schlup

DAVIS, CUSHMAN KELLOGG (16 June 1838–29 November 1900), governor and U.S. senator. Born in Henderson, New York, Davis moved with his parents to Wisconsin, graduated from the University of Michigan in 1857, began law practice in Waukesha, Wisconsin, in 1859, and served in the Civil War. After his return to civilian life, Davis moved to Saint Paul, Minnesota, where he held a seat in the state house of representatives in 1867 and was U.S. attorney from 1868 to 1873. A Republican, Davis served as governor of Minnesota from 1874 to 1876 and as U.S. senator from 1887 until his death in Saint Paul. In this capacity, he sat on various committees, including Pensions, Territories, and Foreign Relations. Davis, who followed the nationalist Republican agenda and favored protective tariffs and a stable currency, expressed particular interest in foreign policy. President William McKinley appointed him to the American delegation that met in Paris in September 1898 to arrange terms of peace formally concluding the Spanish-American War. There he urged the acquisition of the Philippine Islands.

Further Reading: Richard Coy, "Cushman K. Davis and American Foreign Policy, 1887–1900," Ph.D. diss., University of Minnesota, 1965; Kent Kreuter, "The Presidency of Nothing: Cushman K. Davis and the Campaign of 1896," *Minnesota History* 41 (1969): 301–316; Cushman K. Davis Papers, Minnesota Historical Society, Saint Paul.

Leonard Schlup

DAVIS, DAVID (9 March 1815–26 June 1886), Supreme Court justice and U.S. senator. Davis, born in Sassafras Neck, Maryland, was graduated from Kenyon College in Ohio in 1832, and from New Haven Law School in Massachusetts in 1835. He became a judge in Illinois; Abraham Lincoln appeared before him nearly ninety times. Davis managed Lincoln's presidential campaign in 1860, and in 1862 was appointed to the Supreme Court. There Davis wrote several notable opinions, including *Ex Parte Milligan* (1866). Passionately, Davis insisted that military courts, set up where civilian courts were still functioning, had no jurisdiction to try civilians. His tenure on the Supreme Court did not stop his political activity; he actively aided Lincoln's reelection effort in 1864, and was himself mentioned as a candidate for the Liberal Republican nomination in 1872.

During the electoral crisis of 1876–1877, Davis was seriously considered for the fifth, tie-breaking seat on the electoral commission created by Congress (the other members were two Democrats and two Republicans). Fearing that Davis would be too partial to the Democratic claims in the disputed states, the Illinois legislature elected Davis to the U.S. Senate in 1877, a move that quite possibly awarded the election to Rutherford B. Hayes. Davis accepted the seat, resigned from the Supreme Court, and served one undistinguished term before his retirement in 1883. He died in Bloomington, Illinois.

Further Reading: Willard L. King, *Lincoln's Manager: David Davis*, 1960.

Sam S. Kepfield

DAVIS, HENRY GASSAWAY (16 November 1823–11 March 1916),

U.S. senator and railroad builder. Born in Woodstock, Maryland, Davis became wealthy through engaging in banking, coal mining, lumbering, and railroad development. A Union supporter and Republican during the Civil War, he favored industrial growth, sought conciliatory reconstruction policies, and opposed African-American suffrage. Following service as a West Virginia state legislator in the 1860s, he served from 1871 to 1883 as a Democrat in the U.S. Senate. There, for two years, he chaired the Appropriations Committee. In 1881 he began construction of the West Virginia Central and Pittsburgh Railway, which he sold in 1902. He was a delegate to the first two Pan-American conferences (1889 and 1901), and a member of the Intercontinental Railway Survey Commissions from 1890 to 1894. In 1904, at age eighty-one, Davis received the Democratic vice presidential nomination on the ticket headed by Alton B. Parker of New York. From 1901 to 1916 he was chairman of the permanent Pan-American Railway Committee. Davis died in Washington, D.C.

Further Reading: Charles M. Pepper, *The Life and Times of Henry Gassaway Davis*, 1920; *New York Times*, 11 March 1916; John A. Williams, "Davis and Elkins of West Virginia: Businessmen in Politics," Ph.D. diss., Yale University, 1967.

Leonard Schlup

DAVIS, JAMES HARVEY (CYCLONE) (24 December 1854–31 January 1940),

Populist orator. Davis was born near Walhalla, South Carolina, and moved with his parents to Winnsboro, Texas, in 1857. He read law, passed the bar exam, and was twice elected judge of Franklin County, Texas, as a Democrat. He developed into a compelling speaker in several statewide campaigns during the 1880s. A talented writer as well, he helped found the Texas Press Association and became its president in 1882. Davis edited the Mount Vernon *Franklin Herald* that year, and later established the Sulphur Springs *Alliance Vindicator*.

Davis became a lecturer for the Southern Farmers' Alliance in 1884. He was one of the few southern delegates to the Populist Party's first national convention in 1891, where he served on the resolutions and national executive committees. Davis, Ignatius Donnelly, and Thomas Patterson met prior to the Populists' nominating convention of 1892 to draft the Omaha Platform, which became the party's most cherished document. During the 1890s, Davis spoke for the cause in every state west of Pennsylvania and south of Maryland. He engaged in more than a thousand debates, and received the nickname "Cyclone" in an 1894 appearance against Wat Tyler of Kentucky. The reformer Henry Demarest Lloyd described Davis as "tall and thin as a southern pine, with eyes kindled with the fire of the prophet, a voice of far reach and pathos, and a vocabulary almost every word of which seemed drawn from the gospels or denunciatory psalms." Davis's verbal assaults on banks and corporations became legendary. In 1894, he wrote *A Political Revelation*, in which he defended Populism as the true inheritor of the Jeffersonian tradition. Texas Populists nominated him for state attorney general in 1892 and for Congress in 1894. He became the leader of the fusionist (coalition with Democrats) wing of the People's Party in Texas two years later.

Throughout his career, Davis campaigned for prohibition. He returned to the progressive wing of the Democratic Party in 1906, and was elected to Congress, representing an at-large district, in 1914. His vocal opposition to America's entry into World War I, however, cost him

the office. Davis joined the Second Ku Klux Klan in the 1920s, and lost another bid for congressman-at-large in a runoff primary in 1932.
Further Reading: Roscoe C. Martin, *The People's Party in Texas*, 1933; James Harvey Cyclone Davis, *Memoir* (1935); *Dallas Morning News* 1 February 1940.

Worth Robert Miller

DAVIS, RICHARD HARDING (18 April 1864–11 April 1916), war correspondent, journalist, dramatist, and novelist. Davis was born in Philadelphia, Pennsylvania, and attended private preparatory schools and Lehigh University. His fictional Van Bibber sketches in the *New York Evening Sun* brought his first public attention. He went on to chronicle Gilded Age political, military, and social life as the highly skilled impressionist of a society satisfied with itself. His keen eye for superficial details— color, wit, manners, dress—won him wide readership. War correspondence, his most successful métier, celebrated heroic battlefield moments in vivid imagery while satisfying his readers' appetites for the humorous and bizarre. As a gentleman adventurer and man of action, he always stood at the center of his reporting. As a fiction writer and playwright, Davis was more limited. His work revolved around a few basic plots, themes, and stock characters.

Davis's optimism, sentimentality, and insistence on "good form" and the natural aristocracy of birth, breeding, and wealth clashed with twentieth-century irony. In death, he was largely forgotten, although his influence appears in works by Stephen Crane, Jack London, Ernest Hemingway, and others. Davis died in Mount Kisco, New York.
Further Reading: Scott Compton Osborn and Robert L. Phillips, Jr., *Richard Harding Davis*, 1978; Arthur Lubow, *The Reporter Who Would Be King: A Biography of Richard Harding Davis*, 1992; Scott C. Osborn, "Richard Harding Davis: The Development of a Journalist," Ph.D. diss., University of Kentucky, 1953.

James Summerville

DAVIS, WILLIAM OSBORNE (5 August 1837–22 May 1911), publisher and editor. Born in Chester County, Pennsylvania, Davis moved to Bloomington, Illinois, in 1859 at the behest of Jesse Fell, a respected lawyer and friend of Abraham Lincoln. He married Fell's daughter,

Eliza Brown Fell, in 1863. A Quaker, Davis clerked in the Internal Revenue Service in Washington, D.C., during the Civil War. In 1871, he became sole editor and proprietor of the *Bloomington Daily Pantagraph*. Davis shrewdly sensed the temper of the community. He introduced new techniques in gathering and reporting news, turning his Republican newspaper into a respected organ in central Illinois. Davis strongly supported the Spanish-American War, denounced Populism, castigated Altgeldism, and favored protective tariffs. He advocated sound money, nationalistic programs, and an international posture for the United States. His editorials commanded attention across the Midwest. Fiercely independent in his thinking, Davis declined to attend Governor Joseph W. Fifer's inaugural in 1889 because there would be "too much crowd for comfort." He traveled to Europe in 1890 and endorsed Benjamin Harrison for president two years later. In 1893 his daughter, Helen Louise Davis, married Lewis Green Stevenson, son of Vice President Adlai E. Stevenson, a Democrat. Their son, Adlai E. Stevenson II, was born in Los Angeles in 1900. Davis died in Bloomington, Illinois, leaving a legacy in journalism that gained him a place in that profession's hall of fame in the Prairie State.
Further Reading: *Daily Pantagraph*, 23 May 1911.

Leonard Schlup

DAWES, HENRY LAURENS (30 October 1816–5 February 1903), congressman and senator. Born in Cummington, Massachusetts, Dawes was graduated from Yale in 1839 and was admitted to the Massachusetts bar in 1842. He served in the state legislature and as a U.S. attorney, and, from 1857 to 1875, was a Republican member of the federal House of Representatives. Dawes advocated protective tariffs for the textile industry and laid groundwork for creation of the National Weather Service. In 1875, he won election to the Senate, where he served until 1893. There he sponsored the Indian Emancipation Act of 1887, often referred to as the Dawes Severalty Act. The law sought to assimilate Native Americans by dissolving tribal entities and lands. It granted 160 acres to each head of a family, and to protect Native

Americans against unscrupulous land speculators, the government retained a probationary twenty-five-year trust patent. Though billed as a reform, the Dawes Act failed to respect Native American culture, and considerable Indian land was opened to white settlement. In 1934, the law was replaced by the Indian Reorganization Act. Dawes died in Pittsfield, Massachusetts.

Further Reading: Steven J. Arcanti, "To Secure the Party: Henry L. Dawes and the Politics of Reconstruction," *Historical Journal of Western Massachusetts* 5 (1977): 33–45; Fred H. Nicklason, "Early Career of Henry L. Dawes, 1816–1871," Ph.D. diss., Yale University, 1967; Loring Benson Priest, *Uncle Sam's Stepchildren: The Reformation of United States Indian Policy, 1865–1887*, 1942.

Ron Briley

DAWES SEVERALTY ACT. Introduced in February 1886 by Senator Henry L. Dawes, a Massachusetts Republican, the Indian Emancipation Act of 1887, usually called the General Allotment Act or Dawes Severalty Act, was designed to assimilate Native Americans into U.S. political and economic life. Reformers contended that reservations fostered indolence and perpetuated tribal customs which hindered assimilation. The Dawes Act provided for dissolution of Native American tribes as legal entities and the division of tribal lands among individual members. It empowered the president to allot these lands within the reservations, contingent on tribal agreements. The government retained a probationary twenty-five-year trust patent, designed to guard against the sale of the holdings to unscrupulous speculators, after which the individual would have full ownership and title to the land, as well as conferral of U.S. citizenship. The act further provided 160 acres to each head of a family, eighty acres to each adult single person, and smaller plots to others who would leave the reservation.

President Grover Cleveland, whose encouragement helped to assure passage of the measure, signed and praised the Dawes Act. Although the law showed good intentions by attempting to resolve the complex problems surrounding the status of Native American tribes, the legislation was ultimately a failure, both in its endeavor to impose a different culture on Native Americans and in the multitude of legalities generated over the years. It failed to free Native Americans from governmental dependency and opened millions of acres to white settlement. One key difference between Native Americans and African Americans in the Gilded Age was that the former possessed land that whites desired while the latter group did not. Native American degradation continued; promises of a better education and life rang hollow. The butchery at the battle of Wounded Knee in 1890 demonstrated how meaningless these intentions were. The Indian Reorganization Act of 1934 replaced the Dawes Act.

Further Reading: Charles C. Painter, *The Dawes Land in Severalty Bill and Indian Emancipation*, 1887; Leonard A. Carbon, *Indians, Bureaucrats, and Land: The Dawes Act and the Decline of Indian Farming*, 1981; Loring Benson Priest, *Uncle Sam's Stepchildren: The Reformation of United States Indian Policy, 1865–1887*, 1942.

Leonard Schlup

DAY, WILLIAM RUFUS (17 April 1849–9 July 1923), attorney, secretary of state, and Supreme Court justice. Born in Ravenna, Ohio, he was educated there and was graduated from the University of Michigan in 1870. He briefly attended law school at Michigan before establishing a successful practice in Canton, Ohio, in 1872. Active in Republican party politics, Day became a close associate of fellow Canton resident William McKinley. After the latter won the 1896 presidential election, Day was appointed assistant secretary of state. Given elderly Secretary of State John Sherman's diminishing capacities, Day became the de facto secretary. As such, he was involved in Hawaii's annexation in 1898 and in negotiations to assure French and German neutrality in the Spanish-American War. When Congress declared war, Sherman resigned, and Day was officially appointed secretary of state. He soon resigned, however, to head the U.S. delegation to the Paris peace conference. Thereafter, McKinley appointed Day to the U.S. Court of Appeals for the Sixth Circuit, and in 1903 President Theodore Roosevelt appointed him to the Supreme Court. Day served until 1922. He died at Mackinac Island, Michigan.

Further Reading: Joseph E. McLean, *William Rufus Day: Supreme Court Justice from Ohio*, 1946.

R. Volney Riser

DEBS, EUGENE VICTOR (5 November 1855–20 October 1926), labor organizer and, beginning in 1900, five-time Socialist presidential candidate. During the Gilded Age, Debs personified native protest against the ways by which industrial capitalism was blighting lives: dehumanizing the workplace; transforming the family structure; and assaulting the individual sense of self. No Luddite, Debs nevertheless insisted that technological progress must respect traditional rights. To contemporaries, he spotlighted the class struggle without appearing unpatriotic, irreligious, or undemocratic.

Born to Alsatian parents in Terre Haute, Indiana, Debs left public school at age fifteen. He took a railroad laborer's job, eventually rising to locomotive fireman, one of the era's most highly paid workingman's positions. After the Panic of 1873 he secured a clerkship in a wholesale grocery house. Debs joined the local lodge of the Brotherhood of Locomotive Firemen (BLF), which imposed crafts and personal behavior standards as strict as any demanded by management. Debs's early vision of class harmony caused him to rise rapidly within his conservative union. Over the next decade, Debs gradually came to embrace industrial unionism. Accordingly, in 1892, he resigned from the BLF and began organizing the American Railway Union (ARU), composed of nearly all who worked on a railroad. The sole limitation was a discriminatory "whites only" clause, which Debs opposed and which would later haunt ARU strike efforts. The ARU received surprisingly strong support from the start, and a victory over the Great Northern Railroad in May 1894 brought membership rolls to a hundred thousand. Meanwhile, striking workers at the Pullman Car Company near Chicago lobbied ARU members, who, despite Debs's reluctance to do so, voted to boycott all trains that carried sleepers. In July, when a union victory seemed imminent, federal troops intervened. The strike was broken, the ARU was smashed, activists were blacklisted, and Debs was imprisoned for six months in 1895 for defying a court injunction.

Debs emerged as a labor leader without an organization, alienated from old railroad brotherhoods, despising both Samuel Gompers's crafts unionism and the dogmatic Socialist Labor Party (SLP). At the same time, however, he was America's first national working-class hero, and he barnstormed the country. In 1897 he helped form the Social Democracy, which would, with dissident SLP recruits, grow into the Socialist Party in 1901. Debs's concept of socialism crossed America's class boundaries, and probably appealed to as many nonproletarians as workers. Moderate radicals such as Debs offered a reasonable middle path between the reaction and anarchism so evident during the 1890s.

During the Progressive Era, Debs twice received nine hundred thousand votes for President and was sent to the Atlanta Penitentiary for opposing American participation in World War I. He died in Elmhurst, Illinois.

Further Reading: Nick Salvatore, *Eugene V. Debs: Citizen and Socialist*, 1982; Ray Ginger, *The Bending Cross: A Biography of Eugene Victor Debs*, 1949; Scott Molloy, "Eugene Victor Debs and Radical Labor Reform," in Randall M. Miller and Paul A. Cimbala, *American Reform and Reformers*, 1996, 127–138.

James G. Ryan

DEERE, JOHN (7 February 1804–17 May 1886), blacksmith, inventor, and entrepreneur. Born in Rutland, Vermont, Deere received a common school education in Middlebury before serving a four-year apprenticeship as a blacksmith. After moving to Illinois in 1837, he began to experiment with steel plows in partnership with Leonard Andrus. In Moline, he combined the use of imported English steel and ingenuity to develop the first successful American steel plow, suitable to break the heavy, thick sod of the western prairies. He later negotiated with the newly developing American steel industry in Pittsburgh for comparable steel supply.

In 1868 Deere teamed with his son Charles and son-in-law, Stephen H. Velie, incorporating as Deere and Company. Their contribution to agriculture far exceeded the development of the plow; they manufactured farm and agricultural implements, such as cultivators and corn and cotton planters. Deere introduced a new approach to operating a manufacturing business on the prairie, building a line of items and establishing marketing centers and a network of independent retail dealers to sell the products. Deere continued to serve as company president until his death in Moline, Illinois, in 1886.

Further Reading: Rod Beemer, *Inside John Deere: A Factory History*, 1999; John J. Gerstner, *Genuine Value: The John Deere Journey*, 2000.

Ralph G. Giordano

DELANY, MARTIN ROBINSON (6 May 1812–24 January 1885), African-American nationalist and writer. Born in Charles Town, Virginia (now West Virginia), Delany moved in 1832 to Pittsburgh, Pennsylvania. Eighteen years later, he entered Harvard Medical School, where student protests forced his departure. Proud of his heritage, he worked with black self-help organizations, attacked radial prejudice in the North, condemned slavery in the South, and advocated economic self-determination for African Americans. Lured by emigrationist views, he traveled to Africa, where he considered establishing a settlement. (It did not materialize.) Delany recruited African-American troops during the Civil War, served with the Freedmen's Bureau in the post-bellum years, and became involved in Republican politics in South Carolina. He tried to convince philanthropists to purchase land and sell it to African Americans, and continued his belief in self-sufficiency. Becoming disillusioned with white Republicans, Delany joined forces with Democrats, while telling his followers to support whoever would serve their interests. He edited the *Charleston Independent* for a short time in the 1870s. Delany died in Wilberforce, Ohio.

Further Reading: Cyril E. Griffith, *The African Dream: Martin R. Delany and the Emergence of Pan-African Thought*, 1975; Dorothy Sterling, *The Making of an Afro-American: Martin R. Delany*, 1971; Victor Ullman, *Martin Delany: The Beginnings of Black Nationalism*, 1971.

Leonard Schlup

DELEON, DANIEL (14 December 1852–11 May 1914), journalist, editor, organizer, and commanding Socialist Labor Party (SLP) figure. DeLeon made his reputation in revolutionary theory. Supporters have claimed that he offered the Gilded Age's most subtle Marxist analysis of the difficulties in overcoming America's advanced capitalism, thereby foreshad-owing twentieth-century radical socialist and communist thinking. DeLeon propounded the concept of a disciplined party organization that concentrated simultaneously on political action and trade union efforts, while abhorring reformism. Critics have argued that his vision differed little from the socialism of his antecedents and adversaries; his chief legacies were authoritarianism and a determination to rule or ruin every movement in which he participated.

DeLeon's early life is unclear because at times he misrepresented his name, place of birth, ancestry, religious background, and education. Evidence suggests he was born to Sephardic Jewish parents on the island of Curacao. After he received early education at home, his widowed mother took him to Germany. He immigrated to New York City about 1874. In 1876 he was admitted to Columbia University law school on a false claim of possessing a Master of Arts degree from Leyden, and completed the LLB. degree in 1878. He practiced law in Texas, then lectured in international law at Columbia in 1883. Four years later he applied for professional status, was denied, and resigned.

In late 1890 DeLeon joined the small, weak SLP, America's only existing party of socialism. A well-educated, English-language writer of some prominence, he proved valuable to a movement of unassimilated immigrants who conducted meetings in German. His energy, ability, and forceful personality quickly drew attention. Soon he was SLP's gubernatorial candidate. By 1891 he edited its organ, *The People*, a post from which he dominated the movement until his death. Expulsions of critics became commonplace; few rivaled DeLeon at identifying his own policies as the class struggle's cardinal components.

DeLeon also was deeply involved in labor. He proved to be a militant supporter of industrial unionism and an antagonist of Samuel Gompers's crafts-oriented approach. A delegate to the Knights of Labor's leading assemblies between 1893 and 1895, DeLeon led secessionists from that group who reconstituted themselves as the Socialist Trade and Labor Alliance (STLA). In 1896, he won SLP endorsement for the STLA. In so doing, however, he energized an opposing faction that was friendly to tradition-minded unions. Rapidly, they converted a majority of the STLA and sought his removal. Failing to displace DeLeon in July 1899, they withdrew and created a new organization that ultimately became the Socialist Party of America. The SLP never recovered its lost members and prestige, though it continued throughout the twentieth century as a museum piece of American Marxism. DeLeon died in New York City.

Further Reading: L. Glen Seretan, *Daniel DeLeon: The Odyssey of an American Marxist*, 1979; Carl Reeve, *The Life and Times of Daniel DeLeon*, 1972.

James G. Ryan

DE LOME LETTER. In 1898, as tensions between the United States and Spain increased because of Spanish colonialism in Cuba, Enrique Dupuy de Lome served as Spanish ambassador to the United States. His primary mission was to seek a peaceful way of settling the differences between the two countries, and the McKinley administration's desire to avoid war provided him with an opportunity to accomplish this goal. In early February, however, a letter De Lome had written to a friend in Havana was stolen by a Cuban agent and delivered to the newspaper publisher William Randolph Hearst. The missive, which criticized McKinley as weak and at the mercy of party hacks, was printed in Hearst's *New York Journal* on 9 February. It constituted a major coup in Hearst's "yellow journalism" newspaper war against Joseph Pulitzer.

Although De Lome immediately resigned to spare his government further embarrassment, his incautious remarks increased U.S. distrust of Spanish motives just one week before the battleship *Maine* exploded in Havana harbor.

Further Reading: Lewis L. Gould, *The Presidency of William McKinley*, 1980; Julius W. Pratt, *Expansionists of 1898*, 1936; John Tebbel, *America's Great Patriotic War with Spain*, 1996.

Stephen Svonavec

DEMOCRATIC PARTY. The Democrats emerged from the Civil War battered, but still a major political force. Despite being branded traitors during the war, they had fiercely resisted Republican commitment to an expansive national government, national banks, a protective tariff, and, even more, the GOP's determination to emancipate African Americans and raise them to equal citizenship. In the Gilded Age, under leadership of Samuel J. Tilden, Thomas Bayard, and Grover Cleveland, Democrats persisted in their commitment to the traditional Jacksonian ideology of limited government power and equal rights for white males of the producing classes—farmers, artisans, and small shopkeepers—to which they added strong condemnation of the political corruption associated with the Grant era. Their stance brought them much support in the South, among eastern capitalists and bankers hostile to Republican economic policies, and in areas in the lower Middle West populated by people born in the South. It appealed to some good government groups, as well as to the Irish and other white minority ethnic groups in northern cities, repelled by the Republican Party's persistent hostility to Catholics and immigrants. Still, the Gilded Age was an era of extreme frustration for the Democrats, a time when they rarely won national power, despite some of the closest elections in American history. The Republicans' tactic of waving of the "bloody shirt" against Democratic wartime behavior, and electoral college arithmetic told against them. The Democrats lost six of eight presidential elections between 1868 and 1896.

The party had other problems as well. Growing internal strains over policy direction appeared. Some western farm groups demanded support for looser money: greenbacks and, later, the monetization of silver, to raise agricultural prices during a long deflationary era. This appalled eastern capitalists, who feared the impact of cheap money on normal economic activity. Meanwhile, urban ethnic groups, growing in numbers and becoming well organized through such institutions as New York City's Tammany Hall, pressed for increased recognition and for consideration of government-funded social welfare policies helpful to the urban poor. Democratic national conventions became battlegrounds as these groups fought for control, which was usually maintained by eastern and southern blocs against the restive soft money forces and urban political machines.

The economic depression of 1873 provided the Democrats with an opportunity to challenge Republican policies that had laid the country low. In the congressional elections of 1874, the party won the House of Representatives for the first time since before the war. Yet its rise was very brief, for its fortunes ebbed once more. Another opportunity appeared in the early 1890s when Grover Cleveland won the presidency with majorities indicating a significant voter surge to the Democrats and, because of increased numbers of urban voters, perhaps the end of Republican dominance.

Another severe depression hit in 1893, however. The Cleveland administration, true to its heritage, refused to use national authority to ameliorate the condition of unemployed workers and debt-ridden farmers, but did use it to break labor strikes, fearing the latter's dislocating impact on the economy. The result was a voter revulsion against the Democrats in 1894, producing one of history's largest congressional losses for a party in a single election. In 1896, rural Democrats, much influenced by the Populist revolt against conventional economic policies, successfully challenged the weakened eastern wing, nominating the firebrand William Jennings Bryan on a platform calling for unlimited silver monetization and other policies to aid distressed farmers. Bryan conducted an intense, rural-oriented campaign that frightened many urban Democrats and drove them to the Republicans, who effectively claimed themselves friendly to capital and labor alike. The debacle ended an era, for the electoral dynamics of 1896 persisted thereafter, guaranteeing Republican majorities for a generation.

Further Reading: J. Rogers Hollingsworth, *The Whirlagig of Politics: The Democracy of Cleveland and Bryan*, 1963; Paul Kleppner, *The Third Electoral System, 1853–1892: Parties, Voters and Political Cultures*, 1979; R. Hal Williams, " 'Dry Bones and Dead Language': The Democratic Party," in H. Wayne Morgan, ed., *The Gilded Age*, 1970.

Joel H. Silbey

DEMPSEY, JACK (15 December 1862–2 November 1895), professional boxer. Born John Kelly and nicknamed "Nonpareil," he left his native County Kildare, Ireland, for the United States during in his youth. He is often confused with the great heavyweight champion of the 1920s who bore the same name. The latter Jack Dempsey, born William Dempsey, actually adopted the first name of the great early fighter at the beginning of his career to hide his career from his family. The earlier Dempsey began boxing at age twenty and was the first widely recognized world middleweight champion. He won the title in an epic bout with the Canadian George Fulljames in 1884, just two years into his career. Some of his most memorable battles were against George LaBlanche, Billy McCarthy, and Bob Fitzsimmons. In 1891 the latter dethroned Dempsey, who never regained the world title. He finished his career with forty-eight wins, three losses, seven draws, and three no contests. Dempsey died in Portland, Oregon, and was elected to the Boxing Hall of Fame in 1954.

Further Reading: Sam Andre and Nat Fleischer, *A Pictorial History of Boxing*, 1983.

Steve Bullock

DEPEW, CHAUNCEY MITCHELL (23 April 1834–5 April 1928), attorney, railroad president, and U.S. senator. Born in Peekskill, New York, Depew was graduated from Yale College in 1856, was admitted to the bar two years later, and held a variety of local political offices during the 1860s and 1870s. In 1885 he was appointed president of the New York Central & Hudson River Railroad Company, in which capacity he served until 1898. Unsuccessful in his bid to obtain the Republican presidential nomination in 1888, Depew was a U.S. senator from New York from 1899 to 1911. For four congresses he chaired the Committee on Revision of the Laws of the United States. In 1896 he nominated former Vice President Levi P. Morton for president at the Republican National Convention. Depew was defeated in his bid for reelection in 1910. A noted raconteur, speaker, and director of many corporations, he resumed his legal and business pursuits in New York City, where he died.

Further Reading: Chauncey M. Depew, *My Memories of Eighty Years*, 1922; Arthur F. Murray, "The Political Personality of Chauncey Mitchell Depew," Ph.D. diss., Fordham University, 1959; *New York Times*, 6 April 1928.

Leonard Schlup

DESERT LAND ACT OF 1877. Like nearly all laws designed to make ownership of public land easier, the Desert Land Act of 1877 (19 Stat. 377) began with lofty ambitions but soon degenerated into another invitation to commit fraud on the government. By the late 1870s, settlers were rushing onto the Great Plains and into the trans-Rockies West. It was obvious that, at least for the time being, some irrigation would be required. To encourage settlement of "desert lands," Congress provided that anyone could gain title to a section (640 acres) of public land by "conducting water upon the same."

Abuses quickly reached legendary levels. Ditches a few inches long soon scratched the soil; canals linked nothing to nowhere. Cattle companies rounded up field hands to file claims that were soon transferred to an "improvement" company their employer owned. Cattle barons registered deeds, fenced the land, and enjoyed free grazing rights until they were evicted a decade later. The act did, however, encourage formation of some private irrigation outfits in the West. It was repealed in 1891.

Further Reading: Donald J. Pisani, *To Reclaim a Divided West: Water, Law and Public Policy, 1848–1902,* 1992; John T. Ganoe, "The Desert Land Act in Operation, 1877–1891," *Agricultural History* 11 (1937): 142–157.

Sam S. Kepfield

DEWEY, JOHN (20 October 1859–1 June 1952), educator, philosopher, and social activist. Born in Burlington, Vermont, Dewey attended public school, was graduated from the University of Vermont in 1879, and received a doctorate from Johns Hopkins in 1884. For ten years he taught at the University of Michigan. In the fall of 1894 he accepted an appointment as professor and chairman of the department of philosophy, psychology, and pedagogy at the University of Chicago. While at Chicago, he established the famous Laboratory School promoting his theories on "child-centered" learning. As leader of the progressive education movement in America, Dewey circulated his ideas in *The School and Society* (1899) and *The Child and the Curriculum* (1902).

During the twentieth century Dewey became regarded as the nation's preeminent philosopher, publishing *Democracy and Education*

(1916), *Reconstruction in Philosophy* (1920), *Human Nature and Conduct* (1922), and *Individualism: Old and New* (1930). After 1918 Dewey was involved in the Outlawry of War Crusade and headed the commission of inquiry in Mexico City involving the Moscow show trials and Leon Trotsky. Dewey was the first president of the American Association of University Professors and lectured in Japan, China, Turkey, Mexico, the Soviet Union, and South Africa. He died in New York City.

Further Reading: George Dykhuizen, *The Life and Mind of John Dewey,* 1973; Robert Westbrook, *John Dewey and American Democracy,* 1991; Neil Coughlin, *Young John Dewey,* 1975.

Charles F. Howlett

DEWEY, MELVIL (10 December 1851–26 December 1931), librarian, educator, and private resort developer. Dewey was born in Adams Center, New York. Early in life he committed himself to educational reform through librarianship. While a student at Amherst College, he worked on his decimal classification system, the first edition of which he published in 1876. The "Dewey decimal classification system" soon became the standard method for organizing books in libraries. Also, in 1876, Dewey helped organize the American Library Association (ALA) and began serving as first editor of *Library Journal.* In 1881 he started the Library Bureau. Two years later became chief librarian at Columbia College in New York City, where, in 1887, he opened the world's first school of library science. In 1889 he moved his school to Albany, where he accepted a joint appointment as state librarian and secretary to the State University of New York's Board of Regents. In this capacity he created a statewide higher education lobby and built an educational extension system, enrolling New York's public libraries as extension sites. He resigned as secretary in 1899.

Dewey served as ALA president at its very successful World's Columbian Exposition conference (1893), at which the association exhibited a model library whose contents were later published as a selection guide for all American public libraries. In 1894 he and his wife opened the Lake Placid Club, in the Adirondack Mountains of New York. In 1905 several prominent Jewish New Yorkers forced his resignation as state librarian because the club refused them membership. About the same time, a few ALA women forced him out of association activities for sexually harassing females at previous conferences. Dewey spent the remaining years improving the Lake Placid Club, and in 1926 opened a branch of it in southern Florida.

Further Reading: Wayne A. Wiegand, *Irrepressible Reformer: A Biography of Melvil Dewey*, 1996.

Wayne A. Wiegand

DICK, CHARLES WILLIAM FREDERICK

(3 November 1858–13 March 1945), congressman and U.S. senator. Born in Akron, Ohio, Dick attended local schools, then entered the grain and commission business with Lucius C. Miles. From 1886 to 1894, he was Summit County auditor. The following year he opened a law practice in Akron, and later became the senior member of the firm of Dick, Doyle, and Bryan. One of Mark Hanna's political lieutenants in promoting the presidential candidacy of William McKinley in 1896, Dick was secretary of the Chicago headquarters of the Republican National Committee that year. During the Spanish-American War, he went to Cuba, from which he sent President McKinley letters detailing the military, political, economic, geographic, and social conditions of Cuba and the war. Dick served in the U.S. House of Representatives from 1898 to 1904, chairing the Committee on Militia in two Congresses, and in the U.S. Senate from 1904 to 1911, where he once again followed Republican doctrines on national and international issues. He died in Akron.

Further Reading: Akron *Beacon Journal*, 14 March 1945.

Leonard Schlup

DICKINSON, DONALD MCDONALD (17

January 1846–15 October 1917), lawyer and postmaster general. Born in Port Ontario, New York, Dickinson was graduated from the University of Michigan law school in 1867, practiced in Detroit, and became one of the leading attorneys of the Midwest. He supported Horace Greeley for president in 1872, Samuel J. Tilden in 1876, and Grover Cleveland in 1884, 1888,

and 1892. Dickinson, a member of the Democratic National Committee and close friend to Cleveland, accepted the president's offer of the postmaster generalship in 1888, and served until the Democrats left office the following year. Dickinson emerged as one of Cleveland's managers for the presidency in 1892, and refused cabinet portfolios in order to remain in Michigan. He adamantly opposed free coinage of silver and William Jennings Bryan, while endorsing Democratic efforts to reduce tariff duties. In 1896, Dickinson supported the presidential candidacy of Senator John M. Palmer of Illinois on a sound money platform, favored the reelection of President William McKinley in 1900, and offered his encouragement to Theodore Roosevelt's Progressive "Bull Moose" campaign in 1912. After completing some diplomatic assignments and living in retirement, Dickinson died in Trenton, Michigan.

Further Reading: *Detroit News*, 17 October 1917; *New York Times*, 16 October 1917; Robert Bolt, "Donald M. Dickinson and the Second Election of Grover Cleveland," *Michigan History* 49 (1965): 28–39.

Leonard Schlup

DICKINSON, EMILY (10 December 1830–15 May 1886), poet. Born Emily Elizabeth Dickinson, in Amherst, Massachusetts, the daughter of an attorney, Dickinson studied at Amherst Academy and Mount Holyoke Female Seminary. Maintaining close family bonds and cherishing friendships with chosen people, Dickinson gradually came to prefer solitude to society, shrinking from public exposure while valuing and carefully guarding her privacy. She wrote poems in the kitchen pantry and her second-story bedroom of the family "Homestead." Dickinson feared the role of a literary celebrity, and protected herself by accepting the standards of reserve imposed on women by Gilded Age society. Nevertheless, she cultivated connections with authors including Thomas Wentworth Higginson and Helen Hunt Jackson. Despite her reclusive reputation, Dickinson wrote more than a thousand letters, engaging in lively epistolary conversations with close to one hundred correspondents. Her poetry, containing intellectual and emotional thought, was tightly condensed, with short stanzas. Dickinson expressed herself freely in her work, believing her poems would forever remain private or be destroyed upon her death. After her death in Amherst, her beautifully written creations survived. Lavinia Dickinson, while settling her sister's estate, found a box of manuscripts and resolved to display Emily's genius to the world. With the editorial assistance of Mabel Loomis Todd, published collections of Dickinson's poetry appeared in 1890 and 1891. Other additions came later. A product of New England Protestant culture, the anxieties of the Civil War, and the rapid change that occurred in Gilded Age America, Dickinson ranks with Walt Whitman as a preeminent nineteenth-century American poet.

Further Reading: Richard B. Sewall, *The Life of Emily Dickinson*, 2 vols., 1974; Willis J. Buckingham, *Emily Dickinson's Reception in the 1890s: A Documentary History*, 1989; Thomas H. Johnson, ed., *The Complete Poems of Emily Dickinson*, 1960.

Leonard Schlup

DIGGS, ANNIE LEPORTE (22 February 1848–7 September 1916), Populist orator and reformer. Born Ann Maria Thomas LePorte in London, Ontario, Canada, she moved with her family to New Jersey in 1855. After education at home and in public and private schools, she took a job as a newspaper reporter. She moved to Lawrence, Kansas, in 1873 to work in a music store.

Early in her reform career, Diggs advocated temperance and women's suffrage. She was also active in the Kansas Liberal Union, an association of spiritualists, materialists, Universalists, Unitarians, Free Religionists, Socialists, and agnostics. She returned to journalism as a freelance writer, reporting from stops on her speaking tours. In 1890 she became associate editor of the *Topeka* [Kansas] *Advocate*, which she and its editor, Dr. Stephen McLallin, made into the state's leading agrarian reform journal and the newspaper of the Farmers' Alliance movement.

Although eclipsed in history books by Kansas's other female Populist orator, Mary Elizabeth ("Mary Yellin") Lease, Diggs was probably the People's Party most influential woman member. Less crowd-pleasing than Lease, she was much more cerebral. In December 1890 she attended the Ocala, Florida, meeting of the Farmers' Alliance, the first step in organizing a farmer-oriented third party. She also attended the major organizational meetings in Cincinnati (May 1891), St. Louis (February 1892), and Omaha (July 1892).

Throughout the Populist era Diggs remained important in party councils, serving as a member of the Populist National Committee. She was also president of the Kansas Equal Suffrage Association and a delegate to Carrie Chapman Catt's "Organizational Committee" in 1895. Her support of fusion with the Democrats in 1896 caused more-independent minded Populists to denounce her as a "party boss." In fact she was a radical, an "opportunist Socialist," advancing the idea that industries and other enterprises affecting the public should be owned and operated by the public. The only public office she held was Kansas state librarian.

Following Populism's demise, Diggs continued to work as a journalist in Europe and the United States. In 1906 she returned to Kansas to continue her writing, and several years later moved to Detroit, Michigan, to join her son. She died there of muscular dystrophy.

Further Reading: O. Gene Clanton, *Kansas Populism: Ideas and Men*, 1969; Florence Finch Kelly, *Flowering Stream: The Story of Fifty-six Years in American Newspaper Life*, 1939; Wilda M. Smith, "A Half Century of Struggle, Gaining Woman Suffrage in Kansas," *Kansas History* 4 (1981): 74–95.

Robert S. La Forte

DILLINGHAM, WILLIAM PAUL (12 December 1843–12 July 1923), lawyer, governor, U.S. senator. Born in Waterbury, Vermont, Dillingham attended local schools, Newberry Seminary, and Kimball Union Academy. He read law in the Wisconsin office of his brother-in-law, and returned to Vermont to finish his legal studies with his father, then governor (1865–1867). Dillingham was appointed secretary of civil and military affairs in 1866. A Republican, he was elected state's attorney of Washington County, Vermont, in 1872, and served four terms in the legislature (1876–1884). In 1888 he was elected governor of Vermont by the largest plurality up to that time. Twelve years later he won a U.S. Senate seat, filling an unexpired term. He was reelected until his death in Montpelier, Vermont.

Dillingham's career is most notable for his service on the Senate Committee on Immigration, which he chaired from 1903 to 1911. He also headed the U.S. Immigration Commission from 1909 to 1911. Dillingham advocated an openly racist quota system of immigration restriction, designed to reduce the influx of southern and eastern European whites and virtually eliminate people of color. It was enacted as emergency legislation in 1921, made permanent in 1924, and not repealed until 1965.

Further Reading: Henry Steele Wardner, *William Paul Dillingham: An Appreciation*, 1923; John M. Lund, "Boundaries of Restriction: Immigration and Vermont Senator William Paul Dillingham," M.A. thesis, University of Vermont, 1994.

Michael J. Anderson

DINGLEY, NELSON, JR. (15 February 1832–13 January 1899), editor, governor, congressman. Born in Durham, Maine, Dingley studied at Waterville (now Colby) College, was graduated from Dartmouth in 1855, and was admitted to the bar in 1856. That year he became part owner and editor of the *Lewiston Evening Journal* and active in the newly formed Republican Party. An ally of James G. Blaine, Dingley sat in the state legislature from 1861 to 1873, and was speaker for two terms. Elected governor in 1873 and 1875, he extended state railroad regulation. Dingley won an open seat in the U.S. House of Representatives in 1881. There, as a member of the House Ways and Means Committee, he strongly supported the Republican protective tariff. In 1894 he opposed Democratic efforts to reduce duties and declined an offer from President William McKinley to become secretary of the Treasury. Assuming chairmanship of Ways and Means, he spearheaded passage of the 1897 bill that came to be known as the Dingley Tariff. He also played a major role in passage of measures to finance the 1898 war with Spain, and sat on the joint commission named to resolve boundary disputes with Canada.

Further Reading: Donald R. Kennon and Rebecca M. Rogers, *The Committee on Ways and Means: A Bicentennial History, 1789–1989* (1989); Edward Nelson Dingley, *The Life and Times of Nelson Dingley, Jr.* (1902); *Ameri-*

can National Biography, vol. 6 (1999), 615–616; *New York Times* 14 January 1899.

Douglas Steeples

DINGLEY TARIFF OF 1897. During the Gilded Age farmers and industrialists disagreed over the size of import duties. Farmers sought a low tariffs, to reduce the price of manufactured goods they purchased and out of fear that high rates would provoke foreign retaliation which might prevent them from selling staple crops overseas. Industrialists, by contrast, favored a high tariff as protection from import competition and, supposedly, to create jobs.

The Republican Party filled its ranks with industrialists and workers, and thus promoted a high tariff. The Panic of 1893 and the ensuing depression encouraged the Republican argument that Congress should raise the tariff to spark industrial growth and make high wages possible. The 1896 election brought to the Oval Office William McKinley, who in 1890 had guided the McKinley Tariff through Congress. That law had set duties at record highs, but in 1897 McKinley called Congress into special session to boost them yet again. A bill introduced by Nelson Dingley, a Maine congressman, accomplished that goal by setting the average duty on imports at 52 percent of their value.

Further Reading: H. Wayne Morgan, *William McKinley and His America*, 1963; Tom E. Terrill, *The Tariff, Politics, and American Foreign Policy, 1874–1901*, 1973; Lewis L. Gould, "Diplomats in the Lobby: Franco-American Relations and the Dingley Tariff of 1897," *The Historian* 39 (1977): 659–680.

Christopher Cumo

DODGE, GRACE HOADLEY (21 May 1856–27 December 1914), educator and philanthropist. Born in New York City, Dodge received her education primarily at home. Christian dedication moved her to enter a life of service. In 1881, she brought together a group of factory girls for weekly discussion and fellowship. In 1885, she helped in forming an association of working girls' societies in New York City that later became national. Dodge also assisted in founding the Kitchen Garden Association at her Madison Avenue home, which she reorganized into the Industrial Education Association. From 1886 to 1889, she served on the city board of education, and from 1889 until 1911 was treasurer of the newly created Teachers College at Columbia University. Her work in various organizations and appointments to several boards enabled Dodge to become a social welfare worker who sought especially to ease the lives of young women. She died in New York City, bequeathing over a million dollars to charitable causes, including the Young Women's Christian Association, of which she was a leader.

Further Reading: Abbie Graham, *Grace H. Dodge: Merchant of Dreams*, 1926; Marion O. Robinson, *Eight Women of the YWCA*, 1966; *New York Times*, 28 December 1914.

Leonard Schlup

DODGE, GRENVILLE MELLEN (12 April 1831–3 January 1916), U.S. Army officer and congressman. Dodge was born in Danvers, Massachusetts, and received a civil engineering degree from Norwich University in 1848. Four years later, he led a Mississippi & Missouri Railroad survey team across Iowa. During the Civil War, he commanded the Union Army's departments of Missouri and Kansas, fighting guerrilla bands. After the war, Dodge was instrumental in the constructing the Union Pacific Railroad's transcontinental line. He served briefly as a congressman from Iowa (1866–1868). In 1873 he began a long and fruitful collaboration with the financier Jay Gould, overseeing the survey work for thousands of miles of railroad line in the West. When the Spanish-American War ended, President William McKinley appointed Dodge, a loyal and influential Republican Party member, to lead a commission investigating mismanagement charges. Dodge defended his longtime friend, Secretary of War Russell Alger, against critics who accused him of incompetence and corruption. Despite charges that the Dodge Commission was merely a partisan cover-up, the body looked into all aspects of the army's and War Department's actions, and acquitted both entities. Subsequently Dodge worked as a railroad lobbyist in Washington. He died in Council Bluffs, Iowa.

Further Reading: Stanley P. Hirshson, *Grenville M. Dodge: Soldier, Politician, Railroad Pioneer*, 1967.

T. R. Brereton

DODGE, HORACE ELGIN (17 May 1868–10 December 1920), and **DODGE, JOHN FRANCIS** (25 October 1864–14 January 20), bicycle and automobile manufacturers. Born in Niles, Michigan, the Dodge brothers built bicycles in their father's machine shop. Initially an upper-class amusement, the bicycle soon spread as an inexpensive means of travel. In 1894 more than 250,000 were manufactured in the United States; the number increased the following year to 400,000. Use of bicycles was almost universal in Detroit, Michigan, where 80 percent of the city's population raced around town on them. Outnumbered pedestrians feared crossing the streets, and ministers worried about a possible decline in church attendance. One of the fastest and most daredevil racing bicyclists in the country was the Ohioan Barney Oldfield, who in 1902 drove the speed car called "999" on a racetrack in Grosse Pointe, Michigan, against the champion, Alexander Winton of Cleveland, Ohio.

In 1901 the Dodges opened a machine shop in Detroit, to make stove and automobile parts. Known for their toughness and ruggedness, the brothers complemented one another. John was the astute businessman of the partnership, and Horace served as the mechanical genius. An oven that could bake enamel onto steel automobile bodies was among his manufacturing innovations. In 1910, the Dodge Brothers Company established a large automobile parts plant in Hamtramck, Michigan, where their chief customers were Olds Motor Works and the Ford Motor Company. In 1914 the brothers began making automobiles, producing one of the first all-steel cars in America. The first Dodge automobile rolled off the assembly line on 14 November 1914. Chrysler Corporation, founded by Walter P. Chrysler, purchased the Dodge concern in 1928, eight years after the deaths of the brothers.

Further Reading: Jean Maddern Pitrone, *The Dodges: The Auto Family Fortune and Misfortune*, 1981; Caroline Latham and David Agresta, *Dodge Dynasty: The Car and the Family That Rocked Detroit*, 1989.

Leonard Schlup

DOLE, SANFORD BALLARD (23 April 1844–9 June 1926), president of the Hawaiian

Republic and governor of Hawaii. Dole was born at Punahou, Hawaii, to missionaries from New England. He graduated from Williams College in 1868 and joined the Massachusetts bar. He thereupon returned to Hawaii and opened a law office in Honolulu. Advocating closer ties to the United States, Dole won election to the legislature in 1884 and 1886. The next year, he joined the Committee of Thirteen, which forced King Kalakaua to sign the "Bayonet Constitution" that assured continued domination by foreigners and planter elites. Kalakaua appointed Dole to the Hawaiian Supreme Court in 1888. Upon Kalakaua's death, his sister assumed the throne. Determined to reassert native authority, Queen Liliuokalani attempted to promulgate a new constitution in 1893. In response, a planter cabal staged a coup d'état, assisted by U.S. minister John L. Stevens. They declared a provisional government, and appointed Dole president and foreign minister. After initial attempts to secure U.S. annexation failed, the Republic of Hawaii was created on 4 July 1894 and Dole became its only president. Following annexation by the United States, in 1898, President William McKinley appointed him governor; in 1903 President Theodore Roosevelt named Dole federal district judge for Hawaii. Dole died in Honolulu.

Further Reading: Ethel Damon, *Sanford Ballard Dole and His Hawaii*, 1957.

R. Volney Riser

DONNELLY, IGNATIUS (3 November 1831–1 January 1901), agriculturalist and reformer. Donnelly was born in Philadelphia, Pennsylvania, where he attended public schools and was admitted to the bar. After failing as a land speculator, he farmed in Nininger, Minnesota, and between 1863 and 1869 served in Congress, where, as a Republican, he sought land grants for railroads. In 1868, local Republican leaders refused to nominate him for a fourth term, and Donnelly joined the Grange and the Greenback Labor movement. Between 1874 and 1879 as editor of the *Anti-Monopolist*, a newspaper, and as a Minnesota state senator, he abandoned his support of railroads and instead advocated state regulation of them. Don-

nelly repudiated his earlier Republicanism so completely that he now warned of a chasm between rich and poor that was undermining American society.

In 1878 Donnelly again found himself out of office after losing his reelection bid. He returned to journalism, writing essays for the *North American Review* and several books (including the fantasy *Caesar's Column*), whose royalties brought him financial security. Prosperity, however, did not dull Donnelly's desire for reform, and in 1887 he reentered the state legislature, this time a member of the Farmers' Alliance. He helped found the People's Party in 1891, and the next year, wrote the Omaha Platform's stark and famous preamble, which divided the United States into two classes: the haves and the have-nots. In 1896 he opposed fusion with the Democrats, and in 1900 he ran for vice president on the party's independent ticket. The loss returned Donnelly to Nininger, where he edited a newspaper, the *Representative*. He died in Nininger.

Further Reading: Martin Ridge, *Ignatius Donnelly: The Portrait of a Politician*, 1962; John D. Hicks, "The Political Career of Ignatius Donnelly," *Mississippi Valley Historical Review* 8 (1921): 80–132.

Christopher Cumo

DOSTER, FRANK (1 January 1847–25 February 1933), Populist leader and Kansas Supreme Court chief justice. Doster was born in Morgan County, Virginia (now West Virginia), and attended the University of Indiana, Illinois College, and the Benton Law Institute, where he received a degree. In 1871 he set up a practice in Marion Center, Kansas. He won a term in the state legislature in 1872, but lost his bid for reelection in 1874. Originally a Republican, Doster joined the Greenback Party, running as its congressional nominee and for state attorney general. After toning down his views, he was appointed to a judgeship in 1887, and elected later that year to serve a four-year term as judge.

A brilliant iconoclast, Doster promoted the socialistic ideals of John Ruskin, Ralph Waldo Emerson, John Stuart Mill, and Karl Marx, and vigorously attacked both Democrats and Republicans. He became active in the Farmers'

Alliance and Citizens' Alliance of the Populist movement. His efforts culminated in a successful campaign for chief justice of the Kansas Supreme Court in 1897. Though conservative journalists lambasted him, he proved to be more temperate and evenhanded in his work there. In 1902, after losing a reelection bid against a Republican/Democratic coalition candidate, he became an assistant attorney for the Missouri Pacific Railroad. He continued as an activist, supporting women's suffrage and other Populist causes. Doster died of a stroke in Topeka, Kansas, while lobbying for a bill to protect tenants against landlord abuses.

Further Reading: O. Gene Clanton, *Kansas Populism: Ideas and Men,* 1969.

Thomas C. Sutton

DOUBLEDAY, FRANK NELSON (8 January 1862–30 January 1934), publisher. Born in Brooklyn, New York, Doubleday worked twenty years for Charles Scribner's Sons before launching his own publishing house. With Samuel Sidney McClure, he founded the firm of Doubleday & McClure in 1897. Two years later, he took Walter Hines Page and others as partners, reorganizing the firm as Doubleday, Page & Company in 1900. Doubleday remained president until 1927. In 1900 Hines and Page started a monthly magazine, *World's Work,* concerned primarily with political, educational, industrial, and agricultural conditions, especially in southern states. Hines served as its editor until 1913. Doubleday died in Coconut Grove, Florida.

Further Reading: *New York Times,* 31 January 1934; *New York Herald Tribune,* 31 January 1934.

Leonard Schlup

DOUGLASS, FREDERICK (February 1818–20 February 1895), civil rights activist. Born in Talbot County, Maryland, Douglass was the most famous African-American male before and after the Civil War. His campaign work for the Republican Party was rewarded by federal appointments as marshal of the District of Columbia (1877–1881) and recorder of deeds (1881–1886). He also served as assistant secretary on the Santo Domingo Commission in 1871 and, briefly, as president of the ill-fated

Freedman's Bank. Douglass had the courage to order the bank closed once he understood the depth of its mismanagement. Clashes with Radical Republicans during the early Reconstruction years measure Douglass's dedication to black Americans, whose aims and concerns were not held paramount by most politicians. In 1869, he lost ground with women's rights supporters who resented his determination to make black male suffrage a priority. He also was criticized for expressing doubt about the "Exoduster" movement that called on freed persons to homestead in Kansas. In 1872, when nominated as the running mate of presidential candidate Victoria Woodhull, Douglass ignored the call.

In great demand as an elder statesman for Americans of African descent and politically active into his seventies, Douglass denounced the Supreme Court decision that voided the Civil Rights Act of 1875. His proposals for land purchase schemes, labor congresses, and industrial collectives did not reach fruition. Douglass also encountered opposition to his second marriage (to Helen Pitts, who was white). In 1889, however, he was named minister to Haiti, a prestigious diplomatic post. Given a rapturous welcome by Haitians who took pride in their African heritage, Douglass served for two years. In 1893, he was Haitian commissioner at the World's Columbian Exposition even though he recognized the ways in which racist decisions spoiled the fair's nationalistic claims. "The Reason Why the Colored Man Is Not Represented in the World's Columbian Exposition" (1893), an exposé written with Ida B. Wells, was Douglass's last important statement. He died at home in Washington, D.C., after giving a well-received address to a women's rights group.

Further Reading: Philip Foner, *The Life and Writings of Frederick Douglass,* 1950, N. I. Huggins, *Slave and Citizen: The Life of Frederick Douglass,* 1980; William S. McFeely, *Frederick Douglass,* 1991.

Barbara Ryan

DOW, HERBERT HENRY (26 February 1866–15 October 1930), chemist and industrialist. Born in Belleville, Ontario, Canada, Dow spent his early life in Connecticut and Ohio. In

1888, he graduated from the Case School of Applied Science in Cleveland. The following year he relocated to Michigan, where he formed the Midland Chemical Company. By 1894, Dow had developed a commercially successful electrochemical process. That year he established the Dow Process Company, which was incorporated three years later as Dow Chemical. Among other products, the company produced chlorine bleach, sulfur chloride, and chloroform. It flourished in the twentieth century. Dow, a believer in diversification, was a successful businessman in the late nineteenth century and the early twentieth century. He died in Rochester, Minnesota.

Further Reading: Murray Campbell and Harrison Hatton, *Herbert H. Dow: Pioneer in Creative Chemistry*, 1951; Don Whitehead, *The Dow Story: The History of the Dow Chemical Company*, 1968; Herbert H. Dow Papers, Post Street Archives, Midland, Michigan.

Leonard Schlup

DOW, NEAL (20 March 1804–2 October 1897), prohibition agitator. Dow was born in Portland, Maine, and was educated in private and public schools in Maine and Massachusetts. Throughout his adult life he advocated total abstinence. In the 1850s, he led the movement away from moral suasion and toward legal restriction. Dow stitched together a political alliance that enacted the nation's first statewide prohibition law in 1851. Twelve others were quickly passed, partly because Dow traveled widely. The sectional crisis and the Civil War reduced temperence enthusiasm, derailing the movement and Dow's career. From the late 1850s through the 1870s, prohibition laws (including Maine's) were repealed. During the war, Dow rose to brigadier general in the Union Army. When peace returned, he accepted the Republican Party's policy of addressing liquor problems through milder means. Thus, Dow played no part in the birth of the Prohibition Party in 1869 nor in submission of the first national prohibition amendment resolution in 1876. As the revived movement grew, however, Dow returned to his speaking role. He ran for president on the Prohibition Party ticket in 1880. Though the campaign failed miserably,

Dow's involvement made him the cause's elder statesman. He died in Portland.

Further Reading: Frank L. Byrne, *Prophet of Prohibition: Neal Dow and His Crusade*, 1961; Thomas R. Pegram, *Battling Demon Rum: The Struggle for a Dry America, 1800–1933*, 1998; Neal Dow, *The Reminiscences of Neal Dow: Recollections of Eighty Years*, 1898.

Richard F. Hamm

DRAPER, HENRY (7 March 1837–20 November 1882), astronomer and professor. A pioneer in astronomical photography who took the first successful photograph of the spectrum of a star (Vega) in 1872, and eight years later introduced the photography of nebulae, Draper, the son of Professor John William Draper, was born in Prince Edward County, Virginia. He graduated from the University of the City of New York with a medical degree in 1858, and held professorships of natural science, physiology, and analytical chemistry at his alma mater. Beginning with an observatory on his father's New York estate and continuing from his home laboratory in New York City, Draper studied astronomy and achieved outstanding success, especially attracting national attention for his work in stellar spectroscopy. In 1874 he consolidated the photographic endeavors of the federal government's mission to study the transit of Venus. Four years later, Draper coordinated an expedition of astronomers to observe the solar eclipse in Wyoming. Congress awarded him a gold medal for his numerous contributions to science.

Further Reading: Howard Plotkin, "Henry Draper: A Scientific Biography," Ph.D. diss., Johns Hopkins University, 1972; Henry Plotkin, "Henry Draper, the Discovery of Oxygen in the Sun, and the Dilemma of Interpreting the Solar Spectrum," *Journal for the History of Astronomy* 8 (1977):44–51.

Leonard Schlup

DRAPER, LYMAN COPELAND (4 September 1815–26 August 1891), historian and educator. Draper was born in western New York State and attended Granville College and the Hudson River Seminary, which he left in 1837. Working at a variety of jobs and traveling extensively, he spent a large amount of time collecting information and interviewing people. By 1852, he had moved to Madison, Wisconsin, where he hoped to be named state librarian. The position was not available, however, and he became involved in establishing the State Historical Society of Wisconsin. In 1854 he was elected its corresponding secretary and he began to build the society's collection from a meager fifty volumes to over 120,000 by the time he retired in 1886. Elected superintendent of public instruction in 1857, he conducted an extensive study of libraries and schools in the state. Draper made numerous attempts to improve both, but the Civil War shelved his plans. He was happiest when building his extensive manuscript collections of personal histories and interviews. He never published anything but left materials for others. He died in Madison, Wisconsin.

Further Reading: Charles William Conaway, "Lyman Copeland Draper: Father of American Oral History," *Journal of Library History* 1 (1966): 234–241.

Mark E. Ellis

DREXEL, ANTHONY JOSEPH (13 September 1826–30 June 1893), banker and philanthropist. Born and educated in Philadelphia, Pennsylvania, Drexel inherited his father's investment business in 1863. Improvements in national banking and the popularity of railroad securities helped enlarge Drexel's operations in the postbellum period. He maintained business associations with Andrew Carnegie and in 1871 merged with J. P. Morgan, establishing the firm of Drexel, Morgan, and Company, with headquarters on Wall Street in New York City. Morgan and Drexel achieved prominence in American finance in the 1870s and 1880s. Drexel donated huge sums to Philadelphia hospitals, museums, churches, and other charitable organizations. His gift of approximately $3 million resulted in the founding in 1892 of Drexel Institute, an institution of higher learning offering programs in business and technology that admitted students without regard to gender or ethnicity. A Republican and a friend of President Ulysses S. Grant, Drexel was a member of Philadelphia's Reform Club and the Union League. These groups played pivotal roles in supporting civil rights, municipal reform, public education improvements, immigrant welfare, and the restoration of Independence Hall.

Drexel amassed one of the larger fortunes of the late nineteenth century without becoming a typically rapacious robber baron. He died in Carlsbad, Germany.

Further Reading: Dan Rottenberg, *The Man Who Made Wall Street: Anthony J. Drexel and the Rise of Modern Finance*, 2001; Vincent P. Carosso, *The Morgans: Private International Bankers, 1854–1913*, 1987; Alfred D. Chandler, *The Visible Hand: The Managerial Revolution in American Business*, 1977.

Leonard Schlup

DRUG ADDICTION. After the Civil War, drug addiction increased dramatically in the United States. Opium, morphine, chloroform, and cocaine were especially popular. Marijuana was largely unknown outside communities of Mexican immigrants. The federal government did not regulate narcotics until 1909, and only the tariff discouraged opium importation. Although some attempts were made to harvest the opium poppy in the United States, the amount raised failed to supply demand or prove profitable, and most drugs had to be imported from Asia or the Middle East. High addiction rates associated with Chinese laborers led many Americans to erroneously dismiss drug abuse as a foreign problem. It spread, however, to society's most respectable elements.

Although the number of addicts will never be known precisely, some scholars place the figure at about 250,000. A paucity of data and a lack of understanding of the effects of drugs at the time prevent reliable numbers, however. Various factors contributed to increasing narcotic use. From seedy opium dens and houses of prostitution, to the most stylish homes and offices of established physicians, Americans filled their cravings for drugs. Poorly trained doctors freely dispensed opium, morphine, and chloroform for a variety of misunderstood ailments, ranging from nervousness and menstrual problems to dysentery and rheumatism. Pressed by the public to provide instant pain relief, doctors were seldom seen treating patients without their narcotic-filled hypodermic needles. Unregulated patent medicines, which physicians prescribed for their patients, contained a variety of addictive drugs. Before the Pure Food and Drug Act of 1906 and its truth-in-advertising provisions, the contents of patent medicines were largely unknown to practitioner and patient alike. Frequently, members of the rising middle class turned to drugs to alleviate stress and anxiety. In some social circles, narcotics were considered more respectable than working-class alcohol. The promotion of cocaine by Sigmund Freud, and others, as a wonder drug sparked an interest in narcotics among intellectuals for the alleged psychic effects, which included enhanced concentration. Finally, society's marginalized members often turned to drugs. Prostitutes and Civil War veterans who were unable to adjust to peace or injured in the war, used drugs at rates considerably higher than the general public.

American attitudes toward drugs changed quickly after the turn of the twentieth century. As the quality of medical training increased, physicians led the way in recognizing addiction's signs and dangers. Much like prostitution, narcotic use was targeted for elimination in the public health movement of the Progressive Era.

Further Reading: H. Wayne Morgan, *Drugs in America: A Social History, 1800–1980*, 1981; David Must, *The American Disease: The Origins of Narcotic Control*, 1973; Timothy Alton Hickman, "The Double Meaning of Addiction: Habitual Narcotic Use, Social Degradation and Professional Medical Authority," Ph.D. diss., University of California at Irvine, 1997.

Gregory Dehler

DUBOIS, FRED THOMAS (29 May 1851– 14 February 1930), senator, businessman. Born in Palestine, Illinois, DuBois attended public schools, then earned his A.B. at Yale. He was secretary to the Illinois Railway and Warehouse Commission from 1875 to 1876, then went into business in Idaho in 1880. He entered politics in 1882, serving as U.S. marshal until 1886. He was a Republican territorial delegate to Congress from 1887 to 1891, and attended three of the party's national conventions. A leader in anti-Mormon agitation, he helped secure Idaho's statehood in 1890.

DuBois became Idaho's first U.S. senator in 1891. Bolting the Republican Party when it endorsed the gold standard in 1896, he lost his bid for reelection as a silver Republican. Again chosen senator in 1901, he switched to the Democratic Party and changed his residence to the District of Columbia. In 1912 he headed Champ Clark's quest for the Democratic presidential nomination. Later DuBois was an insurance company executive, a civilian member of the Ordnance Board (1918–1920), and a member of the international joint commission to prevent disputes with Canada over the Minnesota boundary waters (1924).

Further Reading: Leo W. Graff, "The Senatorial Career of Fred T. DuBois of Idaho," Ph.D. diss., University of Idaho, 1968; Rufus G. Cook, "The Political Suicide of Senator Fred T. DuBois of Idaho," *Pacific Northwest Quarterly* 60 (1969): 193–204; *Biographical Directory of the Congress of the United States, 1774–1989*, 1989, 933.

Douglas Steeples

DU BOIS, WILLIAM EDWARD BURGHARDT (23 February 1868–27 August 1963), African-American leader, scholar, and researcher. Born in Great Barrington, Massachusetts, where he experienced neither segregation nor poverty, Du Bois was raised in a fatherless home that emphasized education and hard work as keys to success. He first experienced segregation while attending Fisk University in Nashville, Tennessee (1885–1888), and was aghast at the racial prejudice and legal bonds that generated widespread ignorance and abject poverty. At Harvard University, where he became the first African American to earn a Ph.D. (1895), he identified his life mission—to improve the condition of black people—and postulated that political activity and nonviolence were the means to do so. He has been generally recognized as one of the most incisive thinkers and effective platform orators to emerge in the Gilded Age. In the 1890s, Du Bois solidified his belief that the challenge facing the new century was the color line—the relation of the world's darker races to lighter ones. He therefore opposed Booker T. Washington's appeasement of white aggression and demanded the social, economic, educational, and political rights of full citizenship. He focused his solution on a "Talented Tenth," a group of well-educated blacks who would work toward equality with liberal whites. Although largely ignored as a militant radical at the turn of the century, Du Bois later had a significant impact on civil rights by founding the NAACP, writing more than twenty books and one hundred scholarly articles, and pioneering studies of African Americans. He ultimately joined the Communist Party, renounced his American citizenship, and died in Accra, Ghana.

Further Reading: David L. Lewis, *W.E.B. Du Bois: Biography of a Race 1868–1919*, 1994; William Edward Burghardt Du Bois, *The Souls of Black Folks*, 1903.

Berman E. Johnson

DUKE, JAMES BUCHANAN (23 December 1856–10 October 1925), American businessman and philanthropist. Born on a farm east of Durham, North Carolina, Duke became one of the South's wealthiest individuals. By age fourteen, he managed the tobacco factory that his father, Washington, and his three sons had started and had moved to Durham in 1870. In 1884, he opened a factory in New York, and a few years later consolidated the five largest tobacco interests in the United States into the American Tobacco Company; the courts dissolved the company in 1911. Duke then devoted time to the British-American Tobacco Company and to waterpower development projects in Canada and North and South Carolina, and organized the Southern Power Company. He died at his Fifth Avenue home in New York City.

The Duke Endowment, which Duke established in 1924, is used for a variety of educational and charitable purposes. It helped build Duke University, a comprehensive educational institution, in Durham.

Further Reading: John W. Jenkins, *James B. Duke: Master Builder*, 1927; John K. Winkler, *Tobacco Tycoon: The Story of James Buchanan Duke*, 1942; *New York Times*, 11 October 1925.

Jane F. Lancaster

DUNBAR, PAUL LAURENCE (27 June 1872–9 February 1906), author. Born in Dayton, Ohio, Dunbar developed an interest in writing at age twelve, served as chief editor of his high school's student newspaper, and contributed poems to local newspapers prior to his graduation in 1891. The next year he delivered the welcoming address at the annual meeting in Dayton of the Western Association of Writers. In 1893, he published *Oak and Ivy*, a small volume of fifty-six poems, and two years later issued *Majors and Minors*. The endorsement of

William Dean Howells contributed significantly to Dunbar's widespread recognition as a brilliant African-American poet, novelist, short story writer, and essayist. Dunbar became one of the most popular writers in the United States. Known for his dialect poems, intended primarily for a white audience, he enjoyed the distinction of being the first African-American author who supported himself solely through his publications. His life did much to correct misconceptions about African Americans. Dunbar died of tuberculosis in Dayton.

Further Reading: Tony Gentry, *Paul Laurence Dunbar*, 1989; *New York Times*, 10 February 1906.

Leonard Schlup

DUNIWAY, ABIGAIL JANE SCOTT (22 October 1834–11 October 1915), western pioneer, author, and suffragist. Born near Groveland, Illinois, and raised on a farm, she married Benjamin Charles Duniway, an Oregon farmer, in 1853. After an accident with runaway horses left her husband a partial invalid, Abigail Duniway assumed all responsibility for running the farm and caring for the children. To supplement their income, she opened a millinery shop, but the examples of injustice and mistreatment of women propelled her to play a part in the feminist movement. In 1871 she moved to Portland, where she founded *The New Northwest*, a weekly women's-rights newspaper. Duniway traveled by boat, horse, railway, and stagecoach through Oregon, Idaho, and Washington, lecturing on the legal disabilities of women and the necessity for woman's suffrage. In 1873 she helped to found the Oregon Equal Suffrage Association, which she ultimately led. Although a teetotaler, Duniway opposed prohibition and disagreed with the notion of linking woman's suffrage with the temperance movement. Her pioneer background and years of public service brought Duniway national attention. In 1893 she addressed the Congress of Women at the World's Columbian Exposition in Chicago. When Oregon approved woman's suffrage in 1912, Duniway signed the proclamation jointly with the governor and was as the first registered voter in the state. She died in Portland.

Further Reading: Abigail Jane Scott Duniway, *Path Breaking*, 1914.

Leonard Schlup

DU PONT, HENRY (8 August 1812–8 August 1889), manufacturer. Born at Eleutherian Mills, near Wilmington, Delaware, Du Pont graduated from the U.S. Military Academy at West Point, New York, in 1833, assisted his father in the manufacture of gunpowder, and ultimately assumed control of the family business. The demand for munitions during the Civil War transformed his company into a highly prosperous enterprise, and Du Pont emerged as a major recipient of wartime profits. He became the largest landowner in Delaware. By 1881 E. I. Du Pont de Nemours and Company controlled 85 percent of the market for black blasting powder, through the establishment of the powder trust. A former Whig converted to Republicanism, Du Pont attended several GOP national conventions. In 1889 relinquished his position as head of the firm, and died in Wilmington, Delaware, later that year.

Further Reading: John D. Gates, *The Du Pont Family*, 1979; Leonard Mosley, *Blood Relations: The Rise and Fall of the Du Ponts of Delaware*, 1980; Henry Du Pont Papers, Eleutherian Mills Historical Library, Wilmington, Delaware.

Leonard Schlup

DURYEA, CHARLES EDGAR (15 December 1861–28 September 1938), and **JAMES FRANK DURYEA** (8 October 1869–15 February 1967), inventors, businessmen, and manufacturers of bicycles and automobiles. Born in Canton and Washburn, Illinois, respectively, the brothers achieved recognition through their interconnected careers in manufacturing. At Springfield, Massachusetts, in 1893, they conducted a successful test run of a horseless carriage. An improved model in 1895, known as "the Chicago car," constituted the first real automobile in the United States. Charles, flamboyant, eccentric, and domineering, planned and promoted the business while James, practical and steady, designed and built their products. In 1895 the Duryea Motor Wagon Company became the nation's first automobile company; the brothers sold it in 1898. Frank drove the Duryea car in the country's first automobile race (1895). Rivalry between the brothers over recognition marred their final years. Charles died in Philadelphia; Frank, in Saybrook, Connecticut.

Further Reading: Murray Fahnestock, "The Duryeas—American Quandary," *Antique Automobile* 28 (1964): 4–15; Richard P. Scharchburg, *Carriages Without Horses—J. Frank Duryea and the Birth of the American Automobile Industry*, 1993; George W. Mary, *Charles E. Duryea, Automaker*, 1973.

Leonard Schlup

EAKINS, THOMAS COW-PERTHWAIT (25 July 1844–25 June 1916), artist and educator. Probably the most influential painter America has produced, Eakins was born in Philadelphia, Pennsylvania. He attended the city's Central High School, assisted his father in teaching penmanship, and in 1862 enrolled in the Pennsylvania Academy of Fine Arts. Four years later he left for France to study art at the Ecole des Beaux-Arts under Jean-Léon Gérôme. Although Eakins never officially matriculated, he worked in Gérôme's atelier. After completing his studies, he traveled in Europe, remained for a time in southern Spain, produced *A Street Scene in Seville*, and in 1870 returned to Philadelphia. There he maintained a private studio on the top floor at the back of his father's house. A master at painting portraits, historical genre scenes, outdoor sporting events, and realistic surgical operations, Eakins achieved crowning success in 1875 with *The Gross Clinic*, one of the finest American paintings of the nineteenth century, which aroused some controversy and criticism at the time.

In 1878 Eakins became assistant professor of painting and chief demonstrator in anatomy at the Pennsylvania Academy of the Fine Arts; he rose to professor of drawing and painting a year later. His pedagogical beliefs and teaching style often created contention, but Fairman Rogers, chair of the committee on instruction, defended Eakins, who commuted to New York to handle additional teaching assignments. His most accomplished works in the early 1880s were *The Pathetic Song* and *The Swimming Hole*. Forced to resign as director of the Pennsylvania Academy of the Fine Arts in 1886, Eakins faced charges that he had removed a loincloth from a male model in a class filled with female students. Others accused him of rigidity in teaching and exhibiting a dictatorial administrative style, and his brother-in-law orchestrated a campaign of slander and innuendo about Eakins's sexual misconduct. An embittered and depressed Eakins journeyed to the Dakota Territory. In 1887 he returned to Philadelphia, where he continued painting portraits. His later works revealed more sadness and fatalism than his earlier creations. Recognition of his accomplishments grew gradually. In 1893 he received a bronze medal at the World's Columbian Exposition in Chicago. Eakins died at home in Philadelphia.

Further Reading: Lloyd Goodrich, *Thomas Eakins*, 2 vols., 1982; William Innes Homer, *Thomas Eakins: His Life and Art*, 1992; Kathleen A. Foster, *Thomas Eakins Rediscovered*, 1997.

Leonard Schlup

EARP BROTHERS

Earp, Wyatt Berry Stapp (18 March 1848–13 January 1929), was born in Monmouth, Illinois. His career as a lawman began in Lamar, Missouri, in 1870, and progressed to the Wichita, Kansas, police force and then to Dodge City, Kansas, where he served three terms as a deputy U.S. marshal. On 1 December 1879, he arrived in Tombstone, Arizona, where he was an armed guard for Wells Fargo, a deputy sheriff for Pima (later Cochise) County and a deputy U.S. marshal. In the O.K. corral gunfight (26 October 1881) he was a stand-in deputy under his brother, City Marshal Virgil Earp. When Virgil was later ambushed and permanently disabled, and his younger brother, Morgan, was murdered, Wyatt killed three of the suspects and left Arizona. He died in Colma, California.

Earp, Virgil Walter (18 July 1843–19 October 1905), was born in Hartford, Kentucky. A Civil War veteran, Virgil was elected constable of Prescott, Arizona, in 1878. The following year, he was appointed deputy U.S. marshal for Yavapai County. From 1 December 1879 to 29 December 1881, he was deputy U.S. marshal for Pima County, living in Tombstone, where he served as city marshal and police chief. With his brothers Wyatt and Morgan, he participated in the O.K. corral fight (26 October

1881) and received a leg wound. On 28 December 1881, he was shotgunned from ambush and permanently disabled. Virgil was a deputy sheriff when he died in Goldfield, Nevada.

Earp, Morgan S. (24 April 1851–18 March 1882), was born in Pella, Iowa. Beyond his participation in the O.K. Corral fight (26 October 1881), Morgan had a negligible record as a lawman. He rode shotgun for Wells Fargo in the Tombstone area and was deputized occasionally by his brother Virgil. He was a special policeman at the time of the famous fight, in which he was seriously wounded. Morgan was shot in the back, fatally, as he played billiards. The killers escaped in the dark. Earp is buried in Colton, California.

Further Reading: Allen Barra, *Inventing Wyatt Earp: His Life and Many Legends*, 1998; Frank Waters, *The Earp Brothers of Tombstone*, 1960.

Jack Burrows

EAST COAST PLUTOCRACY. Boston's Brahmins, Philadelphia's Gentlemen, New York's Knickerbockers, and the South's plantation class formed an antebellum quasi aristocracy that enjoyed moderate fortunes, lived private lives, performed civic duties, and considered heritage as important as wealth in defining high society's leaders. The unprecedented wealth generated by Civil War and Gilded Age speculation created a plutocracy that displaced these older elites. Nouveaux riches plutocrats rejected noblesse oblige, behaved ostentatiously, and were far more concerned with the size of their fortunes than with their ancestry or accomplishments. Particularly in New York City, where so many powerful millionaires congregated, older society tried to close ranks against them. Yet many prominent families gave the newly rich social legitimacy through marriage. Ultimately their pressure for social position opened places. Some plutocrats ignored elite society altogether. Yet those who entered it seemed exceptionally insecure, and became so perversely obsessed with arranging marriages to British aristocrats that Vice President Theodore Roosevelt once caused the prince of Wales to abandon plans to visit the elite stronghold of Newport, Rhode Island, for fear of embarrassing both nations. The East Coast plutocracy enjoyed high visibility in the era's society-hungry newspapers until the turn of the century, when their extravagant lifestyles became objects of ridicule and disgust.

Further Reading: Nathaniel Burt, *The Perennial Philadelphians*, 1963; Frederic Cople Jaher, "The Boston Brahmins in the Age of Industrial Capitalism," in *The Age of Industrialism in America*, 1968; Frederic Cople Jaher, "Nineteenth Century Elites in Boston and New York," *Journal of Social History* 6 (Fall 1972): 32–77.

Martin T. Olliff

EASTMAN, CHARLES ALEXANDER (OHIYESA) (19 February 1858–8 January 1939), Native American reformer and writer. Born near Redwood Falls, Minnesota, Eastman (his adopted English name) earned an undergraduate degree from Dartmouth College in 1887 and a medical degree three years later from Boston University. He held various federal government positions, including physician at Pine Ridge Agency in South Dakota in the early 1890s, where he witnessed the Wounded Knee massacre, and as outing agent at the Carlisle Indian Industrial School in Pennsylvania in 1899. Nationally known as a lecturer, author, and reformer, Eastman published eleven books and several articles. He helped to organize the Society of American Indians and served as its president. He was Indian secretary of the International Committee of the YMCA from 1894 to 1898. At the beginning of the twentieth century, Eastman was the foremost educated Native American in the United States. He died in Detroit, Michigan.

Further Reading: Charles A. Eastman, *Indian Boyhood*, 1902; Charles A. Eastman, *From the Deep Woods to Civilization*, 1916; Raymond Wilson, *Ohiyesa: Charles Eastman, Santee Sioux*, 1983.

Leonard Schlup

EASTMAN, ELAINE GOODALE (9 October 1863–22 December 1953), writer and reformer. Born in Mount Washington, Massachusetts, Eastman was educated at home and, with her sister Dora, published poetry by her early teens. Their first collection was *Apple Blossoms: Verses of Two Children* (1878). Eastman briefly attended a New York City boarding school, but a decline in the family's finances forced her to go to work. She obtained a teaching position at the Hampton Institute in Virginia, in its Indian department. Her interest piqued, Eastman traveled in the Dakota Territory for several weeks in 1885, and the following year was appointed the first government teacher at the Dakotas' White River camp. By 1890, she was superintendent of all the North and South Dakota Indian schools. Committed to the accepted policy of assimilation, Eastman was nonetheless horrified by the 1890 massacre at Wounded Knee. While caring for the wounded, she met her future husband, Charles Eastman (Ohiyesa), a Sioux physician educated at Dartmouth and Boston universities. The Eastmans publicly condemned the government's actions, and Charles Eastman lost his job. Over the next several years, the couple collaborated on books related to contemporary Native American life. She died in Hadley, Massachusetts.

Further Reading: Ruth Ann Alexander, "Finding Oneself Through a Cause: Elaine Goodale Eastman and Indian Reform in the 1880s," *South Dakota History* 22 (1992): 1–37; *New York Times* 23 December 1953; Elaine Goodale Eastman Papers, Sophia Smith Collection, Smith College, Northampton, Massachusetts.

Kathleen Banks Nutter

EASTMAN, GEORGE (12 July 1854–14 March 1932), businessman, philanthropist, and inventor. Born in Waterville, New York, Eastman attended private and public schools before working in a bank. After observing the shortcomings of the wet-plate photographic process and reading about the new dry-plate process, in 1880 he opened the Eastman Dry Plate Company in Rochester, New York. A year later he persuaded Henry A. Strong, a local manufacturer of whips, to form a partnership and assume the presidency, allowing Eastman to serve as general manager while devoting time to manufacturing. Eastman invented roll film in 1884, and added another partner, William H. Walker, a camera designer, to the reorganized company. He introduced the Kodak camera in 1888, nitrocellulose film in 1889, and the Brownie camera in 1900.

A lifelong bachelor, Eastman, bequeathed most of his fortune of over $100 million to various causes. He contended that money should accompany worthy aims. His philanthropic endeavors extended to education for African

Americans as well as other groups, especially those in Rochester. An adventurer and traveler who enjoyed outdoor life, he lost his enthusiasm for life when he contracted a spinal disease. Eastman committed suicide at his home in Rochester.

Further Reading: Elizabeth Brayer, *George Eastman: A Biography*, 1996; Brian Coe, *The Birth of Photography: The Story of the Formative Years, 1890–1900*, 1976; *Rochester Democrat and Chronicle*, 15 March 1932.

Leonard Schlup

EDDY, MARY BAKER (16 July 1821–3 December 1910), founder of Christian Science. Born Mary Baker on a farm near Bow, New Hampshire, Eddy had chronic illnesses throughout childhood and as a young adult. After spending many years seeking relief through a variety of treatments, she met Dr. Phineas Parkhurst Quimby, who taught that diseases were caused by false religious beliefs. As her recovery process began, she started adapting his teachings to her own ideas. She has been accused of plagiarism, but others have written that loyal followers of Quimby would have "disowned" her and her applications of his teachings. Eddy developed herself into an educator, religious leader, and writer. By 1879, she had formed the Christian Scientist Association and had chartered the Church of Christ (Scientist). Thereafter she created a metaphysical college and, eventually, the worldwide media empire known today. Her church's development can be examined in light of other philosophical and reform movements of the late nineteenth century. Eddy died in Chestnut Hill, Massachusetts.

Further Reading: Robert Peel, *Mary Baker Eddy: The Years of Discovery*, 1966; *Mary Baker Eddy: The Years of Trial*, 1971; *Mary Baker Eddy: The Years of Authority*, 1977.

Ann Mauger Colbert

EDISON, THOMAS ALVA (11 February 1847–18 October 1931), inventor. In addition to the light bulb and the phonograph, Edison's 1,093 patents included fundamental contributions to the telegraph, telephone, typewriter, microphone, motion picture camera, storage battery, and electric railway. The awesome variety of his other accomplishments (his patent total is the largest in history) ranged from mining machinery, Portland cement, the mimeograph, waxed paper, and synthetic chemicals to the dynamo and the system of power distribution. Above all, Edison invented the profession of inventor, initiating the kind of team research and specialization that served as a model for huge industrial research laboratories such as those later organized by General Electric and Bell Telephone.

Born in Milan, Ohio, and educated largely by his mother, Edison began selling candy and newspapers aboard a train at age twelve. In the 1860s he drifted about the country as an itinerant telegrapher, experimenting in his spare time with improvements on the telegraph. Arriving in Boston in 1868, Edison began his career as inventor in earnest, patenting telegraphic devices including relays, repeaters, and a printing telegraph. He later moved to Newark, New Jersey, where he manufactured telegraph instruments and continued his work on double and quadruple transmission systems (sending two or four messages simultaneously over a single wire). In 1876 Edison built a laboratory in Menlo Park, New Jersey. There he invented the phonograph (1878) and the incandescent lamp (1879), and converted Bell's telephone from a crude toy to a commercially practical device (1876). In the early 1880s Edison installed the world's first system of power distribution in a section of New York City. To achieve this, he developed not only a dynamo but all the sockets, switches, fuses, fixtures, and meters. Edison soon established large electrical manufacturing enterprises in both America and Europe. He also began producing phonographs, having greatly improved on his original model. In the late 1880s and early 1890s, working in his newly built laboratory at West Orange, New Jersey—then the largest and best equipped in the world—he and his assistant W. K. L. Dickson developed the first motion picture camera and viewing device.

In 1892, after his electrical industries became part of the merger that formed General Electric, Edison withdrew from the electric light and power business to spend a decade inventing massive machinery for an ore-milling venture that ultimately failed. By the century's end, his interests lay mainly in expanding his roles in the phonograph and motion picture industries. He died in West Orange.

Further Reading: Paul Israel, Edison: *A Life of Invention*, 1998; Neil Baldwin, *Edison: Inventing the Century*, 1994; Wyn Wachhorst, *Thomas Alva Edison: An American Myth*, 1983.

Wyn Wachhorst

EDMUNDS, GEORGE FRANKLIN (1 February 1828–27 February 1919), senator and lawyer. Born in Richmond, Vermont, Edmunds obtained a legal education before moving to Burlington to practice law in 1851. From 1854 to 1862, he served in the state legislature, where, as an antislavery Whig, he assumed leadership roles in both the upper and the lower house. Edmunds entered the U.S. Senate in 1866, appointed to a vacant seat. There he advocated strict enforcement of Reconstruction policies in the South. He initiated the Tenure of Office Act (1867), which led to President Andrew Johnson's impeachment. As Republican chairman of the Judiciary Committee, Edmunds worked to regulate railroads and suppress Mormon polygamy. His most important legislation, the Electoral Commission Act of 1877, enabled select members of the House of Representatives, the Senate, and the Supreme Court to settle the disputed election between Rutherford B. Hayes and Samuel J. Tilden. Edmunds left the Senate in 1891 but continued to practice law, appearing before the Supreme Court in 1895. Edmunds had his public papers destroyed prior to his death in Pasadena, California.

Further Reading: Norbert Kuntz, "Edmunds' Contrivance: Senator George Edmunds of Vermont and the Electoral Compromise of 1877," *Vermont History* 38 (Autumn 1970): 305–315; James Monroe, "The Hayes-Tilden Electoral Commission," *Atlantic Monthly* 72 (1893): 521–538; *New York Times*, 28 February 1919.

Jane M. Armstrong

ELECTORAL CHANGE AND REFORM. Changes in the electoral structure and process during the Gilded Age can be divided into two general categories. Not surprisingly, both are associated with concern for the distribution or redistribution of political power. The first category deals with changes related to post-Reconstruction political realignments. Conceptually the matter involved the identity and comparative strength of the Republican and Democratic parties. In practical terms this usually meant the voting power of African-American males. The second category of change is associated with the growing uneasiness in certain quarters with the dominance of political elites over the political process. Ultimately this trend culminated in the political reforms associated with the Progressive Era. The genesis of reform, however, can clearly be found in the Gilded Age.

During the presidential election of 1868, the Democratic candidate, Horatio Seymour, ran in defense of states' rights, arguing in essence that southern states should retain control over African-American political rights. The Fifteenth Amendment, ratified in 1870, enfranchised black males. Once Reconstruction ended in the mid-1870s, however, white southerners rapidly moved to secure their political dominance in the region. Supreme Court decisions during the 1880s and 1890s did little to contravene these efforts, tending to affirm state control of the political arena. Thus southern states implemented electoral structures to retain white control of the political machinery. They included "Black Codes," "Jim Crow" laws, poll taxes, and literacy tests. The Supreme Court held that these devices did not violate the Fifteenth Amendment.

The integrity of the electoral process gradually became an issue during the Gilded Age. Of particular importance was the degree to which political parties, especially in the large cities of the East and Midwest, controlled voting and elections. In certain areas, party machines substantially managed the electoral process. Voter fraud was common; the dead cast a record number of ballots. Patronage and direct financial support were used to influence individual voters, their churches, and their fraternal organizations.

Adoption of the Australian ballot, in nearly every state by the turn of the century, was one reaction to these abuses. It provided secret voting and made ticket-splitting possible. Another significant development, the Pendleton Act of 1883, created the federal Civil Service Commission. Such legislation limited the ability of political parties to use government employment as a means of controlling votes. These reforms were harbingers of broader electoral reforms in the early twentieth century.

Further Reading: Sean Dennis Cashman, *America in the Gilded Age*, 3rd. ed., 1993; William J. Crotty, *Political Reform & the American Experiment*, 1977; Paul Kleppner, *The Third Electoral System, 1853–1892*, 1979.

Donald E. Greco

ELIOT, CHARLES WILLIAM (20 March 1834–22 August 1926), chemist and university president. Born in Boston, Eliot attended the Boston Latin School and entered Harvard College at age fifteen. He studied chemistry and mathematics, and after earning his A.B. in 1853 taught both subjects at Harvard until 1863. Eliot toured Europe in 1864 and 1867, then returned to Harvard as president in 1869. He obtained further teaching and administrative experience at the newly established Massachusetts Institute of Technology. Eliot's plans for transforming Harvard into a major American university synthesized ideas that were redefining and expanding American higher education. By 1894, the cornerstones of Eliot's new Harvard had been laid: student freedom of choice among elective undergraduate courses, graduate-level scientific research, and advanced studies in professional schools. By the time he retired in 1909, Eliot's commitment to high levels of scholarship and public service were reflected in Harvard's requirement of a bachelor's degree for admission to its graduate schools and emphasis on scientific research among faculty and students.

Eliot's leadership in efforts to raise standards in American higher education was closely linked to his campaign for correcting the failures of popular education. His frequent addresses to departments of the National Education Association (NEA) led to reviews of elementary and secondary education, and efforts to standardize the nation's emerging public school system. Eliot was a leading member of the NEA's famous "Committee of Ten" on secondary school studies (1892–1893), which forged the link between a subject-centered high school curriculum and college entrance requirements. Eliot headed led the NEA's Committee on College Entrance Requirements, whose report in 1899 led to the establishment of the College Entrance Examination Board a year later. He died at his summer home in Northeast Harbor, Mount Desert Island, Maine.

Further Reading: Hugh Hawkins, *Between Harvard and America: The Educational Leadership of Charles W. Eliot*, 1972; Laurence Veysey, *The Emergence of the American University*, 1965; Henry James, *Charles W. Eliot, President of Harvard University*, 1869–1909, 1930.

Kim P. Sebaly

ELKINS, STEPHEN BENTON (26 September 1841–4 January 1911), senator and cabinet member. Born in Perry County, Ohio, Elkins was graduated from the University of Missouri's law department in 1860. After militia service, he practiced law in the New Mexico Territory, and served in the territorial assembly before becoming delegate to Congress (1873–1877). He then founded the town of Elkins, West Virginia, and spent almost a decade developing industry there. Appointed secretary of war by President Benjamin Harrison in 1891, Elkins streamlined the army. He favored increasing benefits to attract more qualified men. He concentrated the army into fewer but larger bases and improved its record keeping, especially regarding Civil War veterans. Elkins improved instruction at West Point and persuaded Congress to increase spending on militia training. Finally, he replaced obsolescent Civil War weapons and built modern coastal defenses.

In 1895 Elkins was named senator from West Virginia. He favored the gold standard, protective tariffs, and railroad regulation. In 1898 he opposed war with Spain. Once fighting began, however, he supported massive action against all Spanish possessions. He later favored statehood, rather than independence, for Cuba. He sponsored the Elkins Act of 1903 and the Mann-Elkins Act of 1910, and remained in the Senate until his death in Washington D.C.

Further Reading: Oscar Doane Lambert, *Stephen Benton Elkins*, 1955.

Stephen Svonavec

ELLIS ISLAND, immigration portal. Situated in New York Harbor, Ellis Island was the principal station for immigrants on the Atlantic coast. Its name comes from Samuel Ellis, who owned it during the late eighteenth century. The federal government purchased it in 1808 for military purposes. It held artillery installations defending the harbor, and was the site of Fort Gibson, an army post. In 1890 President Benjamin Harrison designated the island as the site of a station to enforce new federal immigration laws. More than twelve million immigrants passed through Ellis Island after its opening on 1 January 1892. During the peak years, 1892–1924, about three-quarters of all immigrants to the United States were examined and questioned at the island by officials of the Public Health Service and the Bureau of Immigration. After the National Origins Quota System became permanent in 1924, arrivals at Ellis Island declined. The island was also used for detaining and deporting enemy aliens during wartime. Closed in 1954, it reopened as a museum in 1990. In 1998 the Supreme Court settled a long-standing dispute between New Jersey and New York over the island's sovereignty. The tribunal ruled that New York governed the original island (about three acres), but that New Jersey had title to about twenty-five acres created by landfill over the years.

Further Reading: Thomas Pitkin, *Keepers of the Gate: A History of Ellis Island*, 1975; Pamela Reeves, *Ellis Island: Gateway to the American Dream*, 1991; Wilton Tifft, *Ellis Island*, 1979.

James M. Bergquist

ELY, RICHARD THEODORE (13 April 1854–4 October 1943), economist. Born in Ripley, New York, Ely laid the foundations of institutionalism in American economics when he advanced German historicism. The founders of the institutionalist school, John R. Commons and Wesley C. Mitchell, were students and followers of Ely. The structure of professional economics in the United States bears Ely's stamp as a cofounder, with Edwin R. A. Seligman, of the American Economic Association (1885). Higher education's tenure system can be traced to the academic community's response to Ely's trial at the University of Wisconsin for unpopular positions on strikes, unions, and socialism. Some of Ely's major works include *French and German Socialism in Modern Time* (1883), *The Past and the Present of Political Economy* (1884); *The Labor*

Movement in America (1886), *Outlines of Economics* (1893), and *Property and Contract in Their Relation to the Distribution of Wealth* (1914). He died in Old Lyme, Connecticut.

Further Reading: Benjamin G. Rader, *Academic Mind and Reform: The Influence of Richard T. Ely in American Life*, 1966; John Rutherford Everett, *Religion in Economics*, 1982; *New York Times* 5 October 1943.

David O. Whitten

ENDICOTT, WILLIAM CROWNINSHIELD (19 November 1826–6 May 1900), judge and secretary of war. Born in Salem, Massachusetts, Endicott was graduated from Harvard in 1850 and quickly joined the bar. He failed in bids for elected office, but secured appointment to the Massachusetts Supreme Judicial Court in 1873, from which he resigned in 1882. President Grover Cleveland appointed him secretary of war in 1885, during a naval arms race between Britain and Germany that featured development of the modern battleship, which could destroy brick-and-mortar fortifications. Endicott seized on the vulnerability of America's masonry coastal forts and warned of impending disaster. Congress endorsed the idea of redesigning them and installing armor-piercing artillery, but failed to provide adequate funds to complete the project. Only a handful were reconstructed.

During Endicott's four-year tenure, he established the Infantry and Cavalry School at Fort Leavenworth, Kansas, mandated proficiency examinations for military promotion, and improved conditions and pay for enlisted personnel. One of Endicott's greatest achievements was to modify training procedures to emphasize combat preparedness rather than parade-ground drill. These reforms hastened the military's modernization as the twentieth century approached. After the Cleveland administration ended in 1889, Endicott headed the Peabody Education Fund and the Harvard Alumni Association. He died in Boston.

Further Reading: William C. Endicott, *Memoir of William Crowninshield Endicott*, 1902.

T. R. Brereton

ENGLISH, WILLIAM HAYDEN (27 August 1822–7 February 1896), congressman, Democratic candidate for the vice presidency, banker, and historian. Born in Lexington, Indiana, English served four terms in the U.S. House of Representatives (1853–1861). He then retired and founded the First National Bank of Indianapolis. He returned to politics in 1879 as chairman of the Indiana Democratic Central Committee. He was the unanimous choice as General Winfield Scott Hancock's running mate in the presidential campaign of 1880. Thereafter, English published a *History of Indiana* (1887), *Conquest of the Country Northwest of the River Ohio, 1778–1783* (1896), and *Life of General George Rogers Clark* (2 vols., 1896).

Further Reading: Charles E. Keyser, *The Life of William H. English, the Democratic Candidate for Vice President of the United States*, 1880; John W. Forney, *The Life and Military Career of Winfield Scott Hancock*, 1880; *Indianapolis Sentinel*, 8 and 10 February 1896.

Norman E. Fry

ENTERTAINMENT IN THE WHITE HOUSE. In December 1865, Congress appropriated $30,000 for redecorating the White House. Under President Andrew Johnson, social functions had an unostentatious dignity. On his sixtieth birthday, guests danced in the East Room and ate pineapple glacé. Under Ulysses S. Grant, a new era of elegance began. Julia Dent Grant possessed a flair for entertaining that set new precedents. She recalled her White House years as the happiest of her life. The Grants gave a dinner every Wednesday night and held two receptions each week. The White House wedding of Nellie Grant to Algernon Charles Frederick Sartoris on 21 May 1874 was a brilliant social event at which the guests feasted on spiced oysters, among other delicacies. The Grants' most historic dinner occurred on 3 March 1877, in honor of President-elect and Mrs. Rutherford B. Hayes. There were six wine glasses at every plate, an elaborately decorated State Dining Room, and a ten-foot azalea. The menu included consommé imperiale, filet of beef, breast of pheasant, woodcock patties, salmon, crawfish pudding, goose livers, turkey, sherry, wine, champagne, canvasback duck, and a warm sweet dish for dessert. At midnight Grant whisked Hayes, Secretary of State Hamilton Fish, and Chief Justice Morrison R. Waite into the Red Room, where Hayes secretly took the oath of office.

The Hayeses prohibited the serving of alcohol at their social events. Otherwise, their entertaining rivaled the Grants' extravagance. Lucy Hayes used flowers profusely for all occasions. She and the president started the tradition of having Washington children visit on Easter Monday for egg rolling. When Chester A. Arthur succeeded to the presidency upon James A. Garfield's death in 1881, he refused to move in until the White House had been refurbished, threatening to pay from his own pocket if necessary. A widower and style-setter, Arthur held an auction before 5,000 people gathered. Thereafter, he installed the first elevator and added two new bathrooms. The renovated mansion was as elegant as his dinners. The president's sister, Mary Arthur McElroy, served as official hostess.

Grover Cleveland, the only president to be married in the White House, had the rooms redecorated and painted for his bride. Frances Folsom Cleveland, the youngest First Lady in American history, redesigned the table place cards and had the words "Executive Mansion" printed in silver atop invitations. She held popular Saturday afternoon receptions, so working-women could tour. Upon leaving in 1889, Frances Cleveland notified servants that she and the president would return in four years. Shortly after they did so, their daughter Esther became the first child of a president to be born in the White House. That year's Christmas dinner included blue point oysters, mince pie, tutti-frutti ice cream, and plum pudding.

William McKinley presided over grander state dinners than any of his predecessors. Social responsibilities fell largely on him, his staff, and the wives of cabinet officers because Ida Saxton McKinley was an invalid. At receptions Mrs. McKinley sat in a thronelike chair with the president by her side. McKinley resolved the question of rank at social functions by placing the vice president first before ambassadors. On 12 December 1900, known as "centennial day," McKinley held a morning reception for dignitaries and then opened the doors of the White House to the public, shaking nearly five thousand hands.

Further Reading: Marie Smith, *Entertaining in the White House*, 1967.

Leonard Schlup

ENVIRONMENT. A pivotal era in American environmental history, the Gilded Age was marked by both a massive expansion in the consumption of natural resources and the emergence of conservation sentiment on a national scale. As the population grew from thirty-one million in 1860 to seventy-six million in 1900, the United States changed from a largely agrarian to an industrial economy, a process accompanied by heavy immigration, urbanization, and the adoption of new technologies. The corresponding economic growth, driven by core industries such as steel, railroads, and timber, as well as consumer goods, relied heavily on natural resources. Raw materials and even the land itself were consumed at a greater rate than ever before as new industries and new markets evolved to meet the growing demands of consumers and investors. After John Wesley Powell led the last great exploratory expedition into the American West in 1869, homesteaders, ranchers, miners, and timbermen poured into the region so quickly that the U.S. Bureau of the Census declared the frontier closed in 1890. During the same period eastern cities grew at such a rate that by 1890 one-third of all Americans lived in urban areas, a dozen of which held more than 250,000 people. The ecological consequences of this expansion were apparent in declining wildlife populations, reduced soil fertility and topsoil erosion, the clearing of vast forests for fuel and lumber, and the dramatic scarring of the land resulting from large-scale commercial mining for coal, iron ore, gold, and other minerals. In the industrial cities, air pollution (primarily coal smoke) and water pollution (primarily domestic sewage and industrial effluents) produced health problems among inhabitants already threatened by disease due to high population densities, inadequate medical care, and poverty.

But as species such as the whooping crane, the passenger pigeon, and the bison were being hunted into or near extinction, a countervailing trend emerged as some Americans began to develop a romantic view of the natural world they had left behind in the rush to the cities. Wilderness came to symbolize an idyllic past that was celebrated in the landscape paintings of Albert Bierstadt, the nature writing of John Burroughs, and ultimately Frederick Jackson Turner's monumental 1893 essay "The Significance of the Frontier in American History."

To preserve some remnants of wilderness and to ensure a future supply of natural resources, Congress set aside Yellowstone as the world's first national park in 1872, and in 1891 extended federal protection to the timber reserves that would become the national forests. Private organizations such as the Audubon Society (1886) and the Sierra Club (1892) were formed to advocate preservation of some remaining wilderness; the Boone and Crockett Club was founded (1885) by Theodore Roosevelt and other members of the New York elite intent on putting a stop to the market hunting that had decimated fish, game, and waterfowl populations across the nation. Public figures such as John Muir wrote and spoke out on behalf of nature preservation and the value of wild things, and by the 1890s the foundations of the Progressive Era conservation movement were being laid within government by men such as the Yale-educated forester Gifford Pinchot. The gospel of progress, which encapsulated the Gilded Age faith in material wealth and the blessings of industry, was challenged in a fashion that would not halt environmental degradation in the following decades. For the first time, however, society recognized intrinsic as well as utilitarian values in nature. As a result, the great conservation debates of the early twentieth century were not only over how to develop natural resources most profitably, but also over whether they should be developed at all.

Further Reading: John Opie, *Nature's Nation: An Environmental History of the United States*, 1998; Richard White, *Nature's Metropolis: Chicago and the Great West*, 1991; Donald Worster, ed., *American Environmentalism: The Formative Period, 1860–1915*, 1973.

Derek R. Larson

ETHNICITY AND CULTURAL PLURALISM.
While America has always had significant ethnic diversity, the nation's dramatically changing nature during the late nineteenth century resulted in a vastly altered ethnic landscape. Reconstruction in the South, subjugation of the Amerindian tribes in the West, and increasing immigration from Europe, Asia, and Latin America required that natives and newcomers alike adjust to altered cultural realities. Anglo-American political and social hegemony exerted strong pressures on out-groups to assimilate, but newcomers and marginalized natives fought to retain their own cultural identities, thereby creating a pluralistic culture.

Reconstitution of ethnic parameters in the South and the West began in the 1860s and continued throughout the Gilded Age. The postwar period required that relationships between African Americans and Euro-Americans be reconstructed. Freedmen cooperated with Euro-Americans in the Republican Party and various economic endeavors, but they also sought to create their own parallel institutions such as churches, schools, and benefit organizations for self-empowerment. In the West, sustained military campaigns and economic development undermined Amerindian autonomy, and by the end of the century, federal policy and philanthropic organizations pursued a forced assimilation, which met significant resistance from subject peoples, through the Dawes General Allotment Act and schools such as that at Carlisle, Pennsylvania.

The American West was especially fertile for ethnic pluralism. Euro-Americans and diverse groups of European immigrants displaced Amerindians. Coming to California and then penetrating the interior were Asian peoples: first the Chinese and, by century's end, Japanese and Koreans. Racial stereotyping, economic competition, sojourner status, discriminatory legislation, and vigilante terrorism forced the Chinese especially to create strong cultural institutions in ethnic enclaves such as Chinatowns. Agricultural labor needs in the region gave Mexicans increased work opportunities throughout the Gilded Age, and political turmoil in the Caribbean contributed to increased Cuban immigration.

In the North, accelerating industrial development shifted ethnic demographics as immigration from southern and eastern Europe increased dramatically. Many immigrants were Catholics and Jews who sought to create their own urban political, economic, and social institutions. Nativism reasserted itself, but newcomers created fraternal organizations, religious networks, and economic enterprises that preserved cultural traditions. By 1900, the United States had become a dramatically different place with an even greater ethnic richness.

Further Reading: Leonard Dinnerstein, et al., *Natives and Strangers: A Multicultural History of Americans*, 1997; Ronald T. Takaki, *A Different Mirror: A History of Multicultural America*, 1993; John Higham, *Strangers in the Land: Patterns of American Nativism, 1860–1925*, 1955.

Timothy Dean Draper

EVANS, CHARLES (13 November 1850–8 February 1935), bibliographer and librarian. Born in Boston and orphaned as a boy, Evans was sent to the Boston Asylum and Farm School for Indigent Boys. In 1866 he became an assistant in the library of the Boston Athenaeum, where he was surrounded by scholars and literary figures, including the famous librarian William F. Poole. In 1872, on Poole's recommendation he was appointed as the first librarian of the Indianapolis Public Library. Evans built a collection balanced between general literature and new fiction, and he stressed local and state history materials. At the conference that formed the American Library Association, Evans was elected treasurer. Personality conflicts cost him his Indianapolis position, and subsequent ones in Baltimore and Chicago.

Determined to prove his career was not a total failure, Evans began compiling *American Bibliography: A Chronological Dictionary of All Books, Pamphlets and Periodical Publications Printed in the United States of America from the Genesis of Printing in 1639 Down to and Including the Year 1820 with Bibliographical and Biographical Notes*. The library community reacted skeptically to such a monumental undertaking, but when volumes began appearing every few years, starting in 1903, disdain turned to applause and assistance. Volume 1 covered the years 1639 to 1729; each subsequent volume covered less time as the number of publications expanded geometri-

cally. Evans's final efffort, volume 12 (1934) did not quite get to the year 1800. However, this mammoth bibliography (with subsequent additions and indices by others), which is now commonly referred to as "Evans," remains the standard listing of early American imprints. He died in Chicago.

Further Reading: Edward G. Holley, *Charles Evans: American Bibliographer*, 1963; Lawrence C. Wroth, "Evans's 'American Bibliography': Matrix of Histories," in *Charles Evans, American Bibliography 1639–1729*, 1943.

Philip H. Young

EVANS, HENRY CLAY (18 June 1843–12 December 1921), congressman, commissioner of pensions, businessman, diplomat. Born in Juniata County, Pennsylvania, Evans graduated from a Chicago business school in 1861. After serving in the Civil War, he moved to Chattanooga, Tennessee. There he became president of the Chattanooga Car and Foundry Company, helped organize the city's public school system, and was president of the school board and school commissioner. He served two terms as mayor of Chattanooga in the early 1880s, and in 1888 won election as a Republican to the Fifty-first Congress. His endorsement of the 1890 Federal Elections Bill to safeguard African-American suffrage contributed to his defeat that year in the national Democratic sweep of the House of Representatives. President Benjamin Harrison appointed Evans first assistant postmaster general; he served from 1891 to 1893. Although Evans won a plurality of 748 votes over his opponent, Peter Turney, in the 1894 Tennessee gubernatorial contest, he lost the office in a recount ordered by the Democrat-controlled state legislature. The campaign brought national recognition. In 1896 he ran second to Garret A. Hobart for the Republican vice presidential nomination. President William McKinley selected Evans for commissioner of pensions in 1897. From 1902 until 1905, Evans was U.S. consul general in London. He died in Chattanooga.

Further Reading: Henry C. Evans Papers, Chattanooga-Hamilton County Bicentennial Library, Chattanooga, Tennessee.

Leonard Schlup

EVARTS, WILLIAM MAXWELL (6 February 1818–28 February 1901), lawyer, attorney general, secretary of state, senator. Born in Boston, Massachusetts, Evarts was graduated from Yale and Harvard Law School, and was admitted to the New York bar in 1841. First a Whig, later a Republican, he successfully argued the "Prize Cases" before the Supreme Court during the Civil War. He defended Andrew Johnson during his impeachment trial in 1868, and later became his attorney general. After returning to New York City in 1870, he helped found the New York Bar Association.

Evarts was one of the most widely respected attorneys in America during the 1870s and 1880s. In 1871–1872 he was counsel for the *Alabama* arbitration in Geneva, Switzerland; in 1875 he defended Reverend Henry Ward Beecher in his adultery trial; and in 1876–1877 he advised Rutherford B. Hayes before the Electoral Commission that decided the presidential election. Evarts was Hayes's secretary of state from 1877 to 1881. He opposed French construction of a canal across Panama; negotiated a revision of the Burlingame Treaty of 1868, which had protected Chinese immigrants; and promoted arbitration in international disputes. In 1885 he was elected to the U.S. Senate, where he served until 1889. He died in New York City.

Further Reading: Brainerd Dyer, *The Public Career of William M. Evarts*, 1933; Chester L. Barrows, *William M. Evarts: Lawyer, Diplomat, Statesman*, 1941; Gary A. Pennanen, "The Foreign Policy of William Maxwell Evarts," Ph.D. diss., University of Wisconsin-Madison, 1969.

Dimitri D. Lazo

EWING, JAMES STEVENSON (19 July 1835–7 February 1918), lawyer and diplomat. Born in McLean County, Illinois, Ewing graduated from Centre College, in Danville, Kentucky, in 1858. After reading law in Philadelphia, he moved to Bloomington, Illinois. There he entered a successful law partnership with his double cousin, Adlai E. Stevenson, a local politician who later became vice president of the United States. The Stevenson & Ewing law firm gained a respectable reputation across the Midwest for the next twenty-five years. Ewing tended to be the trial lawyer while Stevenson was more the office lawyer and politician. Ewing worked behind the scenes at the 1892 Democratic National Convention in Chicago, lining up delegates to win Stevenson the vice presidential nomination on the ticket headed by former President Grover Cleveland. During the campaign, Ewing wrote letters to party leaders outlining political strategies and emphasizing the importance of carrying Illinois. He accompanied Stevenson on campaign tours in Kentucky, North Carolina, Indiana, and Illinois. After Cleveland's inauguration in 1893, Ewing was named U.S. minister to Belgium, in which capacity he served until 1897. Ewing died in Bloomington.

Further Reading: *The Daily Pantagraph* [Bloomington], 8 February 1918; James S. Ewing, "Mr. Stevenson, the Democratic Candidate for Vice-President," *The American Monthly Review of Reviews* 22 (1900): 420–424; Leonard Schlup, "Democrats, Populists, and Gilded Age Politics," *Manuscripts* 60 (1998): 27–40.

Leonard Schlup

EXODUSTERS. Several thousand poor African-American tenant farmers from Tennessee, Texas, Mississippi, and Louisiana journeyed to Kansas in 1879 to escape the bondage, unfair credit system, poverty, and political and social injustices of the redeemed South. Among the leaders of the group were Henry Adams, a former soldier, and Benjamin Singleton, a cabinetmaker. Boarding riverboats to head up the Mississippi to the "Negro Canaan," a promised land, the Exodusters believed the national government would furnish them with free land and supplies, and that they would enjoy equality in their new environment. It was rural-to-rural migration. The movement was a qualified success in that African Americans in Kansas were generally better off than their counterparts in southern states.

Further Reading: Nell Irvin Painter, *Exodusters: Black Migration to Kansas After Reconstruction*, 1977.

Leonard Schlup

EX PARTE YARBROUGH (110 U.S. 651). In this Supreme Court case, decided in 1884, the justices upheld a congressional statute that prohibited two or more persons from conspiring to threaten or intimidate citizens seeking to exercise their right to vote for candidates for national office. The case originated with a habeas corpus petition by a group convicted of conspiring to intimidate blacks at the polls. Writing for the court, Justice Samuel F. Miller stated that the Fifteenth Amendment conferred upon blacks the right to vote, and that Congress had the power to protect and enforce that right. The lower court criminal convictions were affirmed, and the writ was denied.

Further Reading: Louis Fisher, *American Constitutional Law*, 3rd ed., 1999, pp. 1105–1106; *U.S. Reports* 110 U.S. 651.

Thomas C. Sutton

FAIRBANKS, CHARLES WARREN (11 May 1852–4 June 1918), senator and vice president of the United States. Born near Unionville Center, Ohio, Fairbanks graduated in 1872 from Ohio Wesleyan University. After attending the Cleveland Law School, he moved to Indiana, where his uncle, the railroad magnate Charles Warren Smith, arranged a position for him with the Indianapolis, Bloomington and Western Railroad. Fairbanks earned a reputation as a successful railroad attorney, made profitable investments, and purchased railroads, becoming a millionaire. He was president of the Terre Haute and Peoria Railroad and vice president of the Ohio Southern. An advocate of the gold standard and protective tariffs, Fairbanks played an active role in Republican politics. He managed Walter Q. Gresham's Republican presidential nomination campaign in 1888. In 1896 Fairbanks delivered the keynote address at the party's national convention, for which he served as temporary chairman, and helped to draft the platform's sound money plank. During the campaign he managed the canvass in Indiana for William McKinley, the presidential nominee.

In 1896 Fairbanks won a seat in the U.S. Senate, and held it until 1905. Neither a great orator nor a power broker, he nevertheless exerted influence because of his close ties to President McKinley. Fairbanks supported proposals for internal improvements, including waterways. He made no enemies and avoided intraparty antagonisms. The president sent Fairbanks to Alaska to resolve the boundary dispute between the United States and Canada. In 1900 Fairbanks, who entertained presidential ambitions, rejected an offer from Republican political leader Mark Hanna to join the ticket. Four years later Fairbanks was elected vice president of the United States, serving under President Theodore Roosevelt from 1905 to 1909. In 1916 Fairbanks was the vice presidential nominee on the Republican ticket headed by Charles Evans Hughes. Fairbanks died in Indianapolis.

Further Reading: *New York Times*, 5 June 1918; Lewis L. Gould, ed., "Charles Warren Fairbanks and the Republican National Convention of 1900: A Memoir," *Indiana Magazine of History* 77 (1981): 358–72; Charles Warren Fairbanks Papers, Lilly Library, Indiana University, Bloomington.

Leonard Schlup

FAIRCHILD, CHARLES STEBBINS (30 April 1842–24 November 1924), banker and secretary of the Treasury. Born in Cazenovia, New York, Fairchild graduated from Harvard College in 1863 and from the its law school two years later. He was elected attorney general of the state in 1875, and under the direction of New York Governor Samuel J. Tilden, he conducted the prosecutions in the "Canal Ring" frauds. Upon Secretary of the Treasury Daniel Manning's resignation in 1887, President Grover Cleveland appointed Fairchild as his replacement, a post he held remained until the Cleveland administration ended in 1889. Fairchild thereupon returned to New York City, where he became a banker and philanthropist. In 1896 he opposed free silver coinage and the presidential nomination of William Jennings Bryan. At the New York State Democratic Convention that year in Rochester, Fairchild was permanent chairman: delegates decided to send a Gold Democrat delegation to Indianapolis to nominate a separate, sound money Democratic ticket. Opposed to woman's suffrage in his later years, Fairchild died in Cazenovia.

Further Reading: *New York Times*, 25 November 1924.

Leonard Schlup

FARMER, FANNIE MERRITT (23 March 1857–15 January 1915), author and teacher of cooking. Born in Boston, Massachusetts, Farmer attended Medford (Massachusetts) High School. Paralysis in her left leg, contracted when she was a teenager, resulted in a permanent limp. In 1887 she enrolled in the Boston Cooking School, where she completed a two-year program. Farmer remained there as assistant principal, and ultimately as head of the school (1894), until 1902, when she opened Miss Farmer's School of Cookery. In 1896 she published *The Boston Cooking-School Cook Book*, a popular work that turned her name into a household word. Farmer emphasized nutritional values of food, a proper diet, specific cooking directions, and new dishes. She died in Boston.

Further Reading: Edward T. James, ed., *Notable American Women, 1607–1950: A Biographical Dictionary*, 1971.

Leonard Schlup

FARMERS' ALLIANCE. In 1875, agrarians on the Texas frontier formed the Farmers' Alliance. It began as a social organization, but its agenda expanded. By 1886 it had one hundred thousand members in Texas alone, and had spread, as the Southern Alliance, throughout the South and West (though not in the Midwest, where the Grange had flourished). That year Robert Humphreys, a white minister, organized the Colored Farmers' Alliance. The next year, Charles W. Macune, the Southern Alliance's new president, proposed that members create an exchange that would loan them money, store their crops, and sell them supplies.

The exchange's collapse did not dampen farmers' enthusiasm. By 1890 the Colored Alliance had a million members, and the Southern Alliance claimed 1.5 million whites. That year the Southern Alliance entered politics, winning both houses of the Nebraska legislature and one house in Kansas. Its success was partly due to flamboyant leaders who delivered fiery speeches. A larger reason was a platform that included railroad regulation, the coinage of silver, female suffrage, a graduated income tax, the secret ballot, direct election of senators, and the eight-hour day. In 1891, Alliance leaders formed the People's Party. Its demands would help shape the political agenda of the Progressive Era.

Further Reading: John D. Hicks, *The Populist Revolt: A History of the Farmers' Alliance and the People's Party*, 1931; Robert C. McMath, *The Populist Vanguard*, 1975; Theodore Saloutos, *Farmer Movements in the South, 1865–1933*, 1960.

Christopher Cumo

FARWELL, JOHN VILLIERS (29 July 1825–20 August 1908), merchant. Born in Steuben County, New York, Farwell moved to Chicago at age nineteen, seeking a career in commerce. At first he worked as a clerk, salesman, and bookkeeper. Ultimately, through fortuitous circumstances, he became president of John V. Farwell and Company in the 1860s. Farwell's business activities made him wealthy. He donated to and worked with social service agencies, including his church; the Illinois Street Mission, which assisted the city's boys; slum rescue projects; and the U.S. Christian Commission. In part because of the influence of the revivalist Dwight L. Moody and that of George Williams, known as the father of the Young Men's Christian Association (YMCA), Farwell gave land for the first YMCA building in Chicago. He also served as U.S. Indian commissioner under President Ulysses S. Grant. Farwell died in Chicago.

Further Reading: *Chicago Daily News*, 21 August 1908; *Chicago Tribune*, 21 August 1908.

Leonard Schlup

FEDERAL ELECTIONS BILL OF 1890. In the early 1870s, Republican Congresses enacted several laws designed to safeguard suffrage rights of newly enfranchised African-American males in the South. Yet continued violence and other intimidation, coupled with growing unwillingness of the administrations of Ulysses S. Grant and Rutherford B. Hayes to intervene, resulted in the steady diminution of black voting and the consolidation of the Democratic Party's hold on the South. After the Republicans lost control of the House of Representatives in 1874, they were powerless to add further legislation to protect the ballot. Because the end of slavery had widened the population base for congressional representation from the former slave states, thereby giving the South a greater number of seats in the House, the systematic barring of black suffrage gave the white southern voter much greater influence than his northern counterpart.

In 1889, when the Republicans gained control of both houses of Congress as well as the presidency under Benjamin Harrison, they welcomed the opportunity to redress this wrong.

Representative Henry Cabot Lodge and Senators George F. Hoar and John C. Spooner devised a bill to tighten federal control over congressional elections. Under its terms, federal circuit courts, on complaint of a hundred or more voters, could appoint bipartisan supervisory boards to oversee registration and elections, and investigators to examine disputed elections and determine winners. The bill said nothing about use of troops or marshals or about state or local elections, but Democrats nonetheless labeled it a "force bill" that would bring back the "bayonet rule" of Reconstruction. The bill narrowly passed the House in July 1890, but it proved a costly issue for the Republicans in the fall elections, which they lost heavily. In the postelection second session of the Fifty-first Congress, the general dispirit among Republicans, plus the abandonment of the bill by several party senators favoring silver legislation, led to the measure's defeat in the Senate.

Further Reading: Richard E. Welch, Jr., "The Federal Elections Bill of 1890: Postscripts and Prelude," *Journal of American History* 52 (1965): 511–526; R. Hal Williams, *Years of Decision: American Politics in the 1890s*, 1978.

Charles W. Calhoun

FELSENTHAL, BERNHARD (2 January 1822–12 January 1908), rabbi. Born at Münchweiler, Bavaria, Felsenthal immigrated to the United States in 1854, settling first in Indiana and then Chicago. There, in 1861, he became the first rabbi of Congregation Sinai. A preeminent figure in the development of Reform Judaism in the Midwest, Felsenthal wielded enormous influence. As a member of the Jewish Publication Society of America, he proposed founding the American Jewish Historical Society. Felsenthal wrote prolifically; his bibliography includes some 315 titles. Interspersed throughout his publications and lectures were the themes of Reform Judaism and Zionism. His attitude toward these movements altered as his experience, knowledge, and judgment deepened over the years. At first he demonstrated no active support for the Jewish Palestinian Crusade, but by 1897 he rallied to its cause. Felsenthal taught that Judaism was both a religion and a national culture; it constituted "the sum total of all the manifestations of the dis-tinctively Jewish national spirit." His convictions, teachings, and writings earned him a significant place in American Jewish life during the Gilded Age.

Further Reading: *New York Times*, 14 January 1908.

Leonard Schlup

FELT, DORR EUGENE (18 March 1862–7 August 1930), inventor and manufacturer. Born in Beloit, Wisconsin, Felt moved in 1882 to Chicago, where he worked for the Pullman Company. In 1886, he constructed the first multiple-column, key-operated calculating machine. Called the Comptometer, it was the first totally accurate adding machine. The following year he formed a partnership with Robert Tarrant to manufacture this invention and others, including in 1889 the Comptograph, the first practical adding and listing machine to come on the market. President of Felt and Tarrant Manufacturing Company until his death, Felt, a Republican, became a prominent figure in the Midwest, served on various boards of directors, lectured on business conditions, and engaged in amateur photography. He died in Chicago.

Further Reading: *Chicago Tribune*, 8 August 1930.

Leonard Schlup

FENGER, CHRISTIAN (3 November 1840–7 March 1902), surgeon, pathologist, and professor. Born in Breininggaard, Denmark, Fenger studied and practiced medicine in Europe and Egypt before immigrating in 1877 to Chicago. There he taught and engaged in pathological work at Cook County Hospital. In 1880 he became curator of the pathology museum at Rush Medical College, and professor of surgery there nine years later. His autopsies, lectures, theory on the bacterial nature of endocarditis, and advocacy of medical education for women attracted national attention. With his meticulous dissections and precise diagnoses, Fenger pioneered in pathology and surgery during the Gilded Age. He died in Chicago.

Further Reading: Edwin F. Hirsch, "Christian Fenger, M.D., 1840–1902: The Impact of His Scientific Training and His Personality on Medicine in Chicago," *Proceedings of the Institute of Medicine of Chicago* 287 (1971): 513–530; "Christian Fenger," *Journal of the American Medical Association* 38 (1902): 718–720.

Leonard Schlup

FERNOW, BERTHOLD (28 November 1837–3 March 1908), historian. Born at Inowrazlaw, Prussia, Fernow began his education with private teachers and in the gymnasiums of Magdeburg and Bromberg, and ended with the study of agriculture in Silesia. He spent two years in the Prussian army before immigrating to the United States in 1862. He enlisted in the Fourth Missouri Cavalry during the Civil War and was commissioned a lieutenant in the Third United States Colored Infantry, which fought in the final Union campaign in Charleston, South Carolina. Fernow farmed in New Jersey and did business in New York City before becoming New York State archivist in 1875, under Secretary of State John Bigelow. He transcribed several volumes of colonial documents and compiled the first edition of New York State archives in 1887. He was forced to resign in 1889 for undisclosed reasons. He wrote on local, New York, and American history and genealogy for several publications and organizations in his later years. His favorite hobby was canoeing, and he wrote magazine articles on that subject. He was unmarried, and died in the national home for disabled soldiers at Togus, Maine.

Further Reading: *National Cyclopedia of American Biography*, vol. 33, 1933.

Richard Digby-Junger

FERRY, ELISHA PEYRE (9 August 1825–14 October 1895), governor and lawyer. Born to French immigrants in Monroe, Michigan, Ferry received a public education, studied law, and was admitted to the Illinois bar in 1845. The following year he moved to Waukegan, Illinois, to practice law, and was later elected the city's first mayor. He served as a presidential elector in the 1852 and 1856 elections, and rose to colonel in the Adjutant General's Office during the Civil War. As reward for his service, President Ulysses S. Grant appointed Ferry surveyor general of the Washington Territory in 1869. Three years later he became territorial governor. During two terms in that office, Ferry oversaw extinction of British title to the San Juan Islands, the final departure of the Hudson's Bay Company from the region, extension of aid to Idaho during the Nez Percé War

(1877), and growth of the statehood movement. After leaving office, he practiced law for several years, briefly served as a bank officer, then won election as Washington's first state governor in 1889. A Republican, he opposed women's suffrage and, because of illness, retired after one term (1893). Ferry spent the remainder of his life in Seattle. Ferry County was named in his honor in 1899.

Further Reading: Hubert Howe Bancroft, *History of Washington, Idaho, and Montana, 1845–1889*, 1890; Edmond S. Meany, *History of the State of Washington*, 1909.

Derek R. Larson

FERRY, THOMAS WHITE (1 June 1827–14 October 1896), representative and senator. Born on Mackinac Island, Michigan, Ferry moved in 1834 to the Grand River, where his family founded the town of Grand Haven. After attending the village school, he joined his father's lumber business, Ferry & Sons, and entered local politics. He was a Republican member of Michigan's lower house from 1850 to 1852, and a state senator in 1856. Elected to the House of Representatives in 1865, he served three terms; he entered the Senate six years later. He led efforts to reform the national banking system and initiated the 1877 revision of the Senate rules. On 9 March 1875, senators elected him as president pro tempore of the Senate, and following Vice President Henry Wilson's death in November, Ferry was considered President Grant's acting vice president. As the Electoral Commission's presiding officer, he supervised bipartisan efforts to resolve the disputed presidential election of 1876, announcing Rutherford B. Hayes's victory over Samuel Tilden on 2 March 1877. Ferry lost his Senate seat to Republican Thomas W. Palmer in 1883, and withdrew from public affairs. He died in Grand Haven.

Further Reading: Lawrence E. Ziewacz, "The Eighty-first Ballot: The Senatorial Struggle of 1883," *Michigan History* 56 (1972): 216–232; *Detroit Free Press*, 15 October 1896.

Jane M. Armstrong

FIELD, DAVID DUDLEY (13 February 1805–13 April 1894), lawyer. Field, the eldest son of a Congregationalist minister and brother of U.S. Supreme Court justice Stephen Field and telegraph promoter Cyrus Field, was born in Haddam, Connecticut. Educated at Williams College, he began practicing law in New York in 1828. Appointed to a state commission to reform legal procedures in 1847, he drew up a standard code for civil procedures, which New York and twenty-four other states adopted by 1873, and a code for criminal procedures, adopted by eleven states. Field believed the legislature, rather than judges, should control legal procedures, which would be uniform throughout the nation. The Field Codes became standard guidelines to courtroom procedure and legal practices. Though a Republican, Field opposed radical Reconstruction, arguing against federal power over the states in *United States* v. *Cruikshank* (1876) and *United States* v. *Reese* (1876). As attorney for Jay Gould, James Fisk, and William Marcy Tweed, Field was one of the country's most highly paid lawyers. His activities on behalf of his clients led New York lawyers to form the Bar Association of the City of New York, which unsuccessfully attempted to expel Field. He died in New York City.

Further Reading: Daun Roell van Ee, "David Dudley Field and the Reconstruction of the Law," Ph.D. diss., Johns Hopkins University, 1974; Stephen N. Subrin, "David Dudley Field and the Field Code: A Historical Analysis of an Earlier Procedural Vision," *Law and History Review* 6 (1988): 311–373; Henry M. Field, *The Life of David Dudley Field*, 1995.

Robert J. Allison

FIELD, JAMES GAVEN (24 February 1826– 12 October 1901), Populist Party politician. Born in Walnut, Virginia, Field attended a classical school, worked as a merchant and teacher, then journeyed to California in 1848 with the army. There he became involved in territorial affairs and was chosen secretary to the convention that framed the state's first constitution in 1850. Field returned to Virginia, read law under his uncle, and was admitted to the bar in 1852. In 1859, he became commonwealth attorney. During the Civil War, he served on the staff of Confederate General Ambrose P. Hill. Field lost a leg on 9 August 1862, at the battle of Slaughter's Mountain. In 1877, he became attorney general of Virginia. After serving for five years, he retired to a private life devoted to agriculture and religion.

Field attended the Populists' 1892 convention, at Omaha, Nebraska, and was nominated as former Union General James B. Weaver's running mate. The choice of the two men was meant in part to signify the replacement of sectionalism with class solidarity. Hoping at least to deny the two major candidates an electoral college majority, the Weaver/Field ticket fell short of its goal. The Populists won a mere twenty-two electoral votes, with less than 5 percent of the popular vote. Field returned to retirement and died nine years later at his home in Gordonsville, Virginia.

Further Reading: *New York Times* 6 July 1892; *National Cyclopaedia of American Biography*, 1904.

Harvey Gresham Hudspeth

FIELD, MARSHALL (18 August 1834–16 January 1906), retail magnate and philanthropist. Born near Conway, Massachusetts, Field dropped out of high school, clerked, and eventually rose to general manager of a Chicago dry-goods firm. A pioneer in the rise of modern department stores, he opened his own venture in 1864, and by 1867 was grossing over $12 million per year. Field rationalized business practices and imposed strict codes of conduct on his employees. He invested in the enterprises of other rising Chicago businesses, including those of Cyrus McCormick and George Pullman. Field was noted for his tough business acumen, strong opinions, and a frugal lifestyle. To some, he was a "robber baron." Female sales clerks worked long hours for low wages, while Field's wealth reached $125 million by 1905. He ardently opposed labor unions, the free silver movement, and radicalism. He battled a hostile Chicago press corps, which accused him of bribery and undue political influence. He helped incorporate the Art Institute of Chicago, the University of Chicago, and the Field Museum of Natural History. Field was credited with the adage "The customer is always right," though he actually said, "Assume that the customer is right until it is plain beyond all question he is not." His business methods are still in use, and Marshall Field's remains a retail powerhouse.

Further Reading: John Tebbel, *The Marshall Fields: A Study in Wealth*, 1947; Rev. Charles Rice, ed., *The Field*

Memorial Library, 1907; Chicago Tribune, 17 January 1906.

Robert E. Weir

FIELD, STEPHEN JOHNSON (November 1816–9 April 1899), Supreme Court justice. Born in Haddam, Connecticut, Field graduated from Williams College (1837), was a partner with a brother in a New York lawfirm, then moved to California in 1849. A Democrat, he specialized in real estate and mining claims, and won a seat in the state legislature the next year. In 1857, he was elected to the state supreme court. President Lincoln appointed him to the U.S. Supreme Court in 1863. There he opposed both federal and state regulation of business as an infringement on property rights. He also supported Chinese immigrants against discriminatory legislation.

Field is most remembered, however, for his tumultuous personal life. Disbarred twice and twice challenged to a duel, he was nearly assassinated by former California chief justice David Terry in 1889, after deciding a complicated and messy divorce case. Field's bodyguard killed Terry. By the 1890s Field, once the Supreme Court's intellectual leader, had become senile. He was persuaded to retire in 1897, having served thirty-four years, eight months, and twenty days, at the time the longest tenure of any justice. He died in Washington, D.C.

Further Reading: Paul Kens, *Justice Stephen Field: Shaping Liberty from the Gold Rush to the Gilded Age*, 1997; Carl Brent Swisher, *Stephen J. Field: Craftsman of the Law*, 1963.

Robert J. Allison

FIELDS, ANNIE ADAMS (6 June 1834–5 January 1915), social welfare advocate and author. Born in Boston, Massachusetts, Adams married James Thomas Fields, head of the Boston publishing house of Ticknor and Fields, in 1854. During the 1880s and 1890s, she published three volumes of poetry and several works of literary reminiscences, including those of her husband, John Greenleaf Whittier, Harriet Beecher Stowe, Nathaniel Hawthorne, and Charles Dudley Warner. She traveled extensively, entertained at numerous social events, and was one of the principal founders in 1879

of the Associated Charities of Boston. In the 1870s she promoted coffeehouses in poor neighborhoods as a temperance measure, and aided individuals living in tenements. Although not an active feminist, she supported woman suffrage. Fields died in her Charles Street home in Boston.

Further Reading: *Boston Transcript*, 6 January 1915; Annie Adams Fields diary, Massachusetts Historical Society, Boston.

Leonard Schlup

FIFER, JOSEPH WILSON (28 October 1840–6 August 1938), governor of Illinois. Born near Staunton, Virginia, Fifer attended public schools, fought in the Union Army, and graduated from Illinois Wesleyan College in 1868. After studying in a law office, he opened a practice in Bloomington, Illinois, in 1869. He won local elections, then served in the Illinois Senate from 1880 to 1884. In 1888, he narrowly defeated Democrat John M. Palmer for governor. During his term (1889–1893), Fifer worked with Democrats to avoid rigid partisanship. He secured the adoption of the Australian ballot, a major reform step toward honest elections. Fifer also supported measures to codify the public school laws and an annexation act for state consolidation of cities. An 1889 compulsory education law, requiring children in both public and parochial schools to be taught in English to age twelve, was the most controversial legislation of his administration. Both German Lutherans and Catholics voiced their opposition. Fifer lost the governorship in 1892 to the Democrat John Peter Altgeld. In 1899, President William McKinley named Fifer to the Interstate Commerce Commission, where he remained until 1906. In an age of political generals, his nickname "Private Joe" provided the common touch that politicians cultivated. He died in Bloomington.

Further Reading: James O. Bennett, *"Private Joe" Fifer*, 1936; Robert P. Howard, *Mostly Good and Competent Men: Illinois Governors, 1818–1988*, 1988; Joseph W. Fifer Papers, Illinois State Historical Library, Springfield.

Robert M. Sutton

FIFTEENTH AMENDMENT. Passed by Congress in February 1869 and ratified on 30 March 1870, the Fifteenth Amendment to the

U.S. Constitution guaranteed to every citizen the right to vote, regardless of race, color, or "previous condition of servitude." It was the last of three Civil War amendments. The former slaves possessed voting rights in the former Confederate states because of the Reconstruction Acts of 1866 and 1867, but most northern states limited suffrage to white males. Only a constitutional amendment could permanently enfranchise African Americans in the former Confederacy, a circumstance deemed absolutely essential to protect the lives, liberties, and property of everyone after the expected recapture of power by the former Confederate elite in the readmitted states.

Proposed suffrage amendments ranged from a federal guarantee of manhood suffrage to impartial suffrage, by which states could impose limitations on the right to vote so long as the limitations were imposed on both white and African-American voters. The latter approach was adopted after a contentious struggle by a lame duck Congress aware that election losses made future action on the question unlikely. During the congressional debate on the amendment, radicals feared that impartial suffrage would allow use of such devices as property or literacy requirements to disenfranchise African Americans, a fear that proved correct.

Further Reading: Michael Les Benedict, *A Compromise of Principle: Congressional Republicans and Reconstruction, 1863–1869,* 1974; Earl M. Maltz, *Civil Rights, the Constitution, and Congress, 1863–1869,* 1990; Xi Wang, "Bondage, Freedom and the Constitution: The New Slavery Scholarship and Its Impact on Law and Legal Historiography" and "Emancipation and the New Conception of Freedom: Black Suffrage and the Redefinition of American Freedom, 1860–1870," *Cardozo Law Review* 17 (1996): 2153–2223.

M. Susan Murnane

FIFTY-SEVEN CENTS. In 1884 Reverend Russell Herman Conwell (1843–1925), pastor of Grace Baptist Church in Philadelphia, Pennsylvania, arrived at his small church building one Sunday morning and found several children in front of the door, unable to enter for lack of chairs and room. He told them that one day there would be larger accommodations with sufficient space for everyone. Conwell thereupon lifted Hattie May Wiatt, a sobbing six-year-old girl from a nearby house, onto his shoulders and walked into the overflowing church, where he secured a place for her in a corner. Two years later, Hattie's parents summoned Conwell to their home, where Hattie had just died. After Conwell conducted the funeral, the girl's grieving mother gave the minister a little bag she had discovered under her daughter's pillow. It contained fifty-seven cents that Hattie had saved to help build the little temple, so more children could attend Sunday school. Converting the fifty-seven cents into fifty-seven pennies, Conwell, an eloquent orator and popular religious leader, offered them for sale to help fund the building project. The idea immediately sparked interest. The pennies were bought for $250. Congregation members returned fifty-four of the fifty-seven pennies, which church officials framed for posterity. From that amount and the generosity of supporters and benefactors challenged by Hattie's vision, and supplemented by the Wiatt Mite Society, the amount of money multiplied over time. Successful fund-raising campaigns resulted in the construction of Temple Baptist Church in Philadelphia, a large Sunday school building, Temple University, and Good Samaritan Hospital. The architect Thomas P. Lonsdale supervised the church's construction. Conwell later placed a commissioned painting of Hattie in the new church, which was completed in 1891 and located on North Broad Street between Montgomery and Norris streets. It was a fitting conclusion to the touching story of a poor little girl who died and left a legacy of fifty-seven cents with which to build a bigger church.

Further Reading: *The Temple Review,* 19 December 1912; *Philadelphia Press,* 2 March 1891; Russell H. Conwell, *The Angel's Lily and the History of Temple University,* 1920.

Leonard Schlup

FILLMORE, MYRTLE (6 August 1845–6 October 1931), and **FILLMORE, CHARLES SHERLOCK** (22 August 1854–5 July 1948), founders of the Unity School of Christianity. Myrtle was born Mary Caroline Page in Pagetown, Ohio, attended Oberlin College, taught school, and briefly operated a private academy.

In 1876, in Denison, Texas, she met Charles S. Fillmore, a native of Saint Cloud, Minnesota, who was distantly related to President Millard Fillmore. Charles had worked widely in the West as a real estate salesman, railroad freight inspector, and assayer. They married in Clinton, Missouri, in 1881, lived in Colorado until 1884, and then moved to Kansas City, Missouri. There they advocated temperance and began a religious periodical, *Modern Thought*, (1889).

The Fillmores were influenced by Emma Curtis Hopkins, E. B. Weeks, and Joseph Adams, advocates of the New Thought movement, and they preached an idealistic healing method within Christianity. Both Fillmores taught tolerance, forgiveness, love, compassion, meditation, true health, and the philosophy that a good, omnipotent God was the only presence and power in the universe, that the love and light of God watched over and uplifted people. Individuals could walk peacefully with each other in perfect harmony. A divinity of humanity encompassed the freedom of people in their personal practices and beliefs. The Fillmores began a prayer ministry in 1890, and named their growing movement Unity. Myrtle functioned as its inspirational leader, especially after healing a person afflicted with tuberculosis in 1888. Charles served as the church's writer, organizer, developer, and marketer. Unity was headquartered in Lee's Summit, Missouri (known as Unity Village) and became for its members a beacon of spiritual light to the world community. The religion expanded rapidly in the twentieth century, claiming 602 churches by 1992 with over two million adherents. Both Fillmores died at Lee's Summit.

Further Reading: T. E. Witherspoon, *Myrtle Fillmore, Mother of Unity*, 1977; J. D. Freeman, *The Story of Unity*, 1978; Neal Vahle, *Torch-Bearer to Light the Way: The Life of Myrtle Fillmore*, 1996.

Leonard Schlup

FILSON CLUB. Ten prominent Kentuckians founded the Filson Club Historical Society in Louisville on 15 May 1884. A private organization, it was named for John Filson (1753–1788), who wrote *The Discovery, Settlement, and Present State of Kentucke* (1784). The club's first president, Reuben Thomas Durrett,

served from 1884 to 1913. The society collects and preserves library and manuscript materials and objects of material culture. It also publishes historical monographs. In 1926, the society began issuing *The Filson Club History Quarterly*, a regional history journal. Over the years, the society has grown from a small club for amateur historians to one of the finest research institutions in the South.

Further Reading: Otto A. Rothert, *The Filson Club and Its Activities, 1884–1922*, 1922; Lowell H. Harrison, "A Century of Progress: The Filson Club, 1884–1984," *The Filson Club History Quarterly* 58 (1984): 381–407; James R. Bentley, "The Filson Club," in John E. Kleber, ed., *The Kentucky Encyclopedia*, 1992, 317–318.

Nelson L. Dawson

FIRESTONE, HARVEY SAMUEL (20 December 1868–7 February 1938), entrepreneur and industrialist. Firestone was born on a farm in Columbiana County, Ohio. Success in livestock trading convinced him to attend business college in Cleveland before taking a sales position with a Columbus carriage manufacturer. The company sent him to Detroit, where he sold buggies for a time; then he moved to Chicago, where he started the Firestone-Victor Rubber Company, which made hard rubber buggy tires. Firestone relocated to Akron, Ohio, in 1900, and with three others founded the Firestone Tire and Rubber Company, joining earlier arrivals B.F. Goodrich (1871) and Goodyear (1898). In 1905 Firestone secured an order for two thousand sets of tires for the visionary automaker Henry Ford. Firestone's company became one of the keys to Akron's industrial growth. Firestone, who headed his company through most of the Great Depression, died at his winter home in Miami Beach, Florida.

Further Reading: Alfred Lief, *Harvey Firestone: Free Man of Enterprise*, 1951; Karl H. Grismer, *Akron and Summit County*, 1952; George W. Knepper, *Akron: City at the Summit*, 1981.

Stephen Paschen

FISH, HAMILTON (3 August 1808–7 September 1893), congressman and cabinet member. Born in New York City, Fish was graduated from Columbia College in 1827. He practiced law, served in the U.S. House of Representatives (1843–1845), was governor of New

York (1849–1851) and U.S. senator (1851–1857). During the Civil War, he served on a prisoner-exchange board. President Ulysses Grant appointed him secretary of state in 1869. In that post Fish concentrated on resolving claims with Great Britain and other powers rising out of the Civil War, most notably the *Alabama* claims. The 1871 Treaty of Washington established binding arbitration and redefined the responsibility of neutrals. The agreement also allowed free navigation of the St. Lawrence River by U.S. vessels. In 1872, Fish negotiated a settlement of the long-standing border dispute with Great Britain in the Pacific Northwest. He also opposed American intervention in Cuba's revolt against Spain. When the Spanish seized the American steamer *Virginius*, bringing arms to Cuban rebels in 1873, and executed fifty-three passengers and crew, Fish successfully defused public outrage and convinced Spain to promptly release the ship and the survivors, and to pay compensation. In internal State Department matters, Fish reduced political influence, instituted competitive examinations, and sought a merit system. Fish left office in 1877. He died in Garrison, New York.

Further Reading: Allen Nevins, *Hamilton Fish: The Inner History of the Grant Administration*, 1937; *New York Times*, 8 September 1893.

Stephen Svonavec

FISKE, JOHN (30 March 1842–4 July 4 1901), historian and philosopher. Born Edmund Fisk Green in Hartford, Connecticut, Fiske was graduated from Harvard in 1863 and wrote several accounts of early New England and the American Revolution. His most influential history work was *The Critical Period in American History* (1888), which argued that the Articles of Confederation nearly destroyed the nation, and that the heroes of the Philadelphia Convention who wrote the federal Constitution saved it. His assertion met no significant challenge before Charles Beard and Merrill Jensen in the twentieth century. Of Fiske's numerous philosophical writings, *Outlines of Cosmic Philosophy* (1874) is best known. Fiske sought a synthesis of Darwinian natural selection with a Christian and theistic cosmology uniting history, science, and religion. Knowledge was

progressive, evolving from the unknown expression of faith to the known data of science; humanity would benefit immeasurably from cosmic and evolutionary endeavor. Hence, Darwinism and Christianity led to an understanding of the same moral law. Fiske represented one of several schools of thought that explored the complex relationships among history, science, and religion.

Further Reading: Milton Berman, *John Fiske; the Evolution of a Popularizer*, 1961; Jennings B. Sanders, "John Fiske," *The Marcus W. Jernegan Essays in American Historiography*, 1937; John Clark Spencer, *The Life and Letters of John Fiske*, 2 vols., 1917.

Donald K. Pickens

FITZGERALD, JOHN FRANCIS (11 February 1863–2 October 1950), congressman, mayor, and businessman. The grandfather of President John F. Kennedy, Fitzgerald was born in Boston, Massachusetts. After being graduated from the Boston Latin School, he held a position in the city's customhouse from 1886 to 1891, and was a member of the Boston Common Council in 1892. A Democrat, he spent the next two years in the Massachusetts Senate. He reigned as boss of the North End of Boston, succeeding his friend Matthew Keany. Fitzgerald served in the U.S. House of Representatives from 1895 to 1901. He was one of only three Catholic congressmen. Fitzgerald favored expansion of the Port of Boston, supported the plan to tax incomes rather than levy higher duties on foreign products, and advocated unrestricted immigration. He delivered a powerful oration on immigration to his colleagues on 27 January 1897 and later discussed the issue with President Grover Cleveland. Fitzgerald chose not to seek renomination to Congress in 1900, concentrating instead on his varied business activities. He served as mayor of Boston from 1906 to 1907 and again from 1910 to 1914. Fitzgerald unsuccessfully sought election to the U.S. Senate in 1916 and to the governorship of Massachusetts in 1922. When he died in Boston, his grandson was already in Congress.

Further Reading: *New York Times*, 3 October 1950; John Henry Culter, *"Honey Fitz": Three Steps to the White House. The Life and Times of John F. (Honey Fitz) Fitzgerald*, 1962; Doris Kearns Goodwin, *The Fitzgeralds and the Kennedys*, 1987.

Leonard Schlup

FITZSIMMONS, ROBERT PROMETHEUS (26 May 1862–22 October 1917), professional boxer. Born in Helston, Cornwall, England, Fitzsimmons moved at a very young age to Australia. There he gained prominence as one of the nation's best fighters before exhibiting his talents in the United States. Fitzsimmons held the world heavyweight (1897–1899), light heavyweight (1903–1905), and middleweight (1891–1897) championships. His most prominent bouts were against Jack Dempsey, Jim Corbett, and Jim Jeffries. Fitzsimmons won the first of his world titles by defeating a very formidable Dempsey in 1891. In 1897, during a much-anticipated heavyweight title contest against Corbett, Fitzsimmons started slowly and was losing badly in the opening rounds. He rebounded, however, and felled the champion with one punch to the abdomen, which became known as his "solar plexus" punch. Two years later, Fitzsimmons lost his crown to Jeffries. Fitzsimmons was inactive late in his career until fighting again in 1903 for the world the light-heavyweight title, which he retained for two years. He compiled a career record of forty wins and eleven defeats. He died in Chicago and was elected to the Boxing Hall of Fame in 1954.

Further Reading: Elliot J. Gorn, *The Manly Art: Bare-Knuckle Prize Fighting in America*, 1986.

Steve Bullock

FLAGLER, HENRY MORRISON (2 January 1830–20 May 1913), industrialist and developer of eastern Florida. Flagler was born in Hopewell, New York, and began his career in the salt business in Saginaw, Michigan, in 1863. Despite initial success, he went bankrupt when demand fell following the Civil War. He moved to Cleveland, Ohio, and became associated with John D. Rockefeller, eventually buying into the partnership that became Rockefeller, Andrews, and Flagler. Experience convinced him that competition was ruinous, so he joined Rockefeller in fixing oil prices. He was instrumental in negotiating rail transport contracts, and is credited with making the rebate and drawback standard procedure. He was one of the original trustees of Standard Oil in 1882, and served as president of the Standard Oil Company of New Jersey. He became interested in Florida development in 1885 and started a project there that would occupy him until his death in West Palm Beach. His Florida East Coast Railway linked Florida rails to existing east coast systems, and provided the capital to establish extensive agricultural experiments and to build luxury hotels along the coast. In 1912 he was successful in linking up to Key West. He, as much as Rockefeller, represents the ambivalent characterization of Gilded Age businessmen as either robber barons or industrial statesmen.

Further Reading: Edward N. Akin, *Flagler: Rockefeller Partner and Florida Baron*, 1999; David Leon Chandler, *Henry Flagler*, 1986.

C. Edward Balog

FLETCHER, ALICE CUNNINGHAM (15 March 1838–6 April 1923), anthropologist and advocate of reform of Native American policy and education. Born in Havana, Cuba, where her parents were visiting, Fletcher attended Brooklyn Female Academy. She helped organize the Association for the Advancement of Women in 1873, and later informally studied under Frederic W. Putnam, the nation's premier archaeologist. While examining artifacts at Harvard University's Peabody Museum of American Archaeology and Ethnology, where she was the first woman fellow, Fletcher met a group of Native Americans. The chance encounter changed her life's direction. In 1881 she camped among the Omahas on their reservation in Nebraska; engaged in scientific studies of Native Americans, particularly their women; and assisted the Omaha people to address a successful petition to Congress for titles to their lands. Fletcher went to Washington to lobby for their cause, became special agent for the Bureau of Indian Affairs to survey lands, and selected the allotment for each family, person, and child. Her friendship with Francis LaFlesche, son of Chief Joseph LaFlesche, led to their ethnological collaboration. In 1890 she adopted Francis as her son.

During her career, Fletcher produced an impressive stream of publications. Her lectures and written works, including *Indian Education and Civilization* (1888), brought her national recognition. On occasion she advised President Grover Cleveland on Native American issues. Fletcher opposed the agency system that considered Natives as wards and confined them to reservations under a federal agent's control. She endorsed the Dawes Act of 1887, an allotment program she later considered a mistake. Seeking to bring Native Americans into society's mainstream, Fletcher relished her role in restructuring Native life. A pioneering ethnologist engaged in fieldwork and the first woman anthropologist of significance in the United States, Fletcher, nicknamed "Her Majesty," steadfastly sought to improve understanding between Anglos and Natives and to tear down barriers of ignorance and mistrust. Living with her Indian friends made her feel like a stranger in her own land. As time went on, however, she believed she heard the echo of pre-Columbian America and sought to make it audible to others. Fletcher died in Washington, D.C.

Further Reading: E. Jane Gay, *With the Nez Perces: Alice Fletcher in the Field, 1889–1892*, 1987; Joan T. Mark, *A Stranger in Her Native Land: Alice Fletcher and the American Indians*, 1988.

Leonard Schlup

FLETCHER, WILLIAM ISAAC (23 April 1844–15 June 1917), pioneer librarian, educator, author, and indexer. Fletcher was born in Burlington, Vermont, and grew up in Winchester, Massachusetts. As a boy, he visited the Boston Athenaeum with his father. Subsequently, he returned alone but was not allowed to stay. This incident helped him develop an outgoing and friendly attitude as a librarian later in life. Though Fletcher never finished high school, he was hired as an assistant librarian in the Winchester Library. By 1861, he joined the Boston Athenaeum, where he was placed in charge of the circulation desk. Fletcher spent considerable time collating new volumes and cataloging books. In 1866, he left to serve as librarian for several towns in Connecticut and Massachusetts.

In September 1883, Fletcher became librarian at Amherst College. Here he joined the American Library Association (ALA), began conducting library education seminars, and was a lecturer in Melvil Dewey's course. Fletcher

was well known as an author and indexer. He completed *Poole's Index to Periodical Literature* as well as his own periodical index in 1893. He edited numerous publications for the ALA, and was its president for 1891–1892. In 1951, he was elected along with forty other librarians to the Library Hall of Fame.

Further Reading: George S. Bobinski, "William Isaac Fletcher, an Early American Library Pioneer Leader," *Journal of Library History* 5 (1970): 101–118.

Mark E. Ellis

FLIPPER, HENRY OSSIAN (31 March 1856–3 May 1940), first black West Point graduate, engineer, and author. Born a slave in Thomasville, Georgia, he attended Atlanta University, and in 1873 was appointed to the U.S. Military Academy. After suffering four years of ostracism, he was graduated in 1877. He served with the segregated Tenth Cavalry Regiment at various Oklahoma and Texas forts. In 1881, he was court-martialed for alleged embezzlement and conduct unbecoming an officer. Found guilty of the latter, he was separated from the army in 1882.

For the next fifty years, Flipper worked as an engineer in the West. Fluent in Spanish and an expert in the law, he was employed by both private companies and the federal government. He volunteered for the Spanish-American War, but attempts in Congress to restore his commission failed. Continuing as an engineer, he met Albert B. Fall, later U.S. senator and secretary of the interior under President Warren G. Harding. Fall made him an assistant, but Flipper was not implicated in the Teapot Dome Scandal. He left the country anyway, working as an engineer in Venezuela from 1923 to 1940. He died in Atlanta, Georgia. In 1976, the army cleared Flipper of the nineteenth-century charges against him, and his bust was unveiled at West Point as an integrated corps of cadets passed in review.

Further Reading: Henry O. Flipper, *The Colored Cadet at West Point*, 1878; Theodore D. Harris, ed., *Black Frontiersman: The Memoirs of Henry O. Flipper, First Black Graduate of West Point*, 1997.

John F. Marszalek

FLOWER, BENJAMIN ORANGE (19 October 1858–24 December 1918), editor and reformer. Born near Albion, Illinois, Flower attended Bible school in Kentucky and grew up in Illinois, Indiana, and Pennsylvania. In 1889 he founded *The Arena*, a monthly review journal headquartered in Boston. With contributions from Stephen Crane, Hamlin Garland, Jack London, and other moralistic and realistic writers, Flower made *The Arena* a platform for individuals espousing reforms, including populism, women's rights, and the single tax. In 1896 the journal endorsed William Jennings Bryan for president. Flower earned the sobriquet "Father of the Muckrakers" for his crusade against concentration of wealth. Following a nervous breakdown in 1895, he founded and coedited *The Coming Age*, which merged with *The Arena* in 1898. Flower wrote numerous articles and books on a variety of subjects. Later he demonstrated interest in psychic research and sought to alert people to what he perceived as the menace of Roman Catholicism. He died in Cambridge, Massachusetts.

Further Reading: Howard F. Cline, "Benjamin Orange Flower and the *Arena*, 1889–1909," *Journalism Quarterly* 17 (1940): 139–50; David Dickinson, "Benjamin Orange Flower: Patron of Realists," *American Literature* 14 (1942): 148–56; *New York Times*, 25 December 1918.

Leonard Schlup

FLOWER, ROSWELL PETIBONE (7 August 1835–12 May 1899), congressman, governor. Born into comfortable circumstance in Theresa, New York, Flower fashioned a career in business, banking, and politics. In 1869, he was administrator of the estate of Henry Keep, president of the New York Central Railroad. Flower's duties brought him to Manhattan, where he was admitted to the New York Stock Exchange in 1873. A power on Wall Street, he was associated most prominently with Brooklyn Rapid Transit and Federal Steel. His means and connections brought him to the attention of New York City Democrats, who endorsed his victorious congressional bids in 1881, 1888, and 1890. Opponents denounced him as a "flamboyant millionaire" and suspected he had grander political ambitions. In 1884, Tammany Hall encouraged him to make a presidential run in hopes of heading off pro-Cleveland sentiment. With Tammany's support, he served as

governor of New York from 1892 to 1895. During his term, the legislature enacted a new banking code; and important revisions were made to the state constitution. In 1894, growing Republican sentiment caused him to forgo renomination. Flower's opposition to William Jennings Bryan's presidential nomination in 1896 put him on the national stage. He headed a New York Gold Democrat delegation to the Indianapolis convention, where he delivered an impassioned address against "populism and anarchy." He died on Long Island, New York.

Further Reading: *New York Herald*, 17 September 1891; *New York Times*, 13 May 1899; *New York Tribune*, 3 September 1896.

Marie Marmo Mullaney

FOLGER, CHARLES JAMES (16 April 1818–4 September 1884), judge and secretary of the Treasury. Born on Nantucket Island, Massachusetts, Folger moved with his parents to Geneva, New York, in 1830, was graduated from Geneva College in 1836, and practiced law locally. Appointed judge of the court of common pleas of Ontario County in 1844, he later was county judge. A former Democrat and Free-Soiler, Folger served as a Republican in the state senate in the 1860s and was an associate judge of the state court of appeals in the 1870s. In 1881, after declining the attorney generalship offered him by President James A. Garfield, Folger joined President Chester A. Arthur's cabinet as secretary of the Treasury. His years in that office coincided with a large reduction of the public debt and the advancement of classified civil service positions within the department. In 1882, Folger was defeated for the New York governorship by Grover Cleveland. Folger died in Washington, D.C.

Further Reading: *New York Times*, 5 September 1884; *New York Evening Post*, 5 September 1884; *Geneva Courier*, 10 September 1884.

Leonard Schlup

FOLKLORE. The word "folklore" was coined in 1846 by the Englishman William John Thoms. In the United States, such prominent writers on Native American mythology as Henry Rowe Schoolcraft, Horatio Hale, and Daniel Garrison Brinton used it. The materials of folklore—particularly local legends, ethnic beliefs, and supernatural tales—were also familiar in American literature as a source for Nathaniel Hawthorne, Washington Irving, and Mark Twain. Folklore that had origins in ancient usage was cited as key evidence of cultural evolution during the Gilded Age. It helped support the idea that industry and nation-states representing "civilization" reflected the natural, inevitable progress from "savagery" and "barbarism," where folklore supposedly developed. Using Native American folklore as evidence, Lewis Henry Morgan's *Ancient Society* (1877) became an influential text by applying the savagery/barbarism/civilization model to the American setting. It was often cited by John Wesley Powell, head of the Bureau of American Ethnology, which was established at the Smithsonian Institution in 1879 to record the "survivals" of native language and folklore.

In 1888, William Wells Newell organized the American Folklore Society, and in 1891 Fletcher Bassett formed a rival organization, the Chicago Folklore Society (later the International Folklore Association). These organizations promoted the study and appreciation of folklore and expanded the kinds of materials considered as folklore to regional-ethnic groups in America such as African Americans, Appalachian inhabitants of old English stock, Pennsylvania Germans, and French Canadians. When Franz Boas of Columbia University replaced Newell as editor of the *Journal of American Folklore* in 1908, he advanced his ideas of cultural relativism, which challenged the ethnocentric, hierarchical assumptions of evolutionism. Boas urged many anthropologists (including Margaret Mead, Ruth Benedict, Melville Herskovits, and Alfred L. Kroeber) to combat the biological bases of racism with research on folklore that would reveal the distinctive, artistic character of cultures.

Folklore was also used during the Gilded Age to create a sense of nationalism. Amid growing immigration and cultural diversity, Theodore Roosevelt called for the creation of a national folk literature in the United States, similar to efforts in Ireland and Germany, that could boost the sense of national tradition. He endorsed John Lomax's collections of cowboy songs and Henry Shoemaker's heroic legends and tall tales of the wilderness as examples of America's unique lore.

Further Reading: Simon J. Bronner, *Folklife: Studies from the Gilded Age*, 1987; Simon J. Bronner, *Following Tradition: Folklore in the Discourse of American Culture*, 1998; William K. McNeil, "A History of Folklore Scholarship Before 1908," Ph.D. diss., Indiana University, 1980.

Simon J. Bronner

FOOD. The Gilded Age brought expanded food options. In the immediate post–Civil War years food was little different for Americans than it had been. It comprised locally produced and quickly consumed comestibles with almost no shelf life. Potatoes, carrots, turnips, and a few other vegetables could be kept for several months, but most vegetables and meat had to be consumed immediately upon harvest or be subjected to preservation by smoking, salting, or drying. The taste and texture of food were profoundly altered by contemporary processing; beef jerky is tough and dry, and sauerkraut has little resemblance to the cabbage used to make it, but some portions of hog kills, especially ham and bacon, acquire attractive characteristics when cured for preservation, and are still popular with consumers.

Railroads changed the way people ate. Local food supplies were supplemented with fruits, vegetables, and meat produced at great distances, at costs low enough to permit shipment over hundreds, even thousands, of miles. As population and demand for food grew on the east coast, wheat cultivation and flour milling moved to the Midwest, where land was abundant and cheap and rail access enabled shipment of flour to distant markets. Corn production spread westward; much of the crop was fed to hogs that would supply the eastern markets with preserved pork. Beef production expanded into the West and cattle, herded to railheads, were shipped by rail to eastern abattoirs. In the 1880s, Chicago became the center of the new American dressed-beef industry. Cattle fattened on western grasslands and ranches were shipped to Chicago, where they were killed in slaughter factories. The edible carcasses were shipped via refrigerated rail cars to markets in the East. Similar refrigerated cars preserved vegetables and fruit shipped from as far away as California to New York and other eastern metropolitan markets. Canning, also introduced in the Gilded Age, altered the contents of the American pantry.

Further Reading: David O. Whitten, *The Emergence of Giant Enterprise, 1860–1914: American Commercial Enterprise and Extractive Industries*, 1983.

David O. Whitten

FORAKER ACT OF 1900. This act of Congress established the principle that the country's new territorial acquisitions did not receive membership in the American union. At issue was a tariff measure that would include Puerto Rico in the U.S. customs and internal revenue systems. Protected tobacco, sugar, and fruit interests argued that Puerto Rico was not part of the United States and was, therefore, subject to tariffs. Senator Joseph B. Foraker, an Ohio Republican, led the successful defense of the modified bill that placed Puerto Rico under the control of Congress and denied it the protections of the U.S. Constitution.

Further Reading: Joseph B. Foraker, *Notes of a Busy Life*, vol. 2, 1916.

Norman A. Graebner

FORAKER, JOSEPH BENSON (5 July 1846–10 May 1917), governor and U.S. senator. Born on a farm near Rainsboro, Ohio, Foraker served in the Civil War, graduated from Cornell University in 1869, and began practicing law in Cincinnati, Ohio, the same year. He held a city superior court judgeship from 1879 to 1882. Republican governor of Ohio from 1886 to 1890, Foraker favored voter registration laws, re-funding the state debt, creating a state board of health, and appointing commissions to reform Cincinnati's police force and public works administration. A U.S. senator from 1897 to 1909, Foraker, known as "Fire Alarm Foraker" for his colorful personality and aggressive verbal attacks on prominent politicians, supported U.S. participation in the Spanish-American War. As chairman of the Committee on the Pacific Islands and Puerto Rico, he sponsored and pushed through to adoption the Foraker Act of 1900, to organize the civil government of Puerto Rico. He was an independent thinker, a constitutional lawyer, a

skilled speaker, and subsequently a conservative who opposed most of President Theodore Roosevelt's policies. Foraker retired amid controversy over certain campaign contributions, and died in Cincinnati.

Further Reading: Joseph Benson Foraker, *Notes of a Busy Life*, 2 vols., 1916; Everett Walters, *Joseph Benson Foraker: An Uncompromising Republican*, 1948; *New York Times*, 11 May 1917.

Leonard Schlup

FORD, HENRY (30 July 1863–7 April 1947), inventor. Ford was born in Dearborn, Michigan, where he attended the public schools between 1871 and 1879, though he believed his real education began in Detroit's machine shops and factories. In 1879 he was apprenticed to a machinist in Detroit and repaired watches for a jeweler at night. The next year he joined the Detroit Drydock Company, the city's largest shipbuilding firm, where he learned how a power plant operated. In 1882 Ford began to repair steam traction engines for farmers at Westinghouse Engine Company in Detroit. During the 1880s he also worked in other factories and on his father's farm. In 1891 Edison Illuminating Company hired him as a night engineer, and two years later promoted Ford to chief engineer.

While at Edison, Ford designed a two-passenger car, and in 1899 he convinced investors in Detroit to loan him $150,000 to create the Detroit Automobile Company, the city's first automobile plant. Ford produced roughly twenty cars before declaring bankruptcy the following year. This failure did not discourage him, and during the twentieth century his name became synonymous with the automobile. At his death in Dearborn, he had built Ford Motor Company into an industrial empire.

Further Reading: Jacqueline L. Harris, *Henry Ford*, 1984.

Christopher Cumo

FORD, JOHN THOMPSON (16 April 1829–14 March 1894), theatrical entrepreneur. Born in Baltimore, Maryland, Ford managed the Holliday Street Theatre there from 1854 to 1879, and completed work on Ford's Theatre on Tenth Street in Washington, D.C., in 1863. Over the next two years, 495 performances were staged under his able management. Following President Abraham Lincoln's assassination in Ford's Theatre on 14 April 1865, Ford and his brother Harry Clay Ford were incarcerated for over a month until exonerated from any complicity in the crime. Public threats prevented Ford from reopening the building, though he had mounted engaging productions, employed modern equipment, and hired first-rate actors. In 1866, Congress paid Ford $100,000 for the theater, and shortly thereafter, the War Department converted the building into government offices. On 9 June 1893 parts of the edifice collapsed, killing twenty-eight persons. Renovation and restoration of Ford's Theatre occurred over the next century. During the Gilded Age, Ford managed theatres in Philadelphia, Richmond, Virginia, and Alexandria, Virginia. He built the Grand Opera House in Baltimore in 1871. His connections with banking and financial concerns, his presidency of the Union Railroad Company, and the vice presidency of the West Baltimore Improvement Association gave him prominence as a successful businessman. Ford also served as trustee of numerous philanthropic institutions. He died in Baltimore.

Further Reading: *Baltimore Sun*, 15 March 1894; *New York Tribune*, 15 March 1894; Edward Steers, Jr., *Blood on the Moon: The Assassination of Abraham Lincoln*, 2001.

Leonard Schlup

FORD, PAUL LEICESTER (23 March 1865–8 May 1902), historian and author. Born in Brooklyn, New York, Ford gained a reputation for his scholarly endeavors that focused on the lives and writings of important figures in U.S. history, including Benjamin Franklin, Thomas Jefferson, John Dickinson, and George Washington. Ford also compiled dozens of minor and major bibliographies. He coedited *Library Journal* from 1890 to 1893, during which time he crusaded for improved library service, urged open stacks for readers, encouraged library specialization, advocated formation of union catalogs, and emphasized interlibrary loan, then a revolutionary concept. In 1894 Ford published his first novel, *The Honorable Peter Stirling*. His second novel, *Janice Meredith*, appeared in 1899. In 1891 the death of his father, Gordon

Lester Ford, a wealthy businessman and political figure, gave Ford and his brother Worthington the opportunity, eight years later, to donate most of the family's valuable library to the New York Public Library. When Malcolm Ford, the disinherited brother, sued unsuccessfully for a share of his father's monetary estate, Paul, under oath in court, blamed Gordon's death on Malcolm, from whom the elder Ford had contracted typhoid fever. Malcolm, humiliated by his financial loss and gradually turning delusional, fatally shot Paul in the latter's New York City home.

Further Reading: Paul Z. DuBois, *Paul Leicester Ford: An American Man of Letters, 1865–1902*, 1977; *New York Evening Post*, 9 May 1902; Paul L. Ford Papers, Manuscript Division, New York Public Library.

Leonard Schlup

FOREIGN POLICY. During the Gilded Age, the United States responded to incidents with little thought to policy although there was a general consistency and the presence of ill-defined and emotional sacred principles such as the Monroe Doctrine. Following the Civil War, the United States addressed diplomatic issues. France withdrew from Mexico and ended its support of Maximilian (1867). In 1871 and 1872, the Treaty of Washington and subsequent arbitration resolved a more difficult problem created by Confederate cruisers constructed in British shipyards. For their attacks on the North's shipping, the United States received $15.5 million in 1872.

Attempted territorial expansion was a common policy theme. Russia happily sold Alaska to the United States for $7.2 million (1867). President Ulysses Grant unsuccessfully tried to annex Santo Domingo (1870). In a partition of the Samoan Islands, the United States received Tutuila with the harbor of Pago Pago (1899). A successful white planter-backed revolution supported by the U.S. minister overthrew the Hawaiian monarchy in 1893 and petitioned Washington for annexation. Incoming President Grover Cleveland blocked approval, and the Republic of Hawaii waited in the wings until 1898, when the spirit of war and growing interest in the Philippine Islands favored annexation by joint resolution of Congress. The

Gilded Age reflected traditional U.S. interest in the Caribbean in the form of bases and an isthmian canal. The Clayton-Bulwer Treaty (1850) with Great Britain handicapped U.S. government action on a canal until approval of the Hay-Pauncefote Treaty (1901). The Venezuela-British Guiana boundary dispute climaxed in 1895 when the Cleveland administration made broad claims for the Monroe Doctrine in urging Britain to arbitrate the boundary. Eventually London accepted arbitration, indicating a growing acceptance of U.S. dominance in the western hemisphere and contributing to a developing Anglo-American rapprochement at century's end.

The 1898 war with Spain over Cuba symbolically marked America's emergence as a world power. The war and the peace (Treaty of Paris, 1898) added Puerto Rico, Guam, and the Philippines to U.S. territory and led to Cuba's becoming a de facto protectorate. Acquisition of the Philippines as stepping-stones to the Asian continent illustrated the belief of some Americans that there was a vast market for their goods in East Asia. Secretary of State John Hay's Open Door notes of 1899 and 1900 were attempts to ensure that the market offered equal commercial opportunity and to preserve Chinese territorial and administrative entity. By 1900, U.S. diplomats focused more on policy defined by such individuals as the naval officer and theorist Alfred Thayer Mahan, Theodore Roosevelt, John Hay, and Henry Cabot Lodge.

Further Reading: Charles S. Campbell, *The Transformation of American Foreign Relations, 1865–1900*, 1976; Robert L. Beisner, *From the Old Diplomacy to the New, 1865–1900*, 2nd ed., 1986; Walter LaFeber, *The New Empire: An Interpretation of American Expansion, 1860–1898*, 1963.

William Kamman

FOREST RESERVE ACT OF 1891. On 3 March 1891, President Benjamin Harrison received congressional authorization to proclaim forest reserves from the public domain. The primary purpose was to protect forested watersheds in the arid West. Congress had debated the issue for two decades, always concerned to enhance western settlement without imposing undue federal authority, especially presidential

authority. Nonetheless, parliamentary finesse and general support for the concept eventually enabled the act to slip through a Congress racing to complete its agenda before adjournment.

On 30 March 1891, President Harrison proclaimed the Yellowstone Park Timberland Reserve. By 1893, Harrison and Grover Cleveland had set aside nearly twenty million acres of forest reserves (renamed national forests in 1905). Cleveland, however, declined to proclaim additional reserves until their purposes were clarified by statute (were they quasi-national parks or were they available for commercial use?), which Congress did with the Forest Service Organic Act of 1897. By 1907, when Congress essentially repealed the Forest Reserve Act, approximately 150 million acres had been set aside.

Further Reading: Harold K. Steen, *The Beginning of the National Forest System*, 1991.

Harold K. Steen

FOREST SERVICE ORGANIC ACT OF 1897. The Forest Reserve Act of 1891 did not include specific language on purposes for the reserves, nor did it provide management authority. Congress immediately set about correcting these deficiencies, but for a variety of reasons, the process required six years. On 4 June 1897, President William McKinley signed the measure, which has several names—Forest Service Organic Act, Forest Management Act, and Pettigrew Amendment. Technically, the act was an amendment to the appropriations bill for the U.S. Geological Survey, but nonetheless the language was clear enough to guide creation and management of forest reserves (renamed national forests in 1905) for seven decades. The act defined the purpose of the reserves as protecting watersheds and timber supplies. Land better suited for agriculture was not to be included. The resources (minerals, forage, timber, water, etc.) were to be used under a permit system that was to assure adequate, long-term protection. The General Land Office in the Department of the Interior provided management until 1905, when authority was transferred to the Department of Agriculture and the Forest Service.

Further Reading: Harold K. Steen, *The U.S. Forest Service: A History*, 1976; Harold K. Steen, ed., *The Origins of the National Forests*, 1992.

Harold K. Steen

FOSS, SAM WALTER (19 June 1858–26 February 1911), poet and librarian. Born in Candia, New Hampshire, Foss graduated from Brown University in 1882, and with William E. Symthe purchased a Lynn, Massachusetts, newspaper that they renamed the *Saturday Union.* Foss supplied material by writing humorous local color stories and verses, stressing optimism and the work ethic. His use of the vernacular voice and the nostalgia of his messages resonated well with the public and gained widespread acceptance. Foss edited the *Yankee Blade* in Boston from 1887 to 1894. Beginning in 1892, five collections of Foss's poems were published. His most popular poem, "The House by the Side of the Road," was taught to schoolchildren for generations. Foss published *Songs of War and Peace* in 1899, and "The Song of the Library Staff," a humorous description of public libraries, in 1906 (reprinted the following year in *Songs of the Average Man*). In 1898 Foss accepted appointment as librarian of the Somerville, Massachusetts, public library. Believing that libraries should be service institutions having open shelves and holding multiple copies of popular books, Foss pioneered a modern concept of the public library and initiated traveling collections to nursing homes, hospitals, schools, and factories. His democratic philosophy of life and librarianship echoed throughout New England and ultimately helped to spark reform in the profession. Foss died in Somerville.

Further Reading: Mary S. Woodman, *Sam Walter Foss: Poet, Librarian, and Friend to Man*, 1922; *Boston Globe*, 27 February 1911; Sam Walter Foss Papers, John Hay Library, Brown University, Providence, Rhode Island.

Leonard Schlup

FOSTER, CHARLES (12 April 1828–9 January 1904), congressman, governor, and secretary of the Treasury. Born near Tiffin, Ohio, Foster left school at age fourteen to work at his father's store. After becoming a partner, Foster expanded his business interests to banking, oil, and other fields, eventually amassing a fortune.

During the Civil War, Foster helped recruit troops for the Union Army but did not serve, opting to run the family business—a decision that later earned him the nickname "Calico Charlie." Foster was elected to Congress in 1870 and was reelected three times before losing in 1878. During his years in the House of Representatives, he helped expose the Sanborn frauds and advised Rutherford B. Hayes during the disputed presidential election of 1876–1877. In 1879 Foster was elected governor of Ohio, and during his two terms reformed the tax code and appointed boards to streamline state institutions. Efforts to regulate the liquor trade failed, however, and led to the defeat of the entire state Republican ticket in 1883. In 1891, President Benjamin Harrison appointed Foster secretary of the Treasury. A bimetallist, he dutifully supported implementation of the Sherman Silver Purchase Act of 1890. He returned to private life in 1893 and saw his personal finances dwindle with that year's panic. Foster died in Springfield, Ohio.

Further Reading: George W. Knepper, *Ohio and Its People*, 1989; Ari Hoogenboom, *The Presidency of Rutherford B. Hayes*, 1988; *Cincinnati Commercial Tribune*, 10 January 1904.

Ed Bradley

FOSTER, JOHN WATSON (2 March 1836–15 November 1917), secretary of state. Born in Pike County, Indiana, Foster graduated from Indiana University in 1855, practiced law, served in the Union Army, and edited the *Evansville Daily Journal*. His endorsement of Ulysses S. Grant for reelection in 1872 led to his appointment as minister to Mexico (1873–1880). During his career, he also was minister to Russia (1880–1881) and to Spain (1883–1884). His Washington law practice specialized in international affairs. President Benjamin Harrison chose him to handle assignments including reciprocity treaties and arbitration. When Secretary of State James G. Blaine resigned in 1892, Harrison appointed Foster to fill the position. Following a successful coup against Queen Liliuokalani of Hawaii in 1893, Foster attempted to push an annexation treaty through the Senate. The effort failed. When Harrison's term ended in 1893, Foster returned to his law practice. In 1898, he advised President William McKinley on Hawaiian annexation. Foster was the father-in-law of Robert Lansing, secretary of state from 1915 to 1920, and grandfather of John Foster Dulles, secretary of state from 1953 to 1959. Foster died in Washington, D.C.

Further Reading: John Watson Foster, *Diplomatic Memoirs*, 2 vols. 1909; Michael J. Devine, *John W. Foster: Politics and Diplomacy in the Imperial Era, 1873–1917*, 1981; *New York Times*, 16 November 1917.

Leonard Schlup

FOSTER, JUDITH ELLEN HORTON AVERY (3 November 1840–11 August 1910), lawyer, prohibitionist, and Republican political figure. Born in Lowell, Massachusetts, Horton graduated from Genessee Wesleyan Seminary, taught school, and married Addison Avery in 1860. She worked as a music teacher in Chicago, and in 1869 married Elijah Caleb Foster, a lawyer, who encouraged her to study law. The Fosters practiced law in Clinton, Iowa. In 1873 Judith Foster founded the Woman's Temperance Society of Clinton and subsequently emerged as an important figure in the Woman's Christian Temperance Union (WCTU). Opposed to Frances Willard's attempt to affiliate the WCTU with the Prohibition Party, Foster, wanting to keep the issue separate from politics, formed the Nonpartisan Woman's Christian Temperance Union. In the 1880s she also created the Woman's Republican Association of the United States, serving as its president. She addressed the Republican National Convention of 1892 in Minneapolis. After moving to Washington, D.C., in 1889, Foster continued her correspondence with Republican leaders and secured appointments that took her around the nation and the world. She published many of her writings and speeches. Foster died in Washington, D.C.

Further Reading: Ruth Bordin, *Women and Temperance*, 1981; Melanie Gustafson, "Partisan Women," Ph.D. diss., New York University, 1993; Rebecca Edwards, "Gender and American Politics," Ph.D. diss., University of Virginia, 1995.

Leonard Schlup

FOULKE, WILLIAM DUDLEY (20 November 1848–30 May 1935), author. Born in New York City, Foulke received the LL.B. from Columbia University in 1871, gained admittance to the bar the next year, and in 1876 moved to Indiana, where he held a seat in the state senate from 1883 to 1885. A member of the U.S. Civil Service Commission from 1901 until 1903, Foulke was an active reformer, editor, and participant in organizations. He published several books, including *Life of Oliver P. Morton* (1889). Foulke died in Richmond, Indiana.

Further Reading: William Dudley Foulke, *Fighting the Spoilsmen: Reminiscences of the Civil Service Reform Movement*, 1919; William Dudley Foulke, *A Hoosier Autobiography*, 1922; *New York Times*, 31 May 1935.

Leonard Schlup

FOURTEENTH AMENDMENT. The Fourteenth Amendment to the U.S. Constitution was initially proposed on 13 February 1866, and was adopted in its final form on 21 July 1868. The amendment, a direct response to the Civil War and its aftermath, consists of five clauses with many subparts. Section 1 placed in the Constitution the first definition of citizenship, constitutionalizing the common-law rule that anyone born under the jurisdiction of the United States was a citizen of the state in which he/she was born and of the United States. This provision filled a void in the original Constitution, overruled the suggestion in *Dred Scott v. Sanford* (1857) that African Americans could never become U.S. citizens, and constitutionalized the definition of citizens adopted by Congress in the Civil Rights Act of 1866. Section 1 also indicated that no state could "abridge" the privileges or immunities of citizens of the United States. Though the framers of the amendment intended that this section would provide both antidiscrimination and substantive protections to U.S. citizens, a 5–4 decision in the Supreme Court's 1873 *Slaughter-House Cases* rendered this clause a nullity.

In addition, Section 1 provided that no state could deprive any "person" of "life, liberty, or property without due process of law" or deny any person "equal protection of the laws." Similar provisions existed in various state constitutions, but the framers of the amendment believed federal enforcement was needed because the states had failed to enforce these provisions. The Supreme Court has held that most of the provisions of the federal Bill of Rights are enforceable against the states through the due process clause. The Court has struck down discrimination based upon race and gender through the protection clause. Much of contemporary constitutional litigation is based upon these two provisions and their implementing statutes.

Sections 2, 3, and 4 of the amendment were extremely important at the time it was ratified, but are largely of historical interest now. They treated the apportionment of members of the House of Representatives, disqualification of certain classes of leaders of the rebellion, the validity of the public debt, repudiation of the debt of the rebellion, and prohibition of compensation for the emancipation of former slaves. Section 5 gave Congress the power to pass legislation to enforce the first four sections.

Further Reading: Michael Kent Curtis, *No State Shall Abridge*, 1986; Akhil Amar, *The Bill of Rights: Creation and Reconstruction*, 1998; Charles Fairman, *Reconstruction and Reunion*, 1971, 2 vol., 1986.

Richard L. Aynes

FRANCIS, DAVID ROWLAND (1 October 1850–15 January 1927), businessman and politician. Born in Richmond, Kentucky, Francis moved to St. Louis in 1866. Within seven years of being graduated from Washington University (1870), he opened a grain commission house, D. R. Francis & Brother. His investments eventually included warehousing, banking, transportation, insurance, and newspapers. A Democrat, he served as mayor of St. Louis from 1885 until 1889, establishing an anticorruption and antitrust record. From 1889 to 1893, he was governor of Missouri. His reforms included introduction of the Australian ballot, standardization of textbooks, grain inspection regulations, the Board of Mediation and Arbitration for strikes, and the state's first antitrust law. During his term, conflicts between the Democratic Party and the Missouri Alliance (absorbed by the Populist Party in 1892) dominated state politics. Francis opposed the Populists and William Jennings Bryan, but played a national role during the 1888 and 1892 Democratic national conventions. He characterized a new type of leader in the Democratic party, rankling old elites, yet his alliance with Grover Cleveland cost him influence. Cleveland appointed him secretary of the interior (1896–1897). From 1916 to 1918 he served as ambassador to Russia. Francis died in St. Louis.

Further Reading: C. Joseph Pusateri, "A Businessman in Politics: David R. Francis, Missouri Democrat," Ph.D. diss., St. Louis University, 1965; Walter B. Stevens, *David R. Francis, Ambassador Extraordinary and Plenipotentiary*, 1991.

Linda Eikmeier Endersby

FRELINGHUYSEN, FREDERICK THEODORE (4 August 1817–20 May 1885), lawyer, senator, and secretary of state. Born in Millstone, New Jersey, Frelinghuysen was graduated from Rutgers in 1836. Admitted to the bar in 1839, he served as state attorney general from 1861 to 1866. Selected to complete an unfinished term in the U.S. Senate from 1866 to 1869, Frelinghuysen returned to the Senate from 1871 to 1877. He was a member of the commission that decided the outcome of the election of 1876. In 1881, President Chester A. Arthur selected him to replace James G. Blaine as secretary of state. Frelinghuysen quickly reversed Blaine's forceful diplomacy with Chile and Peru in the War of the Pacific, and the conflict ended in 1883 without U.S. intervention. Frelinghuysen argued unsuccessfully for abrogation of the Clayton-Bulwer Treaty with Great Britain, and negotiated a canal treaty with Nicaragua that was never ratified. Though he ignored possible opportunities for naval bases in Venezuela and Haiti, he supported reciprocity treaties with Mexico, various Caribbean nations, Hawaii, and Spain, and approved U.S. participation in the Berlin Conference on the Congo (1884–1885), where the American delegate argued for free trade. Frelinghuysen and Arthur had few diplomatic successes. As noted by the historian David M. Pletcher, their tenures fell in an awkward transition period increasingly concerned with foreign trade, security, and prestige, but countered by isolationism and congressional opposition. Shortly after Frelinghuysen left office, he died in Newark, New Jersey.

Further Reading: David M. Pletcher, *The Awkward Years: American Foreign Policy Under Garfield and Arthur*, 1961; Philip Marshall Brown, "Frederick Theodore Frelinghuysen," in Samuel Flagg Bemis, ed., *The American Secretaries of State and Their Diplomacy*, vol. 8, 1928; John F. Hageman, "The Life, Character and Services of Frederick T. Frelinghuysen," *New Jersey Historical Society Proceedings* 9 (1887), 47–75.

William Kamman

FRELINGHUYSEN-ZAVALA TREATY OF 1884.

During the last two decades of the nineteenth century, the U.S. government intensified its efforts to construct and control a canal across Central America. The Clayton-Bulwer Treaty of 1850, in which the United States had agreed to share control of any Central American canal with Great Britain, proved a major obstacle. In 1881, Secretary of State James G. Blaine, motivated by Ferdinand de Lesseps's efforts to build a canal in Colombia's possession of Panama, unsuccessfully attempted to persuade Great Britain to abrogate the treaty. Three years later, Secretary of State Frederick Frelinghuysen negotiated the treaty with Nicaragua that bears his name. The pact secured transit rights for the United States across Nicaragua and clearly violated the Clayton-Bulwer agreement, causing President Grover Cleveland to withdraw the treaty when he took office. The United States nevertheless continued to press for control of any isthmian canal—an interest that paralleled growing U.S. attention to, and intervention in, Latin American affairs.

Further Reading: John Rollins, "Frederick Theodore Frelinghuysen, 1817–1885: The Politics of Diplomacy and Stewardship," Ph.D. diss., University of Wisconsin, 1974.

John D. Coats

FRÉMONT, JESSIE BENTON

(31 May 1824–27 December 1902), writer, and **FRÉMONT, JOHN CHARLES** (21 January 1813–13 July 1890), western explorer and politician. Jesse was born at "Cherry Grove," near Lexington, Virginia, and married John, an army officer, in 1841. They lived in California for some time, although John headed several financed expeditions and journeys to western regions between the Missouri River and the northern boundary of the United States. He was California's first U.S. senator (1850–1851). In 1856,

Frémont, who was born in Savannah, Georgia, and opposed the extension of slavery into territories, won the Republican nomination for president but narrowly lost the election to Democrat James Buchanan. Jessie Frémont achieved distinction as the first wife of a national candidate to play an active role in a campaign. During the Panic of 1873, the Frémonts faced near poverty. President Rutherford B. Hayes appointed John governor of the Arizona Territory, in which capacity he served from 1878 to 1881. Jessie stayed with him for a year before returning east. She wrote professionally, including *A Year of American Travel* (1878) and *Souvenirs of My Time* (1887). John died in New York City. Jessie emerged as a widely known and controversial figure who promoted western expansion and opposed slavery. She died in Los Angeles, California.

Further Reading: Pamela Herr, *Jessie Benton Frémont: A Biography*, 1987; Allan Nevins, *Frémont: Pathmarker of the West*, 1955.

Leonard Schlup

FRENCH, DANIEL CHESTER

(20 April 1850–7 October 1931), sculptor. Born in Exeter, New Hampshire, French was largely self-taught but worked briefly with John Quincy Adams Ward and William Morris Hunt. In 1873 he received a commission to produce the life-size bronze *Minute Man* to commemorate the battle of Concord. While the pose is derived from the ancient *Apollo Belvedere,* the studied historical detail and the suave naturalism are characteristic of French's style. In this re-creation of an ideal early American patriot, French established his reputation at an early age. After living in Italy from 1874 to 1876, he worked in Washington, D.C. and Boston, producing both architectural sculpture and portraits, including a marble bust of Ralph Waldo Emerson (1879) and a bronze seated figure of John Harvard (1884). French studied at Paris in 1886 and 1887, and eventually settled in New York City. His works were displayed at the World's Columbian Exposition in Chicago (1893). His dramatic 1891 *Angel of Death and the Sculptor* was created as a memorial to another sculptor, Martin Milmore. French collaborated with architects in the integration of

sculpture and site. He continued to produce sculpture, including the Lincoln Memorial's colossal seated figure of Abraham Lincoln, which was dedicated in 1922, until he died in Stockbridge, Massachusetts.

Further Reading: M. Cresson, *Journey into Fame: The Life of Daniel Chester French*, 1947; Michael Richman, *Daniel Chester French: An American Sculptor*, 1976.

Ann Thomas Wilkins

FRICK, HENRY CLAY (19 December 1849–2 December 1919), industrialist. Frick was born in West Overton, Pennsylvania, and attended public schools and Otterbein University in Westerville, Ohio, where he studied literature and art but did not take a degree. After working as a store clerk and bookkeeper, Frick in 1870 convinced investors to help him build a coke oven near Pittsburgh, Pennsylvania, the beginning of what would become H. C. Frick Coke Company. In the aftermath of the Panic of 1873, he bought coalfields for a fraction of their value, and by 1879 his fortune had surpassed $1 million. Two years later he met Andrew Carnegie in New York City and persuaded him to invest in his company. In return Carnegie invited Frick to invest in his steel mills, and in 1889 appointed him chairman of Carnegie Brothers. Frick despised labor unions, and in 1892 he used the state militia to crush a strike by the Amalgamated Association of Iron, Steel and Tin Workers at Homestead, Pennsylvania. During the strike a Russian immigrant shot and stabbed Frick, but the wounds were not fatal. In 1901 Frick negotiated the sale of Carnegie's mills to John Pierpont Morgan, a move that created the United States Steel Corporation. Frick donated money to the College of Wooster and Princeton University, and gave 150 acres and $2 million to Pittsburgh. He died in Pittsburgh, and his will bequeathed his $15 million estate to the city.

Further Reading: George Harvey, *Henry Clay Frick, the Man*, 1936.

Christopher Cumo

FRYE, WILLIAM PIERCE (2 September 1830–8 August 1911), congressman and U.S. senator. One of the most prominent Gilded Age legislators, Frye was born in Lewiston, Maine,

graduated from Bowdoin College in 1850, studied law under William Pitt Fessenden, and practiced first in Rockland and then in Lewiston. Thereafter he held various offices in the 1860s, including state legislator, mayor of Lewiston, and attorney general of Maine. He sat in the U.S. House of Representatives from 1871 to 1881, and in the U.S. Senate from 1881 until his death in Lewiston. Frye consistently supported protective tariffs. Known as an "Old Guard" Republican and powerful "wheel horse," he served on important committees such as Rules, Foreign Relations, Appropriations, and Commerce. An ardent expansionist who sought additional territories and a transisthmian canal for the United States, Frye favored the annexation of Hawaii in 1898 and endorsed acquisition of the Philippine Islands. President William McKinley appointed him to the American peace commission that negotiated a treaty to conclude the Spanish-American War; the Senate narrowly ratified the document in 1899. Frye was president pro tempore of the Senate during the Fifty-fourth through the Sixty-second Congresses.

Further Reading: *New York Sun*, 9 August 1911; *Lewiston Evening Journal*, 9–11 August 1911; William P. Frye Papers, Maine Historical Society, Portland.

Leonard Schlup

FUERTES, ESTÉVAN ANTONIO (10 May 1838–16 January 1903), educator and civil engineer. Born in San Juan, Puerto Rico, Fuertes earned a Ph.D. from the University of Salamanca in Spain and an engineering degree in 1861 from Rensselaer Polytechnic Institute in Troy, New York. He worked as an engineer in Puerto Rico and New York City before becoming dean of the department of civil engineering at Cornell University in 1873, where he emphasized laboratory work and a combination of practice and theory. He also wrote numerous scientific articles. Two months after resigning his faculty appointment, Fuertes died in Ithaca, New York.

Further Reading: *New York Times*, 17 January 1903.

Leonard Schlup

FULLER, MELVILLE WESTON (11 February 1833–4 July 1910), chief justice of the U.S. Supreme Court. Born in Augusta, Maine,

Fuller learned political lessons in Jacksonian democracy from his maternal grandfather, Nathan Weston, chief justice of the Maine Supreme Judicial Court. Fuller graduated from Bowdoin College in 1853; read law in the office of a maternal uncle, George Melville Weston, in Bangor, Maine; attended Harvard Law School; and was admitted to the Maine bar in 1855. Thereafter he moved to Chicago, where he practiced law and entered state Democratic politics. Although supportive of the Union during the Civil War, Fuller, who avoided military service, defended states' rights and at times berated President Abraham Lincoln's policies; he condemned the Emancipation Proclamation (1863) as an unconstitutional usurpation of executive power. Intensely partisan, Fuller briefly held a seat in the Illinois House of Representatives, made prudent real estate investments, and achieved prominence.

President Grover Cleveland selected Fuller as chief justice of the U.S. Supreme Court in 1888. Even though Republicans commanded a majority there, a conservative coalition of Democrats and Republicans dominated the rulings. Fuller, a superb administrator, joined the majority view of *Plessy* v. *Ferguson* (1896), accepting the "separate but equal" doctrine of racial segregation. He remained consistently opposed to labor unions, and declined Cleveland's invitation in 1893 to become secretary of state. He accepted assignments to join the international Venezuelan Boundary Commission in 1897 and to serve on the Permanent Court of Arbitration at The Hague four years later. Fuller died in Sorrento, Maine.

Further Reading: James W. Ely, Jr., *The Chief Justiceship of Melville W. Fuller, 1888–1910*, 1995; Willard L. King, *Melville Weston Fuller*, 1950; Walter F. Pratt, "Rhetorical Styles on the Fuller Court," *American Journal of Legal History* 24 (1980): 189–220.

Leonard Schlup

FUNERAL PRACTICES AND DEVELOPMENTS.

The Civil War initiated a change in American funeral customs. Thomas Holmes developed the modern method of embalming, and practiced the procedure upon soldiers killed in battle when families wanted the bodies returned home for burial. President Abraham Lincoln's assassination further publicized embalming. His funeral caravan lasted two weeks and covered seventeen hundred miles. More than seven million persons along the route viewed Lincoln's treated body, for officials removed the coffin from the train and opened it at major stops. Prior to the 1870s, members of the deceased's family and friends performed the tasks consequent to death. Funerals functioned as a neighborhood affair, taking place in the home. Industrialization and immigration, resulting in ethnic and religious diversity, altered mortuary patterns in urban centers. As towns grew, community solidarity lessened in changing neighborhoods, and morticians took increasing responsibility. By 1900, undertakers directed most aspects of funerals. Ornate tombs and large, parklike cemeteries characterized the burials of some segments of Gilded Age America.

The period was a transitional time for funeral directors and burial standards. In the early 1870s, Crane, Breed and Company supplied the first true sheet-metal casket. That material gradually replaced the heavier cast-iron casket. In 1871, Samuel Stein of Stein Patent Burial Casket developed a line of cloth-covered burial cases as the main item of manufacture. Coffins incorporating glass grew in popularity between 1870 and 1890 with the work of George W. Scollay, John Weaver, and Isaac Shuler, Their designs reflected the public's growing desire to display a body in its physical entirety and place it in a handsome setting. In addition, the first crematorium in the United States was built in 1884 at Cedar Lawn Cemetery in Lancaster, Pennsylvania, and the *Embalmers' Monthly* published its first issue in April 1892.

On 14 January 1880, twenty-six undertakers convened at the Hibbard House in Jackson, Michigan, to establish the first funeral directors' organization in the United States. Thomas Gliddon, editor of *The Casket*, delivered the opening address, and Allen Durfee, a well-known Grand Rapids mortician and compounder of embalming fluid, was elected president of the association. The event gave impetus to similar organizations in other states in the 1880s. The movement culminated in formation of the National Funeral Directors Association at Rochester, New York, in June 1882. Its purpose was to enhance the profession, promote quality service to the consumer, and provide a national identity for funeral directors. At the first national convention, held in 1885, delegates selected Charles L. Benjamin, a mortician from Saginaw, Michigan, as first president of the association. With increased standardization of public health rules regarding transportation of the deceased, Gilded Age funeral directors anticipated further advancements in their profession in the twentieth century.

Further Reading: Robert W. Habenstein, William M. Lamers, and Kathleen A. Walczak, *The History of American Funeral Directing*, 5th rev. ed., 2001; Howard C. Raether, *Funeral Service: A Historical Perspective*, 1990; Constance Jones, *R.I.P.: The Complete Book of Death and Dying*, 1997.

Leonard Schlup

FUSION. The term "fusion" refers to an agreement between two or more political parties to back a single ticket. The practice was common in the late nineteenth century, especially in western and southern states where agrarian insurgents made deals with leaders of one "old" party in order to defeat the other. Short-term rewards could be substantial. In 1890 third-party forces challenged Republican power in Kansas. Aided by Democrats, they gained control of the state house of representatives, elected five U.S. congressmen, and sent William A. Peffer to the U.S. Senate. In North Carolina neither the People's Party nor the Republican Party could carry the state; but in 1894, a well-planned cooperation elected a Populist majority in the state senate, a Republican majority in the state house, and three Populists and three Re-

publicans to the U.S. Congress. The fusion legislature chose a Republican to fill an unexpired term in the U.S. Senate and a Populist, Marion Butler, for a full term.

Fusion was less likely to succeed in the deep South, where Democrats controlled most of the election machinery and responded to serious challenges by stuffing ballot boxes. Georgia congressman Tom Watson, perhaps the region's most dynamic Populist, was "counted out" in 1892 and 1894 despite the support of Republicans. Reuben F. Kolb, an Alabama Alliance leader, ran for governor as a "Jeffersonian Democrat" in 1892 and 1894. He enjoyed the support of Populists and a powerful faction of Republicans; yet his fate was the same as Watson's. Fusion made a poor long-term strategy, however, because it represented an ideological compromise. Changing voters' economic thinking was a major goal of both the Farmers' Alliance and the People's Party. Yet Populist leaders such as Alabama's Joseph C. Manning spent so much time reaching across party lines (and fighting election frauds) that they had little opportunity to promote the Subtreasury. Therefore, many agrarian radicals viewed fusion as a type of betrayal. Certainly, the People's Party never recovered from the decision of its leadership to back the 1896 presidential candidacy of Democrat William Jennings Bryan.

Further Reading: John C. Hicks, *The Populist Revolt*, 1931; Lawrence Goodwyn, *Democratic Promise: The Populist Moment in America*, 1976; William Warren Rogers, *The One-Gallused Rebellion: Agrarianism in Alabama, 1865–1896*, 1970.

Paul M. Pruitt, Jr.

GAGE, LYMAN JUDSON (28 June 1836–26 January 1927), banker and secretary of the Treasury. Born in Deruyter, New York, Gage in 1855 moved to Chicago, where he worked as a cashier and bookkeeper in several banks, helped to organize the Honest Money League of the North West, and gained a reputation as a conservative business executive. In 1882, he became vice president of the First National Bank of Chicago; the next year he was elected president of the American Bankers' Association; and was president of the First National Bank (1891–1897). Concerned over the conflicting views of capital and labor during the Gilded Age, Gage earned the respect of both groups. He declined President Grover Cleveland's invitation to join the Democratic cabinet in 1893, but he accepted Republican President William McKinley's offer of the secretaryship of the Treasury in 1897. Vehemently opposed to free silver coinage, Gage worked to secure congressional passage in 1900 of the Gold Standard Act. Gage died in San Diego, California.
Further Reading: *Chicago Daily Tribune*, 27 January 1927; *New York Times*, 27 January 1927.

Leonard Schlup

GALLAUDET, EDWARD MINER (5 February 1837–26 September 1917), educator. Born in Hartford, Connecticut, a son of Thomas Hopkins Gallaudet, educator of the deaf, Edward attended Trinity College. In 1857 the philanthropist Amos Kendall offered him the position of superintendent of the Columbia Institution for the Instruction of the Deaf and Dumb and Blind in Washington, D.C. (renamed Gallaudet College in 1894 to honor Thomas Hopkins Gallaudet). Edward remained at this institution, the first college for the hearing impaired, in an administrative capacity for the rest of his life. The author of more than a hundred articles on education of the deaf, Gallaudet served as president of the Convention of American Instructors of the Deaf from 1895 until his death in Hartford. He gained widespread recognition for his advocacy of using sign language (manualism) in teaching deaf children. Gallaudet University remains a living testimonial to the possibility of higher education for the hearing impaired.
Further Reading: Gallaudet University Archives; Maxine Boatner, *Voice of the Deaf: A Biography of Edward Miner Gallaudet*, 1959; John Vickrey Van Cleve and Barry A. Crouch, *A Place of Their Own: Creating the Deaf Community in America*, 1989.

Leonard Schlup

GALVESTON STORM. In 1900, Galveston, Texas, a city of thirty-eight thousand located on a coastal sandbar, suffered the nation's worst recorded natural disaster. In early September, a powerful hurricane moved through the Caribbean and westward into the Gulf of Mexico. The city's residents paid little heed to newspaper warnings. Galveston began to flood by 5 A.M. on 8 September. Waters rose across the city all afternoon. By evening, the hurricane reached maximum intensity. The local weather bureau recorded the strongest winds at eighty-four miles per hour at 6:15 P.M., just before its wind gauge blew away. By 8 P.M., however, gusts hit an estimated 120 miles per hour. Waters reached a depth of sixteen feet in the city's east end, and for a time the entire island lay beneath the Gulf of Mexico. The tide began to recede shortly before midnight, leaving in its wake a frightful toll of an estimated six thousand dead and $30 million in damages. The city rebuilt, and was the first in the nation to adopt the commission form of local government (1901; it has since been abandoned). It also built the initial portion of a seawall (1902–1904) and grade raising, which lifted the island's elevation to a maximum height of seventeen feet between 1904 and 1910. Merits of these two achievements were proven during a hurricane in 1915, which claimed few lives.
Further Reading: Clarence Ousley, *Galveston in 1900*, 1900; Herbert Molloy Mason, Jr., *Death from the Sea*,

1972; Frank Thomas Harrowing, "The Galveston Storm of 1900," M.A. thesis, University of Houston, 1950.

Casey Edward Greene

GARFIELD ASSASSINATION. James A. Garfield, twentieth president of the United States, encountered his assassin in Washington, D.C.'s Baltimore and Potomac Railroad terminal on 2 July 1881. Charles Guiteau, a self-styled lawyer/politician with neither the education nor the experience to justify either title, sought revenge because he had failed to secure a government position. Stepping up to Garfield from behind, he fired twice. One bullet grazed the left arm; the other penetrated the muscles of the back. Several weeks of uncertainty ensued, as the president's surgeons debated treatment options. More than a dozen consultants offered contradictory opinions. The issue was whether to surgically explore Garfield's wound and remove the bullet, using the latest technology. Alexander Graham Bell brought an induction coil to the executive mansion to pinpoint the bullet's location. The wound was probed several times, without success. An unrelenting fever ensued that was not helped by the severe heat in the capital. The president was moved to the family's New Jersey seashore home, where a network of exhaust fans and dampened Turkish towels approximated the function of an air conditioner. Garfield died at Elberon, New Jersey, on 19 September, of overwhelming infection. As a result, his surgeons suffered the verbal abuse of laymen and professionals. Recollection of Garfield's death influenced the surgeons who attended William McKinley twenty years later.

Further Reading: Robert Reyburn, "The Case of President James A. Garfield: An Abstract of the Clinical History," *American Medicine*, 28 September 1901; Jack C. Fisher, *Stolen Glory*, 2001.

Jack C. Fisher

GARFIELD, JAMES ABRAM (19 November 1831–19 September 1881), congressman and president. Born near Orange, Ohio, Garfield attended Western Reserve Eclectic Institute (later Hiram College) and Williams College, from which he was graduated in 1856. After serving as both teacher and president of Hiram and a Republican member of the Ohio senate, he rose

to major general in the Union Army. From 1863 to 1880, Garfield was a Republican member of the U.S. House of Representative, where he represented the Western Reserve area of northern Ohio. At first deemed too aloof by his colleagues, he won their respect by his learning, oratorical skills, and mastery of financial complexities. In 1871 he was chosen chairman of the House Appropriations Committee. In 1876 he served on the electoral commission deciding the Hayes-Tilden election, where he loyally cast his vote for Hayes, the Republican candidate. In 1880 he received the Republican presidential nomination. A dark horse, he beat out such party "wheel horses" as James G. Blaine, John Sherman, and Ulysses S. Grant, then seeking a third term after a four year absence from the White House. Running against the Democrat Winfield Scott Hancock, on 2 November he was elected president by a margin of fifty-nine electoral votes and 7,368 popular votes, the thinnest popular victory on record.

Troubles, however, were just beginning; he was able to fill his cabinet only on the day of his inauguration. He sought to balance his appointees between the two major Republican factions, the Stalwarts and the Half-Breeds. He appointed Senator James G. Blaine, the Half-Breeds' leader, secretary of state, and—after much maneuvering—chose Stalwart Thomas L. James, the unusually competent postmaster of New York City, to be his postmaster general. The Stalwart leadership, particularly Senator Roscoe Conkling and Vice President Chester Alan Arthur, remained bitter, believing their faction deserved the leadership of the Treasury Department. Such anger was far from assuaged when Garfield appointed William H. Robertson, New York State senator and a Half-Breed, to the collectorship of the New York customhouse, a choice patronage position with its staff of fifteen hundred workers. Both Conkling and his New York colleague in the Senate, Thomas C. Platt, resigned their offices, but to no avail. On 18 May the Senate confirmed Robertson. After a series of weak presidents, Garfield had successfully exercised the prerogatives of his office.

During his brief presidency, Garfield promoted an investigation of the Star Route affair, a scandal centering on postal contracts. He secured the re-funding of the national debt, saving the taxpayers over $10 million. He supported the Readjuster movement in Virginia headed by former Confederate general, railroad promoter, and U.S. senator William Mahone, a move that strengthened Republican power both in the state and in a precariously balanced Senate. As for foreign policy, during his presidency the nation intervened on the side of Peru in its war with Chile, and supported Guatemala in its border dispute with Mexico. In his inaugural address, delivered on 4 March 1881, Garfield promised to end sectionalism, endorsed bimetallism, sought the education of southern blacks, and spoke of a civil service law. He had little chance to execute such policies. On 2 July 1881, he was shot at Washington, D.C.'s Baltimore and Potomac station by Charles Guiteau, a disappointed office seeker who was clearly insane. Garfield died in Elberon, New Jersey.

Further Reading: David M. Pletcher, *The Awkward Years: American Foreign Relations Under Garfield and Arthur,* 1962; Allan Peskin, *Garfield,* 1978; Justus D. Doenecke, *The Presidencies of James A. Garfield and Chester A. Arthur,* 1981.

Justus D. Doenecke

GARFIELD, LUCRETIA RUDOLPH (19 April 1832–14 March 1918), twentieth First Lady of the United States. Born in Garrettsville, Ohio, Lucretia attended Geauga Seminary and was graduated from Western Reserve Eclectic Institute (later Hiram College) in 1854. She was the only woman to give a speech at the graduation ceremony. Garfield was educated in the classics and eventually taught school. She believed a woman's province was in the home, but she loved translating Latin and Greek and keeping her mind active intellectually. As First Lady, Garfield was very concerned about the White House's dilapidated condition. She spent many hours at the Library of Congress researching its history and furnishings, hoping to restore its original splendor. She was never able to carry out these grand plans because she developed a nearly fatal case of malaria. Just as she had recovered, her husband was shot. She spent the next eighty days caring for him; he died despite her heroic efforts. Garfield spent the remainder of her life as the devoted widow. With the funds she received from the public as a result of her husband's death, she built the first presidential memorial library.

Further Reading: Margaret Leech and Harry J. Brown, *The Garfield Orbit,* 1978; Lucretia Rudolph Garfield Papers, Library of Congress; Allan Peskin, *Garfield: A Biography,* 1978.

F. Suzanne Miller

GARLAND, AUGUSTUS HILL (11 June 1832–26 January 1899), governor, senator, and attorney general. Born in Covington, Tennessee, Garland graduated from St. Joseph's College in Kentucky in 1849, gained admission to the bar in 1853, and opened a law practice in Washington, Arkansas. He moved to Little Rock in 1856, and supported John Bell and the Constitutional Union Party in the 1860 presidential election. Garland held seats in both houses of the Confederate Congress during the Civil War, and was a pardoned by President Andrew Johnson in July 1865. Thereupon he returned to law practice in Little Rock. He was governor of Arkansas from 1874 to 1877, opposing debt repudiation and promoting education. Elected as a Democrat to the U.S. Senate, Garland served from 1877 to 1885. He supported tariff revision, sound money, civil service reform, and federal aid to education. As a member of the Senate Judiciary Committee, he earned respect from his colleagues for his knowledge of constitutional issues. Garland resigned in 1885 to become attorney general in the cabinet of President Grover Cleveland. He remained in that post until 1889, urging federal regulation of interstate commerce and establishment of a federal prison system. Garland died of a stroke in Washington, D.C., while addressing the U.S. Supreme Court.

Further Reading: Leonard Schlup, "Augustus Hill Garland: Gilded Age Democrat," *Arkansas Historical Quarterly* 40 (1981): 338–346; *New York Times,* 27 January 1899.

Leonard Schlup

GARLAND, HAMLIN (14 September 1860– 4 March 1940), writer and political activist. Born near West Salem, Wisconsin, Garland grew up on a farm and was intimately familiar with the isolation, hard work, and economic vagaries of life in the upper plains. He may be seen as a transition figure from traditional romanticism to naturalism. He investigated the authentic reality of agricultural life and its subjection to capitalistic exploitation. He strove for an original and distinctively American literary style. To avoid comparison with the milder realism of his fellow American William Dean Howells and the harsher, naturalistic world of Emile Zola, Garland used the word "veritism" to characterize his work. He explored life's sordid aspects by stating the truth as he saw it. He was also one of the first American writers (along with Stephen Crane) to use impressionistic techniques. In midcareer, he drifted back to a romanticization of the Far West in a partial, and puzzling, rejection of his veritism. *Main-Travelled Roads (1891)*, generally recognized as one of the early landmarks of American literary realism, and *Prairie Folks* (1893) display his veritism, while *Her Mountain Love* (1901) is a romantic portrayal of nature's nobility. He associated with great writers including Howells, Mark Twain, Walt Whitman, and Crane, and corresponded with Henry George, Theodore Roosevelt, and William Jennings Bryan. Garland died in Hollywood, California.

Further Reading: Jean Holloway, *Hamlin Garland: A Biography*, 1960; Joseph Carter, "Hamlin Garland," in *American Literary Realism*, 1975; *American Literary Realism, 1870–1910*, vol. 8 (1975), 260–265.

C. Edward Balog

GAY AND LESBIAN AMERICA. Among the persecuted and harassed groups of the Gilded Age were gay men and lesbian women. A report on the population's defective, dependent, and delinquent classes from the 1880 census contained a subdivision on those jailed for a "crime against nature," which meant sodomy and gay sex. Sixty-three persons were listed as being incarcerated for this offense. In 1882 a gay merchant immigrated to the United States after being arrested for homosexual activity in his native land. Believing that homosexuality was a disease, he protested his suffering abroad and his mistreatment in America. He contended that until age twenty-eight he had no suspicion that there were others like him, and he lived in constant anxiety lest he be discovered. In cities there existed a homosexual underground that included transvestites, prostitutes, obscene novels, lesbianism, male homosexual activity in parks and Turkish steam baths, police harassment and raids on gay bars, arrests, venereal disease, sexual exploitation, and suicide. In 1892, when New York City police detective Charles W. Gardener escorted Reverend Charles H. Pankhurst on a tour of vice dens, the latter fled from one house at top speed, shouting that he would not stay there for all the money in the world. That same year Dr. Irving C. Rosse, professor of nervous diseases at Georgetown University, reported a case known to Washington police of a well-connected man who enticed messenger boys to a hotel, where he intoxicated them as a prelude to consensual sex.

The Mazet Committee, composed mostly of upstate Republican legislators, investigated the public offices and departments of New York City's government in 1899 and 1900. New York City Mayor Robert A. Van Wyck, testifying on 16 May 1899, grudgingly admitted that male harlots probably could be found in any big city. Also in New York City, Murray H. Hall, a woman, masqueraded as a man for more than a quarter-century, and figured prominently as a politician. A member of the general committee of Tammany Hall and the Iroquois Club, Hall registered and voted in elections and exercised political influence with Tammany men. She played poker, drank alcoholic beverages, smoked cigars, married two women who kept her secret, and relished her role as a man about town. The discovery of Hall's true sex came after her death from breast cancer that had eaten its way almost to the heart. In 1893 Dr. Ferdinand Eugene Daniel, a Texas editor and physician, asserted that sexual aberrations, alcoholism, insanity, and criminal tendencies were hereditarily transmitted, and that they appeared with alarming frequency among the lower classes. He recommended castration of all criminals and homosexuals. That same year, Dr. Henry Hulst of Michigan suggested hypnosis as a treatment for gays and lesbians.

The West portrayed a different image of male-male relations than has traditionally been chronicled in books, articles, movies, and television. Some men danced together and engaged in homosexual activity while camping, working as cowboys, mining, soldiering, or being confined together, away from home, for long periods of time. In the 1870s a man known as "Mrs. Nash" held the post of company laundress in the Seventh Cavalry. Married to a succession of soldier-husbands while cohabiting with others, Nash's male identity was not revealed until his burial. His widower, a corporal, unable to bear the ridicule and scorn showered on him, committed suicide with a revolver. Documents concerning the Nash episode demonstrated that homosexuality existed to a certain degree among the enlisted men serving in the frontier West.

The difficulties that gays and lesbians experienced in Gilded Age America continued throughout the next hundred years. The 1882 emigrant merchant hoped for better understanding and acceptance in the twentieth century. Building effective community support for laws and policies that promote equal rights for gay, lesbian, bisexual, and transgender people would be a fitting memorial in the twenty-first century for those special men and women who endured hardship, abuse, loathing, discrimination, and death in nineteenth-century America.

Further Reading: Jonathan Ned Katz, *Gay American History*, 1992; John Lauritsen and David Thorstad, *The Early Homosexual Rights Movement (1864–1935)*, 1974.

Leonard Schlup

GEAR, JOHN HENRY (7 April 1825–14 July 1900), congressman. Born in Ithaca, New York, Gear moved with his family in 1836 to Galena, Illinois, and in 1838 to Fort Snelling, Iowa. He seldom attended school, but received an education from his father, an army chaplain. He settled in 1843 in Burlington, Iowa, where he owned a grocery store. His support of small government and a free market resonated with Iowans, who in 1870 elected Gear to the first of three terms in the state legislature. In 1874 he became speaker of the Iowa house of representatives, and in 1876 was the first person to be reelected speaker. That fall he won the first of two terms as governor (1878–1882). Gear's statewide success fueled his ambition for na-

tional office. Although he lost bids for the Senate in 1882 and the House in 1890, he won a seat in Congress in 1886, 1888, and 1892. There he sided with William McKinley of Ohio and displeased farmers by advocating a protective tariff. His conservatism carried him to the Senate in 1895, but he died in Washington, D.C., before the end of his term.

Further Reading: *Iowa State Register*, 15 July 1900.

Christopher Cumo

GENDER POLITICS. Gilded Age struggles to define what constituted appropriate male and female roles were inherently political in the sense that they had a bearing on social relationships and individual possibilities. Negotiation of gender roles was not unique. What made the era distinctive was the extent to which gender struggles spilled over to electoral politics, thus affecting not only understandings of masculinity and femininity, but also the contours of the nation's political system.

The post–Civil War period featured mass male political participation. Whereas earlier both race and gender determined political rights, after the war, gender briefly became the most important determinant of enfranchisement. The Fifteenth Amendment, ratified in 1870, eliminated (on paper but, as Reconstruction waned, ever less in practice) racial restrictions on voting. Like popular fraternal organizations, political parties united men from different walks of life, teaching them that they formed a privileged class relative to women. Late nineteenth-century men looked to electoral politics to help develop their masculine identities. Conversely, they needed to demonstrate a manly character to be taken seriously in electoral politics. In the post-bellum period, this character was seen as having a markedly martial nature. Since men who were stigmatized as effeminate (including prohibitionists, Mugwumps, and anti-imperialists) found it difficult to assert political authority, male political activists struggled to present themselves and their policies as manly. Gender beliefs had a particularly coercive role in debates over war and empire at the turn of the century. They also played a significant role in Redemption: proclaiming the vulnerability of white women,

Southern white supremacists fabricated the myth of the black rapist to justify the disfranchisement of black men and to keep white women from carving out a greater public role.

Although partisan politics commonly was seen as male terrain, activist women hotly contested men's monopoly, despite great opposition. By the 1890s, women participated in a wide range of activities. They debated political issues, wrote and distributed campaign literature, delivered stump speeches, attended rallies and conventions, gathered at the polls on Election Day to influence male voters, formed civic-minded municipal organizations, and lobbied on behalf of numerous reforms, ranging from anti-lynching (Ida B. Wells was prominent in this endeavor) to temperance (Frances Willard, leader of the Woman's Christian Temperance Union, was especially notable in this cause). Women found insurgent third parties, including the Greenback, Prohibition, and Populist parties, most open to their participation, but even the Republican and, to a lesser extent, Democratic parties welcomed women's support, in part because women conveyed an aura of morality. Although women expended much of their political energy in trying to influence men, some women voted—by 1896, four states (Wyoming, Colorado, Utah, and Idaho) had granted full female suffrage and more than twenty others permitted women to vote in local, primarily school board, elections. Women served as state legislators in Colorado and Utah, and they won election and appointments to school boards and municipal offices in several other of states.

In addition, activist women critiqued the assumptions about male honor and valor that had played such a prominent role in politics after the Civil War. In response to women's incursions and their assertions that they aimed to fundamentally change the political system, men committed to a more fraternal style of politics deplored growing female activism, calling it a sign of national degeneracy and a threat to American government. By 1900, the decline of third-party challenges and a reinvigoration of martial ideals of citizenship following the Spanish-American War reduced the prominence of women in political campaigns.

Further Reading: Rebecca Edwards, *Angels in the Machinery: Gender in American Party Politics from the Civil War to the Progressive Era*, 1997; Kristin L. Hoganson, *Fighting for American Manhood: How Gender Politics Provoked the Spanish-American and Philippine-American Wars*, 1998; Paula Baker, "The Domestication of Politics: Women and American Political Society, 1780–1920," *American Historical Review* 89 (1984): 620–647.

Kristin Hoganson

GEORGE, HENRY (2 September 1839–29 October 1897), economist and social reformer. Born in Philadelphia, he was the eldest son of eleven children. He attended private and public schools but dropped out before turning fourteen. In 1858, he moved to California, where he spent two decades working variously as printer, editor, and journalist, chiefly for San Francisco newspapers. In 1879, after a decade of thought and two articles, George published his signature book, *Progress and Poverty*, in which he advanced his theory that only a 100 percent tax on increases in land values could stem the paradoxical growth of both progress and poverty. This tax, he argued, would provide enough revenue to obviate the need for other levies, freeing labor and capital to reap the results of their efforts because improvements to the land were not subject to taxation. The culprit, thus, was not the capitalist system but the unequal distribution of wealth within it.

George spent the rest of his life explaining and defending his theory to national and international audiences. With two million copies of his book in print by 1890, nationalist groups, especially in Ireland and Scotland, were supportive, while American audiences largely rejected George. Although working-class organizations such as the Knights of Labor championed his cause as their own in an era of great labor discontent, George's theories collided with entrenched ideas about contractual rights, private property, and laissez-faire economics. Moreover, his many enemies misunderstood and/or misrepresented his ideas as socialist and communist. In 1886, at the height of his strength in the United States, George placed second in the New York mayoral race behind Tammany Hall's Abram Hewitt, but well ahead of Republican Theodore Roosevelt. In 1897, he again entered the race, primarily to spoil the bid of the Tammany nominee, but died in New York City of a massive stroke, four days before the voting. His other major writings include *Social Problems* (1883), *Protection or Free Trade* (1886), *The Condition of Labor* (1891), *Perplexed Philosopher* (1892), and *The Science of Political Economy* (1898).

Further Reading: Charles Albro Barker, *Henry George*, 1955; John L. Thomas, *Alternative America*, 1983.

Samuel J. Thomas

GEORGE, JAMES ZACHARIAH (20 October 1826–14 August 1897), judge and U.S. senator. A Democrat, George was born in Monroe County, Georgia, and grew up in Carroll County, Mississippi. He served in the Mexican and Civil wars, attaining the rank of brigadier general in the latter. In the postwar period, he practiced law in Carrollton, Mississippi, led the struggle for conservative restoration, and became chief justice of the Mississippi's supreme court. From 1881 until his death, he represented Mississippi in the U.S. Senate. Known as the "Great Commoner" of Mississippi, George endorsed a narrow interpretation of national government power. Defending the South against federal interference highlighted his Senate terms. He supported Mississippi's constitution of 1890 and helped to frame the Sherman Antitrust Act of 1890. He died in Mississippi City, Mississippi.

Further Reading: James Z. George, *The Political History of Slavery in the United States*, 1915; Lucy Peck, "The Life and Times of James Z. George," Ph.D. diss., Mississippi State University, 1964; James Z. George Papers, Mississippi Department of Archives and History, Jackson.

Leonard Schlup

GERM THEORY OF DISEASE. In the 1870s, the European scientists Louis Pasteur and Robert Koch determined that microscopic organisms within the environment, not the environment itself, caused infections. For American reformers, proof of the germ theory of disease justified new public health measures that often placed the welfare of the community above the rights of the individual. Greater knowledge of disease etiology, transmission, and incubation periods led to government-mandated inspections and quarantines. Urban health departments staffed diagnostic laboratories, dispatched nurses to schools and tenement

buildings, and on rare occasions advised officials to cordon off city blocks in order to contain epidemics. The Marine Hospital Service, renamed the Public Health Service in 1912, extended its authority under the Quarantine Act of 1878. Its doctors, stationed at ports of immigration, examined new arrivals for contagious disease. While fewer than 1 percent of Ellis Island immigrants were denied entry due to illness, thousands more spent their first weeks in America quarantined in the island's hospital.

Further Reading: George Rosen, *A History of Public Health*, 1958, rep. 1993; Alan M. Kraut, *Silent Travelers: Germs, Genes, and the Immigrant "Menace,"* 1994; James H. Cassedy, *Medicine in America: A Short History*, 1991.

Jane M. Armstrong

GERONIMO (GOYATHLAY) (ca. 1829–17 February 1909), Chiricahua Apache chief. A Bedonkohe Apache born near present-day Clifton, Arizona, Geronimo later lived among the Chiricahua and Warm Springs Apaches, and spent years raiding and plundering. After Mexicans killed his mother, wife, and children in 1858, he and his followers camped for several years in the Sierra Madre Mountains and executed vengeful raids in Mexico, New Mexico, and Arizona. After Geronimo's final surrender to U.S. Army officials in 1886, which ended most armed resistance to the U.S. reservation policy, he and his band were imprisoned at Fort Pickens in Pensacola, Florida, and later at Mount Vernon Barracks, Alabama, before being sent to Fort Sill, Oklahoma. Geronimo became a farmer and U.S. Indian scout for his village on the east side of Cache Creek. His notoriety brought him invitations to fairs, parades, and pageants, and requests for interviews. A heavy drinker, he died from pneumonia at the Fort Sill Indian hospital and was buried in the Apache cemetery on Cache Creek.

Further Reading: Jason Betzinez, with Wilbur Sturtevant Nye, *I Fought with Geronimo*, 1959; S. M. Barrett, *Geronimo's Story of His Life*, 1906; Angie Debo, *Geronimo: The Man, His Time, His Place*, 1976.

Jane F. Lancaster

GIBBONS, ABIGAIL HOPPER (7 December 1801–16 January 1893), abolitionist and advocate of prison reform. Born in Philadelphia, Pennsylvania, she married James Sloan Gibbons, a Quaker merchant, in 1833. After moving to New York City, Gibbons became interested in social amelioration. Before the Civil War, she concentrated on abolitionism. After the conflict's end, Gibbons sought to locate employment for veterans, convert female convicts to religion, and distribute food to indigent people. She headed the Women's Prison Association from 1877 until her death in New York City. Joining forces with Josephine Shaw Lowell, Gibbons advocated separate penal institutions for women managed by women. Their efforts resulted in an act passed by the New York legislature in 1890 requiring the presence of female prison guards at women's reformatories. Her address to the state legislators on this topic, at age ninety-one, constituted one of her last official acts for the cause of social betterment.

Further Reading: Sarah Hopper Emerson, ed., *Life of Abby Hopper Gibbons, Told Chiefly Through Her Correspondence*, 2 vols., 1897; *New York Times*, 18 January 1893.

Leonard Schlup

GIBBONS, JAMES (23 July 1834–24 March 1921), Roman Catholic cardinal. Born in Baltimore, Maryland, Gibbons was ordained as a priest in 1861; he was assigned first to St. Patrick's parish and later to St. Bridget's, both in Baltimore. Upon the recommendation of Archbishop Martin John Spalding, Gibbons succeeded to the episcopacy in 1868. While in North Carolina in 1876, he wrote the popular book *Faith of Our Fathers*. The next year he became archbishop of Baltimore and was named a cardinal in 1886, installed by Pope Leo XIII in 1887. While in Rome, Gibbons joined a coterie of "Americanizers" of the Roman Catholic Church. The list included Archbishop John Ireland, Bishop John J. Keane, and Monsignor Denis O'Connell. Gibbons remained on friendly terms with American labor, supported the separation of church and state in the United States, favored democratic procedures within the church, and sought to ameliorate differences between Protestants and Catholics. He opposed female suffrage. Among

his published books are *Our Christian Heritage* (1889) and *Ambassador of Christ* (1896). Gibbons died in the cathedral rectory in Baltimore.

Further Reading: John Tracy Ellis, *The Life of James Cardinal Gibbons, Archbishop of Baltimore, 1834–1921*, 2 vols., 1952.

Leonard Schlup

GIBSON, CHARLES DANA (14 September 1867–23 December 1944), illustrator and artist. Gibson was born Roxbury, Massachusetts, but grew up in Flushing, New York. He studied at the Art Students League in New York for two years but in 1885 struck out on his own. After numerous rejections, *Life* magazine accepted one of his submissions in 1886. Gibson quickly became one of the Gilded Age's favorite illustrators. Readers delighted in his witty depictions of American society and politics. During the 1890s his idealized females, with their slim figures, full bodices, chiseled features, and swept-up hair, became known collectively as the Gibson Girl. This composite figure came to represent the ideal American woman of the turn of the century: modern and spirited, yet respectable and proper. The Gibson Girl was not a single woman, but a type who could be modified for a variety of modern situations. Gibson often poked fun at the hypocrisy of societal customs and manners. His elegant style of illustration gave rise to many imitators and admirers, such as Howard Chandler Christy and James Montgomery Flagg. Gibson maintained close ties to *Life*, but his work also appeared in *The Century, Collier's Weekly*, and *Cosmopolitan*. His illustrated works include *The Education of Mr. Pipp* (1899) and *The Americans* (1900). He died in New York City.

Further Reading: Fairfax Downey, *Portrait of an Era as Drawn by C. D. Gibson*, 1936; Henry C. Pitz, *The Gibson Girl and Her America: The Best Drawings of Charles Dana Gibson*, 1969.

Lacey Jordan

GILDED AGE. A period generally considered to run from 1868 to 1901, the Gilded Age witnessed America's transformation from an agricultural, rural, and relatively homogeneous society into a republic marked by industrialization, urbanization, and greater diversity. Domestic developments and foreign policy initiatives reshaped the nation's political landscape, turning an epoch of equilibrium and legislative ascendancy into a distinct time of political realignment, presidential prerogative, and international stature. Many politicians failed to comprehend how these momentous changes were altering society. The period acquired its name from Mark Twain's novel *The Gilded Age: A Tale of Today*, published in 1873 in collaboration with Charles Dudley Warner. Twain and Warner satirized business ethics, fraudulent stock dealings, rampant greed, and financial tycoons affecting legislation. Colonel Eschol Sellers was a duplicitous figure in a corrupt, superficial, and excessively opulent society. The book's depiction of unbridled American materialism and venality warned against ruthless acquisition of enormous wealth and its ostentatious misuse, which resulted almost inevitably in ruinous consequences. Twain and Warner deliberately chose the word "gilded," referring to a bright, sparkling glitter making something appear to be valuable and attractive. Modern dictionaries of the English language define the Gilded Age as the period in the United States characterized by a greatly expanding economy and the emergence of plutocratic influences in government and society.

Admittedly a complex time of contradictions, the Gilded Age for too long was dismissed and misunderstood as a complacent and lackluster era of material excess wedged between the emotional fervor of the Civil War and the reform impulse of the Progressive Era. Historical reassessments since the 1950s, however, have demonstrated that the age gave rise to a spirit of reform and a sense of adventure and accomplishment that later translated into concrete achievements. In fact, the post–Civil War period was an important milestone during which traditions and innovations conflicted, and the foundation was laid for the shaping of modern America in the twentieth and twenty-first centuries.

Further Reading: Sean Dennis Cashman, *America in the Gilded Age*, 1988; Vincent P. de Santis, *The Shaping of Modern America, 1877–1916*, 1989.

Leonard Schlup

GILDED AGE: A TALE OF TODAY. In 1873 the humorist Mark Twain and the New England editor Charles Dudley Warner published a novel, *The Gilded Age: A Tale of Today*. It satirized postbellum America's politics, rampant greed, Wall Street financial chicanery, unchecked western land speculation, business ethics, and corruption at all levels of government. Warning against the ruthless acquisition of wealth and its ostentatious misuse, the book was the first novel of consequence about Washington, and Twain's first extended work of fiction. It established him in the literary world as a keen observer of the national scene rather than a journalist. The authors chose the word "gilded" to signify something displaying or giving a bright, pleasing, or specious aspect while adding unnecessary ornamentation. They intended it to illustrate the outwardly showy but inwardly corrupt nature of American society during their day. Their book named an age in U.S. history characterized by a greatly expanding economy and the emergence of plutocratic influences in government and society.

Twain wanted Thomas Nast, the era's foremost political cartoonist, to handle the book's graphics. When Nast declined the commission because of scheduling and financial considerations, the authors and their publisher, Elisha Bliss, settled on Augustus Hoppin, an illustrator whose specialty was political caricature and who enjoyed wide recognition for his fine detail. Because Hoppin commanded a large salary, Bliss used him sparingly and hired two other successful illustrators, True Williams and Henry Louis Stephens, to assist in drawing the three hundred illustrations. Due to an apparent lack of supervision and communication among the artists, the somewhat lackluster illustrations suffered from inconsistency and a tendency toward symbolism. The team worked from pictures of actual political figures and counterparts thinly disguised by Twain and Warner. Twain insisted that sketches of Colonel Eschol Sellers at all times give him the appearance of a gentlemen. In the end, Twain expressed disappointment with what he perceived as the haphazard and shoddy design of the novel, referring to the "wretched paper and vile engravings" and pronouncing *The Gilded Age* "rather rubbishy looking." Despite some shortcomings in the book, Twain, in a letter to the editor and writer

Thomas B. Aldrich, boasted of the substantial profits from its sales. A theatrical adaptation of the novel appeared in 1874.

Further Reading: Mark Twain and Charles Dudley Warner, *The Gilded Age: A Tale of Today*, 1873; Bryant Morey French, *Mark Twain and The Gilded Age: The Book That Named an Era*, 1965.

Leonard Schlup

GILLETTE, KING CAMP (5 January 1855–10 July 1932), safety razor inventor and manufacturer. Born at Fond du Lac, Wisconsin, Gillette held various jobs in Chicago, New York, and Kansas City prior to perfecting his safety razor and blade. In 1903, the first year the Gillette Safety Razor Company operated, fifty-one razors and fourteen dozen blades were sold; the next year the numbers skyrocketed to ninety thousand razors and fifteen million blades. Known primarily for his invention, Gillette, a Republican, also advocated a socialist community near Niagara Falls, New York. In 1894, during an economic depression, he published *Human Drift*, which set forth his plans for a world corporation, a billion-dollar organization to obliterate commercial strife and eradicate crime. Features of his new social order included large apartment houses where intelligent people would not want for material necessities. Gillette died in Los Angeles, California.

Further Reading: *New York Times*, 11 July 1932.

Leonard Schlup

GILMAN, CHARLOTTE ANNA PERKINS (3 July 1860–17 August 1935), author and reformer. Born in Hartford, Connecticut, the great-niece of Harriet Beecher Stowe and Henry Ward Beecher, early in life Charlotte designed greeting cards and tutored children. Her 1884 marriage to Charles Walter Stetson ended in divorce. In 1900 she married her first cousin, George Houghton Gilman. Charlotte Gilman identified herself with social Darwinist thought as espoused by Lester Frank Ward. Maintaining that men and women shared a common humanity, Gilman argued that females could not reach their fullest potential because of the absence of autonomy. In other words, social imbalance existed whenever women were subservient to men.

Gilman expressed her humanist thoughts in numerous articles, poems, lectures, and books, including *Women and Economics* (1898) and the well-known short story "The Yellow Wallpaper" (1892). By making gender the primary focus of her expression, Gilman contributed to the social thought of her era and delineated the necessity for changing women's roles and positions in society. Suffering from inoperable breast cancer and aware of her impending death, she committed suicide in Pasadena, California, one year after her husband's death. Her farewell note read in part: "When all usefulness is over, when one is assured of unavoidable and imminent death, it is the simplest of human rights to choose a quick and easy death in place of a slow and horrible one."

Further Reading: *New York Times*, 20 August 1935; Mary Armfield Hill, *Charlotte Perkins Gilman: The Making of a Radical Feminist, 1860–1898*, 1980; Charlotte Perkins Gilman, *The Living of Charlotte Perkins Gilman*, 1935.

Leonard Schlup

GILMAN, DANIEL COIT (6 July 1831–13 October 1908), educator and administrator. Gilman was born in Norwich, Connecticut, and graduated from Yale College in 1852. Two years in Europe (1853–1855) greatly influenced his ideas about higher education. He returned to Yale as librarian and professor of geography, and became involved in reorganizing what became the Sheffield Scientific School. It pioneered the "new education" that put scientific methodology on a level footing with traditional classical studies, and a model of combining undergraduate and graduate education.

From 1872 to 1875 Gilman was as president of the University of California at Berkeley, where he sought to spread his ideas about higher education. Opposed by a strong faction wanting a traditional agricultural college, he left in 1875 to become president of the newly founded Johns Hopkins University. There he sought to develop the most dynamic institution of higher intellectual training in America. His successes quickly received international renown. He recruited top professors, many from Europe, and built a university strong at the traditional, undergraduate level but especially outstanding for its education of graduate students.

This concept of the American university structure was influenced by German models but differed in its support for undergraduate as well as graduate education. Gilman nurtured Johns Hopkins University for over twenty-five years, developing curriculum, finding funding for buildings, and coordinating undergraduate and graduate development. He promoted graduate fellowships to assist doctoral students; he used visiting lectureships to supplement the regular faculty's fields; and he nurtured scholarly journals. He helped reorganize Johns Hopkins Hospital and became its director in 1889.

Following his retirement from Johns Hopkins in 1902, Gilman served for two years as president of the new Carnegie Institution in Washington, D.C. His reforms at Hopkins had great influence on development of other American universities. He died in Norwich, Connecticut.

Further Reading: Fabian Franklin, *The Life of Daniel Coit Gilman*, 1910; Abraham Flexner, *Daniel Coit Gilman: Creator of the American Type of University*, 1946; Francesco Cordasco, *Daniel Coit Gilman and the Protean Ph.D.: The Shaping of American Graduate Education*, 1960.

Philip H. Young

GLADDEN, SOLOMON WASHINGTON

(11 February 1836–2 July 1918), religious leader and author. Born in Pottsville, Pennsylvania, Gladden grew up in Oswego, New York. After being graduated from Williams College in 1859, Gladden became a Congregationalist minister and served as pastor of a number of churches in New York and New England. He was drawn to the teachings of Horace Bushnell, who disputed traditional Calvinist doctrine and insisted that the natural goodness of human nature could be nurtured through the creation of a Christian environment. Gladden began writing articles defending Bushnell and other "liberal" theologians. In 1871, he joined the staff of *The Independent*, a New York City-based Congregationalist periodical, where he continued his theological debates. Gladden left in 1875 to become pastor of a church in Springfield, Massachusetts. Having arrived during the Panic of 1873–1877, he increasingly considered the practical implications of his theological positions. In *Working People and Their Employers*, (1876), he suggested that Christian cooperation would lessen the conflict between labor and capital.

Gladden moved to Columbus, Ohio, in 1882 to become minister of the city's First Congregational Church. There he gained prominence as one of the leaders of the Social Gospel movement, which sought to use Christian principles to solve social problems. In dozens of books and articles, he addressed labor conflict, municipal reform, vice, public utilities, religious intolerance, the rise of big business, leisure activities, the Spanish-American War, and many other topics. Though Gladden was not an original thinker, his writings influenced a generation of ministers and reformers. He served a term (1900–1902) on Columbus's city council and helped established the American Economic Association (1885). He died in Columbus.

Further Reading: Jacob H. Dom, *Washington Gladden: Prophet of the Social Gospel*, 1968; Washington Gladden, *Recollections*, 1909; Washington Gladden Papers, Ohio Historical Society, Columbus.

Michael Pierce

GLICK, GEORGE WASHINGTON

(4 July 1827–13 April 1911), governor. Born at Greencastle, Ohio, Glick attended Central Ohio College, read law in the office of Rutherford B. Hayes, and was admitted to the bar in 1850. He moved to the Kansas Territory in 1859 and helped write the Wyandotte Constitution, under which Kansas entered the Union in 1861. During the Civil War began he served in the Union Army. Glick, who in 1868 was the Democratic Party's first candidate for governor of Kansas, was also the first Democratic governor to be elected. He defeated the incumbent Republican prohibitionist, John P. St. John, in 1882. As governor, Glick differed little from his Republican contemporaries, except for his opposition to prohibition. After a hoof-and-mouth disease epidemic, he engineered creation of a state veterinarian and livestock sanitary commission. He was defeated for reelection by John A. Martin in 1884. Glick was nationally known as a breeder of white shorthorn cattle, and organized and served a term as president of the Kansas State Board of Agriculture. He was also an important figure in state and national affairs. A Democratic state legislature placed his sculp-

ture in Statuary Hall of the U.S. Capitol. He died in Atchison, Kansas.

Further Reading: James Humphrey, "The Administration of George W. Glick," *Kansas Historical Collection* 9 (1905–1906): 395–413; Zelma E. McIlvain, "Governor Glick and Prohibition, 1883–1884," M.A. thesis, University of Kansas, 1931; Homer E. Socolofsky, *Kansas Governors*, 1990.

Robert S. La Forte

GLIDDEN, JOSEPH FARWELL (18 January 1813–9 October 1906), farmer, inventor, industrialist. Born in Charleston, New Hampshire, and raised in Orleans County, New York, Glidden bought a six hundred-acre farm near De Kalb, Illinois, in the early 1840s. In 1873, working to improve upon the ideas of others, he developed a double-strand variety of barbed wire and, after litigation with competitors, received a patent in 1874 for what became the standard in a burgeoning wire fence industry. Originally developed for farmers who wanted to keep livestock out of their crops, Glidden's wire, known as "The Winner" because of its performance in patent litigation and in the marketplace, found ready acceptance in the West among cattlemen who needed an inexpensive way to confine their animals to grassland. Glidden and Isaac L. Ellwood established the Barb Fence Company in DeKalb in 1874; in 1876 Glidden sold his interest to a Massachusetts company for $60,000, and until 1891, when his patent expired, received a royalty of $.25 per hundred pounds of wire manufactured. Glidden owned or held an interest in several businesses and properties in and around De-Kalb, and also invested in Texas Panhandle ranchland, usually in partnership with his son-in-law, W. H. Bush. By 1889 Glidden's estimated worth was $1 million. He died in DeKalb.

Further Reading: Henry D. McCallum and Frances T. McCallum, *The Wire That Fenced the West*, 1965; Walter Prescott Webb, *The Great Plains*, 1931; Paul H. Carlson, *Empire Building in the Texas Panhandle: William Henry Bush*, 1996.

William W. Savage, Jr.

GODKIN, EDWIN LAWRENCE (2 October 1831–21 May 1902), editor and writer. Born in Moyne, Ireland, of English heritage, Godkin was educated at the Royal Institute and Queen's College in Belfast. Beginning in 1854, he served as a foreign correspondent for the *London Daily News*, where he documented the Crimean War and defended the Union during the Civil War. In 1865, Godkin became first editor in chief of *The Nation*, an American weekly covering politics, literature, science, and art. Founded by abolitionists, *The Nation* quickly came to reflect Godkin's social conservatism. It favored a more restrictive democracy, opposed black and female suffrage, and supported immigration restriction. After *The Nation* merged with the *New York Evening Post* in 1881, Godkin used the *Post* as a forum against imperialism and institutions he considered corrupt, including New York's Tammany Hall. In 1884, he broke from the regular Republicans and endorsed Democrat Grover Cleveland for president. Though his stance cost Godkin subscribers, he continued to have a profound impact on the intellectual elite, particularly editors impressed by his resistence to the influence of political parties. Godkin died in Brixham, England, shortly after relinquishing his editorial duties.

Further Reading: William M. Armstrong, *E. L. Godkin: A Biography*, 1978; William M. Armstrong, *E. L. Godkin and American Foreign Policy: 1865–1900*, 1973; Henry F. Pringle, "Great American Editors: E. L. Godkin," *Scribner's Magazine* 96 (December 1934): 327–334.

Jane M. Armstrong

GOEBEL, WILLIAM (4 January–1856 February 1900), political leader and governor. Born in Carbondale, Pennsylvania, to German immigrant parents, Goebel grew to maturity in Covington, Kentucky. He became an attorney, then entered politics as a reform-minded Democratic state senator in 1887. Goebel eventually become president pro tem of the Kentucky senate; involvement in a shooting that killed an opponent barely slowed his rise. In 1899, Goebel won the Democratic gubernatorial nomination after a bitter convention fight. His campaign attacked the railroad "trust," but when the results of the election were finally certified, Goebel had lost to Republican William S. Taylor by some two thousand votes. The Democratic majority in the legislature contested the results, however. On 30 January 1900, as those deliberations continued, Goebel was shot. Declared the legal governor the next day by the Democrats, he was sworn in, but soon became the only governor in American history to die in office in Frankfurt as a result of assassination. The secretary of state and two other men were tried and convicted, but eventually all went free on pardons because the trials were so partisan. Goebel's assassination limited the reform movement in the state.

Further Reading: James C. Klotter, *William Goebel: The Politics of Wrath*, 1977; Goebel Family Papers, University of Kentucky Special Collections (microfilm), Lexington; Thomas D. Clark, "The People, William Goebel, and the Kentucky Railroads," *Journal of Southern History* 5 (1939): 34–48.

James C. Klotter

GOLD DEMOCRATS. This ephemeral party of 1896 offered a fig leaf of honor for conservative Democrats who wanted Republican William McKinley, gold standard champion, to triumph over Democratic nominee, but free silver advocate, William Jennings Bryan. President Grover Cleveland's insistence on repeal of the Sherman Silver Purchase Act in 1893 had alienated financially strapped farmers. Protectionist Democrats left after a long, bitter fight over the Wilson-Gorman Tariff of 1894. The Homestead and Pullman strikes, and what prior to 1929 was known as the Great Depression (beginning in 1893), produced more defections. The remnant were called Gold Democrats. With the resounding defeat of a gold plank and a resolution commending the president at the Democratic National Convention in Chicago, gold supporters—out of power for the first time—refused to accept the verdict and formed the National Democratic Party. Its 884 delegates who gathered in Indianapolis on 2–3 September represented forty-one states and three territories, but prominent party regulars stayed away. Besides its raison d'être and praise of Cleveland, other planks of the Gold Democrats' platform included a tariff for revenue only, strict economy in government, liberal pensions for veterans, arbitration of international disputes, continued independence of the Supreme Court, and the supremacy of the law. Senator John M. Palmer of Illinois was nominated for president; his running mate was former Confederate general Simon B. Buckner of Kentucky.

In the election, McKinley defeated Bryan 7,218,039 to 6,511,495, and Palmer secured a trifling 133,435 votes (0.96 percent). But in a race where Republicans outspent Democrats by more than ten to one, the defection of gold standard Democrats deprived Bryan and the old party of its best organizers and money raisers. The 1900 Gold Standard Act demonetized silver, and the National Democratic Party disbanded. The factors usually cited for the Populist Party's demise also made Gold Democrats superfluous—returning prosperity, new Yukon mines' greatly increasing the gold supply, and the Spanish-American War.

Further Reading: J. Rogers Hollingsworth, *The Whirligig of Politics: The Democracy of Cleveland and Bryan*, 1963; Gilbert C. Fite, "Election of 1896," in Arthur M. Schlesinger, Jr., and Fred L. Israel, eds., *History of American Presidential Elections, 1789–1968*, vol. 2 (1971): 1787–1825.

Edward Scott Blakeman

GOLD STANDARD ACT OF 1900. Although the Coinage Act of 1792 had established both gold and silver as specie, silver became undervalued in the United States during the late 1840s, and investors therefore exchanged it for gold in foreign markets. With so little silver in circulation, Congress in 1873 authorized the Treasury to cease minting the silver dollar. The move angered farmers, who favored unlimited silver coinage as a way of inflating the currency and thereby raising food prices. Industrialists, on the other hand, wanted an inelastic money supply and stable prices, and thus opposed any attempt to increase the amount of money in circulation. From their perspective, the Bland-Allison Act of 1878 and the Sherman Silver Purchase Act of 1890 came too close to doing just that. The only way to avert the risk of inflation was to follow Great Britain in adopting the gold standard, which Congress did by passing the Gold Standard Act in 1900. After more than a century of bimetallism, gold alone was specie.

Further Reading: Milton Friedman and Anna Schwartz, *A Monetary History of the United States, 1867–1960*, 1963; Paul Studenski and Herman Krooss, *A Financial History of* the United States, 1952; Gretchen Ritter, *Goldbugs and Greenbacks: The Antimonopoly Tradition and the Politics of Finance in America*, 1997.

Christopher Cumo

GOLDMAN, EMMA (27 June 1869–14 May 1940), anarchist and feminist. Born in a Jewish ghetto in Kovno, Russia (now Lithuania), Goldman left school at the age of thirteen. In 1885, she immigrated to the United States and settled in Rochester, New York. Already influenced by radicalism in Russia, and shocked at the execution of the radicals accused of the Haymarket bombings in Chicago (1887), she became involved in the anarchist movement and met her lifelong companion, Alexander Berkman (1870–1936). During the Homestead strike of 1892, she was implicated in Berkman's unsuccessful attempt to assassinate the industrialist Henry Clay Frick. Over the next twenty years, Goldman lectured on the evils of capitalism, espoused free speech and civil liberties, and was an advocate of birth control and sexual liberation. The U.S. government targeted "Red Emma" for her radical activities and jailed her on several occasions. During the Red Scare of 1919, it deported her and Berkman to the Soviet Union. She left the Soviet Union after she criticized the authoritarian nature of the Bolshevik regime. Goldman died in Toronto, Canada, and was buried in Chicago.

Further Reading: Richard Drinnon, *Rebel in Paradise: A Biography of Emma Goldman*, 1961; Alice Wexler, *Emma Goldman: An Intimate Life*, 1984.

John F. Lyons

GOMPERS, SAMUEL (26 January 1850–3 December 1924), labor leader. Born in London to Jewish immigrants from the Netherlands, Gompers followed his father into the cigar-making trade and moved with his family to New York City in 1863 after U.S. protection depressed London's export business. Among New York's cigar makers, many of whom were refugees of the revolutions of 1848, Gompers was introduced to the ideas of Karl Marx and other socialist thinkers, and joined the Cigar Makers International Union (CMIU). He served as its president from 1874 until 1881, when he and leaders of other craft unions formed the Federation of Organized Trades and Labor Un-

ions (FOTLU). Gompers headed the FOTLU from its inception until 1886, when it merged with dissident Knights of Labor to form the American Federation of Labor (AFL). A loose amalgam of independent unions composed of highly skilled workers, the AFL's primary purposes were to coordinate the activities of member unions, resolve jurisdictional disputes, and generally promote trade unionism. Except for 1895, Gompers served as president of the AFL from its birth until his death in 1924 in San Antonio, Texas.

As AFL president, Gompers became the chief proponent of "pure and simple" trade unionism. Drawing on Marxist ideas and his experience with the CMIU, he argued that the conflict between capital and labor was essentially economic rather than political, that the working class alone could find its own salvation, and that the concentration of capital was inevitable. Rather than using political struggle to challenge industrial capitalism's emergence, as the rival Knights of Labor, did, Gompers insisted that unions should rely on economic tools—strikes, boycotts, benefits, union labels, and collective bargaining—to improve the lives of members. Since unskilled and semiskilled workers had little economic power, the AFL did not organize these workers. Under Gompers's leadership the AFL replaced the Knights of Labor as the nation's most powerful labor organization. Membership grew rapidly from fewer than 150,000 members in 1886 to just under 600,000 in 1900. By 1904, over 1.6 million workers belonged to AFL unions.

Further Reading: Staurt Kaufman, *Samuel Gompers and the Origins of the American Federation of Labor*, 1973; Samuel Gompers, *Seventy Years of Life and Labor*, 1925.

Michael Pierce

GONZALES, BOYER (22 September 1864– 14 February 1934), artist. Gonzalez was born in Galveston, Texas. He studied with the famed artist Winslow Homer, and was influenced by the Dutch painter Hendrik Willem Mesdag. In 1894, Gonzales worked with William J. Whittemore, a watercolorist. The following year, he began creating watercolor scenes of Mexico, inspired by the sea, harbors, ships, and waterfowl. Thereafter, Gonzales, devoted his life to painting and developed his talent; time brought recognition. His oil paintings and watercolors can be found in public and private collections in the United States and Europe. He died in Galveston.

Further Reading: Edward Simmen, *With Bold Strokes*, 1997.

Santos C. Vega

GOODRICH, BENJAMIN FRANKLIN (4 November 1841–3 August 1888), physician, inventor, and businessman. A native of Ripley, New York, Goodrich was educated in Fredonia, New York, and Austinburg, Ohio, then received training in medicine at Cleveland Medical College. He served as a surgeon during the Civil War, taking leave to study surgery at the University of Pennsylvania. After the war, Goodrich practiced medicine in Jamestown, New York, but became interested in business. He worked for a time in the Pennsylvania oil industry, then sold real estate in New York. Finally, he raised enough capital to begin manufacturing rubber in New York.

The board of trade of Akron, Ohio, convinced Goodrich to move his rubber factory in 1870. Twenty-four local businessmen raised funds for the move, and the B. F. Goodrich Company began manufacturing in 1871 in downtown Akron, producing hoses, belts, and hard rubber tires for carriages. By 1890, Goodrich employed more than a thousand workers, launching the period of Akron's most rapid growth. Within the next decade Goodrich was joined in Akron by the Goodyear and Firestone rubber companies. Goodrich served on the city council during 1880–1881 and was its president in 1880. He contracted tuberculosis in the mid-1880s, moved to Colorado for his health, and died in Manitou Springs, Colorado.

Further Reading: Mansel G. Blackford and K. Austin Kerr, *B. F. Goodrich: Tradition and Transformation, 1870–1995*, 1996; Karl Grismer, *Akron and Summit County*, 1952; Samuel A. Lane, *Fifty Years and Over of Akron and Summit County*, 1892.

Stephen Paschen

GORDON, JOHN BROWN (6 February 1832–9 January 1904), U.S. senator and governor of Georgia. Born in Upson County, Georgia, Gordon studied at the University of Georgia and was admitted to the bar in 1853 without having graduated. As a former Confederate Army officer, he unsuccessfully challenged Republican Rufus B. Bullock for governor in 1868. Gordon defeated former Confederate vice president Alexander H. Stephens for U.S. senator in 1873. Gordon served for seven years, seeking both Democratic "redemption" in the South and southern reconciliation with the North. Reelected in 1879, he resigned one year later to promote construction of the Georgia Pacific Railroad. His resignation fueled rumors of a political "deal" that allowed another Democrat, Joseph E. Brown, to succeed him. Although never proven, the charges cost Gordon a loss of prestige from which he never fully recovered. Nevertheless, he managed to win election as governor in 1886. He was reelected two years later, and regained his former Senate seat in 1891. Gordon was long considered a member of the old guard Bourbon "Atlanta Ring," however, and his political career fell victim to the Populist revolt of the 1890s. He retired in 1897. Devoting his final years to lecturing and literary pursuits, Gordon found himself in great demand by northern audiences. Shortly before his death in Miami, Florida, he published a book, *Reminiscences of the Civil War* (1903).

Further Reading: *New York Times*, 10 January 1904; Ellis Paxson Oberholtzer, *A History of the United States Since the Civil War*, 1931.

Harvey Gresham Hudspeth

GORGAS, WILLIAM CRAWFORD (3 October 1854–3 July 1920), sanitarian and surgeon general of the U.S. Army. Born near Mobile, Alabama, Gorgas graduated from the University of the South at Sewanee, Tennessee, in 1875, and four years later from the Bellevue Hospital Medical College in New York City. The next year he began his career as a physician with the U.S. Army Medical Corps. After being stricken with yellow fever, Gorgas recovered and headed the yellow fever camp at Siboney, Cuba (1898), subsequently becoming chief sanitary engineer of Havana after the Spanish-American War. Through the advice and discoveries of others, including Walter Reed and Dr. Carlos J. Finlay, Gorgas freed

Havana of mosquitoes and yellow fever. Shortly thereafter he gained recognition as a sanitary expert, clearing the way for the construction of the Panama Canal. Gorgas died in the Queen Alexandra Military Hospital at Millbank, England.

Further Reading: *London Times*, 5 July 1920; *New York Times*, 5 July 1920; Marie Cook Doughty Gorgas and B. J. Hendrick, *William Crawford Gorgas: His Life and Work*, 1924.

Leonard Schlup

GORMAN, ARTHUR PUE (11 March 1839–4 June 1906), U.S. senator. One of the most prominent Gilded Age Democrats, Gorman was born in Woodstock, Maryland. In 1852 he went to Washington, D.C., to become a congressional page, and eventually rose to postmaster of the Senate. Subsequently he was collector of internal revenue for Maryland's Fifth Congressional District, president of the Chesapeake and Ohio Canal Company, chairman of the Maryland Democratic Central Committee, state legislator in both chambers, and manager of the successful 1884 Democratic presidential campaign. Gorman was U.S. senator from 1881 to 1899 and from 1903 until his death. An old guard leader of the Maryland Democrats, he exercised power through force of character, parliamentary skill, and his cognizance of the importance of committee structure. A member of the powerful Appropriations Committee and the Committee on Rules, he helped enact the Interstate Commerce Act of 1887 and the Public Printing Act of 1894. He opposed civil service reform. Gorman led the filibuster that killed the 1890 Federal Elections Bill, an attempt to safeguard African-American suffrage in the South. He also played a significant role in shaping the Wilson-Gorman Tariff of 1894.

Occupying a middle ground between high protectionists and free traders, Gorman devised a calculated policy based on practical business principles and sectional interests. By adding hundreds of protective amendments, he emasculated the Wilson Bill passed by the House of Representatives and favored by President Grover Cleveland. Gorman's verbal assaults on the chief executive further strained their relationship. Gorman was the Senate majority leader from 1893 to 1895 and minority leader from 1889 to 1893, 1895 to 1898, and 1903 to 1906. An anti-imperialist and an advocate of sound money, Gorman counseled moderation and patience during the free silver enthusiasm of 1896. He championed party loyalty, brought conservative leadership to Senate Democrats, and wielded enormous political power. He died in Washington, D.C.

Further Reading: John R. Lambert, Jr., *Arthur Pue Gorman*, 1953; Peter H. Argersinger, "From Party Tickets to Secret Ballots: The Evolution of the Electoral Process in Maryland During the Gilded Age," *Maryland Historical Magazine* 82 (198): 214–239; Arthur P. Gorman Papers, Maryland Historical Society, Baltimore.

Leonard Schlup

GOULD, JASON (27 May 1836–2 December 1892), capitalist and railroad financier. Born in Roxbury, New York, Gould attended Hobart Academy, clerked in a country store, and learned surveying and mapmaking. By 1860, Gould, with James "Jubilee" Fiske and Daniel Drew, formed a Wall Street brokerage house speculating in gold and stocks, and succeeded in warding off a bid by Cornelius Vanderbilt to take over the Erie Railroad. When Gould tried to corner the gold market (Black Friday, 24 September 1869), he was unsuccessful and lost control of the Erie Railroad. Both events showed Gould to be a sharp trader almost to the point of knavery, a man whose main concerns were his garden and his books. From 1872 to 1883, he tried to build a "Gould System" of railroads in the Southwest by gaining control of several companies. He died in New York City, leaving an estate of $72 million to his six children.

Further Reading: Maury Klein, *The Life and Legend of Jay Gould*, 1988; Julius Godinsky, *Jay Gould: His Business Career, 1867–1892*, 1959; Maury Klein, "In Search of Jay Gould," *Business History Review* 52 (1978): 166–98.

Nicholas C. Polos

GOVERNORSHIPS. Governorships hovered between two very different eras during the Gilded Age. During the early years, especially in the South, governors faced challenges associated with the Civil War and Reconstruction, while in the final years, strong leadership was emerging as a major impetus for the Progressive movement. War-related concerns fueled the political careers of men such as Lucius Fairchild of Wisconsin (1866–1872), who initiated "veterans politics" with his frequent resort to waving the bloody shirt, and Ambrose Everett Burnside of Rhode Island (1866–1869), who obtained prompt acknowledgment and payment of the state's war claims. New, albeit short-lived, opportunities for African Americans enabled Louisiana's Pinckney B. S. Pinchback to become the nation's first black governor in 1872.

The office of governor continued to modernize. South Carolina, the last state to employ legislative appointment of the governor, abandoned it in 1865. Terms of office also became more standardized, and by 1900, one- and three-year terms had virtually disappeared. Similarly, the governor's veto power expanded. In 1860, only twenty-five of thirty-three states permitted the veto, whereas by 1900 all but three of forty-five employed it. Salaries also generally increased. The executive branch became increasingly unwieldy, as legislatures scrambled to address emerging social problems by creating a host of new agencies over which governors could exercise little control. Limits placed on executive ability to remove agency members further contributed to gubernatorial ineffectiveness. Gubernatorial power was also severely limited by the presence of other directly elected executive officers (secretary of state, treasurer, and attorney general).

Following Reconstruction, state government became increasingly corrupt and inefficient. Party bosses, who headed powerful machines and rewarded followers with public offices and political favors, were the real leaders. In New Jersey, for example, every chief executive from 1868 to 1890 had strong, direct ties with the railroad industry at some point in his career. In addition, the period's concern for property rights worked against the regulation of railroads and utility companies.

A subsequent demand for honest, efficient, and responsive administration meant added influence for governors, and fueled careers of several well-known figures. These included Rutherford B. Hayes (1868–1872, 1876–1877)

and William McKinley of Ohio (1892–1896), and Samuel Tilden (1875–1877), Grover Cleveland (1883–1885), and Theodore Roosevelt (1899–1901) of New York. Lesser-known George Stoneham of California (1883–1887) attempted to curb the power and control the rates of the Southern Pacific Railroad. John Peter Altgeld of Illinois (1893–1897) pardoned the three surviving Haymarket prisoners and appointed pioneering social activist Florence Kelley to public office. Hazen Pingree of Michigan (1897–1901) advocated a graduated income tax, the eight-hour day, and direct election of U.S. senators.

Further Reading: Coleman B. Ransone, *The Office of Governor in the United States*, 1956; Leslie Lipson, *The American Governor: From Figurehead to Leader*, 1939; Joseph E. Kallenbach, *The American Chief Executive: The Presidency and the Governorship*, 1966.

Marie Marmo Mullaney

GOWDY, JOHN KENNEDY (23 August 1843–25 June 1918), politician and consul general. Born in Arlington, Indiana, Gowdy fought in the Civil War, owned farmland in Rush County, Indiana, and was chairman of the Rush County Republican Committee in the 1880s. From 1890 to 1897, he chaired the Indiana Republican Committee, during which time he argued extensively with Thomas H. Carter, Republican National Committee chair, over the conduct of Benjamin Harrison's presidential campaign in Indiana, insufficient funds, and an absence of noted speakers, among other matters, which he brought to the attention of the president through an exchange of correspondence. In 1896 Gowdy acquired a national reputation for his efficient organization and the sizable win the GOP achieved in Indiana. The following year, President William McKinley appointed him U.S. consul general at Paris, where he served during the negotiations to end the Spanish-American War and at the time of the Paris Exposition of 1900. In 1905 Gowdy became the first American consular officer to be named an Officer of the Legion of Honor by the French government. Gowdy died in Rushville, Indiana.

Further Reading: *Indianapolis Journal*, 26 June 1918; Leonard Schlup, "Hoosier Republican in the Gilded Age:

John K. Gowdy and the 1892 Presidential Campaign in Indiana," *Tamkang Journal of American Studies* 9 (1992): 1–21.

Leonard Schlup

GOWEN, FRANKLIN BENJAMIN (9 February 1836–14 December 1889), lawyer and railroad president. Born in Mount Airy, Pennsylvania, Gowen attended a Roman Catholic school in Emmitsburg, Maryland, and Beck's Boys Academy in Lititz, Pennsylvania, a Moravian institution. In 1857 he began a long connection with the anthracite industry by managing his father's colliery. The next year he formed a mining partnership that collapsed when coal prices fell. Following his failure as a mine owner, Gowen read law under a Pottsville, Pennsylvania, attorney and was admitted to the bar in 1860.

In 1865 the Philadelphia & Reading Railroad, the region's largest anthracite carrier, chose Gowen as its local counsel in Pottsville. He quickly rose within the company management, and became the firm's president in 1870. He served in that capacity from 1870 to 1880, from 1882 to 1884, and in 1886, and attempted to expand the company from a regional to a major national corporation. He added to his reputation in 1877 when Pennsylvania appointed him special prosecutor in the main case against the Molly Maguires. Following the failure of his expansion plans in the mid-1880s, he slipped into obscurity and returned to private law practice. While in Washington, D.C., preparing to present an antitrust case before the Interstate Commerce Commission, Gowen purchased a revolver and killed himself.

Further Reading: Marvin W. Schlegal, *Ruler of the Reading: The Life of Franklin B. Gowen*, 1947; *The Philadelphia Inquirer*, 15 December 1889; Reading Company Collection, Hagley Museum and Library, Wilmington, Delaware.

John H. Hepp, IV

GRADY, HENRY WOODFIN (24 May 1850–23 December 1889), editor of the *Atlanta Constitution*. A leading proponent of the New South movement to promote reconciliation between the North and the South as the catalyst for southern economic progress, Grady was born in Athens, Georgia. He received his education at the universities of Georgia and Virginia. His program of New South progress rested on white supremacy and segregation, but Grady minimized racial conflicts when he spoke to northern audiences, assuring potential investors of southern goodwill toward African Americans. In his most famous speech "The New South," presented to the New England Society of New York in 1886, Grady depicted the Civil War as a painful period that freed the South from its economically stifling dependence on slavery and agriculture. In defeat's aftermath, he argued, a more democratic and stronger South arose—ready for investment and industrial growth. Although Grady's rhetoric focused on the urban, middle-class South, he also advocated an agricultural program of crop diversification and scientific farming to wean southern farmers from cotton and tobacco and draw them into an expanding global market. At the time of his death in Atlanta, farmers and townsmen across the South memorialized his vision of renewal and progress.

Further Reading: Ferald J. Bryan, *Henry Grady or Tom Watson: The Rhetorical Struggle for the New South, 1880–1890*, 1994; Harold E. Davis, *Henry Grady's New South: Atlanta, a Brave and Beautiful City*, 1990; Raymond B. Nixon, *Henry W. Grady: Spokesman for the New South*, 1943.

Connie L. Lester

GRANGER LAWS. Specific agriculture-related regulatory acts passed in Illinois, Minnesota, Iowa, and Wisconsin in the 1870s were popularly called Granger laws. Similar legislation was considered in Indiana, Michigan, Missouri, Kansas, Nebraska, California, and Oregon. The name derived from agitation for economic reform by the Grange (or Patrons of Husbandry), which had become a political force in the upper Midwest. Organized for social purposes, the Grange claimed to be nonpolitical. Economic distress associated with the Panic of 1873, however, caused many of its local groups to attempt to influence public policy. At times Grangers were joined by urban shippers with similar interests.

The acts referred to as "Granger laws" dealt with railroads and grain storage facilities. The first Granger laws, four in number, were passed in Illinois in 1871. They created a board of railroad and warehouse commissioners, and mandated grain inspection, and regulation of warehouses, railroad passenger fares, and freight rates, especially long- and short-haul discrimination. Enforcement proved difficult, and the act regarding rate discrimination was declared unconstitutional by the Illinois supreme court. In response, in 1873 the Illinois legislature passed a more effective regulation that became a model for measures enacted by other states in the ensuing years. The statute stated that any railroad company charging more than fair or reasonable rates was guilty of extortion, and any railroad making unjust discriminations in rates violated the act. The law detailed what constituted unjust discrimination, and provided fines for violators. Aggrieved shippers were allowed to recover three times the amount of damages suffered. Furthermore, the law required the state railroad commission to remedy abuses and to prepare a schedule of reasonable maximum freight rates.

Granger laws illustrated the growing strength of agrarian reformers during the Gilded Age. They also demonstrated an increased opposition to laissez–faire economic policy, as states asserted their regulatory power in the marketplace. As a result of the Granger laws, the U.S. Supreme Court upheld state police power to regulate private businesses "affected with a public interest" in the *Granger Cases* (1877) and *Munn* v. *Illinois* (1877). Yet railroad regulation, per se, by the states was short-lived; the Supreme Court effectively nullified it in *Wabash, Saint Louis and Pacific Railroad Company* v. *Illinois* (1886) a decade later. In addition, a series of decisions in the 1890s and the early twentieth century further weakened the restraining hand of states.

Further Reading: Ward M. McAfee, "Local Interests and Railroad Regulation in California During the Granger Decade," *Pacific Historical Review* 37 (1968): 51–66; George Hall Miller, *Railroads and Granger Laws*, 1971; Harold D. Woodman, "Chicago Businessmen and the Granger Laws," *Agricultural History* 36 (1962): 16–24.

Robert S. La Forte

GRANT, JULIA BOGGS DENT (26 January 1826–14 December 1902), First Lady. Born near St. Louis, Missouri, Julia married Ulysses S. Grant on 22 August 1848. They spent eight

years in the White House (1869–1877). Mrs. Grant epitomized the Gilded Age with extravagant parties and elaborate style. She was more accessible than previous First Ladies, holding weekly receptions. She helped make the role of the political wife a public one; and she was the first presidential spouse to work with the media and the first to write her memoirs. In retirement, President and Mrs. Grant toured Europe. They subsequently settled in New York City. Following her husband's death in 1885, Mrs. Grant moved to Washington, D.C., where she died.

Further Reading: John Y. Simon, ed., The *Personal Memoirs of Julia Dent Grant*, 1975; Ishbel Ross, *The General's Wife: The Life of Mrs. Ulysses S. Grant*, 1959; *New York Times*, 15 December 1902.

Terri Pedersen Summey

GRANT, ULYSSES SIMPSON (27 April 1822–23 July 1885), general and president. Born in Point Pleasant, Ohio, Grant entered West Point in 1839. After graduation in 1843, he had an undistinguished career and left the army. He reenlisted for the Civil War and rose to fame as the most successful Union leader. His service culminated in promotion to lieutenant general and acceptance of the Army of Northern Virginia's surrender at Appomattox in April 1865. Grant was promoted to general in 1866, served in Washington, D.C., during early Reconstruction, and distanced himself from the increasingly unpopular President Andrew Johnson. He emerged as the 1868 Republican presidential candidate and won election handily.

In the White House from 1869 to 1877, Grant struggled against imposing political, economic, and racial obstacles. Southern hostility toward blacks and Republicans provoked incessant violence. Grant supported use of the army to suppress the Ku Klux Klan and other terrorists. Slackening of such efforts after initial successes had dire effects. Grant's peace policy for Indians placed Quakers and other religious figures as agents, strove to eliminate venality in the Indian Bureau, and advocated restrained responses to the frequent allegations of Indian outrages against whites. He persisted in this policy even after numerous incidents showed how intractable the Indian question remained. Grant promoted education and economic self-sufficiency for African Americans and Indians. To better the lot of laborers and encourage commerce, he backed an eight-hour-day law that provided workers at government installations with the same wages previously earned in ten hours.

Political factionalism and patronage demands bedeviled Grant. He pursued civil service reform unsuccessfully. Grant never mastered the art of selecting high officials. His cabinet and Supreme Court choices often astounded observers or angered important elements in the Republican Party. His indulging relatives with minor appointments drew additional criticism. Disaffection with Grant inspired the Liberal Republican movement that resulted in Horace Greeley's unsuccessful presidential run in 1872.

In foreign affairs, Grant settled the *Alabama* claims, simultaneously improving relations with Great Britain, strained since the Civil War, and establishing the principle of arbitration for resolving international differences. He defused an explosive situation in 1873 when the Spanish interdicted the *Virginius*—reputedly sailing to assist the Cuban independence movement—and executed crew members and passengers. Earlier, Grant had unsuccessfully sought to annex Santo Domingo to the United States. Secretary of State Hamilton Fish proved an able adviser and spared Grant embarrassing missteps in diplomatic matters.

Embarrassments, however, dominated Grant's second term as scandals made constant headlines. His private secretary, Orville E. Babcock, was deeply implicated in the Whiskey Ring that siphoned Internal Revenue funds. Secretary of War William W. Belknap resigned rather than submit to official sanction for brokering trading-post licenses. These spectacular revelations, and lesser ones, gave credence to fears that Grant formerly had ignored: actions of relatives or friends that precipitated the gold panic of 1869 (Black Friday) and dubious transactions in the New York custom house. "Grantism" emerged as a generic label for scandal and corruption, and doomed his third-term aspirations. Formerly detached from routine, Grant responded to the turmoil by involving himself in matters great and small, and keeping the government afloat salvaged his personal reputation. His final presidential achievement was avoiding a constitutional breakdown during the disputed presidential election crisis of 1876–1877.

Grant toured the world from 1877 to 1879. Enthusiastic welcomes restored his political viability at home, and Republican "Stalwarts" eagerly recruited him as their 1880 candidate. Grant lost the nomination after an extended convention fight. He then settled in New York City, where an unscrupulous business partner lost his life savings and Grant developed throat cancer. He triumphed over his ill fortune and illness by willing himself to complete his *Personal Memoirs*—a literary and financial success—only days before his death at Mount McGregor, New York.

Further Reading: John Y. Simon, ed., *The Papers of Ulysses S. Grant*, 1967– ; William S. McFeely, *Grant: A Biography*, 1981; Mark Wahlgren Summers, *The Era of Good Stealings*, 1993.

William M. Ferraro

GRAY, ASA (18 November 1810–30 January 1888), botanist and educator. Born in Sauquoit, New York, Gray earned a medical degree in 1831, studied plants, and developed friendships with prominent botanists, including John Torrey of New York. In 1857, Charles Darwin, the English naturalist, wrote a letter to Gray outlining his theory of the evolution of species by natural selection and sent him an advance copy of *On the Origin of Species*. Thereafter, Gray was Darwin's chief American advocate. In 1842, Gray accepted the Fisher professorship of natural history at Harvard, remaining at the university until his death in Cambridge, Massachusetts. Having become the acknowledged leader of American botanists during the Gilded Age, Gray traveled extensively at home and abroad. He created Harvard's department of botany, published widely, and pioneered in the field of plant geography. He also completed a masterful monograph on the botany of Japan (1859), helped to establish the National Academy of Sciences, served as president of the American Academy of Arts and Sciences from 1863 to 1873, and was a regent of the Smithsonian Institution from 1874 to 1888. Gray was so esteemed among his fellow botanists that in

1885, 180 of them joined to send him letters of congratulation upon his birthday.

Further Reading: *Boston Transcript*, 31 January 1888; *New York Times*, 31 January 1888; A. Hunter Dupree, *Asa Gray: American Botanist, Friend of Darwin*, 1959, 1988.

Leonard Schlup

GRAY, GEORGE (4 May 1840–7 August 1925), U.S. senator and judge. Born in New Castle, Delaware, Gray graduated from Princeton University in 1859, practiced law in New Castle, and served as attorney general of Delaware from 1879 to 1885. He held a seat as a Democrat in the U.S. Senate from 1885 to 1899. In 1880 he nominated Thomas F. Bayard of Delaware for president at the Democratic National Convention in Cincinnati, Ohio. In 1896, Gray supported the Gold Democrat presidential ticket headed by Senator John M. Palmer of Illinois instead William Jennings Bryan's free-silver candidacy. President William McKinley in 1898 named Gray one of the U.S. commissioners to negotiate peace with Spain at Paris and formally conclude the Spanish-American War. After Gray retired from the Senate, McKinley appointed him judge of the U.S. circuit court of appeals. In 1900, the president selected Gray for membership on the Permanent Court of Arbitration at The Hague. A public figure holding strong convictions and a person of unquestioned integrity, Gray earned national attention during the Gilded Age and was called into service by both Democrats and Republicans. He died in Wilmington, Delaware.

Further Reading: Michael Crosslin, "The Diplomacy of George Gray," Ph.D. diss., Oklahoma State University, 1980; *New York Times*, 8 August 1925.

Leonard Schlup

GRAY, ISAAC PUSEY (18 October 1828–14 February 1895), governor and diplomat. Gray was born in Chester County, Pennsylvania, and in 1836 moved with his parents to Ohio. In 1855, he settled in Indiana and practiced law. After service in the Civil War, he entered local politics as a Republican. He served four years in the Indiana state senate (1868–1872) and became its president pro tempore. Indiana's Democratic state senators tried to block the state's ratification of the Fifteenth Amendment to the U.S. Constitution by leaving the chamber, thereby preventing a quorum. Gray locked the doors, counted those in the lobby as present, and declared the amendment properly passed. In 1872 he associated with Liberal Republicans opposing President Ulysses S. Grant, but in 1876 Gray accepted the Democratic nomination for lieutenant governor and won the election. Governor James D. Williams died in office in 1880, and Gray completed Williams's term (1880–1881) and one of his own (1885–1889). He was a prominent but unsuccessful aspirant for the Democratic vice presidential nomination in 1888 and 1892. In the latter year, he campaigned vigorously across Indiana for the Democratic ticket, helping Grover Cleveland carry the state's electoral votes. The president responded by appointing Gray minister to Mexico, where he served from 1893 until his death in Mexico City.

Further Reading: *Indianapolis Journal*, 15 February 1895; Leonard Schlup, "Isaac P. Gray of Indiana and the National Democratic campaign of 1892," *Proceedings of the Indiana Academy of the Social Sciences* 12 (1977): 78–87.

Leonard Schlup

GREAT HOMES. The majestic homes of the newly wealthy built during the postbellum period represented a distinct genre, helped shape American culture, and provide windows into their time. Some were true estates designed to be self-sufficient, with orchards, gardens, and dairy and poultry operations. A few were museums from the beginning. Many reflected the owner's strong personal involvement, while others expressed the proprietor's social stature. In some homes, antiques were used to create period rooms. Their imperial scale and classical ornamentation also recalled homes of the European upper classes in earlier eras. Newport, Rhode Island, became America's leading resort and a center of the arts and architecture. Here lived the China trade merchant William Wetmore, whose stone Château-sur-Mer was the first summer mansion built there. Florence Vanderbilt and her husband, Hamilton McKown Twombly, owned Florham, a hundred-room Georgian Revival masterpiece, in Morris County, New Jersey. Charles McKim, William

Mead, and Stanford White, partners in the foremost architectural firm of the day, helped build it 1897, and Frederick Law Olmsted landscaped it. Italian immigrant laborers made up the construction crew. A carriage house that quartered forty horses; ten greenhouses, an orangerie, and a gate lodge were among the outbuildings. The staff numbered 125, including chauffeurs attired in maroon livery. Mrs. Richard Gambrill chose John M. Carrère and Thomas Hastings, designers of the New York Public Library and the U.S. Senate Office Building, to plan Whiteholme (later Vernon Court), an adaptation of a seventeenth-century French chateau, in Newport. Widely heralded as the most spectacular mansion of its kind in the nation, its beauty and originality brought comparisons with the White House, the Breakers, and other monuments. The marble hall, petit salon, and ballroom were modeled after Marie Antoinette's suites at Versailles. Its formal sunken gardens were inspired by King Henry VIII's Pond Gardens at Hampton Court Palace.

Politicians and regional entrepreneurs generally dwelt in more modest luxury. Among them were of Vice President Adlai E. Stevenson and Supreme Court associate justice David Davis (Bloomington, Illinois) and John Henry Hower, a milling industrialist (Akron, Ohio). The Hower House, built in 1871 and designed in Second Empire Italianate style, had twenty-eight rooms radiating from a large octagonal center hall, capped by a mansard roof and soaring tower. Grovelawn (built in 1893), the residence of Phineas C. Lounsbury, Republican governor of Connecticut from 1887 to 1889, had a windmill, a bowling alley, and a private water supply.

Further Reading: Harry Devlin, *Portraits of American Architecture: A Gallery of Victorian Homes*, 1989; Irvin Haas, *America's Historic Houses and Restorations*, 1966.

Leonard Schlup

GREAT PLAINS STATES. Part of a vast region stretching from the hills near the Appalachian Mountains in the east to the slopes of the Rocky Mountains in the west, this area is characterized by a treeless, often level surface with low rainfall. North and South Dakota, Nebraska, Kansas, Indian Territory, Oklahoma Territory, and Texas were part of the Great Plains during the Gilded Age. When the era began, the plains were the domain of buffalo hunters, outlaws, cowboys, and Native American tribes. The 1862 Homestead Act opened settlement, and between 1850 and 1900 the area's population grew elevenfold. The invention of barbed wire made fencing the land practical. The building of railroads across the Great Plains profoundly affected development of the West, more firmly establishing economic dependence on eastern capital. Native Americans lost their land and were relocated on reservations. During the Gilded Age, cowboys and cattle trading gave way to agricultural settlement, and violence yielded to a society more closely resembling that of the East. Yet the Great Plains exerted a powerful influence on America, achieved primarily through production of a mythic wild West of outlaws and lawmen, and battles between whites and the last remnants of Native American resistance. Reality was the hardship of eking out an existence in a precarious and difficult environment.

Further Reading: Alexander B. Adams, *Sunlight and Storm: The Great American Plains*, 1977; Russell McKee, *The Last West: A History of the Great Plains of North America*, 1974; Walter Prescott Webb, *The Great Plains*, 1931.

Amanda Laugesen

GREELEY, HORACE (3 February 1811–29 November 1872), journalist and presidential candidate. Greeley was born in Amherst, New Hampshire. A passionate reader, he became an apprentice printer instead of finishing school, and in 1831 moved to New York City. There he promoted Whig Party candidates and launched the influential *New York Tribune* (1841). After the Civil War, Greeley was moderate on Reconstruction. An advocate of peace and harmony, he helped post bond for Jefferson Davis. Greeley favored impeaching President Andrew Johnson and supported Ulysses Grant in the 1868 election. Greeley was active in New York State politics, running for a number of offices and feuding with the political machine headed by Roscoe Conkling. Greeley opposed Grant's renomination in 1872. He broke with the regular Republicans and moved to the emerging Liberal Republican Party, which nominated him as its presidential candidate. Attempting to overcome the Civil War stigma, the Democrats also reluctantly nominated him. Greeley campaigned on the slogan of "New Departures." His wife died during the campaign, and he was defeated decisively, carrying only six states with 43.8 percent of the vote. Greeley died in a Pleasantville, New York, sanitarium before Grant's second inauguration.

Further Reading: Jeter Allen Isely, *Horace Greeley and the Republican Party, 1853–1861: A Study of the New York Tribune*, 1965; Glyndon G. Van Deusen, *Horace Greeley: Nineteenth Century Crusader*, 1953.

William C. Binning

GREEN, SAMUEL SWETT (20 February 1837–8 December 1918), librarian. Green helped found the American Library Association, wrote prolifically, and served from 1871 to 1909 as a librarian in Worcester, Massachusetts, the place of his birth and death. He gained international recognition through his innovations in public service, associations with schools, and interlibrary loan procedures. A graduate of Harvard College (1858), he later earned a divinity degree. Green drifted through life until his uncle left money to establish the Free Public Library of Worcester, and stipulated that Green be appointed to its board of trustees. In 1871, he was hired as its librarian, and remained there until his retirement. Dedicated to the principle of courteous public service, Green contended that a librarian should not permit a patron to leave with a question unanswered. In 1872 the Worcester library became the first New England library of size to open on Sundays. Green was an eloquent speaker, a careful organizer, and a lecturer at educational institutions. He tirelessly advocated education for librarianship. In 1913 he published *The Public Library Movement in the United States, 1853–1893*.

Further Reading: Robert Kendall Shaw, *Samuel Swett Green*, 1926; Austin S. Garver, "Samuel Swett Green: An Appreciation," *Library Journal* 34 (June 1909): 269–271; Timothy Rivard, "Samuel Swett Green: Library Pioneer," *Bay State Librarian* (Fall 1984): 7–8.

Terri Pedersen Summey

GREENBACK LABOR MOVEMENT. Gilded Age farmers favored inflating the currency as a way of increasing food prices and lowering the value of their debts. The issuance of Treasury notes, known as Greenbacks, to finance the Civil War did just that. Business figures, however, demanded hard money in the aftermath of the Panic of 1873. In response, leaders of the Indiana and Illinois Granges called a conference to mobilize support for Greenbacks. The farmers who gathered at Indianapolis in November 1874 formed the Independent National Party, known as the Greenback Labor Movement.

Congress's decision in 1875 to redeem Greenbacks in coin after 1 January 1879 had little immediate effect on the party, and it attracted only eighty thousand votes in 1876. Two years later, by contrast, it garnered a million votes and elected fifteen congressmen. In 1880 the party attempted to attract even more votes by broadening its platform to include a graduated income tax, female suffrage, and railroad regulation. But the Specie Resumption Act had taken effect in 1879, inflationists had abandoned Greenbacks in favor of increasing the amount of silver in circulation, and James B. Weaver, a Union general during the Civil War, polled only three hundred thousand votes as the party's presidential candidate. In 1884 it disbanded after receiving only 175,000 votes.

Further Reading: Solon J. Buck, *The Agrarian Crusade*, 1920; Walter T. K. Nugent, *Money and American Society, 1865–1880*, 1968.

Christopher Cumo

GREENBACKISM. Greenbackism was a political ideology that emerged in the post-1865 period and provided the major challenge to gold monometallism and gold and silver bimetallism in the late nineteenth century, though Greenbackers were sometimes associated with the bimetallists. Greenbackers maintained that the price level was a function of the quantity of money in circulation and the demand for its use, rather than the form which money took. They wanted a more flexible currency, one more available to farmers, laborers, and small businessmen—the "producing classes"—at low interest rates. Though they were often accused of favoring inflation, in general they sought to stabilize prices.

Greenbackism had several origins: the writings of Edward Kellogg in the late 1840s and the 1850s; the issuance of legal tender Treasury notes (greenbacks) by the U.S. Treasury to help finance the Civil War; the modification of Kellogg's ideas by Alexander Campbell in 1864, in the form of an interconvertible bond scheme; the ideas of Henry Carey; the proposal of George H. Pendleton to redeem war bonds with greenbacks; and the withdrawal of greenbacks from circulation by Hugh McCulloch, Andrew Johnson's secretary of the Treasury in the immediate postwar period. The first groups to support the greenbacks were drawn from Republican supporters, especially small entrepreneurs. By the late 1860s, the labor movement, especially the National Labor Union, was attracted to greenbackism through the ideas of Alexander Campbell. By the late 1870s and early 1880s the greenback banner was carried by the Greenback Labor Party. Greenbackism's political base had expanded from the working class and small business to include farmers.

Greenbackism made its last appearance in the Farmers' Alliance movement of the late 1880s and the Populist Party of the 1890s. By this time, the major support for greenbackism came from farmers, especially in the South and the West. The election of 1896, with William Jennings Bryan espousing a bimetallic standard, and currency expansion following the discovery of gold a few years later in Alaska and then South Africa, put an end to greenbackism.

Further Reading: Bruce Palmer, *"Man over Money": The Southern Populist Critique of American Capitalism*, 1980; Gretchen Ritter, *Goldbugs and Greenbacks: The Antimonopoly Tradition and the Politics of Finance in America, 1865–1896*, 1997; Robert P. Sharkey, *Money, Class, and Party: An Economic Study of Civil War and Reconstruction*, 1959.

Bruce Palmer

GREENER, RICHARD THEODORE (30 January 1844–2 May 1922), diplomat, educator, lawyer. Greener was born free in Philadelphia, Pennsylvania, and in 1870 became the first African-American graduate of Harvard College. Subsequently he ran two black schools, and helped edit the *New National Era*

and Citizen. He taught at the University of South Carolina from 1873 to 1877. A leading proponent of the "exoduster" movement, Greener later taught law at Howard University. Admitted to the District of Columbia bar in 1877, he opened a law practice and accepted a federal clerkship. Greener's expertise and political connections proved useful in 1880, when an African-American cadet at West Point was found bloodied, unconscious, and fettered. Johnson C. Whittaker claimed to have been beaten in a racist attack sanctioned by school authorities; doubters charged that he had staged the assault. The case became a national cause célèbre. With Greener's help, Whittaker's "guilty" verdict was overturned.

A tireless Republican campaigner, Greener served on James A. Garfield's inaugural executive committee. In 1898, he became the first American consul to Vladivostok, Russia. When a baseless smear campaign ended his diplomatic career in 1905, Greener joined the Niagara Movement. He died in Chicago, Illinois.

Further Reading: Ruth Ann Stewart and David M. Kahn, *Richard T. Greener: His Life and Work*, 1980; Richard T. Greener Papers, Howard University, Harvard University, and the Schomburg Center for Research in Black Culture, New York City.

Barbara Ryan

GREENWICH VILLAGE. This section of New York City was an established community with its own character during the Gilded Age. It attracted reformers, social workers, newspaper reports, painters, authors, idealists, and some of the greatest figures in American arts and letters. Isaac Hull Brown, sexton of the imposing Grace Church, wielded power in fashionable society by knowing everything that occurred in the village. Through accumulated influence and questionable tactics, Brown amassed a sizable personal fortune, accepting gifts from young men, bakers, jewelers, and others. Nearby, between 1876 and 1908, was Huntington Close, the location of Fleischmann's Model Vienna Bakery. Specializing in Old World pastries, coffees, and rolls, Fleischmann's, the city's most elegant coffeehouse, underscored the freshness of its products by distributing unsold baked goods at midnight,

free of charge, to the hungry. Several hundred shabbily dressed people from the streets and flophouses gathered for handouts. This poignant ritual, ultimately known as a breadline, began in the 1880s.

On 11 May 1877, Alexander Graham Bell demonstrated the telephone for startled spectators at the St. Denis Hotel. The Academy of Music, opened in 1854, was New York's first successful opera house and the site of spectacular events. The Worrell Sisters' Theatre at Broadway and Waverly Place introduced the cliff-hanger with John Augustin Daly's play *Under the Gaslight*. Another theater was Wallack's, built in 1861 for Lester Wallack's stock company, on the corner of Broadway and Thirteenth Street. In 1881, when Wallack's troupe moved, the building became the Star Theatre, remaining New York City's most prestigious until its demolition in 1901. William Morris, a German immigrant, founded a talent agency on Fourteenth Street. Moretti's, an Italian restaurant, introduced spaghetti to New Yorkers. The village's leading ethnic eating establishment was Luchow's, a German restaurant. The Union Square Theatre, which opened in 1871, was the setting on 20 August 1883 of the first performance of *Vera, or the Nihilist*, a play by the British playwright, poet, and novelist Oscar Wilde.

Brothels in Greenwich Village were headquartered on Greene Street between Canal Street and Clinton Place. The Slide was a homosexual male pickup bar in the 1890s. The Tenth Street Studio housed leading American artists, including Winslow Homer. Wanamaker's Dry Goods Store, a cast-iron building with rows of columns and arched windows, provided a shopping center. The Condict Building, constructed in 1898 at Bleecker Street, was the only New York City edifice designed by Louis Sullivan. In the 1890s, Madame Katharine Branchard converted run-down row house property at Washington Square into inexpensive rooming houses appealing to struggling artists and writers pursuing their dreams. When Greenwich Village became a bohemian stronghold during the years prior to World War I, Branchard's dwelling received recognition and baptism as "the House of Genius." At the southern end of Fifth Avenue, Washington Square, boasting a majestic arch topped by the founding father's statue, emerged as one of New York City's most fashionable and respected neighborhoods. Increasing social awareness characterized the last years of the nineteenth century in the village. Following the example of Jane Addams in Chicago, Mary K. Simkhovich founded Greenwich House, for settlement work in the city's slums, in 1902. By the turn of the century, Greenwich Village was famous for both its diversity and its community.

Further Reading: Terry Miller, *Greenwich Village and How It Got That Way*, 1990; Edmund T. Delaney, *New York's Greenwich Village*, 1968.

Leonard Schlup

GREGORY, JOHN MILTON (6 July 1822–19 October 1898), clergyman and educator. Born at Sand Lake, New York, Gregory, an 1846 graduate of Union College, was ordained to the Baptist ministry. In the 1850s he shifted his career to education, becoming editor of the *Michigan Journal of Education* and president of Kalamazoo College before serving as the first president of the Illinois Industrial University (University of Illinois) at Urbana-Champaign. There he remained from 1867 to 1880. During his tenure, women gained admission in 1871. Gregory, known as a strong Progressive leader in the Midwest, wrote numerous articles and books, was appointed to commissions and boards, and traveled widely. He spent two years as a member of the U.S. Civil Service Commission, was president of the National Educational Association, and was commissioner at the Vienna Exposition in 1873. He died in Washington, D.C.

Further Reading: John M. Gregory, *The Seven Laws of Teaching*, 1884; Allene Gregory, *John Milton Gregory: A Biography*, 1923; *Washington Post*, 21 October 1898.

Leonard Schlup

GRESHAM, WALTER QUINTIN (17 March 1832–28 May 1895), judge and cabinet officer. Born in Harrison County, Indiana, Gresham attended Indiana University's Preparatory Department, started a law practice in Corydon, Indiana, and served as a Republican in the state house of representatives. He rose to brevet major general in the Union Army, then ran unsuccessfully for Congress in 1866 and 1868. In 1869, President Ulysses Grant appointed him federal district judge for Indiana, a post he held until 1883. In politics, Gresham opposed the dominance of the Indiana Republican Party by Oliver P. Morton and Benjamin Harrison, losing a bid for the U.S. Senate to Harrison in 1880. Three years later, he entered Chester Arthur's cabinet as postmaster general and earned praise for implementing the Pendleton Civil Service Act (1883) and other reforms. Gresham used his department's patronage to aid Arthur's bid for the presidential nomination in 1884, and he enjoyed some support himself as a possible dark-horse nominee. In the fall of 1884 he served briefly as secretary of the Treasury before returning to the bench as judge of the Seventh Circuit, based in Chicago.

Gresham's occasional pronouncements against political corruption, coupled with his sympathetic treatment of strike cases, earned him a reformist image that formed the basis of his candidacy for the Republican presidential nomination in 1888. He lost to Harrison, during whose administration Gresham grew increasingly disenchanted with Republican Party policy, especially the protective tariff. On that issue he broke with the party in 1892 and supported Democrat Grover Cleveland, who appointed him secretary of state during his second term. In the State Department, Gresham followed a traditionalist policy by which he sought to reverse the expansionist thrust of the Harrison years. He blocked the annexation of Hawaii and tried, unsuccessfully, to pull the United States out of the condominium (with German and Britain) controlling Samoa. Toward Latin America he defended the Monroe Doctrine but resisted its redefinition in the interest of expansion. Gresham's foreign policies sparked considerable criticism, which Republicans exploited to popularize their own expansionist ideas. Ill health marred much of his service in the State Department, and he died in office, in Washington, D.C.

Further Reading: Walter Quintin Gresham Papers, Library of Congress; Charles W. Calhoun, *Gilded Age Cato: The Life of Walter Q. Gresham*, 1988; Matilda Gresham, *Life of Walter Quintin Gresham, 1832–1895*, 1919.

Charles W. Calhoun

GRIDLEY, CHARLES VERNON (24 November 1844–5 June 1898), naval officer. Born in Logansport, Indiana, Gridley graduated from the U.S. Naval Academy (1863) and participated in the Civil War. Promoted during the postwar period, he served on several ships, taught seamanship at the Naval Academy, and worked at the Washington Navy Yard. For seven years, he held the position of inspector of the Tenth Lighthouse District in Buffalo, New York. In 1892 Gridley assumed command of the U.S.S. *Marion*, and in 1897 of the U.S.S. *Olympia*, flagship of the Asiatic Squadron. After the outbreak of the Spanish-American War in 1898, Gridley's ship led the American squadron at the battle of Manila Bay. Commodore George Dewey told his flag captain: "You may fire when you are ready, Gridley." Gridley fired several shots before opening rapid fire against the opposing force. The defeat of the Spanish in this naval encounter contributed to the American takeover of the Philippine Islands in 1899. Gridley died at Kobe, Japan, en route to the United States aboard the steamer *Coptic*.

Further Reading: Maxwell P. Schoenfeld, *Charles Vernon Gridley: A Naval Career*, 1983; George Dewey, *Autobiography of George Dewey*, 1913; *New York Tribune*, 6 June 1898.

Leonard Schlup

GRIGGS, JOHN WILLIAM (10 July 1849–28 November 1927), statesman and attorney. Born in Newton, New Jersey, and educated at Collegiate Institute and Lafayette College, Griggs was a talented student and orator. After gaining admittance to the bar in 1871, he formed a law partnership with Socrates Tuttle. In 1875 he was elected to the New Jersey General Assembly, served as a senator from 1882 to 1888, and was president of the state senate in 1886. He was elected governor of New Jersey in 1896. Griggs was appointed attorney general by President William McKinley in 1897. After his service in Washington, he returned briefly to a lucrative corporate law practice in New Jersey. He served as a member of the Permanent Court of Arbitration at The Hague from 1901 to 1908. He died in Paterson, New Jersey.

Further Reading: *New York Times*, 29 November, 1927; W. S. Griggs, *The Genealogy of the Griggs Family*, 1926.

Nicholas C. Polos

GRIMKÉ, CHARLOTTE FORTEN (17 August 1837–22 July 1914), educator and writer. Born a free African American in Philadelphia, Pennsylvania, Forten was an abolitionist in the antebellum years. A graduate of the Salem (Massachusetts) Normal School, she taught in Salem and Philadelphia before moving to the Sea Islands of South Carolina, where from 1862 to 1864 she taught freed persons. In 1865–1871, she worked for the New England Freedmen's Union Commission. In 1878, she married Francis J. Grimké, a minister and former slave from South Carolina. After teaching free children at the Shaw Memorial School in Charleston, South Carolina, Grimké taught at the Preparatory High School in Washington, D.C., before moving to Florida to engage in missionary work with her husband. She wrote essays and poems for publication, always seeking rights and justice for African Americans.

Further Reading: Brenda Stevenson, ed., *The Journals of Charlotte Forten Grimké*, 1988; Dorothy Sterling, ed., *We Are Your Sisters: Black Women in the Nineteenth Century*, 1984.

Leonard Schlup

GRINNELL, GEORGE BIRD (20 September 1849–11 April 1938), ethnographer and conservationist. Born in Brooklyn, New York, Grinnell attended school in Audubon Park, New York, graduated from Yale University in 1870, and immediately joined the paleontologist Othniel C. Marsh on an archaeological expedition to western territories. There he met William F. Cody and Frank J. North, leader of Pawnee scouts. By 1876 Grinnell was the natural history editor of *Forest and Stream*. Eventually he acquired control of the weekly publication, and used it as a forum. He advocated a game warden system to protect wildlife and urged enlargement of forest reserves. He earned a doctorate in paleontology from Yale in 1880 and founded the Audubon Society in 1886. With Theodore Roosevelt and others, Grinnell edited a series of books containing articles on conservation and hunting by members of the sportsmen's Boone and Crockett Club.

Although he lived in New York, Grinnell undertook yearly journeys to the West, captivated by the West's spirit of adventure, rugged life, natural beauty, flora and fauna, and varied culture. He discovered Grinnell Glacier in Montana (1885) and spent much time associating with and writing about Native Americans, especially the Plains people. Some of his articles on Natives appeared in the *Journal of American Folklore*; his books included *Pawnee Hero Stories and Folk Tales* (1889) and *The Story of the Indian* (1895). Because of Grinnell's reputation, President Grover Cleveland dispatched him in 1895 to negotiate a fair treaty with the Blackfoot and Fort Belknap tribes. In 1899 Grinnell and the photographer Edward Curtis accompanied Edward H. Harriman, a railroad tycoon, and an elite crew of scientists and artists on a two-month survey of the Alaskan coast. Harriman conceived, planned, and paid for the trip. Some 126 passengers, including the conservationist John Muir and the writer John Burroughs, traveled on the *George W. Elder*. Grinnell recorded data on the salmon industry, natural resources, and Natives. The expedition brought back one hundred trunks of specimens and more than five thousand photographs and illustrations. Grinnell died in New York City.

Further Reading: Cynthia Parsons, *George Bird Grinnell: A Biographical Sketch*, 1992; *New York Times*, 12 April 1938.

Leonard Schlup

GRISWOLD, WILLIAM MCCRILLIS (9 October 1853–3 August 1899), librarian, bibliographer, and indexer. Born in Bangor, Maine, Griswold graduated from Phillips Exeter Academy in 1871 and from Harvard University in 1875. A person of inherited wealth, he joined the American Library Association in 1881 and, the following year, the staff of the Library of Congress. He clerked in the Copyright Office until 1889 and served for four years as an assistant to Ainsworth Rand Spofford, the librarian of Congress. During the 1880s, Griswold produced and published several periodical indexes, including an index to *The Nation* that covered the period from 1865 to 1880, and cumulative indexes to *Lippincott's Magazine*, *International Review*, and *Scribner's Monthly*.

His *Annual Index to Periodicals* began with nine American magazines, and eventually encompassed several dozen English, French, and German-language periodicals printed in North America and Europe until 1889. In 1890, he moved to Cambridge, Massachusetts, where he compiled a series of annotated bibliographies of books. He published *Passages from the Correspondence and Other Papers of Rufus W. Griswold* in 1898. Griswold died at his summer home in Seal Harbor, Maine.

Further Reading: Rufus Wilmot Griswold Papers, Boston Public Library; *The Nation*, 31 August 1899.

Leonard Schlup

GROESBECK, WILLIAM SLOCUM (24 July 1815–7 July 1897), lawyer and politician. Born in Kinderhook, New York, Groesbeck graduated from Miami University in Ohio in 1835 and gained admittance to the Ohio bar the following year. He became one of the most prominent lawyers in Cincinnati. Elected as a Democrat to the U.S. House of Representatives, Groesbeck served one term (1857–1859). During the postbellum period, he opposed Radical Reconstruction and was one of the attorneys for President Andrew Johnson in the impeachment trial in 1868. In this capacity, he distinguished himself, delivering a powerful defense of the president in his final speech. Groesbeck supported civil service reform and bimetallism. He was an American commissioner at the 1878 International Monetary Conference in Paris. Groesbeck died in Cincinnati, Ohio.

Further Reading: *New York Times*, 9 July 1897.

Leonard Schlup

GRONLUND, LAURENCE (13 July 1846–15 October 1899), socialist and author. Born in Copenhagen, Denmark, Gronlund graduated from the University of Copenhagen in 1865, studied law, and in 1867 immigrated to the United States. In Chicago, he launched a law practice but abandoned it for journalism, joined the Socialist Labor Party, and published *The Coming Revolution: Its Principles* (1878). He espoused German socialism, which differed from the communitarian or utopian socialism associated with the French social philosopher Charles Fourier. Gronlund's vision was mod-

erate and evolutionary; the class struggle did not play a major role in his book *The Cooperative Commonwealth* (1884). Marxist economic determinism did, however, occupy Gronlund's thoughts; he sought eventual revolutionary socialist success in the United States. In 1891 Gronlund published *Our Destiny*, emphasizing socialism's religious foundations. Joining with William Dwight Porter Bliss, Gronlund supported development of a native Fabian Socialist movement. He also favored a society of scholars to spread socialist ideas throughout the country. His final books, *Socializing a State* and *The New Economy: A Peaceable Solution of the Social Problem*, appeared in 1898. Gronlund died virtually penniless in New York City.

Further Readings: Solomon Gemorah, "Laurence Gronlund—Utopian or Reformer?" *Science and Society 33* (1969): 446–458; *New York Journal*, 16 October 1899.

Leonard Schlup

GROSVENOR, CHARLES HENRY (20 September 1833–30 October 1917), congressman. Born in Pomfret, Connecticut, Grosvenor moved with his family to Athens County, Ohio, in 1838. Following service in the Civil War, he opened a law practice and entered politics. A presidential elector in 1872 and 1880, Grosvenor held a seat in the Ohio House of Representatives from 1874 to 1878, and was speaker from 1876 until 1878. In 1884 he won election to the U.S. House of Representatives, where he served from 1885 to 1891 and again from 1893 to 1907. A highly partisan parliamentarian, he earned a reputation for his debating skills, political shrewdness, and devotion to Republican causes. He opposed creation of the Interstate Commerce Commission in 1887 and steadfastly supported tariff protectionism. A delegate to the Republican National Convention in 1896 and 1900, Grosvenor joined Mark Hanna, a Cleveland industrialist, in promoting the nomination of William McKinley for president. Grosvenor advised McKinley during the campaign of 1896. Nicknamed "Old Figgers" because of his penchant for making arithmetical prognostications of election results, Grosvenor was the official statistician of the party, issuing detailed statements of McKinley's strength in each state and forecasting results. Grosvenor often appeared on the Chautauqua lecture circuit and on occasion debated national issues. He favored better regulation of hospitals for the insane. Grosvenor died in Athens, Ohio.

Further Reading: Leonard Schlup, "The Sage of Athens: Charles H. Grosvenor and Presidential Politics in Ohio in 1908," *Ohio History* 105 (1996): 145–156; *Athens Daily Messenger*, 30 October 1917.

Leonard Schlup

GUGGENHEIM, MEYER (1 February 1828– 15 March 1905), financier. Born in Langnau, Switzerland, Guggenheim immigrated to the United States in 1847 and immediately engaged in small merchandising ventures in Philadelphia before investing in railroad stock. In 1872 he established the firm of Guggenheim and Pliaski, which imported Swiss embroideries. He strategically placed his sons in the business, carefully preparing, educating, and integrating them into what became a dynastic enterprise. Becoming interested in mining ventures and the processing of metals, Guggenheim formed the Philadelphia Smelting and Refining Company in 1888. At first the American Smelting and Refining Company, created in 1899, excluded the Guggenheims but, outwitting the trust in various ways, the family captured more than its proportionate share of the ore supply for smelting. The trust capitulated in 1901, and the Guggenheims obtained control of American Smelting and Refining Company. Guggenheim died in Palm Beach, Florida.

Further Reading: *New York Herald*, 17 March 1905; Harvey O'Connor, *The Guggenheims: The Making of an American Dynasty*, 1937; Edwin P. Hoyt, Jr., *The Guggenheims and the American Dream*, 1967; John H. Davis, *The Guggenheims: An American Epic*, 1978.

Leonard Schlup

GUITEAU, CHARLES JULIUS (8 September 1841–30 June 1882), presidential assassin. A former member of the religious Oneida Community in New York State, Guiteau spent most of his life moving from job to job, delivering sermons, and lecturing on behalf of Republican candidates. He published his beliefs in a pamphlet, *The Truth: A Companion to the Bible*. In 1880 he wrote and spoke publicly for the Republican presidential candidate, James A. Garfield, hoping to receive a high diplomatic position in return. Rejection fed Guiteau's growing displeasure with President Garfield's cabinet appointments, which favored supporters of James G. Blaine. By May 1881, Guiteau was convinced that God wanted him to kill Garfield. In June he reedited his pamphlet, knowing his act would make him famous, and bought a fancy handgun. On 2 July 1881, Guiteau shot the president at Washington, D.C.'s railroad station and was arrested on the spot. At his three-month trial, he pleaded not guilty. His attorney, his brother-in-law George Scoville, tried to use the insanity plea. At the time, however, the device was regarded a dodge for the wealthy and the well-connected, and the court rejected the motion. After a half-hour's deliberation, the jury found Guiteau guilty, and he was sentenced to death by hanging.

Further Reading: James C. Clark, *The Murder of James A. Garfield: The President's Last Days and the Trial and Execution of His Assassin*, 1993; Charles E. Rosenberg, The *Trial of the Assassin Guiteau: Psychiatry and the Law in the Gilded Age*, 1968.

Bryan Craig

GULICK, LUTHER HALSEY (4 December 1865–13 August 1918), educator and physical fitness advocate. Gulick was born in Honolulu, Hawaii, and during his early years traveled extensively with his family. He received his education at Oberlin College, where he participated actively in athletics, particularly baseball. After graduation, Gulick held various posts, most importantly in the physical education department at what is today Springfield College in Massachusetts. Cooperating closely with James Naismith during the winter of 1891, Gulick helped devise a basic outline and rudimentary rules for what became known as basketball. He posited a strong connection between physical fitness and religion: a healthy Christian could be a more devoted Christian. Gulick worked with the Young Men's Christian Association until accepting a post with the New York public schools in 1900. In 1903, he became the head of the physical education division in greater New York and revolutionized fitness education. One of Gulick's most lasting achievements was creation of the Camp Fire Girls, which he and his wife, Charlotte, founded in 1910. Gulick spent his later years as a lecturer at New York University and died in New York City.

Further Reading: Ethel Josephine Dorgan, *Luther Halsey Gulick*, 1934.

Steve Bullock

GUTHRIE, LOGAN COUNTY, OKLAHOMA TERRITORY. On 22 April, 1889, the federal government held a land run for approximately 1.9 million acres in the center of Indian Territory. Legally designated as Oklahoma Territory by the Organic Act of 2 May 1890, the land opened for homesteading later became six counties in the state of Oklahoma. One of those is Logan County. On the day of the land run, Guthrie had only two buildings, a Santa Fe Railroad depot and an uncompleted land office. Ten thousand people made the run that day. Frame construction began that afternoon, the first brick building was completed in late May, the electric street railway was in operation in July, and the electric power plant furnished electricity for the railway and for the entire city by August.

Joseph Foucart, born in Arlon, Belgium, in 1848, completed his architectural studies at Ghent in 1865. He worked on several European buildings, including the new city hall in Paris in 1872. At age forty, Foucart immigrated to Texas, and by June 1889, he was in Guthrie. Demonstrating the theories of Eugène Viollet-le-Duc, Foucart's buildings reflect rational planning, structural determinism, and Gothic style (without its most prominent feature, the pointed arch window). Foucart's gloriously eclectic architecture dominated the commercial district of Guthrie in the last decade of the nineteenth century and continues to do so today. Foucart buildings in Guthrie include the Grey Brothers Building (1890), the DeFord Building (1890), the Victor Building (1893), the DeStigner Building (1895), the State Capital Publishing Company (1895), and Guthrie's city hall (1896). Several Guthrie homes have been attributed to Foucart, but only the P. J. Heilman home (1895), a Victorian Gothic with Foucartian variations, has been validated.

Guthrie, first designated as the territorial capitol, attracted building on the scale and of the caliber befitting a *fin-de-siècle* state capital. After the territory achieved statehood in 1907, a series of political maneuvers moved the state capital to Oklahoma City (1910). The move allowed preservation of Guthrie's Victorian architectural treasures. Had Guthrie continued to serve as the capital, the ensuing development would have brought the destruction of Foucart's architectural legacy.

Today, Guthrie's original town site, some four hundred square blocks and the only surviving intact territorial capital in the United States, is a National Historic District. It has the largest collection of Victorian architecture in the United States.

Further Reading: Howard L. Meredith and Mary Ellen Meredith, *Of the Earth: Oklahoma Architectural History*, 1980; Arn Henderson, "Low-Style/High Style: Oklahoma Architectural Origins and Image Distortions," in Howard F. Stein and Robert F. Hill, eds., *The Culture of Oklahoma*, 1993; Arn Henderson, Frank Parman, and Dortha Henderson, *Architecture in Oklahoma: Landmark & Vernacular*, 1978.

Larry D. Griffin

HAGUE PEACE CONFERENCE OF 1899.

The Hague Peace Conference marked the birth of an international body of fixed and broadly recognized principles of law, and created the first standing court to arbitrate disputes between international appellants. In addition, it established precedents in law, arbitration, and international agreement that have affected the design of every supranational body and treaty since 1899. The United States agreed to participate in the first international peace conference because of thirty years of unsuccessful negotiations with the British over property rights at sea. The American delegation consisted of Andrew D. White, a senior diplomat and one of the founders of Cornell University, as head; Frederick W. Holls, an attorney in international law; and Seth Low, president of Columbia University. Captains William R. Crozier and Alfred Thayer Mahan represented the military. The minister to the Netherlands, Stanford Newell, and Assistant Secretary of State David Jayne Hill completed the group.

The conference had three foci. The first concerned arms limitation. The American position was to prevent harm to U.S. defense capabilities and to rely on larger nations to aggressively support the concept of national sovereignty when negotiating armament limitations. The second objective built on Czar Alexander II's request, made in 1874, to establish international rules of war. The conference passed guidelines for treatment of prisoners of war, rules regarding apprehension of sailors from neutral ships, medical care for enemy personnel, and policies on destruction of civilian property. All items interested the United States, and the Americans worked diligently for a consensus. The conference's final focus was on creation of an international court of arbitration. The item resonated strongly with European diplomats and was supported by international peace organizations. After prolonged discussion, the Permanent Court of Arbitration was established at The Hague.

In the United States, reaction to the success of the conference was mixed. Perhaps that of Seth Low was most perceptive. He saw it as not preventing all war, but changing the manner in which war would now be presented. A nation's decision to enter a conflict would now have to seem justified in the forum of public opinion.

Further Reading: Calvin DeArmond Davis, *The United States and the First Hague Peace Conference*, 1962; Alfred Thayer Mahan, *Lessons of the War with Spain and Other Lessons*, 1918.

A. Jacqueline Swansinger

HALE, EUGENE

(9 June 1836–27 October 1918), congressman and senator. Born in Turner, Maine, Hale studied law, passed the bar in 1857, and opened a practice in Ellsworth, Maine. A prominent Hancock County Republican, he served briefly in the state legislature in the late 1860s before winning election to the U.S. House of Representatives in 1868. There he became an ally of James G. Blaine, also from Maine, and the Republican establishment, and during his ten years in the House, he gained a reputation as a high tariff politician and an expert on naval and military affairs. In 1881, the state legislature elected Hale to the U.S. Senate, a seat he held for thirty years. Early in his Senate career, he pushed for aggressive naval expansion as the Civil War–era fleet deteriorated. By 1898, however, Hale was increasingly critical of the American navy and worked to limit arms expenditures. In addition, he openly opposed the Spanish-American War and the annexation of Spanish territory, positions that threatened his popularity at home and earned him the lasting hatred of nationalists such as Theodore Roosevelt. As the Progressives gained political power after 1900, Hale was attacked as a member of the conservative Senate oligarchy; he continued to oppose naval reforms and tariff reciprocity, and he declined to stand for reelection in 1910. He died in Washington, D.C.

Further Reading: *New York Times*, 28 October 1918; Martin Meadows, "Eugene Hale and the Navy," *American Neptune* 22 (1962): 187–193.

Michael J. Connolly

HALFORD, ELIJAH WALKER (4 September 1843–27 February 1938), editor and presidential secretary. Halford was born in Nottingham, England. He was brought to the United States as a young child and became editor of the *Indianapolis Journal*. In 1872, he was named managing editor of the newly established *Chicago Inter Ocean*, promoting its popularity and influence throughout the Midwest. Halford was also was a lifelong Methodist leader. As a young Indianapolis reporter, he covered the progress of the funeral train of President Abraham Lincoln through Indiana in 1865, and as he became more political, remained loyal to Republican Party politics. When Benjamin Harrison of Indianapolis was elected president in 1888, Halford served as his private secretary, corresponding with state and national figures for four years. He died in Leonia, New Jersey.

Further Reading: *Indianapolis Star*, 28 February 1938; E. W. Halford, "General Harrison's Attitude Toward the Presidency," *The Century Magazine* 84 (1912): 305–310.

Ann Mauger Colbert

HALL, CHARLES FRANCIS (1821–8 November 1871), explorer. Born in Rochester, New Hampshire, Hall ran the *Cincinnati Occasional* before the Civil War. Intrigued by earlier arctic missions and financed by the wealthy whaling merchant Henry Grinnell, Hall went to New York and Connecticut to familiarize himself with scientific investigations and explorations. Determined to find a way to the North Pole, Hall in the early 1860s ascertained that Frobisher Strait is a bay. He also charted the Melville Peninsula. In mid-1869, he quarreled with and killed Patrick Coleman, a British sailor, but neither the United States nor Great Britain charged him with the crime. On 12 July 1870, President Ulysses S. Grant signed a congressional appropriation of $50,000 to support Hall's expedition to the arctic frontier. The steamer *Periwinkle* was refitted and renamed *Polaris*. It left New York City with great fanfare on 3 July 1871. Aboard with Captain Hall were sailing master Sidney Buddington, assistant navigator George Tyson, two Eskimo interpreters, Ebierbing and Tookoolito, and sixteen others.

Mutinous passions soon erupted. Nearly two months later, Hall reached the most northern point yet attained by any arctic explorer. Stopped by ice, he sought refuge in Greenland. Upon returning to the stationary *Polaris* on 10 October 1871, he suddenly fell ill. His condition worsened, deteriorating into seizures and paranoia before his death. Shipmates wrapped the body in an American flag and buried Hall's remains near Thank God Harbor. On 12 August 1872, the crew sailed for home, but the *Polaris* was lost on 13 October. The following spring, a Newfoundland whaler rescued many of the starving survivors floating on ice packs. The remaining crew members had found temporary haven on land.

Mystery surrounding Hall's peculiar death and the wreck of the *Polaris* aroused considerable controversy and suspicion. A government investigation whitewashed the entire affair rather than further disgrace Grant's scandal-ridden administration. In 1968 the historian Chauncey C. Loomis succeeded in legally exhuming Hall's remains. An autopsy disclosed the presence of arsenic, making it seem likely that Hall died of poisoning and plausible that Emil Bessels, a German doctor aboard the vessel, or a fellow sailor had committed the act. Another scholar maintained that a killer boarded the ship. Regardless of what actually occurred, Hall's enigmatic death ended the life of an irascible, domineering, and reckless Gilded Age individualist who sought fame for himself and glory for his country.

Further Reading: Chauncey C. Loomis, *Weird and Tragic Shores: The Story of Charles Francis Hall, Explorer*, 1971; Richard Parry, *Trial by Ice: The True Story of Murder and Survival on the 1871 "Polaris" Expedition*, 2001; Bruce Henderson, *Fatal North: Adventure and Survival Aboard USS "Polaris," the First U.S. Expedition to the North Pole*, 2001.

Leonard Schlup

HALL, GRANVILLE STANLEY (1 February 1844–24 April 1924), educator and psychologist. Born in Ashfield, Massachusetts, Hall was graduated from Williams College in

1867 and then read Hegelian philosophy at Union Theological Seminary. Next, he studied under William James at Harvard University, earning a Ph.D. in psychology in 1878. Hall's was the first doctorate awarded in that field in the United States. In 1884 Hall became professor of psychology and pedagogy at Johns Hopkins University, and held the first chair of psychology in the United States. He championed scientific psychology, lectured, published, and founded the *American Journal of Psychology* in 1887. The next year he accepted an appointment, tendered by Jonas Clark, as the first president of Clark University in Worcester, Massachusetts. Hall urged school reform, emphasized children's health necessities, and promoted developmental psychology and psychopathology. Four years after retiring from Clark University, Hall died in Worcester, Massachusetts.

Further Reading: Dorothy Ross, *G. Stanley Hall: The Psychologist as Prophet*, 1972; G. Stanley Hall Papers, Clark University Archives, Worcester, Massachusetts.

Kim P. Sebaly

HALLIDIE, ANDREW SMITH (16 March 1836–24 April 1900), inventor and engineer. Born in London, England, Hallidie studied civil engineering, then immigrated to California in 1853 to seek a fortune in gold. There he designed and built fourteen wire suspension bridges and flumes along the Pacific slope. In 1857, he started a factory that produced the first wire rope on the Pacific coast. The business ultimately became the California Wire Works, of which Hallidie served as president until his death. After successfully experimenting with ropeways for freight transportation, Hallidie thought of means other than horses to pull loaded streetcars up the hilly San Francisco streets. By 1871, he had come up with an underground moving cable and a mechanical gripping device. This subsequently led to the city's famous cable car system. Hallidie was active in many municipal and civic organizations, expressed interest in reform movements, and helped found the San Francisco Public Library. He died in San Francisco.

Further Reading: *San Francisco Chronicle*, 26 April 1900.

Leonard Schlup

HALLOCK, CHARLES (13 March 1834–2 December 1917), journalist, author, and scientist. Born in New York City, Hallock was graduated from Amherst College in 1852. He lived in Canada during the Civil War. Upon his return to the United States, he secured the position of financial editor of *Harper's Weekly*. In 1873 he founded an illustrated magazine, *Forest and Stream*, which dealt with fishing, hunting, and other outdoor recreation. Interested in conservation, Hallock organized the International Association for the Preservation of Game (1874). He founded the town of Hallock, Minnesota, in 1880; collected specimens for the Smithsonian Institution; and wrote numerous books and pamphlets. He died in Washington, D.C.

Further Reading: *Washington Post*, 3 December 1917.

Leonard Schlup

HALSTEAD, MURAT (2 September 1829–2 July 1908), journalist. Born in Paddy's Run, Ohio, Halstead graduated from Farmers' College in Pleasant Hill, Ohio, in 1851, and began a career in journalism. He was editor in chief of the *Cincinnati Commercial* in 1859, and by 1866 controlled it. The paper later merged with the *Gazette*. Halstead's political editorials attracted national attention. Openly critical of the corruption that permeated the administration of Ulysses S. Grant, Halstead joined with a group of editors, known as the "Quadrilateral," to support the Liberal Republican movement in 1872. He later endorsed the presidential candidacies of Rutherford B. Hayes in 1876 and Benjamin Harrison in 1888. Gradually, Halstead turned from an idealistic reformer to a conservative, partisan pragmatist. After the U.S. Senate rejected his nomination as minister to Germany, partly out of political retaliation, Halstead moved to New York City, where he edited the *Brooklyn Standard-Union*. He also wrote articles for prominent magazines, published twenty books on history and politics, and championed imperialism in the late 1890s. He died in Cincinnati.

Further Reading: Donald W. Curl, *Murat Halstead and the Cincinnati Commercial*, 1980; Murat Halstead Papers,

Historical and Philosophical Society of Ohio, University of Cincinnati Library.

Leonard Schlup

HAMLIN, HANNIBAL (27 August 1809–4 July 1891), vice president, congressman, senator, and ambassador. Born in Paris Hill, Maine, Hamlin never attended college, but studied law with the Portland attorney and politician Samuel Fessenden, gaining admission to the bar in 1833. After opening his practice near Bangor, he became a Democratic political leader and served three terms in the state legislature and two in the U.S. House of Representatives (1843–1847). In 1848 Hamlin entered the Senate as a Free Soil Democrat, was one of its more influential antislavery members, and in 1856 joined the Republican Party. Representing its radical wing, he ran with Abraham Lincoln in 1860, and in March 1861 became vice president. Dumped from the ticket in 1864, Hamlin returned to New England as collector of the Port of Boston but resigned in protest over President Andrew Johnson's Reconstruction policies. In 1869, he returned to the Senate as a Radical Republican leader and was an ally of James G. Blaine. Hamlin for a time served as chairman of the Foreign Relations Committee. He was a vocal defender of the spoils system and gained stature as an opponent of the Chinese Exclusion Act of 1879. In reward for his years of service, he was appointed minister to Spain in 1881. He died in Bangor, Maine.

Further Reading: Jean Baker, *Affairs of Party: The Political Cultures of Northern Democrats in the Mid-Nineteenth Century*, 1983; H. Draper Hunt, *Hannibal Hamlin of Maine: Lincoln's First Vice-President*, 1969; Charles E. Hamlin, *The Life and Times of Hannibal Hamlin*, 1899.

Michael J. Connolly

HAMMERSTEIN, OSCAR, I (8 May 1846– 1 August 1919), impresario, inventor. Hammerstein was born in Stett, Poland. The oldest of five children, he studied music at the Berlin Conservatory. At odds with his father after his mother's death, he pawned his violin in 1863, traveled to Hamburg, Germany, and booked steerage passage on a cattle boat to America. In New York City he began work as a cigar maker, and by the end of his life held some one hundred patents relevant to cigar making and for building innovations in his theaters, including an automatic fire-fighting apparatus and a vacuum cleaner. In the 1870s he became an American citizen, began a tobacco trade journal, and speculated in real estate. In 1871 he began his lengthy association with the theater, investing in New York productions and writing plays, operettas, and orchestral pieces for specific theaters. During the 1880s, he made the first of several fortunes, and designed and built the first of more than fifteen innovative theaters and entertainment complexes. Booking mostly plays and variety acts, Hammerstein, a master of publicity, persistently attempted to provide novelty for the public, introduced the first all-African-American act on Broadway, singing waiters, and newsreels ("Vitagraph News").

Hammerstein's greatest ambition was to produce opera, and during the 1890s he sponsored a number of traveling opera companies and produced several operas in English. In 1906 he founded the Manhattan Opera Company. Supervising and designing the building of the Manhattan Opera House and all aspects of his productions, Hammerstein created a rival to the Metropolitan Opera. In addition to the traditional Italian repertoire, the Manhattan Opera Company introduced many works by French and German composers, and presented the American premieres of Richard Strauss's *Elektra*, Claude Debussy's *Pelléas and Mélisande*, Jules Massenet's *Thaïs*, and Gustave Charpentier's *Louise*. Hammerstein brought a stellar cast of European stars to America, including Mary Garden, Nellie Melba, Alessandro Bonci, Maurice Renaud, and Luisa Tetrazzini. Financial troubles in 1910 led his son Arthur to negotiate a deal to sell his father's operatic interests, buildings, and contracts to the Metropolitan Opera for $1.2 million, with the stipulation that Hammerstein would not produce opera in New York, Philadelphia, Boston, or Chicago for ten years. Hammerstein produced operas in London in 1911, and died in New York City eight months before his agreement with the Met expired.

Further Reading: Vincent Sheean, *Oscar Hammerstein I*, 1956; John Frederick Cone, *Oscar Hammerstein's Manhattan Opera Company*, 1966.

Leslie Petteys

HAMPTON, WADE (28 March 1818–11 April 1902), governor and senator. Born in Charleston, South Carolina, Hampton graduated from South Carolina College (1836) before helping manage the family's lands. By the Civil War, he headed the region's largest slaveholding family. Hampton opposed congressional reconstruction and campaigned for Democrat Horatio Seymour for president in 1868. That same year, devastated financially by the war, he declared bankruptcy. His fortunes revived when his political rights were restored in 1872. Four years later, he was the Democratic candidate for governor of South Carolina. Running on a platform of economic retrenchment and political reform, Hampton defeated his Republican opponent in a controversial contest. Reelected in 1878, he resigned when chosen for the U.S. Senate in 1879. As governor, Hampton was known for his efforts to achieve sectional reconciliation and his voiced support for the civil rights of African Americans. While in the Senate, however, he denounced the proposed Federal Elections Bill of 1890 as unconstitutional. Thereafter Hampton's influence within South Carolina's Democratic Party waned. A new breed of Democrats, led by Benjamin Tillman, castigated "aristocrats" and dedicated themselves to rescinding advances made by African Americans. After winning the governorship in 1890, Tillman engineered election of one of his supporters to Hampton's Senate seat. Hampton accepted an appointment as commissioner of railroads in 1893. He retired from public life in 1898 and returned to Columbia, South Carolina, where he died.
Further Reading: Manly Wade Wellman, *Giant in Gray: A Biography of Wade Hampton of South Carolina*, 1949; Hampton M. Jarrell, *Wade Hampton and the Negro: The Road Not Taken*, 1949; William J. Cooper, *The Conservative Regime: South Carolina, 1877–1890*, 1968.

Ed Bradley

HANCOCK, WINFIELD SCOTT (14 February 1824–9 February 1886), general and presidential candidate. Born in Montgomery Square, Pennsylvania, Hancock attended Norristown Academy and West Point, from which he graduated in 1844. In 1861, he was made brigadier general. His Civil War battles included the Peninsular campaign, Antietam, Fredericksburg, Chancellorsville, the Wilderness, and Spotsylvania. He achieved lasting fame at Gettysburg, where his corps repulsed Confederate attacks.

Appointed major general in the regular army in 1866, Hancock commanded the Central Military Department in 1867, in which capacity he fought Plains Indians; the Department of Louisiana and Texas the same year, in which role he fostered civilian rule; the Department of Dakota from 1870 to 1872; the Division of the Atlantic from 1872 to 1886; and the Department of the East in 1886. Never in sympathy with the Reconstruction policies of the Radical Republicans, he received 144 votes at the 1868 Democratic convention.

In 1880, the Democratic Party nominated Hancock for president. He had the advantages of being a heroic Union general possessing southern backing, had made few enemies, and had taken no stand on the major issues of the time. Hancock lost the election by fifty-nine electoral votes and a narrow popular plurality. He died at Governor's Island, in New York City.
Further Reading: Glenn Tucker, *Hancock, the Superb*, 1960; David M. Jordan, *Winfield Scott Hancock: A Soldier's Life*, 1988.

Justus D. Doenecke

HANNA, MARCUS ALONZO (24 September 1837–February 15, 1904) was a national Republican Party leader. Born in New Lisbon, Ohio, Hanna attended public school in Lisbon and later in Cleveland, Ohio, where his family moved when he was fifteen years old. In 1864, he married C. Augusta Rhodes, whose father owned a successful coal and iron shipping business. Hanna joined his father-in-law's firm and became a very successful businessman in his own right. Expanding his interests, he bought a newspaper, became active in banking, and owned a street railway company in Cleveland. The street railway company led him to be active in politics. In 1884, he attended his first Republican National Convention, where he met William McKinley.

In 1888, while supporting John Sherman of Ohio for the presidential nomination, Hanna took a greater interest in McKinley. He became a major financial supporter of McKinley and helped to elect him governor of Ohio in 1891. In 1894, Hanna turned his business interests over to his brother, and devoted full attention to McKinley's political career. Two years later, Hanna helped orchestrate McKinley's presidential nomination, and his own service as Republican National Committee chairman. The platform focused on protective tariffs and the gold standard. Hanna ran the McKinley campaign, raising money from industrial leaders. He hired fourteen hundred campaigners to distribute Republican literature. In an age of political bosses and business-dominated government, "Dollar Mark" Hanna nevertheless received criticism for alleged excesses on both counts. After McKinley took office, Hanna would not accept a cabinet position. Instead, he urged McKinley to appoint Senator John Sherman as secretary of state; Hanna was then appointed to Sherman's Senate seat while remaining a close McKinley confidant.

Hanna did not support the selection of Theodore Roosevelt as McKinley's running mate in 1900. After McKinley's assassination in 1901, however, Hanna worked with the new president. Hanna refused calls to challenge Roosevelt for the Republican nomination in 1904, citing poor health and a desire to "stand pat." He died in Washington, D.C.

Further Reading: Herbert David Croly, *Marcus Alonzo Hanna, His Life and Work,* 1912; Thomas Beer, *Hanna, Crane and the Mauve Decade,* 1941; Clarence Stern, *Resurgent Republicanism: The Handiwork of Hanna,* 1968.

William C. Binning

HANS v. LOUISIANA, 134 U.S. 1 (1890).

In a unanimous decision, the Supreme Court held that the Constitution barred Hans, a Louisiana citizen, from suing the state for bond interest in federal court. Hans claimed an amendment to Louisiana's constitution, prohibiting payment, unconstitutionally impaired contracts. Justice Joseph P. Bradley conceded that, read literally, the Eleventh Amendment only precluded Hans from suing another state, not his home state, for violating the Constitution. The Court had never held that the Eleventh Amendment barred a suit against a state by one of its own citizens. Brad-

ley's ruling protected states from liability in federal court unless they specifically consented to be sued.

Hans was not entirely clear in articulating the basis of a state's immunity from suits brought against it by its own citizens. The bar has been attributed to the Eleventh Amendment, some deeper structural principle of sovereign immunity implicit in the Constitution, or simply a common law protection. In its day, *Hans* restricted the ability of the federal courts to protect contract rights against states. It remains an important part of the Court's jurisprudence on sovereign immunity of states.

Further Reading: James W. Ely, Jr., *The Chief Justiceship of Melville W. Fuller, 1888–1910,* 1995; David P. Currie, "The Constitution in the Supreme Court: The Protection of Economic Interests, 1889–1910," *Chicago Law Review* 52 (1985): 324–388; Richard H. Seamon, "The Sovereign Immunity of States in Their Own Courts," *Brandeis Law Journal* 37 (1998): 319.

Joel K. Goldstein

HANSBROUGH, HENRY CLAY (30 January 1848–16 November 1933),

congressman and U.S. senator. Born near Prairie du Rocher, Illinois, Hansbrough learned printing in California and Wisconsin. He moved to Dakota Territory, where he established the *Grand Forks News* in 1881 and the *Inter-Ocean* at Devils Lake two years later. Mayor of Devils Lake from 1885 to 1888 and a promoter of railway expansion through the northern plains, Hansbrough served on the Republican National Committee from 1888 to 1896, sought the partition of Dakota into two states, and won election to the federal House of Representatives (1889–1891). He served in the U.S. Senate from 1891 to 1909. During the 1890s, he favored protective tariffs to benefit North Dakotans, advocated a flexible currency, opposed monopolies, championed agricultural interests, voted against the Wilson-Gorman Tariff of 1894, supported the Spanish-American War, and endorsed the Treaty of Paris (1898–1899). A fiercely independent public figure who broke with his state's political boss and ultimately with Theodore Roosevelt, Hansbrough grew increasingly more progressive in the twentieth century, championing a number of causes and becoming the grand old man of North Dakota politics. He died in Washington, D.C.

Further Reading: Leonard Schlup, "Henry C. Hansbrough and the Fight Against the Tariff in 1894," *North Dakota History* 45 (1978): 4–9; Leonard Schlup, "Quiet Imperialist: Henry C. Hansbrough and the Question of Expansion," *North Dakota History* 45 (1978): 26–31; *New York Times*, 17 November 1933.

Leonard Schlup

HARDIN, PARKER WATKINS (3 June 1841–14 July 1920), politician and lawyer. Hardin was born in Columbia, Kentucky, and opened a law practice in 1865. Elected Kentucky attorney general in 1879, 1883, 1887, and 1891, he helped to orchestrate the Democratic victory in Kentucky in 1887. Hardin lost the Democratic gubernatorial nomination in 1891 to John Young Brown, and that in 1899 to William J. Goebel. Although Hardin obtained the nomination for governor in 1895, he was defeated in the general election; William O. Bradley, with whom Hardin had debated campaign issues, became the state's first Republican governor. A popular, experienced orator, he was unable to overcome Democratic divisions on the contentious monetary issue. He favored free silver but ran on the gold platform favored by his party's convention. Hardin endorsed Grover Cleveland for president in 1892 and William Jennings Bryan in 1896. He personally knew numerous political leaders and generally supported southern doctrine on tariff reform, reduced taxation, the rights of farmers, and an inflationary currency to reduce debts. Following his final unsuccessful attempt to gain the Democratic nomination for governor, Hardin retired. He died at his daughter's home in Richmond, Virginia.

Further Reading: *Louisville Courier-Journal*, 24 July 1920; *New York Times*, 26 July 1920.

Leonard Schlup

HARLAN, JOHN MARSHALL (1 June 1833–14 October 1911), associate justice of the U.S. Supreme Court. Born in Boyle County, Kentucky, Harlan graduated in 1850 from Centre College, gained admission to the bar in 1853, and later won a Franklin County judgeship (1858). Although a member of Kentucky's slaveholding aristocracy, Harlan supported the Union cause during the Civil War, rising to the position of state attorney general. As a Republican, Harlan ran unsuccessfully for the U.S. Senate in 1872 and for governor three years later. At the Republican National Convention in 1876, Harlan nominated his law partner, Benjamin H. Bristow, secretary of the Treasury in Ulysses S. Grant's cabinet, for president. When the delegates deadlocked, Harlan led Kentucky's delegates to Ohio Governor Rutherford B. Hayes, a crucial step toward Hayes's nomination. In 1877, President Hayes appointed Harlan to the U.S. Supreme Court. Known as one of the court's great dissenters, Harlan, who lectured at the Columbian Law School (George Washington University) from 1889 to 1911, opposed the majority opinion in *Pollock* v. *Farmers' Loan and Trust Company* (1895), which struck down the nation's first peacetime income tax. Harlan's most famous disagreement was in *Plessy* v. *Ferguson* (1896), which set forth the segregationist doctrine of "separate but equal." Harlan called the Constitution color-blind, and predicted the decision would become as infamous as that in the *Dred Scott* case (1857). One of the Supreme Court's longest-serving justices, he participated in numerous cases. Harlan died in Washington, D.C.

Further Reading: Tinsley E. Yarbrough, *Judicial Enigma: The First Justice Harlan*, 1995; Loren P. Beth, *John Marshall Harlan: The Last Whig Justice*, 1992.

Leonard Schlup

HARMON, JUDSON (3 February 1846–22 February 1927), jurist, attorney general, governor of Ohio. Born in Newton, Ohio, Harmon practiced law for seven years before his election to the local superior court, where he served as judge from 1878 until 1887. A loyal Republican during the Civil War, he revolted against Radical Reconstruction and backed the Liberal Republicans and Horace Greeley in 1872. He eventually joined the Democratic Party, and in June 1895, President Grover Cleveland appointed Harmon to succeed Richard Olney as attorney general. He directed prosecutions under the Sherman Antitrust Act until he returned to private practice in 1897. Known as a Tilden-Cleveland conservative, Harmon reentered

Ohio politics as a reform governor, elected in 1909 and 1911. He died in Cincinnati, Ohio.

Further Reading: William Jennings Bryan, *The Memoirs of William Jennings Bryan*, 1925; *Cincinnati Enquirer*, 23 February 1927.

Norman E. Fry

HARPER, WILLIAM RAINEY (24 July 1856–10 January 1906), linguist, biblical scholar, and university president. Born in New Concord, Ohio, Harper earned a B.A. degree in 1870 from Muskingum College, and a Ph.D. from Yale in 1875. Following brief teaching assignments at Masonic College in Macon, Tennessee, and Denison University in Granville, Ohio, Harper arrived in Chicago in 1879, where he taught Hebrew at the Baptist Union Theological Seminary. There he created a Hebrew correspondence course that spread nationwide. Harper began offering his course at Chautauqua in 1883, and by 1887 the popularity of his teaching and his prodigious energy led him to the principalship of Chautauqua's newly formed degree-granting College of Liberal Arts, a position he held until 1896. Harper was appointed professor of Semitic languages at Yale in 1886, and four years later accepted John D. Rockefeller's offer of the presidency of the major new university he planned to build in Chicago. During Harper's energetic fifteen-year tenure as president of the University of Chicago, he wove several new strands into the emerging American university movement: academic quarter sessions, major and minor courses of study, extension programs, summer schools, and a university press. He died in Chicago.

Further Reading: Richard J. Storr, *Harper's University: The Beginnings of the University of Chicago*, 1928; James P. Wind, *The Bible and the University: The Messianic Vision of William Rainey Harper*, 1987; George M. Marsden, *The Soul of the American University*, 1994.

Kim P. Sebaly

HARRIMAN, EDWARD HENRY (20 February 1848–9 September 1909), stock market investor and railroad magnate. Known as the "Colossus of [Rail] Roads," Harriman was born in Hempstead, New York. In the mid-1870s, he teamed with his friend James B. Livingston in an investment firm called E. H. Harriman and Company. A dominant figure on Wall Street, a social baron, and a philanthropist, Harriman once commented that his time was worth "a mule a minute." In his later years, he transformed himself into an audacious transcontinental railroad leader, developing, merging, acquiring, and modernizing railroads from the Union Pacific to the Burlington. Harriman entered the railroad business in 1880; three years later he owned the Sodus Bay & Southern Railroad and had been elected a director of the Illinois Central. No doubt his major business accomplishment was the rebuilding of the Union Pacific Railroad following its bankruptcy in 1893. An efficient and visionary Gilded Age entrepreneur, Harriman ranks with other financial titans of his era, including John D. Rockefeller and Andrew Carnegie. Harriman died in his mansion, "Arden," north of Jersey City, New Jersey.

Further Reading: George Kennan, *Edward Henry Harriman: A Biography*, 1922; Lloyd J. Mercer, *E. H. Harriman: Master Railroader*, 1985; Maury Klein, *The Life and Legend of E. H. Harriman*, 2000.

Leonard Schlup

HARRIS, ISHAM GREEN (10 February 1818–8 July 1897), governor and senator. Born in Franklin County, Tennessee, Harris attended public schools before practicing law locally. He was Tennessee governor from 1857 until he fled the state in 1862, when President Abraham Lincoln appointed Andrew Johnson the military governor. Harris spent three years in the Confederate Army and nearly two in exile in Mexico and England. He returned to Memphis in 1867 and reentered politics. The state legislature in 1877 elected Harris to the U.S. Senate; he won reelection three times. He emerged as leader of Tennessee's Bourbon Democrats, advocating low tariffs, states' rights, bank reforms, limited government, currency expansion, strict constitutional construction, and protection of workers and farmers from exploitation by moneyed interests. He favored currency expansion, condemned the Federal Elections Bill of 1890, and reluctantly accepted the Wilson-Gorman Tariff of 1894. As president pro tempore of the Senate from 1893 until March 1895, he led Silver Democrats against President

Grover Cleveland's demand in 1893 for unconditional repeal of the Sherman Silver Purchase Act of 1890. Harris passionately supported William Jennings Bryan for the presidency in 1896. He died in Washington, D.C.

Further Reading: George W. Watters, "Isham Green Harris: Civil War Governor and Senator from Tennessee, 1818–1897," Ph.D. diss., Florida State University, 1977; Memphis *Commercial Appeal*, 9 July 1897; *Washington Evening Star*, 9 July 1897.

Leonard Schlup

HARRIS, WILLIAM TORREY (10 September 1835–5 November 1909), philosopher and educator. Born near North Killingly, Connecticut, Harris entered Yale in 1854. Disappointed with his studies, but inspired by talks with A. Bronson Alcott, Harris moved to St. Louis in 1857, seeking a career in business. Instead he found one as a public school teacher. Within a decade, Harris became one of the nation's best-known school superintendents and a widely recognized scholar of Hegel. In his thirteen annual superintendent's reports (1868–80) and numerous speeches to the National Education Association, Harris outlined an educational philosophy emphasizing the importance of individual self-help and disciplined study of literature and art, history, geography, mathematics, and grammar. Perhaps the most influential educational leader of the era, Harris challenged the social and economic ideas of Henry George, a foe of industrial capitalism. Harris helped establish the St. Louis Philosophical Society in 1866, and its influential *Journal of Speculative Philosophy* (1867–1889). Harris served as superintendent of schools in Concord, Massachusetts, from 1882 to 1885. President Benjamin Harrison appointed him U.S. commissioner of education in 1889, a position he held until 1906. He died in Providence, Rhode Island.

Further Reading: Kurt F. Leidecker, *Yankee Teacher: The Life of William Torrey Harris*, 1946; Merle Curti, *The Social Ideas of American Educators*, 1935; Edgar B. Wesley, *NEA: The First Hundred Years*, 1957.

Kim P. Sebaly

HARRISON, BENJAMIN (20 August 1833–13 March 1901), senator, president of the United States. Born at North Bend, Ohio, Harrison was graduated from Miami University of Ohio in 1852. He practiced law, served as city attorney of Indianapolis, and won election as reporter of the state supreme court. He rose to colonel during the Civil War, and in the postwar years, his oratory gained recognition for the Republican Party. In 1876 he ran for unsuccessfully for governor. Harrison played a key role in switching the Indiana delegation at the 1880 Republican National Convention to James A. Garfield, and accepted election to the U.S. Senate. In 1884, he had some backing for a possible presidential run, but at the national convention he judiciously threw his support to the eventual nominee, James G. Blaine. Two years later, Harrison lost a reelection bid for the Senate that did not eliminate him as a contender for the Republican presidential nomination in 1888. Harrison's strengths as a candidate included his residence in an important swing state, his war record, his proven campaign skills, and his acceptability to the party's Blaine wing. Nominated on the eighth ballot, Harrison conducted a brilliant front-porch campaign against President Grover Cleveland, avoiding exhausting travel, speaking several times daily to visiting delegations, and receiving excellent press coverage. He won a narrow victory and carried a Republican majority in both the House and the Senate with him.

As president, Harrison took his legislative role more seriously than most of his predecessors, thereby pointing the way for twentieth-century development of the office. Partly because of Harrison's labors, the Fifty-first Congress posted a remarkable record. The carefully crafted McKinley Tariff Act aimed to lower the government's burgeoning budget surplus, afford protection to American producers, and empower the president to negotiate reciprocity treaties to expand the export market. The Sherman Antitrust Act represented a significant step forward in curtailing the growth of monopoly power. The Sherman Silver Purchase Act called for the wider government use of the white metal to back "silver certificates," while averting an inflationary free coinage and maintaining the gold standard's sanctity. The Meat Inspection Act helped open foreign ports to American beef and pork. The Veterans Dependent Pension Act offered aid to a needy segment of the population. Under the Land Revision Act, Harrison set aside twenty-two million acres of national forest reserve. The chief failure on the Republicans' legislative agenda was the defeat of the Federal Elections Bill, which would have provided greater protection to beleaguered black voters in the South. Despite the Republicans' substantial record of achievement, in the midterm congressional elections of 1890 the party lost overwhelmingly to the Democrats.

In tandem with Secretary of State James G. Blaine, Harrison pursued an activist foreign policy. The administration hosted the first Pan-American Conference, designed to improve western hemisphere relations and foster the nation's trade. Under the General Act of Berlin, the United States joined Britain and Germany in a joint protectorate over Samoa. The festering Bering Sea fur seal controversy with Britain neared resolution with the signing of an arbitration treaty in 1892. Harrison avoided overt conflict, but nonetheless stoutly upheld national honor in a dispute with Italy over the lynching of eleven Italian Americans in New Orleans and in another with Chile over the murder of American servicemen in a Valparaiso saloon brawl. At the close of his term, Harrison pushed for the acquisition of Hawaii, but the Senate failed to act on an annexation treaty before he left office.

Harrison traveled widely as president, skillfully using his rhetorical talents from the nation's bully pulpit. Yet he was not without enemies within his own party, particularly among state bosses who disagreed with his patronage policies. Although efforts to block his renomination failed, he lost a rematch with Cleveland in 1892. During Harrison's postpresidential years, he concentrated on his lucrative legal practice, occasionally speaking for the Republican Party. At century's end, he opposed President William McKinley's expansionist policies. Harrison died in Indianapolis.

Further Reading: Benjamin Harrison Papers, Library of Congress; Harry J. Sievers, *Benjamin Harrison*, 3 vols., 1952–1968; Homer E. Sokolofsky and Allan B. Spetter, *The Presidency of Benjamin Harrison*, 1987.

Charles W. Calhoun

HARRISON, CAROLINE LAVINIA SCOTT (1 October 1832–25 October 1892), first lady. "Carrie" Scott, born in Oxford, Ohio, received her formal education at the Oxford Female Institute, a school her father founded. Benjamin Harrison, who had known the family earlier, enrolled as a student at Miami University and became a frequent visitor at the Scott home. They were married in Oxford on 20 October 1853, and moved to Indianapolis in 1854. Over the years, as her husband's law career burgeoned, Harrison became involved in church activities, charitable causes, and women's organizations that were emerging in the city. By 1876, their large home had become a social center that reflected the demands of their increasingly prominent positions. Life in Washington, as the wife of a U.S. Senator, began 4 March 1881. Her husband lost the campaign for reelection in 1886, but they returned to Washington after his successful bid for the presidency in 1888. As First Lady, she turned first to domestic concerns. Their two children, spouses, and grandchildren, plus three members of her family, joined them at the White House, despite the crowded conditions, rats, and rotting floors. She supervised a major renovation and, in the process, assembled numerous remnants of presidential china, furniture, and artifacts for preservation and future use. Her talent for decorative arts, painting, needlework, and gardening enhanced the elegance of the White House for daily living and official functions. Believing that the character of women contributed enormously to the success of the country, she continued to give extensive time and support to women's organizations and civic causes during these last years of her life.

Further Reading: Harry J. Sievers, *Benjamin Harrison: Hoosier President*, 1952, 1959, 1968, Harriet McIntire Foster, *Mrs. Benjamin Harrison*, 1908; Ophia D. Smith, "Caroline Scott Harrison: A Daughter of Old Oxford," *National Historical Magazine* 75 (1941): 4–8, 65.

Nancy Lair

HARRISON, CARTER HENRY I (15 February 1825–28 October 1893), congressman, Chicago mayor, real estate speculator. Born near Lexington, Kentucky, Harrison moved to

Chicago after obtaining a law degree in 1855, and became wealthy from real estate ventures. A regular Democrat, he won election as a Cook County commissioner in 1874 on a nonpartisan, "fireproof" ticket recalling the Chicago fire of 1871. He served in the federal House of Representatives from 1875 to 1879, but found the best outlet for his political ambition as mayor of Chicago. He held four two-year mayoral terms between 1879 and 1887. He lost in 1891, but was reelected in 1893 as the "World's Fair mayor." His murder by a spurned office seeker inspired the Illinois legislature to require the merit system for most public employment. A political master, Harrison appealed to business interests in both major parties because of his entrepreneurial success, and promised to carry his principles to city hall. His sympathy for the views of moderate socialists gained Harrison their support as well. He also carried the ideologically less articulate "saloon interests," the neighborhood institutions that spoke for Chicago's working-class and immigrant populations, which approached 49 percent. Harrison's political coalition of middle- and working-class voters presaged that of the Progressives of the early twentieth century.

Further Reading: Willis J. Abbot, *Carter Henry Harrison: A Memoir*, 1895; Claudius O. Johnson, *Carter Henry Harrison I, Political Leader*, 1928.

Norman E. Fry

HARRISON, CARTER HENRY II (23 April 1860–25 December 1953), lawyer, mayor of Chicago. Born in Chicago, Harrison attended Yale from 1881 to 1883 and received a law degree. A wealthy speculator whose father was Chicago Mayor Carter Henry Harrison I, he could have avoided the rough-and-tumble political life. Instead, he plunged into Chicago politics, serving four consecutive two-year terms as Democratic mayor from 1897 to 1905 and a four-year term from 1911 to 1915. During his first four administrations, Harrison blended bossism and progressive reform. He tolerated the gambling and prostitution dens and the saloons, whose clientele consisted of the working classes and immigrants who voted for him. Harrison favored honest government, but liberally

used patronage and initially opposed civil service reform. In 1896 he accepted the Municipal Voters League plan to elect aldermen on a nonpartisan basis, and in 1902 championed home rule for cities, direct primaries, and the referendum for public policy issues. Civic reformers found him willing to use governmental power to enrich urban life by expanding city services to keep up with growth, and through public ownership of utilities. In 1898, Chicago took control of the street cars from traction magnate Charles Tyson Yerkes, and began building the first fifty-five miles of its famous elevated railway system. He died in Chicago.

Further Reading: Paul M. Green and Melvin G. Holli, *The Mayors: The Chicago Political Tradition*, 1987; Edward Wagenknecht, *Chicago*, 1964; Kenan Heise and Ed Baumann, *Chicago Originals*, 1990.

Norman E. Fry

HARRISON, MARY SCOTT LORD DIMMICK (30 April 1858–5 January 1948), socialite and hostess. Born in Honesdale, Pennsylvania, Lord lived in several northeastern states, received her education at Elmira College in New York, and married Walter Erskine Dimmick, a New York lawyer, who died shortly afterward. Her aunt, Caroline Lavinia Scott, married Benjamin Harrison, who was president of the United States from 1889 to 1893. When the First Lady developed tuberculosis, Mary lived in the White House to help with official duties and correspondence. Following Caroline Harrison's death in 1892, and President Harrison's defeat that same year, Mary kept in touch with the former chief executive, who returned to his Indianapolis home. On 6 April 1896, despite objections of his children, Harrison married Mary Dimmick in Saint Thomas Episcopal Church in New York City. Devoted to music and her husband, Mary Harrison occupied her time with travels, church activities, and social gatherings. Privately, she objected when international arbitration reaffirmed Great Britain's claim to a disputed area with Venezuela, contending that the world would end if England ever had to relinquish control over anything. After her husband's death in 1901, Mary Harrison published a compilation of his papers, *Views of an Ex-President*. She never remarried, and died in New York City.

Further Reading: Carl Sferrazza Anthony, *First Ladies: The Saga of the Presidents' Wives and Their Power, 1789–1961*, 1990; Carole Chandler Waldrup, *President's Wives*, 1989.

Leonard Schlup

HARRITY, WILLIAM FRANCIS (19 October 1850–17 April 1912), lawyer, businessman, and chairman of the Democratic National Committee. Born in Wilmington, Delaware, Harrity graduated in 1870 from Philadelphia's La Salle College, studied law under Lewis C. Cassidy and Pierce Archer in Philadelphia, and in 1880 formed a law partnership with James G. Gordon. Active in Democratic politics on the local and state levels, Harrity attended national conventions and acquired friends. He served as Philadelphia's postmaster from 1885 to 1889, and then as president of the Equitable Trust Company. In 1891 Governor Robert E. Pattison appointed Harrity secretary of state. The following year, as chairman of the Democratic National Committee, Harrity exerted much influence in favor of the presidential nomination of Grover Cleveland, but he subsequently declined a cabinet portfolio. Harrity headed the Pennsylvania delegation to the 1896 Democratic National Convention and received twenty-one votes for vice president. His strong opposition to free silver cost him most of his power and influence, and he was removed from the Democratic National Committee shortly thereafter by the victorious Bryanites. Thereafter, Harrity devoted himself chiefly to his duties as a director of banks, companies, businesses, and railways in Pennsylvania. He died at Overbrook, Pennsylvania.

Further Reading: *New York Times*, 18 April 1912; Leonard Schlup, "William F. Harrity and National Democratic Politics in the Cleveland Era," *Pennsylvania History* 59 (1992): 236–255.

Leonard Schlup

HART, ALBERT BUSHNELL (1 July 1854–16 June 1943), historian. Born in Clarksville (now Clark), Pennsylvania, Hart was graduated from Harvard University in 1880 and went to Europe, where he received the Ph.D. in history from the University of Freiburg in Germany (1883). When Hart returned home, few colleges offered separate courses in history, and fewer still in American history. Throughout a long, distinguished career as professor of history and government at Harvard (1883–1926), Hart pioneered in the organization, teaching, and writing of American history as an academic discipline. Through courses in political and constitutional history, he instilled a love of American history in his students, who included future senators, governors, a president (Franklin D. Roosevelt), and professional historians.

Stressing the use of original documents, Hart produced a wide variety of books, bibliographic aids, maps, and documentary editions. He also was instrumental in establishing the American Historical Association, and served for twelve years as editor of the *American Historical Review*. He died in Boston, Massachusetts.

Further Reading: Samuel Eliot Morison, "A Memoir and Estimate of Albert Bushnell Hart," *Proceedings of the Massachusetts Historical Society* 77 (1966): 28–52; "Historical News," *American Historical Review* 49 (1943): 192–194; Randall C. Farmer, "Albert Bushnell Hart: Guardian of the American Political Tradition," M.A. thesis, Wake Forest University, 1993.

Mary Ann Blochowiak

HARTE, BRET (25 August 1836–5 May 1902), author, editor, poet, and critic. Francis Bret Harte was born in Albany, New York, and reared in Hudson, New York, but he is best remembered as a regionalist chronicler of the California gold rush mining camps. He returned to the east coast, moving to Boston in 1871, after publication and enthusiastic critical and popular reception of his stories and sketches, notably "The Luck of Roaring Camp" and "The Outcasts of Poker Flat." He received a lucrative contract from a Boston publisher, but apparently enjoyed the life of literary celebrity more than that of solitary writer, and failed to meet deadlines. After a brief stint on the lecture circuit and the publication of a disappointing novel, *Gabriel Conroy*, he began writing for the stage, once collaborating with Mark Twain on *Ah Sin*. In 1878, Harte secured appointment as U.S. commercial agent in Crefeld, Germany; in 1880 he was appointed American consul to Glasgow, a position he held until 1885. Harte never returned to the United States. He continued to write short stories while living in Europe and London, publishing a volume nearly every year until his death in London, and reaching American readers through magazines.

Further Reading: Gary Scharnhorst, *Bret Harte*, 1992; Axel Nissen, *Bret Harte: Prince and Pauper*, 2000.

James D. Ivy

HARVEY, WILLIAM HOPE "COIN" (16 August 1851–11 February 1936), writer, publicist, reformer. Born and schooled in Buffalo, West Virginia, and at Marshall College, he opened a law practice in Ohio in 1870. He began a lifelong association with silver when his practice took him to Colorado. There he superintended the Silver Bell mine. Declining silver prices led him to attempt several unsuccessful ventures, including a Mardi Gras in Salt Lake City, before he accepted an offer from silver interests in 1893 to move to Chicago and publish a weekly pro-silver-coinage newspaper. It failed, but months later Harvey vaulted to fame with a profusely illustrated, simply written silverite tract, *Coin's Financial School* (1894). It purportedly told the story of a diminutive expert who established a school of finance at the Art Institute of Chicago, and convinced both silverites and leading gold standard bankers of the merits of bimetallism. The publication quickly sold three hundred thousand copies. It argued that a bankers' conspiracy to reduce the supply, and thus drive up the value of money, through demonetization of silver caused the deflation and grinding depressions of the 1870s–1890s. Harvey's prominence faded after the presidential election of 1896, when William McKinley and the gold standard prevailed. He died in the town he had founded, Monte Ne, Arkansas.

Further Reading: Harry A. Stokes, "William Hope Harvey: Promoter and Agitator," M.A. thesis, Northern Illinois University, 1965; Jeanette P. Nichols, "Bryan's Benefactor: Coin Harvey and His World," *Ohio Historical Quarterly* 47 (1958), 299–325.

Douglas Steeples

HATCH ACT OF 1887. Farm leaders embraced science as a means of improving agriculture, and after 1875 they persuaded state legislatures to create agricultural experiment stations. Yet the stations received little money, and could hire only part-time scientists. Directors begged implements, livestock, and seeds from farmers, land-grant colleges, and the U.S. Department of Agriculture (USDA). They stretched manpower by recruiting farmers to do experiments. In 1883 the states' financial neglect prompted Seaman A. Knapp, a professor at Iowa State Agricultural College, to ask Congress for an annual appropriation for the stations. Washington rejected the request. Only in 1887 did the combined effort of the land-grant colleges, the experiment stations, the USDA, and the National Grange convince Congress to pass the bill of Missouri Representative William H. Hatch. The new law gave each state $15,000 to create or maintain an experiment station. In its provision that the stations do research and communicate the results to farmers, the act laid a foundation for the discovery in the twentieth century of vitamins and antibiotics, the breeding of hybrid corn, and the creation of the extension service.

Further Reading: Alan I. Marcus, *Agricultural Science and the Quest for Legitimacy*, 1985; Norwood A. Kerr, *The Legacy: A Centennial History of Agricultural Experiment Stations, 1887–1987*, 1987.

Christopher Cumo

HATFIELDS AND MCCOYS FEUD. This series of retaliatory murders and other confrontations between two Appalachian Mountain clans became one of the best-known sagas of American history. The fighting began in 1878 over ownership of a hog, but gradually escalated to involve socioeconomic issues and extensive legal proceedings in West Virginia, Kentucky, and the federal court system. The dispute ended in 1889–1890 with imprisonment of several men and the execution of one for crimes associated with "the Feud." The violence occurred in the Tug River Valley, spanning the eastern half of Pike County, Kentucky, and the western part of Logan County, West Virginia (now Mingo County). Contemporary mountaineers attributed the Feud to deep personal animosities between the families, their friends, and their business associates. Outsiders viewed the conflict through the prism of Gilded Age political values, alleging that it was a product and extension of the Civil War: The Mc-

Coys were Unionists; the Hatfields were Confederates. Others saw the dispute through the lens of Victorian society's social concerns, ascribing the disorder to the inadequacy of Appalachian culture. The absence of evangelical Protestantism, strong governmental institutions, and effective schools supposedly produced a value system based on primitive emotionalism, excessive family loyalty, religious fatalism, and widespread acceptance of violence. Modern historians interpret the Feud as a typical consequence of the economic distress, social conflict, and psychological anxiety created when market capitalism, industrialization, and modern values penetrate a traditional culture. The media's continual fabrication of stereotypical images of mountaineer violence, hostility, and ignorance hindered the economic development of eastern Kentucky and southern West Virginia throughout the twentieth century.

Further Reading: Altina L. Waller, *Feud: Hatfields, McCoys, and Social Change in Appalachia, 1860–1900,* 1988.

Michael S. Fitzgerald

HAVEMEYER, HENRY OSBORNE (18 October 1847–4 December 1907), capitalist and sugar refiner. Born in New York City to a family connected to the sugar industry and cousin to William Frederick Havemeyer, a New York mayor, he received little education despite his family's wealth. He soon became involved in the sugar refining business and was president of the Sugar Refineries Company before its dissolution by the courts. In 1891 it reappeared as a reorganized corporation, under a New Jersey charter, as the American Sugar Refining Company. With considerable business acumen and ties to Wall Street, Havemeyer was a powerful personality and Gilded Age captain of industry. Although he consistently supported a reduction of tariff barriers on the importation of raw sugar, he demanded tariff protection for finished sugar products. A collector of European art, Havemeyer enjoyed the good life at his quarter-million-dollar estate on the shore of Great South Bay on Long Island.

Further Reading: *New York Sun,* 5 December 1907.

Leonard Schlup

HAY, JOHN MILTON (12 October 1838–1 July 1905), secretary of state, author. Hay was born in Salem, Indiana, and grew up in Springfield, Illinois. He was graduated in 1858 from Brown University, where his fame and benefaction are remembered through the John Hay Library. He read law in his uncle's Springfield office and, after working for Abraham Lincoln's election, was appointed one of the president's private secretaries. In March 1865, Hay was named secretary to the U.S. legation in Paris, was charge d'affaires in Vienna (1867–1868), and secretary of legation in Madrid in 1869. Following his return to America in 1870, he wrote editorials for the *New York Tribune* until 1875. A successful poet, he published *Pike County Ballads and Other Pieces* (1871) and a novel, *The Bread-Winners* (1884), a satirical, unsigned anti-union tract. With John G. Nicolay, Hay wrote the ten-volume *Abraham Lincoln: A History* (1890). Hay also launched a business career, much enhanced in 1874 by marriage to Clara Stone, daughter of the industrialist Amasa Stone. Industry, marriage, and wise investments multiplied his fortune.

Except for brief service as assistant secretary of state under President Rutherford B. Hayes in 1878, Hay remained out of government until William McKinley appointed him ambassador to Great Britain in 1897. However, a circle of friends, including Henry Adams and Theodore Roosevelt, had kept Hay close to the intellectual and political centers of influence. In September 1898, he was appointed secretary of state in time to support acquisition of the Philippine's. In 1899, he circulated the Open Door Notes to the major powers in an effort to keep China open to trade. His careful diplomacy moderated tensions in the Boxer Rebellion in 1900. The Hay-Pauncefote Treaty (1900), abrogating the Clayton-Bulwer Treaty of 1850, opened the way for U.S. control of an isthmian canal. The Hay-Herrán treaty with Colombia for a canal fell through in 1903, and President Theodore Roosevelt led his own diplomacy in the creation of Panama and construction of the canal. He died in Fells, New Hampshire.

Further Reading: Robert Gale, *John Hay,* 1978; Kenton J. Clymer, *John Hay: The Gentleman as Diplomat,* 1975.

Mario R. DiNunzio

HAYDEN, FERDINAND VANDEVEER (7 September 1828–22 December 1887), naturalist and geologist. Born in Westfield, Massachusetts, Hayden graduated from Oberlin College in 1850, received his M.D. from Albany Medical College in 1853, and then began exploring western territories to collect natural history and geological materials. Ultimately he became an outstanding field geologist, making numerous pioneering expeditions. He found marine Jurassic fossils in the red beds of the Rocky Mountain area, worked for the Department of the Interior from 1867 to 1878, published numerous articles and books, and was elected to the National Academy of Sciences in 1873. Hayden directed several geologic and natural history surveys that assisted in popularizing science. Moreover, through the distribution of photographs Hayden helped influence the way Americans interpreted the West. He died in Philadelphia.

Further Reading: Marlene Deahl Merrill, ed., *Yellowstone and the Great West: Journals, Letters, and Images from the 1871 Hayden Expedition*, 1999; Mike F. Foster, *Strange Genius: The Life of Ferdinand Vandeveer Hayden*, 1994.

Leonard Schlup

HAYES, LUCY WARE WEBB (28 August 1831–25 June 1889), first lady. Born in Chillicothe, Ohio, the daughter of a physician, Webb graduated in 1850 from Wesleyan Female Seminary in Cincinnati. Two years later she married Rutherford B. Hayes, a lawyer. A commitment to Methodism formed her strong views on social issues, including abolitionism. During the Civil War, Hayes journeyed to military hospitals to care for wounded Union soldiers and cheer the homesick, earning the name "Mother Lucy" from men of the Twenty-third Ohio Volunteer Infantry. As wife of Ohio's governor in the postwar period, Hayes accompanied her husband on visits to reform schools and prisons. After he won the disputed presidential election of 1876, Hayes emerged as a popular and generous White House hostess. In 1878 she opened the executive mansion's grounds to neighborhood children for an Easter egg roll on the lawn, an event that continues today. Two years later she accepted the presidency of the Woman's Home Missionary So-

ciety, a Methodist social welfare organization. A teetotaler and member of the Woman's Christian Temperance Union, Hayes acquired the sobriquet "Lemonade Lucy" from disgruntled politicians and Washingtonians who objected to her banning alcoholic beverages from the White House. Hayes normally began the day with a morning prayer service in the family's private quarters. Upon conclusion of President Hayes's single term in 1881, the Hayeses retired to Spiegel Grove, an estate at Fremont, Ohio, where she died. The first First Lady to graduate from college, Hayes impressed people with her knowledge of political figures, intelligence, cheerfulness, and attractive entertaining. With her pronounced beliefs on certain issues and organizational work, Hayes in several ways emerged as a representative of the new woman in Gilded Age America.

Further Reading: Emily A. Geer, *First Lady: The Life of Lucy Webb Hayes*, 1984; Rutherford B. Hayes Presidential Center, Fremont, Ohio.

Leonard Schlup

HAYES, RUTHERFORD BIRCHARD (4 October 1822–17 January 1893), congressman, governor, and president of the United States. Hayes was born in Delaware, Ohio, and educated at private schools, Kenyon College (graduated 1842), and Harvard Law School. In 1845, he returned to Ohio, was admitted to the bar, and opened a practice in Lower Sandusky (now Fremont). In 1850 he moved to Cincinnati, then a booming gateway to the West. During the Civil War, Hayes rose to brevet major general in the Union Army. In 1864, while he was still fighting in Virginia, Ohioans elected him as a Republican member of the House of Representatives. In Congress he was a minor figure but a strict party man who supported Radical Reconstruction. He was reelected in 1866, and chosen governor of Ohio in 1867 and again in 1869.

Hayes preferred administrative tasks in Columbus to legislative duties in Washington. He was a good governor, working vigorously to improve Ohio's prisons, reform schools, and mental asylums. His four years as governor were among his happiest, but he nonetheless gladly returned to private life. Republicans, however, nominated him again for governor in 1875. He reluctantly accepted the challenge and defeated the Democratic incumbent, William Allen. Hayes's Ohio triumphs made him an attractive possibility for the Republican presidential nomination in 1876. At the Cincinnati convention, he outdistanced his chief rivals, James G. Blaine of Maine and Roscoe Conkling of New York, on the seventh ballot. The Democratic nominee, Samuel J. Tilden of New York, also was a reform-minded governor.

After a hotly disputed election in which both sides claimed the electoral votes of Florida, Louisiana, South Carolina, and Oregon, a fifteen-man electoral commission created by Congress declared Hayes the winner. After tense, eleventh-hour negotiations between party managers from both camps, the Democrats, in return for economic and political concessions, agreed to accept the commission's decision. Just a week before the scheduled inauguration, Hayes was officially informed that he had won. His tainted victory foreshadowed the four stormy years of his administration. Confronted during part of his term by a Democratic majority in the House of Representatives, and by a Senate filled with men who refused to accept his leadership, Hayes found little support for his program. Although he had been a loyal Republican, political jealousies coupled with northern antipathy toward his plans for post–Civil War reconciliation frequently left him a man without a party.

Hayes treated the presidency as a moral stewardship. His temperance (no liquor was served at White House social events), and quest for civil service reform epitomized his approach to politics. Hayes vetoed cheap money nostrums and a discriminatory exclusion bill that would have stopped the flow of Chinese immigrants to the United States. He also stood firm when congressional Democrats tried to cripple the government by denying the three branches the appropriations necessary to their survival. His vetoes of seven heavily ridered appropriations bills sent a clear message to the Democrats that their tactics were futile. In general, Hayes's strong stand against Congress revealed an unforeseen strength and political acumen. Despite a tenuous claim to his office,

Hayes proved more popular than most of his detractors. During the 1870s and 1880s Congress had a poor reputation, and Hayes's quiet, firm demeanor proved effective against numerous personal attacks.

After retirement in 1881, Hayes returned to Fremont, Ohio, with his wife, Lucy. He devoted the remaining dozen years of his life to numerous philanthropic and educational activities, and especially enjoyed reunions with his Civil War comrades in arms. He died in Fremont.

Further Reading: Kenneth E. Davison, *The Presidency of Rutherford B. Hayes*, 1972; Ari Hoogenboom, *Rutherford B. Hayes, Warrior & President*, 1995.

Frank P. Vazzano

HAYMARKET TRAGEDY. On 3 May 1886, while strikers at Chicago's McCormick Harvest Works battled scab workers, police fired into the crowd, killing two and wounding more. A small protest against police violence held the next day in Haymarket Square was about to break up of its own accord when police demanded the participants disperse immediately. An unknown assailant hurled a bomb at the police, killing one officer and wounding others. In the ensuing chaos, police fired wildly, wounding each other as well as innocent protesters. Because the three speakers at the rally were prominent local anarchists prone to incendiary language, they and other anarchist writers and organizers became the quarry in a sensational citywide police manhunt. Newspapers across the nation painted threats of anarchist attacks that never came but frayed the nerves of an already panicked public and paved the way for a sensational trial.

The McCormick strike coincided with a national campaign for an eight-hour workday that had set a deadline of 1 May, threatening a general strike. Over three hundred thousand workers struck nationwide, shutting thirteen thousand workplaces. In Chicago, the Federation of Organized Trades and Labor Unions, the Knights of Labor, and the small International Working People's Association (which contained a significant anarchist contingent) cooperated to build a strike of forty thousand in the city. Chicago had also witnessed one of the earliest May Day parades when eighty thousand workers marched on Michigan Avenue. Although the IWPA was the smallest of the three organizations participating in the strike, two of its anarchist leaders, Albert Parsons and August Spies, became prominent in its events, and their fiery rhetoric was enthusiastically distorted by Chicago newspapers.

The Haymarket trial began on 21 June with eight anarchist members of the IWPA (George Engle, Samuel Fielden, Adolph Fischer, Louis Lingg, Oscar Neebe, Albert Parsons, Michael Schwab, and August Spies) accused of murdering police officer Mathias Degan by word, if not by deed. This ridiculous conspiracy theory was accepted by a carefully selected hostile jury and under the watch of an openly biased judge. The prosecutor built on the national hysteria whipped up by newspapers, introducing as evidence explosives of the type he imagined anarchists used, as well as the bloody uniforms of officers injured in the 4 May melee. Two months later, one defendant was sentenced to fifteen years at hard labor and the seven others to death. Despite a nationwide clemency campaign and a petition signed by forty-one thousand Chicagoans, four were executed in November 1887, Parsons and Spies among them. Louis Lingg committed suicide in his prison cell. The remaining three lingered in prison until pardoned by Governor John Peter Altgeld in 1893.

The tragedy in Haymarket Square and the hysterical fear of working-class unrest that followed, further stratified an increasingly urban, industrial, and corporate nation along class lines. Haymarket contributed to the exile of radicals from labor coalitions and the demise of the Knights of Labor, who appealed to "producers" across lines of class, politics, race, and gender. The labor movement's future would lie with the conservative, crafts-based unionism of the American Federation of Labor until the 1930s.

Further Reading: Paul Avrich, *The Haymarket Tragedy*, 1984; Carl Smith, *Urban Disorder and the Shape of Belief: The Great Chicago Fire, the Haymarket Bomb, and the Model Town of Pullman*, 1995.

Adam Hodges

HAY-PAUNCEFOTE TREATY. The U.S. dream of constructing an isthmian canal in the late 1890s was blocked by the Clayton-Bulwer treaty of 1850, which mandated joint Anglo-American control. By 1898, America sought a renegotiation. Great Britain displayed willingness to do so, but demanded universal access. Secretary of State John Hay and British ambassador Lord Julian Pauncefote opened talks in late 1898. A draft, written mainly by Pauncefote, appeared in January 1899. In the Senate, its provisions for nonfortification, a joint declaration of the canal's neutrality, and an invitation to other powers to adhere to the agreement met severe and protracted resistance. Some members of Congress even proposed unilateral abrogation of the Clayton-Bulwer pact. Though Hay threatened to resign over the matter, he remained in office even when the Senate ratified an amended version in December 1900. Britain rejected it in March 1901.

Hoping to salvage an agreement, Hay drafted a new treaty that permitted fortifications, eliminated any reference to other powers, and made the United States the sole guarantor of the canal's neutrality. Although his new draft closely resembled the Senate document, Britain approved it in November 1901 as the best deal possible, and the Senate followed with ratification in December. Under its terms, the United States later constructed the Panama Canal.

Further Reading: Kenton J. Clymer, *John Hay: The Gentleman as Diplomat*, 1975; R. B. Mowat, *The Life of Lord Pauncefote*, 1929.

Stephen Svonavec

HEALTH CARE, HOSPITALS, AND MEDICAL EDUCATION. When the Gilded Age began, children in Chicago had barely a 50 percent chance of surviving to age five. Rapid industrialization and urbanization contributed to wretched sanitation, crowded tenement housing, and dangerous working conditions in poorly paid employment. Infectious diseases regularly swept the nation. Massachusetts established the first board of health in 1869, and by 1900, nearly every town, city, and state boasted such an agency. The boards promoted garbage collection and disposal, milk pasteurization, clean water and efficient sewage systems, improvements in housing and working conditions, vaccination programs, neighborhood dispensaries, and isolation hospitals. By 1898, even though infectious disease remained the leading cause of death, Chicago reported a child's chance of living to age five had increased to 75 percent.

Hospitals, primarily charitable institutions sponsored by public, immigrant, and religious groups for the "deserving" poor and uprooted populations, increased from approximately 120 in 1870 to nearly 4,000 by 1900. The first pathology laboratory opened in 1878 at Bellevue Hospital Medical College in New York City, and bacteriology and the germ theory of disease gained acceptance during the 1880s. By the 1890s, hospitals began to seek paying patients by altering their architecture to appear more homelike and by offering safer medical, nursing, and surgical care through aseptic and antiseptic methods. In the public imagination, the hospital's transformation from the house of death to a community embodiment of civic pride and wealth had begun.

In 1888, Dent v. West Virginia affirmed the right of states to license medical doctors. The Johns Hopkins Medical School, founded in Baltimore in 1893, set new standards for medical education, raising admissions requirements, increasing term length, expanding the curriculum, adding laboratory science and research components, establishing full-time faculties, and requiring a licensing examination upon graduation. As such practices became more widely adopted, the number of medical schools and new graduates began to decrease. At the same time, however, only a few sectarian medical schools were accepting female students. Elizabeth Blackwell and others established women's medical colleges, dispensaries, and hospitals, which flourished as separatist institutions until the century's end. Thereafter, male-dominated orthodox institutions began to admit female students. While barely 300 women physicians had acquired medical degrees by 1870, 7,387 women had earned them by 1900. In 1868, with black students denied access to medical schools, Howard University, in Washington, D.C., opened. By 1900, there were eight black medical schools, and following repeated rebuffs from the American Medical Association, black physicians formed the National Medical Association. Although standards in separatist medical education programs rose, dual levels of funding and quality of health care were institutionalized, relegating blacks and the poor to secondary status.

Further Reading: W. Michael Byrd and Linda A. Clayton, *An American Health Dilemma: A Medical History of African Americans and the Problem of Race, Beginnings to 1900*, 2000; Guenter B. Risse, *Mending Bodies, Saving Souls: A History of Hospitals*, 1999; Regina Markell Morantz-Sanchez, *Sympathy and Science: Women Physicians in American Medicine*, 1985.

Jennifer L. Tebbe

HEALY, JAMES AUGUSTINE (6 April 1830–5 August 1900), religious leader. Born near Macon, Georgia, Healy was the eldest of ten children. He and two of his brothers became the first African-American Catholic priests. His brother Patrick, the first African American to obtain a doctorate, served as president of Georgetown University. Another brother, Michael, became a famous naval officer. James, after being baptized in the Catholic Church, was graduated from Georgetown University, studied at seminaries in Montreal and Paris, and entered the priesthood in Boston. In 1875, he became the first black Catholic bishop, and served the diocese of Portland, Maine, for twenty-five years. In demand as a speaker, Healy generated appeal beyond New England. He was a strong advocate of the poor and Native Americans. Healy used leadership skills to overcome the social restrictions placed on members of his race. He died in Portland.

Further Reading: Cyprian Davis, *The History of Black Catholics in the United States*, 1990; Albert S. Foley, *Bishop Healy: Beloved Outcast*, 1969.

Leonard Schlup

HEALY, MICHAEL AUGUSTINE (22 September 1839–30 August 1904), African-American naval officer. Born near Macon, Georgia, Healey ran away from several schools in his teens to seek adventure on the sea. In 1865 he entered the U.S. Revenue Cutter Service, a forerunner of the Coast Guard. Healy engaged in rescue operations and undertook pioneering explorations, and in 1884–1885 published *The Cruise of the "Corwin,"* a book detailing his exploits. Promoted to captain in

1883, he took command of the *Bear*, a barkentine steamer and flagship of the Bering Sea Force, whose purpose was to apprehend seal poachers and murderers. He commanded it through 1895.

By 1886 the flamboyant Healy was the main federal law enforcement officer in the waters around Alaska and the remote coastal villages. He engineered transportation of reindeer herds from Siberia to Alaska to help an Eskimo population confronted with starvation. He also was judge and jury for criminals. In 1889, 1891, and 1896, Healy faced court-martial proceedings for excessive suppression of mutinies, alleged cruelty to seamen, and periodic episodes of drunkenness. Convicted in 1896, he was demoted to the bottom of the captain's list. In 1900, Healy went back into service to rescue shipwrecked whalers, for which he received praise and citations from the federal government and several private organizations. Healy retired in 1903 as the most famous of Alaska's Revenue Cutter Service captains. He died in San Francisco, California.

Further Reading: Gerald O. Williams, "Michael A. Healy and the Alaska Maritime Frontier, 1880–1902," Ph.D. diss., University of Oregon at Eugene, 1987; Mary Cocke and Albert Cocke, "Hell Roaring Mike: A Fall from Grace in the Frozen North," *Smithsonian* 13 (1983): 119–137; Polly Burrough, *The Great Ice Ship "Bear": Eighty-Nine Years in Polar Seas*, 1970.

Leonard Schlup

HEARST, WILLIAM RANDOLPH (29 April 1863–14 August 1951), publisher, journalist, politician. Born in San Francisco, California, Hearst was tutored at home, attended a New Hampshire preparatory school, and was expelled from Harvard. He apprenticed with the *New York World* and purchased the *New York Evening Journal* in 1895. By lowering the paper's per-copy price and recruiting skilled journalists, Hearst increased its circulation from a few thousand copies to eighty thousand within months. *Journal* articles and stories were written to appeal to workers and immigrants, while attacking political corruption and big business. Hearst stressed the sensational, strange, and horrific. In 1895, he used the Cuban revolution to boost sales further. He dispatched reporters to Cuba, although the pro-revolutionary junta

banned coverage of events in the interior. The *Journal*'s reckless stories, based on junta releases and poor research, focused public attention on the island. When the U.S. battleship *Maine* exploded in Havana harbor on 15 February 1898, the *Journal* immediately claimed Spanish responsibility. Hearst editorialized for American intervention until the U.S. war declaration on 25 April. He then traveled personally to Cuba. The war provided good material for his paper, which sold over one million copies per day by August. Soon the *Journal* surpassed all New York City rivals. During the twentieth century, Hearst was elected to Congress (1903–1907), lost a bid for the Democratic presidential nomination (1904), and expanded his empire dramatically. He died in Beverly Hills, California.

Further Reading: Ben Procter, *William Randolph Hearst: The Early Years, 1863–1910*, 1998; W. A. Swanberg, *Citizen Hearst: A Biography of William Randolph Hearst*, 1961; David Nasaw, *The Chief: The Life of William Randolph Hearst*, 2000.

Michael W. Vogt

HEINZ, HENRY JOHN (11 October 1844–14 May 1919), food processor. Heinz was born in Pittsburgh and began his working career in his father's brickyard. While still a teenager he began to raise vegetables and to market produce in the community. The first packaged food he attempted to sell was horseradish in a glass bottle, under the name "Anchor Brand." The enterprise evolved into Heinz, Noble and Company, which also marketed sauerkraut and pickles. When the firm was driven into bankruptcy in 1875, Heinz and his brother formed a new company, F. and J. Heinz. They concentrated on pickles, but then began to use the new tin-plate cans for the marketing of processed foods including baked beans and some fruits. In 1889 he opened a large processing factory in Allegheny City, across the river of that name from Pittsburgh. To handle the marketing of the mass-produced food, he developed a model warehousing and distribution system that created a nationwide market for the company. In 1896 he introduced his enduring trademark on a label showing a pickle and mentioning his fifty-seven varieties of products (the company produced many more). The company became the country's largest producer of pickles and ketchup. Heinz was an important civic leader in Pittsburgh, and a benefactor of colleges and museums in the city. He died in Pittsburgh.

Further Reading: Robert C. Alberts, *The Good Provider: H. J. Heinz and His 57 Varieties*, 1973; Eleanor Dienstag, *In Good Company: 125 years at the Heinz Table*, 1994.

James M. Bergquist

HEISMAN, JOHN WILLIAM (23 October 1869–3 October 1936), college football coach. Born in Cleveland, Ohio, Heisman revolutionized the game of football. Introduced to college football as a law student, first at Brown University and then at the University of Pennsylvania, he starred as a player at both schools from 1887 to 1892. When he sustained an eye injury at Penn, physicians recommended that he refrain from reading fine print. This ended his law career, and Heisman channeled his energies into coaching. He accepted a position at Oberlin College, beginning a career that spanned thirty-six years. A harsh disciplinarian, Heisman stressed academics and became known for his rousing pregame speeches. He is most remembered for innovations that transformed the game. Historians credit Heisman with promoting the forward pass, and devising new offensive techniques such as the hidden-ball trick, the handoff, the center snap, and the double lateral. Besides Oberlin, he coached for Clemson, Auburn, Georgia Tech, and Rice, and still holds records at several of them for overall winning percentage. In 1900 he led Clemson to its first undefeated regular season with a 6–0 mark. Heisman spent his later years as president of the Downtown Athletic Club in New York City. He is best known in modern times for the trophy bearing his name that the club gives annually to the nation's finest collegiate football player. He died in New York City.

Further Reading: Wiley Lee Umphlett, *Creating the Big Game: John W. Heisman and the Invention of American Football*, 1992.

Steve Bullock

HELLER, MAX (13 January 1860–30 March 1929), religious leader and reformer. Born in Prague, Czechoslovakia, Heller came to the United States in 1879. Enrolling at the Hebrew Union College in Cincinnati, he received his bachelor's and master's degrees in 1882 and 1884, respectively. In 1887 he became rabbi at the largest Reform synagogue in New Orleans, Temple Sinai. Heller quickly established himself as a leading figure in Louisiana by allying himself with middle-class Protestant reformers against the Louisiana State Lottery Company, a powerful gambling business that sought renewal of its charter from the state in 1890. Despite criticism from both his congregation and lottery supporters, Heller successfully lobbied for denial of the new charter as president of the Anti-Lottery League. From 1892 through 1901 he championed the rights of Russian Jewish immigrants and took an increasingly critical view of Louisiana's growing discrimination against African Americans. He died in New Orleans.

Further Reading: Bobbie Malone, *Rabbi Max Heller: Reformer, Zionist, Southerner, 1860–1929*, 1997.

John T. McGuire

HEMPHILL, JOHN JAMES (25 August 1849–11 May 1912), congressman. Born in Chester, South Carolina, Hemphill graduated from the University of South Carolina in 1869, practiced law in Chester, and held a seat in the state legislature from 1876 to 1882. In 1882, he won election as a Democrat to the federal House of Representatives, where he served from 1883 to 1893. There Hemphill became an active spokesman for the South and vehemently denounced the Republican-sponsored Federal Elections Bill of 1890. Unsuccessful in his bid for reelection in 1892, Hemphill practiced law in Washington, D.C., where he died.

Further Reading: *Charleston News and Courier*, 12 May 1912.

Leonard Schlup

HENDERSON, DAVID BREMNER (14 March 1840–25 February 1906), speaker of the U.S. House of Representatives. Born in Aberdeenshire, Scotland, Henderson immigrated with his parents to Illinois in 1846. He attended Upper Iowa University, and during the Civil War suffered a leg wound that necessitated partial amputations over the years. Henderson practiced law in Dubuque, was assistant U.S. attorney for the northern district of Iowa from

1869 to 1871, and served in the federal House of Representatives from 1883 to 1903. His House chairmanships included the committees on militia, the judiciary, and rules. He helped write the Gold Standard Act of 1900. Henderson served as speaker during the Fifty-sixth and Fifty-seventh Congresses (1899–1903), the first speaker from a state west of the Mississippi River. In September 1902, Henderson stunned the nation with the sudden announcement of his retirement, effective upon the conclusion of his term. He had become the target of the Iowa's Progressive reformers. After leaving Congress, Henderson practiced law for a brief time in New York before returning to Iowa. He died in Dubuque, Iowa.

Further Reading: Leonard Schlup, "Defender of the Old Guard: David B. Henderson and Republican Politics in Gilded Age America," *Julien's Journal* 22 (1997): 22–24; Willard L. Hoing, "Colonel David Bremner Henderson: Speaker of the House," M.A. thesis, Iowa State Teachers College, 1956; *New York Times*, 26 February 1906.

Leonard Schlup

HENDRICKS, THOMAS ANDREWS (7 September 1819–25 November 1885), vice president of the United States. Born in Muskingum County, Ohio, Hendricks graduated from Hanover College in Indiana in 1841, practiced law, and won election to the Indiana General Assembly in 1848. He held a seat in the federal House of Representatives from 1851 to 1855. A Democrat, Hendricks served in the U.S. Senate from 1863 to 1869; there he opposed Radical Reconstruction and voted against the conviction of President Andrew Johnson in the impeachment trial of 1868. Hendricks was governor of Indiana from 1873 to 1877. He was vice presidential nominee in 1876 on the unsuccessful ticket headed by Samuel J. Tilden. In 1884, he again accepted his party's vice presidential nomination, running with Governor Grover Cleveland of New York. The Cleveland-Hendricks team proved a winning combination. Hendricks favored tariff reform and limited government, and denounced corruption. He served nine months before dying in Indianapolis.

Further Reading: *New York Times*, 26 November 1885; John W. Holcombe and Hubert M. Skinner, *Life and Public Services of Thomas A. Hendricks*, 1886.

Leonard Schlup

HEPBURN, WILLIAM PETERS (4 November 1833–7 February 1916), congressman. Born in Wellsville, Ohio, Hepburn's moved with his family in 1841 to Iowa City, Iowa, where he attended private schools and was admitted to the bar in 1854. After being a prosecutor, a clerk in the state legislature, a cavalry officer in the Union Army during the Civil War, and a private attorney, Hepburn, a Republican, in 1880 won the first of three consecutive terms in Congress. There he tried to increase military pensions while asserting that Congress spent too much money. After losing a bid for reelection in 1886, Hepburn resumed his law practice until President Benjamin Harrison appointed him Treasury solicitor in 1889. Four years later, Hepburn returned to Congress, this time for eight consecutive terms, and rose to chair the House Committee on Interstate and Foreign Commerce. As a Progressive, Hepburn led campaigns to fund construction of the Panama Canal, strengthen the Interstate Commerce Commission, and pass the Pure Food and Drug Act. After returning to his law practice, Hepburn died in Clarinda, Iowa.

Further Reading: John E. Briggs, *William Peters Hepburn*, 1919; *Des Moines Register and Leader*, 8 February 1916.

Christopher Cumo

HERBERT, HILARY ABNER (12 March 1834–6 March 1919), soldier, congressman, secretary of the navy, and author. A native of Laurinsville, South Carolina, Herbert attended the universities of Alabama and Virginia, was admitted to the Alabama bar, and later rose to colonel in the Confederate Army. During Reconstruction, he considered African Americans unfit for full citizenship, and blamed Republicans for black officeholding. To him, the cornerstone of the Constitution was equality of states, not of persons. These views brought Herbert a seat in Congress in 1876. There he served eight terms, battling agrarian opponents. In some respects a "Bourbon" Democrat, he fought a government grant to the Texas and Pacific Railroad, and helped write a book, *Why the Solid South?*, to discredit the Federal Election Act of 1890. Herbert took a broader view in foreign policy. Though not an imperialist,

from the mid-1880s he advocated naval expansion. On the Naval Affairs Committee, he cooperated with Republicans to secure construction of an armored fleet. In 1893 he became secretary of the navy and increased the buildup. Following his retirement in 1912, he published *The Abolition Crusade and Its Consequences*, a history of the mid-nineteenth century from a southern conservative point of view.

Further Reading: Hugh C. Davis, "Hilary A. Herbert: Bourbon Apologist," *Alabama Review* 20 (1967): 216–225; Hugh B. Hammett, *Hilary Abner Herbert: A Southerner Returns to the Union*, 1976.

Paul M. Pruitt, Jr.

HERRMANN, ALEXANDER (10 February 1844–17 December 1896), magician. Born in Germany, Herrmann traveled widely in Europe as his older brother's assistant in magic performances before immigrating to the United States in 1860. Thereafter he performed his own magic shows throughout much of the world. His engagement in London ran for one thousand nights. In 1876 Herrmann, known as "Herrmann the Great," became a naturalized U.S. citizen. With his personal charm, extraordinary beard, and clever manner of presentation, he attracted large audiences filled with people who often watched his acts several times. He ran his own shows, carried his equipment, and played practical jokes in public to advertise his appearances. By the late 1890s, Herrmann had a solid reputation as a popular entertainer.

Further Reading: H. J. Burlingame, *Herrmann the Magician*, 1897; *New York Tribune*, 18 December 1896.

Marvin D. Cohen

HERSHEY, MILTON SNAVELY (13 September 1857–13 October 1945), candy manufacturer and philanthropist. Born in Derry Church, Pennsylvania, Hershey served an apprenticeship with a Lancaster confectioner, then opened his own candy business in Philadelphia in 1876. He made the product at night and sold it by day from a pushcart to crowds attending the Centennial Exposition. During the 1880s, he worked in numerous cities without achieving independence. He then returned to Lancaster to join with William Henry Lebkicher to form the Lancaster Caramel Company, using fresh milk to improve the candy's quality. Subsequently, Hershey opened plants in other cities, produced "Crystal" caramels, learned to dip caramels in chocolate and add milk to the chocolate coverings, and opened a chocolate company in 1894. He began marketing the milk chocolate Hershey bar in 1900. He built a chocolate plant and a company town, later named Hershey. Sales skyrocketed in the early twentieth century, and the town enlarged to include schools, churches, a hospital, an amusement park, a zoo, and a sports arena. Hershey and his wife also founded an orphanage, which ultimately became the Milton Hershey School. He died in Hershey, Pennsylvania.

Further Reading: Joel Glenn Brenner, *The Emperors of Chocolate: Inside the Secret World of Hershey and Mars*, 1999; James D. McMahon, Jr., *Built on Chocolate: The Story of the Hershey Chocolate Company*, 1999; Katherine B. Shippen and Paul A. W. Wallace, *Milton S. Hershey*, 1959.

Leonard Schlup

HEWITT, ABRAM STEVENS (31 July 1822–18 January 1903), iron manufacturer, congressman, mayor, and philanthropist. Born in Haverstraw, New York, Hewitt in 1842 earned a law degree at Columbia College. There he met Sarah Cooper, the only daughter of the wealthy Peter Cooper; they were married in 1855. He entered business with Cooper's son, Edward. Their partnership, Cooper, Hewitt & Company, successfully pioneered iron manufacture in the United States, and produced the first high-phosphorus, low-carbon steel of commercial value. Hewitt entered politics when he, Samuel J. Tilden, and Edward Cooper sought to oust the corrupt Tweed Ring in New York City. Subsequently, Hewitt was elected to five terms in Congress (1875–1887), where he championed tariff reform, labor, and stable currency. In 1876, he chaired the Democratic National Committee during the disputed Tilden-Hayes presidential election. Ten years later, Hewitt was elected mayor of New York City. He served one term, fighting Tammany patronage and trying to improve municipal services. He wrote the Rapid Transit Bill, which ultimately created New York's mass transit system. After losing a reelection bid,

Hewitt focused on his business and philanthropic interests. His legacy is today reflected most notably in his endowment of Cooper Union for the Advancement of Science and Art. He died in New York City.

Further Reading: Alan Nevins, *Abram S. Hewitt, with Some Account of Peter Cooper*, 1935; "The Late Ex-Mayor Hewitt," *The Nation* 76 (22 January 1903): 67; Abram Stevens Hewitt Papers, Columbia University and New-York Historical Society, New York City.

Janet Butler Munch

HICKOK, JAMES BUTLER "Wild Bill" (27 May 1837–2 August 1876), peace officer, gunfighter, and frontier hero. Hickok was born in Troy Grove, Illinois. He moved to Monticello, on the Kansas frontier, in 1855. There, in 1858, he found employment as a constable before driving wagons and stage coaches over the Santa Fe and Oregon trails. A fervent abolitionist, he fought in the border war between the Free-Soil Kansans and the pro-slavery Missourians, a conflict in which he won the sobriquet "Wild Bill." A Union Army spy and scout, Hickok in 1865 killed a turncoat soldier, Dave Tutt, in Springfield, Missouri's, public square. Thereafter eastern journalists described him as the classic gunfighter. Hickok, who gambled professionally, enjoyed the notoriety. Between 1867 and 1869, he fought in the sporadic Indian wars. A Kansas lawman from 1868 to 1871, he killed four men in the line of duty. When he mortally wounded his own deputy by accident, he lost his position. Thereafter, failing eyesight plagued him and his career degenerated into a miasma of gambling, public intoxication, and arrests for vagrancy. In 1872–1873 he worked briefly for "Buffalo Bill" Cody's Wild West show. Then he wandered to Deadwood, a Dakota Territory mining town. There, a saddle tramp named Jack McCall shot him from behind as he sat playing poker. He was holding aces and eights, "the dead man's hand."

Further Reading: G. A. Custer, *My Life on the Plains or Personal Experiences with Indians*, 1874; Nyle H. Miller and Joseph W. Snell, *Why the West Was Wild*, 1963; Joseph G. Rosa, *Wild Bill Hickok: The Man and His Myth*, 1996.

Maurice Law Costello

HIGGINSON, HENRY LEE (18 November 1834–14 November 1918), banker and philanthropist. Born in New York City, Higginson was reared in Boston. He studied at the Boston Latin School and, briefly, at Harvard. His family sent him to Europe, in 1852 and 1853, to study music. When he realized he could never play professionally, he returned to Boston in 1860. He rose to major in the Union Army, then joined his father and uncle in the brokerage firm of Lee, Higginson and Company. Investing primarily in railroads and mining, the firm prospered. In 1881 Higginson created the first permanent orchestra in the United States. The Boston Symphony Orchestra played its first concerts in the fall of 1881, and until 1918 Higginson supported its deficits from his personal funds. Higginson ran the business operations, leaving the artistic decisions to his conductors. Going from twenty concerts the first year to 112 concerts in the 1888–1889 season, the orchestra became an established cultural institution. In 1885 Higginson established the "Pops" series, featuring young people's concerts, public rehearsals, and professionally written program notes. He also gave generously of his administrative expertise, money, and property to Harvard and to charitable causes. Higginson died in Boston, Massachusetts.

Further Reading: Bliss Perry, *Life and Letters of Henry Lee Higginson*, 1921; M. A. DeWolfe Howe, *Boston Symphony Orchestra, 1881–1931*, 1931; Philip Hart, *Orpheus in the New World*, 1973.

Leslie Petteys

HILGARD, EUGENE WOLDEMAR (5 January 1833–8 January 1916), geologist and chemist. Hilgard was born in Zweibrücken, Bavaria, but reared in Belleville, Illinois. He studied chemistry at the Homeopathic Medical College in Washington, D.C., and at Philadelphia's Franklin Institute, and in 1853 received a Ph.D. in geology from the University of Heidelberg. During the 1860s, he surveyed soils and published his results as *The Geology and Agriculture of the State of Mississippi* (1866) and *The Geology of the Mississippi Delta* (1870). These books founded pedology, the science of soils. Hilgard believed soil improvement was the surest way to increase crop yields, and that agricultural scientists should identify the ideal soil for a crop or rotation of crops. In

1874 he became professor of agriculture at the University of California, and the next year established an experiment station. In 1877 he organized a soil survey of California; two years later, his appointment to the Census Bureau allowed him to expand his survey to the lower South. During the 1880s, other scientists imitated his work, and in 1894 the Department of Agriculture organized a nationwide soil survey. Hilgard retired as the leading soil scientist. He died in Berkeley, California, just as a cornbreeding revolution began to elevate genetics above soil science.

Further Reading: Alfred C. True, *A History of Agricultural Experimentation and Research in the United States, 1607–1925*, 1937; *Experiment Station Record* 34 (1916): 301–303.

Christopher Cumo

HILL, DAVID BENNETT (29 August 1843– 20 October 1910), governor and senator. Born in Havana (now Montour Falls), New York, Hill gained admission to the bar in 1864, held a seat in the New York Assembly in 1871 and 1872, and developed a friendship with Governor Samuel J. Tilden. Hill helped expose Tammany Hall corruption, become mayor of Elmira in 1882, and won election that year as lieutenant governor on Grover Cleveland's state ticket. Hill rose to the governorship when Cleveland became president in 1885, and held the office until 1892. He favored civil and criminal code reform, substitution of electrocution for hanging in capital punishment cases, and establishment of Labor Day, child labor laws, and a state forestry preserve. Hill served in the U.S. Senate from 1892 to 1897. He entertained presidential ambitions and battled with Cleveland over New York patronage. Hill opposed free coinage of silver and the presidential nomination of William Jennings Bryan in 1896, writing: "I am a Democrat still—very still." Four years later he seconded Bryan's nomination at the Kansas City convention but disavowed attempts by some delegates to elevate him to the vice presidential spot on the ticket. Hill He died at his country home, "Wolfert's Roost," near Albany, New York.

Further Reading: *Brooklyn Daily Eagle*, 20 October 1910; *New York Times*, 20 October 1910; Herbert Bass, *"I Am a Democrat": The Political Career of David Bennett Hill*, 1961.

Leonard Schlup

HILL, JAMES JEROME (16 September 1838–29 May 1916), railroad president. Born near Rockwood, Ontario, Hill spent his adult life in Saint Paul, Minnesota. There he became a pivotal figure in transportation and the economic development of Minnesota and the American Northwest, as well as a major force in the national economy. Initially, Hill invested in the steamboat trade on the Mississippi and Red rivers, and in warehousing. In 1877, he headed a group that extended the St. Paul & Pacific Railway to the Canadian border. In the mid-1880s, he constructed the Minneapolis, Manitoba & St. Paul line to western Montana Territory when the area emerged as the country's principal copper-producing region. In 1893, his line, renamed the Great Northern, completed the transcontinental link by reaching Seattle. Under Hill's leadership, the Great Northern, unlike other large rail lines, successfully weathered the Panic of 1893. In alliance with the House of Morgan, Hill obtained control of his bankrupt rival, the Northern Pacific, in 1896. By 1901, he controlled the Great Northern, Northern Pacific, and Chicago, Burlington & Quincy lines. Hill then joined with E. H. Harriman to combine those interests in the Northern Securities Company, which immediately became the nation's largest railway corporation. The Supreme Court ordered its dissolution in 1904, but those "Hill lines" were reunited six decades later. Hill died in Saint Paul.

Further Reading: Michael P. Malone, *James J. Hill: Empire Builder of the Northwest*, 1996; Albro Martin, *James J. Hill and the Opening of the Northwest*, 1976, 1991; James J. Hill Papers, James J. Hill Reference Library, Saint Paul, Minnesota.

W. Thomas White

HILLSBORO CRUSADE. On the evening of 23 December 1873, Dr. Dioclesian Lewis, an author and social/health reformer, lectured on temperance at the Music Hall in Hillsboro, Ohio, birthplace of the Woman's Temperance Crusade. The next morning, under the leadership of Eliza Thompson, wife of a judge and daughter of a former governor, seventy women left the Presbyterian church worship services and walked two by two to Hillsboro's saloons, singing the Woman's Christian Temperance Union hymn, "Give to the Winds Thy Fears." Daily they visited saloons and drugstores that sold liquor. They prayed on floors and knelt on sidewalks before the doorways until most of the sellers of intoxicating beverages capitulated to their demands. The early Ohio crusades received spectacular publicity in the Cincinnati, Chicago, and New York press, as well as in other large cities. Stories and cartoons appeared in *Harper's Weekly*. Lewis addressed groups in Ohio for two weeks in February 1874, repeatedly telling the Hillsboro story. Eliza Daniel Stewart, known as "Mother Stewart," who had worked for the Sanitary Commission during the Civil War, preached to a crowd at Lagonda House and emerged as an inspiring leader of the movement who later joined the Prohibition Party. The Cleveland writer Sarah K. Bolton observed that the female crusaders had driven the liquor traffic out of 250 towns and villages, including Washington Court House, Ohio, and in the process had increased church attendance and decreased court appearances. The women's crusade of 1873–1874 was the culmination of years of women's taking direct action against saloons and the liquor traffic. Because they possessed no direct political power, women used prayer vigils, petition campaigns, demonstrations, and hymn singing to persuade owners of taverns to dispose of their beverages, close their doors, and pursue other occupations.

Further Reading: Eliza Daniel Stewart, *Memories of the Crusade: A Thrilling Account of the Great Uprising of the Women of Ohio in 1873 Against the Liquor Crime*, 1888; Jack S. Blocker, Jr., *"Give to the Winds Thy Fears": The Women's Temperance Crusade, 1873–74*, 1985.

Leonard Schlup

HIRES, CHARLES ELMER (19 August 1851–31 July 1937), druggist, soft drink manufacturer. Hires was born near Roadstown, New Jersey, and after limited schooling, apprenticed in a drugstore in Bridgeton (1863–1867). With borrowed money, he opened his own drugstore in Philadelphia in 1869. After tasting a drink made from sassafras and herbs while on vacation in 1875, Hires began to experiment with sarsaparilla roots, bark, and herbs. He created a potion that he named Hires Root Beer. He popularized it by selling it from a stand at the Philadelphia Centennial Exposition in 1876 and then to soda fountains, employing aggressive advertising. For several years it was sold as packages of bark, roots, and herbs for home brewing, and from 1893, both as a bottled beverage and in three-ounce bottles as a brewing extract. Although Hires had bought a botanical drug firm in 1877, robust root beer sales required his increasing attention. In 1890 he incorporated the Hires Root Beer Company, initially capitalized at $300,000. In 1896, he became interested in producing condensed milk. Over the next twenty years he acquired half a dozen companies, operating twenty-one plants, before he sold out to Nestlé in 1918 and focused entirely on root beer. He died in Haverford, Pennsylvania.

Further Reading: Frank H. Olsen, *Inventors Who Left Their Brands on America*, 1991; *American National Biography*, 10 (1999): 851–852; New York *Times*, 1 August 1937; *Philadelphia Public Ledger*, 1 August 1937.

Douglas Steeples

HISPANIC AMERICANS. During the Gilded Age, immigrant Mexicans helped construct the railroads and labored in the mines, in the fields, and on the ranches. Twenty years before 1868, the United States had taken the Southwest from Mexico. Mexican Americans in California and New Mexico attempted to assimilate while continuing a struggle to preserve titles to their lands, conserve their language, and protect their religious heritage and culture. Other Hispanics, Puerto Ricans and Cubans, also experienced great changes in their ways of living as their lands came under U.S. control. Although the former became a colony, the latter gained independence, except for the Guantánamo Bay naval station.

In the Southwest, New Mexican villages had survived for generations through use of common lands or *ejidos*. The Forest Reserve Act of 1891 set aside thousands of acres as national forests, much of that land was taken from village commons. In 1897, the Supreme Court, in *United States* v. *Sandoval*, rejected town claims to *ejidos*, thereby depriving them of their economic base. Hispanics also suffered as land speculators and politicians exploited natural resources. A shift of forest land from pasturage to business interests deprived them of grazing areas. Nevertheless, a number of Hispanics were active in politics and business. Francisco J. Chávez was elected to the New Mexico territorial legislative council in 1875. He also served as a delegate to the state constitutional convention four years later. Miguel Antonio Otero, Jr., became territorial governor in 1898. Casimiro Barela attended the Colorado constitutional convention in 1875, became a state senator less than twelve months later, and was reelected continuously for forty years. Elfego Baca, a sheriff's deputy in New Mexico, became legendary 1884 for single-handedly overpowering eighty Texans in a shoot-out. In Arizona, Esteban Ochoa built the Southwest's leading freight company before losing out in the 1880s to the railroad. He then served in the territorial legislature and as mayor of Tucson.

During the Gilded Age, Hispanic peoples in the United States developed basic strategies and organizations, such as the Sociedad Alianza Hispano-Americana, necessary for both survival and success as citizens of the United States.

Further Reading: Matt S. Meier and Feliciano Ribera, *Mexican Americans/American Mexicans*, 1993; Maurilio E. Vigil, *Los Patrones: Profiles of Hispanic Political Leaders in New Mexico History*, 1980; David J. Weber, *Foreigners in Their Native Land: Historical Roots of the Mexican Americans*, 1973.

Santos C. Vega

HOAR, GEORGE FRISBIE (29 August 1826–30 September 1904), U.S. senator. One of the preeminent Gilded Age Republicans, Hoar, born in Concord, Massachusetts, graduated from Harvard College in 1846 and its law school three years later. He practiced law in Worcester, Massachusetts, and served in the state legislature during the 1850s. Hoar sat in the federal House of Representatives from 1869 to 1877, and the U.S. Senate from 1877 until his death in Worcester. Appointed a House manager to conduct the impeachment proceedings against former secretary of War William W. Belknap, Hoar was also on the electoral commission that decided the disputed presidential election of 1876. In the Senate, Hoar chaired the Judiciary Committee and was a member of other committees. He wrote two rules concerning decorum in debate, drafted the Presidential Succession Act in 1886, and helped repeal the existing portion of the Tenure of Office Act in 1887. He adamantly opposed the Chinese Exclusion Act and was a strong advocate of civil rights and woman suffrage. Hoar opposed the direct election of senators and the acquisition of the Philippine Islands in 1899. A person of political morality and integrity, Hoar never hesitated to express his views while remaining tolerant of those of others. In an era noted for graft and corruption, Hoar epitomized the honest and dedicated public servant.

Further Reading: *Boston Transcript*, 30 September 1904; George F. Hoar, *Autobiography of Seventy Years*, 2 vols., 1903; Richard E. Welch, Jr., *George Frisbie Hoar and the Half-Breed Republicans*, 1971.

Leonard Schlup

HOBART, ESTHER JANE TUTTLE (30 April 1849–8 January 1941), second lady and presidential hostess. Born in Paterson, New Jersey, "Jennie" Tuttle married Garret A. Hobart, a lawyer, on 21 June 1869. In 1896, he was elected vice president of the United States. After the inaugural ceremonies, the Hobarts leased the Cameron mansion near the White House, where they entertained and developed a close friendship with President William McKinley and his invalid wife. Because of Ida Saxton McKinley's frail health, Jennie Hobart frequently helped with social responsibilities. The first person to designate herself as Second Lady, she greatly enjoyed her Washington society role, and held weekly afternoon receptions. The Hobarts won a dispute concerning protocol with the British ambassador, Sir Julian Pauncefote, who insisted that since he represented Queen Victoria, he should be rated next to the president at social functions. Indifferent to titles, the Hobarts maintained that a vice president should precede all diplomatic personages, thereby establishing a precedent for their successors. Following her husband's death in office in 1899, Mrs. Hobart lived in their home, Carroll Hall, in Paterson. Upon hearing of Mc-

Kinley's assassination in 1901, she immediately traveled to Buffalo to comfort Mrs. McKinley. Jennie Tuttle Hobart died in Haledon, New Jersey.

Further Reading: *New York Times*, 9 January 1941; Jennie Tuttle Hobart, *Memories*, 1930; Jennie Tuttle Hobart, *Second Lady*, 1933.

Leonard Schlup

HOBART, GARRET AUGUSTUS (3 June 1844–21 November 1899), vice president of the United States. Born at Long Branch, New Jersey, Hobart graduated in 1863 from Rutgers College. He subsequently studied law, opened a practice at Paterson, New Jersey, in 1866, and became prominent in business, law, and politics. He held local offices, won election to the state legislature in 1872, and became its speaker two years later. A Republican landslide in 1876 took him to the state senate, where he remained until 1882, serving as its president in 1881 and 1882. From 1880 to 1891, Hobart chaired the New Jersey Republican Committee, and in 1884 he secured a place on the GOP National Committee. A director of several banks that were connected with sixty corporations, he accumulated a fortune. His business sagacity and attendance at Republican national conventions since 1876 earned him a prominent place among northern New Jersey Republicans. In 1895 he managed the successful campaign of John W. Griggs, the first Republican governor of New Jersey since 1869. Hobart, an advocate of tariff protectionism and sound money, was William McKinley's running mate in 1896. Elected vice president, he took office in March 1897. He presided over Senate sessions, worked with Republicans in caucus rooms, and cast the deciding vote against Philippine independence. Friendly with McKinley, Hobart often advised the president on private financial investments. In several ways, Hobart was the nation's first modern vice president. He died at his home in Paterson.

Further Reading: Leonard Schlup, "Republican Nationalist in the McKinley Era: Garret A. Hobart of New Jersey and His Political Career and Letters," *The North Jersey Highlander* 32 (1996): 17–26; David Magie, *The Life of Garret Augustus Hobart*, 1910; *New York Times*, 22 November 1899.

Leonard Schlup

HOGG, JAMES STEPHEN (24 March 1851–3 March 1906), attorney general and governor. Hogg was born near Rusk, Texas, and became the state's first native governor. He attended private schools before publishing newspapers in Longview and Quitman. Hogg studied law, was admitted to the bar, and won election as Wood County attorney in 1878. He then served as U.S. attorney for the Seventh District from 1880 to 1884. Upon becoming Texas attorney general in 1886, Hogg used his office to make the insurance and railroad industries more accountable. He was the first of a series of Progressive governors who gained office with Edward M. House's support, and is regarded as the most effective and most popular of them. His legislature created the Railroad Commission, the first such state regulatory agency. Other aspects of his program, known as the "Hogg Laws," were regulating railroad stock trading, ending land grants to foreign corporations, forcing others to return unused land, and requiring insurance companies to deposit premiums within the state. Hogg also supported higher education. He retired in 1895, moved to Houston, and amassed a fortune through law and oil investments. The historian Joe B. Frantz observed that Hogg is the governor against whom all his successors are judged. Hogg died in Houston.

Further Reading: Robert C. Cotner, *James Stephen Hogg: A Biography*, 1959; Robert C. Cotner, "James Stephen Hogg," *The New Handbook of Texas*, 3 (1996): 652–53; Archie P. McDonald, *"On This Day of New Beginnings": Selected Inaugural Addresses of Texas Governors*, 1979.

Archie P. McDonald

HOLDEN v. HARDY, 169 U.S. 366 (1898). The Utah legislature in 1896 passed a law limiting the hours of those working in underground mines to eight per day. The mine owners sued, and the case reached the Supreme Court. In a 7–2 opinion, the Court found the law a "valid exercise" of state police power. Justice Henry B. Brown, writing for the majority, declared that the Court had previously upheld similar regulations requiring ventilation of mines and the keeping of accurate maps, in case of cave-ins, so as to save lives. If measures for protecting life were permissible, then it followed that regulations to guard the health or morals of the miners were allowed. Brown brushed aside owners' arguments that the law violated the Fourteenth Amendment by abridging the privileges and immunities of citizens, and depriving both employer and laborer of property without due process. However, while laboring above ground for eight hours would not threaten one's health, it did not follow that toiling "for the same length of time" was "innocuous" below ground. Public safety compelled the legislation. Such distinctions apparently allowed the Court to strike down similar hour-limitation laws for bakers a few years later in *Lochner* v. *New York* (1905). Until the Court reversed itself in *Muller* v. *Oregon* (1908), maximum-hours cases would be "perilously close to the legal frontier."

Further Reading: Lawrence M. Friedman, *A History of American Law*, 2nd ed., 1985.

Sam S. Kepfield

HOLLEY, ALEXANDER LYMAN (20 July, 1832–29 January 1882), inventor, engineer, and writer. Born in Lakeville, Connecticut, Holley demonstrated an early aptitude for all things mechanical. After graduating from Brown University in 1853, he worked with railroad engines and did technical publishing. While in England in 1862, he visited a blast converter built on Henry Bessemer's design. Holley was impressed with the technology's potential, and negotiated the American rights for Bessemer's process in 1863. From then until his death, he was the most important American proponent of the Bessemer process, making the rise of the American steel industry possible. Holley's genius lay in his ability to improve existing ideas and equipment. He played a leading role in the construction of nine of the first ten Bessemer converters installed in the United States. In 1872, Holley designed the Edgar Thomson steelworks for Andrew Carnegie. Holley's integration of Bessemer's technique into the larger steel manufacturing process made the mammoth plant the model of industrial efficiency. Plagued by poor health, Holley devoted his later years to improving engineering education. His interest in technical innovation never flagged, as evidenced by the key role he played in introducing the Thomas open-hearth process to the United States in 1880. Holley died in Brooklyn, New York.

Further Reading: Alfred Chandler, *The Visible Hand: The Managerial Revolution in American Business*, 1977; Jeanne McHugh, *Alexander Holley and the Makers of Steel*, 1980.

Kurt Hackemer

HOLLIDAY, JOHN HENRY "DOC" (14 August 1851–8 November 1887), dentist, and frontier gambler. Holliday was born in Griffin, Georgia. His mother died when he was fifteen, and her death, plus his father's rapid remarriage to a much younger woman, left Holliday estranged. After receiving a classical education at the Valdosta Institute, he was graduated from the Pennsylvania College of Dental Surgery in Philadelphia (1872). Holliday practiced in Griffin, then in Atlanta. A persistent cough, and a physician's diagnosis of chronic pulmonary tuberculosis, led him to seek a drier climate in Dallas, Texas. Adept at faro and poker, Holliday virtually abandoned dentistry for a gambling career. In 1878, during a dispute over cards, he killed Ed Bailey with a knife. He was placed under "house arrest" at the Planter's Hotel and, with the aid of Kate Elder, managed to escape a lynch mob. The pair fled to Dodge City, Kansas. There Holliday formed a lasting friendship with Wyatt Earp, the assistant marshal. Holliday gambled, and briefly resumed dental practice, before moving on. His temper, however, brought numerous knife fights and gunfights as he drifted across the West, gambling and drinking in the mining towns of Colorado and New Mexico. In 1880, Holliday followed the Earp brothers to Tombstone, Arizona. The next year, he joined them in the O.K. Corral shootout against the Clanton gang. Suspected in two subsequent revenge killings, Holliday fled Arizona with Wyatt Earp in 1882. He died in Glenwood Springs, Colorado.

Further Reading: Pat Jahna, *The Frontier World of Doc Holliday: Faro Dealer from Dallas to Deadwood*, 1957; John Myers, *Doc Holliday*, 1955; Karen Holliday Tanner, *Doc Holliday: A Family Portrait*, 1998.

Maurice Law Costello

HOLMAN, WILLIAM STEELE (6 September 1822–22 April 1897), congressman. Born near Aurora, Indiana, Holman attended Franklin College for two years and then entered the law. After holding a variety of judicial positions in the 1840s and 1850s, he gained prominence as a Union Democrat during the Civil War and later as a political ally of veterans. For nearly forty years, he was the Democratic contender for the House seat from the Fourth Congressional District of Indiana, serving nonconsecutive terms from 1859 to 1865, 1867 to 1877, 1881 to 1895, and again for one month in 1897, before his death in Washington, D.C. When Democrats controlled the House, he often chaired important committees, such as Appropriations, Indian Affairs, and Public Lands. A master parliamentarian and effective orator, he earned the sobriquets "The Watch Dog of the Treasury" and "The Great Objector" for his careful consideration of appropriations bills and his opposition to expenditures for the Library of Congress and improvements for the nation's capital. His demagogic tactics, nonchalant manner of dressing, negligent appearance, and addiction to tobacco frequently camouflaged his shrewd cognizance of the era's economic issues and his ability to tackle problems successfully. Holman was a Jeffersonian from an agricultural area that, during the Gilded Age, was industrializing and urbanizing.

Further Reading: *Washington Post*, 23 April 1897; *Indianapolis Star*, 23 April 1897.

Leonard Schlup

HOLT, HENRY (3 January 1840–13 February 1926), book publisher. Born in Baltimore, Maryland, Holt graduated from the Columbia University Law School in 1864, and with George Palmer Putnam, thought of publishing books. In 1866, Holt established the publishing firm of Leypoldt and Holt; in 1873 it became Henry Holt and Company, a publisher of school and university textbooks. Among the authors Holt solicited were Henry Adams, John Dewey, and John Fiske. Holt launched the Leisure Hour series in 1872. These books, largely novels, cost a dollar each and included Thomas Hardy's *Far from the Madding Crowd*. Holt also issued a Leisure Moment series, a Leisure Season series, and the American Science series. In addition he did writing of his own. Holt died in New York City, bequeathing an estate of over $1 million.

Further Reading: New York *Times*, 14–16 February 1926; Charles A. Madison, *The Owl Among Colophons: Henry Holt as Publisher and Editor*, 1966; Henry Holt Papers, Princeton University Library.

Leonard Schlup

HOLT, THOMAS MICHAEL (15 July 1831– 11 April 1896), manufacturer, legislator, and governor. Born in Orange (now Alamance) County, North Carolina, Holt was exposed to manufacturing at a young age in his father's cotton factory. He was educated by tutors and later briefly attended the University of North Carolina. He spent a year in Philadelphia as an assistant in a large machine shop. In 1851 he returned home and became a partner in the family cloth-manufacturing business, which eventually became one of the largest companies in North Carolina. By 1890, it employed more than five hundred workers at 434 looms. Holt designed the industrial village at Haw River, which became a prototype for factory towns throughout the South.

Holt served a state senator from 1876 to 1880 and in the House of Commons from 1882 to 1888. He was elected speaker in 1884. Holt favored both agriculture and internal improvements. He became president of the North Carolina Railroad in 1875, and simultaneously headed the state's agricultural society. Elected lieutenant governor of North Carolina in 1888, Holt rose to governor in 1891. He is remembered for his personal popularity. He died in Graham, North Carolina.

Further Reading: C. B. Denson, "An Address in Memory of Thomas M. Holt, Governor of North Carolina," delivered in the hall of the House of Representatives, Raleigh, 27 October 1898; Donald Grant, *Alumni History of the University of North Carolina*, 2nd ed., 1924, 294.

Christian B. Keller

HOMER, WINSLOW (24 February 1836–29 September 1910), artist and illustrator. Born in Boston, Homer became a freelance illustrator after a two-year apprenticeship to a lithographer. During the Civil War, *Harper's Weekly* hired him as a correspondent. Homer quickly became the nation's most noted chronicler of the conflict through a series of acclaimed paintings. By 1865, he was elected a full academician of New York's National Academy of Design, the principal institution for American artists. In 1866 two of his paintings, *Prisoners from the Front* and *The Bright Side*, were chosen as part of the American display for the 1867 Exposition Universelle in Paris. In 1867, Homer began to devote more time to paintings and watercolors, although he would continued to submit illustrations to *Harper's* until 1875. Among his most beloved paintings from this period are his series of school subjects, including the widely reproduced *Crack the Whip*.

In 1881 Homer went to a small English fishing village. There he spent nearly two years depicting the heroic, sculpturesque figures of the English fisherfolk. Soon afterward, he moved to a similarly remote spot on the American coastline, Prout's Neck, Maine. His paintings from the next three decades represent the elemental struggles of the natural world: the surf against the rocky shores, the daring rescue of men and women at sea, and the battles between hunter and hunted. Homer based these watercolors and oils on his own experiences as an outdoorsman, his time at Prout's Neck, and his travels in the Adirondacks, Canada, Florida, and the Caribbean. Working at a distance from the New York art world, the intensely private Homer gained a reputation as a recluse, as a pure American artist whose commitment to artistic realism had been left untainted by the effeminate influence of European art. He died in his Prout's Neck studio, having never married and leaving no heirs.

Further Reading: Marc Simpson, *Winslow Homer: Paintings of the Civil War*, 1988; Bruce Robertson, *Reckoning with Winslow Homer: His Late Paintings and Their Influence*, 1990; Nicolai Cikovsky, Jr., *Winslow Homer*, 1990.

Lacey Jordan

HOMESTEAD STRIKE OF 1892. Andrew Carnegie, owner of steel mills near Pittsburgh, Pennsylvania, had grown up poor, and styled himself a friend of workers. As such, he claimed to endorse unionization, and boasted that his fairness in negotiating with them precluded their need to strike. The reality was otherwise. In 1889 the Amalgamated Association of Iron, Steel and Tin Workers at his plant in Homestead, Pennsylvania, won a strike that gave them wages 33 percent higher than those at nearby mills. When the contract expired in 1892, the Amalgamated was the only union left at a Carnegie mill. While Carnegie secluded himself in Scotland, his partner, Henry Clay Frick, announced in June that he would no longer recognize the union. He surrounded the mill with a barbed wire fence, hired three hundred Pinkertons, and on 2 July closed the mill, intending to reopen it with nonunion workers. Three days later, workers and Pinkertons exchanged gunfire for twenty-four hours, killing nine strikers and seven guards. The Pinkertons' surrender emboldened workers at other mills to join the strike, and not until September was Frick, with help from the state militia, able to reopen the mills. On 20 November the Amalgamated admitted defeat by calling off the strike, and Frick fired and blacklisted its leaders. With the union gone, Homestead workers saw their wages fall 20 percent between 1892 and 1912. Carnegie's geographical distance did not fool the *St. Louis Post-Dispatch*, which branded him a coward. In England the *St. James Gazette* dismissed his pro-labor platitudes as a ruse.

Further Reading: Melvin Dubofsky, *Industrialism and the American Worker, 1865–1920*, 1985; Harold C. Livesay, *Andrew Carnegie and the Rise of Big Business*, 1975; David Montgomery, "Strikes in Nineteenth-Century America," *Social Science History* 4 (1980): 81–104.

Christopher Cumo

HOMOSEXUALITY. The term "homosexuality" first appeared in Germany and became widely known among intellectuals during the 1880s; it is therefore somewhat inappropriate historically as a description of the romantic friendships that flourished among both sexes, particularly among the upper classes, during the period from 1868 to 1901. The poetry and lives of Walt Whitman (1819–1892) and of Emily Dickinson (1830–1886) best characterize the Gilded Age's literary figures. Although their fascination with their own sex is clear to the careful modern reader, their silence on their same-sex desire ("adhesiveness," to Whitman) and their fear of being discovered are equally apparent. Many critics do not mention same-sex desire in discussing either author, demonstrating that silence, fear, and ignorance continued after Gilded Age. The industrial revolution allowed white men to leave home to work; in boardinghouses and on the Western frontier, sexual relationships with other men could flourish. The song "The Ballad of Mrs. Nash" describes a man who passed as female in the West. Women desiring such independence sometimes dressed, and passed, as men, establishing "marriages" with other women in which secrecy about the worker's gender was necessary. In college, women developed intense "crushes" on one another, and sometimes formed lifelong partnerships, rivaling marriage, even when heterosexually married. Some women's friendships were overtly sexual; others were not.

By the end of the Gilded Age, Richard Krafft-Ebbing and other European writers were describing same-sex attraction as symptomatic of mental illness, so that secrecy became more necessary, and internalized homophobia and fear of physical violence more likely for those experiencing same-sex attraction. From at least the 1880s, an urban homosexual culture began to take shape, to be strengthened during and after World War II. Meeting places located in tough areas of cities such as New York, Boston, and Chicago included clubs, restaurants, steam baths, and military bases.

Further Reading: John d'Emilio and Estelle B. Freedman, *Intimate Matters: A History of Sexuality in America*, 1988; Lillian Faderman, ed., *Chloe plus Olivia: An Anthology of Lesbian Literature from the Seventeenth Century to the Present*, 1994; Mary W. Blanchard, "The Soldier and the Aesthete: Homosexuality and Popular Culture in Gilded Age America," *Journal of American Studies* 30 (1996): 25–46.

Robert E. Bennett

HOPKINS, PAULINE ELIZABETH (ca. 1859–13 August 1930), novelist and editor. Born a free African American in Portland, Maine, Hopkins was educated in Boston and wrote her first play, about the Underground Railroad, at age twenty. Known as "Boston's Favorite Colored Soprano" she performed with her parents. Leaving the stage in her thirties, Hopkins became a stenographer and lecturer. She helped establish *The Colored American Magazine* in 1900, publishing short stories, novels, historical sketches, and biographies in this venue. Her best-known work, *Contending Forces: A Romance Illustrative of Negro Life North and South* (1900), discusses activism among middle-class African Americans and the sexual victimization of black women. Hopkins's "Of One Blood," published in *The Colored American* in 1902 and 1903, envisioned a mystic union between Americans of African descent and a powerful, but hidden, race of Egyptian mages. Hopkins resigned from the magazine's editorial board in 1904, possibly for expressing reservations about Booker T. Washington's accommodationist politics. She spent the rest of her life in Boston; any later writing was destroyed by the fire in which she died.

Further Reading: Jane Campbell, *Mythic Black Fiction: The Transformation of History*, 1986; Hazel V. Carby, *Reconstructing Womanhood: The Emergence of the Afro-American Woman Novelist*, 1987; Claudia Tate, "Pauline Hopkins: Our Literary Foremother," in Marjorie Pryse and Hortense J. Spillers, eds., *Conjuring: Black Women, Fiction, and Literary Tradition*, 1985.

Barbara Ryan

HOPPIN, AUGUSTUS (13 July 1828–1 April 1896), illustrator. Born in Providence, Rhode Island, Hoppin attended Brown University and Harvard Law School, briefly practicing law before becoming an illustrator. During the late nineteenth century, his popular and fashionable drawings appeared in *Illustrated American News*, *Putnam's Magazine*, and *Yankee Notions*, as well as in books by Louisa May Alcott, Thomas Bailey Aldrich, Oliver Wendell Holmes, and William Dean Howells. Hoppin's illustrations fit well with the authors' conceptions. His images often glamorized Gilded Age symbols of prosperity. Like Thomas Nast, Hoppin's specialty was political caricature. Because Hoppin commanded high fees, Elisha Bliss, Mark Twain's publisher, divided the illustrations in *The Gilded Age*, (1873), among Hoppin, True Williams, and Henry Louis Stephens. In addition, Hoppin wrote and illustrated amusing works of his own, *On the Nile* (1874) and *Married for Fun* (1885). He died at Flushing, Long Island.

Further Reading: *New York Times*, 3 April 1896.

Leonard Schlup

HORNADAY, WILLIAM TEMPLE (1 December 1854–6 March 1937), zoologist and conservationist. Born near Plainfield, Indiana, Hornaday grew up in Iowa, fascinated with nature and troubled by the killing of animals. Having learned taxidermy while a student at Iowa State College, he left without a degree to make it his career. From 1874 to 1879 he traveled in Florida, South America, and Asia, collecting specimens. In 1882 Hornaday was appointed chief taxidermist of the National Museum. He conducted the last government-sponsored buffalo hunt, to collect twenty skins for the museum, in 1888. His study of the animal's history and habits appeared in the Smithsonian Institution's *Annual Report* in 1889. Hornaday concluded that unregulated hunting, and commercialization of wildlife, fated the buffalo to become extinct. He spent the rest of his life advocating wildlife conservation. Hornaday helped create the National Zoological Park in Washington, D.C., which he directed briefly. He pioneered the use of large open ranges for herd animals such as deer and elk, then left to head the New York Zoological Park (Bronx Zoo) from 1896 to 1926. He died in Stamford, Connecticut.

Further Reading: James Andrew Dolph, "Bringing Wildlife to the Millions: William Temple Hornaday, the Early Years, 1854–1896," PhD. diss., University of Massachusetts, 1975; William Temple Hornaday, "Eighty Fascinating Years: An Autobiography," unpublished manuscript, Hornaday Papers, Wildlife Conservation Society, Bronx, New York; *New York Times*, 7 March 1937.

Gregory Dehler

HOUK, LEONIDAS CAMPBELL (8 June 1836–25 May 1891), congressman and judge. Born near Boyds Creek, Tennessee, Houk opened a law office in 1859 in Clinton, Tennessee. A Union loyalist during the Civil War, he spent two years in military service, was a presidential elector in 1864 for the Lincoln-Johnson ticket, and participated in the constitutional convention of 1865 to reorganize Tennessee's postwar government. He held the post of circuit judge from 1866 until 1870. Devoted to the Republican Party, Houk supported Ulysses S. Grant for president in 1868 and 1872, even favoring him as a Stalwart for a third term in 1880. A presidential elector in 1872 and 1876, Houk was a delegate to virtually every Republican National Convention. He served in the Tennessee legislature from 1873 to 1875. In 1878, Houk won election to the U.S. House of Representatives, where he remained until his death in Knoxville, Tennessee. A nationalist Republican who followed party doctrine, Houk was a southern representative who showed more concern for the plight of poor farmers and the consequences of agricultural depression than many of his northern urban Republican colleagues.

Further Reading: Verton M. Queener, "The East Tennessee Republicans in the State and Nation, 1870–1900," *Tennessee Historical Quarterly* 2 (1943): 99–128; Leonidas C. Houk Papers, Mc Clung Historical Collection, Lawson McGhee Library, Knox County Public Library, Knoxville, Tennessee.

Leonard Schlup

HOWARD, OLIVER OTIS (8 November 1830–26 October 1909), educator and government official. Born in Leeds, Maine, Howard graduated in 1850 from Bowdoin College and from the U.S. Military Academy four years later. A devout Christian, he detested alcohol and profanity, distinguished himself militarily during the Civil War, headed the Freedmen's Bureau in the immediate postwar period, and befriended African Americans. In 1867, he co-founded Howard University in Washington, D.C., serving as its president from 1869 until 1874. Later he commanded the Department of the Columbia in Portland, Oregon, the Department of the Platte in Omaha, Nebraska, and ultimately the Department of the East in New York. Less cordial to Native Americans in the West, Howard was present when Chief Joseph of the Nez Percé declared: "I will fight no more forever." Upon retiring from the army, Howard published books and memoirs. He died in Burlington, Vermont.

Further Reading: John Carpenter, *Sword and Olive Branch: Oliver Otis Howard*, 1964; William McFeely, *Yankee Stepfather: General O. O. Howard and the Freedmen*, 1968; Robert Utley, "Oliver Otis Howard," *New Mexico Historical Review* 62 (1987): 55–63.

Leonard Schlup

HOWE AND HUMMEL. The partners in this notorious, nationally known New York City law firm were William F. Howe (7 July 1828–1 September 1902) and Abraham Henry Hummel (27 July 1850–22 January 1926). Both were born in Boston, Massachusetts. Howe attended King's College in London, England, and studied medicine before winning admission to the New York City bar in 1859. Immediately his colorful personality attracted attention, and he earned the sobriquet "Habeas Corpus Howe." Known especially for defending clients accused of murder, he wore gaudy clothing, bright ties, and a large watch. With consummate theatrical skills, familiarity with the law, and homey statements, Howe captured jurors' sympathy. In 1869, he took into partnership his office boy, Abraham H. Hummel, who secured admission to the bar partly through Howe's connivance. This began the most clever, picturesque, and highly remunerated criminal law firm in Gilded Age America. Their office at Center and Leonard streets in New York City had a huge illuminated sign outside. Unscrupulous and a master of making cases out of slim evidence, Hummel, known as "Little Abe" for his small stature and large bald head, always dressed in black, squandered money at racetracks and in high society, and specialized in divorce, homicide, and sensational cases. He cultivated powerful friends in the underworld and among politicians and wealthy individuals. Not as flamboyant as the masterful Howe, but bound to Howe in their law practice and by a romantic friendship, Hummel was briefly incarcerated in 1907 following his conviction on a conspiracy charge. Released in 1908, he sailed for London, where he died in a Baker Street room; his partner had passed on in New York City, in better circumstances.

Further Reading: *New York Times*, 3 September 1902; *New York Tribune*, 3 September 1902; *Daily Telegraph* (London), 25 January 1926.

Leonard Schlup

HOWE, JULIA WARD (27 May 1819–17 October 1910), suffragist, reformer, and author. Born in New York City, Julia Ward in 1843 married Dr. Samuel Gridley Howe, head of the Perkins Institute for the Blind, in Boston. Torn for years by a troubled marriage, she traveled widely in Europe, wrote poems and plays, and

assumed leadership roles in the women's rights crusade and the peace movement. Her most famous work, "The Battle Hymn of the Republic," appeared in the February 1862, issue of the *Atlantic Monthly*. Founder of the *Woman's Journal* in 1870, she was, for seven years in the 1870s, president of the Massachusetts Woman Suffrage Association, and in the 1880s of the Association for the Advancement of Women. Howe helped establish the New England Woman Suffrage Association and the American Woman Suffrage Association. In 1872 she suggested a Mother's Day in the United States, and thereafter held organized meetings every year in Boston to honor mothers. She died in Oak Glen, Massachusetts.

Further Reading: *New York Times*, 18 October 1910; Julia Ward Howe, *Reminiscences*, 1899; Mary H. Grant, *Private Woman, Public Person: An Account of the Life of Julia Ward Howe from 1819 to 1868*, 1994.

Leonard Schlup

HOWE, TIMOTHY OTIS (24 February 1816–25 March 1883), senator and postmaster general. Born in Livermore, Maine, Howe served three terms in U.S. Senate between 1861 and 1879. He supported Radical Reconstruction of the southern states, favored the African-American suffrage bill for the District of Columbia, spoke against Andrew Johnson's postwar program, and voted for his removal from office. On the "money question," Howe urged redemption of greenback currency, favored a repeal of the law restricting the number of national banks, and supported the Bland-Allison Act of 1878, which introduced the concept of limited bimetallism into the currency system. Howe represented the United States at the Paris Monetary Conference of 1881. During fifteen months as postmaster general, he reduced postage, issued postal notes, and urged postal reform. He died in Kenosha, Wisconsin.

Further Reading: Maurice McKenna, *Fond du lac County, Wisconsin*, 1912; *Milwaukee Sentinel*, 26 March 1883; *Wisconsin State Journal*, 26 March 1883; Timothy Otis Howe Papers, State Historical Society of Wisconsin, Madison.

Norman E. Fry

HOWELLS, WILLIAM DEAN (1 March 1837–11 May 1920), editor and writer. Born in Martin's Ferry, Ohio, Howells became the

Gilded Age's most influential literary critic. He shaped reading tastes and brokered literary reputations for nearly fifty years. Howells extended the New England literary tradition while editing the *Atlantic Monthly* in the 1860s and 1870s. As *Harper's Magazine* editor in 1881, he introduced his readers to such foreign writers as Leo Tolstoy, Ivan Turgenev, Gustave Flaubert, George Eliot and Henrik Ibsen. Close friendships with Mark Twain and Henry James measured Howells's nature and sympathies. Writers he aided include Stephen Crane, Charles Chesnutt, Sarah Orne Jewett, Hamlin Garland, Paul Laurence Dunbar, and Abraham Cahan. A gifted author himself, Howells wrote honed novellas and short stories. Perhaps his best novel is *A Hazard of New Fortunes* (1890), which demonstrates Howells's social conscience during an era of labor unrest. His interest in the form of art and literature that he called "realist" was a response to his desire to see cultural producers combat poverty and injustice. Though naturalists would mock Howells's sense of what constituted "real life" as prim, few appreciated his critical generosity or matched his popular appeal. He died in New York City.

Further Reading: Edwin H. Cady, *The Road to Realism*, 1956; Kenneth S. Lynn, *William Dean Howells: An American Life*, 1971; William Dean Howells papers at Yale, Harvard, and Alfred universities and Miami University of Ohio.

Barbara Ryan

HOWER, JOHN HENRY (22 February 1822–10 May 1916), inventor and businessman. Hower was born in Stark County, Ohio and later moved to Doylestown, Ohio, where he spent most of his childhood and early adulthood. He found his first employment as a teacher while living in Doylestown. In the late 1850s Hower met John F. Seiberling, inventor of the Excelsior mower and reaper; in 1861, Hower and Seiberling, along with Peter Cline, founded the Excelsior Mower and Reaper Works. The Civil War spurred grain production and provided impetus for the farm implement industry's growth. In 1865, Hower and his partners moved their operation to Akron, Ohio, where he was named vice president of the new,

larger factory. The depression of the 1870s crippled the entire industry. Manufacturers farther west survived, but Akron's farm implement industry disappeared by the 1890s. Hower purchased the Selle Gear Company, a maker of carriage hardware, in 1885, and in 1888, the Turner Oatmeal Mill, which was renamed the Hower Company. It was one of several cereal producers to merge into the American Cereal Company, which later became Quaker Oats. Hower died in Akron.

Further Reading: Stephen Paschen, "Hower House," 1993 (pamphlet); Karl H. Grismer, *Akron and Summit County*, 1952.

Stephen Paschen

HOYT, CHARLES HALE (26 July 1859–20 November 1900), journalist and playwright. A popular Gilded Age theater director, producer, humorist, and social critic, Hoyt was born in Concord, New Hampshire. He wrote numerous plays and comedies about life in the United States, treating manners, society, rural areas, and sports, among other topics. His best-known work, *A Trip to Chinatown*, opened at Hoyt's Madison Square Theater in 1891 and toured for over twenty years. Much of his success came from monitoring audience reactions, rewriting plays, and recasting actors and actresses while the production continued in one town. Committed to an insane asylum later in life but subsequently released, Hoyt died in Charlestown, New Hampshire.

Further Reading: *New York Times*, 21 November 1900; Nancy Foell Swortzell, "The Satire of Charles Hoyt," Ph.D. diss., Yale University, 1964.

Leonard Schlup

HUBBELL, JOHN LORENZO (27 November 1853–12 November 1930), western trader. Born in Pajarito, New Mexico, Hubbell attended a Presbyterian school in Santa Fe before serving as clerk and Spanish interpreter for the U.S. military. In 1878, he settled at Ganado, Arizona, establishing a trading post with the Navajos. There he built an empire of freight and mail lines that included over thirty trading centers. Hubbell exercised a powerful influence over local Native Americans, encouraging the Navajo people to produce outstanding work and to specialize in beautiful designs. He helped stimulate interest in Navajo art, rugs, and jewelry by promoting them and functioning as a bridge between two cultures. Travelers flocked to his remote desert location. Guests included the English philosopher Herbert Spencer. Hubbell's hacienda became a museum of Native American artifacts. A Republican who actively participated in politics and advocated statehood for Arizona, woman's suffrage, and prohibition, Hubbell spent two terms in the territorial assembly and was the first senator to represent his county in the state legislature. He gambled recklessly until sustaining a loss of $60,000 in 1896. Hubbell died of a stroke at his home in Ganado. Heirs ran the business at Ganado until 1967, when the National Park Service purchased the site and continued operations, making it the oldest continuously operating trading post on the Navajo reservation.

Further Reading: *Arizona Republic*, 13 November 1930.

Leonard Schlup

HULL HOUSE. The first and most famous settlement house in the United States, Hull House was founded on Chicago's west side in 1889. Its origins reflected the Gilded Age's underside; its development bridged nineteenth-century reform to twentieth-century progressivism; its leadership mirrored the shifting roles of women in American society. Hull House's significance goes beyond the immediate impact it had on the persons it served, encompassing long-range changes in public policy, academic inquiry, the helping professions, and the nation's concept of social justice.

Jane Addams established Hull House because of her horror at human suffering, her faith in social reform, and her impatience with the limits of women's lives. With other college-educated young women, she nurtured a community of single females (plus some males) dedicated to the social good. In the process, they created an intellectual and cultural center at Hull House, professionalized social work, promoted progressive education, and aided development of urban sociology at the University of Chicago.

Hull House adopted a variety of strategies to meet the needs of Chicago's poor, immigrant population of every age. It offered classes in literacy and citizenship, cooking and sewing, literature and music, hygiene and gymnastics, mathematics and art history. It established an employment bureau, a model lodging house, two cooperative housing clubs, a kindergarten, a glee club, a theater, an art gallery, and a restaurant.

Among the first to study the conditions of urban life, its staff became proponents of unions, public parks, and urban planning as well as advocates for legislation concerning child labor, sweatshops, housing, health, and women's rights. Hull House inspired a national settlement house movement, but World War I diverted resources away from domestic reform and brought criticism of Addams's pacifism. By the time she died in 1935, some of Hull-House's functions were being eclipsed by the New Deal. After its old buildings were bulldozed in 1963, Hull House became the coordinator of dispersed social agencies better suited to confront the realities of the modern city. Thus, the original spirit of Hull-House continues to adapt and, thereby, to prevail.

Further Reading: Mary Lynn McCree Bryan and Allen F. Davis, eds., *One Hundred Years at Hull House*, 1990; Elizabeth Lasch-Quinn, *Black Neighbors: Race and the Limits of Reform in the American Settlement House Movement, 1890–1945*, 1993; Eleanor J. Stebner, *The Women of Hull House: A Study in Spirituality, Vocation, and Friendship*, 1997.

Joanne Reitano

HUNT, RICHARD MORRIS (31 October 1827–31 July 1895), architect. Born in Brattleboro, Vermont, Hunt studied at the École des Beaux-Arts in Paris. Upon returning to the United States in 1855, he designed the Tenth Street Studio Building in New York City. A founding member of the American Institute of Architecture and its third president (1888–1891), Hunt helped to organize and set standards for the profession. His reputation skyrocketed as a result of his projects in New York City, such as the Stuyvesant Apartments, the Delaware and Hudson Canal Company Building, the Guernsey Building, the Lenox Library (commissioned by James Lenox, a wealthy merchant), the Tribune Building, the Fifth Avenue mansion of William K. Vanderbilt, and the pedestal base for the Statue of Liberty. Hunt also designed buildings and houses outside New York, including a house for Marshall Field, a Chicago merchant, in the early 1870s. He also did buildings for Princeton College, Case Western Reserve University, Harvard College, the U.S. Military Academy at West Point, the George Vanderbilt mansion ("Biltmore") in Asheville, North Carolina, and various Newport, Rhode Island, "cottages." Chairman of the Board of Architects for the World's Columbian Exposition at Chicago in 1893, Hunt designed the Administration Building. His last major commission was a wing for the Metropolitan Museum of Art in New York City, in the mid-1890s. The widely acclaimed "dean of American architecture" died at Newport, Rhode Island.

Further Reading: Paul R. Baker, *Richard Morris Hunt,* 1980.

Leonard Schlup

HUNT, WARD (14 June 1810–24 March 1886), U.S. Supreme Court associate justice. Hunt was born in Utica, New York, attended Oxford and Geneva academies, and received his LL.D. from Union College in 1828. He did further legal studies at Litchfield Law School in Connecticut, was admitted to the New York bar in 1831, and formed a partnership with former judge Hiram Denie. Hunt began his political career as a Jacksonian Democrat. He was sent to the New York Assembly in 1838, and was elected mayor of Utica six years later. Hunt failed in two attempts to gain a seat on the state supreme court. He helped organize the New York Republican Party, and in 1865, he finally won election to the New York Court of Appeals.

A protégé of the powerful Republican Roscoe Conkling, Hunt in 1872 became President Ulysses Grant's third successful Supreme Court nominee. He served for nine years, writing 149 majority opinions and four dissents. Hunt voted consistently to uphold the egalitarian spirit of the post–Civil War amendments to the Constitution. Ill health prevented him from being one of the Court's more influential members. His firm support of voting rights for African-American males never extended to similar rights for women, as he demonstrated in an

1873 case involving Susan B. Anthony. Hunt retired in January 1882, and died in Washington, D.C.

Further Reading: *New York Times,* 25 March 1886; C. Peter Magrath, *Morrison Waite: The Triumph of Character,* 1963.

Harvey Gresham Hudspeth

HUNT, WILLIAM HENRY (12 June 1823–27 February 1884), jurist, secretary of the navy, diplomat. Hunt was born in Charleston, South Carolina, and admitted to the Louisiana bar in 1844. Although he was a Confederate officer, he opened his house to Union Admiral David C. Farragut when the latter took New Orleans. Hunt supported the Reconstruction policies and constitutional amendments, and his cases centered on interpretation of the Fourteenth Amendment. He entered Louisiana Republican politics in the early 1870s when he provided counsel to Governor William P. Kellogg, and became state attorney general in 1876. When the Republicans were removed from state offices, Hunt became associate justice of the federal Court of Claims. President James A. Garfield named Hunt secretary of the navy in 1881, in part because he was a southerner. Hunt believed the United States needed vessels to protect its citizens and growing trade interests abroad. To create a stronger fleet, he convened a naval advisory board that included Rear Admiral John Rogers. The Rogers board advocated building sixty-eight ships and replacing wood and iron vessels with those of steel. When Garfield died, Hunt accepted the post of minister to russia to avoid serving a Stalwart Republican president. In Russia he fought against anti-Semitism. He died in St. Petersburg, Russia.

Further Reading: Walter Herrick, *American Secretaries of the Navy,* vol., *1775–1913,* ed. Paolo Coletta, 1980; Justus Doenecke, *The Presidencies of James A. Garfield and Chester Arthur,* 1981.

Bryan Craig

HUNTINGTON, COLLIS POTTER (22 October 1821–13 August 1900), financier and railroad magnate. Born at Harwinton, Connecticut, Huntington moved in the early 1850s to California, where he helped launch the state Republican Party in 1856. A planner and policy maker, Huntington raised capital and cultivated political connections to achieve his goal of building the Central Pacific Railroad eastward. Prior to completing the Central Pacific and acquiring the Chesapeake and Ohio Railroad, he purchased some twenty-three railroads in California. His vast fortune, influence, and lobbying techniques could, on occasion, delay legislation detrimental to his business activities even when Congress investigated his dealings. By the time he died at Pine Know Lodge on Raquette Lake in New York State, Huntington had demonstrated the life of self-development in Gilded Age America, leaving a railroad network that shortened distances and unified the western and eastern states.

Further Reading: *New York Times*, 15, 17, and 18 August 1900; David Lavender, *The Great Persuader*, 1970.

Leonard Schlup

IMMIGRATION. The rejection by the British government of colonial demands for a more open immigration policy was one of the causes of the American Revolution. The Declaration of Independence charged King George III with attempting to keep the colonies depopulated, refusing to recognize naturalization acts passed by colonial assemblies, and restricting the westward movement of settlements. The framers of the U.S. Constitution made the foreign born ineligible for only one office in the federal government, that of president.

In 1790, Congress passed the first federal laws that loosely defined a uniform rule for the naturalization of immigrants: any fully white person who resided for two years within the limits and under the jurisdiction of the United States was eligible. In 1801, Congress changed the residency requirement to five years, where it remains today. The federal government kept no official records of immigration until 1820, and it was not until 1850 that the Census Bureau distinguished between foreign- and native-born citizens. In 1864, Congress established the Bureau of Immigration.

Between 1820 and 1993, 60.7 million immigrants came to the United States. In the period before the Civil War, the large majority of the immigrants, over 80 percent, were from northern and western Europe. Except for the French and Irish, many were Protestant and most were farmers. The great change came between 1880 and World War I, when the large majority of immigrants came from southern and eastern Europe and most were Catholics or Jews. (Since the 1960s, most immigrants have been from western hemisphere countries, and since the 1980s, from the Philippines, Korea, and China.)

In 1875, Congress enacted the first federal statute to regulate immigration by preventing entry by criminals and prostitutes. The period from 1880 to the mid-1960s has been characterized as the "restrictionist era" in immigration policy. Beginning with the Chinese Exclusion Act of 1882, Congress actively administered and controlled immigration. This law suspended entry of Chinese workers for ten years, and barred all foreign-born Chinese from acquiring citizenship. For the first time, a national group was excluded from the United States.

In 1917, over a presidential veto, the Immigration Act of 1917 was passed, requiring immigrants over age sixteen to prove they could read and write in some language. Those who could not meet that requirement were sent back. This same statute also barred Asiatics (defined as persons from India, Indochina, Afghanistan, Arabia, and East India) from entry. The ban had nothing to do with literacy, but it was nevertheless added.

The Immigration Act of 1921, also known as the Quota Act or the Johnson Act, introduced a system of national quotas. The quota was determined as a percentage of the number of immigrants from the country in question at the time of a designated national census. The annual number of immigrants allowed from each nation was set at 3 percent of the foreign-born of that nationality, as recorded in the 1910 census. The 1921 law also set an annual limit of 350,000 on all European immigration, and set quotas for countries in the Near East and Africa, as well as Australia and New Zealand. No quotas were imposed on immigrants from nations in the western hemisphere. In 1924, the year the 1921 Quota Act expired, and Congress passed the harsher National Quota (Johnson-Reed) Act, which set quotas at 2 percent of the foreign-born from a given nation in the 1890 census. The new statute also provided that, beginning in 1927, the overall European quota limit would be 150,000, proportioned by the distribution of the foreign-born in the 1920 census.

In 1990, Congress passed the most liberal immigration bill since the Quota Act of 1921. The Immigration Act of 1990 set the overall annual quota at 700,000 for the period 1992–1994, and a permanent annual level of 675,000 immigrants beginning in 1995. It established a three-track preference system for family-sponsored, employment-based, and diversity immigrants. (Diversity immigrants are persons from countries with low sending rates.) Of the 675,000 visas, 480,000 are allocated on the basis of family preference criteria.

Further Reading: Roger Daniels, *Coming to America: A History of Immigration and Ethnicity in American Life*, 1990; Robert E. Long, ed., *Immigration to the United States*, 1992; Leonard Dinnerstein and David M. Reimers, *Ethnic Americans: A History of Immigration*, 4th ed., 1999.

Rita J. Simon

IMMIGRATION RESTRICTION LEAGUE.

Founded in 1894 by Charles Warren, Robert deCourcy Ward, and Prescott Farnsworth Hall, all Boston Brahmins of the Harvard class of 1889, the Immigration Restriction League sought to save the United States from infiltration by the "new" immigrants from southern and eastern Europe who began arriving in the United States in great numbers in the 1880s. Within a year of its founding the League had established branches throughout the country. Over the period of its existence until the 1930s, it included as its spokespersons leading intellectuals, business executives, and representatives of the craft unions. The presidents of Harvard (A. Lawrence Lowell) and Stanford (David Starr Jordan) were actively involved, as were the social scientists John R. Commons, Edward A. Ross, and Franklin Giddings. The publisher Henry Holt, Senator Henry Cabot Lodge of Massachusetts, Immigration Commissioner Francis Walker, and, in 1909, Madison Grant, author of *The Passing of the Great Race in America* (1916), became some of the League's strongest proponents.

At its founding, the League asked the American public whether they wanted their country to be peopled by British, German, and Scandinavian stock, who were historically free, energetic, and progressive, or by Slavs, Latins, and Asiatics, races who were historically downtrodden, atavistic, and stagnant. Francis Walker called them "beaten men from beaten races." In addition to advocating sharp restrictions on the "new" immigrants, the League joined with groups that supported literacy requirements and eugenic testing for admission to the United States. In the 1920s, the League adopted explicit racist language and ideology that supported the preservation of the "Teutonic" race. It spread its message in university classrooms, settlement houses, meetings of business and labor union leaders, Congressional hearings, and thousands of newspapers and magazines all over the country.

Further Reading: Alan M. Kraut, *The Huddled Masses: The Immigrant in American Society, 1880–1921*, 1982; John Higham, *Strangers in the Land: Patterns of American Nativism, 1860–1925*, 1955.

Rita J. Simon

IMPERIALISM.

Imperialism exists when a stronger nation or group attempts to impose control over weaker peoples. This control may be formal (via annexation, protectorate, or military occupation) or informal (via economic control, cultural domination, or threat of intervention). Official political or military personnel normally administer formal empire. Informal imperialism may result from the actions of businesses, missionaries, teachers, or other nonstate actors. The United States practiced both formal and informal imperialism during the Gilded Age. The most commonly noted instances of formal imperialism occurred in association with the Spanish-Cuban-American-Filipino War. After ostensibly going to war to free Cuba from Spanish control, the United States annexed a wide-ranging island empire. Hawaii, Puerto Rico, and the Philippines were acquired formally between August 1898 and February 1899. Little or no direct military force was utilized in Hawaii or Puerto Rico, but three years of brutal guerrilla fighting was required to subdue Filipino resistance. In addition to seizing these official colonies, the United States imposed a protectorate on Cuba.

These acts of imperial domination were not unprecedented cases of the United States' imposing itself militarily and culturally on weaker, nonwhite peoples during the Gilded Age. Indeed, the final military suppression of the Sioux on the Great Plains and the Apache in the Southwest constituted a clear precedent for turn-of-the-century actions. A decisive power advantage and accompanying assumptions of racial superiority characterized U.S. actions in these cases. U.S. interactions with Native Americans also provide insights into the process of informal and cultural imperialism. Once they were confined to reservations, Native Americans were pressured to adopt American agriculture, religion, language, and dress—in short, American culture. White reservation officials exerted much of this pressure, but missionaries and teachers were also prominent purveyors. By pressing for a superior American way—be it capitalism, Christianity, or Western medical practices—U.S. representatives sought to remake cultures in Cuba, the Philippines, China, Latin America, Asia, and Africa.

A variety of motives prompted U.S. imperialism. Policy makers acted to protect U.S. security; business and political leaders pursued export markets; missionaries believed they were doing God's will; and other expansionists viewed the challenges of imperial administration as a way to strengthen the moral fiber of American society. Although idealistic and cynical motives were not mutually exclusive, the assumptions of racial and cultural superiority that underpinned them were ethnocentric and patronizing, and the actions themselves elicited hostile, nationalistic responses from the peoples at whom they were directed. In view of U.S. motives, imperial institutions, and outcomes, imperialism American style was not particularly innocent or unique.

Further Reading: Edward P. Crapol, "Coming to Terms with Empire: The Historiograhy of Late Nineteenth-Century American Foreign Relations," in Michael J. Hogan, ed., *Paths to Power: The Historiography of American Foreign Relations to 1941* (2000), 79–116; Joseph A. Fry, "Phases of Empire: Late Nineteenth-Century U.S. Foreign Relations," in Charles W. Calhoun, ed., *The Gilded Age: Essays in the Origins of Modern America* (1996), 261–288.

Joseph A. Fry

INCOME TAX. Congress enacted a tax on personal incomes in 1861 as a temporary measure to help finance the Civil War, and repealed it following the conflict's end. The depression of the 1890s brought the first government deficits since the war and presented a need for increased tax receipts. The duties imposed by the Wilson-Gorman Tariff of 1894 promised to compound the problem because certain items that had generated large revenues were placed on the free list. Others carried such high duties that imports would be excluded from the domestic market, further reducing receipts. Congress responded by amending the tariff bill to include an income tax provision, graduating upward from an annual levy of 2 percent on incomes of $4,000. The Supreme Court struck down the tax the following year in *Pollock* v. *Farmers' Loan and Trust Co.* (157 U.S. 429, 158 U.S. 601). Not until ratification of the Sixteenth Amendment in 1913 did the federal government gain clear authority to tax incomes.

Further Reading: R. G. Blakey and G. C. Blakey, *The Federal Income Tax*, 1940; Robert Stanley, *Dimensions of Law in the Service of Order: Origins of the Federal Income Tax, 1861–1913*, 1993; Charles Vuille Stewart, "The Formation of Tax Policy in America, 1893–1913," Ph.D. diss., University of North Carolina at Chapel Hill, 1974.

Douglas Steeples

INDUSTRIALIZATION. The Gilded Age's industrialization can best be characterized as a transformation of scale—an immense growth in wealth and status for many and a corresponding increase in poverty and disenfranchisement for many more. The World's Columbian Exposition, held at Chicago in 1893, celebrated the triumphs of modern technology. It did not, however, address the economic exploitation of persons, resources, and land.

The Civil War created a seemingly insatiable demand for goods and evolving technology. Following post-Reconstruction economic troubles (including a recession and a railroad strike in 1877), the nation found itself enjoying unmatched prosperity as the economy turned from a focus on subsistence level to one on "capital" goods that added to consumption and growth. At the beginning of the Gilded Age, the United States became a net exporter for the first time. By 1890, the nation led the world in iron and steel production. New industries and techniques fueled a national process of growth and expansion. A catalyst of this growth, and of much social change as well, was the railroad. Its demand for rails revolutionized the steel industry. It also transformed the nation by creating time zones in 1883, in order to increase efficiency.

This was merely one feature of a standardization process, which by 1890 included a common gauge for width on the nation's 160,000 miles of track. Improved agricultural techniques allowed fewer people to provide more food to a growing nonagricultural population. By 1887, for the first time, farmers were no longer the majority of the American people. Surplus populations gravitated to urban areas, leading to even more development and production.

New and more efficient corporate structures, such as vertical integration, increased capital availability, produced goods more cheaply and efficiently. New marketing and sales processes also emerged, including direct catalog and mail-order sales, pioneered by Montgomery Ward in 1872. Wanamakers in Philadelphia became the first fully integrated department store in 1876. In response to the increasing power and growth of corporations, the Knights of Labor and the American Federation of Labor emerged and grew to prominence during this period. The era was also marked by extreme, violent disputes between labor and management. The famous Homestead Strike in Pennsylvania in 1892 ended in a pitched battle between workers and management-hired Pinkerton guards. Indeed, industrialization transformed the workforce's very nature. Women became one quarter of the working population by 1900. Immigrants also composed a higher percentage of the workforce and were a noticeable presence in urban areas.

Further Reading: Nell Irvin Painter, *Standing at Armageddon: The United States, 1877–1919*, 1987; Robert Weibe, *The Search for Order, 1877–1920*, 1967.

Jerome D. Bowers II

INGALLS, JOHN JAMES (29 December 1833–16 August 1900), senator. Born in Middleton, Massachusetts, Ingalls was graduated in 1855 from Williams College and opened a law practice in Atchison, Kansas, in 1860. In 1872 he ran for the U.S. Senate as a Republican, but trailed until bribery charges damaged his opponent. During three terms he solidified his ties with other Republicans by denouncing southern Democrats for having left the Union during the Civil War. In his final term he rose to be president pro tempore of the Senate. As the 1890 election approached, Ingalls surprised colleagues by supporting the Farmers' Alliance in its call for a graduated income tax, direct election of senators, female suffrage, and unlimited coinage of silver. This agrarian radicalism, from a figure who had never before advocated reform, neither brought farmers to his side nor divided his opponents, and Ingalls lost the election. He retired to Las Vegas, New Mexico, where he wrote articles for magazines and newspapers and worked to compiled his family's genealogy. He died in Las Vegas and was buried in Atchison, Kansas, where the town council erected a statue in his honor.

Further Reading: Charles Burleigh, *The Genealogy and History of the Ingalls Family in America*, 1903; *Topeka Daily Capital*, 17 August 1900.

Christopher Cumo

INGERSOLL, ROBERT GREEN (11 August 1833–21 July 1899), lawyer and lecturer. Born in Dresden, New York, Ingersoll gained fame as "the agnostic" who gave witty and critical lectures on Christianity's errors and contradictions. A Democrat-turned-Republican by the Civil War, he gained recognition in 1876 as a delegate to the party's national convention, where he gave the presidential nominating speech for James G. Blaine. Blaine lost the nomination, but won an immortal nickname when Ingersoll dubbed him the "plumed knight." The speech marked Ingersoll as one of America's greatest orators. He worked as a litigation lawyer in government cases, but he was in constant demand to debunk religion with lectures such as "Some Mistakes of Moses" and "Why I Am an Agnostic."

Further Reading: Orvin P. Larson, *American Infidel: Robert G. Ingersoll, A Biography*, 1962; Frank Smith, *Robert G. Ingersoll: A Life*, 1990; *New York Times*, 22 July 1899.

Norman Fry

IN RE DEBS, 158 U.S. 564 (1895). The Supreme Court unanimously upheld a federal injunction against obstruction of interstate mail shipments during the Pullman Strike of 1894. Eugene V. Debs and other American Railway Union leaders had been found guilty of contempt of court for disregarding the injunction. They petitioned for writ of habeas corpus to challenge their custody. Justice David J.

Brewer's opinion denied the writ, and upheld broad federal power to remove obstructions to interstate commerce and mail transportation. The Constitution, Brewer reasoned, conferred on the federal government plenary powers over interstate commerce and the mail; Congress had exercised them. Although the Court did not cite a statute authorizing an injunction, it held that the executive could remove obstructions to mail delivery by force or through the courts. The decision reflected a broader vision of the utility of injunctions. Although criticized as reflecting a bias toward propertied classes and as inconsistent with *United States* v. *E. C. Knight Company* (1895), such explanations oversimplify distinctions between the two and the different doctrines involved.

Further Reading: James W. Ely, Jr., *The Chief Justiceship of Melville W. Fuller, 1888–1910*, 1995; John R. Schmidhauser, *The Supreme Court as Final Arbiter in Federal-State Relations, 1789–1957*, 1958; David P. Currie, "The Constitution in the Supreme Court: The Protection of Economic Interests, 1889–1910," *University of Chicago Law Review* 52 (1985): 324–388.

Joel K. Goldstein

INSULAR CASES. These cases concerned Congress's powers to impose tariffs over newly acquired territories following the Spanish-American War. The cases involved the Constitution's uniformity clause, which stipulates uniformity of application of all federal taxes and duties throughout the United States. The clause also restricts the federal government's taxing of items exported from any particular state. If this were interpreted to mean that no tariffs could be imposed on the territories, it might well have spelled a quick end to imperialist designs, for free trade between the territories and the United States was feared as a path to bankruptcy of American farmers.

DeLima v. *Bidwell* (182 U.S. 1 1901). This case concerned whether the territories acquired in the Spanish-American War could continue to be considered "foreign," and thus subject to the Dingley Tariff, after being formally ceded by Spain. In 1901 the court ruled 5–4, with Justice Henry B. Brown writing for the majority, that Puerto Rico and the other territories (primarily the Philippines) could not be considered foreign

after being ceded, and therefore were not subject to the Dingley Tariff. Dissenting justices were Joseph McKenna, George Shiras, Jr., Edward D. White, and Horace Gray.

Downes v. *Bidwell* (182 U.S. 244 1901). In 1900, Congress passed the Foraker Act, which provided a tariff for goods traded between the United States and its territory of Puerto Rico, pegging the rate at 15 percent of the amount levied against similar articles imported from foreign countries. The issue was whether Congress could administer the territories in a manner different from both its relations with foreign powers and its relationship to the states. Writing for a 5–4 majority, Justice Brown defended the legality of the Foraker Act. He distinguished between limitations of the Constitution and placement of the flag on territories, stating that the Constitution did not extend to the territories until so determined by Congress. Brown favored giving Congress the latitude to acquire and administer territory in building the American empire. His opinion went against the legal principles of the *Dred Scott* case, in which Congress was restricted from selectively admitting territories as states on the demand that they not legalize slavery. Dissenting in this case were Chief Justice Melville Weston Fuller and justices John Marshall Harlan, David Josiah Brewer, and Rufus W. Peckham.

Dooley v. *United States* (182 U.S. 222). Also involving the legality of the Foraker Act, this case concerned whether the law violated the export clause. As in *Downes* v. *Bidwell,* Justice Brown wrote for the 5–4 majority in 1901 that the export clause was not violated, and upheld the lower tariff on goods imported from Puerto Rico. Dissenting, as in *DeLima* v. *Bidwell*, were justices White, Gray, Shiras, and McKenna.

Further Reading: Owen M. Fiss, *History of the Supreme Court of the United States,* vol. 8, *Troubled Beginnings of the Modern State, 1888–1910*, 1993, 234–251; *U.S. Reports* 182 U.S. 1.

Thomas C. Sutton

INTERNATIONAL BIMETALLISM. A debate over the merits of bimetallism took place in the United States from 1873 to 1896. During its early years, the nation had used gold and silver coins as legal tender, but a high price of silver relative to the official rate kept silver coins out of circulation after the 1830s. In 1862, under the duress of fighting the Civil War, the federal government switched to paper money. It returned to the gold standard in 1873 and to bimetallism in 1878, with the coining of silver in limited amounts. Adherents of bimetallism fell into three groups. Silver producers wanted a market for their product. Inflationists expected silver coins to expand the money supply. International bimetallists believed a fixed rate of exchange between gold and silver would simplify trade between countries on the gold standard and countries on the silver standard. They argued that if all countries adopted bimetallism, the exchange rate would remain stable within acceptable limits. Francis A. Walker, president of the Massachusetts Institute of Technology and a prominent economist, led the fight for international bimetallism. World conferences in 1878, 1881, and 1892 failed to agree on a bimetallic international monetary system. As a result, European nations gradually moved to a monetary system based on gold alone. Bimetallic advocacy in the United States culminated with William Jennings Bryan's unsuccessful 1896 presidential campaign. America adopted a gold standard in 1900.

Further Reading: Francis A. Walker, *International Bimetallism*, 1897.

Donald R. Stabile

INTERNATIONAL MONETARY CONFERENCE OF 1878.

By an act of 28 February 1878, the U.S. Congress invited the nations of Europe to an international monetary conference, to be held in Paris on 10–20 August. America sought an agreement establishing gold and silver as the basis for the international monetary system and to fix for all countries a rate of exchange between the two metals. At the time, European nations followed the gold standard or the silver standard, or used both metals as money. Because the relative value of gold and silver fluctuated, countries engaged in international trade had an interest in establishing a uniform monetary system. England had long followed the gold standard, but used silver in its Asian colonies. An international monetary conference in 1867 had created a union among France, Belgium, Italy, and Switzerland based on the gold standard. Germany had converted from silver to gold in 1871. The United States strongly favored bimetallism at this time, and fear that gold might become the international monetary standard motivated the call for the conference. In Paris, however, participants could agree only that each country should be free to set its own monetary standard.

Further Reading: *Proceedings, the International Monetary Conference of 1878,* 1879.

Donald R. Stabile

INTERNATIONAL MONETARY CONFERENCE OF 1881.

After the International Monetary Conference of 1878 refused to accept bimetallism as the basis for the international monetary system, France and the United States invited the governments of Europe to another conference. It was held in Paris for thirteen sessions from 19 April to 8 July 1881. Its purpose was to reconsider establishing an international bimetallic monetary system. The United States proposed that bimetallism in international trade be established through an agreement that all countries would permit the free coinage of gold and silver in coins of uniform weight, with a fixed ratio in value between gold and silver. At the time, America adhered to bimetallism. Because foreign trade kept draining its gold reserves, the U.S. government wanted to make international settlements with both silver and gold. Bimetallism would work only if all countries agreed to follow it. England and Germany were committed to the gold standard, however, and the conference adjourned without taking action. Another international monetary conference to promote international bimetallism was held in Belgium in 1892, but it, too, ended without an agreement. America officially adopted the gold standard in 1900.

Further Reading: *Proceedings, the International Monetary Conference of 1881,* 1887.

Donald R. Stabile

INTERSTATE COMMERCE ACT OF 1887.

Gilded Age farmers accused railroads of price discrimination and giving rebates to industrialists but not to farmers. During the

1870s, they convinced five states to create commissions to regulate railroads, but these commissions did little. To make matters worse, the Supreme Court ruled in *Wabash, St. Louis, and Pacific Railroad Co.* v. *Illinois* (1886) that they had usurped a power of Congress. State regulatory failure prompted the National Grange to campaign for federal control. In 1887 Congress passed the Interstate Commerce Act, which outlawed pools, rebates, and the practice of charging less per mile for a long haul than for a short one. It required shippers to publish rate schedules and charge fairly. It created a commission to supervise the industry, but left enforcement to the courts, whose conservative judges sided with shippers rather than farmers. In 1897 the Supreme Court, in the *Maximum Freight Rate* case, forbade the Interstate Commerce Commission to set rates, and in the *Midlands* case, it permitted shippers to offer discounts on long hauls. The commission's weakness led the People's Party in 1892 to urge Congress to nationalize the railroads. The party's demise after 1896 left the problem for twentieth-century Progressives.

Further Reading: Gabriel Kolko, *Railroads and Regulation, 1877–1916*, 1965; Richard D. Stone, *The Interstate Commerce Commission and the Railroad Industry* 1991; Joshua Bernhardt, *The Interstate Commerce Commission*, 1989.

Christopher Cumo

ISTHMIAN CANAL. A passage connecting the Atlantic and Pacific oceans had long been a seafarer's dream. Two obstacles to its construction by the United States vanished when a French canal company, licensed by Colombia, collapsed in 1889, and when the Hay-Pauncefote Treaty of 1901 abrogated British rights to a joint canal venture, previously provided for in the Clayton-Bulwer Treaty (1850). Nicaragua and Panama, then a Colombian province, provided feasible routes. When Theodore Roosevelt's canal terms proved unsatisfactory to Colombia, a rebellion erupted in November 1903. American marines discouraged reestablishment of Colombian authority, and prompt recognition of the Republic of Panama cleared the way for Roosevelt to negotiate with the new nation. By the Hay–Bunau-Varilla Convention of 1904, the United States agreed to pay Panama $10 million and an annual rental fee of $250,000 in exchange for a ninety-nine-year lease on a ten-mile-wide canal zone. The canal, completed in 1914 despite yellow fever outbreaks and difficult terrain, was one of the great engineering feats of the age. To Roosevelt's fury, Woodrow Wilson later paid Colombia $25 million in what some considered "conscience money." The United States, after intense debate, finally relinquished control in a treaty with Panama negotiated under President Jimmy Carter in 1977.

Further Reading: David McCullogh, *The Path Between the Seas: The Creation of the Panama Canal, 1870–1914*, 1977; Gerstle Mack, *The Land Divided: A History of the Panama Canal and Other Isthmian Canal Projects*, 1944.

Mario R. DiNunzio

JACKSON, HOWELL ED-MUNDS (8 April 1832–9 August 1895), U.S. senator, appellate court judge, Supreme Court associate justice. Born in Paris, Tennessee, Jackson was graduated from the Cumberland School of Law then opened a practice in 1856. He served Confederacy and subsequently was pardoned by President Andrew Johnson. Jackson later became an arbitration court judge. He lost a state supreme court election in 1878, but was sent to the legislature two years later. His opposition to debt repudiation helped secure his election to the U.S. Senate in 1881. There he supported the Blair Education Bill. Jackson's strong opposition to the Tenure of Office Act led Democratic President Grover Cleveland to appoint him to the Sixth Circuit Court of Appeals in 1886. Jackson's 1892 decision in *In re Greene* later served as the legal foundation for the Supreme Court's 1895 ruling in *United States* v. *E.C. Knight Company*, which all but nullified the Sherman Antitrust Act. Jackson's 1893 ruling in *United States* v. *Patrick*, upholding the conviction of three Tennesseeans charged with violating the Civil Rights Act, hastened his appointment to the Supreme Court in that year. There he served just twenty-nine months. Jackson is frequently remembered for his deathbed dissent favoring a federal income tax in *Pollock* v. *Farmer's Loan and Trust Company*. He died near Nashville, Tennessee.
Further Reading: Harvey Gresham Hudspeth, "Forgotten Whig: The Life and Times of Howell Edmunds Jackson, 1832–1895," Ph.D. diss., University of Mississippi, 1994.

Harvey Gresham Hudspeth

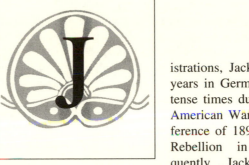

JACKSON, JOHN BRINCKERHOFF (19 August 1862–20 December 1920), diplomat. Born in Newark, New Jersey, Jackson graduated from the U.S. Naval Academy in 1883 and began the practice of law in 1889. The next year he commenced a long career in diplomatic service with an appointment by President Benjamin Harrison; later he received one from President Grover Cleveland. Under four administrations, Jackson spent twelve years in Germany that included tense times during the Spanish-American War, the Hague Conference of 1899, and the Boxer Rebellion in China. Subsequently Jackson served in Greece, Bulgaria, Persia, Cuba, and Romania. His long experience in Europe made his services valuable to the State Department and several presidents. Jackson died in Switzerland.
Further Reading: *New York Times*, 21 December 1920.

Leonard Schlup

JACKSON, SHELDON (18 May 1835–2 May 1909), missionary, educator, and Alaska advocate. Born and raised on a farm near Minaville, New York, Jackson "gave his life to Christ" during his boyhood. After graduation from Union College and Princeton Theological Seminary, he was ordained in 1858 by the Presbytery of Albany, New York. Because of his poor eyesight and extremely small stature, his church superiors dissuaded him from foreign missionary work. In 1859, after a one-year mission assignment to the Choctaw Indians, Jackson moved to Minnesota, and for the next ten years carried out various church organizational responsibilities in addition to his pastorate at Rochester, Minnesota (1864 to 1869). In 1869, eager for even greater Christian responsibilities, Jackson accepted appointment as superintendent of the Board of Domestic Missions (National or Home Board) in the Rocky Mountain District. From his Denver base, surrounded by the booming post–Civil War West, Jackson set about establishing Presbyterian churches in embryo towns extending from the Southwest to Montana.

The manner in which the self-styled "Rocky Mountain Superintendent" relentlessly drove himself—well publicized in his newspaper, the *Rocky Mountain Presbyterian*—astonished his east coast superiors. In 1877 their applause turned to perturbation when, without their approval, he steamed north to southeastern Alaska and established a Presbyterian mission at Wrangell. Within a few years he became the paramount spokesman for the vast territory. America's spreading net of transcontinental railroads and Pacific steamships greatly facilitated his missionary and educational endeavors. Working with Senator Benjamin Harrison, Jackson pushed through the Alaska Organic Act of 1884; his appointment as Alaska's general agent for education (stationed in Washington, D.C.) followed. Utilizing U.S. Revenue cutters, Jackson made annual inspection tours of the enormous District of Alaska, where he had scattered common schools for Native youth. All too familiar with whites' exploitation of Native Americans, Jackson labored to sequester their remarkable material culture. Shaken by liquor's devastating impact on Alaska's indigenous population, he vainly fought to keep the entire territory dry.

With the security of a civil service sinecure and widespread backing from the Friends of the Indians and Christian women, Jackson gave lectures and published opinions on Alaska's enormous potential that reached tens of thousands. His bitter feuds with two Alaska governors, John H. Kinkead and Alfred P. Swineford, revealed an unfortunate degree of self-righteousness. His mixture of religious funds with public money in his common schools incurred criticism—often quite unjustified. Jackson's introduction of the Siberian reindeer to augment the Eskimo food supply remains controversial, as does so much else about this amazingly peripatetic Christian educator. He died in Asheville, North Carolina.

Further Reading: Norman J. Bender, *Winning the West for Christ*, 1996; Ted C. Hinckley, *The Americanization of Alaska*, 1972; Robert L. Stewart, *Sheldon Jackson*, 1908.

Ted C. Hinckley

JAMES, HENRY JR. (15 April 1843–28 February 1916), novelist. Born in New York City, James was the son of the Swedenborgian theologian Henry James, Sr., and the brother of William James, philosopher and founder of pragmatism. Along with many other writers of his time, he criticized the crass materialism of industrial wealth during the Gilded Age. What sets him apart from his contemporaries, however, is that he spent most of his life in England. Thus his criticism of new American manners was focused on the encounter of the new "ugly Americans" with the culture of the Old World. *Roderick Hudson* (1876) and *Daisy Miller* (1879) portrayed the inability of Americans who had foresaken solid Puritan values for the new mores of industrialism to accommodate themselves to sophisticated Europe. James viewed the new American society as vulgar, devoid of beauty, and lacking an appreciation for history, obsessed with the new, no matter how superficial. Disenchanted with his own culture, he became a lifelong expatriate, and died in London, England. Nonetheless, he is widely considered to be one of America's greatest men of letters.

Further Reading: Leon Edel, *Henry James: A Life*, 1985; F. O. Matthiessen, *Henry James: The Major Phase*, 1963.

C. Edward Balog

JAMES, JESSE WOODSON (5 September 1847–April 1882), probably the most famous criminal in U.S. history. Born 5 September 1847 in Centerville, Missouri, Jesse James and his equally ruthless older brother, Frank, grew up amid the border warfare between free-state Kansans and pro-slavery Missourians. During the Civil War, the brothers participated in massacres of civilians; they robbed their first train in 1864. Unlike regular Confederate soldiers, guerrillas received no amnesty after the war, and returned home as outlaws. Frank, who had served briefly as a soldier in Ben McCulloch's Confederate army, turned himself in to the federals at Louisville, Kentucky, and was immediately paroled. Jesse, in a futile surrender attempt, was critically wounded by federal troops near Lexington, Missouri, in 1865, but escaped. A year later the Jameses joined the four Younger Brothers. Using guerrilla tactics of surprise and terror, they robbed banks and trains regularly, killing anyone who stood in their way. Missouri's governor, Thomas T. Crittenden, offered rewards of $5,000 each for Jesse and Frank. Their new comrade Bob Ford took up the offer. He killed Jesse in St. Joseph, Missouri. Six months later, Frank turned himself in to Governor Crittenden. Tried three times, once for murder and twice for armed robbery, he was acquitted each time. He lived thirty-three years longer, eventually giving guided tours. James was murdered by Robert and Charles Ford in St. Joseph, Missouri.

Further Reading: Duane Schultz, *Quantrill's War: The Life and Times of William Clarke Quantrill*, 1996; William A. Settle, Jr., *Jesse James Was His Name*, 1966; T. J. Stiles, *Jesse James*, 1994.

Maurice Law Costello

JAMES, WILLIAM (11 January 1842–26 August 1910), philosopher, psychologist, founder of pragmatism. Born in New York City, James was the son of Henry James, Sr., a Swedenborgian theologian, and brother of the novelist Henry James, Jr. He was drawn to science and studied medicine at Harvard, receiving his M.D. in 1869. Soon after becoming an instructor in anatomy and physiology there in 1873, he moved to the new fields of psychology and, eventually, to philosophy. James departed from late nineteenth-century Darwinian determinism in his conviction that free will and consciousness contributed to the functioning of the mind. This view of thought as a process led to his famous lecture delivered in 1897 ("Philosophical Conceptions and Practical Results"), in which he identified his point of view as pragmatism. He acknowledged his connection to Charles Sanders Peirce, but Peirce pointedly separated himself from James's individualistic form of pragmatism in favor of his own version, which pursued collective habits of behavior that Peirce henceforth termed "pragmaticism." For James the mind was a teleological instrument creating ideas whose validity would be judged by their concrete results. If the results created a satisfactory relationship with reality, then they were true. An idea was a hypothesis to be tested in the laboratory of everyday experience. Thus, the search for truth was a dynamic process in which an idea was made true by its consequences (i.e., by events). Pragmatism still claims a solid core of support in the American philosophical community. James died in Chocorua, New Hampshire.

Further Reading: A. J. Ayer, *The Origins of Pragmatism: Studies in the Philosophy of Charles Sanders Peirce and William James*, 1968; William James Papers, Houghton Library, Harvard University.

C. Edward Balog

JAMESON, JOHN FRANKLIN (19 September 1859–28 September 1937), historian. A native of Somerville, Massachusetts, Jameson was graduated from Amherst College in 1879 and received the Ph.D. in history from Johns Hopkins University in 1882. He remained at Hopkins for six years as a faculty member, then taught at Brown University from 1888 to 1901. Jameson took special interest in younger members of the profession, encouraging and guiding their scholarship and compiling lists of doctoral dissertations in progress. He also wrote *The History of Historical Writing* (1891).

Jameson helped found the American Historical Association (AHA) and its publication, the *American Historical Review*, the primary vehicle for expanding scholarship in the field. He served as the *Review*'s managing editor from 1895 to 1901. Jameson proposed a program for the systematic collection, organization, and publication of source materials. He chaired the Historical Records Commission, and edited the letters of Phineas Bond, Stephen Higginson, and John C. Calhoun. In 1899 the AHA established a public archives commission, and in 1901 called for a national hall of records. Thereafter, Jameson concentrated on developing federal and state government archives. He died in Washington, D.C.

Further Reading: Victor Gondos, Jr., *J. Franklin Jameson and the Birth of the National Archives, 1906–1926*, 1981; "John Franklin Jameson," *American Historical Review* 43 (1938): 243–252; Morey David Rothberg, "Servant to History: A Study of John Franklin Jameson, 1859–1937," Ph.D. diss., Brown University, 1982.

Mary Ann Blochowiak

JEFFERSON, JOSEPH III (20 February 1829–23 April 1905), actor. Born in Philadelphia, Pennsylvania, Jefferson began acting early in life, joined various stock companies, and journeyed to Europe, Australia, and South America to observe theatrical performers. Although he played numerous roles in theaters across the United States, Jefferson gained national attention and widespread popularity for his portrayal of the title role in the stage version of Washington Irving's *Rip Van Winkle*. His success was immediate, a magical blend of personality and portrayal. Jefferson began performing the part in September 1866, at New

York City's Olympic Theater. He played Rip almost exclusively for the next fifteen years while touring the country extensively. These productions turned Jefferson into an institution; he epitomized the best of the American theater of his day. The critic William Winter commented in 1892 that Jefferson was the Gilded Age's most beloved actor. Jefferson enjoyed a patrician lifestyle and owned estates in Buzzards Bay, Massachusetts, Palm Beach, Florida, and New Iberia, Louisiana. President Grover Cleveland was his neighbor and fishing companion at Buzzards Bay. Jefferson's acting career, which spanned seven decades, ended in 1904. He died in Palm Beach, Florida.

Further Reading: Joseph Jefferson, *The Autobiography of Joseph Jefferson*, 1890; William Winter, *Life and Art of Joseph Jefferson*, 1893.

Leonard Schlup

JENNEY, WILLIAM LE BARON (25 September 1832–15 June 1907), architect. The October 1871 fire that destroyed Chicago, where most of the buildings were wooden, lured many of the most innovative architects. They made the city the Gilded Age's architectural capital, birthplace of the skyscraper, and home of the "Chicago School." William Le Baron Jenney, who built the world's first skyscraper in 1883–1884, was a key figure in all three developments. Jenney was born in Fairhaven, Massachusetts, and graduated from Phillips Academy in Andover. He sailed around the world before entering the Harvard Engineering School. Further study in Europe led Jennny to embrace the French classical tradition. During the Civil War, he served with the Army Corps of Engineers. Jenney designed churches and residential and commercial buildings. In his domestic and noncommercial design, he preferred the Gothic Revival style in the 1860s and 1870s, then in the 1880s adopted the Romanesque Revival. He received greatest acclaim for inventing the revolutionary steel and wrought-iron skeleton frame method of construction, which permitted him to erect tall buildings while increasing space and light. Jenney trained talented architects, including Louis Sullivan. He died in Los Angeles.

Further Reading: Carl W. Condit, *The Rise of the Skyscraper*, 1952; William Le Baron Jenney, *Principles and Practice of Architecture*, 1869; Theodore Turak, "William Le Baron Jenney: A Nineteenth Century Architect," Ph.D. diss., University of Michigan, Ann Arbor, 1966.

Charles W. Macune, Jr.

JIM CROW LAWS. The term "Jim Crow," perhaps coined by the minstrel performer Thomas Rice, symbolized the legal segregation of African Americans after the Civil War. Though laws requiring racial segregation had appeared in the South as early as 1868, it was not until the mid-1880s that a systematic separation of the races was in place. By then most southern states prohibited blacks from sharing public facilities, including trains, streetcars, steamboats, hotels, restaurants, barbershops, beauty parlors, and theaters. The 1896 Supreme Court decision in *Plessy* v. *Ferguson* upheld this system of "separate but equal," and made Jim Crow the law of the land. Essentially the laws showed in a public manner the inferior position of African Americans in American society.

Further Reading: C. Vann Woodward, *The Strange Career of Jim Crow*, 1955, 3d ed., 1974; William L. Van DeBurg, *Slavery and Race in Popular Culture*, 1984.

Kelly McMichael Stott

JOHNSON, ANDREW (29 December 1808–31 July 1875), senator and president of the United States. Born in Raleigh, North Carolina, he never went to school and was apprenticed to a tailor when barely ten years old. After running away from his master, he settled in Greeneville, Tennessee, where he practiced his trade. After becoming councilman and mayor, in 1835 and 1839 he was elected to the state assembly as a Democrat. He served until 1841, when he entered the state senate. Elected in 1843 to the federal House of Representatives, Johnson served there until 1853. He became governor in 1853. He won a U.S. Senate seat in 1857, and remained loyal during the secession crisis, the only senator from a seceding state to do so. The Lincoln administration appointed him military governor of Tennessee in 1862.

Johnson was nominated and elected to the vice presidency on the National Union ticket in 1864; he became president following Lincoln's assassination. A former slave owner and racist, he favored the speedy restoration of the seceded states without onerous conditions. This conservative restoration, not Reconstruction, policy so affronted the Republican majority in Congress that in 1868 he was impeached, ostensibly for violating the Tenure of Office Act; he was acquitted by one vote. After unsuccessfully seeking the Democratic nomination for president in 1868, he returned to Tennessee in search of vindication. In 1869 Johnson failed in his quest for a Senate seat, suffered defeat again in 1872 in a race for congressman at large, and finally succeeded in securing reelection to the Senate in 1874. Considering that the Radical Rupublicans had never forgiven him and the former secessionists bitterly opposed him, this victory was most gratifying. In 1875 he entered the Senate, thirty-five members of which seven years earlier had voted to convict him. Sworn in at the special session of March 1875, Johnson delivered a slashing speech condemning President Ulysses Grant's interference in Louisiana, where General Philip Sheridan had ejected five elected assemblymen from their seats. Before the regular session of Congress convened, Johnson died near Carter's Station, Tennessee.

Further Reading: Hans L. Trefousse, *Andrew Johnson: A Biography*, 1989; Lately Thomas, *The First President Johnson*, 1968; Robert Winston, *Andrew Johnson, Plebeian and Patriot*, 1928.

Hans L. Trefousse

JOHNSON COUNTY WAR. The 1892 war or invasion of Johnson County, 250 miles north of Cheyenne, Wyoming, was one of the last western vigilante conflicts. Local cattle barons, already suffering from reduced profits because of speculation, overgrazing, and bad weather, felt increasingly threatened by cattle rustlers. Determined to end cattle thieving, forty-six vigilantes (calling themselves the Invaders or Regulators), led by Frank Wolcott and Frank H. Canton, prepared to invade Johnson County, then surprise and shoot down their primary suspects. The Invaders trapped and killed two men near Buffalo—Nate Champion and Nick Ray—before the locals were able to organize and form a posse. The U.S. Cavalry intervened to prevent further casualties. Following nine months of delays, the case against the Invaders was dismissed because prosecution proved too

expensive. The unsuccessful invasion polarized the state and became the major issue in the political campaign of 1892.

Further Reading: Asa S. Mercer, *The Banditti of the Plains*, 1894; Helena H. Smith, *War on Powder River*, 1966.

Kelly McMichael Stott

JOHNSON, ELIZA MCCARDLE (4 October 1810–15 January 1876), First Lady. Eliza McCardle was born in Leesburg, Tennessee. On 17 May 1827, she married Andrew Johnson in Warrensburg, Tennessee, and subsequently helped advance his education. During his political ascendancy, she remained in Greeneville, Tennessee, raising their five children. In April 1865, after Johnson became president of the United States, Eliza moved to Washington, D.C. During her time in the White House, she did not function as First Lady, leaving most of the work to her two daughters, Martha Johnson Patterson and Mary Johnson Stover. She spent most of her time in the upstairs living quarters, reading, doing needlework, and visiting with family and friends, behavior that led to speculation that she used illness to avoid the public eye. In March 1869, following the end of Andrew Johnson's presidential term, the family returned to Greene County, Tennessee, where they remained until their deaths.

Further Reading: Lewis L. Gould, ed., *American First Ladies: Their Lives and Their Legacy*, 1996; Betty Boyd Caroli, *First Ladies*, 1987; New York *Times*, 17 January 1876.

Terri Pedersen Summey

JOHNSON, SAMUEL WILLIAM (3 July 1830–21 July 1909), agricultural chemist. Born in Kingsboro, New York, Johnson moved during childhood to Watertown, where he was graduated from Lowville Academy. He completed his education by studying chemistry at Yale College and the University of Munich, but took no degree from either. His pietist upbringing motivated Johnson to choose a practical career as an agricultural chemist, which he launched in 1852 with several essays in *Country Gentleman*, a farm journal. Three years later he became professor of agricultural chemistry at Yale. There he demonstrated to farmers the value of chemistry by publishing fertilizer analyses which revealed that manufacturers often exaggerated the amount of nitrogen, phosphorus, and potassium in their products. In 1868 and 1870 he published *How Crops Grow* and *How Crops Feed*, respectively. These became standard agricultural textbooks during the Gilded Age and were translated into Russian, Swedish, Italian, Japanese, and German. In 1875 he helped found the Connecticut Agricultural Experiment Station, which he directed between 1877 and 1899, and in 1878 he became president of the American Chemical Society. After his retirement in 1900, Johnson remained in New Haven, where he died.

Further Reading: Margaret W. Rossiter, *The Emergence of Agricultural Science: Justus Liebig and the Americans, 1840–1880*, 1975; H. S. Klooster, "Liebig and His American Pupils," *Journal of Chemical Education* 33 (1956): 493–497.

Christopher Cumo

JOHNSTOWN FLOOD (31 May 1889). A storm began in Kansas and Nebraska on 28 May 1889. It moved eastward through Indiana, Kentucky, and Tennessee for two days. The U.S. Signal Service warned the mid-Atlantic states of threatening weather on 29 May. Johnstown, Pennsylvania, a company town of the Cambria Iron Works, had a population of ten thousand persons. Workers were mostly immigrants from Germany, Hungary, Italy, Poland, Russia, Sweden, and Wales. The Little Conemaugh and the Stony Creek rivers join to form the Conemaugh River. Johnstown stands on the flood plain at the junction of these two rivers, which drain 657 square miles. Town expansion narrowed the channels, and Johnstown experienced yearly floods.

On Friday, 31 May 1889, as the townspeople prepared for usual, expected high water, fourteen miles away men worked to shore up the South Fork Dam on Lake Conemaugh. The lake belonged to the South Fork Fishing and Hunting Club, of which Andrew Carnegie and Henry Clay Frick were members. The Signal Service estimated that eight inches of rain had fallen during the previous twenty-four hours. Shortly after 3 P.M., the dam buckled. At 4:07 P.M., a wall of water forty feet high and half a mile wide, weighing twenty million tons and possessing the force of Niagara Falls, hit Johnstown at forty miles per hour. In ten minutes the Johnstown Flood concluded its immediate devastation.

Victims numbered 2,209, 396 of them children under the age of ten; 777 were never identified. Ninety-nine entire families were among the victims. One body was found in Steubenville, Ohio. The flood destroyed 1,600 homes and 280 businesses, and damage was estimated at $17 million. More than one hundred newspapers and magazines sent reporters to the area. Eighteen foreign countries and the United States contributed more than $3 million in relief funds. On 5 June 1889, Clara Barton and the American Red Cross arrived in Johnstown to relieve their first major disaster.

Within five years, the town had recovered. Individuals filed suits against the South Fork Fishing and Hunting Club, but survivors received no awards from courts that judged the dam break was an act of God. Floods continued to inundate Johnstown for the next forty-seven years. Only after the loss of additional property and lives did flood prevention efforts prevail.

Further Reading: David McCullough, *The Johnstown Flood*, 1968; Richard O'Connor, *Johnstown: The Day the Dam Broke*, 1957; David Beale, *Through the Johnstown Flood: By a Survivor*, 1890.

Larry D. Griffin

JONES, JAMES KIMBROUGH (29 September 1839–1 June 1908), senator and Democratic Party chairman. Born in Marshall County, Mississippi, Jones moved with his father to Dallas County, Arkansas, in 1848. After serving in the Confederate Army, he returned to his plantation to farm, practiced law in Washington, Arkansas, and held a seat in the state senate from 1873 to 1879. Elected as a Democrat to the federal House of Representatives in 1880, Jones remained in the lower chamber for two terms, then moved to the U.S. Senate, where he served until 1903. He fought for tariff reform, opposed the Dingley Tariff of 1897, espoused the cause of free silver, attended the Memphis Convention in 1895, denounced imperialism, and sought to protect the rights of Native Americans. He chaired the Democratic National Committee in the presidential campaigns of 1896 and 1900. After being defeated for reelection in 1902, Jones practiced law in Washington, D.C., until his death there.

Further Reading: Leonard Schlup, "Senator James K. Jones and Presidential Politics in 1900," *Tamkang Journal of American Studies* 10 [1993]: 1–23; *Little Rock Gazette*, 2 June 1908; Farrar Newberry, *James K. Jones, the Plumed Knight of Arkansas*, 1913.

Leonard Schlup

JONES, JOHN PERCIVAL

JONES, JOHN PERCIVAL (27 January 1829–27 November 1912), U.S. senator. Born in Herefordshire, England, Jones grew up in Cleveland, Ohio. He moved in 1849 to California, where he held local offices. In 1867, Jones settled in Nevada and rapidly became superintendent of several mines. Investments in the Crown Point mine's stock made him a millionaire, allowing him to start a railroad from Santa Monica, California, to Salt Lake City, and to exert influence on Nevada's political life. Nevada legislators elected Jones, a Republican, to the U.S. Senate, where he served continuously 1873 to 1903. His career centered primarily on free silver and mining legislation, and he chaired a congressional monetary commission in 1876. In addition to silver coinage, he supported protective tariffs, favored antitrust legislation, and endorsed his party's foreign policy. In 1893, when President Grover Cleveland asked Congress to repeal the Sherman Silver Purchase Act, Jones participated in a filibuster. His speech filled more than 450 printed pages. Silverites immediately hailed it as a compendium on the subject. Almost religiously, Jones believed the white metal would remedy the nation's troubles. In 1894, he joined the Populists. Two years later he endorsed the fusion of Populists and Silver Republicans with Democrats under the leadership of the Democratic presidential nominee, William Jennings Bryan, and campaigned for the ticket. When the Gold Standard Act of 1900 closed the debate, Jones returned to the Republicans. He died in Los Angeles.

Further Reading: Leonard Schlup, "Nevada's Doctrinaire Senator: John P. Jones and the Politics of Silver in the Gilded Age," *Nevada Historical Society Quarterly* 36 (1993): 246–262; John P. Jones, *The Money Question*, 1894; *Los Angeles Times*, 28 November 1912.

Leonard Schlup

JONES, MARY HARRIS "MOTHER"

JONES, MARY HARRIS "MOTHER" (ca. 1 May 1830–30 November 1930), social activist and union organizer. Born in Cork, Ireland, Jones immigrated to Toronto, Canada, where she grew up as the daughter of a railroad laborer. After being graduated from normal school, she worked as a teacher in Michigan and then as a seamstress in Chicago until her shop was destroyed by the great fire of 1871. Her husband and four children died of yellow fever in 1867. Sympathetic to working-class immigrants, particularly coal miners, Jones joined forces with Terence Powderly and the Knights of Labor. She also was a member of the United Mine Workers (UMW) and a founder of the Industrial Workers of the World. In the early 1890s she met Eugene V. Debs and became a Socialist, contributing articles to the journal *Appeal to Reason*. In 1897, Jones participated in a strike called by the UMW and eventually became a union organizer, earning the sobriquet "the Miner's Angel." She ignored middle-class ideals of womanly behavior, regularly using her voice to excoriate modern capitalism. Frequently arrested, she persistently condemned Gilded Age industrialists as "robber barons," and labeled wage work as a new form of slavery.

Jones did not limit her activities to labor agitation, however. Living in the South and working in its textile mills, she became an outspoken critic of child labor, in 1903 leading an army of protesters to demand child protective legislation. Jones also supported women's empowerment, but distanced herself from the suffrage movement, declaring that legal rights would not advance the cause of working-class women. Before she died at Silver Spring, Maryland, she claimed to be one hundred years old.

Further Reading: Donna R. Gabaccia, "Mary Harris Jones: Immigrant and Labor Activist," in Ballard C. Campbell, ed., *The Human Tradition in the Gilded Age and Progressive Era*, 2000; Priscilla Long, *Mother Jones: Woman Organizer, and Her Relations with Miners' Wives, Working Women, and the Suffrage Movement*, 1976; Elliott

J. Gorn, *Mother Jones: The Most Hated Woman in America*, 2001.

Mary L. Kelley

JONES, MATILDA SISSIERETTA JOYNER (5 January 1868–24 June 1933), African-American singer. Born in Portsmouth, Virginia, Joyner studied at the Providence Academy of Music in Rhode Island and at the New England Conservatory in Boston. She married David R. Jones in 1883, and five years later she made her singing debut in New York City. Known as the "Black Patti" and "Madame Jones," she sang in concert, opera, and vaudeville halls in solo recitals or with groups, such as the Patrick Gilmore Band. On 15 July 1888 she became the first African-American singer to appear on stage at Wallack's Theatre in New York City. While singing in Europe, she observed that Europeans recognized the soul of a person instead of the color of skin.

Jones appeared at Madison Square Garden in 1892, sang for President Benjamin Harrison at the White House that year, entertained at Carnegie Concert Hall, and performed in 1893 at the World's Columbian Exposition in Chicago. Widely acclaimed as the premier African-American singer of her time, she possessed a remarkable soprano voice and a commanding presence. She formed her own company of singers who performed a mix of genres ranging from opera to ragtime as they toured the country. Performing almost exclusively for white audiences, Jones ceased working in the early twentieth century. She lived in penniless obscurity until her death in Providence, Rhode Island. Her success as a major black concert and theatrical pioneer on the American stage in the Gilded Age helped African Americans gain more acceptance as serious artists.

Further Reading: Willia E. Daughtry, *Sissieretta Jones: Profile of a Black Artist*, 1972.

Leonard Schlup

JONES, THOMAS GOODE (26 November 1844–28 April 1914), attorney, politician, and federal judge. Born in Macon, Georgia, Jones lived in Montgomery, Alabama, served in the Confederate Army, and was admitted to the Alabama bar. He established himself as an attorney for the Louisville and Nashville Railroad. A conservative Democrat, Jones won election in 1884 to the state legislature; two years later he was its speaker. Jones opposed the Farmers' Alliance and labor unions. In 1890, he became governor; most historians agree his reelection two years later was the result of stolen Black Belt ballots. No mere reactionary, Jones combined paternalism with due process. He sought to hold sheriffs accountable for lynchings, and opposed the convict-lease system, yet used troops to put down a coal strike in 1894. After leaving office, Jones sought to disfranchise blacks, but spoke against the "grandfather clause" employed in the Alabama constitution of 1901. Appointed in 1901 to the federal bench with Booker T. Washington's recommendation, Jones opposed peonage and racist contract labor laws, but he was criticized for his pro-railroad rulings. To the end, he defended both economic privilege and constitutionalism. Jones died in Montgomery, Alabama.

Further Reading: Brent Jude Aucoin, "Thomas Goode Jones, Redeemer and Reformer: The Racial Policies of a Conservative Democrat in Pursuit of a 'New' South," M.A. thesis, Miami University, 1993; Pete Daniel, *The Shadow of Slavery: Peonage in the South, 1901–1969*, 1973; William Warren Rogers, *The One-Gallused Rebellion: Agrarianism in Alabama, 1865–1896*, 1970.

Paul M. Pruitt, Jr.

JORDAN, DAVID STARR (19 January 1851–19 September 1931), university president and director of the World Peace Foundation. Born near Gainsville, New York, Jordan received degrees from Cornell University in 1872 and Indiana Medical College in 1875. He accepted a teaching position in natural history at Northwestern Christian University (now Butler University), where he used the scientific method to study social reform. Jordan moved to Indiana University in 1879, and was its president from 1885 to 1891. From 1891 to 1913, Jordan was Stanford University's first president. During his tenure, he challenged the belief that military conflict was a natural aspect of Darwinian selection. Deeply affected by his older brother's death in the Civil War, Jordan linked his scientific teachings to the peace crusade. In 1896, President Grover Cleveland appointed him head of the American division of a commission on the fur seal problem in the Bering Sea, and in 1898 he was one of the vice presidents of the Anti-Imperialist League. Upon retirement from Stanford, he headed the World Peace Foundation, founded by the textbook publisher Edward Ginn, and chaired the Emergency Peace Federation. He died in Stanford, California.

Further Reading: David Starr Jordan, *The Days of a Man*, 1922; Edward McNall Burns, *David Starr Jordan: Prophet of Freedom*, 1953; Luther William Spoehr, " 'Progress' Pilgrim: David Starr Jordan and the Circle of Reform, 1891–1931," Ph.D. diss., Stanford University, 1975.

Charles F. Howlett

JOURNALISM. The Civil War changed newspapers by showing that news mattered more than well-written opinion, and by introducing novel technologies for publishing the product. The Gilded Age was known for its development of sensationalism; such an approach to news writing and display emerged from the public's growing appetite for the latest information. The removal of editorials from the front page encouraged an industry standard of objectivity and a drive for readers and greater market share. Advertising revenue hastened the change from party-owned to private organs.

Although modesty marked the early attempts to professionalize journalism, by century's end, large urban dailies engaged in sometimes vicious circulation battles. What came to be called "yellow journalism" began as a feud by publishers William Randolph Hearst and Joseph Pulitzer over a comic strip character. The phrase captured not only early efforts at printing in color but also the sensational approaches that had come to market individual newspapers among many competitors in most urban centers. At the same time, the press in less populous areas learned lessons in developing readership loyalties. Frequently the inside pages, which contained feature material and advertising, were printed in advance, then completed with sufficient news to fill the front and back pages.

The degree to which a newspaper engaged in circulation battles or used prepackaged feature material reflected a profit calculation. The largest printing companies had already learned that a successful newspaper could be an avenue to both wealth and mass influence. Indeed, many publishers saw their products as stepping-stones to political power. When newspapers started printing separate sections, they began to resemble magazines. As some magazines became commentators on the political scene, they started to resemble newspapers. Sunday papers quickly transformed themselves into vehicles for the latest fiction. Realism surfaced in literary circles, and some realists were introduced to the form in newspapers and by writing the news.

By century's end, cheap postal rates made the mailing of publications feasible. Sensationalism and the development of illustrations gave cheap American magazines amazing vitality and quality.

Further Reading: Gerald J. Baldasty, *The Commercialization of News in the Nineteenth Century*, 1992; David T. Z. Mindich, *Just the Facts: How Objectivity Came to Define American Journalism*, 1998; William David Sloan et al., *The Media in America*, 1996.

Ann Mauger Colbert

JUDAISM. Judaism comprised two main population groups and divided into three organized religious bodies during the Gilded Age.

With roots in Western Europe, especially Germany, the first group was able increasingly to enter corporate life, amass wealth, wield political influence, and participate in philanthropy. Jewish communities were diffused across the American map by 1868, in the legacy of German Reform. Influenced by the Enlightenment, they flourished. Many, for example, allowed for some worship on Sunday and in English. Not all their foods or practices were kosher.

Anti-Semitism was sufficiently strong to impose a relatively low ceiling on Jewish aspiration. Jews were excluded from most Gentile-dominated universities, social clubs, and elite circles. Thus in 1893 the Union League Club in New York excluded even the "uptown" Jews. They developed their own agencies, hospitals, and clubs. "Cultural anti-Semitism" colored the writings of notables such as Henry Adams. Yet overt persecution was rare and harassment was generally bearable. Reform leaders such as Rabbi Isaac Mayer

Wise at Hebrew Union College in Cincinnati spoke of America as the new Israel, Zion.

Eastern Europeans, the second cluster, whose members settled in dense communities in New York and a few other large cities, came in great numbers after pogroms around 1881. They arrived from shtetls, small rural villages, or ghettos, in larger European cities. While their rabbis were learned in studies of Torah, Talmud, and other documents of faith, most of the people had had no opportunity to participate in "high culture" and were at first, apparently at least, not candidates for much participation in what historians associate with Gilded Age life—except as victims.

Most of the observant Jews among them clung to Orthodox ways and instituted hundreds of shuls, usually small synagogues. Often snubbed by the more adapted Jews, they were critical of emergent Reform. Not all were observant. Many reacted against Orthodoxy, deserted the synagogue, closed the Torah, did not "keep kosher" or follow the traditional laws, and invented non-religious forms of community life.

Obviously, not all Jews could be congenially gathered under one institutional canopy. The landmark events for nascent Reform were a meeting that issued the Pittsburgh Platform in 1885 and the founding of the Central Conference of American Rabbis in 1889. While defining the movement, the rabbis engaged in often-bitter disputes. Still, they gave coherence and a common voice to the movement's members.

The Orthodox tended to have more difficulty organizing beyond local synagogues, but in 1898 rabbis did initiate an organization. Those who found Orthodoxy too constraining and Reform alienating, converged around "Historical" or, eventually, Conservative Judaism, best expressed at Jewish Theological Seminary in New York. It retained what seemed meaningful in the tradition, but also allowed for some cultural accommodation of a sort milder than that of Reform.

If "Gilded Age" implied grossness and corruption, Judaism offered few notorious examples. Its communities often claimed the lowest crime rates in respect to physical violence. But Progressive reformers found other kinds of crime among commercial interests. Charges that vice reigned were often the result of misunderstanding, sometimes willful, among prejudiced officials. Observers of day-to-day life in urban communities were impressed at the law-abiding character of most Jews.

Jewish entrepreneurs became specialists in some areas of expansion during this period. The department store management, typified by the leadership of Julius Rosenwald at Sears, Roebuck and Company was one of these. Another was modern banking, with characteristic leaders such as Jacob H. Schiff, who arrived in 1868 to set a pace in the banking industry, philanthropy, in efforts to "Americanize" downtowners.

Most Jews were too busy establishing themselves in their new country to participate on levels of finance and political or cultural power to be seen as central to the Gilded Age plot. Sociologists would have described them as members of "marginal" groups, along the way toward becoming "mainstream" among faith groups and in American culture.

Further Reading: Nathan Glazer, *American Judaism*, 1972; Howard Sacher, *A History of the Jews in America*, 1992; Israel Goldberg, *The Jews in America: A History*, 1972.

Martin E. Marty

JUILLIARD v. GREENMAN (110 U.S. 421).

In 1884, the U.S. Supreme Court ruled on an 1878 act of Congress which stipulated that Civil War legal tender notes must be kept in circulation and not withdrawn. Writing for the majority, Justice Horace Gray upheld the law's constitutionality by noting that Congress possessed the authority to provide a uniform national currency and thus could make notes legal tender without basing its actions on the war power authorization. In a vigorous dissent, Justice Stephen J. Field warned of the potential dangers of any doctrine that granted the government "the power to alter the conditions of contracts."

Further Reading: Bernard Schwartz, *A History of the Supreme Court*, 1993.

Leonard Schlup

KASSON, JOHN ADAM (11 January 1822–18 May 1910), congressman. Born in Charlotte, Vermont, Kasson attended an academy in Burlington, Vermont, and graduated second in his class from the University of Vermont in 1842. He established a law practice in Des Moines, Iowa, and won election to the state legislature in 1868 and 1870 as a Republican. Between 1873 and 1877 he served in Congress, where he voted for the Coinage Act of 1873 and the Civil Rights Act of 1875. In 1877 he left to be ambassador to Austria-Hungary, then in 1881 he returned to the House, where he helped draft the Civil Service Act (Pendleton Act) of 1883. During the 1880s he negotiated treaties to maintain the neutrality of the Congo and to confirm America's claim, along with those of Germany and Great Britain, to Samoa. In 1898 President William McKinley sent Kasson to Alaska to redraw the boundary between it and Canada, but the effort failed. Kasson resigned in 1901. He remained in Washington, D.C., where he died.

Further Reading: Edward Younger, *John A. Kasson: Politics and Diplomacy from Lincoln to McKinley*, 1955.

Christopher Cumo

KEAN, JOHN (4 December 1852–4 November 1914), businessman and politician. Born near Elizabeth, New Jersey, Kean studied at private schools and attended Yale College before graduating from Columbia University's law school in 1875. Preferring to engage in business, farming, banking, and manufacturing concerns instead of the law, he was director or president of several corporations, including the Manhattan Trust Company and the Elizabethtown Gas Company. He won election as a Republican to the federal House of Representatives, holding a seat from 1883 to 1885 and 1887 to 1889. In 1891, he chaired the New Jersey Republican Committee. Unsuccessful in securing the governorship in 1892, Kean helped revise New Jersey's judicial system and subsequently served in the U.S. Senate from 1899 until 1911. He died in Ursino, New Jersey, leaving a legacy as a member of one the state's prominent political families.

Further Reading: *New York Times*, 5 November 1914.

Leonard Schlup

KEELER, WILLIAM HENRY (3 March 1872–1 January 1923), professional baseball player. Born in Brooklyn, New York, Keeler reached adulthood weighing only 140 pounds and standing five feet, four inches tall. Predictably nicknamed "Wee Willie," he is still regarded one of the greatest players in the game's history. An outstanding defensive fielder, he never hit for power. By perfecting his "hit-'em-where-they-ain't" strategy, he compiled startling statistics. In nineteen seasons, spent primarily in Baltimore and New York, Keeler compiled a .341 lifetime average, twelfth highest in major league history. In 1897, Keeler had his highest average, .424, the third best ever. That same season he set baseball's hitting streak record by batting safely in forty-four consecutive games, a feat surpassed only by Joe DiMaggio in 1941. Keeler's achievement remains the National League standard a century after he set it, although Pete Rose tied it in 1978. After Keeler retired, he attempted to remain in the game by coaching. Like Rogers Hornsby after him, however, Keeler could not impart his skills to other players. Financial difficulties marred his later years, and he died in Brooklyn. When the Hall of Fame was established after his death, Keeler was an early inductee.

Further Reading: Lee Allen and Thomas Meany, *Kings of the Diamond*, 1965; Ira L. Smith, *Baseball's Greatest Outfielders*, 1954.

Steve Bullock

KEIFER, JOSEPH WARREN (30 January 1836–22 April 1932), lawyer, congressman, army officer, and banker. Born in Clark County, Ohio, Keifer was a major general when mustered out of the Union Army in June 1865. He served in the Ohio Senate in 1868 and 1869, and in 1873 became president of the Lagonda National Bank of Springfield, Ohio. Keifer was a delegate to the Republican National Convention in 1876 and served four consecutive terms, from 1877 to 1885, in the U.S. House of Representatives. His support of the Fourteenth and Fifteenth amendments and of African-American suffrage, as well as strong Grand Army of the Republic (GAR) connections, made him a member of the party's Stalwart faction. He was speaker of the House during the forty-seventh Congress (1881–1883). Once called a called "professional veteran," he commanded the Ohio GAR in 1871 and 1872, served as an officer during the Spanish-American War in 1898, and was first commander in chief of the Spanish War Veterans during 1900 and 1901.

Further Reading: Charles B. Galbreath, *History of Ohio*, 1925; Benjamin F. Prince, *Standard History of Springfield and Clark Country, Ohio*, 1922; H. B. Fuller, *Speakers of the House*, 1909.

Norman E. Fry

KELLEY, OLIVER HUDSON (7 January 1826–20 January 1913), agriculturalist and reformer. Kelley was born in Boston, Massachusetts, where he attended public schools. In 1864 he became a clerk in the Department of Agriculture, and two years later President Andrew Johnson sent him to gather information about rural conditions in the South. In 1867, in response to the poverty and isolation Kelley saw there, he created the Patrons of Husbandry, known as the Grange, and served as its first secretary. During the next year he traveled throughout the Midwest to recruit members. In 1874 he could count more than twenty thousand local chapters and a million members. By then the Grange had grown beyond being a fraternal organization to advocate railroad regulation, cooperative marketing, and scientific agriculture. In 1875 Kelley published *Origins and Progress of the Order of the Patrons of Husbandry*, but thereafter turned his attention to land speculation in northern Florida, resigning in 1878. He made little money, however, and until his death subsisted in Washington, D.C., on a pension from the Grange.

Further Reading: Solon J. Buck, *The Granger Movement*, 1913; Charles M. Gardner, *The Grange—Friend of the Far-*

mer, 1949; D. Sven Nordin, *Rich Harvest: A History of the Grange, 1867–1900*, 1974.

Christopher Cumo

KELLOGG, JOHN HARVEY (26 February 1852–14 December 1943), physician and health advocate. Born in Livingston County, Michigan, Kellogg received the M.D. in 1875 from Bellevue Hospital Medical College in New York City. Editor of the Seventh-Day Adventist monthly *Good Health* from 1879 until his death, Kellogg gained prominence as a health reformer. He sought to improve dietary habits, advocated vegetarianism, emphasized biologic living and proper exercise, and urged the drinking of eight to ten glasses of water daily. Kellogg served as superintendent of the Battle Creek Sanitarium from 1877 until his death. He studied abdominal surgery in Vienna and London, where he worked under Dr. Lawson Tait. Kellogg performed 165 successive abdominal surgeries without a fatality and 22,000 other operations. He and his wife developed multigrain biscuits named "granola." Later he and his brother Will experimented with mastication of food and produced wheat flakes that their competitor, Charles W. Post, countered with his "Grape Nuts." Kellogg also propagated imitation meats and peanut butter. In 1895, he launched the American Medical Missionary College in Chicago as an institute to promote biologic living. Kellogg died in Battle Creek, Michigan.

Further Reading: Richard W. Schwarz, *John Harvey Kellogg, M.D.*, 1970; James C. Whorton, *Crusaders for Fitness: The History of American Health Reformers*, 1982; John Harvey Kellogg, *Home Hand-book of Domestic Hygiene and Rational Medicine*, 1900.

Leonard Schlup

KELLY, JOHN (20 April 1822–1 June 1886), congressman and Tammany Hall leader. Born in New York City, Kelly attended parochial schools before going into business and Democratic politics. He served in the U.S. House of Representatives from 1855 to 1858, and as sheriff of the city and county of New York from 1859 to 1862 and 1865 to 1867, respectively. In 1868, alleged ill health led him to withdraw a bid to capture the mayoral office, to which the voters elected A. Oakley Hall. In

1876, Kelly was an appointed comptroller of New York State. A delegate to several Democratic National Conventions, he became head, or Grand Sachem, of Tammany Hall in 1873 and subsequently was a powerful urban boss until his retirement in 1882. Kelly died in New York City.

Further Reading: *New York Times*, 2 June 1886; *New York Tribune*, 2 June 1886; *New York Herald*, 2 June 1886.

Leonard Schlup

KELLY, MICHAEL JOSEPH (31 December 1857–8 November 1894), professional baseball player. Born in Troy, New York, Kelly acquired the moniker "King" because of his regal stature on the baseball diamond. He played sixteen professional seasons, primarily in Chicago and Boston. A professional by the age of twenty, Kelly was one of the game's most versatile players. He was an outfielder, but his skills allowed him to excel at almost any position on the field, particularly catcher. One of the first superstars, Kelly was universally loved by fans. His Irish background help fill ballparks with immigrants, particularly in Boston. Exceptionally clever, Kelly was one of the first to utilize signs between the pitcher and catcher, and the hit-and-run play. He played a prominent role in the players' revolt of 1890 and led the Boston club to the only pennant awarded in the rival Players League. In addition to his exceptional diamond skills, Kelly was also known for a his love of nightlife, which probably contributed to his early death. In his final few seasons, he made only sporadic appearances, rarely displaying his earlier dominance. Kelly capitalized on his name recognition in his later years by opening a tavern in Boston, where he died soon after his retirement. He was elected to the Baseball Hall of Fame in 1945.

Further Reading: Marty Appel, *Slide, Kelly, Slide: The Wild Life and Times of Mike "King" Kelly, Baseball's First Superstar*, 1999.

Steve Bullock

KENNA, JOHN EDWARD (10 April 1848–11 January 1893), U.S. congressman and senator. Born near St. Albans, Kanawha County (now part of West Virginia), Kenna grew up in rural Missouri and fought with the Confederate Army. After the Civil War, he returned to West Virginia, and was admitted to the bar in 1870. He entered Democratic politics, emerging as an early leader of the "Kanawha Ring," young, war-impoverished professionals attracted to Charleston by the elusive "Kanawha coal boom." Chosen county attorney in 1872, Kenna was elected to the federal House of Representatives in 1876, defeating the "Redeemer" Democratic incumbent. He served from 1877 to 1883. On the Commerce Committee, he helped draft legislation that ultimately became the Interstate Commerce Act of 1887. Elevated to the U.S. Senate in 1883, Kenna sought more railroad regulation and loyally supported President Grover Cleveland. Described as a "powerful orator," he was able to maintain the support of West Virginia's "backwoods" population with his wit and humor as well as feats of physical strength. He died in Washington, D.C. His statue represents West Virginia in the Capitol's Statuary Hall.

Further Reading: *National Cyclopaedia of American Biography* 1 (1892): 299; Leonard Schlup, "West Virginia Constitutionalist: John E. Kenna and Relations Between the Senate and President," *Journal of the Alleghenies* 31 (1995): 99–110.

Harvey Gresham Hudspeth

KENNA, MICHAEL (20 August 1857–9 October 1946), saloonkeeper and political boss. Born in Chicago, Illinois, Kenna, known as "Hinky Dink," joined with John Joseph "The Bath" Coughlin in the 1890s. Together they bossed Chicago's First Ward during forty years of the city's rapid growth. Kenna, a cigar-smoking teetotaler, made or unmade judges, mayors, controllers, and police chiefs. He opened the fabulous Workingmen's Exchange, a colorful and at times tempestuous saloon that boasted the largest and coolest beer for five cents. Known as "the little fellow" because of his short stature, Kenna set a fixed price of fifty cents for a vote and took good care of his constituents and cronies. As a perennial Democratic ward committeeman and as alderman from 1897 until 1925, Kenna was a crude parliamentarian whose every word, despite his rugged syntax, was like a royal edict. He played at municipal skullduggery to his own profit and was unaffected by reform, sharing political power over the Loop district with Coughlin in an era of magnificent corruption. "The Hink" died in his suite at the Blackstone Hotel in Chicago.

Further Reading: Lloyd Wendt and Herman Kogan, *Bosses in Lusty Chicago: The Story of Bathhouse John and Hinky Dink,* 1967; *New York Times,* 10 October 1946.

Leonard Schlup

KENNEDY, PATRICK JOSEPH (14 January 1858–18 May 1929), brass finisher, saloon keeper, hotelier, liquor importer, and political figure. The paternal grandfather of President John F. Kennedy, Patrick Kennedy was born in East Boston, Massachusetts, where he ultimately established a political grip on its precincts. He ran a miniature welfare state by helping Irish Americans with food and drinks, asking for their votes in return. Kennedy doled out offices, jobs, and favors. Although he disliked campaigning, he won elections by landslide majorities, serving in the Massachusetts House of Representatives from 1886 to 1892 and the senate for two terms thereafter. In 1888, he seconded the nomination of President Grover Cleveland at the Democratic National Convention. At various times, Kennedy was Boston elections commissioner and fire commissioner, as well as a hotelier. He founded P. J. Kennedy and Company, a liquor importing enterprise. Kennedy helped organize the Columbia Trust Company in 1895, and subsequently served as its president. A realistic politician and reserved man, Kennedy, who sported a curled moustache, was a successful businessman and founder of a political dynasty. He died in Boston.

Further Reading: Doris Kearns Goodwin, *The Fitzgeralds and the Kennedys,* 1987; Richard J. Whalen, *The Founding Father: The Story of Joseph P. Kennedy,* 1993.

Leonard Schlup

KENT, WILLIAM (5 March 1851–18 September 1918), editor and mechanical engineer. Born in Philadelphia, Pennsylvania, Kent received his engineering degree from Stevens Institute of Technology in Hoboken, New Jersey, in 1876. From 1877 until 1882 he edited the *American Manufacturer and Iron World,* and worked as a mechanical engineer for Schoenberger & Company in Pittsburgh. In 1882, Kent became manager of the Pittsburgh office of Babcock and Wilcox, manufacturers of boilers, and also joined William F. Zimmerman to form the Pittsburgh Testing Laboratory. Subsequently, Kent moved to New York City as superintendent of sales and test engineer for Babcock and Wilcox. He also obtained patents. Other positions Kent held after 1887 included general manager of the United States Torsion Balance and Scale Company, associate editor of *Engineering News,* and dean of Syracuse University's College of Applied Science. In addition, Kent established a private consulting engineering practice in New York, wrote books, and helped to found the American Society of Mechanical Engineers. In 1895, his *Mechanical Engineers' Pocket-Book* became the first modern reference handbook for the profession; it had gone through nine editions before the author's death at Gananoque, Ontario, Canada.

Further Reading: *New York Times,* 19 September 1918.

Leonard Schlup

KERN, JOHN WORTH (20 December 1849–17 August 1917), political figure. Born in Alto, Indiana, Kern graduated from the University of Michigan's law school in 1869, practiced law Kokomo, Indiana, and served as city attorney from 1871 until 1884. He won election in 1884 as reporter of the Indiana Supreme Court. Kern held a state senate seat from 1893 to 1897, and was city solicitor of Indianapolis from 1897 to 1901. A supporter of union labor and an opponent of free silver, Kern backed William Jennings Bryan for president in 1896. In 1900 and 1904, Kern ran unsuccessfully as the Democratic candidate for governor of Indiana. He surfaced as Bryan's vice presidential running mate in 1908, but the Democratic ticket went down to defeat. Kern served in the U.S. Senate as a Progressive from 1911 to 1917. He died in Asheville, North Carolina.

Further Reading: Claude G. Bowers, *The Life of John Worth Kern,* 1918; *Indianapolis News,* 18 August 1917.

Leonard Schlup

KERR, MICHAEL CRAWFORD (15 March 1827–19 August 1876), congressman and speaker of the U.S. House of Representatives. Born in Titusville, Pennsylvania, Kerr graduated in 1851 from the law department of Louisville University in Kentucky. He practiced law in New Albany, Indiana, while holding local and state political offices. Elected as a Democrat to the U.S. House of Representatives, he served from 1865 to 1873 and again from 1875 until his death. Kerr opposed Radical Reconstruction policies and the scandalous excesses of President Ulysses S. Grant's administration. Although an electoral defeat in 1872 interrupted continuous service in the lower chamber, Kerr scored a political comeback in 1874. He was speaker of the House during the Forty-fourth Congress. Kerr died at Rockbridge Alum Springs, Virginia.

Further Reading: *New York Times*, 20 August 1876.

Leonard Schlup

KEY, DAVID MCKENDREE (27 January 1824–3 February 1900), senator, postmaster general, and judge. Born in Greene County, Tennessee, Key spent most of his life practicing law and politics. He served the Confederacy during the Civil War until wounded and captured at Vicksburg. After the conflict, he received a pardon from his friend President Andrew Johnson. Key was an active Democrat, twice serving as a presidential elector and participating in the Tennessee constitutional convention of 1870. In 1875 Key was appointed to the U.S. Senate, where he served until 1877. While there, he gained a reputation as an advocate of sectional reconciliation, helping to enact legislation to aid help the southern states economically. His actions assisted in making the Compromise of 1877. President Rutherford B. Hayes appointed him postmaster general shortly after his inauguration. Key, the only Democrat in the cabinet, resigned in May 1880 to become a U.S. district judge in Tennessee. There he earned a reputation for impartiality and justice. He retired in 1894 and died in Chattanooga, Tennessee.

Further Reading: David M. Abshire, *The South Rejects a Prophet: The Life of Senator D. M. Key, 1824–1900*, 1967; *Chattanooga Times*, 4 February 1900; David M. Key Papers, Chattanooga Public Library, Chattanooga, Tennessee.

Terri Pedersen Summey

KIDD v. _PEARSON_ (128 U.S. 1). A narrow interpretation of commerce resulted from this U.S. Supreme Court opinion of 22 October 1888; the vote was 8–0. Associate Justice Lucius Q. C. Lamar wrote the majority report. At issue was an Iowa law that prohibited the manufacture of intoxicating liquors for shipment to other states, which was challenged as state infringement of interstate commerce. The Court held that the Iowa statute constituted a legitimate police power regulation rather than an interference with federal commerce. The justices distinguished between commerce and manufacturing, upholding the law on the assumption that it pertained to the regulation of manufacturing. They feared that to decide otherwise could vest Congress with absolute control over all aspects of production. The restricted conception of commerce as defined here and in other cases under Chief Justice Melville Weston Fuller corresponded to the laissez-faire theory of governmental functions that prevailed during the Gilded Age, in contrast to the broad construction of commerce applied years earlier by Chief Justice John Marshall.

Further Reading: Bernard Schwartz, *A History of the Supreme Court*, 1993.

Leonard Schlup

KIRKWOOD, SAMUEL JORDAN (20 December 1813–1 September 1894), senator. Born in Hartford County, Maryland, Kirkwood attended a private school in Washington, D.C., was admitted to the bar, and practiced law first in Ohio and then in Iowa. A Republican, he served in the Iowa legislature and as governor. In 1866 he entered the U.S. Senate to complete the term of James Harlan, who had left to become secretary of the interior. In 1875 the Republican Party again nominated Kirkwood for governor of Iowa, though he had not sought the office. He won, but resigned in 1877 to return to the Senate. In 1881 President James A. Garfield appointed him secretary of the interior, but Garfield's assassination led Kirkwood to resign the next year so President Chester A. Arthur could appoint someone of his choice. After losing a House race in 1886, Kirkwood retired to Iowa City, Iowa, where he died.

Further Reading: Dan E. Clark, *Samuel Jordan Kirkwood*, 1917; Herbert Hake, "The Political Firecracker: Samuel J. Kirkwood," *Palimpset* 56 (1975): 2–14.

Christopher Cumo

KITCHIN, WILLIAM HODGE (22 December 1837–2 February 1901), editor, lawyer, and politician. Born in Lauderdale County, Alabama, Kitchin moved to North Carolina, served in the Confederate Army, and practiced law. As a Democrat, he won a seat in the federal House of Representatives in 1878. Although he championed greenbackism and income tax, Kitchin marked his single term mainly by engaging in verbal arguments with Republican Representative Daniel Russell. An outspoken white supremacist, advocate of silver coinage, and opponent of protective tariffs, Kitchin utilized his hometown weekly, the *Democrat*, to rebuke President Grover Cleveland's sound money policies, castigate eastern business and banking concerns, and vehemently denounce black suffrage. In 1894 he announced his conversation to the Populist Party, a temporary political expedient. He later rejoined the Democrats, claiming that he had never been away. Kitchin died in Scotland Neck, North Carolina.

Further Reading: Eric Anderson, *Race and Politics in North Carolina, 1872–1901: The Black Second*, 1981; *Scotland Neck Commonwealth*, 7 February 1901; H. Larry Ingle, "A Southern Democrat at Large: William Hodge Kitchin and the Populist Party," *North Carolina Historical Review* 45 (1968): 178–194.

Leonard Schlup

KLONDIKE GOLD RUSH. In 1897 and 1898, an estimated one million people from around the world planned to travel to Canada's Northwest Territory to find gold. The rush included twelve stampedes to locales in Alaska and Canada during 1898, and nine more through 1902. The initial discovery occurred on 17 August 1896; George Washington Carmack and "Skookum" (Strong) Jim Mason found a large quantity of coarse gold on Rabbit Creek (later named Bonanza), in what came to be called the Klondike District. The 130-square-mile area is bounded by the Klondike River to the north, the Yukon River to the west, and the Indian River to the south; the port of Dawson was founded where the Klondike meets the Yukon. Carmack left news of gold in the wake of his journey to Forty Mile to register claims, and prospectors stampeded the Klondike District. Word of rich finds did not reach the outside world until in 1897, with the arrival of the S.S. *Excelsior* in San Francisco on 14 July and the S.S. *Portland* in Seattle on 17 July. Then newspapers around the world reported how the Klondike had made many everyday men and women rich.

An estimated one hundred thousand people headed north either by the "rich man's" all-water route (San Francisco or Seattle to St. Michael, then up the Yukon to Dawson) or by the water-land-water route (Seattle to Dyea or Skagway, over the Chilkoot or White Pass, across lakes, and down the Yukon to Dawson). About a thousand arrived in Dawson before "freeze up" in 1897 and another thirty thousand after "break-up" in 1898—only to discover that every foot of the forty-five-square-mile, primary gold-bearing area (laced by creeks with names like Allgold, Eldorado, Gold Bottom, and Gold Run) had been staked in September 1896. During the summer of 1898, the great rush to the Klondike shifted to the golden sands of Nome on the Bering Sea, with eight thousand gold seekers leaving Dawson in August. The Klondike continues to produce sizable amounts of gold.

Further Reading: Alaska Geographic Society, *Dawson City*, 1988; Ken DeRoux, *All That Glitters: A Centennial Exhibition on the Alaska-Yukon Gold Rushes*, 1996; Pierre Burton, *Klondike Fever*, 1958.

Art Petersen

KNIGHTS OF LABOR. Founded in Philadelphia, Pennsylvania, on 31 December 1869 by garment workers led by Uriah S. Stephens, the Knights of Labor (KOL) started as a clandestine ritualistic assembly. It grew gradually until the railway strike of 1877 convinced workers in eastern states to seek a larger movement. In 1878 delegates convened in Reading, Pennsylvania, where they selected Stephens as first Grand Master Workman. A year later Terence

V. Powderly replaced him. Membership was open to all gainfully employed persons over eighteen years of age (with the exception of certain professional groups), regardless of ethnic origin, sex, or race.

The KOL was an industrial union headed by a General Assembly. Farmers dominated the organization in the West; trade unionists for the most part filled the ranks in the East. With a motto that an injury to one was the concern of all, the Knights attempted to advance their idealistic goals through educational means. They frowned on strikes but supported boycotts and arbitration, and advocated adoption of a graduated income tax, an eight-hour day, equal pay for equal work, abolition of child and convict labor, and elimination of private banks. In 1886 the Knights boasted 135 producers' cooperatives and seven hundred thousand members. The Haymarket Riot of 1886, for which the KOL was not responsible, generated public distrust of strikes and agitators. Membership fell to one hundred thousand by 1890, most of them residing in small towns and agricultural areas, and in 1900 the union was practically extinct. Causes of its downfall included factional disputes, excessive centralization, mismanagement, loss of financial resources through unsuccessful strikes, and the emergence of the American Federation of Labor. John R. Sovereign of Iowa, editor of a farm journal, replaced Powderly in 1893.

Further Reading: Kim Voss, *The Making of American Exceptionalism: The Knights of Labor and Class Formation in the Nineteenth Century*, 1994; Robert E. Weir, *Beyond Labor's Veil: The Culture of the Knights of Labor*, 1996; Craig Phelan, *Grand Master Workman: Terence Powderly and the Knights of Labor*, 2000.

Leonard Schlup

KNOTT, JAMES PROCTOR (29 August 1830–18 June 1911), congressman and governor. Born in Raywick, near Lebanon, Kentucky, Knott, after serving as a Democratic legislator and attorney general in Missouri, returned to his hometown of Lebanon, Kentucky to practice law following a brief imprisonment for failing to swear allegiance to the Union. Subsequently elected to Congress six times (1867–1871, 1875–1883), Knott opposed Radical Reconstruction and protectionism. He won lasting fame for his witty 1871 "Duluth" speech, in which he ridiculed federal aid to a proposed railroad. Elected governor of Kentucky in 1883, Knott pressed the General Assembly to abolish tax immunities for corporations, to tax or abolish lotteries, and to give "teeth" to the Railroad Commission. All of these innovations were ignored, but the legislature did respond to the governor's plea for an overhaul of the state's tax assessment system by creating a Board of Equalization. Although reform-minded, Knott as governor was quite oblivious to the state's rampant lawlessness and indirectly contributed to it through a generous pardoning record. After leaving office in 1887, Knott was a special assistant to the attorney general and a delegate to the 1890–1891 constitutional convention. In his later years he achieved wide acclaim as an educator at Centre College. He died in Lebanon.

Further Reading: Robert M. Ireland, "J. Proctor Knott," in Lowell H. Harrion, ed., *Kentucky's Governors, 1792–1985*, 1985, 96–100; Hambleton Tapp, "James Proctor Knott and the Duluth Speech," *The Register of the Kentucky Historical Society* 70 (1972): 77–93.

Edward Scott Blakeman

KOHLSAAT, HERMAN HENRY (22 March 1853–17 October 1924), editor. Born in Albion, Illinois, Kohlsaat spent his youth in Galena, Illinois, operated lunchrooms in Chicago, and supported the Republican Party. He became part owner of the *Chicago Daily Inter-Ocean* in 1891, and publisher of the *Chicago Times-Herald* in 1895, renaming it the *Record-Herald* in 1901. Kohlsaat endorsed the protective tariff and the gold standard. He claimed authorship of the gold plank in the Republican Party's platform in 1896. Kohlsaat took satisfaction in knowing presidents and other prominent political leaders. His sudden death occurred in Washington, D.C.

Further Reading: H. H. Kohlsaat, *From McKinley to Harding: Personal Recollections of Our Presidents*, 1923; *Chicago Tribune*, 18 October 1924.

Leonard Schlup

KOHUT, ALEXANDER (22 April 1842–25 May 1894), Judiac scholar and rabbi. Born in Félegyháza, Hungary, Kohut earned a doctorate in 1864 from the University of Leipzig, was ordained in 1867, and then began a rabbinical career that won him recognition over the next two decades. He arrived in New York City in 1885 to accept a position at Ahavath Chesed (Central Synagogue). A traditionalist, Kohut became embroiled in a spirited debate with Kaufmann Kohler, the Reform rabbi of Temple Beth-El. The next year Kohut teamed with others to establish the Jewish Theological Seminary of America, whose purpose was to train Conservative rabbis and teachers to counterpoise the reform work of Rabbi Isaac M. Wise of Cincinnati, Ohio. Kohut was a brilliant orator and dedicated scholar who expressed interest in education and social welfare. He died in New York City.

Further Reading: Moshe Davis, *The Emergence of Conservative Judaism: The Historical School in Nineteenth Century America*, 1965; Robert E. Fierstien, *A Different Spirit: The Jewish Theological Seminary of America, 1886–1902*, 1990.

Leonard Schlup

KROEGER, ALICE BERTHA (2 May 1864–31 October 1909), librarian and educator. Born in St. Louis, Missouri, Kroeger attended public schools there, and upon graduating from high school became a clerk at the St. Louis Public Library. She worked there from 1882 through 1889. She left to enroll in the New York State Library School, and in July 1891, she received her diploma. Melvil Dewey recommended her for a position at the Drexel Institute of Art, Science and Industry in Philadelphia, where she served as librarian and organized the new School of Librarianship. She spent the rest of her life in Philadelphia as director of that school. Kroeger was an active member in the American Library Association, a frequent speaker, and a contributor to the literature of the field. In 1902 she compiled *Guide to the Study and Use of Reference Books: A Manual for Librarians, Teachers and Students*, which has become a standard in the field, with subsequent editors building on her foundation.

Further Reading: *Library Journal* 34 (November 1909): 518.

Terri Pedersen Summey

KU KLUX KLAN. The Ku Klux Klan of the Reconstruction era became the principal means to restore and maintain white supremacy in the former Confederate states, through terrorizing African Americans and rendering the Republican Party powerless. The Klan was not a unified organization, nor even a loose confederation. It and related organizations, such as the Knights of the White Camellia in Louisiana, however, had a common purpose and used similar tactics. They were secret paramilitary organizations that attracted members from across the social and economic spectrum of white society. Usually masked, Klansmen used intimidation and violence in behalf of the Democratic Party, the planter class, and white supremacy.

The first organization known as the Ku Klux Klan was the creation of six Confederate veterans in Pulaski, Tennessee, in the spring of 1866. Their original intentions were innocent, but in a few weeks they began to intimidate local blacks, especially those who violated the community's racial code. The Klansmen created a ritual that helped attract new members. In 1867, two prominent Tennessee Democrats saw the Klan's potential as a means for mobilizing the Democratic vote. Former Confederate general Nathan Bedford Forrest was chosen as Grand Wizard, the only person to hold that office. In 1868 the Klan expanded to other southern states, and acts of violence against white Republicans and blacks proliferated. The impact of Klan violence was especially obvious during the 1868 presidential election in Georgia and Louisiana. Klan members were also determined to assert economic control over blacks and punish those who had achieved some success. Many conservative whites were displeased by the Klan's excesses, and in 1869 Forrest announced drastic restrictions on Klan activity. Mob action continued, however, forcing a reluctant President Ulysses Grant to ask Congress for legislation to enforce the rights guaranteed by the Fourteenth and Fifteenth amendments. Congress passed a series of Enforcement Acts, culminating in the so-called Ku Klux Act of 1871, which empowered the president to suspend habeas corpus in order to cope with Election Day violence. Despite immense obstacles, the Justice Department successfully prosecuted accused Klansmen. Grant sent troops into nine South Carolina counties. Although there were only a few hundred convictions, the federal government had demonstrated its intent. A combination of federal action and white revulsion at the violence brought a sharp decline in Klan activity by 1872.

Further Reading: Allen W. Trelease, *White Terror: The Ku Klux Klan Conspiracy and Southern Reconstruction*, 1971; Eric Foner, *Reconstruction: America's Unfinished Revolution, 1863–1877*, 1988.

James R. Sweeney

KYLE, JAMES HENDERSON (24 February 1854–1 July 1901), minister and U.S. senator. Born near Xenia, Ohio, Kyle briefly attended the University of Illinois at Urbana, graduated from Oberlin College in Ohio in 1878, and studied at the Western Theological Seminary in Allegheny, Pennsylvania. He served as pastor of Congregational churches in Utah before moving to Yankton, South Dakota, where he was identified at one time or another with Democrats, Republicans, and Populists. A member of the U.S. Senate from 1891 to 1901, Kyle chaired the Committee on Education and Labor in three Congresses and sought the establishment of the University of the United States. From 1898 to 1901, he headed the National Industrial Commission, a group created by Congress to investigate the nation's industrial status. He died in Aberdeen, South Dakota.

Further Reading: *Daily Argus-Leader* (Sioux Falls), 2 July 1901; *New York Times*, 2 July 1901; Harold Quinion, "James H. Kyle, United States Senator from South Dakota, 1891–1901," *South Dakota Historical Collections* 13 (1926): 311–321.

Leonard Schlup

LABOR AND UNIONS. During the Gilded Age, the lives of American workers were transformed, and organized labor established itself as a major force in the nation's life. The number of workers engaged in manufacturing rose from fewer than one million in 1860 to six million in 1900. Employers introduced new machinery and work methods that diluted traditional artisan skills, and American workers competed with millions of European immigrants for unskilled jobs. As periodic economic crises swept the land, high levels of unemployment, low wages, long hours, and poor working conditions sparked the organization of a labor movement, and repeated strikes and protests.

Before the Civil War, labor unions were invariably local and composed of skilled white male workers. Because of industrialization, improved communications, and the growth of corporations, these skilled workers formed national organizations during the war years. In Baltimore in 1866, a number of national and local unions united into the National Labor Union, but by 1872 internal strife left it moribund. Subsequently, during the economic depression of 1873–1878, unions faced an employers' offensive that severely weakened labor organizations. In the summer of 1877, however, railroad workers, on strike in response to a 10 percent pay cut, engaged in the largest and most violent labor uprising the nation had yet witnessed. The job action cost many lives and ended only after intervention by federal troops. During the 1880s, the Noble and Holy Order of the Knights of Labor, founded in 1869 by Philadelphia garment cutters, became the preeminent labor organization in America. During its first decade, the Knights was a small, secret regional organization, but from 1881, under the leadership of Terence V. Powderly, the Knights dropped all secrecy and substantially increased their membership. By the spring of 1886 the Knights, who more than any other labor organization of the time sought to include the unskilled, women, and African Americans, embraced seven hundred thousand workers, about 10 percent of the industrial labor force. The Knights sought to replace the wage system through the establishment of cooperative factories and stores, and played a major role in the largely unsuccessful struggle for an eight-hour workday. The movement culminated in a nationwide strike on 1 May 1886. After a series of strike defeats and internal conflict, membership declined, and by the 1890s, the Knights ceased to function.

Thereafter, the more conservative American Federation of Labor (AFL) emerged as the major labor organization. The AFL was founded in December 1886 in Columbus, Ohio, by a group of craft unions who elected Samuel Gompers, leader of the cigar makers union, president. Under his dominating ideology, stressing "pure and simple" trade unionism, AFL membership reached 850,000 in 1901. Simply put, AFL unions increasingly believed that workers could best secure higher wages and better working conditions not through political reform but through union strength at the workplace. Partly due to ideological prejudice, and partly to protect the wages of its members by keeping potential competitors out of the labor market, many AFL unions excluded immigrants, blacks, and women from membership.

Another economic depression in the 1890s brought major problems for the labor movement. Often with government assistance, employers used force to break unions and defeat strikes. In 1892, at Andrew Carnegie's Homestead steelworks in Pennsylvania, the powerful steelworkers' unions were crushed after a strike that saw sixteen people killed in a gun battle between strikers and armed guards. Two years later, in Pullman, Illinois, striking workers belonging to the American Railway Union, the nation's largest union, were defeated after intervention by federal troops and the arrest of their leader, Eugene V. Debs. In spite of these defeats, in 1901, 1.1 million, mostly skilled, workers, nearly 10 percent of the industrial labor force, belonged to unions. With most industrial workers still working long hours for low pay and at the mercy of the market and employers, the conflict between labor and capital continued into the next century.

Further Reading: Leon Fink, *Workingmen's Democracy: The Knights of Labor and American Politics*, 1983; Melvyn Dubofsky, *Industrialism and the American Worker, 1865–1920*, 3rd ed., 1996.

John F. Lyons

LABOR EXCHANGE. Founded in 1889 by Giovanni Battista DeBernardi of Independence, Missouri, the Labor Exchange attempted to unite farmers and workers in a single cooperative movement designed to preserve their preindustrial status as independent producers and property owners. During the depression triggered by the Panic of 1893, the Labor Exchange attracted considerable attention from urban craftsmen and farmers who had been active in the Knights of Labor and the Farmers' Alliance. By late 1898, there were more than 325 locals of the Labor Exchange scattered across the country, doing business in at least thirty-three states and claiming fifteen thousand members. Hoping to build an alternative to the modern capitalist marketplace, these locals promoted the direct exchange of goods between producers by circumventing corporate middlemen and by issuing their own paper currency or scrip in accordance with the "DeBernardi Plan" of cooperation.

An immigrant from Turin, Italy, DeBernardi had come to America in 1858 and settled on a farm in Missouri, where he rose to prominence in the Grange and the Greenback Party. The failure of those agrarian movements prompted him to launch the Labor Exchange and to popularize his ideas by publishing a utopian novel in 1890. Proclaimed the "textbook of the Labor Exchange," *Trials and Triumph of Labor* helped spread DeBernardi's cooperatives between 1894 and 1898. The return of prosperity, however, led to the Labor Exchange's swift decline. DeBernardi's death in 1901 sealed its fate.

Further Reading: Michael Magliari, "Producerism's Last Gasp: G. B. DeBernardi and the Labor Exchange Movement, 1889–1901," in Paola Sensi-Isolani and Anthony Tamburri, eds., *Italian Americans: A Retrospective on the Twentieth Century* (2001), 1–28.

Michael Magliari

LA FARGE, JOHN FREDERICK LEWIS JOSEPH (31 March 1835–14 November 1910), writer and artist. Born in New York City, La Farge enjoyed a privileged childhood provided by his wealthy French Catholic parents. He graduated from Mount Saint Mary's College in Emmitsburg, Maryland, in 1853, and began a law career. European travels later in the 1850s, however, turned a fondness for art into an unquenchable desire. After inheriting money, he abandoned the law. He worked under William Morris Hunt in Rhode Island, but was dissatisfied with Hunt's techniques. Through experimentation and his skills, La Farge emerged on his own, painting still lifes and landscapes, and doing book illustrations. In 1875, he was commissioned to redesign the interior of Trinity Church in Boston. The result won him national recognition as a decorative artist, and heralded the beginning of the American Renaissance. Thereafter La Farge earned his livelihood through decorative commissions, selling watercolors, teaching, speaking, and writing. Later his reputation declined because of scandals, legal problems, quarrels with his family, and his eccentric behavior. He died in a mental institution in Providence, Rhode Island. Modern scholarship has rehabilitated his tarnished image as America's old master.

Further Reading: Royal Cortissoz, *John La Farge: A Memoir and a Study*, 1911; *New York Times*, 15 November 1910; La Farge Family Papers, Department of Manuscripts and Archives, Sterling Memorial Library, Yale University.

Leonard Schlup

LAISSEZ-FAIRE. This is the theory that upholds the autonomous character of the economic order, maintaining that government should intervene as little as possible in the direction of economic affairs. Laissez-faire is based on the argument that the natural economic order, when undisturbed by artificial stimulus or regulation, tends to secure the maximum well-being for the individual and the community. The French meaning of the expression is "leave alone" or "let it be." Opposition to mercantilism and state paternalism motivated Adam Smith, a Scottish economist and professor of moral philosophy, to advocate that trade should be free of government restrictions. Smith did not espouse laissez-faire in an absolute sense; rather, he found a place for governmental activity in public works. He published *The Wealth of Nations* in 1776. Other eighteenth- and nineteenth-century exponents of laissez-faire were the English economists, Jeremy Bentham and John Stuart Mill. The philosophy of individualism permeated Gilded Age America. National leaders declined to intervene to offset recessionary times in the 1870s and the economic depression in the mid-1890s, yet laissez-faire principles and doctrines were nowhere embodied fully in legislation. The national government continued to levy tariffs to protect domestic manufacturers.

Further Reading: Sidney Fine, *Laissez-Faire and the General Welfare State: A Study of Conflict in American Thought, 1865–1901*, 1957; J. W. McConnell, *Basic Teachings of the Great Economists*, 1943; Louis P. Cain and Jonathan R. T. Hughes, *American Economic History*, 1997.

Leonard Schlup

LAMAR, LUCIUS QUINTUS CINCINNATUS (17 September 1825–23 January 1893), representative, U.S. senator, secretary of the interior, and Supreme Court justice. Born near Eatonton, Georgia, Lamar was graduated from Emory College in 1845 and later studied law. He moved in 1849 to Oxford, Mississippi, where he was a lawyer, a mathematics professor, and a pro-slavery Democrat. In 1852, he moved to Corrington, Georgia, and was elected to the state legislature in 1853. He returned to Mississippi in 1855 and won a seat in the U.S. House of Representatives in 1857, but resigned in 1860 as the Civil War approached. He drafted Mississippi's ordinance of succession and served as an officer in the Confederate Army and a special commissioner to Russia.

Lamar returned to the House in 1873. The following year, he called for sectional reconciliation and emerged as a leader of the New South. In 1876, after helping Mississippi Democrats regain control of the state government, he won election to the Senate, then defied his state legislature's instructions by opposing the

free silver movement. He remained in the Senate until 1885, when President Grover Cleveland named him secretary of the interior. Two years later, senators confirmed his appointment to the Supreme Court despite concerns over his health and his Confederate past. Lamar died in Macon, Georgia.

Further Reading: James B. Murphy, *L. Q. C. Lamar: Pragmatic Patriot*, 1973; Wirt A. Cate, *Lucius Q. C. Lamar: Secession and Reunion*, 1935; John F. Kennedy, *Profiles in Courage*, 1955.

Jane M. Armstrong

LAMB, MARTHA JOANNA READE NASH (13 August 1829–2 January 1893), author, editor, and historian. Born in Plainfield, Massachusetts, Martha Nash attended public schools and had a brief career as a mathematics teacher. In 1852, she married Charles A. Lamb. The marriage did not last, however, and in 1866, she moved to New York City, where she wrote a series of children's books, a novel, and several magazine articles. Her two-volume *History of the City of New York: Its Origin, Rise and Progress* (1877–1881), established her literary reputation. Because of the depth of her research, which included colonial documents, old newspapers, and manuscripts, her work gained attention. In May 1883, she purchased the *Magazine of American History* and made it successful, serving as both writer and editor. She also secured contributions by other authors. Much of her work was reprinted in two books, *Wall Street in History* and *Unpublished Washington Portraits*. During her lifetime, she achieved a reputation for scholarly work that was not normally accorded a woman, and two presidents invited her to the White House. Lamb died in New York City.

Further Reading: Daniel Van Pelt, "Mrs. Martha J. Lamb," *Magazine of American History* 29 (1893): 126–130; *New York Times*, 3 January 1893.

Terri Pedersen Summey

LAMONT, DANIEL SCOTT (9 February 1851–23 July 1905), secretary of war and financier. Born in McGrawville, New York, Lamont left Union College to enter journalism. He purchased an interest in the *Democrat*, a Cortland County newspaper, became its editor, and later helped publish the *Albany Argus*. During the 1882 New York gubernatorial campaign, Lamont worked for the Democratic candidate, Grover Cleveland. The next year, Cleveland placed Lamont on his staff. Cleveland won the presidency in 1884, and in 1885 Lamont accompanied him to Washington. There he served as the president's private secretary, increasing the position's importance to its present level. It was he, not Cleveland, who declared public office a public trust. During Cleveland's second administration (1893–1897), Lamont was secretary of war. No other cabinet officer knew of the president's cancer surgery aboard a private yacht in 1893. Lamont announced the virtual end of Native American warfare, worked to improve his department's efficiency, disapproved of the annexation of Hawaii, and directed the policing of Chicago during the 1894 Pullman Strike. A conservative Democrat, he vehemently opposed William Jennings Bryan's presidential nomination in 1896. Thereafter Lamont helped direct two major corporations. He died in Millbrook, New York.

Further Reading: Sister Anne Marie Fitzsimmons, "The Political Career of Daniel S. Lamont," Ph.D. diss., Catholic University of America, 1965; *New York Times*, 24 July 1905; Daniel S. Lamont Papers, Manuscript Division, Library of Congress.

Leonard Schlup

LANGDELL, CHRISTOPHER COLUMBUS (22 May 1826–6 July 1906), law professor and educator. Langdell was born in New Boston, New Hampshire, and paid for his education at Exeter Academy and Harvard College by working in textile mills in Manchester, New Hampshire. He entered Harvard Law School when he was twenty-five, working in the library to support himself. After three years, he moved to New York to practice. He returned to Cambridge in 1869 as dean of the Harvard Law School and an endowed professor. He revolutionized the study of law, teaching legal principles by using actual cases instead of lecture, recitation, and memorization. Langdell also hired legal scholars, rather than practicing lawyers, to conduct classes. Although controversial at first, his methods were standard in most American law schools by the time he re-

tired in 1895. He died in Cambridge, Massachusetts.

Further Reading: Christopher Langdell Papers, Harvard Law School Library, Cambridge, Massachusetts; Christopher Columbus Langdell, *A Selection of Cases on the Law of Contracts*, 1871; Charles W. Eliot, "Langdell and the Law School," *Harvard Law Review* 33 (1919): 518.

Robert J. Allison

LANGSTON, JOHN MERCER (14 December 1829–15 November 1897), political leader, professor of law, and diplomat. Born free in Louisa County, Virginia, the son of Ralph Quarles, a wealthy white planter, Langston was orphaned in 1834 and thereafter boarded with various white and black families in Ohio. He graduated from Oberlin College in 1849, joined the African-American civil rights movement, and sought black suffrage. The first African-American graduate of Oberlin's theological department (1853), Langston eschewed the ministry because of organized religion's widespread reluctance to oppose slavery. In 1854 he was admitted to the Ohio bar, held various local political offices in Oberlin, and raised hundreds of African-American volunteers for service in the Civil War. In 1864 he won election as first president of the National Equal Rights League.

Langston favored a Reconstruction plan based on "impartial justice," organized Republican Union Leagues, and worked to secure rights for freed persons. In 1869 he became professor of law and first dean of the law department at Howard University. President Ulysses S. Grant appointed him to the board of health of the District of Columbia in 1871. Langston served as U.S. minister and consul general to Haiti from 1877 to 1885. The first African American elected official in the nation and the first of his race from Virginia elected to the House of Representatives (1890–1891), he acquired a national reputation for his work, ideas, and goals to better the lives of blacks. Later he practiced law in the nation's capital, remained active in education and politics, and predicted that African Americans ultimately would secure their rights in the courts. He published his autobiography, *From the Virginia Plantation to the National Capitol*, in 1894. Langston died in Washington, D.C.

Further Reading: William Cheek and Aimee Lee Cheek, "John Mercer Langston: Principle and Politics," in Leon

Litwack and August Meier, eds., *Black Leaders of the Nineteenth Century*, 1988; John Mercer Langston Papers, Fisk University Library, Nashville, Tennessee.

Leonard Schlup

LARNED, JOSEPHUS NELSON (11 May 1836–15 August 1913), librarian and historian. Larned was born in Chatham, Canada, and raised in Buffalo, New York. In 1859, he became editor (with Mark Twain) of the *Buffalo Express*, where he specialized in writing political editorials. In 1872, Larned was elected city superintendent of education, and supported compulsory school attendance. From 1877 to 1897, he headed the library of the Young Men's Association in Buffalo. He believed free education and free access to books would build democracy, and quickly became a leader in the new public library movement. His was the first library to fully implement the Dewey classification system. He opened the stacks, established a reference service, created children's programs, cataloged the pamphlet collection, and opened the library on Sunday. He urged that libraries supply wholesome literature for uplifting the populace, not light fiction merely for entertainment. Larned believed the fundamental problems of the American political system dealt with new issues of labor, wealth, and class structure. He compiled an enormous bibliography on American history and published a study of morality through the ages. He died in Orchard Park, New York.

Further Reading: Betty Young, "Josephus Nelson Larned and the Public Library Movement," *Journal of Library History* 10 (1975): 323–340; Sidney Herbert Ditzion, "The Social Ideas of Library Pioneer Josephus Nelson Larned, 1836–1913," *Library Quarterly* 13 (1943): 113–131; "Josephus Nelson Larned," in Emily Miller Danton, *Pioneering Leaders in Librarianship*, 1972.

Philip H. Young

LEASE, MARY ELIZABETH CLYENS (11 September 1853–29 October 1933), Populist orator and writer. Born in Ridgeway, Pennsylvania, Clyens attended St. Elizabeth's Academy, a local Catholic school. She taught for five years before her marriage in 1873 brought her to a farm in rural Kansas. After a decade the farm failed and the family moved to Wichita. There Lease tended her children, took in washing and began studying law. She later claimed that she was admitted to the Kansas bar in 1885, the same year she began lecturing for the Irish National League and for woman suffrage. A member of the Knights of Labor, she spoke before the state convention of the Union Labor party in 1888 and went on to be an editor of the party's newspaper, the *Wichita Independent*.

Increasingly recognized as a gifted orator, Lease soon started speaking on behalf of the Farmers' Alliance. She became one of the most popular as well as controversial figures in the newly formed People's Party, making more than 160 speeches during the Kansas campaign of 1890. The following year she took her message into the West and the South. A member of the committee that organized the People's party on a national level, Lease proudly seconded the 1892 nomination of James B. Weaver as the party's presidential candidate and campaigned for the Populist ticket across the South and the West. In 1893 she was appointed chair of the Kansas State Board of Charities but soon lost the job when she refused the governor's order to dispense jobs to Democrats as well as Populists. An ardent antifusionist Populist, Lease was steadfast in her refusal to link the Populist cause with the post–Civil War Democratic party. Her intransigence cost Lease her standing in the People's party as well, especially after she attempted to prevent the 1896 presidential nomination of William Jennings Bryan. In 1895 she published *The Problem of Civilization Solved*, in which she called for the free coinage of silver, nationalization of the railroads and the white colonization of the tropics. Her book as well as her defection from the People's party brought her to the attention of Joseph Pulitzer, who hired Lease as a feature writer for the New York *World*. Beginning in 1897, she made New York City her home, still occasionally speaking on behalf of such causes as woman suffrage, prohibition and birth control. She died in Callicoon, New York.

Further Reading: Michael Lewis Goldberg, *An Army of Women: Gender and Politics in Gilded Age Kansas*, 1997; Betty Lou Taylor, *Mary Elizabeth Lease: Kansas Populist*, M.A. thesis, Wichita State University, 1951; Mary Elizabeth Lease Papers, Kansas State Historical Society, Topeka.

Kathleen Banks Nutter

LEE, FITZHUGH (19 November 1835–28 April 1905), soldier and governor. Born in Fairfax County, Virginia, Lee was graduated from the U.S. Military Academy in 1856, rose to major general in the Confederate Army, and promoted sectional reconciliation after the Civil War. After he campaigned for Grover Cleveland in the 1884 presidential election, Democrats in Virginia chose him to run for governor. Lee proved the ideal candidate to wrest the governorship from the Readjusters, a third party biracial coalition. Lee symbolized the Lost Cause, the cult of the Confederacy, which was gaining popularity in Virginia. He became the first of twenty-one consecutive Democratic governors (1886–1970). Not an activist, he spent much time dealing with problems relating to the state debt and inadequate revenues. He also demonstrated a strong interest in public education for both races. In 1896, President Cleveland appointed Lee consul general in Havana, Cuba. Two years later, when the United States went to war with Spain, he was commissioned a major general of volunteers. Retiring from service in 1901, he was active in planning the Jamestown Exposition in 1907. He died in Washington, D.C.

Further Reading: Harry W. Readnour, "Fitzhugh Lee: Confederate Cavalryman in the New South," in Edward Younger and James T. Moore, eds., *The Governors of Virginia, 1860–1978,* 1982; Harry W. Readnour, "General Fitzhugh Lee: A Biographical Study," Ph.D. diss., University of Virginia, 1971.

James R. Sweeney

LEGAL TENDER CASES. These were three related U.S. Supreme Court cases.

Hepburn **v.** *Griswold* (75 US 8 Wallace 603). *Hepburn* addressed the question of whether Congress can create a new form of legal tender and apply it to payment for past debts. In a 4–3 decision in 1870, Chief Justice Salmon Chase ruled that new tender could be applied only to new debt. Using new tender as payment for previous debts violated existing contracts, which were signed with the understanding that payment would be made with existing currency or coin. A significant element in this case was the number of justices involved in the ruling. The combination of retirements and recent legislation expanding the Court from eight to nine seats weakened the *Hepburn* ruling, setting the stage for subsequent cases concerning the Legal Tender Act of 1862.

Knox **v.** *Lee* **and** *Parker* **v.** *Davis* (12 Wallace 457). Consideration of these cases resulted in reversal of the *Hepburn* ruling. In *Knox* v. *Lee,* the question involved compensation of a property owner for seizure by the Confederacy during the Civil War. A Mrs. Lee of Pennsylvania owned a flock of sheep in Texas that was confiscated in 1863 under the Confederacy's Sequestration Act. In a suit filed in federal district court, Mrs. Lee contended that the value of her flock was greater in specie than in an equivalent amount of greenbacks, and that she should be paid the difference. The trial judge instructed that Mrs. Lee be paid in legal tender, in accordance with the Legal Tender Act. As to the question of whether Mrs. Lee was due compensation for the seizure of her flock, the Court referred to its ruling in *Texas* v. *White* (1869), which determined that all contractual agreements executed in any of the states must be honored, and that seizures and other acts of the Confederacy should be considered invalid.

Parker v. *Davis* concerned the demand by Parker for payment in gold for property purchased from him by Davis. The Massachusetts Supreme Judicial Court set the stage for the U.S. Supreme Court's eventual ruling by stipulating that payment to Parker could be made "either in coined money of the United States or in the Treasury notes of the United States." On 1 May 1871, Justice William Strong wrote for a 5–4 majority that the Legal Tender Act was constitutional, and that all contracts prior to its passage could be honored with legal tender payment. Strong argued that no constitutional distinction existed between honoring debts incurred after passage of the Legal Tender Act and honoring prior debts. Invalidation of the act on this basis would cause grave disruption of business agreements, and perpetuate the injustice of using two distinct types of payment based on when a contract was invoked. Strong also argued that the coining of money is a constitutional power of Congress, but that the type of money created was not to be taken literally (i.e., coins of gold or other precious metals).

Further Reading: Charles Fairman, *History of the Supreme Court of the United States*, vol. 6, *Reconstruction and Reunion 1864–1888*, 1971, 703–719, 740–771.

Thomas C. Sutton

LEGAL TRAINING. Lawyers typically learned their craft by apprenticing themselves to practitioners in the field. After a period of study, a prospective lawyer was examined by a committee of attorneys, who then either admitted the applicant to the bar or required additional study. In 1898, not even one fourth of lawyers in the nation had graduated from college. Some colleges had opened law schools to offer legal training, usually requiring a year or more of specialized study. Persons unable to qualify for college admission could enroll in them. By the end of the nineteenth century, some states were raising the qualifications, requiring a high school diploma before admission to law school.

Further Reading: Robert Stevens, *Law School: Legal Education in America from the 1850s to the 1980s*, 1983; Robert Stevens, "Two Cheers for 1870: The American Law School," *Perspectives in American History* 5 (1971): 405–548.

Robert J. Allison

LEIDY, JOSEPH MELLICK (9 September 1823–30 April 1891), natural historian, human and comparative anatomist, paleontologist, microscopist. Leidy spent his entire life in Philadelphia. He received an M.D. degree from the University of Pennsylvania in 1844. After a brief and unsatisfactory career as a physician, he spent the rest of his life working at Penn and Philadelphia's Academy of Natural Sciences. He published more than six hundred papers, books, and monographs, some of them "epoch making" classics, many of them beautifully illustrated. In 1853 he became professor of anatomy at Penn, and later wrote a standard medical textbook of anatomy. A master microscopist, Leidy demonstrated the power of this analytic tool in forensic pathology and histology. In 1846, he described trichina larvae in ham, thereby discovering the source of trichinosis, a serious and sometimes lethal affliction of hu-

mans, and he advocated heating pork products to eliminate the source of infection.

Leidy was the first to describe the dinosaur in America (1858), assigning to it the familiar, modern, bipedal form. Indeed, America's love affair with the dinosaur begins with Leidy. From tons of fossil material sent to him, mostly from the Midwest, he described more than three hundred extinct beasts, some unlike anything ever seen. Leidy identified the prehistoric camel, rhinoceros, hippopotamus, saber-toothed cat, and numerous early species of the horse, all from North America. He was librarian, chief curator, and then president of the Academy of Natural Sciences of Philadelphia. During the Civil War, Leidy was a surgeon and pathologist at Satterlee General Hospital in Philadelphia, and a member of the Sanitary Commission. He was also a founder and head of Penn's biology department, professor of natural history at Swarthmore College, and the head and chief curator of the Wagner Free Institute of Science in Philadelphia.

The winner of numerous prizes and member of many scientific societies, Leidy has been called the father of American vertebrate paleontology, protozoology, and parasitology. He was also a gifted botanist, zoologist, mineralogist, entomologist, and helminthologist. Despite his astonishing achievements and encyclopedic knowledge, he is virtually unknown today.

Further Reading: Leonard Warren, *Joseph Leidy, the Last Man Who Knew Everything*, 1998; Henry F. Osborne, "Biographical Memoir of Joseph Leidy, 1823–1891," in *Biographical Memoirs. National Academy of Sciences*, 1913.

Leonard Warren

LELAND, CYRUS, JR. (15 June 1841–30 August 1917), Entrepreneur and politician. Born in Prairie du Sac, Wisconsin Territory, Leland grew up in Troy, Kansas. He served in the Union Army, became the leading merchant in northeastern Kansas, and entered Republican politics. He served in the state legislature at various times and headed the Doniphan County Commission for twenty-five years, but was mainly known for his role as Republican Party leader. He served on the Republican National Committee for sixteen years (1884–1900), often on the executive committee. Leland was an ardent foe of agrarian reform movements, and by the later 1880s, he led the faction that dominated Kansas politics. He served as state collector of internal revenues (1889–1893) and Missouri Valley pension agent (1897–1901). His greatest accomplishment came in 1896 when he was one of several chairmen of William McKinley's successful presidential campaign. Leland personified rural party bosses who helped direct Republican Party affairs on the state level during the late nineteenth century. He died in St. Joseph, Missouri.

Further Reading: Robert S. La Forte, "The Making of a Rural Boss: Cy Leland, Jr., and the Doniphan County Railroad Bond Default," *Heritage of the Great Plains* 17 (Summer 1984): 19–29; Robert S. La Forte, "Cyrus Leland, Jr., and the Lawrence Massacre: A Note and Document," *Kansas History* 9 (Winter 1986/1987): 175–181.

Robert S. La Forte

LEONARD, WILLIAM ANDREW (15 July 1848–21 September 1930), bishop of the Protestant Episcopal Church. Born in Southport, Connecticut, Leonard graduated from Berkeley Divinity School in 1871, ordained deacon of the Protestant Episcopal Church that year, and advanced to the priesthood in 1872. He founded the Brooklyn Free Library and served as rector of St. John's Church in Washington, D.C., from 1880 to 1889; in the latter year he was elected bishop of the Ohio diocese. His accomplishments included building the cathedral in Cleveland, Ohio, and strengthening the programs and divinity school at Kenyon College. Leonard published several books, including *History of the Christian Church* (1878) and *Witness of the American Church to Pure Christianity* (1894). He died in Gambier, Ohio.

Further Reading: *Cleveland Plain Dealer*, 22 September 1930.

Leonard Schlup

LESLIE, FRANK (29 March 1821–10 January 1880), engraver and pioneer in illustrated newspaper publication. Born Henry Carter in Ipswich, England, he learned wood engraving while working at the *Illustrated London News*, where he adopted his nom de plume. He emigrated to New York City in 1848, and seven years later founded *Frank Leslie's Illustrated Newspaper* (1855–1922), one of America's first influential news weeklies. Leslie devised a method for illustrating current events by subdividing double-paged drawings into numerous blocks that could be distributed among many engravers and later reassembled; every large engraving house eventually adopted the system. Profits and fame peaked during the Civil War, when Leslie's artists sent back battlefield illustrations and circulation reached two hundred thousand. In the Gilded Age, personal problems, poor time management, and lavish living undermined his success. He went bankrupt in 1877, and *Harper's Weekly* superseded his journal for the remainder of the century. His second wife, Miriam Florence Leslie, whom he married in 1874, skillfully managed his business interests after his sudden death in New York City. The flamboyant "Empress of Journalism" pulled the paper out of debt by jettisoning small, unprofitable ventures, and eventually left a $2 million estate to the woman suffrage cause.

Further Reading: Budd Gambee, *Frank Leslie and His Illustrated Newspaper 1855–60*, 1964; Madeline Stern, *Queen of Publishers' Row: Mrs. Frank Leslie*, 1965; *New York Times*, 11 January 1880.

Jon Sterngass

LEUPP, FRANCIS ELLINGTON (2 January 1849–19 November 1918), journalist. Born in New York City, Leupp graduated from Williams College in 1870 and from the Columbia Law School two years later. In 1885, he moved to Washington, D.C., where he became a correspondent for the *New York Evening Post*, in charge of its Washington bureau, and simultaneously represented *The Nation* until 1904. In this capacity, Leupp achieved a distinguished reputation among Washington correspondents, making his daily rounds of executive departments, Congress, and the White House while gaining the confidence of political figures. From 1892 to 1895, he also edited *Good Government*, the official newspaper of the National Civil Service Reform League. Interested in Native Americans, Leupp visited western reservations. In 1895, Secretary of the Interior Hoke Smith sent Leupp to the Southern Ute area as a confidential agent in preparation for negotiating a treaty pertaining to their land. Leupp served on the Board of Indian Commissioners in 1896 and 1897. He died in Washington, D.C.

Further Reading: *New York Evening Post*, 20 November 1918; *New York Times*, 20 November 1918.

Leonard Schlup

LEVERING, JOSHUA (12 September 1845–5 October 1935), businessman, active Southern Baptist layman, and prohibitionist leader. A lifelong Baltimorean, Levering briefly played a national role in the events that destroyed the influence of the leading Gilded Age prohibitionist organization, the Prohibition Party, and brought to the forefront the cause's principal Progressive Era voice, the Anti-Saloon League. The wealth provided by his family's coffee importing business afforded Levering leisure to devote to his favorite causes: the Southern Baptist Church, Sabbatarianism, and prohibition. During the early 1890s, the Prohibition Party embroiled itself in fierce internecine conflict over fundamental issues of strategy and constituency. Levering sided with its conservative wing, which sought to attract support from dry middle-class Protestant voters. The Prohibition Party split at its 1896 national convention, and Levering emerged as the presidential nominee of his faction, which retained control of the party's name and what remained of its organization. Both fragments did poorly in the national election, but the principles for which Levering stood crystallized in the rising Anti-Saloon League.

Further Reading: Jack S. Blocker, *Retreat from Reform*, 1976; *New York Times*, 6 October 1935.

Jack S. Blocker, Jr.

LEWELLING, LORENZO DOW (21 December 1846–3 September 1900), Populist governor of Kansas. Born in Salem, Iowa, Lewelling served in the Union Army, was graduated from Whittier College in Salem, Iowa, and soon headed both boys' and girls' reform schools. He moved to Wichita, Kansas, in 1886 to become a dairy and produce merchant. Lewelling joined the Populist Party in 1890 and gave the keynote address at its 1892 state convention, advocating coalition (or fusion) with Democrats. Followers rallied behind his candidacy for the gubernatorial nomination. Democrats subsequently endorsed Lewelling, who carried the election. Both Republicans and Populists claimed to have carried the state House of Representatives in 1892. When Republicans physically seized the chamber and both sides began arming themselves, Lewelling, a Quaker and a pacifist, backed down in the potentially violent "Kansas Legislative War" of 1893. He outraged opponents in 1893 by issuing his famous "Tramp Circular," asking metropolitan police commissioners to ignore vagrancy laws during the depression of the 1890s. Lewelling was a strong public speaker and a noted advocate of the moral humanism of Populism. He lost his bid for reelection in 1894 when Democrats, angry at the Populist endorsement of woman suffrage, fielded a separate ticket in 1894. Lewelling served as an Iowa railroad commissioner in 1897 and 1898, and as a state senator from 1897 until his death in Arkansas City, Kansas.

Further Reading: O. Gene Clanton, *Kansas Populism: Men and Ideas*, 1969; *The Kansas Blue Book*, 1900.

Worth Robert Miller

LEWIS, DIOCLESIAN (3 March 1823–21 May 1886), temperance reformer and physical education pioneer. Born near Auburn, New York, Lewis studied medicine and homeopathy. He preached the philosophy of individual improvement through self-discipline and its application to social problems exacerbated by industrialization and urbanization. Lewis lectured on the necessity of temperance and physical activity for a healthy lifestyle for both sexes and all age groups. He supported women's rights, started a school for girls in Massachusetts, wrote several books and pamphlets, and established an institute for physical education in Boston. A prominent spokesman for better health and reform in Gilded Age America, Lewis died in Yonkers, New York.

Further Reading: Mary F. Eastman, *Biography of Dio Lewis*, 1891; Mabel Lee, *A History of Physical Education and Sports in the U.S.A.*, 1983; Dio Lewis, *Prohibition a Failure*, 1875.

Leonard Schlup

LEXOW COMMITTEE. Scandals and allegations of corruption tarnished the New York City Police Department's reputation during the latter part of the Gilded Age. The city, overwhelmed by expanding slums, a high crime rate, a vast underworld of pickpockets, gamblers, and prostitutes, and frequent rioting, adopted certain policing reforms before the Civil War. Still, officers were selected through cronyism and political patronage. Social problems increased as the population swelled past the one million mark in the 1870s. In 1885 more than 134,000 homeless people slept in dingy precinct cellars without toilets. Widespread police dishonesty plagued the force of approximately twenty-five hundred men in the 1880s. Common illegal practices included the selling of police captaincies and the paying of tithes to police officials by gamblers and pimps. Reverend Charles Pankhurst thundered against police depravity from his pulpit.

In 1894, at the same time that consolidationists favored an initiative to usher in a new metropolis of good government led by the city's best individuals, the state senate created a committee to investigate the New York City Police Department. Headed by Republican Senator Clarence Lexow, a prominent lawyer and businessman from Rockland County, and an advocate of municipal reform, the committee issued a scathing report detailing major criminal activity within the organization while listing sensational accusations of turpitude and brutality against the Tammany-controlled police force. Outcomes included the election of reform mayor William L. Strong and the appointment of reform Police Commissioner Theodore Roosevelt, a strong leader known for his unimpeachable honesty and integrity. The latter secured his appointment in 1895, the year that public disapproval of the police department forced cancellation of its annual parade. He zealously initiated strict and effective measures that helped restore confidence. Roosevelt adopted the Bertillon system of identifying criminals by the measurements of their bone structures, closed the precinct basements to indigents, removed notorious offenders, and hired ethnic minorities. He also appointed the first woman, Minnie Gertrude Kelly, and in this and other ways set the standard for the modern New York City Police Department.

Further Reading: Edwin G. Burrows, *Gotham: A History of New York City to 1898*, 1998; H. Paul Jeffers, *Commissioner Roosevelt: The Story of Theodore Roosevelt and the New York City Police, 1895–1897*, 1994.

Leonard Schlup

LIBERAL REPUBLICANS. During President Ulysses S. Grant's first administration (1869–1873), widespread discontent with presidential leadership manifested itself as a movement to reform the Republican Party. Sources were many: dismay over Grant's proposal to annex Santo Domingo, impatience with his failure to foster sectional reconciliation by swiftly ending Reconstruction, and irritation at an appointment policy that favored spoilsmen over reformers. Liberals first surfaced in Missouri under the leadership of Carl Schurz, an idealistic German immigrant and Civil War veteran. By early 1872, anti-Grant feeling had spread, and the Liberals called a convention to nominate a candidate. The delegates who gathered at Cincinnati in May, however, were a motley group with varied and even contradictory interests. Their presidential nominee, Horace Greeley, editor of the *New York Tribune*, was identified with many positions certain to antagonize key voter groups. When the Democrats, of whom Greeley had long been an outspoken critic, later endorsed him, their opportunism was all too obvious. Grant, renominated by the Republicans, easily won reelection, and the Liberal Republican movement collapsed. Most insurgents soon returned to the Republican Party, positioning themselves as an independent faction that urged the party to abjure spoils politics, and to adopt civil service reform and a low-tariff policy.

Further Reading: John G. Sproat, *"The Best Men": Liberal Reformers in the Gilded Age*, 1968; William S. McFeely, *Grant: A Biography*, 1981.

Gerald W. McFarland

LIBRARY OF CONGRESS. During the Gilded Age, the Library of Congress underwent significant change. Ainsworth Rand Spofford, Librarian of Congress from 1864 to 1897, built it into a national institution. Through his efforts, the copyright law of 1870 required all copyright applicants to submit two copies of their work to the library, resulting in a bombardment of books, pamphlets, photographs, and other items. Confronted with a shortage of shelf space, Spofford persuaded national legislators of the necessity for a new edifice, for which Congress in 1873 authorized a competition to sketch architectural plans. In 1886 Congress approved the design offered by John L. Smithmeyer and Paul J. Pelz in Italian Renaissance style. Two years later, General Thomas Lincoln Casey, chief of the Army Corps of Engineers, oversaw the construction with Bernard R. Green as his main assistant. In 1892 Casey's son, Edward Pearce Casey, assumed supervision of the interior work. Philip Martiny, a French-born sculptor who had worked with Augustus Saint-Gaudens, made the decorative sculptures that adorn the balustrades of the majestic stairway. The building opened to the public on 1 November 1897. Hailed as for its size, cost, and safety, the Library of Congress went through additional renovations in the twentieth century.

Further Reading: John Young Cole, *Jefferson's Legacy: A Brief History of the Library of Congress*, 1992.

Leonard Schlup

LILIUOKALANI, QUEEN (2 September 1838–11 November 1917), queen of Hawaii, musician, and composer. Born Lydia Kamakaeha, in Honolulu, Liliuokalani was educated at missionary schools, including the Royal School for the Hawaiian elite. Her brother, King David Kalakaua, named her heir to the Hawaiian throne in 1877. While a princess, she visited the countryside to meet the people, supported a school for young Hawaiian girls, and established a bank for women. She disliked the Bayonet Constitution of 1887 that removed the monarch's power and put it into the hands of the cabinet, and reduced native Hawaiian voting rights. She also opposed the 1887 treaty that gave the United States exclusive rights to use Pearl Harbor.

On 29 January 1891, Liliuokalani became queen upon her brother's death. At the time the Hawaiian economy was in a depression because the McKinley Tariff of 1890 added duties to its sugar exports. The legislature was fragmented between parties that supported either the monarchy or a more democratic form of government. For this reason, the queen encountered

difficulty trying to appoint a stable cabinet. In 1893, believing that she had native support, Liliuokalani tried to rescind the Bayonet Constitution and rule by decree, as her ancestors had done. A pro-American committee of public safety arrested her on 16 January and deposed her the next day.

Liliuokalani was found guilty of treason by a military commission and sentenced to five years at hard labor and a $5000 fine, but Sanford Dole, head of the provisional republican government, commuted the sentence to imprisonment. She hoped for the monarchy's restoration because President Grover Cleveland opposed the actions that led to her deposition. However, the provisional government remained in power, and she stayed under arrest from January 1895 to October 1896 at Iolani Palace and at her home at Washington Place. After the government freed her, she traveled frequently to America and tried to obtain monetary compensation for her lost crown lands.

Liliuokalani played a wide range of musical instruments and wrote traditional Hawaiian songs. One of her most famous songs was "Farewell to Thee" ("Aloha Oe," 1898). She died at Washington Place in Honolulu. A unique Victorian woman, Liliuokalani was a strong supporter of native customs and rights, as well as of the education of women.

Further Reading: Helena G. Allen, *The Betrayal of Liliuokalani*, 1982; Ralph S. Kuykendall, *The Hawaiian Kingdom, 1874–1893*, 1967; Queen Liliuokalani, *Hawaii's Story by Hawaii's Queen*, 1898.

Bryan Craig

LINCOLN COUNTY WAR. Between February 1878 and February 1879, the community of Lincoln, New Mexico, was embroiled in a battle between two elite factions. Lawrence G. Murphy and James H. Dolan fought John Tunstall, John Chisum, and Alexander McSween for the control of government contracts for beef and other provisions. Murphy's supporters initially waged a legal battle, but after Tunstall was murdered, violence erupted and climaxed in the "five-day battle." The Murphy-Dolan faction laid siege to McSween and his supporters. The governor sent troops from nearby Fort Stanton, but, showing partiality toward Dolan, the soldiers stood by and watched as McSween and four other men were killed. Though violence subsided, Lincoln County remained in conflict for several years. One of the most notorious participants in the war was William H. Bonney, later known as "Billy the Kid."

Further Reading: John P. Wilson, *Merchants, Guns, and Money: The Story of Lincoln County and Its War*, 1987; Frederick W. Nolan, *The Lincoln County War: A Documentary History*, 1992; Robert M. Utley, *High Noon in Lincoln: Violence on the Western Frontier*, 1987.

Kelly McMichael Stott

LINCOLN IMAGE. The Lincoln image in the American mind began to take shape on the day President Abraham Lincoln died in 1865. Struck down by an assassin's bullet at his moment of triumph, Lincoln became an epic figure, remembered, memorialized, and celebrated. His funeral entourage, the apotheosis of the martyred chief executive, initiated the transformation process. The composite representation of ideas, ideals, and policies identified with Lincoln was nurtured as Gilded Age Americans refashioned and molded his persona. The sage of Springfield emerged as a leader who synthesized conflicting views, preserved the Union, abolished slavery, won the Civil War, and in the end lost his life as the conflict's symbolic final casualty. His idealization enabled various groups, including industrialists and biographers, to employ a variety of different aspects of the Lincolnian perception. In addition, prints served to make Lincoln an emblem of popular and political culture throughout the remainder of the century.

Many citizens saw Lincoln as the personification of the self-made man in an era of rags-to-riches success stories. African Americans also responded to his memory. Politically, Lincoln combined the philosophy of Alexander Hamilton with the principles of Thomas Jefferson, successfully uniting these two divergent strands while forging a strong government within the limits of the Declaration of Independence. Numerous politicians reshaped his glory and laid claim to his mantle. Lincoln's genius as a motivator and his humility were interconnected in Gilded Age thought. Campaigns, speeches, written words, and other forms of ex-

pression gave Lincoln a secure place in the people's imagination, and his influence extended well beyond his time.

Further Reading: Merrill D. Peterson, *Lincoln in American Memory*, 1994; Harold Holzer et al., *The Lincoln Image: Abraham Lincoln and the Popular Print*, 2001; J. David Greenstone, *The Lincoln Persuasion: Remaking American Liberalism*, 1993; Roy P. Basler, *The Lincoln Legend: A Study in Changing Conceptions*, 1935.

Leonard Schlup

LINCOLN, MARY ANN TODD (13 December 1818–16 July 1882), wife of the sixteenth president of the United States. Born in Lexington, Kentucky, Todd was educated at John Ward's Academy, and in 1832 attended Madame Mentelle's boarding school in Lexington. These twelve years placed her at the forefront of American women in terms of education. Her intellectual interests included politics; her father, Robert Smith Todd, was a Whig politician. In 1839 Todd lived with her sister in Springfield, Illinois, where she met Abraham Lincoln. They were married on 4 November 1842. She was First Lady from 1861 until 1865. The position was difficult because her half brothers fought for the Confederacy. The strain of public scrutiny was compounded by her son Willie's death from typhoid in 1862. After he died, she was criticized for her unmitigated sorrow in a time of national crisis, and her mental state deteriorated. President Lincoln was shot on 14 April 1865 as Mary sat by his side in Ford's Theatre. In 1868 Mrs. Lincoln traveled to Europe; she returned to the United States in 1870, when Congress granted her a pension. In 1875 she was committed to a mental hospital in Illinois by her son Robert Todd Lincoln, but released a few months later with the assistance of Myra Bradwell, one of the nation's first female lawyers. She then lived in France until 1880. She died in Springfield, Illinois.

Further Reading: Justin G. Turner and Linda Levitt Turner, *Mary Todd Lincoln: Her Life and Letters*, 1972; Ruth Randall, *Mary Lincoln: Biography of a Marriage*, 1953.

Lisa De Palo

LINCOLN, MARY JOHNSON BAILEY (8 July 1844–2 December 1921), writer, teacher, and lecturer. Born in South Attleboro, Massachusetts, Bailey graduated from Wheaton Female Seminary in 1864 and married David A. Lincoln the following year. She directed the Boston Cooking School from 1879 until 1885. In addition, Lincoln cofounded the *New England Kitchen Magazine* and served as its culinary editor while writing columns. Also active in the New England Woman's Press, Lincoln developed baking powder, wrote books, and lectured, often while preparing food on stage. Through her writings and ideas, she helped to build self-esteem for Gilded Age women and offered tributes to their work and other activities.

Further Reading: *Boston Herald*, 3 December 1921; Laura Shapiro, *Perfection Salad*, 1986.

Leonard Schlup

LINCOLN, ROBERT TODD (1 August 1843–26 July 1926), secretary of war and railroad official. Born in Springfield, Illinois, he was the eldest son of Abraham and Mary Todd Lincoln. Lincoln was graduated from Harvard University in 1864 and briefly served on the staff of General Ulysses Grant. After studying at Harvard Law School, he was admitted to the Illinois bar in 1867 and became a wealthy corporate lawyer. Although Lincoln shunned politics, in 1881 he accepted appointment as secretary of war in President James A. Garfield's cabinet. There Lincoln sought to limit white settlement on Indian lands and to secure pay increases for enlisted personnel. Most of Lincoln's War Department work proved routine, though he did remove many longtime but ineffective officials. Lincoln transferred the Weather Bureau from the War Department to the Agriculture Department. General William Hazen unfairly criticized him for failing to resupply A. W. Greely's polar mission, but Hazen's court-martial conviction after Lincoln left office vindicated the secretary. The only Garfield cabinet member to serve throughout the subsequent administration of President Chester A. Arthur, Lincoln left office in March 1885. From 1889 to 1893, he was minister to Great Britain. Uninterested in the law after his son's death in London, Lincoln headed the Pullman

Company from 1887 to 1911. He died in Manchester, Vermont.

Further Reading: John S. Goff, *Robert Todd Lincoln: A Man in His Own Right*, 1969.

Stephen Svonavec

LIND, JOHANNA "JENNY" MARIA (6 October 1821–2 November 1887), singer. Lind was born in Stockholm, Sweden, and received vocal training there and in Paris. She sang in Berlin, Copenhagen, Vienna, London, and throughout Italy before coming to the United States in 1849 at P. T. Barnum's invitation. While on tour, she married Otto Goldschmidt, and the two returned to Europe in 1852. He wrote an oratio, *Ruth*, in 1869, which she sang in Hamburg and London. In London she trained female singers in the Bach Choir between 1876 and 1883, and was professor of singing at the Royal College of Music between 1883 and 1886. She gave her last public concert in 1883. She died in Malvern, England.

Further Reading: Elisabeth Kyle, *The Swedish Nightingale: Jenny Lind*, 1966.

Christopher Cumo

LINDSAY, WILLIAM (4 September 1835–15 October 1909), senator. Born near Lexington, Virginia, Lindsay settled in Clinton, Kentucky, in 1854, gained admission to the bar in 1858, and served in the Confederate Army. He held a seat in the state senate from 1867 to 1870 and again from 1889 to 1893. Elected as a Democrat to the U.S. Senate, Lindsay remained there from 1893 until 1901, when he chose not to seek renomination. During his Senate years, he favored tariff revision, limited government, and sound money. His position as a conservative Gold Democrat put him in conflict with presidential candidate William Jennings Bryan in 1896. Lindsay died in Frankfort, Kentucky.

Further Reading: Leonard Schlup, "William Lindsay and the 1896 Party Crisis," *Register of the Kentucky Historical Society* 76 (1978): 22–33; *Louisville Courier-Journal*, 16 October 1909; William Lindsay Papers, University of Kentucky Library, Lexington.

Leonard Schlup

LITERATURE. Gilded Age literature is identified by its efforts to come to terms with the new industrial society that was emerging following the Civil War. The name of the era is taken from the novel *The Gilded Age* (1873) by Mark Twain and Charles Dudley Warner. They satirized the acquisitive modern businessperson, and society in general, as superficial, material-istic, and corrupt. Shortly after the Civil War ended, the local-color school of writers ap-peared. Members included Bret Harte with his stories of the West, Joel Chandler Harris and his Georgia folk tales, and Sarah Orne Jewett's descriptions of a decaying social order in New England. Mark Twain began his career as a lo-cal colorist, penning stories about the West and the Mississippi River. His work also repre-sented a new perspective in literature that in-cluded other regional writers—the perspective of realism. All the forces that were transform-ing American life—industrialism, immigration, science, and social dislocation—influenced writers to look more closely at the environment and its impact on society and behavior, and to reject romantic nostalgia. Horatio Alger typified a transition to realism in that his stories, espe-cially the Ragged Dick series, clearly portray the negative aspects of modern urban life, yet still hold out the hope that perseverance and hard work will bring personal and material suc-cess. Alger appealed to those who clung to the old values of individualism and diligence. Hamlin Garland's *Main Travelled Roads* (1891) depicted the loneliness and deprivation of farming life on the plains in a consistent, more realistic manner. Stephen Crane's *Mag-gie, a Girl of the Streets* (1893) described slum life in New York City. The most influential re-alistic novelist of the age was William Dean Howells. His *Rise of Silas Lapham* (1885) ex-posed the less flattering side of a self-made businessman. Howells's later work dealt with the social strife and labor demonstrations of the 1890s.

While realists tried to portray the common-place in life, naturalists moved beyond this to explore the darker side of life. They viewed man as merely another animal, shaped by en-vironment and engaged in a constant struggle to survive. Stephen Crane's *Red Badge of Courage* (1895), Frank Norris's *McTeague* (1899) and *The Octopus* (1901), and Jack Lon-don's short stories set in the Yukon and the South Pacific all emphasized this theme. Gilded Age literature was a rich and accurate reflec-tion of the nation's efforts to understand the new, dynamic culture created by so many concurrent forces. The writings provide insight into the effort to reconcile industrial capitalism with the American tradition of democratic individualism.

Further Reading: H. Wayne Morgan, *American Writers in Rebellion: From Mark Twain to Dreiser*, 1965; Vernon L. Parrington, *Main Currents in American Thought*, vol. 3: *Beginnings of Critical Realism, 1860–1920*, 1930; Donald Pizer and Earl Harbert, eds., *American Literature to 1900*, 1987.

C. Edward Balog

LITTLE BIG HORN, BATTLE OF. The first of several failed attempts in 1876 to remove Lakota Sioux to the Great Sioux Reservation, the battle (near today's Crow Agency, Mon-tana) pitted Lakotas, Northern Cheyenne allies, and a few others against Lieutenant Colonel George A. Custer and his Seventh Cavalry reg-iment. Custer's fate is well known. He and all 210 men in his battalion perished on 25–26 June 1876. Less well known are the Valley and Reno-Benteen fights, also part of the battle. Major Marcus Reno, Custer's second in com-mand, initiated hostilities on 25 June by attack-ing the Indian village nestled in Little Big Horn Valley. Ultimately warriors drove off Reno's battalion. The soldiers scrambled in confusion to high bluffs across the river. There Captain Frederick Benteen, returning with his battalion from scouting upriver, met Reno and stopped to assist him. The two groups consolidated on the bluffs, where warriors laid siege into the next day.

Custer's battle took place some four miles to the north. After ordering Reno's attack, Custer veered right and rode unopposed across high bluffs on the opposite bank. Entering a broad coulee, he organized into two wings. The left rode to the coulee mouth. Across the river lay the north end of a now nearly empty village. Reno's assault had attracted the warriors, and sent noncombatants fleeing north. Facing little resistance, Custer elected to pursue the non-combatants. Both wings withdrew farther north. The left wing again went to the river, the two wings afterward deploying about a mile apart. Belatedly learning of Custer, warriors left

Reno, arriving in bunches as the two wings maneuvered. Seeing only the right wing at first, most began to pressure it. After light exchanges, a company of the right wing charged, but Lame White Man's counterattack drove it back in confusion. Panic spread to the entire right wing. Some twenty survivors made it to the left wing, now on "Last Stand Hill."

About 105 soldiers—half the battalion—remained. Minutes later, a company rushed on foot toward the river, hoping to divert attention from several riders who galloped south for help. However, the riders were killed and the company collapsed, the survivors fleeing into a rugged ravine. Warriors soon overran the hill, spilling into the ravine, where fighting ended. Eyewitness accounts indicate the decisive fighting—from the right wing's collapse to the end—lasted scarcely a half hour.

Afterward, warriors returned to the Reno-Benteen field, where soldiers successfully kept their antagonists at bay. Learning of another force—General Alfred Terry's column—the Indians struck camp late on 26 June. That evening, Terry's advance scouts arrived. Some fifty, with Reno and Benteen, died, bringing the Seventh Regiment's losses to about 260 dead. Indian deaths are hard to pinpoint, but forty to fifty is a reasonable estimate.

Further Reading: Richard A. Fox, *Archaeology, History, and Custer's Last Battle: The Little Big Horn Reexamined*, 1993; Charles M. Robinson III, *A Good Year to Die: The Story of the Great Sioux War*, 1995.

Richard A. Fox

LITTLE LORD FAUNTLEROY SUITS FOR BOYS. Proper dress played an important role in Victorian America, an era strongly conscious of the niceties of good form and the many gradations of social position. Even the simplest costumes were far from plain. The lavish trimmings reflected an age in which women and children were considered as ornamental, a perfect complement to the overstuffed parlors and the plethora of ostentation and richness that characterized nineteenth-century taste. A particularly interesting period in the evolution of boys' clothing for the upper echelons of society occurred in the late 1880s. Boys normally wore dresses until they were about four or five years old. Thereafter discerning mothers dressed their sons in kilt skirts, trousers, or Buster Brown suits. A new style appeared following the 1886 publication of the Anglo-American writer Frances Hodgson Burnett's *Little Lord Fauntleroy*. The author based her fictional creation on her own son, Vivian. Reginald Bathurst Birch's superb illustrations for the book started the Little Lord Fauntleroy fashion craze, which continued through the turn of the century. Boys often wore their hair in long "sausage" curls and dressed in fancy black or dark blue velvet suits, lace collars, black stockings, pants reaching to the knee or below, broad-brimmed, plumed sailor hats, and a colorful silk sash. The Fauntleroy suit was a status symbol. Children dressed this way could not work in factories or mines, or on the farm. Moreover, putting on a Fauntleroy outfit was complicated; most boys needed assistance. Accordingly, Fauntleroyism was an instant statement of family wealth and status during the last fifteen years of American Victorianism.

Further Reading: Frances Hodgson Burnett, *Little Lord Fauntleroy*, 1886; Historical Boys' Clothing web site.

Leonard Schlup

LLOYD, HENRY DEMAREST (1 May 1847–28 September 1903), Progressive reformer and publicist. Lloyd, born in New York City, was a prime critic of America capitalism, a supporter of democracy and of labor unions, opposed to industrial trusts, and a devotee of the dictum that social progress was always religious. He applauded labor cooperatives at home and abroad, and of such champions of democracy as Giuseppe Mazzini, the Swiss Confederation, and New Zealand. His best-known work was his diatribe against the Standard Oil trust, *Wealth Against Commonwealth* (1894). In politics, he supported such Progressive reformers as William Jennings Bryan and Eugene V. Debs, a socialist. He died in Chicago.

Further Reading: Caro Lloyd, *Henry Demarest Lloyd*, 2 vols., 1912; Alun Muslow and Owen R. Ashton, *Henry Demarest Lloyd's Critiques of American Capitalism, 1881–1903*, 1995; Henry Demarest Lloyd Papers (microform), State Historical Society of Wisconsin, Division of Archives and Manuscripts, Madison.

Paolo E. Coletta

LOCKWOOD, BELVA ANN BENNETT MCNALL (24 October 1830–19 May 1917), teacher, attorney, and suffragist. Born in Royalton, New York, Lockwood was educated in rural schools and received a degree from Gennessee College. She moved to Washington, D.C., in 1866 to open a school and become politically active. In order to make a difference, Lockwood decided to become a lawyer. She helped secure the passage of the Arnell Bill in 1872. After several attempts, Lockwood entered the National University Law School. Upon completing the course, she was denied her diploma until she protested to President Grant. In order to practice in the federal court system, she helped the Lockwood Bill become law in 1879. Lockwood became the first female attorney admitted to practice before the U.S. Supreme Court, and sponsored the first southern black in 1880. Her successful law practice specialized in claims against the government. In the 1884 presidential election, Lockwood was the candidate of the National Equal Rights Party. She was a strong advocate of world peace, attending the First World Peace Conference in 1886 and serving on the nominating committee for the Nobel Peace Prize. A founding member of the Universal Franchise Association, Lockwood was also active in the National Woman Suffrage Association. During her lifetime, Lockwood made a great strides in the women's movement, and through her lectures and activities brought the cause of rights for women to the attention of the nation.

Further Reading: Belva Lockwood, "My Efforts to Become President," *Lippincott's Monthly Magazine* 41 (February 1888): 215–229; Julia Davis, "Belva Ann Lockwood: Remover of Mountains," *American Bar Association Journal* 65 (1979): 924–928; Julia Hull Winner, "Belva A. Lockwood: That Extraordinary Woman," *New York History* 39, no. 1 (1958): 321–340.

Terri Pedersen Summey

LODGE, HENRY CABOT (12 May 1850–9 November 9, 1924), U.S. senator and author. Born in Boston, Massachusetts, Lodge was graduated from Harvard College in 1871 and its law school in 1874. While Lodge was completing his studies, Henry Adams offered him the assistant editorship of *North American Review*. While working there (1873–1876), he received Harvard's first doctorate in political science. He published a number of essays and books, including *A Short History of the English Colonies in America* (1881). Lodge was elected to the Massachusetts House of Representatives in 1879, and to Congress in 1886. An effective and frequent speaker in the House, he promoted a force bill to establish federal supervisors over polling places in the South, and called for civil service reform. He also helped draft the Sherman Antitrust Act of 1890. As U.S. senator from 1893 to 1924, he voted against the direct election of Senators and woman suffrage. Possessing a strong interest in international affairs, he advised Theodore Roosevelt on foreign policy, served on the Alaskan Boundary Commission, and later opposed U.S. entry into the League of Nations. During the early 1920s, his influence peaked as the senior Republican in the Senate and chairman of the Foreign Relations Committee. He also served as one of the American representatives at the Washington Naval Conference in 1921. He died in Cambridge, Massachusetts.

Further Reading: C. S. Groves, *Henry Cabot Lodge, the Statesman*, 1925; John A. Garrity, *Henry Cabot Lodge: A Biography*, 1953.

William C. Binning

LOGAN, JOHN ALEXANDER (9 February 1826–26 December 1886), U.S. senator and vice presidential nominee. Born on a farm near Murphysboro, Illinois, Logan attended local schools, served in the Mexican War, and studied law at the University of Louisville. He practiced in Benton, and later Egypt, Illinois, and held a seat as a Jacksonian Democrat in the state legislature. An ally of Senator Stephen A. Douglas, Logan served in the U.S. House of Representatives from 1859 until 1862. At first reticent about the Civil War, he eventually denounced both secession and abolitionists, and fought notably as a War Democrat. He campaigned in 1864 for President Abraham Lincoln's reelection, helped organize the Grand Army of the Republic, and conceived the idea of Memorial Day. He won a congressional seat as a fervent Republican convert in 1866, mercilessly attacking President Andrew Johnson. Logan served in the House of Representatives

from 1867 until his election in 1871 to the U.S. Senate. There he sat from 1871 to 1877 and again from 1879 until his death in Washington, D.C. Supporting Ulysses S. Grant's presidency, Logan, a resident of Chicago, benefited from patronage. In 1884, he was nominated for the vice presidency on the Republican ticket headed by James G. Blaine of Maine, which lost to the Democrats. Logan wrote two books.
Further Reading: James P. Jones, *John A. Logan: Stalwart Republican from Illinois*, 1982; *Chicago Tribune*, 27 December 1886.

Leonard Schlup

LONDON, JACK (12 January 1876–22 November 1916), author. London was born John Griffith in San Francisco, California. More than any other American fiction writer of the Gilded Age, he applied the doctrine of the survival of the fittest to the human condition. He wrote more than fifty books, including fiction, essays, and journalism. His two most famous novels, *The Call of the Wild* (1903) and the *Sea Wolf* (1904), though published after the turn of the century, reflect the dominance of Darwinian ideas in literary circles during the 1890s. London translated Darwinism into the vernacular through rousing adventure stories, dime novels, and socialistic essays. Nature was indifferent to humanity, and humanity was but a part of the great evolutionary struggle for survival. One might perceive an apparent contradiction, however, between his portrayal of life as a struggle in which the strong inevitably triumph, and his personal commitment to a revolution of the disadvantaged against the strong. His early stories range in locale from the Yukon to the South Pacific to northern California. He spent the last years of his life on his ranch in Glen Ellen, California, where he died of kidney disease at age forty.
Further Reading: Andrew Sinclair, *Jack: A Biography of Jack London*, 1977; Joan D. Hedrick, *Solitary Comrade: Jack London and His Work*, 1982.

C. Edward Balog

LONE WOLF (1820–1879), Kiowa chief. A respected warrior, Lone Wolf joined Ten Bears of the Comanche, Lean Bear of the Southern Cheyenne, and others, in a delegation to meet President Abraham Lincoln in Washington, D.C., in 1863. Following the death of Little Mountain in 1866, Lone Wolf emerged as the compromise choice as principal chief over Satanta, head of the war faction, and Kicking Bird, who led the peace contingent. In 1867, Lone Wolf signed the Treaty of Medicine Lodge, which created the boundaries of the conjunctional Comanche and Kiowa reservation in Indian Territory (Oklahoma). The Kiowa refusal to adhere to the covenant compelled General Philip H. Sheridan to take Lone Wolf as a prisoner of war. Although agreeing to peace in 1872, the next year, following the killings of his son and nephew by soldiers, Lone Wolf turned to armed conflict. He fought Texas Rangers and federal army troops under General Nelson A. Miles and Colonel Ranald S. Mackenzie during the Red River War of 1874–1875. The Kiowa attacked buffalo hunters at Adobe Walls in June 1874. Defending Palo Duro Canyon in September proved formidable for the Native Americans, who lost lives, ponies, and tepees to Mackenzie's forces. Lone Wolf surrendered at Fort Sill, Indian Territory, in February 1875. Exiled to Fort Marion, Florida, he contracted malaria and returned to his homeland, where he died.
Further Reading: Carl Waldman, *Biographical Dictionary of American Indian History to 1900*, rev. ed., 2001.

Leonard Schlup

LONG, JOHN DAVIS (27 October 1838–28 August 1915), governor and cabinet member. Born in Buckfield, Maine, Long studied at Harvard Law School, and was admitted to the Massachusetts bar in 1861. A Republican, he served as speaker of the state assembly from 1875 to 1878, and as governor from 1880 to 1882. He sat in the federal House of Representatives from 1883 to 1889, and in 1897, was appointed secretary of the navy by President William McKinley. Throughout his term, Long sought to improve the material condition and efficiency of the navy. He obtained congressional approval for expanding the government's navy yards and the acquisition of new dry docks and coaling facilities, especially in the Pacific. The major event of Long's tenure was the war with Spain in 1898. Once the battleship *Maine* was destroyed in Havana harbor in February 1898,

Long worked diligently to prepare for war. Co-operating closely with his aggressive assistant secretary, Theodore Roosevelt, Long implemented contingency plans to quickly engage the Spanish. During the hostilities, Long ably managed a rapidly expanding navy. When peace came, he continued his efforts to improve the navy's strength, asking Congress to continue the construction of a strong, modern fleet. He resigned in 1902 and later died in Hingham, Massachusetts.

Further Reading John Long, *The New American Navy*, 1903; Scott Mraz, "Recognition Long Overdue," *Naval History* 12 (June 1998): 24–26.

Stephen Svonavec

LORIMER, WILLIAM (27 April 1861–3 September 1934), Republican Party boss. Born in Manchester, England, Lorimer entered Chicago politics in 1884, and began organizing his district's traditionally Democratic Irish, Bohemian, and Russian Jewish working-class immigrants. He won support through the machine politician's usual method: building a network of friendships, patronage, and favors to develop a strong personal following. Lorimer regarded politics as a business, and his organization had strong ties with the traction magnate Charles Tyson Yerkes, the electrical utility builder Samuel Insull, and the banker John R. Walsh. Lorimer protected and advanced their corporate interests in the Chicago City Council and in the Illinois General Assembly. He acquired great power in Illinois Republican politics, frequently allying with downstate Republican politicians against Chicago reformers, and was the determining influence in nominations for state and federal, as well as city, offices. From 1895 to 1901, and from 1903 to 1909, Lorimer represented the Second District of Illinois in the House of Representatives. In 1909, a bipartisan group in the Illinois General Assembly elected Lorimer to the U.S. Senate. Charges of corruption in his election, however, led to Lorimer's ouster in 1912, even though two Senate investigatory committees had supported his retention. He died in Chicago.

Further Reading Joel A. Tarr, *A Study in Boss Politics: William Lorimer of Chicago*, 1971; William T. Hutchinson, *Lowden of Illinois*, 2 vols., 1957.

Joel A. Tarr

LOUDENSLAGER, HENRY CLAY (22 May 1852–12 August 1911), businessman and political figure. Born in Mauricetown, New Jersey, Loudenslager attended public schools in Paulsboro, New Jersey. From 1872 to 1882 he worked in the produce commission business in Philadelphia. County clerk of Gloucester County, New Jersey, from 1882 to 1892, Loudenslager was elected as a Republican to the U.S. House of Representatives, representing New Jersey's First Congressional District from 1893 until his death at his home in Paulsboro. During the political contests of 1906, 1908, and 1910, he served as secretary of the Republican Congressional Campaign Committee. Loudenslager, a party regular who supported House Speaker Joseph G. Cannon, devoted most of his attention to pension legislation. He chaired the Committee on Pensions in the Fifty-fourth through Sixty-first Congresses. Loudenslager maintained a strong personal and political association with President William Howard Taft.

Further Reading *New York Times*, 13 August 1911.

Leonard Schlup

LOWELL, JAMES RUSSELL (22 February 1819–12 August 1891), professor, poet, and U.S. ambassador. Born in Cambridge, Massachusetts, Lowell was graduated from Harvard University in 1838, and from its law school in 1840. His literary career began in 1843 with his editorship of *The Pioneer*. Subsequently, he taught at Harvard from 1855 to 1872, and 1874 to 1886. Lowell also edited the *Atlantic Monthly* between 1857 and 1861. His political views became widely known during the Mexican War, when he argued that the conflict was a slaveholders' plot to annex territory. In a series of satiric poems, *The Biglow Papers*, he attacked those who hid behind the cloak of Manifest Destiny. Later he supported the Union cause. After the Civil War, Lowell's poetry and criticism continued to influence literary perceptions and style. One of his best-known poems, "Ode Recited at the Harvard Commemoration" (1865), bore testament to his respect for scholarship and culture. In the 1880s, Lowell deplored the growing sense of alienation from culture and criticism. The overemphasis on method and textual criticism, he argued, had obscured the essence of beauty and civilizing qualities found in literature. From 1877 to 1880, he served as ambassador to Spain, and then to England from 1880 to 1885. He died in Cambridge.

Further Reading: Merle Curti, *The Growth of American Thought*, 1943; Martin Duberman, *James Russell Lowell*, 1966; *The Writings of James Russell Lowell*, 10 vols., 1891; Thomas Wortham, ed., *James Russell Lowell's The Biglow Papers: A Critical Edition*, 1977.

Charles F. Howlett

LOWELL, PERCIVAL (13 March 1855–12 November 1916), astronomer and author. Born in Boston, Massachusetts, Lowell was graduated from Harvard in 1876. He wrote articles and books, and founded an observatory at Flagstaff, Arizona Territory, in 1894, to search for life on Mars. Controversy surrounded some of his observations and writings, especially his contention that the Martian surface contained canals. Yet his findings, published works, and photographic telescopes were enthusiastically received by many persons who had once considered astronomy and the origin of the solar system as dull and overly complex. Lowell predicted the existence of an undiscovered planet, and began his search in 1905. His death, at the observatory in Flagstaff, came before the discovery of Pluto in 1930. Although modern scientists have criticized much of his work, his founding of and bequest to the Lowell Observatory stand today as lasting legacies.

Further Reading: William Graves Hoyt, *Lowell and Mars*, 1976; David Strauss, "The 'Far East' in the American Mind, 1883–1894: Percival Lowell's Decisive Impact," *Journal of American-East Asian Relations* 2 (1993): 217–241; David Strauss, "Percival Lowell, W. H. Pickering, and the Founding of the Lowell Observatory," *Annals of Science* 51 (1994): 37–58.

Leonard Schlup

LYNCHING. America's Gilded Age was the golden age of lynching, the illegal killing of a person by a mob. In the early post-Civil War period, lynching was primarily a western phenomenon that victimized mostly whites. Between 1882 and 1888, 595 whites were lynched, as opposed to 440 African Americans. As the frontier faded in the 1890s, lynching became concentrated in the South and focused on African Americans. In 1892, some 230 to 240 people were lynched, almost three-fourths of them black. Within a decade, that figure rose to more than 90 percent blacks. All told, about eight hundred blacks were lynched in the violent decade of the 1890s.

Lynching, like the bloody race riots of the period, can be understood in the context of growing racism and the determination of white southerners to suppress blacks. Persons of all classes and genders took part in lynchings, though most of the perpetrators were young working-class males. Most mobs accused their victims of some crime and wrested their prey from law enforcement officials or jails. The crime most often cited as justifying the lynchings of blacks was the rape of white women. However, only about 25 percent of the blacks lynched were accused of rape.

Several blacks were lynched for such trivial charges as sassing a white person, engaging in politics, or simply being unduly successful. Furthermore, many innocent African Americans were killed as rampaging mobs searched for persons accused of crimes. As the century neared its end, quiet and quick private hangings of blacks tended to give way to public spectacles attended by thousands of whites. Frenzied crowds burned blacks alive, and engaged in fiendish tortures that lasted for hours. After lynchings, white youths scrambled to retrieve dismembered body parts, treating them as souvenirs. The primary purpose of lynching was to terrorize all African Americans and perpetuate the American caste system that had been weakened by Reconstruction. Since extralegal violence had widespread southern support, few lynchers were arrested and fewer still were convicted.

Further Reading: Ida B. Wells, *A Red Record*, 1892, rep. 1997; W. Fitzhugh Brundage, *Lynching in the New South*, 1993; E. Stewart Tolnay and E. M. Beck, *A Festival of Violence: An Analysis of Southern Lynching, 1880–1930*, 1995.

David W. Southern

MACCORKLE, WILLIAM ALEXANDER (7 May 1857–24 September 1930), West Virginia governor. Born in Lexington, Virginia, MacCorkle received a law degree from Washington and Lee University

in 1879. After moving to Charleston, West Virginia, MacCorkle joined the "Kanawha Ring," consisting of young professionals impoverished by the Civil War and attracted by the 1870s coal boom. MacCorkle was admitted to the bar in 1880. By then, under Congressman John Kenna's leadership, the "ring" had become the dominant political faction within the state Democratic Party. MacCorkle soon found himself Charleston's prosecuting attorney, and was elevated to Arthur B. Fleming's gubernatorial staff in 1890. He became governor in 1893, largely by appealing to the state's pro-southern element. He had first gained fame by physically assaulting a Republican official who had denounced Jefferson Davis. At the same time, MacCorkle gained "backwoods" support through courting Anderson "Devil Anse" Hatfield of Logan County. As governor, he subsequently repaid Hatfield by preventing his extradition to Kentucky to answer for twenty murders associated with the Hatfield-McCoy feud. In the 1894 elections, the GOP captured the state legislature, and spent the next two years preparing the way for Republican Governor George W. Atkinson to succeed MacCorkle in 1897. MacCorkle was elected to the state senate in 1910. Before his death, he wrote a number of books, including *Recollection of Fifty Years of West Virginia.*

Further Reading: *National Cyclopaedia of American Biography* 12 (1904): 432.

Harvey Gresham Hudspeth

MACDOWELL, EDWARD ALEXANDER (18 December 1861–23 January 1908), composer. Born in New York City, MacDowell early displayed talent for art and music, studied in France and Germany, and remained in Europe for eight years. There he wrote music, taught piano, performed in concerts, and published his compositions. When he returned to the United States in 1888, MacDowell possessed an international reputation as a composer. He settled in Boston. Popular for his orchestral works and tone poems that featured melodic lines and conveyed emotion, he emerged as perhaps the best and most renowned American composer and symphonist during the late nineteenth century. Two of his pieces were *Indian Suite* (1895) and *Woodland Sketches* (1896). In 1896, President Seth Low of Columbia University hired MacDowell as the university's first professor of music. MacDowell clashed with the institution's new president, Nicholas Murray Butler, over administrative policies, and resigned in 1904. Overcome by depression, complicated by injuries sustained from having been hit by a New York City cab, MacDowell degenerated physically and mentally, suffering from aphasia and aging rapidly. Having lost his will to live, he died in New York City in his mid-forties. Shortly thereafter, his wife started a colony for musical artists at their home in Peterborough, New Hampshire, which continues to serve as MacDowell's monument to Gilded Age music.

Further Reading: John F. Porte, *Edward MacDowell,* 1922; T. P. Currier, *Edward MacDowell (As I Knew Him),* 1915; Marian MacDowell, *Random Notes on Edward MacDowell and His Music,* 1950; Edward A. MacDowell Papers, Manuscripts Division, Library of Congress.

Leonard Schlup

MACUNE, CHARLES WILLIAM (20 May 1851–3 November 1940), agrarian reformer. Born in Kenosha, Wisconsin, Macune grew up in Freeport, Illinois. In 1874–1875 he edited a Democratic, fervently anti-Radical Reconstruction, weekly newspaper in Burnet, Texas. In 1879, he began a career, which continued off and on for the next forty-four years, as a physician. By 1886, with a successful medical practice, Macune had bought farm properties and a newspaper in Cameron, Texas, and become a member of the state Farmers' Alliance. Between 1886 and 1889, Macune organized the National Farmers' Alliance and served for three years as its president. The Alliance offered a program of nonpartisan economic cooperation and reform. From 1889 to 1893, he edited the *National Economist*, a weekly in Washington, D.C., advocating such radical reforms as the subtreasury plan to establish federal government-owned and -operated warehouses for surplus agricultural commodities. When Congress failed to support agrarian proposals, Macune helped organize the Populist Party in 1891–1892. By 1896, disgusted with the party, he abandoned politics. He returned to Texas and launched a law practice. He later became a Methodist minister. Macune died in Fort Worth, Texas.

Further Reading: Robert C. McMath, Jr., *Populist Vanguard: A History of the Southern Farmers' Alliance*, 1975; Lawrence Goodwyn, *Democratic Promise: The Populist Moment in America*, 1976; Charles W. Macune, Jr., "The Wellsprings of a Populist: Dr. C. W. Macune Before 1886," 90 (1986): 139–158.

Charles W. Macune, Jr.

MACVEAGH, ISAAC WAYNE (19 April 1833–11 January 1917), lawyer, attorney general, diplomat. Born in Phoenixville Pennsylvania, MacVeagh rose to prominence as a Philadelphia lawyer and general counsel to the Pennsylvania Railroad. In 1877, President Rutherford B. Hayes appointed him to a commission that was to find a political settlement leading to removal of federal troops from Louisiana. MacVeagh supported the Democratic government over the Republicans. He was part of the Republican Party faction that supported civil service reform and the Pendleton Act of 1883. Because President James A. Garfield wanted a balanced cabinet, he named Mac-Veagh attorney general in 1881. There he helped Postmaster General Thomas L. James build a case against government officials involved in fraudulent mail-route contracts. However, MacVeagh left office by November, before any case went to trial, because he did not want to serve Stalwart Republican President Chester A. Arthur. MacVeagh backed

Grover Cleveland in the 1892 presidential race, and Cleveland named him minister to Italy in 1893. He served until 1897. In 1903, Theodore Roosevelt appointed him chief counsel for the United States and Venezuela in an international boundary dispute before the International Court of Justice at The Hague. He argued for arbitration, not force, to resolve the country's debt issue. By World War I, he initially supported noninvolvement, but grew upset over German submarine attacks.

Further Reading: Alan Peskin, *Garfield*, 1978; Richard Welch, Jr., *The Presidencies of Grover Cleveland*, 1988.

Bryan Craig

MAGEE, CHRISTOPHER LYMAN (14 April 1848–8 March 1901), businessman and political leader. Born in Pittsburgh, Pennsylvania, Magee began his political rise by holding various local offices, including city treasurer for four years in the early 1870s. In 1882, he became chairman of the executive committee of the Republican Party in Allegheny County. Awash in business interests, and having built a political machine with William Flinn, a public contractor, Magee was a powerful factor in Pennsylvania politics for twenty years. In 1892, he led the delegates for President Benjamin Harrison at the Republican National Convention in Minneapolis. Magee also owned a newspaper, maintained real estate holdings, and functioned as the Pennsylvania Railroad's political agent. He served as president of the Consolidated Traction Company, held stock in more than fifty enterprises in Pittsburgh, and was a director of fifteen local banks and insurance companies. Magee donated liberally to local organizations and charities, and left an estate of approximately $4 million at the time of his death in Pittsburgh.

Further Reading: *Pittsburgh Press*, 9 March 1901; *Pittsburgh Dispatch*, 9 March 1901.

Leonard Schlup

MAHAN, ALFRED THAYER (27 September 1840–1 December 1914), naval historian, strategist, and proponent of U.S. imperialism. Born at West Point, New York, Mahan attended Columbia College, and then the U.S. Naval Academy at Annapolis, where in 1859 he graduated second in his class. During the Civil War he served with the South Atlantic Blockading Squadron. In 1883 Mahan published *The Gulf and Inland Waters*, which analyzed U.S. naval operations during the Civil War. The book impressed Captain Stephen Luce. In 1885, Luce, then president of the newly established Naval War College at Newport, Rhode Island, invited Mahan to lecture there on naval tactics and history. In 1890 Captain Mahan published his lectures under the title *The Influence of Sea Power upon History, 1660–1783*. It is a history of British naval development in its most crucial period, a treatise on war at sea, and a ringing defense of a large navy. The book had particular influence in Britain and Germany, but Mahan's lectures and magazine articles on current strategic problems also won an ever-widening audience in the United States.

Mahan argued that the United States needed a strong navy to compete for the world's trade. He contended there was no instance of a great commercial power long retaining its leadership without a large navy. He also criticized traditional U.S. "single ship commerce raiding" (the *guerre de course*), which could not win control of the seas. Mahan advocated building a seagoing fleet, an overbearing force that could beat down an enemy's battle line. Its strength had to be in battleships operating in squadrons. Mahan believed in the concentration of forces, urging that the fleet be kept in one ocean only. He also called for establishing naval bases in the Caribbean and in the Pacific. Mahan had his shortcomings: he overlooked new technology, such as the torpedo and the submarine, and he was not concerned with speed in battleships.

An important apostle of the new navalism, Mahan retired from the Navy in 1896 to devote full time to writing. He died in Washington, D.C.

Further Reading: C. G. Reynolds, *Famous American Admirals*, 1974; Robert Seager II, *Alfred Thayer Mahan: The Man and His Letters*, 1977; R. W. Turk, *The Ambitious Relationship: Theodore Roosevelt and Alfred Thayer Mahan*, 1987.

Spencer C. Tucker

MAHONE, WILLIAM (1 December 1826–8 October 1895), railroad president, soldier, and senator. Born in Southampton County, Virginia, Mahone was graduated from Virginia Military Institute in 1847. In 1853 he became chief engineer for the Norfolk and Petersburg Railroad, and by 1861, he controlled it. Mahone rose to major general in the Confederate Army. After the war, he added the Southside and Virginia and Tennessee railroads to his empire. Mahone played an important role in Virginia politics from Reconstruction until his death. His support was vital to the election of Gilbert Walker, a moderate Republican, as governor in 1869. Walker repaid Mahone by backing legislation that consolidated Mahone's railroads into the Atlantic, Mississippi and Ohio. When Mahone lost control of it during the 1870s, he turned full attention to politics. Supporting a partial repudiation of the state's antebellum debt, he helped found a new political party, the Readjusters, in 1879. It won control of the legislature that year, and the governorship in 1881, sponsoring a program of reform legislation. The party elected Mahone to the U.S. Senate, where he served from 1881 to 1887. His vote determined which party would control the Senate in 1881. In return for patronage and committee assignments, he chose the Republicans, an act that enraged many Virginians. After the Readjuster Party's collapse, Mahone built the Virginia Republican Party machine. He unsuccessfully sought the governorship in 1889, and died in Washington, D.C.

Further Reading: Nelson M. Blake, *William Mahone of Virginia: Soldier and Political Insurgent*, 1935; Allen Moger, *Virginia: Bourbonism to Byrd 1870–1925*, 1968; William Mahone Papers, Duke University Special Collections Library, Durham, North Carolina.

James R. Sweeney

MAINE, SINKING OF. On the night of 15 February 1898, the battleship *Maine* exploded in Havana harbor, killing 260 and leading directly to war between the United States and Spain. At 6,648 tons, the *Maine* rated as a battleship, but actually was an armored cruiser. The War Department supposedly had sent the *Maine* to protect American interests, but actually to pressure Spain to change its colonial policies in Cuba. Clearly Spain resented the provocation. On 28 March a naval inquiry reported that an external mine had caused the explosion, implying Spanish responsibility. Careful examination in 1911, by an army/navy board, confirmed the finding. Although the precise cause will probably never be established, Admiral Hyman Rickover and his staff cited stress studies of metal in underwater explosions to conclude in 1976 that spontaneous combustion of bituminous coal in one of the ship's bunkers had ignited ammunition in an adjacent magazine. If indeed an external mine existed, one might imagine Cuban rebels, rather than Spaniards, as the source. The loss provided a rallying point for Americans who wanted war, and the cry "Remember the *Maine*—to hell with Spain!" One day after the board of inquiry's report, President William McKinley sent Madrid an ultimatum that led to the U.S. declaration of war on 25 April.

Further Reading: Michael Blow, *A Ship to Remember*, 1992; Hyman Rickover, *How the Maine Was Destroyed*, 1976; John Edward Weems, *The Fate of the Maine*, 1985.

Spencer C. Tucker

MANDERSON, CHARLES FREDERICK (9 February 1837–28 September 1911), U.S. senator. A native of Philadelphia, Manderson moved to Canton, Ohio, in 1856, and was admitted to the bar in 1859. The next year, he became Canton city attorney. In 1861, he enlisted in the Union Army as a private; by 1865, having seen action at Shiloh, Stone River, and Murfreesboro, he had risen to brigadier general. Manderson returned to Canton after the war, but in 1869 moved to Omaha, Nebraska. He rose quickly in legal and political circles, becoming Omaha city attorney and a delegate to the 1871 and 1875 constitutional conventions. In 1883, the Nebraska legislature sent him to the U.S. Senate, and reelected him without opposition in 1889. Manderson became president pro tempore of the Senate in 1891, and championed army reform, increased pensions for veterans, and irrigation in the West. He retired from public life in 1895, and served as general solicitor for the Burlington Railroad. He was president of the American Bar Association in 1900–1901. Manderson died at sea.

Further Reading: *Publications of the Nebraska State Historical Society* 9 (1902): 333–361; *New York Times*, 29 September 1911.

Sam S. Kepfield

MANHOOD. The stereotypical image of the Victorian male as a sexually repressed patriarch misrepresents the wide variety of male behaviors and conceptions of manhood during the Gilded Age. In fact, there were many alternative and competing behaviors and attitudes that together formed the private and emotional world of American men. The total adult male population of the United States in 1896 was 19 million, of whom 5.5 million belonged to fraternal groups; the Odd Fellows had the largest membership (810,000). An article by W. S. Harwood in the May 1897 issue of the *North American Review* characterized the last three decades of the nineteenth century as the "Golden Age of Fraternity." Rituals and socialization fulfilled a need among men for bonding and for reaffirming symbols in a transitional society that witnessed reform crusades, women's suffrage agitation, urbanization, and the Social Gospel movement.

Such internal struggles and shifting paradigms were crucial to American males' understanding of themselves, for masculinity was largely a cultural construct. Industrialization substituted machinery for skilled labor, and brought unskilled women and children to the factory. Their presence often undermined the traditional paths to manhood among skilled male workers. One consequence of economic growth and structural change was the physical distance and separation of men from the home and domesticity during much of the day, contributing to a decline of paternal authority while simultaneously fostering the overriding presence of women teachers and mothers, thereby affecting the development of young males. Gender roles were thus transformed by the husband's departure from the domestic scene and the average wife's preoccupation with raising children during working hours, without fathers who were gainfully employed by factories or businesses in industrialized cities. Male farmers in rural areas, on the other hand, worked long days but were at home. Native American male youths retained their familial structure and periodic manhood rituals on reservations.

In addition, a "manliness ethos," personified by Theodore Roosevelt, characterized the Gilded Age. In an era of vocal veterans' groups, western frontiersmen, rugged individualism, fraternities, athletic games, entrepreneurs, political debates, and the image of the self-made man, American men faced the stern realities of competition that absorbed their emotional energies. They sought careers that shaped personal identities while assuming an active interest in the political process. Their attitudes toward work, leisure, intimacy, home, family, community, style, clothing, courtship, education, religion, and manners contributed to the male experience and the culture of manhood during the Gilded Age.

Further Reading: Mark C. Carnes, *Secret Ritual and Manhood in Victorian America*, 1989; Mark C. Carnes and Clyde Griffen, eds., *Meanings for Manhood: Constructions of Masculinity in Victorian America*, 1990; E. Anthony Rotundo, *American Manhood: Transformations in Masculinity from the Revolution to the Modern Era*, 1994.

Leonard Schlup

MANILA, BATTLE OF (1 May 1898). This was a key battle in the Spanish-American War. Unlike the army, the U.S. Navy was ready for the conflict. On 27 April 1898, Commodore George Dewey ordered his Asiatic Squadron of five cruisers and two gunboats to sail from near Hong Kong to the Philippines. Ignoring the threat of mines, the squadron steamed into Manila Bay at midnight on 30 April. On 1 May, the force attacked Spanish Admiral Patricio Montojo's four cruisers and three gunboats. Montojo had anchored his ships off the fortified naval yard at Cavite, where land batteries supported them. Many of the Spanish ships were wooden hulled, however, and the squadron was inferior to the American one in both armament and drill. In a six-hour-long engagement, Dewey destroyed all seven Spanish ships. The United States suffered only eight sailors wounded, while Spain lost 361 killed or wounded. Dewey's ships then shelled the naval yard into surrender. The Americans took possession, and then blockaded Manila. In June, U.S. troops arrived, and in August, Manila surrendered. Control of the ocean allowed the United States to wrest an empire from Spain. Washington took the Philippines as a bargaining chip, but ultimately decided to keep the islands. The decision had profound implications for the United States, ultimately leading to the 1941 confrontation with Japan.

Further Reading: Michael Blow, *A Ship to Remember*, 1992; G. J. A. O'Toole, *The Spanish War*, 1984; David F. Trask, *The War with Spain in 1898*, 1981.

Spencer C. Tucker

MANNING, DANIEL (16 May 1831–24 December 1887), secretary of the Treasury. Born in Albany, New York, Manning left school early to help his widowed mother support the family. In 1856 he became a reporter for the Albany *Argus*, assuming its presidency in 1873. Meanwhile, he had also forged a successful business career, entered politics, and established himself as a major figure in the New York State Democratic Party. A friend and protégé of Samuel J. Tilden, Manning chaired the party's state committee in the early 1880s, working against Tammany Hall's efforts to control the party statewide. He also backed the career of Governor Grover Cleveland, playing a considerable role in the latter's successful run for the presidency in 1884. As a reward for his efforts, Manning was appointed secretary of the Treasury. During his tenure (1885–1887), Manning echoed Cleveland's sound-money and low-tariff principles; his reports included arguments for the retirement of greenbacks and the cessation of government purchase of silver. A relentless worker, Manning resigned because of ill health. He died in Albany.

Further Reading: Allan Nevins, *Grover Cleveland: A Study in Courage*, 1932; Richard E. Welch, Jr., *The Presidencies of Grover Cleveland*, 1988; *New York Times*, 25 December 1887.

Ed Bradley

MANNING, JOSEPH COLUMBUS (21 May 1870–19 May 1930), Populist organizer and state legislator. Born in Clay County, Alabama, as a teenager Manning traveled for a year selling books in Texas, at that time a Farmers' Alliance hotbed. In 1891 Manning moved to Atlanta, where he worked as a journalist and came under the influence of the agrarian radical Tom Watson. The next year, Manning was sent to Alabama as a People's Party organizer. He was a formidable stump speaker but found Alliance members committed to the gubernatorial candidacy of "Jeffersonian Democrat" Reuben F. Kolb. Bowing to necessity, he backed Kolb twice in 1892 and 1894, only to see him twice cheated of election by Democratic officials in predominantly black counties. Manning would have preferred to promote the Subtreasury or other aspects of the Omaha Platform but instead decided to lead the fight to secure "a free ballot and a fair count." A member of the 1894–1895 Alabama legislature, Manning helped organize a convention at which Kolb's forces joined the People's Party. Manning's larger strategy was to promote a congressional investigation of the Alabama voting frauds. To this end he gave speeches in New York and other cities; in 1895 he formed the Southern Ballot Rights League. Congress was not interested, however, and by the fall of 1896, as the People's Party began to collapse, he joined the Republicans. Over the next decades, Manning became a critic of white supremacy Democrats who had disfranchised blacks and poor whites alike. After 1909 he worked with members of the National Association for the Advancement of Colored People. He died in New York City.

Further Reading: Paul M. Pruitt, Jr., "Joseph C. Manning, Alabama Populist: A Rebel Against the Solid South," Ph.D. diss., College of William and Mary, 1980; William Warren Rogers, *The One-Gallused Rebellion: Agrarianism in Alabama, 1865–1896*, 1970.

Paul M. Pruitt, Jr.

MARQUIS, ALBERT NELSON (10 January 1855–21 December 1943), editor and publisher. Born on a farm in Brown County, Ohio, Marquis moved to Cincinnati in 1876 and in 1884 to Chicago, where he established a publishing company. It issued the first Chicago business directory in 1884, and Marquis traveled the nation looking for book manuscripts. He decided in the mid-1890s to compile a biographical directory of notable Americans by using the re-

sponses from his questionnaires to write brief sketches of the individuals. From the beginning, he declined to exclude distinguished Americans on the basis of race, ethnicity, or religion. In 1899, he published the first volume of *Who's Who in America*, a Gilded Age success story that continues into the twenty-first century. Marquis died in Evanston, Illinois.

Further Reading: *New York Times*, 22 December 1943.

Leonard Schlup

MARSH, OTHNIEL CHARLES (29 October 1831–18 March 1899), paleontologist. Marsh was born in Lockport, New York, received a B.S. from Yale College in 1860, and a Ph.D. from Yale's Sheffield Scientific School in 1862. Four years later he became professor of paleontology at Yale, where he remained for the rest of his life. In addition to his professorial duties, between 1882 and 1892 Marsh held the first appointment as paleontologist of the U.S. Geological Survey. Marsh's fossil expeditions between 1870 and 1873 in the northwestern United States won him fame. There he discovered fossil horses and primates, and eighty dinosaur species. Perhaps most spectacular was his discovery of the first toothed bird, which established an evolutionary link between dinosaurs and modern birds. These finds, which are in Yale's Peabody Museum, were the strongest evidence for evolution to that date, and Charles Darwin, a founder of the theory of evolution by natural selection, rejoiced over them. Marsh slowed the pace of his work during his final years, though he remained one of Yale's most respected professors. He died in New Haven, Connecticut, secure in the knowledge that he had helped make evolution the core idea of biology.

Further Reading: Charles Schuchert and Clara M. LeVene, *O. C. Marsh: Pioneer in Paleontology*, 1940.

Christopher Cumo

MARTÍ, JOSÉ JULIAN (28 January 1853–19 May 1895), Cuban revolutionary patriot, political leader, poet, and journalist. Born in Havana, Cuba, Martí was exiled for his pro-independence activities against Spain, but returned following the amnesty of 1878. His agitation continued, however, and again he was forced to leave. He settled in New York in 1881. For fourteen years he rallied support for his cause. Widespread sympathy for Cuban independence existed in the United States. To Martí, political independence required a change of spirit as well; he recognized the importance and social potential of Cuba's nonwhite populations, and this motivated his concepts during the 1880s. On 24 February 1895, the "Grito de Bayre" (the Cry of Bayre) opened the war of independence against Spain. Martí returned to Cuba when the Cuban Revolutionary Party, which he had founded, began its final struggle. He was killed four months later, at Dos Ríos, Oriente Province, but his legacy continued through his writings. In "Our America" (1891), Martí distinguished between two very different Americas, North America, which clung to a European worldview, allowed full participation and citizenship only to people of European descent. "Our America" (Latin America) offered the possibility of creating an original synthesis by blending the European culture with the indigenous and African peoples in the hemisphere.

Further Reading: Franklin W. Knight and Colin A. Palmer, eds., *The Modern Caribbean*, 1989; José Martí, "Nuestra América," *La Rèvista Ilustrada* (The Illustrated Review), 10 January 1891; Deborah Wei and Rachael Kamel, eds., *Resistance in Paradise: Rethinking 100 Years of U.S. Involvement in the Caribbean and the Pacific*, 1998.

Santos C. Vega

MARTIN, JOHN ALEXANDER

MARTIN, JOHN ALEXANDER (10 March 1839–2 October 1889), governor and Republican leader. Born in Brownsville, Pennsylvania, Martin was an apprentice on the town newspaper. In 1857, he moved to Atchison, Kansas Territory, where he purchased the *Squatter Sovereign* and made it a staunchly antislavery journal, renamed *Freedom's Champion*. Only twenty years old, Martin helped organize the Republican Party in Kansas in 1859. That July he was elected secretary of the Wyandotte Convention, which wrote the Kansas constitution. He served in the first state senate in 1861, before joining the Union Army, and remained active in party affairs throughout his life. After the Civil War, he returned to Atchison and resumed editing the *Champion*. In 1884 and 1886, Martin was elected governor. During his tenure, Kansas sustained a period of unprecedented growth and prosperity, even though his last year in office witnessed the beginning of the drought and depression that spawned the subsequent farmers' revolt.

Martin's administration anticipated the Progressive movement. He championed property tax equalization, legal and judicial reform, highway improvements, establishment of a school for mentally handicapped youth, and a state-operated silk farm. As tacit leader of the reform faction, he advocated a state corporation law to attack business abuses and the monopoly problem; played a role in helping secure the right for women to vote in school, school bond, and municipal elections; and supported governmental reorganization, adding several boards and commissions to state government. His two terms were beset by labor problems stemming from strikes against various Kansas railroad lines by the Knights of Labor. Martin used the state militia, reorganized into the Kansas National Guard, to keep order. He was also forced to deal with a number of county seat struggles, including the so-called "Stevens County War" of 1887. Martin died in Atchison, Kansas.

Further Reading: Dorothy Liebengood, "Labor Problems in the Second Year of Governor Martin's Administration," *Kansas Historical Quarterly* 5 (1936): 191–207; Matthew A. Raney, "The Early Political and Military Career of Governor John Alexander Martin of Kansas," M.A. thesis, Kansas State University, 1991; Homer Socolofsky, *Kansas Governors*, 1990.

Robert S. La Forte

MASTERSON, WILLIAM BARCLAY (BARTHOLOMEW) "BAT"

MASTERSON, WILLIAM BARCLAY (BARTHOLOMEW) "BAT" (24 November 1853–25 October 1921), lawman, gambler, and newspaperman. Born in Quebec, Canada, Masterson moved with his family to Illinois. As a young man he went to the frontier, first working as a buffalo hunter and living a life of hard drinking and gambling. While serving briefly as an army scout in 1874, Masterson was involved in a controversial incident concerning a dance hall girl, in which he killed a local army sergeant. He quickly gained a reputation as a gunman. He went to Dodge City, Kansas, then a wild cattle town that derived its income from gambling and saloons. In 1876 and 1877 he won election as sheriff. Through the 1870s and 1880s, Masterson worked intermittently as a lawman, most famously with Wyatt Earp in cleaning up Dodge City, as well as Colorado mining camps. Masterson supplemented his income through gambling, and despite lore to the contrary, this was his primary occupation. As places such as Dodge City became respectable, he relied totally on gambling for a living. An interest in sports, particularly boxing, took up increasingly more of his time, and in 1901 he moved to New York City, to begin a career as a newspaperman for the *Morning Telegraph*. He continued this work until his death in New York City.

Further Reading: Robert K. DeArment, *Bat Masterson: The Man and the Legend*, 1979.

Amanda Laugesen

MATTHEWS, CLAUDE (14 December 1845–28 August 1898), cattle breeder and governor. Born in Bethel, Kentucky, Matthews graduated from Centre College in Danville, Kentucky, in 1867, and shortly thereafter began breeding livestock in Indiana. He also developed an interest in Democratic politics. Matthews was elected to Indiana's lower legislative chamber in 1876 and as secretary of state in 1890. He served as governor from 1893 to 1897, a time of severe depression in the nation. During his administration, he contended with a coal strike, the election of a Republican legislature in 1894, and amendments to the state's tax laws. A proponent of free silver coinage, on the early ballots Matthews received the votes of Indiana's delegation as a favorite son for the presidential nomination at the 1896 Democratic National Convention. A Democrat in a nominally Republican state, Matthews gained national prominence during the Gilded Age. He died in Veedersburg, Indiana.

Further Reading: Indianapolis *Sentinel*, 29 August 1898.

Leonard Schlup

MATTHEWS, STANLEY (21 July 1824–22 March 22 1889), Supreme Court justice. Born in Cincinnati, Ohio, Matthews was graduated from Kenyon College in 1840 and returned home to practice law. An antislavery Democrat, he briefly the *Cincinnati Herald*. Before the Civil War, he served on a state court, in the state senate, and was appointed U.S. attorney for the Southern District of Ohio (1858–1861), where he enforced the 1850 Fugitive Slave Law. In the Union Army, Matthews rose to lieutenant colonel, and was initially superior officer to his college friend Rutherford B. Hayes. Matthews accepted a seat on the Superior Court of Cincinnati in 1863. In 1876, he served as a member of the electoral commission that was charged with investigating vote fraud in Louisiana, and that later awarded the votes to Hayes. He presented the Republican case to the National Electoral Commission, and aided in negotiating the Compromise of 1877. He was rewarded with an appointment to the Senate seat vacated by John Sherman. Nominated to the Supreme Court by Hayes in 1879, Matthews did not win approval until May 1881. On the Court, his jurisprudence was eclectic. He wrote the decision in *Yick Wo* v. *Hopkins* (118 U.S. 356, 1886), which expanded the concept of equal protection under the Fourteenth Amendment. Yet he held in *Hurtado* v. *California* (110 U.S. 516, 1884) that an indictment was not an essential element of due process. He died in Washington, D.C.

Further Reading: *New York Times*, 23 March 1889; Matthews Papers, in the Rutherford B. Hayes Presidential Center, Fremont, Ohio.

Sam Kepfield

MATTHEWS, WILLIAM (29 March 1822–15 April 1896), bookbinder and author. Born in Aberdeen, Scotland, Matthews received his education in London and was apprenticed to a bookbinder. He immigrated to New York City in 1843 and, three years later, established a bindery at 74 Fulton Street. In 1854 Matthews became head of the bindery department at the publishing firm of D. Appleton Company, retiring in 1890. Known for his good workmanship, meticulous craft, and thoroughness, Matthews was an active member of the Grolier Club; in 1885 he delivered a lecture, "Modern Bookbinding Practically Considered," that was published by the club in 1899. He wrote articles for magazines and encyclopedias. Matthews also served as president of the Flatbush Water Works Company. His death in Brooklyn

Heights, New York, was occasioned by the shock of having been run down by a bicycle.

Further Reading: Brander Matthews, *Bookbindings Old and New*, 1895; *New York Tribune*, 16 April 1896; *New York Times*, 16 April 1896.

Leonard Schlup

MATZELIGER, JAN ERNEST (15 September 1852–24 August 1889), African-American inventor. Born in Paramaribo, Dutch Guiana (now Suriname), Matzeliger immigrated to Lynn, Massachusetts, in 1878 and worked at the Harney Brothers shoe factory. He recognized the necessity for building a machine that could duplicate fingers on the hands of lasters. After practicing and experimenting on crude models in the 1880s, Matzeliger finally completed his fourth product, inventing a lasting machine that fitted the leather and fed nails into position. It was a time-saving success, revolutionizing the production of shoes. Overwork and years of poverty eventually took their toll, and Matzeliger succumbed to tuberculosis at an early age. He died in Lynn.

Further Reading: Charlemae Hill Rollins, *They Showed the Way: Forty American Negro Leaders*, 1964.

Leonard Schlup

MAY DAY. For centuries, Europeans had celebrated the beginning of May as a springtime folk festival. In Gilded Age America, class conflict helped to turn the tradition into something more. The first May Day observance emerged from the movement for shorter working hours. Labor organizations demanded a schedule that allowed for eight hours of work, eight of sleep, and eight of recreation. At the American Federation of Labor (AFL) convention in 1884, George Edmonston introduced and helped pass a resolution calling for a universal strike for the eight-hour day on 1 May 1886. Between four hundred thousand and five hundred thousand workers struck, but the events of Haymarket Square on 4 May tarnished May Day. The AFL nevertheless revived the idea at its 1888 convention, advocating mass strikes on 1 May 1890. In 1889, the Marxist International Socialist Congress voiced support, turning May Day into a worldwide celebration of change, struggle, and worker solidarity.

Throughout the 1890s, May Day became increasingly popular in Europe. In the United States however, after the designation of Labor Day as a national holiday in 1894, its popularity dwindled. For many U.S. workers, Labor Day came to symbolize Americanism, whereas May Day seemed European and radical. By 1901, the AFL had stopped endorsing May Day strikes and instead supported Labor Day, thus ending May Day's official position within organized labor.

Further Reading: Philip S. Foner, *May Day: A Short History of the International Workers' Holiday 1886–1986*, 1986; Sidney Fine, "Is May Day American in Origin?" *The Historian*, 16 (Spring 1954): 121–34.

S. Paul O'Hara

MAYO, WILLIAM JAMES (29 June 1861–28 July 1939), and **CHARLES HORACE MAYO**, (19 July 1865–26 May 1939), physicians and founders of the Mayo Clinic. Born respectively in LeSueur and Rochester, Minnesota, William and Charles Mayo were the sons of a prominent physician who maintained a medical practice in Rochester. In 1883, William Mayo graduated from the University of Michigan Medical School; his younger brother earned his medical degree from Northwestern University in Chicago in 1888. They practiced medicine with their father. William focused his attention on pelvic and abdominal surgery, while Charles handled eye, ear, nose, throat, bone, brain, neck, and nerve surgery. Utilizing the advances of modern medicine, the Mayo brothers attracted national attention during the Gilded Age and Progressive Era. The Mayo Clinic in Rochester, Minnesota, formally acquired its name in 1914. Both men served as president of various medical and surgical associations of their day. Charles died in Chicago; his brother, in Rochester.

Further Reading: Papers of William and Charles Mayo, Mayo Foundation Historical Collection, Rochester, Minnesota; Helen Clapesattle, *The Doctors Mayo*, 1941; Clark W. Nelson, *Mayo Roots: Profiling the Origins of the Mayo Clinic*, 1990.

Leonard Schlup

MAYORS AND LOCAL GOVERNMENTS. The shifting of authority was a distinctive characteristic of American city government.

The overarching development in the decades after the mid-nineteenth century was the sharp decline of the municipal council in the larger cities and abolition of their numerous committees that had supervised the administrative functions of the city. The New York City charters of 1871 and 1873, the Brooklyn charter of 1880, and the Boston charter of 1885 deprived their councils of important powers. As reformers had sought, by 1900 power and responsibility came to be concentrated in the mayor. Aldermen, most of whom were elected annually or biennially, no longer exerted authority over citywide issues and became influential as ward or neighborhood representatives.

No uniform structure of municipal government existed; cities had in common only an independently elected mayor—a uniquely American practice—and a council. By 1880, the mayor was generally empowered to appoint heads of administrative departments, as in the Philadelphia charter of 1887. However, conducive to weak-mayor government were charter provisions requiring council confirmation of appointments, a bicameral council, independently elected administrative officers, and the appointment or election of boards and commissions, which took hold in the third quarter of the nineteenth century. The Brooklyn charter of 1880, providing for the highest level of concentration of executive authority, was the first of its kind. Seth Low, an ardent believer in a strong and responsible mayor, became the first mayor of Brooklyn (1881–1885) to have unlimited authority to appoint department heads. He was definitely responsible for the whole administration—his "cabinet" was responsible to him—because the terms of his chief administrators were made coterminous with his own. New York, Boston, and Buffalo were cities that early adopted the "Brooklyn Plan," which provided for a unicameral council. (In the 1890s cities veered toward unicameralism.) In the last decades of the nineteenth century, the mayor's office gained still further strength: proposal of the annual budget, genuine influence on municipal legislation (stemming from his messages on ordinances and from veto power), the item veto, and extension to a two-year term. There also were "strong"

mayors—among them Carter Harrison, Sr., of Chicago (1879–1887), Josiah Quincy III of Boston (1895–1899), and Samuel ("Golden Rule") Jones of Toledo (1897–1904)—whose leadership added dimension to the office.

Further Reading: Maury Klein and Harvey A. Kantor, *Prisoners of Progress: American Industrial Cities, 1850–1920*, 1976; Constance Green, *American Cities in the Growth of the Nation*, 1965; Richard D. Bingham and David Hedge, *State and Local Government in a Changing Society*, 1990.

Bernard Hirschhorn

MCALLISTER, (SAMUEL) WARD (28 December 1827–31 January 1895), lawyer and author. Born in Savannah, Georgia, McAllister won admittance to the Georgia bar before moving to California and, ultimately, New York. Wealthy from his business ventures, Ward relished managing social events and dinners. He organized a series of dances known as the "patriarchs" in 1872, introduced "Dutch treats" to society, and wrote *Society as I Have Found It* (1890). He traveled extensively at home and abroad, and coined the term "the Four Hundred" on 1 February 1892, on the occasion of a grand ball hosted by Mary Dahlgren Paul Astor, wife of William Waldorf Astor, a capitalist and diplomat. McAllister died in New York City.

Further Reading: *New York Times*, 1 February 1895.

Leonard Schlup

MCBRIDE, JOHN (25 July 1854–9 October 1917), labor leader and politician. Born in Wayne County, Ohio, McBride worked in the area's coal mines as a boy. He helped organize the Ohio Miners Union in 1882, and served as its president until 1889. Convinced that state and regional unions could not be effective in a national economy, McBride worked to create a national miners union throughout the 1880s. He succeeded in 1890 when he led formation of the United Mine Workers of America (UMWA). As its president, he sought to reach a nationwide agreement with mine operators to insulate miners' wages from competition. McBride saw politics as essential to labor's goals. A Democrat, he sat in the Ohio House of Representatives from 1883 until 1887; he was defeated when he ran for Ohio secretary of state in 1886. From 1890 to 1892, he headed the Ohio Bureau of Labor Statistics. After the failure of the nationwide coal strike of 1894, McBride severed his connection with the Democrats and led the formation of an Ohio labor-Populist alliance, which advocated collective ownership of the means of production. In December 1894, McBride defeated Samuel Gompers for the presidency of the American Federation of Labor (AFL) by calling for the Federation to enter partisan politics. Illness marred his presidency, as did allegations of corruption, internal divisions within the AFL, and the federation's poor financial state. Gompers narrowly defeated McBride in 1895, and McBride retired from the labor movement. He operated a small business in Globe, Arizona, until his death.

Further Reading: *New York Times*, 10 October 1917; Charles A. Madison, *American Labor Leaders: Personalities and Forces in the Labor Movement*, 1950; John H. M. Laslett, *Labor and the Left: A Study of Socialist and Radical Influences in the American Labor Movement, 1881–1924*, 1970.

Michael Pierce

MCCLURE, SAMUEL SIDNEY (17 February 1857–21 March 1949), editor and publisher. Born in Frocess, County Antrim, Ireland, McClure immigrated to Indiana with his mother and three brothers in 1866, and graduated from Knox College in Illinois in 1882. He obtained employment in Boston editing a monthly magazine, *The Wheelman*, financed by Albert A. Pope, a manufacturer of bicycles. By the mid-1880s, McClure had worked briefly as junior editor of *The Century* and had formed his own literary syndicate, gathering stories and poems from writers in both America and Europe. *McClure's Magazine* began in 1893, the year of the financial panic, and eventually enjoyed great success. Two who bought stock in the magazine were the scientist Henry Drummond and the English fiction writer Arthur Conan Doyle. McClure's hiring of Ida M. Tarbell, a prominent writer, biographer, and later muckraker, was a major accomplishment. After Frank Nelson Doubleday left the company to form a publishing house with Walter Hines Page, McClure established McClure, Phillips &

Company, to publish books, in 1899. McClure died in the Bronx, New York.

Further Reading: Peter Lyon, *Success Story: The Life and Times of S. S. McClure*, 1963; *New York Times*, 23 March 1949; *New York Herald Tribune*, 23 March 1949.

Leonard Schlup

MCCREARY, JAMES BENNETT (8 July 1838–8 October 1918), governor, congressman, and senator. Born in Madison County, Kentucky, McCreary earned a law degree from Cumberland University in Tennessee. Following service in the Confederate cavalry, he was speaker of the Kentucky House of Representatives before his election as governor (1875–1879). A weak executive, McCreary dwelt on the legal minutiae and committed himself only on popular issues. A paragon of Southern Democratic conservatism, he won a reduction in interest rates and property taxes, creation of a state board of health, and a higher assessment of railroad property for tax purposes. As a congressman from 1885 to 1897, McCreary supported measures for agriculture, tariff reform and reciprocity, and free coinage of silver. He also wrote the bill providing for the Pan-American Congress, which encouraged reciprocal commercial relations among twenty nations. He attended the Brussels Monetary Conference as one of five U.S. delegates in 1891–1892. A fervent bimetallist, McCreary helped nominate William Jennings Bryan at three national conventions. After serving a term in the U.S. Senate (1903–1909), the erstwhile conservative provided active leadership when again elected governor of Kentucky (1911–1915), and secured a lasting reputation as a progressive. McCreary died in Richmond, Kentucky.

Further Reading: Hambleton Tapp and James C. Klotter, *Kentucky: Decades of Discord, 1865–1900*, 1977; Nicholas C. Burckel, "James B. McCreary," in Lowell H. Harrison ed., *Kentucky's Governor's, 1792–1985*, 1985, 88–92.

Edward Scott Blakeman

MCDOWELL, MARY ELIZA (30 November 1854–14 October 1936), settlement house director and reformer. Born in Cincinnati, Ohio, McDowell moved with her family to Chicago in time to assist victims of that city's 1871 fire. She taught Sunday school classes in a Methodist church during the 1870s. In 1878, she heard Frances E. Willard, corresponding secretary of the Woman's Christian Temperance Union (WCTU), address a group of young Chicago women. Impressed with Willard and the temperance work of the youth branches, McDowell joined, and began organizing new groups. By 1887, she was the national director of the WCTU's youth branches. She took a year off to attend the Chicago Kindergarten Training School, taught for a short time in New York City, and in 1891 returned to Chicago to become the kindergarten teacher at Hull House.

McDowell committed the rest of her life to the settlement house movement. Its philosophy, then being enunciated by Jane Addams, offered a way to put her religious beliefs into action. Addams, who soon became a close friend and confidante, recommended McDowell for the directorship of a new settlement being established by students and professors connected with the University of Chicago. It was located in "Packingtown," a working-class district southwest of the stockyards and meatpacking plants. McDowell seized the opportunity, and in 1894 moved to a cold-water flat on Ashland Avenue. By century's end the residents of the University of Chicago Settlement sponsored a wide array of clubs and classes for neighborhood people, and McDowell had raised enough money to build a combined gymnasium and auditorium, and to start planning the three-story permanent building that the settlement would construct in 1905. McDowell continued as director until 1923, combining settlement work with the promotion of labor unions, welfare legislation, and sanitary reform. From 1923 until 1927 she served in Mayor William Dever's reform administration as Commissioner of Public Welfare. She died in Chicago.

Further Reading: Howard E. Wilson, *Mary McDowell, Neighbor*, 1928; Caroline M. Hill, comp., *Mary McDowell and Municipal Housekeeping*, 1938; Mary E. McDowell/University of Chicago Settlement Papers, Chicago Historical Society.

Louise Carroll Wade

MCGEE, WILLIAM JOHN (17 April 1853–4 September 1912), geologist and anthropologist. Born near Farley, Iowa, McGee early in life showed interest in aboriginal artifacts and burial mounds. After joining the American Association for the Advancement of Science, he published two papers in the *American Journal of Science* in 1878. Over the next four years, he explored northeastern Iowa's topography. In 1883 McGee went to work for the U.S. Geological Survey, producing geologic maps, projecting the uses of petroleum, and engaging in stratigraphy. Emerging as a pioneer in geomorphology, McGee recorded observations of the 1886 earthquake in Charleston, South Carolina, assisted in founding the Geological Society of America in 1888, served as president of the American Anthropological Association from 1898 to 1900, headed the Bureau of American Ethnology from 1894 to 1903, wrote approximately thirty reports on Native Americans, and later was a contributor to the *National Geographic Magazine*. An advocate of natural resources conservation, McGee died in Washington, D.C.

Further Reading: Frank Hall Knowlton, *Bulletin of the Geological Society of America* 24 (1913): 18–29; Hazel McFeely Fontana and Bernard L. Fontana, *Trails to Tiburon: The 1894 and 1895 Field Diaries of W. J. McGee*, 2000; W. J. McGee, "Explorations by the Bureau of American Ethnology in 1895," *National Geographic Magazine* 7 (1896): 77–80.

Leonard Schlup

MCGHEE, FREDERICK LAMAR (1861–9 September 1912), lawyer and African-American activist. Born in Aberdeen, Mississippi, McGhee studied under the guidance of Presbyterian missionaries at Knoxville College in Tennessee, read law with Edward H. Morris in Chicago, and gained admission to the Illinois bar in 1885. He moved to St. Paul, Minnesota, in 1889, and became a highly skilled criminal lawyer with a biracial clientele. McGhee was the first African American admitted to the Minnesota bar and the first person of color who argued cases before the Minnesota Supreme Court. Known for his eloquence, intelligence, and endeavors to curtail racial discrimination, McGhee helped revive the Afro-American League, an organization founded in 1890 to promote social equality. In 1898, the reconstituted Afro-American Council assumed a more conciliatory posture. McGhee aligned with

Booker T. Washington in the latter's program of industrial education and economic chauvinism. Years later, McGhee assisted in initiating the Niagara Movement, a group opposed to Washington's conservative views. A Democrat in an era when Republicans counted on traditionally reliable African-American political support, McGhee rejected imperialism and condemned U.S. military attempts to crush Filipino insurrectionists. McGhee insisted that blacks should protest most loudly against the oppression of others. He died in St. Paul.

Further Reading: Earl Spangler, *The Negro in Minnesota*, 1961; August Meier, *Negro Thought in America*, 1880–1915, 1963.

Leonard Schlup

MCGILLYCUDDY, VALENTINE TRANT O'CONNELL (14 February 1849–6 June 1939), physician and agent for Native Americans. Born in Racine, Wisconsin, McGillycuddy earned a degree from the Detroit College of Medicine in 1869, worked as a recorder and surgeon with the U.S. Survey of the Great Lakes from 1871 to 1874, and accepted General George Crook's invitation to serve as a cavalry surgeon in 1876. As assistant post surgeon at Fort Robinson, Nebraska, McGillycuddy treated Crazy Horse's wife for tuberculosis and befriended Native Americans. He attended Crazy Horse upon the latter's death in 1877. While meeting with federal officials in Washington in 1879, McGillycuddy complained to Secretary of the Interior Carl Schurz about mistreatment of Natives. Schurz immediately chose McGillycuddy as agent for the Pine Ridge Sioux reservation in South Dakota, where he remained from 1879 to 1886. These years represented the pinnacle of his career. He built new schools, installed a Native police force to maintain peace, and removed corrupt white traders. Regrettably, arguments and confrontations with Red Cloud marred his otherwise successful tenure.

In 1886 President Grover Cleveland dismissed McGillycuddy, a Republican, for insubordination after he refused to replace his chief clerk with a Democrat. McGillycuddy, active in the movement for Dakota statehood and the division of the territory into two states, signed South Dakota's constitution. He served as assistant adjutant general for South Dakota from 1889 to 1898. When a new religious fervor, the Ghost Dance, preached by Wovoka, a Paiute from Nevada, threatened to disrupt harmony, McGillycuddy counseled inaction, believing that the movement would subside on its own. General John R. Brooke spurned McGillycuddy's prudent offer to negotiate between the Sioux and the army. The massacre at Wounded Knee occurred on 29 December 1890. Had McGillycuddy been agent at the time instead of D. F. Royer, the catastrophe might have been averted. McGillycuddy died in San Francisco, California.

Further Reading: Julia Blanchard McGillycuddy, *Blood on the Moon: Valentine McGillycuddy and the Sioux*, 1990; Robert M. Utley, *The Indian Frontier of the American West, 1846–1890*, 1987.

Leonard Schlup

MCKEE, ROBERT (1830–ca. 1900), journalist. Born in Fleming County, Kentucky, McKee displayed a flair for journalism at an early age. A Jacksonian Democrat, he joined the Confederate Army and served in Alabama. There, in 1869, he founded the *Selma Southern Argus*. McKee detested Republican racial and economic policies. To him, subsidies for railroads represented the special privilege that Democrats had always resisted. McKee was equally harsh on Democrats who acquiesced in Republican schemes. He soon developed a following among the yeoman farmers who made up the Democratic voters in northern Alabama's hill country. A coalition of planters and industrialists had come to dominate the post-Reconstruction Democratic party by means of carefully controlled county and state conventions. Its leaders worried that McKee was inspiring the independent candidates who ran in the late 1870s, thus risking division of the white vote. Probably in an effort to co-opt him, in 1878 Governor Rufus W. Cobb offered to make McKee his private secretary. To the surprise of many, he accepted, serving Cobb as well as his successor, Edward A. O'Neal. McKee opposed privileges given to coal mine owners, who leased the bulk of Alabama's convicts. Leaving office just as the Farmers' Alliance came to prominence, McKee sympathized with the plain folk who were its members. In the 1890s, he edited newspapers in Alabama and California, but never attained his former influence.

Further Reading: Samuel L. Webb, "A Jacksonian Democrat in Postbellum Alabama: The Ideology and Influence of Journalist Robert McKee, 1869–1896," *Journal of Southern History* 62 (May 1996): 239–274; Allen Johnston Going, *Bourbon Democracy in Alabama, 1874–1890*, 1992.

Paul M. Pruitt, Jr.

MCKENNA, JOSEPH (10 August 1843–21 November 1926), U.S. congressman, circuit court judge, attorney general, Supreme Court justice. Born in Philadelphia, Pennsylvania, McKenna grew up in Benecia, California. In 1865, he was graduated from the law department of Benecia Collegiate Institute. One year later, he became district attorney for Solano County. Elected as a Republican to the state House of Representatives in 1874, McKenna reached the U.S. Congress in 1884. In Washington, he became a loyal lieutenant of the railroad magnate and senator Leland Stanford, who secured McKenna an appointment as judge on the Ninth U.S. Judicial Court in 1892. Five years later, President William McKinley named McKenna attorney general. Upon the retirement of Stephen Field in late 1897, McKinley named McKenna to fill the vacancy on the Supreme Court. McKenna served on the High Court for twenty-seven years, the sole McKinley appointee. In 633 written opinions, McKenna left at best a mixed record on government regulation of private enterprise. He was gently forced into retirement in 1925, and died twenty-two months later at his home in Washington, D.C.

Further Reading: "Attorney General McKenna," *The Green Bag* 9 (July 1897): 289–290; Brother Matthew McDevitt, *Joseph McKenna: Associate Justice of the United States*, 1946.

Harvey Gresham Hudspeth

MCKENZIE, ALEXANDER JOHN (1 April 1851–22 June 1922), political boss. Born in Beaverton, Ontario, Canada, McKenzie moved at age sixteen to Dakota Territory. In 1873 he settled in Bismarck, where he manufactured carbonated beverages. McKenzie held the post of sheriff of Burleigh County from 1875 until

1886. He was by then a celebrated and influential citizen, with a personal following that allowed him to build political power and a machine to dictate the course of the region's political life. Known to Chief Sitting Bull, and every American president from Ulysses S. Grant to Warren G. Harding, McKenzie worked to establish universities at Grand Forks and Fargo, encouraged Congress to divide the area into two states for admission in 1889, and dominated the convention that adopted the North Dakota state constitution. Candidates for local, state, and federal offices normally owed their election to his support; much state legislation required his approval before enactment; and he held a seat as a Republican national committeeman from North Dakota for two decades. A shrewd businessman, "Alexander the Great" died a millionaire in Saint Paul, Minnesota, where he had lived for years.

Further Reading: *Bismarck Daily Tribune*, 23 June 1922; Kenneth J. Carey, "Alexander McKenzie: Boss of North Dakota, 1883–1906," M.A. thesis, University of North Dakota, 1949; David B. Baglien, "The McKenzie Era: A Political History of North Dakota from 1880 to 1920," M.A. thesis, North Dakota State University, 1955.

Leonard Schlup

MCKINLEY, ASSASSINATION OF. On 6 September 1901, President William McKinley stood in a reception line at Buffalo's Pan-American Exposition, protected by the Secret Service, police, and military. Nobody spotted a self-proclaimed anarchist, Leon Czolgosz, who approached with a concealed revolver and fired twice at close range. Surgeons responded promptly and operated at once; they discovered and repaired two holes in McKinley's stomach. For six days, the president appeared to be recovering satisfactorily. Then suddenly his condition deteriorated, and he died on the eighth day, stunning the nation. The surgical team, considered heroic at first, was quickly declared incompetent by the press. Nearly every historical interpretation of the McKinley era has concluded that botched surgery cost the nation its leader. A modern review of the medical records shows that McKinley's death had little to do with his surgery, where it was done, when it was done, how it was done, or who did it. The tragedy had everything to do with failing to recognize a blast injury to the pancreas and adjacent organs, resulting in major body fluid shifts, gradual contraction of the plasma volume, eventual heart failure, and death. The president perished from a kind of shock not yet understood in 1901. The surgeons erred because of their naïveté, not because of neglect. Their combined efforts were as appropriate and sophisticated as any surgeon could offer at the time. The political impact of McKinley's murder was enormous: the anarchist movement was driven underground, Theodore Roosevelt became president, America moved from the Gilded Age to the Progressive Era, and the Secret Service's responsibilities expanded. During the century that followed, medical science achieved significant advances in knowledge and technology. Today a traumatic injury similar to McKinley's would rarely lead to death.

Further Reading: Jack C. Fisher, *Stolen Glory: The McKinley Assassination*, 2001.

Jack C. Fisher

MCKINLEY, IDA SAXTON (8 June 1847–26 May 1907), First Lady. Born in Canton, Ohio, Saxon attended local elementary schools and Brooke Hall in Pennsylvania. While working as a cashier in her father's bank, she met William McKinley, a Canton lawyer, whom she married in 1871. The death of her mother and of second daughter in 1873, compounded by the death of her first daughter two years later, devastated Ida McKinley. The tragedies threw her into depression accompanied by epileptic seizures and phlebitis; eventually she required a paid personal care attendant when her husband was absent. Thrown into the social whirl of Washington when her husband served in the U.S. House of Representatives, and of Columbus when he held the Ohio governorship, Ida McKinley, a querulous invalid under medical treatment, attempted to entertain guests with the help of friends, staff, and caterers. Her nervous ailments and sedentary existence at times caused irritability and melancholy, and she sought relief by crocheting slippers and making black neckties for her husband. As First Lady from 1897 to 1901, she kept the White House filled with flowers while remaining most of the time in her bedroom. Ignoring protocol at state dinners, she sat beside the president, who gently placed a napkin over her face during a seizure and summoned a maid or niece to escort her out of the room. After sustaining mortal gunshot wounds in 1901 at Buffalo, New York, President McKinley lived a week, his wife by his side. Upon her return to Canton, where she died, the former First Lady busied herself writing letters and visiting her husband's grave. Although the McKinley home in Canton, Ohio, made famous by his front porch campaign speeches, no longer stands, the Saxton-McKinley House, where Ida lived as a girl and was married, is today a museum and the headquarters of the National First Ladies' Library, covering all First Ladies from Martha Washington to the present.

Further Reading: Margaret Leech, *In the Days of McKinley*, 1959; H. Wayne Morgan, *William McKinley and His America*, 1963; *Canton Repository*, 27 May 1907.

Leonard Schlup

MCKINLEY TARIFF. One of the most renowned pieces of legislation passed by the extremely active Fifty-first, or "Billion-Dollar," Congress (1889–1891), this tariff also became misunderstood, misconstrued, and misrepresented, largely because there was not enough time before its replacement to demonstrate its effects. In contrast to the 1888 Democratic call for tariff rate reductions, the Republicans remained adamant about protection. Given the mixed results of the 1888 national contest, it arguably was not clear what the public wanted in relation to this or any other issue addressed by the respective party platforms. Nonetheless, with a Republican constitutionally installed in the White House and Republicans in narrow but viable control of both houses of Congress, the party proceeded to claim a mandate.

The task of devising a new protective tariff fell to the chairman of the House Ways and Means Committee, William McKinley of Ohio. The problem was to frame a measure that would provide protection for critical sectors of a rapidly developing national economy while not adding to a large and growing Treasury surplus. The endeavor was made more complex by the efforts of Secretary of State James G. Blaine, with President Benjamin Harrison's backing, to establish the principle of reciprocity, and thus his desire not to give in a tariff law what could be negotiated in a reciprocal agreement. After the addition of literally hundreds of amendments, the McKinley Tariff became law in October 1890. Perhaps its most noteworthy features, in addition to joining protectionism with reciprocity, were those providing a complex schedule of duties for wool and protection for the nascent tin industry, while offsetting any revenue raised by these and other increases by providing for duty-free raw sugar and accompanying compensation for the relatively few American producers. Although balanced so as to not add to the national surplus, the overall thrust of the new law was to raise rates slightly above previous levels. Aware that the general public impression was that the cost of almost everything would rise due to this new tariff, the Democrats played to that misconception. The result was that the Republicans suffered major losses in the 1890 congressional elections, one of them being the legislation's principal architect, William McKinley. The act itself was superseded in 1894.

Further Reading: F. W. Taussig, *The Tariff History of the United States*, 8th ed., 1967 reprint; Tom E. Terrill, *The Tariff, Politics, and American Foreign Policy, 1874–1901*, 1973.

James L. Baumgardner

MCKINLEY, WILLIAM

MCKINLEY, WILLIAM (29 January 1843–14 September 1901), congressman, governor, president of the United States. Born in Niles, Ohio, McKinley attended the Poland (Ohio) Academy and Allegheny College. He enlisted in the Twenty-third Ohio Volunteer Regiment in June 1861, and emerged from the Civil War a brevet major. McKinley studied law briefly at the Albany Law School, and with a practitioner, then settled in Canton, Ohio. His first elective office was prosecuting attorney of Stark County. He served in Congress from 1877 to 1891, except for a brief period in 1884–1885. A moderate Republican on most issues, he favored civil service reform, briefly supported bi-

metallism, and became a noted spokesman for tariff protection. He was known for honesty, diligence, and an ability to harmonize conflicting interests. McKinley lost the election of 1890 owing to a gerrymandered district and a backlash against protection. He won the governorship of Ohio in 1891 and 1893 with substantial tallies. As governor, he favored tax reform, including levies on corporations, and used the militia to maintain public order during labor troubles.

Leaving the governorship early in 1896, he set in motion the organization he had been building to secure the Republican presidential nomination. He was a leading national figure in the party, especially after he conducted several speaking tours on behalf of Republican candidates in the congressional elections of 1894. His long-standing support of the tariff worked to his advantage in the hard times a of the mid-1890s, and he easily defeated favorite son candidates on the first ballot at the June national convention. McKinley refused to duplicate the barnstorming of his unexpected rival, Democrat William Jennings Bryan, a champion of free silver as an answer to the depression. Instead, he organized the "front porch campaign," in which hundreds of delegations of faithful Republicans came to Canton to hear him speak. McKinley emphasized tariff protection and gold-backed currency to end business uncertainty and to restore prosperity. He also radiated sobriety, common sense, and safety. He won 271 electoral votes to Bryan's 176, and was the first presidential candidate since 1872 to receive a majority of the popular count.

The new administration focused on restoring business confidence and prosperity with the Dingley Tariff of 1897. Foreign affairs, however, unexpectedly consumed the president's attention as he sought to end the devastating war in Cuba that had raged since 1895. His goals were to compel Spain to grant autonomy to the island, and to alleviate the suffering of the Cuban people. He had some success in the fall of 1897, but dramatic events such as the De Lome letter and the destruction of the battleship *Maine* in Havana harbor thwarted his diplomacy. The war that followed, forced Spain from the hemisphere and gained independence for Cuba under temporary American tutelage. The United States became a world power after it annexed Hawaii, and acquired the Spanish possessions of Puerto Rico and the Philippine Islands in the peace settlement. McKinley gained popularity by successfully prosecuting the war and elevating the country's status. He sought reelection in 1900 with a new running mate, Theodore Roosevelt, after Garret Hobart died in 1899. The ticket received 292 electoral votes to 155 for William Jennings Bryan, and 7,219,828 popular votes to 6,358,160.

McKinley was inaugurated a second time on 4 March 1901, prepared to face an agenda of domestic issues that included tariff reciprocity and trust reform. Fate decreed otherwise. An anarchist shot him on 6 September 1901, during his visit to the Pan-American Exposition in Buffalo, New York. He died there on 14 September. His legacies included a greatly strengthened presidency and an America with world responsibilities, and well prepared to enter the world economy.

Further Reading: Margaret Leech, *In the Days of McKinley*, 1959; H. Wayne Morgan, *William McKinley and His America*, 1963; Lewis L. Gould, *The Presidency of William McKinley*, 1980.

H. Wayne Morgan

MCLAURIN, JOHN LOWNDES (9 May 1860–29 July 1934), U.S. representative and senator. Born in Red Bluff, South Carolina, McLaurin studied at Bethel Military Academy in Virginia, Swarthmore College in Pennsylvania, and Carolina Military Institute before attending the University of Virginia School of Law. Admitted to the bar in 1883, he began a practice in Bennettsville, South Carolina. He soon became one of the first men of means and position to join Benjamin Tillman's political movement. In 1885 McLaurin won election to the state legislature. Chosen state attorney general in 1891, he secured a congressional seat the following year. Governor Tillman, addressing an 1892 campaign rally, referred to McLaurin as "Little Curly Headed Joe," a nickname that remained for the rest of McLaurin's career. An authority on fiscal matters,

McLaurin soon drifted away from his mentor. In a savage public letter issued in 1894, he openly broke with Tillman. Elected to the Senate in 1897, he served in an uneasy relationship with his former mentor, by then also a member. The breach between the two grew even wider. Tillman subsequently alleged that McLaurin's vote in favor of Philippine annexation in 1899 was secured through bribes from the cotton textile industry. This resulted in a celebrated fistfight on the Senate floor on 22 February 1902. The altercation led to McLaurin's decision not to seek reelection. Retiring in March 1903, McLaurin spent his remaining years engaged in agricultural pursuits on his Bennettsville estate. He briefly reentered public life in 1914, as state senator and, later, warehouse commissioner. He died on his estate.

Further Reading: *New York Times*, 30 July 1934; William J. Cooper, Jr., *The Conservative Regime: South Carolina, 1877–1890*, 1968.

Harvey Gresham Hudspeth

MCMILLIN, BENTON (11 September 1845–8 January 1933), congressman, governor of Tennessee, diplomat. Born in Monroe County, Kentucky, McMillin attended Philomath Academy in Tennessee before the Civil War. The son of a planter, he had two brothers serving in the Confederate Army, and he hoped to fight for the South as well. Due to his young age, however, he was effectively prevented from doing so by his parents. McMillin was nevertheless taken prisoner by Union forces after he refused to swear an oath of allegiance. Imprisoned for one winter, he was finally released back to his parents due to poor health. Attending the University of Kentucky at war's end, McMillin studied law and was admitted to the bar. In 1871, he opened a law practice in Celina, Clay County, Tennessee. Taking an early interest in politics, he won election to the state house of representatives in 1874. A member of the legislative session that returned Andrew Johnson to the Senate in 1875, McMillin was commissioned one year later to serve as a special judge of the circuit court.

Elected to the U.S. House of Representatives in 1878, McMillin spent the next two decades in Congress. As a congressman, his greatest achievement was his sponsorship of the first general income tax bill introduced in peacetime. Though unsuccessful at the time, it nevertheless helped lay the groundwork for the ratification of the Sixteenth Amendment in 1913. Declining nomination for an eleventh term in 1898, McMillin chose instead to stand for election as governor of Tennessee. During his two two-year terms in office, he manifested a distinct interest in public education. He also established a sinking fund for the retirement of bonded indebtedness, and he saw to it that the state capitol building was refurbished. The most dominant issue for McMillin's administration was the continuing debate over prohibition. Declining nomination for a third term, McMillin retired from office in 1903. The issue, however, ultimately led to his failure to be elected U.S. senator in 1911. Appointed Woodrow Wilson's minister to Peru in 1913, he served in that post until 1919, when he was appointed to a similar position in Guatemala. Retiring in 1922, he died in Nashville.

Further Reading: *New York Times*, 9 January 1933; Robert E. Corlew, *Tennessee: A Short History*, 1981.

Harvey Gresham Hudspeth

MCQUAID, BERNARD JOHN (15 December 1823–18 January 1909), Catholic bishop and educator. Born in New York City, McQuaid entered the priesthood, and became an energetic and capable ecclesiastical administrator and organizer of Catholic schools. Although recognized as a leader of urban congregations, McQuaid devoted considerable time to parochial education. He was a firm advocate of Christian academies over public schools. Known for stern discipline, authoritarian methods, and conservative thought, McQuaid founded St. Bernard's Seminary in 1893. He opposed the Knights of Labor, berated secret societies, and disavowed American Catholicism's liberal tendencies. McQuaid established numerous parishes within his New York jurisdiction and built homes for the elderly, recreational facilities, orphanages, and a Young Men's Catholic Institute. An educational pioneer and leading Catholic spokesman in Gilded

Age America, McQuaid died in Rochester, New York.

Further Reading: Norlene M. Kunkel, *Bishop Bernard J. McQuaid and Catholic Education*, 1988; Frederick J. Zwierlein, *The Life and Letters of Bishop McQuaid*, 3 vols., 1925–1927; *New York Times*, 19 January 1909.

Leonard Schlup

MEDICINE. Following the Civil War, military medical facilities yielded to a proliferation of civilian general hospitals, mental institutions, and tuberculosis sanatoriums, as well as a number of segregated and faith-based hospitals. Aspiring physicians studied in Europe or received domestic educations of varying quality. American medical schools, once easily chartered, became more rigorous when they attempted to emulate the high standard set by the Johns Hopkins University in 1876. Medical associations recognized the emerging specialties of neurology, psychiatry, and pharmacology. Chiropractors, osteopaths, and nutritionists gained popularity and professional status, and nurses were trained to serve in hospital, industrial, residential, and school settings. Louis Pasteur's work with pathogenic microorganisms opened medicine's bacteriological era. Late nineteenth-century scientists discovered the causes of typhoid, tuberculosis, cholera, malaria, and other communicable illnesses. Advances in disease etiology supported government-sponsored quarantines, vaccination programs, and efforts to detect contagions at ports of immigration. Social reformers, influenced by the public health movement, attempted to improve urban living conditions. Better indoor heating, ventilation, and plumbing extended life expectancies from forty years in 1850 to fifty years by 1900.

Further Reading: James H. Cassedy, *Medicine in America: A Short History*, 1991; Richard Harrison Shryock, *Medicine in America: Historical Essays*, 1966.

Jane M. Armstrong

MELLETTE, ARTHUR CALVIN (23 June 1842–25 May 1896), governor of South Dakota. Born in Henry County, Indiana, Mellette earned the LL.B. degree from Indiana University. He served briefly, in the state legislature before moving to Dakota Territory in January 1879. While serving as a register of public lands, he attended a Thanksgiving Day political gathering at Yankton, the territorial capital. There a plan emerged to separate the well populated southern half of the territory from the sparsely settled, frigid northern half, creating two states. The meeting led to four constitutional conventions in southern Dakota from 1882 to 1889; at them, Mellette emerged as a leader in composing a lengthy document that reflected his deep suspicion of legislative prerogatives. The constitution of South Dakota also expressed regional Democratic attitudes that soon appeared in the Omaha Platform of the People's Party. The handiwork of Mellette more than any other individual, it became the organic law for the state and he became the first elected governor. Mellette left several legacies. He and those around him belied the myth that most political leaders in the West were incompetents, charlatans, and thieves. The detailed constitution he drafted left an imprint of populism, and soon made South Dakotans pioneers in implementing such practices as direct democratic initiative and referendum, primary elections, and statutory controls over corporations. Mellette's persona was unexciting, sometimes morose, and on occasions even suicidal. Yet, while serving as governor of the territory, and then of the state (1889–1893), he presented a demeanor of propriety, integrity, and thoroughgoing dedication to northern Great Plains development. Mellette died in Pittsburg, Kansas.

Further Reading: William O. Farber, "From Territorial Status to Statehood: Arthur Calvin Mellette," in Herbert T. Hoover and Larry J. Zimmerman, *South Dakota Leaders*, 1989, 163–184; Herbert S. Schell, *History of South Dakota*, 1975.

Herbert T. Hoover

MELLON, THOMAS (3 February 1813–3 February 1908), judge and banker. Born at Camp Hill Cottage near Omagh, Lower Castleton, County Tyrone, Ireland, Mellon came with his parents to the United States in 1818, settling on a Pennsylvania farm. He graduated in 1837 from the Western University of Pennsylvania (now University of Pittsburgh), opened a law practice in 1839, invested wisely in real estate, and served as assistant law judge of the Court

of Common Pleas from 1859 to 1869. The next year, he opened the private banking house of Thomas Mellon and Sons. In 1885 Mellon completed his autobiography, *Thomas Mellon and His Times*. He died in Pittsburgh. Mellon's son, Andrew W. Mellon, was secretary of the Treasury from 1921 until his resignation in 1932, holding this cabinet portfolio during the presidential administrations of Warren G. Harding, Calvin Coolidge, and Herbert Hoover.

Further Reading: *New York Times*, 4 February 1908; David Losloff, *The Mellons: The Chronicle of America's Richest Family*, 1978; Burton Hersh, *The Mellon Family: A Fortune in History*, 1978.

Leonard Schlup

MENCHES, CHARLES E. (10 June 1859–3 December 1931), businessman. Born in Canton, Ohio, Menches worked as a trapeze artist for the Robinson Circus from 1879 to 1885. Two years later he and his younger brother, Frank, formed a partnership that endured until 1931. Their businesses during the Gilded Age included the Piedmont Café in Canton, a cigar factory in Canton, and Summit Lake Park in Akron. In 1885, at their concession stand at the Erie County Fair in New York, the Menches brothers substituted beef for pork in their popular sausage patty; added brown sugar, coffee, and other ingredients to camouflage the taste; and placed the product in a bun. They christened this sandwich the "hamburger" after Hamburg, New York, the site of the fair. The birth of the hamburger profoundly impacted American food habits in the twentieth century. At the Saint Louis World's Fair in 1904, the Menches invented the ice cream cone. In the early twentieth century, they operated the Liberty Theatre, the Novelty Rubber Company, the Liberty Hotel, the Premium Cone and Candy Company, and the Premium Popcorn Works in Canton and Akron. Charles Menches died in Akron.

Further Reading: *Akron Beacon Journal*, 4 December 1931.

Leonard Schlup

MERCER, HENRY CHAPMAN (24 June 1856–9 March 1930), archaeologist, historian, ceramist, and collector. Born in Doylestown,

Pennsylvania, Mercer graduated from Harvard University in 1879 and subsequently studied at the University of Pennsylvania Law School. Having inherited wealth, he lived the life of a gentleman scholar, studied history, traveled extensively, took photographs of various places, collected cultural artifacts, and meticulously recorded his observations. In 1880 Mercer helped establish the Bucks County Historical Society. From 1891 to 1897 he worked for the department of archaeology and paleontology in the University of Pennsylvania Museum, served as associate editor of *American Naturalist* (1893–1897), and published *Hill Caves of the Yucatan* (1896). In 1898, Mercer organized the Moravian Pottery and Tile Works in Doylestown; there he manufactured handcrafted pictorial tiles that were used in buildings throughout the nation. Often expressing his discoveries in his work, Mercer insisted that his tiles express both beauty and purpose. He played an important role in revitalizing ceramic tile use in architecture, and founded a museum that today perpetuates his memory and houses displays of the furnishings, folk art, and implements of early America, including Native American artifacts. He died in Doylestown.

Further Reading: Cleota Reed, *Henry Chapman Mercer and the Moravian Pottery and Tile Works*, 1987; Henry C. Mercer Papers, Spruance Library, Bucks County Historical Society, Doylestown, Pennsylvania.

Leonard Schlup

MERTS AND RIDDLE COACH AND HEARSE COMPANY. In 1859, at Ravenna, Ohio, the brothers-in-law Charles Merts and Henry Warner Riddle formed the Merts and Riddle Coach and Hearse Company (which operated as Riddle Coach and Hearse Company after Merts retired in 1891). A fire at the carriage works in 1871 burned the plant and damaged several adjacent buildings; losses were estimated at $40,000. A greater conflagration occurred in 1903. The owners rebuilt and persevered in both instances. Merts and Riddle hearses were considered the nation's best during the postbellum period. They were used in the funeral processions of presidents William McKinley and Warren G. Harding, and probably of James A. Garfield. The company closed

in 1925. Many Riddle conveyances survive as glossy museum exhibits.

Further Reading: Larry L. Miller, ed., *Days of Yore: A Portage Panorama*, 2002; Riddle archives and catalogs, Portage County Historical Society, Ravenna, Ohio.

Leonard Schlup

METCALF, WILLARD LEROY (1 July 1858–9 March 1925), artist. Born in Lowell, Massachusetts, Metcalf apprenticed under the landscape painter George L. Brown in Boston, and studied at the Boston Normal Art School and the Académie Julian in Paris. He drew illustrations of the Zuni in New Mexico and Arizona in 1884, painted with the French Impressionist Claude Monet in 1885 and 1886, and sketched scenes in Algeria and Morocco in 1887. Metcalf taught painting classes at Cooper Institute in New York City from 1893 to 1903, and shared studios with Robert Reid and William H. Howe. In 1898 Metcalf became a member of "The Ten," an independent group of artists that included John Henry Twachtman, Childe Hassam, and William Merritt Chase. They distanced themselves from the Society of American Painters and the National Academy of Design. A heavy drinker who endured marital problems, Metcalf became increasingly addicted to alcohol by century's end. Despite his despondency, Metcalf continued to paint, producing several nature and landscape masterpieces in the twentieth century while winning numerous awards. A loner who enveloped his life in painting, drinking, fishing, and a few artistic colleagues, Metcalf died in New York City.

Further Reading: Patricia Jobe Pierce, *The Ten*, 1976; Elizabeth de Veer and Richard J. Boyle, *Sunlight and Shadow: The Life and Art of Willard L. Metcalf*, 1987.

Leonard Schlup

METCALF, WILLIAM (3 September 1838–5 December 1909), steel manufacturer. Born in Pittsburgh, Pennsylvania, Metcalf graduated in 1858 from Rensselaer Polytechnic Institute in Troy, New York; worked as general superintendent of Fort Pitt Foundry, a Pittsburgh ironworks (1859–1865); and supervised the company's production of armaments for the Union Army during the Civil War. In 1869 he became a partner in the steel firm of Miller,

Metcalf & Parkin, which earned a reputation for quality steel while steadily increasing production. In 1896, Metcalf published *Steel: A Manual for Steel Users*. The next year he founded the Braeburn Steel Company, a producer of cast crucible steel, serving as president until his death in Pittsburgh. A member of numerous mining, scientific, and engineering societies, Metcalf played an important role in the emerging professional organizations for engineering in Gilded Age America.

Further Reading: *Pittsburgh Dispatch*, 6 December 1909; *Pittsburgh Post*, 7 December 1909; John Ingham, *Making Iron and Steel: Independent Mills in Pittsburgh, 1820–1920*, 1991.

Leonard Schlup

METEOROLOGY. Meteorology in the Gilded Age featured the expansion of observational systems and government service under the U.S. Army Signal Service and the Department of Agriculture. Congress established the U.S. Weather Bureau on 9 February 1870. It also created a federal storm warning service that year, from which Cleveland Abbe expounded meteorological theory. Originally part of the Signal Service, on 1 July 1891 the Weather Bureau became part of the Department of Agriculture, thereby formalizing the link between meteorology and agriculture. Soon the budget for governmental meteorological services topped $1 million. The Weather Bureau employed one thousand individuals by 1897. Most of their experience came from on-the-job training. They served as station attendants, whose duties included reading instruments, launching balloons, and wiring data to Washington. It was an era dominated by government service in meteorology. The editor Charles Dudley Warner penned the observation that "everybody talks about the weather, but nobody does anything about it" in the *Hartford Courant* in 1890. On 30 June 1940, the U.S. Weather Bureau was transferred to the Commerce Department.

Further Reading: Robert M. Friedman, *Appropriating the Weather: Vilhelm Bjerknes and the Construction of a Modern Meteorology*, 1989; James R. Fleming, *Meteorology in America, 1800–1870*, 1990.

Leonard Schlup

MICHELSON, ALBERT ABRAHAM (19 December 1852–9 May 1931), physicist. Born in Strelno, Prussia (now Poland), Michelson grew up in San Francisco, California. In 1873 he was graduated from the U.S. Naval Academy, where he taught physics until 1879. He then was a physics professor at the new Case School of Applied Sciences in Cleveland, Ohio (1883–1889). There he investigated wave motion. Physicists knew sound was a wave that could not travel through a vacuum; it required a medium, such as the atmosphere. Yet light was a wave that traveled through space, where no medium was apparent. Physicists believed they had not yet discovered the medium, which they dubbed "the ether," and attempted to identify. Michelson reasoned that the ether was stationary and would produce a drag on the earth as it rotated. Light traveling against the ether should move more slowly than light moving perpendicular to it. In 1887, Michaelson and Edward W. Morley tested this hypothesis at Cleveland's Western Reserve University, but failed to detect a difference in light's speed, whatever its direction. The speed of light, it seemed, was constant, an idea that laid the foundation for Albert Einstein's special theory of relativity. Michelson's work brought him the Nobel Prize in physics in 1907, making him the first American Nobel laureate in a science. The California Institute of Technology's most distinguished scientist, Michelson died in Pasadena.

Further Reading: Bernard Jaffe, *Michelson and the Speed of Light*, 1960; Gerald Holton, "Einstein, Michelson, and the 'Crucial Experiment,' " *Isis* 60 (1969): 133–197.

Christopher Cumo

MILES, NELSON APPLETON (8 August 1839–15 May 1925), U.S. army officer and commanding general of the army. Born near Westminster, Massachusetts, Miles was educated informally and acquired military knowledge from a former French army colonel. During the Civil War he recruited volunteers, was wounded four times, and participated in all important battles, save one, involving the Army of the Potomac. Frequently cited for courage, he became a major general of volunteers, commanding a corps of twenty-six thousand men at age twenty-six. Following the war, Miles was briefly responsible for guarding Jefferson Davis at Fort Monroe. In July 1866, he became a permanent colonel in the regular army. In the Indian wars that followed, Miles was associated with almost every major campaign. He defeated the Cheyennes, Kiowas, and Comanches; he dispersed the Sioux. In 1877, Miles captured Chief Joseph and his band of Nez Percé after an epic 160-mile pursuit. In 1886, as a brigadier general he ended depredations by Apaches under Geronimo. From 1888 to 1890, Miles commanded the Department of the Pacific, and in 1890 became a major general. In 1891–1892 he headed forces that crushed the Sioux at Wounded Knee. In 1894, while commanding the Department of the Missouri with headquarters in Chicago, Miles was ordered by President Grover Cleveland to put down the Pullman strike.

In 1895, Miles became by seniority the commanding general of the army. During the war against Spain, he oversaw volunteer units. He favored a period of training and a later invasion of Cuba, but public opinion demanded an immediate assault on the island; the result was near chaos. Miles commanded five thousand men in a late July 1898 invasion of Puerto Rico, a well-planned and -executed operation that contrasted sharply with the earlier landing on Cuba. With few U.S. casualties, Miles's force had almost eliminated Spanish resistance on Puerto Rico when hostilities ended in mid-August. In 1901 Miles opposed a number of Secretary of War Elihu Root's reform measures, including establishment of a general staff, which Congress nonetheless passed. He retired in 1903 at age sixty-four, as required by law. He died in Washington, D.C.

Further Reading: Virginia Johnson, *The Unregulated General,* 1962; Nelson Miles, *Personal Recollections and Observations by General Nelson A. Miles,* 1896; Robert Wooster, *Nelson A. Miles and the Twilight of the Frontier Army,* 1993.

Spencer C. Tucker

MILLARD LETTER. In the August 1897 issue of *The Arena,* Charles C. Millard, a resident of Wichita, Kansas, published an open letter to eastern capitalists. He noted that entrepreneurs from the East owned western businesses, houses, public buildings, facilities of the Young Men's Christian Association, farms, and even churches on which there were mortgages. Evidence of eastern mortgages appeared everywhere in broken or boarded-up windows. Defending westerners as practical people willing to wear rags and economize to make interest payments, Millard objected to eastern financial policy, politics, and religion. He added that the East could never own the people. He discussed silver coinage as a moral issue, sacred dogma, economic panacea, political necessity, and social manifestation, observing that neither Democrats nor Republicans had offered a solution through tariffs or other sensible measures. He urged eastern financiers to join with the West in the free silver movement. He also reminded creditors that whatever added to western prosperity would increase the value of their holdings, and that the interests of the two regions were identical.

Millard was not a politician; rather, he was an average citizen who demonstrated no prejudice against Gilded Age plutocrats and rejected the notion that all financiers were corrupt. He proved an effective spokesman for his region's interests. Millard believed that if eastern industrialists comprehended the situation in the West and the South, they would realize that a different approach would be to their economic advantage. Millard claimed no partisan interest, offering plain facts that he believed could be easily verified. He predicted that continuation of existing financial policies would bring disaster to the East as well as the West.

Further Reading: Charles C. Millard, "An Open Letter to Eastern Capitalists," *The Arena* 18 (1897): 211–217.

Leonard Schlup

MILLER, GEORGE AUGUSTUS, SR (29 January 1856–12 July 1932), railroad executive. Born in Boston, Massachusetts, Miller was educated in local schools before becoming an apprentice in the machine shops of the Boston and Maine Railroad. After moving to

Florida in 1883, he was foreman on the Jacksonville, Tampa and Key West Railroad, then joined the Florida East Coast Railroad (FEC) when it was building connections between the Florida Keys and the mainland. During this golden age of rail development in Florida, Miller directed the FEC machine shops in St. Augustine, as general foreman, master mechanic, and finally superintendent of motive power and machinery. In tribute to Miller's leadership, the FEC repair facilities in St. Augustine were named the Miller Shops. He died in St. Augustine.

Further Reading: George Augustus Miller, Jr., Papers, Archives, Auburn University Library, Auburn, Alabama.

David O. Whitten

MILLER, HARRIET MANN (25 June 1831–25 December 1918), author and ornithologist. Born in Auburn, New York, Mann in 1854 married Watts Todd Miller and moved to Brooklyn, New York. Talented at storytelling, she published numerous short articles in various magazines and newspapers, including *Youth's Companion*, *The Independent*, and the *Chicago Tribune*. Using the pseudonym Olive Thorne Miller, she offered "sugar-coated pills of knowledge" for children. Some of Miller's collections of stories for young people include *Our Little Newsboy and Other Stories* (1879) and *Tales from Storyland* (1890). Miller's love of ornithology led her to observe and write about birds. Her first adult book, *Bird-Ways*, appeared in 1885. Three years later she wrote *In Nesting Time*, followed in 1892 by *Little Brothers of the Air* and in 1894 by *Bird-Lover in the West*. Between 1870 and 1915, Miller produced seven hundred articles and twenty-four books. A lecturer and humanitarian, she condemned the destruction of birds, denouncing male hunters who lost "sight of the terror and pain of the victims" and berating women who wore "the beautiful plumage of a delicate winged creature, whose sweet life of song and joy was rudely cut short." Concerned for the environment and the preservation of wilderness and natural resources, Miller in many ways was ahead of her time in the conser-

vation movement. She supported women's clubs as a means of elevating women in American society. Miller died in Los Angeles, California.

Further Reading: *Los Angeles Times*, 26 December 1918; Harriet M. Miller Papers, Manuscripts Division, Library of Congress.

Leonard Schlup

MILLER, KELLY (18 July 1863–29 December 1939), mathematician, sociologist, and writer. Born in Winnsboro, South Carolina, Miller earned undergraduate and graduate degrees from Howard University and in 1887 did postgraduate work in mathematics at the Johns Hopkins University, thereby becoming the first African-American mathematics graduate student. In 1889 he began teaching mathematics and, some years later, sociology at Howard. In 1895, Miller addressed the Walt Whitman Fellowship on Whitman's position in African-American literature and thought. A noted essayist and writer of books, Miller was one of the founders of the American Negro Academy in 1897. He also published a syndicated column in black newspapers. In 1896 Miller published *Race Traits and Tendencies of the American Negro*, in which he contended that African Americans might be underdeveloped, but they were not genetically inferior to other races. He promoted African-American education, crusaded for racial equality, accepted lawful protest, shunned rigid, dogmatic theories, and maintained that black migration to the North and congested urban conditions had detrimentally affected the morals and values of African Americans. Known as a "philosopher of the race question," Miller gained prominence as a pioneering advocate of the systematic study of African Americans, urging that Howard University become a national center for black studies. Miller died at his home in Washington, D.C., leaving an incomplete autobiography but a powerful legacy of African-American achievements in the late nineteenth and early twentieth centuries.

Further Reading: Bernard Eisenberg, "Kelly Miller: The Negro Leader as a Marginal Man," *Journal of Negro History* 45 (1960): 182–197; August Meier, "The Racial and

Educational Philosophy of Kelly Miller, 1895–1915," *Journal of Negro Education* 29 (1960): 121–127.

Leonard Schlup

MILLER, LEWIS (24 August 1829–17 February 1899), inventor and educator. Born in Greentown, Ohio, Miller was educated at Plainfield Academy in Illinois. After beginning as an apprentice in 1851, he became rose to superintendent and partner of Aultman, Miller & Company, a farm implement manufacturer in Akron, Ohio. Miller patented the Buckeye mower and reaper in 1856, and followed with many other patents for farm implements over the next few decades. Aultman, Miller & Company, also known as the Buckeye Works, produced twenty thousand harvesting machines a year by 1881. Miller also pioneered sales innovations such as exact operating scale models for salesmen to show dealers and farmers. He was involved in many other manufacturing interests and banks in Akron and Canton between the 1860s and his death. Miller was a founder and sponsor of the Chautauqua Movement. He also financially supported and served on the boards of Mount Union College (where he was president), Ohio Wesleyan University, and Allegheny College. He was a member of the Akron board of education and the public library board. His daughter, Mina, married the inventor Thomas Alva Edison in 1886. He died in New York City.
Further Reading: Ellwood Hendrick, *Lewis Miller: A Biographical Essay*, 1925; John H. Vincent, *The Chautauqua Movement*, 1886; Karl Grismer, *Akron and Summit County*, 1952.

Stephen Paschen

MILLER, WARNER (12 August 1838–21 March 1918), paper manufacturer and U.S. senator. Born in Hannibal, New York, Miller graduated in 1860 from Union College in Schenectady, and then taught school. After military service during the Civil War, he operated the Warner Miller and Company paper mill in Herkimer, New York, developing new processes for manufacturing the product. He also was president of the American Paper and Pulp Association and a member of the New York State Assembly in the mid-1870s. After holding a seat in the federal House of Representatives from 1879 to 1881, Miller served as a Republican in the U.S. Senate from 1881 until 1887. Nationalistic in his views, Miller favored Chinese exclusion, encouraged the development of the merchant marine, and advocated protective tariffs. In 1888 he lost a bid for the New York governorship to Davis Bennett Hill. He died in New York City.
Further Reading: *New York Times*, 22 March 1918.

Leonard Schlup

MILLER, WILLIAM HENRY HARRISON (6 September 1840–25 May 1917), U.S. attorney general. Born in Augusta, New York, Miller graduated from Hamilton College in 1861, served in the Union Army, and was admitted to the bar in 1865. He moved to Fort Wayne, Indiana, in 1866. Shortly thereafter, Benjamin Harrison invited Miller to join the Indianapolis law firm of Harrison and Hines. When Harrison assumed the presidency in 1889, Miller became attorney general and one of the president's closest advisers. Miller carefully investigated the records of individuals nominated for federal judicial appointments during Harrison's term. Among Miller's assistants was William Howard Taft, the solicitor general. Upon the conclusion of Harrison's years in the White House in 1893, Miller rejoined his law firm in Indianapolis, remaining active in the practice until 1910. He died in Indianapolis.
Further Reading: *Indianapolis Star*, 26 May 1917; *Indianapolis News*, 26 May 1917.

Leonard Schlup

MILLS BILL. President Grover Cleveland devoted his entire State of the Union message in December 1887 to a call for tariff reform through reduction. The House Committee on Ways and Means, chaired by Roger Quarles Mills of Texas, immediately began work on a proposal to cut duties. Introduced in March 1888, the measure sought reductions averaging about 7 percent, falling mostly on raw materials. It reflected the sectional interests of the South, whose representatives dominated the committee. Severe cuts in rates on finished metal products, crockery, wood, glass, finished iron and steel, and woolen goods would fall heavily on the North. Retention of duties on low-grade cotton fabrics, continued protection of rice, and light reductions for sugar and iron ore favored southern interests. The bill thus fell short of tariff reforms proposed by President Cleveland. Debate ran from 17 April to 21 July, when the House approved the bill 162–149. Tariff reform was the central issue in the election of 1888. With Cleveland's defeat, the measure was lost and momentum for tariff reform halted.

Further Reading: Joseph Allan Nevins, *Grover Cleveland: A Study in Courage*, 1932; Tom E. Terrill, *The Tariff, Politics, and American Foreign Policy, 1874–1901*, 1973.

Douglas Steeples

MILLS, ROGER QUARLES (30 March 1832–2 September 1911), congressman and U.S. senator. Born in Todd County, Kentucky, Mills relocated to Texas in 1850, and began practicing law at Corsicana in 1852. He supported John C. Breckinridge for president in 1860, and served in the Confederate Army. After the Civil War he farmed and practiced law. In 1872, Mills won election as a Democrat to the U.S. House of Representatives, where he served from 1873 until his resignation in March 1892. During these years, Mills voiced the views of white southerners on Reconstruction, supported federal assistance for railroads and harbors in Texas, and favored an increase of currency circulation. He expressed his views in articles in the *North American Review* and *The Forum*, and focused attention on tariff reduction, which, he contended, would stimulate trade and benefit consumers. The Mills bill to lower tariff rates surfaced as an issue in the presidential campaign of 1888. Although Mills was not a strong proponent of silver coinage, he won the U.S. Senate seat formerly held by John H. Reagan in 1892. Mills served until 1899, when he chose not to seek reelection. He died in Corsicana.

Further Reading: *Dallas Morning News*, 3 September 1911; Roger Q. Mills Papers, Dallas Historical Society, and Eugene C. Barker Texas History Center, University of Texas at Austin.

Leonard Schlup

MILLS, SUSAN LINCOLN TOLMAN (18 November 1825–12 December 1912), educator.

Born in Enosburg, Vermont, Tolman graduated from Mount Holyoke Seminary in 1845 and three years later married Cyrus T. Mills, a Presbyterian minister. After working as missionaries in Ceylon and later as teachers in Hawaii, Susan Mills and her husband in 1871 founded Mills Seminary in Oakland, California, in 1871. There she served in several capacities, including dean of faculty and ultimately, in 1909, president of the institution, which California had chartered as a college in 1885. Mills was primarily responsible for the growth and stability of the school, the first woman's college on the west coast. Under her leadership new buildings were added to the campus, and she convinced the architect Julia Morgan to design some of them. Mills also recruited faculty, raised academic standards, taught classes, and paved the way for the institution's financial security. She died at Mills College.

Further Reading: E. O. James, *The Story of Cyrus and Susan Mills*, 1953; Susan Mills Papers, Mills College Library, Oakland, California.

Leonard Schlup

MILWAUKEE RIOTS OF 1886. Fragmentation within labor and ethnic groups in Milwaukee, Wisconsin, affected the approaches people took toward improving their living conditions. In the 1880s, German Americans ranked as the largest and most influential population segment in the city, and they dominated local politics. By 1886 the Knights of Labor and Paul Grottkau's Central Labor Union helped to bring diverse elements together. The Knights in Milwaukee, under Robert Schilling, numbered sixteen thousand, crossing skilled and unskilled lines. Grottkau, a German-born socialist who edited the newspaper *Arbeiter Zeitung*, epitomized, in the minds of many conservative Wisconsin businessmen, the immigrant agitator whose appeals to American workingmen had inflamed the growing capital-labor conflicts. Both organizations favored the eight-hour day, but Grottkau was more militant, demanding ten hours of pay.

In April 1886, organized labor in Milwaukee intensified its struggle. Local assemblies of the Knights and the Central Labor Union merged to establish the Eight Hour League, and promised to strike on 1 May. At first the strike developed sporadically, but as it grew, business leaders feared its consequences. They requested state aid, and Governor Jeremiah Rusk arrived in Milwaukee by train from Madison. He conferred with Chandler P. Chapman, adjutant general of Wisconsin's twenty-four-hundred-member National Guard, and Captain Charles King, member of a prominent Milwaukee family. Demonstrators escalated their activities after half a dozen Polish Kosciusko Guards fired over the heads of the crowd, an unauthorized action that momentarily scattered protestors but inflamed their bellicosity. A brick hit the head of Captain Francis J. Borchardt, commander of the Kosciusko unit.

While the state solidified its position, tactical differences divided workers. In public addresses, Grottkau advocated belligerency, urging his followers to close the city's businesses and industries. Schilling, by contrast, met with Rusk, suggested a National Guard withdrawal, and beseeched Knights, in an appeal for law and order, to clear the streets. After Rusk declined to recall the Guard, the Knights basically withdrew from the strike. When rioters neared the Bay View mills on 5 May, a Major Traeumer gave the order to fire, a volley that killed five people, two of whom were not belong part of the mob. Strikers thereupon dispersed. Although disorder continued briefly, the shootings led to a restoration of law and order. Thereafter, authorities arrested and convicted thirty-seven individuals, including Grottkau. The state had broken the strike, without reductions in hours or raises in wages.

Further Reading: Jerry M. Cooper, "The Wisconsin National Guard in the Milwaukee Riots of 1886," *Wisconsin Magazine of History* 55 (1971) 31–48.

Leonard Schlup

MINES AND MINING. From 1868 to 1901, gold and silver mining prospered as never before or since, and copper and coal mining came of age. In the United States, the industry began in the late 1820s in Georgia and North Carolina. It then gained worldwide fame with the 1849 California gold rush. Just before the Civil War, two rushes occurred in areas that would become Colorado and Nevada. On this foundation, postwar mining prospered.

In the years following the opening of the Comstock mines, prospectors scurried around Nevada, developing silver mining districts and camps throughout the state. Discovery of Leadville's silver lodes in 1877–1878 brought huge numbers of miners to Colorado. For the next decade, Colorado was the leading mining state, a mineral treasure house. The San Juan, Cripple Creek, and Aspen mines became famous. Cripple Creek gold revitalized the state after the silver crash of 1893, and continued Colorado's mining preeminence well past 1900. Colorado was joined by Utah, Montana, and Idaho as major mining states during the 1880s. Montana shifted from gold to silver, and finally to copper mining. The Butte copper deposits were the richest yet found, and after a classic fight between companies, the Anaconda Company came to dominate the district and even the state. Utah emerged just a little later with its copper, and finally Arizona joined the "big three" producers. These developments affected industry, urbanization, communication, transportation, and the national economy. Rushes to the Klondike in 1898 and to western Nevada in the early 1900s ended the era.

The consequences of western mining on the mining industry were profound. The development of water pumps, tramways, and power drills, and the use of electricity were revolutionary. Because of the western mining experience, Congress passed the Mining Act of 1872. Meanwhile, mining lawyers found the industry a "gold mine" of disputes and cases. For the industry, the evolution of the professions of mining engineering and geology placed mining beyond the old saying, "You can't tell beyond the pick at the end of the mine." Mining engineers, such as Theodore Comstock, founder of the Arizona School of Mines, and James D. Hague brought professionalism to what had been the "school of hard knocks."

In each western state, mining influenced all aspects of development, from promotion to transportation to agriculture and politics. Mining men became governors and senators, and funded political parties. Some, such as Horace Tabor and John W. Mackay, became celebrated for their wealth and lavish lifestyles. Mining camps and towns became famous, or infamous, with growth of the "silver issue." Overproduction of silver against limited use, especially as gold replaced silver for coinage, depressed the commodity's price. Miners protested heatedly in the 1870s and 1880s, demanding federal government support. While they received some help by the government's buying silver and coining silver dollars, the government refused to guarantee a price. When the panic of 1893 hit the country, easterners and others blamed it on the purchase of silver. The repeal of the Sherman Silver Purchase Act collapsed the price to the 50 cents an ounce. Depression gripped the silver states, resulting in wholehearted support for "free silver" and William Jennings Bryan in the 1896 election. Both lost.

With less glamour and excitement, coal mining developed in Pennsylvania and nearby states, and also in such western states as Colorado and Utah. Coal districts and towns were dominated by companies from the very start, making them completely different from their western cousins. They were the scenes of some of the early management-labor conflicts that turned violent. The same pattern unfolded in the West by century's end. As individual opportunity declined, Western miners squared off against owners. The latter emerged triumphant in both regions.

Further Reading William Greever, *The Bonanza West*, 1963; Duane A. Smith, *Mining America*, 1987.

Duane A. Smith

MOLLY MAGUIRES, alleged Irish and Irish-American terrorist organization. Between 1846 and 1854, approximately 1.2 million Irish immigrated to the United States, only to encounter discrimination by nativists, anti-Catholic polemicists, more established immigrant groups, and unscrupulous employers. Family, church, saloons, and fraternal organizations such as the Ancient Order of Hibernians (AOH) offered some solace. The isolated anthracite coal mining villages of northeastern Pennsylvania were notorious for violence and unsolved murders. They were equally infamous for harsh working conditions, low wages, and long hours. Between 1868 and 1874 John Siney was active in organizing Irish workers into the Workingmen's Benevolent Association (WBA), and it struck area mines. In 1873, rumors circulated that Irish miners belonged to the Molly Maguires, an alleged ultrasecret terrorist group (whose name derives from a legendary opponent of British landlords in Ireland). In that year, Franklin Gowen, president of the Philadelphia and Reading and Lehigh Valley Railroad conglomerate, which controlled many of the area's mines, hired Pinkerton Agency detective James McParlan to infiltrate the Mollies. McParlan claimed that a vast, interlocking conspiracy existed across the region, involving the AOH, saloonkeepers, and miners. The Mollies, he alleged, were responsible for murders of mine superintendents, police officers, and local citizens opposed to unions. The first arrests came in May 1876, and by 1879, nineteen convicted ringleaders had been hanged.

Evidence for the Molly Maguires' conspiracy rests almost entirely on McParlan's testimony. Many Irish Americans accused Gowen and McParlan of inventing the conspiracy in order to crush the WBA, whose five-month "long strike" in 1875 vexed Gowen. They also charged the pair with exploiting anti-Irish xenophobia. All those arrested were Irish, most were miners who had participated in strikes, and several were members of the Irish Land League. The WBA declined precipitously after 1876, and recruitment for heavily Irish organizations like the Knights of Labor was hindered by Molly Maguire innuendoes. The existence of the Molly Maguires remains problematic, but in the Gilded Age, references to them fueled anti-Irish discrimination, and were used to justify crackdowns against radicals and labor advocates of all sorts.

Further Reading: Anthony Bimba, *The Molly Maguires*, 1989; Sidney Lens, *The Labor Wars*, 1974; Cleveland Moffett, "The Overthrow of the Molly Maguires," *McClure's Magazine* 14 (1894): 90–100.

Robert E. Weir

MONEY, HERNANDO DE SOTO (26 August 1839–18 September 1912), U.S. congressman and senator. Born in Zeiglersville, Mississippi, Money graduated from the University of Mississippi law department in 1860, and was subsequently admitted to the bar. He rose to lieutenant during the Civil War. An active Democrat, he was elected mayor of Winona in 1873 and served until his elevation to the federal House of Representatives two years later. He spent the next decade there, retired in 1884, and was returned in 1892. He served until elevation to the Senate. Taking his Senate seat in 1897, Money remained until 1911. There he became an influential member of the Foreign Relations Committee and briefly served as Senate minority leader. Perhaps Money's most notable achievement came when he underwent a dramatic transformation from fervent war advocate to noted anti-imperialist. Accepting a commission as colonel in the Fifth Immune Regiment, U.S. Volunteers, in 1899, Money reconsidered his support of American imperialism. He found himself within a distinct minority, however, for the Senate voted overwhelmingly to ratify the treaty granting the United States ownership of the Philippines, Guam, and Puerto Rico. Money died at his home in Biloxi, Mississippi.

Further Reading: *New York Times*, 19 September 1912; *A Guide to the [Mississippi] Hall of Fame*, 1978; Leonard Schlup, "Hernando De Soto Money: War Advocate and Anti-Imperialist, 1898–1900," *Journal of Mississippi History* 55 (1988): 315–340.

Harvey Gresham Hudspeth

MONOMETALLISM. Throughout monetary history, monometallism has meant use of gold as the money standard, with the mint buying only gold bullion to be coined into specie; anything else that circulated as money was defined in terms of the legal gold content of the unit of money. In modern Western history, including the Gilded Age, use of both gold and silver, or bimetallism, has been the legality but use of one or the other has often been the actuality. Between 1873 and passage of the Gold Reserve Act of 1900, the United States was legally bimetallic, but only gold was freely bought and coined; only a limited amount of silver was accepted.

Further Reading: Milton Friedman and Anna Jacobson Schwartz, *A Monetary History of the United States 1867–1960*, 1963.

Edwin Dale Odom

MONTEZUMA, CARLOS (ca. 1867–31 January 1923), Native American physician and activist. One of the first Native Americans to earn a medical degree and practice medicine on reservations, Montezuma was born to Yavapai parents in the Superstition Mountains of central Arizona. His native name was "Wassaja." After Pimas abducted him to Mexico, Carlos Gentile, a photographer, purchased the boy, christened him "Carlos Montezuma," and moved with him to Chicago. Under the tutelage of his guardian, a Baptist minister named William Steadman, Montezuma graduated from the University of Illinois at Urbana-Champaign with a chemistry degree. By 1889, he had completed his training at the Chicago Medical College. That same year Thomas Jefferson Morgan, commissioner of Indian Affairs, appointed Montezuma to the position of clerk and physician at Fort Stevenson in the Dakota Territory. From 1893 to 1896, he served as physician at the assimilationist Carlisle Indian School in Pennsylvania, under the leadership of Richard Henry Pratt. Montezuma subsequently entered private practice and engaged in political activism. He crusaded for citizenship rights, political autonomy, and economic empowerment for Native Americans. When his health deteriorated, Montezuma returned to Arizona, where he died on the Fort McDowell Reservation.

Further Reading: Harvey Markowitz, ed., *American Indian Biographies*, 1999; Frederick Dockstader, *Great North American Indians*, 1977.

Leonard Schlup

MOODY, DWIGHT LYMAN (5 February 1837–22 December 1899), itinerant evangelist. Born in Northfield, Massachusetts, Moody was converted to religious enthusiasm through his Sunday school teacher. He became a prosperous shoe salesman shortly after moving to Chicago in 1856, but focused on popular religious life. Though he never sought ordination, he contributed to the work of the Young Men's Christian Association and other evangelistic efforts in Chicago. In 1873, Moody organized a small-scale preaching excursion to Great Britain with the choir director and hymnist Ira Sankey. The tour proved a dramatic success, providing a new vision for urban evangelism. They returned home famous and in considerable demand. For the rest of his life, Moody led campaigns in American and British cities, preaching his simple message of the "Three R's: Ruin by Sin, Redemption by Christ, and Regeneration by the Holy Ghost." He founded schools for boys and girls, and in 1889 helped establish a Bible institute in Chicago. The latter was renamed Moody Bible Institute after his death in Northfield, and became a center for the emerging fundamentalist movement in the early twentieth century. Although Moody eschewed broader social issues, he was one of the last evangelists to enjoy support from a wide spectrum of Protestants, who would soon be divided by debates between theological conservatives and modernists.

Further Reading: William G. McLoughlin, *Modern Revivalism*, 1959; J. F. Findlay, *Dwight L. Moody: American Evangelist*, 1837–1899, 1969; S. M. Gundry, *Love Them In*, 1982.

Gillis J. Harp

MOREY LETTER. In the national election of 1880, James A. Garfield, the Republican presidential candidate, tiptoed around the combustible Chinese immigration question. A political bombshell exploded on 20 October when *Truth*, a New York City newspaper, published a letter he purportedly had written on 23 January to H. L. Morey of Lynn, Massachusetts. It declared that individuals or companies had a right to buy labor where they could get it most cheaply, an implicit endorsement of Chinese immigration. Garfield was initially uncertain if he had written it. After searching his files, he emphatically denounced the Morey letter as a forgery.

Republicans groaned about the distribution of millions of printed handouts, whose lethal wording could anathematize Garfield to westerners. California's Democratic newspapers had long stigmatized Garfield as friendly to Chinese labor. Republican reaction ranged from seeking revenge to treating the letter as comedy. A New York court confirmed that the letter was a fabrication after detectives hired by the GOP found no evidence of Morey's existence. Possibly the author was Kenward Philp, a political prankster and *Truth* journalist. Although influential in some areas, the Morey letter was only one of several factors that affected the election's outcome.

Further Reading: Ted C. Hinckley, "The Politics of Sinophobia: Garfield, the Morey Letter, and the Presidential Election of 1880," *Ohio History* 89 (1980): 381–399; Herbert J. Clancy, *The Presidential Election of 1880*, 1958.

Leonard Schlup

MORGAN, JOHN PIERPONT (17 April 1837–31 March 1913), financier. Born in Hartford, Connecticut, Morgan attended schools there and in Boston. He studied mathematics at the University of Göttingen in Germany, and then was a banker in several firms between 1856 and 1871. In the latter year, Morgan and Anthony J. Drexel founded a brokerage house; Drexel died in 1893, and the firm was renamed J. P. Morgan & Company in 1895. As a financier, Morgan hoped to consolidate the railroads. After selling much of his stock in the New York Central Railroad to English investors in 1879, he persuaded them in 1885 to lease the New York, West Shore & Buffalo Railroad, thus creating one of the largest lines east of the Mississippi River. Also in 1885, Morgan convinced Pennsylvania Railroad investors to buy the South Pennsylvania Railroad. In 1886, he added to the holdings of the Philadelphia & Reading Railroad, and in 1888 to the Chesapeake & Ohio.

The Panic of 1893 turned Morgan's attention to the solvency of the U.S. Treasury. In 1895, the Treasury's gold reserves dipped below $100 million for the second time in three years, frightening foreign investors. Morgan halted the exodus of gold by selling $62 million of Treasury bonds, half of them abroad. His profits from this sale provoked public outrage and a congressional investigation; Morgan refused to tell the committee the size of his profits. With equal ambition Morgan entered the steel industry, financing the Federal Steel Company in 1898, and the National Tube Company and the American Bridge Company the next year. By 1901, however, he realized that Andrew Carnegie's mills had become more efficient than his, and feared Carnegie would undercut his prices. Morgan defused the crisis by buying out Carnegie for $480 million. The new corporation, United States Steel, was the world's largest. Morgan thereby closed the Gilded Age with a fortune that few could approach. At his death in Rome, his art collection was worth $50 million, and his estate surpassed $68 million in value. His financial houses in New York City and Philadelphia, Pennsylvania, alone were worth nearly $30 million.

Further Reading: Frederick Lewis Allen, *The Great Pierpont Morgan*, 1949; Ron Chernow, *The House of Morgan: An American Banking Family and the Rise of Modern Finance*, 1991; Vincent P. Carosso, *The Morgans: Private International Bankers, 1854–1913*, 1987.

Christopher Cumo

MORGAN, JOHN TYLER (20 June 1824–11 June 1907), attorney, soldier, and U.S. senator. Born in Athens, Tennessee, Morgan grew up in Alabama, was admitted to the Alabama bar in 1845, and rose to brigadier general in the Confederate cavalry. He played a central role in the elections of 1874 and 1876, which ended Republican Reconstruction in Alabama. He entered the U.S. Senate in 1877, and was reelected four times, becoming the state's most important public figure. He sought to restore southern autonomy and to promote states' rights, low tariffs, expanded silver currency, and an income tax. He opposed the Interstate Commerce Act, the Sherman Antitrust Act, and every attempt to protect African-American rights. Morgan consistently appealed to race in his efforts to form and maintain a solid South. His foreign-policy views, however, often conflicted with southern opinion. Morgan endorsed territorial expansion in Hawaii, Cuba, Puerto Rico, and the Philippines. The incorporation of nonwhites into the body politic did not deter him. He gave priority to enhanced southern export markets and additional southern states. Morgan was the era's foremost champion of a transisthmian canal across Nicaragua, which he saw as the key to the conversion of the Gulf of Mexico into an American lake.

Further Reading: Joseph A. Fry, *John Tyler Morgan and the Search for Southern Autonomy*, 1992; "Joseph A. Fry, An Unlikely 'Friend' to Native Americans: John Tyler Morgan and Gilded Age Indian Policy," *Hayes Historical Journal* 11 (1993): 5–18.

Joseph A. Fry

MORMONISM. The Church of Jesus Christ of Latter-day Saints, the Reorganized Church of Jesus Christ of Latter-day Saints, and a number of smaller churches are based on the teachings of Joseph Smith (1805–1844). Most Latter-day Saints followed Brigham Young (1801–1877) to the West. By 1930, the Mormons had established at least 742 settlements, principally in Utah but also in all mountain western and Pacific coast states, Canada, Mexico, Hawaii, and Samoa. In 1860, many who remained in the Midwest called Joseph Smith III (1832–1914), eldest son of Joseph Smith, to the presidency of the Reorganized Church, which eventually established its headquarters in Independence, Missouri. Intent on building the Kingdom of God on Earth in preparation for Christ's return, Young's followers laid out towns and organized wards (congregations) and stakes (units of a number of wards). Between 1864 and 1874 they established cooperatives and communitarian United Orders, and they boycotted non-Mormon businesses. Young died in 1877, and his successor, John Taylor (1808–1877), lifted the boycott in 1882.

Opposed to the Latter-day Saints' political, social, and economic control and to polygamy, Congress passed laws in 1862, 1874, 1882, and 1887 that led to imprisonment of more than one thousand men and women, limited the authority of local governments, disfranchised women, and confiscated the church's secular properties. The Supreme Court approved the laws in decisions such as *United States* v. *Reynolds* (1879) and *United States* v. *Late Corporation* (1890). The Edmunds Act (1882) established the Utah Commission, which supervised elections in Utah and provided a model for independent regulatory commissions.

Threatened with the confiscation of church properties, Taylor's successor, Wilford Woodruff (1807–1898), announced the end of plural marriage in 1890. The Mormons dissolved their political party in 1891, and cooperated in organizing national political parties, chambers of commerce, and business enterprises. Proclamations by presidents Benjamin Harrison and Grover Cleveland returned the church's property, and Congress admitted Utah as a state in 1896.

Further Reading: Leonard J. Arrington, *Great Basin Kingdom: An Economic History of the Latter-Day Saints, 1830–1900*, 1958; Dale F. Beecher, "Colonizer of the West," in Susan Easton Black and Larry C. Porter, eds., *Lion of the Lord: Essays on the Life & Service of Brigham Young*, (1995): 172–208; Roger D. Launius, *Joseph Smith III: Pragmatic Prophet*, 1988.

Thomas G. Alexander

MORRILL, JUSTIN SMITH (14 April 1810–28 December 1898), representative and senator. Born in Stratford, Vermont, Morrill obtained a secondary-school education before becoming a successful merchant, farmer, and politician. As a Whig, he won election to the House of Representatives in 1854, but soon joined the Republican Party. While combating Mormon polygamy, he sponsored the Morrill Tariff Act of 1861 and the Internal Revenue Act of 1862. His best-known legislation, the 1862 Morrill Land Grant Act, established public colleges in every state. Elected to the Senate in 1866, Morrill sought to improve Washington's physical landscape. From his position on the Committee on Public Buildings and Grounds, he guided the completion of the Washington Monument, and sought to have the Library of Congress and the Supreme Court constructed at their current Capitol Hill locations. Morrill died in Washington, D.C., during his sixth Senate term.

Further Reading: Coy F. Cross, *Justin Smith Morrill: Father of the Land-Grant Colleges*, 1999; William B. Parker, *The Life and Public Services of Justin Smith Morrill*, 1924, rep. 1971; John H. Florer, "Major Issues in the Congressional Debate of the Morrill Act of 1862," *History of Education Quarterly* 8 (1968): 459–478.

Jane M. Armstrong

MORRISON, WILLIAM RALLS (14 September 1824–29 September 1909), congressman and Interstate Commerce Commission member. Born on a farm at Prairie du Long, near Waterloo, Illinois, Morrison attended McKendree College in Lebanon, Illinois. In 1855, he began practicing law in Waterloo, held local offices, and served in the Illinois House of Representatives. After rising to colonel in the Union Army, he was elected as a Democrat to the U.S. House of Representatives. Morrison served from 1863 to 1865 and again from 1873 until 1887, during which time he normally sat on powerful committees, including Ways and Means, Public Lands, and Expenditures. Although unsuccessful in an 1885 endeavor to obtain a U.S. Senate seat, Morrison gained national attention in 1887 when President Grover Cleveland appointed him to the Interstate Commerce Commission, on which he served until 1897, and was chair from 1892 until his term ended. He thereupon resumed his law practice in Waterloo, where he died.

Further Reading: David E. Robbins, "The Congressional Career of William Ralls Morrison," Ph.D. diss., University of Illinois at Urbana-Champaign, 1963.

Leonard Schlup

MORSE, EDWARD SYLVESTER (18 June 1838–20 December 1925), biologist and museologist. Born in Portland, Maine, Morse studied zoology under Louis Agassiz, worked at the Peabody Academy of Science, and helped establish the *American Naturalist* in 1868. From 1871 to 1874, Morse was professor of zoology and comparative anatomy at Bowdoin College. In 1875 he published the textbook *First Book in Zoology*. Two years later, he went to Japan to teach zoology at Imperial University in Tokyo. After returning to the United States in 1880, Morse became director of the Peabody Museum in Salem, Massachusetts, where he remained until 1916. The museum improved under his stewardship: organized displays attracted widespread attention; and financial contributions made it possible to enlarge the building. He served as president of the American Association for the Advancement of Science in 1886. In 1888 Morse published *Japanese Homes and Their Surroundings*. Two years later, he placed his superb collection of Japanese pottery in the Boston Museum of Fine Arts. Morse was the first American to receive the medal of the Order of the Rising Sun, awarded in 1890 by the emperor of Japan, twenty-three years after the Meiji Restoration.

Known for his jocundity and speaking abilities, Morse died in Salem, Massachusetts.

Further Reading: Dorothy Wayman, *Edward Sylvester Morse: A Biography*, 1942; Edward S. Morse Papers, Peabody Essex Museum, Salem, Massachusetts.

Leonard Schlup

MORTON, JULIUS STERLING (22 April 1832–27 April 1902), secretary of agriculture. Born in Adams, New York, Morton attended the University of Michigan but was expelled before graduation in 1854 because of a dispute with the institution's president. The faculty ultimately granted his A.B. in 1858. In 1854 he moved to Nebraska and began editing a newspaper, the *Nebraska City News*, in 1855. A conservative, he advocated a small federal government and a free market. In contrast to farmers, Morton opposed railroad regulation and courted support from the Chicago, Burlington & Quincy Railroad in his campaigns for governor and Congress. Although Morton never held elected office, President Grover Cleveland appointed him secretary of agriculture in 1893. Like his predecessor, Jeremiah Rusk, Morton left the department's oversight to Edwin Willits, the assistant secretary and former president of Michigan Agricultural College. In keeping with his conservatism, Morton insisted that Willits do nothing to enlarge the department. The restriction frustrated the department's scientists, who welcomed the activism of Morton's successor, James Wilson. In 1897 Morton returned to Nebraska City, where he continued to write newspaper articles and to speak at Farmer's Institutes. He died in Lake Forest, Illinois, with a greater reputation among businessmen than among farmers.

Further Reading: James C. Olson, *J. Sterling Morton*, 1972; Alfred C. True, *A History of Agricultural Experimentation and Research in the United States, 1607–1925*, 1937.

Christopher Cumo

MORTON, LEVI P. (16 May 1824–16 May 1920), vice president of the United States, governor, and banker. Born in Shoreham, Vermont, Morton became a successful Boston merchant. At twenty-seven he joined fortunes with Junius Spencer Morgan, father of J. P. Morgan. A close friend of President Ulysses S. Grant, Morton helped settle the *Alabama* claims in 1871 and was deeply involved in the resumption of specie payments in 1879. He was elected to Congress as a Republican in 1878 and 1880. Appointed ambassador to France (1881–1885), he played a role in acquiring the Statute of Liberty. Morton was nominated for the vice presidency in 1888, and campaigned for tariff protectionism. Despite losing the popular vote, the Benjamin Harrison-Levi P. Morton ticket won in the electoral college. The gentlemanly Morton, as the Senate's presiding officer, refused to adequately push the Federal Elections Bill of 1891, which Harrison had championed, delaying African-American civil rights for decades. Harrison dropped Morton from the ticket in 1892. Two years later, Morton was elected governor of New York (1895–1897), and promoted civil service and ballot reform. He also helped create Greater New York City, where he died.

Further Reading: Robert McElroy, *Levi Parsons Morton: Banker, Diplomat, Statesman*, 1930; Irving Katz, "Investment Bankers in American Government and Politics: The Political Activities of William W. Corcoran, August Belmont, Levi P. Morton and Henry Lee," Ph.D. diss., New York University, 1964; Homer E. Sokolofsky and Allan B. Spetter, *The Presidency of Benjamin Harrison*, 1987.

Robert S. La Forte

MORTON, OLIVER PERRY (4 August 1823–1 November 1877), governor of Indiana and U.S. senator. Born in Salisbury (Saulsbury), Indiana, Morton gained fame as a founder of the Republican Party in Indiana and a wartime governor (1861–1867) who ardently supported the Union cause. A U. S., senator from 1867 until his death, he became well known as a radical Republican and "bloody shirt" politician. He favored harsh Reconstruction for the South, worked for the passage of the Fifteenth Amendment, closely advised southern Republicans, and participated in the impeachment of President Andrew Johnson. He sought the Republican presidential nomination in 1876, but his soft-money tendencies, opposition to civil service reform, and extreme partisanship made the less controversial Rutherford

B. Hayes a better choice. Morton died in Indianapolis.

Further Reading: William D. Foulke, *Life of Oliver P. Morton*, 1899; Charles M. Walker, *Sketch of the Life, Character, and Public Services of Oliver P. Morton*, 1878; *Indianapolis Journal*, 2 November 1878.

Norman E. Fry

MOSES, PHOEBE ANN (ANNIE OAKLEY) (9 August 1860–3 December 1926), sharpshooter, show business personality. Born on a farm near Greenville, Ohio, Moses learned to shoot in childhood. She helped support her family by hunting, and at age fifteen defeated the marksman Frank Butler in a match at North Star, Ohio. She married Butler in 1876 and began using "Annie Oakley" as her stage name. She was "adopted" in 1884 by the Sioux leader Sitting Bull, who gave her the name "Little Sure Shot" (Watanya Cicilia), and later that year she and Butler joined Buffalo Bill's Wild West, touring with William F. Cody through the 1901 season. Injuries sustained in a train wreck interrupted her career, and she toured only intermittently until World War I, when she and her husband began visiting army camps to offer marksmanship instruction. An automobile crash in 1922 led to her retirement. She died in Greenville, Ohio.

Further Reading: Shirl Kasper, *Annie Oakley*, 1992; Glenda Riley, *The Life and Legacy of Annie Oakley*, 1994.

William W. Savage, Jr.

MOST, JOHANN JOSEPH (5 February 1846–17 March 1906), anarchist. An illegitimate child of an impoverished family in Augsburg, Germany, Most endured an unhappy youth due to his mother's death, a cruel stepmother, and a disfiguring jaw infection. As an adult, he roamed central Europe, joined the International Workingmen's Association in 1867, and became active in Germany's Marxist Social Democratic Party. Most edited socialist newspapers, delivered spirited speeches, and wrote songs for the working class. He published the anarchist newspaper *Freiheit* (Freedom), and exiled himself to London. There he offended Karl Marx by professing that laborers could establish a classless society immediately after assuming power instead of having to grapple with a temporary proletarian dictatorship. After his release from prison for having praised the assassination of Czar Alexander II of Russia in 1881, Most arrived on 12 December 1882 in New York City, where fellow anarchists escorted him to Cooper Union. There he gave a fiery oration against government, religion, and capitalism.

Most rejected the theory of anarchism advanced by Benjamin R. Tucker, an ardent defender of individual anarchism. Over the years he became known as the main American exponent of the anarchism associated with Peter Kropotkin, a Russian revolutionary, scientist, and sociologist who preached anarchist morality. Most believed the American bourgeoisie would neither permit social reform nor tolerate wage earners' achieving governmental control democratically. He called for violent revolution, emphasizing that workers would arise once they understood the hopelessness of their situation and had witnessed terrorism against capitalist industrialists. In 1883 Most helped write the "Pittsburgh Manifesto," which appealed for unification of all revolutionary socialist organizations. In his "Beast of Poverty" speech that same year, he envisioned the hanging of Jay Gould and other capitalists and the founding of a utopian cooperative commonwealth. Two years later, while working at a dynamite factory in New Jersey, he published a book on making bombs, *The Science of Revolutionary Warfare*. It instructed anarchists how to destroy the country's infrastructure at ten cents per copy. Most's words and deeds terrified mainstream Americans. Following his discharge from jail for inciting riots, Most shared a lecture tour with the anarchist Emma Goldman in 1890, and six years later they jointly published *Defended by Anarchists*. Most applauded Leon Czolgosz's assassination of President William McKinley in 1901. He concluded in his last years that the American working class would not take up arms, and thereupon repudiated terrorism, outraging many followers. He died in Cincinnati, Ohio, while touring on the lecture circuit.

Further Reading: Frederic Trautmann, *The Voice of Terror: A Biography of Johann Most*, 1980.

Leonard Schlup

MUGWUMPS. Mugwumps were Republicans who in 1884 rebelled against their party's presidential nominee, James G. Blaine, and endorsed the Democratic candidate, Grover Cleveland. The bolters, most of whom were well-educated professionals and businessmen from New England and New York, rejected the spoils politics that Blaine supposedly represented. Their positive program—civil service reform, lower tariffs, and sound money—was characteristic of classical nineteenth-century liberalism. The strategy seemed to succeed in 1884. Despite the Mugwumps' small numbers, the fact that Cleveland won the election by carrying New York State by a very narrow margin gave credence to the view that he owed his victory to their backing. Once in office, Cleveland found it difficult to please both regular Democrats, who were eager for spoils, and Mugwumps, who asserted that merit rather than party loyalty should determine appointments. In 1887, Cleveland's advocacy of lower tariffs won some applause from Mugwumps, and in the 1890s a few of his strongest admirers among the insurgents became Democrats of the sound money, anti-Bryan type. After a final flurry of activity at century's end, as anti-imperialists opposed to the McKinley administration's goal of annexing the Philippines, the Mugwumps disappeared as an organized force.

Further Reading: Gerald W. McFarland, *Mugwumps, Morals, and Politics, 1884–1920*, 1975.

Gerald W. McFarland

MUHLENBERG, WILLIAM AUGUSTUS (16 September 1796–8 April 1877), Episcopal clergyman. Born in Philadelphia, Pennsylvania, Muhlenberg graduated from the University of Pennsylvania in 1815, then studied under Jackson Kemper, a missionary Episcopal bishop. In 1820, Muhlenberg became rector of Saint James Church in Lancaster, Pennsylvania. Noted for his interest in civic affairs, he worked to inaugurate a system of public schools and to establish a public library. He reinvigorated his church to make it more appealing to diverse urban groups and to render services to the community. Later he founded what later became Saint Paul's College on Long Island, and was appointed rector of the Church of the Holy Communion in New York City (1846). Muhlenberg gained attention for his beliefs in the social ideals of Christianity, progressive education, and medical care; he introduced a boys' choir, used certain Catholic ritual traditions to make Episcopal services more attractive, and set up a housing project on Long Island. By adapting to Gilded Age social conditions, Muhlenberg became one of the most influential leaders of the Episcopal Church. He died at Saint Johnland on Long Island, New York.

Further Reading: Anne Ayres, *Life and Work of William Augustus Muhlenberg*, 1894; Alvin W. Skardon, *Church Leader in the Cities: William Augustus Muhlenberg*, 1971.

Leonard Schlup

MUIR, JOHN (21 April 1838–24 December 1914), naturalist, explorer, conservationist. Born in Dunbar, Scotland, Muir immigrated with his family to a frontier farm near Portage, Wisconsin, in 1849. In 1861, he entered the University of Wisconsin, where he encountered the ideas of Ralph Waldo Emerson and Henry David Thoreau. Leaving after two and a half years, Muir took to the roads and fields of America to study in what he called the "University of the Wilderness." In 1868, he moved to Yosemite Valley in California, and set about exploring the Sierra Nevada. Alarmed by the destruction being wrought by loggers and sheepherders, Muir began writing articles on conservation for national magazines. They were instrumental in the establishment of Yosemite National Park in 1890. In 1892, Muir helped found the Sierra Club as an institution to fight for the protection of nature, and began publishing books such as *The Mountains of California* (1894) to further the cause. His desire to preserve untouched wilderness led him into conflict with Gifford Pinchot and the utilitarian wing of the conservation movement. Muir died in Los Angeles, California.

Further Reading: John Muir, *Story of My Boyhood and Youth*, 1913; Thurman Wilkins, *John Muir: Apostle of Nature*, 1995; David Traxel, *1898: The Birth of the American Century*, 1998.

David Traxel

MULLIGAN LETTERS. Between 1864 and 1876, letters from Republican Senator James G. Blaine of Maine to the Boston businessman Warren Fisher, Jr., revealed that Blaine had used his influence while speaker of the House of Representatives to benefit the Little Rock and Fort Smith Railroad. One of Fisher's employees, James Mulligan, told a congressional committee on 31 May 1876 that he had the letters. The revelation led a committee member to adjourn the proceedings by claiming illness. That afternoon Blaine took the letters, and on 5 June read them before the House in an attempt to defend himself. Blaine thought he had settled the matter, though his detractors branded him "the continental liar." Publication of the letters in 1884 may have contributed to Blaine's narrow loss to Grover Cleveland in the presidential race.

Further Reading: Leonard D. White, *The Republican Era, 1869–1901*, 1958; Allan Nevins, *Grover Cleveland: A Study in Courage*, 1932; Richard E. Welch, Jr., *The Presidencies of Grover Cleveland*, 1988; Marvin Rosenberg and Dorothy Rosenberg, "The Dirtiest Election," *American Heritage* 13 (1962): 4–9, 90–99.

Christopher Cumo

MUNN v. *ILLINOIS* (94 U.S. [4 Otto] 113, 24 L.Ed. 77). Cereal plants mature and can be harvested only once a year. When this occurs for a commercially valuable product, such as wheat, the temporary surplus depresses prices. Only owners of large storage facilities and the elevators needed to process the large mass of grains were truly able to profit from the year-round demand for food. Often these operators used their seasonal advantage to force farmers to pay exorbitant prices to store their perishable produce. Facing growing pressure from farm organizations, such as the Illinois State Farmers Association and the National Patrons of Husbandry, the Illinois General Assembly passed a law in 1871 which established maximum rates that granaries and elevators could charge commercial farmers. In addition, these businesses were required to obtain licenses to operate.

In 1872, grain elevator operator Ira Munn was found in violation of the law. Munn challenged the statute, claiming it violated the U.S. Constitution by usurping the powers of Congress to regulate commerce, provided under Article I of the Constitution, and because the law denied his firm the "due process" guaranteed under the Fourteenth Amendment. The Cook County court, which initially heard the case, decided against Munn. This ruling was later supported by the Illinois Supreme Court and, finally, the U.S. Supreme Court in 1877. In delivering the majority opinion, Chief Justice Morrison Waite opened private utilities to public regulation when he wrote, "Property does become clothed with a public interest when used in a manner to make it of public consequence, and affect the community at large." In addition, the high tribunal found that states, and not the federal government, had the foremost right to regulate these public interests.

Further Reading: Harry N. Scheiber, "The Road to Munn: Eminent Domain and the Concept of Public Purpose in State Courts," *Perspectives in American History* 5 (1971): 329–402; C. Peter Magrath, "*Munn v. Illinois*: A Foot in the Door," *American Heritage* 15, no. 2 (1964): 44–48, 88–92.

David Blanke

MUNSEY, FRANK ANDREW (21 August 1854–22 December 1925), publisher and editor. Born near Mercer, Maine, Munsey managed a Western Union office in Augusta, Maine, before developing interests in politics and publishing. After financial setbacks, Munsey successfully marketed his periodical, *Golden Argosy*, in 1882, and wrote novels for new material. He supported James G. Blaine for president in 1884, moved to New York City, and started the monthly *Munsey's Magazine* in 1891. He established his own distribution company, advertised widely, and ultimately reduced the price of *Munsey's* to a dime. By 1898 he claimed the largest magazine circulation in the world. Munsey branched out to purchase, absorb, or create newspapers and other magazines, such as *Godey's Ladies Book* (1898), becoming wealthy in the process. A Republican who hoped for an ambassadorship, Munsey made enemies over the years due to his ethics and business-centered rules for personal and professional conduct. He died virtually alone in New York City.

Further Reading: George Britt, *Forty Years—Forty Millions: The Career of Frank A. Munsey*, 1935; *New York Sun*, 22 December 1925.

Leonard Schlup

MURCHISON LETTER. The three presidential campaigns of the 1880s are remembered for the narrow vote margins separating the two major candidates, and for three sensational letter episodes. Each sought to tilt the election results: the 1880 Morey letter, the 1884 Mulligan letters, and, in the 1888 contest between Democratic incumbent President Grover Cleveland and the Republican Benjamin Harrison, the melodramatic Murchison letter. "Charles F. Murchison" was in fact George Osgoodby, an inconspicuous southern Californian who, under the fictitious name, asked Great Britain's minister to the United States, Lionel Sackville-West, his preference in the election. "Murchison" received the stunningly candid reply that, given the incumbent's advocacy of tariff reduction, Sackville-West favored him. When the GOP publisher Harrison Grey obtained the damning handwritten reply—on official stationery—he immediately publicized it. New York's Irish, who loathed England and had voted against the Republican James G. Blaine in 1884 in part because of the "Rum, Romanism, and Rebelllion" canard, reversed their vote of four years earlier. New York City, and thus the state, which had supported Cleveland in 1884, swung back into the Republican column and Harrison became president. Seemingly much ado about nothing, the Murchison letter underscored the swelling electoral power of non-WASP urban Americans.

Further Reading: Ted C. Hinckley, "Pomona's Call to Fame," *California Historical Quarterly* 37 (June 1958): 171–179, and "George Osgoodby and the Murchison Letter," *Pacific Historical Review* 27 (November 1958): 359–370.

Ted C. Hinckley

MUSCULAR CHRISTIANITY. Muscular Christianity proclaimed that young men, particularly educated Protestant males, could be strong physically and spiritually. The notion flourished in the preparatory academies and Ivy League colleges of the Northeast, and also flowered in Dixie. Evangelical Muscular Christianity arose because of the rapid acceptance of sport in Gilded Age America, especially as it encouraged opportunities for the Young Men's Christian Association (YMCA) on college campuses. In the 1894 dedication address at the Springfield College Training School gymnasium, the noted psychologist G. Stanley Hall endorsed Muscular Christianity, a popular theology widespread in YMCAs that deemed physical robustness to be an essential element of Christian life. The idea paralleled earlier teachings of Thomas Arnold, father of the British poet/essayist Matthew Arnold, whose educational practices combined athletic activity to foster team spirit and manliness with a strong sense of moral purpose. Arnold's followers stressed that the best and most moral Christians were those with sound bodies.

The Muscular Christianity movement also mirrored to some extent the early nineteenth-century work of Friedrich Ludwig Jahn, who unified exercise and sport with German history and tradition. His follower Charles Follen led the movement in antebellum America, organizing the Round Hill School at Harvard. German Americans established a gymnastic institution called the Turnverein in Cincinnati, Ohio, in 1848. Later known as the Turners, these groups developed nationally and organized picnics, games, and celebrations of German culture. The physical education pioneer Dio Lewis, a reformer and author of a book on digestion, also promoted Muscular Christianity after the Civil War. Believing poor eating habits led to bad health and possible social disorder, Lewis and other fitness advocates formulated a connection between reshaping the body and restructuring society. Lewis championed exercise for all ages and both sexes, including the swinging of Indian clubs, to combat poor posture. By the century's end, Dr. Luther H. Gulick, an educator and author, had transformed the YMCA into the epitome of Muscular Christianity. It became the largest organization of urban gymnasiums and fitness centers. During the early twentieth century, evangelical Christians disengaged themselves from sport, but they reestablished their ties after World War II. The Reverend Billy Graham and other fundamentalists spearheaded the renewed appeal. Graham's ministry included the appearance of sports heroes in his televised crusades.

Further Reading: Donald E. Hall, ed., *Muscular Christianity: Embodying the Victorian Age*, 1994; Tony Ladd and James A. Mathisen, *Muscular Christianity: Evangelical Protestants and the Development of American Sport*, 1999; Clifford Putney, *Muscular Christianity: Manhood and Sports in Protestant America, 1880–1920*, 2001.

Leonard Schlup

MUSIC AND MUSICIANS. An American musical identity emerged during the Gilded Age. Few nations have experienced such a variety of influences in so short a time: the tunes of a diverse immigrant population, a wide variety of entertainment venues, and a formative business role. During the 1840s European artists began touring throughout the United States. After the Swedish soprano Jenny Lind's well-publicized and financially successful tour, sponsored by P. T. Barnum in 1850–1851, the number of European and American-born traveling virtuosi escalated, a trend that continued through the 1890s. Americans came to know the violinist Henri Wieniawski, the pianist Anton Rubinstein, and the composers Johann Strauss, Peter Ilyich Tchaikovsky, and Antonin Dvorak. American musicians who toured extensively included the pianists Louis Moreau Gottschalk and Julie Rive-King, the singers Clara Louise Kellogg, Lillian Nordica, and Emma Cecilia Thursby, and the conductors C. F. Theodore Thomas and Patrick Gilmore.

After the Civil War, Americans participated in music festivals where choral and orchestral groups presented large-scale works in a series of concerts. The Music Teachers National Association, established in 1876, reported over half a million students taking piano lessons in 1887. Although a federal report indicated fewer than 250 public school systems were teaching music in 1886, most private schools offered it and private instruction was available throughout the nation. Reviews and educational articles were published in the nationally distributed periodicals *Etude*, *Musical America*, *Musical Courier*, and *The Musician*.

The omnipresent dichotomy of wealth versus idealism appeared in music as well. Affluent residents of New York City supported musical forms and institutions featuring traditional European concert music, and catering to a limited audience: the Philharmonic Society, the Academy of Music, and the Metropolitan Opera House. By 1890 most towns and cities in the United States had a community band. The conductor John Philip Sousa decried artistic snobbery and wanted to create music for the millions. He and his band toured tirelessly, presenting outstanding soloists and programming his own compositions, original works, and transcriptions drawn from the symphonic, operatic, and popular repertoire.

African Americans and women assumed a more visible role in America's musical life. The Fisk University Jubilee Singers introduced spirituals to white audiences in Europe and America. Sissieretta Jones toured regularly and gave solo recitals, including a White House appearance before President Benjamin Harrison. James Bland had many songs published during the 1870s and 1880s, including "Carry Me Back to Old Virginny" (1875). Women composers included Amy Marcy Cheney Beach, Margaret Ruthven Lang, and Carrie Jacobs Bond; administrators and patrons included Jeannette Thurber, Clara Baur, and Ettie Crane. Because women were excluded from performing in orchestras, except as harpists, a number of all-female orchestras appeared during the 1880s.

Gilded Age America had a wide variety of entertainment venues. Vaudeville, or variety shows, eventually replaced the minstrel show as the most popular and characteristic form of American stage entertainment. Opening in 1865 in New York City, Tony Pastor's Opera House was the first permanent home for vaudeville shows. In 1878 the American public heard its first Gilbert and Sullivan operetta, and traveling companies performed works by Victor Herbert and John Philip Sousa. Ragtime music became a national craze in 1898, and lasted for two decades. As the center for publishers of popular songs moved to New York City by 1890, the term Tin Pan Alley was coined to refer to the publishing firms centered around 28th Street. Songs composed and popularized during the Gilded Age include "O Little Town of Bethlehem," "Rock-a-bye Baby," "America the Beautiful," "The Band Played On," "Hot Time in the Old Town," "Love Makes the World Go Round," "Stars and Stripes Forever," and the "Maple Leaf Rag."

Further Reading: Joseph A. Mussulman, *Music in the Cultured Generation*, 1971; Charles Hamm, *Music in the New World*, 1983; Nicholas E. Tawa, *The Way to Tin Pan Alley*, 1990.

Leslie Petteys

NAISMITH, JAMES (6 November 1861–28 November 1939), inventor of basketball. Born in Almonte, Ontario, Naismith spent his youth as a student at McGill University and Presbyterian College in Montreal. Following graduation from the latter in 1890, he taught physical education at what later became Springfield College in Springfield, Massachusetts, from 1890 to 1895. In 1891, Naismith created the game of basketball as a diversion for his students during the winter months. Early players used peach baskets instead of hoops and had to climb a ladder to retrieve balls after scoring. Not until nearly twenty years later did the open-bottom hoops in use today emerge on a wide scale. During the game's formative years, Naismith experimented with various rule changes, including the number of players on each team. Initially, he concluded that nine players on each team should play simultaneously, but eventually settled on the current number of five. He also spent several years as director of physical education, first at the Young Men's Christian Association in Denver, and then at the University of Kansas (1898–1937). He died in Lawrence, Kansas, and was posthumously elected to the Basketball Hall of Fame in 1959.

Further Reading: Bernice Larson Webb, *The Basketball Man: James Naismith*, 1973.

Steve Bullock

NAST, THOMAS (27 September 1840–7 December 1902), cartoonist and artist. Nast was born in Landau, Germany, and with his parents moved to New York City. He attended public schools there, studied art at the National Academy of Design, and worked for *Leslie's Illustrated News*. While there, he obtained some technical training from Sol Eyting, a draftsman, and started to do political cartoons on the milk scandal and urban evils. He drew for *Harper's Weekly*, the *Sun Courier*, and the *New York Illustrated News*. Having studied the methods of English illustrators, he adopted Fletcher Harper's concept of "pictures of ideas rather than pictures of events." His Civil War pictures were so successful that President Abraham Lincoln praised him. Drawings such as "After the Battle," "Emancipation," "On to Richmond," and "Compromise with the South" cemented his reputation. He painted Andrew Johnson as a bully and dictator. His "Boss" Tweed and original "Santa" Christmas illustrations (1870–1886) made him wealthy and famous. Nast's usual target was the Democratic Party, which he considered a group of "corruptionists" composed of Irishmen, Catholics, and southerners.

Nast possessed a malicious streak and displayed strong feelings against Horace Greeley, Ben Butler, the Populist Party, and politicians in general. He was both original and clever. It was he who first drew the Democratic donkey and the Republican elephant, but he did not invent the "Tammany Tiger." Nast's later years were chaotic. He bought an estate in New Jersey, lost his money through bad investments, went to Europe several times, left *Harper's Weekly*, and started his own *Nast's Weekly*, which failed quickly. He tried sketching his lucrative Christmas illustrations with some small success. Finally, he accepted President Theodore Roosevelt's appointment as consul general at Guayaquil, the principal port of Ecuador. He died there from yellow fever.

Further Reading: Lynda Pflueger, *Thomas Nast, Political Cartoonist*, 2000; David Shirley, *Thomas Nast: Cartoonist and Illustrator*, 1998; *New York Times*, 8 December 1902.

Nicholas C. Polos

NATION, CARRY (25 November 1846–9 June 1911), temperance reformer and activist. Born Carry Amelia Moore in Garrard County, Kentucky, she received little formal education due to an intestinal disorder that left her a semi-invalid. Her first husband, Charles Gloyd, a physician, was an alcoholic who died within twenty-four months of their marriage. In 1877 she married David Nation, a minister, editor, and lawyer, but this union ended in divorce. Carry Nation assumed an active role in the Woman's Christian Temperance Union in Kansas during the 1890s. In May 1900, she aggressively stormed three saloons in Kiowa, Kansas, and in December of that year she attacked the Hotel Carey bar in Wichita. Her violent activism galvanized the dry supporters in the state. Addressing the Kansas legislature, Nation told members that because they had refused her the vote, she used a rock. Newspaper cartoons often depicted her with hatchets, and anti-prohibitionist and conservative publications attempted to portray her as an outlaw. Her fervent work left its mark on Gilded Age social history. Nation died at a hospital in Leavenworth, Kansas.

Further Reading: Carry A. Nation, *The Use and Need of the Life of Carry A. Nation*, 1909; Robert L. Taylor, *Vessel of Wrath: The Life and Times of Carry Nation*, 1966; Robert S. Bader, *Prohibition in Kansas: A History*, 1986.

Leonard Schlup

NATIONAL AMERICAN WOMAN SUFFRAGE ASSOCIATION.

This organization was formed in 1890, after much lobbying from women who belonged to the two prominent groups that had been seeking female enfranchisement since before the Civil War. The National Woman Suffrage Association (NWSA) had worked toward a federal amendment, and was led by Susan B. Anthony and Elizabeth Cady Stanton. The American Woman Suffrage Association, which had represented more affluent women and sought the same goal through state-by-state amendment campaigns, was guided by Lucy Stone and Henry B. Blackwell. The NAWSA agreed to combine both approaches. As the twentieth century began, agitation increased; by 1914 women could vote in eleven states. Many young women formed a radical union that used public tactics to bring attention to the issue, and the NAWSA found itself no longer in the vanguard.

Further Reading: Sara Hunter Graham, *Woman Suffrage and the New Democracy*, 1996; William Leach, *True Love and Perfect Union*, 1989; Kirk H. Porter, *A History of Suffrage in the United States*, 1969.

Ann Mauger Colbert

NATIONAL ASSOCIATION OF COLORED WOMEN.

Founded in 1896, the National Association of Colored Women (NACW) was the first successful national African-American organization. Freed from slavery, black women established thousands of local clubs and associations during the Gilded Age. However, in 1893 the Board of Lady Managers of the Chicago Columbian Exposition refused to accept the participation of African-American women's groups, giving the excuse that they had no national organization to represent them. In 1895 two rival national organizations were established. Each held its first convention in Washington, D.C., during July 1896, at which time they united and elected Mary Church Terrell president. Although individual clubs adhered to many different political philosophies, Terrell supported Booker T. Washington and his accommodationist policies. The platform adopted at the first NACW conference in Nashville in 1897 stressed self-help and racial self-defense. Under the slogan "Lifting As We Climb," NACW affiliates founded and supported homes for the aged, orphanages, day care centers, community centers, clinics, and homes for young working women. They also organized anti-lynching campaigns and opposed segregation laws. Most members belonged to an educated, middle-class elite, and regarded their mission as racial uplift and social service.

In 1902 the NACW claimed four hundred clubs, organized into both state and regional federations. By 1924 the organization had expanded to one hundred thousand members in over a thousand clubs. The NACW's national departments reflected a broad range of social, cultural, and political concerns, including temperance, humane and rescue work, domestic science, juvenile courts, suffrage, religion, music, literature, mothers clubs, kindergartens, working women, and professional women.

Further Reading: Dorothy Salem, *To Better Our World: Black Women in Organized Reform, 1890–1920*, 1990; Charles H. Wesley, *The History of the National Association of Colored Women's Clubs: A Legacy of Service*, 1984.

L. Mara Dodge

NATIONAL GEOGRAPHIC SOCIETY.

The world's largest scientific and educational institution was founded in January 1888 when thirty-three gentlemen of science and letters met in Washington, D.C., to form a society to broaden geographical knowledge. Its first elected president was Gardiner Greene Hubbard, a Boston lawyer and humanitarian who had helped organize the first telephone company for Alexander Graham Bell, his son-in-law. The first *National Geographic* magazine was published in October 1888 as a slim, technical journal with an unassuming terra-cotta cover. Two hundred charter members perused such articles as "The Classification of Geographic Forms by Genesis" and similar abstract discussions. Hubbard hoped for a magazine that would appeal to intelligent laymen as well as geographers, but died before fulfilling his dream.

Bell succeeded his father-in-law as president in 1898, and devoted his immense energy and intellect to improving the journal. He made two key decisions that would profoundly affect the Society's future course. The first appealed to persons genuinely interested in the organization's work by offering the publication to those who to became members, as opposed to selling it on newsstands. Second, Bell decided to hire a full-time editor to enliven the magazine and promote membership. Gilbert H. Grosvenor, a twenty-three-year-old schoolteacher, transformed the *National Geographic* magazine from a staid professional journal into a medium for presenting the world in all its glory, thereby making a lasting impression on American journalism. Membership in the Society now exceeds nine million; worldwide readership numbers about forty-five million.

Society sponsorship of expeditions and research projects began early. The first National Geographic expedition, in 1890–1891, explored and mapped Mount St. Elias on the southern Alaska-Canada border, in the process discovering Mount Logan, Canada's highest peak. The Society has since supported over six thousand scientific research projects. The twentieth century saw the National Geographic Society move into television, cartography, book publishing, geography education, and electronic media.

Further Reading: C. D. B. Bryan, *The National Geographic Society: 100 Years of Adventure and Discovery*, 1987, 1997.

Dorothy Garrett Lerda

NATIONAL GRANGE.

In 1866 President Andrew Johnson sent Oliver Kelley of the U.S. Department of Agriculture (USDA) to the South to gather information about rural conditions. In response to the poverty and isolation of southern farmers, Kelley founded the Patrons of Husbandry, known as the Grange, in 1867. Beginning as a social and educational organization, by 1874 the Grange had 1.5 million members, and its agenda had grown to include cooperative marketing, railroad regulation, and public funding of agricultural science. During the 1870s the Grange convinced five states to create commissions to regulate railroads. These commissions, despite their ineffectiveness, laid a foundation for creation of the Interstate Commerce Commission in 1887. That year the Grange joined the USDA, land-grant colleges, and agricultural experiment stations in persuading Congress to begin funding the experiment stations. Thereafter the Grange's political activism declined as members put their energies into establishing cooperatives and building rural community through 4-H clubs.

Further Reading: Solon J. Buck, *The Granger Movement*, 1913; Charles M. Gardner, *The Grange—Friend of the Farmer*, 1949; D. Sven Nordin, *Rich Harvest: A History of the Grange, 1867–1900*, 1974.

Christopher Cumo

NATIONAL NEGRO BUSINESS LEAGUE.

In an effort to stimulate growth within the African-American community, Booker T. Washington summoned approximately four hundred business leaders and concerned individuals to a meeting in Boston, Massachusetts, on 23 and 24 August 1900, to form a trade organization known as the National Negro Business League. Similar in purpose to a chamber of commerce, the consortium Washington envisioned would encourage and inspire members to move forward economically. This coalition, the first such confederation for businesspeople based on race, attracted delegates representing thirty-four states. By 1907, over three hundred branches of the National Negro Business League had been established across the nation. With the support of Andrew Carnegie and the dominating influence of Washington, the association focused attention on the growth and stability of African-American businesses in the United States.

Further Reading: John H. Burrows, *The Necessity of Myth: A History of the National Negro Business League,* 1988.

Leonard Schlup

NATIVE AMERICANS. After the Civil War, Congress authorized a peace commission to end military campaigns being waged against several tribal nations. The Treaty of Medicine Lodge (1867), with Southern Cheyenne, Arapaho, and Kiowa from the southern plains; the Treaty of Fort Laramie (1868), with the Lakota; and the Treaty of Fort Sumner (1868), with the Navajo continued the pre–Civil War policy of isolating and separating Indians from the rest of the country's population. These treaties failed to maintain peace. Throughout the American West, Indians and whites renewed warfare. Arizona Territory citizens attacked the Apache at Camp Grant. In 1870, Major Eugene M. Baker massacred Heavy Runner's Blackfeet in Montana. Crazy Horse and Sitting Bull joined forces in 1876 to vanquish George A. Custer's military command at the Little Big Horn, and in 1878 army regulars nearly annihilated Dull Knife and Little Wolf's Northern Cheyenne bands, which had left Indian Territory and were attempting to return to their Montana homeland.

The Indians' legal status made these confrontations displeasing to a large number of citizens. The Civil War ended slavery but did not change the "trust relationship," whereby the government made decisions for both individuals and tribes. Tribesmen remained wards under U.S. guardianship; their communities continued as dependent nations operating under reduced autonomy. Demographics revealed that this paternalistic arrangement failed the Indians. During this era of national growth, indigenous populations declined. The 1900 census reported only 237,196 Indians. Small reservations with shrunken populations were found in states and territories from Florida to California and Maine to Arizona Territory. The numbers were highest on the northern Great Plains, the southern Great Plains (especially Indian Territory), and the Southwest. Reservations with the largest territory and population were those of the Navajo, Cherokee, Creek, Blackfeet and Sioux. The latter two were divided into several smaller reserves in 1888 and 1889, respectively.

Economic conditions on the reservations varied from communities that were self-sufficient to those dependent on treaty rations; there also were differences among residents living on the same reservation. Environmental conditions, resource potential, treaty stipulations, and access to local markets all contributed to the success or failure of each reservation's economy. Prosperous Cherokee farms dotted their reservation; Comanches leased their lands to outside cattle operators. Navajos herded sheep and bartered wool products with local traders. San Carlos Apache sold hay and cordwood to the U.S. Army post at Camp Grant until the post closed. Many Northwest coastal communities fished and made a niche for themselves in local industry; Lakota farming efforts failed due to drought.

Tribal educational opportunities also differed. Cherokees and Creeks operated their own successful schools until Oklahoma statehood, but Indian-controlled operations were the exception. Churches sponsored many post–Civil War reservation schools serving few students. The impetus for the churches came from President Ulysses S. Grant's policy, in where individual denominations were assigned specific reservations as an exclusive domestic mission field. As part of their duties, churches began day schools, and some eventually built boarding schools. When Congress pushed Indian assimilation even harder in 1887 with the passage of the General Allotment Act (Dawes Act), the United States initiated an extensive program of constructing schools on reservations. Off-reservation federal industrial boarding schools, such as that at Carlisle, Pennsylvania, also were built. Education of Indian children was intended as a step toward assimilation.

Conversion to Christianity accompanied the educational process. By the end of the Civil War, Catholics, Baptists, and Presbyterians had done the most work; initiation of Grant's policy brought many more churches onto the reservations. When Grant's policy ended, many churches stayed. They made some headway converting tribesmen, even bringing select individuals into their operations as lay ministers, catechists, and, in some cases, ordained ministers. Their task was not easy, for missionaries opposed tribal philosophies and traditional leaders. At the same time the Native American Church challenged the orthodox denominations.

Many former abolitionists joined Indian reform movements. Non-Indian groups lobbied for Indian issues and changes in congressional policy. Helen Hunt Jackson became a leading reformer of the era with her book *A Century of Dishonor* (1881). The Indian Rights Association was one of the most prominent advocacy groups monitoring government actions. The Boston Indian Citizenship Committee advocated Indian citizenship, which was intended to bring the tribesmen into the American mainstream and protect them in the court system. Beginning in the 1880s, the Lake Mohonk conference of the Friends of the Indian served as a clearinghouse for the reform organizations as they united to influence legislation. Many believed that Indian citizenship should be tied to land allotment of the reservations. These concepts became the nation's policy after the passage of the General Allotment Act of 1887.

Further Reading: Frederick E. Hoxie, *A Final Promise: The Campaign to Assimilate the Indians*, 1984; Henry Eugene Fritz, *The Movement for Indian Assimilation, 1860–1890*, 1963.

Richmond L. Clow

NATIVE AMERICAN WOMEN. During the Gilded Age, Native American women centered their lives around food, clothing, shelter, and family, regardless of tribe. They erected and dismantled housing; cut wood; washed clothes; fetched water daily; planted seeds; cultivated crops; prepared and cooked food; made pots, tools, rugs, and baskets; processed and decorated animal hides; herded and sheared sheep; spun and wove wool; and raised children. Cradleboards were a functional way to carry babies, and Native mothers had their offspring at their sides as they performed daily tasks. Consequently Native children learned and performed the arts of living early. The entire extended family nurtured infants, older children, and adolescents. Grandmothers participated in child rearing, teaching moral behavior, reciting tribal histories, and sharing sacred ceremonial rituals.

A tribe's lifestyle and location influenced the types of dwellings it inhabited. Nomadic Natives needed easily assembled and dismantled housing structures. Moving required a carrier or travois that held the long tepee poles and heavy hides. Women organized the relocation operations, including packing and pulling the travois. Plains women were the sole designers, makers, and erectors of tepees. Agricultural peoples enjoyed more permanent domiciles, such as pueblos in the desert Southwest. Men and women jointly constructed pueblos, compartmentalized complexes consisting of one or more flat-roofed structures of stone or adobe, arranged in terraces and housing a number of families. Women generally applied the adobe surfaces to the shelters. Upon completion, they were the unit owners.

Although men were the primary agriculturists, women owned the harvest. Women of the buffalo-hunting tribes fully utilized the animals. They skinned and scraped a warm skin, stripped the meat, and set it out to dry. A proficient woman could process three buffalo a day, totaling three hundred pounds of dried meat and pemmican. The Navajos maintained a division of property. The hogan, sheep, and goats belonged to women. Horse saddles and jewelry were men's. A Navajo woman could divorce her husband by placing his saddle outside the hogan door.

Nationally prominent Gilded Age Native American women included Emily Pauline Johnson (Tekahionwake), a Canadian Mohawk writer, performer, and activist; Lizzie Cayuse, a Nez Percé spokeswoman; Sarah Winnemucca, a Northern Paiute who was a mesmerizing advocate for Native rights; Alice Lee Jemison, a Seneca naturalist; Nampeyo, a Hopi artist who invented new designs in pottery ware and reconstructed from archaeological evidence forms that had not been produced for centuries; Laura Minnie Cornelius Kellogg, an Oneida orator and linguist; Susan LaFlesche Picotte, a graduate of the Woman's Medical College of Philadelphia and the first female Native American physician; Susette La Flesche Tibbles (Bright Eyes), a popular speaker, writer, and proponent of Native rights; and Gertrude Simmons Bonnin (Zitkala Sha), a Sioux teacher, musician, and author.

Gilded Age Anglo culture did not comprehend the honor, status, and wealth accorded Native American women for their industry and expertise. Nor did Anglos recognize other powers Native women held, such as arranging marriages, consulting on peace and war, leading special ceremonies, directing tribal movements, and speaking on issues in council. Wearing elaborate clothing and jewelry further signified a woman's status within her realm. Native women's independence contrasted sharply with white women's general dependence on their husbands. The principles upon which most Native societies were organized conferred upon women a status very different from that of their white counterparts. Native women possessed the security of a tribe or indigenous nation committed to care for them if they were orphaned or widowed, and to protect them from male mistreatment. A Native wife never submitted entirely to her husband. These freedoms prompted twentieth-century white feminists to look partly to Amerindian models for the rhetoric of reform.

Further Reading: Rayna Green, *Women in American Indian Society*, 1992; Gretchen M. Bataille and Laurie Lisa, eds., *Native American Women: A Biographical Dictionary*, 2nd ed., 2001; Carolyn Niethammer, *Daughter of the Earth: The Lives and Legends of American Indian Women*, 1996.

Leonard Schlup

NATURALISM. During the Gilded Age, the rural, agricultural United States was becoming an urban, industrial society. This change would be completed essentially within a single generation. The principles and formal philosophies that had guided American society since its founding were inevitably questioned in terms of both their validity and their applicability to modern, faster-paced times. The static worldview of the colonial culture and the Enlightenment-based culture of the early national period no longer served the needs of the new society. Science seemed to offer the key to a new worldview, since it presented the prospect of objective, dispassionate, and therefore true, information. The scientific perspective dominated contemporary thought, and society was beginning to be viewed in biological terms. Charles Darwin's theories of evolution permeated all aspects of American thought and culture. Naturalism was never really the dominant philosophy, however, in that this would suggest the disappearance of the traditional American emphasis on individualism and popular democracy, but it engendered spirited debates about the nature of man and society.

The English sociologist Herbert Spencer was possibly the most influential purveyor of this organic, dynamic view of society. In reality, naturalism represented yet another form of determinism in which individual actions were insignificant when compared with the larger evolution of the social organism. Supporters of the new society, dominated by a few wealthy industrialists, clearly favored this interpretation as a justification for their actions because they could now claim that natural laws, and not their own actions, were responsible for the immense social changes disrupting society. Although William James retained his strong sense of individualism, his evolutionary views of the brain and its functions were clearly influenced by naturalism. Other individuals affected by this dynamic conception of the world included Oliver Wendell Holmes, with his principles of legal realism; the sociologist William Graham Sumner; and the economist Thorstein Veblen. Naturalism generated substantial debates in religion, history, and literature as well. At the end of the Gilded Age, there was a resurgence of a commitment to individual capacities to effect social and political, as well as individual, change. The impact of naturalism on American thought, however, was so powerful that it was impossible to ignore.

Further Reading: Paul Boller, *American Thought in Transition: The Impact of Evolutionary Naturalism, 1865–1906*, 1969; Ralph Henry Gabriel, *The Course of American Democratic Thought*, 1956; Morton White, *Social Thought in America: The Revolt Against Formalism*, 1957.

C. Edward Balog

NELSON, KNUTE (2 February 1843–28 April 1923), politician, first Norwegian-American citizen in Congress. Born in Evanger, Norway, Nelson was brought to the United States at age six. He attended school in Wisconsin and, after service in the Civil War, read law in Madison. In 1867 he was admitted to the bar and elected to the state assembly as a Republican. In 1871, he moved to Minnesota, where he sat in the state senate from 1874 to 1878. Elected to Congress in 1882, he served three terms before returning to his law practice.

Nelson was attractive to Minnesota Republicans as a broker between immigrant Norwegians and "Yankee" elites. A low tariff stance was his only deviation from solid Republican conservatism. Combating the Populist tide, he was elected governor in 1892 and reelected two years later. He resigned in 1895 when he was chosen U.S. senator, a position he held until death. He wrote the Nelson Bankruptcy Act of 1898 and was interested in Native Americans and the Alaska territory. A champion of McKinley, Nelson responded to Progressivism by adopting a moderate course: championing the legislation that created the Department of Commerce and Labor (1902), advocating a federal income tax, helping establish the Interstate Commerce Commission, and fighting against weakening of the Sherman Antitrust Act, while strongly opposing the Adamson Act (1916). He died en route from Washington, D.C. to his home in Alexandria, Minnesota.

Further Reading: Millard L. Gieske and Steven J. Keillor, *Norwegian Yankee: Knute Nelson and the Failure of American Politics, 1860–1923*, 1995; Martin W. Odland, *The Life of Knute Nelson*, 1926.

Michael J. Anderson

NEVADA, EMMA (7 February 1859–20 June 1940), opera singer. Nevada was born Emma Wixom at Alpha, near Nevada City, California. She studied voice under Alfred Kelleher at Mills Seminary (Mills College) in Oakland, California, and graduated in 1876. While touring Europe and singing in London, she adopted the stage name of Emma Nevada. During this early time of struggle, she accepted monetary assistance from Marie Hungerford Mackay, wife of a Nevada millionaire. Nevada's success as an opera singer in Europe and the United States attracted widespread attention. She appeared in *La Sonnambula* in New York City in 1884. The following year, in Paris, she married Raymond Spooner Palmer, an English physician. Upon her return to the United States in the late 1880s for additional performances, she received a warm welcome in Nevada and sang at Virginia City. A favorite of the British royal family, Nevada died in Liverpool, England.

Further Reading: *New York Times*, 22 June 1940.

Leonard Schlup

NEW ENGLAND STATES. During the period 1870–1900, the six northeasternmost states declined in relative importance even as they continued to grow in most respects. Constituting only 2.2 percent of the continental land area (Alaska aside), the region contained 8.8 percent of the nation's population in 1870 and 7.4 percent in 1900. Population growth (60.3 percent) not only lagged behind that of the nation (90.9 percent), but also was geographically skewed: Massachusetts and Rhode Island surpassed the national rate (and Connecticut the regional rate), while Maine, Vermont, and New Hampshire fell short of both. By 1900, Massachusetts accounted for half of New England's population; Connecticut had joined that state and Rhode Island as predominantly urban. Boston had risen from seventh to fifth among the nation's cities, but most other ranking New England cities had lost place. As of 1900, the New England states, except Maine and Vermont, exceeded national percentages in foreign-born and children of foreign-born. Irish, French Canadian, and English Canadian immigrants were most numerous. Only in Connecticut were Germans prominent. The "new immigrants" had not yet had their major impact.

Lacking ores and fossil fuels, and disadvantaged in location, New England experienced a relative decline in manufacturing during the period: from 1850 to 1900 it fell from 27.8 percent to 14.4 percent of the nation as a whole. (On a per capita basis, though, Rhode Island, Connecticut, and Massachusetts still ranked 1–2–3 in the value of manufactures.) Given the nature of the region's industries, the earlier exploitation of abundant waterpower, and the paucity of local fuels, all six states continued to rank above average in dependence on waterpower in 1900. The three northernmost did so markedly, at a time when steam (77.4 percent) far surpassed water (15.3 percent) as a source of power nationwide. New England states ranked highest in light manufacturing, such as factory-produced boots and shoes; cotton, woolen, and worsted goods; and metal products. New England agriculture declined during the late nineteenth century. Improved acreage fell off markedly; production of grains (except oats and barley), even more so. Sheep and beef cattle became less numerous; while dairy cattle increased. Cheese and butter output dropped; fluid milk production jumped. Fruits and vegetables were increasingly important, as well as broad-leaf wrapper tobacco in Connecticut, which by 1900 ranked eighth in tobacco production.

In politics, New England leaned markedly toward the Republicans during the period 1868–1892, and overwhelmingly so from 1893 to 1900, when an economic depression (1893) and the Democrats' presidential nomination of William Jennings Bryan (1896) worked to the advantage of the GOP. Democrats did carry Connecticut, the region's only closely contested state, in four of the seven presidential contests between 1868 and 1892, but no other northeastern state in any national election from 1868 to 1900. Gubernatorial elections usually went to the Republicans, including some in which Democrats led but fell short of a constitutionally required majority, which resulted in legislative selection of winners. Given regionwide Republican dominance of state legislatures, in which supportive rural areas were overrepresented, such contests almost always resulted in GOP victories. The Republicans' grip on legislatures virtually assured triumphs in elections to the U.S. Senate. Democrats enjoyed greater success in elections to the House of Representatives, but still lost most.

Further Reading: *Twelfth Census of the United States. 1900*; *Congressional Quarterly's Guide to U.S. Elections, 1975*.

Samuel T. McSeveney

NEWMAN, ANGELIA LOUISE FRENCH THURSTON KILGORE (4 December 1837–15 April 1910), reformer, Methodist churchwoman, and lecturer.

Born in Montpelier, Vermont, Thurston studied at Montpelier Academy, taught school, and attended Lawrence University in Wisconsin for one term. At age eighteen, in Madison, Wisconsin, she married Frank Kilgore, who died within a year. In 1859 she wed David Newman, a dry goods merchant. Newman's poor health improved following their move in 1871 to Lincoln, Nebraska, where she assumed an active role in the Women's Foreign Missionary Society. She contributed essays to its magazine, and worked to raise money for missionary endeavors in India.

Effective on the lecture circuit and encouraged by Bishop Isaac W. Wiley to express her religious opinions, Newman orchestrated a campaign against polygamy. She asserted that a harem was no substitute for the home and that Mormonism did not constitute a religion. Adopting a cause already well publicized by Ann Eliza Webb Young, the twenty-seventh wife of the Mormon leader Brigham Young, Newman took her message throughout the Midwest and Northeast. Although the Edmunds Act of 1882 outlawed polygamy, the Mormon Church did not officially rescind the practice until 1890. Continuing to outline the Mormon threat, Newman assumed the superintendency of the Mormon Department of the Woman's Christian Temperance Union, established in 1886. A petition of 250,000 signatures, collected by Newman and her colleagues, persuaded members of Congress to cancel the enfranchisement of women in the Utah Territory, arguing that men with multiple wives were using woman's suffrage to uphold Mormon rule. This cancellation occurred in 1887 with the Edmunds-Tucker Act. Newman thereupon stationed herself in Washington, testified before the Senate Education and Labor Committee, and organized efforts to create a refuge and rehabilitation center in Salt Lake City for Mormon women shunted aside as a result of federal legislation. She was instrumental in winning a $40,000 congressional appropriation to aid in this effort.

From 1883 to 1892, Nebraska governors appointed Newman a delegate to the National Conference of Charities and Correction. She was also active in the Women's Relief Corps and the National Council of Women. After her husband's death in 1893, Newman visited Hawaii, where she engaged in missionary work. A Republican, she supported protective tariffs, sound money, and the imperial policies of President William McKinley, who was a Methodist. Newman died in Lincoln, Nebraska.

Further Reading: *Nebraska State Journal*, 16 April 1910; Laura E. Tomkinson, *Twenty Years' History of the Woman's Home Missionary Society of the Methodist Episcopal Church, 1880–1900*, 1903.

Leonard Schlup

NEW SECTIONALISM.

In an article that appeared in *The Forum* in 1894, Dr. Lindley Miller Keasbey (1867–1946), professor of political science at the University of Colorado, warned against "the Money Power of the Eastern States." His essay, "The New Sectionalism," defined silver coinage as a moral issue, sacred dogma, political principle, economic necessity, and intensely personal question. He described honest farmers striving to pay their debts and provide a decent living for their families. A Democrat who later taught at the University of Texas before retiring to Tucson, Arizona, Keasbey berated eastern capitalists who sought to enslave western people and "snatch the very bread from their mouths" and "shackle them more closely" to eastern interests. He claimed that the United States was too large and diverse to be ruled by any one area or dominated by one class; therefore, sectionalism must become the essence of America's body politic, replacing localism. He further emphasized that the East had to recognize that the basis of representation consisted not so much in the states as in the country's natural economic sections.

Further Reading: Lindley M. Keasbey, "The New Sectionalism: A Western Warning to the East," *The Forum* 16 (1894): 578–587.

Leonard Schlup

NEZ PERCÉ WAR.

This conflict commenced in 1877 when Nez Percé Native Americans, under Chief Joseph, refused to leave their land in Oregon's Wallowa Valley, near the Washington and Idaho borders. After a group of warriors attacked settlers, Joseph retreated with approximately eight hundred of his people across to Wyoming and ultimately into Montana, traveling more than one thousand miles to seek safety in Canada. Colonel Nelson A. Miles caught them near the international boundary. They surrendered following a five-day battle. General William T. Sherman exiled the Nez Percé, as prisoners of war, to Fort Leavenworth, Kansas, before transferring them to what is now Oklahoma.

Further Reading: Scott M. Thompson, *I Will Tell of My War Story: A Pictorial Account of the Nez Percé War*, 2000; Bruce Hampton, *Children of Grace: The Nez Perce War of 1877*, 1994.

Leonard Schlup

NORRIS, BENJAMIN FRANKLIN

(5 March 1870–25 October 1902), novelist and journalist. Born in Chicago, Illinois, Norris grew up in California. He attended the Belmont School, studied art and drawing in London and Paris at the Atelier Julien in 1887, and then took a program in literature at University of California. Norris covered the Boer War for the *San Francisco Chronicle*, *Chicago Inter-Ocean*, and *Harper's Weekly* for a short time. After returning to San Francisco in 1896, he wrote for *The Wave*, a literary weekly, and completed his *Moran of the Lady Letty*, a maritime love story, in 1898, the year he began writing for *McClure's Magazine*. In a short life, Norris produced many fine novels; only his *A Man's Women* was not very successful. After 1900 he wrote his trilogy titled *Epic of the Wheat*, which consisted of *The Pit* (1903), *The Wolf*, and *The Octopus* (1901). The latter, on the Mussel Slough tragedy, helped his reputation. He did for the San Joaquin Valley what Owen Wister did for Medicine Bow. His *Deal in White, The Circle, Vandever and the Brute*, and *Responsibilities of a Novelist* were published posthumously. Norris died in San Francisco, California.

Further Reading: Franklin Walker, *Frank Norris: A Biography*, 1932; *San Francisco Chronicle*, 26 October 1902; *San Francisco Examiner*, 26 October 1902.

Nicholas C. Polos

NORRIS, MARY HARRIOTT (16 March 1848–14 September 1918), educator and writer. Born in Boonton, New Jersey, Norris graduated from Vassar College in 1870. During her life she published several novels that combined romanticism with morality and instruction. When she wrote *Dorothy Delafield* in 1886, Norris hoped that readers would "gain fresh inspiration." She also produced several textbooks. After serving for sixteen years as principal of a private school that she had founded in 1880 in New York City, Norris became dean of women and assistant professor of English at Northwestern University in 1898. There she organized a self-governing association for students, lectured on religion, emphasized personal hygiene, and started a library. Upon completing one academic year at Northwestern, she returned to writing, and died in Morristown, New Jersey, leaving a progressive legacy for the advancement of women and humanity.

Further Reading: *New York Times*, 23 September 1918.

Leonard Schlup

NORTHEN, WILLIAM JONATHAN (9 July 1835–25 March 1913), governor, educator, agricultural reformer, and writer. Born in Jones County, Georgia, Northen was graduated from Mercer University in 1853, taught, and served in the Confederate Army. After the Civil War, he championed scientific innovations in agriculture. After terms as a Georgia state representative and senator, Northen won the Democratic nomination for governor in 1890, and with the backing of the Farmers' Alliance, won unopposed. Alliance support was critical that year: as six of Georgia's ten congressional seats went to Alliance men, as well as 168 of the 218 seats in the state legislature. Northen was reelected in 1892. He supported some of the Alliance/Populist agenda, notably free coinage of silver and strict railroad regulation, but opposed government ownership and the Subtreasury plan. He advocated reduced taxes, educational reform and biracial planning committees, and he spoke out repeatedly against lynching. Northen led the drive to establish a state college for African Americans in 1891, Georgia Industrial College at Savannah. He devoted his later years to writing and editing. Northen died in Atlanta.

Further Reading: James F. Cook, *The Governors of Georgia, 1754–1995*, 1995; James Calvin Bonner, "The Gubernatorial Career of W. J. Northen," M.A. thesis, University of Georgia, 1936; *Atlanta Constitution*, 26 March 1913.

Hutch Johnson

NORWEGIAN IMMIGRATION. Norwegians immigrated to Gilded Age America for several reasons. First, inexpensive land prices attracted many. The Homestead Act of 1862 and treaties with Native Americans opened additional territories for settlement. Second, the strict Norwegian social system pushed emigrants outward. Third, large numbers of Norwegians left their homeland because increasing population, industrial machinery, low wages, and mountainous terrain unsuitable for farming contributed to a paucity of employment opportunities. Unlike that of the early nineteenth century, extensive Norwegian emigration in the 1870s often consisted of young, unmarried individuals. By the late 1880s, the profile of the average immigrant shifted from member of a rural family unit to a single man from an urban center. Large numbers of Norwegians flocked to Minnesota, where they found conditions to their liking. By 1875, Norwegians comprised 30 percent of the total population of Polk and Clay counties. The Norwegian population of Duluth increased dramatically, from 242 in 1870 to 7,500 in 1900. By the mid-1880s, Norwegian migration to Minnesota shifted to the cities, including Minneapolis and Saint Paul.

Further Reading: Arlow W. Andersen, *The Norwegian-Americans*, 1975; Ingrid Semmingsen, *Norway to America: A History of the Migration*, 1978; Lowell J. Soike, *Norwegian Americans and the Politics of Dissent, 1880–1924*, 1991.

Leonard Schlup

NURSING. Social needs spurred an evolution in nursing during the Civil War. Previously, nurses had been untrained, and often members of religious orders. Clara Barton (1821–1912) and Mary Ann Bickerdyke (1817–1901) responded to Union Army appeals for help in caring for the sick and wounded. Dorothea Lynde Dix (1802–1887) was appointed superintendent of female nurses, and charged with recruiting and equipping a nurse corps. Dix organized two thousand capable, enthusiastic female volunteers. President Jefferson Davis recognized Sally Tompkins's (1833–1916) service by naming her a captain in the Confederate Army. Harriet Tubman (1820–1913), an abolitionist and compassionate black nurse, led care at the Colored Hospital, Fort Monroe, Virginia. Barton organized the American Red Cross. The demand for educated nurses promoted women's emancipation.

The Woosley sisters, Abby, Jane, and Georgeanna, who had served in the war, influenced the development of professional training. Louisa Lee Schuyler (1837–1926) is recognized as the originator of the first American training school for nurses (ca. 1874). Melinda Anna (Linda) Richards (1841–1930) was America's first trained nurse. The English nurse Florence Nightingale (1820–1910) encouraged schools in the United States to prepare nurses rather than physicians' assistants. Nightingale revolutionized both the care of the sick and the education of women. Her system of training became institutionalized by 1873 with the establishment of three schools: Bellevue Hospital Training School in New York City, Connecticut Training School in New Haven; and Boston Training School at Massachusetts General Hospital. Hospitals, which had grown from 178 in 1872 to 2000 in 1900, recognized the economic advantage of the trained nurses. Schools of nursing grew in number from four to more than four hundred by century's end. Leaders in nursing education included Isabel Hampton Robb (1860–1910) and Mary Adelaide Nutting (1858–1948).

Lavinia L. Dock (1858–1956) organized the first national nursing organization, the American Society of Superintendents of Training Schools of Nursing, in 1893. Isabel Hampton Robb and Sophia Palmer formed the Nurses Associated Alumnae of the United States and Canada in 1896. Lillian Wald (1867–1940) and her friend Mary Brewster established the Henry Street Settlement; it became the Visiting Nurse Service of New York, which cared for the sick and the poor in their homes, and helped lead to modern public health nursing. In 1900 the International Council of Nurses was formed to support global nursing care. The *American Journal of Nursing* was founded in 1900, and continues today as the official publication of the American Nurses Association. The Gilded Age moved nursing from the Dark Ages to modern times, resulting in education and a career option for women, while advancing the nursing care of patients worldwide.

Further Reading: Philip A. Kalisch and Beatrice J. Kalisch, *The Advance of American Nursing*, 1995; Josephine A. Dolan, *Nursing in Society, a Historical Perspective*, 1978; Sister Charles Marie Frank, *The Historical Development of Nursing*, 1953.

Martha A. Conrad

OATES, WILLIAM CALVIN

(1 December 1835–9 September 1910), soldier, lawyer, and politician. Oates was born in Pike County, Alabama, where he led a roving life before practicing law. Not a fervent secessionist, he nevertheless rose to regimental commander in the Confederate Army and lost his right arm. Oates returned to his law practice and entered politics as a Bourbon Democrat and pillar of white supremacy. He endorsed ballot-box stuffing, and bribery and intimidation of black voters. Elected to Congress in 1880, he served seven terms, opposing such legislation as the Blair bill and the Interstate Commerce Act. Oates won the Democratic gubernatorial nomination in 1894. He defeated his opponent, the quasi-Populist Reuben F. Kolb, partly through election fraud. As governor of Alabama, Oates was forced to borrow money to finance a state government crippled by the Panic of 1893. He served as a brigadier general during the Spanish-American War. At the Alabama constitutional convention of 1901, he argued against the total disfranchisement of blacks. In 1905, he published a well-regarded memoir, *The War Between the Union and the Confederacy*. He died in Montgomery, Alabama.

Further Reading: John Sparkman, "The Kolb-Oates Campaign of 1894," M.A. thesis, University of Alabama, 1924; Paul M. Pruitt, Jr., "Joseph C. Manning, Alabama Populist: A Rebel Against the Solid South," Ph.D. diss., College of William and Mary, 1980; William Warren Rogers, *The One–Gallused Rebellion: Agrarianism in Alabama, 1865–1896*, 1970.

Paul M. Pruitt, Jr.

OCALA MEETING OF 1890.

One of the Gilded Age's most dynamic agrarian organizations was the Farmers' Alliance, which numbered 1.5 million whites and 1 million blacks at its peak. In 1890, its leaders met in Ocala, Florida, to define an agenda, at the heart of which was the Subtreasury plan. The plan called on Congress to establish warehouses for crops and to loan farmers up to 80 percent of a crop's value at 1 percent interest. In addition to the Subtreasury plan, the Alliance wanted Congress to abolish national banks in order to diminish the clout of bankers, whom the Alliance believed enriched themselves on wealth that farmers and workers had created. Other reforms included inflating the currency by unlimited coinage of silver, a graduated income tax, tariff reduction, direct election of senators, nationalization of the railroads, and female suffrage. These demands formed the core of the Omaha Platform, which the People's Party issued in 1892. Although they failed during the Gilded Age, these reforms helped shape the Progressive agenda during the twentieth century.

Further Reading: Robert C. McMath, *The Populist Vanguard*, 1975; Theodore Saloutos, *Farmer Movements in the South, 1865–1933*, 1960.

Christopher Cumo

OCHOA, ESTEBAN

(17 March 1831–October 1888), merchant and civic leader. Born in Chihuahua, Mexico, Ochoa was raised on the Nuevo Mexico frontier. Through the Treaty of Guadalupe Hidalgo (1848), the United States acquired the region, including what became Arizona Territory in 1863. Ochoa studied for business in Missouri before moving to Tucson, where he created an extensive freight business. Mexicans were the majority of Arizona's population through the 1870s. By the 1880s Mexican immigrants formed a large percentage of the labor force in the Arizona mines, smelters, and railroad yards. To take advantage of the expanding Arizona mining activities, Ochoa organized Tully, Ochoa, and Company, which became the leading freight company in the Southwest. Ochoa's education and experience made him a natural spokesman for the Mexican-American population of southern Arizona. He acted as intermediary between the Mexican-American society and the Anglo population and culture.

Ochoa and a few other Mexican Americans won election to the territory legislative assembly in the years before 1880. In addition, he was elected mayor of Tucson. Ochoa did much to establish a public school system in the Arizona Territory. With the coming of the railroad to Tucson on 25 March 1880, Ochoa's freight business of pack trains was doomed to end.

Further Reading: Manuel P. Servin, *The Mexican-Americans: An Awakening Minority*, 1970; David J. Weber, ed., *Foreigners in Their Native Land: Historical Roots of the Mexican Americans*, 1973.

Santos C. Vega

OCHS, ADOLPH SIMON (12 March 1858–8 April 1935), journalist and publisher. Born in Cincinnati, Ohio, Ochs moved during childhood to Tennessee. With little schooling, he worked as an office boy for the *Knoxville Chronicle* and spent two extra hours daily with the foreman. Here he learned all branches of the newspaper trade. Using borrowed money, he purchased the failing *Chattanooga Times* in 1878. While still a young adult, he became one of the town's leading citizens.

In 1896, Ochs bought the nearly bankrupt *New York Times*. Despite vicious competition from "yellow" papers, based on gossip and hyperbole and selling for a penny, Ochs defeated rivals. He insisted that his editors publish only "the news fit to print," thereby giving the *Times* a slogan it still uses. He subordinated editorialization to solid reporting and eliminated clearly fraudulent advertising. During the Spanish-American War, he lowered the price to a penny per copy, thereby attracting readers who normally would have bought a competing paper. When Ochs relinquished direct editorial control in 1904, he was known for saving America's most influential newspaper and uplifting professional journalism. He died during a visit to his beloved Chattanooga.

Further Reading: Doris Faber, *Printer's Devil to Publisher: Adolph S. Ochs of the New York Times*, 1996; Stephen J. Ostrander, "All the News That's Fit to Print: Adolph Ochs and the *New York Times*," *Timeline* 10 (1993): 38–53.

Christian B. Keller

OGLESBY, RICHARD JAMES (25 July 1824–24 April 1899), soldier and governor. Oglesby, born in Oldham County, Kentucky, was orphaned when his parents succumbed to cholera. With an uncle he traveled to Decatur, Illinois, where he did manual labor and later read law. He served in the Mexican War, practiced law, ran unsuccessfully for Congress as a Republican in 1858, and was elected to the state senate in 1860. He soon resigned to take a colonel's commission in the Union Army, was severely wounded in battle, and rose to major general. He resigned in 1864 to run for governor of Illinois. Oglesby returned to his law practice after one term. Elected governor again in 1872, he had agreed in advance to step down in favor of his lieutenant governor. The legislature then chose him to replace Senator Lyman Trumbull, now out of favor with Republicans for his role in the Liberal Republican revolt in 1872. After one Senate term, Oglesby was again elected governor in 1884. In office, he granted clemency appeals, reducing the sentences of two of the accused in the Haymarket bombing of 1886, but he refused to commute the death sentences of five others. He lost another Senate bid in 1891.

Further Reading: Richard J. Oglesby Papers, Illinois State Historical Library, Springfield; Mark A. Plummer, "Richard J. Oglesby, Lincoln's Rail-Splitter," *Illinois Historical Journal* 80 (1987): 2–12.

Mario R. DiNunzio

O'HANLON, VIRGINIA (20 July 1889–13 May 1971), educator. Born in New York City, O'Hanlon gained national attention at age eight when she questioned the existence of Santa Claus. Taking her father's advice, she sent a letter to the *New York Sun*'s "Question and Answer" column, asking for the truth. Charles Anderson Dana (1819–1897), editor of the *Sun*, assigned the response to Francis Pharcellus Church (1839–1906), who had covered the Civil War for the *New York Times* and usually wrote unsigned, somewhat sardonic, editorials on controversial theological subjects. Church's famous reply appeared on Tuesday, 21 September 1897. He told Virginia there was a Santa Claus, existing as certainly as love and generosity and devotion exist. Church went on to write of a world without Santa as one lacking Virginias, childlike faith, poetry, and romance. His popular editorial swept the nation at the end of the Gilded Age. Over the years it was translated into numerous languages and distributed worldwide. The *Sun* reprinted it annually until going out of business in 1949. Meanwhile, O'Hanlon married Malcolm Douglas in 1915 and earned a doctorate in education in 1930 from Fordham University. She had a productive career as a teacher and principal. She died in Valatie, New York.

Further Reading: *New York Times*, 14 May 1971; *New York Sun*, 21 September 1897.

Leonard Schlup

OHIO IDEA (PENDLETON PLAN).

By 1867, leading Democrats were searching for issues to reunite the Democratic Party and return it to national power. George H. Pendleton, a former Ohio congressman, suggested a focus on postwar financial issues. Pendleton's plan was a response to the Republican policy of removing greenbacks from circulation in order to return the country to specie payments. The immediate result was hardship for debtors, farmers, and some laborers who found it more difficult to pay off debt and make a living in a deflationary system. Pendleton called for the end of contraction and the payment of five–twenty war bonds in greenbacks. He selected only those bonds because they had no stipulation on how they were to be paid and bondholders had purchased them with the paper currency. The plan was designed to save the government money, increase the currency supply in the Midwest and South, and lessen the power of the national banks, which held many of those bonds as collateral for banknotes. Payment of those bonds, therefore, would have replaced banknotes with greenbacks and forced the national bank system, which Pendleton saw as an unfair monopoly of financial power, to collapse. This side effect was perfectly acceptable for Pendleton, and allowed him to argue that he was being consistent with the party's Jacksonian heritage. In the end, Pendleton saw his plan as a short and relatively painless means of paying the war debt and eventually returning the country to specie payments.

The Democrats adopted much of the Ohio Idea in their national platform in 1868, but Pendleton, the front-runner for the presidential nomination that year, was thwarted by the hard money Bourbon Democrats. As in 1864, the hopelessly divided party gave itself no chance of victory.

Further Reading: Chester M. Destler, *American Radicalism, 1865–1901: Essays and Documents*, 1963; Max Shipley, "The Background and Legal Aspects of the Pendleton Plan," *Mississippi Valley Historical Review* 24 (1937): 329–340; Thomas S. Mach, " 'Gentleman George' Hunt Pendleton: A Study in Political Continuity," Ph.D. diss., University of Akron, 1996.

Thomas S. Mach

O.K. CORRAL, GUNFIGHT AT THE.

On 26 October 1881, the three Earp brothers, Wyatt, Virgil, and Morgan, along with John H. "Doc" Holliday, confronted Ike and Billy Clanton, and Tom and Frank McLowery in a vacant lot on Fremont Street in Tombstone, Arizona. This was the storied gunfight at the O.K. corral, a tragic bloodletting that, like Custer's battle at the Little Bighorn, has become a defining moment in western history. The fight resulted from a deal between Ike Clanton, Frank McLowery, and Wyatt Earp that soured. Ike and Frank agreed to set up three outlaws so Wyatt, a candidate for sheriff of the newly formed Cochise County, could capture them. He believed the "glory" of the capture would assure his election. In return, he would give the $3500 reward to Ike and Frank. The plot miscarried, and Ike blamed Wyatt. Ike "called down the thunder" and fled when the shooting began. The McLowery boys and Billy Clanton were killed, and Virgil and Morgan Earp were wounded. The O.K. corral gunfight passed into the language as the prototype for unfocused Western violence and helped to create the gunfighter myth. There were also more immediate results. Two months later, on 28 December, Virgil was gunned down from ambush and permanently disabled. On 18 March 1882, Morgan was shot in the back and killed as he played billiards in Hatch's Saloon on Allen Street in Tombstone. Wyatt then took the law into his own hands, killing three men he believed to be guilty, including a rustler chief, Curly Bill Brocious.

Further Reading: Paula Mitchell Marks, *To Die in the West*, 1989.

Jack Burrows

OKLAHOMA LAND RUSH OF 1889. Prominent "Boomers," such as David L. Payne and William L. Couch, urged federal officials during the Gilded Age to open land for white settlement. On 2 March 1889, Congress passed the Indian Appropriation Act, proclaiming that three million acres of unassigned lands belonged to the public domain. Thousands of persons, mostly from Kansas and Missouri, gathered on the Arkansas and Texas borders of Oklahoma Territory on 22 April to seek parcels of land and file for ownership. They came by Santa Fe Railroad, covered wagons, and horseback. Settlers who jumped the gun to claim prime places earned the sobriquet "Sooners." Guthrie and Oklahoma City became cities of ten thousand individuals in one day. Because all of Oklahoma except the panhandle had previously been set aside for displaced Natives, uprooted Native Americans in 1889 included the Osage, Quapaw, and Cherokee tribes. Once the initial scramble abated, some people, learning of the scarcity of water and provisions, returned home.

Further Reading: Stan Hoig, *The Oklahoma Land Rush of 1889*, 1984; Kathlyn Baldwin, *The 89ers: Oklahoma Land Rush of 1889*, 1981.

Leonard Schlup

OLCOTT, HENRY STEEL (2 August 1832–17 February 1907), cofounder of the Theosophical Society. Born in Orange, New Jersey, and reared in New York City, Olcott became interested in spiritualism, wrote books and essays on farming, practiced law in New York City, and contributed articles to newspapers. In 1875 he met Helena P. Blavatsky (1831–1891), a Russian-born religious philosopher. That year, they and others established the Theosophical Society, of which Olcott served as president for the remainder of his life. Also in 1875 he published *People from the Other World*. Olcott's interest in the occult, recovering ancient wisdom, Asian cultures, and esoteric spiritual ideas marked his role as a missionary in Gilded Age America. He lectured widely and punctuated his remarks with concrete examples. Olcott and Blavatsky traveled together, including journeys to India. In 1880 they converted to Buddhism. Olcott died in New York City.

Further Reading: Howard Murphet, *Yankee Beacon of Buddhist Light: Life of Colonel Henry S. Olcott*, 1988; Bruce F. Campbell, *Ancient Wisdom Revived: A History of the Theosophical Movement*, 1980.

Leonard Schlup

OLDS, RANSOM ELI (3 June 1864–26 August 1950), automobile manufacturer. Born in Geneva, Ohio, Olds grew up in Lansing, Michigan, where he worked in his father's steam engine business, P. F. Olds & Son. After assuming the role of general manager from his father and brother, Olds emphasized smaller and easier to operate engines using a gasoline burner, an idea that significantly increased the company's sales. By the mid-1890s, Olds controlled the company. In 1887, he tested a three-wheeled vehicle, and later developed a more elaborate and powerful "horseless carriage." After viewing various models at the World's Columbian Exposition at Chicago in 1893, Olds turned his attention to devising an internal combustion gasoline engine, which he and Madison F. Bates patented in 1896. In 1897 he organized the Olds Motor Vehicle Company, which two years later became the Olds Motor Works. By the turn of the century, Olds was producing a small, highly popular car for $650. By 1902 the Olds Motor Works had become the leading domestic automobile company. Olds gradually turned his attention to developing a powered lawnmower, investing in real estate, boating, and traveling. He died at his home in Lansing.

Further Reading: Glenn A. Neimeyer, *The Automotive Career of Ransom E. Olds*, 1963; George S. May, *R. E. Olds: Auto Industry Pioneer*, 1977; *Lansing State Journal*, 27 August 1950; *New York Times*, 27 August 1950; Ransom E. Olds Papers, Historical Collections Library, Michigan State University, East Lansing.

Leonard Schlup

OLMSTED, FREDERICK LAW (26 April 1822–22 August 1903), landscape designer, urban planner, and theorist. Born in Hartford, Connecticut, Olmsted became America's most influential landscape designer. His writings and his designs for parks, gardens, and communities demonstrated his belief that landscape could be an important civilizing influence. His most important early project, in collaboration with Calvert Vaux, was Central Park in New York City (1858–1877), where footpaths, bridle paths, carriage roads, and scenic effects that included settings for gatherings and concerts, were made available to urban dwellers. Olmsted's largest project, the "Emerald Necklace," developed for Boston (1879–1881), linked a ten-mile-long string of parks.

As planners, Olmsted and Vaux's most important project was the design for Riverside, Illinois (1868), in which curvilinear streets enhanced the picturesque nature of the community and discouraged the use of suburban streets as main thoroughfares. Olmsted and Vaux dissolved their partnership in 1872. The prolific Olmsted designed university campuses and domestic gardens, and was also involved in many projects for parks and grounds, including those of the U.S. Capitol in Washington (1874), George Vanderbilt's estate "Biltmore" in North Carolina (1888), and the World's Columbian Exposition in Chicago (1893). He collaborated on several projects with the architect H. H. Richardson. Olmsted and Vaux coined the term "landscape architecture." Olmsted died in Waverly, Massachusetts.

Further Reading: Charles C. McLaughlin, ed., *The Papers of Frederick Law Olmstead*, 6 vols., 1977–1992; M. Kalfus, *Frederick Law Olmstead: The Passion of a Public Artist*, 1990; Charles E. Beveridge and Paul Rocheleau, *Frederick Law Olmstead: Designing the American Landscape*, 1998.

David G. Wilkins

OLNEY COROLLARY TO THE MONROE DOCTRINE.

With the Monroe Doctrine forming the cornerstone of American foreign policy in the western hemisphere, any threat of European intervention regularly met with opposition from Washington. Such was the case in a long border dispute between Great Britain and Venezuela. In 1895, Secretary of State Richard Olney proposed that the United States mediate the issue, but the British rejected his offer. An angry President Grover Cleveland then sent Congress a message, written primarily by Olney, containing a blistering attack on the British position. It strongly warned Britain not to take aggressive action in the western hemisphere, regardless of circumstances. This message greatly

expanded the Monroe Doctrine because the United States now claimed that matters such as border disputes were issues of national security, and thus subject to U.S. interest. Faced with the strong American position, Britain agreed to binding arbitration, as did Venezuela.

Further Reading: Dexter Perkins, *A History of the Monroe Doctrine*, 1963; Gerald G. Eggert, *Richard Olney: Evolution of a Statesman*, 1974.

Stephen Svonavec

OLNEY-PAUNCEFOTE TREATY OF 1897.

The Olney-Pauncefote convention of January 1897 had its origins in a long-standing boundary dispute between British Guiana and Venezuela. Britain rejected U.S. demands for arbitration until President Glover Cleveland, in December 1896, threatened military intervention. Britain then agreed to arbitration, with the understanding that areas occupied by Venezuela and Britain for fifty years be exempted. The resulting Olney-Pauncefote Treaty provided that conflicting claims go before a tribunal of six members, three from each country. The convention failed to pass the Republican-dominated Senate. In February 1897, Britain and Venezuela reached their own agreement on arbitration.

Further Reading: Henry James, *Richard Olney and His Public Service*, 1923; Gerald G. Eggert, *Richard Olney: Evolution of a Statesman*, 1974.

Norman A. Graebner

OLNEY, RICHARD

(15 September 1835–8 April 1917), lawyer, U.S. attorney general, and secretary of state. Born in Oxford, Massachusetts, Olney was schooled at Leicester Academy and in 1856 graduated from Brown University. After attending Harvard Law School (1858) and passing the bar in 1859, he entered the Boston law office of Judge Benjamin F. Thomas. Olney built a distinguished clientele among major railroads and other corporations, as well as prominent persons. A lifelong Democrat, he was elected to one term in the Massachusetts legislature (1873) but had no other political success. He was relatively unknown when Grover Cleveland chose him as attorney general in 1893. Olney inherited a case against the sugar trust (*United States* v. *E. C. Knight Company*) from the Harrison administration, and although

he had strong reservations about the Sherman Antitrust Act, continued the case as a test. The Supreme Court decision (1895), distinguishing between commerce and manufacturing, reflected an argument Olney had made a few years earlier. He believed the income tax to be constitutional but was unsuccessful in arguing the *Pollock* v. *Farmers' Loan & Trust Company* and *Hyde* v. *Continental Trust Company* (both 1895). Olney feared Jacob Coxey's march on Washington in 1894 and moved to halt similar "armies" farther west by approving, in selected cases, the use of federal troops to prevent their seizure of trains. In 1894 he recommended the use of an injunction and the dispatch of federal troops to Chicago to move trains carrying mail, thus breaking the railroad strike, led by Eugene Debs, supporting Pullman Company workers.

When Secretary of State Walter Q. Gresham died, Olney moved his position on 10 June 1895. With Cleveland's support, he challenged the British to settle the long-standing Venezuela-British Guiana boundary dispute, explaining U.S. interest with broad Monroe Doctrine claims. The eventual agreement to arbitrate the boundary contributed to developing Anglo-American rapprochement and recognition of growing U.S. dominance in the western hemisphere. When the Cuban insurrection against Spain reemerged in 1895, Olney withstood congressional pressure for recognizing a state of war, but did suggest reforms and offered Washington's good offices to attain them. Spain was not moved, and the Cuban question remained for the McKinley administration. When the conservative Cleveland-Olney faction lost control of the Democratic Party to the Bryanites in 1896 and the Republicans gained the presidency, Olney retired to private law practice. He remained interested in national affairs and was a favorite-son nominee for president in 1904. Later, President Woodrow Wilson offered him an ambassadorship to Great Britain and an appointment on the Federal Reserve Board, both of which he declined. He died in Boston.

Further Reading: Gerald G. Eggert, *Richard Olney: Evolution of a Statesman*, 1974; Henry James, *Richard Olney and His Public Service*, 1923; Montgomery Schuyler, "Richard Olney," in Samuel Flagg Bemis, ed., *The American Secretaries of State and Their Diplomacy*, vol. 8, 1928.

William Kamman

OMAHA PLATFORM OF 1892. A platform adopted by the People's or Populist Party, its immediate forerunners appeared at the December 1889 (St. Louis) and December 1890 (Ocala, Florida) national conferences of the Southern Farmers Alliance as well as the May 1891 (Cincinnati) founding convention of the People's Party and another Alliance meeting in February 1892 (St. Louis). Considered Populism's holy writ, the Omaha Platform contained a preamble, three planks (money, transportation, and land), and a series of resolutions. The preamble, written by the novelist Ignatius Donnelly, offered an apocalyptic indictment of Gilded Age politics and society. It argued that corruption dominated public life and governmental injustice bred two classes (tramps and millionaires), and blamed a vast conspiracy that jeopardized the republic's future. In the money plank, Populists called for a government-operated currency system, free coinage of silver, a circulating medium of at least $50 per capita (which meant greenbacks), a graduated income tax, a postal savings bank, and the Subtreasury plan of the Southern Farmers Alliance. In transportation, Populists advocated government ownership of railroads and of the telephone and telegraph systems. The land plank denounced speculation, sought prohibition of land ownership by aliens, and demanded that the government reclaim railroad- and corporation-owned lands in excess of actual needs for actual settlers. Ten resolutions, pointedly not part of the platform but expressing the convention's sentiment, championed the secret ballot, direct election of senators, single terms for president and vice president, the initiative and referendum, pensions for Union Army veterans, the eight-hour day for government workers, and restriction of immigration. They also endorsed a Knights of Labor strike then in progress, and denounced government subsidies to corporations and private corporate armies (Pinkertons).

The Omaha Platform was a consensual document. Controversial statements favoring female and universal suffrage from earlier platforms were deleted. Inclusion of the planks on government ownership and the Subtreasury plan apparently was a quid pro quo deal between their western and southern proponents, respectively. Previous third parties had agitated for all of the platform's issues except the Subtreasury plan. The 1896 Populist national platform repeated much of the Omaha document, incorporated some of the resolutions into the body of the platform, added a few new items, and deleted endorsement of the Subtreasury plan. Much of the Omaha Platform, especially the appended resolutions, became law in the early twentieth century.

Further Reading: Gene Clanton, *Congressional Populism*, 1998; Lawrence Goodwyn, Democratic Promise, 1976; John D. Hicks, *The Populist Revolt*, 1931.

Worth Robert Miller

OPEN DOOR POLICY. Formally enunciated by Secretary of State John Hay in 1899 and 1900, the Open Door policy in China was based on three principles: equality of commercial opportunity, territorial integrity, and administrative efficiency. By the late nineteenth century, Japan and the western European powers had carved much of China into separate spheres of influence. Permanent partition of China might ruin American hopes for further trade with that country. Under the terms of the Open Door policy, each country would agree not to deny others access to its sphere of influence. This would give equal trading and development rights in China to all. Although Hay announced in March 1900 that his recommendations had been approved by other nations, there were no sanctions to enforce such a policy. Russia extended its sphere of influence in Manchuria during the Boxer Rebellion of 1900. In the Taft-Katsura Agreement of 1905, the Root-Takahira Agreement of 1908, and the Lansing-Ishii Agreement of 1917, the United States recognized Japan's growing power and special interests in east Asia. During the Washington Conference of 1921–1922, the Open Door policy was reaffirmed. In 1932, however, when Japan occupied Manchuria and established the puppet state of Manchukuo, the United States lodged the only protest.

Further Reading: J. Israel, *Progressivism and the Open Door: America and China, 1905–1921*, 1971; L. C. Gardner, *Imperial America*, 1976; E. S. Rosenberg, *Spreading the American Dream*, 1982.

Xiaojian Zhao

ORANGE RIOT OF 1871. Tensions between Protestants and Catholics originated in the theological disputes of the sixteenth century. Protestantism, in the form of the Anglican Church, swept England that century, though Ireland remained Catholic. Anglicans rejoiced on 12 July 1690, when their coreligionist William of Orange claimed the British crown by defeating the Catholic James II at the battle of the Boyne. Thereafter Catholics and Protestants used its anniversary as an excuse for quarreling. The potato famine of the mid-nineteenth century brought large numbers of Irish, and the quarrel, to the United States. By 1870, the Irish had staffed the New York City police department for a generation, and that 11 July they did little to quell a riot that left five dead. The next year members of the Irish Hibernian Society announced their intent to disrupt the annual Protestant parade. Police Superintendent James J. Kelso not only refused to protect the paraders, he ordered them not to march. But on 10 July, the governor of New York and the mayor of the city countermanded the order, and the next day seven hundred police and five thousand militia escorted one hundred marchers. Religious leaders on both sides appealed for calm, but a shoot-out between the militia and Catholics left thirty-nine dead and more than ninety wounded.

Further Reading: Dennis Clark, *Hibernia America: The Irish and Regional Cultures*, 1986.

Christopher Cumo

ORGANIC ACT OF 1884. Between 1867 and 1883, members of Congress introduced two dozen civil government bills for Alaska, but they aroused scant interest and were stillborn. The Presbyterian missionary Dr. Sheldon Jackson finally served as a catalyst to prompt congressional action. Jackson had first come to Alaska in 1877 and established Protestantism there. He subsequently became an effective spokesman for Alaska and in May 1883 persuaded the General Assembly for Alaska of the Presbyterian Church to draft a memorial to the Congress urging establishment of a civil government and creation of industrial schools for the Natives. Having found an ally in Senator Benjamin Harrison of Indiana, Jackson undertook a campaign of lecturing, publishing, and lobbying in the contiguous states on behalf of Alaska, and maintained extensive contacts with federal officials. In 1883 representatives had introduced four civil government bills in the House, and on 4 December, Senator Harrison introduced his own measure, S.B. 153. During the following month he reconciled the provisions of his bill with related measures.

The Senate passed the Harrison version in January 1884, and the House, four days later. The 1884 Organic Act made Alaska a civil and judicial district with a court headquartered in Sitka. It mandated a clerk who also was to serve as ex-officio secretary and treasurer of the district; a district attorney, a U.S. marshal, and four deputy marshals; four commissioners and a governor. The president was to appoint all these officials with the advice and consent of the Senate. The general laws of the state of Oregon were to be in force in Alaska as far as they were applicable and not in conflict with the act or federal law. This rudimentary legislation served Alaska until Congress passed the Organic Act of 1912.

Further Reading: 23 Sta.L. 24, 1884; Claus-M. Naske, *A History of the Alaska Federal District Court System, 1884–1959*; and *The Creation of the State Court System*, 1985.

Claus-M. Naske

ORNITHOLOGY. As American science matured and diversified in the postbellum period, its practitioners sought to forge boundaries and organize themselves into specialized national societies. The first ornithological society in the United States was formed in the early 1870s in Cambridge, Massachusetts, under the leadership of William Brewster, Ruthven Deane, and Henry W. Henshaw. On 26 September 1883, twenty-four leading ornithologists convened in the library of the American Museum of Natural History in New York City to establish the American Ornithologists' Union (AOU). Participants included Professor Joseph A. Allen, El-

liott Coues, and William Brewster. The ornithological community in Gilded Age America remained heterogeneous and inclusive, but boundaries started to solidify with the AOU's creation. The union functioned not only as a society for studying and appreciating birds but also as a means of certifying a member's scientific accomplishments. Local and regional organizations quickly developed across the nation.

In 1885 Allen, a noted zoologist, accepted an offer to become a curator of birds and mammals at the American Museum of Natural History, under the leadership of its president, Morris K. Jesup. Allen turned the department into a national center for scientific research, recruiting Frank M. Chapman as his assistant in 1888. Smaller museums across the nation also commenced work in ornithology, collecting specimens and hiring curatorial staffs. The AOU grew with little tension until a major scandal threatened to dissolve the group in 1896 and 1897. A founding leader, the former army surgeon Robert W. Shufeldt, was compelled to address charges of having an affair with his young Norwegian housekeeper and of blackmailing his wife, Florence Audubon Shufeldt, granddaughter of the naturalist John James Audubon, to prevent her from divorcing him. Shufeldt's misogynistic outbursts further aggravated the explosive situation. AOU members regarded Shufeldt's scandalous behavior as unbecoming a gentleman and grounds for revoking his membership. The incident badly divided ornithologists. Those who ranked Shufeldt among the most accomplished scientific ornithologists clashed with colleagues who demanded his expulsion. The AOU appeared to be a gentlemen's club and scientific fraternity, but some of its adherents interpreted the group as one in which the moral conduct of its associates was unimportant. On 8 November 1897, the ten council members of the AOU deliberated and reached a consensus resolution stating that evidence sustained the charges against Shufeldt but that the AOU possessed "no jurisdiction" in the case.

In the decades following the Civil War, as industrialization and urbanization increasingly reshaped the landscape, many Americans sought adventure and aesthetic gratification through avian pursuits. By 1900 the official membership of the AOU stood at 748, but many more devotees joined local Audubon societies, purchased field guides, read the AOU's journal *Auk*, and kept records of species they encountered in the wild. Bird-watching exemplified an increasing public interest in ornithology throughout the period.

Further Reading: Mark V. Barrow, Jr., *A Passion for Birds: American Ornithology After Audubon*, 1998; Frank M. Chapman and T. S. Palmer, eds., *Fifty Years' Progress of American Ornithology, 1883–1933*, 1933; Frank B. Webster, "Practical Taxidermy," *Ornithologist and Oologist* 10 (1885): 137–139.

Leonard Schlup

ORTH, GODLOVE STEIN (22 April 1817–16 December 1882), congressman. Born near Lebanon, Pennsylvania, Orth attended Pennsylvania College in Gettysburg before studying in a law office there. After gaining admission to the bar in 1839, he moved to Lafayette, Indiana, to practice law and enter politics. Orth helped organize the Republican Party there. In 1862, he won election to the federal House of Representatives, serving from 1863 to 1871, 1873 to 1875, and from 1879 until his death. During these years he endorsed the Thirteenth, Fourteenth, and Fifteenth amendments to the Constitution, supported strong Reconstruction measures, favored President Andrew Johnson's impeachment, helped James G. Blaine become speaker of the House, advocated annexation of Santo Domingo, and helped reorganize the diplomatic and consular system. Orth also was a spokesman for tariff protectionism, pensions for veterans, and a sound monetary system. President Ulysses S. Grant appointed him envoy extraordinary and minister plenipotentiary to Austria-Hungary, where he remained from 1875 to 1876. Shortly after Orth received his party's gubernatorial nomination in 1876, rumors spread of his connection with swindlers who had speculated in Venezuelan bonds and claims. Orth's steadfast reticence on the subject aroused the suspicions of a hostile Democratic press and reformist Indiana Republicans. He ultimately withdrew from the contest because of public pressure. A House investigatory committee later concluded that Orth had no criminal involvement. Orth died in Lafayette.

Further Reading: O. B. Carmichael, "The Campaign of 1876 in Indiana," *Indiana Magazine of History* 9 (1913): 276–297; *Indianapolis Sentinel*, 17 December 1882; Godlove S. Orth Papers, Indiana Historical Society Library, Indianapolis.

Leonard Schlup

O'SULLIVAN, MARY KENNEY (8 January 1864–18 January 1943), labor organizer. Born in Hannibal, Missouri, the daughter of Irish immigrants, Kenney attended local schools until age fourteen. Then her father died, and she became the sole support of her invalid mother, going to work in a local bookbindery. She and her mother moved to Chicago in the late 1880s. There, in response to the low wages and long hours faced by women in the trade, Kenney formed Women's Bindery Workers Union No. 1 in 1890. She became an active resident of Chicago's famed settlement, Hull-House, and went on to organize wage-earning women working in the garment trade. In 1892 the American Federation of Labor appointed Kenney its first woman organizer, a position she held for six months. Despite the many objections to trade unions, especially for women, she organized women collar makers in New York and shoe workers and garment makers in Massachusetts. After her marriage in 1894, she moved to Boston and continued her trade union work there, organizing women silk weavers and garment makers. She was a founder of the National Women's Trade Union League in 1903 and was appointed as an industrial safety investigator for the newly created Massachusetts State Board of Labor and Industries in 1914. O'Sullivan retired in 1934 and died in West Medford, Massachusetts.

Further Reading: Kathleen Banks Nutter, *The Necessity of Organization: Mary Kenney O'Sullivan and Trade Unionism for Women, 1892–1912*, 2000; Mary Kenney O'Sullivan Papers, Schlesinger Library, Radcliffe College.

Kathleen Banks Nutter

OTERO, GABRIELLA MARTÍNEZ (1850–4 September 1905), nun. Otero was born in what is now Tucson, Arizona. She was twenty when the Sisters of St. Joseph of Carondelet arrived to set up schools and a convent for females. Otero became well acquainted with them and their charitable work. More nuns came, and schools, orphanages, and hospitals were built in the Arizona Territory. On 15 August 1877, Otero was one of four young Hispanic women who entered the newly formed novitiate. She and the other young women assisted in teaching children from nearby ranches. Otero taught Spanish, drawing and painting, and the piano, harp, guitar, and violin. On weekends she joined other teaching sisters to relieve the nursing sisters at St. Mary's Hospital. In 1880, she took final and perpetual vows, choosing the religious name of Sister Clara of the Blessed Sacrament. Quietly going about her duties, she was considered a very gentle and holy person. She died in Tucson.

Further Reading: Arizona Historical Society Museum, *Arizona Women's Hall of Fame*, 1988; *Tucson Citizen*, 23 May 1920.

Santos C. Vega

OTIS, HARRISON GRAY (10 February 1837–30 July 1917), editor and publisher. Born in Washington County, Ohio, Otis fought in the Union Army, then held various jobs in the postwar period. In 1880, he moved to Los Angeles, California, where he commenced a long career as editor and publisher of the *Los Angeles Times*. He successfully battled for construction of a federally funded deep-water harbor at San Pedro, opposing the attempt by Collis P. Huntington, president of the Southern Pacific railroad in the 1890s, to locate the harbor at Santa Monica. Otis served in the Philippines during the Spanish-American War and the Filipino insurrection from 1898 to 1899. In 1903 he joined Edward H. Harriman, a railroad entrepreneur, and Henry E. Huntington of the Pacific Electric Company in forming a real estate syndicate known as the Los Angeles Suburban

Homes Company. Otis died in Hollywood, California.

Further Reading: *San Francisco Chronicle*, 31 July 1917; *Los Angeles Times*, 31 July 1917; Richard C. Miller, "Otis and His Times," Ph.D. diss., University of California at Berkeley, 1961.

Leonard Schlup

OWENS, COMMODORE PERRY (29 July 1852–10 May 1919), western lawman, adventurer. Owens was born on a farm in eastern Tennessee. After hunting buffalo in Texas in the early 1870s, Owens became sheriff of Holbrook, Territory of Arizona. Holbrook was a wild and woolly town, and nearby the Graham-Tewksbury feud, a classic cattlemen-sheepmen's war, raged. In 1886, the notorious Hash Knife outfit from Texas moved herds of wild cattle into Holbrook. Rustling, horse theft, and drunkenness abounded. Among the cowboys were members of the notorious Blevins gang, including Andy Cooper, Mose Roberts, Sam Houston Blevins, and John Blevins. Cooper was wanted for murder. On 4 September, the four men were gathered at the Blevinses' house in Holbrook. Owens, newly elected sheriff and sporting blond shoulder-length hair, goat hide chaps, and a wide-brimmed sombrero, appeared with a warrant for Cooper's arrest. Rifle in hand, he approached the house. In the shootout that followed, Cooper, Roberts, and Sam Houston Blevins were killed. John Blevins was wounded. Owens remained unscathed. The shooting of fourteen-year-old Sam Houston Blevins haunted Owens, even though the boy had approached him with a pistol. Hailed at first as a hero, he saw the town eventually turn against him. Embittered, Owens became a wanderer, turning to different pursuits, including saloon keeper. He died in northern Arizona and is buried in Flagstaff.

Further Reading: Larry D. Ball, *Desert Lawmen: The High Sheriffs of New Mexico and Arizona, 1846–1912*, 1992.

Jack Burrows

PABST, FREDERICK (28 March 1836–1 January 1904), brewer, was born in Germany and emigrated to the United States at age eleven. As a teenager, he worked in hotels and restaurants in Chicago, then was a crew member and ship captain on steamers on the Great Lakes. In 1862 he married Maria Best, daughter of Phillip Best, owner of a large Milwaukee brewing firm. In 1864 he entered a partnership with his father-in-law, and in 1866, upon Best's retirement, Pabst and another Best son-in-law took over the brewery's management. In 1873 Pabst became president of the company, whose name was changed to Pabst Brewing Company in 1889. Pabst was a leader in turning brewing into a major industry, applying scientific and technological innovations. The company pioneered many modern techniques of advertising and marketing, in order to broaden distribution for a national market. In 1875, it became one of the first to bottle beer for consumers. By 1893 the Pabst Brewing Company was the largest producer of beer in the nation, selling over a million barrels annually. (It was surpassed by its archrival in Milwaukee, the Schlitz Brewing Company, in 1902.) Pabst had great influence on the Milwaukee economy; the brewing company was the city's largest property owner at the turn of the century. Pabst died in Milwaukee.

Further Reading: Thomas C. Cochran, *The Pabst Brewing Company*, 1948; Bayrd Still, *Milwaukee: The History of a City*, 1948; Stanley W. Baron, *Brewed in America: A History of Beer and Ale in the United States*, 1962.

James M. Bergquist

PACHECO, ROMUALDO (31 October 1831–23 January 1899), governor, congressman, and diplomat. Born José Antonio Romualdo Pacheco in Santa Barbara, California, Pacheco attended an English school in Hawaii and later learned navigation on one of his stepfather's ships. After California's admission to the Union in 1850, he turned his attention to politics and government, holding local judicial positions and a state senatorial seat. Originally a Democrat, he switched political affiliation due to his abhorrence of slavery and his loyalty to the Union. Elected lieutenant governor in 1871, Pacheco became governor when Newton Booth left for the U.S. Senate. In office from 27 February to 9 December 1875, Pacheco, California's first native chief executive, pardoned sixty prisoners. He recommended a statewide policy on irrigation, advocated increased expenditures for public schools, supported the development of the Yosemite Valley, and sought to build a harmonious society among California's heterogeneous residents. He also encouraged fair wages for honest labor. Although he sought the gubernatorial nomination in 1875, intraparty divisions caused him to withdraw. He served in the U.S. House of Representatives from 1879 to 1883, chairing the Committee on Private Land Claims in the Forty-seventh Congress. In 1890 President Benjamin Harrison summoned Pacheco to serve as envoy extraordinary and minister plenipotentiary to several Central American republics. After his return in 1893, he lived quietly in retirement. He died in Oakland, California.

Further Reading: Peter Thomas Conmy, *Romualdo Pacheco, 1831–1899: Distinguished Californian of the Mexican and American Periods*, 1957; Ronald Genini and Richard Hitchman, *Romualdo Pacheco: A Californio in Two Eras*, 1985; R. Hal Williams, *The Democratic Party and California Politics, 1880–1896*, 1973.

Leonard Schlup

PACKARD, JAMES WARD (5 November 1863–20 March 1928), automobile manufacturer. Born in Warren, Ohio, Packard graduated in 1884 from Lehigh University in Pennsylvania with a degree in mechanical engineering. He found employment with the Sawyer-Mann Electric Company of New York City and quickly obtained patents, including one for the Packard lamp in 1889. The next year, with his brother, he incorporated the Packard Electric Company in Warren and subsequently became general superintendent of the New York and

Ohio Company, which manufactured incandescent lamps and transformers. From this foundation the Packard Motor Car Company grew in the late 1890s. It produced forty-nine automobiles in 1900, demonstrating several of them at the first National Automobile Show in New York City that November. The cars quickly gained a reputation for quality, and in 1903 the Packards transferred production from Warren to a new facility in Detroit, Michigan. Packard died in Cleveland, Ohio.

Further Reading: *New York Times*, 21 March 1928; Beverly Rae Kimes, ed., *Packard: A History of the Motor Car and the Company*, 1978.

Leonard Schlup

PAGE, WALTER HINES (15 August 1855– 21 December 1918), journalist and diplomat. Born in Cary, North Carolina, Page studied at Randolph-Macon College and did graduate work at Johns Hopkins University. In 1880 he went to work for the *St. Joseph Gazette* in Missouri. The following year, he set out on an investigative tour of the South. Major newspapers in New York, Chicago, and Boston published his findings, which brought him a position with the *New York World* from 1881 to 1883. He then returned to North Carolina as editor of the Raleigh *State Chronicle*. During his two-year stint in Raleigh, Page stressed the New South themes that he would trumpet the rest of his journalistic career: improvements in southern education and agriculture, industrial development, and sectional reconciliation. He also reviled the southern obsession with the Lost Cause and cursed the malignant legacy of slavery. His passion was to bring the backward South into the national mainstream of progress. In 1885 Page returned to New York, where he became a freelance writer, publishing articles in newspapers and magazines such as *Atlantic Monthly, Harper's, The Century,* and *The Independent*. Two years later he went to work for *The Forum*. As its editor from 1891 to 1895, Page gained a reputation for editorial excellence that took him to the prestigious *Atlantic Monthly* in 1895. In 1899 he became a partner in the publishing house of Doubleday, Page, and Company, and the next year he founded *The World's Work*, which he edited for thirteen years.

Ever conflicted by his dual identity as southerner and American, Page served as an influential interregional ambassador, constantly explaining the North and the South to one another. In the turbulent 1890s he opposed Populism and supported imperialism, but gradually became a reformer in the early 1900s. On the race issue, Page believed that blacks had a flawed ancestry and were not ready for suffrage, but he also condemned extreme southern white supremacists, denounced lynching, and called for improved, if separate and industrial, education for blacks. In 1913 Page's friend President Woodrow Wilson named him ambassador to Great Britain, where he served until 1918. An engaging writer, Page produced hundreds of articles and reviews, three books, and volumes of letters. His published letters were a journalistic sensation in the 1920s. He died at Pinehurst, North Carolina.

Further Reading: John Milton Cooper, Jr., *Walter Hines Page: The Southerner as American, 1855–1918*, 1977; Burton J. Hendricks, *The Training of an American: The Earlier Life and Letters of Water Hines Page*, 1928; Walter Hines Page Papers, Duke University, and Houghton Library, Harvard University.

David W. Southern

PAGO PAGO NAVAL STATION. With the establishment in 1869 of an American steamship line between San Francisco and Australia, the port of Pago Pago in the Samoan Islands became a desirable location for a coaling station. The administration of President Ulysses S. Grant showed interest in the port, and in 1878 secured a treaty giving the United States the right to establish a station and a naval base. However, Great Britain and Germany signed their own agreements with the Samoans that same year, and Pago Pago quickly became the center of a three-nation dispute. In 1889, they agreed to jointly supervise a nominally independent Samoa, but fighting among the natives on the islands effectively nullified the agreement and prevented development of Pago Pago. Finally, under the 1899 Berlin General Act, Germany and Britain renounced in favor of the United States all Samoan land east of 171°

west longitude. This area included Pago Pago, the present-day capital of American Samoa.

Further Reading: George H. Ryden, *The Foreign Policy of the United States in Relation to Samoa*, 1933; Richard P. Gilson, *Samoa, 1830–1900: The Politics of a Multi-Cultural Community*, 1970; Charles S. Campbell, *The Transformation of American Foreign Relations, 1865–1900*, 1976.

Ed Bradley

PAINE, CHARLES JACKSON (26 August 1833–12 August 1916), businessman and yachtsman. Born in Boston, Massachusetts, Paine graduated from Harvard College in 1853, gained admittance to the bar three years later, and fought in the Civil War. During the postwar era, he was prominent in the management of the Atchison, Topeka and Santa Fe and the Chicago, Burlington and Quincy railroads. Best known as a yachtsman, Paine built or purchased several America's Cup winners. With his sportsmanship, fairness, monetary investments, and influence on yacht design, Paine, typically clad in plain clothes and a straw hat, won international attention in business affairs and yachting. Committed to a sound currency, he supported William McKinley for the presidency in 1896. The next year President McKinley selected Paine, along with Senator Edward O. Wolcott of Colorado and former Vice President Adlai E. Stevenson, to serve on a bimetallic monetary commission charged with sounding out European leaders on a possible international agreement on bimetallism. The commission members failed in their endeavor. Three years later Congress passed the Gold Standard Act. Paine died in Weston, Massachusetts.

Further Reading: Leonard Schlup, "Charles J. Paine and the Bimetallic Monetary Commission of 1897," *Tamkang Journal of American Studies* 9 (1993): 1–18; *Boston Transcript*, 14 August 1916; *New York Times*, 15 August 1916.

Leonard Schlup

PALMER, ALICE ELVIRA FREEMAN (21 February 1855–6 December 1902), educator. Born in Colesville, New York, Freeman attended Windsor Academy and graduated in 1876 from the University of Michigan. In 1879, she accepted the chairmanship of the history department at Wellesley College, and was president of Wellesley College from 1881 to 1888.

Functioning as her own dean and secretary, Freeman established an administrative structure for the institution, raised standards of admission, and fostered the student Christian Association. She also encouraged educated women to associate collectively, and in 1882 helped form the Association of Collegiate Alumnae, later renamed the American Association of University Women. Pioneering work marked Freeman's tenure at Wellesley.

In 1887, Freeman married George Herbert Palmer (1842–1933), professor of philosophy at Harvard College. Her marriage irritated both feminists and antifeminists. Although she had abandoned a career in higher education to reside with her husband, Palmer relished her new role. In 1889 she accepted a position on the Massachusetts State Board of Education. From 1892 to 1895, she spent twelve weeks a year as dean of women at the University of Chicago. Never a proponent of universal college education, Palmer held firmly to her orthodox Presbyterianism. She supported woman's suffrage but did not lobby for the cause, assisted in organizing the Woman's Building at the Chicago World's Fair of 1893, and traveled to Europe. She enjoyed ornithology and photography while carefully setting limitations on her activities due to fragile health. Palmer died in Paris. Her life was a bridge between those who favored new roles for women and those who held to traditional expectations.

Further Reading: George H. Palmer, *The Life of Alice Freeman Palmer*, 1908; Alice F. Palmer Papers, Wellesley College Library, Wellesley, Massachusetts.

Leonard Schlup

PALMER, BERTHA HONORÉ (22 May 1849–5 May 1918), civic advocate, social leader, and reformer. Born in Louisville, Kentucky, Palmer grew up in Chicago. An 1867 graduate of the Visitation Convent School in Georgetown, D.C., she married Potter Palmer, a wealthy Quaker known as the "first merchant prince of Chicago," in 1870. After losing most of their buildings in the Chicago fire of 1871, they rebuilt. Prominent in Chicago society, Palmer, identified with the city's "upward movement," endeavored to bring artistic and cultural refinements to the city. Dedicated to reform, unions, and philanthropy, she joined the Chicago Woman's Club, frequently visited Hull-House, and disliked the militancy in the woman suffrage crusade. In 1893 she chaired the Board of Lady Managers of the World's Columbian Exposition and developed plans for a Woman's Building at the fair. The artist Mary Cassatt painted murals for the edifice. Other women helped in designing the interior, which included the first gas range. Palmer traveled and presented her views on numerous international and national issues, such as local government corruption. A Democrat, she accepted President William McKinley's appointment as the sole female on the American board of commissioners to the 1900 Paris Exposition. In 1910 she moved to Osprey, Florida, where she died.

Further Reading: Ishbel Ross, *Silhouette in Diamonds: The Life of Mrs. Potter Palmer*, 1960; Donald L. Miller, *City of the Century: The Epic of Chicago and the Making of America*, 1996; Bertha H. Palmer Papers, Chicago Historical Society.

Leonard Schlup

PALMER, DANIEL DAVID (7 March 1845–20 October 1913), founder of chiropractic. Born near Toronto, Ontario, Canada, Palmer later relocated to Iowa. He became interested in medicine, philosophy, science, health, healing, and therapy, developing a concept that disease is caused by interference with nerve functions and that manipulation of body joints can restore them to normal. Living in Davenport, Iowa, afforded Palmer proximity to Kirksville, Missouri, a center for osteopathy. In his office in the Ryan Building, Palmer performed his first spinal adjustment on a patient, Harvey Lillard, on 18 September 1895. Another patient, Samuel H. Weed, a clergyman and scholar of Greek history, called the practice "chiropractic." Palmer's first two students graduated in 1898; the school later was renamed the Palmer Institute and Chiropractic Infirmary, and after 1902 he left its direction to his son, B. J. Palmer, a recent graduate. The elder Palmer journeyed to Oregon and California, where he taught classes; upon his return to Davenport, he was convicted of practicing medicine without a license, for which he spent nearly a month in jail. Following a bitter feud with his son, and their subsequent reconciliation, Palmer moved to the west coast, wrote, lectured, and traveled. His death in Los Angeles ended the enigmatic and controversial career of the first chiropractor, on whom some Gilded Age contemporaries derisively pinned the term "quack."

Further Reading: *Los Angeles Times*, 21 October 1913; Verne Gielow, *Old Dad Chiro: A Biography of D. D. Palmer*, 1981; Dennis Peterson and Glenda Wiese, *Chiropractic: An Illustrated History*, 1995; Palmer Papers, Daniel David Palmer Health Sciences Library, Davenport, Iowa.

Leonard Schlup

PALMER, JOHN MCAULEY (13 September 1817–25 September 1900), governor and senator. Born in Scott County, Kentucky, Palmer grew up in Illinois. He was elected state senator in 1851, and helped form the Illinois Republican Party. He rose to major general in the Union Army during the Civil War. As a friend of Abraham Lincoln, Palmer received that high rank despite his lack of military experience. In February 1865 he became commander of the Department of Kentucky. Palmer's encouragement of emancipation brought him into deep conflict with the Kentuckians. He resigned from the army in April 1866 and was indicted by the Kentucky courts in November 1866 for aiding the escape of slaves. The indictment was later voided. Palmer reentered politics after the war, serving as the Republican governor of Illinois from 1869 to 1873. He became disenchanted with the Republican Party and joined the Liberal Republicans in 1872, and eventually the Democrats. Palmer was defeated as a Democratic candidate for governor in 1888 but won election to the Senate in 1891. A conservative, he was the presidential candidate of the Gold Democrats in the 1896 election. He died in Springfield, Illinois.

Further Reading: George Thomas Palmer, *A Conscientious Turncoat: The Story of John M. Palmer, 1817–1900*, 1941.

Damon Eubank

PAN-AMERICAN CONFERENCE OF 1889. At Secretary of State James G. Blaine's invitation, delegations from eighteen Latin American countries traveled to the United States for the Pan-American Conference of 1889. After touring over forty cities, the delegates assembled in Washington to consider matters of substance. Blaine offered, and the Latin delegations promptly rejected, proposals for compulsory arbitration of disputes and lower tariffs. The representatives clearly believed the U.S. initiatives were a thinly veiled attempt to dominate the hemisphere economically. The delegations did manage to approve a series of individual reciprocity treaties to expand trade, improve communication, and better transportation, but the Republican-controlled Senate rejected the treaties in favor of protectionist policies.

Blaine's call for cooperation reflected an established desire for hemispheric accord, and the failure of the 1889 conference did not kill that impulse. Instead, subsequent efforts organized the International Bureau of American Republics (renamed the Pan-American Union in 1910). The conference, Bureau, and Union set a precedent for other inter-American conferences and for the establishment of the Organization of American States in 1948.

Further Reading: Arthur P. Whitaker, *The Western Hemisphere Idea: Its Rise and Decline*, 1954; Clifford Clasey, "The Creation and Development of the Pan American Union," *Hispanic American Historical Review* 13, no. 4 (1933): 437–456.

John D. Coats

PAN-AMERICAN EXPOSITION AT BUFFALO (1901).

The Philadelphia Centennial Exposition, the World's Columbian Exposition (1893), and the Cotton States and International Exposition (1895) inspired Buffalo, New York's, business elite to organize a similar extravaganza to promote their city. The sponsors particularly wished to encourage Latin American trade and to demonstrate the hydroelectric power available from Niagara Falls. The fair ran from May to November, and its theme was "progress of the New World during the 19th century." Highlights included a 375-foot electric tower and Thomas A. Edison's new wireless telegraph. Buildings on the midway were devoted to ethnography, agriculture, electricity, and other subjects selected to demonstrate, in the words of the exposition committee, "America's rise to the apex of civilization." Although promoters received funds from both federal and state governments, rainy weather and poor press reviews reduced crowds. Other nations of the hemisphere also participated.

Financial prospects improved as attendance swelled in the summer. A great crowd was anticipated for President's Day, 5 September, when President William McKinley promised a public address to endorse trade reciprocity with Latin America. On the second day of his visit, while shaking hands in the Temple of Music, he was mortally wounded by two pistol shots fired by Leon Czolgosz. As McKinley's condition worsened, the fair closed. Following the president's death on Saturday, 14 September, the gates reopened until the close on 2 November. More than eight million people visited the exposition, but it suffered a deficit of $3 million, and the subscribers to its stock lost money. Nor did the fair do for Buffalo what its promoters had hoped. Its impact on improved relations with Latin America was negligible. Tragically, its most lasting historical association was with McKinley's murder and the accession of Theodore Roosevelt, a dynamic young leader facing a challenging new century.

Further Reading: Lewis L. Gould, "Buffalo, 1901: Pan-American Exposition," in John E. Findling, ed., *Historical Dictionary of World's Fairs and Expositions*, 1990.

James Summerville

PANIC OF 1873.

The September Panic, most spectacularly the collapse of Jay Cooke and Company, which had been financing construction of the Northern Pacific Railroad, touched off the first cyclical depression (1873–1879) during the long-wave deflation of the 1870s–1890s. It may very well have been the case that the tightening of credit which occurred as business expanded had made railroads (heavy borrowers) and their financiers vulnerable. Dangerous financial practices (the employment of short-term capital for long-term purposes) and weaknesses in the banking system (the absence of a central bank; the pyramiding of reserves in New York City institutions; and tightness in the money supply, especially during harvest periods) also contributed. Although financiers moved quickly to calm financial markets, business cutbacks triggered by the panic led to a depression unusual for its long duration and limited declines in production.

The hard times affected politics in various ways. The money question, which had emerged during the Civil War, was addressed under changed circumstances by administrations and congresses. (The Coinage Act of 1873, demonetizing silver, had already become law.) In 1874, Congress enacted an "inflation bill," which was nullified by the veto of President Ulysses Grant, and a free-banking measure. One year later, the Resumption Act pledged to resume specie payments in 1879 but also contained provisions to mollify supporters of free banking and greenbacks. Then in 1878, Congress passed, over President Rutherford B. Hayes's veto, the Bland-Allison Act, providing for limited coinage of silver. The period also witnessed the emergence of the Antimonopoly, Greenback, and Greenback Labor political parties. Finally, the depression contributed to the Democrats' recapture of the House of Representatives in the midterm elections of 1874, though their failure to win the Senate and (two years later) the presidency resulted in divided government rather than Democratic dominance.

In a larger sense, the depression of 1873 accelerated the weakening of ideas of class harmony and the hardening of class lines in a nation undergoing profound economic and social changes. Widespread unemployment led workers to rally for public works and relief, spending rejected by "reform" city governments. Sometimes their demonstrations were suppressed by police (as in New York City). Many of the unemployed took to the road as tramps, triggering the enactment of laws to rid localities of vagrants. Labor-management conflict intensified in industries and coalfields and on railroads, climaxed by the Great Strike of 1877, which involved disorder, bloodshed, and destruction of property, as well as the employment of citizens' groups, state militias, and federal troops to restore order and subdue the discontented.

Further Reading: Rendigs Fels, *American Business Cycles, 1865–1897,* 1959; Walter T. K. Nugent, *Money and American Society, 1865–1880,* 1968; Eric Foner, *Reconstruction: America's Unfinished Revolution, 1863–1877,* 1988.

Samuel T. McSeveney

PANIC OF 1893. This panic set off the final cyclical depression (1893–1897) during the long-wave deflation of the late nineteenth century, marked by social unrest and political conflict. The economy sank during 1893–1894 (with major business failures during February and May 1893 creating panic conditions), partially recovered in 1894–1895, and again contracted during 1896, before resuming sustained growth during 1897. President Grover Cleveland, a Democrat, blamed deteriorating economic conditions and declining Treasury gold reserves on the Sherman Silver Purchase Act of 1890, and in 1893 insisted on terminating monthly purchases of silver. He secured repeal but alienated inflationist southern and western congressmen. Subsequent concerns over gold reserves led the administration, which could not gain congressional cooperation, to sell bonds for gold (1893, 1894, 1895, 1896). The third sale, negotiated with J. P. Morgan, intensified criticism of the president. Cleveland also sought to reduce the McKinley Tariff's protective rates. Although the Senate weakened the House reform measure, any tinkering with the tariff during hard times was politically dangerous. The Wilson-Gorman Tariff (1894) provided for a federal income tax, but this provision, supported primarily by southerners and westerners, was declared unconstitutional by the Supreme Court one year later.

The depression led to efforts to address the plight of the unemployed and of workers. A number of unemployed "armies" descended on Washington, D.C., demanding public works and monetary inflation. Some municipalities sought to assist the unemployed in various limited ways. Labor-management strife erupted in 1894, in the bituminous coalfields, on the Great Northern Railroad, and at the Pullman Palace Car Company near Chicago. In the latter struggle, railroad management, rival labor unions, and the federal government defeated Eugene V. Debs and the American Railway Union.

Republicans capitalized on discontent to score sweeping gains in the midterm elections of 1894. Two years later, southern and western Democrats repudiated their party's northeastern leadership to nominate William Jennings Bryan, running on a free silver platform, for president. The People's (Populist) Party endorsed Bryan, as did Silver Republicans, while Gold Democrats supported the National Democratic Party or the Republican nominee, William McKinley. The Republicans completed their capture of the national government, which they would dominate for years, and led the nation into an era of prosperity, during which they firmly established gold as the monetary standard.

Further Reading: Rendigs Fels, *American Business Cycles, 1865–1897*, 1959; Milton Friedman and Anna Jacobson Schwartz, *A Monetary History of the United States, 1867–1960*, 1963; Gretchen Ritter, *Goldbugs and Greenbacks: The Antimonopoly Tradition and the Politics of Finance in America: 1865–1896*, 1997.

Samuel T. McSeveney

PARKER, ALTON BROOKS (14 May 1852–10 May 1926), judge and presidential nominee. Born in Cortland, New York, Parker graduated from the Albany Law School in 1873, practiced in Kingston, New York, and successfully managed the gubernatorial campaign of David B. Hill and the entire Democratic state ticket in 1888. Parker secured various judicial appointments for the next seven years. In 1897 he was elected chief justice of the Court of Appeals by a landside. Choosing the bench over other offices, Parker, a conservative who supported the gold standard, offered liberal opinions in labor cases, avoided intraparty factionalism, endorsed the presidential candidacies of William Jennings Bryan in 1896 and 1900, and emerged as the Democratic nominee for president in 1904. He lost badly to President Theodore Roosevelt. Parker subsequently practiced law in New York City, where he died.

Further Reading: Leonard Schlup, "Alton B. Parker and the Presidential Campaign of 1904," *North Dakota Quarterly* 49 (1981): 48–60; *New York Times*, 11 May 1926; *New York Tribune*, 11 May 1926.

Leonard Schlup

PARKER, ELY SAMUEL (HASANOANDA) (1828–30 August 1895), U.S. commissioner of Indian affairs. Born into the Wolf Clan on the Tonawanda Reservation near Indian Falls, New York, the son of a Seneca chief, Parker took the name "Ely" after a Baptist teacher in the area, and attended the Baptist Mission School and the Yates and Cayuga academies. Afterward he read law, worked as an interpreter, was a tribal representative for meetings with federal officials, studied civil engineering, and supervised public works projects in Galena, Illinois. There he met Ulysses S. Grant. Commissioned a captain—he later attained the rank of brigadier general in the Union Army—Parker served as Grant's military secretary, in which capacity he witnessed General Robert E. Lee's capitulation at Appomattox Court House, Virginia, in 1865. Parker recorded the terms of surrender, wrote the official documents, and distributed copies.

In 1869 President Grant selected Parker, by now his close friend, to head the Office of Indian Affairs, where he remained until 1 August 1871. Parker was the first Native American to hold that federal position. His ideas were associated with the administration's peace plan, which sought to assimilate and educate the Natives. Parker contended that the government had to deliver on its promises. Because treaties had been violated or had failed to achieve goals, he advocated the termination of the treaty system. In an era when Native Americans could not become U.S. citizens and were rarely seen in the professions, Parker was an extraordinary figure, a warrior in two worlds who used his talents and intellect to overcome racism and bigotry in order to serve his people and his country. In 1876 he accepted an assignment with the New York City Board of Commissioners. Parker died in Fairfield, Connecticut. On 18 December 2000, Kevin Gover, assistant secretary of the Bureau of Indian Affairs in the Department of the Interior, formally opened the Ely S. Parker Building, the Bureau of Indian Affairs's new facility in Reston, Virginia, with the unveiling of a plaque honoring Parker's contributions.

Further Reading: William H. Armstrong, *Warrior in Two Camps: Ely S. Parker, Union General and Seneca Chief*, 1978; Ely S. Parker Papers, American Philosophical Society Library, Philadelphia, Pennsylvania.

Leonard Schlup

PARKER, QUANAH (ca. 1852–23 February 1911), Comanche Indian chief. In his early life, this son of Cynthia Ann Parker, a white captive, and Peta Nocona, a Quahada Comanche chief, herded buffalo, raided Texas settlements, and warred with the Utes and other tribes. By 1875, however, Parker supported the Comanches' surrender to U.S. officials at Fort Sill. He cooperated with agents, superintendents, and Washington officials, and the commissioner of Indian affairs named him principal chief in 1899. A progressive who wanted the Comanches to farm and learn European ways, Parker supported private allotment of reservation land and often discussed the government's Indian policies with officials in Washington. He also helped negotiate the Jerome Agreement (1892) and served as a judge on the Court of Indian Offenses, a position he lost because of his polygamy. Parker, who had a town site and railroad terminus named for him, rode in Theodore Roosevelt's inaugural parade, attended the inauguration of Oklahoma's first state governor, and was the featured attraction at state fairs, stock shows, and parades. Native Americans and whites, including a British ambassador, visited his ranch near Cache, Oklahoma, and hundreds attended his funeral at Post Oak Mission in Oklahoma.

Further Reading: William T. Hagan, *Quanah Parker, Comanche Chief*, 1993, and *United States-Comanche Relations*, 1990; *Daily Oklahoman*, 25 February 1911.

Jane F. Lancaster

PARKHURST, CHARLES HENRY (17 April 1842–8 September 1933), clergyman and civic reformer. Born in Framingham, Massachusetts, Parkhurst graduated from Amherst College in 1866. He studied philosophy and theology at Halle and Leipzig in Germany. His aptitude for the ministry became apparent when he was pastor of the Congregational church at Lenox, Massachusetts, where he served for five years (1874–1879). In 1880 Parkhurst was appointed pastor of the Madison Square Presbyterian Church in New York City, a post he held until 1918. Mindful of an urban congregation composed mostly of young men, Parkhurst in 1892 assailed police protection of vice and crime under Tammany Hall. He pounded municipal corruption throughout 1893, supported by many civic organizations and newspapers. In January 1894, a Republican-controlled state

legislature appointed a committee chaired by Senator Clarence E. Lexow to inquire into Parkhurst's charges. Meanwhile, in the mayoral election of 1894, Parkhurst was the foremost campaigner for the Republican and fusion ticket. William L. Strong's victory by 45,187 votes over Hugh J. Grant, the Democratic nominee, was widely seen as a triumph for Parkhurst. His preaching influenced the climate of reform in other American cities. He died in the Atlantic City, New Jersey.

Further Reading: Charles H. Parkhurst, *Our Fight with Tammany*, 1895, and *My Forty Years in New York*, 1923; M. R. Werner, "That Was New York: Dr. Parkhurst's Crusade," *New Yorker* (19 November 1955): 201–222 and (26 November 1955): 99–139.

Bernard Hirschhorn

PARSONS, LEWIS BALDWIN (5 April 1818–17 March 1907), lawyer and political figure. Born in Genesee County, New York, Parsons graduated from Yale in 1840 and from Harvard's law school four years later. After moving to Illinois, he was city attorney for Alton from 1846 to 1849. Subsequently he served as attorney, treasurer, and finally president of the Ohio and Mississippi Railroad between 1854 and 1878. Parsons ran unsuccessfully as the Democratic nominee for lieutenant governor of Illinois in 1880 with former Senator Lyman Trumbull as the gubernatorial standard-bearer. From 1895 to 1898, Parsons was president of the Illinois Soldiers and Sailors Home. He died in Flora, Illinois.

Further Reading: *New York Times*, 18 March 1907; Lewis B. Parsons Papers, Illinois State Historical Library, Springfield.

Leonard Schlup

PARSONS, LUCY ELDINE (1853–7 March 1942), writer, labor activist, and anarchist spokeswoman. Born near Waco, Texas, of African-American, Native American, and Hispanic ancestry, Lucy met Albert Parsons, a former Confederate scout and journalist, in 1870 and reportedly married him the following year. Miscegenation laws forced them to leave Texas in 1873. Ultimately they resided in a poor German-American neighborhood in Chicago, where they witnessed unemployment, workplace exploitation, and growing labor protests. In 1876 the Parsonses began their collaboration with the Workingmen's Party. After her husband affiliated with the Social Democratic Party of North America, Lucy came in contact with the doctrines of Karl Marx. Opposed to the capitalist system, Parsons joined the Chicago Working Women's Union in 1879, supported woman suffrage, sought equal pay for equal work, and concluded that a revolution of workers against owners of capital would end economic woes. She advocated a woman's right to divorce, to practice birth control, and to remain free from rape, describing American women as "slaves of slaves." In 1885–1886 she helped organize seamstresses to agitate for an eight-hour day.

Expressing her opinions in numerous published articles, Parsons contributed pieces to *The Socialist, Labor Defender*, and *The Alarm*, the weekly newspaper of the International Working People's Association. In an 1884 *Alarm* essay, "To Tramps," Parsons urged impoverished individuals contemplating suicide to learn how to detonate explosives, so as to take other people with them. In May 1886, as she and her husband were withdrawing from the commotion at Haymarket Square in Chicago, police arrested and detained them. Released but placed under surveillance and tormented for her racial origins, Parsons dressed in black at her husband's trial, which ended in a guilty verdict. She toured Ohio, Connecticut, and New Jersey to seek sympathy for him, plead for leniency, and urge commutation of his death sentence, while justifying anarchism as a remedy for the country's economic plight. Following her husband's hanging in November 1887, Parsons devoted the next half-century to agitation for the underprivileged. She also helped create the International Labor Defense and the Industrial Workers of the World. She died in Chicago. Parsons was the first African-American woman to play a prominent role in American leftist activities. Viewing racial oppression as mainly a class question, Parsons, whose complexion enabled her to pass for Spanish, contended that socialism would eliminate racism and sexism.

Further Reading: Lucy E. Parsons, *The Life of Albert R. Parsons, with a Brief History of the Labor Movement in America*, 1889; Carolyn Ashbaugh, *Lucy Parsons: Ameri-*

can Revolutionary, 1976; *Chicago Tribune*, 8 and 9 March 1942.

Leonard Schlup

PASCO, SAMUEL (28 June 1834–13 March 1917), senator. Born in London, England, Pasco immigrated as a child to Massachusetts, attended public schools in Charlestown, and graduated from Harvard College in 1858. He moved to Jefferson County, Florida, in 1859 to head an academy, and later served in the Confederate Army. Florida achieved home rule under President Andrew Johnson's Reconstruction plan, and the Democratic regime appointed Pasco clerk of the circuit court in 1866. When Radical Reconstruction began in 1868, the Republicans removed Pasco. He thereafter practiced law and remained an ardent Democrat. From 1872 until 1900 he served at various times on the state and national Democratic committees, and was the state committee chairman in 1876–1877 when the "compromise" ended nineteenth-century Republican rule in Florida. Elected a state representative in 1884, he was the House speaker briefly in 1887, and took a U.S. Senate seat that May. During his two terms, Pasco served on the Military and Claims committees, chairing the latter after 1893. Upon leaving the Senate in 1899, he held a seat on the Isthmian Canal Commission until 1904. Pasco died at Tampa, Florida.

Further Reading: James J. Horgan, *Samuel Pasco of Pasco County*, 1987; *New York Times*, 14 March 1917.

Hutch Johnson

PATTISON, ROBERT EMORY (8 December 1850–1 August 1904), lawyer, banker, governor. Born in Quantico, Maryland, Pattison moved with his family to Philadelphia during his childhood. He was admitted to the Philadelphia bar in 1872. After being frustrated in early bids for public office, he won election as Philadelphia's controller in 1877 and 1880. Having reformed the office and rescued the city from bankruptcy, he was elected governor in 1882. A Democrat, Pattison was committed to economy and reform; he reduced the state's debt and tried to check the rising power of corporations, especially railroads and canal companies. Constitutionally ineligible to succeed himself, in 1887 he accepted appointment as a member of the U.S. Pacific Railway Commission, authorized by Congress to investigate the methods by which railroads received federal aid. As chair of the commission, Pattison wrote its minority report, which remains a valuable contribution to the financial history of the land-grant railroads. Reelected governor in 1890, Pattison devoted his second term to the reduction of taxation and to municipal reform. He achieved adoption of the secret ballot in 1891, but was unsuccessful in reducing labor-management tensions. When the Homestead strike broke out in 1892, Pattison called in the state militia to restore order. He failed in a bid for governor in 1902. Pattison died in Philadelphia.

Further Reading: *New York Times*, 2 August 1904; *Philadelphia Press*, 2 August 1904; *Philadelphia Public Ledger*, 2 August 1904.

Marie Marmo Mullaney

PEACE JUBILEE BANQUET. On 19 October 1898, some Gilded Age personalities gathered at the Auditorium in Chicago to celebrate the successful conclusion of the Spanish-American War. It was a nonpartisan affair emphasizing national unity, the obliteration of sectional divisions, and emergence of the United States as a world power. Illinois Governor John R. Tanner welcomed the guests. President William McKinley delivered the keynote address, a speech on American foreign policy and the conduct of the brief military conflict. Former Vice President Adlai E. Stevenson used the occasion to outline his views on the presidency and to convey his support of the war. He added that nations, like individuals, were their brothers' keepers. To have remained deaf to the stricken and starving would have brought the dread judgment of history.

Further Reading: Adlai E. Stevenson, *Something of Men I Have Known*, 1909; *Chicago Daily Tribune*, 20 October 1898.

Leonard Schlup

PEACE MOVEMENT. The years immediately following the Civil War saw the ideal of a world without war regain considerable momentum. Between 1865 and 1900, peace efforts were associated with practical aspects of inter-nationalism. A lengthy campaign for the arbitration of international disputes enabled the peace movement to develop a highly organized structure, giving widespread credence to the cause. The antebellum nonresistant tradition resurfaced with the establishment in 1866 of the Universal Peace Union, headed by Alfred Love, a Philadelphia merchant. Under his direction, and largely through its journal, *The Peacemaker*, the union supported reforms to improve society, including temperance and the suffragist crusade. Seeking as much visibility as it could, the union gained the support of nearly two hundred prominent public figures, including former President Ulysses S. Grant as a titular vice president.

While Love's Universal Peace Union continued the nonresistant motif of socially concerned pacifism, the mainstream peace movement acquired a more sophisticated approach—a worldly view reflecting America's increasing role in international affairs. As a result of improved methods of transportation and communication, a more cosmopolitan approach to world peace developed. A small group of lawyers and businessmen attempted to collaborate with sympathetic European peace workers in lobbying governments to establish judicial and arbitral means of settling disputes. The movement was mainly an urban, northeastern endeavor, and its advocates concentrated their efforts on the development of a legal system that would assist the United States in its rise to world power and, simultaneously, insulate it from European political entanglements.

During the Gilded Age, peace advocates received increasing support from business, the legal profession, and government elites for alternatives to war. Business magnates such as Andrew Carnegie, university presidents such as Nicholas M. Butler of Columbia and David Starr Jordan of Stanford, and legal experts including James Brown Scott valued arbitration, Anglo-American cooperation, and mechanistic means for organizing an industrial world of Great Power interdependence. Close to 130 new international nongovernmental organizations—and the appearance of the term "international organization"—were established in the half-century following the Civil War.

Specialized organizations took shape in the 1880s. Among them were the International Arbitration League (1880), and the National Arbitration League (1882), led by Robert McMurdy, an educator. The new peace constituencies in America examined the implications of international arbitration. The peace movement of the Gilded Age argued for the necessity of Great Power cooperation and control of the underdeveloped world. Old-line organizations such as the American Peace Society and Universal Peace Union continued to influence public opinion as in the past. A growing preference for institutional and professional associations, rather than personal and voluntary ones, characterized the practical and cosmopolitan expansion of post-Civil War peace efforts.

Further Reading: Charles Chatfield, *The American Peace Movement: Ideals and Activism*, 1992; Warren F. Keuhl, *Seeking World Order: The United States and International Organization to 1920*, 1969; David S. Patterson, *Toward a Warless World: The Travail of the American Peace Movement, 1887–1914*, 1976.

Charles F. Howlett

PEARY, ROBERT EDWIN (6 May 1856–20 February 1920), explorer. Born in Cresson, Pennsylvania, Peary graduated from Bowdoin College in 1877, worked as a draftsman for the U.S. Coast and Geodetic Survey (1879–1881), and displayed interest in the proposed Nicaraguan canal project. In 1881 he obtained a commission as a civil engineer in the navy, leading survey teams through the jungles of Nicaragua between 1885 and 1888. After a private trip to Greenland in 1886, Peary decided to explore the arctic. He undertook expeditions to Greenland in the 1890s, proving that it was an island. His staff consisted of his wife, Josephine Diebitsch Peary; an African American named Matthew Henson; Peary's future rival, Dr. Frederick Cook; the Norwegian skier Eivind Astrup; and Langdon Gibson, a noted ornithologist. The meteorologist and largest monetary sponsor, John Verhoeff, mysteriously disappeared in 1892. Peary dubbed himself the "Delineator of Greenland," a sobriquet that the Greenland explorer Adolphus W. Greely, chief of the U.S. Army Signal Corps, disputed, demanding that Peary stop using it. Peary led North Pole expeditions from 1898 to 1902,

which gave him expertise on long dogsled journeys over the polar icecap and cost him most of his toes. In 1900 he discovered Cape Morris Jesup, Greenland's northernmost point of land, which he named for a museum benefactor and president of the Peary Arctic Club. Generally credited with the discovery of the North Pole in 1909, Peary died in Washington, D.C.

Further Reading: Thomas D. Davies, *Robert E. Peary at the North Pole*, 1989; John Edward Weems, *Peary: The Explorer and the Man*, 1967; Robert E. Peary Papers, National Archives, Washington, D.C.

Leonard Schlup

PECKHAM, RUFUS WHEELER (8 November 1838–24 October 1909), lawyer and U.S. Supreme Court justice. Born in Albany, New York, Peckham was the scion of a family prominent in the law. After attending private schools and reading law in his father's office, Peckham was admitted to the New York State bar in 1859. Over the next thirty-five years he developed both a substantial corporate practice and an important involvement in state Democratic affairs. In 1883, Peckham was elected to the New York Supreme Court, the state's trial court. Three years later he moved to the state's highest court, the Court of Appeals. President Grover Cleveland, a political associate, nominated Peckham for the Supreme Court on 3 December 1895; Peckham was confirmed on 12 December. Peckham's first prominent opinion, *Allgeyer* v. *Louisiana* (1897), established the "freedom of contract" principle as a significant limitation on state regulation of business. He died near Albany.

Further Reading: Richard Skolnik, "Rufus Peckham," in Leon Friedman, *Justices of the United States Supreme Court*, vol. 3, 1969.

John T. McGuire

PEFFER, WILLIAM ALFRED 10 September 1831–6 October 1912), journalist and senator. Born in Cumberland County, Pennsylvania, Peffer, a Republican, fought in the Union Army during the Civil War and was admitted to the Tennessee bar in 1865. He practiced at Clarksville until 1869, when he moved to Kansas, where he farmed and practiced law. He also took up journalism, successively editing the *Fredonia Journal*, Coffeyville *Journal*, and Topeka's *Kansas Farmer*. He was elected to the Kansas Senate in 1874. Beginning in the late 1880s, Peffer promoted the interests of the Southern Farmers Alliance. He left the GOP for the People's Party in 1890, and Kansas Populists elected him to the U.S. Senate in 1891. In *The Way Out* (1890) and *The Farmer's Side* (1891), Peffer called for monetary reform and argued that only the national government could alleviate farm distress.

As the Populists' first senator, Peffer came to symbolize the new party, and opposition cartoonists produced unflattering portrayals of his long beard and collarless shirts. He was renowned for his earnest, but long-winded and excessively statistical, speeches. He took control of the Populists' state paper, the *Topeka Advocate*, in 1895. Peffer strongly opposed fusion with Democrats, which Kansas Populists adopted in 1892 and 1896. Whereas he advocated the full Populist program as set out in the Omaha Platform of 1892, fusionists increasingly emphasized free silver. In 1897, Kansas Populists replaced Peffer in the U.S Senate with the fusionist William A. Harris, and Peffer sold his interest in the *Topeka Advocate*.

Prohibitionists nominated Peffer for governor in 1898. In a series of articles published in the GOP-oriented *Chicago Tribune* in 1899, he emphasized divisions within the Populist movement, between ex-Democrats and ex-Republicans, over the role of the national government, arguing that they eventually led to dissolution of the Populist Party. Peffer published *Americanism and the Philippines* and campaigned for the GOP national ticket in 1900. He died in Grenola, Kansas.

Further Reading: Peter H. Argersinger, *Politics and Populism: William Alfred Peffer and the People's Party*, 1974; William A. Peffer, *Populism: Its Rise and Fall*, 1992; O. Gene Clanton, *Kansas Populism: Men and Ideas*, 1969.

Worth Robert Miller

PEIRCE, CHARLES SANDERS (10 September 1839–19 April 1914), philosopher, mathematician, logician. A native of Cambridge, Massachusetts, Peirce was employed by the U.S. Coast and Geodetic Survey for thirty years and achieved international recognition as an astronomer. He published a single book (*Photo-*

metric Researches, 1878), but wrote many journal articles on logic and mathematics. He helped found pragmatism, and he was instrumental in the study of signs (which he called semiotics). Peirce was a member of the Metaphysical Club at Harvard during the 1870s; there he discussed philosophy with William James, Francis E. Abbot, and Chauncey Wright. Peirce formulated the name "pragmatism" in his 1878 article "How to Make Our Ideas Clear." His pragmatism was based on the principle that knowledge was fallible and constantly being developed toward a community of belief, and that this persistent inquiry would lead to truth. Truth, then, consisted in the universals held by the community. Peirce was particularly influential in his efforts to establish the hypothesis (which method he called abduction) as a method in the search for truth, because it was a posteriori and scientific rather than a priori and formal. He broke with William James when James began to emphasize individualism over the community in discovering truth. To emphasize their differences, Peirce began to refer to his philosophy as "pragmaticism" rather than pragmatism. In addition to his work in philosophy, he made significant contributions to mathematics, logic, physics, astronomy, and psychology. Peirce possessed one of the most original and significant minds of his generation and was a true polymath. He died in Milford, Pennsylvania.

Further Reading: J. Brent, *Charles Sanders Peirce: A Life*, 1993; Philip P. Weiner, ed., *Values in a Universe of Change: Selected Writings of Charles S. Peirce*, 1958.

C. Edward Balog

PENDLETON ACT (1883), also known as the Civil Service Reform Act of 1883. Shortly after President James A. Garfield's election in 1880, Democratic Senator George H. Pendleton of Ohio began to push for civil service reform. He introduced two bills that were based on earlier, aborted reform efforts. The first called for reform in the civil service appointment system, and the second prohibited political assessments of government employees. Pendleton accepted an alternative bill proposed to him by Dorman B. Eaton, secretary of the New York Civil Service Reform Association, which he then introduced in the Senate in place of his own bill. After numerous amendments, the Senate, and ultimately the House, enacted the measure, creating a three-person bipartisan Civil Service Commission. Its role was to implement competitive examinations for those seeking government positions. In addition, jobs were to be apportioned among the states on a population basis. One of the successful amendments ended the practice of forced contributions to the party in power. At the time of the act's passage, only 10 percent of government posts were covered by the new law, but it gave the president the discretion to place additional positions under the merit system as he wished. As a result, the figure steadily grew during the Gilded Age as presidents sought to protect their appointees.

Many factors contributed to the law's success. Pendleton saw this type of reform as a significant new interpretation of traditional Jacksonianism. While it clearly undermined the spoils system, the reformed system promised to open more offices to the common man rather than to just an elite group of politically powerful or well-connected men. Contributing factors included the continuing partisan struggle for power, the conscientious reform efforts of men like Eaton, and the assassination of President James A. Garfield by a deranged office seeker. Many Republicans and Democrats alike only grudgingly accepted reform in light of the growing public consensus, and Pendleton's own constituency thanked him by replacing him with another Democrat at the end of his first term.

Further Reading: Ari Hoogenboom, *Outlawing the Spoils: A History of the Civil Service Reform Movement, 1865–1883*, 1961; Adelbert B. Sageser, *The First Two Decades of the Pendleton Act: A Study of Civil Service Reform*, 1935; Thomas S. Mach, " 'Gentleman George' Hunt Pendleton: A Study in Political Continuity," Ph.D. diss., University of Akron, 1996.

Thomas S. Mach

PENDLETON, GEORGE HUNT (29 July 1825–24 November 1889), representative, senator and civil service reformer. Born in Cincinnati, Ohio, Pendleton was a leader of the Democratic Party's midwestern faction for much of the nineteenth century. He helped head the extreme Peace Democrats in Congress dur-

ing the Civil War, and along with men such as Clement Vallandigham, gave only limited support to the struggle, believing the Union's restoration was not possible through bloodshed. In the 1864 presidential campaign, Pendleton ran as General George B. McClellan's running mate. Losing both the election and his House seat, he spent almost fifteen years out of public office, but not out of public life. Seeking a return to political prominence and a possible presidential nomination, Pendleton fostered the "Ohio Idea": to pay off the portion of the Civil War debt held in five–twenty bonds with paper currency rather than coin. The plan gained significant support in the Midwest and portions of the South because it was perceived as a Jacksonian attack against a privileged group of wealthy easterners who owned most of the bonds. Though this plan propelled Pendleton to the position of frontrunner in the 1868 Democratic nomination process, eastern Bourbon Democrats thwarted his bid.

In 1879, after a decade as president of the Kentucky Central Railroad and continual party service, Ohio Democrats rewarded Pendleton with a U.S. Senate seat. Serving one term (1879–1885), Pendleton fathered the first major civil service reform legislation, the Pendleton Act of 1883. It created the Civil Service Commission and developed the merit system within the federal bureaucracy. Seemingly against party ideology, Pendleton argued that the patronage system had long since stopped serving the Jacksonian ideals of democracy and opportunity. The law's competitive examinations were designed to prevent government positions from being filled by an elite group of politicos and power brokers, once again opening them to the common man. While the means had changed from Jackson's day, the goal remained the same. Though the bill passed, most Democrats opposed it, and Ohio Democrats expressed their dissatisfaction with Pendleton's interpretation of Jacksonianism by failing to return him to the Senate. After leaving office, Pendleton served as minister to Germany from 1885 until his death in Brussels, Belgium.

Further Reading: G. M. D. Bloss, *Life and Speeches of George Hunt Pendleton*, 1868; Thomas S. Mach, " 'Gentleman George' Hunt Pendleton: A Study in Political Continuity," Ph.D. diss., University of Akron, 1996; *New York Times*, 26 November 1889.

Thomas S. Mach

PENNOYER, SYLVESTER (6 July 1831–30 May 1902), governor, editor, and teacher. Born in Groton, New York, Pennoyer was educated at Home Academy and Harvard Law School. After graduating in 1854, he moved to Portland, Oregon. There he rose to county superintendent of schools by 1860. In 1862, Pennoyer entered the lumber business and developed an interest in politics; by 1868 he was editor of the state's major Democratic newspaper, the *Oregon Herald*. Though soundly defeated in the Portland mayoral race in 1885, Pennoyer drew statewide attention as an outspoken opponent of Chinese labor. He was nominated by the Democrats in the 1886 gubernatorial election, which he won. As governor, he supported antimonopoly legislation, expanded public schools, and advocated the graduated income tax, while opposing repeated attempts to finance Portland's municipal water system with tax-exempt bonds. Backed by the Democratic and Union parties, he won a second term in 1890 and joined the newly formed Populist Party in 1892, becoming a national figure through his vocal support of Coxey's Army, the silver standard, and presidential candidate William Jennings Bryan. Pennoyer was elected to a two-year term as mayor of Portland in 1896, running on the Populist and Democratic tickets, and retired to his nearby ranch when the term expired. He died in Portland.

Further Reading: Harvey W. Scott, *History of the Oregon Country*, 1924; M. C. George, "Political History of Oregon from 1876–1898 Inclusive," *Quarterly of the Oregon Historical Society* 3 (1902): 109–122.

Derek R. Larson

PENROSE, BOIES (1 November 1860–December 31, 1921), Republican Party leader and U.S. senator. Born in Philadelphia, Pennsylvania, Penrose graduated magna cum laude from Harvard University in 1881 with a degree in political economy. After college, he became an attorney. He was coauthor of *The City Government of Philadelphia* (1887). At first, he had an interest in reform, but he soon turned to practical politics and came to know the Republican Party leaders. In 1884, he was elected to the lower house of the state legislature. He served in the state senate from 1887 to 1897. In 1895, Penrose lost a bid for the Republican nomination for mayor of Philadelphia. In 1897, with the support of Republican state party leader, Matthew Quay, Penrose was elected to the U.S. Senate, where he served until his death. He had an interest in tariff issues and was generally opposed to the Progressive reform agenda. He supported the direct primary in Pennsylvania. After Quay's death, Penrose took over the Pennsylvania party organization. He also played a significant role at the Republican National Conventions from 1904 to 1916. Penrose had an interest in outdoor physical activity, especially big game hunting. He was not given to public speaking. He focused on maintaining his large statewide organization and was not involved in many of the national issues of his day. Never married, Penrose died in Washington, D.C.

Further Reading: Walter Davenport, *Power and Glory: The Life of Boise Penrose* 1931.

William G. Binning

PENSION ACT OF 1890. The Fifty-first, or "Billion-Dollar," Congress (1889–1891) was one of the most active in American history. Of the major legislation it enacted, perhaps the least remembered is the Dependent and Disability Pension Act, which became law in June 1890. At the time, however, much attention and praise accompanied its passage, as well as much debate about its generous terms. Though it represented a major victory for the Grand Army of the Republic, the era's premier veterans' organization, the act had less than a glorious past and became law as much or more for political reasons than for any desire that Civil War soldiers and sailors receive just compensation for injuries received in the line of duty.

As early as 1862, Congress had attempted to make provision for individuals who suffered physical disability as a result of military service, as well as for their dependents. Taking advantage of the generous allowances of the Pension Bureau, an increasing number of individuals had their names added to the pension rolls on the basis of at best questionable, and at worst outright fraudulent, claims. The resultant drain on the Treasury was made even greater by the willingness of Congress to enact, for political benefit, thousands of private bills granting pensions to individuals whose claims had been so spurious that even the Pension Bureau had rejected them.

Despite this congressional largesse, many veterans and their relatives wanted even more governmental generosity, and threw their support behind the Republican Party in 1888 with that objective in mind. To their satisfaction, the Republican-controlled Congress passed the Pension Act. By it, virtually every veteran with any kind of physical disability, regardless of its origin, became eligible for a pension, as did anyone who could lay claim to being a veteran's dependent. Consequently, it arguably became a service as opposed to a veteran's benefit. Either way, it quickly solved the vexing problem of the surplus that the Treasury had been running for several years.

Further Reading: Mary P. Dearing, *Veterans in Politics: The Story of the G.A.R.*, 1952; Stuart McConnell, *Glorious Contentment: The Grand Army of the Republic, 1865–1900*, 1992.

James L. Baumgardner

PERIODICALS. The Gilded Age began with what was called a mania for starting magazines and ended with the introduction of the first mass-market periodicals and culture in American history. The annual number of new titles increased four and a half times between 1865 and 1885, from seven hundred at the conclusion of the Civil War to some thirty-three hundred twenty years later. Circulations climbed in the postwar years from antebellum figures of fifty thousand or less. *Ladies Home Journal* claimed an almost exclusively female readership of 270,000; *Youth's Companion* of 385,000; and the mail-order house *People's Literary Companion*, half a million in 1885. The most prestigious periodicals included *Scribner's*, *Harper's*, and *Lippincott's*, produced by their respective publishing houses, and *Atlantic Monthly*, *North American Review*, *Galaxy*, *Nation*, and *Century*. *Harper's Weekly* had the most advertising during the 1870s and 1880s. Leading writers such as Mark Twain were pub-

lished, but Gilded Age magazines were mostly associated with the personality of their editors, opinionated men such as Edwin L. Godkin, George William Curtis, Dr. Josiah G. Holland, Richard Watson Gilder, William Dean Howells, and Allen Thorndike Rice. Most writers were poorly paid and remained obscure; rare exceptions included Bret Harte, Rebecca Harding Davis, and Helen Hunt Jackson.

The prestigious magazines were able to maintain their market positions into the 1890s, but the growth of Sunday newspapers, especially their literary supplements, had a serious impact during the 1880s. The urbanization and suburbanization of late nineteenth-century America created a new professional-managerial class with information needs previously unknown to magazine publishers. The result was a new type of publication, the mass-market magazine, which sought to answer the new challenges of everyday life and sell as many copies as possible. The first of these was *Munsey's*, founded by Frank A. Munsey in 1889. *Munsey's* circulation languished for several years until its price was reduced to a dime per copy in September 1893. Coupled with content directed toward the professional-managerial class, including a feature called "Artists & Their Work" under a photograph of an undraped female in an artistic setting, and a new distribution network based upon speedy transcontinental trains, *Munsey's* circulation climbed from forty thousand before its price change to seven hundred thousand by 1897. Munsey sold 2.1 million magazines—*Munsey's* and three of his other titles—in March 1906.

Munsey's was challenged by *McClure's*, founded by Samuel S. McClure in 1893. The circulation of *McClure's* climbed to over four hundred thousand by 1902, and the magazine was able to command the previously unheard-of price of $400 for a single-page display advertisement. Although it never surpassed *Munsey's* in circulation, *McClure's* had the most advertising of the mass-market magazines, at least once in excess of 200 pages, and a reputation for muckraking that began in 1900. *Cosmopolitan*, which was founded in 1886, was the first magazine to sell for 15 cents per copy. The *Ladies Home Journal*, founded in 1883, achieved a circulation of half a million by the turn of the century and sold for a nickel per issue for a time in the early 1890s. Although several were named after their publishers, the mass-market magazines became best known for their articles and authors. All of them were eclectic in content, with literary, science, fashion, sports, photographic, celebrity, and other departments, feature articles, and ads that introduced readers to brand name goods and services. Each monthly issue provided information on culture, current events, and consumption to its professional-managerial readers and families, creating the first homogeneous mass audience for culture and entertainment. Interestingly, they ignored the lower classes, which had to wait until the advent of motion pictures, radio, and so-called confession magazines for their mass culture. Gilded Age periodicals stigmatized women, their primary readership, and ignored the deteriorating state of race relations in the country. Still, they charted the course for the mass cultures of the twentieth century and initiated the Age of Information.

Further Reading: Richard Ohmann, *Selling Culture: Magazines, Markets, and Class at the Turn of the Century*, 1996; Matthew Schneirov, *The Dream of a New Social Order: Popular Magazines in America, 1893–1914*, 1994; John Tebbel, *The American Magazine: A Compact History*, 1969.

Richard Junger

PERKINS, GEORGE CLEMENT (23 August 1839–26 February 1923), politician and businessman. Born in Kennebunkport, Maine, Perkins received a meager education and took to the sea as a cabin boy at age twelve. He arrived in San Francisco in 1855 and immediately headed for the goldfields, eventually becoming a store clerk at Oroville. Through savings and careful investment, he was able to buy the store three years later, and developed secondary interests in mining, milling, and banking. A Republican, Perkins was elected to the state senate in 1869; there he met Charles Goodall, who became his partner in the Pacific Coast Steamship Company when Perkins left the senate in 1876. Shortly thereafter, the company dominated Pacific coastal trade, and its success helped Perkins win the California gu-

bernatorial race in 1879. During his term, limited to three years by the 1879 California state constitution, Perkins oversaw the state's penal institutions and the expansion of the higher education system. He ran unsuccessfully for the U.S. Senate in 1886, but was appointed to the seat upon Leland Stanford's death in 1893. As a senator, Perkins drew on his seafaring experiences to become an expert on naval and trade issues. He remained in the Senate until 1915, and was active in California civic affairs and fraternal organizations until his death in Oakland.

Further Reading: Hubert Howe Bancroft, *History of California*, vol. 7, 1884; Theodore H. Hittell, *History of California*, 1897.

Derek R. Larson

PETTIGREW, RICHARD FRANKLIN (23 July 1848–5 October 1926), U.S. senator. Born in Ludlow, Vermont, Pettigrew attended Beloit College and studied law at the University of Wisconsin before settling in Dakota Territory in 1870. A lawyer and surveyor active in community affairs, real estate, and railroads, he became a Republican leader in Dakota politics. He was a territorial delegate to Congress (1881–1883), sought to control patronage, and accused Territorial Governor Nehemiah Ordway of corruption. Pettigrew proposed statehood for the southern division of the territory. He won election to the U.S. Senate, where in 1891 he teamed with Charles D. Wolcott of the U.S. Geological Survey to sponsor an amendment permitting the president to issue proclamations setting aside forest reservations. The rise of agrarian unrest and his own business failures led Pettigrew to walk out of the Republican National Convention in 1896, along with Silver Republicans opposing the party's sound money platform. He thereupon joined the Populist Party, affirming his support of free coinage of silver, measures to alleviate high railroad rates, and laws to reduce the influence of special interest groups. During William McKinley's presidency, Pettigrew inveighed against the gold standard, bankers, big business, and the annexation of Hawaii. He became a leader in opposing U.S. control of the Philippine Islands. Pettigrew also accused Republican

Senator Marcus A. Hanna of bribery. Following his defeat for reelection in 1900, Pettigrew practiced law for a decade in New York City. He died in Sioux Falls, South Dakota.

Further Reading: *New York Times*, 6 October 1926; Richard Franklin Pettigrew, *Triumphant Plutocracy: The Story of American Life from 1870 to 1920*, 1921.

Leonard Schlup

PETTUS, EDMUND WINSTON (6 July 1821–27 July 1907), soldier, lawyer, U.S. senator. Born in Limestone County, Alabama, and educated at Clinton College in Tennessee, Pettus practiced law at Gainesville, Alabama, rose to brigadier general in the Confederate Army, and returned to the law after the Civil War. In politics he was a "redeemer" and supported the post-Reconstruction alliance between large landowners and urban businessmen. Between 1876 and 1896 he worked behind the scenes, holding no elective offices but serving as a delegate to Democratic National Conventions. In 1896, veteran U.S. senator James Pugh lost favor with the Bourbon establishment and Pettus emerged as his successor. As a senator, Pettus questioned the constitutionality of the grandfather clause, but supported the state Democratic goal of disfranchising blacks and poor whites. He died in Hot Springs, North Carolina.

Further Reading: Thomas M. Owen, *History of Alabama and Dictionary of Alabama Biography*, 1921; Allen W. Jones, "Political Reform and Party Factionalism in the Deep South: Alabama's 'Dead Shoes' Senatorial Primary of 1906," *Alabama* 26 (1973): 3–32.

Paul M. Pruitt, Jr.

PHARMACY AND DRUGS. After the Civil War, Americans treated their ailments with a variety of therapies. Herbal remedies remained popular, and use of homeopathic medicines flourished. Physicians prescribed drugs, and pharmacists compounded them from the 1820 *United States Pharmacopoeia*, the standard for purity and strength of medicinal drugs. Pharmacists also provided prescriptions and chemical supplies to physicians and consumers. Outside professional apothecary practice, patent medicine use flourished at the same time that itinerant medicine show operators traveled the countryside vending their products, which often were based on accessible pharmacopoeial reci-pes. Biologics and antisera were developed toward the end of the century, technological products from the germ theory and concepts of immunity. Relationships among pharmacy, medicine, science, industry, academe, and politics became competitive in regard to consumer attitudes and beliefs, and public safety.

Drug manufacturing, distribution, and advertising grew into complex interrelated networks, enabled by mechanization that led to mass production and promoted competition. Trains and mail-order catalog networks increased the flexibility and speed with which drug products were delivered to consumers. Innovations in dosage form design, such as tablets, and changes in packaging requirements expanded advertising opportunities. Manufacturers specialized, as did wholesalers and retail druggists. Drug trade associations organized as protection groups and imposed restrictions related to issues such as trademark infringement, counterfeit labels, product purity, and adulteration of chemical supplies. Proprietary entrepreneurship became an institutionalized drug industry.

Pharmacy education begun with proprietary schools in the 1820s, appeared in public institutions in 1868. The research-based University of Michigan was the first of many land-grant institutions to establish a pharmacy course. Separated from the drug industry, academic specialization promoted custodial responsibilities of drug knowledge, quality, and supply. As professional pharmacy associations reorganized because of specialization, the separation of academic and industrial chemists and pharmacy-based practitioners occurred. By 1900 the drug industry's reputation was questionable. Due in large part to patent medicine abuses and quackery, adulteration and mislabeling of drugs became a primary concern of the American public. The twentieth century would showcase legislation enacted to control the purity of chemical supplies, leading to the 1906 Pure Food and Drug Act.

Further Reading: Glenn Sonnedecker, *Kremers and Urdang's History of Pharmacy*, 1976; James Harvey Young, *The Toadstool Millionaires*, 1961.

Shirley Stallings and Michael Montagne

PHELPS, SHERMAN D. (20 July 1814–13 November 1878), banker, businessman, and mayor. Born in Simsbury, Connecticut, Phelps was a banker in Binghamton, New York, and founder of the Binghamton Water Works and the Binghamton Gaslight Company. He won election as mayor on a fusion ticket, serving from 1872 to 1876. A Victorianist, Phelps selected Isaac G. Perry, chief architect for the New York State Capitol Building in Albany during its final seventeen years of construction, to design and build his home, a two-story mansion, that was one of the finest examples of post–Civil War Victorian (Second Empire) architecture. Completed in 1870, it showcased the opulence, plenitude, and exuberance of Gilded Age America. The home's interior featured large rooms, sixteen-foot ceilings, nine majestic fireplaces with towering ornamentals, tall doorways, magnificent chandeliers, judiciously positioned mirrors, and walnut, rosewood, maple, and golden oak woods. The main hall, paved with Italian marble, connected all the first floor rooms. Its most imposing feature was a black walnut staircase. The mansion's exterior was rosy-red brick with gray stone trim, floor-length windows, and a mansard roof of blue-gray slate. An intricately designed iron fence enclosed the estate, which remains open for tours. Phelps died in Binghamton.

Further Reading: *Binghamton Morning Republican*, 14 November 1878.

Leonard Schlup

PHILANTHROPY. The philanthropists of the 1890s were confident that an increase of useful knowledge could largely prevent oppressive societal ills. John D. Rockefeller, Sr., who was particularly interested in promoting education and medical research, exemplified the attitude. Following his gift in 1882 to Spelman Seminary, a school for black women in Atlanta (renamed Spelman College in 1924), Rockefeller made donations to the new University of Chicago in 1889 (it opened in 1892) and the Rockefeller Institute for Medical Research in New York (founded in 1901 and renamed Rockefeller University in 1965). He pioneered new approaches in gift-giving, such as "wholesale" contributions to large institutions, expert administration, and matching grants. In 1901 he created a permanent grant-making trust: the Rockefeller Foundation, formed in 1913, concentrated on public health and medical education.

In postbellum America, a number of other universities named after their enormously wealthy businessmen benefactors came into being, including Cornell in 1868, Clark in 1887, Vanderbilt in 1875, Johns Hopkins in 1876, and Stanford in 1885. George Peabody of Massachusetts established the Peabody Education Fund in 1867 to assist and encourage the impoverished South to develop state public school systems for primary education and to establish normal schools for teacher training.

In this age of big business, municipal library expansion was unprecedented, and Andrew Carnegie uniquely influenced this growth. Following his offer, made in 1881, to Pittsburgh to build a library (the Carnegie Library of Pittsburgh was founded in 1895), his numerous other gifts also went largely for library construction, by the end of 1898 totaling almost $6 million. In 1901 Carnegie committed $5.2 million to build sixty-five branch libraries for the New York Public Library. The New York Public Library itself was formed in 1895 when the Astor and Lenox libraries and the Tilden Trust were combined. The Enoch Pratt free Library in Baltimore and the Walter L. Newberry and John Crerar Libraries in Chicago were established by bequests in 1886, 1886, and 1889, respectively.

Urban growth had affected the quality of children's lives markedly: the streets became the focus for children of tenement districts. From 1880, as cities underwent even greater change, philanthropic efforts to improve daily life became more forceful. In 1892 there were ninety-two charity organizations and affiliated societies in the United States to systematize the work of the large number and great variety of beneficent associations of various cities. There was the college, university, or neighborhood settlement movement and the inclusion of sociology in the university curriculum, as well as the laboratory training provided by the New York Summer School for Philanthropic Work, begun in 1898 by the Charity Organization Society of the City of New York.

Philanthropists influenced municipal government. New York's Association for Improving the Condition of the Poor helped bring tenement-house legislation in 1895. Louisa Lee Schuyler, a social welfare reformer who led the State Charities Aid Association from 1872 to 1891, fought for professional administration of charitable institutions in New York State and New York City. In many cities, philanthropists were drawn to movements for playgrounds (women were generally the most conspicuous supporters), wholly free public libraries, and children's free home libraries. At the Civic Philanthropic Conference held in 1897 at Battle Creek, Michigan, reforms for the immigrant poor were proposed: slum clearance, improvements in public education, and provision for kindergartens, technical schools, and cultural institutions. The consensus was that urban philanthropic advances of the period were chiefly a force for good.

Further Reading: Ron Chernow, *Titan: The Life of John D. Rockefeller, Sr.*, 1998; George Iles, "The Art of Large Giving," *Century* 53 (1897): 767–779; Charles Mulford Robinson, "Improvement in City Life: Philanthropic Progress," *Atlantic Monthly* 83 (1899): 524–537.

Bernard Hirschhorn

PHILIPPINE-AMERICAN WAR (1899–1902). Under the Treaty of Paris, which ended the Spanish-American War, Spain ceded the Philippines to the United States, which imposed military rule rather than granting the islands their independence. Emilio Aguinaldo and other Filipino revolutionaries, who had aided the United States against Spain in hopes of securing Philippine independence, understandably felt betrayed. In June 1898, they proclaimed the Republic of the Philippines and established a provisional government, with Aguinaldo as president, at Malolos on Luzon. Not until February 1899, however, did hostilities between the Americans and Filipinos actually begin. Not equipped to wage a conventional war, the Filipinos resorted to guerrilla warfare by November 1899. American forces quickly realized that in order to win the war, they would have to do more than defeat the conventional Filipino forces. As a result, civic action programs were established throughout the Philippines to improve transportation, education, and public

health. On 23 March 1901, Brigadier General Frederick Funston led a company of native scouts on a daring raid and captured Aguinaldo at his jungle headquarters. Afterward, Aguinaldo swore an oath of allegiance to the United States and urged his fellow insurgents to surrender, but sporadic fighting continued for another year. Upon the end of the war in 1902, U.S. civil government replaced the military government, and William Howard Taft, later U.S. president, became the first civil governor. The Commonwealth of the Philippines was created in 1935, but it was not until 1946, after World War II, that the islands formally became independent.

Further Reading: Brian M. Linn, *U.S. Army and Counterinsurgency in the Philippine War*, 1989, and *The Philippine War*, 2000.

Alexander M. Bielakowski

PICKERING, EDWARD CHARLES (19 July 1846–3 February 1919), astronomer. Born in Boston, Massachusetts, Pickering graduated from Harvard in 1865 with an engineering degree. As professor of physics at the Massachusetts Institute of Technology (1866–1877), he set up a laboratory for instructional purposes. From 1877 until his death in Cambridge, Massachusetts, Pickering directed the Harvard College observatory. His particular interests were using photography to explore the night skies, inventing photometers, conducting research in spectroscopy, and establishing an observatory in Peru. His activities led to the discovery in 1889 of the first spectroscopic binary. For fourteen years, beginning in 1905, Pickering was president of the American Astronomical Society. In that post he obtained, from various sources, funds to distribute as research grants to qualified astronomers. Pickering gained international recognition for his research, publications and achievements in astrophysics.

Further Reading: Howard Plotkin, "Edward C. Pickering," *Journal for the History of Astronomy*, 21 (1990): 47–58; Howard Plotkin, "Edward C. Pickering and the Endowment of Scientific Research in America, 1877–1918," *Isis* 69 (1978): 44–57; Edward Charles Pickering Papers, Harvard University Archives, Cambridge, Massachusetts.

Leonard Schlup

PICOTTE, SUSAN LA FLESCHE (17 June 1865–18 September 1915), physician and reformer. The youngest daughter of Omaha chief Joseph La Flesche by his first wife, Susan was graduated from Hampton Institute in 1886, and in 1889 from the Woman's Medical College of Pennsylvania (with support of the Connecticut branch of the Women's National Indian Association). She served as government physician at the Omaha agency school for four years, until illness forced her resignation. Upon recovery, she married Henry Picotte, a Sioux, and practiced medicine first at Bancroft, and later at Walthill, Nebraska. She lobbied for required medical inspection of schools and for sanitary ice cream dishes, spoons, and school drinking fountains. She also fought tuberculosis, alcoholism, the housefly, and the common drinking cup. She chaired the State Health Committee of the Nebraska Federation, and organized the Thurston County Medical Association, a new Presbyterian church and a hospital for Walthill. Politically astute, she headed a delegation to Washington, D.C., where she secured her tribe's right to rent or lease its lands and handle its own monies.

Further Reading: Benson Tong, *Susan LaFlesche Picotte, M.D.: Omaha Indian Leader and Reformer*, 1999; Valerie Sherer Mathes, "Susan La Flesche Picotte, M.D.: Nineteenth-Century Physician and Reformer," *Great Plains Quarterly* (1993): 172–186; Valerie Sherer Mathes, "Dr. Susan LaFlesche Picotte: The Reformed and The Reformers," in L. G. Moses and Raymond Wilson, *Indian Lives: Essays on Nineteenth and-Twentieth Century Native American Leaders*, 1985.

Valerie Sherer Mathes

PIERCE, GILBERT ASHVILLE (11 January 1839–15 February 1901), author, territorial governor, and U.S. senator. Born in East Otto, New York, Pierce fought in the Civil War, began practicing law in Valparaiso, Indiana, and held a seat in the Indiana legislature. For twelve years thereafter he was associate editor and managing editor of the *Chicago Inter-Ocean*. During this time, Pierce displayed his literary talents, publishing *The Dickens Dictionary* in 1872. His two novels, *Zachariah, the Congressman* (1876) and *A Dangerous Woman* (1883), dealt with Washington's political life. One of his plays, *One Hundred Wives* (1880), played for two seasons, with De Wolf Hopper as the leading actor.

Active in Republican Party politics, Pierce attended the Republican National Convention at Chicago in 1884 to encourage the nomination of President Chester A. Arthur. On 2 July 1884, Arthur appointed Pierce governor of Dakota Territory, in which capacity he served until 15 November 1886. Upon the admission of North Dakota to the Union, he won election to the U.S. Senate, where he held a seat from 1889 to 1891. Unsuccessful in his bid for reelection due to intraparty squabbling, Pierce moved to Minneapolis, Minnesota, where he purchased the *Minneapolis Tribune* and became its chief editor. Although he accepted President Benjamin Harrison's appointment as minister to Portugal in 1893, he held the post for only three months before submitting his resignation for health reasons. He died in Chicago.

Further Reading: *Minneapolis Tribune*, 16 February 1901; Leonard Schlup, "Gilbert A. Pierce and Republican Party Politics in the Harrison Era," *Nanzan Review of American Studies* 19 (1997): 85–99.

Leonard Schlup

PILLSBURY, JOHN SARGENT (29 July 1828–18 October 1901), manufacturer, statesman, philanthropist, "father of the University of Minnesota." Born and schooled in Sutton, New Hampshire, Pillsbury moved in 1855 to St. Anthony's Falls, Minnesota, to enter the hardware business. After 1875 he focused on lumber and real estate, and especially on the flour-milling firm he had established in Minneapolis with his nephew, Charles A., and his brother, George, in 1872. Charles A. Pillsbury & Company led in milling innovation, introducing steel rollers to replace millstones. The company grew to be the world's largest miller. Pillsbury helped raise three regiments during the Civil War, was state senator (1863–1875), and was elected as a Republican in 1876 to the first of three terms as governor. As governor he defeated an agrarian effort to repudiate state railroad construction bonds. He continued support of the state university begun while he was senator, improved public schools and care for the insane, sought construction of a penitentiary, and fought grasshoppers devastating Minnesota's farms. He personally paid for the university's science building in 1889. For his service, extending from his selection as a regent in 1863, he was made a life regent in 1895. Pillsbury gave away most of his fortune before his death in Minneapolis.

Further Reading: James Gray, *The University of Minnesota, 1851–1951*, 1951; William J. Powell, *Pillsbury's Best: A Company History from 1869*, 1985; *American National Biography*, 17 (1999): 522–524.

Douglas Steeples

PILLSBURY, PARKER (22 September 1809–7 July 1898), reformer and women's rights advocate. Born in Hamilton, Massachusetts, Pillsbury devoted his life to social reform. From the Garrisonian abolitionism of his youth, until his death in Concord, New Hampshire, he labored for various causes. Pillsbury resisted an early call to the ministry because of what he viewed as the Congregational Church's hypocrisy on the slavery issue. During the postbellum period, he advocated African-American suffrage, temperance, political reform, and international peace. It was women's rights to which he gave his longest service. He helped draft the constitution of the American Equal Rights Association, served as vice president of the New Hampshire Woman Suffrage Association, and worked with Susan B. Anthony and other suffragists in promoting their cause. He also published tracts on reforms and wrote *Acts of the Anti-Slavery Apostles* (1883).

Further Reading: Stacey M. Robertson, *Parker Pillsbury: Radical Abolitionist, Male Feminist*, 2000; *Concord Evening Monitor*, 7 July 1898.

Leonard Schlup

PINCHBACK, PINCKNEY BENTON STEWART (10 May 1837–21 December 1921), lawyer and political figure. Pinchback was born a free person of mixed race in Macon, Georgia. He attended school in Cincinnati, Ohio, worked as a steward on a Mississippi River boat, and fought in the Union Army. An early advocate of African-American rights, he helped found the Louisiana Republican Party and urged the government to extend the franchise to blacks. During the postwar period, he was a member of the Louisiana constitutional

convention and the state senate. Because Pinchback was elected as the latter body's president pro tempore, he became lieutenant governor upon the death of the incumbent, Oscar J. Dunn. From 9 December 1872 to 13 January 1873, Pinchback briefly was acting governor after the impeachment and conviction of Governor Henry Clay Warmoth, a carpetbag official. Pinchback was elected congressman-at-large and U.S. senator during this time, but Democrats challenged both outcomes, denying Pinchback his seat. White supremacy's return in the South after 1877 ended Pinchback's political career. He spent the remainder of his life investing in successful business ventures. In 1897, he moved his family to Washington, D.C., where they joined the African-American social elite. Pinchback died in Washington, having spent most of his fortune maintaining his status.

Further Reading: James Haskins Pinckney, *Benton Steward Pinchback*, 1973; W. E. B. Dubois, *Black Reconstruction in America*, 1962; Lerone Bennett, *Black Power USA*, 1967.

Abel Bartley

PINCHOT, GIFFORD (11 August 1865–4 October 1946), conservationist, politician. Born in Simsbury, Connecticut, to a wealthy merchant family, Pinchot graduated from Yale in 1889, then went to Europe, the first American to study scientific forestry. He attended the French National Forestry school in Nancy, and returned to the United States convinced that trees were a renewable crop like any other. In January 1892, Pinchot took charge of the forest on George W. Vanderbilt's estate, "Biltmore," in North Carolina, using it to demonstrate the strengths of scientific management and preparing an exhibition on the subject for the World's Columbian Exposition in Chicago (1893). In 1896, he was secretary of the National Forest Commission, and in 1897 he worked for the secretary of the interior. The next year Pinchot was appointed head of the government's Division of Forestry, where his utilitarian philosophy led to conflict with John Muir, a preservationist. In 1909, he was involved in a controversy with Secretary of the Interior Richard Ballinger over the use of public lands, which led to his firing by President William Howard Taft in 1910. He later served as Republican governor of Pennsylvania (1923–1927, 1933–1935). He died in New York City.

Further Reading: Gifford Pinchot, *Breaking New Ground*, 1947; David Traxel, *1898: The Birth of the American Century*, 1998; M. Nelson McGeary, *Gifford Pinchot: Forester-Politician*, 1960.

David Traxel

PINGREE, HAZEN STUART (30 August 1840–18 June 1901), businessman, mayor, and governor. Born near Denmark, Maine, Pingree served in the Union Army, then moved in 1865 to Detroit, Michigan, where he became a wealthy shoe manufacturer. In 1889 Pingree won election as Republican reform mayor of Detroit. He was reelected three times, serving for seven years altogether. Beginning as a structural reformer, he centralized power and responsibility in the mayor's office in order to achieve the Mugwump goals of honest, efficient, and economical government. As early as his first administration, Pingree was building an impressive record as a social reformer that had no parallel in late nineteenth-century urban America and that made him enormously popular with working-class and immigrant groups. He called for the adoption and expansion of an electrified street railway system; was sympathetic toward, and successfully pushed for, the termination of the street railway strike of 1891, and, during the depression that followed the Panic of 1893, alleviated economic distress by expanding the opportunities for employment in the public sector. The 3-cent fare—his principal issue—stirred discussion in the nation's municipalities.

In 1896 Pingree was elected governor of Michigan; he won a second term in 1899. As he had done while mayor, he redistributed the tax burden between individual property owners and corporations by taxing the property of both at the same rate. Additionally, Pingree pressed a bill through the legislature that provided for the nation's first statewide appraisal of corporate property as a basis for taxation. An overpoweringly conservative legislature defeated

his other reform measures, and he decided not to seek a third term in 1900. He died in London.

Further Reading: Melvin G. Holli, "Hazen S. Pingree: Urban and Pre-Progressive Reformer," Ph.D. diss., University of Michigan, 1966; Hazen S. Pingree, "Detroit: A Municipal Study," *Outlook* 55 (1887): 437–442.

Bernard Hirschhorn

PINKERTON DETECTIVE AGENCY. Allan Pinkerton (1819–1884), General George McClellan's intelligence chief during the Civil War, founded in 1850 what became in the Gilded Age the first national detective agency. Pinkerton's sons William and Robert assumed control of the business during the late 1870s and early 1880s. Allan Pinkerton developed new and highly effective methods of infiltration and of examining evidence. During a period when almost all police at the local level had only scant training, the Pinkerton Detective Agency applied the new technologies of photography and telegraphy to locate fugitives throughout the nation, assembling massive files of mug shots and Bertillon measurements. By the 1880s, it also assisted European police forces in apprehending criminals from London to Constantinople. During the Gilded Age, railroads and banks employed the Pinkertons to combat robberies by marauding gangs, including Jesse James's and Butch Cassidy's "Wild Bunch," in the poorly policed West. Pinkerton agents frequently worked undercover on trains and streetcars to detect conductors' pocketing of fares.

From the 1870s, the agency was significantly involved in protecting strikebreakers and in labor espionage. Allan Pinkerton achieved his most spectacular infiltration success after a Pennsylvania coal producer hired him in 1873 to suppress the Molly Maguires, an Irish miners' secret society suspected of committing acts of violence and sabotage against management. Gaining the confidence of leaders of the society, Pinkerton's undercover agent James Mc-Parlan provided testimony that resulted in their hanging. McParlan's success greatly encouraged employers' use of labor spies. In 1892 the agency's image was badly tarnished after three hundred Pinkerton agents hired to guard strike-breakers at Carnegie Steel's immense Home-stead, Pennsylvania, works became involved in a bloody gun battle with strikers and their sympathizers, resulting in serious casualties on both sides.

Further Reading: James Mackay, *Allan Pinkerton: The First Private Eye*, 1996; James D. Horan, *The Pinkertons: The Detective Dynasty That Made History*, 1967; Wayne G. Broehl, Jr., *The Molly Maguires*, 1964.

Stephen H. Norwood

PINKHAM, LYDIA ESTES (9 February 1819–17 May 1883), social reformer and medicine manufacturer. Born in Lynn, Massachusetts, Estes married Isaac Pinkham in 1843. Over the years Pinkham, a friend of Frederick Douglass, became involved in teaching school, antislavery crusades, temperance movements, Swedenborgianism, phrenology, women's rights, spiritualism, and fiat money. After the Panic of 1873, when her husband, a real estate speculator, lost his fortune, she started selling an herb medicine that she had been concocting for years as a remedy for various physical disorders. It was first available in Lynn in 1875. The following year, Pinkham obtained a registered label with the patent office. Purchasing newspaper space, distributing handbills, traveling, writing advertisements, and engaging in other shrewd business tactics, the Pinkhams soon marketed a profitable product known as Mrs. Lydia E. Pinkham's Vegetable Compound. Some persons journeyed for miles to purchase bottles, and others used the postal system. By 1898, Pinkham's compound had become the most widely advertised product in the country. The advertisements included her portrait, and appealed to emotion. Pinkham died in Lynn.

Further Reading: Elbert Hubbard, *Lydia E. Pinkham*, 1915; R. C. Washburn, *The Life and Times of Lydia E. Pinkham*, 1931.

Leonard Schlup

PITCAIRN, JOHN, JR. (10 January 1841–22 July 1916), businessman. Born in Johnstone, Scotland, Pitcairn immigrated to the United States with his parents, settling in Pittsburgh, Pennsylvania. He began his career with the Pennsylvania Railroad, eventually heading the Philadelphia division. His success led to business affiliations with several giants of enterprise, including John D. Rockefeller, Richard Mellon, Henry Phipps, and Henry Clay Frick. In 1883, Pitcairn joined with John B. Ford in founding the Pittsburgh Plate Glass Company (PPG). Pitcairn served as president from 1896 to 1906, a period of growth and diversification for the company. By 1900, PPG had ten plants and produced 65 percent of the plate glass made in the United States. In 1889, Pitcairn purchased a parcel of land in a wooded area outside Philadelphia on which he built the family estate, "Cairnwood." A devoted follower of the Swedish revelator Emmanuel Swedenborg, Pitcairn believed in responsibility to family, work, and society. He died in Philadelphia.

Further Reading: Richard R. Gladish, *Uncommon Entrepreneur: John Pitcairn, Founder of Pittsburgh Plate Glass and Bryn Athyn, Pennsylvania*, 1989; *New York Times*, 23 July 1916.

Leonard Schlup

PLATT AMENDMENT. After the Spanish-American War, the United States had to decide how to deal with Cuba, whose independence, the stated goal of the war, had been guaranteed in the Teller Amendment. While some, such as Senator Stephen Benton Elkins, favored statehood, in 1901 Cuba was granted its independence. However, to ensure American interests in the new nation, Republican Senator Orville H. Platt of Connecticut introduced an amendment to the Army Appropriations Act of 1901 that placed severe restrictions on the new Cuban government. The amendment limited the Cubans' ability to negotiate treaties or contract debts that could lead to foreign intervention; provided for American intervention if the United States feared a threat to Cuban independence; and forced Cuba to acknowledge all acts and laws passed by the United States while in possession of the island. The terms of the amendment were then included in the new Cuban constitution and in a 1903 treaty between the United States and Cuba. Under its terms the United States intervened in Cuban affairs four times before treaty renegotiations in 1934 did away with the effects of the amendment.

Further Reading: Alexander De Conde, *A History of American Foreign Policy*, 2nd ed., 1971.

Stephen Svonavec

PLATT, ORVILLE HITCHCOCK (19 July 1827–21 April 1905), U.S. senator. Born in Washington, Connecticut, Platt practiced law in Meriden, Connecticut, for almost thirty years. Before the Civil War he was a fervent abolitionist, and affiliated with the Whig, Free Soil, and Know Nothing parties before joining the Republicans. After holding local and state offices, Platt was elected to the U.S. Senate, where he advanced a nationalist Republican agenda from 1879 until his death. He supported the Federal Elections Bill, tariff protectionism, sound money, copyright laws, annexation of Hawaii, and the Treaty of Paris of 1898. The Platt Amendment in 1901 authorized the United States to intervene to preserve Cuban independence, to keep order, and to maintain a naval base on the island, thus giving the United States a quasi protectorate over Cuba. During the 1890s, Platt wielded sufficient power to rank among the five most influential Republican senators. He was a member of several important Senate committees, such as Judiciary and Finance. Although a conservative, Platt, a loyal Republican, worked well with the progressive President Theodore Roosevelt. He died in Meriden, Connecticut.

Further Reading: *Hartford Courant*, 22 April 1905; *New York Times*, 22 April 1905; Louis A. Coolidge, *An Old-Fashioned Senator: Orville H. Platt of Connecticut*, 1910; Edwina C. Smith, "Conservatism in the Gilded Age: The Senatorial Career of Orville H. Platt," Ph.D. diss., University of North Carolina at Chapel Hill, 1976; Orville H. Platt Papers, Connecticut State Library, Hartford.

Leonard Schlup

PLATT, THOMAS COLLIER (15 July 1833–6 March 1910), senator, political boss. Born in Owego, New York, Platt began his political career in 1859 as county clerk there, and held minor posts until 1870. Joining the "Stalwart" wing of the Republican Party, he was a close associate of Roscoe Conkling. Platt served in the House of Representatives from 1875 to 1879, and became a U.S. senator in 1881. He and Conkling resigned from the Senate later that year to protest control of New York patronage by the Garfield, "Half-Breed" wing of the party. The ploy backfired when the legislature refused to reelect them. Platt regained some stature in 1888 as a supporter of Benjamin Harrison. With the election of Levi Morton as governor in 1894, Platt acquired his greatest influence, winning control of the state Republican machinery and the state legislature. He was elected to the U.S. Senate again in 1897 and 1903.

Platt was nicknamed the "Easy Boss" for his skill in compromise and easing party conflict. Famous, if not notorious, were his Sunday conferences in the Fifth Avenue Hotel lobby, where he met party leaders and supplicants in the "Amen Corner." In 1896 Platt proposed the Greater New York bill to charter all communities bordering on New York Harbor under one municipal government. Opposed upstate, the bill passed in 1897, when Platt won support from Tammany Democrats looking to the increased patronage of a larger city. Platt supported Theodore Roosevelt for governor in 1898 only because party scandals in the administration of Governor Frank S. Black required a new face and the unsullied reputation of the war hero. The alliance was an uneasy one, and Platt worked diligently to elect Roosevelt vice president in 1900 to get him out of New York and out of his hair. However, when Roosevelt became president, he controlled federal patronage in New York, and Platt's power faded.

Further Reading: Harold F. Gosnell, *Boss Platt and His New York Machine*, 1924; Richard L. McCormick, *From Realignment to Reform: Political Change in New York State, 1893–1910*, 1981; Sean Dennis Cushman, *America in the Gilded Age*, 1988.

Mario R. DiNunzio

PLESSY, HOMER ADOLPH (17 March 1862–1925), African-American shoemaker and lawsuit plaintiff. Plessy, born free in New Orleans, Louisiana, was light-skinned, seven-eighths white. He gained national attention after the Louisiana legislature enacted a law, drafted by Murphy Foster, requiring segregated railway cars in 1890. The next year a small band of influential African-American and Creole professionals in New Orleans formed the Citizens' Committee to Test the Constitutionality of the Separate Car Law and hired Albion W. Tourgée, a prominent white New York attorney, to challenge the legislation. Their strategy called for a person of mixed blood to violate the statue, which would permit Tourgée to question its arbitrariness. Because Plessy, a mannerly, well-attired shoemaker, could pass for white, he surfaced as the perfect candidate in 1892.

On 7 June, Plessy purchased a first-class ticket for the white section on an East Louisiana Railroad train running between New Orleans and Covington, Louisiana. An unknown member of this well-orchestrated plan notified the conductor and police, who asked Plessy to move to the colored section. He refused, thereby setting in motion the chain of events (as well as a precedent for Rosa Parks in 1955 when she declined to surrender her bus seat to a white man in Montgomery, Alabama).

Arrested by Detective Chris C. Cain and jailed for sitting in the "whites' " car on the train, Plessy, released on a $500 bond, argued in court that the Separate Car Act violated his civil rights as well as the Thirteenth and Fourteenth amendments to the U.S. Constitution. Judge John Howard Ferguson, a Massachusetts lawyer, ruled that Louisiana could lawfully regulate railroad companies that operated solely within the state. Found guilty, Plessy in 1893 appealed to the state supreme court, which upheld Ferguson's decision. On 18 May 1896, in a milestone case in American legal history, the United States Supreme Court in *Plessy* v. *Ferguson* found Plessy culpable, deciding, with one dissenting vote, that Louisiana constitutionally could mandate separate but equal accommodations on intrastate railroads. The tribunal thereby established a doctrine used as a legal foundation to justify many other racially discriminatory "Jim Crow" actions by state and local governments to separate blacks and whites socially. Essentially the majority opinion institutionalized segregation in the United States until 1954. After the case ended, Plessy drifted into anonymity, eventually becoming a collec-

tor with the People's Life Insurance Company. He died in New Orleans.

Further Reading: Charles A. Lofgren, *The Plessy Case: A Legal-Historical Interpretation*, 1988; Brook Thomas, ed., *Plessy v. Ferguson: A Brief History with Documents*, 1996.

Leonard Schlup

PLESSY v. *FERGUSON* (163 U.S. 537). Decided by the Supreme Court in 1896, *Plessy* v. *Ferguson* upheld the constitutionality of a Louisiana law mandating "separate but equal" railroad cars for African-American passengers. The case established a precedent allowing for increasingly harsh "Jim Crow" laws, which legalized racial segregation until *Brown* v. *Board of Education of Topeka* overturned the doctrine in 1954. Legal and social advances made by blacks during Reconstruction came under pressure in the 1880s as the Radical Republicans faded from prominence. Throughout the South, Jim Crow laws legalized segregation. In Louisiana, the black community organized against one such law, which mandated separate but equal railroad cars for the white and "colored" races. They arranged for a test case to be argued by Albion Tourgée, a lawyer and author who had long defended African-American rights.

On 7 June 1892, Homer A. Plessy, nearly white in appearance but of one-eighth African blood, refused to move to the "colored" car of a train. When his case came to trial, Louisiana courts upheld the law, and the issue reached the U.S. Supreme Court, as *Plessy* v. *Ferguson*, in 1896. Tourgée contended that the law was inconsistent with the Thirteenth and Fourteenth amendments, that segregation subjugated blacks to a form of slavery, forcing them into a lower caste than whites. The law was clearly intended to advance white supremacy, Tourgée added. It also accorded too much responsibility to untrained railroad operators, who were responsible for determining which passengers must ride in the "colored" car. The court disagreed, and on 18 May 1896, Justice Henry B. Brown delivered the majority opinion that the "separate but equal" doctrine was constitutional. The sole dissenter, Justice John Marshall Harlan, eloquently anticipated the impending advance of Jim Crow, predicting that segregated rail cars would lead to segregation in many other public facilities, until the races scarcely mingled at all. Harlan argued that in the eyes of the law, no citizen was superior to any other, but he failed to influence other members of the court. In the wake of *Plessy* v. *Ferguson*, southern states enacted, and the courts upheld, laws segregating not only railroad cars but schools and other public places as well.

Further Reading: Brook Thomas, ed., *Plessy v. Ferguson, a Brief History with Documents*, 1997; Charles A. Lofgren, *The Plessy Case: A Legal-Historical Interpretation*, 1987; C. Vann Woodward, "The Birth of Jim Crow," *American Heritage* 15 (1964): 52–55, 100–103.

Kevin B. Witherspoon

PLUMB, PRESTON B. (12 October 1837–20 December 1891), journalist and U.S. senator. Born in Delaware County, Ohio, Plumb attended Kenyon College, helped establish Emporia, Kansas, and founded the *Kansas News* (*Emporia News*), before studying law. After gaining admittance to the bar, he became the first reporter of the state supreme court. In 1867 and 1868, Plumb served in the Kansas House of Representatives, and the first year was its Speaker. In 1877 he won election to the U.S. Senate, where he served until his death. A member of the Committee on Public Lands, Plumb became its chair in 1881, and in 1891 helped pass the Land Law. He advocated free silver, worked toward retirement of the national debt, and backed legislation returning unused railroad land grants to the public domain. A prohibitionist, in 1881 he offered the first proposal for a constitutional amendment banning alcohol. Considered a "western" senator and sectional defender, Plumb exerted significant influence. He died in Washington, D.C.

Further Reading: William Elsey Connelley, *The Life of Preston B. Plumb, 1837–1891*, 1913; *Memorial Addresses on the Life and Character of Preston B. Plumb*, 1892; *New York Times*, 21 December 1891.

Terri Pedersen Summey

POKAGON, SIMON (1830–27 January 1899), Potawatomi leader, orator, and writer. Born in Michigan, Pokagon studied at Notre Dame Academy in Indiana, Oberlin Collegiate Institute, and Twinsburg Academy in Ohio. Christened a Roman Catholic, he demonstrated interests in theology, research, writing, poetry, and the organ. He wrote for magazines, spoke five languages fluently, published his poems, and addressed groups on the history, culture, and conditions of Native Americans. As principal chief of the Potawatomi, Pokagon persuaded the U.S. government to pay his tribe an old treaty land claim of $150,000. He met twice with President Abraham Lincoln and once with President Ulysses S. Grant to improve relations between the Potawatomi and whites, and to assert Native American rights. His booklet *The Red Man's Greeting*, printed on birch bark, was exhibited in 1893 at the World's Columbian Exposition in Chicago, where he delighted visitors with descriptions of Native American life. The publication of his book *Ogimawkwe Mitigwaki: Queen of the Woods*, which retold his courtship of his first wife, appeared in 1899. Pokagon quite possibly was the most educated Native American of his time. He died near Hartford, Michigan.

Further Reading: Simon Pokagon, "Future of the Red Man," *Forum* 23 (1897): 698–708; Simon Pokagon, "Indian Superstitions and Legends," *Forum* 25 (1898): 618–629; Carl Waldman, *Biographical Dictionary of American Indian History to 1900*, rev. ed., 2001.

Leonard Schlup

POLITICAL MACHINES. Party organizations or machines (confederations or coalitions) and bosses (brokers of both political parties) were heavily involved in urban politics during the last four decades of the nineteenth century. Machines differed from political parties in that they were not guided by principles, instead working primarily for their own interests. Neither were they restrained by party members; voters had only to vote as instructed.

The economic expansion that followed the Civil War created vast opportunities for making money. Big corporations evolved; businessmen were valued. Concurrently, professional politicians discovered in the growing cities the ingredients that enabled them to make a business of politics: the lack of municipal services, the spoils system—the lifeblood of the machine—fragmentation in city government resulting in diffusion of responsibility, the intrusion of national issues into municipal elections to strengthen party loyalty (voting for a Democrat or a Republican), and a feverish demand for public works and other services. Police departments, business organizations (notably public service corporations), and raids on the city treasuries became the principal generators of graft.

Party structure from 1870 to 1900 remained fragmented; for example, nominations for district aldermen originated at the ward level. In Chicago and Boston, the strength of ethnic minorities enhanced the importance of ward leaders. The vigorous two-party system in Chicago during the late nineteenth century precluded any one machine from becoming a prevailing force. Indeed, no Chicago leader could claim the title of city boss, nor was any centralized machine equipped to rule either party. In Boston, no citywide figure dominated ward leaders; they vigilantly guarded their rights. Additionally, within the ward itself, rivalry and competition eroded the party organization's unity. In cities such as New Orleans, St. Louis, Cleveland, Boston, and Chicago, the citywide leader made no attempt to resolve ward conflicts.

Big-city chieftains chose to think of themselves as "leaders"; their detractors customarily regarded them as "bosses." James McManes, who took control of the Philadelphia Gas Ring in the late 1860s, led the Republican machine; he won control of the votes of workers in city departments and exerted authority over the municipal legislature. Yet he was the leader only of the Seventeenth Ward; as in many other large cities, power was shared among ward leaders. Hugh McLaughlin led the Democratic machine in Brooklyn, New York, for four decades. Nevertheless, he faced challenges from Democratic politicians of consequence in 1875, 1878, 1880, and 1893, and was compelled to negotiate with the rival Jefferson Hall faction during the 1880s. Isaac Freeman Rasin controlled the Democratic Party in Baltimore from the mid-1880s until 1895. He dominated city government, but seven-time (thirteen-year) mayor Ferdinand C. Latrobe, a lawyer from a distinguished family, was a popular and independent figure. Christopher A. Buckley, the acknowledged leader of the Democratic Party in

San Francisco during the 1880s, was confronted with intraparty challenges and from a rival group named the Precinct and County Democracy. Buckley's tenure as party leader was only eight years. George B. Cox ran Cincinnati's Republican organization during the 1890s, but he lost power in 1897 following an election debacle. Edward R. Butler had no secure control of St. Louis's Democratic Party; in the 1887 municipal election, his faction was but one of three. Butler's power was essentially confined to the Nineteenth Ward.

In sum, so-called bosses were open to attack, and even in New York, none of them ever directly governed the city.

Further Reading: Samuel P. Orth, *The Boss and the Machine*, 1919; Thomas Harrison Reed, "The Triumph of the Machine," in *Municipal Government in the United States* 1926, 104–16; rev. ed., 1934, 104–16; Jon C. Teaford, *The Unheralded Triumph: City Government in America, 1870–1900*, 1984.

Bernard Hirschhorn

POLITICS OF HERITAGE AND MYTH-MAKING IN THE AMERICAN WEST.

For the East in the Gilded Age, the West was a place of outlaws and gunmen, Native Americans, and spectacular landscapes. Dime novels and Buffalo Bill's Wild West shows portrayed a mythic West for popular consumption. It offered a vision of a nation defined by its frontier experience and united beyond the Civil War's sectional strife in taming the land and its indigenous peoples. Yet the power of this myth, a product of the Gilded Age, obscured the fact that many westerners made their own history, myths, and heritage for different, yet equally powerful, reasons. Creating a usable past reflected a desire of westerners to celebrate their lives and experiences. Through writing their local histories and autobiographies, creating pioneer associations and historical societies, and erecting monuments and memorials, westerners sought to make a past that typified their section. This tied them to their new homes and helped define their communities. They created a local heritage, generating stories that turned a process of conquest into the celebratory triumph of Anglo-Saxon civilization.

An illustration of the politics of heritage in the West concerned the women of the Sacagawea Statue Association, who campaigned to have a statue of the Native American woman, who guided Meriwether Lewis and William Clark across the Rocky Mountains, made and displayed at the Lewis and Clark Centennial Exposition of 1905 in Portland, Oregon. They remade her as a prototypical woman pioneer who helped civilize the West, more white than Native American, and a symbol of the women's suffrage campaign that many of these women embraced. The campaign and statue illustrated not just that women participated in creating a Western heritage but also that this heritage became fundamentally political in its rewriting of race and conquest.

Further Reading: Amanda Laugesen, "Making Western Pasts: Historical Societies of Kansas, Wisconsin, and Oregon, 1870–1920," Ph.D. diss., Australian National University, 2000; S. Elizabeth Bird, *Dressing in Feathers: The Construction of the Indian in American Popular Culture*, 1996.

Amanda Laugesen

POLK, LEONIDAS LAFAYETTE (24 April 1837–11 June 1892), agrarian crusader, editor, and alliance leader. Born in Anson County, North Carolina, Polk, a slaveholder and a Whig, was elected to North Carolina's lower house in 1860. He fought in the Confederate Army, and in 1864, ran in abstentia for his former seat and won. Polk served in the North Carolina constitutional convention of October 1865, then farmed on a full-time basis. In 1873 he subdivided his farm and turned it into a town, starting a newspaper to promote it. When the Patrons of Husbandry (the Grange) appeared in North Carolina, Polk joined and rose quickly through its ranks. The Grange spearheaded a move to create a state department of agriculture, and from 1877 to 1880 Polk served as its first commissioner. In 1881 he was elected secretary of the North Carolina Agricultural Society, and opened an agricultural implement store in Raleigh. His business failed in 1883, and he turned full time to developing and selling his patent medicine, Polk's Diphtheria Cure. In 1885 he started the *Progressive Farmer*, which became the premier agricultural journal in the Southeast. As its editor he led the successful fight for an agricultural and mechanical college.

Polk joined the Farmers' Alliance in 1887, and the *Progressive Farmer* became the alliance's official paper. He was elected secretary of the North Carolina Alliance in 1887 and held that office until 1890. He was elected first vice president of the Southern Farmers' Alliance in 1887, chaired its executive committee in 1888, and became president of the National Farmers' Alliance and Industrial Union (NFA&IU) in December 1889, a position he held until his death. Polk helped to lead much of the Alliance membership in North Carolina and the NFA&IU into the Populist Party in 1891 and 1892. He was its popular, but undeclared, candidate for the presidential nomination in 1892, when he died suddenly in Washington, D.C. Throughout his career, Polk combined commitment to both New South economic development goals and farmers and farming. He never changed his lifelong conviction of African-American inferiority, taking a typical if paternalistic attitude toward black people.

Further Reading: Stuart Noblin, *Leonidas Lafayette Polk, Agrarian Crusader*, 1949; Lawrence Goodwyn, *Democratic Promise: The Populist Moment in America*, 1976; Leonidas Lafayette Polk Papers, Southern Historical Collection, University of North Carolina at Chapel Hill.

Bruce Palmer

POLLOCK v. FARMERS LOAN AND TRUST COMPANY (157 U.S. 429; 15 S. Ct. 673; 39 L. Ed. 759; rehearing 58 U.S. 601; 15 S. Ct. 912; 39 L. Ed. 1108). The Civil War income tax expired in 1872. A minority of agrarians and Populists agitated to revive it, but protectionist tariffs produced large federal budget surpluses throughout the 1870s and 1880s. A modest 2 percent tax on personal income above $4,000, and on all corporate income, was included in the Wilson-Gorman Tariff in 1894, to replace revenue lost from tariff reduction. The income tax was immediately challenged in court. In January 1895, *Pollock* v. *Farmers Loan and Trust Company* was filed in the Southern District of New York, as a shareholder suit to enjoin the corporation from paying taxes. The Supreme Court agreed to hear an expedited appeal. The case was aggressively litigated, and despite its procedural irregularity and the weight of prior precedent, a bitterly divided Supreme Court held in May that a tax on income from property was equivalent to a tax on property—a direct tax that must be apportioned among the states according to population. The decision received wide criticism as judicial usurpation in defense of powerful property interests.

Further Reading: Sidney Ratner, *American Taxation: Its History as a Social Force in Democracy*, 1942; Edwin R. A. Seligman, *The Income Tax: History, Theory, and Practice of Income Taxation* 2nd. ed., 1914; Robert Stanley, *Dimensions of Law in the Service of Order: Origins of the Federal Income Tax, 1861–1913*, 1993.

M. Susan Murnane

POOLE, WILLIAM FREDERICK (24 December 1821–1 March 1894), librarian. Born in Salem, Massachusetts, Poole graduated from Yale College in 1849. While there, he was the librarian of Brothers in Unity, a society whose substantial library included almost ten thousand volumes. Realizing that there was no easy access to the contents of the library's magazines, he prepared and published an index that came to be valued by libraries in the United States and abroad. From 1852 to 1856, Poole was librarian of the Boston Mercantile Library Association, where he created a dictionary catalog. From 1856 to 1869, he headed the Boston Athenaeum, one of the largest libraries in the country, reclassifying all its holdings and publishing a catalog. Poole organized the Public Library of Cincinnati, Ohio, from 1869 to 1874. From 1874 to 1887, he was librarian of the Chicago Public Library, which grew to have the largest circulation of any public library in the nation. From 1887 to 1894, he organized and headed the Newberry Library of Chicago. Poole died in Evanston, Illinois.

Poole participated in the conference that founded the American Library Association, and from 1885 to 1887 was its second president. In 1888 was president of the American Historical Association. Poole is best known for the continuation of the index to periodicals that he began in college. In 1882, with a team of over fifty contributing librarians, he brought out *Poole's Index to Periodical Literature*, the precursor of all modern indices to periodicals. Subsequent updates continued to bear Poole's name for many years.

Further Reading: William Landram Williamson, *William Frederick Poole and the Modern Library Movement*, 1963;

William E. Foster, "Five Men of '76," *Bulletin of the American Library Association* 20 (October 1926): 3–13.

Philip H. Young

POORE, BENJAMIN PERLEY (2 November 1820–29 May 1887), newspaper correspondent, editor, and author. Born near Newburyport, Massachusetts, Poore moved with his family to Washington, D.C. in 1827, traveled abroad with his parents in 1831, spent six years in Boston, then returned to Washington in 1854, where he was a correspondent for several newspapers for three decades (1854–1887), during which he became as a well-known personality. During the same period, he served as editor of the *Journal of Agriculture* and of the first issue of the *Congressional Directory* (1865). He also compiled several lists of U.S. government documents, including *A Descriptive Catalogue of the Government Publications of the United States: September 5, 1774–March 4, 1881*, published in 1885. Poore was a prolific author, writing at least ten books during the latter half of the nineteenth century, including *Perley's Reminiscences of Sixty Years in the National Metropolis* (1886). He died in Washington.

Further Reading: J. J. Currier, *History of Newburyport, Massachusetts, 1764–1909*, 2 vols., 1909; *New York Times*, 29 May 1887.

Mark E. Ellis

POPULISM. After the Civil War, agriculture began to decline as the nation urbanized and industrialized. The average price of wheat and cotton decreased. By 1889 corn was selling for 10 cents a bushel in Kansas, and farmers were burning it for fuel. The widening difference between income and expenses forced many farmers to mortgage their land or borrow money from eastern sources, creating suspicions between western and southern debtors, on the one hand, and eastern creditors and bankers, on the other. Nearly a third of America's farms were mortgaged by the end of the 1890s. Fewer farmers owned the land they worked. Especially hard hit was the rural South, where by 1900 income had fallen to 51 percent of the national average. Unable or unwilling to comprehend the new world market, farmers blamed the railroads, bankers, and financiers for their economic ills and social distress. They pressed for an expanded money supply and the coinage of silver with which to pay their debts and combat deflation. They raised free coinage of silver to a sacred dogma and moral imperative.

The sectional struggle between debtor and creditor, intensified by agricultural depressions, led the agrarian protest movement to take political action. Populism flowered as a large democratic mass movement in the late nineteenth century. The People's Party made its national debut in 1891 at a convention in Cincinnati, Ohio. In their national platforms of 1892 and 1896, Populists favored government ownership or effective regulation of the railroads and communication lines, a graduated income tax, direct election of U.S. senators, establishment of a postal savings system, free and unlimited coinage of silver at the ratio of sixteen to one with gold, the adoption of the secret ballot, restrictions on immigration, a shorter work day for industrial labor, the reduction of tariff rates, and the initiative and referendum. Regrettably, free silverism came to dominate the Populist agenda, and the party's merger with Democrats in 1896 around the presidential candidacy of William Jennings Bryan blurred political goals and diminished its distinctiveness.

Although Populism enjoyed some state successes from 1890 to 1900, its program was essentially national. Populism developed strong bases in virtual one-party states, where Republicans (in the South) and Democrats (on the Great Plains) were weak. In certain states, such as Iowa, Democrats managed to absorb Populist sentiment and form farmer-labor coalitions. Fifty Populist congressmen were elected from in sixteen states and one territory between 1891 and 1903. By calling attention to the growing power of monopolies, sectional disparities, and economic disadvantages from which farmers suffered, Populists performed an admirable service for the nation. Many of their political proposals became law during the presidential administrations of Theodore Roosevelt and Woodrow Wilson. Populism was a positive and humane force in American politics. Its adherents stood for human rights, opposed imperialism, and distrusted big business. As bearers of a reform message, Populists were ahead of their time in Gilded Age America.

Further Reading: Gene Clanton, *Congressional Populism and the Crisis of the 1890s*, 1999; Jeffrey Ostler, *Prairie Populism: The Fate of Agrarian Radicalism in Kansas, Nebraska, and Iowa, 1880–1892*, 1993; Robert McMath, *American Populism: A Social History*, 1993.

Leonard Schlup

POPULIST MANIFESTO (1895). The election of Populists to the U.S. House and Senate in 1891, 1893, and 1895 brought increasing pressure on Congress to alleviate the agricultural depression. Some members of both major parties viewed free silver as the panacea that would halt Populist growth. Fearful of losing the silver issue, James B. Weaver, the Populist presidential candidate in 1892, presented a manifesto to the Populist congressional delegation in February 1895. In it, he urged Populists to focus exclusively on the currency question. Initially several members resisted, arguing that they already held the field on the issue, because it had been in their platform since 1892. Moreover, they feared the manifesto would narrow the currency problem to the question of free silver alone, while rank-and-filers still supported other options. Nevertheless, only William A. Peffer, the senator from Kansas, refused to sign the manifesto, which was endorsed by party chair Herman E. Taubeneck. Released to the press on 14 February 1895, the Populist Manifesto laid the groundwork for fusion efforts in the 1896 presidential campaign.

Further Reading: Peter H. Argersinger, *Populism and Politics: William Alfred Peffer and the People's Party*, 1974; Lawrence Goodwyn, *Democratic Promise: The Populist Moment in America*, 1976; William A. Peffer, *Populism: Its Rise and Fall*, 1992.

Connie L. Lester

PORTER, JAMES DAVIS (17 December 1828–18 May 1912), educator, governor. Born at Paris, Tennessee, Porter was graduated from the University of Nashville, studied law at Cumberland University, practiced law, and served a term in the state legislature before the Civil War. He served in the Confederate Army as chief of staff to Major General Benjamin F. Cheatham. Porter returned to his law practice after the war, and in 1870 was elected a state circuit court judge. A Whig before secession, Porter ran as the Democratic gubernatorial nominee in 1874, defeating the Republican Horace Maynard. In his two terms, he favored sound fiscal policies, railroad and business development, and educational growth. Among his accomplishments was acquiring the grounds and buildings for the Peabody Normal College, of which he was president (1902–1909) when it merged with the University of Nashville to become the George Peabody College for Teachers. Prominent in the Nashville business community in the 1880s and 1890s, Porter served for four years as president of the Nashville, Chattanooga, and St. Louis Railroad. He also was assistant secretary of state from 1885 to 1887, and minister to Chile in 1893–1894. Porter died at his home in Paris, Tennessee.

Further Reading: Wallis Beasley, *The Life and Educational Contributions of James D. Porter*, 1950; C. E. Little, *George Peabody College for Teachers*, 1912; *Nashville Banner*, 20 May 1912.

Hutch Johnson

PORTER, JOHN ADDISON (17 April 1856–15 December 1900), journalist and secretary to the president. Born in New Haven, Connecticut, Porter graduated with honors from Yale College in 1878, studied law in Cleveland, Ohio, and returned to New Haven to become a journalist. He worked for local newspapers while doing graduate work in American history at Yale. In the early 1880s Porter was a reporter for New York and Washington newspapers, and in 1886 organized the Arlington Publishing Company in Washington, D.C. Three years later he became the sole proprietor and editor in chief of the *Hartford Evening Post*, which in the 1890s he made an influential proponent of Republican principles. Porter represented Hartford in the state legislature in 1891, attended the Republican National Conventions of 1892 and 1896, and was an unsuccessful contender for the Republican gubernatorial nomination in 1894, 1896, and 1898. During this time, he wrote a number of books and magazine articles. When William McKinley assumed the presidency in 1897, he selected Porter to serve as secretary to the president, a position he

held until poor health forced him to resign in May 1900. He and the president formed a close personal and professional association over these three years. Porter died in Pomfret, Connecticut.

Further Reading: *New York Times*, 16 December 1900; Porter letters in the William McKinley Papers, Manuscripts Division, Library of Congress.

Leonard Schlup

POST, GEORGE BROWNE (15 December 1837–28 November 1913), architect, designer, and engineer. Born in New York City, Post graduated from New York University in 1858. He was a consulting architect for the Equitable Life Insurance Building (1868–1870; now destroyed), the first office building designed with a passenger elevator (which was crucial to development of the skyscraper). Post designed the ten-story Western Union Building (1872–1875; destroyed), and the method of framing he used in the New York Produce Exchange (1881–1884; destroyed) was an important step in the development of the full skeleton framing that became the construction norm. Other significant skyscrapers designed by Post are the Post Building (1880–1881), built in a U-shape to allow for maximum light, and the Mills Building (1881–1883). Post's designs were eclectic, as can be seen in the French-style Williamsburgh Savings Bank in Brooklyn, New York (1869–1875) and the home built for Cornelius Vanderbilt II (1879–1882, addition 1892–1894; destroyed), which made the French Renaissance château style popular. The Park Building in Pittsburgh (1896) features a row of monumental terra-cotta telamones just below the cornice. Post also designed elegant homes for many wealthy clients.

Buildings such as the Pulitzer (World) Building (1889–1890; destroyed), with its gilded dome, and the Manufacturing and Liberal Arts Building (1891–1892; destroyed), the largest structure at the World's Columbian Exposition in Chicago (1893), exemplify the grand, highly decorated, and eclectic Gilded Age style. Post died in Bernardsville, New Jersey.

Further Reading: L. Mausolf, "A Catalog of the Works of George B. Post: Architect," Ph.D. diss., Columbia University, 1983; D. Balmori, "George B. Post: The Process of Design and the New American Architectural Office

(1868–1913)," *Journal of the Society of Architectural Historians* 46 (December 1987): 342–355.

Ann Thomas Wilkins

POSTON, CHARLES DEBRILLE (20 April 1825–24 June 1902), Arizona pioneer, government official, and mining entrepreneur. Born near Elizabethtown, Kentucky, Poston read law in Nashville, Tennessee, and secured a position as clerk of the state supreme court. He possessed a restless nature, however, and after moving to California, he headed an expedition in 1854 to explore the newly acquired Gadsden Purchase. Thereafter he settled in Arizona, founded Yuma, and prospected for silver. Poston installed himself as patriarch at Tubac, befriended the area's Native Americans, supported the Union during the Civil War, and urged President Abraham Lincoln to create the Territory of Arizona. Congress did so in 1863. Poston mapped the new territory, became superintendent of Indian affairs, and in July 1864 won election, as a Republican, as the territory's first congressional delegate. He served from 5 December 1864 to 3 March 1865. Defeated for reelection later in 1865 and again in 1866, he gained admission to the bar in 1867 and then traveled abroad to study irrigation projects in China, Egypt, and India, hoping ultimately to develop irrigated agriculture in Arizona. Poston also was a foreign correspondent for the *New York Tribune* prior to returning to the United States in 1876. For the next two decades, he held minor government offices in Arizona, Texas, and Washington, D.C., such as register of the U.S. land office at Florence, Arizona. In 1894, Poston wrote a series of articles for the *Overland Monthly* of San Francisco. After financial misfortunes, he lived in obscurity and poverty until 1899, when the territorial legislature recognized his role as Arizona's "first citizen" and voted him a pension. He died in Phoenix, leaving a legacy of compassion for Native Americans, a frontier spirit, and dreams of Arizona's future greatness. Poston is remembered as the "Father of Arizona."
Further Reading: Charles D. Poston, *Apache-Land*, 1878; A. W. Gressinger, *Charles D. Poston, Sunland Seer*, 1961; Benjamin Sacks, *Be It Enacted: The Creation of the Territory of Arizona*, 1964.

Leonard Schlup

POTTER, BEATRIX (28 July 1866–22 December 1943), children's author, conservationist. Born in London, England, to a wealthy family, Potter was educated by governesses. She passed the time alone, with a menagerie of animals for company, at homes in Scotland and the Lake District. She was inspired by them to draw and create stories. When she could not find an established professional scientist to write the text for an illustrated book she wished to create on local plant life, she decided to try her hand at publishing greeting cards based on her animal drawings. In 1890 Potter went to Hildesheimer and Faulkner with her work. *A Happy Pair*, a book that included illustrations of rabbits, resulted. In 1893, Potter elaborated on the theme by writing a picture letter to a child of a former governess. It proved the basis for something grander. In 1901 Potter privately published 250 copies of *The Tale of Peter Rabbit*. Frederick Warne & Company displayed interest in publishing the book in 1902, and in 1903, Warne published *The Tale of Squirrel Nutkin*. Over the next decade, Potter bought farms in the Lake District and became a breeder of Herdwick sheep and a conservationist of the region's natural beauty. She worked with the National Trust, using her writing income to buy land to donated to the organization, and willed it more than four thousand acres. Potter's literary legacy included more than a dozen beloved children's books.
Further Reading: Leslie Linder, *A History of the Writings of Beatrix Potter*, 1971.

Lisa De Palo

POWDERLY, TERENCE VINCENT (22 January 1849–24 June 1924), labor leader and public official. Born in Carbondale, Pennsylvania, Powderly left school at age thirteen to work on the railroads. In 1876 he was initiated into the secret labor organization the Noble and Holy Order of the Knights of Labor. With the title "grand master workman," Powderly became its leader in 1879. In 1881 the Knights dropped their secrecy and allowed all "producers" to join, excluding only bankers, lawyers, liquor dealers, and stockbrokers. More than any previous labor organization, the Knights opened their membership to the unskilled, women, and blacks, and by 1886 had approximately eight hundred thousand members.

Besides being a labor leader, Powderly was active in politics. Under the Greenback Labor Party banner, he was mayor of Scranton, Pennsylvania, for three two-year terms (1878–1884). He was a member of the Socialist Labor Party between 1880 and 1882, but later repudiated socialism, opposed strikes, and favored arbitration with employers. In 1886 he disavowed the national labor strikes that sought the eight-hour day, and condemned the radicals who had been arrested after a bomb exploded at a rally in Haymarket Square in Chicago. Thereafter, due to internal factionalism and an employer offensive, the membership of the Knights drastically declined. As internal opposition to Powderly's conservative policies grew, he was forced from office in 1893. The following year he was admitted to the bar in Pennsylvania and undertook a number of unsuccessful business enterprises. He joined the Republican Party and campaigned for William McKinley for president in 1896. Powderly was commissioner general of immigration (1897–1902) and head of the Division of Information of the Immigration Bureau (1907–1921). He wrote widely on the labor movement and his role in it, including *Thirty Years of Labor: A History of the Organization of Labor Since 1860* (1889). Powderly died in Washington, D.C.

Further Reading: Vincent J. Falzone, *Terence V. Powderly, Middle Class Reformer*, 1978; Richard Oestreicher, *Solidarity and Fragmentation: Working People and Class Consciousness in Detroit, 1875–1900*, 1986.

John F. Lyons

POWELL, JOHN WESLEY (24 March, 1834–23 September 1902), scientist and government official. Powell was born in Mount Morris, New York; grew up on family farms in Ohio, Wisconsin, and Illinois; and rose to major in the Union Army. At the battle of Shiloh, he lost his right arm. Powell then taught geology at Illinois Wesleyan College, and in 1867 and 1868 made two scientific expeditions to the Rocky Mountains of Colorado. In 1869 and 1871 he explored the Colorado River canyons. A product was his *Explorations of the Colorado River of the West and Its Tributaries* (1875), a book often reprinted and still available. His fine writing and lecturing skills on the popular topic established his reputation.

Powell became director of the U.S. Geographical Survey of the Rocky Mountain Region. Rival surveys in the field, best known by the names of their directors and in the aggregate as the Great Surveys, were the Hayden Survey (U.S. Geological and Geographical Survey of the Territories), the King Survey (U.S. Geological Exploration of the Fortieth Parallel); and the Wheeler Survey (U.S. Geographical Surveys West of the One Hundredth Meridian). Powell was an able bureaucrat. He helped found the Cosmos Club in Washington, D.C., and campaigned for the consolidation of the Great Surveys. This took place in 1879 with the creation of the U.S. Geological Survey. In that year Powell was appointed the first director of the Bureau of American Ethnology, and in 1881 became the second director of the Geological Survey. He incurred the enmity of westerners by publishing *Lands of the Arid Regions*, in which he advocated radical changes in land settlement patterns. In 1894 he resigned as director of the Geological Survey, but continued active until his death in Haven, Maine.

Further Reading: William Culp Darrah, *Powell of the Colorado*, 1951; Richard A. Bartlett, *Great Surveys of the American West*, 1964; William H. Goetzmann, *Exploration and Empire*, 1966.

Richard A. Bartlett

PRAGMATISM. Pragmatism was the characteristically American philosophical response to the upheaval of the Gilded Age. Its roots can be found in the work of Charles S. Peirce, who is credited with coining the term. It is most closely associated with a group of intellectuals connected to Harvard and the Metaphysical Club, including Peirce, Josiah Royce, John Fiske, Francis Abbot, William James, and Oliver Wendell Holmes. The term has been applied to a range of philosophical perspectives, but it may be viewed generally as an attempt to find a middle ground between the extremes of scientific empiricism and rationalistic monism. The goal was to define the process of establishing truth. This ranged from the community consensus of belief favored by Peirce to the open universe and individualism of James. All were influenced by evolutionary convictions that life itself was an experiment and that the physical world was the result of natural selection. For pragmatism, the validity of an idea, the test of truth, consisted in its meaning (i.e., concrete results when put into practice). The impact of pragmatism is readily identifiable in subsequent efforts to analyze and define society, including instrumentalism, legal realism, institutionalism, and the New History.

Further Reading: A. J. Ayer, *The Origins of Pragmatism: Studies in the Philosophy of Charles Sanders Peirce and William James*, 1968; Bruce Kuklick, *The Rise of American Philosophy*, 1977; Louis Menand, *The Metaphysical Club: A Story of Ideas in America*, 2001.

C. Edward Balog

PRATT, RICHARD HENRY (6 December 1840–15 March 1924), military officer and educator. Born in Rushford, New York, Pratt served in the Union Army during the Civil War. In 1875, he took approximately seventy Native American prisoners of the 1874–1875 Red River War to Fort Marion Military Prison at Saint Augustine, Florida. There he established an educational program for them. In 1879, he taught Native Americans at the Hampton Institute in Virginia, a training school for African Americans. That same year the War Department authorized Pratt to establish the first off-reservation federal Native American boarding school at Carlisle, Pennsylvania. Congress formally authorized the institution and appropriated funds in 1882. As superintendent, Pratt instituted an "outing" system by which students lived and worked for periods of time with families in the vicinity. He sought to teach Native Americans to earn a place for themselves off their reservations, a process of acculturation. For the rest of his life, Pratt promoted his assimilationist views. He died in San Francisco, California.

Further Reading: *New York Times*, 16 March 1924.

Leonard Schlup

PRESIDENCY. The Gilded Age presidency faced two major challenges: the post–Civil War reconstruction and the social consequences of massive industrialization. The period was characterized by a weak presidents, an assertive Congress, and a competitive national political party system. Lincoln's war policies were based on a fairly easy reconstruction policy that would allow the seceded states to return to the Union as soon as possible. The Gilded Age began, however, with the continuation of Republican and Union Army rule in parts of the South. The occupation ended with the disputed election of Rutherford B. Hayes in 1876 and the deal Democrats made to end the deadlock in the House of Representatives. Inexorably, the GOP abandoned the blacks in the South and the protections afforded to them by the federal government in the Thirteenth, Fourteenth, and Fifteenth amendments.

Republican presidents strongly supported the development of industrial capitalism and adopted a laissez-faire attitude toward federal regulation of the economy. The major Democrat of the Gilded Age, Grover Cleveland, represented the conservative elements of that party and often adopted similar positions. The reforming elements of both parties made substantial progress in municipal and state elections. Not until Theodore Roosevelt, however, would a president be identified with the critics of capitalism and the forces of progressive social reform. The Gilded Age presidency emphasized personal probity, modest expectations, and a deferential attitude toward Congress. The era is generally judged to be one of the nadirs in the development of the executive branch of government.

Further Reading: H. Wayne Morgan, *From Hayes to McKinley*, 1969; Allen Nevins, *Grover Cleveland: A Study in Courage*, 1932; Michael P. Riccards, *The Ferocious Engineer of Democracy*, vol. 1, 1997.

Michael P. Riccards

PRESIDENTIAL ELECTION OF 1868. The presidential election of 1868 was the first post–Civil War contest. Abraham Lincoln's untimely death left the country with the uncertain leadership of President Andrew Johnson. The era's salient issue was the treatment of the former Confederate states. The Radical Republicans opposed Johnson's lenient stand on the South's reentry to the Union. In the midterm election of 1866, Johnson challenged the Radical Republicans by supporting conservative congressional candidates, most of them Democrats. His efforts were unsuccessful. Thereafter Republicans passed tough Reconstruction legislation and the House impeached Johnson in 1868. A single vote in the Senate spared him from removal.

In the 1868 presidential battle, the Republicans held their convention in May at Chicago, where they nominated the popular general Ulysses S. Grant. They adopted an ambiguous platform calling for black suffrage in the South, but leaving that issue to state discretion in the North. On the fourth ballot, they selected Indiana House of Representatives speaker Schuyler Colfax as Grant's running mate, rejecting the radical Benjamin Wade. The Democrats, who met in the new Tammany Hall building in New York City in July, did not have a clear front-runner. Aspirants included Chief Justice Salmon P. Chase and George Pendleton, who promoted the "Ohio Idea," which proposed paying off bonds with greenbacks. After eighteen ballots, they nominated the convention chair, New York governor Horatio Seymour, a reluctant candidate. The platform advocated an end to Reconstruction and endorsed the Ohio Idea. Seymour's running mate, General Francis P. Blair, had earlier written a letter arguing that Reconstruction legislation should be voided.

Grant made few public statements beyond the slogan "Let us have peace." Seymour was more active, but he was not enthusiastic about the Ohio Idea. Loyalty to the Republicans was seen as an expression of loyalty to the Union. Business interests, particularly eastern bankers and railroad promoters, helped finance the party's campaign. Grant won easily, collecting 214 electoral college votes to Seymour's 80. The popular contest was closer: 3,012,833 to 2,703,249 votes. Grant's total might have been below Seymour's without the African-American vote. After the election, the Fifteenth Amendment was added to the Constitution, guaranteeing the right to vote regardless of "race, color, or previous condition of servitude." President Grant was not a skilled politician, and he surrounded himself with a weak cabinet.

Further Reading: John Hope Franklin, "Election of 1868," in Arthur M. Schlesinger, Jr., ed., *A History of Presidential Elections*, vol. 2, 4 vols. 1971; William S. McFeely, *Grant: A Biography*, 1981.

William C. Binning

PRESIDENTIAL ELECTION OF 1872. The presidential election of 1872 focused on the performance of President Ulysses S. Grant's administration. The national economy was strong. Certain sectors, particularly manufacturing, banking, and railroads, prospered during Grant's first term. Western farmers, however, had not done as well. The administration was viewed by many as corrupt and incompetent, although the major scandals of Grant's presidency did not break until the second term. Republicans had added the Fifteenth Amendment to the Constitution, giving African Americans the right to vote. Federal troops remained in the South. A number of leading Republicans, concerned about Grant's favorable treatment of business, lack of interest in reform, and mediocre cabinet appointments, formed the opposition Liberal Republicans. Malcontents from Missouri called for a convention to be held at Cincinnati in May 1878. The resulting platform favored free trade mildly, and advocated universal amnesty in the South and supremacy of civil over military rule. The new party condemned land grants to railroads, and favored civil service reform and elimination of corrupt politics and special privilege. Its laissez-faire economic program offered little to restrain the excesses of the emerging industrial capitalist economy.

Liberal Republicans had difficulty picking a presidential nominee. The most earnest reformers favored Charles Francis Adams, minister to Great Britain during the war. Distant and aloof, however, he would not actively seek the nomination. The new party finally nominated New York newspaperman Horace Greeley and Governor B. Gratz Brown of Missouri. Republican regulars met at Philadelphia in June, and renominated Ulysses Grant without opposition. Vice President Colfax was dropped for Senator Henry Wilson of Massachusetts. The regular Republicans did not challenge the new liberal party on most issues, and paid lip service to civil service reform and their "obligations" to "loyal women." The Democrats gathered in

Baltimore in July and reluctantly endorsed the Liberal Republicans' Greeley-Brown ticket. Some, however, could not accept Greeley as their party's nominee. He had long been a Republican propagandist.

The economy continued to be strong during the election. The Liberal Republicans were not well organized, and the press painted Greeley as an eccentric. Grant, though cast as a spoilsman and drunkard by opponents, won easily, without campaigning. He captured 286 of the 366 electoral votes, and garnered 6,467,679 popular votes to Greeley's 2,834,761. Greeley died soon after the election. Republicans gained seats in the House. Grant's second term endured an economic crash and the exposure of widespread corruption in the administration.

Further Reading: William Gillette, "Election of 1872," in Arthur M. Schlesinger, Jr., ed., *A History of Presidential Elections*, vol. 2, 4 vols., 1971; Martin E. Mantell, *Johnson, Grant and the Politics of Reconstruction*, 1973.

William C. Binning

PRESIDENTIAL ELECTION OF 1876. The presidential election of 1876 pitted the Republican governor of Ohio, Rutherford B. Hayes, against the Democratic governor of New York, Samuel J. Tilden. Both were reform-minded, particularly Tilden, who had vaulted to prominence by attacking Manhattan's notoriously corrupt Tweed Ring. Beyond party affiliation, there was little to choose between the two; each seemed to personify the country's reform mood after the scandals of the Grant administration. A deceptively dull campaign preceded the most controversial election in American history. Three southern states, Florida, Louisiana, and South Carolina, submitted dual sets of votes, one for each candidate. Oregon's vote, too, was questionable because a Republican officeholder there—in violation of the Constitution—served as an elector.

Conflicting returns were troublesome enough, but the situation was complicated by the absence of any procedure to determine which ballots were valid. Tilden had already beaten Hayes by more than 250,000 popular votes and led in the electoral count, 184 to 165, but the four disputed states represented twenty electoral votes. Hayes would win only if he captured all of them. Congress compromised its way to a solution in January 1877. The House and the Senate agreed create a fifteen-man commission (five members each from the House, the Senate and the Supreme Court). The Democratic House named Henry Payne of Ohio, Eppa Hunton of Virginia, and Josiah Abbot of Massachusetts, all Democrats; and Republicans George F. Hoar of Massachusetts and James A. Garfield of Ohio as its representatives. The Republican Senate selected three members of that party—Oliver P. Morton of Indiana, Frederick Frelinghuysen of New Jersey, and George F. Edmunds of Vermont—and Democrats Allen G. Thurman of Ohio and Thomas F. Bayard of Delaware. Given the equal number of Democrats and Republicans representing Congress, both sides hoped that a fair judgment could be assured through the appointment of two Republican justices, William Strong and Samuel F. Miller; two Democrats, Nathan Clifford and Stephen Field; and an independent, David Davis. However, when the Illinois legislature elected Davis to the U.S. Senate, he stepped aside, and Joseph P. Bradley, a Republican, took his place.

The Electoral Commission began its work on 1 February 1877. For a month the commissioners examined the returns and heard arguments from lawyers representing both candidates. First Florida, then Louisiana and Oregon, and finally South Carolina were declared for Hayes. In each instance, the partisan vote was eight to seven. Democrats were understandably outraged, and cried foul. For several days, rumors of revolution and the threat of a congressional filibuster that would prevent an official counting of the election returns swept the capital. Finally, after last-minute bargaining, partisans on both sides agreed that Hayes would be president. In return, Republicans assured the Democrats that Hayes would remove the last federal troops from the South, thereby ending formal Reconstruction, appoint a southern Democrat to the cabinet, and commit federal monies to rebuilding the ravaged region. Although many Democrats felt their man had won the election of 1876, it was Hayes who took the oath of office as the nation's nineteenth president.

Further Reading: Ari Hoogenboom, *Rutherford B. Hayes, Warrior and President*, 1995; Keith Ian Polakoff, *The Pol-*

itics of Inertia: The Election of 1876 and the End of Reconstruction, 1973; C. Vann Woodward, *Reunion and Reaction: The Compromise of 1877 and the End of Reconstruction*, 1951.

Frank P. Vazzano

PRESIDENTIAL ELECTION OF 1880. In 1880, the Republican Party nominated Congressman James A. Garfield for president and Chester Alan Arthur, former collector of the New York Customhouse, as his running mate. Democratic standard-bearers were, respectively, General Winfield Scott Hancock, hero of Gettysburg, and William H. English, War Democrat, banker, and former congressman from Indiana. Other candidates included Greenbacker James B. Weaver and Prohibitionist Neal Dow. Like Garfield and Hancock, both had been Civil War generals.

In its platform, the Grand Old Party stressed the emancipation of African Americans, endorsed a protective tariff, and promised debt reduction, pensions for Union veterans, and improvement of seacoasts and harbors. It opposed polygamy, unlimited immigration of Chinese, and federal land grants to railroads and corporations. In his acceptance letter, Garfield endorsed sound money, moderate tariff protection, and a free ballot. His civil service policy was ambivalent; he promised both to consider merit and to consult local party leaders. The Democrats backed Chinese exclusion and "a tariff for revenue only"; their platform addressed civil service reform (in vague terms), southern "home rule," and opposition to government "centralization." Hancock's acceptance letter abounded in platitudes.

Hancock ran a modest campaign, staying at a military base on Governor's Island in New York Harbor and simply endorsing his party's platform. He blundered by ineptly calling the tariff a mere "local matter." Democrats revived the Crédit Mobilier scandal and one involving a Washington paving company, claiming Garfield was compromised by both. Furthermore, they said, Garfield had refused to pay a laundry bill, spurned a poor solider who sought relief, and stolen bedding from a southern widow. A forged letter, supposedly written by Garfield to one H. L. Morey of Lynn, Massachusetts, rep-

resented the Republican candidate as favoring Chinese immigration and as claiming that any employer had the right to obtain labor as cheaply as possible.

The Republicans, in turn, asserted that during the Civil War, Hancock had plotted to march on Washington and depose Lincoln. Moreover, the Democratic nominee had directed a swindle in the oil industry, issued fraudulent bonds in Louisiana, and hauled down the American flag while entertaining former Confederate general P. G. T. Beauregard. Garfield had to spend much of his time mollifying the Stalwart faction of his party, for Roscoe Conkling had been reluctant to back the ticket. According to the "Treaty of Fifth Avenue," Garfield promised to recognize every party faction when appointments were made, and there would be a particular—though unspecified—plum for the banker and congressman Levi P. Morton.

In many ways, the campaign reflected the typical Gilded Age alignment, with Democrats assured of a solid South and border states, Republicans capturing the North and Middle West, and such "swing" states as Ohio and Indiana playing a crucial role. In the end, the election was one of the closest in American history. The Republicans captured the electoral college 214 to 155, but their popular vote margin was only 7,368 out of 9.2 million votes cast, 0.10 percent. They won the House 147 to 135. The Senate was deadlocked, although Arthur, as vice president, could cast the deciding vote.

Further Reading: Herbert J. Clancy, *The Presidential Election of 1880*, 1958; Justus D. Doenecke, *The Presidencies of James A. Garfield and Chester A. Arthur*, 1981; Leonard Dinnerstein, "1880," in Arthur M. Schlesinger, Jr., ed., *Running for President: The Candidates and Their Images*, 1994, pp. 345–383.

Justus D. Doenecke

PRESIDENTIAL ELECTION OF 1884. The victory of the Democrat Grover Cleveland over the Republican James G. Blaine indicated the limitations of appeals to the issues and rhetoric of the Civil War and Reconstruction. Cleveland became the first Democratic president to be elected in twenty-eight years. The election was close; a shift of six hundred votes in one state would have changed the outcome. It was in many ways a typical Gilded Age contest, with emotions running high and scandals darkening each man's prospects.

Cleveland was a strong candidate. In youth he had overcome personal adversity and was self-made in the good Victorian sense. Rather indifferent to Civil War results, he was honest, having quarreled with New York's Tammany Hall leader John Kelly over patronage. Cleveland had experience as mayor of Buffalo and governor of New York, and a reformer's dedication to ending corruption in political office. James G. Blaine led a divided Republican Party. After a fierce convention struggle between the Half-Breeds and the Stalwarts, GOP patronage factions, Blaine faced the scorn of the Mugwumps, independent Republicans who supported Cleveland from 1884 to 1897. Blaine was politically well experienced, personally charming, and a solid family man, but his career was marked by rumors of corruption. The Mulligan letters were a typical example. Written by Blaine and held by James Mulligan of Boston, they discussed how in 1869 Blaine, who was then speaker of the House of Representatives, received a generous and secret commission for selling bonds for the Little Rock and Fort Smith Railroad. The issue was a major factor in the presidential campaign in 1884. The "Plumed Knight" also had other distractions from his campaign for the White House.

New York State provided the margin of victory. The Irish Americans supported Cleveland. Leading a delegation of clerics, Reverend Samuel D. Burchard publicly called the Democrats the party of "Rum, Romanism, and Rebellion." Even through his mother and sister were Roman Catholics, Blaine, for some unknown reason, did not rebuke Burchard or disavow the remark. Quickly, the Democrats spread the news that Blaine had countenanced a slander on the Catholic Church. Blaine later said the incident cost him the election.

Cleveland had a near disaster. During the campaign, Republicans charged that he had fathered a child out of wedlock. In typical fashion, Cleveland told his campaign workers to tell the truth. As a young man, Cleveland had courted a young woman who had several other male companions. As a result, no one knew who the father of the child really was, but the mother thought Cleveland would make a good husband. He did not marry her, but for a number of years gave her child-support payments.

The election result was close. Cleveland carried New York by fewer than twelve hundred votes. The candidacies of Ben Butler of the National Greenback Party and John P. St. John of the Prohibition Party reduced Blaine's total in New York and New Jersey. Although Cleveland's popular majority was less than twenty-five thousand in a total vote of more than ten million, he had 219 electoral votes, and Blaine, 182. In addition to New York, Cleveland carried the South, New Jersey, Connecticut, and Indiana. The Democrats had captured the White House.

Further Reading: Allan Nevins, *Grover Cleveland: A Study in Courage*, 1933; David S. Muzzey, *James G. Blaine: A Political Idol of Other Days*, 1934; Eugene H. Rosenboom, *A History of Presidential Elections*, 2nd ed., 1964.

Donald K. Pickens

PRESIDENTIAL ELECTION OF 1888. As the incumbent, Grover Cleveland had little trouble securing the 1888 Democratic presidential nomination. His reelection bid, however, was immediately placed in jeopardy by the selection of Allen G. Thurman as his running mate. Although Thurman was a beloved and revered stalwart of the party, his advanced age (seventy-four) and poor health made him a bad choice, particularly because he would be expected to shoulder a major share of campaigning for the ticket. The Republican nomination ultimately went to Benjamin Harrison of Indiana. Of several candidates for the party's nod, John Sherman of Ohio initially emerged as front-runner. Sherman's main concern was a belated entry into the contest by the 1884 standard-bearer, James G. Blaine. By the time Sherman realized Blaine presented no threat, however, Harrison's supporters had secured the prize for their man.

Harrison soon proved the much more formidable of the two major presidential contenders. While Cleveland dallied and refused to campaign actively, and Thurman finally had to stay home, Harrison adopted an extremely effective "front-porch" approach. In this effort, he was backed by a Republican war chest the Democrats could not hope to match. He also was aided by an illustrious family name, a solid war record, and the lack of a major political record to defend. The only prominent office he had held prior to his nomination was one inconsequential term as a U.S. senator. Given the relatively static nature of the state-by-state support for the two parties during this era, Republicans knew from the outset that they needed to put together some combination of the swing states of Connecticut, New York, New Jersey, and Indiana, while the Democrats were aware that they had to hold New York to achieve victory. Accompanied by unprovable charges that Indiana was bought by Republicans from among eighteen to twenty thousand "floating" votes alleged to be available there, Harrison carried his home state. Cleveland lost New York amid a chorus of Democratic complaints about Republican vote-buying and vote swapping between state leaders of the two parties.

The one obvious reason for the election's outcome was that the Republicans had conducted a well-organized, strongly financed, effective campaign that stood in sharp contrast to the bumbling, lackluster effort of the Democrats. Illustrative was the handling of the tariff, the one issue clearly dividing the two parties. Although Cleveland had sought to introduce the idea of rate reduction as a means of dealing with a mounting federal budget surplus, the Republicans, quickly wrapping themselves in the mantle of protectionism, managed to neutralize the issue by raising the twin bogeys of ruinous free trade and divisive sectionalism.

Although Cleveland received a popular ballot plurality in excess of ninety thousand, Harrison won the electoral vote 233 to 168, and with it the presidency. Cleveland's loss of New York's thirty-six electoral votes spelled defeat for him in 1888, just as carrying that state four years earlier had given him the victory. In light of the questionable settlement of the 1876 contest, Harrison's 1888 victory is the only clear example in either the nineteenth or the twentieth century of the presidency gained via the electoral college despite an opponent's greater popular vote.

Further Reading: Harry J. Sievers, *Benjamin Harrison: Hoosier Statesman*, 1959; John Edgar McDaniel, Jr., "The Presidential Election of 1888," Ph.D. diss., University of Texas at Austin, 1970.

James L. Baumgardner

PRESIDENTIAL ELECTION OF 1892. The election of 1892 was a culminating event in the history of American populism. The Populist Party, with James B. Weaver as its presidential nominee, captured approximately 8 percent of the national vote for that office. The Panic of 1873 had provided the seedbed for the growth of a populist movement, which originated among farmers who had been driven from the land by foreclosures, as well as small businessmen who had been bankrupted by their inability to secure extensions of further credit. The period featured the growing strength of a powerful class of financiers and industrialists, who seemed to stop at nothing to maximize profits. Farmers, workers, and small business operators sought a national government that would afford them some protection from what they saw as the unbridled forces of the new industrialism. Those forces included, the Populists believed, the political bosses in both the Republican and the Democratic parties. The Republican Party's Mark Hanna of Ohio personified bossism. He was determined to prevent the return to political power of Democrats and their candidate, Grover Cleveland, vanquished in a bid for a second White House term in 1888.

In 1884, Cleveland had won a bitter campaign, securing the votes of farmers and critics of unbridled capitalism. Four years later he had lost to Benjamin Harrison, the Republican candidate, although he had secured almost 100,000 more popular votes. The Panic of 1890 led to Democratic midterm congressional victories, as the public punished the Republicans for their higher tariff policy, which led to a deflationary spiral and, among other casualties, to the failure of the Union Pacific Railroad. Cleveland, who had retreated after his 1888 defeat to a prosperous law practice, got back into the political fray by denouncing the free coinage of silver.

For the 1892 election, the Populists drafted

a radical platform that included nationalization of railroads, and the telephones and the telegraph systems. James Weaver was nominated as their presidential candidate by acclamation. In the end, aided by a sense of crisis that was furthered by such violent labor disputes as the strike at Andrew Carnegie's Homestead Steelworks, Cleveland's bid to recapture the While House was successful. He won by 364,000 votes over his nearest opponent, the incumbent Benjamin Harrison. The Populists, although defeated, showed great strength in the farm states, polling almost 40 percent of the vote in Nebraska and winning control of a number of state legislatures and governorships.

Further Reading: Page Smith, *The Rise of Industrial America: A People's History of the Post-Reconstruction Era*, 1984; George H. Knoles, *The Presidential Campaign and Election of 1892*, 1942.

John B. Anderson and Patrick Foley

PRESIDENTIAL ELECTION OF 1896. The presidential election of 1896 took place during a severe economic depression. The incumbent, Grover Cleveland, had divided his party. Republicans had scored major victories in the 1894 congressional elections, and their leaders expected to recapture the White House. Their convention met in St. Louis, and chose William McKinley of Ohio on the first ballot. Author of the Tariff of 1890, McKinley presented protection as the solution to the depression. He was cool to temperance advocates, hoping to prevent ethnocultural concerns from taking center stage. Shortly before the convention, he and his advisers decided to write into the platform a commitment to "the existing gold standard." Though the platform also included a promise to establish a bimetallic standard (gold and silver) through international agreement, it failed to satisfy a group of western Republicans who, led by Henry Teller of Colorado, walked out when the platform was adopted.

At the Democratic convention in Chicago, a majority of the delegates favored silver coinage, and William Jennings Bryan had made himself well known. A delegate from Nebraska and not a declared candidate for the presidential nomination, Bryan served on the platform committee. He presented the closing argument on

behalf of silver before the convention. Bryan's speech has become the standard example for capturing a convention through oratory. He claimed later that he only expressed delegate sentiments, but his address electrified the audience by proclaiming that mankind must not be crucified on a cross of gold. The speech gave Bryan the presidential nomination on the fifth ballot. Arthur Sewall of Maine, a successful businessman who supported silver, was his running mate.

Dubbed the "Boy Orator of the Platte," Bryan hoped to unite all silver advocates behind his banner. A new party, officially the National Silver Party, but usually called Silver Republicans because nearly all were former members of the GOP, met in St. Louis at the same time as the Populist convention. The Silver Republicans enthusiastically endorsed Bryan, Sewall, and silver. Many Populists, however, feared they would lose their identity if they did the same. In the end, the Populist convention named its own vice-presidential candidate, Thomas E. Watson of Georgia, hoping Sewall would withdraw; then the convention endorsed Bryan. Though he united the silver forces behind his candidacy, Bryan failed to unite all Democrats. A group labeling itself National Democrats, but usually called Gold Democrats by others, nominated two former Civil War generals, one northern and one southern, and focused their campaign solely on drawing Democratic votes away from Bryan.

Public interest was high and the campaign was closely fought. The McKinley campaign raised $10–$16 million; Bryan collected only $300,000. Republican campaigners deluged the nation with pamphlets and political gewgaws—including the first campaign buttons—but McKinley ran a traditional campaign by remaining at home in Canton, Ohio, and delivering speeches from his front porch. Bryan took his cause directly to the voters. He traveled eighteen thousand miles and delivered three thousand speeches, especially in the crucial Middle West; in the course of his travels, he earned the nickname "the Great Commoner" for his unassuming ways.

The campaign focused on federal economic policy. McKinley defended the gold standard, but concentrated especially on the protective tariff as the best means to restore prosperity. Bryan emphasized silver but did not ignore the tariff, income tax, and other reforms. Voters turned out in extraordinary numbers—up to 95 percent of those eligible in some states, and nearly 80 percent for the nation as a whole. In the end, Republican tariff arguments and fears of inflation gave McKinley the edge among voters in urban and industrial areas (especially among the middle class but including many workers) and among more prosperous farmers in the eastern Midwest, the Northeast, and the Pacific coast states. Bryan took 6.5 million votes (46.7 percent of the total) to 7.1 million (51.1 percent) for McKinley. The electoral vote was more lopsided, 271 for McKinley to 176 for Bryan. Bryan supporters pointed to fraud and intimidation in some areas and claimed the election was stolen, but McKinley's victory actually marked a long-term shift in voter loyalties. From 1877 through 1892, neither major party could achieve a majority. After the mid-1890s, the Republicans held an unquestioned national majority until the early 1930s.

Further Reading: Paul W. Glad, *McKinley, Bryan and the People*, 1964; Richard Jensen, *The Winning of the Midwest: Social and Political Conflict, 1888–1896*, 1971; Stanley L. Jones, *The Presidential Election of 1896*, 1964.

Robert W. Cherny

PRESIDENTIAL ELECTION OF 1900. The nation enjoyed economic prosperity during President William McKinley's first term. The protective Dingley Tariff received most credit, because the Gold Standard Act, a key part of the 1896 Republican campaign, did not go into effect until 1900. Monopolies and trusts multiplied, and the United States unexpectedly emerged as a force in global politics, entering the Spanish-American War, acquiring Puerto Rico and the Philippines, and demanding an interoceanic canal.

The Republican National Convention met at Philadelphia in June. McKinley's renomination was assured. The only uncertainty was his running mate. Vice President Garret Hobart had died, and McKinley left his replacement to the convention. Mark Hanna wanted Cornelius Bliss, who refused the offer. There was a boom

for the governor of New York, Theodore Roosevelt. He had become quite popular because of his Rough Riders during the Spanish-American War. New York political boss Thomas Platt helped orchestrate the nomination of Roosevelt to get him out of New York politics. Mark Hanna unsuccessfully tried to block it.

The Democrats held their convention in Kansas City, Missouri, in July. William Jennings Bryan, the party nominee in 1896, was the obvious choice again. He was unwilling to give up his free coinage of silver position for this election. The issue created divisions, and became a plank of the party platform by a single vote. Bryan, who had supported the Spanish-American War, was critical of U.S. imperialism, particularly in the Philippines. Adlai E. Stevenson was selected as Bryan's running mate. A faction of the divided Populist Party also supported Bryan. The Socialist Party appeared, with the durable Eugene V. Debs as its nominee.

Bryan downplayed free silver and focused on imperialism. Since that did not ignite voter interest, he turned to the issue of the trusts and special privilege. Mark Hanna managed McKinley's campaign, collecting a war chest of over $2.5 million from big business alarmed by Bryan's positions. President McKinley was unwilling to campaign, but Roosevelt did so actively. Hanna also hit the campaign trail, and generally made a good impression. The Republican campaign focused on the good economy, with the slogans "Let well enough alone" and "a full dinner pail." McKinley did better than he had in 1896. In 1900, he collected 292 electoral votes to Bryan's 155. The Republicans captured more western states than they had in 1896. McKinley garnered 7,218,491 votes to Bryan's 6,356,734. Six months after his inauguration, McKinley was assassinated in Buffalo, New York, and Theodore Roosevelt succeeded him.

Further Reading: H. Wayne Morgan, *William McKinley and His America*, 1963; Louis W. Koenig, *Bryan: A Political Biography of William Jennings Bryan*, 1971.

William C. Binning

PRESIDENTIAL HOMES. Gilded Age presidential homes reflected the personality, hospitality, comfort, social stability, and times of the occupants. Andrew Johnson's Greeneville, Tennessee, "Homestead" was a two-story, ten-room brick house built about 1850. Ulysses S. Grant's home in Galena, Illinois, on Bouthillier Street was a two-story, Italianate structure of brick erected in 1859–1860 and later enlarged. "Spiegel Grove" (spiegel is the German word for "mirror"), was the home of President Rutherford B. Hayes. Located in Fremont, Ohio, the thirty-three-room mansion with a broad veranda, epitomized nineteenth-century Victorian architecture. Hayes moved there in 1873. Iron gates used at the White House during his presidency marked the entrances to the two-and-one-half-story brick residence after he left office. On the grounds today is the Rutherford B. Hayes Presidential Center, the first presidential library. James A. Garfield's two-and-one-half-story home, "Lawnfield," had been built in 1832 by James Dickey. Garfield purchased it in 1876 and added a front porch, from which he conducted his 1880 presidential campaign. Chester A. Arthur, a Vermont native, moved to New York City in 1853 and lived in what became known as the Arthur House, a five-story brownstone row house on Lexington Avenue, in what was then a fashionable area, most of his adult life. From 1891 to 1904, Grover Cleveland spent summers on Buzzards Bay, Cape Cod, Massachusetts, in "Gray Gables," a two-story clapboard cottage situated on Monument Point. After he left the presidency, Cleveland resided on Hodge Road in Princeton, New Jersey, from 1897 to 1908. He named the house "Westland" to honor a close friend and Princeton professor, Andrew F. West. Completed in the mid-nineteenth century by Commodore Robert F. Stockton, the two-and-one-half-story stone structure, covered with yellow stucco, had twin parlors on the first floor.

Benjamin Harrison contracted with the architect H. T. Brandt to design a brick, sixteen-room Italianate house, with a picket fence along the front sidewalk. Completed in 1875, the home on North Delaware Street was near his Indianapolis law office. William McKinley's personal residences have all been destroyed over the years. A memorial building marks his birthplace in Niles, Ohio. The McKinley Museum, including a science center, a planetarium, and the Ramsayer Research Library, is near his tomb in Canton, Ohio. Theodore Roosevelt lived at Sagamore Hill on Cove Neck Road in Oyster Bay, New York, overlooking Long Island Sound. He named the estate for the Native American chief Sagamore Mohannis, who had owned the land two hundred years earlier. Roosevelt thoroughly enjoyed the solidly constructed Victorian frame-and-brick home of twenty-two rooms containing multiple fireplaces.

Further Reading: (David Kruh and Louis Kruh, *Presidential Landmarks*, 1992; William G. Clotworthy, *Presidential Sites: A Directory of Places Associated with Presidents of the United States*, 1998, and *Homes and Libraries of the Presidents*, 1995.

Leonard Schlup

PRESIDENTIAL SUCCESSION ACT OF 1886.

Vice President Chester A. Arthur's succession to the presidency in 1881, upon James A. Garfield's assassination, and the death of Vice President Thomas A. Hendricks in 1885, left the vice presidential office vacant for much of the 1880s. When Hendricks died, Congress had not yet chosen its leaders, which meant the House had no speaker and the Senate no president pro tempore. Because the existing 1792 succession law named no one beyond that point, an apprehensive Grover Cleveland declined to attend his vice president's funeral in Indianapolis.

Soon thereafter, the Forty-ninth Congress approved a remedy, introduced by Massachusetts Senator George F. Hoar. President Cleveland, who did nothing to initiate or speed the legislation, signed the measure on 19 January 1886. The new act provided a long line of succession. It extended from the vice president, secretary of state, secretary of the Treasury, and on through other cabinet-level executive departments, in order of their creation by Congress. Any new president had to meet eligibility qualifications under the Constitution, and could not be currently facing impeachment proceedings. The law provided for orderly transfer of power while upholding electoral verdicts. It allowed cabinet members, who normally belonged to the president's party, to succeed to the presidency rather than possibly be supplanted by a legislator affiliated with the political opposition. The law remained in force until 1947.

Further Reading: Ruth C. Silva, *Presidential Succession*, 1968.

Leonard Schlup

PRINTING ACT OF 1895. The Printing Act of 1895 initiated major changes in the depository library system and the description and collocation of public documents. It consolidated existing laws dealing with the printing, binding, and distribution of documents, and enlarged the categories of materials eligible for depository libraries. The legislation codified free public access to federal government information materials that were of public interest or educational value, except those strictly for administrative purposes, classified under national security, or constrained by privacy considerations. It stated specifically that government publications were for public use without charge.

This legislation specified two publications for the delineation and arrangement of public documents. First, it required that a "comprehensive index of public documents" be prepared "at the close of each regular session of Congress." *The Catalogue of the Public Documents of the . . . Congress and of All Departments of the Government of the United States* fulfilled this stipulation. Second, the measure called for a catalog listing the publications printed during a month, where they were obtainable, and their price. *The Monthly Catalog of United States Government Publications* met this requirement. Dr. John Griffith Ames, superintendent of documents from 1881 to 1893, compiled the *Comprehensive Index to the Publications of the United States Government*. In addition, he introduced the practice of serial set numbering and assumed responsibility for the issuance of the *Checklist of United States Public Documents, 1789–1909*.

The 1895 act also transferred the position of superintendent of public documents in the Department of the Interior, a position created in 1869, to the Government Printing Office, established in 1861 by the Printing Act of 1860. The 1895 enactment renamed the position superintendent of documents and expanded the respon-

sibilities of the officeholder. With amendments, the Gilded Age statute remained in force until the Depository Library Act of 1962.

Further Reading: Joe Morehead, *Introduction to United States Government Information Sources*, 5th ed., 1996.

Leonard Schlup

PRISONS. During the Gilded Age, American prisons witnessed two major changes: the creation and institutionalization of industry in prison and the first calls for reform. Between 1868 and 1900, prison industry became so important that states invented ways to use and profit from inmate labor. Some employed a contract system, whereby prison officials leased the labor of convicts to outside contractors who provided the raw materials and machinery, and supervised the work of the inmates, while prison guards ensured that no inmates tried to escape. States also used the piece-price system, under which a contractor paid a prearranged amount to the prison for goods after supplying the prison with raw materials. Other arrangements included the state-account system and the state-use system. In the former, states sold prison-produced goods on the open market and inmates received a very small share of the profits. Under the latter, other state entities (e.g., hospitals and state offices) used goods produced by inmate labor. Finally, states also had inmates produce goods used by the prison. Prison agriculture quickly became a necessary part of institutional life, especially since growing and harvesting crops involved hard labor for inmates.

The Gilded Age featured the first prison-reform agitation. In 1870, for example, the National Congress on Penitentiary and Reformatory Discipline met in Cincinnati, Ohio. Organized by noted penologists, the gathering provided a national forum for correctional experts. Some sought to create reformatories as the foundation of a "new penology." Championed by Zebulon R. Brockway, then warden of the Elmira State Reformatory in New York State, it stressed individualized treatment, indeterminate sentences, inmate education, and parole. The "reformatory movement," as it was known, flourished between 1870 and 1910, spearheaded by Brockway's policies. Reforms included educational training for inmates, designated library hours, lectures by faculty members, and vocational training workshops.

While some of the programs established at Elmira quickly spread to other states, the reformatory movement as a whole ultimately failed. In most cases, prison officials never implemented Brockway's reforms, and by 1910, they fell into disfavor. The experiment did, however, leave its mark on prisons; indeterminate sentences, conditional release (parole), educational programs for inmates, and rehabilitation became the foundation for correctional policy in later decades. The Gilded Age was a period of contrasts in U.S. prisons. At the very time when "new penology" proponents believed that education, religion, meaningful work, and self-governance should come into the prison, opponents, especially conservative administrators and politicians, argued that "stern discipline" was the best way to control inmates. They continued to advocate time-honored regimentation and harsh discipline. Meanwhile, prison industry became one of the most important features of institutional life, one that continues to the present.

Further Reading: Michael Foucault, *Discipline and Punishment*, 1978; Adam J. Hirsch, *The Rise of the Penitentiary: Prisons and Punishment in Early America*, 1992.

John J. Sloan III

PROCTOR, REDFIELD (1 June 1831–4 March 1908), governor, secretary of war, and senator. Born in Proctorsville, Vermont, Proctor graduated from Dartmouth College in 1851, earned a degree from the Albany (New York) Law School eight years later, and fought in the Union Army. Thereafter, he practiced law in Rutland, Vermont, and ran a marble company. He held seats in both houses of the state legislature in the 1860s and 1870s, and was elected lieutenant governor in 1876 and governor in 1878. When President Benjamin Harrison took office in 1889, he appointed Proctor secretary of war. Proctor sought to build modern guns for fortification and field service, improve the pay and rations of enlisted men, and organize the Record and Pension Division. He resigned in 1891 to become U.S. senator, and subsequently won elections in 1892, 1898, and 1904.

He endorsed protective tariffs and the gold standard. He also proposed to limit the presidency and vice presidency to a single six-year term each. In 1898 Proctor undertook a fact-finding tour of Cuba. Upon his return, he delivered a ringing denunciation of Spanish colonialism. The speech strengthened interventionist sentiment, and helped precipitate the Spanish-American War. Proctor delighted in the brief conflict and approved the Treaty of Paris that followed. He died in Washington, D.C.

Further Reading: *Montpelier Evening News*, 5 March 1908; Chester W. Bowie, "Redfield Proctor: A Biography," Ph.D. diss., University of Wisconsin at Madison, 1980; Redfield Proctor Papers, Proctor Free Library, Proctor, Vermont.

Leonard Schlup

PROCTOR'S SPEECH. On 17 March 1898, Republican Senator Redfield Proctor of Vermont, secretary of war under President Benjamin Harrison, delivered a crucial and persuasive speech on the Senate floor. Yellow journalists had alleged Spanish oppression in Cuba, and Proctor had journeyed there to ascertain the situation. He reported firsthand on Spanish atrocities he had witnessed. His rhetoric aroused indignation against Spain and fueled the flames of war. Proctor described the brutality of General Valeriano Weyler and his reconcentration policy. He detailed unsanitary conditions, starvation, death in the streets, polluted earth and water, and disease, stating that these matters had to be seen to be appreciated. His words had a profound and instant impact on the nation, and greatly influenced Senate and public opinion. They strengthened and increased American interventionist sentiment. The religious commentator Lyman Abbott recorded in his memoirs that Proctor's address aroused a storm of irresistible humanitarian indignation. Five weeks later, the United States declared war against Spain.

Further Reading: Michelle B. Davis and Rollin W. Quimby, "Senator Proctor's Cuban Speech: Speculations on a Cause of the Spanish-American War," *Quarterly Journal of Speech* 55 (1969): 131–141; Chester W. Bowie, "Redfield Proctor: A Biography," Ph.D. diss., University of Wisconsin at Madison, 1980; Redfield Proctor, *The Condition of Cuba: It Is Not Peace, nor Is It War*, 1898.

Leonard Schlup

PROHIBITION AND PROHIBITION PARTY. Prohibition was a reform issue that predated the Gilded Age and was not resolved until the Progressive period, despite the activities of the Prohibition Party. Many Americans, especially those of Anglo-Saxon and old immigrant stock, saw liquor as an unmitigated evil that needed to be outlawed. As early as the 1850s, many temperance advocates embraced prohibition of the manufacture and sale of liquor as the solution to the liquor problem and pressured states to ban liquor. Before the Civil War, thirteen states banned liquor, but such laws proved short-lived. At the opening of the Gilded Age, only three prohibition states survived; and in those states the policy was poorly enforced. Throughout the period, there was a constant agitation for the creation of state prohibition laws or state constitutional prohibition; by the end of the period, the number of prohibition states had doubled to six. Strangely, this agitation was mostly carried on by reformers not directly associated with the Prohibition Party.

The Prohibition Party was the leading male temperance organization of the Gilded Age. An 1869 convention launched the party as an alternative to the major parties, which drys believed largely ignored temperance reform. The mainline party faithful feared that the drys' efforts could destroy the current party system and give birth to a new political era dominated by prohibitionism. The new party never succeeded in its grandiose plan to reshape the system, in part because it did not grow as its adherents hoped it would. Its members came primarily from the temperance wing of the Republicans, and it had effective organizations only in the northeastern and midwestern states. Though it failed to become a true national organization, the party grew from the 1870s through the 1890s. Where the Republicans retreated on the issue, the Prohibition Party gained votes, reaching its electoral zenith in 1892, when it gleaned 2.2 percent of all votes cast.

The emergence of Populism ended the Prohibition Party's electoral appeal. Throughout its history, the party was beset with factionalism and bedeviled as to what other issues (such as woman suffrage) to embrace or reject. Thus, it followed a vacillating course. At times, it was very narrow-gauge, focusing exclusively on the prohibition issue. At other times, it attempted to become broad-gauge. For instance, in the early 1890s, the party was active in seeking a grand reform coalition with the Populists and Knights of Labor. Moreover, because it asked men to abandon their party affiliation in an age where party affiliation was extremely strong, it remained marginal, unable to achieve it stated goal.

The Prohibition Party's chief accomplishment was proselytizing; through its platforms, candidates, and publications, bringing the liquor issue to the public's attention. The party also refined prohibitionist ideas and programs, dedicating the movement to total criminalization of liquor and rejecting lesser restrictions on the trade. Its stated goal was national prohibition, but paradoxically the party supported state prohibition efforts, and even local efforts to ban liquor sales as means to that end. Even so, the Prohibition Party was never able to defeat the liquor interests in the political arena or curtail the sale of liquor to any great degree. By the middle of the 1890s, the party was widely perceived to be a failure, a perception that fueled the creation of a new organization, the Anti-Saloon League.

Further Reading: Jack Blocker, Jr., *Retreat from Reform: The Prohibition Movement in the United States, 1890–1913*, 1976; Thomas R. Pegram, *Battling Demon Rum: The Struggle for a Dry America, 1800–1933*, 1998; D. Leigh Colvin, *Prohibition in the United States: A History of the Prohibition Party and the Prohibition Movement*, 1926.

Richard F. Hamm

PROMONTORY, UTAH. Advocates of Manifest Destiny had long favored building transcontinental railroads to lure Americans west. Such lines would stimulate western farming and would bind the territory between the Atlantic and Pacific oceans into a single culture. The first transcontinental rail link became reality on 10 May 1869 at Promontory, Utah, when the Central Pacific, stretching 689 miles east from Sacramento, California, joined the Union Pacific, which spanned 1,086 miles west from Omaha, Nebraska. The crew that connected them included Americans of Irish, Chinese, Mexican, African, and English ancestries. A gold spike commemorated the event, though the final spike was steel, a far more durable metal. It was wired to a telegraph line so Americans throughout the country could hear it being pounded. Leland Stanford, former governor of California, swung the hammer to drive the spike, but missed. Despite Stanford's gaffe, the telegrapher sent the message "Done," and Americans cheered. During the next quarter-century, four more lines crossed the United States.

Further Reading: George R. Taylor and Irene Neu, *The American Railroad Network*, 1956; George Kraus, *High Road to Promontory*, 1969.

Christopher Cumo

PROSTITUTION. Despite sporadic campaigns to curb or eliminate prostitution, it was an ubiquitous institution of the Gilded Age. Earlier efforts to contain the activity to informally sanctioned red light districts had reduced its visibility in many neighborhoods, but those measures did not significantly reduce the number of women engaged in the trade. Estimates suggest that 5 to 10 percent of women in New York City were prostitutes, and that the proportion increased in times of economic depression.

Prostitution played a significant role in the western states and territories. Protected by businessmen and local governments that profited from its revenues, and informally sanctioned by the U.S. Army, it employed a significant fraction of women working outside the home. Few ever achieved the wealth and respectability of the mythical queens of the saloons, but despite the exploitation, ostracism, and danger they faced, prostitutes occasionally managed to earn a living and acquire some property and standing in their communities.

Recent scholarship has complicated considerably the eastern prostitute's image as a victim of the white slave traffic. While coercion (as well as assault, murder, disease, suicide, substance abuse, and legal sanction) played a role in the lives of many prostitutes, for others prostitution may have appeared to be least deplorable among a very limited and repressive set of economic choices. Many participants remained in the life for only a few years, or worked part-time to supplement their meager incomes.

Further Reading: Barbara Meil Hobson, *Uneasy Virtue: The Politics of Prostitution and the American Reform Tradition*, 1987; Timothy J. Gilfoyle, *City of Eros: New York City, Prostitution, and the Commercialization of Sex, 1790–1920*, 1992; Anne M. Butler, *Daughters of Joy, Sisters of Misery: Prostitution in the American West, 1865–90*, 1985.

James D. Ivy

PROTECTIONISM. The most popular tariff policy among Republicans during the Gilded Age, protectionism sought to employ high customs duties on foreign imports—especially manufactures—to prevent them from competing in the domestic market. Protectionism had roots in Alexander Hamilton's Treasury program of 1789 and Henry Clay's "American System" of the 1820s. Though resisted by Democrats, it was most influential as the United States industrialized between 1868 and 1897. Protectionism shaped the McKinley and Dingley tariffs of 1890 and 1897, respectively, blocking tariff reduction in 1894. After 1901 it lost favor to reciprocal trade agreements through which American manufacturers could obtain duty-free raw materials and duty-free access to foreign markets for their products.

Further Reading: Clarence A. Stern, *Protectionist Republicanism: Republican Tariff Policy in the McKinley Period*, 1971; Paul Wolman, *Most Favored Nation: The Republican Revisionists and U.S. Tariff Policy, 1897–1912*, 1992.

Douglas Steeples

PROTESTANT THOUGHT AND CHURCHES. Grounded in the traditions of the Reformation, Pietism, and early American Puritanism, Gilded Age Protestants exhibited a number of character traits linking together the diversity of their mainline denominations (Congregationalists, Baptists, Presbyterians, Episcopalians). First, they generally regarded the Bible as God's definitive communication to humankind. Because Scripture is "God-breathed," they argued, its pages must be free from error in everything it teaches, for God does not lie. Second, they believed that the objective gospel—the message that Christ's death and resurrection bring forgiveness of sins and salvation—must be appropriated subjectively through an individual, personal faith in Christ. This emphasis on personal conversion (and its corporate counterpart, revivalism) was best exemplified in the ministry of Dwight L. Moody, who transformed American revivalism into a gentle offering of the love of God through the proclamation of the simple gospel. Third, they believed personal transformation through the gospel immediately suggested a social, moral, and political agenda that enshrined Christian virtue, thereby ensuring the perpetuity of God's chosen nation. From these sentiments arose the social reforms of Frances Willard's temperance movement and the Woman's Christian Temperance Union, the Sabbatarian movement, and fellowships such as the Salvation Army and the Young Men's Christian Association (both British imports), which responded to the social and economic blight that accompanied industrialism.

Though Protestants championed their cause against those outside their ranks—Roman Catholics, Mormons, and Spiritists—a greater enemy arose from within. Due to a substantial reliance on Scottish Common Sense epistemology, American Protestants were confident of the unity between the two "books" of God: the Bible and nature. When new theories such as Darwinism and higher Biblical criticism began to question this cherished unity, American Protestants, rather than reexamining the foundations of their epistemology (as many Continental Protestants did), generally responded in one of three ways. A handful, such as Princeton's president James McCosh, who embraced a form of evolution, cautiously adopted the new learning within the structures of conservative orthodoxy. Slightly more popular was an uncritical embrace of the new learning combined with an acceptance of Protestant theological liberalism, which denied the existence of the supernatural, miracles, and hell, and called into question both the exclusivity of Christianity and the unity of the Bible. Though largely confined to the academy and the well-educated, these views began to circulate among American Protestants through popular preachers such as Henry Ward Beecher and Phillips Brooks, as well as through sensational "heresy trials" of left-leaning seminary professors such as Charles A. Briggs of Union Seminary in the early 1890s. The great majority of American Protestants, however, resisted the new learning, remaining loyal to their Bibles and their ministries.

A new Protestant theology, which represented a popular alternative to the older conservative orthodoxies, came to their aid: Dispensational Premillennialism. Developed by the Irish Protestant John N. Darby at mid-century, and popularized through annual, interdenominational gatherings such as the Niagara Bible conferences and Moody's Northfield (Massachusetts) Bible conferences, Dispensational Premillennialism offered American Protestants a fresh view of history (Christ could return at any moment), an impetus to moral purity and missions ("Are you ready for his return? Is the world ready?"), and a literal hermeneutic of biblical interpretation that shielded their theology from the new learning. By 1900, it was increasingly clear that constituencies in each of the mainline denominations were moving in different theological directions, a trend that would culminate in the Fundamentalist-Modernist controversy, splitting the mainline denominations in the generation after World War I.

Further Reading: Paul A. Carter, *The Spiritual Crisis of the Gilded Age*, 1971; George M. Marsden, *Fundamentalism and American Culture*, 1980.

Robert Caldwell

PUBLIC LIBRARIES. When the Boston Public Library (BPL) opened its doors in 1852, it created a model followed by most public libraries established thereafter. Democracy required an informed citizenry, BPL organizers argued, and using local tax dollars to make "good" books and "useful knowledge" accessible to the public constituted a civic responsibility. It would also, they said, help citizens educate themselves beyond the primary grades. Within a generation, 250 more public libraries were founded. Most had grown out of social libraries, and most were located in the Northeast.

Several factors contributed to the spread of public libraries in the late nineteenth century: a growing economy, an expanding population, rapid industrialization, mechanization of the printing and paper industries, and shifting attitudes about government's responsibility to educate citizens. In this environment, an emerging library profession lobbied for more public libraries. In 1876, for example, Melvil Dewey helped establish the American Library Association; published his decimal classification system to uniformly organize library collections; began editing a new periodical, *Library Journal*, which functioned as a forum for developing a professional discourse; and started a library supplies company. By 1900, America boasted over one thousand public libraries, most of which practiced a "library science" that emphasized efficient service and management, and delegated to other professionals the authority to identify the "good" books that libraries would collect. More than twenty state library commissions and a similar number of state library associations added their voices.

By that time, the steel magnate Andrew Carnegie had articulated a philosophy that challenged all wealthy Americans to support self-improvement institutions such as libraries. Although many took up his challenge (between 1890 and 1896, philanthropists donated $34 million to fund public libraries), Carnegie led the charge. By the time he died in 1919, he had contributed $41 million to construct 1,679 public library buildings in 1,412 communities. To qualify, a community had only to provide a suitable site and promise annual support of 10 percent of the construction grant.

Despite the best intentions of librarians to provide good reading for the greatest number at the lowest cost, throughout the Gilded Age (and after) patrons routinely sought mostly popular fiction. Although professional guides such as the *Catalog of A.L.A. Library* (1893) recommended that collections contain no more than 20 percent fiction, in 1901 popular fiction still constituted 65 to 75 percent of books that public libraries circulated.

Further Reading: Sidney H. Ditzion, *Arsenals of a Democratic Culture: A Social History of the American Public Library Movement in New England and the Middle Atlantic States from 1850 to 1900*, 1947; Wayne A. Wiegand, *The Politics of an Emerging Profession: The American Library Association, 1876–1917*, 1986; Abigail A. Van Slyck, *Free to All: Carnegie Libraries and American Culture, 1890–1920*, 1995.

Wayne A. Wiegand

PUCK. The nation's premier magazine of humor and political satire during the late nineteenth century, *Puck* was published in New York City between 1877 and 1918. For much of its long run, the magazine was under the artistic domination of its chief founder, the Vienna-born cartoonist Joseph Keppler (1838–1894), who earlier had published a German-language version in St. Louis. In September 1876, he and Adolf Swaezmann, business manager of *Leslie's Illustrated*, founded a second German-language *Puck* in New York. In March 1877, they launched the more famous English version with a different text and an editorial page written especially for a middle-class American audience. Over the next decade, the magazine's staff grew to more than four hundred, and included several cartoonists who achieved preeminence. Unlike its St. Louis predecessor, the English-language *Puck* focused more on issues and trends in nation, state, and city than on international affairs. In 1879, the incorporation of full-color lithography further enhanced its quality and appeal. Through its biting and often savvy, if biased, editorial columns and its generally high literary quality, due largely to its longtime editor, Henry C. Bunner, the magazine developed into an important mirror and molder of public opinion.

Although typically Democratic in national politics, by the early 1880s *Puck* was a respected voice of independent (later Mugwump) political ideas, a relentless and feared critic of political corruption, and a source of frequent anticlerical polemics, particularly against the Catholic Church in the mid-to-late 1880s. Its paid circulation peaked at a very respectable ninety thousand, and its cartoons rivaled those of Thomas Nast, who worked for *Harper's*. *Puck* has long been a valuable, albeit underutilized, primary source for researchers and teachers of the Gilded Age.

Further Reading: Richard Samuel West, *Satire on Stone: The Political Cartoons of Joseph Keppler*, 1988; Richard Marschall, "What Fools These Mortals Be: The History of the Comic Strip . . . Parts 1 and 2," *The Comics Journal* 57 (June 1980): 134–139, and 58 (September 1980): 84–87.

Samuel J. Thomas

PUGH, JAMES LAWRENCE (3 May 1819–9 March 1907), lawyer and politician. Born near Waynesboro, Georgia, Pugh was educated in Alabama and Georgia. Admitted to the Alabama bar in 1841, he practiced in Eufaula. Pugh was elected to Congress as a Democrat in 1858, but resigned when Alabama seceded. After brief military service, Pugh was chosen for the Confederate Congress; unlike many of his House colleagues, he was reelected in 1863. He took an active part in opposing Republican power. Chairman of the Democratic National Convention in 1874, he was a prominent member of Alabama's 1875 constitutional convention. As such, he helped to build the Bourbon system of limited government and emphasis upon white supremacy. Pugh ran unsuccessfully for the U.S. Senate in 1878, but two years later was elected to fill the unexpired term of George S. Houston, who had defeated him. In the Senate, Pugh deviated from the states' rights faith by backing the Blair Bill, supporting creation of the Interstate Commerce Commission, and seeking federal aid for Alabama's rivers and harbors. He was also an ardent supporter of free silver. His sympathy for the Farmers' Alliancemen and Populist rebels contributed to his defeat in 1896 by the Bourbon candidate Edmund Pettus. After leaving office, Pugh lived out the rest of his life in Washington, D.C.

Further Reading: Thomas M. Owen, *History of Alabama and Dictionary of Alabama Biography*, 1921; Austin L. Venable, "Alabama's 'War of the Roses,'" *Alabama Review* 8 (1955): 243–259; Mary Jane Davidson, "James Lawrence Pugh: A Half Century in Politics," M.A. thesis, Auburn University, 1971.

Paul M. Pruitt, Jr.

PULITZER, JOSEPH (10 April 1847–29 October 1911), journalist and newspaper publisher. Born in Mako, Hungary, the German-speaking Pulitzer immigrated to the United States in 1864. After service in the Union Army, he journeyed to St. Louis, which had a sizable German population. There he studied law, made friends with the Radical Republican Carl Schurz, and was hired as a reporter for the *Westliche Post* in 1868. He joined with Schurz and other Missouri Republicans to form the Liberal Republican Party in 1871. The defeat of Horace Greeley for president in 1872 so disheartened Pulitzer that he became a lifelong Democrat.

Pulitzer worked as a newsman, politician, and lawyer until he purchased the *St. Louis Dispatch* at a foreclosure sale and merged it with the *Post* in 1878. The combined newspaper, which specialized in reform stories and sensationalism, lived up to its promise of opposing all fraud and shams and serving no party but the people, although it was Democratic by choice. It was one of St. Louis's most influential and profitable newspapers when Pulitzer expanded his horizons and purchased the failing *New York World* in 1883. Pulitzer remade the morning *World* into a voice of social conscience. He assailed what he called the vulgar wealthy and watered-stock aristocracy of New York, and exposed such horrors of immigrant tenement life as high infant mortality, starvation, and other "slum tragedies" that were ignored by other newspapers. Pulitzer championed Grover Cleveland's election in 1884, making the *World* one of the leading Democratic voices in the country. In 1887, he hired away a twenty-one-year-old *Pittsburgh Dispatch* reporter named Elizabeth Cochrane, who called herself Nellie Bly, and helped her become the best-known female newswriter of the century.

Aided by faster and more far-reaching trains, Pulitzer was able to distribute his *Sunday World* to eight surrounding states before breakfast by 1886, and the paper's total circulation grew to over 740,000 by 1896. Blindness and poor health forced Pulitzer to run his newspaper empire through memoranda for much of his life, but he maintained control over editorial content and finances through intermediaries. William Randolph Hearst's purchase of the *New York Evening Journal* in 1895 ignited the greatest newspaper circulation war in American history. Hearst considered the *World* "old journalism," and competed with Pulitzer through the art of ballyhoo or self-promotion to attract new readers and by luring away many of Pulitzer's best reporters, editors, and contributors with higher salaries. Among his conquests was R. F. Outcault, creator of the first continuing newspaper comic strip, "The Yellow Kid," and the *Sunday*

World staff, which Hearst hired in its entirety in 1896.

There were nearly forty war correspondents covering rebel insurgents in Cuba by 1897. The *World* and the *Journal* agreed that the McKinley administration was reacting too slowly to the Cuban crisis, but that was all until the U.S.S. *Maine* exploded in Havana harbor on 15 February 1898. Sensationalistic coverage in the *World* sold five million copies over the following week, but Pulitzer lost money for the year. The Hearst-Pulitzer competition made the Spanish-American War the first media war in American history. The Hearst press slowly eclipsed Pulitzer's circulation around the turn of the twentieth century, but his newspapers continued to be profitable. Pulitzer endowed a journalism school at Columbia University, one of the first in the country, and annual prizes in journalism and writing that were named for him after his death. He died in Charleston, South Carolina.

Further Reading: George Juergens, *Joseph Pulitzer and the New York World*, 1966; W. A. Swanberg, *Pulitzer*, 1967.

Richard Digby-Junger

PULLMAN, GEORGE MORTIMER (3 March 1831–19 October 1897), industrialist. Pullman was born in Brocton, New York, where he attended school until age fourteen. He designed a sleeping car for railroad passengers, and later dining, chair, and vestibule cars. In 1867 he founded the Pullman Palace Car Company and, over time, constructed a town named for himself south of Chicago to house his workers. Pullman fancied himself an enlightened capitalist, and spent $1.2 million building a trade school in his town. When the economy slumped in 1893, however, he slashed wages by as much as 40 percent, without reducing rents or prices in Pullman. Workers petitioned him to restore wages in 1894. When he fired three of them, American Railway Union president Eugene V. Debs called a nationwide strike that idled 260,000 workers. Pullman, fearing mass sabotage, requested federal aid. In response, President Grover Cleveland sent troops to Chicago; they killed thirteen persons and wounded more than fifty on 4 July. The strike collapsed after the arrest of Debs and other union leaders. Despite its failure, the strike revealed Pullman's ruthlessness. He died in Chicago, his wealth intact but his philanthropic image tarnished.

Further Reading: Stanley Buder, *Pullman: An Experiment in Industrial Order and Community Planning, 1880–1930*, 1967; Almont Lindsey, *The Pullman Strike: The Story of a Unique Experiment and of a Great Labor Upheaval*, 1942; *Chicago Daily Tribune*, 20 October 1897.

Christopher Cumo

PULLMAN STRIKE. One of the greatest challenges posed by organized labor in the Gilded Age was the Pullman strike, when several hundred thousand railroad workers stopped train traffic for weeks in the summer of 1894. Pullman came in the wake of large, vicious, and ultimately unsuccessful strikes among steelworkers in Homestead, Pennsylvania, and hardrock miners in the Coeur d'Alene Mountains of Idaho. Taken together, these three events demonstrated the intensity of class conflict during the Gilded Age. If the "southern question" was the topic of mid-nineteenth-century America, surely the "labor question" was one issue that helped define the Gilded Age.

The depression of 1893–1898 was the worst in U.S. history until that time. The Pullman Palace Car Company laid off many workers and cut others' wages by between 25 and 40 percent—without reducing the rents in the company-owned town where many Pullman workers lived.

Thousands of Pullman workers belonged to the recently formed American Railway Union (ARU). Led by Eugene V. Debs, the ARU was created to challenge the exclusive craft union model of the railroad brotherhoods; the ARU would organize all workers, regardless of skill, so long as they toiled in the railroad industry—with the important exception of African Americans, who were denied membership. On 26 June 1894, after Pullman workers struck, the 150,000-member ARU called a nationwide boycott of all railroads that carried Pullman cars. An additional one hundred thousand workers recognized this boycott, and another quarter-million were affected by it. By the end of June, railroad traffic nationwide was seriously affected, most importantly in Chicago, the hub of the nation's transportation network.

Workers were not the only ones organized. Twenty-six railroad companies formed the General Managers Association (GMA) in order to help the Pullman Company defeat the strike. The GMA announced that any worker who refused to handle a Pullman car would be fired. Furthermore, the GMA appealed to the federal government, claiming that the strike interfered with the delivery of the U.S. mail (railroads started joining mail and Pullman cars together). Subsequently, Attorney General Richard Olney secured a sweeping injunction from the federal courts on the grounds of protecting the mail against the ARU's boycott. On Independence Day, federal troops, supported by state militia forces, arrived in Chicago, ignoring the protest of Governor John Peter Altgeld, who denounced President Grover Cleveland's handling of the situation. Thirteen strikers were killed and more than fifty wounded in fighting. In twenty-six states across the nation, violent clashes left a total of thirty-four people dead and millions of dollars in property destroyed.

In the aftermath, the strike was broken and the ARU was destroyed. Debs and other leaders were held in contempt of court and served six months in jail. In prison, Debs converted to socialism; he would become the most influential socialist in American history. The Pullman strike placed the public on notice that labor conflicts were becoming increasingly national and industrial in scope, and demonstrated the extent to which solidarity had developed as a result of fierce class conflict in the Gilded Age.

Further Reading: Stanley Buder, *Pullman: An Experiment in Industrial Order and Community Planning, 1880–1930,* 1967; William H. Carwardine, *The Pullman Strike,* 1894; Samuel Yellen, *American Labor Struggles,* 1969.

Peter Cole

PUTNAM, FREDERIC WARD (16 April 1839–14 August 1915), anthropologist and museologist. Born in Salem, Massachusetts, Putnam, at age seventeen, became curator of ornithology at the Essex Institute in Salem, and entered the Lawrence Scientific School at Harvard University. There he studied under the prominent naturalist Louis Agassiz. Putnam held appointments with various museums and scientific surveys over the next two decades. In 1874 he accepted the post of curator of the Peabody Museum at Harvard University and in 1886 that of Peabody professor of American archaeology and ethnology, remaining as professor from 1886 to 1909. He also served as curator of the American Museum of National History in New York from 1894 to 1903. Putnam's work in museum administration, field investigation, and academe, plus his memberships in numerous professional organizations, helped define anthropology as a standardized scientific branch of knowledge. In 1893 Putnam directed the anthropological division of the World's Columbian Exposition in Chicago. His expeditions in Ohio led to the excavation and restoration of Serpent Mound. He died in Cambridge, Massachusetts.

Further Reading: *Boston Transcript,* 16 August 1915; Alfred M. Tozzer, "Frederic Ward Putnam, 1839–1915," in *Biographical Memoirs National Academy of Sciences* 16 (1935): 125–52; Frederic W. Putnam Papers, Peabody Museum Archives, Harvard University.

Leonard Schlup

**QUAY, MATTHEW STAN-
LEY** (30 September 1833–28
May 1904), Republican senator,
party national chairman, and
powerbroker. A lifelong Penn-
sylvanian, Quay was born in
Dillsburg, graduated from Jef-

ferson College, and was admitted to the Beaver
County bar in 1854. He won the Congressional
Medal of Honor during the Civil War and subsequently attracted veterans en masse to his political camp. Quay began his postwar career as
a subordinate in Simon Cameron's political machine, and took over Republican state leadership about 1886. Together with Cameron before
him and Boies Penrose after him, he helped administer the state's dynasty of party bosses
(1867–1921). Like the others, Quay cared more
about power, organization, and patronage than
about program. Although the economy of his
state dictated that he be a tariff advocate, his
direct role in Senate legislation was not extensive. He was a member of the committees on
Commerce, Territories, Indian Affairs, and
Manufactures, and chaired the Committee on
Public Buildings and Grounds. Here Quay
could expedite or delay construction of all new
federal buildings. He quickly discovered the
potential power in this office. Since senators
and congressmen were always clamoring for
new (and more) post offices in their districts,
he could speed a post office project through
channels in exchange for a legislator's promised votes on issues important to him.

Quay first served as a state legislator, then as
treasurer and secretary of the Commonwealth
of Pennsylvania before his election to the U.S.
Senate, where he served from 1887 to 1904.
Head of the state Republican Party in 1886, he
became national chairman in 1888. He provided
pivotal influence in that year's elections. Although Benjamin Harrison was a minority president (by one hundred thousand votes), Quay
managed to capture nineteen House seats from
southern states for the Republican Party, more
than in any year since Reconstruction. For the
first time in sixteen years the Republicans controlled both Congress and the presidency.

Quay's leadership was crucial
to legislation in the "Billion
Dollar Congress" of 1890. He
gained more respect in the South
than any other Republican of his period because
he prevented the Federal Elections Bill from
coming to a vote. Its tabling angered President
Harrison, led to the most bitter internal quarrel
the Republican Party experienced in its first
hundred years, and contributed to Harrison's
defeat in 1892.

Under Quay's leadership, Pennsylvania became the most solidly Republican and most
boss-dominated state during the late nineteenth
century. As a result of his tactics, it sent a
Republican-dominated delegation to Congress
every two years and provided Republican elec-
tors every four. Along with Thomas C. Platt of
New York, Quay introduced a new style of
bossism, one with a power base in the individual states, replacing party reliance on federal
patronage. Quay died in Beaver, Pennsylvania.
Further Reading: James A. Kehl, *Boss Rule in the Gilded
Age: Matt Quay of Pennsylvania*, 1981; Robert G. Crist,
ed., *Pennsylvania Kingmakers*, 1985.

James A. Kehl

QUIGG, LEMUEL ELY (12 February 1863–
1 July 1919), journalist and congressman. Born
near Chestertown, Maryland, and educated in
the Wilmington, Delaware, public schools,
Quigg entered journalism at an early age. After
working briefly for the *New York Times*, he became editor of the *Times* of Flushing, Long Island, in 1883, and the following year joined
Whitelaw Reid at the *New York Tribune*. There,
for the next decade, he wrote political articles.
A press agent for the Republican National
Committee in 1892, Quigg expressed loyalty to
Thomas C. Platt of New York, head of the Republican Party machine in the state and city. In
1894, Quigg won election to the U.S. House of
Representatives to fill the vacancy created by
the resignation of John R. Fellows's. Twice re-

elected, he chaired the Committee on Expenditures in the Department of State. Quigg advocated a gold standard and U.S. intervention in Cuba. He was president of the New York County Republican Committee from 1896 to 1900. In 1898, the year he suffered defeat for reelection, Platt dispatched Quigg to persuade Theodore Roosevelt, former assistant secretary of the navy and popular Spanish-American War hero, to run for governor of New York. After losing political prominence under Republican governor Benjamin B. Odell, Quigg became an attorney. He died in New York City.

Further Reading: *New York Times*, 3 July 1919; Harold F. Gosnell, *Boss Platt and His New York Machine*, 1924; L. J. Lang, ed., *The Autobiography of Thomas Collier Platt*, 1910.

Leonard Schlup

QUINCY, JOSIAH PHILLIPS (28 November 1829–31 October 1910), author and historian. Born in Boston, Massachusetts, Quincy graduated from Harvard in 1850, gained admittance to the Massachusetts bar in 1854, traveled abroad, and returned to Quincy, Massachusetts. There he wrote poetry, stories for magazines, fiction, and political articles. Quincy contributed much biographical material to the Massachusetts Historical Society and its *Proceedings*. His varied interests and reading habits embraced spiritualism, biography, science, government, economics, sociology, psychic phenomena, and Shakespeare. He died in Quincy.

Further Reading: *Boston Transcript*, 1 November 1910.

Leonard Schlup

QUINTARD, CHARLES TODD (22 December 1824–15 February 1898), Episcopal bishop and physician. Born in Stamford, Connecticut, Quintard received the M.D. degree from New York University Medical College. Before the Civil War, he held a psychology professorship at the Memphis Medical College, edited the *Memphis Medical Recorder*, and, after completing ministerial studies in 1856, was rector of Calvary Church in Memphis. An eloquent, thoughtful orator, Quintard served in the Confederate Army as both surgeon and chaplain. Elected bishop of Tennessee in 1865, he

worked thereafter for over three decades to reunite the northern and southern branches of his church. In 1877, President Rutherford B. Hayes named Quintard a member of the Board of Visitors to the U.S. Military Academy. In addition to other duties, Quintard traveled extensively, engaged in missionary work, and helped to establish preparatory schools. He also preached in England, and labored relentlessly to secure financial support for the second founding of the University of the South at Sewanee, Tennessee, which constituted his most significant achievement in higher education. Indeed, he personally selected many of the building sites. Quintard was vice chancellor of the institution for nearly six years before his retirement in 1872. He died in Meridian, Georgia.

Further Reading: A. H. Noll, *Doctor Quintard*, 1905; G. R. Fairbanks, *History of the University of the South*, 1905; Richard N. Greatwood, "Charles Todd Quintard (1824–1898): His Role and Significance in the Development of the Protestant Episcopal Church, in the Diocese of Tennessee and in the South" (Ph.D. diss., Vanderbilt University, 1977).

Leonard Schlup

QUINTON, AMELIA STONE (31 July 1833–23 June 1926), reformer. Quinton, influenced by the religious teachings of her grandfather, began doing humanitarian work in New York's charity asylums, infirmaries, prisons, and women's reformatories. She conducted weekend Bible classes for sailors and served as state organizer for the Woman's Christian Temperance Union. In 1879, she moved to Philadelphia, where she joined with Mary Lucinda Bonney to protest white encroachment in Indian Territory, in violation of federal treaties. Quinton also helped establish the Women's National Indian Association. She soon became the driving force of the organization, researching and writing leaflets, addressing missionary groups, meeting with federal Indian officials, and establishing new state associations and auxiliaries. She served as the association's secretary from 1881 to 1887, president from 1887 to 1905, and honorary president for the next twenty years. She also chaired its missionary department.

Further Reading: Valerie Sherer Mathes, *Helen Hunt Jackson and Her Indian Reform Legacy*, 1990, and "Nineteenth Century Women and Reform: The Women's National Indian Association," *American Indian Quarterly* (Winter 1990): 1–18; Amelia Stone Quinton letters, Huntington Library, San Marino, California.

Valerie Sherer Mathes

RACE AND AMERICAN LITERATURE.

RACE AND AMERICAN LITERATURE. Strict attention to race became an unfortunate means of maintaining social boundaries during the sweeping changes of the Gilded Age. Postwar anxiety about status, fed by the newly emerging "science" of eugenics, encouraged a brutal system of racial segregation. Reconstruction's promise of freedom and equality was soon abandoned, and African Americans, stripped of their newly acquired civil rights, lived in the shadow of forced labor, the chain gang, and the lynch mob. The literature of the era reveals this national preoccupation with the color line. Not surprisingly, the divide between white and black dominated literary conversations about race, but authors also considered racial boundaries by employing figures like the barbarous cannibal, the noble savage, and the grasping foreigner. After the Civil War, the reading public sought texts that evoked the clear racial boundaries of the antebellum South. Much of the work of George W. Cable, Charles Chesnutt, Paul Laurence Dunbar, Joel Chandler Harris, and Mark Twain focused on pre–Civil War America. Naturally, the blacks portrayed in these works were usually slaves who could do little to combat the status quo.

As the century progressed, however, many writers began to dismantle the black plantation character in favor of a more complex representation of race relations. For instance, Mark Twain's *The Adventures of Huckleberry Finn* (1884) uses the friendship between a white boy and a runaway slave to question the national belief system that devalued black freedom and dignity. Twain's *Pudd'nhead Wilson* (1894) features a popular literary trope of the time: a black character who can pass for white and defy the supposedly sacrosanct race barrier. African-American authors would often employ such a "tragic mulatto" character to reveal the hypocrisy and brutality necessary to maintain an arbitrary color line. Charles Chesnutt's novels draw on the trials of interracial families to question the logic of segregation. Frances Harper's *Iola Leroy* (1892) focuses on a mulatto woman whose suffering moves her to promote racial equality through education.

But perhaps the greatest revolution in America's literary construction of race came in nonfiction writing. In 1897, W. E. B. Du Bois began publishing essays that insisted on a new place for African Americans in U.S. history. As the nation entered the twentieth century, representations of African Americans in literature had moved from slave characters who fulfilled white expectations to strong individuals whose voices could critique, and eventually transform, America's self-definition.

Further Reading: Bernard Bell, *The Afro American Novel and Its Tradition*, 1987; Leonard Cassuto, *The Inhuman Race: The Racial Grotesque in American Literature and Culture*, 1997; Eric Sundquist, *To Wake the Nations: Race in the Making of American Literature*, 1993.

Anna Mae Duane

RAILROAD REGULATION. To farmers, railroads symbolized the worst abuses of the industrial order. They increased rates at harvest time and offered rebates to industrialists, but not to agrarians. Atop the railroads stood a managerial elite whose fortunes contradicted the agrarian notion of broad wealth distribution. Railroads had no desire to restrain themselves, so farmers sought government regulation. During the 1870s, the Grange convinced five states to establish rate commissions. The effort drew strength from the Supreme Court, which confirmed, in *Munn* v. *Illinois* (1877), the states' authority to do so. The victory proved illusory, however. Governors appointed opponents of regulation to these commissions, and in 1886 the Supreme Court, in *Wabash, Saint Louis, and Pacific Railroad Company* v. *Illinois*, ended the practice. Railroads crossed state lines, and only Congress could monitor interstate trade. After the *Wabash* decision, the Grange and Farmers' Alliance lobbied Congress to create the Interstate Commerce Commission (ICC) in 1887. The railroads had no more to fear from it, however, because it lacked power to enforce its decisions. The ICC's impotence led the People's Party to propose nationalization of the railroads. The idea contradicted a private property tradition in the United States and did not become law during the Gilded Age. The need for railroad regulation confronted Progressives during the twentieth century.

Further Reading: Gabriel Kolko, *Railroads and Regulation, 1877–1916*, 1965.

Christopher Cumo

RAILROAD STRIKE OF 1877. The Panic of 1873 and the ensuing depression led railroad presidents to slash wages. Workers struck in West Virginia on 16 July 1877, because the Baltimore and Ohio cut pay by 10 percent. When President Rutherford B. Hayes ordered troops to West Virginia three days later to protect the railroad, workers in Maryland and Pennsylvania joined the strike. In Baltimore, the state militia killed eleven and wounded forty. Pennsylvania Railroad president Thomas Scott dispatched his own armed men to augment the state militia that gathered at Pittsburgh on 21 July. A shoot-out there killed five soldiers and forty civilians. Strikers retaliated by igniting the railroad yard. In Chicago, federal troops ended a general strike by threatening to use artillery. Over two weeks, the turmoil engulfed fourteen states, spreading as far south as Galveston, Texas, and as far west as San Francisco, California. More than a hundred persons were killed, and property damage totaled millions of dollars. The first national strike, it set the pattern for federal military aid to business. The Gilded Age's most savage confrontation between labor and capital, it presaged similar violence at Chicago in 1886, at Homestead, Pennsylvania, in 1892, and at Pullman, Illinois, in 1894.

Further Reading: David O. Stowell, *Streets, Railroads and the Great Strike of 1877*, 1999; Jerry M. Cooper, "The Army as Strikebreaker: The Railroad Strikes of 1877 and 1894," *Labor History* 18 (1977): 179–196; Robert V. Bruce, *1877: Year of Violence*, 1989.

Christopher Cumo

RAILROAD STRIKE OF 1888. The railroad strike of 1888 lasted ten and a half months and extended from Chicago to Denver. It spotlighted tensions among labor, management, and the government as well as within labor itself. Accordingly, it is an excellent barometer of the class struggle during the Gilded Age. The strike against the Chicago, Burlington and Quincy Railroad (CBQ) was called by engineers over wages, seniority, and grievance procedures. Representing the elite of the railroad workers, the Brotherhood of Locomotive Engineers (BLE) was led by Peter M. Arthur, who preferred arbitration to confrontation and was nicknamed "King Arthur." By contrast, Eugene V. Debs, humble advocate of the common folk, headed the Brotherhood of Locomotive Firemen (BLF). Despite long-standing differences with Arthur, Debs brought both the firemen and the switchmen into the strike. Terence V. Powderly's Knights of Labor, however, angry over the engineers' recent refusal to support them, acted as strikebreakers and the company imported additional workers from points east. CBQ president Charles Elliott Perkins, a fierce opponent of unions, refused to negotiate and hired Pinkertons to control the strikers. Violence erupted, several workers were killed, and trains were disabled. When Perkins secured an injunction from Judge Walter Q. Gresham, Arthur withdrew BLE support for the strike.

In essence, this broke the strike, but thousands of firemen and switchmen stood firm for several more months. In the end, labor was badly defeated. For Debs, the lesson was the need to reorganize across craft lines. Arthur temporarily lost (but later regained) his credibility, and Perkins confirmed his reputation as labor's enemy. Nonetheless, the cost of the strike was so great that it compelled the CBQ to improve some employee policies. Relations within labor, as well as those among labor, management, and the government, were in flux.

Further Reading: John A. Hall, *The Great Strike on the "Q,"* 1889; Donald L. McMurray, *The Great Burlington Strike of 1888*, 1956; Charles H. Salmons, *The Burlington Strike: Its Motives and Methods*, 1889.

Joanne Reitano

RAILROADS. Railroads were the principal transport during the Gilded Age. In their rapid growth and immensity they epitomized the rising industrial order. In 1868, most railroads lay east of the Mississippi River, where they linked midwestern farmers to eastern markets. The Baltimore and Ohio, for example, joined St. Louis to Baltimore, and the New York Central connected Chicago and New York City. The network of track was densest in the Northeast and along the Great Lakes. By comparison, track was sparse in the South, though it stretched as far as Tampa, Florida. By 1868, the United States had roughly thirty-five thousand miles of track. As large as this network was, it doubled between 1868 and 1873. The most impressive achievement during these years was the linking of the Union Pacific and the Central Pacific in May 1869 as the first transcontinental railroad. By 1890, two lines flanked it on either side. To the south lay the Southern Pacific and the Santa Fe, and to the north stretched the Northern Pacific and the Great Northern. The transcontinental lines underscored the vastness of America's railroad system. Between 1879 and 1883, workers laid an average of eight thousand miles per year, and between 1880 and 1889, they put down more than seventy-three thousand miles. By 1900, the United States had nearly two hundred thousand miles, three-quarters of the track it would ever have, and more miles than Great Britain and continental Europe, including Russia. But these tracks did not all have the same width, known as gauge; in 1868, five gauges were used on more than a thousand miles each. In the South, tracks had five-foot gauge, whereas in the North most tracks had four-foot, nine-inch gauge; the New York and Erie railroads used six-foot, and the Grand Trunk had five-foot, six-inch. By 1890, however, all railroads used four-foot, nine-inch gauge.

Whatever the gauge, steel track lasted eight times longer than iron rail. In 1862, the Pennsylvania Railroad had been the first to lay steel track, though its high cost slowed the transition from iron to steel. In 1868, iron cost $83.13 per ton, whereas steel sold for $166 per ton. Only after 1883 was steel cheaper than iron. Thereafter all track laid was steel. Between 1880 and 1889, the percentage of track in steel jumped from 30 to 80 percent.

The expansion, improvement, and consolidation of railroads owed much to investments of land and money. By 1871, the state legislatures and Congress had given the railroads 49 million and 131 million acres of land, respectively. By 1880, private investors had poured more than $4.6 million into the railroads. By 1897, the value of railroad stocks and bonds exceeded $10 billion, ten times the national debt. This money created a managerial elite that included Collis P. Huntington, Charles Crocker, Mark Hopkins, and Leland Stanford, the organizers of the Central Pacific, and Jay Gould, James J. Hill, and Cornelius Vanderbilt, the presidents of the Northern Pacific, the Great Northern, and the New York Central railroads, respectively. Investors in the Union Pacific reaped as much as 1200 percent in a year.

Less spectacular but no less real was the fact that railroads gained an average of 1.9 percent in productivity per year between 1870 and 1890. During these years, the average cost of hauling one ton of freight one mile decreased from $1.65 to 75 cents.

Further Reading: George R. Taylor and Irene Neu, *The American Railroad Network*, 1956; James A. Ward, *Railroads and the Character of America, 1820–1887*, 1986; Robert L. Frey, ed., *Railroads in the Nineteenth Century*, 1988.

Christopher Cumo

RAMSEY, ALEXANDER (8 September 1815–22 April 1903), senator and cabinet member. Born near Harrisburg, Pennsylvania, Ramsey attended Lafayette College and was admitted to the Pennsylvania bar in 1839. A Whig congressman from 1843 to 1847, he served as territorial governor of Minnesota between 1849 and 1853, and governor from 1860 to 1863. As a Republican, Ramsey was U.S. senator from Minnesota between 1863 and 1875, chairing the Committee on Post Offices and Post Roads and contributing to postal reform. He accepted appointment as secretary of war in President Rutherford B. Hayes's cabinet in 1879.

Ramsey's two-year tenure in the War Department came at a time when military appropriations were dwindling and the nation gave little attention to the armed forces. Even the

Indian wars, long the army's primary focus, were beginning to wind down, with the main difficulties in the Southwest. As a result, little of consequence occurred while Ramsey was in office. He attempted to improve departmental administration by having Congress approve the position of assistant secretary, but otherwise left little mark on the department.

From 1882 to 1886, Ramsey chaired the Edmunds Commission, which examined the question of Mormonism and polygamy in Utah. President of the Minnesota Historical Society from 1849 to 1863 and 1891 to 1903, Ramsey died in St. Paul.

Further Reading: William J. Ryland, *Alexander Ramsey: Frontier Politician*, 1941.

Stephen Svonavec

RANCHING. From its origins in southern Texas in the early eighteenth century, cattle ranching spread quickly throughout the Great Plains after the Civil War. Ranching drew strength from the continuing displacement of Native Americans, virtual extermination of the bison, and a postwar railroad-building boom. Mass production of beef between 1865 and 1890 qualified ranching as an industry, on a par with manufacturing in the eastern United States. Before barbed wire became generally available in the early 1880s, open-range ranching predominated. Thereafter, the business changed substantially, characterized by improved breeding practices and decreased reliance on cowboy labor. The northern Plains became a feeding ground to complement the breeding ground of the southern Plains. The promise of huge profit at the Chicago market led to the overstocking of northern ranges, and thus enormous losses of livestock during the winter of 1886–1887, which diminished entrepreneurial spirit and brought a new fiscal conservatism to the ranching business.

Further Reading: Edward Everett Dale, *The Range Cattle Industry*, new ed., 1960; Ernest Staples Osgood, *The Day of the Cattleman*, new ed., 1954; Louis Pelzer, *The Cattlemen's Frontier*, 1936.

William W. Savage, Jr.

RANDALL, SAMUEL JACKSON (10 October 1828–13 April 1890), speaker of the House of Representatives. Born in Philadelphia, Pennsylvania, and educated at the University Academy in Philadelphia, Randall served on the Philadelphia Common Council and in the Union Army. In 1862, he was elected as a Democrat to the U.S. House of Representatives, a seat that he held continuously until his death. As Philadelphia's only Democratic representative, he found himself linked to his constituents who were mechanics, artisans, and laborers. Throughout his tenure in the House, Randall was an ardent protectionist, supporting tariffs on foreign imports. From 1876 to 1881, he served as speaker of the House of Representatives and found himself in the minority against the Republican machine. He was also a leading figure in the Crédit Mobilier investigations. During his last few years in Congress, Randall opposed tariff revision. It has been said that he represented the interests of his state and constituents to a fault, a position that ultimately led him to forgo several opportunities to gain national power and to stand alone in his final years against Grover Cleveland and changes in the philosophies and practices underlying American tariffs. He died in Washington, D.C.

Further Reading: Frank B. Evans, *Pennsylvania Politics, 1872–1877: A Study in Political Leadership*, 1966; Albert V. House, Jr., "The Political Career of Samuel Jackson Randall," Ph.D. diss., University of Wisconsin, 1935.

Jerome D. Bowers II

RANHOFER, CHARLES (7 November 1836–9 October 1899), chef. Ranhofer, who made French cookery fashionable among the aspiring upper class throughout the United States, was born in St. Denis, a suburb of Paris, France, into an Alsatian family of chefs and hoteliers. He served an apprenticeship in M. Fleuret's pastry shop on Boulevard de la Madeleine in Paris and spent another year as a chief baker there. Ranhofer produced state dinners for Prince Hénin of Alsace from 1852 until 1856. After immigrating to New York City, Ranhofer worked for the Russian consul, M. Duvernois, in Washington, D.C., and in Auguste Lefevre's restaurant in New Orleans. In 1860 Ranhofer revisited France to work at the Tuilleries Palace of Napoleon III, then returned to New York the following year. Between 1862 and 1898 he commanded the kitchens of the world-famous Delmonico's restaurant, except for 1876–1879, when he operated the Hôtel Américaine in Enghien-les-Bains, a Paris suburb. Ranhofer invented baked Alaska and perfected lobster newberg. In 1895 he codified his conception of haute cuisine in an eleven hundred-page cookbook, *The Epicurean*. He was a founding member and honorary president of the Société Culinaire Philatropique, and served with other benevolent societies. He died in New York City.

Further Reading: Lately Thomas, *Delmonico's: A Century of Splendor*, 1967; *New York Daily Tribune*, 12 October 1899; *New York Times*, 11 October 1899.

Martin T. Ollif

RANSOM, MATT WHITAKER (8 October 1826–8 October 1904), U.S. senator and diplomat. Born in Warren County, North Carolina, Ransom graduated from the University of North Carolina having already passed the bar. He had early success as a lawyer and politician, and rose to major general in the Confederate Army. Ransom won election to the U.S. Senate in 1872 as successor to Zebulon Vance. There he won fame for his key roles in securing the Compromise of 1877 and defeating the Federal Election Bill of 1890. He also was chairman of the committee that created the designs for Washington's Potomac Park, and a member of the Democratic National Committee from 1876 to 1895. A faithful Democrat to the end of his political career, Ransom reminded his party and the nation of the important role of the postwar South in his famous 1875 senatorial speech, "The South Faithful to Her Duties." Ransom lost his Senate seat after the Populists and Republicans allied in 1895. Immediately thereafter President Cleveland appointed him minister to Mexico, where he arbitrated the long-standing dispute between Mexico and Guatemala. In 1897 he returned to the United States and resumed his law practice in Weldon, North Carolina, where he died.

Further Reading: Matthew Whitaker Ransom Papers, Southern Historical Collection, University of North Carolina, Chapel Hill; Clayton C. Marlow, *Matt W. Ransom, Confederate General from North Carolina*, 1996; Richard G. King, *Matt W. Ransom: United States Minister to Mexico, 1895–1897*, 1983.

Christian B. Keller

RAPIER, JAMES THOMAS (13 November 1837–31 May 1883), congressman. Born in Florence, Alabama, the son of free parents, Rapier studied in Nashville, Tennessee, and in Canada. He returned to Tennessee in 1864, and delivered a speech at the Tennessee Negro Suffrage Convention. Two years later he moved to the city of his birth, winning a seat at the first Republican state convention in Montgomery. Cautious and diplomatic, Rapier advocated moderation, for he recognized the tenuous threads that tied together the coalition of African Americans and pro-Union whites. After the Ku Klux Klan chased him from his home in 1868, he fled to the Montgomery, where he remained in near seclusion for months. Nominated for secretary of state in 1870, Rapier lost the general election. In 1871, he founded the Alabama Negro Labor Union and secured appointment as assessor of internal revenue for the Montgomery District. The next year, he successfully campaigned in the Black Belt for the Second District congressional seat, securing victory by a margin of three thousand votes over Confederate veteran William Oates. During his single term (1873–1875), Rapier sought to improve education in the South, supported civil rights laws, and led a campaign for passage of a bill to make Montgomery a port of delivery. Thereafter Rapier lost electoral contests because of fraud, violence, and intimidation. Following his appointment in 1877 as collector of internal revenue for the Second Alabama District, Rapier espoused emigration and encouraged African Americans in the South to relocate to the West. He died in Lowndes County, Alabama.

Further Readings: Loren Schweninger, *James T. Rapier and Reconstruction*, 1978; Eugene Feldman, *Black Power in Old Alabama: The Life and Stirring Times of James T. Rapier*, 1968.

Leonard Schlup

RAUSCHENBUSCH, WALTER (4 October 1861–25 July 1918), minister and reformer. Rauschenbusch was born in Rochester, New York, attended a gymnasium in Germany from 1879 to 1883, and received a bachelor's degree from the University of Rochester in 1884. He was graduated from the Rochester Theological

Seminary and ordained in 1886. His first ministry was to poor immigrants at the Second German Baptist Church in New York City. There he observed urban workers' plight and began to form ideas of Christian social activism. In 1886, he supported "single-tax" reformer Henry George's mayoral campaign. In 1891–1892, Rauschenbusch visited England, where he met Sidney and Beatrice Webb and learned of the Fabian social-reform movement. Rauschenbusch resigned his ministry in 1897 for a professorship of New Testament interpretation at Rochester. There he elaborated his "Social Gospel" philosophy, arguing that the ideals of Jesus as reflected in the New Testament obliged Christians to deal with the social problems of their time. He criticized both capitalist society and Christian churches that stressed only personal salvation. Although many regarded Rauschenbusch as a radical, his model of society envisioned a mild, non-Marxian socialism. *Christianity and the Social Crisis* (1907) provides the fullest statement of his views. He died in Rochester.

Further Readings: Paul M. Minus, *Walter Rauschenbusch, American Reformer*, 1988; Donovan E. Smucker, *The Origins of Walter Rauschenbusch's Social Ethics*, 1994.

James M. Bergquist

RAVENEL, HARRIOTT HORRY RUTLEDGE (12 August 1832–2 July 1912), author. Born in Charleston, South Carolina, Rutledge married St. Julien Ravenel, a physician and chemist, in 1851. During General William T. Sherman's march through South Carolina during the Civil War, Harriott Ravenel fought heroically to save her home and possessions from fire. She published her reminiscences of the ordeal in *South Carolina Women in the Confederacy* (1903). Ravenel began writing stories in the late 1870s. Her close friend was the writer Mary Boykin Miller Chesnut (1823–1886). Ravenel published her first book, *Eliza Pinckney*, in 1896. Five years later, she wrote a biography of her maternal grandfather, *The Life and Times of William Lowndes of South Carolina, 1782–1822*. Ravenel, active in Charleston's social life, was a member of the Daughters of the Confederacy and of the South Carolina Society of Colonial Dames, of which she served as president from 1896 to 1898. She died in Charleston.

Further Readings: *Charleston News and Courier*, 3 July 1912; Harriott H. Ravenel Papers, South Carolina Historical Society, Charleston.

Leonard Schlup

RAWLINS, JOSEPH LAFAYETTE (28 March 1850–24 May 1926), politician and lawyer. Eulogized as the "Father of Utah" for his role in guiding Utah to statehood, Rawlins was born in Salt Lake County and educated at the University of Deseret and Indiana University. While serving as Salt Lake City attorney, he realized that Utah would have to reject polygamy and organize around the national political parties in order to gain admission to the Union. Rawlins played a central role in building Utah's Democratic Party in 1891 and was elected as a territorial delegate to the U.S. Congress the following year. There he championed Utah's interests, free silver, and the legal restoration of the Mormon Church following the 1887 Anti-polygamy Act. Rawlins's most significant legislative contribution was the 1893 Enabling Act, which established the process by which Utah became a state in 1896. Defeated in his 1894 reelection bid, Rawlins successfully campaigned for the Senate in 1896, where he served until 1902. He then returned to Salt Lake City to practice law, and remained involved in politics and with the University of Utah until his death.

Further Readings: Joseph L. Rawlins, *The Unfavored Son: The Autobiography of Joseph L. Rawlins*, 1956; Joan Harrow, "Joseph L. Rawlins, Father of Utah Statehood," *Utah Historical Quarterly* 44 (1976): 59–75.

Derek R. Larson

RAYNER, JOHN BAPTIS (13 November 1850–14 July 1918), African-American Populist leader. Born in Raleigh, North Carolina, the son of a white Whig officeholder and a slave mother, Rayner attended Raleigh Theological Institute (Shaw University) and Saint Augustine's Normal and Collegiate Institute. He moved to Texas in 1880, supported prohibition during the Gilded Age, and joined the People's (Populist) Party in 1890. Within four years he had become that party's foremost African-

American spokesman in the Lone Star State. Rayner served on the Populist state executive committee, urging the party faithful to adopt positions beneficial to African Americans, who shared financial burdens in common with white debtor farmers. A preacher, a perceptive political observer, an effective speaker, a writer for newspapers, a fund-raiser, an opportunist, and an educator, Rayner was probably the most significant African-American southern Populist in the later nineteenth century. After Populism's defeat, he reversed himself on a number of issues, including a sudden endorsement of the poll tax, thereby ending his career on an erratic and contradictory note. Rayner died in Calvert, Texas.

Further Readings: Gregg Cantrell, *Feeding the Wolf: John B. Rayner and the Politics of Race, 1850–1918*, 2001, and *Kenneth and John B. Rayner and the Limits of Southern Dissent*, 1993.

Leonard Schlup

REAGAN, JOHN HENNINGER (8 October 1818–6 March 1905), Confederate postmaster general, U.S. congressman and senator, Texas Railroad Commission chairman. Reagan was born in Sevier County, Tennessee. He studied briefly at Nancy and Boyd's Creek academies and the Southwestern Seminary, then worked as a tanner and plantation manager in Tennessee and Mississippi before moving to Nacogdoches, Texas, in 1839. Reagan served as judge in Henderson County and in the state legislature before being elected to Congress (1857–1861). He supported secession, and represented Texas in Montgomery, Alabama, when the Confederate States of America was formed. Confederate President Jefferson Davis appointed Reagan postmaster general in 1861. Following the Civil War, Reagan was imprisoned at Fort Warren, Massachusetts, from May until December 1865, then returned to Texas. He received amnesty and was elected to represent the First Congressional District of Texas in 1875; he remained in the House until elected to the Senate in 1887, and was instrumental in the passage of legislation creating the Interstate Commerce Commission. Reagan resigned from the Senate in 1891 to become head of the Texas Railroad Commission, an office he held until 1903. He

unsuccessfully sought the Democratic nomination for governor in 1894.

Further Readings: Ben H. Procter, *Not Without Honor: The Life of John H. Reagan*, 1962, and, "John Henninger Reagan," *The New Handbook of Texas* 5 (1996): 464–466; Carl H. Moneyhon, *Republicanism in Reconstruction Texas*, 1980.

Archie P. McDonald

REAGAN* v. *FARMERS' LOAN & TRUST COMPANY (154 U.S. 362). This was a suit by the Farmers' Loan and Trust Company against Texas railroad commissioners John H. Reagan, William P. McLean, and L. L. Foster; Texas Attorney General Charles A. Culberson; the International & Great Northern Railroad Company; and its receiver, Thomas N. Campbell. The action sought to restrain the railroad commissioners from enforcing certain rates and regulations, and to inhibit the attorney general from suing for penalties arising from failure to conform to or obey such rates and regulations. In 1891, the Texas legislature had passed an act to establish a railroad commission with the power to adopt necessary rates, charges, and regulations to govern freight and passenger tariffs, to correct abuses and prevent unjust discrimination in freight rates and tariffs on the Texas railroads, and to enforce these rules and prescribed penalties through the courts. On 26 May 1894, the U.S. Supreme Court upheld the right of the courts to review the fixing of rates by the Texas Railroad Commission acting under state law. Writing for the majority, Justice David J. Brewer declared: "It has always been a part of the judicial function to determine whether the act of one party . . . operates to divest the other party of any rights of person or property. In every constitution is the guaranty against the taking of private property for public purposes without just compensation."

Further Readings: Charles Warren, *The Supreme Court in United States History*, Vol. 3, *1856–1918*, 1999.

Leonard Schlup

REAM, VINNIE (25 September 1847–20 November 1914), sculptor. Born in Madison, Wisconsin, Vinnie Ream excelled at art throughout childhood. In 1863, she was inspired to become a sculptor after observing Clark Mills working in his studio at the U.S. Capitol. She soon became his student and secured several important portrait commissions. These provided access to President Abraham Lincoln, who granted her daily half-hour sittings during which she studied him working at his desk. She was just completing her bust of Lincoln when he was assassinated. In 1866, Ream won a $10,000 contract from the federal government to create a full-length marble statue of Abraham Lincoln for the Capitol rotunda (completed in 1871). The eighteen-year-old Ream was the first woman to receive a government commission for sculpture. Her youth, gender, and limited artistic experience called her abilities into question. In addition, she was accused by the journalist Jane Grey Swisshelm and other critics of obtaining the commission through the use of "her feminine wiles." Ultimately the commission stood, and Ream produced a more authentic image of Lincoln than any of the other competitors. She traveled to Rome in 1869 to have the Lincoln statue transferred into marble, and remained in Europe for two years, studying and carving portrait busts.

In 1875, Ream won a federal commission for a bronze statue of Admiral David G. Farragut for Farragut Square in Washington, D.C. (completed in 1881). After Ream's marriage to a Navy lieutenant, Richard L. Hoxie, on 28 May 1878, her professional work declined. She accompanied her husband to his various posts and was active in society and charity work. She resumed sculpting in 1906, when the state of Iowa commissioned a statue of Governor Samuel Kirkwood (completed in 1913) for Statuary Hall in the U.S. Capitol. She died in Washington, D.C., while at work on her final commission, a bronze statue of the Cherokee leader Sequoyah (commissioned in 1912), also for Statuary Hall.

Further Readings: Glenn V. Sherwood, *Labor of Love: The Life and Art of Vinnie Ream*, 1997; Richard Hoxie, *Vinnie Ream*, 1908; Joan A. Lemp, "Vinnie Ream and Abraham Lincoln," *Woman's Art Journal* 6 (1985/1986): 24–29.

Charlene G. Garfinkle

RECONSTRUCTION. The effort to restore the seceded states to the Union and to provide integration of the freed persons began even during the Civil War. In 1865 President Andrew Johnson attempted to carry out his plan of "restoration," an effort to return the southern states without any significant concessions. The results of his policy not only virtually remanded the freed persons to a condition not far removed from slavery, but also set up extremely conservative regimes in the South. Congress countered with the Fourteenth Amendment, which Johnson opposed with all his might. Then Congress passed the Reconstruction Acts, which placed the southern states under military rule, and required them to institute African-American suffrage and to ratify the Fourteenth Amendment before they could be restored to the Union. This process started in 1867–1868 and established radical regimes in the southern states. Texas, Georgia, Virginia, and Mississippi, states which had not fully complied with the acts, were forced to accept the Fifteenth Amendment as well, and by 1870, all the seceded states had been restored.

Although the radical regimes in the South were accused of incompetence and corruption, the latter probably unavoidable at a time of mammoth graft in the North, they succeeded in establishing public schools and various charitable institutions in the South. Nor was the term "black Reconstruction" justified, for African Americans were generally in a minority and power was in the hands of "scalawags" and "carpetbaggers," southern Republicans and migrants from the North, respectively. As time went on, however, the Reconstruction governments could not sustain themselves. The blacks lacked economic power; the whites had recourse to social pressure and terror, especially through the Ku Klux Klan; and the federal government did little in the long run to sustain radical regimes.

By 1877, only South Carolina, Louisiana, and Florida still had Republican administrations, although they were often challenged by rival governments. In the contested presidential election of 1876, disputed returns arrived from these three states, and only after a series of compromises, involving economic promises to the South as well as the withdrawal of troops from the statehouses, did the Democrats finally permit the inauguration of Rutherford B. Hayes.

The result was the collapse of Reconstruction and the gradual worsening of the condition of the blacks. Only the three amendments—the Thirteenth, abolishing slavery; the Fourteenth, granting citizenship and equal rights to African Americans; and the Fifteenth, mandating black suffrage—remained to make possible a reversal of this trend some one hundred years later.

Further Reading: Eric Foner, *Reconstruction, 1863–1877: America's Unfinished Revolution*, 1988; Kenneth M. Stampp, *The Era of Reconstruction, 1865–1877*, 1965; John Hope Franklin, *Reconstruction After the Civil War*, 1961.

Hans L. Trefousse

RECREATION AND LEISURE. The Gilded Age was an exciting period for recreation and leisure in America. Population shifts produced severe social problems for the urban population, much of which was working class. Areas and opportunities for recreation and leisure were minimal in the cities. Because of this and other social changes, several recreation and leisure movements emerged or gained strength during the Gilded Age.

America's fondness for sports continued during this period. In 1869, Rutgers and Princeton played the first known intercollegiate football game, and interest in the sport grew quickly. The National Baseball League was formed during the 1870s. James A. Naismith developed basketball in 1891. The Young Men's Christian Association (YMCA) established some 260 large gymnasiums around the country and fueled American youth's interest in sports and exercise. Other areas of recreation and leisure expanded. Parks and playgrounds flourished during this period. The first state and county parks were established. The first designated national park, Yellowstone, was founded in 1872. Though the primary purpose of national and state parks at this time was the preservation of national resources, the value of recreational use soon followed. During the last decades of the nineteenth century, Americans began to enjoy national forests and state parks for hiking, fishing, hunting, and camping. The children's playground movement began when playgrounds were established in several major cities. Settlement houses in New York City and Chicago's Hull House, established in slum sections to aid the poor, were started in the 1880s, and provided recreation among their services. Other popular recreation pastimes for Americans included bicycling, first introduced in the 1870s, roller-skating, archery, croquet, and lawn tennis.

Commercial amusements also became more popular during this period. In various forms, theater expanded in popularity. Other types of entertainment attracting many people during their increased leisure time were dime museums, dance halls, shooting galleries, bowling alleys, billiard halls, beer gardens, saloons, and amusement parks. Auto racing became a spectator amusement when the first motor-vehicle race was run at Chicago in 1895.

Further Reading: Richard Kraus, *Recreation and Leisure in Modern Society*, 5th ed., 1998; Reynold Edgar Carlson, Theodore R. Deppe, and Janet R. MacLean, *Recreation in American Life*, 2nd ed., 1972.

Paul Keenan

RED CLOUD (May 1821?–10 December 1909), Lakota Sioux chief. Red Cloud was born along Blue Water Creek in what is today Garden County, Nebraska. He became a great warrior of the Oglala tribe, one of the seven Western or Lakota Sioux tribes that dominated much of the northern Great Plains during the late nineteenth century. Red Cloud's prowess against such enemy tribes as the Crows and Pawnees earned him forty coups. On 21 December 1866, he engineered the famous Fetterman massacre, which handed the U.S. Army its worst defeat against the Indians until the fateful battle of the Little Bighorn. The Fetterman battle, one of several fought during the so-called Red Cloud War, compelled the federal government to close the Bozeman Trail through Wyoming's Powder River country to pioneers hoping to reach the booming Montana goldfields. Thus, Red Cloud became the only Native American leader to win a major war against the United States. Red Cloud won for his people the favorable Treaty of Fort Laramie of 1868, which gave the Sioux an enormous reservation in Dakota Territory, which included the Black Hills until the defeat of the Lakota tribes in the Great Sioux War of 1876–1877.

Red Cloud spent his remaining years as a "treaty Indian," living at the Red Cloud Agency in northwestern Nebraska until 1877 and at the Pine Ridge Reservation in South Dakota until his death. He remained active during most of these years, opposing a reduction in the size of the Great Sioux Reservation in 1889 and unsuccessfully working to defuse the tensions caused by the Ghost Dance movement, which led to the bloody battle of Wounded Knee Creek in 1890. Although his fame was somewhat eclipsed by such Sioux leaders at the Little Bighorn as Crazy Horse and Sitting Bull, some historians have considered him the most important Gilded Age tribal leader.

Further Reading: Robert W. Larson, *Red Cloud: Warrior Statesman of the Lakota Sioux*, 1997; R. Eli Paul, ed., *Autobiography of Red Cloud: War Leader of the Oglalas*, 1997; James C. Olson, *Red Cloud and the Sioux Problem*, 1965.

Robert W. Larson

REDEMPTION. The Bourbons, as southern conservatives were called, labeled the period of their restoration to power "redemption" to signify alleged liberation from "radical Reconstruction." The era was marked by extreme penury that resulted in cutbacks of public services, especially schooling. A revolt in Virginia against the Redeemers' insistence on paying the huge interest on the state debt resulted in a "Readjuster" movement led by General William Mahone that for a while reduced these payments. The Readjusters even collaborated with the Republicans but, in the long run, could not overcome racist opposition. While shortchanging public services, the Bourbons were very interested in industrializing the South, and courted northern investment. Neglecting agrarian interests, they soon faced farmers' revolts that, after displacing some Redeemers in 1890, were met in the end by appeals to white solidarity. While poor whites tended to gain more power, the blacks, largely sharecroppers, eventually lost what little they had. Although they were not immediately disfranchised, the suffrage was gradually restricted by such measures as an "eight box" ballot law in South Carolina and poll taxes. Republican strength in the South declined very rapidly and the federal courts, de-

claring parts of the Ku Klux Act and the Civil Rights Act of 1875 unconstitutional, refused to interfere. By the 1890s, segregation laws were becoming more and more prominent, and were confirmed in 1896 by the Supreme Court in *Plessy* v. *Ferguson*. And though since Reconstruction there had always been a few southern blacks in Congress, the last such congressman for two generations left the House in 1901. The Solid South had been created, and blacks reduced to impotence for the next several decades.

Further Reading: C. Vann Woodward, *The Origins of the New South, 1877–1913*, 1951; Howard N. Rabinowitz, *The First New South, 1865–1920*, 1992.

Hans L. Trefousse

REED, THOMAS BRACKETT (18 October 1839–7 December 1902), speaker of the House of Representatives. Born in Portland, Maine, Reed was graduated from Bowdoin College in 1860. He studied law, and then served in the Union Navy before launching a law practice in Portland. In the late 1860s he served three terms in the Maine legislature, and was the state's attorney general from 1870 to 1873. In 1876 he won the first of twelve elections as a Republican to the U.S. House of Representatives. There Reed rose rapidly, principally through hard work and great skill in parliamentary maneuver. He had both high intelligence and a pungent wit that made him a respected and feared antagonist in debate. When Reed arrived in Congress, the Republicans had begun to move away from sectional issues lingering after Reconstruction. They were turning to an activist government program to foster economic growth through a protective tariff, a stable currency, and subsidies for business. Reed supported this new emphasis, and he took an early interest in reforming the House rules, in some measure to circumvent the Democrats' obstructionism.

House Republicans elected Reed speaker in the Fifty-first Congress (1889–1891), but their majority was razor-thin. Democrats moved to block legislation through the time-honored device of being present but refusing to vote. Boldly attacking this "disappearing quorum," Reed forced a rules change that permitted the clerk to mark members as present, thereby achieving a quorum. The Democrats were livid, but Reed stood his ground, also sparking their ire by refusing to entertain dilatory motions. He earned the sobriquet "Czar Reed," but the revised procedures he enforced, collectively known as the Reed Rules, expedited House business. As a result, the congressional Republicans posted an unprecedented activist record, passing the McKinley Tariff, the Sherman Antitrust Act, the Sherman Silver Purchase Act, the Meat Inspection Act, and many others. In 1896 Reed sought the Republican presidential nomination but had little chance against William McKinley. He opposed McKinley's imperialist foreign policy, but rather than openly break with his party, he resigned from Congress in 1899. He died in Washington, D.C.

Further Reading: William A. Robinson, *Thomas B. Reed: Parliamentarian*, 1930; Richard Stanley Offenberg, "The Political Career of Thomas Brackett Reed," Ph.D. diss., New York University, 1963.

Charles W. Calhoun

REED, WALTER (13 September 1851–22 November 1902), physician and U.S. Army officer. Reed was born in Belroi, Virginia. Privately educated, he earned a medical degree from the University of Virginia in 1869. Six years later he received a U.S. Army Medical Corps commission. After a lengthy assignment in Arizona, in 1890 he was transferred to Baltimore and allowed to pursue graduate medical study at the Johns Hopkins Hospital. Here Reed developed an interest in bacteriology, and with it earned a teaching position at the Army Medical School in Washington, D.C., in 1893.

Reed's principal research pursuit was the transmission of disease. In 1898 he headed a team that sought to determine the cause of typhoid fever, and found that flies were a principal means by which the disease was spread. This work led Reed to an interest in yellow fever, which had long plagued the Gulf coast. Previous studies had assumed a bacterial infection caused it, but Reed thought otherwise. In 1900 he was assigned to Havana, Cuba, where he headed a commission charged with studying yellow fever. In his experiments, Reed followed the unorthodox theory of mosquito-borne trans-

mission. His suspicions—based partially on his typhoid fever research—were correct. He developed a vaccine that eradicated yellow fever from the United States. Shortly after his return to Washington, D.C., Reed died of acute appendicitis.

Further Reading: Howard A. Kelly, *Walter Reed and Yellow Fever*, 1906; William B. Bean, *Walter Reed: A Biography*, 1989.

T. R. Brereton

REICK TELEGRAM. Historians, including Julius W. Pratt, Walter LaFeber, and Philip S. Foner, have long debated the role played by the business community in allegedly hastening the Spanish-American War. One piece of evidence, the Reick telegram, appears in President William McKinley's papers. William Charles Reick, the influential city editor of the *New York Herald*, dispatched a telegram on 25 March 1898 to John Russell Young, a newspaperman whom McKinley had named librarian of Congress. It declared that major corporations would welcome war as a relief of suspense. One cryptic figure, ostensibly the *Herald*'s owner, James Gordon Bennett, agreed. Bennett, ostracized from proper Gilded Age society after urinating in his fiancée's fireplace, resided in Paris, France, and on a yacht. Absent from historical analysis are the unanswered questions of when the telegram reached the White House and what influence, if any, it had on McKinley's decision for war. Did the president react solely to events or to pressure as well? Could one cable coming from outside his cabinet have swayed his judgment? McKinley was an able commander in chief who followed a consistent policy toward Cuba. Lewis L. Gould's careful study shows the Reick telegram was overrated. It was merely one piece of information that flowed into the White House prior to the declaration of war.

Further Reading: Lewis L. Gould, "The Reick Telegram and the Spanish-American War: A Reappraisal," *Diplomatic History* 3 (1979): 193–99; Julius W. Pratt, *Expansionists of 1898: The Acquisition of Hawaii and the Spanish Islands*, 1936; Walter LaFeber, *The New Empire: An Interpretation of American Expansion, 1860–1898*, 1963.

Leonard Schlup

REID, WHITELAW (27 October 1837–15 December 1912), journalist, politician, and diplomat. Born near Xenia, Ohio, Reid graduated in 1856 from Miami University in Ohio. During the Civil War, he was a correspondent for the *Cincinnati Gazette* and the *Cleveland Herald*. Reid secured an appointment as librarian of the House of Representatives, where he remained from 1863 to 1866. Disenchanted by President Abraham Lincoln's wartime leadership, Reid promoted Secretary of the Treasury Salmon P. Chase for the Republican presidential nomination in 1864. Four years later, he joined the staff of the *New York Tribune*, serving under Horace Greeley and editor John Russell Young. Reid managed Greeley's unsuccessful presidential campaign in 1872 as the Liberal Republican-Democratic nominee. Following Greeley's death less than a month after the election, Reid bought control of the *Tribune*. Under Reid, circulation increased considerably. A new building containing modern typesetting technology, the addition of major reporters and commentators, and the thorough coverage of the Grant administration's scandals contributed to the growing importance of the *Tribune* as a national organ of opinion, without the sensationalism that characterized the newspapers of William Randolph Hearst and Joseph Pulitzer.

Reid built a conservative and responsible newspaper, and he began the tall building movement in New York City by erecting the Tribune Building. Personally close to several Republican presidential candidates, Reid opposed Democrat Grover Cleveland and New York Republican bosses Thomas C. Platt and Roscoe Conkling. From 1889 to 1892, Reid served as minister to France. He accepted the Republican vice presidential nomination in 1892 on the ticket headed by President Benjamin Harrison, who lost the election to former President Cleveland. President William McKinley appointed Reid, a moderate imperialist, to the American commission that negotiated the Treaty of Paris, which formally ended the Spanish-American War (1898). In 1905, President Theodore Roosevelt named Reid ambassador to Great Britain. The author of several books and articles, Reid died in London, England.

Further Reading: Bingham Duncan, *Whitelaw Reid: Journalist, Politician, Diplomat*, 1975; Royal Cortissoz, *The Life of Whitelaw Reid*, 2 vols., 1921; *New York Tribune*, 16 December 1912; Whitelaw Reid Papers, Manuscript Division, Library of Congress.

Leonard Schlup

RELIGION. The historian Henry F. May noted that the majority religion, Protestantism, in 1871 presented a massive, almost unbroken front defending the social status quo. He was speaking chiefly of northern white Protestantism, which was culturally dominant. African-American Protestants were segregated both by white Protestants and by their own choice. Both the renewed "freedmen's churches" dating from before the Civil War and new denominations took shape. Their faith did not represent a defense of the status quo, marked as it was by prejudice against them. Following pogroms in eastern Europe after 1881, great numbers of immigrant Jews arrived, adding significant numbers to the socially better-placed pre–Civil War Jewish newcomers from Germany in particular. These new arrivals, however, were poor and often subject to anti-Semitism. Roman Catholicism was coming into its own, after half a century of immigration from Germany and after the Irish potato famines of the late 1840s. Catholics were still left in the position of challenging the social status quo then dominated by Protestants. Southern Protestants were busy fighting the effects of Reconstruction, which they resented, or nursing their wounds from their loss in the war; Methodists, Baptists, Presbyterians, and Congregationalists were most prominent in the culture. Protestant leadership in the South had adapted to an emergent society that was marked by "robber barons," opponents of labor unions, and defenders, on social Darwinist grounds, of laissez-faire economics and, often, stigmatization of the poor.

The postbellum period was marked by the presence of enormously popular leaders who took the ancient Christian message and used some of its themes to assure members of their denominations that Gilded Age's celebration of economic competition, and the growth of corporate life unconfined by antitrust measures, were pleasing to God. Phillips Brooks in Boston and Henry Ward Beecher in Brooklyn were among those who sanctioned the world as it was. Laypeople such as John D. Rockefeller, and many others of great wealth, profited from these sanctionings and began a tradition of philanthropy that helped churches. As decades passed, both new theology and the Social Gospel developed. From the ranks of those who advocated these came calls for efforts to bring in God's Kingdom through reorganization of society. By the end of the Gilded Age, and after two financial panics that were setbacks to the complacent, the prophetic and critical voices of religion had again begun to be heard. Protestantism, along with emergent minority faiths, was ready to address what has come to be called the era of Progressivism.

Further Reading: Henry F. May, *Protestant Churches and Industrial America*, 1949; Charles Howard Hopkins, *The Rise of the Social Gospel in American Protestantism, 1865–1915*, 1940.

Martin E. Marty

REMINGTON, FREDERIC (4 October 1861–26 December 1909), artist, writer, and illustrator. Remington was born in Canton, New York, and attended Yale University (1878–1880) but did not graduate. Eschewing the course of European study popular among aspiring young artists, he instead went west in 1881, living in Montana and Kansas. In 1885, he returned to New York City, and worked as an illustrator. Documenting his travels in the West in a profusion of pen-and-ink drawings, he quickly gained a reputation as a talented illustrator for *Harper's Weekly*. He continued to travel throughout the West, and in 1888 he illustrated Theodore Roosevelt's serialized articles in *The Century Illustrated Magazine*. By 1890, Remington had become the preeminent illustrator of the American West, and he was able to purchase a large home, "Endion," in New Rochelle, New York. He next turned his attention to painting and writing. Here, as in his illustrations, Remington favored subjects from the West—cowboys, Native Americans, soldiers, and gunfights. In 1891 he was elected an associate member of the National Academy of Design.

In 1895 Remington took up yet another medium, sculpture. That year he began work on his first and most popular bronze sculpture, *The Bronco Buster*, a cast of which was later given to Theodore Roosevelt by the Rough Riders. The same year marked publication of Remington's first book, *Pony Tracks*. Near the end of his career, Remington began a series of nocturnes that were among his most enthusiastically received works of art. These subdued moments of frontier life often appear under the veil of moonlight, as in *Fired On* (1907, National Museum of American Art, Smithsonian Institution). Remington died in Ridgefield, Connecticut.

Further Reading: Michael Edward Shapiro and Peter Hassrick, *Frederic Remington: The Masterworks*, 1988; James K. Ballinger, *Frederic Remington*, 1989; Alexander Nemerov, *Frederic Remington and Turn-of-the-Century America*, 1995.

Lacey Jordan

REMINGTON, PHILO (31 October 1816–4 April 1889), manufacturer. Born in Litchfield, New York, Remington spent his youth on the family farm and in his father's shop and foundry in Ilion, New York. Interested in mechanics, he assumed charge of the family-run armory upon his father's death in 1861. After the Civil War, he reorganized the corporation under the name of E. Remington & Sons, serving as its president until his death in Silver Springs, Florida. In addition to making pistols, Remington began manufacturing a typewriter in 1873 and introduced it in 1876 at the Centennial Exposition in Philadelphia. The Remington Sewing Machine Company began operations in 1882.

Further Reading: *New York Tribune*, 5 April 1889; K. D. Kirkland, *History of Remington Firearms*, 1988.

Leonard Schlup

REPEAL OF THE SHERMAN SILVER PURCHASE ACT IN 1893. In 1890, the Sherman Silver Purchase Act had authorized the secretary of the Treasury to redeem Treasury notes in gold or silver. As long as the government had enough gold, the danger of inflation remained minimal. A decline in gold reserves, however, might prompt the Treasury to redeem notes in silver, which would cause inflation if the amount of silver added to circulation increased the money supply faster than the growth of goods and services. The possibility alarmed industrialists, who wanted an inelastic currency and stable prices, as they watched the Treasury's gold supply fall from $200 million to $117 million between January 1890 and June 1891. The inflation threat worsened in 1892 when the People's Party demanded unlimited coinage of silver and the Senate passed a bill to do just that (though it died in the House).

In May 1893, the news that gold reserves had slipped below $100 million triggered a panic. That August, President Grover Cleveland called Congress into special session to repeal the Sherman Silver Purchase Act and thereby end the possibility of adding silver to the money supply through redemption. Congress agreed that October, a decision that enraged inflationists, who elevated the unlimited coinage of silver to the dominant issue of the 1896 election.

Further Reading: Milton Friedman and Anna Schwartz, *A Monetary History of the United States, 1867–1960*, 1963; Paul Studenski and Herman Krooss, *A Financial History of the United States*, 1952.

Christopher Cumo

REPEAL OF THE TENURE OF OFFICE ACT IN 1887.

In 1869, during the presidency of Ulysses S. Grant, a Republican Congress changed the 1867 Tenure of Office Act to allow presidents to dismiss officials for any reason, not simply misdeeds. If the Senate refused to concur, the dismissed officeholder was not restored to his office, but the president could appoint a new official. Conflict flared when Grover Cleveland, a Democrat, removed over six hundred officials without giving notice of his reasons for the removals. He had, however, previously promised that he would remove officeholders only for dishonesty, incompetence, or partisanship. In protest, the Republican Senate held up his appointments, then began demanding, under the Tenure of Office Act, that cabinet members provide documentation on the offices under dispute. Cleveland ordered his cabinet not to comply, and months of controversy followed. Finally Congress repealed the law. Cleveland thereby won an important victory for the independence of the executive branch. In 1926, the Supreme Court declared the Tenure of Office Act unconstitutional in the case of *Vide Meyers* v. *United States*.

Further Reading: John F. Marszalek, "Grover Cleveland and the Tenure of Office Act," *Duquesne Review* 15 (Spring 1970): 206–219, repr. in Joel Silbey, ed., *The First Branch of American Government*. 4 vols., 1991, vol. 1, pp. 206–219; Louis Fisher, "Grover Cleveland Against the Senate," *Congressional Studies* 7 (Winter 1979): 11–25; *Vide Meyers* v. *United States* (262 U.S. 52).

John F. Marszalek

REPUBLICAN PARTY.

In 1868, the Republican Party enjoyed a commanding position in American politics. Yet by the mid-1870s the Democrats had achieved parity, and the two parties remained locked in equilibrium for the next two decades. The era's political history reflects the Republican Party's successful struggle to reassert its national preeminence. Although neither party was a monolith, Republicans generally acquiesced in a common set of beliefs that grew more coherent over time. They favored a loose constitutional interpretation that permitted an activist national government to foster economic growth. Their chief policies were a protective tariff and "sound" money based on gold, with silver and paper currency subordinate. Much more than the small-government Democrats, they supported federal expenditures. At the state level, activist Republicans tended to favor moralistic legislation, such as temperance laws, and "Americanization" of immigrants.

When Ulysses S. Grant entered the White House in 1869, Reconstruction problems persisted. Republican governments in the South, some tainted by charges of corruption and all menaced by aggressive white Democrats bent on regaining control, failed to meet the Republicans' original expectations. Indeed, a group of self-styled reformers opposed Grant's determination to uphold these regimes. These malcontents, equally dismayed by the president's patronage policies, which ignored them, opposed him in 1872, backing Horace Greeley under a Liberal Republican banner. Also nominated by the Democrats, Greeley lost overwhelmingly. Grant's reelection did not, however, solidify a national majority. During his second term, disenchantment with Reconstruction grew and was compounded by revelations of corruption in high places. Moreover, the Panic of 1873 sparked a deep depression, and many suffering voters blamed the Republican Party. In the 1874 elections, it lost its majority in the House for the first time since before the Civil War.

In 1876 Republicans passed over leaders James G. Blaine and Roscoe Conkling and to instead nominated Governor Rutherford B. Hayes of Ohio. Hayes's irreproachable ethics and endorsement of sectional reconciliation and civil service reform made him a strong candidate, but he nonetheless fell 250,000 popular votes behind Democrat Samuel J. Tilden. Both parties, however, claimed electoral victory. The dispute, centered in three southern states, finally moved Congress to create a special commission, which awarded the election to Hayes. Hayes entered the White House under a cloud, but his popularity rose when prosperity returned in the late 1870s. He had, however, pledged to serve only one term.

Although the revitalized economy brightened the Republicans' prospects for 1880, the party was divided, largely over Hayes's attempts to implement civil service reform. His efforts to clean up the New York Customhouse threatened the well-oiled machine of Senator Roscoe Conkling, whose Stalwart faction favored nominating former president Grant. Opposing them, the Half-Breeds backed Blaine. A deadlocked convention turned to Ohio's James A. Garfield and selected Conkling lieutenant Chester A. Arthur as the vice presidential candidate. Together they campaigned on two themes: the mistreatment of southern blacks and the protective tariff, which Republicans touted as the key to prosperity. Garfield defeated Democrat Winfield Scott Hancock, but fell to an assassin's bullet in 1881.

Garfield's successor, Arthur, steered an independent course with policies that sometimes seemed closer to the Democrats' ideas. He favored modest tariff reduction and vetoed internal improvement bills. Although a better president than most observers had expected, he failed to win the nomination in 1884, which

went to Blaine. Blaine's candidacy was dogged by doubts about his personal probity, especially among the so-called Mugwumps, reform Republicans who backed his rival, Grover Cleveland. Blaine campaigned vigorously on economic issues, especially the protective tariff, and came within a hair's breadth of winning.

Out of power, the Republicans grew more united by espousing activist economics. Cleveland's 1887 annual message calling for a low tariff helped rally Republicans behind protectionism. The next year they nominated Benjamin Harrison, who emphasized the issue in a highly effective front-porch campaign. He defeated Cleveland, and the Republicans carried a majority in both houses of Congress.

Holding both the presidency and Congress for the first time in more than a decade, the Republicans proceeded to pass many important laws, including the McKinley Tariff Act, the Sherman Antitrust Act, the Sherman Silver Purchase Act, the Dependent Pension Act, the Meat Inspection Act, and expenditures for the navy, internal improvements, and other projects. The chief failure was the defeat of the Lodge Federal Elections bill, aimed at augmenting federal protection for the right to vote. At the state level, some midwestern Republican legislatures passed temperance legislation and English-language mandates for schools. While all this activism fulfilled much of the Republican agenda, voters in the 1890 congressional elections balked, giving an overwhelming majority to the Democrats. Two years later, Grover Cleveland crushed Harrison in a rematch, thereby suggesting a Democratic majority.

Such was not to be. The Panic of 1893 sent the economy into the deepest depression of the century, and Cleveland and the Democrats seemed powerless to deal with the crisis. Republicans again touted their prescriptions for a strong economy and trounced the Democrats in the 1894 midterm elections. Two years later, William McKinley, who personified the Republicans' tariff protectionism, swamped William Jennings Bryan and his free-silver panacea. The elections of 1894 and 1896 were critical ones, when masses of Democrats moved to the Republican Party and stayed, except for the anomalous Woodrow Wilson years, until another economic upheaval at the end of the 1920s created another seismic shift in Americans' political allegiance.

Further Reading: Robert W. Cherny, *American Politics in the Gilded Age,* 1997; Robert D. Marcus, *Grand Old Party,* 1971; H. Wayne Morgan, *From Hayes to McKinley,* 1969.

Charles W. Calhoun

REVELS, HIRAM RHODES (27 September 1827–16 January 1901), U.S. senator and college president. Born in Fayetteville, North Carolina, Revels studied at Quaker Seminary in Indiana, Drake County (Ohio) Seminary, and Knox College in Galesburg, Illinois. In 1845 he was ordained a minister in the African Methodist Episcopal Church in Baltimore, Maryland. During the Civil War he helped organize two black regiments in Maryland and briefly served as an army chaplain. Later he helped establish African-American schools in Mississippi. In 1868 Revels was elected an alderman in Natchez. The next year he went to the Mississippi state senate. In January 1870, the legislature elected him as a Republican to the U.S. Senate, making him the first African American to serve there. Revels sat on the Committee on Education and Labor and the District of Columbia Committee. He never pushed for any significant legislation that could affect the black community. Revels's term expired in 1871. He was president of Alcorn Agricultural College in Mississippi, the first land-grant college in the United States for African-American students, from 1876 to 1882. He died in Aberdeen, Mississippi.

Further Reading: Lerone Bennett, *Black Power USA: The Human Side of Reconstruction, 1867–1877,* 1967; W. E. B. Du Bois, *Black Reconstruction in America, 1860–1880,* 1964; Julius Thompson, *Hiram R. Revels, 1827–1901: A Biography,* 1982.

Abel A. Bartley

RICE, CHARLES ALLEN THORNDIKE (18 June 1851–16 May 1889), editor, journalist, and publisher. Born in Boston, Massachusetts, kidnapped as a child by his divorced mother, and raised in Europe, Rice earned degrees from Oxford. He returned to the United States with inherited wealth and in 1876 purchased the moribund *North American Review* for $3,000.

Rice reinvigorated the periodical. He moved its offices from Boston to New York, transformed it into a monthly, and enlarged the list of contributors. He solicited essays from prominent individuals offering opposing viewpoints on timely topics, including woman's suffrage, religion, politics, diplomacy, social issues, and economics. In 1889 Andrew Carnegie's article "Wealth" appeared in the *Review.* Rice's editorial stewardship of thirteen years resulted in increased circulation and profits for the *North American Review.* A bachelor of varied interests, including the ownership of a western ranch and large art collection, Rice advocated election reform and favored the Australian ballot. In 1886 he edited and published *Reminiscences of Abraham Lincoln.* Three years later President Benjamin Harrison selected Rice to serve as minister to Russia. While preparing for the assignment, Rice died suddenly in his New York City home.

Further Reading: *New York Times,* 17 May 1889.

Leonard Schlup

RICHARDSON, HENRY HOBSON (29 September 1838–27 April 1886), architect. Richardson, born in St. James Parish, Louisiana, was one of the most important, influential, and prolific architects of the late nineteenth century. After a year at the University of Louisiana, Richardson entered Harvard College, from which he graduated in 1859. He then studied in Paris in the ateliers of several architects and attended courses at the École des Beaux-Arts. In Paris he learned to appreciate the monumental historicizing architecture popular at the time, but when he returned to America, he gradually developed his own interpretation of the Romanesque, which became popularly known as Richardsonian Romanesque.

His public buildings in this style—Trinity Church and its rectory in Boston (1872–1881), the New York State Capitol in Albany (1876–1879), the Allegheny County courthouse and jail in Pittsburgh (1884), and the Marshall Field Building in Chicago (1885–1887)—are grand in scale and massive in effect, in part because of Richardson's use of a surface of heavily rusticated stone over masonry. His subtle use of Romanesque detail enhances the bold masses of his structures. The Allegheny County buildings reveal Richardson's ability to fulfill the needs of the specific program in plan and in design; the contrast established between the regularity of the courthouse and the irregular masses of the jail is surely his intentional comment on the contrast between governmental order and lawlessness. His models in two new building types, the small civic library and the suburban railroad station, were highly influential on later architects, and his use of shingles in a series of handsome houses encouraged development of the popular Shingle Style.

To ensure the unity of the arts so important for the Gilded Age, Richardson worked with artists such as John La Farge, who designed the interior decoration for Trinity Church, and with Frederick Law Olmsted, the most important landscape architect of the epoch. Richardson's interiors often feature an array of fine materials, and he designed the furniture for some of his public buildings. The massive presence of his buildings in the period directly following the disruptive Civil War may help explain the widespread popularity of the Richardsonian Romanesque. Richardson died in Brookline, Massachusetts.

Further Reading: Mariana G. Van Rensselaer, *Henry Hobson Richardson and His Works*, 1888; James F. O'Gorman, *H. H. Richardson: Architectural Forms for an American Society*, 1987, and *Living Architecture: A Biography of H. H. Richardson*, 1997.

David G. Wilkins

RICHARDSON, JAMES DANIEL (10 March 1843–24 July 1914), congressman, editor, Masonic leader. Born in Rutherford County, Tennessee, Richardson attended local schools and Franklin College. After serving the Confederacy during the Civil War, he read law and began practicing at Murfreesboro in 1867. As a Democrat, Richardson won a seat in the Tennessee House of Representatives in 1871, and was chosen its speaker. He held a state senate seat from 1873 to 1874, and was elected to the U.S. House of Representatives in 1884. There he served ten consecutive terms (4 March 1885–3 March 1905). Richardson was chairman of the Democratic Congressional Committee. In 1893 his colleagues chose him to head

the project that became the ten-volume *Compilation of the Messages and Papers of the Presidents* (1896–1899). He later edited the two-volume *A Compilation of the Messages and Papers of the Confederacy* (1905). Throughout Richardson's career he held Masonic offices and Masonic studies. He left Congress to devote his energies to serving Masonry and in 1883 published *Tennessee Templors*, a biographical account of leading Masons. Richardson was largely responsible for the construction of the Scottish Rite Temple in Washington D.C. He died at Murfreesboro.

Further Reading: James D. Richardson Papers, #3700, Southern Historical Collection, University of North Carolina at Chapel Hill; P. M. Hamer, *Tennessee: A History*, 1933; *New York Times*, 25 July 1914.

Hutch Johnson

RIDDLEBERGER, HARRISON HOLT (4 October 1844–24 January 1890), senator. Born in Edinburgh, Virginia, Riddleberger received a limited education, then fought in the Confederate Army. At war's end, he returned home to edit the *Tenth Legion Banner*. He also studied law, was admitted to the Virginia bar, and opened a practice in Woodstock. Riddleberger soon took an active interest in local politics. Elected to the state legislature in 1871, by 1879 he had emerged as a leader in William Mahone's "Readjuster" movement and in the controversy over how best to settle the state's postwar debt. Rejecting the conservatives' pleas for maintaining fiscal orthodoxy, Riddleberger joined Mahone and others in calling for a more flexible policy. Blacklisted from the Democratic organization, Riddleberger helped create the Readjuster Party. Forming an uneasy alliance with the Republicans, the Readjusters captured the state legislature in 1879. Elected to the state senate in this landslide, Riddleberger was, for the next decade, one of the state's most powerful men. The Mahone-dominated senate passed Riddleberger's bill to readjust the state debt. The act, denounced by conservatives as repudiation, cemented its author's relationship with Mahone, who helped secure his protégé's election as Virginia's junior U.S. senator in December 1881. Personal independence soon alienated Riddleberger from his mentor and fellow senators, however. He retired in March 1889 and died in Winchester, Virginia.

Further Reading: *New York Times*, 25 January 1890; Allen W. Moger, *Virginia: Bourbonism to Byrd*, 1968.

Harvey Gresham Hudspeth

RIIS, JACOB AUGUST (3 May 1849–26 May 1914), Progressive journalist, author, social reformer, and photographer. Born in Ribe, Denmark, Riis was educated at home by his father, an instructor in Latin and a newspaper printer. He apprenticed as a carpenter before immigrating to New York City in 1870. There he did a variety of jobs until hired as a journalist in the late 1870s. He worked for the *New York Tribune* (1877–1888) and the *New York Evening Sun* (1888–1899). Riis is remembered for campaigning against the wretched and filthy conditions in New York City's slums. His first book, *How the Other Half Lives* (1890), exposed the unsanitary conditions surrounding the city's poor. Additional books, articles, photo essays, and lectures brought to light the debilitating conditions faced by low-income families. Riis worked tenaciously to organize relief and assistance for New York City's poor. He campaigned alone early in his career, but eventually gained an influential ally in New York governor (and later president) Theodore Roosevelt. His active reform career met an obstacle in 1904 when Riis was diagnosed with heart disease. Despite his failing health, he continued to work, write, and lecture until his death at Barre, Massachusetts.

Further Reading: Edith P. Mayer, *The Story of Jacob A. Riis*, 1974; *New York Times* 27 and 28 May 1914; James B. Lane, *Jacob A. Riis and the American City*, 1974.

Michael W. Vogt

RILEY, JAMES WHITCOMB (7 October 1849–22 July 1916), poet. Riley was born in Greenfield, Indiana, and spent his adult life in nearby Indianapolis. He left school at sixteen, became a sign painter, and later traveled with a patent medicine salesman. Eventually he returned to Greenfield as literary editor for the local newspaper, and began writing poetry. He achieved notoriety in 1873 by submitting a poem to the *Kokomo Dispatch*, reputed to be a lost work by Edgar Allan Poe, in an effort to prove that for a poem to become popular, it had to be written by someone who was already famous. The hoax cost Riley his job, and he moved to Indianapolis to work for the *Indianapolis Journal*. During this period (1877–1885) he published *When the Frost Is on the Punkin* in book form in 1883, establishing his reputation as a dialect poet. His characters such as Little Orphan Annie and The Raggedy Man represented a simpler life to his Gilded Age readers, who were trying to adjust to the complex, industrial society that was forming in America. Riley was a very popular reader of his own works from the lecture platform. A lifelong bachelor, he spent the remainder of his life in Indianapolis, where he died.

Further Reading: Jeannette Covert Nolan, *James Whitcomb Riley, Hoosier Poet*, 1941; James Whitcomb Riley Papers, Archives of the Indiana Historical Society, Indianapolis.

C. Edward Balog

RINGO, JOHN PETERS (3 May 1850–14 July 1882), rustler and gunman, was born in Green Fork, Indiana. The only record of his schooling is a brief period at Horace Mann Elementary School in San Jose, California. Quiet and gentlemanly when sober, Ringo made a vicious drunk. In 1869 or 1870, he went to Texas, joined the Scott Cooley gang of outlaws, and participated in two murders. After a brief time in jail, by 1879 he was in Arizona. There he offered to buy a man named Louis Hancock a drink of whiskey. When Hancock insisted on beer, Ringo shot him. In Arizona, Ringo became a member of the Clanton gang of rustlers and was noted for challenging John H. "Doc" Holliday to a gunfight. An alcoholic who suffered fits of depression, Ringo shot himself to death in the Foothills of the Chiricahua Mountains of southern Arizona. Ringo was largely the creation of Walter Noble Burns, an author who portrayed the outlaw as a Hamlet-like figure, tragic and darkly handsome, a man born for better things who recklessly threw his life away. That image, though proven false, still obtains.

Further Reading: Jack Burrows, *John Ringo: The Gunfighter Who Never Was*, 1987.

Jack Burrows

ROACH, JOHN (25 December, 1813–January 10, 1887), shipbuilder. Born in Mitchelstown, County Cork, Ireland, Roach came to the United States at age sixteen to work in the iron industry. He developed a reputation for building marine engines, and boldly expanded his business during the Civil War. After the conflict, Roach realized that the future of shipbuilding lay in iron vessels. He again expanded his business by buying out several competitors. In 1871, he moved from New York City to Chester, Pennsylvania, where he rebuilt an existing facility to concentrate all shipbuilding functions in one place. Roach's integrated manufacturing process made him the largest and most efficient builder of iron vessels in the United States. From 1873 to 1885, Roach turned out more iron ships than all of his major competitors combined. Roach's downfall was the direct result of federal politics. Because he had successfully completed a series of government contracts in the 1860s and 1870s, the navy encouraged Roach to bid on the building of the nation's first four steel warships in 1883. The Chester shipyard's efficiency allowed Roach to underbid his competitors, and he was awarded all four contracts. Construction began, but an incoming Democratic administration questioned the ethics of Roach's contracts, and made it more difficult for Roach to be paid for work completed. Roach ultimately forfeited the contracts for three of the four ships and entered receivership. He died in New York City.
Further Reading: Leonard Alexander Swann, *John Roach, Maritime Entrepreneur: The Years as Naval Contractor, 1862–1886*, 1965.

Kurt Hackemer

ROACH, WILLIAM NATHANIEL (25 September 1840–7 September 1902), U.S. senator. Born in Washington, D.C., Roach attended Georgetown University and clerked in the Quartermaster's Department during the Civil War. In 1879, he moved to Larimore, Dakota Territory. A member of the territorial house of representatives in 1885 and a prominent businessman, he was unsuccessful as the Democratic gubernatorial candidate in the first state election in 1889 and again in 1891. Roach served six years in the U.S. Senate from 1893 to 1899; there he battled for the interests of agricultural North Dakota while generally opposing high tariff protectionism. Vehemently denouncing the annexation of Hawaii in 1898 and the acquisition of the Philippines the following year, Roach used political, economic, constitutional, racial, geographical, and historical arguments to document his opposition to overseas expansion. An anti-imperialist who supported President Grover Cleveland's foreign policy, Roach lost his bid for reelection. He subsequently discontinued his North Dakota business pursuits to retire to Washington, D.C. Roach died in New York City.
Further Reading: Leonard Schlup, "William N. Roach: North Dakota Isolationist and Gilded Age Senator," *North Dakota History* 57 (1990): 2–11.

Leonard Schlup

ROBBER BARONS, a pejorative term for Gilded Age business leaders who were conspicuous for their ruthlessness, shady practices, evasions of the law, and avarice. The stereotype was applied, notably, to such figures as the Central Pacific Railroad builders Collis P. Huntington, Leland Stanford, Charles Crocker, and Mark Hopkins; the financiers Jay Gould and James "Jubilee Jim" Fisk; and industrialists George Pullman and John Davison Rockefeller. It was fixed in popular thought and historical writing during the twentieth century by writers advocating closer regulation of business.
Further Reading: Gustavus Myers, *History of the Great American Fortunes*, 1910; Matthew Josephson, *The Robber Barons*, 1935; Thomas C. Cochran, "The Legend of the Robber Barons," *Pennsylvania Magazine of History and Biography*, 74, 1950: 307–321.

Douglas Steeples

ROBERTS, ELLIS HENRY (30 September 1827–8 January 1918), editor, congressman, and financier. Born in Utica, New York, Roberts graduated from Yale in 1850 and four years later became sole editor of the *Utica Morning Herald*, an influential Republican newspaper. As a state legislator after the Civil War, he favored black suffrage and aligned himself politically with Roscoe Conkling. Serving in the U.S. House of Representatives from 1871 to 1875, Roberts, a member of the Ways and Means Committee, advocated the refunding of the national debt, redemption of bonds, reduction of war taxes, and protective tariffs to shield American industries from foreign competitors. On more than one occasion, he advised President Ulysses S. Grant on financial matters. A feud with Conkling, a Stalwart, over the spoils of office cost Roberts, a Half-Breed, his House seat in 1874. On 1 April 1889 President Benjamin Harrison appointed Roberts assistant U.S. treasurer, in which capacity he served until 1893, when he accepted the presidency of the Franklin National Bank of New York. In 1897 President William McKinley chose Roberts to be treasurer of the United States, a position he held until 1905. He died in Utica.

Further Reading: *New York Times*, 9 January 1918; *Utica Daily Press*, 9 January 1918.

Leonard Schlup

ROBERTS, GEORGE BROOKE (15 January 1833–30 January 1897), railroad president. Born in Lower Merion Township, Pennsylvania, Roberts attended local schools before graduating from Rensselaer Polytechnic Institute in 1849. He began working for the Pennsylvania Railroad two years later as a rodman, and spent the remainder of his life with that company. He rose quickly through the engineering and managerial ranks. He was named a director in 1869, and first vice president following the death of his mentor, J. Edgar Thomson, in 1874. Six years later Roberts was elected president of the Pennsylvania, a position he retained until his death. Roberts continued the aggressive expansion policy established by his predecessors and increased the railroad's track mileage by nearly 50 percent, from 6,092 miles in 1879 to 8,922 in 1896. Perhaps his single most significant acquisition was the Philadelphia, Wilmington and Baltimore (1881), which gave the Pennsylvania a through route between New York and Washington. Under his leadership, the Pennsylvania undertook a systematic program of improvements to increase capacity throughout its system.

Further Reading: George H. Burgess and Miles C. Kennedy, *Centennial History of the Pennsylvania Railroad Company*, 1949; *Philadelphia Public Ledger*, 1 February 1897; Penn Central Collection, Hagley Museum and Library, Wilmington, Delaware.

John H. Hepp IV

ROCKEFELLER, JOHN DAVISON (8 July 1839–23 May 1937), industrialist, philanthropist. John D. Rockefeller was a pioneer and pacesetter in the rise of big business in the United States. His name became synonymous with oil, cartel, trust, holding company, corporate leadership, personal wealth, and, later, philanthropy. Rockefeller was born in Richford, New York. His family later moved to Ohio, and in 1853, he was graduated from Cleveland High School. Rockefeller immediately began work with a large firm of commission merchants. In 1859, he formed a partnership handling a variety of commodities. During the boom years of the Civil War he prospered, but his entrepreneurial passion shifted to refining and exporting petroleum from the nearby Pennsylvania oil region. In 1863, he and four partners constructed their first refinery in Cleveland. Overproduction by the late 1860s drove weaker refineries out of business, but Rockefeller prospered by developing a carefully managed, cost-efficient, vertically integrated company. In 1870, he and one of his partners, Samuel Andrews, converted their operation into the Standard Oil Company of Ohio, a joint-stock company. By then Rockefeller had concluded that competition was ruinous, and envisioned a giant cartel of producers.

Rockefeller wasted little time creating a cartel. By 1872 his Standard Oil had absorbed practically all of Cleveland's refineries, becoming an industrial giant. In the 1870s and 1880s the company developed a near monopoly of the U.S. petroleum industry's piping, refining, and marketing. Rockefeller created the Standard Oil Trust in 1881, a system of centralized management in which a board of trustees held the stock of all of the subsidiary companies nad eliminated price competition. As popular and political opposition to giant monopolies intensified in the 1880s and 1890s, the resourceful Rockefeller developed newer means of maintaining his company's domination. In 1899, full control over the component companies was transferred to a holding company, Standard Oil (New Jersey), which he headed.

Unprecedented wealth allowed Rockefeller to concentrate on philanthropy. A devout, lifelong Baptist and lay leader, he donated more than half a billion dollars to colleges, hospitals, asylums, libraries, foreign missions, temperance work, and the Baptist Education Society. He established the University of Chicago in 1889, and between 1901 and 1918, he created four of the country's principal philanthropic institutions, the Rockefeller Institute for Medical Research, the General Education Board, the Rockefeller Foundation, and the Laura Spelman Rockefeller Memorial Foundation. He died in Ormond, Florida.

Further Reading: Ron Chernow, *Titan: The Life of John D. Rockefeller, Sr.*, 1998; Allan Nevins, *Study in Power: John D. Rockefeller, Industrialist and Philanthropist*, 2 vols., 1953; David Freeman Hawke, *John D.: The Founding Father of the Rockefellers*, 1980.

Charles W. Macune, Jr.

ROCKHILL, WILLIAM WOODVILLE (1 April 1854–8 December 1914), diplomat. Born in Philadelphia, Pennsylvania, Rockhill graduated from a military school in France in 1873, and then became a pioneering Orientalist scholar. He explored China and Tibet between 1888 and 1892, and published several books, including *Diary of a Journey in Mongolia and Tibet in 1891 and 1892* (1894) and *The Life of the Buddha* (1884). Rockhill held diplomatic posts in China, Korea, Greece, Romania, Serbia, Russia, and Turkey, under Democratic and Republican administrations, from 1884 to 1913. He served as assistant secretary of state from 1896 to 1897. Secretary of State John Hay secured Rockhill's appointment in Washington as director of the International Bureau of American Republics (1899–1905). In 1899 and 1900, Rockhill played significant roles in formulating the Open Door Notes and in the Boxer Rebellion peace negotiations. He ended his career as foreign adviser to Chinese President Yuan Shih-kai. Rockhill died in Honolulu, Hawaii.

Further Reading: Paul A. Varg, *Open Door Diplomat: The Life of W. W. Rockhill*, 1952; Peter W. Stanley, "The Making of an American Sinologist: William W. Rockhill and the Open Door," *Perspectives in American History* 2 (1978): 419–460; *New York Times*, 9 December 1914; William W. Rockhill Papers, Houghton Library, Harvard University.

Leonard Schlup

ROMANCE OF REUNION. As the Gilded Age opened, Americans held to wartime agendas, rather than on extending the olive branch to wartime enemies. By the 1870s, however, the refrain for sectional peace could be heard increasingly, especially from northern Democrats and even some Republicans, tired of Reconstruction's sacrifices. Many thought a heartfelt reunion could cement national bonds more thoroughly than laws and military occupation. President Ulysses Grant himself had campaigned with the slogan "Let Us Have Peace," offering a vague plea for both sectional unity and biracial coexistence in the South. In 1872, Horace Greeley challenged Grant for being too hesitant to embrace the Union's former foes. Greeley lost, but helped popularize the idea in the North.

By the 1880s, northern culture had begun to sentimentalize the South. No longer seen through the prism of conflict, the region now conjured a vision of simplicity and romance. Tourists discovered charming and health-restoring locales in the South and came to imagine "picturesque" qualities of the region's black population. Likewise, literature and drama were now filled with heartrending accounts of the travails of white southerners, especially southern white women. Indeed, the "romance of reunion" emerged as a central theme, as southern ladies frequently became the objects of northern white men's affection. Through this literary device, the North could again project its triumph over the South, in a marriage between a northern man and a southern woman. The new unity appreciated southern ways, including racial intolerance. Not all Americans embraced romantic reconciliation, however. Many Union veterans continued to "wave the bloody shirt," reminding comrades of Confederate treason and the political righteousness of the Republican Party. African Americans, too, worked to preserve war memories that emphasized the evils of slavery and continued exploitation of southern blacks. White southerners also preserved memories of the conflict and Confederate traditions through the ideas of the "Lost Cause." Yet even they showed increasing willingness to meet and come together with northerners, if not by condoning real or imagined marriages, then by telling stories of Confederate heroism to any audience willing to listen.

And by the 1890s, more northerners did seem willing to accept such accounts. Northern politicians and writers, and even veterans, increasingly paid tribute to the courage displayed by white soldiers on both sides. Americans increasingly disregarded the causes and conflicts that had led to war. By the time of the Spanish-American War, the nation had forged a new "romance of reunion," celebrating the martial qualities of white men around the country, while it relegated African Americans to second-class status.

Further Reading: David Blight, *Race and Reunion: The Civil War in American Memory, 1863–1915*, 2001; Paul Buck, *The Road to Reunion*, 1937; Nina Silber, *The Romance of Reunion: Northerners and the South, 1865–1900*, 1993.

Nina Silber

ROOSEVELT, ALICE HATHAWAY LEE

(29 July 1861–14 February 1884), first wife of Theodore Roosevelt. A relative of the Cabots and the daughter of an influential Boston lawyer, Alice Lee was part of Boston society before her marriage. After their wedding in 1880, the Roosevelts were active in New York society. She was his hostess for his first year in Albany as a state assemblyman, and remained in New York City during his subsequent terms. Alice Lee Roosevelt died there after giving birth to their first child, on the same day as the death of her mother-in-law.

Further Reading: David McCullough, *Mornings on Horseback: The Story of the Young Theodore Roosevelt and His Family*, 1981; Michael Teague, "Theodore Roosevelt and Alice Hathaway Lee: A New Perspective," *Harvard Library Bulletin* 23, no. 3, 1985, 225–238.

Victoria Kalemaris

ROOSEVELT, EDITH KERMIT CAROW

(6 August 1861–30 September 1948), second wife of Theodore Roosevelt. A childhood friend of Theodore Roosevelt's, Edith grew up with the Roosevelt family. After their marriage in 1886, she was a wife, mother, companion, and hostess. Her husband's political career took the family to Washington, D.C., and Albany, New York, and they maintained a residence at Sagamore Hill in Oyster Bay, New York. Edith

raised six children, managed the various households, and supervised several family moves. A graduate of Miss Comstock's School in New York City, she remained interested in intellectual pursuits throughout her life. While living in Washington, D.C., she was a member of Henry Adams's intellectual circle, and was active in an Albany women's intellectual club while her husband was governor of New York. After Theodore Roosevelt assumed the presidency of the United States in 1901, Edith Roosevelt supervised a renovation and expansion of the White House. She made several changes in the role of the First Lady, including hiring a social secretary. She died at Sagamore Hill, having outlived her husband and three of her sons.

Further Reading: Sylvia Jukes Morris, *Edith Kermit Roosevelt: Portrait of a Lady*, 1980.

Victoria Kalemaris

ROOSEVELT, JAMES

(16 July 1828–8 December 1900), lawyer, financier, and railroad president. James Roosevelt, the father of President Franklin D. Roosevelt, was born at Hyde Park, New York. He was graduated from Union College in 1847 and from Harvard Law School in 1851. Business opportunities lured him from his law practice, however, and ultimately he became president of the Louisville, New Albany, and Chicago Railroad and of the Lake George Steamboat Company, and vice president of the Delaware and Hudson Canal Company. Roosevelt also sought to develop the transportation system of the South, and had mining interests in the Northwest. A philanthropist, he served on boards of social and charitable organizations, and was an alternate New York state commissioner to the World's Columbian Exposition in 1893.

Roosevelt knew President Grover Cleveland and, on one occasion, took young Franklin to the White House. The chief executive placed his hand on the lad's shoulder and whispered that he hoped he would never grow up to become president and have to endure the burdens of that office. James Roosevelt died in New York City.

Further Reading: Peter Collier and David Horowitz, *The Roosevelts: An American Saga*, 1994; Geoffrey C. Ward,

Before the Trumpet: Young Franklin Roosevelt, 1882–1905, 1985; Nathan Miller, *The Roosevelt Chronicles,* 1979.

Richard Harmond

ROOSEVELT, THEODORE (27 October 1858–6 January 1919), governor of New York, vice president and president of the United States. Born in New York City, Roosevelt graduated from Harvard University in 1880, read law, traveled abroad, and published historical works. He held a state assembly seat from 1882 to 1884, and then lived on a North Dakota ranch until 1886, in an effort to recover from the deaths of his mother and his first wife and to build his physical strength. He was an unsuccessful candidate for mayor of New York in 1886. From 1889 to 1895, he was a remarkably effective U.S. Civil Service Commission member. From 1895 to 1897, Roosevelt headed the New York City Board of Police Commissioners. In 1897 President William McKinley appointed him assistant secretary of the navy, a position that brought him national recognition and enabled him to prepare the American navy for war with Spain. A belligerent expansionist, Roosevelt resigned in 1898 to help organize a volunteer regiment popularly known as the Rough Riders. As colonel of this expedition, he led the charge up San Juan Hill in Cuba.

His military heroics catapulted Roosevelt into the governorship of New York (1899–1901). His reform administration alarmed the state's political bosses, particularly Thomas C. Platt, who wanted Roosevelt placed safely in an innocuous office that would not threaten their interests. Delegates to the 1900 Republican National Convention chose the highly popular Roosevelt as President William McKinley's running mate. Roosevelt barnstormed the nation, criticizing Democratic nominee William Jennings Bryan for his anti-imperialist stand while upholding McKinley's foreign and domestic policies and endorsing the Republican platform. The McKinley-Roosevelt ticket swept the nation on election day.

Inaugurated vice president on 4 March 1901, Roosevelt suddenly succeeded to the presidency at age forty-two on 14 September, when McKinley died. The youngest American chief executive, he served as president from 1901 to 1909, pushed through a domestic program of reform, and won the Nobel Peace Prize. His administration ended the Gilded Age and began the Progressive Era. Roosevelt built on the activist conception of the White House, turning it into a place of moral and political leadership. After an unsuccessful attempt in 1912 to recapture the presidency on the Progressive "Bull Moose" ticket, Roosevelt continued writing on and addressing national and international issues until his death at Oyster Bay, New York.

Further Reading: William Henry Harbaugh, *Power and Responsibility: The Life and Times of Theodore Roosevelt,* 1961; Nathan Miller, *Theodore Roosevelt: A Life,* 1992; *New York Times,* 7 January 1991; Edmund Morris, *The Rise of Theodore Roosevelt,* 1979.

Leonard Schlup

ROOT, ELIHU (15 February 1845–7 February 1937), cabinet member, senator. Born in Clinton, New York, Root graduated from New York University Law School in 1876 and practiced in New York City, becoming one of the most respected attorneys in the nation for the force of his argument and his courtroom skills. Successful in corporate law, he also assisted in the defense of the political boss William Marcy Tweed in his celebrated trial of 1873. Always a conservative, Root was active much of his life in the New York Republican Party, and served as U.S. attorney for the New York City area from 1883 to 1885. He presided over the state constitutional convention of 1894, and later he was adviser to Governor Theodore Roosevelt. Root made his debut in national affairs as William McKinley's secretary of war in 1899. He directed modernization of the army, establishing the general staff system and the Army War College. After the victory over Spain, Root named General Leonard Wood as military governor of Cuba and pressed for the protection of American interests on the island, reserving the right of U.S. intervention. Root also shaped the relationship between America and newly acquired Puerto Rico, and set rules for the occupation of the Philippines. After resigning in 1903, Root returned to serve as secretary of state from 1905 to 1909, and he won a Senate seat in 1909. Leaving office in 1915, he remained influential in politics, philanthropy, and the law. Root died in New York City.

Further Reading: Philip C. Jessup, *Elihu Root*, 2 vols., 1938; Richard Leopold, *Elihu Root and the Conservative Tradition*, 1954.

Mario R. DiNunzio

ROUGH RIDERS. Shortly after Congress declared war on Spain in April 1898, President William McKinley called for 125,000 volunteers to support the regular army. The summons fit perfectly with the plans of Theodore Roosevelt, who persuaded Secretary of War Russell A. Alger to appoint him lieutenant colonel for service under General Leonard Wood. Resigning as assistant secretary of the navy, Roosevelt took charge of recruiting what became the First U.S. Cavalry Volunteers. The possibility of serving with Roosevelt drew over twenty thousand applicants for about one thousand positions. From several possibilities the name Rough Riders was chosen, and accompanied the regiment to fame. Successful applicants, who ranged from western cowboys and Indians to Harvard football players and New York socialites, gathered for training in San Antonio, Texas, in May. They were quickly shaped into a force that, Roosevelt boasted, could outfight Caesar's Tenth Legion. Their contribution to victory at Kettle Hill and San Juan Hill in July confirmed Roosevelt's words. The Rough Riders suffered the heaviest casualties of any American unit in Cuba—one third of its numbers dead, wounded, or struck down by disease—and they returned home heroes. For his role, Roosevelt was belatedly awarded the Congressional Medal of Honor in 1998.

Further Reading: Virgil Jones Carrington, *Roosevelt's Rough Riders*, 1971; Peggy Samuels and Harold Samuels, *Teddy Roosevelt at San Juan: The Making of a President*, 1997; Dale L. Walker, *The Boys of 98: Theodore Roosevelt and the Rough Riders*, 1998.

Mario R. DiNunzio

RUM, ROMANISM, and REBELLION. Senator James G. Blaine of Maine failed to gain the Republican nomination for president in 1876 and 1880, losing to the Ohioans Rutherford B. Hayes and James A. Garfield, respectively. He won the nomination in 1884 and battled Grover Cleveland for the White House.

Both courted business leaders, bankers, and workers. To that end, Blaine wooed the Irish, reminding them that his mother was Catholic and criticizing the British. For some reason, Blaine neglected the strategy when seven hundred clergy visited him on 31 October at Republican headquarters in New York City. There the Reverend Samuel Dickinson Burchard mocked the Democrats as a party of "rum, Romanism, and rebellion." Blaine failed to distance himself from the insult, allowing Democrats to accuse him of supporting it. His failure to counter this charge may have cost him the election. Although Cleveland gained 219 of 401 electoral votes, he won the popular vote by fewer than thirty thousand.

Further Reading: Leonard D. White, *The Republican Era, 1869–1901*, 1958.

Christopher Cumo

RUSK, JEREMIAH MCLAIN (17 June 1830–21 November 1893), agriculturalist. Rusk was born on a farm in Deerfield, Ohio, where he attended the public school. In 1853 he settled in Viroqua, Wisconsin, and launched a political career as a Republican. He served as sheriff, coroner, state legislator, and state comptroller. In 1870 he won a seat in Congress, and in 1881 he was elected to the first of four gubernatorial terms. In that post, he helped organize Farmers' Institutes, at which he spoke frequently. In 1889, President Benjamin Harrison appointed him secretary of agriculture, though Rusk delegated the department's oversight to Edwin Willits, the assistant secretary and former president of Michigan Agricultural College. During Rusk's tenure, animal scientists at the department identified the pathogen that causes Texas fever in cattle and the tick that transmitted it. These discoveries, plus the finding that the *Anopheles* mosquito carries malaria, led U.S. Army physician Walter Reed in 1900 to identify the *Aedes* mosquito as the carrier of yellow fever.

In 1893 Rusk handed the department to the new secretary, Julius Sterling Morton, and returned to his farm in Viroqua, where he died.

Further Reading: A. Hunter Dupree, *Science in the Federal Government*, 1957; Alfred C. True, *A History of Ag-*

ricultural Experimentation and Research in the United States, 1607–1925, 1937.

Christopher Cumo

RUSKIN COLONIZATION. Julius Augustus Wayland (26 April 1854–11 November 1912), a socialist, established a newspaper, *The Coming Nation,* in Greensburg, Indiana, in 1893. He used it to found the Ruskin Colonies in Tennessee and Georgia in 1894. Wayland and his followers conceived of Ruskin as a response to the concentration of wealth and economic power in Gilded Age America. Ruskin was designed as an ecumenical socialist community to spark a national cultural and economic transformation—both a grandiose plan and a cooperative commonwealth. Approximately five hundred white individuals, mostly Protestants from the Midwest and Northeast, pursued agendas in their utopian environment. Ultimately the dissolution of Ruskin as a communitarian experiment in the South resulted from several factors, including numerous organizational ambiguities, economic exigencies, socialized domesticity, the nebulous status of women in the colony, and an impoverished community's attempt to survive in a prosperous nation after 1897. Wayland failed to realize his bold dream of communitarian socialism because Ruskin exemplified too much a part of the American society he wanted to change. Nevertheless, Ruskin ranked within the larger trends in American radicalism at the turn of the century. In 1895, having left the colony, Wayland started *Appeal to Reason* in Kansas City, Kansas.

Further Reading: W. Fitzhugh Brundage, *A Socialist Utopia in the New South: The Ruskin Colonies in Tennessee and Georgia, 1894–1901,* 1996.

Leonard Schlup

RUSSELL, CHARLES MARION (19 March 1864–24 October 1926), artist, author, and humorist. Born in Saint Louis, Missouri, Russell became a cowboy in Montana in 1880. During the bitterly cold winter of 1886–1887, he lived as a wrangler on a ranch. In reply to the owners who inquired about the condition of their surviving cattle, Russell took a small piece of cardboard and drew an eloquent watercolor sketch depicting a thin, starving cow encircled by hungry wolves, titling it "Waiting for a Chinook." He sent the sketch along with his report. Newly impoverished neighbors quickly related to the popular drawing. Soon thereafter, postcards of the sketch were dispatched throughout the country and other parts of the world. It also became known as "The Last of the Five Thousand." In 1888 Russell spent the summer with the Bloods, a northern band of the Blackfoot. He learned their language, customs, and legends, growing to respect the Native Americans. He gained their trust, adopted their long hair and clothes, and remained steadfastly sympathetic to their cause in the face of white discrimination and brutality. Russell's *Studies in Western Life,* a portfolio of twenty-one color pictures, appeared in 1890. Seven years later he started publishing short stories that captured and recorded the West's pioneering spirit. He died at Great Falls, Montana.

Further Reading: Ramon F. Adams and Homer E. Britzman, *Charles M. Russell: The Cowboy Artist. A Biography,* 1948; Robert L. Gales, *Charles Marion Russell,* 1979; Peter H. Hassrick, *Charles M. Russell,* 1989.

Leonard Schlup

RUSSELL, CHARLES TAZE (16 February 1852–31 October 1916), founder of the Watch Tower Bible and Tract Society. Born in Allegheny, Pennsylvania, Russell early in life searched for his individual spirituality and concept of religion. He believed in Jesus Christ's return as a spiritual presence and predicted that God's kingdom on earth would occur by 1914. In 1879, Russell started publishing *Zion's Watch Tower and Herald of Christ's Presence.* Continuing to refine his theology throughout his life, while keeping his basic eschatology constant, he disavowed the doctrine of the Trinity. He affirmed Jehovah as God's personal name, and traveled extensively throughout the United States and Europe, claiming no special revelation. Russell suggested that the world was declining in the age of industrialization and nationalism, and contended that Christian teaching had fragmented among too many selfish denominations. In 1886 he published the first volume of *Millennial Dawn.* At Pittsburgh, Pennsylvania, he organized the Watch Tower Bible and Tract Society in 1884, serving as its head until his death. His supporters, variously known as Russellites, Bible Students, Millenarians, or Millennial Dawnists, acquired the name Jehovah's Witnesses after 1931. Russell died in Pampa, Texas.

Further Reading: Jerry Bergman, *Jehovah's Witnesses and Kindred Groups: A Historical Compendium and Bibliography*, 1984; M. James Penton, *Apocalypse Delayed: The Story of Jehovah's Witnesses*, 1985; Melvin D. Curry, *Jehovah's Witnesses: The Millenarian World of the Watch Tower*, 1992.

Leonard Schlup

RUSSELL, LILLIAN (4 December 1861–6 June 1922), actress and singer. Russell was born Helen Louise Leonard in Clinton, Iowa. In 1865, her family moved to Chicago, where she completed her formal education at the Park Institute, a finishing school. Following her parents' divorce in 1877, Leonard, with her mother and sisters, went to New York City, where she began her singing career in 1879 with a chorus part in Edward E. Rice's production of Gilbert and Sullivan's *H.M.S. Pinafore*. In 1880, she made her debut for the impresario Tony Pastor, who renamed his new star Lillian Russell. She worked under Pastor's management until 1893. Among her greater theatrical successes were *The Princess Nicotine* (1893) and *An American Beauty* (1896). During the 1890s, Russell became close friends with the legendary Diamond Jim Brady. Their relationship (apparently platonic) and lavish lifestyle were well chronicled by the press and seemed to personify the extravagance of the Gilded Age. In 1899, she recorded her most famous song, "Come Down, My Evenin' Star," with burlesque comics Joe Weber and Lew Fields. In 1905, Russell made her debut in vaudeville while continuing to work on the musical stage. Her only film appearance was in *Wildfire* (1915), opposite Lionel Barrymore. Her name has remained synonymous with the Gilded Age stage. She died in Pittsburgh, Pennsylvania.

Further Reading: John Burke, *Dust in Diamonds: The Flamboyant Saga of Lillian Russell and Diamond Jim Brady in America's Gilded Age*, 1972; Lois Rather, *Two Lilies in America: Lillian Russell and Lillie Langtry*, 1973; Albert Austen, "Chamber of Diamonds and Delight: Actresses, Suffragists, and Feminists in the American Theater,

1890–1920," Ph.D diss., State University of New York, Stony Brook, 1981.

Ron Briley

RUSSELL, WILLIAM EUSTIS (6 January 1857–16 July 1896), lawyer, mayor, governor. Born in Cambridge, Massachusetts, Russell earned degrees from Harvard College and Boston University Law School. Despite Republican sentiments of his college classmates, he was a staunch supporter of the presidential bid of the Democratic reformer Samuel J. Tilden in 1876. Russell was elected to the Cambridge Common Council in 1881, the Board of Aldermen in 1882 and 1883, and the mayoralty in 1884. He followed a "pay as you go" approach to municipal finances, and enforced the local prohibition laws despite his personal opposition. Although he refused the Democratic nomination for Congress in 1886, he received the first of five Democratic nominations for governor in 1888. Defeated in 1888 and 1889, he won in 1890, 1891, and 1892. Governor Russell's achievements include repeal of the poll tax, passage of a collateral inheritance tax, an anti-sweatshop bill, and several pro-labor measures. A tireless foe of protectionism and free silver, he remained a force in national Democratic politics after his retirement from state office. In June 1896, at President Grover Cleveland's request, he accepted election as a delegate to the Democratic National Convention in Chicago, where with other leading Gold Democrats he conducted a vigorous though unsuccessful fight against free silver. He died in St. Adelaide, Quebec, Canada.

Further Reading: William Russell Papers, Massachusetts Historical society, Boston; Geoffrey Blodgett, *The Gentle Reformers: Massachusetts Democrats in the Cleveland Era*, 1966; New York *Times*, 17 July 1896.

Marie Marmo Mullaney

RUSSIAN-AMERICAN RELATIONS. Czarist Russia and the United States enjoyed good relations preceding the Gilded Age. The era of cordiality began with the Crimean War (1853–1856) and intensified during America's Civil War. The U.S. purchase of Alaska in 1867 marked the high point. In addition, symmetry of experience fostered sympathy. Both countries had endured social revolution with the freeing of serfs and slaves; they also had overcome regional insurrection (in Poland and the South). The governments in St. Petersburg and Washington were carving national territories out of their respective continents. Statesmen from each nation shared an antipathy for British power. Consequently, some pundits in the late 1860s predicted that the western republic and the eastern autocracy would enter into formal alliance.

Contrary to such expectation, bilateral relations became strained during the waning decades of the nineteenth century. The decline in mutual confidence was caused by American impatience (on diplomatic and popular levels) with anti-Jewish pogroms and other persecutions in the empire. The pogroms compelled hundreds of thousands of Jews to seek refuge in America. Their impecuniousness on arrival alternately provoked anxiety and contempt among nativists, who worried that charitable organizations might be overwhelmed by a flood of unassimilable people. American protests over Russian mistreatment of Jews were dismissed by czarist officials as constituting reckless interference in the domestic affairs of a sovereign state. Meanwhile, heightened awareness in the United States of the scale of political repression against dissidents in Russia, and the brutality of its far-flung penal system, led to impassioned support of anti-czarist activists. Mark Twain expressed the view of many when he declared that czardom deserved the "remedy" of dynamite.

Incipient Russian-American rivalry for influence in the Far East produced further complications. This concern in the United States was dissipated by Japan's startling victory over czarist forces in the 1904–1905 war, which strengthened the disdain felt by Americans, including President Theodore Roosevelt, for Russian institutions and backwardness.

Further Reading: Norman Saul, *Concord and Conflict: The United States and Russia, 1867–1914*, 1996; Frederick Travis, *George Kennan and the American-Russian Relationship, 1865–1924*, 1990.

David Mayers

RUSSIAN MENNONITES. In the 1870s and 1880s, approximately one-third of Russia's

Mennonites moved to North America, hoping to reproduce their exclusively religious settlements. The United States offered economic opportunity and religious freedom but did not permit the immigrants to duplicate the closed ethnic-faith communities they had established within the Russian empire. To prepare for their relocation and to examine political and social conditions in Gilded Age America, the Mennonites sent twelve representatives to seek out places for settlement. Included in this group were Paul and Laurence Tschetter, Tobias Unruh, Andreas Schrag, and Leonard Sudermann. They met with American Mennonite leaders to obtain advice, and seemed particularly attracted to South Dakota, Kansas, Illinois, Nebraska, Minnesota, and Pennsylvania. In 1873 the Tschetters and Unruh conferred with President Ulysses S. Grant at his summer home near New York City. The chief executive recommended that Congress consider setting aside land for Mennonite settlement. Secretary of the Interior Columbus Delano concurred. Congressional legislators debated the "Mennonite Bill," but in 1874 the Senate rejected it.

Despite the setback, by mid-1874 Russian Mennonites began arriving in large numbers, totaling some ten thousand people over the next decade. Elder Jakob Buller in 1874 led the entire Alexanderwohl church membership from Molotschna, Russia, to board the *Cimbria* and *Teutonia*, their ultimate destination Goessel, Kansas. The Russian Mennonites recognized America's promise and the opportunity to develop their faith. They were fortunate, too, in that some railroads, such as the Santa Fe, sold them land. Between the 1870s and mid-1890s, crop prices dropped, resulting in depressed times for American agriculture. Generally, however, Mennonites were not among the poorest of Plains farmers. Wheat constituted their main staple at a time of expanding production, which led to reasonably prosperous Mennonite communities. The goals of the Russian Mennonites were to reestablish their families, serve their communities, and worship in their churches. In the process, they contributed much to the nation by turning prairie land into farms, developing hard winter wheat, and expanding food production for the United States and the world.

Mennonites became loyal citizens and productive members of their neighborhoods and regions. Due to their Russian heritage, they possessed a strong sense of obligation to government and society, respecting American political institutions. Russian immigrants brought a great deal to American Mennonitism: vision, a sense of history, experience, and the ability to create schools and newspapers. These individuals added strength to the Mennonites' agrarian, conservative philosophy of private property, reaffirming the group's class pattern.

The newcomers also provided an indomitable understanding of pacifism. Most of all, the Russians and Prussians brought choice, variety, and voluntarism to American Mennonitism. The Russian Mennonites' experience in Gilded Age America constituted an important dimension in social and religious history.

Further Reading: Theron F. Schlabach, *Peace, Faith, Nation: Mennonites and Amish in Nineteenth-Century America*, 1988; Royden K. Loewen, *Family, Church, and Market: A Mennonite Community in the Old and the New Worlds, 1850–1930*, 1993; Georg Liebbrandt, "The Emigration of the German Mennonites from Russia to the United States and Canada in 1873–1880," *Mennonite Quarterly Review* 6 (1932): 205–226, and 7 (1933) 5–41.

Leonard Schlup

SAINT-GAUDENS, AUGUSTUS

SAINT-GAUDENS, AUGUSTUS (1 March 1848–3 August 1907), sculptor and painter. Born in Dublin, Ireland, and raised in New York City, Saint-Gaudens was apprenticed in 1861 to a cameo cutter. Several years later he began working with Jules Le-Brethon, a shell cameo cutter, under whom he produced the *Head of Hercules* (c. 1867, Cornish, N.H., Saint-Gaudens National Historic Site). He also studied drawing, initially at the Cooper Union in New York and later at the National Academy of Design. In 1867 he went to Paris, where he worked as a cameo cutter until he was admitted to the École des Beaux-Arts in 1868 and began studying with François Jouffroy. The subtlety of Saint Gaudens's relief sculptures is surely due to his early training as a cameo cutter. In 1870 Saint-Gaudens traveled to Rome, where he worked on his marble sculpture *Hiawatha* (1872–1874; Palm Beach, Fla., private collection), which was inspired by Longfellow's poem. He continued to produce cameos, and he was commissioned by William Maxwell Evarts to copy famous ancient sculptures.

Saint-Gaudens returned to America in 1872, and in 1875 he established a studio in New York City. There he became acquainted with the painter John La Farge and the architect Stanford White, and began working for Tiffany Studios. Beginning in late 1876, he worked in conjunction with other artists, under La Farge's direction, on the mural paintings for Trinity Church in Boston. He took an active role with other artists in denouncing the conservatism of the National Academy of Design. His works in the late 1870s included a portrait relief of Francis Davis Millet (1879; New York, Metropolitan Museum) and his first large public work, the monument to David Glasgow Farragut (1877–1881; Madison Square Park, New York City), which symbolized American heroism. The architect Stanford White designed the pedestal, decorated with Saint-Gaudens's reliefs *Loyalty* and *Courage*. From 1881 to 1883,

Saint-Gaudens produced elegant sculpture used as interior decoration for the homes of Cornelius Vanderbilt II and Henry Villard in New York City. In this context he combined his interest in classical sculpture with the influence of the fashionable Art Nouveau style. The Abraham Lincoln monument (1884–1887; Chicago, Lincoln Park) and *The Puritan* (1883–1886, Springfield, Mass.) were among his most popular works. The bronze memorial to Robert Gould Shaw and the Massachusetts Fifty-fourth Regiment (1884–1897; Boston Commons), which combines relief sculpture with the equestrian monument, honors the Civil War hero and his regiment of black soldiers.

At this time Saint-Gaudens was producing other major works, such as the brooding Adams Memorial commissioned by Henry Adams (1886–1891; Washington, D.C., Rock Creek Cemetery). In addition to his major public commissions, he continued to produce portrait busts and reliefs, such as the low relief of John Singer Sargent's sister, Violet Sargent (1890; Washington D.C., National Museum of American Art). The influence of Saint-Gaudens on American sculpture and sculptors was great. He taught at the Art Students League from 1888 to 1897 and founded the National Sculpture Society in 1893. He died in Cornish, New Hampshire.

Further Reading: John H. Dryfhout and Beverly Cox, *Augustus Saint-Gaudens: The Portrait Reliefs*, 1969; John H. Dryfhout, *The Work of Augustus Saint-Gaudens*, 1982; Kathryn Greenthal, *Augustus Saint-Gaudens: Master Sculptor*, 1985.

Ann Thomas Wilkins

SALARY GRAB ACT. In late February 1873, Representative Benjamin F. Butler of Massachusetts offered an amendment to the Civil Appropriations bill that generously increased salaries for members of Congress, the president, and other top federal officials to offset spiraling living expenses in Washington, D.C. The controversial proposal made the pay raises retroactive for the entire Forty-second Congress. The House of Representatives hotly debated the amendment on economic grounds, and several congressmen feared for their political survival. Nevertheless, the appropriations bill emerged from conference committee with salary increases intact. House opponents accepted the conference report to secure other components of the bill and to avoid another congressional session. The Senate swallowed the report with less difficulty. An outraged public christened it a "salary grab" and denounced the lawmakers for fattening their wallets without apparent thought for lowly civil service clerks or the nation's laboring classes. Several legislators returned their bonus pay to the Treasury or donated the sum to charity. At the next election, voters, not easily mollified, unseated nearly all incumbents who took the back pay. Congress repealed the salary increases for all but the president and Supreme Court justices early in the next session. The salary grab heightened suspicions about the integrity of politicians.

Further Reading: Mark Wahlgren Summers, *The Era of Good Stealings*, 1993; Margaret Susan Thompson, *The Spider Web: Congress and Lobbying in the Age of Grant*, 1985.

William M. Ferraro

SALMON, LUCY MAYNARD (27 July 1853–14 February 1927), historian. Born in Fulton, New York, Salmon worked her way through the University of Michigan at Ann Arbor, studying history under Charles Kendall Adams and graduating in 1876. For the next five years she taught and served as principal of a high school in McGregor, Iowa, then returned to Ann Arbor to earn a master's degree in history in 1883. Four years later, she became the first history instructor at Vassar College in Poughkeepsie, New York, and secured an appointment as full professor in 1889. She remained at Vassar for the rest of her professional career. Dedicated to the concept that learning was a joint venture between teacher and student, she used the seminar method for her advanced classes, encouraged the reading of daily newspapers, introduced a course in historical methodology, and served as department chair. Salmon stressed the necessity for a good library

on campus, published widely, worked for civic improvements, supported civil service reform and woman suffrage, and was an active member of the American Historical Association. She died in Poughkeepsie, New York.

Further Reading: Louise Fargo Brown, *Apostle in Democracy: The Life of Lucy Maynard Salmon*, 1943; Rebecca Lowrie, *Lucy Maynard Salmon*, 1951.

Leonard Schlup

SALVATION ARMY. The Salvation Army began in the United States on 10 March 1880, when Commissioner George Scott Railton and seven Salvationist women arrived at Castle Garden in New York City. They were sent under the direction and guidance of General William Booth, the founder of the Salvation Army in England. Although it was difficult for the organization to gain acceptance by the American public, the Salvation Army moved across the country with remarkable speed. As Railton and his officers were establishing operations in the major cities along the east coast and in St. Louis, Missouri, Major Alfred Wells arrived in San Francisco, California, in January 1881, to begin west coast operations. During this time Salvationists' energies were chiefly expended in fighting for the right of free speech on the streets. In spite of opposition, the Salvation Army was successful, and soon established its social work programs. In 1885, the first prison brigade, offering aid to released prisoners, opened in Hartford, Connecticut. Four years later, the Army's slum work began in America. In the program officers, a majority of them women, went into the worst sections of the major cities to live, assisting people, through education, to live successfully in poor conditions. The Salvation Army was able to attract the support and funds of the wealthy to sustain this program. Urban living conditions were changed for the better.

Between 1890 and 1900, the Salvation Army initiated several programs in the United States: day nurseries (1890) providing care for children; food and shelter depots (1891), providing cheap lodgings, meals, and clothing; the Salvation Army Labor Bureau (1894), a job placement service centralized at the Army's national headquarters in New York City; salvage brigades (1896), which became the industrial homes under the Men's Social Department; and farm colonies (1898), an attempt to put rehabilitated persons on western farms to become self-sufficient. During times of crisis, the Salvation Army has offered assistance. Its work with the national armed forces began with establishment of the Naval and Military League in 1896. Assistance to the military continued during World War I, World War II, and the Vietnam War.

The Salvation Army played an important role in the development of the United States during the Gilded Age. Although it was not generally accepted in the beginning, its social programs created better urban conditions and rehabilitated many people. Because of the early success of the Salvation Army's programs worldwide, it is currently recognized as a social, charitable, and religious organization.

Further Reading: Norman H. Murdoch, *Origins of the Salvation Army*, 1996; E. H. McKinley, *Marching to Glory: The History of the Salvation Army in the United States, 1880–1992*, 1992; Stephen Brook, *God's Army: The Story of the Salvation Army*, 1999.

Scott Bedio

SAMOAN PARTITION (1899). When King Malietoa of Samoa died in August 1898, the civil war that erupted over sucession to the throne brought in Germany, Great Britain, and the United States. After a cease-fire, the three powers sent a commission to the region. Its report confirmed that the existing tripartite system established by the 1889 Berlin Conference was unsound, and recommended dismantling the monarchy and creating a provisional government. Germany and Britain signed a partition agreement in November 1899. The United States was now open to the idea of partition, having just acquired the Philippines, Puerto Rico, Guam, and Hawaii. Secretary of State John Hay supported the Anglo-German negotiations as long as Pago Pago remained in U.S. hands, because the government wanted the harbor. On 2 December 1899, the three powers signed an agreement that gave Germany the western half of the islands, and the United States the eastern half that included Pago Pago. Great Britain left Samoa and received Tonga,

the German part of the Solomon Islands, and German rights in West Africa. After Senate ratification of the agreement, the U.S. Navy took direct control of the eastern islands by April 1900. The region's importance never materialized, however, because the United States possessed Pearl Harbor, in Hawaii. The partition illustrated American willingness to increase U.S. colonial holdings in the Pacific.

Further Reading: Paul M. Kennedy, *The Samoan Tangle*, 1974.

Bryan Craig

SANFORD, HENRY SHELTON (15 June 1823–21 May 1891), diplomat and businessman. Born in Woodbury, Connecticut, Sanford graduated from the Episcopal Academy in Cheshire, Connecticut, in 1839; attended Washington College (now Trinity College) in Hartford, Connecticut, for one year; and earned a doctor of laws from the University of Heidelberg in 1849. After serving as a secretary in the American legations in St. Petersburg, Berlin, and Paris during the late 1840s and early 1850s, he pursued a series of Latin American business ventures until the outbreak of the Civil War. President Abraham Lincoln appointed Sanford U.S. minister to Belgium, where he served from 1861 until President Ulysses S. Grant's inauguration in 1869.

From 1869 until his death in Healing Springs, Virginia, Sanford sought consciously but with mixed results to achieve a solid and lasting historical reputation. He lost vast sums of money in speculative investments in the South, the most important of which were the development of citrus groves and the founding of the town of Sanford, Florida. He successfully lobbied the Chester A. Arthur administration to extend diplomatic recognition to King Leopold II's International African Association (later the Congo Free State) in 1884. He also served as an associate U.S. delegate to the West African Conference of 1884–1885 in Berlin and as a member of the American delegation to the Antislavery Conference of 1889–1890 in Brussels. These Gilded Age activities made him a central figure in both the formation of late nineteenth-century U.S. policy for Africa and the development of the modern Florida citrus industry.

Further Reading: Joseph A. Fry, *Henry S. Sanford: Diplomacy and Business in Nineteenth-Century America,* 1982; Richard J. Amundson, "The Florida Land and Colonization Company," *Florida Historical Quarterly* 4 (1966): 153–168.

Joseph A. Fry

SAN JUAN HILL. On 1 July 1898, this was the site of the climactic land battle of the Spanish-American War. Defended by entrenched Spanish troops, San Juan heights, including San Juan Hill and Kettle Hill, stood between American forces and their objective, the city of Santiago, Cuba. In the face of withering rifle fire and shrapnel-spitting artillery shells, an infantry division commanded by Brigadier General Jacob F. Kent attacked San Juan Hill, while nearby and to the right Theodore Roosevelt had already led a contingent of the Rough Riders, and men from two regiments of black troops, in an assault on Kettle Hill. Roosevelt's forces took their objective despite heavy casualties, and at his command, the troops rushed to join the attack that had begun on San Juan Hill. The combined American forces captured the hill after intense fighting in suffocating tropical heat. Their success set the stage for a siege of Santiago, which the Spanish surrendered on 17 July. The victory at San Juan heights cost more than seventeen hundred American casualties.

Further Reading: Anastasio C. M. Azoy, *Charge! Story of the Battle of San Juan Hill,* 1961; David F. Trask, *The War with Spain in 1898,* 1981.

Mario R. DiNunzio

SANTO DOMINGO AFFAIR (1870). The corruption that permeated government in post–Civil War America extended to foreign affairs. The most notorious case was the aborted attempt to annex the Caribbean island of Santo Domingo in 1869–1870. National security considerations—possession of the harbor at Samana Bay—might have justified its acquisition, but this consideration was not uppermost in the minds of such highly placed figures as President Ulysses S. Grant's personal secretary, Orville Babcock. A member of the notorious Whiskey Ring, which bilked the U.S. Treasury

of millions of dollars, Babcock joined the American speculators William Cazeneau and Joseph Fabens to conspire with Dominican President Buenaventura Báez to annex the Dominican Republic and assume its debt of $1.5 million. If the Senate refused to ratify the treaty, a second treaty would have sold Samaná Bay for $2 million. Báez, Cazeneau, and Fabens would profit from the rise in the value of their property, as well as from subsequent American investment in the island. Given Babcock's influence with Grant, Santo Domingo might have been annexed in 1870 as another step toward making the Caribbean an American lake. Despite the president's enthusiastic support, however, the treaty ran afoul of Charles Sumner of Massachusetts, chairman of the Senate Foreign Relations Committee. Exposing the corrupt bargain between Baez and the two American schemers, Sumner managed to defeat the annexationist lobby, first in his committee and then in a Senate vote in June 1870, when the annexation treaty failed to win a two-thirds majority.

Further Reading: David C. MacMichael, "The United States and the Dominican Republic, 1871–1949: A Cycle in Caribbean Diplomacy," Ph.D. diss., University of Chicago, 1964; Samuel G. Howe, *Letters on the Proposed Annexation of Santo Domingo,* 1871; Sumner Welles, *Naboth's Vineyard: The Dominican Republic, 1844–1924,* 1928.

Lawrence S. Kaplan

SARGENT, AARON AUGUSTUS (28 September 1827–14 August 1887), United States senator and advocate of woman suffrage and Chinese exclusion. Born in Newburyport, Essex County, Massachusetts, and apprenticed to a cabinetmaker, Sargent held various minor jobs before relocating in 1850 to Nevada City, California, where he ultimately surfaced as owner of the *Nevada Daily Journal*. Admitted to the bar in 1854, he practiced his profession and held a number of local and state political offices. Elected as a Republican to the United States House of Representatives, he kept a seat from 1861 to 1863 and again from 1869 to 1873. He authored the Pacific Railroad Act of 1862, which served as the authority to build the transcontinental railroad, completed in 1869. Sargent was a member of the United States

Senate from 1873 to 1879, during which time he chaired the Committee on Mines and Mining in the Forty-Fourth Congress and the Committee on Naval Affairs in the Succeeding Congress. In 1876 he led a congressional investigation on the effects of Chinese immigration to the United States and was the Senate's most prominent advocate of Chinese exclusion. In 1878 Sargent introduced the twenty-nine words that later became the Nineteenth Amendment to the Constitution of the United States. He and his wife, Ellen Clark Sargent, chair of the National Women's Suffrage Association, championed voting rights for women. Sargent made a political mistake by not seeking re-election in 1878. Upon the conclusion of his senatorial term, Sargent resumed his law practice in San Francisco, California, until appointed envoy extraordinary and minister plenipotentiary to Germany in 1882, in which capacity he remained for two years. He declined President Chester A. Arthur's offer to appoint him to minister of Russia. Unsuccessful in 1885 in an endeavor to secure Republican senatorial nomination, Sargent continued to practice law. He died in San Francisco, California.

Further Reading: Christine Freeman, "1827–Aaron Augustus Sargent–1887: Nevada County's International Citizen," *Nevada County Historical Society Bulletin* 32 (1978): 13–21.

Leonard Schlup

SARGENT, JOHN SINGER (12 January 1856–25 April 1925), artist. Born in Florence, Italy, to American parents, Sargent lived most of his life in Europe, but refused to renounce his heritage even when offered a knighthood by King Edward VII of Great Britain. By the end of the nineteenth century, American critics often described the self-effacing Sargent as one of the most successful expatriate artists.

As a young man, Sargent studied painting in Paris at the atelier of Carolus-Duran. From Carolus-Duran, Sargent learned the methods of modern portraiture and bravura brushwork, which, combined with an appreciation for the art of the Old Masters, brought him international recognition at a young age. Parisians admired Sargent's ability to re-create the visual world and to capture momentary effects of light and movement. In scenes such as *El Jaleo* and in portraits such as *The Daughters of Edward Darley Boit*, Sargent's seemingly effortless brushwork appeared to record a momentary vision, or impression, witnessed by the artist—an aesthetic aligned with the most avant-garde movement of his day, French Impressionism. With his 1885 tour de force *Carnation, Lily, Lily, Rose*, Sargent combined the floral effusion of British Aestheticism with the Impressionist methods of plein-air painting that he had observed while working beside his friend Claude Monet.

Sargent's career took an unexpected turn when his elegant yet sensuous portrait of Virginie Gautreau, titled *Madame X*, caused a scandal at the Salon of 1884. Artist and subject were dismayed as Paris audiences mocked this image of the young American "professional beauty" with one strap of her gown hanging seductively off a shoulder. Encouraged by a fellow expatriate, the writer Henry James, Sargent subsequently moved to London, where he established a portrait practice that far outpaced his previous work. His bravura brushwork transformed wealthy women, such as Mrs. Hugh Hammersley, into glamorous, somewhat attenuated figures, dressed in the height of fashion and surrounded by elegant furnishings. His oeuvre provides a brilliant record of Gilded Age fashions and mannerisms.

Sargent's passion during his last decades was the plein-air watercolors and oils made during his travels to Italy, Austria, and Switzerland, where he had traveled as a youth. He also devoted much of his mature career to a series of murals for the Boston Public Library, *The Triumph of Religion* (1890–1919). For the entrance hall to the library's special collections, Sargent produced a series of murals that record a progressive history of religious experience, a series of images meant to trace the rise of a personal and individual relationship with God. Sargent died in London on the eve of his planned departure for Boston, having completed another set of murals for the city's Museum of Fine Arts.

Further Reading Marc Simpson, H. Barbara Weinberg, and Richard Ormond, *Uncanny Spectacle: The Public Ca-*

reer of the Young John Singer Sargent, 1997; Elaine Kilmurray and Richard Ormond, John Singer Sargent: The Early Portraits, 1998; Sally M. Promey, Painting Religion in Public: John Singer Sargent's Triumph of Religion at the Boston Public Library, 1999.

Lacey Jordan

SATANTA (SET-TAIN-TE) (c. 1820–11 October 1878), Kiowa tribal leader. Also known as White Bear and "The Orator of the Plains," Satanta was born on the northern Plains but later migrated to the southern Plains with his people. Much of his adult life was spent in conflict with settlers heading west across Kiowa land and U.S. soldiers sent to protect them. Satanta participated in raids along the Sante Fe Trail in the early 1860s and in 1866, and became the leader of the Kiowa who favored armed resistance against U.S. military forces. He and Satank, another Kiowa leader, signed the 1867 Treaty of Medicine Lodge with the federal government. Under its provisions, the Kiowa were assigned to a reservation in the western part of Indian Territory. The treaty allowed the Kiowa to hunt on buffalo lands south of the Arkansas River, as long as the animals' numbers justified it. In return, the Kiowas were required to give up their claims in Colorado, Kansas, and New Mexico. As the railroads pushed west across Kansas and white buffalo hunters slaughtered the animals south of the Arkansas River, conflict was inevitable. Satanta complained that Major Joel Elliott commanded a squadron of the Seventh Cavalry which killed the animals for sport. He was quoted as saying that the good Indian received nothing; only the independent Indian was rewarded.

Satanta scorned renewed peace efforts, and under his leadership Kiowa raids were renewed. Beginning in 1868, Satanta and Satank led sorties into northern Texas, where cattle ranchers and white hunters were steadily reducing the number of buffalo and hastening the day when all Kiowa would be restricted to the reservation in Indian Territory. Major General Philip H. Sheridan was put in charge of chastising the Indians. In May 1871, Satanta and his warriors attacked an army wagon train carrying supplies between Fort Belknap, Texas, and Fort Richardson, Texas. A number of teamsters were killed. Satanta and Satank were pursued to Fort Sill, Indian Territory, arrested, put in chains, and sent to Texas, to be tried for murder. Satank was killed trying to escape while being transported to prison, and Satanta was sentenced to death. The arrest and conviction of Satanta and Satank were due in a large part to the testimony of Laurie Tatum, Indian agent at Fort Sill. Yet it was Tatum's intervention, along with that of humanitarian groups and Indian leaders, that caused his death sentence to be reduced to life imprisonment, on the condition that he remain on the Kiowa reservation. On 19 August 1873, Satanta was released from prison.

Kiowa raids continued in 1874, however, and Satanta led many of them. The army was now able to move large numbers of troops by train, and with the army after them and the buffalo now gone, the Indians began to return to the reservation. Satanta went to the Cheyenne Agency, where he was placed under arrest and sent to Fort Sill. He was returned to the Texas prison on 17 September 1874. The details surrounding Satanta's death are unclear. However, it appears that, depressed because his life sentence, was now imposed, he jumped from the prison hospital at Huntsville, Texas, ending his life. In 1963, after many requests by relatives, the Texas legislature allowed Satanta's remains to be returned to Oklahoma and reinterred at Fort Sill.

Further Reading: Duane Champagne, The Native North American Almanac, 1994; Francis Paul Prucha, American Indian Treaties: The History of a Political Anomaly, 1997; Wilbur Sturtevant Nye, John R. Wunder, and Nick Eggenhofer, Bad Medicine and Good: Tales of the Kiowas, 1969.

Troy R. Johnson

SCHIFF, JACOB HENRY (10 January 1847–25 September 1920), banker and financier. Born in Frankfurt, Germany, Schiff immigrated to the United States in 1865 and entered the brokerage business. Naturalized in 1870, he married the daughter of Solomon Loeb, a principal of Kuhn, Loeb and Company, and joined the firm in 1875. When Loeb retired in 1885, Schiff became head of the firm, which grew into the second largest investment house in the country, surpassed only by that of J. P. Morgan. Much of Schiff's business involved financing the expanding American railroad system. He had transactions with James J. Hill, Edward H. Harriman, and Alexander J. Cassatt. When, at century's end, competition for the control of western railroads developed between the Hill interests and those of Harriman, Schiff associated with Harriman, while the House of Morgan allied with Hill. Schiff was especially active in attracting Scottish and English investors to support American railroad ventures.

From early in his career Schiff was a community leader in New York City, endowing the Jewish Theological Seminary. In the 1890s he attempted to persuade American diplomatic representatives to speak out against the persecution of Jews in Russia and eastern Europe. During the Russo-Japanese War (1904–1905), his dislike of czarist Russia and his interest in Japan led him to become one of the principal financiers of the Japanese government. After 1900, Schiff was the banker for some of the largest American corporations, including the Western Union Telegraph Company, American Telephone and Telegraph, and Westinghouse. He died in New York City.

Further Reading: Cyrus Adler, *Jacob H. Schiff: His Life and Letters*, 2 vols., 1928; Gary Dean Best, *To Free a People: American Jewish Leaders and the Jewish Problem in Eastern Europe, 1890–1914*, 1982.

James M. Bergquist

SCHUMACHER, FERDINAND (30 March 1822–15 April 1908), entrepreneur and temperance activist. Born in Celle, Germany, Schumacher immigrated to the United States with his brother, Otto, in 1850. He leased water rights on the Ohio and Erie Canal in Akron in 1856, milling rolled oats and other grain products there. During the Civil War, the Union Army purchased large quantities of his oatmeal. By the conflict's end, Akron's economy was booming, and Schumacher was the town's richest man. Former Union soldiers made his products popular after the war, and his firm expanded into markets across the country. The gigantic Jumbo Mills complex, completed in the 1870s, culminated this growth, but the prosperous years came to an end because of a series of disastrous mill fires. Schumacher suffered huge financial losses. In 1886, he merged his

business with the Akron Milling Company to form F. Schumacher Milling. Schumacher consolidated with the American Cereal Company in 1891, and the firm later became the Quaker Oats Company. Schumacher was president of American Cereal until 1899. A temperance leader, he established two temperance hotels in Akron, the Windsor and the Clarendon, in the 1880s, and spent thousands of dollars developing the model temperance town of Harriman, Tennessee. Schumacher was a strong supporter of the Universalist Church. He died in Akron, Ohio.

Further Reading: Karl Grismer, *Akron and Summit County*, 1952; Harrison John Thornton, *The History of the Quaker Oats Company*, 1933; George W. Knepper, *Akron: City at the Summit*, 1981.

Stephen Paschen

SCHURMAN COMMISSION. To decide whether to keep Spain's former colony of the Philippines following the end of the Spanish-American War, President William McKinley toured the nation's heartland from 11 to 21 October 1898, and was confirmed in his decision to do so. He asked Jacob Gould Schurman, president of Cornell University, to head a five-man commission of inquiry—three civilians, two members of the military—to go to the islands. Schurman demurred, saying he opposed overseas expansion. McKinley claimed he did, too, but saw no alternative. Schurman sailed for the islands just as Emilio Aguinaldo, a leading Tagalog nationalist, demanded that the United States honor its promise of independence for the Philippines. Schurman offered Filipinos a plan of civil government with extensive native participation. Because General Elwell S. Otis would not grant the Filipino insurgents an armistice—as Schurman suggested he do—the plan was abandoned and hostilities continued. When McKinley supported Otis, Schurman about-faced and did likewise, even though he told McKinley that he opposed Otis's plan to crush the insurgents. McKinley recalled the two other civil members of the commission. When Schurman refused to return to the islands, the President replaced him with an Ohio judge named William Howard Taft.

Further Reading: Margaret Leech, *In the Days of McKinley*, 1959; H. Wayne Morgan, *William McKinley and His*

America, 1963; David F. Trask, *The War with Spain in 1898*, 1981.

Paolo E. Coletta

SCHURZ, CARL (2 March 1829–14 May 1906), German-American immigrant leader, general, senator from Missouri, and secretary of the interior. Born in Liblar, near Cologne, Germany, Schurz came to America in 1852 after participating in the Revolution of 1848, during which, after an adventurous escape from the Prussians, he rescued his professor, Gottfried Kinkel, who had been condemned to life imprisonment for his part in the uprising.

A masterful practitioner of ethnic politics and opponent of slavery, Schurz was nominated for lieutenant governor of Wisconsin before he had become a naturalized citizen. After chairing the Wisconsin delegation to the Chicago convention that nominated Abraham Lincoln, he was charged with securing much of the German vote for the Republicans, and was appointed minister to Spain by the Lincoln administration. In 1862 he was commissioned brigadier general, and later major general. Moving to St. Louis after the war to edit the *Westliche Post*, Schurz was elected U.S. senator in 1869. Although originally a radical Republican, he broke with President Ulysses S. Grant because of the latter's effort to annex the Dominican Republic, his failure to introduce viable civil service reform, and his adherence to Radical Reconstruction in the South.

One of the founders of the Liberal Republicans, Schurz presided over their convention at Cincinnati in 1872 and reluctantly supported Horace Greeley. After his defeat for reelection, he continued to devote himself to reform politics, and in 1877 was appointed secretary of the interior by Rutherford B. Hayes. In this position, he distinguished himself by introducing civil service tests, rooting out corruption, attempting to save natural resources, and reforming the Indian service. At the close of the Hayes administration, he moved to New York, where he became active in the civil service movement and municipal reform. Joining the Mugwumps in supporting Grover Cleveland against James G. Blaine in 1884, he abandoned the Republicans and thereafter pursued independent poli-tics. Although he backed William McKinley in 1896, Schurz broke completely with that administration after 1898 because of his violent opposition to imperialism. Toward the end of his life, he resumed his advocacy of the freedmen, an effort he had downplayed while opposing President Grant. He died in New York City, a role model for his fellow German Americans, whom he had taught to Americanize while retaining their German heritage.

Further Reading: Hans L. Trefousse, *Carl Schurz: A Biography*, 1982, 1999; Claude Moore Fuess, *Carl Schurz, Reformer 1829–1906*, 1932.

Hans L. Trefousse

SCIENCE. Gilded Age scientists were institution builders. They established agricultural experiment stations, medical schools and libraries, the National Board of Health, and the National Bureau of Standards. In 1879 the Smithsonian Institution created the Bureau of American Ethnology, and in 1890, the Astrophysical Observatory. Not to be outdone, in 1884 the U.S. Department of Agriculture (USDA) founded the Bureau of Animal Industry, in 1890 the Weather Bureau was transferred from the War Department, and in 1903 the bureaus of Chemistry, Plant Industry, and Soils were established. It added the Division of Economic Ornithology and Mammalogy in 1886 and the Office of Experiment Stations in 1888. These institutions highlighted the importance of the life sciences.

Asa Gray, a physician and botany professor at Harvard University, published *The Manual of the Botany of the Northern United States*, which ultimately went through eight editions and became the standard reference work in botany. During the 1870s Othniel C. Marsh, a paleontologist at Yale University, buttressed evolution by discovering a succession of fossil horses and the first toothed bird, an evolutionary link between dinosaurs and modern birds. More useful was the USDA's discovery in 1893 of the pathogen that caused Texas fever in cattle and of the tick that transmitted the pathogen. The work on Texas fever underscored American science's practicality, which was also evident in geology. During the 1860s the soil scientist Eugene W. Hilgard mapped the soils of Mississippi, in an effort to identify the best soil types for particular crops. In this work, he founded pedology, the science that describes the origins and types of soil. The USDA and agricultural experiment stations followed Hilgard's lead by beginning a national mapping of soils in 1894. In the meantime, in 1875 Hilgard had become director of the California Agricultural Experiment Station, where he focused on discovering the principles of soil fertility. During the 1880s, agricultural scientists throughout the United States undertook similar work.

Of the physical sciences, chemistry was more practical than physics. Agricultural chemists analyzed soils, fertilizers, and livestock feeds, and industrial chemists manufactured paints and dyes. In physics the principal challenge was an abstract one: to discover the ether, which physicists believed to be the medium for light. The failure of Albert A. Michelson and Edward W. Morley to do so in 1887 at Western Reserve University in Cleveland, Ohio, led Albert Einstein to discard the search for ether and to regard the speed of light as constant, thus laying a foundation for his special theory of relativity.

Further Reading: Robert V. Bruce, *The Launching of Modern American Science*, 1987; A. Hunter Dupree, *Science in the Federal Government*, 1957.

Christopher Cumo

SCIENCE AND TECHNOLOGY MUSE-UMS.

Science and technology museums advanced scientific knowledge, preserved historical ideas and artifacts, and presented information to encourage scientific learning among the general public. The second half of the nineteenth century proved to be a volatile period for museums. By century's end, many institutions combined education and entertainment through research and display. Science and technology museums took many forms, including zoos, aquariums, botanical gardens, planetariums, and industrial sites, as well as more traditional museums dedicated to natural history, anthropology, and the physical sciences.

Nineteenth-century industrial fairs pushed museums to concentrate on the public as they focused on increasing industrial education, enhancing the role of science in industry, and exposing the public to scientific and technological advances. Exhibitions such as the 1893 World's Columbian Exposition, added substantially to natural history collections. Technology and industry found a place next to science as proper subjects for museums during the Gilded Age. Natural history museums served as places of popular education, outpacing art museums in attendance and applicability to everyday life. The American Museum of Natural History, founded in New York City in 1869, served as a model of true public service.

Gilded Age entrepreneurs founded several museums. In Chicago, Marshall Field gave his name and money to the Field Museum of Natural History, to house biological and anthropological specimens from the 1893 Columbian Exposition. Andrew Carnegie brought natural history to Pittsburgh in 1896 with the Carnegie Museum of Natural History, a leader in natural history display and research.

The increasing number and size of science museums in the Gilded Age coincided with changes in the roles and institutional settings for science and technology in American society. Major technical schools appeared and universities established engineering and science schools, with curricula distinct from traditional liberal arts. Science and technology development became "institutionalized" in the new research laboratories, such as that of Thomas Edison at Menlo Park, New Jersey.

Further Reading: Edward P. Alexander, *The Museum in America: Innovators and Pioneers*, 1997; Silvio A. Bedini, "The Evolution of Science Museums," *Technology and Culture* 6 (1965): 1–29; Victor Danilov, *America's Science Museums*, 1990.

Linda Eikmeier Endersby

SCOTT, THOMAS ALEXANDER

(28 December 1823–21 May 1881), railroad executive, lobbyist, and corporate innovator. Born in Fort Loudoun, Pennsylvania, Scott rose from stationmaster to vice president of the Pennsylvania Railroad. He helped transform it into the world's largest corporation after the Civil War. Competition for midwestern freight business drove Scott and the Pennsylvania's president, J. Edgar Thomson, to seek control of several small midwestern lines. A desire to run them efficiently and remove direct stockholder oversight led Scott in 1870 to secure a charter for

the Pennsylvania Company, the nation's first holding company. The following year he created the southern Railway Security Company, which purchased controlling interests in thirteen southern railroads running from Washington, D.C., to New Orleans. Scott's ambitions were transcontinental: he served briefly (1871–1872) as president of the Union Pacific, and from 1872 to 1880 was president of the Texas and Pacific, securing for the latter generous land grants from Congress in 1871. That same year Scott created the South Improvement Company, designed to block John D. Rockefeller and Standard Oil from controlling oil shipments through Pennsylvania.

The Panic of 1873 eroded Scott's empire. Stockholders repeatedly investigated the Pennsylvania's financial condition thereafter. Scott's crafty lobbying of southern state legislatures for charters and subsidies, and the elevation of his key associates to important political positions in southern states, contributed to charges that the Reconstruction governments were corrupt "carpetbagger" regimes. Under these criticisms Scott, who became president of the Pennsylvania Railroad in 1874, eventually divested the Pennsylvania of most southern holdings. An attempt to gain additional subsidies, the "Scott Plan," was pivotal to the presidential election compromise of 1877, but never achieved final passage. Wage cuts and unsafe operating policies led to strikes in 1877, which were especially destructive to the Pennsylvania system. Conflict with President Rutherford B. Hayes over Scott's call for federal troops to suppress the strikes ended Hayes's support for railroad subsidies. In 1878, Scott was forced to concede Rockefeller's victory in the oil wars. He resigned from the presidency of the railroad in 1880 and died a year later near Darby, Pennsylania.

Further Reading: James A. Ward, *J. Edgar Thomson, Master of the Pennsylvania*, 1980; C. Vann Woodward, *Reunion and Reaction*, 1951; *New York Times*, 22 May 1881.

Lloyd Benson

SEARS, RICHARD WARREN (7 December 1863–28 September 1914), business executive. Born in Stewartville, Minnesota, Sears established a mail-order watch company in 1886.

Five years later, after having sold it, he formed a partnership with Alvah Curtis Roebuck that became Sears, Roebuck, and Company, a mail-order business headquartered in Chicago. Roebuck left the firm in 1895, and Sears thereupon took two new partners, Aaron Nusbaum and Julius Rosenwald. Under the Sears's management, his recognition of the public's desire for inexpensive manufactured goods, his imitation of the methods of Aaron Montgomery Ward, and his clever advertising led the company to enjoy spectacular growth, reaching a sales volume of $10 million in 1900. Sears died in Waukesha, Wisconsin.

Further Reading: Boris Emmet and John E. Jeuck, *Catalogues and Counters: A History of Sears, Roebuck, and Company*, 1950; Gordon L. Weil, *Sears, Roebuck, U.S.A.: The Great American Catalog Store and How It Grew*, 1977; *Chicago Daily Tribune*, 29 September 1914.

Leonard Schlup

SEAVER, EDWIN PLINY (24 February 1838–7 December 1917), educator and school administrator. Born in Northborough, Massachusetts, Seaver attended Harvard College, where he earned an A.B. with honors in 1864, and an A.M. in 1867. He also received an LL.B. degree from Harvard in 1870 but chose education as a career. Tutor and assistant professor of mathematics at Harvard from 1867 to 1874, he then served for six years as headmaster of English High School in Boston, Massachusetts. In 1880, Seaver was named superintendent of the Boston public school system, a position he held until his retirement in 1904. Between 1877 and 1907 he wrote several secondary textbooks on arithmetic, algebra, and trigonometry, as well as a mathematical handbook and articles on school administration and curriculum. Highly respected, Seaver epitomized the Progressive spirit in education and school administration so popular during the Gilded Age. He guided the Boston school system through dramatic growth and significant changes in organization, curriculum, and demographics. He advocated elective studies for high school students, the infusion of democratic principles into the curriculum, and greater administrative efficiency and responsiveness. He died in New Bedford, Massachusetts.

Further Reading: Michael B. Katz, "The Emergence of Bureaucracy in Urban Education: The Boston Case, 1850–

1884. Part II." *History of Education Quarterly* 8 (Fall 1968): 319–357; *New Bedford Evening Standard [Times]*, 8 December 1917; *Boston Evening Transcript*, 8 December 1917.

Robert L. Osgood

SECRET SERVICE. Presidential security was first considered a priority of state during the Civil War. President Abraham Lincoln was guarded by the Union Army and the Metropolitan Police. After the war, Congress established the U.S. Secret Service to combat counterfeiting. Prior to 1906, presidential protection remained an unsanctioned task. All presidents were vulnerable, though some felt more conscious of potential danger than others. Lincoln was oblivious to his protective detail, as were most presidents who followed him. Grover Cleveland was the exception; he and his wife genuinely feared personal attack. They were targets of press criticism when it was discovered that the Secret Service had been guarding both the White House and their summer home in Massachusetts.

The United States lost three presidents to assassin's bullets within thirty-six years. In 1901, despite the presence of three Secret Service "operatives," a man with a hidden revolver mortally wounded William McKinley at a Buffalo, New York, reception. An outraged American public, demanding better protection for its leaders, pressured Congress to give the Secret Service broader powers. Numerous legislative proposals, as well as nearly five years of debate, followed. The sticking point was the creation of a federal police force, a step that had been avoided since the republic's creation. Finally, in 1906, Congress enacted legislation that assured the Secret Service's protective function; necessary funding came in 1907. The agency remained within the Department of the Treasury.

Theodore Roosevelt, who disdained visible protection, assigned his detail to various investigations on his behalf. For example, he sent agents to the Chicago stockyards to ascertain if Upton Sinclair had exaggerated conditions there in his book *The Jungle*. Knowledge of these abuses led to formation of the Federal Bureau of Investigation. When Roosevelt visited Panama's Canal Zone in 1908, becoming the first sitting president to travel beyond the nation's borders, the Secret Service accepted international responsibility. Following the election of William Howard Taft as president in 1908, the Secret Service began to guard presidents-elect. In 1917, the agency extended protection to the president's immediate family. Today the Secret Service maintains a force of two thousand agents in Washington, D.C., and at 116 field offices.

Further Reading: Richard B. Sherman, "Presidential Protection During the Progressive Era: The Aftermath of the McKinley Assassination," *The Historian* 46 (1983): 1–20; Jack C. Fisher, *Stolen Glory*, 2001.

Jack C. Fisher

SECTIONALISM. Sectionalism can be defined as the primacy of region being the lens through which interests and attitudes are perceived and acted upon in politics, economic policies, and social relations. From this perspective, the Gilded Age in many ways simply continued the sectional politics that had earlier driven the United States into the Civil War. In that sense, sectionalism both reflected the historical inheritance of that conflict and was reinvigorated by its consequences.

Viewed from the broadest perspective, the United States was divided into three great sections: the cotton South, the industrializing Northeast and Great Lakes littoral, and the grain- and mineral-producing Plains and mountain West. In terms of historical inheritance, the Civil War and Reconstruction hardened antagonism between the white residents of the former states of the Confederacy and the remainder of the Union. One result was that former Confederate and Union veterans often comprised a quarter or more of all members of Congress. At times, in fact, party caucuses in the U.S. House of Representatives and Senate resembled nothing so much as the rival army encampments of the Civil War, with almost all Confederate veterans in the Democratic Party and the large majority of Union veterans lining up with the Republicans.

However, while the shedding of blood during the Civil War certainly reinforced sectional feeling during the Gilded Age, regional attitudes were also reinvigorated by the dominance of the northern developmental program during the period. Three great policies underpinned northern industrialization; all of them tended to redistribute wealth between the regions, particularly from the southern plantation economy to the northern manufacturing belt. First, the tariff protected northern industry from foreign competition, forcing export-oriented southern producers both to pay higher prices for manufactured goods in the domestic market and to accept lower prices for cotton and tobacco on the world market. Second, the gold standard, by imposing a steady deflation upon the national economy, similarly redistributed wealth from the credit-starved South and West to the capital-rich Northeast. Third, the emergence of an unregulated national market, a developmental precondition for the modern business enterprise that administered the huge industrial corporations of the period, facilitated a redistribution of wealth by striking down interstate barriers to trade between the manufacturing belt and the peripheral agricultural sections. All of these policies lined up Republicans and Democrats on opposite sides in ways almost identical to the partisan divisions between Confederate and Union veterans.

As an overarching feature of American society and politics, sectionalism strengthened throughout the Golden Age. In particular, regional polarization in politics was consolidated by the presidential nomination of William Jennings Bryan at the 1896 Democratic National Convention. In the ensuing "Battle of the Standards" between Bryan and William McKinley, the Republican nominee, the Republicans reinforced their dominant position in the Northeast and Midwest while the Democrats emerged in an even stronger position in the South. The resulting party alignment was destined to structure American politics for another six decades, until the Barry Goldwater-Lyndon Johnson presidential contest in 1964.

Further Reading: Richard Bensel, *Sectionalism and American Political Development, 1880–1980*, 1984; Paul H. Buck, *The Road to Reunion, 1865–1900*, 1937; Vincent P. De Santis, *Republicans Face the Southern Question, The New Departure Years, 1877–1897*, 1959.

Richard Bensel

SEGREGATION. As Southern whites "redeemed" state governments during Reconstruction, they increasingly relied on coercion and intimidation to keep blacks in an inferior position. On one hand, the Ku Klux Klan (KKK) violently suppressed those attempting to exert their civil rights and suffrage. On the other hand, state and local authorities enacted laws that socially separated blacks from whites. The purpose was to instill a palpable sense of inferiority. The federal government offered blacks little protection or inspiration, and the United States Supreme Court consistently issued rulings legally sanctioning segregation. In the *Slaughterhouse Cases* (1873) the court ruled the responsibility of enforcing the 14th Amendment rested not with the federal government, but with the states. In 1876 the court held that federal laws against violence to blacks applied only to the states, not to individuals. Congress attempted to ban segregation as it was emerging with the Civil Rights Act (1875), but the high tribunal ruled in 1883 that it only applied to state-run facilities, not privately-owned enterprises. Since the states refused to legislate or enforce laws, African Americans had no legal protection and nowhere to turn for succor.

Segregation nevertheless spread slowly and sporadically over the South as long as whites felt secure in their political and social control. In the mid-1880s that sense broke under the stress of volatile and divisive politics. As white Democrats dissolved into conservative Bourbons and radical Populists, they neared hysteria in their fear that black Republicans would capture control of the state governments and overturn the racial order. Whites responded with a violent regime of repression. Lynching, the most favored method of coercing blacks, increased dramatically. When Ida B. Wells published accounts of hangings in her Memphis newspaper, her printing press was destroyed by rowdies and she was forced to take refuge in the North. Jim Crow laws were enacted to completely separate Southern society into superior white and inferior black facilities. In 1896 the Supreme Court ruled in *Plessy* v. *Ferguson* that segregation was legal as long as the separate facilities were equal. Lack of any enforcement provision, however, prevented equality. By

1900 the South was racially divided in every imaginable facility, including restaurants, railroads, bathrooms, water fountains, hotels, schools, jails, and theaters, just to name a few. Poll taxes, literacy tests, and grandfather clauses disenfranchiseed blacks and prevented them from gaining any measure of political control.

Many blacks responded to the harsh economic realities of tenant farming and segregation by migrating to Northern cities, such as Chicago. Where segregation was hardening in the South it was growing a little less restrictive in the North. Prior to the Civil War, the North was very much segregated even though it had a small black population. Blacks, for example, could not vote or serve on juries and some states even blocked blacks from entering altogether. After the war the North began desegregating some public facilities, such as railroad cars and theaters. The North did provide a safe haven where blacks such as Ida B. Wells and W.E.B. Du Bois could speak out against segregation and lynching more freely. Moreover, the black markets in the urban North provided economic opportunities unimaginable in the South. Still housing, occupations, and schools remained racially segregated in the North well into the twentieth century. Segregation in the schools was declared unconstitutional in 1954 with U.S. Supreme Court decision in *Brown* v. *the Board of Education*. The court ruled that separate was inherently unequal and hence a violation of constitutional rights. Segregation was banned by the federal Civil Rights Act of 1964. The right to vote was guaranteed the following year with the Voting Rights Act (1965). Legal segregation of housing ended with the Housing Rights Act of 1968.

Further Reading: Leon F. Litwack, *Trouble in Mind: Black Southerners in the Age of Jim Crow.* New York, 1998; Jerrold M. Packard, *American Nightmare: The History of Jim Crow.* New York, 2002; C. Van Woodward, *The Strange Career of Jim Crow.* 2nd rev. ed. New York, 1966.

Gregory Dehler

SEIGNIORAGE. Seigniorage is the difference between what a governmental treasury receives for a unit of metal when it is coined into specie and what it had cost when it was bought as bullion. Neither government gains nor losses from this process have been significant throughout history, even during the period from 1878 to 1893, when the commercial price of silver was declining substantially and the U.S. Treasury was required by law to purchase a limited amount of silver, coin it into legal tender silver dollars, or issue Treasury notes redeemable in either silver or gold.

Further Reading: Milton Friedman and Anna Jacobson Schwartz, *A Monetary History of the United States, 1867–1960,* 1963.

Edwin Dale Odom

SEWALL, ARTHUR (25 November 1835–5 September 1900), shipbuilder, railroad magnate, bank president, and vice presidential candidate. Born in Bath, Maine, Sewall in 1854 founded a shipbuilding company with his brother Edward. Upon Edward's death in 1879, the firm became Arthur Sewall & Company. Over the next fifty years, the firm produced eighty wooden sailing ships, more than any other person in the United States. At various times, he also served as president of the Eastern Railroad and the Central Railroad, and headed the Bath National Bank. As eastern imperialist, tariff protectionist, and sound money advocate, Sewall seemed an illogical choice to team with William Jennings Bryan in 1896. Yet Sewall's endorsement of free silver shortly before the Democratic National Convention caught Bryan's attention and that of the delegates, who selected the Maine banker for their vice presidential candidate. Sewall afforded geographical balance and demonstrated the belief of one businessman that an inflated currency would stimulate the nation's depressed economy. Having held only a position on the Bath city council, Sewall was politically unknown to the nation in 1896. After a barnstorming campaign, Bryan and Sewall lost handily to William McKinley and hard money. Republicans in Maine triumphed with large majorities. Sewall died in Stony Point, Maine.

Further Reading: Leonard Schlup, "Bryan's Partner: Arthur Sewall and the Campaign of 1896," *Maine Historical Society Quarterly* 16 (1977): 189–211; *Bath Times,* 6 September 1900.

Leonard Schlup

SEWALL, LUCY ELLEN (26 April 1837–13 February 1890), physician. A native of Boston, Massachusetts, Sewall in 1856 met Dr. Marie Elizabeth Zakrzewska, a physician and advocate of women's rights, under whom she studied at the New England Medical College. Sewall received her M.D. in 1862, and then spent a year in England and France. She returned to Boston to accept an appointment as physician at the New England Hospital for Women and Children, where she excelled in her commitment to health care. Because of the discriminatory barriers imposed on female physicians during the Gilded Age, Sewall encountered much opposition. Nevertheless, she steadfastly persevered to provide medical treatment to women of all classes and races and to encourage young women to enter the medical profession. A person of determination and dedication, Sewall traveled by horse and carriage to treat patients in her private practice. She declined to charge fees to impoverished patients. Battling frail health, she relentlessly counseled women, treated the ill, and broke new ground for reforms. Sewall died in Boston, leaving a legacy as a capable and knowledgeable servant who upheld the Hippocratic Oath as a code for all who practiced medicine.

Further Reading: Sophia Jex-Blake, *Medical Women: A Thesis and a History*, 1886; Shirley Roberts, *Sophia Jex-Blake*, 1993; *Boston Post*, 19 February 1890.

Leonard Schlup

SEWARD, GEORGE FREDERICK (8 November 1840–28 November 1910), diplomat and businessman. Born in Florida, New York, Seward, nephew of Secretary of State William Henry Seward, attended Union College in Schenectady, New York. After fifteen years of consular service, he was appointed U.S. minister to China in 1876. Controversy erupted when he supported western construction of a railway and advised the promoters how to bypass Chinese opponents of the venture, including officials who claimed that Seward had deceived them about the railroad and that the transaction violated the Burlingame Treaty of 1868. Democrats in the U.S. House of Representatives investigated Seward's handling of the project and raised impeachment charges, but Republicans halted the proceedings on technicalities. Seward served until 1880. An advocate of westernization for China who warned against anti-Chinese sentiment in California and Chinese exclusion, Seward wrote *Chinese Immigration in Its Social and Economical Aspect* in 1881. After returning to the United States, he served as president of the Fidelity and Casualty Company of New York from 1893 to 1910. He died in New York City.

Further Reading: Paul H. Clyde, "Attitudes and Policies of George F. Seward, American Minister in Peking, 1876–1880," *Pacific Historical Review* 2 (1933): 387–404; David L. Anderson, *Imperialism and Idealism: American Diplomats in China, 1861–1898*, 1985; George Frederick Seward Papers, New York Historical Society, New York City.

Leonard Schlup

SEYMOUR, HORATIO (31 May 1810–12 February 1886), political leader and presidential candidate. Born in Pompey Hill, New York, Seymour attended the American Literary, Scientific & Military Academy, studied law, and was admitted to the New York bar in 1832. A Democrat, he was elected governor of New York during the Civil War (1863–1865), and by 1868 was known nationally. He presided over that year's Democratic nominating convention in New York City, favoring Salmon P. Chase's nomination for president. On the twenty-second ballot, a deadlocked convention turned to Seymour to run against the Republican Ulysses S. Grant. During the campaign Seymour broke with conservative Democrats by virtually repudiating the party's platform on debt redemption and taxation issues. Though he initially allowed others to speak for him, in October, following Republican victories in four early states, Seymour made a campaign tour through the upper Midwest. He called for an end to Reconstruction and a greater focus on government economy. However, Seymour carried only eight states and lost by over three hundred thousand votes out of nearly six million cast. Following his defeat, Seymour served on a number of state commissions and rejected efforts by fellow New Yorkers to draft him for presidential runs in 1876 and 1880, and a for Senate seat in 1874. He supported efforts by Samuel Tilden to reform Tammany and served as an elder statesman in the Democratic Party until his death in Utica, New York.

Further Reading: Stewart Mitchell, *Horatio Seymour of New York*, 1938.

Stephen Svonavec

SHAFTER, WILLIAM RUFUS (16 October 1835–12 November 1906), army officer. Born in Galesburg, Michigan, Shafter taught school until 1861, when he helped organize the seventh Michigan Regiment. His Civil War record was distinguished by his winning the Medal of Honor for his exploits at Fair Oaks, his command of the Seventeenth Colored Infantry, and his promotion in March 1865 to brevet brigadier general.

Remaining in the army, he continued to lead black units who fought the Apache, Comanche, Kiowa, and Kickapoo in the Southwest. Shafter also mapped the Llano Estacado. Promoted to colonel of the First Infantry in 1879, he led that regiment during the Ghost Dance campaign of 1890 and the Pullman strike of 1894. As a brigadier general (from 1897), he was named commander of the U.S. army sent to Cuba in 1898. Obesity and illness plagued him, and his record was mixed. He quarreled with the press and some subordinates, including Theodore Roosevelt, who criticized Shafter's supposed lack of aggressiveness, splintering of his army, and logistical difficulties. To Shafter's credit, he had led sixteen thousand men to Cuba, had pushed the enemy back onto Santiago, and had received their surrender—all within less than one month. Shafter retired in 1899 a major general, and died at the Presidio in California.

Further Reading: Paul H. Carlson, *"Pecos Bill": A Military Biography of William R. Shafter*, 1989; Graham Cosmas, *An Army for Empire: The United States Army in the Spanish-American War*, 1971; Robert M. Utley, *Frontier Regulars: The United States Army and the Indian, 1866–1891*, 1973.

Malcolm Muir, Jr.

SHAW, ALBERT (23 July 1857–25 June 1947), publisher and editor. Born in Paddy's Run (now Shandon), Ohio, Shaw graduated from Iowa (now Grinnell) College in 1879 and earned a doctorate in history and political science in 1884 from Johns Hopkins University. There he met Woodrow Wilson, J. Franklin Jameson, Richard T. Ely, and Herbert Baxter Adams, and participated in the scholarly community. From 1884 to 1891, Shaw was head editorial writer for the *Minneapolis Tribune*, also contributing articles to the *Century Illustrated Monthly Magazine* and publishing books. His credentials opened doors to academic positions, which he considered from time to time. In the end, his most significant editorial contribution to Gilded Age America was starting an American edition of the *Review of Reviews*, which had been founded in 1890 in London by the reformer and journalist William T. Stead. In April 1891, Shaw launched the American version. He made the magazine more attractive to American readers by adding illustrations and political cartoons, and using a higher grade of paper. A progressive Republican, Shaw retained complete control over the editing and management of the *Review*, also writing the section "The Progress of the World." The *Review of Reviews*, widely read between 1893 and 1910, left its mark on American periodical journalism in the Gilded Age and thereafter. Shaw died in New York City.

Further Reading: Lloyd J. Graybar, *Albert Shaw of the Review of Reviews: An Intellectual Biography*, 1974; *New York Times*, 26 June 1947; Albert Shaw Papers, New York Public Library.

Leonard Schlup

SHAW, ANNA HOWARD (14 February 1847–2 July 1919), minister, physician, women's suffrage orator. Shaw was born in Newcastle-upon-Tyne, England, but grew up in Michigan. Her early education consisted mostly of home studies. At age fifteen, she became a teacher at the request of local officials; by twenty-four, Shaw was an ordained Methodist minister. In 1873, after two years of preaching, she enrolled at Albion College. Thereafter she went on to graduate studies at Boston University's School of Theology, beginning in 1876. After graduation, she spent seven years as a full-time minister in a small Methodist church in East Dennis, Massachusetts. She also became responsible for a second parish in nearby Dennis, while studying medicine at Boston Medical School. In 1885, upon earning her M.D., Shaw felt a greater calling. She moved to Boston and became involved in the women's suffrage movement. Joining the ranks of great suffragists such as Susan B. Anthony, Elizabeth Cady Stanton, and Carrie Chapman Catt, Shaw toured the United States, delivering sermons as well as speeches on suffrage, temperance, and prohibition. Her involvement with the National American Woman Suffrage Association, of which she was later president, and her tireless efforts paved the way for women's rights in the United States. Shaw delivered over ten thousand speeches, lectures, and sermons. She died in Moylan, Pennsylvania.

Further Reading: Anna Howard Shaw, *The Story of a Pioneer*, 1915; Eve Merriam, *Growing Up Female in America: Ten Lives*, 1971.

Christopher D. Marinaro

SHEAKLEY, JAMES (24 April 1829–11 December 1917), governor of Alaska. Born in Sheakleyville, Pennsylvania, Sheakley taught in rural schools and learned the cabinetmaking trade, but never worked at it. He went to California and prospected for gold between 1851 and 1855, then returned to Pennsylvania, where he entered the dry goods business and later the oil industry. He served a single term as a Democrat in the U.S. House of Representatives from 1875 to 1877. He then became U.S. commissioner and superintendent of schools in Wrangell, Alaska, from 1887 to 1893, and was admitted to the Alaska bar in 1888. A churchgoing Presbyterian, Sheakley allied himself with Sheldon Jackson and his supporters. In 1892, President Grover Cleveland appointed Sheakley governor of Alaska, a position he held until 1897. Afterward he moved to San Francisco, where he worked with the city's board of trade. There he lectured widely on Alaska, touting the trade opportunities. In 1900, Sheakley moved to Pennsylvania to become mayor and justice of the peace in Greenville, where he died.

Further Reading: Evangeline Atwood and Robert N. DeArmond, *Who's Who in Alaskan Politics*, 1977; Ted C. Hinckley, *The Americanization of Alaska, 1867–1897*, 1972.

Claus-M. Naske

SHELL MANIFESTO. As the South Carolina statewide elections approached in 1890, the populist Democrat Benjamin Tillman's followers were determined to seize control of the state Democratic Party and elect the next governor. On 24 January 1890, they published a manifesto stating their intentions. Signed by Farmers' Association president (and future Congressman) George Washington Shell, the document, in fact prepared by Tillman, accused South Carolina's conservative "Bourbon" regime of wealthy planters and businessmen of denying political power to the state's poor, small-farmer majority. The manifesto called for a Farmers' Association convention in March to nominate a full ticket for the upcoming elections. To avoid the stigma of appearing outside the Democratic machinery, the manifesto stipulated that the nominees would be subject to the next Democratic state convention's approval, pledging to abide by its ultimate decision. Tillman sought to sidestep normal party procedure and still enter the gubernatorial race far ahead of any conservative rival. Inviting sympathetic Democrats to attend the 27 March convention in Columbia, he hoped the Farmers' Association could force Tillman on the state party. Tillman easily won the endorsement of most of participants. Subsequently capturing the Democratic nomination, he went on to take that November's general election. He won reelection in 1892. Having in the meantime rewritten the state constitution to disenfranchise most African-American voters, Tillman served in the U.S. Senate from 1895 until his death in 1918.

Further Reading: William J. Cooper, Jr., *The Conservative Regime: South Carolina, 1877–1890*, 1968; Elmer D. Johnson and Kathleen Lewis Sloan, eds., *South Carolina: A Documentary History of the Palmetto State*, 1971.

Harvey Gresham Hudspeth

SHERIDAN, PHILIP HENRY (6 March 1831–5 August 1888), army officer. Born (exact location uncertain) to an Irish immigrant family on its way to Ohio, Sheridan graduated from the U.S. Military Academy in 1853. During the Civil War, he enjoyed a meteoric rise because of his combat performance at Perryville, Stones River, and Missionary Ridge. Selected to head the cavalry of the Army of the Potomac, Sheridan led his troopers from Yellow Tavern to Appomattox. Following Reconstruction duty in the Gulf states, Sheridan commanded the Department of the Missouri from 1867 to 1883. He orchestrated successful campaigns against the tribes of the central Plains, including the Cheyenne, Comanche, and Sioux, and was promoted to lieutenant general in March 1869. He also served as the U.S. observer with the German army during the Franco-Prussian War. On 1 November 1883, Sheridan followed William T. Sherman as commander in chief of the U.S. Army. In this position, he advocated bolstering the National Guard and the country's coastal defenses. Suffering from heart troubles, he died barely two months after his promotion to general on 1 June 1888. He died in Nonquitt, Massachusetts.

Further Reading: Paul Andrew Hutton, *Phil Sheridan and His Army*, 1985; Roy Morris, Jr., *Sheridan: The Life and Wars of General Phil Sheridan*, 1992; Philip H. Sheridan, *Personal Memoirs of P. H. Sheridan*, 1888.

Malcolm Muir, Jr.

SHERMAN ANTITRUST ACT. The Republican-controlled Fifty-first, or "Billion-Dollar," Congress (1889–1891) addressed a number of issues, of which antitrust came closest to achieving bipartisan status. Fittingly, the legislation produced by this concern proved to be of far-reaching importance. Of the various forms of organization conceived by the business moguls of the late nineteenth century, the trust was of greatest concern to the general public. Designed to curtail competition, it was considered a menace to consumer interests because of the potential to create higher prices for the diverse range of goods involved. It therefore was no surprise that the 1888 platforms of both major parties, as well as of some minor ones, expressed antitrust sentiments. If there appeared to be a public mandate concerning any issue, it was to address the monopolistic tendency embodied in the trust and similar combinations. Senate Bill No. 1, submitted in early December 1889 by John Sherman of Ohio, proposed antitrust legislation. Although a number of other such measures were submitted for congressional consideration, and others, particularly senators George F. Hoar of Massachusetts and George F. Edmunds of Vermont, did much

of the work in shaping the bill, the one that finally emerged carried Sherman's name. It passed the Senate with only one negative vote and the House with no opposition, although a considerable number of the representatives chose not to vote. It became law in early July 1890.

Though a number of states had passed similar legislation, the Sherman Antitrust Act was the first such measure to be enacted by Congress. So sweeping that it failed to differentiate among combinations that were common to the business community of the era, the vagueness of its terms were declared by some doubters to have been deliberate. Ignored was the fact that Congress had no experience in designing such laws and no precedent upon which to rely. Although enforcement of the act in line with its obvious intent remained lax for a number of years following its passage, it nonetheless provided a solid basis for more vigorous federal efforts in the twentieth century to protect the public from the worst excesses of monopolistic practices.

Further Reading: Hans B. Thorelli, *The Federal Antitrust Policy: Origination of an American Tradition*, 1974.

James L. Baumgardner

SHERMAN, JOHN (10 May 1823–22 October 1900), U.S. senator, cabinet official, brother of William T. Sherman, and leading Republican authority on financial affairs. Born in Lancaster, Ohio, Sherman gained admission to the Ohio bar in 1844. A founding father of the Republican Party in Ohio, he campaigned on a free-soil platform. He served in the U.S. House of Representatives from 1855 to 1861 and chaired the Ways and Means Committee in 1859. When President Abraham Lincoln in 1861 chose Ohio Senator Salmon P. Chase to become secretary of the Treasury, the state's legislators selected Sherman to replace Chase. Sherman held a seat in the United States Senate from 1861 to 1877, took the lead in drafting the Reconstruction Act of 1867, voted to remove President Andrew Johnson from office, and headed the Finance Committee. In 1873 he urged Congress to discontinue coinage of silver dollars. Sherman served as secretary of the Treasury under President Rutherford B. Hayes (1877–1881). He worked with congressional leaders to assure passage of the Bland-Allison Act of 1878.

One of the ablest leaders of his generation, Sherman repeatedly lost his party's presidential nomination. He hoped a deadlocked GOP convention would turn to him as a compromise in 1880. That honor instead went to James A. Garfield. Sherman thereupon returned to the Senate, where he remained from 1881 to 1897. He displayed greatest delegate strength at the national convention in 1888, but failed to win the nomination. Although intelligent and capable, Sherman exuded dullness and coldness. Known as the "Ohio Icicle," he often had to compete against the popular James G. Blaine of Maine.

Sherman contributed greatly to his state and the country. In 1890, he helped write the Sherman Silver Purchase Act, which he endorsed halfheartedly, and introduced a bill that materialized, after amendments and revisions offered mainly by Senator George F. Hoar of Massachusetts and Senator George F. Edmunds of Vermont, as the Sherman Antitrust Act. It made combinations in restraint of trade illegal. In 1894, having set a record for longevity in the Senate, Sherman began experiencing periodic memory lapses. In 1897 President William McKinley elevated him to secretary of state, thereby creating a Senate opening for the wealthy Cleveland industrialist Mark Hanna, McKinley's campaign manager. Sherman, suffering from a loss of hearing and the onset of senility, endured a lackluster year in the cabinet. At times he could not recognize acquaintances or concentrate for prolonged periods on his responsibilities. Accepting recommendations from close colleagues that he leave office for health reasons, Sherman resigned in 1898. He allowed anti-imperialists in 1899 to use his name in their crusade against overseas expansion. Sherman died in Washington, D.C., having had a remarkable career of forty-three continuous years of public service.

Further Reading: John Sherman, *Recollections of Forty Years in the House, Senate, and Cabinet: An Autobiography*, 2 vols., 1895; Theodore Burton, *John Sherman*, 1906; Winfield S. Kerr, *John Sherman: His Life and Public Services*, 2 vols., 1907.

Leonard Schlup

SHERMAN SILVER PURCHASE ACT OF 1890. After the late 1840s, the amount of silver in circulation had declined. It was undervalued in the United States and thus was exchanged overseas for gold. In 1873 Congress responded to the dearth of silver by directing the Treasury to stop minting the silver dollar. Industrialists favored an inelastic currency and applauded the measure, though farmers wanted unlimited coinage of silver to inflate the currency and, with it, food prices. In 1890 Congress passed the Sherman Silver Purchase Act as a compromise. The act, fashioned by Senator John Sherman of Ohio, directed the Treasury to buy 4.5 million ounces of silver per month with Treasury notes printed for this purpose. The secretary of the Treasury could redeem the notes in silver or gold, and because he did so in gold, the act did not add silver to the money supply. The act, therefore, was a victory for industrialists rather than farmers.

Further Reading: Milton Friedman and Anna Schwartz, *A Monetary History of the United States, 1867–1960*, 1963; Paul Studenski and Herman Krooss, *A Financial History of the United States*, 1952.

Christopher Cumo

SHERMAN, WILLIAM TECUMSEH (8 February 1820–14 February 1891), army general and brother of John Sherman. Born in Lancaster, Ohio, Sherman attended the U.S. Military Academy from 1836 to 1840. In the Civil War, he became a national figure during the Atlanta campaign and the marches to the sea and through the Carolinas. In 1869, Sherman was named commanding general of the army, replacing U. S. Grant upon his election to the presidency. Almost immediately Sherman and Grant quarreled over the commanding general's control of the general staff, a dispute never resolved during his career. Sherman strongly supported construction of the transcontinental railroad, and continued uncompromising warfare against the Native Americans in the West. In 1871, he began extended service as regent of the Smithsonian Institution. In 1874, angered over reductions in the army and his inability to influence military policy, he moved the army's headquarters to St. Louis in protest, completing his memoirs there in 1875. He established a professional school for officers at Fort Leavenworth, Kansas, in 1881. When he retired in 1884, many Republicans urge him to become their presidential nominee. He responded: "I will not accept if nominated and will not serve if elected." He spent his retirement years as one of the era's most popular after-dinner speakers. He died in New York City.

Further Reading: John F. Marszalek, *Sherman: A Soldier's Passion for Order*, 1994; Robert G. Athearn, *William Tecumseh Sherman and the Settlement of the West*, 1956; William T. Sherman Papers, Library of Congress.

John F. Marszalek

SHIRAS, GEORGE, JR. (26 January 1832–2 August 1924), Supreme Court justice. Born in Pittsburgh, Pennsylvania, Shiras graduated from Yale in 1853 and established a local law practice. He ultimately became one of the most successful attorneys in western Pennsylvania, devoting nearly four full decades to private practice. Reportedly, there was hardly a major case in which he was not involved as legal counsel. Shiras rejected many offers to enter public service. The most famous occurred in 1881, when he had an opportunity to be U.S. senator. Shiras rejected the offer, angering the Republican Party machine. President Benjamin Harrison noted his political independence and named him to the Supreme Court in 1892, despite opposition from Pennsylvania's congressional delegation. Shiras served for the next ten years and four months, often casting the crucial swing vote in cases involving state regulation of the economy. His record was decidedly mixed, but ultimately, it was Shiras's role in the 1895 case of *Pollock* v. *Farmers Loan and Trust Company* that established his historical reputation. A first vote on the case was kept confidential, and many suspected Shiras of having switched sides, thereby "Shirasing" one of the major pieces of Gilded Age social reform legislation. Despite public denials by his family and his congressman, Shiras and his reputation never fully recovered from the accusations. He resigned in 1903 and, two decades later, died in Pittsburgh.

Further Reading: *New York Times*, 3 August 1924; *The Green Bag*, 1892.

Harvey Gresham Hudspeth

SHOUP, GEORGE LAIRD (15 June 1836–21 December 1904), first governor of Idaho, U.S. senator. Born in Kittanning, Pennsylvania, Shoup rose to colonel in the Union Army during the Civil War. In 1866 he was a founder of Salmon, Idaho, engaged in the mercantile business there, and began stock raising. Shoup started his political career as a Lemhi County commissioner, and in 1872 became county superintendent of schools. In 1874 he was elected as a Republican to the territorial legislature, and later (1879–1880) served one term on the territorial council. At this time Shoup became active in national Republican politics, serving as a delegate to the 1880 Republican National Convention and as a member of the Republican National Committee (1880–1884, 1888–1892). President Benjamin Harrison appointed him territorial governor in 1889. In that office, Shoup worked tirelessly for statehood. He helped organize the constitutional convention that met in July 1889 and later lobbied in Washington. After statehood was granted in 1890, Shoup was elected the first governor. When, in 1891, the legislature threatened to deadlock over the choice of Idaho's first senators, Shoup allowed himself to be a candidate and won a four-year term, beginning in March 1891. He served for a decade, backing the gold standard and opposing expanded silver coinage, despite Idaho's being a silver producer. His defeat in 1900 was due, at least in part, to that opposition. He died in Boise, Idaho.

Further Reading: Leonard J. Arrington, *History of Idaho*, 1994; David L. Crowder, "Pioneer Sketch: George Laird Shoup," *Idaho Yesterdays* 33 (1990): 18–23.

Michael J. Anderson

SIBLEY, JOSEPH CROCKER (18 February 1850–19 May 1926), congressman. Born in Friendship, New York, Sibley taught school, studied medicine, engaged in the oil refinery business in Franklin, Pennsylvania, and undertook manufacturing and agricultural pursuits. Elected as a Democrat to the U.S. House of Representatives, he served from 1883 to 1895 and again from 1899 to 1901, having been unable to hold his House seat in the Republican years 1894 and 1896. A Gilded Age politician who switched allegiance from the Democrats and Populists to the Republicans, Sibley returned to the House as a Republican in 1901. He remained there until 1907. He died near Franklin, Pennsylvania.

Further Reading: *New York Times*, 20 May 1926.

Leonard Schlup

SIERRA CLUB. Founded in May 1892 and led by the legendary conservationist John Muir (1838–1914), the Sierra Club began with 182 charter members. They sought to "explore, enjoy, and protect" the earth, and Muir became "father of the national park system." Early prominent members included the scientist Joseph Le Conte (1823–1901), who studied geology with the naturalist and systematist Louis Agassiz (1807–1873), who was a paleontologist at Harvard University; the mountaineer and conservationist Edward Taylor Parsons (1861–1914), and William E. Colby (1875–1964), an environmentalist who assisted in establishing the club's outings programs.

In its first conservation campaign, the Sierra Club successfully took on stockmen and others who sought to reduce the boundaries of Yosemite National Park, which had been created by an act of Congress in 1890. Although the club's founders could not match the financial power of the special interests trying to exploit Yosemite, they mobilized overwhelming public support and won this critical battle.

In 1893, the Sierra Club began to issue the *Sierra Club Bulletin*, and President Benjamin Harrison established a thirteen-million-acre Sierra Forest Reserve. Six years later, Congress created Mount Rainier National Park through legislation based on a Sierra Club statement. In 1903, President Theodore Roosevelt and Muir visited Yosemite. Together they planned the foundation of Roosevelt's innovative conservation program. During the twentieth century, the Sierra Club earned a solid reputation as America's leading environmental champion.

Further Reading: Terry Gifford, ed., *John Muir: His Life and Letters and Other Writings*, 1996; Stephen R. Fox, *The American Conservation Movement: John Muir and His Legacy*, 1986; Andrew J. Feldman, *The Sierra Club Green Guide*, 1996.

Leonard Schlup

SILVER CONVENTIONS OF 1893 AND 1895. In November 1893, the American Bimetallic League held a convention in Chicago, organized by the silver lobbyist William H. Harvey. Although the three-day meeting accomplished little, the election of several high-ranking Populists to convention offices signaled free silver's growing popularity. Prominent Populists serving in convention offices or on committees included George Washburn, Ignatius Donnelly, H. E. Taubeneck, and William V. Allen. By November 1894, Taubeneck had moved the party farther from its agrarian roots and issued a repudiation of what he characterized the wild theories of the Omaha Platform, in an apparent realignment of the People's Party with the silverites.

In June 1895, the largest and most successful silver convention opened in Memphis, Tennessee. Spearheaded by Senator Isham G. Harris of Tennessee, convention planners billed the event as a nonpartisan demonstration of silver support. Between two thousand and twenty-seven hundred Silver Democrats and Populists from across the South and the Plains states attended. Democrats clearly dominated the proceedings, with Ben Tillman and William Jennings Bryan playing prominent roles. Almost lost among the Democratic luminaries on the convention platform was the lone Populist, Marion Butler of North Carolina. Democrats controlled all convention offices, and Populists gained a single representative on the important resolutions committee only after John McDowell of Tennessee complained about the party's lack of representation. The meeting ended with the Democrats controlling the silver issue.

Further Reading: John M. Eisenberg, Jr., "A House Divided: Silver Democrats and Their Party," *West Tennessee Historical Society Papers* 29 (1975): 86–99.

Connie L. Lester

SILVER REPUBLICANS, 1896. Party designations in 1895 and 1896 blurred over the currency question. Senator Henry M. Teller of Colorado, for instance, would leave the Republican Party if it did not declare for silver. He would not discuss the financial question unless free coinage was considered also, and said he would try to defeat appropriations bills if President Grover Cleveland sought to issue more bonds. Meanwhile, the Democratic free silverite, William Jennings Bryan, demanded fusion with the Populists and urged sympathizers to bolt if their party conventions supported gold. Early in June 1896, Teller visited the Illinois Democratic state convention, seeking Governor John Peter Altgeld's endorsement, and Bryan attended the Republican National Convention as a special correspondent of the *Omaha World-Herald*. Beaten on a minority report on silver in the Republican committee on resolutions, Teller stood ready to depart. When the committee agreed to presidential nominee William McKinley's request that a pledge to promote international agreement on free coinage be added to the money plank, Teller, tears streaming down his face, did bolt, followed by various others, mostly westerners. Instead of joining Democrats or Populists, however, Silver Republicans created their own organization—and went nowhere.

Further Reading: Paolo E. Coletta, *William Jennings Bryan Vol. 1: Political Evangelist, 1860–1908*, 1964; Elmer Ellis, *Henry Moore Teller*, 1941, and "The Silver Republicans in the Election of 1896," *Mississippi Valley Historical Review* 18 (March 1932): 519–534.

Paolo E. Coletta

SIMPSON, JERRY (31 March 1842–23 October 1905), U.S. congressman. Born in Westmoreland County, New Brunswick, Canada, Simpson was mostly self-educated. He began working as a seaman on a lake vessel at fourteen, and over the next twenty years, held multiple positions, captaining several ships. During the Civil War he served briefly in the Union cause. In 1879 he left the Great Lakes area for Kansas, ultimately settling near Medicine Lodge. Simpson, who failed as farmer, sawmill operator, cattleman, and businessman, finally accepted the job of marshal of Medicine Lodge. His great ability was political agitation, especially for the era's third-party movements. Once a Republican, he later allied with the Greenback Party, the Single Tax movement, the Union Labor Party, the Farmers' Alliance movement, and the People's Party. He was twice defeated in congressional races (1886 and 1888) before Populism swept him into office in 1890.

Like many agrarian reform leaders interested in office, Simpson was never a strenuous adherent to party ideology. He was an accomplished and clever speaker, with a quick wit. He is best remembered by the nickname he assumed as the result of an intended slur by a young newspaperman, who responded to a Simpson remark that his opponent wore silk stockings by claiming that Simpson wore none. Henceforth, he became "Sockless Jerry Simpson." In addition to winning election to Congress in 1890, he was reelected in 1892 and 1896, but lost in 1894 and 1898. As a congressman, Simpson entered few bills and spoke sparingly. He was best in give-and-take debate, excelling in repartee. His commitment to Populism has been questioned by some. He was a fusionist, believing the movement's future lay in joining with Democrats. Thus, he eagerly supported William Jennings Bryan's nomination in 1896. Simpson was an advocate of monetary inflation and opposed expansionism. He did much to energize Kansas farmers in the 1890s, but otherwise his impact was negligible.

After leaving Congress, Simpson moved to Wichita, Kansas, where he published *Jerry Simpson's Bayonet* for several years. He then took up residence in Roswell, New Mexico, where he ranched and speculated in land. He returned to Wichita to be treated for a chronic heart ailment, and died there a few weeks later.

Further Reading: Karel D. Bicha, "Jerry Simpson: Populist Without Principle," *Journal of American History* 54 (1967): 291–306; O. Gene Clanton, *Kansas Populism: Ideas and Men*, 1969; Elvis E. Fleming, " 'Sockless' Jerry Simpson: The New Mexico Years, 1902–1905," *New Mexico Historical Review* 69 (1994): 49–69.

Robert S. La Forte

SITTING BULL (c. 1831–15 December 1890), Hunkpapa Lakota spiritual leader and statesman. *Tatanka Iyotanka*, literally "stubborn buffalo sitting on its haunches," was born somewhere between Fort Pierre and the Grand River in present-day South Dakota. At age fourteen he became a warrior, counting his first coup during a skirmish with Crows on the Powder River. Sitting Bull's stature in Hunkpapa warrior societies rose rapidly. In 1857, the Strong Hearts made him a society war chief. Later that year he became a Hunkpapa war chief. The 1860s brought whites in ever more numbers to the Great Plains, and turmoil to Plains Indians. Some Lakotas counseled accommodation; others, especially Sitting Bull, violently resisted white intrusions. In 1868, leaders of some Lakota tribes signed the Treaty of Fort Laramie, agreeing to reservation life. Other Lakota, including Sitting Bull, refused. Nontreaty chiefs, worried about unity, sensed the need for a supreme leader. In 1869, in an unprecedented move for an egalitarian people, they created the office of Lakota head chief, to which they elected Sitting Bull.

For seven years, Sitting Bull's bands roamed in relative isolation through the Powder River country. In 1875, the U.S. Army delivered an ultimatum: return to the reservation by 31 January 1876, or be forcibly removed. Sitting Bull did not respond, precipitating events that led to the battle of the Little Big Horn. Beyond warrior age, Sitting Bull fought only briefly in this battle. His greatest achievement was galvanizing his people, including many treaty Lakota, and Northern Cheyenne allies. Together they utterly routed the Seventh U.S. Cavalry. After the Little Big Horn, Sitting Bull led many of his followers to Canada. He surrendered at Fort Buford, Dakota Territory, in 1881, settling at Standing Rock Reservation. Treated as a celebrity, he traveled widely, including an 1885 stint with Buffalo Bill Cody's Wild West Show. Sitting Bull became embroiled in reservation politics, embracing the Lakota ways at every turn. While planning a Ghost Dance on Grand River, he was confronted and killed by Lakota police.

Further Reading: Robert M. Utley, *The Lance and the Shield: The Life and Times of Sitting Bull*, 1993; Stanley Vestal, *Sitting Bull: Champion of the Sioux*, 1932.

Richard A. Fox

SIXTEEN TO ONE RATIO. The Coinage Act of 1792 had established both gold and silver as legal tender, and had set the value of gold at fifteen times that of silver. In 1834 Congress raised the value of gold to sixteen times that of silver, and thereafter one could therefore exchange sixteen ounces of silver for one ounce of gold at the Treasury. Although the currency was bimetallic in principle, in 1873 Congress directed the Treasury to stop minting the silver

dollar because so little silver was in circulation. The move angered farmers, who spent much of the Gilded Age advocating unlimited coinage of silver at a 16:1 ratio; that is, the money supply would have sixteen times more silver than gold, to reflect the relative value of each metal. Despite farmers' efforts, the Gold Standard Act of 1900 dropped silver as legal tender and thereby ended the possibility of returning it to circulation at a 16:1 ratio.

Further Reading: Milton Friedman and Anna Schwartz, *A Monetary History of the United States, 1867–1960*, 1963; Paul Studenski and Herman Krooss, *A Financial History of the United States*, 1952; Paul W. Glad, *The Trumpet Soundeth: William Jennings Bryan and His Democracy, 1896–1912*, 1960.

Christopher Cumo

SLAUGHTERHOUSE CASES (83 U.S. [16 Wall] 36, 21 L. Ed. 394, 1873). The strategic location of New Orleans made it the center of the beef slaughtering industry at the end of the Civil War, but its numerous small unsanitary packers aggravated the city's endemic public health problems. In 1869, Louisiana's legislature chartered a monopoly corporation, the Crescent City Live-Stock Landing and Slaughter-House Company, to construct facilities for all butchers in the city without discrimination. Established butchering interests, harmed by loss of their favored market position, sued under the newly ratified Fourteenth Amendment on the grounds that the monopoly charter violated their right to earn a living from honest employment. Louisiana's supreme court held the slaughterhouse monopoly a proper exercise of a state's inherent power to make reasonable regulations in the interest of public health and welfare.

A divided U.S. Supreme Court affirmed the Louisiana supreme court in April 1873, in the first significant judicial interpretation of the Fourteenth Amendment. The Court defined the privileges and immunities protected by the amendment so narrowly as to defeat the its purpose of securing meaningful freedom for the newly emancipated African Americans. Three dissenting justices argued that the amendment profoundly changed the federal structure because the national government became the guarantor against state interference with all of the rights and privileges associated with state citizenship, including the right to engage in employment subject only to reasonable regulation. They contended that creation of a monopoly was not essential to ensuring the public health, and constituted an impermissible exercise of state power. The rationale of the dissent was the first expression of a doctrine later known as "substantive due process," by which the Supreme Court invalidated progressive social legislation deemed to interfere with individual liberty.

Further Reading: Eric Foner, *Reconstruction: America's Unfinished Revolution 1863–1877*, 1984; Herbert Hovenkamp, *Enterprise and American Law: 1836–1937*, 1991; Mitchell Franklin, "The Foundations and Meaning of the Slaughterhouse Cases," *Tulane Law Revue* 18 (1943): 1–88, 218–262.

M. Susan Murnane

SMALLS, ROBERT (5 April 1839–23 February 1915), congressman. Born in Beaufort, South Carolina, Smalls, an African American, moved to Charleston in 1851, and held various jobs on the waterfront. During the Civil War, he piloted the cotton steamer *Planter* past Confederate coastal defenses and into possession of the Union fleet. A member of the state constitutional convention in 1868, Smalls held a seat in the lower house from 1868 to 1870, and in the upper chamber from 1870 to 1874. Elected to the U.S. House of Representatives as a Republican in 1874, Smalls was accused of having accepted a bribe from a printer; Democratic Governor William D. Simpson pardoned him in a political bargain. Smalls was defeated in 1878 and 1880, but successfully contested the latter race due to Democratic fraud. He replaced George D. Tillman, and served from 19 July 1882 to 3 March 1883. Though gerrymandered out of his seat, Smalls was elected again to fill the vacancy created by the death of the incumbent, Edmund W. M. Mackey. Smalls remained in the House from 18 March 1884 until 3 March 1887. He was collector of the port of Beaufort from 1889 to 1913. Having fought long for African-American rights, Smalls grew disillusioned during the segregated era. He died in Beaufort.

Further Reading: Okon Edet Uya, *From Slavery to Public Service: Robert Smalls, 1839–1915*, 1971; Edward A. Miller, Jr., *Gullah Statesman: Robert Smalls from Slavery to Congress, 1839–1915*, 1995.

Leonard Schlup

SMITH, HOKE (2 September 1855–27 November 1931), lawyer and politician. Born in Newton, North Carolina, Smith read law in Atlanta, Georgia, and was admitted to the Georgia bar. Adjusting to the urban, industrial life of the New South, he established himself as a plaintiff's champion, winning many damage suits against railroads and developing an enduring suspicion of corporate power. Following the example of Henry W. Grady, Smith chose the newspaper business as a means of developing political influence. In 1887 he was chief purchaser of the *Atlanta Journal*; while continuing to practice law, he worked to make it an organ of low-tariff, anticorporate democracy. In the process, Smith built a following among Georgia farmers. He shied away from radicalism, however, supporting Grover Cleveland in 1888 and 1892. He was rewarded with appointment as secretary of the interior. There he proved a loyal and vigorous administrator until 1896, when he resigned after deciding to support William Jennings Bryan for president.

After a decade of practicing law and charitable work, Smith reentered politics in a way that illustrates the ambiguities of southern Progressivism. Hostility to railroads was on the rise in Georgia, and Smith ran for governor in 1906 as a proponent of stricter railroad regulation. However, to ensure victory, he made a bargain with the agrarian boss Tom Watson to bring about disfranchisement of black voters. Formerly Smith had been a paternalist and a racial moderate; now he ran a racist campaign and as governor threw his influence behind a disfranchising amendment that passed in 1907. All the same, he was an effective reformer, supporting measures to strengthen the railroad commission, enhance public education, abolish the convict lease system, and bring about prohibition of alcoholic beverages. Smith later served in the U.S. Senate (1911–1921). He died in Atlanta.

Further Reading: Dewey W. Grantham, Jr., *Hoke Smith and the Politics of the New South*, 1958.

Paul M. Pruitt, Jr.

SMITH, JAMES (12 June 1851–1 April 1927), U.S. senator and political boss. Born in Newark, New Jersey, Smith attended St. Mary's College in Wilmington, Delaware, before embarking on a business career. Ultimately, he became president of the Federal Trust Company of Newark and for years owned the *Newark Advertiser* and later the *Newark Star*. Although prominent and wealthy through his business operations, Smith became a powerful Democratic boss of his state, beginning with local offices and culminating with his election to the U.S. Senate in 1892. He served there from 1893 to 1899 and chaired the Committee on the Organization, Conduct, and Expenditures of Executive Departments. Rumors circulated that he had speculated in sugar stocks in 1894, an accusation he denied. After leaving office, Smith engaged in banking, newspaper publishing, and the manufacture of leather. His power waned during the Progressive Era, and he lost a bid to return to the Senate in 1911. He died in Newark.

Further Reading: *Newark Evening News*, 2 April 1927.

Leonard Schlup

SMITH, JOSEPH FIELDING (13 November 1838–19 November 1918), president of the Mormon Church. Nephew of the founder Joseph Smith, Joseph F. Smith was born in Far West, Missouri; migrated with his mother and Brigham Young to Utah in 1848; and rose rapidly in the church hierarchy. He was president of the European mission in 1874, 1875, and 1877. Also active in politics, Smith served on the municipal council of Salt Lake City and later in both chambers of the territorial legislature before moving to Hawaii in 1884 to escape prosecution for polygamy. In 1887 he traveled to Washington to urge Congress to grant statehood to Utah. Eleven years later he became second counselor to the church president; in 1901 he was first counselor, and later that year was chosen president. He died in Salt Lake City.

Further Reading: *Deseret Evening News*, Salt Lake City, 19 November 1918.

Leonard Schlup

SMYTH v. AMES (169 U.S. 466), Supreme Court decision. State regulation of railroad rates was the primary issue in *Smyth* v. *Ames*, specifically, whether the Eleventh Amendment gives states total immunity from suits. The case was well known in its day, in part for the involvement of two nationally known attorneys, William Jennings Bryan and James C. Carter. In a unanimous decision of seven justices (Stephen Johnson Field had resigned, and Chief Justice Melville Weston Fuller did not participate), the court ruled in 1898 that individual state agencies and officers are not protected under the amendment.

An 1893 Nebraska statute required railroads to provide public access at specific rates. The railroads contended that they were not profiting from the arrangement, and sued for just compensation. Justice John Marshall Harlan, in the opinion for the court, invoked the Fourteenth Amendment in defense of the suit, determining that state officers could be held liable for claims of denial of equal protection and due process, which were two of the contentions of the railroad suit. To the question of what specifically determined just compensation, Harlan struggled to develop a method for determining fair return, without significant result. The primary question of what was meant by "just compensation" thus remained unanswered.

Further Reading: Owen M. Fiss, *History of the Supreme Court of the United States*, Vol. 8, *Troubled Beginnings of the Modern State, 1888–1910*, 1993, 207–216.

Thomas C. Sutton

SOCIAL DARWINISM. In 1859, the English naturalist Charles Darwin published *On the Origin of Species*, positing the theory of evolution by natural selection. In each generation more organisms are born than will survive to leave offspring. Moreover, organisms differ in inherited traits, and those with the most advantageous traits have the greatest probability of surviving long enough to reproduce. Darwin's friend Thomas Huxley condensed natural selection into the phrase "survival of the fittest," and in this form Herbert Spencer, an English philosopher, transformed the idea into social Darwinism to justify capitalism. In a free market, skilled workers will supplant unskilled laborers, and shrewd entrepreneurs will trump obtuse rivals. Capitalism therefore guaranteed progress, and government should not interfere by regulating business or dispensing charity. In the United States, Spencer's ideas coincided with the emergence of an industrial elite. After 1872, *Popular Science Monthly* championed social Darwinism, and William Graham Sumner of Yale University equated unfettered capitalism with social progress. John D. Rockefeller likened his elimination of industrial rivals to pruning a rosebush. In 1901 Andrew Carnegie summarized the tenets of social Darwinism in *The Gospel of Wealth*.

Further Reading: Carl N. Degler, *In Search of Human Nature: The Decline and Revival of Darwinism in American Social Thought*, 1991.

Christopher Cumo

SOCIAL GOSPEL MOVEMENT.

The rise of industry drew attention to urban poverty. Although some religious leaders, notably Reverend Henry Ward Beecher of New York, dismissed the poor as casualties of industrialization, others saw a duty to uplift them. After 1870, the Young Men's Christian Association spread throughout cities, and in 1880 the Salvation Army came to the United States. Russell Conwell's Baptist Temple in Philadelphia, Pennsylvania, had a night school for factory workers and clerks that later grew into Temple University. The Catholic Church built schools and soup kitchens in Irish and Italian slums. These religious organizations established gymnasiums, libraries, schools, lecture rooms, and outreach services to improve the lives of the urban underclass.

Walter Rauschenbusch of Colgate-Rochester Theological Seminary provided an intellectual foundation for activism. He challenged Christians to build a Kingdom of God in which workers earned a fair wage and retained their dignity. He defended their right to unionize, and complained that class distinctions shamed all persons. The Beatitudes, not social Darwinism, should define workplace behavior. Rauschenbusch was not alone. In 1891 Pope Leo XIII defended labor unions and condemned employers who impoverished their workers.

Further Reading: Sidney Ahlstrom, *A Religious History of the American People*, 1972; Susan Curtis, *A Consuming Faith: The Social Gospel and Modern American Culture*, 1991; Henry May, *Protestant Churches and Industrial America*, 1949.

Christopher Cumo

SOCIALIST LABOR PARTY.

The Socialist Labor Party was a vehicle for political debate among Marxists who discussed the proper approach to challenging corporate capitalism in the late nineteenth century. German immigrants brought Marxian socialism to the United States in the 1850s, and two decades later Lassallean socialists organized the Social Democratic Party of North America. Dissidents left that party in 1876 to develop an organization that would support strikes by industrial laborers and engage in political activity. Initially, they called their organization the Workingmen's Party. A year later they renamed it the Socialist Labor Party of North America (SLP). Its political slogan suggested its mission and methodology: "Science the Arsenal, Reason the Weapon, Ballot the Missile."

Over the next few years membership increased from three thousand to an estimated ten thousand. The rank and file were immigrants, largely Jewish needle trade workers from eastern Europe in lower Manhattan. Only 10 percent were native-born. For the first two decades, the United German Trades and the United Hebrew Traders Association dominated the organization. SLP membership declined with the appearance of a new radical labor group, the International Working People's Association, established in 1883. The SLP responded by recruiting Daniel De Leon, a lecturer in international law at Columbia University.

From 1890 until his death, De Leon, a Jewish immigrant from the Dutch West Indies, dominated the SLP with his controversial leadership. He attacked the Knights of Labor and the American Federation of Labor by creating the Socialist Trade and Labor Alliance. His decision to do so alienated many colleagues and led to protracted intraparty warfare. By 1899 the party had split into two factions. While some remained loyal to De Leon, many turned to Morris Hillquit, who organized a coup against De Leon at the party's Rochester, New York, convention in January 1900. Dissidents abandoned De Leon and the SLP, formed the Socialist Party of America, and nominated native-born Eugene V. Debs as their presidential candidate. For the next decade, De Leon's ideologically rigid political stance resulted in the SLP's becoming more of a sect than a functioning political party.

Further Reading: John H. M. Laslett and Seymour Martin Lipset, eds., *The Failure of a Dream? Essays in the History of American Socialism*, 1974; Albert Fried, *Socialism in America: From the Shakers to the Third International. A Documentary History*, 1970; John Patrick Diggins, *The Rise and Fall of the American Left*, 1973.

David O'Donald Cullen

SOLID SOUTH. The phrase refers to the united support of the southern states for Democratic Party candidates, especially in presidential elections, after Reconstruction. "Solid South" specifically refers to the eleven former Confederate states. These states gave their electoral votes to the Democratic candidate in every presidential election from 1876 to 1920. In the latter year Republican Warren G. Harding carried Tennessee. In 1928 the Republican candidate, Herbert Hoover, carried five states of the old Confederacy.

Future speaker of the House Schuyler Colfax first used the phrase "Solid South" in 1858 when he referred to a vote in which all the southerners and about twenty northerners opposed a resolution approving existing legislation against the African slave trade. The phrase became popular in 1876, however, when former Confederate General John S. Mosby shocked southern whites by announcing his support for the Republican presidential candidate, Rutherford B. Hayes. In a letter he questioned what the South would do if Hayes were elected and a Solid South opposed him. During the campaign the phrase was repeated in the *New York Tribune*. Thomas Nast added to its popularity in his *Harper's Weekly* cartoons by referring to the Solid South and using such negative images as a wolf and a snake to characterize it. During the Gilded Age many white southerners believed that voting Democratic was a way of demonstrating racial solidarity and keeping faith with those who had given their lives for the Confederacy. Insurgent movements such as the Populists were vulnerable to Democrats' accusations that they divided the votes of whites, making it possible for black and white Republicans to regain the power they had enjoyed during Reconstruction.

Further Reading: Hans Sperber and Travis Trittschuh, *American Political Terms*, 1962; William Safire, *The New Language of Politics*, 1972; Florence Elliott and Michael Summerskill, *A Dictionary of Politics*, 1966.

James R. Sweeney

SOUSA, JOHN PHILIP (6 November 1854–6 March 1932), conductor, composer, author. Born in Washington, D.C., Sousa began his musical training in 1861. His father, who played with the U.S. Marine Band, persuaded his son to become an apprentice with the band in 1868 rather than join the circus. Young Sousa left the band in 1875 to work as a freelance conductor, composer, arranger, and violinist in Philadelphia. Appointed as the fourteenth conductor of the U.S. Marine Band in 1880, Sousa enlarged it and improved its repertoire, performance standards, and reputation. In 1892, frustrated by the lack of both a commission and a salary, Sousa resigned and formed a professional civilian band. The New Sousa Band, managed by David Blakely, who had arranged tours for the conductors Patrick Gilmore and Theodore Thomas, toured at least six months of every year until 1931, traveling over a million miles. In addition to the American tours, the band made four European excursions between 1900 and 1905, and a sixteen-month world trip in 1910–1911. Sousa programmed a mix of classical and popular music, and featured outstanding soloists such as the violinist Maud Powell and the soprano Estelle Liebling.

Dubbed the "March King" by a European journalist, Sousa, who composed 136 marches including "Liberty Bell" (1893), "The Washington Post" (1889), and "Stars and Stripes Forever" (1897), created a type of American composition that was universally recognized and admired. In addition, he penned fifteen operettas, seventy songs, over one hundred instrumental works, and more than three hundred arrangements and transcriptions, as well as three novels, an autobiography, and several articles between 1873 and 1931. During the 1890s Sousa had a bass tuba made to his specifications, which came to be called the sousaphone. An active lobbyist for composers' rights and copyright reform, Sousa served as an officer in the Authors' and Composers' Copyright League of America. He died in Reading, Pennsylvania.

Further Reading: Kenneth Berger, *The March King and His Band*, 1957; Paul E. Bierley, *John Philip Sousa*, 1973; and Jon Newsom, ed., *Perspectives on John Philip Sousa*, 1983.

Leslie Petteys

SOUTHERN ALLIANCE. The Southern Farmers' Alliance, the largest agricultural movement in southern history, was a product primarily of declining agricultural conditions in commercial crop producing areas of the South, particularly the fall in commodity prices and consequent loss of land by small farmers. In response to these conditions, the Texas Alliance, appearing in the late 1870s, by 1884 was promoting cooperative ideas learned from the Grange and antimonopoly politics learned from the Greenbackers. Between 1886 and 1889, the Texas Alliance spread east to the remainder of the South, and northward to Kansas. Women were encouraged to join but African-American farmers could not, although the Southern Alliance did work with the Colored Farmers' Alliance, organized in 1886. State cooperative exchanges organized by the Southern Alliance quickly failed, but local cooperative efforts in marketing, purchasing, and some manufacturing often succeeded for a while.

Between 1889 and early 1892, the Southern Alliance entered politics, first as Democrats and then as Populists. These moves undermined the organization, and by 1893 not much was left of it, though here and there a few Alliances and Alliance cooperatives remained.

Further Reading: Robert C. McMath, Jr., *Populist Vanguard: A History of the Southern Farmers' Alliance*, 1975; Nelson A. Dunning, ed., *Farmers' Alliance History and Agricultural Digest*, 1891; Lawrence Goodwyn, *Democratic Promise: The Populist Moment in America*, 1976.

Bruce Palmer

SPALDING, ALBERT GOODWILL (2 September, 1850–9 September 1915), professional baseball player and retailer. Born in Byron, Illinois, Spalding realized his talent for baseball at an early age. He began his eight-year major league career in 1871 with Boston's National League club. In 1875 he became the first pitcher to win over two hundred games, averaging more than forty per season. He racked up fifty victories in both 1874 and 1875. In 1876, Spalding made a surprising jump to the Chicago team, where his playing career ended several years later. He went on to become the Chicago club's president from 1882 to 1891. Spalding was instrumental in crushing the players' revolt in 1890, and his efforts were invaluable to the preservation of the National League.

In 1876, with his brother James, Spalding had organized one of the first, and the largest, sporting-goods businesses in the United States. They eventually secured a tight monopoly and became quite wealthy as a result. Spalding, who died in Point Loma, California, was posthumously elected to the Baseball Hall of Fame in 1939.

Further Reading: Peter Levine, *A. G. Spalding and the Rise of Baseball*, 1985.

Steve Bullock

SPANISH-AMERICAN WAR. Spain's brutal attempts to suppress a revolt in Cuba that had begun in February 1895 were widely covered in the American press, and aroused great public outrage over the deaths of more than one hundred thousand women, children, and old men. Americans had been critical of European failure to halt recent Turkish massacres of Armenians, and now similar atrocities were happening just ninety miles off their own coast. There was also resentment that a European monarchy still held possessions in the New World, and the hope by some expansionists that this rich island could fall under American control. President William McKinley successfully put pressure on the Spanish government to halt the offenses against Cuban civilians, and to grant the island some form of self-government. But on 15 February 1898 the U.S. battleship *Maine* blew up in Havana harbor from a still mysterious cause, killing 266 crewmen. After the *Maine*'s sinking, popularly blamed on Spain, pressure for war became irresistible. On 19 April, Congress passed resolutions recognizing Cuban independence, demanding Spanish withdrawal from the island, and authorizing the president to use force to achieve these goals. Also passed was the Teller Resolution, which stated that the United States would make no attempt to annex Cuba. Spain declared war on the United States on 23 April, and Congress declared war on 25 April, retroactive to 21 April.

Commodore George Dewey had prepared the American Asiatic Squadron for immediate action under orders from Assistant Secretary of the Navy Theodore Roosevelt. On 1 May, his ships steamed into Manila Bay, site of the capital of Spain's Philippine possessions, and in five hours of fighting the squadron destroyed the antiquated Spanish fleet while losing none of its own vessels. Dewey did not have the troops necessary to take and hold Manila, however, and had to wait for reinforcements. The city did not surrender until mid-August.

The Spanish fleet in the Atlantic at first proved more difficult to locate, but was finally discovered in the harbor at Santiago, Cuba. The American navy established a blockade, but asked for army assistance in capturing Santiago, to drive the Spanish ships out so they could be engaged. Unfortunately, the army, whose peacetime strength had been only twenty-eight thousand officers and men, was having a difficult time organizing, equipping, and training the more than two hundred thousand volunteers and National Guard troops who had rushed to the colors. An invasion force of eighteen thousand men was finally landed near the end of June. It included both African-American and white regular units, National Guard formations, and outfits such as the First Volunteer Cavalry (Rough Riders), led by Theodore Roosevelt and Leonard Wood. Conditions were uncertain and chaotic, but on 1 July an assault was made on Santiago's defenses at San Juan Hill and El Caney that proved victorious, though at a heavy cost in American casualties.

Two days later the Spanish fleet tried to escape from the harbor at Santiago, but it was destroyed in a running battle along the coast. A landing was made on Puerto Rico on 25 July, and good progress in conquering the island was being made when, on 12 August 1898, Spain asked for an armistice and the fighting stopped. The war had lasted only ten weeks, at the cost of over five thousand American deaths, the great majority from disease. The Treaty of Paris ending the war was signed 10 December 1898, and it awarded the United States Guam, Puerto Rico, and the Philippine Islands. This brief struggle established the United States as a world power, and set it on the course of empire.

Further Reading: David F. Trask, *The War with Spain in 1898*, 1981; David Traxel, *1898: The Birth of the American Century*, 1998.

David Traxel

SPARKS, WILLIAM ANDREW JACKSON

(19 November 1828–7 May 1904), congressman and General Land Office commissioner. Born near New Albany, Indiana, Sparks grew up in Macoupin County, Illinois, graduated from McKendree College in 1850, and opened a law practice in Carlyle, Illinois. An active Democrat, he won election to the U.S. House of Representatives in 1874, a time of economic stagnation and plummeting agricultural prices. He was reelected three times. Sparks sponsored legislation to remonetize silver, advocated governmental regulation of railroads, and opposed high protective tariffs. He contended that the power to count and determine the 1876 disputed electoral vote rested with the people under the Tenth Amendment, and could be resolved constitutionally by the House of Representatives. Sparks chaired the House Committee on Public Lands and the Committee on Military Affairs.

Declining to seek another term in 1882, Sparks returned to his law practice in Carlyle. In 1885 President Grover Cleveland appointed Sparks commissioner of the General Land Office, a division of the Interior Department. Opposed to powerful schemers seeking to plunder the public domain, Sparks endeavored to reform the Land Office. He met stiff opposition from railroad interests, cattle barons, land speculators, and some congressmen. His zealous crusade ultimately cost him his job in November 1887. Involved with several financial institutions having heavy investments in various interests, Sparks owned a considerable amount of real estate in his last years. He died in Saint Louis, Missouri.

Further Reading: Leonard Schlup, "Prairie Politician: William Andrew Jackson Sparks and the Politics of Honor During the Gilded Age," *Illinois Historical Journal* 88 (1995): 117–134; John B. Rae, "Commissioner Sparks and the Railroad Land Grants," *Mississippi Valley Historical Review* 25 (1938): 211–230; *Carlyle Union Banner*, 8 May 1904.

Leonard Schlup

SPECIE RESUMPTION. Congress issued Treasury notes, known as greenbacks, to finance the Civil War. Though the return of peace in 1865 ended the need for them, Congress hesitated to retire them for fear that farmers would protest the move as deflationary. In the absence of swift congressional action, the surplus of greenbacks caused a system of two prices: one for transactions in gold, and a higher price for transactions in greenbacks. In other words, a dollar was worth more in coin than in paper. But until the exchange rate was 1:1, greenbacks could not be redeemed at full value. Rapid economic growth after the Civil War brought the demand for money in line with supply, and in 1875 Congress passed the Resumption Act, which authorized the Treasury to redeem greenbacks in coin after 1 January 1879.

As Congress feared, the act exacerbated the debate between supporters of hard and soft money. Whereas business leaders favored gold as specie in order to maintain an inelastic currency, farmers favored the printing of greenbacks or the coining of silver to inflate the money supply. The Greenback Labor Movement, the Farmers' Alliance, and the People's Party all advocated inflation, though without success.

Further Reading: Walter T. K. Nugent, *Money and American Society, 1865–1880*, 1968; Irwin Unger, *The Greenback Era: A Social and Political History of American Finance, 1865–1879*, 1964.

Christopher Cumo

SPEED, JOSHUA FRY (14 November 1814–29 May 1882), merchant and businessman. Born in Jefferson County, Kentucky, and educated at St. Joseph's College in Bardstown, Kentucky, Speed moved to Springfield, Illinois, where he managed the A. Y. Elis and Company general store. There he met Abraham Lincoln on 15 April 1837. The two shared a bed in an upstairs room for the next three years, developing a lifelong close friendship that was damaged only briefly by the slavery issue. While Lincoln matured as a lawyer and politician, Speed returned to Kentucky, helped edit a newspaper, engaged in farming, and served in the state legislature. During the Civil War, President Lincoln asked the pro-Union Speed to handle certain assignments, and in 1864, he appointed Speed's brother, James, attorney general of the United States. In 1870, Joshua Speed and fellow businessman James Henning developed a highland section of Louisville, known as Cherokee Triangle, on land once owned by the parents of President Zachary Taylor. This eastern suburb attracted such prominent citizens as Judge William B. Fleming, the philanthropist Daniel G. Parr, and J. Stoddard Johnston, Kentucky secretary of state from 1875 to 1879. Speed died in Louisville, Kentucky.

Further Reading: *Louisville Courier-Journal*, 30 May 1882; Susan Krause, "Abraham Lincoln and Joshua Speed, Attorney and Client," *Illinois Historical Journal* 89 (1996): 35–50.

Leonard Schlup

SPINDLETOP. On 10 January 1901, at 10:30 A.M. the Spindletop oil well near Beaumont, Texas, spewed black gold approximately two hundred feet into the air, covering everything for acres and creating joyous bedlam. It was the first American oil gusher, an event that changed the world. It dramatically increased Beaumont's population and quickly created fortunes. The discovery proved what geologists had long suspected about the existence of petroleum reservoir deposits in the Lone Star State. Samuel M. Jones, a former mayor of Toledo, Ohio, who witnessed the oil strike, correctly gauged its significance when he remarked that liquid fuel would be the fuel of the twentieth century.

Further Reading: James Anthony Clark and Michel Thomas Halbouty, *Spindletop: The True Story of the Oil Discovery that Changed the World*, 2000; Roger L. Shaffer, *Spindletop Unwound*, 1997.

Leonard Schlup

SPOFFORD, AINSWORTH RAND (12 September 1825–11 August 1908), librarian. Born in Gilmanton, New Hampshire, Spofford moved to Cincinnati in 1845 to sell and publish books. By 1859 he had become chief editorial writer for the *Cincinnati Daily Commercial*. After going to Washington in 1861 to cover Abraham Lincoln's inauguration, Spofford accepted the position of assistant librarian of Congress, which he held until Lincoln appointed him librarian of Congress on 31 December 1864. Between 1865 and 1870 Spofford lobbied Congress to pass six acts to turn his place of work into a functioning national library. The first (1865) allocated additional funding to expand the library's quarters in the Capitol. The second (1865) amended copyright law to shift requisite deposits to the library. The third (1866) transferred the forty-thousand-volume Smithsonian Institution Library to the Library of Congress. The fourth (1867) provided money to purchase Peter Force's one-hundred-thousand-volume Americana collection. The fifth (1867) forged new international exchange agreements with foreign countries. The sixth (1870) centralized all U.S. copyright registration and deposits in the Library of Congress.

The impact of all this legislation was immediate. By 1875 the Library of Congress had run out of shelf space, and Spofford quickly began to lobby Congress for a separate building. Not until 1897, however, was the new building completed and opened to the public. Spofford was a collection builder more than a library manager, however, and when Congress held hearings in 1896 to discuss the library and its internal organization just before it moved into new quarters, he decided to resign his position as librarian of Congress and become chief assistant librarian with major responsibility for collections. He remained in that position until his death in Washington, D.C.

Further Reading: John Y. Cole, *Ainsworth Rand Spofford: Bookman and Librarian*, 1975.

Wayne A. Wiegand

SPOILS SYSTEM. From Thomas Jefferson until the election of Andrew Jackson, the presidential administrations maintained a similar political stripe and government jobholders were secure in their positions. In Jackson's inaugural speech, he suggested to the American people that government workers had been in office too long and held a position of privilege. His reason for replacing some (between 11 and 20 percent) was, he argued, to democratize the government. Jackson believed the ordinary man, endowed with common sense, could adequately fulfill the functions required of these offices. William Marcy, senator from New York, gave the practice its name when he noted, in an 1832 speech, that to the victor went the spoils. The spoils system was used to control the executive offices of the government, recompense party faithful, and maintain partisan support. In addition, in its most egregious form, the system included the use of political assessments upon officeholders to fill the war chests of the dominant party. When the Whig Party gained control of the executive branch in 1841, government officials were replaced almost to a man, and the practice continued throughout much of the Gilded Age.

The spoils system spilled over into the states and became the mechanism for the creation of numerous state political machines. After sporadic and ineffectual attempts at reform during Reconstruction and the early Gilded Age, George H. Pendleton, a Democratic senator from Ohio, was able to push through Congress the first major civil service reform legislation, known as the Pendleton Act of 1883. Ironically arguing that the reform would reinstate the Jacksonian ideal of opening government jobs to the larger populace rather than solely to a politically connected aristocracy, Pendleton succeeded in creating the Civil Service Commission to administer competitive examinations for 10 percent of all federal government jobs. By the mid-twentieth century, the number of jobs covered by this reform approached 90 percent, relegating the spoils system to the pages of history.

Further Reading: Carl R. Fish, *The Civil Service and the Patronage*, 1963; Paul P. Van Riper, *History of the United States Civil Service*, 1958; Robert Maranto, *A Short History of the United States Civil Service*, 1991.

Thomas S. Mach

SPORTS. Sports experienced vigorous growth during the Gilded Age. Existing sports became more common and new activities emerged. Developments during this era set the foundation for many of today's sports.

Thoroughbred horse racing enjoyed renewed popularity. The Travers Stakes, the Belmont Stakes, the Preakness, and the Kentucky Derby all started within ten years of the end of the Civil War. In New York an owner-dominated Jockey Club, founded in 1865, supervised the sport along with a state agency. For the first time jockeys became celebrities. African-American jockeys like Isaac Murphy, however, lost status by the era's end. Gambling remained popular as pari-mutuel betting gained favor. Harness racing under the aegis of the National Trotting Association drew large audiences.

In the late 1860s baseball became a national sport. An existing association split into professional and amateur divisions following the appearance in 1869 of the first all-professional team, the Cincinnati Red Stockings. Owners organized the National League of Professional Baseball Clubs in 1876. It and the American Association, which permitted drinking and Sunday games, enjoyed major league status through the 1880s. The two best teams played for the world championship. By decade's end, many of the best players, dissatisfied with their pay and status, joined a new league, the eventual failure of which left the National League as the sole major league through the 1890s.

Boxing gained some respectability as John L. Sullivan emerged in the 1880s as the greatest heavyweight. He retained his supremacy with bare knuckles in several highly publicized matches, but in 1892 lost to James Corbett in a gloved affair. Sullivan never fought the black boxer Peter Jackson. Many communities still forbid even the more refined style.

Rowing contests, introduced on the intercollegiate level in the 1850s, continued to attract attention, especially among collegians whose teams occasionally challenged those of Oxford.

A number of sports made their appearance. Croquet had a national association. In 1875 Mary Outerbridge introduced English lawn tennis, by way of Bermuda, to Staten Island and American society. American men's tennis championships took place at the Newport (Rhode Island) Casino, starting in 1881.

Women began to compete for the national championship six years later. By 1900 courts could be found in nearly every city. By the end of the century Americans were playing golf on the outskirts of many communities. The high-wheeled bicycle enjoyed popularity especially among members of the League of American Wheelmen in the 1880s. The safety bicycle made the sport feasible for all but the poorest in the 1890s. Of all the organized sports, only yachting and polo remained exclusively for the rich.

In addition to competing in rowing and baseball, collegians took up variations of rugby and soccer. American football emerged in the early 1880s when Walter Camp of Yale introduced the line of scrimmage and a system of downs. When players began to tackle below the waist, offenses turned to mass-motion plays, including the flying wedge, first employed in 1891. This type of game produced numerous injuries and deaths.

By the end of the century a few colleges competed in basketball, a sport developed by James Naismith and first played in 1891 in Springfield, Massachusetts, at the training school for the Young Men's Christian Association, an organization that sponsored many sporting events. Senda Berenson, the director of physical education at Smith College, introduced a modified form of the game for women. Most colleges had track and field contests.

Numerous athletic clubs were organized in the larger towns and cities. The Amateur Athletic Union, formed in 1888, supervised these players. An American delegation dominated track and field at the first modern Olympics, held at Athens in 1896.

Further Reading: Benjamin G. Rader, *American Sports: From the Age of Folk Games to the Age of Televised Sports*, 3rd ed., 1983; Steven A. Riess, *City Games: The Evolution of American Urban Society and the Rise of Sports*, 1991.

Peter C. Stewart

SPOTTED TAIL [SINTE GLESKA]

SPOTTED TAIL [SINTE GLESKA] (1833–5 August 1881), Lower Brulé Sioux leader and peace proponent. Born either near the Makizita (White River) in west central South Dakota or near Fort Laramie in Wyoming, Spotted Tail obtained his name because he wore a raccoon tail, a gift from a fur trapper, when dressed for war and ceremonials. Installed as war leader at age thirty and wearing a shirt adorned with over one hundred locks of hair representing numerous coups, he ultimately became civil leader, the highest rank among the Brulé. By the 1860s, Spotted Tail was chief spokesman for all the Brulé bands. He united fragmented leagues and worked to keep his people together after he and others signed the Treaty of Fort Laramie in 1868. Two years later Spotted Tail traveled to Washington, D.C., to confer with President Ulysses S. Grant and the Seneca commissioner of Indian Affairs, Ely Parker. He urged national leaders to undertake gradual cultural change among Native Americans. In 1873 he visited the Black Hills mining camps following the discovery of gold to ascertain the value of the mineral, which resulted in his demand of $60 million for the sale of the area, a price rejected by the federal government.

Spotted Tail directed his followers toward degrees of tolerance toward and acceptance of whites (Wasichus) and acculturation policies. Contemplating long-range goals, he warned the Lakota to cope with changing situations and accept Wasichus skills, such as clerking and translating, or face extinction. To demonstrate his commitment to bicultural education, Spotted Tail dispatched four sons and two grandchildren to the Carlisle Indian Industrial School in Pennsylvania. During the Sioux War of 1876–1877, Spotted Tail and his group remained on the reservation. Like Red Cloud, he excelled in diplomacy. He negotiated a surrender of the Sioux militants and his nephew, Crazy Horse, in 1877. Some belligerents who never forgave him for the consequences of that arrangement plotted his overthrow. One of these conspirators, Crow Dog, assassinated Spotted Tail at Rosebud, South Dakota, while he was returning home from a council meeting that had voted to send him to Washington, D.C., thereby ending the life of one of the nineteenth century's most brilliant Native American leaders. In a landmark 1883 opinion, the U.S. Supreme Court ruled in *Ex Parte Crow Dog* that state and federal courts possessed no jurisdiction on Native land. Crow Dog was set free.

Further Reading: John G. Bourke, *On the Border with Crook*, 1891; Sidney L. Harring, *Crow Dog's Case: Amer-*

ican *Indian Sovereignty, Tribal Law, and United States Law in the Nineteenth Century*, 1994; Carl Waldman, *Who Was Who in Native American History*, 1990.

Leonard Schlup

SPRECKELS, CLAUS (9 July 1828–26 December 1908), manufacturer and businessman. Born in Lamstedt, Germany, Spreckels immigrated to Charleston, South Carolina, in 1846, and purchased grocery stores in Charleston, New York City, and San Francisco. He organized the Bay Sugar Refining Company in 1863, established the California Sugar Refinery in 1867, and benefited considerably from the 1876 reciprocity treaty between the United States and the Hawaiian Islands. A shrewd capitalist who bought, merged, or drove his competitors out of business, Spreckels was known as the "Sugar King." He fought the eastern Sugar Trust in the late 1880s, and his Western Beet Sugar Company in Watsonville, California, produced seven hundred tons of sugar daily by 1892. Spreckels financed the Pajaro Valley Railroad in 1895 and became president of the San Francisco & San Joaquin Valley Railroad that same year. He also constructed the first skyscraper in San Francisco; the Spreckels Building (Central Tower) was located at the corner of Market and Third streets. In 1899, he launched the Independent Electric Light and Power Company, which was followed by the Independent Gas and Power Company two years later. Spreckels died in San Francisco.

Further Reading: Jacob Adler, *Claus Spreckels: The Sugar King in Hawaii*, 1966; *San Francisco Chronicle*, 27 December 1908.

Leonard Schlup

SPRINGER v. UNITED STATES (102 U.S. 586). This case addressed the question of what constitutes direct taxation, authorized by the Constitution. It resulted in a unanimous 1881 Supreme Court ruling that a federal income tax, imposed in 1864, did not qualify, and was therefore unconstitutional. The case began with a suit by a Mr. Springer against the United States for its having seized his land after Springer refused to pay the levy. Justice Noah Swayne, writing for the court, stated that capitation and real estate taxes were the only direct taxes authorized under the Constitution. Income taxes were therefore held unconstitutional. Subsequent events demonstrated the ruling's strength, in that the income tax did not begin until passage of the Sixteenth Amendment in 1913.

Further Reading: Owen M. Fiss, *History of the Supreme Court of the United States, Vol. 8, Troubled Beginnings of the Modern State, 1888–1910*, 1993, pp. 88–89; Akhil Reed Amar and Alan Hirsch, *For the People: What the Constitution Really Says About Your Rights*, 1998, p. 221; *U.S. Reports* 102 U.S. 586.

Thomas C. Sutton

SPRINGER, WILLIAM MCKENDREE (30 May 1836–4 December 1903), congressman and judge. Born near New Lebanon, Indiana, Springer graduated from Indiana University in 1858 and practiced law in Springfield, Illinois. He served one term as a Democrat (1871–1872) in the Illinois House of Representatives. From 1875 to 1895, he sat in the U.S. House of Representatives, where in various sessions he chaired the committees on Claims, Elections, Territories, and Banking and Currency. A prominent politician who gained power by virtue of his seniority and expertise on issues, Springer enjoyed a favorable reputation. After his defeat for reelection in the Republican landslide of 1894, he opened a law practice in the nation's capital. President Grover Cleveland appointed him U.S. judge for the Northern District of Indian Territory, and later chief justice of the U.S. Court of Appeals of Indian Territory, in which capacities her served from 1895 to 1900. Springer died in Washington, D.C.

Further Reading: *Illinois State Register* (Springfield), 5 December 1903.

Leonard Schlup

SQUIRE, WATSON CARVOSSO (18 May 1838–7 June 1926), U.S. senator. Born in Cape Vincent, New York, Squire graduated from Wesleyan University in Middletown, Connecticut, in 1859, completed a program at the Cleveland (Ohio) Law School, and served in the Civil War. He moved to Seattle, Washington Territory, in 1879. Appointed territorial governor by President Chester A. Arthur, Squire held this position from 1884 to 1887. Upon the state's admission to the Union in

1889, he was elected as a Republican to the U.S. Senate. He served from 1889 to 1897, when he unsuccessfully sought another term. In the Senate, he chaired in some sessions the committees on Coast Defenses and Transportation Routes to the Seaboard. After leaving politics and retiring from law, he managed properties in Seattle, ultimately becoming president of the Union Trust Company and the Squire Investment Company. Squire died in Seattle.

Further Reading: *New York Times*, 8 June 1926.

Leonard Schlup

ST. JOHN, JOHN PIERCE (25 February 1833–31 August 1916), governor and prohibitionist leader. Born in Brookville, Indiana, St. John was admitted to the Illinois bar in 1860. He rose to lieutenant colonel in the Union Army during the Civil War, then practiced law in Olathe, Kansas. There he also entered politics and the temperance movement, becoming well known for his oratory. He served a term in the state senate (1873–1877), then declined renomination in 1876. Two years later, while heading Kansas's Temperance Union, St. John was elected governor as a Republican. During two terms, he pushed prohibition vigorously, even though he had promised to refrain from making it a legislative issue. Unwisely, prohibition's opponents, believing it would fail as a constitutional amendment, placed it on the ballot. There it won by four percentage points in 1880. St. John's commitment to abstinence was based on his father's problem with alcohol and his own observations of constituents. Also during his tenure, he headed the Kansas Freedmen's Relief Association, organizing support for black "exodusters" from the South.

St. John was defeated when he ran for a third time in 1882. In 1884, he accepted the Prohibition Party's nomination for president of the United States. He attracted only 1.5 percent of the total vote, but his twenty-five thousand in New York allowed the claim that he swung the state's electoral vote to Grover Cleveland. St. John remained a spokesman for prohibition and for the Prohibition Party's general commitment to reform. Having long advocated women's suffrage, he now supported free silver, direct election of senators, and government ownership of railroads. He also opposed race-based immigration restriction. St. John died in Olathe, Kansas.

Further Reading: Robert Smith Bader, *Prohibition in Kansas: A History*, 1986; Emil Pocock, "Wet or Dry? The Presidential Election of 1884 in Upstate New York," *New York History* 54 (1973): 174–190; Homer Socolofsky, *Kansas Governors*, 1990.

James G. Ryan

ST. LOUIS CYCLONE OF 1896. A contemporary account called the tornado of Wednesday, 27 May 1896, the most disastrous storm of modern times. In about twenty minutes, eighty-mile-per-hour winds, followed by heavy rain, passed through and leveled much of an area two miles by three miles in the city of St. Louis, Missouri, as well as much of East St. Louis, Illinois. Among the hardest hit areas of the Missouri city were the fashionable Lafayette Square and Compton Heights neighborhoods, as well as the poorer Mill Creek Valley. Accounts of the extent of loss of life and property vary, with numbers ranging from 125 to 400 dead, and up to $50 million in property damage. An extensive local relief effort was launched, with approximately forty thousand persons ultimately receiving assistance. While many accounts laud the benevolence and effectiveness of the relief efforts, some sources note the misplaced pride of the city fathers in refusing assistance offered by other cities, and the unevenness of aid distribution.

Further Reading: James Neal Primm, *Lion of the Valley: St. Louis, Missouri, 1764–1980*, 3rd ed., 1998; Julian Curzon, *The Great Cyclone at St. Louis and East St. Louis, 1896*; *St. Louis Post-Dispatch*, special tornado ed., 3 June 1896.

Emily Miller Troxell

STAHL, HENRY (15 August 1835–16 August 1923), professor and researcher. Born in Bonwiller, France, Stahl, educated in Strassburg, immigrated to Erie, Pennsylvania, at age eighteen. He was a professor of modern languages at Allegheny College in Meadville before moving to northwestern Virginia in 1860. After serving in the Union Army during the Civil War, Stahl made his permanent home in Parkersburg, West Virginia, where he taught music and penmanship. During the late nineteenth

century, he acquired a national reputation for antiquarian researches, especially those pertaining to prehistoric Native Americans and Blennerhassett Island. Stahl gathered, classified, and interpreted artifacts, and also lectured on his findings. He viewed cultural change in terms of shifting technologies, with Western industrial society representing the peak of cultural advancement. His ethnocentric view typified much of Gilded Age scientific thought. He died in Parkersburg.

Further Reading: Blennerhassett Museum Archives, Parkersburg, West Virginia.

Leonard Schlup

STALWARTS AND HALF-BREEDS. Although party loyalty was strong during the Gilded Age, intraparty disputes were also intense. The Republican Party was particularly vulnerable to factional infighting, as can be seen in the bitterly divided national conventions from 1872 to 1884 and in the patronage battles that rent the Hayes and Garfield administrations. Attempting to clarify these confusing conflicts, historians have conventionally divided the Republicans into three factions: Mugwumps, Half-Breeds, and Stalwarts.

Mugwumps are easy to identify. They were those self-styled reformers who joined the Liberal Republican bolt of 1872 or who, in 1884, refused to support the presidential aspirations of James G. Blaine.

Half-Breeds and Stalwarts are more difficult to pin down. In fact, contemporaries never used the term Half-Breed to describe a distinct, national party faction. It had brief currency only in the context of New York state politics, about 1881, to describe those who opposed the leadership of the state's Republican boss, Roscoe Conkling, and it soon faded from even that local usage. Historians who needed some term to characterize the anti-Grant faction of the party later resurrected it, but its members, goals, and principles were so vaguely (and contradictorily) defined as to render it virtually meaningless. It was, for example, supposed to have been led by Blaine and to include Rutherford B. Hayes, John Sherman, and James A. Garfield. Yet Blaine and Sherman were lifelong rivals, and Hayes and Blaine were not even on speaking terms. Furthermore, Half-Breeds were supposed to be more interested in policy than in patronage, but just what policies they pursued was left unclear. The term should be expunged from the historical lexicon.

The label Stalwart is somewhat more legitimate. Originally utilized to characterize those Republicans who advocated strong Reconstruction policies, it metamorphosed into a generic description of those who supported the political fortunes of Ulysses S. Grant, particularly at the Republican National Convention of 1880. Among the most prominent members were the leading machine politicians of the larger northern states: Roscoe Conkling, Thomas Platt, and Chester A. Arthur of New York; Simon and Donald Cameron of Pennsylvania; John Logan of Illinois; and Zachariah Chandler of Michigan. The conspicuous presence of these party bosses gave the faction a sinister, somewhat corrupt reputation. Blaine, himself no saint, described them as the party's desperate bad men, bent on loot and booty.

Of the 306 delegates who stalwartly stood by Grant throughout the thirty-six ballots of the 1880 convention, a less lurid group portrait can be drawn. It reveals that there were genuine, legitimate differences that distinguished the Grant supporters from their rivals. The most striking distinction was geographic. An overwhelming percentage of Stalwart delegates came from Democratic districts in the former slave states and in the large northern cities. Faced with strong Democratic opposition, they were compelled to concentrate on party loyalty and organization, and to cling to such tried-and-true issues as the Bloody Shirt.

Non-Stalwarts, secure in their Republican bastions of New England and the Midwest, had the luxury of experimenting with promising new issues, such as the tariff and civil service reform. The future of the party would belong to them.

Republican factional differences, therefore, were not meaningless squabbles over patronage or personalities, but reflected genuine strategic choices based on political realities.

Further Reading: Allan Peskin, "Who Were the Stalwarts? Who Were Their Rivals? Republican Factions in the Gilded Age," *Political Science Quarterly* 99 (1984–1985):
703–716; Vivian B. Schrack, "A Search for the 'Half-Breeds,' " Ph.D. diss., Pennsylvania State University, 1968.

Allan Peskin

STANDARD OIL CORPORATION. Founded in Cleveland, Ohio, in 1870 by John D. Rockefeller and Samuel Andrews, Standard Oil Company quickly became one of the nation's largest, wealthiest, and most influential manufacturing corporations. It epitomized the rise of big business in the Gilded Age, the reasons for its success, its benefits, and its liabilities. Rockefeller, a commodities merchant, and four partners entered Pennsylvania's booming oil business by building a refinery in Cleveland in 1863. By 1865 the remaining partners, Rockefeller and Andrews, operated the largest of the city's thirty refineries. As petroleum prices steadily dropped during the late 1860s, weaker refineries folded, but Rockefeller prospered through careful cost accounting, using the latest equipment, recruiting able managers, obtaining lower railroad freight rates, and vertical integration. In 1870, Rockefeller, Andrews, and Henry M. Flagler converted their operation into Standard Oil of Ohio, a joint stock company.

Dismissing competition as ruinous, Rockefeller built a cartel. By 1872 his Standard Oil had absorbed most of Cleveland's refineries and become an industrial giant. Five years later, the company dominated the piping, refining, and marketing of American petroleum, holding a position close to monopoly. Additional steps toward vertical integration began in the 1880s with the purchase of oil-producing properties. Rockefeller created the Standard Oil Trust in 1881. It featured a board of trustees who held the stock of all subsidiary companies, and managed prices.

Public and legislative hostility to monopoly, reflected in the Sherman Antitrust Act of 1890 and an 1892 Ohio supreme court decision prohibiting trusts, forced the company to divide its properties among subsidiaries in various states. Ever resilient, Rockefeller and his partners then continued Standard Oil's centralized management operation through interlocking company directorates. In 1899, full control over twenty companies was transferred to a holding company, Standard Oil (New Jersey), headed by

Rockefeller. Federal prosecution continued against Standard Oil of New Jersey, however, by then one of the richest and most powerful holding companies in the world. In 1911, under the provisions of the Sherman Antitrust Act, the U.S. Supreme Court ordered the company's dissolution, compelling its component thirty-three subsidiaries to become separate, independent, competing companies. Some of those successors, including Exxon, Mobil, Standard Oil of California, Atlantic Richfield, Standard Oil of Indiana, and Standard Oil of Ohio, remain among the world's largest petroleum companies.

Further Reading: Ralph W. Hidy and Muriel E. Hidy, *History of Standard Oil Company [New Jersey]: Pioneering in Big Business, 1882–1911*, 1955; Bruce Bringhurst, *Antitrust and the Oil Monopoly: The Standard Oil Cases, 1890–1911*, 1979; David Chalmers, "From Robber Barons to Industrial Statesmen: Standard Oil and the Business Historians," *American Journal of Economics and Sociology*, 20 (1960): 47–58.

Charles W. Macune, Jr.

STANDING BEAR, LUTHER

STANDING BEAR, LUTHER (1868?–19 February 1939), Brulé Sioux author and film actor. Raised at the Spotted Tail Agency and Rosebud Reservation in South Dakota, Standing Bear was a member of the first group of Indian students to attend Carlisle Indian Industrial School in Pennsylvania. Employed temporarily at the Rosebud Agency school, he later performed in Wild West shows, worked briefly for a dry goods company in Sioux City, and at 101 Ranch in Oklahoma, before moving to California in 1912 to join a group of Indians working for film producer Thomas Ince. Standing Bear appeared in Hollywood movies, joined a lecture circuit, and instructed Boy Scouts and Girl Scouts.

He wrote numerous essays and articles and four books, published by Houghton Mifflin: *My People, the Sioux* (1928), which is largely autobiographical; *My Indian Boyhood* (1931); *Land of the Spotted Eagle* (1933); and *Stories of the Sioux* (1934).

Further Reading: Richard N. Ellis, "Luther Standing Bear: 'I Would Raise Him to Be an Indian,'" in *Indian Lives: Essays on Nineteenth- and Twentieth-Century Native Americans*, ed. L. G. Moses and Raymond Wilson, 1985.

Valerie Sherer Mathes

STANDING BEAR v. CROOK

STANDING BEAR v. CROOK (25 *Federal Cases*, 695, 700–701). Tried in the U.S. circuit court for the District of Nebraska in 1879, this case was a catalyst for Indian reform. Ponca chief Standing Bear and his followers were arrested, by orders of General George Crook, for leaving Indian Territory without permission. Defended by lawyers hired by the newspaper editor Thomas Henry Tibbles, the Poncas were freed by Judge Elmer Dundy's decision that Indians were "persons" under the law and entitled to habeas corpus. Standing Bear and the Omaha Indians Francis La Flesche and his sister Susette, the chief's interpreter and later the wife of Tibbles, accompanied him on a speaking tour, galvanizing supporters. They established the Omaha Ponca Relief Committee and the Boston Indian Citizenship Committee, precursors to national Indian reform organizations. *The Ponca Chiefs: An Indian's Attempt to Appeal from the Tomahawk to the Courts* (1880) by Tibbles, and *A Century of Dishonor* (1881) by the New England author Helen Hunt Jackson, publicized the issue. The reputation of Massachusetts senator Henry L. Dawes, a member of a committee investigating Ponca removal, was greatly enhanced. He later sponsored the 1887 Dawes Act, which allotted reservation land in severalty.

Further Reading: Valerie Sherer Mathes, "Helen Hunt Jackson and the Ponca Controversy," *Montana, the Magazine of Western History* 39 (1998): 42–53; and "Helen Hunt Jackson and the Campaign for Ponca Restitution, 1880–1881," *South Dakota History* 17 (1987): 23–41.

Valerie Sherer Mathes

STANFORD, LELAND

STANFORD, LELAND (9 March 1824–21 June 1893), railroad entrepreneur, governor, philanthropist, and U.S. senator. Born in Watervliet, New York, Stanford opened a law practice in Wisconsin in 1848. Four years later he moved to California, eventually settling in Sacramento and engaging in mercantile endeavors. Along with Collis Huntington, Mark Hopkins, and Charles Crocker, Stanford invested in a plan to build the Central Pacific Railroad, of which he was president in 1863. The partners, known as the "Big Four," celebrated their success in northwestern Utah at Promontory Point in 1869, with the transcontinental connection between their line and the Union Pacific. Stanford held the governorship of California in 1862 and 1863. Elected as a Republican to the U.S. Senate, in three Congresses he chaired the Committee on Public Buildings and Grounds. Stanford retained his seat from 1885 until his death, but otherwise played a minor role in Washington. In 1884 the death of his only child, Leland, Jr., from typhoid fever nearly shattered Stanford and his wife, Jane Lathrop Stanford. To honor the memory of the sixteen-year-old youth, the Stanfords in 1885 founded the Leland Stanford, Junior, University, a co-educational institution that opened six years later. The gift marked a milestone in higher education in Gilded Age America, for the institution today stands in the first rank of world universities. Stanford died in Palo Alto, California.

Further Reading: Norman E. Tutorow, *Leland Stanford: Man of Many Careers*, 1971.

Leonard Schlup

STANTON, ELIZABETH CADY (12 November 1815–26 October 1902), social reformer and advocate of women's rights. Born in Johnstown, New York, Cady graduated in 1832 from the Troy Female Seminary and married Henry Brewster Stanton, an attorney, in 1840. Elizabeth Stanton teamed with Lucretia C. Mott and other women to hold a women's rights convention at Seneca Falls, New York, in 1848, which began the modern movement for women's equality. Active in the crusade for abolition of slavery prior to the Civil War, Stanton was committed in the postwar period, in writings, lectures, and actions, to the causes of temperance, woman suffrage, the women's rights agenda, and other reforms. She served as president of the National Woman Suffrage Association (1869–1890) and co-editor of *Revolution*, an organ for the advancement of women. Stanton died in New York City.

Further Reading: Elizabeth Cady Stanton, *Eighty Years and More: Reminiscences, 1815–1897*, 1898, 1993; Elisabeth Griffith, *In Her Own Right: The Life of Elizabeth Cady Stanton*, 1984; Alma Lutz, *Created Equal: A Biography of Elizabeth Cady Stanton, 1815–1902*, 1940.

Leonard Schlup

STAR ROUTE. In the lightly populated vastness of the far West, mail service was necessarily slow and expensive. To expedite it, Congress provided extra financial incentives for routes conducted with "certainty, celerity and security," a formula that was usually indicated by three asterisks (***) or stars—hence "star routes." During the administration of President Rutherford B. Hayes, Second Assistant Postmaster General Thomas J. Brady, in collusion with Arkansas Republican Senator Stephen W. Dorsey, inflated the costs of these routes. Brady, Dorsey and several of Dorsey's relatives allegedly pocketed the difference. When Dorsey became chairman of the Republican National Committee in 1880, rumors swirled that some of this star route money had found its way into the party's campaign coffers. The matter was investigated during the administration of President James A. Garfield by Postmaster General Thomas L. James, and the conspirators were brought to trial. In their defense, ably presented by Robert G. Ingersoll, they maintained their innocence of wrongdoing, insisting that they were merely exploiting ambiguities in the system. The jury agreed and set them free, but historians have not yet reached a conclusive verdict on the affair.

Further Reading: Earl J. Leland, "The Post Office and Politics, 1876–1884: The Star Route Frauds," Ph.D. diss., University of Chicago, 1964.

Allan Peskin

STARR, BELLE (5 February 1848–3 February 1889), outlaw. Known as "The Bandit Queen," Belle Starr was born Myra Belle Shirley near Carthage, Missouri. The rebellious daughter of poor parents, she left home at age eighteen to marry the outlaw Cole Younger and travel with his gang. This group included his cousins Frank and Jesse James. Belle quickly learned how to use a weapon and was rumored to have joined her husband and his gang on numerous crime sprees. Younger was caught by the authorities shortly after Belle gave birth to their daughter, and sentenced to twenty-five years in a penitentiary. Belle had a series of seven lovers and common-law husbands throughout her life, all of whom were criminals and five of whom predeceased her. Belle was charged with several crimes, including horse theft and robbery, although she was sentenced to prison only once, for a nine-month term (1883). According to legend, Belle cut a notorious figure. She is said to have enjoyed wearing men's clothing, arming herself with several ornate pistols, and riding in a handsome saddle. Her prowess with a gun was thought to be remarkable, and she often displayed her skills at county fairs. Her life of outlawry, however, apparently brought enemies. Two days before her forty-first birthday, she was found dead, face down in the road, shot in the back. She was buried in Texas with her favorite six-shooter, in a ceremony attended by both whites and Cherokees, with whom she had become friendly in her later years.

Further Reading: Burton Rascoe, *Belle Starr, the Bandit Queen*, 1941.

Jessica Matthews

STATUE OF LIBERTY (LIBERTY ENLIGHTENING THE WORLD). This large copper statue of a woman, 152 feet tall, stands on Liberty Island, formerly known as Bedloe's Island, in New York Harbor. An example of repoussé work, hammered metal shaped over a mold, it consists of three hundred copper sheets and weighs about one hundred tons. The French historian Edouard de Laboulaye wanted to give the United States a gift with political significance, and suggested a monument that represented liberty. Frédéric Bartholdi designed the statue, chose its site, and raised funds for the project in France and the United States. Alexandre Gustave Eiffel built the statue's supporting framework, using the most recent technology. The American Committee for the Statue of Liberty collected $200,000 (of the needed $300,000) for the project, which was considered one of the greatest fund-raising efforts of the nineteenth century. On 4 July 1884, the French presented the statue to the minister of the United States in Paris. After it was shipped to the United States, President Grover Cleveland dedicated the monument on 28 October 1886, and unveiled it before representatives of both countries. The statue became a national monument in 1924 and is America's symbol of liberty and welcome to the op-

pressed. The National Park Service maintains it.

Further Reading: Christian Blanchet and Bertrand Dard, *Statue of Liberty: The First Hundred Years*, 1985.

Jane F. Lancaster

STEALEY, ORLANDO OSCAR (4 January 1842–29 December 1928), journalist and pioneering congressional correspondent. Born in Jeffersonville, Indiana, Stealey became a congressional correspondent for the Louisville *Courier-Journal* in 1884 and continued into the twentieth century as one of Washington's senior correspondents. During his tenure, the number of Washington correspondents tripled, as accurate congressional reporting became more important to out-of-town newspapers. Stealey prided himself on personally knowing nine-tenths of the congressmen and senators he covered. His friend and office mate for many years was the colorful *Cincinnati Gazette* correspondent Henry Boynton. Stealey's newspaper was Democratic; Boynton's, Republican. The two helped one another behind the scenes as much as they assailed one another's politics in print. Stealey also helped defend Boyton in 1884 when the latter was accused of bribing House Speaker Joseph W. Keifer. Stealey helped establish the Gridiron Club, a "club without a clubhouse" organization of Capitol and government reporters in Washington, D.C., in 1886. He lobbied to increase the pay of congressional correspondents, once noting that his telephone budget was so low that extra calls cost him three weeks' salary each year. Stealey also helped found the National Press Club in 1908. He died in Washington, D.C.

Further Reading: O. O. Stealey, *Twenty Years in the Press Gallery*, 1906; Donald Ritchie, *Press Gallery: Congress and the Washington Correspondent*, 1991.

Richard Junger

STEPHENS, URIAH SMITH (3 August 1821–13 February 1882), labor leader. Born in Cape May, New Jersey, Stephens had a meager early education. He wanted to be a Baptist minister, but the Panic of 1837 prevented him from obtaining the necessary education. Instead, he taught school locally, was a tailor in Philadelphia, and visited California, the West Indies,

Central America, and Mexico. In 1869 Stephens was a founder of the Noble Order of the Knights of Labor, which became one of the earliest unions in the United States. By 1886, its membership had soared to almost a million members. Stephens was the first "grand master workman" of the cooperative movement, in essence a Utopian reformer, an idealist whose ambition was to establish district assemblies all over the nation and in Europe. In 1878 Stephens was an unsuccessful Greenback candidate for Congress, and because of internal strife, resigned as a labor leader. He died in Philadelphia, Pennsylvania.

Further Reading: Samuel Eliot Morrison and Henry Steele Commager, *Growth of the American Republic*, Vol. 2 (1942), 155–157; N. J. Ware, *The Labor Movement in the United States, 1860–1895*, 1929; *Public Ledger* (Philadelphia), 15 February 1882.

Nicholas C. Polos

STETSON, FRANCIS LYNDE (23 April 1846–5 December 1920), lawyer. Born in Keeseville, New York, Stetson graduated from Williams College in 1867 and the Columbia Law School two years later. In 1880, he resigned his position as assistant corporation counsel for New York City to form a law partnership, which took different names over the years. Especially interested in corporate entities, Stetson became legal adviser and personal counselor to John Pierpont Morgan, prominent Gilded Age financier and railroad magnate. Well known on Wall Street and in eastern financial centers as a sound money Democrat, Stetson supported New York governors Samuel J. Tilden and Grover Cleveland for president. Serving as a friend and adviser to President Cleveland, Stetson declined offers of cabinet positions to remain with his law firm, with which Cleveland was associated during the four-year interregnum between his two nonconsecutive presidential terms. Stetson was present at the White House meeting when Morgan's syndicate contracted with the national government to sell gold to offset the depleted reserves and relieve the pressure on the U.S. Treasury. Stetson was also active in the affairs of the Episcopal Church and Williams College. He died in New York City.

Further Reading: Allan Nevins, *Grover Cleveland: A Study in Courage*, 1933; *New York Times*, 6 December 1920.

Leonard Schlup

STEUNENBURG, FRANK (8 August 1861–30 December 1905), governor. Born in Keokuk, Iowa, Steunenburg attended Iowa State Agricultural College, learned the printing trade, and worked for several years on leading daily newspapers. In 1885, with W. J. Casey, he bought the *Knoxville Express*. Steunenburg moved to Idaho in 1886, and with his brother bought the *Caldwell Tribune*. He was one of the youngest members at the Idaho constitutional convention, and sat in the state legislature. He was elected governor in 1896 and 1898. During the Coeur d'Alene tension between the miners and the mine owners, Steunenburg summoned the National Guard and requested federal authorities. His anti-labor actions led to a congressional investigation, and he returned to Caldwell, where he entered the banking business and started a lumber company. His short career ended when he was killed by a bomb placed by Albert E. Horsley, alias Harry Orchard, a professional dynamiter. Although Orchard received a death sentence, it was eventually commuted to life imprisonment.

Further Reading: George W. Fuller, *A History of the Pacific Northwest*, 1931; Laurie Clayton, "The U.S. Army and the Labor Radicals of the Coeur d'Alene: Federal Military Intervention in the Mining Wars of 1892–1899," *Idaho Yesterdays* 37 (1993): 12–29.

Nicholas C. Polos

STEVENS, JOHN LEAVITT (1 August 1820–8 February 1895), journalist, author, and diplomat. Born in Mount Vernon, Maine, Stevens was educated at Maine Wesleyan Seminary and Waterville Classical Institute. An ordained Universalist clergyman, he edited and published the *Kennebec Journal* with James G. Blaine. One of the founders of the Republican Party in Maine, Stevens was elected to the state's house of representatives in 1865 and its senate in 1868. He received diplomatic appointments as minister to Uruguay and Paraguay in

1870, and as minister to Sweden and Norway in 1877. By 1889, Stevens was a seasoned diplomat when he was appointed Minister to the Hawaiian Islands. Americans had been a political and economic force there for decades and had developed a profitable sugar trade with the United States. The McKinley Tariff of 1890 destabilized the sugar industry, however, and contributed to the overthrow of the corrupt Hawaiian monarchy in 1893. A provisional government of wealthy American landowners seized power and advocated annexation of the islands by the United States. Stevens proclaimed the legitimacy of the new government and directed the landing of 150 marines at Honolulu to protect American lives and property. With his approval, Sanford Ballard Dole's provisional government dispatched a commission to Washington, D.C. to negotiate annexation. The outgoing administration of Benjamin Harrison submitted an annexation treaty to the Senate. Grover Cleveland's incoming administration, did not support the annexation request, and after conducting an investigation, unsuccessfully attempted to restore the monarch. The provisional government recalled Stevens, accusing him of exceeding his authority and collusion with the revolutionists. A Senate investigation cleared Stevens, and he continued to advocate his cause in the press and through publication of his book *Picturesque Hawaii* (1894). Stevens died in Augusta, Maine, before his recommendations were finally effected in 1898.

Further Reading: William Adam Russ, Jr., *The Hawaiian Revolution*, 1959; *New York Times*, 9 February 1895; John Leavitt Stevens Papers, Maine Historical Society, Portland.

Janet Butler Munch

STEVENSON, ADLAI EWING (23 October 1835–14 June 1914), vice president of the United States. One of the Gilded Age's most versatile politicians, Stevenson was born in Christian County, Kentucky. In 1852 he and his family moved to Bloomington, Illinois. Stevenson attended Centre College in Kentucky, read law in Bloomington, and opened a practice in Metamora, Illinois, in 1858. He held local offices during the Civil War. In 1869 Stevenson

formed a law partnership in Bloomington with his double cousin James Stevenson Ewing. Stevenson was also president of the McLean County Coal Company. Elected as a Democrat to the U.S. House of Representatives in 1874 and 1878, and narrowly defeated for reelection in 1876 and 1880, Stevenson represented a rural Republican constituency. He made politics out of the issue of nonpartisanship. In Congress, Stevenson favored soft money, low tariffs, economy in government, and electoral college reform. In 1885 President Grover Cleveland selected Stevenson as first assistant postmaster general; in that office he removed thousands of Republican postmasters. This earned the wrath of civil service reformers but made valuable political allies who catapulted him into second place on the national ticket with Cleveland in 1892.

Stevenson, a political moderate and accomplished raconteur, did not antagonize diverse Democratic Party elements and found himself a compromise choice. He concentrated much of his 1892 campaign in the South, where farmers distrusted Cleveland's hard money views and Populists had wide political appeal. Stevenson replied to southern Democrats' complaints with assurances of federal investment in the area, locally controlled elections, tariff reductions, and party patronage. He contributed to the Democratic victory and helped to carry the South and Illinois. In 1896, near the end of his term as vice president, Stevenson belatedly sought the Democratic presidential nomination, counting on a deadlocked convention. Highly divisive issues, such as the unlimited coinage of silver, defied compromise, and Stevenson, a skilled neutralist, lost the nomination to the militant silverite William Jennings Bryan.

In 1897 President William McKinley appointed Stevenson to the Bimetallic Monetary Commission, a group that sought unsuccessfully to convince European leaders to accept international bimetallism at an established ratio. The following year, Stevenson backed McKinley's decision to ask Congress for a declaration of war against Spain in order to end oppression in Cuba. He won the Democratic vice presidential nomination in 1900 on the ticket headed by

Bryan because he was the most available political figure in the party to provide harmony. His ability to survive in both the Cleveland and the Bryan camps during the same decade gave him a rare political distinction. In 1900 he campaigned against trusts and imperialism.

Stevenson ran a close, but unsuccessful, race for governor of Illinois in 1908. A cautious centrist and coalition Democrat, he sought harmony in an era of change and intense partisanship, offered soothing words to heal intraparty dissension, and refused to indulge in personal vendettas. The quintessential Gilded Age gentleman, he reportedly never made a personal enemy of a political adversary. Stevenson functioned as a transitional figure between the conservative tradition of Democracy under Cleveland and the progressive outlook of Bryan and Woodrow Wilson. In the end, his most lasting contribution was the founding of a political dynasty. He died in Chicago, Illinois.

Further Reading: Adlai E. Stevenson, *Something of Men I Have Known*, 1909; Leonard Schlup, "The Political Career of the First Adlai E. Stevenson," Ph.D. diss., University of Illinois at Urbana-Champaign, 1973, and "The American Chameleon: Adlai E. Stevenson and the Quest for the Vice Presidency in Gilded Age Politics," *Presidential Studies Quarterly* 21 (1991): 511–529.

Leonard Schlup

STEVENSON, LETITIA BARBOUR GREEN (8 January 1843–25 December 1913), president general of the Daughters of the American Revolution and social organizer. Born in Allegheny, Pennsylvania, Letitia attended a New York City finishing school for girls. Following her father's death in 1863, she moved with her mother, Mary Peachey Fry Green, to Chenoa, Illinois, the home of Letitia's married sister, Julia Green Scott. There, on 20 December 1866, Letitia married Adlai Ewing Stevenson, a Metamora lawyer, whom she had met earlier at Centre College in Danville, Kentucky. The Stevensons eventually lived in a large Victorian home on Franklin Square in Bloomington, Illinois.

The mother of four children, Stevenson assumed active roles in local, state, and national social organizations. A women's rights advocate, she was the first president of the Women's Club of Bloomington. She also was one of the founders of the Congress of Mothers, which later became the Parent Teachers Association. As the wife of the vice president from 1893 to 1897, she kept a high profile in official Washington society: entertaining, greeting guests, traveling the nation, campaigning with her husband, attending rallies, and visiting Alaska. In addition, Stevenson belonged to the Colonial Dames of America and to the Women's Clubs of America. Recognized for her participation in the Daughters of the American Revolution (DAR), and serving four terms as its second president general in the 1890s, Stevenson worked to make the DAR an effective organization to help heal the Civil War breach between northern and southern women, in order to reunite Gilded Age America. In 1897 she accompanied her husband to Europe in his capacity as a member of the Bimetallic Monetary Commission. There she met Queen Victoria and several European political leaders. Stevenson died in Bloomington.

Further Reading: *In Memoriam—Letitia Green Stevenson [and] Adlai Ewing Stevenson*, 1914; *The Daily Pantagraph* (Bloomington), 26 December 1913; Adlai Ewing Stevenson I Collection, Elizabeth Stevenson Ives Papers, Illinois State Historical Library, Springfield.

Leonard Schlup

STEWART, WILLIAM MORRIS (9 August 1827–23 April 1909), lawyer and senator. Born in Galen, New York, Stewart grew up in Trumbull County, Ohio. He attended Farmington Academy in Ohio, studied law at Yale University, and was admitted to the California bar in 1852. Elected district attorney general in 1853, he wrote the state's first rules and regulations for quartz mining. Stewart quickly gained fame for his expertise in mining law, and in 1859 he moved to Downieville, Nevada. There he became active in politics, and was elected to the territorial council and the 1863 constitutional convention. When Nevada entered the Union in 1864, Stewart, a staunch Republican, was elected to the U.S. Senate, where he served until 1875. Formulator of the "one-lode" theory in mining law, he wrote the Reconstruction plan, a bill for amnesty and universal suffrage, national mining laws, and the Fifteenth Amendment. He also defended Chinese immigration at a time when few western politicians did. Stewart later became interested in the silver issue, irrigation laws, and building the Pacific Railroad. He refused an appointment to the Supreme Court. He retired from the Senate in 1875 but was reelected twelve years later and served until 1905. Stewart gave a winning argument in the dispute with Mexico over the Pious Fund, before the Permanent Court of Arbitration at The Hague, in 1902. A lifelong fried of Leland Stanford, he was one of the first trustees of Stanford University. He died in Washington, D.C.

Further Reading: George R. Brown, ed., *The Reminiscences of William Morris Stewart of Nevada*, 1908; *San Francisco Call*, 24 April 1909; *San Francisco Chronicle*, 24 April 1909.

Nicholas C. Polos

STODDARD, CHARLES WARREN (7 August 1843–23 April 1909), author and educator. Born in Rochester, New York, Stoddard converted to Roman Catholicism in 1867, traveled through Hawaii, wrote letters for newspapers, and composed poems. He engaged in homosexual activity with young Hawaiian men. His experiences in Tahiti (1870) resulted in the popular *South-Sea Idyls* (1873). During the next four years, he toured Europe and the Middle East, met Mark Twain and other literary figures, and sampled bohemianism in Munich, Germany. Stoddard experienced a restless life, drifting from one situation to another. In 1885 he published a religious book titled *A Troubled Heart and How It Was Comforted at Last*. From 1889 to 1902, he taught literature at the Catholic University of America in Washington, D.C. He established friendships with many Gilded Age notables, including John Hay and Henry Adams. Stoddard, who was obese, suffered a fatal heart attack in Monterey, California.

Further Reading: Robert L. Gale, *Charles Warren Stoddard*, 1977; Roger Austen, "Stoddard's Little Tricks in South-Sea Idyls," *Journal of Homosexuality* 8 (1983): 73–83; Roger Austen, *Genteel Pagan: The Double Life of Charles Warren Stoddard*, 1991.

Leonard Schlup

STONE, LUCY. (13 August 1818–18 October 1893), reformer and journalist. Born in West Brookfield, Massachusetts, Stone graduated from Oberlin College in 1847, thus becoming the first woman in Massachusetts to hold a bachelor's degree. She lectured for the Massachusetts Anti-Slavery Society in 1848 and organized the first national women's right convention, at Worcester, Massachusetts, two years later. Stone married Henry Brown Blackwell in 1855, but kept her maiden name. Subsequently, married women who kept their maiden names were called "Lucy Stoners." Her fervent efforts as an abolitionist and women's rights activist melded in 1869 when she and her husband established the American Woman Suffrage Association, which worked to advance women's suffrage and African Americans' civil rights. Stone was a key administrator in the organization from 1870 to 1890. She founded the *Woman's Journal* in 1870; it would advance the movement for the next forty-seven years. The American Woman Suffrage Association joined forces with Susan B. Anthony and Elizabeth Cady Stanton's National Woman Suffrage Association to become the National American Woman Suffrage Association in 1890. Stone died in Dorchester, Massachusetts. After her death, her daughter, Alice Stone Blackwell, continued her mother's fight for reform.

Further Reading: Alice Stone Blackwell, *Lucy Stone*, 1930; Elinor Rice Hays, *Morning Star: A Biography of Lucy Stone, 1818–1893*, 1961.

Lisa De Palo

STONE, MELVILLE ELIJAH (22 August 1848–15 February 1929), journalist. Born in Hudson, Illinois, Stone worked as a reporter for various Chicago newspapers in the 1860s, ran an iron foundry, and held positions of leadership in several local, state, and national organizations. A Republican, he directed relief efforts in Chicago after the great fire of 1871. In 1875 Stone and two partners, Percy Meggy and William Dougherty, founded the *Chicago Daily News*, which during the next decade became the city's most popular newspaper. As editor, Stone practiced investigative journalism, sought to root out public corruption, and endeavored to view Chicago as one large family. Scoffing at laissez-faire economic notions, the wealthy Stone supported social welfare and public works. He retired in 1888 and sailed to Europe, but by 1892 he had returned and had assumed the presidency of the Globe National Bank of Chicago. Later he accepted the position of general manager of the Associated Press in New York City, where he died.

Further Reading: Melville E. Stone, *Fifty Years a Journalist*, 1921; Donald J. Abramoske, "The Founding of the *Chicago Daily News*," *Journal of the Illinois State Historic Society* 59 (1966): 341–353; *New York Times*, 16 February 1929.

Leonard Schlup

STONE, WILLIAM JOEL (7 May 1848–14 April 1918), U.S. representative and senator, governor of Missouri. Born near Richmond, Kentucky, Stone attended the University of Missouri at Columbia before opening a law practice in 1869. He served as Columbia city attorney and county prosecutor before winning election to Congress in 1884. He served in the House as a Democrat from 1885 to 1891. He ran for governor of Missouri in 1892, winning largely because of long-established agrarian ties. Stone nevertheless presided over a pro-business administration that effectively hindered efforts to regulate corporations. He first gained national attention as a leader of Missouri's Silver Democratic faction. Stone later served in William Jennings Bryan's first campaign for president in 1896. In 1900, Bryan named Stone vice chairman of the Democratic National Committee, a position he held until 1904.

Stone won election to the U.S. Senate in 1903. Surviving subsequent allegations that as governor he had deliberately concealed an illegal campaign contribution to his successor, Stone remained in the Senate until his death. There he acquired the nickname "Gumshoe Bill" for his ability to work behind the scenes. Chairing the Foreign Relations Committee, he supported efforts by Secretary of State Bryan to keep America out of the European war. A devout pacifist, Stone emerged as one of the "Willful Twelve" who opposed America's declaration of war against Germany in 1917. By the time of his death in Washington, D.C., however, Stone had become one of the Wilson administration's strongest supporters.

Further Reading: Lawrence O'Christensen, *A History of Missouri*, Vol. 4, *1875–1919*, 1997; *New York Times*, 15 April 1918.

Harvey Gresham Hudspeth

STORER, FRANCIS HUMPHREYS (27 March 1832–30 July 1914), chemist and professor. Born and educated in Boston, Massachusetts, Storer was a chemist with the U.S. North Pacific exploring expedition in 1853–1854. In 1855, he earned his B.S. degree from Harvard University. After studying chemistry abroad for two years, he accepted the appointment as chemist of the Boston Gas Light Company. He held it until 1871, when President Charles William Eliot of Harvard, a noted chemist and Storer's brother-in-law, appointed him dean of the Bussey Institution and professor of agricultural chemistry. There he pursued research on cereals, fruits, soils, wood, vegetables, and fertilizers. He also founded and edited the *Bulletin of the Bussey Institution*. Storer published abstracts, reviews, books, and a series of works relating to chemistry; his most significant work, *Agriculture in Some of Its Relations with Chemistry*, appeared in 1887. Storer's substantial research constituted an important development in the field of chemistry during the Gilded Age. He retired in 1907, but retained an active interest in the profession until his death in Boston.

Further Reading: *Boston Transcript*, 30 July 1914.

Leonard Schlup

STRATEMEYER, EDWARD (4 October 1862–10 May 1930), writer. Born in Elizabeth, New Jersey, Stratemeyer graduated from a local high school and began writing stories. In 1888 he secured an appointment as assistant editor of *Young American*. After moving to Newark, New Jersey, in 1890, to operate a newspaper and stationery store, Stratemeyer wrote popular fiction, mysteries, westerns, and dime novels for publication. He published his first book, *Richard Dare's Venture*, in 1894. The following year he started editing *Young Sports of America*. In 1898 Stratemeyer achieved additional success with the publication of *Under Dewey at Manila*, firmly establishing himself by the turn of the century as an author of books for boys. He created the Rover Boys series in 1899, and within a decade had produced more than two dozen series. Some of the best-known of the Stratemeyer Literary Syndicate series included the Hardy Boys, Nancy Drew, and the

Bobbsey Twins, the longest-running series of books for children, which began in 1904. Stratemeyer died in Newark, New Jersey.

Further Reading: Deidre A. Johnson, *Edward Stratemeyer and the Stratemeyer Syndicate*, 1993; *New York Times*, 12 May 1930; Stratemeyer Syndicate Archives, New York Public Library.

Leonard Schlup

STRATTON, CHARLES SHERWOOD (4 January 1838–15 July 1883), entertainer. Better known by his stage name, Tom Thumb, Stratton was born in Bridgewater, Connecticut. His body stopped growing when he was seven months old; he was only twenty-five inches tall and weighed a mere fifteen pounds until early adulthood. When he was four years old, the entertainment entrepreneur P. T. Barnum "discovered" and signed him to perform at his American Museum in New York City. Barnum rechristened Stratton as General Tom Thumb and trained him as a comic performer. In 1844, Barnum and Tom Thumb journeyed to England, where the young boy, whom Barnum passed off as much older, thrilled London audiences and reportedly charmed Queen Victoria. His success led Thumb's working-class parents to insist that they be made full partners in their son's revenues, although Barnum retained control of business decisions. Thumb moved on to France, imitating Napoleon Bonaparte before King Louis Philippe. From 1852 through 1856, he temporarily retired, but entertainment revenues soon had him touring again. In 1863, Thumb married Mercy Lavinia Warren Bump, and the popular couple was invited by President Abraham Lincoln to a White House reception in their honor. Thumb and Lavinia performed nationally and internationally until the diminutive entertainer, one of Barnum's greatest, died in Middleboro, Massachusetts.

Further Reading: Countess M. Lavinia Magri, *The Autobiography of Mrs. Tom Thumb*, ed. A. H. Saxon, 1979; Philip B. Kurnhardt, Jr., *P. T. Barnum, America's Greatest Showman*, 1995.

Ron Briley

STRAUS, OSCAR SOLOMON (23 December 1850–3 May 1926), diplomat and cabinet secretary. Born in Otterberg, Rhenish Bavaria, Strauss immigrated with his family to the United States in 1854. They settled in Georgia, but moved to New York City after the Civil War. Straus received a B.A. from Columbia University in 1871, and graduated from its law school in 1873. He practiced law in New York City, but in 1881 entered the family business, which sold glass and chinaware. The family opened a china shop in the R. H. Macy Company department store, which it later came to own. Straus served as minister to Turkey from 1887 to 1889 and 1898 to 1900. President Theodore Roosevelt named Strauss in 1902 to the International Court of Arbitration at The Hague. In 1906, he became secretary of commerce and labor, the first Jew to be named to a cabinet position. In 1909–1910 he served again as ambassador to Turkey. He ran unsuccessfully for governor of New York in 1912, on the Progressive ticket. Throughout his career, he urged diplomatic efforts by the United States in relief of Jews persecuted in eastern Europe. Following World War I, he served as an adviser to Woodrow Wilson at the Paris Peace Conference of 1918–1919, and was particularly interested in securing the rights of Jews in the newly established state of Poland. He died in New York City.

Further Reading: Naomi Cohen, *A Dual Heritage: The Public Career of Oscar S. Straus*, 1969; Gary Dean Best, *To Free a People: American Jewish Leaders and the Jewish Problem in Eastern Europe, 1890–1914*, 1982.

James M. Bergquist

STRAUSS, LOEB "LEVI" (26 February 1829–27 September 1902), entrepreneur and inventor of "blue jeans." Born in Buttenheim, Bavaria, as Loeb Strauss, he immigrated to New York City in 1847 to join his family in the dry goods business. After obtaining American citizenship, he changed his name to Levi. He journeyed to San Francisco in 1853, in response to the Californai gold rush, intending to sell dry goods to prospectors. His company acquired a reputation for quality products. The introduction of denim jeans (originally called "waist overalls"), with copper rivets at the crucial wear points, came in response to miners' needs for strong and sturdy pants and overalls. Strauss patented the process in 1873 with Reno, Nevada, tailor Jacob Davis. Strauss was a charter member of the San Francisco Board of Trade and an active supporter of the local Jewish community and its first synagogue. Most historical records of Strauss and his company were destroyed by fire in the aftermath of the great San Francisco earthquake of 1906.

Further Reading: Cliff Gromer, "Outdoors Levi's Jeans," *Popular Mechanics* 176 (May 1999): 94–97.

Ralph G. Giordano

STRONG, JOSIAH (19 January 1847–28 April 1916), pastor, author, and reformer. Born in Naperville, Illinois, Strong graduated from Western Reserve College in Hudson, Ohio, in 1869 and was ordained a Congregational minister in 1871. He was pastor of the First Congregationalist Church of Sandusky, Ohio, from 1876 to 1881, then became secretary of the Ohio Home Missionary Society. In his book *Our Country: Its Possible Future and Its Present Crisis*, published in 1885, Strong contended that Anglo-Saxon America had an opportunity to play a profound role in world regeneration, but also listed eight perils to the country's mission: immigration, Mormonism, socialism, alcoholism, materialism, Catholicism, burgeoning urbanism, and temporal challenges to the public school system. Strong's writing catapulted him to national prominence, and led to his selection as general secretary of the Evangelical Alliance in 1886, a position he used to promote social reform. In 1893, he published *The New Era*, a best-seller. Five years later he established the League for Social Service, to conduct research and educate Americans about social issues. His many contributions to the Social Gospel movement gave him his greatest renown in the late nineteenth century. Though maintaining that God had trained the Anglo-Saxon race in America for a supreme role in the future, Strong was by inclination neither an imperialist nor a racist. In fact, he frequently condemned European imperialism and U.S. enlargement of its navy. Strong wanted to apply Christian principles to uplift all nations. He emphasized that the United States had a manifest mission, embedded in social Christianity, to promulgate peace, justice, and economic advancement. Strong died in New York City.

Further Reading: Dorothea R. Muller, "Josiah Strong and American Nationalism: A Reevaluation," *Journal of American History* 53 (1966): 487–503; *New York Times*, 29 April 1916.

Leonard Schlup

STRONG, WILLIAM (6 May 1808–19 August 1895), U.S. Supreme Court justice. Born in Somers, Connecticut, Strong attended Munson Academy and Plainfield Academy before graduating from Yale University in 1828. After reading law, he was admitted to the Pennsylvania bar in 1832. Strong served two terms (1847–1851) in Congress as a Democrat, and then returned to private practice. After joining the newly formed Republican Party, he won election as an associate justice of the Pennsylvania Supreme Court in 1857, serving for eleven years. Thereafter Strong opened a law office in Philadelphia, where he reportedly was making $30,000 a year when Ulysses S. Grant named him to the U.S. Supreme Court in 1870. Strong's elevation to the high bench, and that of Joseph P. Bradley, came shortly after the Court's initial ruling in *Hepburn* v. *Griswold*, one of the *Legal Tender Cases*. The justices reheard it once Bradley and Strong had been confirmed. Although they initially had declared the federal government's use of greenbacks to satisfy prior debts unconstitutional, they now reversed themselves, with both new justices among the five-man majority. Bradley and Strong were to play an equally controversial role in the decision to name Rutherford Hayes winner of the bitterly contested 1876 presidential election. Strong retired in December 1880 and devoted his remaining years to legal and religious endeavors, serving as president of the American Tract Society. He died in Lake Minnewaska, New York.

Further Reading: *New York Times*, 20 August 1895.

Harvey Gresham Hudspeth

STUART, GRANVILLE (27 August 1834–2 October 1918), rancher, miner, and writer. Born in Clarksburg, Virginia (now West Virginia), Stuart and his older brother James located gold in Montana in 1858 and opened a mercantile business in 1863, eventually expanding it to include a store, a lumberyard, a quartz mill, and a mine. He entered a cattle ranching partnership with Samuel T. Hauser and A. J. Davis in

1879, forming DHS Ranch with Stuart as manager. It grew into one of the largest ranches before going bankrupt in the late 1880s. Stuart was one of the leaders of Stuart's Stranglers, a vigilante movement to suppress cattle rustlers in central Montana. At various times he served as president of the state's Stock Growers Association, and of the historical society. In 1891 Governor Joseph K. Toole named Stuart state land agent. As such, he chose lots for schools and engaged in surveying. President Grover Cleveland appointed him envoy extraordinary and minister plenipotentiary to Paraguay and Uruguay, where he remained from 1894 to 1897. Returning to Montana in 1899, Stuart ran a boardinghouse in Butte and in 1905 was head librarian for that city's public library. He gained widespread attention for his written work, contributing numerous articles to newspapers and keeping journals and diaries of his western adventures. Stuart died in Missoula, Montana.

Further Reading: Granville Stuart, *Pioneering in Montana: The Making of a State, 1864–1887*, ed. Paul C. Phillips, 1977; Paul Robert Treece, "Mr. Montana: The Life of Granville Stuart, 1834–1918," Ph.D. diss., Ohio State University, 1974; Granville Stuart Papers, Montana Historical Society Archives, Helena.

Leonard Schlup

STUCKI, JACOB (23 January 1857–10 May 1930), clergyman, missionary, and educator. Born at Diemtigen, Switzerland, Stucki immigrated to the United States in 1873, and gained American citizenship in 1882. He became a divinity student at Mission House College and Seminary in Plymouth, Wisconsin. There he came under the influence of Reverend Henry Kurtz, professor of theology, who had been saved from freezing to death by Native Americans. In 1884 the German Reformed Church sent Stucki as a missionary, teacher, and assistant to Reverend Jacob Hauser. Stucki assumed the administrative duties of Black River Falls Mission upon Hauser's retirement in 1885, and remained there for forty-six years. Known by the Winnebagoes as "Angel White Man," he meticulously translated several parts of the Bible into the difficult Winnebago language. He directed the Winnebago Indian School, which had opened in 1878. Encouraging Native Americans to help themselves, Stucki developed an appreciation and understanding of the Winnebago mentality and culture. Although the violence and injustice done to indigenous peoples could never be redressed, Stucki refused to accept the popular insensitive attitudes about Native Americans. Stucki died at Black River Falls Mission.

Further Reading: Theodore P. Bolliger, *The Wisconsin Winnebago Indians and the Mission of the Reformed Church*, 1922; John P. Von Grueningen, ed., *The Swiss in the United States*, 1940; Arthur V. Casselman, *The Winnebago Finds a Friend*, 1932.

Leonard Schlup

STUDEBAKER, JOHN MOHLER (10 October 1833–16 March 1917), wagon and automobile manufacturer. Born in Adams County, Pennsylvania, Studebaker grew up on poor farms in Ohio and Indiana, and received little education. After a successful sojourn to California, where he sought his fortune in gold mines and worked with local blacksmiths, Studebaker moved to South Bend, Indiana, where he purchased his brother Clement's interest in a wagon-making company. The Civil War increased the need for wagons; the company prospered, and in 1868 was incorporated as the Studebaker Brothers Manufacturing Company. By 1875, sales reached $1 million. Studebaker wagons became standard throughout the Midwest for farmers, and presidents in Washington often rode in Studebaker carriages. The company, financed by J. Pierpont Morgan's resources after the Panic of 1893, reorganized and expanded considerably. In 1901, Studebaker assumed the presidency of the company and without hesitation started producing electric vehicles, and ultimately automobiles powered by gasoline. Rising from rags to riches in post–Civil War American, Studebaker left an important legacy for the American automotive industry. He died in South Bend.

Further Reading: *New York Times*, 18 March 1917; Donald T. Chritchlow, *Studebaker: The Life and Death of an American Corporation*, 1996; Studebaker Corporation Archives, Studebaker National Museum, South Bend, Indiana.

Leonard Schlup

STURGIS, RUSSELL (16 October 1836–11 February 1909), architect, historian, and critic. Sturgis was born in Baltimore, Maryland, and trained in the office of Leopold Eidlitz and at the Munich Academy of Fine Arts and Sciences. He was a practicing architect, as well as a promoter and popularizer of the arts as an essential part of a civilized society. He designed several buildings for the Yale University campus in New Haven, including the High Victorian Gothic Farnham Hall (1869–1870). Sturgis's Austin Building in New York City (1876) reveals his understanding of and interest in current trends in architecture. After he retired in the mid-1880s, he wrote extensively on the arts, and published the first important study on the work of America's greatest Renaissance Revival architects, the firm of McKim, Mead, and White (1895). Sturgis's interests encompassed all the visual arts, including the decorative arts, and he wrote and edited books, dictionaries, encyclopedias, and journals. He was a founder of the Metropolitan Museum of Art in New York City and a supporter of one of the first institutions dedicated to the study of architecture and the preservation of architectural materials, the Avery Architectural Memorial Library at Columbia University. Sturgis died in New York City.

Further Reading: Russell Sturgis, *A Dictionary of Architecture and Building, Biographical, Historical, and Descriptive*, 1901–1902; *How to Judge Architecture*, 1903; and *The Interdependence of the Arts of Design*, 1905.

David G. Wilkins

SUBTREASURY PLAN. Throughout the Gilded Age farmers attempted to improve their living standards by raising crop prices. The difficulty of increasing prices during a time of agricultural surplus and of integrating farming into international markets did not dissuade farm leaders from persisting. The most popular proposal for increasing food prices came from Charles W. Macune, president of the Southern Farmers' Alliance. In 1887, he proposed the Subtreasury Plan, which asked Congress to establish warehouses for crops and to loan farmers up to 80 percent of a crop's value at 1 percent interest. The plan offered cash-poor farmers immediate credit and the ability to hold a crop until its price rose. In addition, it would inflate the currency because it called on Congress to print money to meet farmers' demand

for these loans. Although Alliance members embraced the Subtreasury Plan, Congress rejected it in 1890. The failure convinced Alliance leaders that the traditional parties would not implement farm reforms and led them to create a third party, the People's Party, which promoted the Subtreasury Plan and other reforms.

Further Reading: Robert C. McMath, *The Populist Vanguard*, 1975; Theodore Saloutos, *Farmer Movements in the South, 1865–1933*, 1960.

Christopher Cumo

SUCCESS MANUALS, literary genre. In the broadest sense this genre included fiction, inspirational biographies, and the marriage manuals that emphasized small families and companionate relationships. In a more narrow sense, success manuals were a style of nonfiction written predominantly for the lower middle class, whose members were anxious about and vulnerable to rapid changes in the American economy and society. The books were produced mainly by educators and ministers influenced by the works Benjamin Franklin, Ralph Waldo Emerson, and Henry Ward Beecher. Success manuals glorified rural life and traditional American traits, such as hard work, devotion, diligence, frugality, and honesty. Almost invariably, they claimed the country boy's clean morals and physical advantages would trump the city boy's superior intellect. In this they catered to the rural market, where success manuals were peddled by traveling salesman on a subscription basis. Success manuals romanticized poverty as the ideal environment for achievement, though at the same time they presented it as the equivalent of secular sin. Despite the increasing corporate nature of American life, writers of success manuals stressed the importance of the individual in determining his or her own future.

The success manual genre was highly formalistic, and authors frequently plagiarized one another. There was little practical advice, and the manuals should not be considered "how-to" books. Authors preferred tried-and-true maxims to detailed instructions. Success writers sought to inspire their readers to seek achievement, and they were deeply concerned that younger

American men had become complacent. They rarely measured success solely in financial terms; instead, these authors believed it could be gauged by one's character, virtues, and ability to strive for self-improvement in the face of adversity. Moreover, they preached success in a democratic manner, arguing that inherited wealth and education were not necessary elements.

In all, about 144 success manuals were published between 1870 and 1910. Most famous among them were Russell Conwell's, *Acres of Diamonds* (1870), Thomas Haines and Levi Yaggy's, *The Royal Path of Life* (1876), Orison Marden's, *Pushing to the Front* (1894), and Samuel Smiles's, *Self Help* (1860) and *Duty* (1880). The better-selling success manuals sold over two hundred thousand copies in the United States. Generally, the books cost half a week's wages. They were often large and heavy with gilded edges, and could reach eight hundred pages in length. In addition, numerous pamphlets and sermons were published in the Gilded Age. The best-seller, Elbert Hubbard's *A Message to Garcia* (1899), sold over forty million copies. Success manuals were an important component in acceptance of the emerging industrial system in American society.

Further Reading: Judith Hilkey, *Character Is Capital: Success Manuals and Manhood in Gilded Age America*, 1997; Richard M. Huber, *The American Idea of Success*, 1971; Paulette D. Kilmer, *The Fear of Sinking: The American Success Formula in the Gilded Age*, 1996.

Gregory Dehler

SULLIVAN, JOHN LAWRENCE (12 October 1858–2 February 1918), professional boxer. Sullivan was born in Boston, the son of Irish immigrants. Although he trained as a tinsmith, and then as a mason, Sullivan was unhappy with both occupations. His massive size and strength suggested that he might have a future as a prizefighter. Sullivan began his professional career in 1870, with very little experience. Not one to rely on fancy footwork and maneuvers, he was a powerful puncher who usually disposed of his opponents in early rounds. By 1882, Sullivan had captured the heavyweight championship of the world, defeating Paddy Ryan. He retained that title until his only loss in 1892, against James Corbett in a monumental battle. Sullivan's fight with Corbett was most important for being the first heavyweight championship bout in which the fighters used gloves. Sullivan finished his career with a 43–3–1 record, with twenty-nine of his victories obtained by knockout. He was an Irish-American hero at a time when Irish Americans endured persecution in the United States. Although financial records are incomplete and unclear, Sullivan was most likely the first athlete to earn over $1 million. He spent his later years as an actor and vaudeville performer, where his popularity grew immensely. He died in Abington, Massachusetts.

Further Reading: Michael T. Isenberg, *John L. Sullivan and His America*, 1988.

Steve Bullock

SULLIVAN, LOUIS HENRI (3 September 1856–14 April 1924), architect. Born Louis Henry Sullivan in Boston, Massachusetts, Sullivan studied architecture at the Massachusetts Institute of Technology under the supervision of William Robert Ware and Eugene Letang. He later was an apprentice in Philadelphia to Frank Furness and George Hewitt. After leaving Pennsylvania, Sullivan journeyed to Chicago, following the great fire in 1871. In 1881, after spending time in Paris and as a freelance decorative designer in Chicago, he teamed with Dankmar Adler to establish the firm of Adler and Sullivan. Sullivan's skyscraper designs and prominent buildings in various parts of Gilded Age America earned him a national reputation. Among his artistic successes were the Rothschild Building (Chicago, 1880), the Troescher Building (Chicago, 1884), the Ryerson Building (Chicago, 1884), the Auditorium Building (Chicago, 1886–1890), the Walker Warehouse (Chicago, 1888), the Wainwright Building (St. Louis, 1890), the Guaranty Building (Buffalo, New York, 1894–1896), and the Schlesinger-Mayer Department Store (Chicago, 1898–1904). On occasion he experienced financial difficulties and became a prolific writer. Known as "the prophet of modern architecture," Sullivan was a founding member of the Western Association of Architects in 1884. He died in Chicago.

Further Reading: Sherman Paul, *Louis Sullivan: An Architect in American* Thought, 1962; Robert Trombly, *Louis Sullivan: His Life and Work*, 1986.

Leonard Schlup

SULZER, WILLIAM (18 March 1863–6 November 1941), politician. Born in Elizabeth, New Jersey, Sulzer moved to New York City with his family when a teenager. After serving as a cabin boy, Sulzer came home, attended Columbia Law School, and became an attorney. In 1889 he won his first political office, being elected to the New York State Assembly. Four years later his Democratic colleagues elected him speaker, a position he held until 1895; then he went to the U.S. House of Representatives, where he served nine terms. Sulzer was elected governor of New York in 1912, only to be impeached and removed from office the next year. He died in New York City.

Further Reading: *New York Times*, 7 November 1941.

John T. McGuire

SUMNER, WILLIAM GRAHAM (30 October 1840–12 April 1910), sociologist. Born in Paterson, New Jersey, Sumner attended public schools, graduated from Yale College in 1863, and became an Episcopal priest, first in New York and later in New Jersey. Light clerical duties left time to found and edit a journal, *The Living Church*, and to translate German theological treatises into English. In 1872 his scholarship won Sumner the chair of the political and social science department at Yale. Despite disapproval of Noah Porter, Yale's president, Sumner used Herbert Spencer's *The Principles of Sociology* as a textbook. Social Darwinism shaped Sumner's economic views. He believed in competition, and advocated free trade in an era of protectionism. He applauded the growth of large corporations and denounced government intervention in the economy. He held that charity weakened its recipients, and touted Americans who prospered through thrift and diligence.

Sumner's defense of social Darwinism provided a scholarly rationale for the ruthlessness of American business practices and government passivity during the Gilded Age. His status as a leading sociologist brought him the presidency of the American Sociological Society. In this capacity, he went to New York City to deliver an address, but collapsed in a hotel and died in a hospital in Englewood Cliffs, New Jersey.

Further Reading: Bruce Curtis, *William Graham Sumner*, 1981; William Graham Sumner, *Essays of William Graham Sumner*, 2 vols., 1934.

Christopher Cumo

SUNDAY, WILLIAM ASHLEY (19 November 1862–6 November 1935), baseball player and evangelist. Born in Ames, Iowa, "Billy" Sunday was raised in an orphan's home before taking work at various times as a farmer, janitor, stable boy, and furniture maker. Good with a glove and fleet of foot, Sunday began playing professional baseball with the Chicago White Stockings in 1883. He also played for Pittsburgh and Philadelphia. He became an evangelical Christian and retired in 1891 to pursue a career as a preacher. Sunday was one of the most sought-after speakers in the country from the mid-1890s into the 1920s, and huge crowds gathered to hear his sermons. He appealed to the masses with simple language, employing both his working-class roots and his baseball experience in colorful and captivating sermons. His hallmark was a vibrant, acrobatic delivery, and he worked his audiences into a frenzy by striding across the stage and throwing out key points with a pitcher's windup. His message called for solid family values and traditional Protestant morals; he condemned dancing, smoking, and drinking. His popularity peaked in 1916 during a successful crusade for prohibition. Though he faded from prominence in the 1920s, Sunday continued to preach with great enthusiasm until ill health overwhelmed him shortly before his death.

Further Reading: Lyle Dorsett, *Billy Sunday and the Redemption of Urban America*, 1991; Larry D. Engelmann, "Billy Sunday: 'God, You've Got a Job on Your Hands in Detroit,' " *Michigan History* 55 (1971): 2–21.

Kevin B. Witherspoon

SWEET, WILLIS (1 January 1856–9 July 1925), congressman and free-coinage advocate. Born in Alburg Springs, Vermont, Sweet attended the University of Nebraska at Lincoln, and moved to Moscow, Idaho, in September 1881. There he practiced law, held judicial appointments, and was first president of the University of Idaho's board of regents. When Idaho achieved statehood in 1890, Sweet won election as a Republican to the U.S. House of Representatives, serving until 1895. He steadfastly supported the free and unlimited coinage of silver, a popular view in mining-oriented Idaho. He based his plan for consolidating American silver forces on tactics practiced by the Irish home-rule advocate Charles Stewart Parnell. Sweet wanted to make the pro-silver conglomeration in Congress powerful enough to block all other measures until enactment of silver legislation. The Republicans' nomination of William McKinley, high priest of protectionism, for president in 1896 angered Sweet. He and several other Silver Republicans boycotted the national convention. Sweet ultimately acquiesced in the selection of William Jennings Bryan as the apostle of the white metal. From 1903 to 1905, Sweet was Puerto Rico's attorney general. He also edited a newspaper in San Juan until his death.

Further Reading: Leonard Schlup, "Idaho Republican: Willis Sweet and the Crusade for Free Silver in the 1890s," *Research Journal of Philosophy and Social Sciences* (2001): 15–39; *Idaho Daily Statesman* (Boise), 10 July 1925; *El Mundo* (San Juan), 10 July 1925.

Leonard Schlup

SWETT, JOHN (31 July 1830–22 August 1913), educator. Known as the father of California's public school system, Swett was born in Pittsfield, New Hampshire, taught school in New England, and moved in 1853 to California. There he served as superintendent of the San Francisco public school system from 1892 to 1896. Swett basically developed the foundation of public education in the state. He edited an educational journal for California, expanded institutes and workshops for teachers, sought professional standards for teachers, and served as state superintendent. Some of his controversial ideas included support of physical education and a commitment to coeducation, endeavoring to make California's public school system free to everyone. Honest and moral, Swett deplored racial prejudice. His two published works were *History of the Public School System in California* (1872) and *Public Education in California: Origin and Development with Personal Reminiscences of Half a Century* (1911). Swett died at his Hill Girt Farm near Martinez, California.

Further Reading: Nicholas C. Polos, *John Swett: California's Frontier Schoolmaster*, 1978; *San Francisco Examiner*, 23 August 1913.

Leonard Schlup

SWIFT, GUSTAVUS FRANKLIN (24 June 1839–29 March 1903), entrepreneur. Born near Sandwich, Massachusetts, Swift demonstrated early interests that would make his name synonymous with meatpacking. In 1872 he entered into partnership with James A. Hathaway, a Boston meat dealer, and eventually established headquarters at Albany and Buffalo, New York, and Chicago. He employed an engineer who designed a refrigerated railroad car, allowing circulating fresh air to pass over ice, thereby cooling shipments of meat to distant places. Among Swift's competitors were Philip D. Armour and Nelson Morris. Thrifty and honest, Swift demanded cleanliness in his plants; incorporated his business in 1885 as Swift and Company; expanded his packing plants to newer cattle centers, including Kansas City, Missouri, Omaha, Nebraska, and Saint Paul, Minnesota; and developed by-products, such as oleomargarine, soap, and fertilizer, from previously discarded animal parts. He was also a generous philanthropist. In 1902, with Jonathan Ogden Armour and Edward Norris, Swift formed the National Packing Company, a combination later dissolved by court order. He died in Chicago.

Further Reading: *Chicago Daily Tribune*, 30 March 1903; L. F. Swift and Arthur Van Vlissingen, Jr., *The Yankee of the Yards: The Biography of Gustavus Franklin Swift*, 1927.

Leonard Schlup

SWINEFORD, ALFRED P. (14 September 1836–26 October 1909), journalist, businessman, civil servant, and governor of the District of Alaska. Born in Ashland, Ohio, Swineford worked as a printer's apprentice in several Midwestern states. In Wisconsin he passed the bar, but never practiced law. In Michigan he joined boomers advocating the ill-fated state of Superior (Michigan's Upper Peninsula). During the Civil War he was a Copperhead Democrat. In 1870, he won a single term in Michigan's legislature. His vigorous editorship of the *Marquette Mining Journal* facilitated his 1874 election as mayor of Marquette. That position terminated the following year, and in 1883 he became commissioner of mineral statistics. Since 1874, he had published, first in his newspaper and then as annual volumes, *The Mining Resources of Lake Superior.*

Swineford's friendship with President Grover Cleveland's sister, Cynthia Cleveland, may have facilitated his appointment as governor of Alaska. Shortly after arriving at Sitka in 1885, he joined with Reverend Sheldon Jackson and Reverend John G. Grady to publish the weekly *Alaskan.* His enthusiasm—he soon advocated Alaska's statehood—quickly collided with missionary plans for acculturating Native Alaskans. Swineford, seeking to outflank the churchmen's influence in Washington, D.C., tried to build a political following among Alaska's white settlers. Alaska's immensity, its tiny and scattered population, and congressional apathy defeated him. His muckraking attacks on the Alaska Commercial Company monopoly proved almost as futile, as did his efforts to redress eviction of Juneau's Chinese by mobs of miners in 1886. In 1889 the Harrison administration ended his governorship. From 1893 to 1898 Swineford worked for the federal land office. In 1898 he returned to Alaska, and lived to see Alaska win territorial status in 1906. He died at Juneau, Alaska.

Further Reading: Ted C. Hinckley, *Alaskan John G. Brady*, 1982, and *The Canoe Rocks*, 1996; Leonard Schlup, "The Arrogant Rogue and the Hypocrite," *Alaska History* 8 (Spring 1993): 14–18.

Ted C. Hinckley

TAFT, ALPHONSO (5 November 1810–21 May 1891), judge, secretary of war, attorney general, diplomat. Born in Townshend, Vermont, Taft attended local schools, Amherst Academy, and Yale College, and was admitted to the Connecticut bar in 1838. Rigorous competition led him to move to Cincinnati, Ohio. There his second wife, Louisa Torrey, bore him four surviving children, including a future president, William Howard Taft. In 1865 Alphonso Taft was appointed to Cincinnati's superior court, to which he won two subsequent elections. He resigned to enter private practice in 1872, but President Ulysses S. Grant named him secretary of war in 1876. Just three months later he was shuttled to the attorney general's post, where he drafted the bill creating the commission that settled the disputed Hayes-Tilden presidential election of 1876. Taft was a conservative who twice failed in bids to become governor of Ohio. In 1882, President Chester A. Arthur appointed him minister to Austria-Hungary (1882–1884) and Russia (1884–1885). There being no major problems, he did nothing while overseas. He died in Cincinnati, Ohio.

Further Reading: Lewis Alexander Leonard, *Life of Alphonso Taft*, 1920; Eugene P. Lyle, Jr., "Taft, A Career of Big Tasks: I. His Boyhood and College Days," *The World's Work* 14 (July 1907): 9135–9144; "Portrait" [Alphonso Taft], *Harper's Weekly* 53 (16 January 1904): 24.

Paolo E. Coletta

TAFT COMMISSION. On 7 April 1900, President William McKinley named federal district judge William Howard Taft to head the Second Philippine Commission and establish a civil government for the islands. Under Secretary of War Elihu Root's watchful eye, the commission acted as the legislative body of the archipelago after 1 September 1900. It organized municipal administration, and improved the police, civil service, and educational systems. Eventually, natives were permitted to sit on the commission. Provisions of the Bill of Rights, save trial by a jury of one's peers and the right to bear arms, were granted to the indigenous peoples. Except where insurgent activity continued, on 21 June 1901 military government was terminated—to take effect on 4 July 1901.

Further Reading: Charles B. Elliott, *The Philippines and the End of the Military Regime: America Overseas*, 1916; Margaret Leech, *In the Days of McKinley*, 1959; Daniel R. Williams, *The United States and the Philippines*, 1924.

Paolo E. Coletta

TAFT, WILLIAM HOWARD (15 September 1857–8 March 1930) judge, president of the United States, and chief justice of the Supreme Court. Taft, born in Cincinnati, Ohio, was graduated from Yale University in 1878 and was admitted to the bar, after studying at the Cincinnati Law School, in 1880. Almost continuously he held appointed offices from 1881 to 1909: assistant prosecutor of Hamilton County, Cincinnati's prosecuting attorney; local collector of internal revenue; assistant county solicitor; judge of the state superior court; solicitor general of the United States; federal circuit court judge; president of the Second Philippine Commission; and the first civil governor of the Philippines. Tall and corpulent, Taft often fell asleep after meals and was quite slow in reaching decisions. The product of a moderately wealthy family, he was an ardent Republican, and quite conservative. Because of his judicial rulings in labor cases, he acquired a reputation as an injunction judge. He served as secretary of war from 1904 to 1908, and president of the United States from 1909 to 1913. Taft was professor of law at Yale University from 1913 to 1921. Appointed chief justice of the Supreme Court in the latter year, he held that office until his retirement in 1930, making him the only person in American history to head both the executive and judicial branches of government. He died in Washington, D.C.

Further Reading: Paolo E. Coletta, *The Presidency of William Howard Taft*, 1973; Henry F. Pringle, *The Life and Times of William Howard Taft*, 2 vols., 1939.

Paolo E. Coletta

TAGGART, THOMAS (17 November 1856–6 March 1929), hotel proprietor, banker, and politician. Born in County Monaghan, Ireland, Taggart grew up in Xenia, Ohio, and later moved to Indianapolis. He quickly became involved in Democratic politics, serving as auditor of Marion County, Indiana, from 1886 to 1894. Taggart chaired the Democratic county committee in the 1880s and the state committee the following decade. As mayor of Indianapolis from 1895 to 1901, he emphasized economy in government, general enforcement of liquor laws, and the importance of good city parks. As Democratic National Committee chairman in 1904, he directed the unsuccessful presidential campaign of Alton B. Parker. Taggart died in Indianapolis.

Further Reading: James Phillip Fadely, *Thomas Taggart: Public Servant, Political Boss, 1856–1929*, 1997; *Indianapolis Star*, 7 March 1929.

Leonard Schlup

TAMMANY HALL. Prototypical of urban political machines, Tammany Hall was the executive committee of the Democratic Party in New York County (Manhattan). To remain entrenched in power, it promoted party government, controlled nominations, and made winning elections a prime and continuous activity. It cooperated with city Republican partisans and with both state parties, mined the sources of patronage jobs and graft, and, with assistance and favors, cultivated its constituency's allegiance. William Marcy Tweed, who became the permanent chairman of the executive committee and the grand sachem of Tammany Hall in 1863, and was elected to the state senate in 1867, propelled John T. Hoffman, a former Tammany Democrat mayor, to the governorship in 1868. A. Oakey Hall, a Democrat and a member of the Tweed Ring, was mayor of New York from 1869 to 1873. "Boss" Tweed won a new charter from the state legislature in 1870 that gave the mayor absolute power to appoint the comptroller and heads of departments, and created the Board of Special Audit, to which Tweed was subsequently appointed. By 1871, Tweed had reached the zenith of his power. His downfall later that year resulted from disclosures of the Tweed Ring's plunder. The reformers elected Republican William F. Havemeyer mayor in 1872.

The Tammany Hall faction competed for power in the 1870s and 1880s. "Honest John" Kelly, its first Irish-American leader (1873–1882), created a party machine to counteract defiant aldermen: a system of assembly district leaders and precinct captains. He assessed nominees for elective office, also pressuring them, as well as lesser elected officials to contribute to Tammany's election campaigns. Richard Croker, Kelly's protégé, formally became the Tammany leader in 1884. A fervent believer in the spoils system, he was the most powerful chieftain in New York yet. He was truly a "boss," though not even he had absolute power. He established a controlling influence over the Board of Aldermen, ruled over the whole Democratic Party, and relinquished to his district leaders power over city offices in their districts, thereby helping to make assembly districts important.

In 1894 the Lexow investigation of Tammany's corrupt extralegal authority sparked a coalition of antimachine Democrats and Republicans. That year their reform candidate, William L. Strong, a Republican who garnered the nonpartisan vote, badly defeated Grant. In the mayoral election of 1897, Croker's candidate, Robert A. Van Wyck, won handily over Seth Low (Citizens Union) and Benjamin F. Tracy (Republican). With Croker in charge of mayoral appointments, district leaders became heads of departments. Tammany now had power over Greater New York for four years.

Further Reading: M. R. Werner, *Tammany Hall*, 1928; Jon C. Teaford, "Finis for Tweed and Steffens: Rewriting the History of Urban Rule," in Stanley I. Kutler and Stanley H. Katz, eds., *Reviews in American History* 10 (1982): 133–49.

Bernard Hirschhorn

TARIFF. A tariff is a schedule or system of duties imposed by a government on imports or exports. During the Gilded Age, one of the most consistent economic credos was the advocacy of protective tariffs for American industry. Republicans reintroduced the issue of protective tariffs in the election of 1860. A year later, the Civil War, and the huge sums required to wage it, ensured its passage in Congress. In the latter half of 1861, in 1862, and again in 1864, the tariff was increased to protect domestic producers from the taxes collected to pay for the war. The war transformed a Republican temptation into full-scale seduction. By the time the war ended, protection for a short period had become a long-term policy. After the war, internal taxes were eliminated, but the tariff remained. The years from 1867 to 1872 saw a vigorous prosperity in manufacturing and a buildup of excess government revenue. This led Congress to consider a tariff reduction. In 1872, an across-the-board cut of 10 percent was passed, but following the onset of depression in 1875, it was rescinded. In 1890, and again in 1897, the tariff was increased.

Frank W. Taussig's close examination of the tariffs passed between 1867 and 1909 shows no demonstrable proof that protection directly increased domestic production, nor did it lead to a decline in the price of goods produced at home. Instead, protection became an article of faith sustained by the Republican Party, regardless of any economic benefit to the population, to the government, or even in some cases to the industry it was meant to protect. More recent analysis has argued that manufacturers grew frustrated with the ineffective tariffs devised by politicians and developed greater confidence in economic experts. This shift in the thinking of manufacturers led to the creation of a scientific methodology for tariff formation, later espoused by the Taft and Wilson administrations.

The Democratic Party began to play with the idea of tariff reduction in the 1880s as foreign trade rose and the income of workers declined. But effective political action to reduce the tariff did not occur until the Progressive era. The Underwood-Simmons Tariff, during the Wilson administration, was the first serious reduction since the Civil War, and was based on the argument that competition from foreign manufacturers would aid American consumers and check the growing power of American manufacturers.

Further Reading: Frank W. Taussig, *The Tariff History of the United States*, 1931; William H. Becker, *The Dynamics of Business-Government Relations*, 1982; G. R. Hawke, "The United States Tariff and Industrial Protection in the Late Nineteenth Century," *Economic History Review* 28 (1975): 84–99.

A. Jacqueline Swansinger

TATE, JAMES W. (2 January 1831–?), Kentucky state treasurer. Born in Franklin County, Kentucky, Tate spent his entire career working in government. Affable and extroverted, he secured appointed positions as assistant secretary of state (1854–1855, 1859–1863) and assistant clerk of the state House of Representatives (1865–1867). In 1867, as a Democrat, he was elected state treasurer; for the next two decades he was reelected every two years with only token opposition. Nicknamed "Honest Dick," Tate was among the most respected Kentucky politicians until mid-March 1888, when he suddenly disappeared. Witnesses later recalled that he had left his office carrying satchels of gold and silver coins and rolls of paper money. An investigation revealed that Tate had misappropriated upwards of $250,000. Making no distinction between public and private funds, he had lent money to government officials and others, and had speculated in mines and real estate. Impeached by the House of Representatives, he was tried in absentia, convicted, and removed from office. He never returned to Kentucky, and his whereabouts remained a mystery.

The so-called Tate defalcation aggravated the growing mistrust of government officials. When delegates assembled in 1890 and 1891 to write a new state constitution, the Tate experience was fresh in their minds. This fourth constitution prohibited the governor and other top officials from succeeding themselves in a second term. The ban remained in effect for more than a century.

Further Reading: Emmet W. Mittlebeeler, "The Great Kentucky Absconsion," *Filson Club History Quarterly* 27 (1953): 336–351.

Thomas H. Appleton, Jr.

TAUBENECK, HERMAN E. (?–?), chair of the People's Party National Committee (1891–1896). Taubeneck first rose to public attention in 1891, following his election to the Illinois General Assembly as one of three Independents whose votes would be decisive in determining the election for the U.S. Senate seat. As the legislative session bogged down in a protracted fight, Taubeneck won the gratitude of the agrarian reformers by his refusal to abandon their nominee, A. J. Streeter. Taubeneck's identification with the agrarian movement rested on his affiliation with the Farmers' Mutual Benefit Association; he had joined the Grange in 1876, but he had no association with the Farmers' Alliance. Indeed, he strongly disagreed with many of the principles advocated by Alliance members. Nevertheless, as a result of his actions in the Illinois legislature, Taubeneck rose to chair the Populists' National Committee at the party's organizing convention in Cincinnati, Ohio. Opponents suggested that Taubeneck's conservatism undermined the aims of the more agrarian element of the party, and certainly he played a critical role in championing free silver as the focus of the Populist movement. In 1896, the party repudiated his efforts and removed him from the chairmanship.

Further Reading: Peter H. Argersinger, ed., *Populism, Its Rise and Fall, William A Peffer*, 1992; Roy V. Scott, *The Agrarian Movement in Illinois, 1880–1896*, 1962.

Connie L. Lester

TAUSSIG, FRANK WILLIAM (28 December 1859–11 November 1940), economist. Taussig's name is synonymous with the economics of international trade theory and tariffs. A proponent of Alfred Marshall's neoclassicism, Taussig, born in St. Louis, Missouri, used his professorship at Harvard (1882–1935) to encourage American economics away from marginalism and institutionalism, and toward Cambridge neoclassicism. When Taussig surrendered his chair at Harvard, it was assumed by Joseph Schumpeter. Taussig's books include *The Tariff History of the United States* (1888), *Some Aspects of the Tariff Question* (1915), and *International Trade* (1927). Many of Taussig's noteworthy contributions to economics appeared in the *American Economic Review*—"The Interpretation of Ricardo" (1893), "The Relation Between Interest and Profits" (1894)—and the *Quarterly Journal of Economics*—"Some Aspects of the Tariff Question" (1889). He died in Cambridge, Massachusetts.

Further Reading: *New York Times*, 12 November 1940.

David O. Whitten

TAYLOR, GRAHAM (2 May 1851–26 September 1938), minister, educator, settlement house director, and civic reformer. Born in Schenectady, New York, Taylor graduated from the Theological Seminary of the Reformed Church in American at New Brunswick, New Jersey. During the 1870s, he served a Dutch Reformed church in rural New York, and in 1880 he moved to an inner-city Congregational church in Hartford, Connecticut, where he could experiment with Dwight L. Moody's evangelistic techniques. Hartford Theological Seminary took notice, and asked him to teach practical theology and prepare students for city missionary work. In 1892, the Chicago Theological Seminary chose Taylor to head its innovative department of Christian sociology. He accepted, and held that position until his retirement in 1924.

When Taylor moved his wife and four children to Chicago, he planned to live in a social settlement. The family and four seminary students launched Chicago Commons in 1894. Helped by other residents, they developed clubs, classes, a day nursery and kindergarten, and a weekly forum where neighborhood men discussed social and economic issues. In 1899, Taylor constructed a five-story building for the settlement. He started *The Commons*, a monthly magazine devoted to the settlement house movement, and was active in Chicago's Civic Federation and Municipal Voters' League in the 1890s. Early in the twentieth century Taylor and Charles Henderson of the University of Chicago developed a training school for social workers, and Taylor wrote a weekly column for the *Chicago Daily News* from 1902 until his death at Ravinia, Illinois.

Further Reading: Graham Taylor, *Pioneering on Social Frontiers*, 1930; Louise C. Wade, *Graham Taylor: Pioneer for Social Justice*, 1964; Graham Taylor Papers, Newberry Library, Chicago.

Louise Carrol Wade

TAYLOR, HANNIS (12 September 1851–27 December 1922), lawyer, diplomat, and legal scholar, was born in New Bern, North Carolina. Taylor completed a year at the University of North Carolina at Chapel Hill, read law, moved to Alabama, and was admitted to the bar there in February 1872. Over the next two decades he served as legal and financial adviser to the Mobile city government. He also researched legal history, in 1889 publishing the first volume of his *Origins and Growth of the English Constitution*. The book was a critical and a commercial success. On public policy, Taylor supported Henry Grady's New South program of industrial growth and sectional reconciliation. At that time, like most New South men, he was a Democrat. In 1893 President Grover Cleveland appointed him minister to Spain. Taylor had no diplomatic experience, spoke no Spanish, and did not fully understand Spanish resentment of America's New World interests. During his four years as minister, Taylor became increasingly imperialistic, unhappy with Cleveland's Cuban policy of nonintervention.

Following the Spanish-American War, Taylor twice ran for Congress—only to find that scholarly discussions of foreign policy did not move Alabama voters. In 1902 he secured a post in Washington with the Spanish Treaty Claims Commission; the following year he served on the Alaska Boundary Commission. By then he identified strongly with Theodore Roosevelt's nationalistic progressivism. A second volume of Taylor's *Origins and Growth . . .* appeared in 1898; he also produced articles and books synthesizing scholarship on the history of constitutional law. As counsel in *Cox* v. *Wood* (1918) Taylor challenged the World War I conscription law, and was much criticized. He died in Washington, D.C.

Further Reading: Tennant S. McWilliams, *Hannis Taylor: The New Southerner as an American*, 1978; *Cox* v. *Wood*, 247 *United States Reports* 3–7 (1918).

Paul M. Pruitt, Jr.

TAYLOR, ROBERT LOVE (31 July 1850– 31 March 1912), congressman and governor. Born in Carter County, Tennessee, Taylor studied in New Jersey and at the Buffalo Institute (Milligan College), in Milligan, Tennessee. Having read law before entering politics as a Democrat, he was elected to Congress in 1878, but defeated in 1880 and 1882. With strong rural support, he won his party's nomination for governor in 1886. He defeated his Republican opponent—his brother, Alfred Alexander Tay-

lor—in a colorful campaign called the "War of the Roses." Though Taylor retained his farmer followers, his appointments and policies took a decidedly New South cast. He favored tax and prison reform, and championed the Blair Bill, which offered federal aid to education. He alienated his party's conservative wing, but won a second term despite its opposition. After retiring in 1891, Taylor spent several profitable years on the lecture circuit, then won the governor's office for a third time in 1896, as a silverite. By then, party regulars viewed him as one who might moderate agrarian radicalism in Tennessee. Taylor achieved his long-sought goal of a U.S. Senate seat in 1907, winning the nomination in the state's first primary election. He served until his death, in Washington, D.C.

Further Reading: Daniel M. Robison, *Bob Taylor and the Agrarian Revolt in Tennessee*, 1935; Roger L. Hart, *Bourbons and Populists: Tennessee, 1870–1896*, 1978; Rupert B. Vance, "Tennessee's War of the Roses," *Virginia Quarterly Review* 16 (1940): 413–424.

Hutch Johnson

TELLER AMENDMENT. The Teller Amendment, named for Colorado Senator Henry M. Teller, was part of a Senate resolution passed 19 April 1898, authorizing use of U.S. military force to terminate Spanish sovereignty in Cuba and end an existing revolution on the island. It stated that the United States would not exercise sovereignty over the island or people of Cuba. The resolution precipitated the Spanish-American War when put into effect on 22 April 1898.

Further Reading: *Congressional Record*, 55th Congress, 2nd Session, 1898; Samuel Flagg Bemis, *A Diplomatic History of the United States*, 1947; Julius W. Pratt, *A History of United States Foreign Policy*, 1965.

Michael W. Vogt

TELLER, HENRY MOORE (30 May 1830– 23 February 1914), senator and secretary of the interior. Born in Allegheny County, New York, Teller attended academies in Alfred and Rushford, New York, was admitted to the New York bar, and then moved to Colorado in 1861. There he practiced mining law in Central City for the next fifteen years, and helped organize the Colorado Central Railroad. A confirmed antislavery Republican, he became one of the territory's best orators, and after statehood, turned that reputation into a Senate seat. He served from 1876 to 1882 and supported western interests on Indian and land policy. In 1882 President Chester A. Arthur named him secretary of the interior, a post in which he actively promoted the mining industry.

In 1885 Teller returned to the Senate, where he served until 1909, and became interested in the silver issue. He understood that the Colorado mining economy depended on the federal government's coinage of silver. He defended the Sherman Silver Purchase Act (1890) and fought its repeal in 1893. Three years later he left the Republican Party when the national convention endorsed the gold standard. As a Democrat, Teller defended states' rights. He opposed federal management of western resources, including Gifford Pinchot's forest reserves, believing them impediments to economic development. Though he was better known for oratory than for legislation, his most notable achievement was the 1898 Teller Amendment, which pledged U.S. support for an independent Cuba. He died in Denver, Colorado.

Further Reading: Henry M. Teller Papers, Colorado Historical Society, Denver; Elmer Ellis, *Henry Moore Teller, Defender of the West*, 1941.

Brad F. Raley

TERRELL, MARY CHURCH (23 September 1863–24 July 1954), civil rights activist. Born in Memphis, Tennessee, in relative affluence, "Mollie" Church graduated in 1884 from Oberlin College. In 1891, she married Robert Terrell, who later became a federal judge. Elected president of the National Association of Colored Women in 1896, over the more radical Ida B. Wells, Terrell promoted day care, mothers' clubs, and homes for elderly African Americans. Guided by the intellectual premises of the "black club women," Terrell became the first African-American woman to serve on the Washington, D.C., Board of Education (1895–1901). She introduced "Douglass Day" to encourage black students to take pride in their heritage.

In 1898, Terrell asked the National American Woman Suffrage Association to include black women in its efforts. Thirty years of lecturing to audiences of both races in Europe and the United States, including the Jim Crow South, led to publication of her essays in the *Boston Globe, Chicago Defender, Voice of the Negro,* and *North American Review.* Initially supportive of the "Tuskegee Machine" run by Booker T. Washington, who helped her husband to a judgeship, Terrell was an early convert to the more interventionist agenda of the National Association for the Advancement of Colored People. She died in Annapolis, Maryland.

Further Reading: Mary Church Terrell, *A Black Woman in a White World*, 1940; Paula Giddings, *When and Where I Enter: The Impact of Black Women on Race and Sex in America*, 1984; Terrell Papers, Library of Congress.

Barbara Ryan

TESLA, NIKOLA (10 July 1856–7 January 1943), electrical engineer. A Serbian born in Smiljan, Croatia (then part of the Austro-Hungarian Empire), Tesla studied at the Austrian Polytechnic University and in Prague, Czechoslovakia, before working in a telegraph office in Budapest, Hungary. He discovered the principle of the rotating magnetic field produced by two or more alternating currents out of step with each other. In 1882 he built the first successful alternating-current induction motor while working as an engineer for the Continental Edison Company in Paris.

Seeking greater opportunity, Tesla immigrated to New York in 1884 to work for Edison's Electric Company, which was, however, committed to direct-current electrical systems. Establishing his own company, Tesla developed and patented alternating-current, single- and polyphase induction motors for generating, transmitting, and utilizing electric current. In time his polyphase system came to generate and transmit nearly all of the world's electricity. By 1891 he had become one of the world's most celebrated scientists. Tesla's system illuminated the Chicago World's Columbian Exposition of 1893 and was employed to light the city of Buffalo in 1896. He invented the Tesla coil, a step-up transformer converting low-voltage high current to high-voltage low current at high frequencies, that subsequently was employed in radio and television. Negligent in patenting his inventions, Tesla spent the rest of his life in laboratory research, conducting imaginative, wide ranging-experiments with electricity. He died in New York City. His career reflected the Gilded Age's fascination with science, technology, and big business opportunities.

Further Reading: Margaret Cheney, *Tesla, Man Out of Time*, 1981; Inez Hunt and Wanetta Draper, *Lightning in His Hand: The Life Story of Nikola Tesla*, 1964; Nikola Tesla, *My Inventions: The Autobiography of Nikola Tesla*, 1982.

Charles W. Macune, Jr.

TEXAS v. *WHITE* (7 Wallace 700). A major issue following the Civil War concerned the status of legal matters in the rebellious states during and after the war. Specifically, did the rebellious state maintain the same status as states that did not rebel? In what is considered to be his most enduring statement, in December 1868 Chief Justice Salmon Chase wrote for the court majority that the Constitution, in all its provisions, sees an indestructible Union, composed of indestructible states. Chase made it clear that while the governments of the rebellious states turned against the federal government, this did not mean that the states themselves had withdrawn from the Union.

Texas v. *White* involved the question of whether federal bonds held by Texas before the war could be redeemed by private contractors on the basis of agreements made between them and the Confederate state government during the war. Because of the high interest rate involved in these agreements, Texas refused payment, and sued White and his associates, who held the bonds and sought redemption based on the original contracts. The constitutional issue involved whether Texas had the right to sue in federal court to recover losses from contracts signed by the state government during the war. By declaring that the state status of Texas remained unchanged, Chase ruled that Texas did have the right to sue. The government of Texas during the war, however, was declared illegal, and on that basis the Court ruled that the bond contracts were invalid. The decision was a 5–3 majority, with Justices Robert Cooper Grier, Noah H. Swayne, and Samuel F. Miller dissenting.

Further Reading: Charles Fairman, *History of the Supreme Court of the United States*, Vol. 6, *Reconstruction and Reunion, 1864–1888*, 1971, pp. 628–672; Louis Fisher, *American Constitutional Law*, 3rd ed., 1999, pp. 343–346.

Thomas C. Sutton

THAYER, JOHN MILTON (24 January 1820–19 March 1906), U.S. senator and governor. Born in Bellingham, Massachusetts, Thayer graduated from Brown University in 1841 and gained admittance to the bar the following year. He became a Republican in 1857 because he opposed the extension of slavery into the territories, especially Nebraska, to which he had moved in 1854. After service in the Union Army, he held a seat in the U.S. Senate from 1867 to 1871. A Radical Republican during Reconstruction, he advocated strong measures against the South, opposed President Andrew Johnson, supported President Ulysses S. Grant, and utilized his knowledge of Native American affairs to advise his colleagues on the subject. In 1875, President Grant appointed Thayer governor of Wyoming Territory, where he served until 1879. Seven years later he was elected the seventh governor of Nebraska, and he won reelection in 1888. As governor he followed the wishes of the state's Republican leaders.

Although not a candidate for a third term in 1890, Thayer challenged the election of James E. Boyd, a native of Ireland, contending he had not completed the naturalization process. Thayer at first refused to vacate the office when his term expired, but finally yielded to pressure on 15 January 1891. The Nebraska Supreme Court removed Boyd on 5 May 1891, allowing Thayer to return until a settlement could be reached. On 8 February 1892 the U.S. Supreme Court reversed the state's action, declared Boyd an American citizen, and reinstated him as governor. In the mid-1890s Thayer, a hard-money proponent, and William Jennings Bryan, a free silverite, engaged in a series of debates over the currency issue. Thayer died in Lincoln, Nebraska.

Further Reading: Earl G. Curtis, "John Milton Thayer," *Nebraska History* 29 (1948): 134–150; *Nebraska State Journal*, 20 March 1906.

Leonard Schlup

THAYER, WILLIAM MAKEPEACE (23 February 1820–7 April 1898), minister, editor, and author. Born in Franklin, Massachusetts, Thayer earned an undergraduate degree from Brown University in 1843. He taught school in his native state, studied theology with the Reverend Jacob Ide, and preached at Edgartown and Ashland, Massachusetts, before throat trouble ended his full-time ministerial career. As editor of *The Nation* from 1864 to 1868, a member of the Massachusetts General Court, and secretary of the Massachusetts State Temperance Alliance from 1860 to 1876, Thayer gained national attention. In his books, he stressed morals and the gospel of virtue and success. Among his Gilded Age publications were *Success and Its Achievers* (1891), *Turning Points in Successful Careers* (1895), *Men Who Win* (1896), and *Women Who Win* (1896). He died in Franklin, Massachusetts.

Further Reading: *New York Tribune*, 8 April 1898.

Leonard Schlup

THEATER AND ALLIED ARTS. The Gilded Age was one of great change for the American theater. Transcontinental railroads stimulated the growth of new theatrical markets along major lines and initially strengthened established regional theaters, particularly in the far West. The opening of the California Theatre, one of the nation's finest, in 1869 marked this process and reinforced the position of San Francisco as that region's theatrical center.

Most significant theatrical activity, however, remained in the East, where William Warren, Jr.'s, Boston Museum and Louisa Lane (Mrs. John) Drew's Arch Street Theatre in Philadelphia stood out as two of the best. New York City continued to be the theater capital, with James W. Wallack and Sons' Lyceum and John Augustin Daly's Theatre setting the age's artistic standard. Edwin Booth's Theatre and J. M. Steele MacKaye's Madison Square Theatre represented the cutting edge of theater and scenic technology.

Ultimately, the railroads contributed to further centralization of theatrical power in New York, as New York-based touring shows, complete with stars, supporting casts, and scenery, began to undermine most resident regional stock companies during the 1870s. By 1895, New York was the only American city still hosting important stock companies, and even these suffered as the traditional repertory system gave way to the "extended run," with successful new shows sometimes playing for more than one hundred consecutive performances. The practice made it economically difficult to employ stock actors not involved in the ongoing production. Taking advantage of these changes, a group of eastern businessmen headed by Charles Frohman and known collectively as "The Syndicate" virtually monopolized theatrical production and tour booking from 1896 until 1915.

Under these conditions the actor's lot declined, and not surprisingly, the best were associated with the few remaining resident companies. Edwin Booth, credited with popularizing the "natural" school of acting, is often considered the finest tragic actor of the age, followed by John McCullough and Booth's partner, Lawrence Barrett. Ada Rehan and Anne Hartley (Mrs. G. H.) Gilbert of Augustin Daly's company, both excelling in comic roles, stood out as the most popular actresses of the period. Even great talent, however, could not sustain the stock companies in the face of changing conditions, and most of the finest actors ended their careers either touring or retiring early.

With the extended run came a new emphasis on playwriting, as managers sought hit plays that could attract large audiences for sustained engagements. Bronson Howard, who achieved fame with *Saratoga* in 1870, is usually identified as America's first professional playwright. Other notable figures include William Gillette, author of the Civil War-based plays *Held by the Enemy* and *Secret Service*; James A. Herne, whose *Margaret Fleming* and *Shore Acres* set the standard for nineteenth-century American realism; and the prolific William Clyde Fitch, who in 1900–1901 had ten plays in professional production. Though realism dominated professional playwriting in America, comic writers such as Edward Harrigan, noted for his faithful portrayals of immigrant life, achieved some success, and *Uncle Tom's Cabin*, a melodrama adapted by numerous authors from Harriet Beecher Stowe's novel, remained the most popular and most produced play of the era, with fifty companies touring this show simultaneously. Under the grip of The Syndicate, American playwriting ceased to flourish around the turn of the century.

Other popular forms of theatrical activity included burlesque, which, following the success of Lydia Thompson's "British Blondes" in 1869, shifted its emphasis from parody to feminine sexuality and to vaudeville, variety shows composed of short, unrelated comic acts, which became a popular family entertainment in the 1880s. Finally, the 1866 premiere of *The Black Crook* marked the decline of the romantic ballet and established a vogue for dance "extravaganzas" incorporating song, large-scale spectacle, and lavish special effects. These forms remained popular well into the twentieth century.

Further Reading: Oscar G. Brockett, *History of the Theatre*, 8th ed., 1998; Arthur Quinn, *A History of the American Drama from the Civil War to the Present Day*, 2nd ed., 1949.

James Harley

THOMAS, THEODORE (11 October 1835–4 January 1905), conductor, educator, violinist. Born in Esens, Germany, Thomas immigrated with his family to the United States in 1845. In New York, Thomas, who had begun playing the violin at the age of two, performed with local theater and opera orchestras, and became a member of the New York Philharmonic Society in 1854. With the pianist William Mason he formed a chamber ensemble that presented monthly concerts in New York City and toured from 1855 to 1870.

Thomas considered himself a concert-hall educator, and through his work as a conductor he created an audience for symphonic music. He organized and conducted his first orchestra in 1862. The Theodore Thomas Orchestra was the first to introduce the American public to important new works by Richard Wagner, Antonin Dvorak, Franz Liszt, Johann Strauss, and Johannes Brahms, as well as works by American composers. To keep his orchestra together and ensure high performance standards, Thomas organized outdoor summer concerts and gave 1,227 programs in New York's Central Park from 1868 to 1875. In 1869 he began

yearly tours with his orchestra and guest soloists, including a transcontinental excursion in 1883. In addition to working with his own orchestra, Thomas conducted the Brooklyn Philharmonic from 1862 to 1891 and the New York Philharmonic Society Orchestra from 1877 to 1891. As part of his educational mission, Thomas began a series of young people's concerts and workingman's concerts in New York in 1884. He also organized and conducted the musical activities at the first biennial Cincinnati May Festival in 1873, the 1876 Centennial Exhibition in Philadelphia, and the World's Columbian Exposition at Chicago in 1892. Thomas organized a number of choral and music festivals in New York and other cities on his tour route, which became known as the "Thomas highway." From 1878 to 1880 he organized and directed the Cincinnati Musical College, declining an invitation to become the conductor of the London Philharmonic in 1880.

With the founding of the National Conservatory in New York, Thomas accepted the post of musical director and president of the short-lived American Opera Company. It toured from 1885 to 1887, featuring operas sung in English by American-born singers. Although the company received much critical acclaim and audience support, without the great European stars it was unable to attract the financial support of wealthy patrons.

In 1891, a group of prominent citizens invited Thomas to organize and conduct the Chicago Symphony, the second full-time orchestra in the United States. After forty years of conducting more than seven thousand concerts and opera performances in more than two hundred cities, Thomas died in Chicago.

Further Reading: Theodore Thomas Collection, Newberry Library, Chicago; Theodore Thomas, *A Musical Autobiography*, ed. George P. Upton, 1905; Ezra Schabas, *Theodore Thomas: America's Conductor and Builder of Orchestras, 1835–1905*, 1989.

Leslie Petteys

THOMAS, WILLIAM HANNIBAL (4 May 1843–15 November 1935), African-American preacher, lawyer, journalist, and author. Descended from free mulattoes, Thomas was born free in Pickaway County, Ohio. He performed farm labor, attended school briefly, and in 1859 broke the color barrier at Otterbein University in Westerville, Ohio. His enrollment led to a race riot, and Thomas soon left the school. Initially denied entrance to the Union Army in 1861 because of his color, Thomas labored as a servant before being allowed to fight. In February 1865, he received a gunshot wound in his right arm that led to its amputation. After the war, Thomas studied theology, contributed to religious newspapers, and raised money for African-American schools. In the early 1870s, he went south to run a freedmen's school in Rome, Georgia, and later served on the faculty at Clark University in Atlanta. Thomas next moved to Newberry, South Carolina, where he practiced law, and was appointed trial justice and colonel in the state militia. In the contested 1876 campaign Thomas was elected as a Republican to the state legislature. He lost his seat when Governor Wade Hampton and the "Bourbon" Democrats took office in 1877.

In 1878 President Rutherford B. Hayes appointed Thomas U.S. consul at São Paulo de Luanda, Portuguese West Africa (now Angola). Over the next two decades he moved to Boston and published widely. In 1886 Thomas launched a magazine, *The Negro*, which failed. In 1890 he published *Land and Education*, urging African Americans to help themselves though prayer, education, and land acquisition. During the 1890s Thomas grew increasingly critical of his race. His pessimism appeared full blown in 1901, when he published *The American Negro*. In this work Thomas distanced himself from other African Americans and attacked the race, especially women, relentlessly. No contemporary white critic assaulted the race with as much crude venom, blaming blacks, not whites, for the "Negro problem." *The American Negro* received widespread national attention. It appealed to white racists and served to unify African Americans against one whom they deemed an infamous hypocrite and traitor. Thomas died in obscurity in Columbus, Ohio.

Further Reading: John David Smith, *Black Judas: William Hannibal Thomas and the American Negro*, 2000.

John David Smith

THOMSON, JOHN EDGAR (10 February 1808–27 May 1874), railroad president. Born

in Springfield, Pennsylvania, Thomson had little formal education, but his father, a surveyor, taught him engineering. After working for a number of railroads, Thomson joined the Pennsylvania as chief engineer in 1847. He was named president in 1852, when the railroad was struggling to complete its line over the Allegheny Mountains to Pittsburgh. Under Thomas, the Pennsylvania eventually became one of the most profitable and most powerful railroads in the United States. After purchasing the state system of railroads and canals in 1857, the Pennsylvania extended its route westward from Pittsburgh to Chicago. In the 1870s, it also expanded along the eastern seaboard by purchasing a line to New York Harbor and building a branch between Baltimore and Washington. In addition, the Pennsylvania under Thomson started a transatlantic steamship line based in Philadelphia and invested heavily in southern railroads. Thomas made the Pennsylvania into a well-managed, highly profitable, aggressive corporation. His vision for the railroad largely shaped the Pennsylvania throughout the Gilded Age. Thomas was also active in Philadelphia's public life, serving as a member of the Fairmont Park Commission. He died in Philadelphia.

Further Reading: George H. Burgess and Miles C. Kennedy, *Centennial History of the Pennsylvania Railroad Company*, 1949; *Philadelphia Public Ledger*, 29 May 1874; Penn Central Collection, Hagley Museum and Library, Wilmington, Delaware.

John H. Hepp IV

THURMAN, ALLEN GRANBERRY (13 November 1813–12 December 1895), U.S. senator and Democratic vice presidential nominee. Born in Lynchburg, Virginia, Thurman spent his boyhood in Ohio, opened a law practice at Chillicothe in 1835, and in 1844 won a seat as a Democrat in the U.S. House of Representatives (1845–1847). He supported his party on most issues except internal improvements and frequently revealed his bias against African Americans, on occasion referring to them as "degraded beings." In 1851 voters elected Thurman to the Ohio Supreme Court, where he served one term. A Union Democrat during the Civil War, Thurman seemed more willing to prosecute the war, while criticizing some of President Abraham Lincoln's policies, than to emancipate the slaves. Defeated for the Ohio governorship in 1867, he secured election the next year to the U.S. Senate, where he castigated the Reconstruction policies of President Ulysses S. Grant, opposed the Fifteenth Amendment, and carefully shifted his positions on the vexatious currency question. He displayed only mild enthusiasm for civil service reform and urged a peaceful resolution to the disputed presidential election of 1876. Unsuccessful in his bid for a third senatorial term, Thurman in 1881 resumed his law practice in Columbus and accepted his appointment by President James A. Garfield to the International Monetary Conference in Paris. Known as "Old Roman," Thurman, at age seventy-five, emerged as Grover Cleveland's vice presidential running mate, a choice by the president's advisers that dismayed voters but provided geographical balance for the ticket. The Cleveland-Thurman slate lost to the Republican Benjamin Harrison. A Jeffersonian and Jacksonian in political philosophy, Thurman adhered to a strict constructional interpretation of the Constitution regarding national government prerogatives. He died in Columbus.

Further Reading: John S. Hare, "Allen G. Thurman: A Political Study," Ph.D. diss., The Ohio State University, 1933; *New York Times*, 13 December 1895; *Columbus Evening Press*, 13 December 1895; Allen G. Thurman Papers, Ohio Historical Society Library, Columbus.

Leonard Schlup

THURSTON, JOHN MELLEN (21 August 1847–9 August 1916), U.S. senator. Born in Montpelier, Vermont, Thurston relocated with his parents to Madison, Wisconsin, in 1854; graduated from Wayland University at Beaver Dam, Wisconsin; and gained admission to the bar in 1869. Shortly thereafter he opened a law practice in Omaha, Nebraska. After holding various local government positions, Thurston was appointed assistant attorney of the Union Pacific Railroad in 1877 and its general solicitor in 1888. A presidential elector on the Republican ticket of Garfield and Arthur in 1880, Thurston served in the U.S. Senate from 1895 to 1901; he chose not to seek reelection. During the political controversy over the contentious currency issue in the 1890s, Thurston, a sound money politician, debated the Democrat William Jennings Bryan, the exponent of free silver. Thurston chaired the Senate Committee on Indian Affairs. In 1901 he accepted a presidential appointment as U.S. commissioner to the Saint Louis Exposition. He died in Omaha, Nebraska.

Further Reading: *New York Times*, 10 August 1916.

Leonard Schlup

THWAITES, REUBEN GOLD (15 May 1853–22 October 1913), historian and librarian. Born in Dorchester, Massachusetts, Thwaites was tutored at home by his mother in Madison, Wisconsin, and in 1874 and 1875 did graduate study at Yale College. From 1876 to 1886, he served as managing editor of the *Wisconsin State Journal*. He is best remembered, however, as superintendent of the Wisconsin State Historical Society, his career position. Thwaites systematized and enriched the society's library holdings, and insisted that it promote public education by collecting local history materials. Under his guidance its publications, including his own studies of Indians, fur traders, and others with memories of a vanishing pioneer past, became models for other western states. Thwaites wrote the standard state history, *The Story of Wisconsin*, fourteen other books, and more than one hundred articles and addresses. He edited over 160 books as well, many of unique historical documents, such as *The Jesuit Relations and Allied Documents*. Thwaites also held ranking positions in the American Historical Association and the American Library Association. He died in Madison, Wisconsin.

Further Reading: Frederick Jackson Turner, *Reuben Gold Thwaites: A Memorial Address*, 1914; Clifford L. Lord, *Reuben Gold Thwaites and the Progressive Historical Society*, n.d.

Philip H. Young

TILDEN, SAMUEL J. (9 February 1814–4 August 1886), governor, lawyer, presidential candidate. Tilden was born to a comfortable New Lebanon, New York, family. He received a law degree in 1841 from the City College of

New York. Active in local politics, Tilden was elected to the state legislature while concurrently building a reputation as a trial lawyer specializing in railroad litigation. Tilden opposed Abraham Lincoln's election, and worked in Washington, D.C., during the Civil War organizing Democratic opposition to the Radical Republicans in Congress. After the war Tilden headed the New York State Democratic committee (1866–1874). He earned distinction battling graft and corruption in New York City and helped expose the illegal activities of city boss William Marcy Tweed. Tilden's increasing political stature propelled him to the governor's seat (1875–1877). His reputation as a reformer earned him the Democratic nomination for president against the Republican Rutherford B. Hayes in 1876. Tilden received a plurality of 250,000 popular votes. A partisan commission, however, awarded twenty-two disputed electoral votes from four states to Hayes, thus securing him the presidency. Tilden retired to a Yonkers, New York, estate in 1879. He died there, leaving $5 million to build free public libraries, but heirs successfully broke the trust and took most of the money.

Further Reading: Alexander C. Flick, *Samuel Jones Tilden*, 1939; Lloyd Robinson, *The Stolen Election: Hayes Versus Tilden, 1876*, 1968.

Michael W. Vogt

TIMBER AND STONE ACT (21 Stat. 89). In 1878 Congress, having provided for the sale of virtually all other types of public lands, on 3 June passed the Timber and Stone Act to dispose of timberlands in the Pacific states (California, Oregon, Nevada, and Washington Territory). Not surprisingly, just as cattle raisers abused the Homestead and Desert Land acts, so lumber companies took advantage of the loose procedures under this law. They pressured lumberjacks to file claims, then assign them to their employers. Companies thereby amassed large holdings of timberlands.

Further Reading: Paul W. Gates, *History of Public Land Law Development*, 1968.

Sam S. Kepfield

TIMBER CULTURE ACT (18 Stat. 451). This legislation of 3 March 1873 amended land laws to provide that any person who planted trees on forty acres (later reduced to ten acres) for ten years would receive title to that land. Initially, the act proved quite popular, and over nine million acres were entered in Kansas, Nebraska, and the Dakotas alone between 1873 and 1880. The law was based on the theory that planting more trees on the semiarid Great Plains would increase rainfall, thus improving the area's agricultural potential. In this respect, it was an eastern concept writ large—that the Plains constituted an inferior region that could be made truly habitable only by remaking it in the image of the Atlantic coastal states. The act ultimately proved of questionable value in patenting land, for title to only nine million acres was actually proved up by 1904. The act was repealed in 1891.

Further Reading: Gilbert C. Fite, *The Farmer's Frontier*, 1966; Paul Wallace Gates, *History of Public Land Law Development*, 1968.

Sam S. Kepfield

TIMKEN, HENRY (16 August 1831–16 March 1909), inventor and industrialist. Born in Bremen, Germany, Timken immigrated to St. Louis, Missouri, as a child, and later became an apprentice wagon and carriage builder. By age twenty-four, he had his own carriage factory, earning a reputation for quality construction and modern, efficient manufacturing techniques. Timken rose to captain in the Union Army. Shortly after the Civil war he achieved national recognition and financial success with a system of carriage springs designed to cushion the ride over rough roads. He received twelve carriage patents, retired wealthy at the age of fifty-six, and spent five years traveling and relaxing before launching the project for which he is remembered today.

Timken tried to develop carriage bearings modeled after the ball bearings that helped sustain the bicycle craze of the 1880s. Although fine for bicycles, ball bearings were not sturdy enough for heavy wagons. Roller bearings could support more weight, but they could not resist the lateral forces exerted when carriages navigated curves. In 1898, Timken received two patents for improved bearings that employed tapered rollers assembled to resist forces from any direction. In the same year, he was invited to judge the first U.S. automobile race, which took place in Chicago. Timken foresaw that the automobile would eventually replace the carriage, so he urged his sons William and Henry to move the bearing company closer to steel producers in Pittsburgh and to automakers in Cleveland and Detroit. In 1901, the sons opened a bearing manufacturing facility in Canton, Ohio, where the international company is still headquartered. At the time of Timken's death in San Diego, California, his company employed twelve hundred workers and produced more than 850,000 bearings a year. Timken was inducted into the National Inventors Hall of Fame in 1998. By then the company had grown to employ twenty-one thousand people worldwide and reported sales of $2.6 billion.

Further Reading: *Los Angeles Daily Times*, 17 March 1909.

Jim Quinn

TODD, MABEL LOOMIS (10 November 1856–14 October 1932), author and editor. Born in Cambridge, Massachusetts, Todd was educated in private schools in Cambridge and Georgetown, D.C. She also studied at the New England Conservatory of Music. After her marriage in 1879, Todd moved to western Massachusetts when her husband was appointed to the Amherst College faculty. There, she soon became closely acquainted with the college's treasurer, Austin Dickinson, and, through him, came to be friends with his reclusive sisters, Lavinia and Emily. When Emily Dickinson died in 1886, her sister found more than eight hundred poems written by Emily over the years. Lavinia turned to Todd in the hopes that some of the poems might be published. By 1891 Todd, along with Thomas Wentworth Higginson, had published the first two volumes of the poetry of Emily Dickinson. Alone, she compiled a third volume in 1896, by which time she had also brought out two collections of Dickinson's correspondence. In addition, Todd published several of her own works, both fiction and nonfiction, including *Total Eclipses of the Sun* (1894). She died on Hog Island, Maine.

Further Reading: Polly Longsworth, *Austin and Mabel: The Amherst Affair and Love Letters of Austin Dickinson*

and Mabel Loomis Todd, 1999; Sharon N. White, "Mabel Loomis Todd: Gender, Language and Power in Victorian America," Ph.D. diss., Yale University, 1982.

Kathleen Banks Nutter

TOMBSTONE. Founded and named in 1879 by Edward Schieffelin, a prospector, whose friends warned that he would find his grave rather than mines, Tombstone, a community in the southeastern part of the Arizona Territory, grew rapidly during its early years. Because of silver mining booms, approximately fifty-five hundred people resided there by 1882. Nicknamed "The Town Too Tough to Die," Tombstone became synonymous with lawlessness in the West. The notorious O.K. Corral gunfight occurred there in 1881 when the Earp brothers clashed with the Clantons and McLaurys. Underground water flooded the mineshafts in 1883. Ten years later, when mining activities slowed, the population started to decrease. Along with the facts and fiction surrounding the Superstition Mountain near Apache Junction, the prospector Jacob Waltz, and the eccentric Elisha Reavis, better known as the "Madman of the Superstitions," Tombstone and other historic sites in that region offer a rich experience in Gilded Age frontier life for modern tourists.

Further Reading: Walter N. Burns, *Tombstone: An Iliad of the Southwest*, 1999; William B. Shillingberg, *Tombstone, Arizona Territory: A History of Early Mining, Milling and Mayhem*, 1999; Robert J. Allen, *The Story of Superstition Mountain and the Lost Dutchman Mine*, 1971.

Leonard Schlup

TOMPKINS SQUARE RIOT OF 1874. During the nineteenth century, urban workers came to depend on the factory for their livelihood. After the Civil War, industry grew more rapidly than did the power to regulate it. In flush times the imbalance did not hurt workers, but in a depression they lacked a safety net. During the last third of the century, workers urged state and federal governments to give them jobs in lean years. In 1873 a depression threw millions out of work in the United States. Those in New York City petitioned the city to hire them for public works, but civic leaders refused even to meet with them because some of the jobless advocated unions and socialism. Suspicion of them led officials to refuse them a permit to rally at Tompkins Square. Police, however, told them of the refusal only after seven thousand unemployed had packed the square. Before the crowd could disperse, mounted police charged it, clubbing immigrant women and children. Police commissioner Abram Duryée praised the violence as "the most glorious sight I ever saw," but labor leader Samuel Gompers denounced it as "an orgy of brutality."

Further Reading: David Montgomery, *The Fall of the House of Labor: The Workplace, the State, and American Labor Activism, 1865–1925*, 1987.

Christopher Cumo

TOWNE, CHARLES ARNETTE (21 November 1858–22 October 1928), lawyer, congressman, and free silverite. Born near Pontiac, Michigan, Towne graduated from the University of Michigan in 1881 and gained admittance to the bar in 1885. Five years later, he moved to Duluth, Minnesota. From 1893 to 1895, he was that state's judge advocate general. In 1894, Towne won election as a Republican to the U.S. House of Representatives, where he championed free silver. His House speech of 8 February 1896 on the subject was published in pamphlet form and distributed widely. He ran unsuccessfully for reelection as an independent in 1896 and 1898. Towne obtained the 1900 vice presidential nomination of the Silver Republicans and Populists, but subsequently declined both in order to allow the Democratic presidential contender, William Jennings Byran, to head three tickets with Adlai E. Stevenson as his running mate. Minnesota governor John Lind appointed Towne to fill a Senate vacancy, and he served as a Democrat from 5 December 1900 to 28 January 1901. Towne's speech on his last day, advocating Philippine independence, attracted wide attention. He then moved to New York City, where he practiced law, served in the U.S. House of Representatives from 1905 to 1907, and remained active in Democratic politics. Towne died in Tucson, Arizona.

Further Reading: Leonard Schlup, "Charles A. Towne and the Vice-Presidential Question of 1900," *North Dakota History* 44 (1977): 14–20; *Minneapolis Journal*, 23 October

1928; Charles A. Towne, "Reasons for Democratic Success," *Forum* 30 (1900): 275–285.

Leonard Schlup

TRACY, BENJAMIN FRANKLIN (26 April 1830–6 August 1915), lawyer and secretary of the navy. Born in Owego, New York, Tracy studied law on his own and was admitted to the bar at age twenty-one. He won elections as Tioga Country district attorney and as state assemblyman. During the Civil War, he rose to brigadier general and was nominated for the Congressional Medal of Honor. After the war, Tracy resumed his law practice. He served both as U.S. district attorney for the Eastern District of New York and as chief justice of the state court of appeals. In 1889, President Benjamin Harrison appointed Tracy secretary of the navy, partly to placate Thomas Platt, leader of the Republican Party in New York and Tracy's mentor. Tracy and Harrison soon became close friends. Tracy helped modernize the navy. Inspired by the writings of Alfred Thayer Mahan, he called for the construction of battleships and for extraterritorial naval bases. He also strengthened the Naval War College's independence. Tracy organized the first U.S. Navy "squadron of evolution." His efforts ensured that the navy was prepared for the coming war with Spain. Tracy left office in 1893 and devoted the rest of his life to legal work. In 1897 he was an unsuccessful candidate for mayor of New York City, where he died.

Further Reading: Walter R. Herrick, "General Tracy's Navy," Ph.D. diss., University of Virginia, 1962; and "Benjamin F. Tracy," in *American Secretaries of the Navy*, Vol. 1, *1775–1913*, ed. Paolo E. Coletta, 1980.

Spencer C. Tucker

TRADE AND COMMERCE. Between 1868 and 1901 the American economy nearly quadrupled its industrial production. Agriculture, the second largest economic activity, grew at only half that rate. Population doubled through immigration. Wealth became increasingly concentrated in the hands of private financial capitalists who encouraged consolidation, centralization, and the development of managerial capitalism. This transformation affected the country's social, economic, and political organization.

The rapid advent of the rail transportation network fueled the growth of steel mills, mining, smelting, management, accounting, and financial activities. Railroad growth furthered a huge extension of the marketplace, cheaper transportation rates, and the development of a constantly growing commercial agricultural sector. The railroads' geographic scale and scope initiated new styles of management and new structures to account for costs and revenues. These new managerial forms linked ideas of national markets and international exports to a need for government action to facilitate trade, or to intervene in support of either the industrialist or the farmer.

Government policy teetered between these two economic blocs. Congress created a regressive tax policy favoring savers and investors by increasing the consumer tariff. It also aided commercial growth through its reluctance to put limits on business activities. The Constitution implied power in the states to protect the health, welfare, and morals of citizens, an interpretation reflected in the Granger laws, which mandated equal rail fares for all users. However, by the 1880s this broad view of state power was breached. By 1900, state regulation was subordinate to federal law, and Congress and the president limited the ability of government at any level to regulate business.

A third economic activity of the Gilded Age was the growth of individual economic/financial bankers. Financing the Civil War, and later capitalizing the railroads, gave American bankers a greater role. J. P. Morgan was the supreme example of this breed. The house of Morgan grew to serve as a substitute for a central bank. Unregulated capitalism marked the era.

The rapid growth of manufacturing, agriculture, mining, and construction led in the 1890s to an aggressive search for more markets. This effort coincided with government's push to develop the navy. Alfred Thayer Mahan's *Influence of Sea Power upon History* (1890) reflected the wish to extend influence through markets, naval bases, and the dissemination of the American conception of freedom.

Further Reading: Alfred D. Chandler, *The Visible Hand*, 1977; David F. Noble, *America by Design*, 1977; Ron Chernow, *The House of Morgan*, 1990.

A. Jacqueline Swansinger

TREATY OF PARIS. The 1898 Treaty of Paris officially ended the Spanish-American-Cuban War, launched an era of American imperialism, and signaled the emergence of the United States as a formidable world power. It also initiated a number of diplomatic problems that vexed the United States throughout the twentieth century. Under the treaty's terms, Cuba gained its independence, and the United States annexed Puerto Rico and Guam, and purchased the Philippines from Spain for $20 million.

The United States Senate ratified the treaty on 6 February 1899, by a 57–27 vote, one more than the required two-thirds majority, after much lobbying by President William McKinley. The surprising support of Democrat William Jennings Bryan, McKinley's longtime rival, may have influenced a few key voters. More significant was news that the Filipinos had revolted against the United States, which ensured that the treaty would pass.

The United States struggled to control each of the nations obtained through this treaty. The Filipinos, led by Emilio Aguinaldo, engaged the Americans in guerrilla warfare that, over three years, proved more costly in American casualties and expense than the Spanish-American-Cuban War. Although the Treaty of Paris called for Cuban independence, the U.S. Congress stifled that independence with the Platt Amendment, passed in 1901 and ultimately written into the Cuban Constitution. The Platt provision allowed the United States to intervene in Cuban affairs whenever Cuban independence was threatened, as well as to maintain a military base at Guantánamo Bay. American attempts to meddle in Cuban affairs were met with resistance until 1934, when both Cuba and the United States abrogated the Platt Amendment. Puerto Rico and Guam, while beneficiaries of association with the United States, also have wrestled with the issue of status: whether to become states or independent nations, or to remain something in between.

Through the Treaty of Paris, the imperial powers of Spain and, more important, the United States, imposed their will upon less powerful nations. None of the former Spanish colonies were represented at the peace talks, though clearly the Cubans and Filipinos, at least, played a role in defeating the Spaniards. The treaty enhanced America's global power status, but it also saddled the nation with possessions that proved difficult and costly to control, and led some nations to question the sincerity of the traditionally proclaimed American ideals of independence and self-determination.

Further Reading: Walter LaFeber, *The American Age: U.S. Foreign Policy at Home and Abroad*, Vol. 1, *To 1920*, 1994; John William Tebbel, *America's Great Patriotic War with Spain*, 1996; David Traxel, *1898: The Birth of the American Century*, 1998.

Kevin B. Witherspoon

TREATY OF WASHINGTON (1871). It took some years after the end of the Civil War for the United States and Great Britain to settle their differences in the Treaty of Washington. Tensions had existed since the American Revolution, but excepting the War of 1812, they were never as severe as during the Civil War. Grievances were abundant on both sides. The United States resented Whitehall's pro-Confederate stance, and while no formal recognition or alliance was made, Britain built ships for the Confederacy, notably the *Alabama*, which had disrupted American shipping during the war. Anglophobic American politicians, led by Senator Charles Sumner, claimed that British behavior had prolonged the war by two years. The British for their part were angry at American sympathy for the Fenian Brotherhood that in 1866 attacked Canada from Vermont, in pursuit of Irish independence. The dispatch of American troops to the Canadian border to stop the invasion appeared to the British to be a halfhearted effort, made all the more suspect by American demands for Canada as compensation for Britain's damage to American commerce during the war.

These mutual grievances were the subject of a joint commission that framed the Treaty of Washington on 8 May 1871. Britain expressed its regrets for allowing Confederate raiders to leave British shipyards to be outfitted abroad. Both countries agreed to establish a tribunal to determine claims. Ultimately, the United States accepted payment of a modest $15.5 million, a solution that was credited to the statesmanship of Secretary of State Hamilton Fish.

Further Reading: Allan Nevins, *Hamilton Fish: The Inner History of the Grant Administration*, 1936; Rupert C. Jarvis, "The *Alabama* and the Law," *Transactions of the Historic Society of Lancaster and Chesire*, 3 (1959): 181–198; Adrian Cook, *The Alabama Claims: American Politics and Anglo-American Relations, 1865–1872*, 1975.

Lawrence S. Kaplan

TRUEBLOOD, BENJAMIN FRANKLIN (25 November 1847–26 October 1916), educator, editor, peace activist. Born in Salem, Indiana, Trueblood graduated from Earlham College in 1869. That fall he became professor of classics at Penn College in Iowa, and by 1879 was its president. Yearning for a role in the peace movement, Trueblood resigned in 1890 to become an overseas agent for the Christian Arbitration and Peace Society. In 1892, he left Europe to become secretary of the American Peace Society. Trueblood's twenty-three-year tenure there made him a leading member of the national peace movement. Along with the society's president, Edwin D. Mead, Trueblood helped attract men of wealth, social standing, and organizing ability. He sought to make the peace movement a more respectable endeavor.

Under his guidance, society membership grew from four hundred to close to eight thousand members, and subscribers to its journal, *The Advocate of Peace*, rose dramatically from fifteen hundred to over eleven thousand. Trueblood wrote most of the editorials and many of the articles. Though adding few new ideas to peace thought, Trueblood promoted support for the Hague Peace Conferences, the Permanent Court of Arbitration, and arbitration treaties. He publicized his views in *The Federation of the World* (1899). He also urged that the Permanent Court of Arbitration be made into a World Court. Trueblood represented the American Peace Society at many of the Universal Peace Congresses held in Europe. He also assisted in organizing the Lake Mohonk (New York) Conferences on International Arbitration, held from the 1890s to the World War I period. He died at Newton Heights, Massachusetts.

Further Reading: Calvin D. Davis, *The United States and the First Hague Peace Conference*, 1962, and *The United*

States and the Second Hague Peace Conference, 1976; David S. Patterson, *Toward a Warless World: The Travail of the American Peace Movement, 1887–1914*, 1976.

Charles F. Howlett

TRUMAN, JOHN ANDERSON (5 December 1851–3 November 1914), farmer and livestock dealer. John A. Truman, indomitable father of President Harry S Truman, was born in Jackson County, Missouri, the son of a minor slaveholder. He moved to Lamar in 1882, and to Harrisonville three years later. An astute horse and mule trader and dealer with a quick temper, Truman earned a reputation as a person who never passed a cow without trying to purchase the animal. He was also interested in politics. In 1884, he won a $75 bet on the outcome of the presidential election. A strong-willed and fiercely loyal Democrat, Truman conveyed his political passion to his son, Harry, who in 1892 attended a local Democratic rally with his father, wearing a white "Cleveland and Stevenson" cap proclaiming his support of the national Democratic ticket. Ironically, sixty years later President Truman endorsed the presidential candidacy of Illinois governor Adlai E. Stevenson, grandson of Vice President Adlai E. Stevenson, whom both Trumans admired for his shrewd political instincts. In fact, President Truman confessed in his memoirs that the first Stevenson possessed more political savvy than his namesake. John Truman died in Kansas City, Missouri.

Further Reading: Richard Lawrence Miller, *Truman: The Rise to Power*, 1986; David McCullough, *Truman*, 1992; Leonard Schlup, "The Political Letters of the Second Adlai E. Stevenson to Harry S Truman in 1952," *Manuscripts* 44 (1992): 205–218.

Leonard Schlup

TRUMBULL, LYMAN (12 October 1813–25 June 1896), senator and lawyer. Born in Colchester, Connecticut, Trumbull spent most of his life in Illinois political and legal circles. He played key roles during the Civil War and Reconstruction, and enjoyed a second career during the Gilded Age. As an anti-Nebraska Democrat, he defeated Abraham Lincoln for a U.S. Senate seat in 1855 and served until 1873. As an ally, Trumbull worked for Lincoln's presidential nomination in 1860. He chaired the Senate Judiciary Committee and wrote the Thirteenth Amendment and the Civil Rights Act of 1866. He opposed Andrew Johnson's Reconstruction policies, but he was one of only seven Republicans who voted for acquittal at Johnson's trial. By 1872, Trumbull, disenchanted with Reconstruction, Grant, and the Republican establishment, joined the Liberal Republican Party and competed for its presidential nomination. After the failure of the Liberals, he returned to the Democratic Party, serving as a legal counsel for Samuel Tilden in the disputed election of 1876. He established a law practice in Chicago, and was an unsuccessful Democratic candidate for governor of Illinois in 1880. Trumbull grew increasingly radical in his political and economic views and by 1890 supported Populist ideas. In 1895 he worked with Clarence Darrow, defending Eugene Debs against charges arising from the Pullman strike. He died in Chicago.

Further Reading: Mark M. Krug, *Lyman Trumbull: Conservative Radical*, 1965; Ralph J. Roske, *His Own Counsel: The Life and Times of Lyman Trumbull*, 1979; Horace White, *Lyman Trumbull*, 1913.

Mario R. DiNunzio

TRUSTS. A trust is a legal arrangement, rooted in English law, granting one person control, or nominal ownership, of property to be managed in the interest of another. The term assumed a new meaning during the era of falling prices, ruinous competition, and recurring depressions between the 1870s and the 1890s. America's emerging corporations initially used agreements fixing prices or dividing markets to ease competition. These were inherently fragile, however, for they failed to end attempts to win market advantages through evasion and they lacked effective mechanisms for enforcement. John D. Rockefeller's formation of the Standard Oil Trust in 1879 offered a new twist. Participating companies exchanged shares of their stock for certificates of ownership in the trust, in proportion to their size. In turn, a group of trustees fixed prices, production, and markets. Standard controlled 90 percent of the nation's refining capacity. Its form and domination stabilized the industry and stimulated popular use of the term "trust" to denote big business and monopoly.

After New Jersey and several other states began in 1888 to legalize holding companies, they became the favored means of business combination. Incorporated to own the stock of other firms and thereby unite them, they included such monopolies as the American Sugar Refining Company, the Distilling and Cattle Feeding Company, and the American Tobacco Company. Business consolidation boomed with recovery from the depression of the 1890s. Annually, 301 corporations became parts of giant firms between 1898 and 1902, 14 percent through acquisition and the rest through holding company growth. Nearly all were monopolistic in intent. Displacing other forms of combination, they, too, became targets of antitrust feeling that attended the rise of big business during the Gilded Age.

Further Reading: John Moody, *The Truth About the Trusts*, 1904; Naomi R. Lamoreaux, *The Great Merger Movement in American Business, 1895–1904*, 1985; Stuart Bruchey, *Enterprise: The Dynamic Economy of a Free People*, 1990.

Douglas Steeples

TUCKER, BENJAMIN RICKETSON (17 April 1854–22 June 1939), anarchist. Born in South Dartmouth, Massachusetts, Tucker studied at the Massachusetts Institute of Technology, reading works of philosophers, economists, historians, political scientists, and social reformers. In 1872 he met Josiah Warren and William B. Greene, pioneers of individual anarchism, and converted to their cause. Between 1881 and 1908 he published a broadsheet, *Liberty*, which served as a clearinghouse for unorthodox thought. He also honed his polemic skills working for the *Boston Globe* and later serving as editor of *Engineering Magazine* in New York City. Tucker's outspoken individual anarchism brought little trouble with the law. He disapproved of violence, deplored the methods of Johann Most and Alexander Berkman, and carefully distinguished his brand of anarchism from the anarchist communism of Mikhail Bakunin. In 1899, Tucker addressed the Chicago Civic Federation's Conference on Trusts, using the forum to discuss the anarchist

position on monopolies in the United States. After vigilantes destroyed his New York headquarters in 1908, Tucker removed to France. He died in Pont Ste. Devote, Monaco.

Further Reading: Benjamin R. Tucker, *Instead of a Book, by a Man Too Busy to Write One*, 1893; J. J. Martin, *Men Against the State*, 1953; E. M. Schuster, *Native American Anarchism*, 1932; *New York Times*, 23 June 1939.

Leonard Schlup

TURNER, FREDERICK JACKSON (14 November 1861–14 March 1932), historian. Born in Portage, Wisconsin, Turner received B.A. and M.A. degrees from the University of Wisconsin (1884, 1888), and the Ph.D. from The Johns Hopkins University (1890). A brilliant speaker, as a graduate student he was an instructor in rhetoric and oratory and history, but preferred the latter. Appointed assistant professor at Wisconsin in 1889, he took charge of the history program later that year. During the 1890s, he became a member of the group that guided the American Historical Association, and began to train graduate students who spread his ideas. Talented and ambitious, Turner realized that the history of western America was neglected, and decided to specialize in it. He developed a course in American economic and social history, and in 1895 renamed it "History of the West." It became a prototype for many courses elsewhere.

In 1893 Turner delivered a paper at the meeting of the American Historical Association titled "The Significance of the Frontier in American History." He maintained that the cheap lands of the American West and the movement of people to occupy them largely explained American history and accounted for the nation's democratic institutions and people. The imminent exhaustion of the public lands, he suggested, might have far-reaching consequences. This frontier hypothesis became a popular explanation of American development and character that was debated throughout the twentieth century. Turner also suggested that the interaction of settlers with the environment produced sections of the country whose spokesmen negotiated with each other to shape national policy. Of Turner's four books elaborating these ideas, *The Significance of Sections in American History* won the 1932 Pulitzer Prize. A professor at Harvard from 1910 to 1924, Turner died in Pasadena, California.

Further Reading: Allan G. Bogue, *Frederick Jackson Turner: Strange Roads Going Down*, 1998.

Allan G. Bogue

TURNEY, PETER (27 September 1827–28 October 1903), Tennessee Supreme Court chief justice and governor. Born in Jasper, Tennessee, Turney was admitted to the bar in 1848 and opened a practice in Winchester. He also became an early advocate of secession. When voters rejected the idea in February 1861, Turney called for Franklin County to join the Confederacy as part of Alabama. When Tennessee left the Union, he rose to colonel in the Confederate Army. Turney later opposed Governor William G. "Parson" Brownlow's Radical Reconstruction politics. After Tennessee's Redemption in 1870, Turney was elected to the state supreme court; he was elevated to chief justice sixteen years later. Bourbon Democrats elected him governor in 1892. His major accomplishment during his first term was signing legislation ending Tennessee's convict leasing system and providing land for a state penitentiary. Running for reelection in 1894, Turney at age sixty-seven did little campaigning and was initially declared the loser by 750 votes. Contesting the results, he charged the Republicans with allowing African Americans to vote without showing their poll tax receipts. After lengthy debate, the Democratic-controlled legislature declared Turney the winner by two thousand votes. Turney nevertheless found his administration crippled by his questionable election. He retired from politics in 1897 and never again sought elective office. He died in Winchester.

Further Reading: Robert E. Corlew, *Tennessee: A Short History*, 1981.

Harvey Gresham Hudspeth

TURPIE, DAVID (8 July 1828–21 April 1909), U.S. senator. Born in Hamilton County, Ohio, Turpie graduated in 1848 from Kenyon College in Gambier, Ohio. He began practicing law in Logansport, Indiana, in 1849, and served as state legislator and local judge in the 1850s.

After moving to Indianapolis in 1872 to practice law, Turpie once again served in the Indiana House of Representatives, and became U.S. district attorney. Elected as a Democrat to the U.S. Senate to succeed Benjamin Harrison, he served from 1887 to 1899, a respected midwestern Democrat who carefully voiced his opinions. Turpie chaired the Committee on the Census in the Fifty-third Congress. He died in Indianapolis.

Further Reading: *Indianapolis Journal*, 22 April 1909; David Turpie, *Sketches of My Own Time*, 1903, 1975.

Leonard Schlup

TURPIE-FORAKER AMENDMENT OF 1898. On 11 April 1898, President William McKinley delivered his message to Congress regarding the Spanish-Cuban conflict. Although he asked for authority to use armed force to bring hostilities to an end, the president did not make Cuban independence a U.S. policy goal. This prompted heated congressional debate. House Democrats introduced a resolution that included U.S. recognition of Cuba, but it was defeated, while a call for military action passed overwhelmingly. The Senate Foreign Relations Committee echoed House sentiments. Democratic Senator David Turpie of Indiana, however, introduced an amendment, actually drafted by Ohio Republican Joseph Foraker, specifically calling for Cuban independence. At the same time Republican Henry Teller of Colorado introduced a similar amendment. The Senate resolution included both the Turpie-Foraker and the Teller amendments. A conference committee dropped the former, and the final act of Congress authorizing military action in Cuba included only the Teller language.

Further Reading: *Congressional Record*, 55th Congress, 2nd session; Paul S. Holbo, "Presidential Leadership in Foreign Affairs: William McKinley and the Turpie-Foraker Amendment," *American Historical Review* 72 (1967): 1321–1335.

Dimitri D. Lazo

TURPIE RESOLUTION OF 1894. In 1893 a political coup deposed the reigning monarch of the Hawaiian Islands, Queen Liliuokalani, and the new provisional government promptly drafted an annexation treaty with the United States. President Benjamin Harrison submitted this treaty to the Senate in February 1893, only a few weeks prior to the inauguration of President Grover Cleveland. Unlike his predecessor, Cleveland opposed both annexation and ratification of the treaty. In January 1894 Senator David Turpie, a Democrat from Indiana and a leading anti-annexationist, drafted a Senate resolution embodying Cleveland's sentiments. It further stipulated that any foreign intervention in the Hawaiian Islands would be seen as an "unfriendly act" by the United States. The Senate ultimately passed an amended version of the Turpie Resolution on 31 May 1894 by a vote of 55–0, with thirty abstentions.

Further Reading: *Senate Miscellaneous Documents*, 53rd Congress, 2nd session; Thomas J. Osborne, *Empire Can Wait: American Opposition to Hawaiian Annexation, 1893–1898*, 1981.

Dimitri D. Lazo

TUSKEGEE INSTITUTE. A manual training school established by the Alabama legislature in February 1881 as the Tuskegee Normal and Industrial Institute, this private, nonsectarian institution of higher learning opened that July under the leadership of Booker T. Washington, an influential African-American reformer and educator. He headed the school until his death in 1915. Washington stressed character development and the training of African-American students in practical trade skills. Industrial education, consisting in part of carpentry, masonry, and printing, at first comprised the main curriculum. George Washington Carver, a botanist and scientist, taught at Tuskegee from 1896 until his death in 1943. In 1898, he published a pamphlet titled *Feeding Acorns to Livestock*. Built on the solid reputations of Washington and Carver, Tuskegee acquired a worldwide reputation. By the year 2000, the university had an enrollment of three thousand students.

Further Reading: Louis R. Harlan, *Booker T. Washington: The Wizard of Tuskegee, 1901–1915*, 1983; Max Bennett Thrasher, *Tuskegee: Its Story and Its Work*, 1900; Booker T. Washington, ed., *Tuskegee and Its People: Their Ideals and Achievements*, 1906.

Leonard Schlup

TUTWILER, JULIA STRUDWICK (15 August 1841–24 March 1916), educator and prison reformer. Born in Greene Springs, Alabama, Tutwiler attended the well-known Greene Springs School, Vassar College, and, in 1873–1874, the Institute of Deaconesses at Kaiserswerth, Germany. An idealist, she shared the goals of the emerging women's movement. Although she sought teaching credentials, she also desired self-fulfillment through good works. Tutwiler's opportunity came in 1881, when she was appointed head of what would become the Alabama Normal School, a teachers college at Livingston. She remained there until 1910, establishing a reputation as an educator and a mentor. In addition, she campaigned for coeducation at state universities, and arguably was the main force behind the University of Alabama's admission of women in the 1890s. Also a proponent of industrial education, she helped found a technical school for women at Montevallo in 1895.

Always energetic, Tutwiler was a dedicated member of the Woman's Christian Temperance Union (WCTU). Tutwiler worked for its prison reform department, seeing firsthand the brutalities that marked Alabama's use of the convict lease system. As a state WCTU officer, Tutwiler developed a knack for lobbying the legislature—where she encountered many of her Greene Springs friends. Overcoming inertia and vested interests, she succeeded in establishing night schools for convicts; she also supported reforms that improved prisoners' health and safety. She died in Birmingham, Alabama.

Further Reading: Anne Gary Pannell and Dorothea E. Wyatt, *Julia Tutwiler and Social Progress in Alabama*, 1961; Paul M. Pruitt, Jr., "The Education of Julia Tutwiler: Background to a Life of Reform," *Alabama Review* 46 (July 1993): 199–226.

Paul M. Pruitt, Jr.

TWEED, WILLIAM MARCY (3 April 1823–12 April 1878), politician. Born in New York City to a middle-class family, Tweed left public school to learn chair making, saddle making, and bookkeeping. While a New York City Volunteer fireman, he was elected Seventh Ward alderman in 1851 and served until 1853. In that office he began taking graft. Elected to Congress in 1853, Tweed influenced other political appointments and secured election of

Democratic candidates through voter fraud. His congressional term ended in 1855. In New York City he solidified his political power and channeled more city funds into his own pockets. "Boss" Tweed ran his political machine from Tammany Hall, Democratic Party headquarters. He dominated city and state politics from 1866 until 1871, while stealing millions of dollars from local government accounts. During his career, he also served as a member of the board of supervisors for New York County, state senator, school commissioner, deputy street commissioner, chairman of the Democratic Central Committee of New York County, and director or officer of several banks and businesses.

Tweed's downfall came with the construction of a new city courthouse. A series of editorials and cartoons printed in the *New York Times* during 1870–1871 exposed the graft associated with Tammany Hall. Eventually indicted, tried, and convicted, Tweed died of pneumonia in New York City while serving his jail sentence.

Further Reading: Dennis Tilden Lynch, *Boss Tweed*, 1931; Seymour Mandelbaum, *Boss Tweed's New York*, 1965; Sean D. Cashman, *America in the Gilded Age*, 1988.

Michael W. Vogt

TWICHELL, JOSEPH HOPKINS (27 May 1838–20 December 1918), clergyman. Born in Southington, Connecticut, Twichell graduated with a law degree from Yale University in 1859. He studied for two years at Union Theological Seminary before enlisting in the Union Army, where he was a chaplain. Ordained to the Congregational ministry in 1863, he attended Andover Theological Seminary after the Civil War. Thereafter, he served for forty-six years as pastor of the Asylum Hill Congregational Church at Hartford, Connecticut. In this capacity, Twichell became known as a leader in the religious and intellectual life of the city, counting among his friends the literary giant and member of his church Mark Twain, writing numerous magazine articles, and editing the correspondence of John and Margaret Winthrop, early colonial settlers. He belonged to numerous social organizations, traveled widely at home and abroad, and accompanied Twain

on one of his European sojourns. Twitchell earned a reputation throughout New England for his integrity, commitment, and intelligence. He died in Hartford.

Further Reading: *The National Cyclopedia of American Biography* 29 (1941): 283.

Leonard Schlup

TYLER, MOSES COIT (2 August 1835–28 December 1900), historian of American literature. Tyler was born in Griswold, Connecticut. He attended the University of Michigan briefly, then studied at Yale College, Yale Theological Seminary, and Andover Seminary. After a short career as a minister, in 1867 he accepted a post as professor of English literature at Michigan, having already turned to lecturing and writing articles on health, religion, and politics. Despite working as literary editor of *The Christian Union* in 1873–1874, he devoted himself to a life of teaching and scholarship. His two-volume *History of American Literature* (1878), a pioneering study, established his status in American intellectual life. He also wrote an early historical revisionist biography of Patrick Henry (1887). Tyler went Cornell University in 1881 as the first chair of American history established at an American university. His *Literary History of the American Revolution* (1897) was a pathbreaking intellectual history. Tyler also made an important contribution to the development of the profession of historian as a founding member of the American Historical Association (1884) and in helping to establish its journal, the *American Historical Review*. Tyler died in Ithaca, New York.

Further Reading: Howard M. Jones, *The Life of Moses Coit Tyler*, 1933; Michael Kammen, "Moses Coit Tyler: The First Professor of American History in the United States," *History Teacher* 17 (November 1983): 61–87.

Amanda Laugesen

TYPEWRITER. Although typewriter patents date back to 1714, it was in 1868 that Christopher L. Sholes, Carlos Glidden, and Samuel W. Soule, all from Milwaukee, Wisconsin, received a patent for a machine with understrike type bars. An improved Sholes product in 1872, promoted by James Densmore and George W. N. Yost, typed only in capital letters and introduced the QWERTY keyboard (named after the top row of letters). In 1874 Densmore teamed with Philo Remington to offer the first Remington typewriter to the public. In a letter to Densmore, Yost, and Company on 19 March 1875, humorist Mark Twain complained that people were constantly writing to him to inquire about his typewriter, which Twain described as a "curiosity-breeding little joker." The caligraph appeared on the American market in 1880. James Hammond's typewriter went into production in 1884. Reverend Thomas Oliver in 1892 produced the Oliver typewriter, the first practical visible-writing machine. Three years later John T. Underwood formed the Underwood Typewriter Company. The Underwood Number 1 of 1895, designed by German inventor Franz X. Wagner, was considered to be the first modern typewriter. The frontstrike design made the type fully visible as it was being typed. The four Smith brothers manufactured a typewriter in 1904. Although Thomas Edison obtained the first electric typewriter patent in 1872, practical application of electric power to a typewriter did not occur until early in the twentieth century. The production of typewriters marked another technological advancement during Gilded Age America.

Further Reading: Richard N. Current, *The Typewriter and the Men Who Made It*, 1954; Wilfred A. Beeching, *Century of the Typewriter*, 1974; George C. Mares, *The History of the Typewriter*, 1985.

Leonard Schlup

UHL, EDWIN FULLER (14 August 1841–17 May 1901), lawyer and diplomat. Born in Rush, New York, Uhl graduated in 1862 from the University of Michigan, formed a law partnership in 1866 with Lyman D.  Norris in Ypsilanti, Michigan, and won election as county prosecuting attorney in 1871. He then moved to Grand Rapids to become a partner in Norris and Uhl, one of the most successful and respected law firms in Michigan. Uhl served as president of the Grand Rapids National Bank for twenty years and as mayor of that city from 1890 to 1892. In 1894, President Grover Cleveland appointed Uhl assistant secretary of state. Because of Secretary of State Walter Q. Gresham's illness, Uhl handled numerous responsibilities, including the successful arbitration of a boundary dispute between Brazil and Argentina. After serving as ambassador to Germany from 1896 to 1897, Uhl resumed his law practice in Grand Rapids and near Grand Rapids built a beautiful country home called "Waldheim," where he died.

Further Reading: *Grand Rapids Democrat*, 18 May 1901; *Grand Rapids Evening Press*, 18 May 1901; *Grand Rapids Herald*, 18 May 1901.

Leonard Schlup

UNITED MINE WORKERS OF AMERICA. Formed in 1890 by the merger of the National Association of Miners and Mine Laborers and National Trade Assembly 135 of the Knights of Labor, the United Mine Workers of America (UMWA) was the first nationwide miners union and the largest craft union in late nineteenth-century America. In an industry plagued by overproduction, the UMWA sought a labor-management agreement to insulate wages from the ravages of competition. Unlike other unions, the UMWA saw the market, rather than employers, as the chief obstacle to its members' prosperity. Though initial attempts at agreement proved partially successful, the Panic of 1893 created a glut of coal that destroyed the union's wage scale. The UMWA's most powerful weapon was the strike, which could cut supply and raise prices, thereby allowing operators to increase miners' wages. The union launched two nationwide strikes in the 1890s. The first, in 1894, idled 180,000 of the nation's 240,000 bituminous coal miners, but the union was unable to establish an agreement. The second, in 1897, proved successful and brought creation of the Central Cooperative Field, a union-operator agreement that regulated wages in western Pennsylvania, Ohio, Indiana, and Illinois. Membership increased dramatically from twelve thousand in 1895 to over one hundred thousand by century's end.

Further Reading: Chris Evans, *The History of the United Mine Workers of America*, 1914, 1918; Andrew Roy, *A History of Coal Miners in the United States*, 1905.

Michael Pierce

UNITED STATES MILITARY. Following the Civil War, both the army and the navy were dramatically reduced in size. Both also returned to their traditional antebellum missions: frontier constabulary for the army and commerce protection for the navy. The navy dispersed into foreign squadrons around the world while the army turned its attention to supervising the rapidly expanding frontier and pacifying the Plains Indians. The army's traditional constabulary role expanded to meet national needs, first during Reconstruction and later during periods of labor unrest. Though these missions played an important role in defining each service for the rest of the Gilded Age, this was also a period of great change.

Both services had officers who were convinced the American military must modernize to meet potential European foes. Both services experimented with professionalization, in part because it was relatively cheap and therefore did not attract much outside attention. Naval professionalization organized itself around the U.S. Naval Institute (1873), the Office of Naval Intelligence (1882), and the Naval War College

(1884), which provided forums for ideas, information, and advanced education. The army's professionalism efforts took shape through the Artillery School (1868), the Engineering School of Application (1885), and, most important for its long-term impact, the Infantry and Cavalry School at Fort Leavenworth (1881), which later evolved into the Command and General Staff College. Both services saw the rise of professional journals to disseminate new ideas.

Modernization took a bit longer. The navy led the way by authorizing and constructing steel warships in the early 1880s. Finding justification for a large battle fleet in the writings of Naval War College instructor Alfred Thayer Mahan, especially his *The Influence of Seapower upon History, 1660–1783* (1890), by the turn of the century the navy had rapidly expanded and turned itself into a significant force. The army's modernization was not nearly as dramatic, but important changes occurred nevertheless. In 1882, the army instituted a mandatory retirement age of sixty-four, thus making room for younger officers who had absorbed the lessons of professionalism. The *Infantry Drill Regulations of 1891* made open-order fighting official doctrine, and the adoption of the Krag-Jorgenson rifle gave the service its first magazine-fed, bolt-action rifle firing smokeless powder. Major technical advances were made in the coastal artillery as the army prepared for a war it would never fight.

The Spanish-American War put both services to the test in 1898. The navy performed reasonably well, although the conflict pointed out clear areas for improvement. The army fared much worse, with notable lapses in command and control, logistics, and manpower policy. Those lapses led to far-reaching reforms from 1901 to 1903, under Secretary of War Elihu Root, that were instrumental in preparing the army for modern warfare.

Further Reading: James L. Abrahamson, *America Arms for a New Century: The Making of a Great Military Power*, 1981; Robert Wooster, *The Military and United States Indian Policy, 1865–1903*, 1988; Lance C. Buhl, "Maintaining 'An American Navy,' 1865–1889," in Kenneth J. Hagan, *In Peace and War: Interpretations of American Naval History, 1775–1984*, 1984.

Kurt Hackemer

UNITED STATES v. E. C. KNIGHT COMPANY (156 U.S. 1 [1895]). In 1890 the U.S. Congress passed the Sherman Antitrust Act, the first federal measure that attempted to curb abusive business monopolies. In 1892 the American Sugar Refining Company acquired the stock of all its major competitors. The federal government sued the company, claiming a violation of the Sherman Act. In late 1894, the Supreme Court considered the government's appeal of a lower court's dismissal of the lawsuit. In an 8–1 decision announced in January 1895, Chief Justice Melville Fuller upheld the dismissal. Fuller held that antitrust actions could not be brought against manufacturing monopolies. He reasoned that manufacturing constituted an activity within a state and thus did not come under the congressional regulation of interstate commerce.

Further Reading: Charles W. McCurdy, "The Knight Sugar Decision of 1895 and the Modernization of American Corporation Law, 1869–1903," *Business History Review* 53 (1979): 304–342.

John T. McGuire

UNITED STATES v. WONG KIM ARK (169 U.S. 649). This case pertained to the definition of American citizenship. Born in San Francisco in 1873 to Chinese natives, Wong Kim Ark departed for China in 1894 to visit his parents, who had moved there four years earlier. In August 1895, he returned to the United States on the steamship *Copic*, but the collector of the port of San Francisco barred him from reentering, on the premise that he was not an American citizen. Wong Kim Ark petitioned the U.S. Supreme Court, admitting that his parents were of Chinese descent and subjects of the emperor of China but claiming that he was a U.S. citizen under the Fourteenth Amendment. The question before the court involved whether a child born in the United States of non-American citizens becomes a citizen of the United States at birth. After a thorough analysis of the history of American jurisprudence relating to citizenship, the High Court focused on the first sentence of the Fourteenth Amendment: "All persons born or naturalized in the United States, and subject to the jurisdiction thereof, are citizens of the United States and of the State wherein they reside." On 28 March 1898, by a 7–2 vote, the justices recognized that although originally enacted and ratified to implement the citizenship of free African Americans, the amendment applied to other races as well. While Congress could legally restrict or enlarge naturalization laws, no authority or legal entity could rescind rights conferred by the Constitution. Accordingly, Wong Kim Ark possessed American citizenship by virtue of his birth on American soil.

Further Reading: Charles J. McClain and Laurene Wu McClain, "The Chinese Contribution to the Development of American Law," in *Entry Denied: Exclusion and the Chinese Community in America, 1882–1943*, ed. Sucheng Chan, 1991.

Leonard Schlup

UPTON, EMORY (27 August 1839–15 March 1881), army officer and reformer. Born in Batavia, New York, and a graduate of the U.S. Military Academy in 1861, Upton made a reputation during the Civil War as one of the army's brightest young officers. Convinced the war had been unnecessarily bloody, he devoted himself to devising and implementing a new system of tactics. His ideas and influence can be seen in manuals adopted in 1867 and 1873, although he never felt they addressed the army's needs adequately. In 1875, Upton was sent to observe military organization in Europe and Asia for two years. He returned an advocate of a professional army, preferably along Prussian lines, making his case for reform in *The Armies of Asia and Europe* (1878). When his ideas were rejected, he began writing "The Military Policy of the United States," a scathing indictment of the citizen-soldier ideal. Depressed and suffering from severe headaches, Upton committed suicide at the Presidio in San Francisco. His unfinished manuscript circulated unofficially throughout the officer corps for twenty years. It ultimately came to the attention of Secretary of War Elihu Root, involved in his own reform efforts after the Spanish-American War. Impressed, Root incorporated many of Upton's ideas into his reforms and ordered the army to publish the manuscript in book form in 1904.

Further Reading: Stephen E. Ambrose, *Upton and the Army*, 1964; Peter Smith Mitchie, *Life and Letters of General Emory Upton*, 1885; Richard C. Brown, "Emory Upton, the Army's Mahan," *Military Affairs* 17 (1953): 125–31.

Kurt Hackemer

URBANIZATION. One dimension of urbanization is demographic: the population of the United States grew from 38,558,371 in 1870 to 76,212,168 in 1900, a percentage increase of 97.65; the urban population (number of places of 2,500 or more) grew from 9,902,361 in 1870 to 30,214,832 in 1900, a percentage increase of 305.13. In the 1880s, rapid urbanization was most pronounced in the largest cities. Indeed, by this time the city had established itself as a guiding force in the nation's economic, social, political, cultural, and intellectual life. Although urbanization was nationwide, regional differences in urban growth persisted. In 1900 the Northeast still had the largest concentration of urban population: twelve cities of one hundred thousand people or more. In the Great Plains, urbanism took root fast. In the South, though there were only nineteen cities in 1890, three showed respectable population growth, the largest being New Orleans, followed by Louisville and Atlanta.

The causes of rapid urban expansion included industrialization and technological changes, the mechanization of agriculture, the growth of the railroad system, migration from farming areas to the city, and an extraordinary rise in European immigration. During the 1890s, however, a prolonged depression and reduced fares on steam railroads to the suburbs accounted for slower growth of large cities. The physical dimension of late nineteenth-century urbanization rendered the "walking city" of the 1840s and the 1850s obsolete. By the 1880s, urban mass transit, such as horse-drawn street railways and cable cars, strengthened the outward movement of the affluent to the periphery, exemplifying the mobility that caused large cities to become segmented. Peripheral growth also led to the establishment of urban parks: Chicago in the 1870s and Boston beginning in 1893, for example. Most important, the electric streetcar (trolley), in use by 1890, hastened the rate of suburbanization. By 1900, New York's suburbs contained a million people; more of

Boston's people lived outside the city than within it. Annexation increased the city populations, the major consequence being spatial expansion triggering urban sprawl. Dispersion into the suburbs, particularly observable in the 1890s, reached as far as fifty square miles or more.

Further Reading: Arthur Meier Schlesinger, *The Rise of the City, 1878–1898*, 1933; H. J. Fletcher, "The Drift of Population to Cities," *Forum* 19 (1895): 737–747; F. J. Kingsbury, "The Tendency of Men to Live in Cities," *Journal of Social Science* 33 (1895): 1–19.

Bernard Hirschhorn

URBAN POLITICAL PARTICIPATION.

Voting among white males reached its zenith during the Gilded Age. Some historians see this period as the halcyon days of political participation, especially in cities. It was a time of fierce partisanship fueled by a system of patronage through which newly arrived immigrants received jobs and favors (sometimes including forms of welfare) in return for Election Day support. Perhaps most famously, in New York City the Irish rose to power through a political machine built around the Democratic Party (known as Tammany Hall). Bosses who had built it, and similar creations in other major metropolitan areas, asserted their power within each urban ward, making personal contact with citizens central to their work. In response to purported corruption and graft, patrician Republican reformers, known as Mugwumps, argued for civil service and experiments with new types of city government that would disempower city bosses. Such reformers inspired innovations of the Progressive Era, including settlement houses, the initiative and referendum, and the forum movement. Historians and political scientists still debate whether the Gilded Age machines ensured democratic participation in any meaningful way. Some stress their giving new immigrants political voice; others echo reformers by emphasizing the period's financial irregularities.

Further Reading: William Riordon, *Plunkitt of Tammany Hall*, 1905; Richard Hofstadter, *The Age of Reform*, 1955; Michael McGerr, *The Decline of Popular Politics*, 1986.

Kevin Mattson

URBAN PUBLIC TRANSIT.

The late nineteenth century witnessed large-scale development of local mass transit, one of the primary engines of urban growth in America. Only a handful of cities boasted networks of horse-drawn streetcars until after the Civil War. The system contracted during the conflict, when the government requisitioned horses. Rebuilding slowed when the "Great Epizootic" of 1872, a wave of equine influenza, hit America's cities. Streetcar companies hastened to find an alternative to horsepower, which was expensive and inefficient, and urban dwellers considered manure both unsightly and dangerous to public health.

Over the period from 1873 to 1880, Andrew Hallidie in San Francisco perfected the cable car. It ran on embedded track, exactly like its predecessor, but was steam-powered. An underground cable, exposed near the street surface, ran beneath cars through the center of the tracks. The underbody of the cars had a gripping device that attached to the cable. The forward movement of the cable, powered by a massive underground steam engine somewhere along the route, propelled the car. Chicago became the first metropolis to emulate San Francisco, opening its own cable network in 1882. Through the 1880s, fifty-nine companies developed lines in twenty-seven cities.

In 1888 Frank Sprague launched a streetcar line in Richmond, Virginia, that used an overhead copper wire carrying an electric current for locomotive power. This system, much cheaper than cable, spread rapidly, and street railways carried 5.8 billion passengers across the country by 1902. As late as 1890, however, horses still trod three quarters of street railway mileage, because of the great expense of cable systems.

The period also saw pioneering efforts at elevated and underground mass transit in a very few cities. Elevated steam train lines opened in New York in 1877, and by 1893, carried half a million passengers per day. Chicago was the only other metropolis to develop an extensive elevated network, opening it in 1892 and premiering the first elevated electric cars in 1895. Boston offered the first subway for electric streetcars, intended to circumvent traffic only in the central business district, during 1897; construction of the next subway system began in New York during 1900.

Further Reading: Brian J. Cudahy, *Cash, Tokens, and Transfers: A History of Urban Mass Transit in North America*, 1990.

Adam Hodges

URBAN RELIGION. With urban growth and the influx of "new immigrants," American religious culture took on added diversity. Not only did greater numbers of Catholics and Jews transform American religious life, but the new urban environment required all to address the material as well as the spiritual life of the faithful.

Late nineteenth-century urban Protestants faced significant new challenges, including congregations' outgrowing church facilities, the spread of liberal theology and modernist philosophy, and changes wrought by industrial capitalism. Protestantism responded in a variety of ways. Institutional churches, such as Philadelphia's Baptist Temple, expanded their ministries to include educational, vocational, child-care, and social activities. University of Chicago instructors advocated a social as well as an evangelical mission for the church. Religiously affiliated organizations, such as the Salvation Army, along with local rescue missions and settlement houses, served the needs of the materially deprived and spiritually bereft. By the century's close, such endeavors contributed to the Social Gospel movement so eloquently espoused by Washington Gladden and Walter Rauschenbusch.

American Catholicism also had to respond to the new urban culture, especially since many immigrant Catholics flocked to the cities to toil in factories. While the conservatives frowned on labor organizations as secretive and socialist, liberal clerics supported endeavors such as the Knights of Labor and Henry George's single tax. Like their Protestant counterparts in the Woman's Christian Temperance Union, urban Catholic women urged a religiously inspired reform agenda for urban America through the National League of Catholic Women. The American church increasingly created an urban infrastructure around parochial schools, hospitals, and orphanages.

Even more than Catholics, American Jews belonged to the urban milieu. By one estimate, 135,000, or one-third of American Jewry, lived on New York City's Lower East Side alone. Often led by those belonging to the Reform branch of Judaism, they created strong institutions in the late nineteenth century, including the Union of American Hebrew Congregations, Hebrew Union College, the Hebrew Sheltering Society, United Hebrew Trades, and the Young Men's Hebrew Association. In addition, Jewish Americans in the city linked their own agenda to a national perspective.

With smaller numbers and less influence, members of other American religious groups also shaped the urban environment. Churches became the major organizational structure in African-American institutional life, with links to benefit societies, youth organizations, and temperance groups. Islamic and Hindu congregations appeared in major cities, and the Chinese joss house served as a principal cultural and spiritual venue for most Chinatowns.

Further Reading: Martin E. Marty, *Modern American Religion*, vol. 1, 1986; Josiah Strong, *The Challenge of the City*, 1907; Washington Gladden, *Applied Christianity: Moral Aspects of Social Questions*, 1886.

Timothy Dean Draper

URBAN WEST. The 1860 federal census ranked only two western cities, San Francisco (15) and Sacramento (67), among the nation's one hundred largest. By 1910, the Mountain and Pacific divisions had nine of the nation's hundred largest cities: San Francisco (11), Los Angeles (17), Seattle (21), Denver (27), Portland (28), Oakland (32), Spokane (48), Salt Lake City (57), and Tacoma (64). As western cities developed into national commercial and transportation hubs, urban development became even more critical to the region's infrastructure. The 1890 census listed the rural population of the Pacific division as 7 percent lower than the national average, and only the Northeast had a higher proportion of urban residents. By 1910, a majority of the Pacific population lived in urban areas. The mountain West was 6 percent more rural than the entire nation in 1890; only the Northeast and Great Lakes were more urban.

The urban character of the late nineteenth-century West contradicts the popular image of that region's past. The historian Gerald Nash has termed the region an "urban oasis," a space of vast emptiness (much of it desert) dotted with town and city life. Such a description bet-ter fits the census data than does rural frontier mythology.

Further Reading: Campbell Gibson, *Population of the 100 Largest Cities and Other Urban Places in the United States: 1790 to 1990*, 1998; Richard Slotkin, *The Fatal Environment: The Myth of the Frontier in the Age of Industrialization, 1800–1890*, 1998; Gerald D. Nash, ed., *The Urban West*, 1980.

Adam Hodges

VANCE, ZEBULON BAIRD

(13 May, 1830–14 April 1894), governor and senator. Born in Buncombe County, North Carolina, Vance practiced law during the 1850s. He served in both the North Carolina and U.S. lower

houses, and during the Civil War was elected governor (1862–1865). After a brief wartime internment, Vance was pardoned, but when he was elected to the U.S. Senate in 1870, he was prevented from taking his seat. He retained much popularity, and won the 1876 North Carolina gubernatorial race. Vance supported railroad expansion, school construction, repudiation of the Reconstruction state bonds, and reconciliation with the North. He was again elected to the Senate in 1879, and served there until 1894. Vance found himself continually in confrontation with the Republican majority, yet was widely recognized as a supporter of national reconciliation. He fought the McKinley Tariff, expansion of the Internal Revenue Service, the Civil Service Act, and the repeal of the Sherman Silver Act. A supporter of President Cleveland in most matters, Vance opposed him on civil service reform and the internal revenue system. Vance used his influence back home to fight the North Carolina Farmers' Alliance and its subtreasury plan. He died in Washington, D.C.

Further Reading: Clement Dowd, *Life of Zebulon B. Vance*, 1897; Zebulon B. Vance Papers, State Department of Archives and History, Raleigh, North Carolina; Alan B. Bromberg, "The Worst Muddle Ever Seen in N.C. Politics: The Farmers' Alliance, the Subtreasury, and Zeb Vance," *North Carolina Historical Review* 56 (1979): 19–40.

Christian B. Keller

VANDERBILT, CORNELIUS

(27 November 1843–12 September 1899), financier. Vanderbilt was the grandson of Cornelius Vanderbilt, majority owner of the New York Central & Hudson River Railroad, the Lake Shore & Michigan Southern Railroad, the Michigan Central Railroad, and the Canada Southern Railway. The younger Vanderbilt was born near New Dorp, Staten Island, New York, and attended private schools in New York City. After an apprenticeship as a clerk and banker, he joined his grandfather as assistant treasurer of the New York and Harlem Railroad, where he rose to treasurer, vice president in 1880, and president in 1886. Meanwhile, in 1883 he had become president of the New York Central & Hudson River Railroad, the Michigan Central Railroad, and the Canada Southern Railway. His father's death in 1885 left Vanderbilt responsible for investing the family fortune. In addition to his work, Vanderbilt was chairman of the Metropolitan Museum of Art (1887–1899) and a trustee of Columbia University (1891–1899). He established a Y.M.C.A. in New York City, served on the advisory boards of several Protestant churches, and gave Yale University $1.5 million. He died in New York City.

Further Reading: *New York Times*, 13 September 1899.

Christopher Cumo

VAN WYCK, AUGUSTUS

(14 October 1850–8 June 1922), judge and gubernatorial candidate. Born in New York City, Van Wyck attended Phillips Exeter Academy and the University of North Carolina at Chapel Hill. He practiced law briefly in Richmond, Virginia, and then returned to New York, where he was elected judge of the Superior Court of Brooklyn. Subsequently he transferred to the New York Supreme Court. Although he was active in politics and the brother of Mayor Robert Van Wyck, his choice as Tammany Hall's gubernatorial candidate in 1898 surprised many. His opponent was the Republican Theodore Roosevelt, fresh from his exploits on San Juan Hill. Although the election was expected to result in a Democratic victory, the war hero Roosevelt won by a slim 17,786-vote margin. Tammany boss Richard Croker's attempt to interfere in the reappointment of New York City judge Joseph F. Daly had angered Republicans and Democrats alike, and eroded support for Van Wyck. The Roosevelt triumph dealt a blow to

Tammany's attempts to dominate state politics the way it ruled the city. After his loss, Van Wyck resumed his law practice and did not pursue political office again. He died in New York City.

Further Reading: DeAlva Stanwood Alexander, *A Political History of the State of New York*, Vol. IV (1882–1905), 1923; *New York Tribune*, 9 November 1898; *New York Times*, 9 June 1922.

Janet Butler Munch

VAN WYCK, ROBERT ANDERSON (27 July 1847–15 November 1918), judge and mayor. Born in New York City, Van Wyck was graduated from Columbia Law School, practiced law, and rose from city court judge to chief judge of that court. With Tammany Hall's backing, Van Wyck, a Democrat, was elected the first mayor of greater New York in 1897. In 1898, the city was consolidated into its current borough form of government. Van Wyck took his orders from Tammany boss Richard Croker, and massive patronage, graft, vice, and malfeasance marked his administration. The notorious Ice Trust Company scandal caused Van Wyck the most trouble. The city had granted a company a virtual monopoly to land its ice on city docks, eliminating competition and forcing up prices, and the mayor himself held company stock valued at $678,000. Though the bar called for Van Wyck's removal from office, he was ultimately cleared of all charges. The scandal, however, was a blow to Tammany and discredited Van Wyck's administration. In 1900, he lost the mayoral election to the Republican candidate Seth Low, who ushered in municipal reform. After leaving office, Van Wyck resumed his law practice. He died in Paris, France.

Further Reading: Mazet Committee, *Investigation of Offices and Departments of the City of New York by a Special Committee of the Assembly . . .* , 1899; *New York World*, 17 October 1901; *New York Times*, 16 November 1918.

Janet Butler Munch

VEBLEN, THORSTEIN (30 July 1857–3 August 1929), social theorist and critic. Veblen was born in Cato Township, Wisconsin, to Norwegian parents who later moved to Minnesota. He studied philosophy and economics at Carleton College, and received a doctorate from Yale in 1884. An itinerant professor, Veblen taught at the University of Chicago, Stanford, the University of Missouri, and the New School for Social Research. He was famous for being dismissed due to controversial sexual affairs. Although later recognized for his celebration of engineers against the predatory nature of businessmen, Veblen was best known during the Gilded Age for his book *The Theory of the Leisure Class* (1899). In it he honed his skills in economic anthropology and provided trenchant criticism of the nouveau riches. To Veblen, America's new ruling class served no economic function but simply displayed its wealth through "conspicuous consumption"—one of Veblen's most famous and enduring terms. *The Theory of the Leisure Class*, with its mix of social criticism and modern irony, elevated Veblen to the status of major social critic. He died in Palo Alto, California.

Further Reading: Thorstein Veblen, *The Theory of the Leisure Class*, 1899; Joseph Dorfman, *Thorstein Veblen and His America*, 1934; John Patrick Diggins, *Thorstein Veblen, Theorist of the Leisure Class*, 1999.

Kevin Mattson

VENEZUELA BOUNDARY DISPUTE (1895–1899). Although the boundary between the Republic of Venezuela and British Guiana (territory taken over by Britain from the Dutch in 1814) had apparently been long established, in the 1880s Venezuela claimed half of the colony as its own and broke off diplomatic relations with London. Influenced by the propaganda efforts of a paid American agent of the Venezuelan government and by the desire to regain political favor in the midst of a severe economic depression by twisting the British lion's tail, Secretary of State Richard Olney sent a dramatic dispatch to London in July 1895. It accepted Venezuelan territorial claims at face value, demanded that the dispute be referred to international arbitration, and insisted that the Monroe Doctrine had for all practical purposes made the United States sovereign throughout the western hemisphere.

After several months of consultation, Lord Salisbury, British prime minister and foreign secretary, politely responded that although the Monroe Doctrine deserved respect, it had not been recognized as international law and that arbitration was inappropriate to the case. President Grover Cleveland reacted with new threats against Britain, and Salisbury's cabinet—concerned with crises in South Africa and the Near East—persuaded the prime minister to agree to arbitration. Olney agreed, in turn, to exempt from the process those areas occupied by British settlers for fifty years or more, and in 1899 the commission (two Britons, two Americans, one Venezuelan) awarded nine-tenths of the disputed land to Britain. Resolution of the dispute, which had briefly threatened war between Britain and the United States, helped lead to an era of Anglo-American rapprochement.

Further Reading: A. E. Campbell, *Great Britain and the United States, 1895–1903*, 1960; J. A. S. Grenville, *Lord Salisbury and Foreign Policy*, 1964; Bradford Perkins, *The Great Rapprochement: England and the United States, 1895–1914*, 1968.

Walter L. Arnstein

VERRILL, ADDISON EMERY (9 February 1839–10 December 1926), zoologist. Born in Greenwood, Maine, Verrill was one of the best-known and most productive American systematic zoologists during the Gilded Age. He received the B.S. from Harvard in 1862. From 1864, when he was appointed professor of zoology in the Sheffield Scientific School of Yale University, until his forced retirement in 1907, he taught zoology and geology, lectured, and published more than three hundred articles and books. Verrill collected specimens, described more than one thousand marine invertebrates, and defined the terminology pertaining to zoology and invertebrate paleontology for the 1890 edition of *Webster's International Dictionary*. His zealous life and prodigious work earned him an enviable reputation among colleagues and the general public. Verrill died in Santa Barbara, California.

Further Reading: George Elliot Verrill and Amy Christian Doane Verrill, *The Ancestry, Life and Work of Addison E. Verrill of Yale University*, 1958.

Leonard Schlup

VICE PRESIDENCY. Nine men held the vice presidential office from 1869 to 1901. All, except Thomas A. Hendricks and Adlai E. Stevenson, were Republicans. Three vice presidents—Henry Wilson, Hendricks, and Garret Hobart—died in office, and two—Chester A. Arthur and Theodore Roosevelt—succeeded to the presidency upon the death of their predecessor. For approximately twelve years during the Gilded Age, the nation was without a vice president, and no constitutional mechanism existed to fill the vacancy.

With the exceptions of Senator Wilson and Governor Theodore Roosevelt, Gilded Age vice presidents had not been elected by the people or their legislators on a statewide basis before taking the vice presidential oath. Certainly better qualified individuals could have been vice president, but prominent leaders in positions of importance refused to relinquish their authority and influence for a powerless office, known as a graveyard for politicians instead of a stepping stone to the presidency. A sectional calculus also highlighted presidential and vice presidential politics in Gilded Age America. Both parties emphasized geographical balance in their postwar choices. Democrats needed some large northern states to add to the party's monopoly of southern electoral votes. If a northerner from an eastern state such as New York headed the ticket, then a Midwest political figure from Ohio, Indiana, or Illinois was usually sought for the vice presidency and vice versa, with Ohio playing a pivotal role. Other considerations involved placating factions within the parties, such as the Garfield-Arthur combination in 1880.

Presidential candidates at the time did not dictate their choices for vice president; convention delegates and party leaders made that decision based on several factors. Gilded Age vice presidents, like most of their predecessors and successors, were often politically ignored by the president but accepted socially, and were not invited to attend Cabinet sessions. Important decisions were made without their advice, and the office became what the president wished it to be during his administration. Without question the American vice presidency has been a curiosity in political history.

Further Reading: Jules Witcover, *Crapshoot: Rolling the Dice on the Vice Presidency*, 1992; Sol Barzman, *Madmen and Geniuses: The Vice Presidents of the United States*, 1974; Leonard Schlup, "The Vice Presidency: An Essay on

Duties and Selection," *Review of the Ohio Council for the Social Studies* 28 (1992): 15–22.

Leonard Schlup

VICTORIA, QUEEN OF GREAT BRITAIN

(24 May 1819–22 January 1901), British monarch. Born in London, England, Victoria ascended to the throne in 1837, at age eighteen. The death of her husband, Prince Albert, in December 1861 led to her relative seclusion as the "Widow of Windsor" and to a short-lived movement to supplant the monarchy with a republic. Behind the scenes, however, the queen continued to exercise influence on clerical and diplomatic appointments as well as occasional cabinet appointments. From the mid-1870s, her public appearances increased, and her Diamond Jubilee (1897) coincided with the height of her popularity as a symbol of longevity, matriarchy, and domesticity, as well British imperial unity.

Americans continued to regard the British monarchy with ambivalence. On the one hand, they took pride that America's revolution had established a republic, and they welcomed antimonarchical movements elsewhere. On the other hand, they came increasingly to look on the queen as an exemplary woman. Robert Todd Lincoln, American minister to Britain from 1889 to 1893, described her as a fount of wisdom and of common sense. The queen in turn was fascinated by a variety of Americans, including P. T. Barnum, Buffalo Bill Cody, and Whitelaw Reid, who was appointed special "Diamond Jubilee" emissary by President William McKinley. Victoria's sympathy toward the United States was based on the belief that Prince Albert's last act (in the *Trent* affair) had preserved peace between the two nations, and on the friendly reception that her eldest son, the future Edward VII, had received in the United States during his visit in 1860. She subsequently used her influence to encourage Britain to resolve the *Alabama* claims by arbitration.

Victoria's death on the Isle of Wight, England, ended the longest reign in British history. Congress adjourned and White House flags flew at half-staff. On the day of her funeral, the New York stock market closed, and President McKinley and his entire cabinet attended memorial services at St. John's Episcopal Church in Washington. Her reign symbolized the age known as the Victorian era.

Further Reading: Walter L. Arnstein, "Queen Victoria and the United States," in *Anglo-American Attitudes*, ed. Fred Leventhal and Roland Quinalt, 2000; Mary Leoffelholz, "Crossing the Atlantic with Queen Victoria: American Receptions, 1837–1901," in *Remaking Queen Victoria*, ed. Margaret Homans and Adrienne Munich, 1997; Jerrold M. Packard, *Farewell in Splendor: The Passing of Queen Victoria and her Age*, 1995.

Walter L. Arnstein

VICTORIAN WEST.

Among the labels the period from 1868 to 1901 carried, Mark Twain's blessings gave the edge to "Gilded Age." A less parochial and more inclusive designation "Victorian" also describes the standards and values accepted in the United States. To those living in the eastern states, the West appeared to be a distinct region. The first wave of settlers in the West, attracted by possibilities for mineral, cattle, and land exploitation, seemed to confirm that distinction. The stereotypical, grubbing farm homesteader, the romanticized cowboy, and rough miners of a male-dominated society were not images easily associated with the Gilded Age.

As settlement by a more stable population came to dominate the West, new arrivals brought the intellectual, religious, and social baggage of their former homes in the East. Cattle towns such as Dodge City, Kansas, and mining communities like Denver, Colorado, went through a transition stage, displaying the characteristics of a Dr. Jekyll and Mr. Hyde struggle. The Eastern, or Victorian, orientation came to prevail.

Victorianism included shared values, attitudes, material development, and social, economic, religious concepts, as well as the fabric of day-to-day activities, recreation, manners, and family and class roles. Economically, the exploitative and monopolistic drive of the Wyoming Stock Growers' Association was similar to that of Wall Street tycoons. A free grant of privilege, so cynically sought by the eastern capitalist as the first rung on the ladder of success, exemplified in the railroad land grants, was pursued and obtained by men like Robert M. Wright in his appointment to the post of settler of Fort Dodge—different only in scale and locale. The policies that led to reckless speculation resulting in the economic collapse of the 1890s were followed in Dodge City as it was in the East, and with the same disastrous effect.

The overarching understanding that life is real and earnest, with its stuffy posturing, was accepted across the American culture. Gender and family roles that led to the "Cult of True Womanhood" was as much alive on the prairies as in Boston. Just as the homesteading wife in Dakota Territory confessed a desire to live like women in Syracuse, New York, so the permanent settlers copied the fashions, fads, and follies of the East. Women's dress fashions were quickly taken from print media and pattern books. When the craze for croquet swept eastern cities, croquet courts were laid out on the prairie buffalo grass. Before the end of the cattle-driving business, the favorite recreation of Dodge City and Caldwell, Idaho, had become roller-skating. Opera houses sprang up across the West and presented popular, sweetly sentimental morality plays performed by eastern traveling troupes on their way back home. When Oscar Wilde visited America, he was received with the same reaction in all states.

For men the social institution that epitomized the Gilded Age most clearly was the type of fraternal secret order known as the lodge. Lodges in the East and the West ordered their exotic regalia from the same suppliers. Young dudes in Wichita, Kansas, presented formal calling cards on New Year's Day and danced the latest "racket" and "fanciers" with their favorite belle.

By the turn of the century, Dodge citizens and Denverites were attempting to erase evidence of past, wilder, more exciting times, and the Victorian West had completely won the day.

Further Reading: C. Robert Haywood, *Victorian West: Class and Culture in Kansas Cattletowns*, 1991.

C. Robert Haywood

VILAS, WILLIAM FREEMAN (9 July 1840–27 August 1908), lawyer, postmaster general, secretary of the interior, and U.S. senator. Born in Chelsea, Vermont, Vilas grew up in Madison, Wisconsin, and graduated from the University of Wisconsin and the Albany (New York) Law School. He was admitted to the Wisconsin bar in 1860. During the Civil War he rose to lieutenant colonel in the Union Army. After the war, he helped revise statutes and reedit the first volumes of the *Wisconsin Reports*. He also was a professor of law (1868–1885) and regent (1881–1885, 1898–1905) at the University of Wisconsin.

Vilas rose quickly in the state Democratic Party. His reputation as an orator and his devotion to Bourbon principles attracted eastern establishment attention. After Vilas chaired the 1884 Democratic National Convention, President Grover Cleveland appointed him postmaster general. Being part of the first Democratic administration since the Civil War and heading a patronage-sensitive cabinet department embroiled Vilas in a controversy over civil service reform. In 1888 he was named secretary of the interior, and he streamlined the department's organization. After the first Cleveland administration, he returned to Madison and helped lead the state party's dominant Bourbon faction. When the Democrats won control of the state in 1890, the legislature selected Vilas as U.S. senator. He played a major role in Cleveland's 1892 victory and defended the administration's hard money stance against both the Populists and the rising Silver Democrats. When William Jennings Bryan won the 1896 nomination, Vilas wrote the platform for the national Gold Democrats. Not returned to the Senate by the legislature, Vilas devoted the remainder of his life to business, law, and service to the University of Wisconsin. He died in Madison, Wisconsin.

Further Reading: Horace Samuel Merrill, *William Freeman Vilas: Doctinaire Democrat*, 1954; Alan Nevins, *Grover Cleveland*, 1932.

Michael J. Anderson

VILLARD, HENRY (10 April 1835–12 November 1900), journalist, railroad promoter, and publisher. Born Ferdinand Heinrich Gustav Hilgard in Speyer, Bavaria, and educated at the universities of Munich and Würzburg, Villard immigrated to the United States in 1853. Serving as secretary of the American Social Science Association from 1868 to 1871 gave him the chance to study banking. After investing in the Oregon & California Railroad, he negotiated with other local railroad and steamship companies, formed a transportation monopoly, and then actively encouraged settlement of the Northwest. The approaching Northern Pacific, chartered to build a transcontinental railroad, threatened Villard's interests when it refused to use his railroad lines. Villard outmaneuvered his competition by raising millions in a blind trust to buy controlling interest in the Northern Pacific. He completed the transcontinental railroad in 1883. Ten years later, he abandoned his railroad investments and returned east, where he purchased the *New York Evening Post* and founded the newspaper's supplement *Nation*. Villard died in Dobbs Ferry, New York.

Further Reading: Alexandra Villard de Borchgrave and John Cullen, *Villard: The Life and Times of an American Titan*, 2001; Henry Villard, *Memoirs of Henry Villard: Journalist and Financier, 1835–1900*, 1904; Dietrich G. Buss, *Henry Villard: A Study of Transatlantic Investments and Interests, 1870–1895*, 1978.

Janet Butler Munch

VINCENT, HENRY AND LEOPOLD (LEO)

(Henry, 1 January 1862–29 October 1935; Leo, 20 December 1863–28 March 1955), reform editors. Born in Tabor, Iowa, the Vincents founded the *American Nonconformist* in 1879. The newspaper successively supported the Greenback Labor, Union Labor, and Populist parties. The Vincents moved it to Winfield, Kansas, in 1886. Republicans blamed them for the explosion, in nearby Coffeyville, of a bomb addressed to the *Nonconformist* office in 1888. Union Laborites charged Republicans with a conspiracy to discredit them. The legislature's 1891 investigation proved inconclusive. The Vincents helped found the state's original Populist organization, which carried local elections of 1889. In 1891, the Vincents moved to Indianapolis, hoping to turn their paper into a national Populist organ. Henry edited the Populist-oriented (Chicago) *Searchlight* and Jacob Coxey's *Sound Money* in the mid-1890s. In 1894, he published *The Story of the Commonweal*, the official history of Coxey's Army. Leo became editor of the *Oklahoma Representative* and chairman of the Oklahoma Territory Populist Party in 1894. In 1897, he founded the

Colorado Representative. Both Vincents supported Bellamy Nationalism and became active in the Socialist Party after the turn of the century. Henry Vincent died in Ypsilanti, Michigan. Leo died in San Leandro, California.

Further Reading: Worth Robert Miller, *Oklahoma Populism* (1987); Harold R. Pie, "Henry Vincent: Populist and Radical-Reform Journalist," *Kansas History* 2 (1979): 14–25.

Worth Robert Miller

VINCENT, JOHN HEYL

(23 February 1832–9 May 1920), minister and educator. Born in Tuscaloosa, Alabama, Vincent grew up in Pennsylvania. There he taught school and, following study at the Wesleyan Institute in Newark, New Jersey, began his career as an ardent supporter of Sunday schools. While serving as pastor for several congregations in Illinois, he developed the first uniform Sunday school curriculum for Protestant churches in 1865. He became general agent of the Sunday School Union of the Methodist Episcopal Church in 1866, and served as editor of the *Sunday School Journal* from 1868 to 1888. Vincent's Sunday school movement leadership flowered in the teachers' assemblies that he and Lewis Miller, a wealthy inventor and Methodist Sunday school leader, organized at Lake Chautauqua, New York in 1874. By 1878, the popular summer school program had expanded into year-round correspondence programs of general education organized under the Chautauqua Literary and Scientific Circle and the Chautauqua University, of which he served as chancellor from 1883 to 1898. He was elected bishop of the Methodist Episcopal Church in 1888, a position he held until his retirement in 1904. Vincent died in Chicago.

Further Reading: Jeffrey Simpson, *Chautauqua: An American Utopia*, 1999; Edward A. Trimmer, "John Heyl Vincent: An Evangelist for Education," Ed.D. thesis, Teachers College, Columbia University, 1986; Richard K. Bonnell, "The Chautauqua University: Pioneer University Without Walls, 1883–1898," Ph.D. diss., Kent State University, 1988.

Kim P. Sebaly

***VIRGINIUS* INCIDENT.** This was a violation of American sovereignty on the high seas, on 31 October 1873, during the Cuban revolution against Spain (1868–1878). The steamer *Virginius* was sailing in Jamaican waters, flying the American flag while illegally running weapons, when it was captured by a Spanish gunboat, the *Tornado*. The ship, towed into the harbor at Santiago de Cuba, was actually owned by Cubans, and at the time of the incident was illegally registered. Its commander, Captain Joseph Fry, and seven other U.S. citizens were among sixty persons subsequently executed as pirates by the Spanish government in Cuba as filibusters—civilians engaging in unauthorized warfare against a sovereign power. The Spanish actions severely strained relations with the United States. A compromise eased tensions temporarily. Spain agreed to pay the families of the executed Americans compensation totaling $80,000 and to release the surviving American officers and crew, thereby avoiding outright war with the United States or intervention in the ongoing Cuban crisis. The *Virginius* was wrecked off Cape Fear, North Carolina, during the return voyage to the United States, thus ending her use for trade or smuggling.

Further Reading: Alexander De Conde, *A History of American Foreign Policy*, 2nd ed., 1971; William S. McFeely, *Grant: A Biography*, 1981.

Jerome D. Bowers II

VOORHEES, DANIEL WOLSEY (26 September 1827–10 April 1897), U.S. senator. Born in Liberty Township, Ohio, Voorhees graduated from Asbury (now DePauw) University at Greencastle, Indiana, in 1849 and in 1857 began practicing law in Terre Haute. He served as a Democrat in the U.S. House of Representatives from 1861 to 1865, briefly from 1865 to 1866, and again from 1869 to 1873. Subsequently he won election to the U.S. Senate, where he sat from 1877 to 1897. During these two decades, Voorhees favored a large and freely circulating currency, believed that tariff protection hurt farmers, distrusted eastern money powers, and usually supported President Grover Cleveland on divisive intraparty matters. As chairman of the Committee on Finance, he led the Senate in the successful repeal of the Sherman Silver Purchase Act in 1893 during a special congressional session. Generous and sympathetic, Voorhees was known as a good stump speaker and orator. He died in Washington, D.C.

Further Reading: *Evening Star* (Washington), 10 April 1897; Henry D. Jordan, "Daniel Wolsey Voorhees," *Mississippi Valley Historical Review* 6 (1920): 532–555; Leonard S. Kenworthy, *The Tall Sycamore of the Wabash, Daniel Voorhees*, 1936.

Leonard Schlup

VOORHEES, FOSTER MACGOWAN (5 November 1856–14 June 1927), lawyer, state legislator, and governor. Born in Clinton, New Jersey, Voorhees graduated from Rutgers and Princeton. In his three terms as a Republican assemblyman, he helped aid the financially troubled city of Elizabeth; played a major role in framing a law that increased the cost of liquor licenses; and helped defeat a bill to tax railroads at the same rate as other property. Elected to the state senate in 1893, he rose to the positions of majority leader and senate president. In 1895 Voorhees chaired an investigating committee that exposed statehouse fraud. In 1898, he became acting governor upon Governor John Griggs's appointment as U.S. attorney general, and was elected governor later that year. He served one term (1899–1902) and was regarded as a reformer. He signed a bill establishing a state village at Skillman for the care of epileptics, created the State Board of Children's Guardians (seen by many as one of the most progressive institutions of the period), and funded the completion of the Rahway Reformatory. He refused to sign a 1901 bill allowing a corporation to extend its charter for up to fifty years at any time simply by filing a certificate with the secretary of the state. Although a fiscal conservative, he was committed to the use of state revenues for the strengthening public schools. He supported direct election of U.S. senators. Constitutionally ineligible to succeed himself, he left office in 1902. He died in High Bridge, New Jersey.

Further Reading: Voorhees Papers, New Jersey State Library, Trenton; Paul A. Stellhorn and Michael J. Birkner, eds., *The Governors of New Jersey*, 1982; *New York Times*, 15 June 1927.

Marie Marmo Mullaney

WABASH, ST. LOUIS & PA-CIFIC RAILROAD COM-PANY v. ILLINOIS (118 U.S. 557). This 1886 U.S. Supreme Court case involved the constitutionality of an Illinois law that prohibited long-in-short-haul clauses in all contracts pertaining to transportation. The High Court, exercising the prerogative of judicial review, invalidated the statute, claiming that the measure infringed on the constitutional control that Congress possessed over interstate commerce. This opinion weakened the Court's earlier ruling in the 1877 *Granger Cases* and established nebulous areas where neither the federal government nor the states could have jurisdiction.

Further Reading: Bernard Schwartz, *A History of the Supreme Court*, 1993.

Leonard Schlup

WAGNER, ARTHUR LOCKWOOD (16 March 1853–20 June 1905), U.S. Army officer. Born in Ottawa, Illinois, Wagner graduated from West Point in 1875 near the bottom of his class, but nevertheless went on to become the preeminent army intellectual of his day. After brief service in the West, he was assigned in 1886 to the Infantry and Cavalry School at Fort Leavenworth, Kansas, where he became involved in the army's nascent reform movement. During his thirty-year career, Wagner wrote over three dozen articles and books in which he challenged the army to pursue a more enlightened, progressive combat and educational methodology. His principal works—*The Service of Security and Information* (1890) and *Organization and Tactics* (1894), were used as texts at Fort Leavenworth and supported as the army's tactical modernization.

Wagner's pioneering work at the Infantry and Cavalry School helped establish the credibility of officer education beyond West Point. While at Fort Leavenworth, he was instrumental in revising the army's combat doctrine to reflect recent advances in tactics and military technology. He left the school in 1897 to head

the Military Information Division, and was largely responsible for conceiving the army's plans for the invasion of Cuba during the Spanish-American War. In 1899 he was transferred to the Philippines, and served as adjutant general of the Department of Northern Luzon. Upon returning to the United States in 1902, he was selected to direct the army's first use of military maneuvers for training purposes. In 1903 he won an assignment to the Army War College and the new General Staff, during which he overhauled the army's educational system. Wagner died in Asheville, North Carolina, on the day he was to be promoted to brigadier general.

Further Reading: T. R. Brereton, *Educating the Army: Arthur L. Wagner and Reform, 1875–1905*, 2000.

T. R. Brereton

WAITE, DAVIS HANSON (9 April 1825–27 November 1901), newspaperman, lawyer, and governor. Born in Jamestown, New York, Waite attended local public schools and studied law in his father's office. He then lived in several states where he practiced law, edited newspapers, engaged in the mercantile business, and served as a high school principal. Originally a Jacksonian Democrat, he became a Republican because of his antislavery views, serving that party in the Wisconsin and Kansas legislatures.

In 1879, Waite settled in Leadville, Colorado, to practice law and prospect for silver. A year later, he moved to nearby Aspen to edit the *Aspen Times* and the *Aspen Chronicle*. In 1891 he launched the *Aspen Union Era*, which became a vehicle for his increasingly reformist views and his growing attraction to the Populist movement. In 1892, he attended both the Populist convention in St. Louis, where the new party's platform was adopted, and its gathering in Omaha, which nominated the James B. Weaver-Field ticket. That same year, Waite was elected as Colorado's only Populist governor; he received decisive support from the state's working miners and farmers. His two-year term was tumultuous. A radical reformer, especially when the silver boom in Colorado ended, he advocated sending the state's silver to Mexico to be minted and used in Colorado as legal currency. These "fandango dollars" contributed to his controversial reputation, which grew significantly in 1894. Waite brought the state militia to Denver in 1894, during the so-called City Hall War, to deal with members of the Fire Board and the Police Board who refused to vacate their posts, even though he had legally removed them. His intervention in the Cripple Creek strike on the side of mine employees that same year added to his image as an antimonopolist with unconventional currency views. However, more moderate reforms were also enacted under Waite: women's suffrage and an eight-hour day for government workers.

Waite's radicalism denied him a second term, however. The Populist governor, called "Bloody Bridles" Waite by his opponents because he claimed in a widely publicized speech that it would be "better that blood should flow to the horses' bridles than our national liberties should be destroyed," was defeated in 1894. He died in Aspen, Colorado.

Further Reading: John Robert Morris, "Davis Hanson Waite: The Ideology of a Western Populist," Ph.D. diss., University of Colorado, 1965; Harold Kountz, Jr., "Davis H. Waite and the People's Party in Colorado," M.A. thesis, Yale University, 1944; James Edward Wright, *The Politics of Populism: Dissent in Colorado*, 1974.

Robert W. Larson

WALD, LILLIAN D. (10 March 1867–1 September 1940), nurse and social activist. Born in Cincinnati, Ohio, Wald graduated from the New York Hospital Training School for Nurses in 1891 and briefly attended the Woman's Medical College in New York City. In 1893, she established a visiting nurse service for immigrant families living on New York City's Lower East Side. Funded by philanthropists, Wald moved the service into the Henry Street Settlement in 1895, and it served as a model institution in the social settlement movement. Her nurses promoted healthy lifestyles while they inspected tenement buildings, schools, and industrial settings for disease-causing agents.

An advocate for the urban poor, Wald worked for health, education, and labor reform.

In 1904, she founded the National Child Labor Committee with Florence Kelley. In later years, Wald instituted a public health training program in the American Red Cross, founded the National Organization for Public Health Nursing, and helped secure creation of the U.S. Children's Bureau. She died in Westport, Connecticut.

Further Reading: Phyllis Povell, "Lillian Wald: Social Force in America," *Vitae Scholasticae* 6 (1987): 91–104; Robert Duffus, *Lillian Wald: Neighbor & Crusader*, 1938; Lillian Wald, *The House on Henry Street*, 1915.

Jane M. Armstrong

WALKER, MADAM C. J. (23 December 1867–25 May 1919), hair-care entrepreneur, businesswoman, and philanthropist. Born Sarah Breedlove on a Delta, Louisiana, cotton plantation, the orphaned Breedlove held various jobs and endured a financially difficult youth. During the 1890s, she suffered from a scalp ailment and experimented with homemade remedies to alleviate the condition and resulting loss of hair. In 1905 she moved to Denver, Colorado, and founded her own business, selling a scalp conditioning and healing formula. The next year she married Charles Joseph Walker, a Saint Louis newspaper sales agent. In 1910 she moved her company to Indianapolis, Indiana. An advocate of African-American women's independence and of business opportunities for them, Walker epitomized the successful businesswoman of late nineteenth- and early twentieth-century America. She said: "I got myself a start," adding that there was "no royal flower-strewn path to success." Walker was the first self-made woman millionaire in the United States. She died at Villa Lewaro in Irvington-on-Hudson, New York.

Further Reading: A'Lelia Bundles, *On Her Own Ground: The Life and Times of Madam C. J. Walker*, 2001; Madam C. J. Walker Papers, Indiana Historical Society, Indianapolis.

Leonard Schlup

WALKER, MOSES FLEETWOOD (7 October 1857–11 May 1924), baseball player and author. Born to mulatto parents in Mount Pleasant, Ohio, Walker grew up in Steubenville. In 1879, he enrolled in Oberlin College. As a catcher on the varsity baseball team, Walker was the first African American to play inter-collegiate baseball. In 1881, he transferred to the University of Michigan, ostensibly to study law but in reality because he was more interested in pursuing baseball opportunities with the Wolverines. Walker signed a professional baseball contract with the Toledo Blue Stockings of the Northwestern League in 1883. The following year, when Toledo joined the American Association, Walker became the first black major leaguer. Between 1884 and 1889, he played for professional teams in Toledo, and Cleveland, Ohio; Waterbury, Connecticut; and Syracuse, New York. His career ended in August 1889, when the Syracuse Stars of the International League (which was considered a major league at the time), gave in to segregationist pressure both within and outside the baseball establishment, and released him. Although Walker was hitting only slightly above .200 at the time, he was viewed as a good defensive catcher who could handle pitchers. Walker was the last African American to play in the International League until the post–World War II period and Jackie Robinson.

Walker's later years were troubled. In 1891, he was acquitted of killing a man outside a Syracuse bar. Afterward, he returned to Steubenville, where he worked as a railway mail clerk. In 1898, he was arrested for mail fraud and spent a year in jail. In 1908, Walker became a racial theorist, publishing *Our Home Colony: The Past, Present, and Future of the Negro Race in America*. It challenged the integrationist views of Booker T. Washington, advocating black emigration to Africa as the answer to America's white racism. However, while preaching Afrocentrism, Walker was purchasing an opera house in Cadiz, Ohio, where he provided films and live entertainment for racially mixed audiences. He died in Cleveland.

Further Reading: Moses Fleetwood Walker File, Oberlin College Archives, Oberlin, Ohio; David W. Zang, *Fleet Walker's Divided Heart: The Life of Baseball's First Black Major Leaguer*, 1995; Phil Dixon and Patrick Hannigan, *The Negro Baseball Leagues, 1867–1955*, 1992.

Ron Briley

WALLACE, LEW (10 April 1827–15 February 1905), politician and author. Born Lewis Wallace at Brookville, Indiana, Wallace read voraciously as a youth. He practiced law in Indianapolis and Covington, served in the Union Army, and accepted a teacher's advice to consider a literary occupation. For over twenty-five years, Wallace held a number of diplomatic and governmental positions, including governor of New Mexico Territory (1878–1881). While in Santa Fe, he wrote *Ben-Hur: A Tale of the Christ* (1880), a romance for which he is most famous. This book became one of the most popular works of American fiction in the late nineteenth century. Under Presidents James A. Garfield and Chester A. Arthur, Wallace was ambassador to Turkey (1881–1885). He died in Crawfordsville, Indiana.

Further Reading: Robert E. Morsberger and Katharine M. Morsberger, *Lew Wallace: Militant Romantic*, 1980.

Leonard Schlup

WALLER, THOMAS MACDONALD (1840–25 January 1924), governor. Born Thomas MacDonald Armstrong in New York City, he lost his parents and a brother by 1848, sold newspapers, and worked as a cabin boy on a fishing vessel. Thomas K. Waller, a New London, Connecticut, merchant, adopted him, and the boy assumed Waller as his surname. He served in the Civil War, formed a law partnership in New London, and held a seat in the state legislature in the 1860s. In the early 1870s, he was Connecticut's secretary of state, and mayor of New London from 1873 to 1879, sponsoring a progressive program for civic improvements. In 1883, Waller won the governorship, and the following year seconded Grover Cleveland's presidential nomination. Cleveland appointed him consul general in London, England, where he remained from 1885 to 1889. At the 1896 Democratic National Convention in Chicago, Waller adamantly opposed free silver coinage. As head of the Connecticut delegation, he walked out of the convention in protest against the silver wing of the party and William Jennings Bryan's presidential nomination. Waller endorsed the hard money Gold Democratic ticket headed by John M. Palmer of Illinois. Known as "the Little Giant from Connecticut" for his powerful speaking and debating abilities, Waller maintained an active interest in

Democratic politics in the post-Bryan era. He died in New London, Connecticut.

Further Reading: *New York Times*, 25 January 1924; *New London Day*, 25 January 1924; *New Haven Journal-Courier*, 26 January 1924.

Leonard Schlup

WANAMAKER, JOHN (11 July 1838–12 December 1922), merchant, postmaster general, and philanthropist. Born in Philadelphia Pennsylvania, Wanamaker had only three years' formal schooling. He spent most of his life in retailing, starting at age thirteen as errand boy for a bookstore. In 1861, he opened a men's clothing store, Oak Hall, with his brother-in-law Nathan Brown. Through a series of partnerships, Wanamaker expanded his business. In 1876 he opened the Grand Depot, the largest retail establishment in Philadelphia at the time. When he added dry goods the next year, Wanamaker effectively converted his clothing store into Philadelphia's first department store. He quickly became the city's leading merchant and expanded regularly throughout the late nineteenth century. In 1896, he purchased the famous A. T. Stewart store in New York City. In the early twentieth century, he greatly expanded both his New York and his Philadelphia outlets.

In 1889, Wanamaker was appointed postmaster general by President Benjamin Harrison. During his tenure, the post office issued its first commemorative stamps (honoring the World's Columbian Exhibition). Wanamaker was a devout evangelical Christian and gave much of his time and money to Presbyterian churches and the Young Men's Christian Association. Wanamaker died in his city house in Philadelphia.

Further Reading: Henry Adams Gibbons, *John Wanamaker*, 1926; Herbert Ershkowitz, *John Wanamaker: Philadelphia Merchant*, 1999; John Wanamaker Collection, Historical Society of Pennsylvania, Philadelphia.

John H. Hepp IV

WARD, AARON MONTGOMERY (17 February 1843–7 December 1913), businessman and urban conservationist. Born in Chatham, New Jersey, Ward grew up in Niles, Michigan. At age eight, he began earning his keep as a store clerk and salesman. He moved to Chicago immediately after the Civil War, and later worked as a traveling salesman. By 1871, Ward was back in Chicago. His rural experiences suggested that an industrious Chicago wholesaler could meet the needs of rural consumers. Ward entered the crowded mail-order business. He published his first price list and began operations, only to see the Great Fire of 1871 take his entire investment. Upon reopening the following year, Ward made two significant changes. First, his long-time friend, George Thorne, joined the firm as a partner. In addition, Ward married Thorne's sister-in-law, Elizabeth Cobb, in February 1872. Both connections solidified the strong links between the Ward and the Cobb families. This bond was pivotal because the Cobbs were influential leaders of the growing consumer cooperative movement founded by rural Midwestern commercial farmers and organized through the National Patrons of Husbandry (the Grange). In the spring of 1872, Ward made his first overture to Grange patronage when he spoke at a mass rally and picnic in Bloomington, Illinois. Testimonials by prominent Grangers were key to the success of Ward's catalog that fall. The firm's self-anointed status as the Grange's original supply house—most certainly untrue, given that the Grange purchasing activities began as early as 1868—reflects the importance of this relationship.

With its pecuniary wagon firmly hitched to the Grange's star, Montgomery Ward & Co. expanded dramatically in size and scope. From its inception with $1600 in venture capital and a thirty-six-page catalog, by 1887 Ward's book had expanded to 350 pages and the firm was earning more than $1 million in annual sales. Competition was fierce, but Ward retained the trust and patronage of his rural clientele. Though he retired from active management in 1901, he remained involved in the affairs of Chicago. Earning a reputation as the lakefront watchdog, Ward worked to prevent development on the broad expanse of Chicago's Lake Michigan shoreline, immediately south of the Chicago River. He died in Highland Park, Illinois.

Further Reading: Frank Latham, *1872–1972, a Century of Serving Customers: The Story of Montgomery Ward*, 1972; *Chicago Tribune*, 8 December 1913.

David Blanke

WARD, HENRY AUGUSTUS (9 March 1834–4 July 1906), naturalist and professor. Born in Rochester, New York, Ward received informal education until he met the naturalist Louis Agassiz, who encouraged him to study at Harvard College. Ward did so briefly but then went to Europe, where he studied at the School of Mines in Paris and collected rocks and minerals. Keeping a diary of his activities and writing letters to relatives and associates, Ward emerged as a public figure upon his return to the United States in 1859. Two years later he secured an appointment as professor of natural sciences at the University of Rochester, a post he held until 1876. He traveled extensively, trained students in the science of ecology, became an entrepreneur, encouraged museum building across the United States, and was the main supplier of museum specimens in America. He died in Buffalo, New York, after being accidentally hit by an automobile.

Further Reading: Susan Sheets-Pyenson, "Henry Augustus Ward and Museum Development in the Hinterlands," *University of Rochester Library Bulletin* 38 (1983): 21–59; Henry A. Ward Papers, Department of Rare Books and Special Collections, Rush Rhees Library, University of Rochester.

Leonard Schlup

WARD, JOHN MONTGOMERY (3 March 1860–4 March 1925), professional baseball player, manager, and executive. Born in Bellefonte, Pennsylvania, Ward attended Pennsylvania State University, where he excelled both as a scholar and as a baseball player. Beginning in 1878, he spent seventeen seasons in the major leagues. As a player, he had several outstanding years as a pitcher, leading the league in wins, winning percentage, and strikeouts in 1879 before suffering an arm injury. Ward then switched to shortstop for the majority of his career and performed admirably, leading the league in stolen bases in 1887 and 1892, and in hits in 1890. His career earned run average of 2.10 still ranks among the best in history.

Beyond his playing career, Ward was a staunch advocate of players' rights. At a time when team owners had almost complete control over their players' professional destinies, Ward risked his own career by defending the rights of players to have some control over their professional environment. He was instrumental in establishing the Players' League in 1890, although the venture soon ended in financial disaster. After retiring in 1894, Ward utilized his law degree from Columbia University to continue his quest to protect players from domineering owners. He died in Augusta, Georgia, and was posthumously elected the Baseball Hall of Fame in 1964.

Further Reading: David Q. Voight, *American Baseball: From Gentleman's Sport to the Commissioner System*, 1966; Cynthia Bass, "The Making of a Baseball Radical," *Review of Baseball History* 2 (Fall 1982): 63–65.

Steve Bullock

WARD, JOHN QUINCY ADAMS (29 June 1830–1 May 1910), sculptor. Born in Urbana, Ohio, Ward studied sculpting under Henry Kirke Brown in Brooklyn, New York, and learned to depict American themes with direct naturalism. His works *The Indian Hunter* and *The Freedman* brought him national prominence. In addition to models of political figures, Ward executed several public monuments, including some for New York City's Central Park and the Gettysburg National Military Park. Some of his finest public statues were of George Washington, General Lafayette, Horace Greeley, and James A. Garfield. Ward journeyed in 1872 to Europe, was influenced by French sculpture, and later collaborated with the architect Richard Morris Hunt. Ward, a trustee of the Metropolitan Museum of Art who sat on New York City's advisory committee of fine arts at the 1893 World's Columbian Exposition, was elected in 1898 to the National Institute of Arts and Letters. Active in numerous New York City social clubs, he was an outdoorsman whose country house at Peekamoose in the Catskill Mountains was a convenient meeting place for people of arts and letters. He died in New York City, having bridged the transition from neoclassicism to naturalism.

Further Reading: Lewis I. Sharp, *John Quincy Adams Ward: Dean of American Sculpture*, 1985; *New York Times*, 2 May 1910.

Leonard Schlup

WARD, LESTER FRANK (18 June 1841–18 April 1913), sociologist, social theorist, and critic. Born in Joliet, Illinois, Ward grew up in

Illinois and Iowa. He served in the Union Army, then earned degrees from Columbian College (now George Washington University). In 1881, Ward joined the U.S. Geological Survey; its director, John Wesley Powell, allowed him to pursue his own research and writing. Ward grew increasingly interested in the application of science to social problems. An enthusiastic secularist, he first edited a short-lived periodical appropriately titled the *Iconoclast*. He had been influenced by the deism of Thomas Paine and the Gilded Age freethinker Robert G. Ingersoll, and grappled with Darwin and evolutionary theory. After reading Auguste Comte's *Cours de philosophie positive* in 1875, Ward revised his earlier prospectus for a grand study of biology and sociology. Appearing in two massive volumes in 1883, *Dynamic Sociology* (first titled the *Great Panacea*) established Ward's reputation as a social theorist and critic of laissez-faire. Ward was one of the first and most serious critics of the arguments of William Graham Sumner. In subsequent works, Ward developed his central argument that attacked natural law justifications of individualism and championed intelligent human control of social development. His mature thought was a complex blend of Comtean scientism, Darwinian evolutionary rhetoric, and Whiggish state interventionism. He died in Washington, D.C.

Further Reading: Robert C. Bannister, *Sociology and Scientism: The American Quest for Objectivity, 1880–1940*, 1987; Gillis J. Harp, *Auguste Comte and the Reconstruction of American Liberalism, 1865–1920*, 1995; Edward Rafferty, "Apostle of Human Progress: The Life of Lester Frank Ward, 1841–1913," Ph.D. diss., Brown University, 1999.

Gillis J. Harp

WARNER, ADONIRAM JUDSON (13 January 1834–12 August 1910), economist, businessman, and congressman. Born in Wales, New York, Warner attended Beloit College in Wisconsin and New York Central College. After Civil War service, he gained admittance to the Indiana bar but never practiced law. In 1866, he moved to Marietta, Ohio, where he engaged in the oil, coal, and railroad businesses. He also built the Marietta and Cleveland Railroad. Denouncing the demonetization of

silver in 1873, Warner four years later published *The Appreciation of Money*. A Democrat, he served in the U.S. House of Representatives from 1879 to 1881 and again from 1883 to 1887, sponsoring free-coinage bills. Warner helped consolidate the American Bimetallic Union, and became its president in 1895. In 1896, he encouraged Democrats to nominate Senator Henry M. Teller of Colorado, a Silver Republican, for the presidency. After the presidential nomination that year of William Jennings Bryan, Warner fully endorsed the Democratic ticket and campaigned vigorously for the platform and free silver. In his later years, Warner occupied himself with street railway construction in the nation's capital, railroad improvements in Ohio, and transportation and power development in Georgia, where he organized the Gainesville Railway Company. Warner died in Marietta, Ohio.

Further Reading: *Daily Times* (Marietta), 13 August 1910; *Cincinnati Enquirer*, 14 August 1910.

Leonard Schlup

WARNER, CHARLES DUDLEY (12 September 1829–20 October 1900), editor, essayist, and novelist. Born in Plainfield, Massachusetts, and reared in Cazenovia, New York, Warner received a bachelor's degree from Hamilton College in 1851. He published articles and *The Book of Eloquence* (1851) while still a student, then worked as a railroad surveyor in Missouri after graduation. He next earned a law degree from the University of Pennsylvania. Warner practiced law in Chicago before moving in 1860 to Hartford, Connecticut, to edit the *Evening Press*. Its merger with the *Hartford Courant* in 1867 brought financial success. Warner penned essays on his boyhood, rural life, and travel. He also published four novels, but only *The Gilded Age* (1873), which he wrote with Mark Twain, is much read. (It was a critical and commercial failure at the time.) Warner enjoyed better fortune with biographies of Washington Irving and John Smith (both 1881), and with an edited collection *Library of the World's Best Literature* (1896–1897). Warner's enduring fame came from his stewardship of the *Hartford Courant*, which he elevated to an elite daily, and for his editorship of *Harper's Mag-*

azine, to which he also contributed columns and essays. He died in Hartford, Connecticut.

Further Reading: *Hartford Courant*, 22 October 1900; Annie A. Fields, *Charles Dudley Warner*, 1904; Thomas R. Lounsbury, ed., *The Complete Writings of Charles Dudley Warner*, 1904.

Robert E. Weir

WARREN, FRANCIS EMROY (20 June 1844–24 November 1929), senator, territorial governor, and mayor. Born in Hinsdale, Massachusetts, Warren attended the local secondary academy before enlisting in the Union Army during the Civil War. In 1868, he moved to Wyoming, where he raised livestock and, as a prominent businessman and Republican mayor, helped develop the city of Cheyenne. Following terms as territorial governor and treasurer, he was elected Wyoming's first state governor in 1890, but left the position in order to fill a U.S. Senate seat later that year.

As a Republican senator (1890–1893, 1895–1929), Warren successfully lobbied for his constituents' interests. He obtained federal aid in subduing Wyoming cattle rustlers, sponsored arid-land reclamation bills, and fought to keep army posts in his state. He supported efforts to reorganize the military, and in 1898 was instrumental in creating the Spanish-American War's Rough Rider cavalry regiments. Chairman of several committees, he became one of the most powerful members of Congress. Warren died in Washington, D.C.

Further Reading: Anne C. Hansen, "The Congressional Career of Senator Francis E. Warren from 1890 to 1902," *Annals of Wyoming* 20 (1948): 3–49, 131–158; Murray L. Carroll, "Governor Francis E. Warren, the United States Army and the Chinese Massacre at Rock Springs," *Annals of Wyoming* 59 (1987): 16–27; Leonard Schlup, "A Taft Republican: Senator Francis E. Warren and National Politics," *Annals of Wyoming* 54 (1982): 62–67.

Jane M. Armstrong

WARSHIPS OF THE NEW STEEL NAVY.
Following the Civil War, the U.S. Navy entered a dreary period. The majority of the nation's ships were laid up or sold, and Congress refused to authorize any new vessels. Meanwhile, the rest of the industrialized world embarked on a period of naval improvement that quickly made American vessels obsolescent. In 1881 and 1882, with congressional support, the navy convened two naval advisory boards to explore expansion. The result was a bill, passed on 3 March 1883, authorizing the construction of three cruisers and a dispatch boat. All four vessels would be built in private shipyards, of using American steel, a first for the navy and the catalyst for a close cooperation between the government and the steel industry that has been characterized as a key development in the origins of the military-industrial complex.

The three cruisers (the *Atlanta, Boston*, and *Chicago*) and the dispatch boat (the *Dolphin*) became known as the ABCD ships. Although based on purchased British plans, they were not as technically sophisticated or as powerful and well armed as their foreign counterparts. They were intended to fulfill the traditional American naval strategy of commerce raiding, not to participate in fleet battle actions. Their construction was marred by controversy, with the navy finally building the three cruisers. However, their very existence signaled the beginning of the reconstruction of the American fleet and, ultimately, a major shift in naval policy. Over the next two decades, dozens of new steel warships were authorized and built, culminating in the construction of a respectable American battle fleet by the early twentieth century. In April 1902, at the close of the Gilded Age, the U.S. Navy was the fourth largest in the world, behind Great Britain, France, and Russia. It was modern and balanced, containing vessels of all sizes and capabilities, all built of American steel, and all owing their origins to the ABCD ships.

Further Reading: Benjamin Franklin Cooling, *Gray Steel and Blue Water Navy: The Formative Years of America's Military Industrial Complex 1881–1917*, 1979; Mark R. Shulman, *Navalism and the Emergence of American Sea Power, 1882–1893*, 1995.

Kurt Hackemer

WASHBURNE, ELIHU BENJAMIN (23 September 1816–23 October 1887), politician and diplomat. Born in Livermore, Maine, Washburne attended Harvard Law School and joined the Massachusetts bar in 1840. That year he moved to Galena, Illinois, to practice law and invest in western lands. He was elected to the U.S. House of Representatives as a Whig in

1852. He served in Congress for sixteen years, as a Republican after 1854. During the Civil War he promoted the military and political career of a fellow Galena citizen, Ulysses S. Grant. As president, in March 1869, Grant appointed Washburne secretary of state, then selected him, twelve days later, as U.S. minister to France. During an eight-year ministry, Washburne witnessed the downfall of Napoleon III and France's defeat in the Franco-Prussian War of 1870–1871. He was the only foreign diplomat to remain in Paris throughout the German siege and the period of the French Commune. Upon his return to the United States in 1877, he settled in Chicago, devoting his last years largely to literary pursuits. He died in Chicago.

Further Reading: Gaillard Hunt, *Israel, Elihu, and Cadwallader Washburne*, 1925; Elihu B. Washburne, *Recollections of a Minister to France, 1869–1877*, 1877; *Chicago Tribune*, 24 October 1887.

Norman A. Graebner

WASHINGTON, BOOKER TALIAFERRO

(5 April 1856–14 November 1915), education leader. Born into slavery in Hale's Ford, Franklin County, Virginia, Washington moved with his family after emancipation to Malden, West Virginia, where he packed salt and mined coal until 1871. The next year he enrolled in Hampton Normal and Agricultural Institute, which emphasized character, morality, cleanliness, proper speech, manners, debate, and public service. He graduated in 1875, with honors in agriculture. Between 1875 and 1881, Washington taught school in Malden, briefly attended Wayland Seminary, and taught Native Americans at Hampton. In 1881, he became principal of a newly chartered teachers college for blacks in Tuskegee, Alabama.

Washington solicited financial support from local citizens and purchased a campus on the edge of town. Tuskegee stressed Hampton's values while focusing on industrial education. The curriculum included carpentry, cabinetmaking, printing, shoemaking, dairying, farming, homemaking, and tinsmithing. Students made and sold bricks to supplement the institution's income while Washington traveled the country, raising funds. Washington created a black community, complete with a hospital, nursing program, and agricultural experiment station, that was populated by small farmers, business professionals, and laborers. In 1900 he founded the National Negro Business League to coordinate black business and economic advancement. He preached hard work, thrift, saving, and property ownership along with developing institutions as an alternative to forcing integration. He meshed the school's goals with the desires of average blacks. In 1892 Tuskegee held the first annual conference to teach farmers the latest agricultural techniques.

On 18 September 1895 Washington delivered the keynote address at the Cotton States and International Exposition in Atlanta, Georgia, which catapulted him into the national spotlight and outlined his public philosophy on racial progress. He encouraged blacks to remain in the South and concentrate on moral and social uplift, patiently accommodating their interest to the southern political and cultural landscape. Washington believed it necessary to develop an economic base before blacks struggled for social equality.

Pilloried by black intellectuals who believed that he was surrendering to white racists, Washington muted much of the criticism through his influence over the black press. He was a master fund-raiser and promoter who traveled the North securing financial support from wealthy whites, such as Henry H. Rogers, Andrew Carnegie, John Wanamaker, Robert Ogden, William H. Baldwin, Collis Huntington, and Julius Rosenwald. Washington also developed close political ties to presidents William McKinley, Theodore Roosevelt, and Willaim Howard Taft. His critics did not know that he led a double life, financially supporting court challenges to all-white juries in Alabama, segregation on public transportation, and disenfranchisement of blacks. Privately, he shared the goals of the National Association for the Advancement of Colored People, fearing only that it might threaten his own considerable power within the black community. He died at Tuskegee.

Further Reading: Booker T. Washington Papers, Library of Congress; Louis Harlan, *Booker T. Washington: The Making of a Black Leader, 1865–1901*, 1972; August

Meier, *Racial Ideologies in the Age of Booker T. Washington*, 1963.

Abel A. Bartley

WASHINGTON INAUGURAL CENTENNIAL. Three days of celebration (29 April–1 May 1889) commemorated the centennial anniversary of George Washington's inauguration as the nation's first president. Attending the New York City celebration were President Benjamin Harrison, Vice President Levi P. Morton, cabinet officials, members of Congress, several Supreme Court justices, many governors, former presidents Rutherford B. Hayes and Grover Cleveland, and other dignitaries. On 30 April, a national holiday, artillery salutes echoed across Gotham. President Harrison sat in Washington's pew at St. Paul's Chapel, where the Episcopal bishop of New York, Henry Codman Potter, contrasted the Gilded Age with Washington's times. Potter's sermon, which annoyed Harrison, not only criticized Gilded Age materialism but also berated selfish government officeholders, admonished partisan practices, and mourned the lack of statesmanship. Speaking at the Federal Subtreasury Building, the site of Washington's inaugural, Harrison commented that self-seeking had no public observance or anniversary. The president and others later reviewed troops, attended open-air concerts, watched parades, dined at banquets, and gazed at fireworks.

Some upper-class society figures presented an image of the George Washington they cherished, a man too cultivated and refined for raw democracy. They yearned for the glorious days of Virginia's aristocracy, when everybody knew his place. Groups claiming Washington and Revolutionary War veterans as ancestors gathered for gala balls and glorious banquets along the east coast. In New York City, the Metropolitan Opera House was filled with women dressed in luxurious gowns decked with diamonds and pearls, expensive table settings, gourmet food, and exquisite music and dances. America's high society romanticized aristocracy in an era of increasingly blurred class lines.

Spectators witnessing Manhattan observances purchased souvenirs marking the occasion. When the sculptor Augustus Saint-Gaudens could not devote full attention to designing the official centennial medallion, he turned the work over to his assistant, Philip Martiny, a brilliant sculptor who had executed some carvings for the Cornelius Vanderbilt II mansion on Fifth Avenue. He eagerly accepted the assignment and received a formal commission to create models. The medal was struck in silver and bronze with a likeness of President Washington on the front. It was a fitting tribute to a cherished chief executive's memory.

Further Reading: Homer E. Socolofsky and Allan B. Spetter, *The Presidency of Benjamin Harrison*, 1987; Karal Ann Marling, *George Washington Slept Here: Colonial Revivals and American Culture, 1876–1986*, 1988.

Leonard Schlup

WASHINGTON, MARGARET MURRAY (9 March 1865–4 June 1925), educator. Born in Macon, Mississippi, Murray graduated from Fisk University in 1889. She then accepted appointment as an English instructor at Tuskegee Institute in Alabama, and in 1890, she became dean of women and director of the department of domestic sciences. Active in the endeavor to uplift her race, Washington assumed a leadership role in the African-American women's club movement; in 1895, she founded the Tuskegee Woman's Club. Some of her other achievements included establishing rural schools, teaching women the importance of home life, and promoting the improvement of prison conditions. Washington was vice president (1895) and subsequently president of the National Federation of Afro-American Women, which merged in 1896 with the National Association of Colored Women. She served the merged organization as secretary of the executive board. In 1902, she married Booker T. Washington, the noted African-American educator and leader. She died at her home in Tuskegee.

Further Reading: Margaret Murray Washington, "The Advancement of Colored Women," *Colored American Magazine* 6 (1905): 183–189; Wilma King Hunter, "Three Women at Tuskegee, 1885–1922: The Wives of Booker T. Washington," *Journal of Ethnic Studies* 4 (1976): 76–89; Margaret Murray Washington Papers, Frissell Library, Tuskegee, Alabama.

Leonard Schlup

WATSON, THOMAS EDWARD (5 September 1856–26 September 1922), congressman, vice presidential and presidential candidate. The Civil War impoverished the wealthy and slaveholding Watson family, leaving young Watson, born in Thomson, Columbia County, Georgia, with a strong sense of resentment couched in terms of rebellion and agrarian reform. He read law sporadically while teaching in rural schools, receiving his license in 1875. Watson's oratorical prowess, as well as his pugnacious attitude, quickly won him statewide fame. His disdain for northern industrialists, who appeared to be taking over the region, led him to enter politics as a reformer bent on restoring the South to its former agricultural glories. Watson was elected to the Georgia legislature in 1882 as a Democrat, and served until 1883.

Watson later joined the Farmers' Alliance and served in the U.S. House of Representatives under its banner in 1891–1892. During his term, he championed numerous reforms, including the first resolution for the rural free delivery of mail. In the turbulence of 1892 and 1894, Watson failed to reclaim his seat. Nevertheless, his cries against the expansion of industrial America attracted the attention of the People's Party, which named him its vice presidential candidate in 1896. After his defeat, Watson abandoned politics, devoting time to his law practice in Thomson, and to writing history and biography, publishing a magazine, and engaging in the newspaper business. In 1904, however, he returned to the political arena, serving as the Populist candidate for president, and standing again for his party in 1908. Embittered by his failure to reform the South, Watson turned against his egalitarian ideals, and espoused a rabidly anti-Semitic, anti-Catholic, and antiblack agenda. He was elected as a Democrat to the U.S. Senate in 1920, but died in Washington, D.C., before completing his term.

Further Reading: C. Vann Woodward, *Tom Watson: Agrarian Rebel*, 1938; Charles Crowe, "Tom Watson, Populists and Blacks Reconsidered," *Journal of Negro History* 55 (April 1970): 99–116.

Kimberly K. Porter

WATTERSON, HENRY (16 February 1840–22 December 1921), editor. Born in Washington, D.C., Watterson, served sporadically in the Confederate military, but he published the *Rebel*, its most popular newspaper. Later he edited the *Cincinnati Evening Times* (1865) before moving to Nashville to revive the *Nashville Republican Banner*. There Watterson enunciated his well-known "New Departure" program for the postwar South: accept the Thirteenth, Fourteenth, and Fifteenth amendments, forget the past, and work for a new, industrialized region. Watterson's success in Nashville prompted the owners of the *Louisville Daily Journal* to invite him to become its editor. Watterson accepted, and began a vigorous competition with the *Louisville Courier*, which was owned by Walter N. Haldeman, a Civil War acquaintance. In November 1868, Watterson proposed a consolidation; so began the *Louisville Courier-Journal* under their joint ownership.

Writing for the paper, Watterson earned a reputation as one of the nation's most colorful journalists. Master of the vivid phrase—his most famous was the World War I malediction "To Hell with the Hohenzollerns and Hapsburgs"—Watterson was a fervent but maverick Democrat. An ardent supporter of Samuel J. Tilden in 1876, he often differed with Grover Cleveland, William Jennings Bryan, and Woodrow Wilson. An old-style Jeffersonian Democrat, Watterson accepted many Progressive programs but remained opposed to prohibition, women's suffrage, and the League of Nations, which he denounced as "Wilson's Folly." Watterson was an isolationist, but an ardent nationalist who came to accept the necessity of war with Germany. He died in Jacksonville, Florida.

Further Reading: Joseph F. Wall, *Henry Watterson: Reconstructed Rebel*, 1956; Henry Watterson, *Marse Henry: An Autobiography*, 1919; Ronald R. Alexander, "Henry Watterson and World War I," *The Filson Club History Quarterly* 52 (1978): 251–262.

Nelson L. Dawson

WEAVER, JAMES BAIRD (12 June 1833–6 February 1912), third-party presidential nominee and congressman. Born in Dayton, Ohio, Weaver attended public schools in Michigan and Iowa, and earned a degree from the Cincinnati Law School in 1856. Civil War heroics made him a general, and opened a career in Iowa Republican politics. After securing minor offices in the 1870s, Weaver found his ambitions blocked and his reform ideas rejected by Republican leaders. He then joined the Greenback Party, won its presidential nomination in 1880, and, through fusion with the Democrats, was elected to Congress in 1878, 1884, and 1886. There he unsuccessfully championed financial reform, railroad regulation, and direct election of senators.

During the 1890s, Weaver helped organize the Populist Party. He received its presidential nomination and more than a million popular votes in 1892. Thereafter, he promoted fusion with Free Silver Democrats. His moderating financial views, oratorical and organizational skills, close ties to Democrats, and ruthless behavior helped bring the two parties together in the 1896 presidential campaign for William Jennings Bryan. As the Populists subsequently collapsed, Weaver gradually drifted into the Democratic Party and the obscurity of local politics. He died in Des Moines, Iowa.

Further Reading: Frederick Emory Haynes, *James Baird Weaver*, 1919; Peter H. Argersinger, *Populism and Politics*, 1974; Thomas Colbert, "Political Fusion in Iowa: The Election of James B. Weaver to Congress in 1878," *Arizona and the West* 20 (1978): 25–40.

Peter H. Argersinger

WELCH, WILLIAM HENRY (8 April 1850–30 April 1934), medical scientist and educator. Born in Norfolk, Connecticut, the son of a physician Welch graduated in 1870 from Yale College and five years later from the College of Physicians and Surgeons in New York City. Thereafter he studied in Germany. Once back in the United States, Welch established at Bellevue Hospital in New York the first teaching laboratory in pathology in the United States. In 1884 he accepted a professorship of pathology tendered by President Daniel Coit Gilman of Johns Hopkins University. Anxious to become part of a new departure in American medicine, Welch welcomed the assignment with its emphasis on research. He also persuaded his friend William Halsted, a cocaine addict, to

kick the habit. Halsted ultimately became head of surgery at Johns Hopkins University and one of the greatest surgeons in late nineteenth-century America. At First opposed to the admission of women to the medical school, Welch eventually succumbed to the power, money, and influence that dictated coeducation. With his medical researches and discoveries and prominent position in Baltimore, Welch by 1900 had become a national figure in medicine and reformer of medical education who achieved continuing success and recognition in the twentieth century. He died in the Johns Hopkins Hospital in Baltimore.

Further Reading: Simone Flexner and James T. Flexner, *William Henry Welch and the Heroic Age of American Medicine*, 1941; Donald Fleming, *William H. Welch and the Rise of Modern Medicine*, 1987; William H. Welch Papers, Welch Library, Johns Hopkins Medical School, Baltimore, Maryland.

Leonard Schlup

WELLINGTON, GEORGE LOUIS (28 January 1852–20 March 1927), congressman and senator. Born in Cumberland, Maryland, Wellington received little schooling, and at eighteen became a bank clerk. He entered public life in 1882 when he was chosen Allegany County treasurer. His service as a Republican National Convention delegate in 1884 and 1888 led President Benjamin Harrison to appoint him assistant U.S. treasurer at Baltimore in 1890. Wellington won a seat in the House of Representatives in 1894. There he successfully managed the gubernatorial campaign of his former employer, Lloyd Lowndes. Wellington also led a bipartisan coalition that broke the power of Arthur P. Gorman's political machine in 1895. Chosen state committee chairman that same year, Wellington positioned himself to be the Maryland legislature's choice for U.S. senator in 1896. In office he gained national attention for opposing the McKinley administration's plan to annex the Philippines. In 1900, he broke with his Republican president and actively campaigned for the Democratic candidate, William Jennings Bryan. Having accumulated political enemies, Wellington did not seek reelection in 1902. He supported the Bull Moose presidential candidacy of Theodore Roosevelt in 1912. One year later, Wellington lost his final bid for public office as a Progressive Party candidate for the Senate. He died in Cumberland, Maryland.

Further Reading: *New York Times*, 21 March 1927; George Wellington, *The People of the Philippine Islands Should Be Given the Right of Self-Government*, 1900.

Harvey Gresham Hudspeth

WELLMAN, SAMUEL THOMAS (5 February 1847–11 July 1919), engineer and inventor. Born in Wareham, Massachusetts, Wellman attended Norwich University in Vermont, served in the Union Army, and assisted in operating the first crucible steel furnace in the United States in 1867. He constructed the first commercially successful open-hearth furnace in America for the Bay State Iron Works at Boston. In 1873 Wellman moved to Cleveland, Ohio, where for sixteen years he served as chief engineer and superintendent of the Otis Steel Works. His endeavors resulted in nearly one hundred patents. Among his prominent inventions in the 1880s and 1890s were the electric open-hearth charging machine and the electromagnet for handling pig iron and scrap steel. In 1890, Wellman and his brother Charles established the Wellman Steel Company, which later became the Wellman-Seaver Engineering Company, with Samuel Wellman as president. Consolidation with a firm in Akron, Ohio, led to the Wellman-Server-Morgan Company, of which Wellman headed until his retirement in 1900. He was active in a number of engineering and technical societies and was president of the American Society of Mechanical Engineers in 1901. He died in Stratton, Maine.

Further Reading: *Cleveland Plain Dealer*, 12 July 1919.

Leonard Schlup

WELLMAN, WALTER (3 November 1858–31 January 1934), journalist and explorer. Born in Mentor, Ohio, Wellman moved to Akron, Ohio, in 1880. The next year, in partnership with his brother Frank, he started the *Akron Daily News,* a Republican paper. The paper was short-lived because of a bitter feud between Walter Wellman and his competitor, Carson Lake, publisher of the *Sunday Gazette.* One day Wellman printed an editorial defaming Lake's public and private character: "There is the creature and it has a tape worm for a soul," wrote Wellman. Lake immediately filed suit for libel, and Wellman fled to Cincinnati, where he founded the evening *Cincinnati Post.* From 1884 until 1911, Wellman served as the Washington correspondent of the *Chicago Herald* and its successor, the *Chicago Record-Herald.* In 1888, he backed Benjamin Harrison for the presidential nomination. On a trip to the Bahamas in 1891, Wellman claimed he located the exact landing spot of Christopher Columbus in 1492, on Watlings Island (today San Salvador). Interested in the North Pole, Wellman undertook expeditions by foot and airship in the 1890s and early twentieth century, but failed to reach his goal. Despite setbacks, he discovered new lands on treks by foot into the Arctic region. In 1910, Wellman became the first person to attempt to cross the Atlantic Ocean by air. Although all these adventures ended in failure, he was an early aeronaut and inspired others who succeeded him. Wellman died in New York City.

Further Reading: *Akron Beacon Journal*, 2 February 1934; *New York Times*, 1 February 1934.

Leonard Schlup

WELLS, DAVID AMES (17 June 1828–5 November 1898), economist. Born in Springfield, Massachusetts, Wells graduated from Williams College in 1847. Appointed special commissioner of the revenue in 1866, he sought to reshape the nation's tax structure, and shifted his tariff position from protection to free trade. Wells published numerous works on such economic issues as free trade, sound money, laissez-faire, and quantitative investigation. His *Practical Economics* appeared in 1885. Identified as a Liberal Republican in 1872, in opposition to President Ulysses S. Grant, Wells ran unsuccessfully as a Democrat for a seat in the U.S. House of Representatives from Connecticut in 1876 and 1890. His ambition to serve as secretary of the Treasury eluded him. Wells died in Norwich, Connecticut.

Further Reading: Fred B. Joyner, *David Ames Wells: Champion of Free Trade*, 1939; Tom E. Terrill, "David A. Wells, the Democracy, and Tariff Reduction, 1877–1894," *Journal of American History* 56 (1969): 540–555; David A. Wells Papers, Springfield Public Library, Springfield, Massachusetts.

Leonard Schlup

WELLS-BARNETT, IDA BELL (16 July 1862–25 March 1931), lecturer and activist. Born in Holly Springs, Mississippi to slave parents, Wells attended Rust College until her parents' deaths in 1878, then taught school to support her younger siblings. In 1884, her forcible removal from the "ladies' car" on a train launched her career of activism. Writing of her unsuccessful suit against the railroad, she turned to journalism, and eventually became editor of the *Memphis Free Speech*. After a good friend was lynched in Memphis in 1892, Wells wrote editorials attacking the myth that lynching was caused by black men's rape of white women. Driven out of Memphis, she moved to New York City. There Wells continued her crusade against lynching and all other forms of injustice, and also made two lecture tours of the British Isles. She married and settled in Chicago in 1895, and played key roles in founding such groups as the NAACP. Combining activism with motherhood, Wells-Barnett joined Susan B. Anthony in the fight for woman suffrage, established a black settlement house, investigated lynchings and race riots, published both pamphlets to expose injustice and two newspapers, fought against segregation of schools in Chicago, met with presidents to protest federal inaction against lynchings, became an ardent supporter of the Republican Party, and ran for the Illinois Senate in 1930. She died in Chicago.

Further Reading: Linda O. McMurry, *To Keep the Waters Troubled: The Life of Ida B. Wells*, 1999; Alfreda Duster, ed., *Crusade for Justice: The Autobiography of Ida B. Wells*, 1970.

Linda O. McMurry

WELSH, HERBERT (4 December 1851–28 June 1941), artist, publicist, and reformer. Born in Philadelphia, Welsh graduated from the University of Pennsylvania in 1871, took an interest in municipal reform, and wrote several books on Native Americans. He published *City and State*, a weekly newspaper, from 1895 to 1904. He denounced boss rule and advocated arbitration to settle international disputes. Welsh vigorously opposed America's acquisition of the Philippines in 1899, and was an active conservationist. His most important achievement began in December 1882, when he helped organize the Indian Rights Association. Headquartered in Philadelphia and committed to private donations for support, the nonsectarian, nonpartisan organization promoted favorable public sentiment, proper government treatment, and enhanced education. It encouraged settlement on individual landholdings, and ultimately citizenship. Welsh helped lead the organization for thirty-four years. He exposed schemes to defraud Native Americans, and worked to root out dishonesty and inefficiency fostered by the Indian Service's spoils system. Welsh died in Riverton, Vermont.

Further Reading: William T. Hagan, *The Indian Rights Association: The Herbert Welsh Years, 1882–1904*, 1985; Herbert Welsh, *Allotment of Lands: Defense of the Dawes Indian Severalty Bill*, 1887; *New York Times*, 30 June 1941.

Leonard Schlup

WESTINGHOUSE, GEORGE (6 October 1846–12 March 1914), inventor and manufacturer. Born in Central Bridge, New York, Westinghouse served in both the army and the navy during the Civil War. In the fall of 1865 he studied for three months at Union College, then returned to his father's farm implement shop to work with machines and inventions. Westinghouse's first patent, in 1865, was for a rotary steam engine. His first major invention was an air brake for railroad cars, patented in 1869 and improved thereafter, permitting safe, high-speed rail travel. In 1880, he turned to switches and signals, buying many patents, and in 1882 formed the Union Switch and Signal Company. An interest in electrical circuits grew out of this work, and others followed—in natural gas transmission, electricity production and transmission, electrical motors and meters, and more. After perfecting use of different pressures and pipe diameters to make gas transmission safe, Westinghouse learned in 1885 of a French system for transmitting high-voltage, single-phase, alternating current electricity. He employed engineers, purchased Nicola Tesla's patents and talents, and within months developed an improved system using two-phase current and transformers to step up and step down power.

Westinghouse Electric Company was born in

1886. That year two neighborhoods were experimentally lighted, as was the Chicago World's Columbian Exposition in 1893. Westinghouse lost control of his companies in the Panic of 1907. Though better at improving the ideas of others for practical use than at originating ideas, through his four hundred patents and corporate creations he left an indelible mark. Westinghouse died in New York City.

Further Reading: Barbara Ravage, *George Westinghouse: A Genius for Innovation*, 1997; Steven W. Usselman, "From Novelty to Utility: George Westinghouse and the Business of Innovation During the Age of Edison," *Business History Review* 66 (1992): 251–304; *American National Biography* 23 (1999): 83–85.

Douglas Steeples

WHEELER, WILLIAM ALMON (30 June 1819–4 June 1887), congressman and vice president of the United States. Wheeler was born in Malone, New York. He graduated from Franklin Academy in Malone and attended the University of Vermont for two years. He then returned to Malone, where he read law and was admitted to the New York bar in 1845. Before the Civil War he served as county district attorney, state assemblyman, state senator, and U.S. representative, then retired briefly. Election to New York's constitutional convention in 1867 rekindled his interest in politics, and he was returned to Congress from 1868 to 1874. At a time when legislators were disgracing themselves through one scandal after another, Wheeler proved utterly immune to financial temptations. His reputation for probity made him an easy choice for the vice presidency on the 1876 Republican ticket with Rutherford B. Hayes. They won, but their joy and reputations were diminished because of the disputed election.

Wheeler never truly enjoyed the vice presidency. The death of his wife, Mary, in 1876 saddened him so that he seemed to lose much of his zest for politics, and even for life. He absented himself from Washington and his vice presidential duties for long stretches, although he remained on warm terms with the president. Even after his retirement in 1881, Wheeler maintained epistolary ties with the Hayes family.

Further Reading: Frederick J. Seaver, *Historical Sketches of Franklin County*, 1918; Frank P. Vazzano, "Who Was William A. Wheeler?" *Hayes Historical Journal: A Journal of the Gilded Age* 9 (1993): 5–23; James T. Otten, "Grand Old Partyman: William A. Wheeler and the Republican Party, 1850–1880," Ph.D. diss., University of South Carolina, 1976.

Frank P. Vazzano

WHIPPLE, HENRY BENJAMIN (15 February 1822–16 September 1901), Episcopal bishop and advocate of Native American rights. Born in Adams, New York, Whipple attended Oberlin College, studied theology under William D. Wilson of Albany, and received ordination as an Episcopal priest in 1850. He served as rector in Rome, New York, and Chicago, Illinois, prior to becoming the first bishop of Minnesota in 1859. Whipple gained international attention through his missionary work with Native Americans. Involvement with various tribes convinced him that the national government had mismanaged their affairs and reneged on its treaty obligations. Through correspondence, travels, and lectures, Whipple urged federal officials to improve Native Americans' conditions. He wanted protection from white encroachment, cessation of liquor traffic, and creation of adequate reservations with suitable schools. Whipple's campaign earned him the wrath of frontiersmen and land seekers, but philanthropic and Christian organizations applauded his efforts. His opposition to fraud won him the sobriquet "Straight Tongue." In 1897, Whipple attended the Lambeth Conference as presiding bishop of the Protestant Episcopal Church. He died in Faribault, Minnesota.

Further Reading: Phillips Endecott Osgood, *Straight Tongue: A Story of Henry Benjamin Whipple, First Episcopal Bishop of Minnesota*, 1958; *New York Times*, 17 September 1901; Henry B. Whipple Papers, Minnesota Historical Society, Saint Paul.

Leonard Schlup

WHISKEY RING, criminal conspiracy. This was a secret association of federal government officials and more than thirty Midwestern liquor distillers who collaborated to defraud the federal government of tax revenues on distilled spirits. Benjamin H. Bristow, Ulysses S. Grant's third secretary of the Treasury (1874–1876), discovered that many of his subordinates in the Treasury Department were helping the distillers file false reports and taking kickbacks from the tax abatements granted to them. The scandal also centered around their efforts to bribe journalists, shop owners, and others, as well as to threaten and blackmail them, in order to keep their own actions out of both the public's and government's eye. Nevertheless, the story broke in the St. Louis newspapers.

Bristow's secret investigation revealed that the chief clerk of the Treasury, Orville E. Babcock (Grant's private secretary), and General John McDonald (St. Louis supervisor of revenues and Grant's close friend) were among those involved. His findings resulted in the seizure of sixteen distilleries in Chicago, St. Louis, and Milwaukee on 10 May 1875, and the subsequent indictment of over 240 people.

Many of those involved believed taxes on liquor were excessive. Ironically, most of the actions were common knowledge (among a public who shared their views), and it was the status of the individuals and the importance of the industry that originally prevented measures from being taken against them. It was also commonly believed that much of the money was funneled back into the Republican Party and its campaign funds. Grant, in an attempt to save the reputation of his friend and shed the image of scandal, desired to attend the trial of his secretary, Babcock, but was persuaded to do otherwise by members of his cabinet. Still wishing to help, he used his influence and sent a personal affidavit to St. Louis for consideration in the trial. Babcock was summarily acquitted while one hundred others were found guilty. Most of the latter, however, were soon pardoned. Under pressure, Babcock resigned his White House post, but was later appointed as a lighthouse inspector, a very profitable position.
Further Reading: William S. McFeely, *Grant: A Biography*, 1981; Mark W. Summers, *The Era of Good Stealings*, 1993.

Jerome D. Bowers II

WHISTLER, JAMES MCNEILL (11 July 1834–17 July 1903), artist.

Though born in Lowell, Massachusetts, Whistler later proclaimed himself a southerner and Baltimore, Maryland, his birthplace. After three years at West Point (1851–1854), in 1856 Whistler embarked upon an artistic career and enrolled in the atelier of Charles Gleyre in Paris. In Paris he befriended the young Realists Henri Fantin-Latour and Alphonse Legros, as well as Gustave Courbet. Whistler left Paris for London in 1859, and over the next decade gradually abandoned his Realist sympathies in favor of an aesthetic notion of "art for art's sake." He first drew critical attention with the controversial exhibition of *The White Girl* (1862, National Gallery of Art, Washington, D.C.) at the Salon des Refusés of 1863. Instead of the literary narratives found in many Victorian paintings, *The White Girl* presented Whistler's model, his common-law wife, Jo Hiffernan, standing on a bear skin in the artist's studio, gazing at nobody in particular and holding the remnants of a bouquet of flowers loosely in her hand. In this painting Whistler rejected the effusion of detail and anecdote prevalent within British art in favor of a Realist, modern scene of a model in his studio. In later renaming the painting *Symphony in White, No. 1*, Whistler emphasized the decorative, rather than the Realist, elements of the composition.

The musical titles of subsequent paintings, called "symphonies," "nocturnes," and "harmonies," suggested that, more than anything else, his works were to be appreciated as aesthetic arrangements of color and form. Although Whistler looked on his paintings as "arrangements" rather than strict reproductions of his sitters' likenesses, he became widely admired as a portraitist. His rendition of his mother, *Arrangement in Grey and Black* (1872, Louvre, Paris), is one of the most often reproduced images in American art. Also among Whistler's most important contributions to American art is the interior he designed for Frederick Richards Leyland, *Harmony in Blue and Gold: The Peacock Room* (1876–1877, Freer Gallery of Art, Washington, D.C.). Begun as an addition to an otherwise completed decorative scheme, this project soon transformed the dining room in Leyland's London home into feathery layers of blues, greens, and golds. An ardent admirer of Japanese and Chinese art, here Whistler created an Asian-inspired environment for Leyland's collection of Chinese blue-and-white porcelain. Working largely without his patron's approval, Whistler found in the end that Leyland was unwilling to pay for the project. They broke off relations in 1877, but not before Whistler had immortalized their feud within the decoration in the form of two quarreling peacocks.

Whistler's argumentative personality took a litigious turn in 1878 when he sued the critic John Ruskin for libel. The respected Ruskin had derided Whistler's evocative *Falling Rocket: Nocturne in Black and Gold* (1875, Detroit Institute of Arts) as an insult to the public. At the trial, Whistler took the stand to defend his work not as the result of hours of labor but as the expression of a lifetime's knowledge. He capitalized on trial publicity to become one of the most widely recognized Gilded Age figures, known for his ubiquitous "butterfly" signature and his peacock-like tuft of gray hair. He died in London.

Further Reading: Linda Merrill, *The Peacock Room: A Cultural Biography*, 1998; Richard Dorment and Margaret F. MacDonald, *James McNeill Whistler*, 1995; David Park Curry, *James McNeill Whistler at the Freer Gallery of Art*, 1984.

Lacey Jordan

WHITE, ANDREW DICKSON (7 November 1832–4 November 1918), historian, university president, and diplomat. Born in Homer, New York, White received a degree from at Yale in 1853. He then toured Europe and served as unpaid attaché to the U.S. minister to Russia. He earned an A.M. degree from Yale in 1857, and became professor of history and English literature at the University of Michigan. Following another trip to Europe, White served in the New York Senate from 1864 to 1867. There he persuaded other senators, including Ezra Cornell, to use the state's Morrill Land Grant monies to establish a comprehensive nonsectarian state university. White was president of that university, Cornell, from 1866 to 1885, with frequent absences to serve in diplomatic posts. The Cornell plan, featuring coeducation, integration of science and technology in the liberal arts curriculum, faculty involvement in administration, and an elective system of courses, helped shape the idea of the American university. He served as commissioner to Santo Domingo in 1871 and

minister to Germany from 1879 to 1881. Widely recognized as a scholar, White was the first president of the American Historical Association (1884–1885). He served as minister to Russia from 1892 to 1894, while completing his major work, *A History of the Warfare of Science with Theology in Christendom* (1896). White returned to Germany as ambassador in 1897 to 1902. His final posting was as head of the U.S. delegation to the First Hague International Peace Conference in 1899. He died in Ithaca, New York.

Further Reading: Glen C. Altschuler, *Andrew D. White— Educator, Historian, Diplomat*, 1979; Andrew D. White, *Selected Chapters from the Autobiography of Andrew D. White*, 1939.

Kim P. Sebaly

WHITE, ELLEN GOULD HARMON (26 November 1827–16 July 1915), religious leader and health advocate. Born near Gorham, Maine, and briefly educated in Portland, until a severe nasal injury left her a partial invalid seldom free from pain, Harmon, a Methodist, became a Millerite. In 1846 she married minister James White, a minister who regarded her as a prophetess possessing visionary gifts. Together they toured the nation preaching millenarianism and observing the seventh-day Sabbath. They moved to Michigan in 1855 and organized the Seventh-Day Adventist Church. Ellen's tenuous health worsened over the years due to several ailments and recurrent bouts of depression. In 1866 the Whites opened the Western Health Reform Institute, which emphasized proper diet and natural remedies, in Battle Creek, Michigan. Although she stopped experiencing daytime visions in the 1870s, White continued cultivating Adventism. After her husband's death in 1881, she and her son Willie carried their message to Europe, Australia, and New Zealand in the 1880s and 1890s. Upon returning to America in 1900, she lived on a farm near Saint Helena, California, where she died. Known as the "Lord's Messenger," White wrote hundreds of pamphlets, books, and articles. Her popular work, *Steps to Christ*, appeared in 1892.

Further Reading: Roy E. Graham, *Ellen G. White, Co-Founder of the Seventh-Day Adventist Church*, 1985; Ronald L. Numbers, *Prophetess of Health: Ellen G. White and the Origins of Seventh-Day Adventist Health Reform*, 1992.

Leonard Schlup

WHITE, GEORGE HENRY (18 December 1852–28 December 1918), congressman. White, the first African-American U.S. congressman, was born on a farm in Rosindale, North Carolina. Through personal determination, he worked himself up from poverty. White graduated from Howard University in 1877, studied law, and gained admission to the North Carolina bar in 1879. He practiced in the town of New Bern. White also was principal of the State Normal School, and served in both chambers of the state legislature during the 1880s. He served as solicitor and prosecuting attorney for the Second Judicial District from 1886 to 1894. From 1897 to 1901, White represented his district in the U.S. House of Representatives, where he condemned racial injustice and sponsored anti-lynching bills. He declined to seek reelection in 1900. White died in Philadelphia, Pennsylvania.

Further Reading: George W. Reid, "A Biography of George H. White, 1852–1918," Ph.D. diss., Howard University, 1974; Benjamin R. Justesen, *George Henry White: An Even Chance in the Race of Life*, 2001.

Leonard Schlup

WHITE, HELEN MAGILL (28 November 1853–28 October 1944), educator. Born in Providence, Rhode Island, White graduated in 1873 from Swarthmore College, of which her father, Edward Magill, was president. In 1877, she received a Ph.D. from Boston University, the first doctorate conferred on a woman in the United States. White subsequently studied in England at the University of Cambridge for four years. From 1883 to 1887, she directed Howard Collegiate Institute in Massachusetts. Over her professional career, she held teaching positions at various prepatory schools, but would have preferred an academic post at a coeducational institution of higher learning. In 1890 she married Andrew Dickson White, retired president of Cornell University. White accompanied her husband to his diplomatic stations in Saint Petersburg (1892–1894) and Berlin (1897–1903). Upon her return to the United States, White continued her intellectual pursuits and social endeavors. She died in Kittery Point, Maine.

Further Reading: Glenn C. Altschuler, *BetterThan Second Best: Love and Work in the Life of Helen Magill*, 1990; Geraldine J. Clifford, *Lone Voyagers: Academic Women in Coeducational Universities, 1870–1937*, 1989; Helen Magill White Papers, Division of Rare Books and Manuscript Collections, Cornell University Library, Ithaca, New York.

Leonard Schlup

WHITE, HENRY (29 March 1850–15 July 1927), diplomat. Born in Baltimore, Maryland, White spent much of his youth in Europe, becoming more familiar with its customs and schools than with Gilded Age life in the United States. His long diplomatic career began in 1883 when President Chester A. Arthur appointed him secretary of the American legation in Vienna, to work under Alphonso Taft. White later served as first secretary in London, under ambassadors James Russell Lowell, Edward John Phelps, and Robert Todd Lincoln. There he helped resolve Canadian fishing and sealing controversies. In 1893 President Grover Cleveland replaced him, but White acted unofficially as Secretary of State Richard Olney's representative in the settlement of Venezuela's boundary dispute with Great Britain. After the Republicans regained the presidency in 1897, President William McKinley gave him his former job as first secretary in London. White served for eight years under ambassadors John Hay and Joseph Choate. White aided in resolving the Alaskan boundary and paved the way for the abrogation of the Clayton-Bulwer Treaty of 1850, thus allowing negotiations that produced the Hay-Pauncefote Treaty of 1901, which secured exclusive U.S. control over an isthmian canal. White advised Secretary of State John Hay on the 1900 Boxer Rebellion, an attempt by Chinese revolutionaries to expel foreigners. In addition, White corresponded with Hay on the Open Door policy, designed to secure equal commercial opportunity in China and avoid discriminatory tariffs and other commercial barriers by foreign powers in regions of China under their influence.

In 1905, President Theodore Roosevelt appointed White ambassador to Italy. President Woodrow Wilson appointed White to the commission that helped negotiate the Versailles

Peace Treaty in 1918. White died in Lenox, Massachusetts. Considered the dean of American diplomats, he held distinctly progressive and liberal opinions on international affairs and saw diplomacy as an art that allowed nations to help one another to mutual advantage.

Further Reading: Allan Nevins, *Henry White: Thirty Years of American Diplomacy*, 1930; *New York Times*, 16 July 1927; Henry White Papers, Manuscripts Division, Library of Congress.

Leonard Schlup

WHITE, HORACE (10 August 1834–16 September 1916), journalist. Born in Colebrook, New Hampshire, White graduated from Beloit College in Wisconsin in 1853. An abolitionist who admired Abraham Lincoln, White joined the staff of the *Chicago Tribune*, a Republican newspaper, and worked as its Washington correspondent during the Civil War. In 1865 White became editor in chief of the newspaper. In this capacity, he berated President Andrew Johnson's mild Reconstruction policies and transformed his own conservative stand on African-American suffrage into unrestrained political and social liberalism. White castigated governmental interference in American society and opposed protective tariffs. In 1872 he aligned himself with the Liberal Republican rebellion against President Ulysses S. Grant, but he abhorred the embarrassing presidential nomination of the protectionist Horace Greeley.

The Chicago fire in 1871 cost White part of his fortune, and he resigned the *Tribune*'s editorship in 1874. Two years later he moved to New York City, where he linked his career to Henry Villard, a close friend, by assisting in the management of the latter's railroad interests and financial empire. Villard in return provided White with funds to purchase the *New York Evening Post* and the *Nation*. White thereupon persuaded Carl Schurz and Edwin L. Godkin to join forces with him in an editorial triumvirate. Schurz resigned in 1883. Godkin and White emerged as journalistic giants, turning their daily newspaper and weekly magazine into nationally recognized organs known for their independent thought, literary standards, and laissez-faire ideas. White exposed political corruption, supported the Mugwumps, and en-

dorsed Grover Cleveland's presidential candidacy. He opposed free silver, denigrated the nomination of William Jennings Bryan for president in 1896, attacked President William McKinley's overseas expansion policy, and coalesced with anti-imperialists for Filipino independence. White's books, editorials, and essays marked a distinctive period in the late nineteenth century and played a role in shaping the historiography of Gilded Age America. White died in New York City.

Further Reading: Joseph Logsdon, *Horace White: Nineteenth Century Liberal*, 1971; *New York Evening Post*, 18 September 1916; Horace White Papers, Illinois State Historical Library, Springfield.

Leonard Schlup

WHITE, STEPHEN MALLORY (19 January 1853–21 February 1901), U.S. senator. Born in San Francisco, California, White graduated from Santa Clara College in 1871, and practiced law in Los Angeles. He favored restriction of Chinese immigration, antitrust laws, and railroad regulation. A Democrat, he sat in the state senate and won election in 1893 to the U.S. Senate, where he served one term. White opposed repeal of the Sherman Silver Purchase Act in 1893. Backed by Harrison Gray Otis, Republican publisher of the *Los Angeles Times*, White sought to prevent the Southern Pacific Railroad from gaining a monopoly of the Santa Monica traffic, and helped secure federal construction of a harbor at San Pedro instead of Los Angeles. In 1898 White emerged as a ranking anti-imperialist. After leaving office, he practiced law and served on the city Chamber of Commerce and Bar Association. He died in Los Angeles.

Further Reading: Stephen M. White Papers, Stanford University Library, Stanford, California; *Los Angeles Times*, 22 and 23 February 1901; Curtis E. Grassman, "Prologue to Progressivism: Senator Stephen M. White and the California Reform Impulse, 1875–1905," Ph.D. diss., University of California at Los Angeles, 1971; Edith Dobie, *The Political Career of Stephen Mallory White*, 1927.

Leonard Schlup

WHITMAN, WALT (31 May 1819–26 March 1892), poet. Born in West Hills, in the town of Huntington, New York, Whitman attended what was then the only public school in Brooklyn, leaving in 1830. During the 1830s and 1840s he worked for Brooklyn and Manhattan newspapers as a compositor and editor, taught school on Long Island between 1836 and 1841, and was on the staff of the *Brooklyn Daily Eagle* from 1846 to 1848. In Washington, D.C., Whitman held clerkships in the attorney general's office from 1865 to 1872 and in the Treasury Department from 1873 to 1874. *Leaves of Grass*, published in 1855, was the major part of his work. In *Democratic Vistas* (1871), Whitman deplored rampant corruption in the political and economic life of postbellum America, but deferred the realization of democracy to the distant future. Nonetheless, he revealed in this work a more deferential attitude toward governmental authority, increasing confidence in the two-party system and in presidential power, and an acceptance of capitalistic expansion. His collections of poems of the early 1870s, *Passage to India* (1871) and *Song of the Exposition* (1871), praised technology. Although shaken by the depression of 1873–1879, he retained his belief in business, and by 1879 his observations of flourishing industrial cities had strengthened his faith in capitalism, leading him to assert that material wealth was essential to democracy.

Whitman supported the postwar presidents. Vigorously opposed to the impeachment of Andrew Johnson, he agreed with Johnson's Reconstruction policy that sought to heal the breach between the Union and the conquered South. He admired Ulysses S. Grant, overlooking the shortcomings of his presidency, as evidenced in his poem "Nay, Tell Me Not Today the Publish'd Shame" (1873). Though white Southern rule was revived as a result of the Compromise of 1877, Whitman respected Rutherford B. Hayes, thinking that the president might play a part in unifying the nation. Immediately following the shooting of James A. Garfield on 2 July 1881, he wrote "The Sobbing of the Bells," a poem expressing national bereavement. Whitman saw merit in Grover Cleveland, the conservative pro-business Democrat, celebrating his election victory in the poem "Election Day, November 1884," in which he maintained that presidential contests were wholesome. Above all, Whitman was persistent in his reverence for the Union war cause and the fallen Abraham Lincoln, giving memorial lectures about nineteen times between 1879 and 1890. Whitman died in Camden, New Jersey.

Further Reading: Justin Kaplan, *Walt Whitman: A Life*, 1980; David S. Reynolds, *Walt Whitman's America: A Cultural Biography*, 1995; Gary Schmidgall, *Walt Whitman: A Gay Life*, 1997.

Bernard Hirschhorn

WHITNEY, ANNE (2 September 1821–23 January 1915), sculptor, poet, and reformer. Born in Watertown, Massachusetts, Whitney was brought up believing in the equality of the sexes and the races. Privately educated, she eventually joined Boston literary society, the abolitionist movement, and the campaign for women's rights. Whitney hoped to influence social change through her poetry and published a volume of collected verse, *Poems*, in 1859. Her interests soon turned to sculpture, however. She carved works of social commentary, including *Lady Godiva* (1860) and *Africa* (1863–1864), before sailing for Europe in 1867 to study art. In Rome, she continued creating politically charged sculptures, such as *Roma* (1869) and *Toussaint L'Ouverture* (1870). Whitney lived abroad twenty-five years, but visited the United States regularly. In 1873, she won a commission from the state of Massachusetts for a full-length statue of Samuel Adams, produced in marble for Statuary Hall in the U.S. Capitol, and in bronze for Boston's Dock Square.

Whitney's fight against social injustice became more personal when, in 1875, she won a blind national competition for a public statue of Senator Charles Sumner, but was denied the award when it became known that she was a woman. Whitney and her longtime companion, Abby Adeline Manning, returned permanently to Boston in 1893. Whitney's final major sculpture was the 1902 realization in bronze of her original model of Senator Charles Sumner, which was erected in Harvard Square through private subscription. Whitney was one of many American women artists of the period to choose a career over family obligations, and one of a few to select sculpting as a career to inspire social justice in class, race, and gender through her art. Whitney died in Boston.

Further Reading: Elizabeth Rogers Payne, "Anne Whitney: Nineteenth Century Sculptor and Liberal," unpublished manuscript in the Anne Whitney Papers, Wellesley College Library, Wellesley, Massachusetts, and "Anne Whitney, Sculptor," *Art Quarterly* 25 (1962): 244–261; Lisa B. Reitzes, "The Political Voice of the Artist—Anne Whitney's 'Roma' and 'Harriet Martineau,' " *American Art* 8 (1994): 45–65.

Charlene G. Garfinkle

WHITNEY, WILLIAM COLLINS (5 July 1841–2 February 1904), lawyer, financier, secretary of the navy. Born in Conway, Massachusetts, Whitney graduated from Yale in 1863, attended Harvard Law school (1863–1864), and was admitted to the New York bar in 1865. He became a successful lawyer and a force in local politics. As an associate of Samuel J. Tilden, he helped oppose the Tweed Ring and served as corporation counsel for New York City from 1875 to 1882. Whitney is credited with effectively reorganizing the office. He also built a fortune in the street railway business. In politics Whitney was one of the early and important members of the County Democracy, founded to oppose the influence of Tammany Hall, and helped make it a potent Democratic organization within the state. He helped Grover Cleveland secure the Democratic nomination for governor in 1882 and played a prominent role in his nomination for president in 1884.

With Cleveland's election, Whitney went to Washington as secretary of the navy and was one of the president's closest advisers. Whitney presided over the beginnings of the transformation of the U.S. Navy. He reorganized the department's administration and increased its efficiency. He successfully worked for the expansion and modernization of the fleet, and convinced Congress to curtail expenditures on outdated wooden ships. He opposed, though with less success, the practice of political hiring at the navy yards. However, his opposition to an independent role for the new Naval War College headed by Alfred Thayer Mahan meant that the transformation of strategy and policy would be left to his successor. After Cleveland's defeat in 1888, Whitney returned to private life. Although he played a role in Cleveland's nomination and election in 1892, and fought the free silver movement at the Democratic Convention in 1896, he refused any further public office. He devoted the remainder of his life to business, society, and horse breeding.

Further Reading: Mark D. Hirsch, *William C. Whitney: Modern Warwick*, 1948; Allan Nevins, *Grover Cleveland*, 1932; Walter R. Herrick, Jr., *The American Naval Revolution*, 1966.

Michael J. Anderson

WHITTAKER, JOHNSON C. (23 August 1858–14 January 1931), West Point cadet, teacher, and lawyer. Whittaker was born a slave on the James Chesnut plantation near Camden, South Carolina. His mother served as a maid to Mary B. Chesnut during the diarist's visits to her father-in-law's home. In 1874, Whittaker attended the briefly integrated University of South Carolina; two years later, he obtained a West Point appointment. The only black man there for several years, he found himself ostracized by the cadets. On 6 April 1880, during reveille, he was found in his room, unconscious, arms and legs bound, hair gouged, and ears slashed. He told of three masked men attacking him during the night, threatening to kill him if he did not leave the academy. Suspicious authorities hastily summoned a board of inquiry, which found him guilty of self-mutilation, and an 1881 court-martial, that he demanded to clear himself, agreed. Both proceedings received wide national attention. The judge advocate general threw out the decision in 1882, but Secretary of War Robert Todd Lincoln ejected Whittaker from the academy anyway, allegedly for failing an oral examination in June 1880. Whittaker became a teacher in South Carolina and Oklahoma, and died in Orangeburg, South Carolina. President Bill Clinton posthumously awarded him an army commission in 1994.

Further Reading: John F. Marszalek, *Court-Martial: A Black Man in America*, 1972, paperback ed. retitled as *Assault at West Point*, 1994; court of inquiry and court-martial records, R.G. 153, National Archives.

John F. Marszalek

WILCOX, ELLA WHEELER (5 November 1850–30 October 1919), poet. Born in Johnstown Center, Wisconsin, Wheeler spent an unproductive year at the University of Wisconsin in 1867. She then devoted her life to writing poetry and fiction. In 1884 she married a businessman, Robert Marius Wilcox. Her early poems appeared in Gilded Age periodicals including *Peterson's Magazine* and *Arthur's Home Magazine*. After a Chicago publisher rejected her *Poems of Passion* (1882) as immoral, newspapers, quickly capitalized on the event, bringing her much publicity. Another Chicago publishing house immediately accepted the work, which sold sixty thousand copies in the first two years. A love poet who also tackled alcoholism and prostitution, Wilcox added fiction to her literary repertoire. Among these works were *Sweet Danger* (1892) and *An Ambitious Man* (1896). Although her style and content did not impress critics, Wilcox composed verses for a broad popular audience. Her poetry reached the pages of such magazines as *Ladies' Home Journal, Munsey's Magazine, Woman's Home Companion*, and *Good Housekeeping*. A student of theosophy, a world traveler, and a woman known for her flamboyant personality, she penned poems that gave consolation and inspiration to millions of readers. Wilcox died in Short Beach, Connecticut.

Further Reading: Jenny Ballou, *Period Piece: Ella Wheeler Wilcox and Her Times*, 1940; *New York Times*, 31 October 1919.

Leonard Schlup

WILCOX, ROBERT WILLIAM KALANI-HIAPO (15 February 1855–23 October 1903), Hawaiian rebel leader and territorial delegate. Born in Kahalu, Honuaula, on the island of Maui, Hawaiian Islands, Wilcox attended the Haleakala Boarding School at Makawao, and taught school at Honuaula. He won election in 1880 to the Hawaiian legislature as a representative from Wailuku, and pursued an academic course under the Kalakaua Studies Abroad program at the Royal Military Academy at Turin, Italy, from 1881 to 1885. After being recalled by the Hawaiian government in 1887, Wilcox temporarily moved to San Francisco, California, where he worked as a surveyor. In 1888 he returned to Hawaii, and with some three hundred armed men, attempted to unseat the government. Unsuccessful, the scrappy Wilcox, wearing his Italian officer's uniform, led another revolutionary coup assault in 1889, commanding an army of 150 Hawaiians and Europeans. Wilcox and his men briefly occupied government buildings across the street from Iolani Palace, the royal domain. Tried for high treason, Wilcox was acquitted by a Hawaiian jury convinced of governmental usurpation. Wilcox's two failed rebellions sought to overturn the "Bayonet Constitution," of June 1887, which sharply curbed the monarchy's powers, allowed whites to vote, diminished the political voice of native Hawaiians, and transformed King Kalakaua, the "Merry Monarch," into a powerless figurehead. This document, which the all-white Hawaiian League forced the king to sign, had never been put to the people in a referendum.

Wilcox, elected to the legislature as a representative from Honolulu in 1890 and from Koolauloa two years later, gained additional prominence in 1895 as an insurgent committed to Queen Liliuokalani's restoration. The uprising began with an exchange of shots at Diamond Head, but Wilcox and his Kamehameha Rifles were easily subdued. After the melee, he emerged as a popular hero. Arrested, court-martialed, and sentenced to death, Wilcox escaped execution upon the commutation of his sentence to thirty-five years, and ultimately by the pardon afforded him by President Sanford B. Dole in 1898, the year of Hawaii's annexation to the United States. Elected as the first delegate from Hawaii to the U.S. House of Representatives, Wilcox served from 1900 to 1903. A powerful orator, a charismatic leader, and a newspaper editor who possessed a genuine concern for people, Wilcox fought against what he considered to be injustices to Hawaiians by the planter-business oligarchy. He died in Honolulu.

Further Reading: Ralph S. Kuykendall, *The Hawaiian Kingdom*, 3 vols., 1938–1967; Albertine Loomis, *For Whom Are the Stars? Revolution and Counterrevolution in Hawaii, 1893–1895*, 1976; A. Grove Day, *History Makers of Hawaii: A Biographical Dictionary*, 1984.

Leonard Schlup

WILLARD, FRANCES ELIZABETH CAROLINE (28 September 1839–17 February 1898), educator, journalist, and temperance leader. Born in Churchville, New York, Willard received most of her early education under her mother's tutelage at her wilderness home near Janesville, Wisconsin. Following a year of study at Milwaukee Female College in 1856, and graduation from Northwestern Female College in Evanston, Illinois, in 1859, Willard taught at several academies in Illinois and Pennsylvania. She took a study tour of Europe and the Middle East from 1868 to 1870. When she returned to the United States, she was appointed president of Evanston College for Ladies, the new women's department of Northwestern University. An effective writer and speaker, Willard resigned in 1873 to become an organizing member of the Woman's Christian Temperance Union (WCTU). She was elected WCTU national corresponding secretary in 1874, and became the organization's moving force. She served as president from 1879 to 1896, and as president of the world organization in 1891. Active in women's suffrage and numerous other social reform movements, Willard helped organize the Prohibition Party in 1882 and the Populist Party a decade later. She was elected president of the National Council of Women in 1888. Willard died in New York City.

Further Reading: Ruth Bordin, *Frances Willard: A Biography*, 1986; Carolyn De Swarte Gifford, ed., *Writing Out My Heart: Selections from the Journal of Frances E. Willard, 1855–96*, 1995.

Kim P. Sebaly

WILLIAMS, DANIEL HALE (18 January 1858–4 August 1931), surgeon. Born in Hollidaysburg, Pennsylvania, Williams received a degree from the Chicago Medical College in 1883. He worked to provide additional hospital facilities for residents of Chicago, and sought training schools for African-American doctors and nurses. With the opening in 1891 of Provident Hospital in Chicago, which had an interracial staff, Williams realized his dream. He served on Provident's surgical staff for most of the period between 1891 and 1912. There, on 9 July 1893, he performed the world's first successful open-heart operation. The patient, James Cornish, an African-American laborer, had been stabbed in the chest. Although medical opinion did not recommend incisions for this type of wound, Williams remained convinced that without surgery, the patient would die. Cornish recovered fully from the procedure. Williams spent the period 1893–1898 as surgeon in chief at the Freedmen's Hospital in Washington, D.C. In 1899, he was named professor of clinical surgery at the black Meharry Medical College in Nashville, Tennessee. Williams gained recognition as the first African American to serve on the Illinois State Board of Health. He died in Idlewild, Michigan.

Further Reading: Helen Buckler, *Daniel Hale Williams, Negro Surgeon*, 1968; Lewis R. Fenderson, *Daniel Hale Williams: Open-Heart Doctor*, 1971; Lillie Patterson, *Sure Hands, Strong Heart: The Life of Daniel Hale Williams*, 1981.

Leonard Schlup

WILLIAMS, GEORGE HENRY (26 March 1823–4 April 1910), U.S. senator and attorney general. Born in New Lebanon, New York, Williams practiced law, served as a judge in Iowa, and later moved to Oregon. There he opened a law firm in Portland, acquired the *Oregon Statesman*, and received a presidential appointment as chief justice of Oregon's territorial court (1853–1857). Williams joined the Republican Party in 1864. That year the Oregon state legislature elected him to the U.S. Senate, where he served from 1865 to 1871. Williams supported the Radical Republicans, introduced the Tenure of Office Act of 1867, and advocated the impeachment of President Andrew Johnson. He backed Ulysses S. Grant for the presidency, and secured a diplomatic appointment to the Joint High Commission with Great Britain, which resulted in the Treaty of Washington of 1871.

After failing in a bid for reelection to the Senate, Williams accepted President Grant's appointment as attorney general, a post he held from 1872 until 1875. On 1 December 1873, the president surprised the nation by nominating Williams for the chief justiceship of the Supreme Court. Almost immediately Williams came under attack as insufficiently qualified.

On 7 January 1874 he withdrew his name, citing the flood of calumny that had disparaged him. He practiced law in Washington for a short time before returning to Portland, where he died.

Further Reading: *New York Times*, 5 April 1910; *Portland Morning Oregonian*, 5 April 1910; Sidney Teiser, "Life of George H. Williams: Almost Chief Justice," *Oregon Historical Quarterly* 47 (1946): 256–280, 417–440; George H. Williams Papers, Oregon Historical Society, Portland.

Leonard Schlup

WILLIAMS, JOHN STUART

WILLIAMS, JOHN STUART (29 June 1818–17 July 1898), soldier and senator. Born in Montgomery County, Kentucky, Williams attended Houston Seminary and Miami University in Ohio before practicing law in Paris, Kentucky. He commanded a Kentucky regiment during the Mexican War and later served as a state legislator and as an observer for the U.S. government during the Crimean War. During the Civil War, Williams rose to brigadier general in the Confederate Army. He reentered the state legislature in 1873. He narrowly lost the Democratic nomination for governor in 1875 to James B. McCreary, partly because of allegations about his private morals. In 1876 he was defeated in a U.S. Senate bid by James B. Beck. Finally, in 1879 Williams won a Senate seat when William McCreery retired and Williams roundly defeated Robert Boyd for the nomination. Allegations of a political "deal" concerning that nomination and legislative inactivity marked Williams's term, and he lost his bid for renomination. Williams died and is buried in Winchester, Kentucky.

Further Reading: Hambleton Tapp and James C. Klotter, *Kentucky: Decades of Discord*, 1977; John David Preston, *The Civil War in the Big Sandy of Kentucky*, 1984.

Damon Eubank

WILLIAMS v. MISSISSIPPI

WILLIAMS v. *MISSISSIPPI* (170 U.S. 213). This was one of a series of legal cases concerning whether state laws were being used to exclude blacks from jury service. Writing for a unanimous court in 1898, Justice John Marshall Harlan declared that a jury statute, which on its face appeared nondiscriminatory, should be held in violation of the Fourteenth Amendment if in its application a consistent pattern of preventing blacks from serving on juries was found. Harlan affirmed the principle of *Strau-*der v. *West Virginia*, 100 U.S. 303 (1879), which denounced racial discrimination in jury selection. Despite the strong declarations against discrimination in this and ten similar cases, the court failed to set aside a single conviction handed down by juries from which blacks had been excluded.

Further Reading: Owen M. Fiss, *History of the Supreme Court of the United States*, Vol. 8, *Troubled Beginnings of the Modern State, 1888–1910*, 1993, pp. 372–373; Benno C. Schmidt, Jr., "Juries, Jurisdiction, and Race Discrimination: The Lost Promise of *Strauder* v. *West Virginia*," *Texas Law Review* 61 (1983): 1401.

Thomas C. Sutton

WILSON, HENRY

WILSON, HENRY (16 February 1812–22 November 1875), senator and vice president. Originally named Jeremiah James Colbath, Wilson was born in Farmington, New Hampshire. In 1855, his antislavery views led him to the Republican Party. That same year he became a U.S. senator from Massachusetts, and served until 1873.

Wilson's opposition to President Andrew Johnson's Reconstruction policies made him a well-known Radical Republican. He supported a movement, led by Representative George Hoar of Massachusetts, to create a federal labor commission. Wilson simultaneously called for banking policies and structures that would serve business interests, but fought government subsidies to the railroads. He thereby became identified as supporting small farmers. Wilson was adamant about the wording of the rewritten Southern states' constitutions, seeking to ensure that African Americans were protected. He opposed the Fifteenth Amendment on the grounds that it did not adequately provide for sustained property rights and future education of blacks. Wilson's commitment to social justice led to his introduction of a bill in 1868 advocating female suffrage in the District of Columbia. In 1870, he challenged the Senate to protect both the Native American tribes and Chinese Americans from the abuses caused by western expansion and growing capitalism. Wilson also argued for civil service reform, advocated temperance, called for immigration with protected rights, sought federal relief for victims of the Chicago fire, and hoped to use public funds to ensure that every American had a home.

Wilson was a prolific author and Senate historian. His most notable work, begun in 1872, was *History of the Rise and Fall of the Slave Power in America*, completed posthumously and published in 1877. Wilson's moral convictions and upstanding reputation were seen as a benefit to President Ulysses S. Grant's scandal-laden and corruption-prone first term. They earned Wilson nomination to the vice presidency, though he suffered somewhat from his close, albeit inadvertent connection to the Crédit Mobilier affair. He died in Washington, D.C., twelve days after suffering a stroke while in the Capitol.

Further Reading: Ernest McKay, *Henry Wilson, Practical Radical: A Portrait of a Politician*, 1971; Thomas Russell and Elias Nason, *The Life and Public Services of Honorable Henry Wilson*, 1872; *New York Times*, 23 November 1875.

Jerome D. Bowers II

WILSON, JAMES (16 August 1835–26 August 1920), agriculturalist. Born in Ayrshire, Scotland, Wilson came with his family to Traer, Iowa, in 1855 and established a dairy and sheep farm. He studied agriculture and history at Iowa College in Iowa City, but did not receive a degree. In 1867 he won a seat in the state legislature, where he served three terms as a Republican and rose to speaker. He advocated state support of agricultural education and experiment stations. Between 1873 and 1877 and again between 1883 and 1885, he served in Congress. After leaving office, Wilson published more than fifty essays in agricultural journals and newspapers. They enhanced his reputation as a progressive farmer and won him appointment in 1890 as professor at Iowa State College and director of the Iowa Agricultural Experiment Station. In only six years Wilson doubled the station's state appropriations and number of scientists. In 1896 he supported William McKinley for president, and the next year McKinley appointed him secretary of agriculture. In 1901 Wilson enlarged the department by adding the bureaus of Chemistry, Plant Industry, and Soils. In addition, he advocated greater federal funding for the experiment stations and a greater role for the Department of Agriculture in overseeing them, ideas Congress would enact in 1906. He headed the department until 1913, longer than any other commissioner or secretary. He died in Traer, Iowa.

Further Reading: Alfred C. True, *A History of Agricultural Experimentation and Research in the United States, 1607–1925*, 1937.

Christopher Cumo

WILSON, JAMES FALCONER (19 October 1828–22 April 1895), representative and senator. Born in Newark, Ohio, Wilson in 1853 formed a law partnership in Fairfield, Iowa, and helped found the state Republican Party. Elected to the U.S. House of Representatives, he served from 1861 to 1869. There he promoted the civil and political equality of African Americans. He also chaired the Judiciary Committee for six of his eight years. He maintained a close personal friendship with President Ulysses S. Grant, but declined to serve as his secretary of state. He did, however, accept Grant's appointment as a government director of the Union Pacific Railroad. In 1882 Wilson won election to the U.S. Senate and secured a second term six years later. His tenure lacked the achievements that had marked his years in the House; many outstanding issues that had propelled him into the national spotlight had been resolved by the late 1880s. Wilson helped frame the Interstate Commerce Act of 1887, favored protective tariffs, and endorsed bimetallism. A teetotaler who belonged to the Sons of Temperance, he defended prohibition. Wilson held a Whiggish view of the presidency. A highly moralistic person who at times fell victim to Gilded Age political culture, he was more inclined to conform than to criticize a postwar era beset by a crisis of values. He died in Fairfield, Iowa.

Further Reading: Leonard Schlup, "Republican Loyalist: James F. Wilson and Party Politics, 1855–1895," *Annals of Iowa* 52 (1993): 123–149; *Fairfield Daily Ledger*, 23 April 1895; *Iowa State Register*, 23 April 1895.

Leonard Schlup

WILSON, THOMAS WOODROW (29 December 1856–3 February 1924), educator, politician, and future president of the United States. Wilson was born in Staunton, Virginia, and spent his childhood living throughout the South. He was graduated from Princeton University in 1879, and received a Ph.D. from Johns Hopkins in 1885. He taught at Bryn Mawr, Johns Hopkins, Wesleyan, and, after 1890, Princeton. His dissertation and most important work, *Congressional Government*, was published in 1885. It argued that the committee system in Congress and the supremacy of the legislative branch over the executive branch thwarted governmental efficiency by decentralizing authority and obscuring debate. By contrast, he found the English system to be a model of open discussion and accountability. Wilson continued to publish, but the quality of his scholarship and the originality of his interpretations steadily declined.

As a southerner, Wilson was naturally drawn to the Democratic Party, but he repudiated the predominant states' rights doctrine of his native section. Although a conservative proponent of laissez-faire economics, he also rejected William Jennings Bryan's populistic politics. Only in 1908, after deciding to seek political office, did Wilson adopt more progressive views. He died in Washington, D.C.

Further Reading: John Morton Blum, *Woodrow Wilson and the Politics of Morality*, 1956; Arthur S. Link, *Wilson: The Road to the White House*, 1947.

Gregory Dehler

WILSON, WILLIAM LYNE (8 May 1843– 17 October 1900), educator, congressman, cabinet officer. A native of West Virginia, Wilson was graduated from Columbian College in Washington, D.C., in 1860 and fought in the Confederate cavalry. In 1871 he began a law practice in Charles Town (now Charleston) and was soon active in local Democratic politics. A presidential elector in 1881, he served as president of the University of West Virginia from 1882 to 1883. In the latter year, Wilson began the first of six terms as a U.S. representative. He quickly became a leading opponent of protective tariffs (save for West Virginia coal), which he believed burdened farmers and laborers, and resembled the hated taxes that had provoked the American Revolution. Favoring Jeffersonian limited government, he nevertheless viewed the trusts as menaces to be curbed. In response to Grover Cleveland's plea for reduced tariffs, Wilson introduced the Mills bill in 1888. Following its failure to pass, he led opposition to the 1890 McKinley Tariff. Wilson became chairman of the House Ways and Means Committee in 1893, and introduced the reform bill ultimately enacted as the Wilson-Gorman Tariff of 1894. Defeated in 1894, along with legions of Democratic colleagues, he became postmaster general. In 1896, he accepted the presidency of Washington and Lee University in Lexington, Virginia, where he remained until death.

Further Reading: Festus P. Summers, *William L. Wilson and Tariff Reform: A Biography* (1953); *American National Biography* 23 (1999): 602–604; Thomas R. Tull, "The Shift to Republicanism: William L. Wilson and the Election of 1894," *West Virginia History* 37 (October 1975): 17–33.

Douglas Steeples

WILSON-GORMAN TARIFF Of 1894. Introduced in the House of Representatives on 19 December 1893 by West Virginia Representative William Lyne Wilson, the bill in its initial form aimed to fulfill 1892 Democratic election promises to reduce customs duties. It easily passed the House, 204–140. As approved, it cut rates on manufactures moderately and placed iron ore, coal, sawed lumber, pig copper, wool, hemp, flax, and raw sugar on the free list. An amendment, imposing a 2 percent annual tax on personal and corporate incomes over $4,000, pleased agrarian radicals. In the Senate, Republicans joined protectionist Democrats, led by Arthur Pue Gorman of Maryland, to roll back House cuts. Ultimately, protectionists added 634 amendments. After a futile struggle, the House submitted to the Senate revisions. Duties on manufactures fell by only a fifth, to 40 percent. Raw sugar gained a 40 percent protective rate, despite revelations during legislative debates of sugar-trust influence peddling. Only raw wool, hides, lumber, pig copper, and a few minor items remained on the free list. A disgusted President Grover Cleveland let the bill become law without his signature. The income tax remained, until the Supreme Court struck it down in 1895.

Further Reading: Paul Wolman, *Most Favored Nation: Republican Revisionists and U.S. Tariff Policy, 1897–1912*, 1992; Tom E. Terrill, *The Tariff, Politics, and American*

Foreign Policy, 1874–1901, 1973; Festus P. Summers, *William L. Wilson and Tariff Reform*, 1953.

Douglas Steeples

WINDOM, WILLIAM (10 May 1827–29 January 1891), U.S. representative, senator, secretary of the Treasury. Windom was born in Belmont County, Ohio, and moved in 1855 to Minnesota territory, where he became involved in Republican politics. He represented Minnesota in the U.S. House of Representatives from 1859 to 1869, and in the Senate from 1870 to 1881 and again from 1881 to 1883. He supported moderate railroad regulation, pushing for a federal bureau to collect data and publicize rates, but opposed setting of rates. Unsuccessfully, Windom sought his party's presidential nomination in 1880. Appointed President James A. Garfield's secretary of the Treasury in 1881, he financed government bonds that were due on 1 July at a lower interest rate, thereby saving taxpayers over $10 million. He left the cabinet in November 1881 after regaining his Senate seat. Windom became President Benjamin Harrison's Treasury secretary in 1889. He supported protective tariffs and limited bimetallism. Windom suffered a fatal heart attack while addressing the New York Board of Trade and Transportation in New York City.

Further Reading: Robert Salisbury, *William Windom: Apostle of Positive Government*, 1993, and "William Windom, the Republican Party, and the Gilded Age," Ph.D. diss., University of Minnesota, 1982; *New York Times*, 30 January 1891.

Bryan Craig

WINNEMUCCA, SARAH (THOCME-TONY or SHELL FLOWER) (c. 1844–17 October 1891), Indian rights activist. Born near Humboldt Lake in Nevada, this Paiute Indian woman sought improved conditions for her tribe and other Native Americans, and better relations with whites. After learning English and Spanish as a youth on a ranch in San Joaquin, California, and later in the home of Major William Ormsby in Genoa, Nevada, she taught and interpreted for her people. Winnemucca appeared on stage, wrote letters, and presented lectures in the West and East about the plight of Native Americans under the federal reservation policy. She asked officials in Washington, including President Rutherford B. Hayes, to allot reservation land and give titles and citizenship to Indians. Supported by philanthropists in the East, her autobiography, *Life Among the Piutes: Their Wrongs and Claims*, was published there in 1883. Winnemucca died at her sister's home in Monida, Montana, and was buried near Henrys Lake in Idaho. Although her efforts brought few improvements to the Paiutes, General Otis Howard, for whom she served as guide, scout, and interpreter during the Bannock Indian War (1878), stated that her service to the United States government earned her equality with Pocahontas.

Further Reading: Gae Whitney Canfield, *Sarah Winnemucca of the Northern Paiutes*, 1983; *New York Times*, 27 October 1891.

Jane F. Lancaster

WINSOR, JUSTIN (2 January 1831–22 October 1897), librarian and historian. Born and reared in Boston, Winsor gained renown as superintendent of the Boston Public Library (1868–1877). He was the first to employ statistical data about the collections' use. Winsor believed a library should facilitate citizens' self-improvement and combat low culture. Light fiction could entice them into the building, where they would naturally move to uplifting literature. In 1876, he helped found the American Library Association, and served as its first president. In 1877, Winsor became director of Harvard University Library. It was an era of change in higher education, from the old, lecture-recitation classroom to a research and publication model. Winsor opened the stacks, improved the catalog, established a reserve system, and campaigned for electric lighting to permit evening use. He spread his concept of the academic library as "the centre of the university system." Winsor also pursued historical and cartographical research and writing, and served as an early president of the American Historical Association. His combination of leadership and historical writing made him the era's ideal academic librarian.

Further Reading: Wayne Cutler and Michael H. Harris, *Justin Winsor: Scholar-Librarian*, 1980; William A. Koelsch, *A Profound Though Special Erudition: Justin Winsor as Historian of Discovery*, 1983; William E. Foster,

"Five Men of '76," *Bulletin of the American Library Association* 20 (October 1926): 3–13.

Philip H. Young

WINTON, ALEXANDER (20 June 1860–21 June 1932), automotive pioneer, manufacturer, inventor. Born in Grangemouth, Scotland, Winton immigrated to the United States and moved to Cleveland, Ohio, in 1884. He manufactured an improved bicycle of his own design, but abandoned the successful business as his interest turned to the horseless carriage. In 1898, he sold the first mass-produced, standard-model automobile in America. Although Winton held more than one hundred patents, mainly for engine improvements, promotional efforts may have been his most notable achievement. He became a celebrity in 1899 when he completed a widely publicized five-day drive from Cleveland to New York City, intended to prove that the car was not a passing fad. Nationally syndicated newspaper accounts of the trek standardized the name "automobile" for the vehicle. In 1900, he embraced racing as a way to promote interest in cars, and that year he became the first American to compete in European auto races. In 1901, he became the fastest man in America when he achieved 57.8 miles per hour in his racer, "The Bullet." Although Winton was one of America's largest, most successful automakers, sales peaked at 2,450 vehicles in 1916. His expensive, top-quality cars lost popularity after Henry Ford and others introduced cheaper models. Winton's engine works evolved into the General Motors Diesel Engine Division.

Further Reading: Richard Wager, *Golden Wheels: The Story of the Automobiles Made in Cleveland and Northeastern Ohio, 1892–1932,* 1975; *New York Times,* 23 June 1932.

Jim Quinn

WISE, ISAAC MAYER (26 March 1819–20 March 1900), religious leader. Born in Steingrub, Bohemia, Wise came to the United States in 1846 after several years of rabbinical training. Settling in Cincinnati, Ohio, in 1854, he quickly became a prominent leader in the burgeoning Reform Jewish movement. His goal centered on bringing Judaism into the American mainstream. He first translated the Hebrew prayer book into English, calling the translation *Minhag America.* In 1873 Wise established the Union of American Hebrew Congregations, and in 1875 he was named president of the Hebrew Union College in Cincinnati, which became the center of Judaic studies in the United States. In 1887 Wise helped formulate the set of principles, which came to be known as the "Pittsburgh Platform," that functioned as the guiding set of Reform Jewish beliefs until the 1930s. Wise died in Cincinnati, widely mourned by American Jews.

Further Reading: Sefton D. Temkin, *Isaac Mayer Wise: Shaping American Judaism,* 1992.

John T. McGuire

WISTER, OWEN (14 July 1860–21 July 1938), author. Born in Germantown, Pennsylvania, Wister received his education at private schools in the United States, England, and Switzerland. At Harvard University, from which he graduated in 1882, he formed a lasting friendship with Theodore Roosevelt. Ill health led Wister to seek relief in the West. After graduating in 1888 from Harvard Law School, he practiced in Philadelphia, but the lure of western adventure grew insurmountably strong. He repeatedly journeyed to the West, recording his observations of cowboys and life there. The first of his published western tales appeared in 1892. Wister combined various stories in *Red Men and White* in 1896, *Lin McLean* in 1898, and *The Jimmyjohn Boss* two years later. He dedicated *The Virginian: A Horseman of the Plains* (1902), set in the Wyoming Territory during the late 1870s and 1880s, to President Theodore Roosevelt. Wister's works created the basic western myths and themes later popularized by Zane Grey, Max Brand, and others. Wister died in Saunderstown, Rhode Island.

Further Reading: Fanny Kemble Wister, ed., *Owen Wister Out West: His Journals and Letters,* 1958; Darwin Payne, *Owen Wister: Chronicler of the West, Gentleman of the East,* 1985; Edward G. White, *The Eastern Establishment and the Western Experience: The West of Frederic Remington, Theodore Roosevelt, and Owen Wister,* 1968.

Leonard Schlup

WOLCOTT, EDWARD OLIVER (26 March 1868–1 March 1905), attorney, senator. Born in

Longmeadow, Massachusetts, Wolcott was schooled in Chicago and Cleveland, and served briefly in the Union Army. He was graduated from the law department of Harvard University in 1875. He followed his brother to Blackhawk, Colorado, where he taught briefly, then moved to Georgetown and developed a thriving law practice. Wolcott began public service as Georgetown's district and town attorney in 1876, moved to Denver in 1879, served three years as a Republican state senator, and held a U.S. Senate seat from 1889 to 1901.

A conservative, Wolcott was sensitive to mining interests. In his early years, he favored the free coinage of silver. Rather than bolt the party with Silver Republicans in 1896, however, he remained loyal and endorsed bimetallism by means of an international agreement. President McKinley chose him to head the 1897 commission selected to seek such an arrangement. Wolcott unsuccessfully sought reelection to the U.S. Senate in 1901, 1902, and 1903. He then emphasized his law practice, prospering from work for major corporations including the Denver & Rio Grande Railroad.

Further Reading: Thomas Dawson, *Life and Character of Edward Oliver Wolcott*, 2 vols. (1911); *Dictionary of American Biography* 20 (1936): 441–442; *Biographical Directory of the Congress of the United States: Bicentennial Edition* (1989), 2078.

Douglas Steeples

WOMAN SUFFRAGE. The right of women to vote in elections constituted the first stage in the struggle for political equality. In 1647 Margaret Brent, a prosperous Maryland landowner, was the first woman in the North American colonies to demand the vote. At the Seneca Falls Convention in 1848, Elizabeth Cady Stanton insisted on the approval of a resolution stating that it was a woman's duty to secure the sacred franchise. The abolitionist crusade paved the way for the women's rights movement in the United States. Women learned to organize, hold public meetings, conduct petition drives, and address groups. Campaigns to free slaves and liberate females flourished together, and for many women a philosophy of their place in society evolved during the process. After the Civil War, the Fourteenth Amendment in 1868 de-fined "citizens" and "voters" as "male," raising the question of whether women were considered citizens of the United States. The Fifteenth Amendment in 1870 further excluded women, giving the vote to African-American men but not to females.

In 1869 Stanton and Susan B. Anthony in New York organized the radical National Woman Suffrage Association (NWSA) to agitate for a constitutional amendment. Conservative feminists, such as Lucy Stone and Julia Ward Howe, favored state laws to enfranchise women. They established the American Woman Suffrage Association (AWSA) in Boston. The two groups merged in 1890 to form the National American Woman Suffrage Association (NAWSA) under Stanton's leadership. In 1872 officials arrested Anthony for attempting to vote for Ulysses S. Grant in the presidential election. Three years later the U.S. Supreme Court ruled in *Minor* v. *Hapersett* that citizenship did not in itself confer suffrage rights. In 1878 sponsors introduced a woman's suffrage amendment in the U.S. Congress, and in 1890 Wyoming became the first state to permit woman suffrage. In 1919, after years of petitioning, protesting, and picketing, Congress passed the Nineteenth Amendment, which the requisite number of states ratified by 1920. Other nations granting women the right to vote during the period from 1918 to 1921 included Canada, Czechoslovakia, Germany, Ireland, the Netherlands, Poland, and Sweden. New Zealand had extended that right in 1893. The attention and triumphs achieved by Gilded Age women in their endeavor to secure the vote crystallized into a successful outcome in the twentieth century.

Further Reading: Olivia E. Coolidge, *Women's Rights: The Suffrage Movement in America, 1848–1920*, 1966; Ellen DuBois, *Feminism and Suffrage: The Emergence of an Independent Woman's Movement in America 1848–1969*, 1978.

Leonard Schlup

WOMAN'S CHRISTIAN TEMPERANCE UNION (WCTU). The WCTU was the largest (with over 150,000 dues-paying members in 1890) female reform organization of the age and the first directed and controlled solely by women. Led by Frances Willard, this largely white, middle-class, Protestant organization kept prohibitionism alive when the political structure was hostile to it. The WTCU also helped convince a generation of conservative women that they should seek suffrage. The WCTU grew out of a spontaneous series of attacks on saloons by bands of praying women during the winter of 1873–1874. Inspired by the Social Gospel, and fearful of the effects of alcohol on their families and their society, middle-class women launched moral suasion crusades against saloons, exhorting the proprietors and patrons to abandon liquor. These crusades occurred in over nine hundred communities and revealed the possibilities of women's power. Quickly, women organized temperance groups to channel energy into the antiliquor struggle. In 1874, these local organizations federated into the Woman's Christian Temperance Union.

From 1879 to her death in 1898, Frances Willard, dominated the WCTU. Her dynamism and charisma influenced the WCTU rank and file. Willard endorsed two slogans ("do everything" and the "home protection ballot") that guaranteed the WCTU's influence would extend beyond the issue of temperance. Thus, the WCTU sought stronger laws against the liquor trade, changes in divorce law, better administration of prisons, child protection laws, changes in the laws that set the minimum age for sexual consent, antiprostitution policies, and greater rights for organized labor. Willard cleverly blended maternalist concerns for home and family with what she saw as the practical necessity of woman's suffrage. Without the vote, women could not protect the home from corrupting influences.

Absence of the franchise limited the WTCU's political program to lobbying legislators and circulating petitions. Even so, it was quite successful in seeing much of its agenda enacted. Less successful were the WCTU's attempts to build political coalitions, first with the Prohibition Party and later with the Populists and Knights of Labor. Nonetheless, the WCTU pioneered highly effective lobbying techniques designed to secure support for local- and state-level prohibition. This expertise would prove useful as the battle for prohibition in the new century shifted to Congress. During the Progressive Era, the WCTU would work with another prohibition organization, the Anti-Saloon League, in exerting pressure that would result in national prohibition.

Further Reading: Ruth Bordin, *Woman and Temperance: The Quest for Power and Liberty, 1873–1900*, 1981, and *Frances Willard: A Biography*, 1986; Thomas R. Pegram, *Battling Demon Rum: The Struggle for a Dry America, 1800–1933*, 1998.

Richard F. Hamm

WOMEN IN AMERICAN LIFE. During the Gilded Age, women moved toward a more prominent role in society. A woman's movement, which culminated during the twentieth century, was growing. Changes occurred at various levels and times. Before the Civil War, teaching was predominantly a male occupation. Fifteen years later, over two-thirds of the nation's teachers were women, providing them with an income, a forum, and an opportunity to shape young minds. As more colleges became coeducational, women benefited from expanding educational opportunities in numerous fields. Susan Jane Cunningham, to cite one example, studied at several American and European institutions. In 1869 she helped found Swarthmore College's astronomy and mathematics departments; she headed those divisions until her retirement, as full professor, in 1906. In 1888 Swarthmore awarded her an honorary doctorate of science, the first degree of this kind that it gave. Cunningham in 1891 became one of the first six female members of the New York Mathematical Society (later the American Mathematical Society).

Northern white women without educational credentials and professional attainments sought employment in textile mills, clothing industries, cigar manufacturing, retail sales, and offices. Some ceased earning a wage after marriage. Immigrant women in the late nineteenth century usually toiled as domestic servants. They also spent long hours sewing and knitting at home in order to earn more cash. When Chinese workingmen arrived in the United States, only a few Chinese women were permitted to enter the country. This created a severe social imbalance in the Chinese-American community. Many poor Chinese girls were enslaved and sold as prostitutes. Most immigrant women often felt conflicted at first between their desire to be Americanized and their sense of cultural pride and family loyalty. As a result, they established organizations and institutions to maintain their identities and traditions. In 1888 a congressional act granted citizenship to Native American women who married white men. African-American women normally found agricultural labor in the South and domestic and laundry positions in northern states. Some moved to Kansas and various western regions to escape poverty.

Geographic and regional characteristics influenced women's lives and choices of employment. The industrial North, the agricultural South, the developing West, and affluent neighborhoods of the East produced varying lifestyles. The appearance of women's journals and newspapers, including *The Woman's Journal* and *The Revolution*, formed cohesive bonds. The suffrage crusade laid the foundation for the Nineteenth Amendment in 1920. In 1869 Wyoming's territorial legislature granted women full voting rights. Utah followed suit the next year. In 1883 Washington's legislators gave women the vote, but the territory's Supreme Court rescinded the measure in 1887, the year Congress abolished woman's suffrage in Utah. Washington in 1888 again passed a suffrage law, only to have it blocked a second time. A Washington state referendum in 1889 defeated women's suffrage. In 1890 Wyoming entered the Union as the first state permitting full suffrage for women. A Colorado referendum in 1893 allowed women the vote. In 1896 Utah and Idaho opened the electoral process to women. The remaining battle would be fought in the twentieth century.

By 1880 over four million women, one out of every seven, worked for pay outside their homes. The majority of them were young, unmarried immigrants who typically labored sixty to eighty hours per week, often under noisy, crowded, unsanitary, and dangerous conditions. Female employees in factories without proper ventilation were prone to lung and bronchial diseases and other health problems. With industrialization, the sharp sex-segregated division between private and public life began to break down, but sexual harassment followed women from the patriarchial family into the schools and the workplace, often limiting their mobility, and usurping their rights to human dignity, bodily integrity, and a sense of identity.

Further Reading: Linda K. Kerber et al., eds., *U.S. History as Women's History: New Feminist Essays*, 1995; Nancy F. Cott, ed., *No Small Courage: A History of Women in the United States*, 2000; Linda K. Kerber and Jane S. DeHart, eds., *Women's America: Refocusing the Past*, 5th ed., 1999.

Leonard Schlup

WOMEN'S CLUBS. The women's club movement accomplished a great deal in local, state, and national areas during the Gilded Age. It expanded women's outlook, provided training in public speaking, and gave members experience in presiding over meetings. It fostered intimacy among various groups, and promoted interaction between their coalition and other social and political organizations. It served as an intermediate institution between family, on the one hand, and the woman's complex public sphere, on the other. The women's club movement sharpened members' resourcefulness and served as an educational forum for both women and men. Too frequently all American clubwomen have been equated with the General Federation of Women's Clubs, a league founded in 1890 and claiming a predominantly white, middle-class, Protestant membership. In reality, women's clubs crossed class, religious, and racial lines. Jewish, Mormon, African-American, and Native American women formed clubs. They were diverse and multicultural sisterhoods. In 1896 African-American clubwomen named their federation the National Association of Colored Women. The National Council of Jewish Women began operations in 1893. The Association of Working Girls' Clubs was founded in 1885 and changed its name in 1897 to the National League of Women Workers.

Many local newspapers in the 1890s featured "women's editions" and columns written by clubwomen. The circulation of women's club publications, such as *Far and Near* and *Club Worker*, helped to keep clubs informed of one another's activities. By 1900, approximately two million women participated in club work in every state and in the Arizona and Oklahoma territories. Leading members of women's clubs included Julia Ward Howe, Elizabeth Stuart Phelps Ward, Amelia E. Barr, Ella Wheeler Wilcox, Jennie Cunningham Croly, Mary E. Woolley, Mrs. Henry Ward Beecher, Mrs. Everett C. Brown, Mrs. Anthony W. Smith, Jr., Mrs. Frank A. Pattison, and Mrs. John D. Sherman.

The contributions of women's clubs to social welfare, public service, and practical community projects grew increasingly important during the late nineteenth century. They worked for the betterment of their own homes and those in the community, sponsored literacy programs, encouraged pure food legislation, sought improved public and vocational schools, and lobbied for clean milk, fresh markets, sanitary streets, and a safer environment. Some clubs wanted to preserve America's natural heritage, protect forests and birds, promote public parks, beautify towns by planting trees, enhance educational opportunities for children, establish libraries, advance the work of juvenile courts, support the arts, foster child labor laws, preserve historic landmarks, and campaign for limiting the hours of labor for women. With their shared experiences, reading, writing, and agendas, clubwomen formed a coterie that played significant cultural roles in reinventing the United States during the Gilded Age.

Further Reading: Karen Blair, *The Clubwoman as Feminist: True Womanhood Redefined, 1868–1914*, 1980; Anne Ruggles Gere, *Intimate Practices: Literacy and Cultural Work in U.S. Women's Clubs, 1880–1920*, 1997.

Leonard Schlup

WOMEN'S EDUCATION.

The Gilded Age produced numerous advances in formalized educational opportunities for women. In 1873, Bennett College in Greensboro, North Carolina, was established as an African-American woman's college. After Abby W. May and her followers won election to the Boston School Committee, they used their influence to help create the Girls' Latin School in Boston in 1877. Five years later Spelman College in Atlanta, Georgia, was developed to provide educational opportunities to former female slaves.

By 1894 Vassar, Wellesley, Bryn Mawr, Radcliffe, Barnard, Smith, and Mount Holyoke colleges had opened specifically for women. They served as models for future women's colleges. Female institutions of higher learning emphasized course work, exercise, and sports. Around 1900, the Catholic Church founded a number of women's colleges in the Midwest. Universities across the nation inched toward coeducation. Normal schools thrived as providers of teacher education. By 1880, 80 per cent of America's schoolteachers were women. The Women's Education Association stood at the forefront of women's educational needs. Most women in the Gilded Age who pursued graduate training planned for lives as scholars. In 1877, Helen Magill became the first woman in the United States to earn the Ph.D., receiving the degree from Boston University. Between 1877 and 1900, women obtained 229 doctorates in America; more than half came from Yale, Chicago, Cornell, and New York universities.

Further Reading: Helen Lefkowitz, *Alma Mater: Design and Experience in the Women's Colleges from Their Nineteenth-Century Beginnings to the 1930s*, 1984; Barbara Miller Solomon, *In the Company of Educated Women: A History of Women and Higher Education in America*, 1985; Linda Eisenmann, ed., *Historical Dictionary of Women's Education in the United States*, 1998.

Leonard Schlup

WOMEN'S EDUCATIONAL AND INDUSTRIAL UNION (WEIU).

In 1877, Dr. Harriet Clisby founded the WEIU in Boston as an organization that would simultaneously serve the needs of women of all classes. For the middle- and upper-class women associated with the WEIU, the organization provided an opportunity to channel their social concerns, as they established a variety of programs that sought to address the needs of Boston's working-class women and girls. Vocational training, an employment bureau, and social activities were just a few of the programs established. As the WEIU entered the twentieth century, it increasingly focused on cooperation with other organizations, including trade unions, as it agitated for the passage of protective labor legislation. Though the WEIU spread to other cities in the industrial Northeast, including Buffalo, New York, the Boston organization remained the strongest and has remained active into the twenty-first century.

Further Reading: Sarah Deutsch, "Learning to Talk More like a Man: Boston Women's Class-Bridging Organizations, 1870–1940," *American Historical Review* 97 (1992): 379–404; Robert B. Jennings, "A History of the Educational Activities of the Women's Educational and Industrial Union from 1877–1927," Ph.D. diss., Boston College, 1978; Women's Educational and Industrial Union records, Schlesinger Library, Radcliffe College, Cambridge, Massachusetts.

Kathleen Banks Nutter

WOMEN'S NATIONAL INDIAN ASSOCIATION

(1879–1951). When railroads and settlers entered Indian Territory in violation of federal treaties, Mary Lucinda Bonney, founder of the Chestnut Street Female Seminary, Amelia Stone Quinton, and others initiated a petition drive in protest. Thus began the WNIA which, by century's end had auxiliaries in almost forty states. Along with the male-dominated Indian Rights Association (1882), and the Lake Mohonk Conference of the Friends of the Indian (1883), the WNIA dictated government Indian policy.

These middle- and upper-class evangelical Christian women formed a network of standing committees and departments; published a monthly periodical, *The Indian's Friend*; engaged in petition drives; wrote leaflets; and publicly spoke on behalf of the Indians. The WNIA's Missionary Department built hospitals and sponsored the medical education of Indian women, including Susan La Flesche.

Further Reading: Valerie Sherer Mathes, *Helen Hunt Jackson and Her Indian Reform Legacy*, 1990, 119–157, and "Nineteenth Century Women and Reform: The Women's National Indian Association," *American Indian Quarterly* 14 (1990): 1–18; Helen M. Wanken, "Woman's Sphere and Indian Reform: The Women's National Indian Association 1879–1901," Ph.D. diss. Marquette University, 1981.

Valerie Sherer Mathes

WOMEN'S REFORMATORIES.

Social feminists during the Gilded Age campaigned for penal institutions oriented toward the particular characteristics and needs of women. Although France and Great Britain had established prisons specifically for women earlier in the nineteenth century, in the United States it was not until 1870 that Michigan opened a shelter for female inmates to receive moral and industrial training. Four years later the Indiana Reformatory Institution became the first completely independent and physically separate penitentiary for women in America. The Massachusetts Reformatory Prison for Women began operations in 1877, followed by the New York House of Refuge for Women in 1887 and the Western House of Refuge at Albion, New York, in 1893. In all, twenty women's reformatories opened in the years between 1870 and 1935. They tended to be in rural areas and to offer domestic settings in cottages. Reformatories mirrored the changing conception of female prisoners at the turn of the century. Increasingly women offenders were seen as "wayward" individuals who, under direction, could return to proper societal behavior; some of them could be paroled as domestic servants. Women's reformatories contained educational facilities, workshops, gymnasiums, and classrooms where inmates learned basic skills and health care.

A crusade to replace male wardens and officers with females occurred simultaneously. In 1877 the Indiana Reformatory dismissed its male board of trustees, replacing them with women. Over the next two decades, female doctors and managers achieved prominent positions, so that by 1900 women had largely gained control over the administrative functions of female reformatories. Among these leaders were Eliza Mosher at Framington Reformatory and Sarah Smith at Indiana Reformatory. The women's reformatory undertaking was intertwined with the national movement for prison reform, which included goals to clean up prison conditions, evaluate methods of punishment, eliminate painful indignities, and promote prison hygiene. Leading penal reformers of the time were Enoch Cobb Wines, Zebulon Brockway, Theodore W. Dwight, William M. F. Round, Benjamin F. Sanborn, Samuel Gridley Howe, and Ellen Cheney Johnson. The campaign to transform American corrections and establish women's reformatories constituted a significant part in the reform agenda of the late nineteenth century.

Further Reading: Lucia Zedner, "Wayward Sisters: The Prison for Women," in *The Oxford History of the Prison,* ed. Norval Morris and David J. Rothman, 1995; Estelle B. Freedman, *Their Sisters' Keepers: Women's Prison Reform in America, 1830–1930,* 1981; John W. Roberts, *Reform and Retribution: An Illustrated History of American Prisons,* 1997.

Leonard Schlup

WOODHULL, VICTORIA CLAFLIN (23 September 1838–10 June 1927), broker, publisher, spiritualist, candidate for U.S. president, and advocate for women's suffrage and free love. Mrs. John Biddulph Martin, widow of a wealthy English banker, venerated at death for her charitable works and her role in the suffrage movement, was also the spirited and much maligned Victoria Claflin Woodhull. Labeled "Saint Vickie," "Mrs. Satan," and the "Queen of Prostitutes" over her lifetime, Victoria Woodhull colorfully refracted what Gilded Age writers euphemistically called the "Woman Question." Shocking her Victorian contemporaries with her bold advocacy of "free love" during her 1872 presidential campaign, this beautiful, yet radical, spokeswoman for causes both great and silly divided both the ranks of the suffrage movement and, for a short period, two of its leaders, Elizabeth Cady Stanton and Susan B. Anthony. Despite Woodhull's bohemian behavior, her life reveals much about post-Civil War America, with its mushrooming industrialization and subsequent impact upon the social freedoms women were beginning to enjoy.

Born in Homer, Ohio, as an adolescent, Claflin fine-tuned her skills in her parents' disreputable medicine show, delighting audiences with self-hypnotic trances and clairvoyant fortune-telling. In 1853, not yet sixteen but already a cameo beauty, she married Canning Woodhull, a Chicago physician; their union produced two children but eventually ended in divorce. Despite being saddled with a drunken husband and rationalizing her philosophy of free love, Woodhull bewitched Colonel James Harvey Blood (though he later became her second husband, she never totally abandoned her first husband, and cared for him in her home until his death), who introduced her to a variety of reform causes that captured her interest in the decade to come. In 1868, with her sister Tennessee's assistance, Woodhull attracted Commodore Cornelius Vanderbilt's eye and support to set the two up in their own Wall Street brokerage house of Woodhull, Claflin and Co. After considerable success in the world of finance, Woodhull entered the political domain. *Woodhull and Claflin's Weekly* (begun in 1870) served as a vehicle for her controversial ideas. In 1871, her testimony before a congressional committee on women's suffrage brought her to the attention of the leaders of the National Women's Suffrage Association and led her to establish her own political party and run for president. Shortly before the elections, she was jailed on charges of sending obscenity through the mails, specifically her publicizing the adulterous affair of Henry Ward Beecher (America's most famous preacher of the time) with a married woman. Woodhull's attack on one of America's most venerated idols, numerous court battles and expenses, and Vanderbilt's support resulted not only in her defeat at the polls but also in the eviction of her family from their rented four-story mansion in the Murray Hill section of New York City and, probably, her ultimate decision to permanently leave the country and divorce her colonel.

Close to the age of forty, Woodhull attracted the attention of the banker John Biddulph Martin at her first 1877 London lecture, and married him six years later. Having avidly followed her activities, Martin remained supportive of his wife's travels, speeches, and publications despite his family's opposition to their relationship. Advancing "humanitarian government" and social justice through her publication the *Humanitarian,* Woodhull-Martin established respectability, outlived her husband, and continued until her death in Brendon's Norton (a small village in the Cotswolds) at eighty-eight to voice reform.

Further Reading: Mary Gabriel, *Notorious Victoria: The Life of Victoria Woodhull—Uncensored,* 1998; Ted C. Hinckley and Susan Koester, "Victoria Claflin Woodhull," in *American Portraits: History Through Biography,* ed. Donald W. Whisenhunt, 1994; Victoria Woodhull-Martin Papers, Morris Library Special Collections, Southern Illinois University, Carbondale, Illinois.

Susan H. Koester

WOODS, WILLIAM BURNHAM (3 August 1824–14 May 1887), Supreme Court justice.

One of the least-known members of the High Court, Woods confined his contributions to equity cases. Born in Newark, Ohio, he studied at Western Reserve College and Yale. He returned to Newark to study law, and rose quickly from mayor to state legislator (as a Democrat). In the Civil War, Woods rose to brevet major general in 1866 with the Union forces. Afterward, he settled in Alabama, became a Republican, and was elected to the Middle Chancery Court. In 1869, President Ulysses S. Grant appointed Woods to the Fifth Circuit Court of Appeals. Although a proponent of black rights, he was equally concerned with states' rights. Woods wrote the original opinion in the *Slaughterhouse Cases*, which would later limit the Fourteenth Amendment's grants of privileges and immunities to those which were consistent with state law. He also fashioned an early version of the "separate but equal" doctrine later upheld in *Plessy* v. *Ferguson*. Woods was appointed to the Supreme Court in 1880, where he penned few notable opinions. He overturned the Ku Klux Klan Act of 1871 in *United States* v. *Harris*, on a states' rights theory. He died in Washington, D.C.

Further Reading: Louis Filler, "William B. Woods," in Leon Friedman and Fred L. Israel, eds., *The Justices of the United States Supreme Court 1789–1969: Their Lives and Major Opinions*, vol. 2, 1969; *New York Times*, 15 May 1887; Thomas E. Baynes, Jr., "Yankee from Georgia: A Search for Justice Woods," *Supreme Court Historical Society Yearbook* (1978): 31–42.

Sam Kepfield

WOOLWORTH, FRANK WINFIELD (13 April 1852–8 April 1919), merchant. Born in Rodman, New York, Woolworth attended the local one-room school and then, briefly, a Watertown, New York, business college. At age nineteen, he began his career by working as an unpaid clerk. After holding several retail positions, in 1879 Woolworth opened a store in Utica, New York, that sold only items priced at five cents. This first store failed, closing after three months, but it convinced Woolworth that low-priced, high-volume merchandising would work. On 21 June 1879, he opened a "five and ten cent" store in Lancaster, Pennsylvania, and this time succeeded. Woolworth financed his first two stores by borrowing from his last em-ployer, William H. Moore, and later expanded his retail operations through a variety of partnerships with Moore and others. Throughout the late nineteenth century, Woolworth continually opened new stores. By 1895, he operated twenty-eight stores with combined annual sales of over $1 million. In 1912, he and his partners formed F. W. Woolworth Company to consolidate their retail holdings. The next year, construction was completed on the Woolworth Building in New York City, the world's tallest structure until 1930. At the time of his death, the company operated over one thousand stores.

Further Reading: Karen Plunkett-Powell, *Remembering Woolworth's: A Nostalgic History of the World's Most Famous Five-and-Dime*, 1999; John K. Winkler, *Five and Ten: The Fabulous Life of F. W. Woolworth*, 1940; *New York Times*, 9 April 1919.

John H. Hepp IV

WORKING GIRLS' CLUBS. From 1884 to 1928 a national movement of Working Girls' Clubs evolved to meet the needs of young, white, unmarried females in urban, industrialized America. The idea, which started in a New York City silk factory, spread to other cities, resulting in formation of an Association of Working Girls' Clubs in 1885 and a National League of Women Workers in 1897. The clubs brought together middle-class sponsors and working-class members. Unlike many other organizations of the time, however, the clubs went beyond the typical patron-client relationship to foster a sense of cross-class sisterhood limited, to be sure, by controversies over labor unions. Although sponsors provided seed money and served as administrators, club members played active roles in raising money, managing affairs, and defining agendas. The clubs performed various functions, such as singing, sewing, collecting food for the poor, pursuing culture, and attending lectures. These activities helped build community, compensate for the alienation of the urban environment, and counteract the prevailing negative stereotypes of working women. The clubs always possessed a moralistic component and, in their final years, became increasingly social in orientation as the members began defining themselves in terms more of race and ethnicity than of class.

During their heyday in the 1890s, the Working Girls' Clubs developed concrete strategies to ameliorate members' daily lives: classes in job-related skills, savings plans, mutual benefit associations, employment bureaus, cooperative housing, lunch programs, and even a profit-sharing children's clothes company. Although their function and focus changed over time, Working Girls' Clubs provided an innovative model of cross-class cooperation as they tried to negotiate some of the dilemmas facing nineteenth-century urban women.

Further Reading: Priscilla Murolo, *The Common Ground of Womanhood: Class, Gender and Working Girls' Clubs, 1884–1928*, 1997; Joanne Reitano, "Working Girls Unite!" *American Quarterly* 36 (Spring 1984): 112–134; Anne Firor Scott, *Natural Allies: Women's Associations in American History*, 1992.

Joanne Reitano

WORLD'S COLUMBIAN EXPOSITION.

This was a world's fair held in Chicago, Illinois, from 1 May to the end of October 1893 to commemorate the four hundredth anniversary of Christopher Columbus's arrival in America. Nearly five years in its planning, and the subject of intensive promotion and hype, the exposition embodied both the promise of and the problems inherent in the Gilded Age. Chicago, rebuilt dramatically after the great fire of 1871, was home to over 1.5 million residents by 1893, at least one-third of whom were recent immigrants. Hordes of unemployed laborers vied for work at the massive exposition, whose 633-acre site essentially rebuilt the South Chicago lakeside at a total cost of over $27 million. The fair's design was directed by Daniel Burnham and Frederick Law Olmsted, and some of the day's top architectural firms contributed buildings. The site was divided into an industrial/ historical section, dominated by Burnham's glittering White City and Court of Honor, and a smaller area for amusements, known as the Midway Plaisance. Many nations contributed buildings and exhibits, as did scores of manufacturers and government agencies. Over 27.5 million visitors from far and near crowded the fair. The Midway Plaisance proved far more popular than the fair's industrial, historical, or architectural splendors, with crowds flocking to see such curiosities as the newly in-vented Ferris wheel, a tower made of chocolate, an ice railway, a full-sized alabaster buffalo, hot-air balloon ascensions, and exotic anthropological exhibits of dubious accuracy. One of the biggest draws was the belly dancer "Little Egypt."

The White City stimulated the "City Beautiful" city planning movement in the fair's aftermath, and was home to numerous intellectual conferences. The fair also pioneered such advances as the kinetograph, elevated railroads, moving sidewalks, and large-scale electrical generation. In many respects, though, it represented the triumph of commercial and leisure culture. Were it not for the Midway Plaisance, the exposition would have lost money. Heterosocial crowds spent lavishly there, even though exhibit and ride prices were steep.

The fair was supposed to highlight American unity, stimulate patriotism, and showcase American ingenuity. Although this effort achieved some success, the fair also underscored deep internal social tensions. By the time it opened, the United States was sliding into a severe economic depression, and unemployed workers demonstrated outside the exposition site. On the fair's closing day, Chicago mayor Carter Harrison was assassinated; by May 1894, Chicagoans and the nation were more concerned by the traumatic Pullman strike and boycott than with the splendors of the already crumbling White City.

Further Reading: R. Reid Badger, *The Great American Fair*, 1979; John Kasson, *Amusing the Million*, 1978; Richard Schneirov, *Labor and Urban Politics*, 1998.

Robert E. Weir

WOUNDED KNEE MASSACRE.

Wounded Knee, on the Pine Ridge Reservation in southwestern South Dakota, twice has attracted international attention, becoming one of the most noteworthy sites related to the history of Indian-white relations history in North America: first for the senseless killing on 29 December 1890; then for seventy-one days of occupation by protesters during the spring of 1973. The term "massacre" is most used with regard to the 1890 tragedy to suggest a deliberate effort by U.S. troops to destroy all Native Americans in sight. "Affair" is an alternative to imply an emotional reaction by young troopers out of control. "Battle" is used mainly by officials and military historians to defend the award of Congressional Medals of Honor to men who did most of the killing. Under any descriptive term, Wounded Knee conjures an image of tragedy through the entire history of Indian-white relations across the United States.

It also evokes a memory about causes in a complex backdrop of events: an influx of immigrants into the West after 1840, the destruction of U.S. Army units at the Grattan Massacre (1854) and the Fetterman Massacre (1866), the federal recognition of the Great Sioux Reservation, comprising more than sixty million acres, through terms in the Treaty of Fort Laramie of 1868, its violation by a gold rush into the Black Hills, a tribal reaction in the Great Sioux War of 1876 that included the deaths of George Custer and troops in the U.S. Seventh Cavalry, the dispersion of tribal forces followed by the illegal seizure of more than thirty-eight million acres in the great reservation by Congress in 1877, its further reduction into four Lakota reservations in 1889, and a confrontation of interests that led to the death of Sitting Bull as a symbol of resistance on 15 December 1890. Even without the specter of the Ghost Dance, a confrontation between U.S. troops and unsettled Lakotas was inevitable. The arrival of Big Foot, a Minnconjou with a record of diplomacy instead of militant resistance, with a following of northern Lakotas alarmed federal troopers. Big Foot's presence became a catalyst even though he appeared to be near death from pneumonia.

Several aspects of the tragedy that followed on 29 December 1890 must always remain mysterious. One is what precipitated erratic gunfire by federal troops—their fear, desire to avenge the destruction of the Seventh Cavalry during the Custer fight in 1876, the display of weapons by some tribal members, or a call for resistance by the spiritual leader Yellow Bird. Another unanswered question pertains to which side first opened fire, a matter that never can be settled. A third is how many died. The count of twenty-five dead and thirty-nine wounded among federal troops seems certain, but the death toll of Indians never can be determined. Federal representatives picked up 153 bodies the day after the attack. Later, an official news

organ printed by the Oglala Indian Training School at Pine Ridge contained impressions of elders. One estimate was 340 killed, including one hundred tribal soldiers; another was 370 casualties, including 120 men with weapons. Tribal elders have recounted how survivors hid a majority of bodies in woodpiles during the winter, to be recovered in spring for traditional burials. None who created written records could say how many died or which tribes were most represented in the casualty lists. As well as Oglala Lakotas, perhaps some were members of all tribes represented by more than eight hundred people arrested by federal troops as prisoners of war and forced into settlement at the east end of the Pine Ridge Reservation.

One abiding consequence of Wounded Knee in 1890 was the poisoning of Indian-white relations that has abided into the twenty-first century. Another was the creation of an abiding memory about the cultural imperialism and territorial aggression featured throughout most of the history of federal Indian policy.

Further Reading: Robert M. Utley, *Frontier Regulars: The Unites States Army and the Indian, 1866–1891*, 1974; *The Lance and the Shield: The Life and Times of Sitting Bull*, 1993; *The Last Days of the Sioux Nation*, 1963.

Herbert T. Hoover

WOVOKA (JACK WILSON) (c. 1858–1932), Paiute messiah. Following the death of his father, a prophet, Wovoka, a native of Nevada, lived with the Wilson family who practiced evangelical Presbyterianism. In 1889, during a solar eclipse, Wovoka experienced a vision in which he died, went to heaven, saw those who had died before him, and spoke to God, who instructed him to set war aside and live in peace with the white people. Wovoka was shown a special "Ghost Dance" to be performed repeatedly on five successive nights until a new world, returning the old days of glory and all their friends, ancestors, and relatives, would replace the old one dominated by whites. Western tribes, subjected to reservation life and subsisting on meager rations, willingly accepted this new dance and religion, which blended Mormonism, the Shaker religion, Catholicism, and Presbyterianism. Although women participated fully in the Ghost Dance, some government officials mistook it for a war dance. Tragically, the more militant posture of the Sioux tribe and their use of the "Ghost Shirts," which were supposedly impervious to bullets, led to the 1890 Massacre at Wounded Knee.

Further Reading: James Mooney, *The Ghost-Dance Religion and the Sioux Outbreak of 1890*, 1965; Robert M. Utley, *The Last Days of the Sioux Nation*, 1963.

Valerie Sherer Mathes

WRIGHT, CARROLL DAVIDSON (25 July 1840–20 February 1909), social economist and statistician. Born in Dunbarton, New Hampshire, Wright read law, served in the Union Army, moved to Reading, Massachusetts, and won two state senate elections. In 1873, Governor William B. Washburn selected Wright to head the Massachusetts Bureau of Statistics of Labor, the first such organization in the country. Retaining the position until 1888, Wright gathered statistics during a period of economic development. In 1883, he organized the National Convention of Chiefs and Commissioners of Bureaus of Statistics of Labor, and served as president for twenty years. Preferring conciliation between business and labor, he traveled widely, earned a national reputation, and published *The Relation of Political Economy to the Labor Question* (1882), *The Industrial Evolution of the United States* (1895), and *Outline of Practical Sociology* (1899). In 1885 President Chester A. Arthur appointed Wright the first commissioner of the newly established U.S. Bureau of Labor in the Department of the Interior, a post he held for two decades. Wright chaired the commission to investigate the cause of the 1894 Pullman Strike, helped to complete the eleventh census, lectured as professor of statistics and social economics at Columbian (George Washington) University, and was president of the American Statistical Association from 1897 until his death in Worcester, Massachusetts.

Further Reading: *Springfield* (Mass.) *Daily Republican*, 21 February 1909.

Leonard Schlup

WRIGHT, ROBERT MARR (2 September 1840–4 January 1915), town builder and merchant. Wright was born in Brandensburg, Maryland, and went west in 1856. He spent seven years in various enterprises on the Santa Fe Trail before settling at Fort Dodge, Kansas, where he played a major role in supplying material to the troops in the Indian conflicts. As president of the Dodge City Town Company, Wright helped charter Dodge City. With his partner, Charles Rath, Wright established the largest mercantile store, with branches extending into Texas. The firm was a major dealer in buffalo products—hides, meat, and bones—and nurtured the expansion of the buffalo trade that eventually caused the demise of the great herds. In Dodge City there was scarcely a community project or business of which Wright was not a part. His store was for years the major banking facility in the region. Wright led in promoting the Texas-Kansas cattle trade. He used his leverage, as a member of the state legislature, and his wide acquaintance in Kansas and Texas, to keep the southwestern corner of Kansas open to Texas cattle from 1876 to 1886.

As an advocate of the trade that demanded the presence of "sinful" and "bawdy" distractions, he fought on the state and local levels to keep the reformers and prohibitionists out of Dodge. When the cattle trade ended, that cause was lost. Wright refused to acknowledge the changing nature of the economy and, like others, overexpanded his holdings and speculated in land and railroads. When Dodge was plunged into a "boom and bust" economy, he and the town were caught in the forerunner of the Panic of 1893. Following the depression that came at the end of the Kansas-Texas trade, Wright and the lifestyle of a cattle town he had fought for were largely discredited and Wright became a forgotten man. He died in Dodge City.

Further Reading: C. Robert Haywood, *The Merchant Prince of Dodge City: The Life and Times of Robert M. Wright*, 1998; Robert M. Wright, *Dodge City: The Cowboy Capital and the Great Southwest*, 1913; *Dodge City Globe*, 4 January 1915.

C. Robert Haywood

YELLOW JOURNALISM.

This name referred to a sensationalized type of what was termed "new journalism," a successful effort to popularize newspapers and gain a mass urban audience from the 1880s to 1900. Hallmarks included screaming headlines; displays of line drawings and photographs, as technology improved to permit their use; emotion-laden news accounts; journalistic stunts; crusades; and exposés of social injustices. It took its name from the use of colored ink in printing the first comic strip, "The Yellow Kid," which originally appeared in Joseph Pulitzer's *New York World* and later in William Randolph Hearst's *New York Journal*. Both Pulitzer and Hearst were intimately associated with yellow journalism in their personal rivalry to run the largest-circulation newspaper in New York City, the nation's journalism center. Their competitive drive to break circulation records by selling more than a million copies of their newspapers per day is credited in part with bringing about the Spanish-American War in 1898.

Decried by the upper classes and opinion leaders, yellow journalism represented an understandable, if lamentable, development in an era of growing urbanization when working people bought newspapers on the street for a penny a copy and advertisers sought a mass audience. Purporting to look after the interests of the common person as well as to entertain, it served as a socializing influence for new Americans. Although it resorted to fake stories and inaccuracies, it prepared the way for the more serious investigative journalism of the Progressive muckrakers. Yellow journalism opened the door for women to work on newspapers, because they were hired as "sob sisters" and "stunt girls" to write flamboyant copy that lured readers. Above all, it demonstrated the use of technological advances in printing that made the newspaper a powerful social force in a new age of mass communication.

Further Reading: W. David Sloan and James D. Startt, eds., *The Media in America*, 4th ed., 1999; W. A. Swanberg, *Citizen Hearst*, 1961.

Maurine H. Beasley

YELLOWSTONE NATIONAL PARK.

Private ownership and destruction of places of beauty had angered the public since at least the 1830s. The response took concrete form in the creation of the first national park in the region of the Upper Yellowstone River, primarily in northwest Wyoming. This land of incredible wonders—hot springs, geysers, a large, high-altitude lake, and a beautiful canyon—had been vaguely described in the press since the days of John Colter, who had been with Lewis and Clark, and the mountain man Jim Bridger. It was, however, the coming of the Northern Pacific Railroad in the 1870s that prompted scientists, railroad executives, and Montana citizens to advocate a national park as a method of preventing private claims to this spectacular region. On 1 March 1872, President Ulysses S. Grant signed into law the Enabling Act, creating for the first time a park "for all the people."

Further Reading: Aubrey Haines, *The Yellowstone Story*, 1977; Richard A. Bartlett, *Nature's Yellowstone*, 1974; Richard A. Bartlett, *Yellowstone: A Wilderness Besieged*, 1985.

Richard A. Bartlett

YOUNG, DENTON TRUE "CY"

(29 March 1867–4 November 1955), professional baseball player. Born in Gilmore, Ohio, Young was arguably the greatest pitcher of his era. Nicknamed "Cyclone" early in his career, later shortened to "Cy," he pitched for twenty-two seasons beginning in 1890, compiling a record of 511 wins and 316 losses, both major league records. Pitching primarily for Cleveland in the National League and Boston in the American League, Young won an astounding twenty or more games in thirteen of his first fourteen seasons, and ended his career with a stellar 2.62

earned-run average. A century later he still holds major league records for complete games (749) and innings pitched (7,354). Young hurled more than four hundred innings in five seasons and more than three hundred in eleven other seasons. He pitched on nearly every third day during his career, and in 1904, he strung together a remarkable forty-four consecutive scoreless innings. Probably best known in modern times for lending his name posthumously to the major league award given every year to the best pitcher in baseball, Young died in Newcomerstown, Ohio.

Further Reading: Ellery H. Clark, Jr., *Boston Red Sox: 75th Anniversary*, 1975, and *Red Sox Forever*, 1977.

Steve Bullock

YOUNG, ELLA FLAGG (15 January 1845–26 October 1918), educator. Born in Buffalo, New York, Flagg married William Young, a Chicago merchant, in 1868. District superintendent of the Chicago schools from 1887 to 1899, she studied under John Dewey and received a doctorate in 1900 from the University of Chicago, where she taught until 1904. Young was a member of the Equal Suffrage Association, and helped to organize women teachers across the nation. She associated in social work with Jane Addams, and published articles and books, including her doctoral dissertation, *Isolation in the School* (1900). A person who detested procrastination and inefficiency, Young resisted political interference in the schools and spoke frequently at meetings of educational associations. The educational system changed rapidly during the time of her professional career, and she actively promoted her reform agenda. She died in Chicago.

Further Reading: J. T. McManis, *Ella Flagg Young and a Half-Century of the Chicago Public Schools*, 1916; *Chicago Daily News*, 26 October 1918; *Chicago Sunday Tribune*, 27 October 1918.

Leonard Schlup

YOUNG MEN'S CHRISTIAN UNION OF BOSTON. Founded by Harvard students in 1851 as a religious study group, the Young Men's Christian Union (YMCU) evolved into a social, intellectual, and religious organization for men during the Gilded Age. In 1876 Nathaniel Bradlee designed its Boylston Street building in High Gothic style. Oliver Wendell Holmes appeared before the YMCU on 1 June 1893 to read Scripture and deliver an address. Adolph E. Nordquest, an advocate of physical exercise, kept in proper condition at the YMCU's gymnasium, where he met John Y. Smith and Thomas E. White, Gilded Age athletes. With its gymnasium and library, the YMCU functioned as an exercise facility for strengthening bodies and improving health, as a religious and benevolent organization, and as a social meeting place. In 2000 the Boston YMCU received a loan of $8.5 million for renovations.

Further Reading: Young Men's Christian Union file, Simmons College Archives, Boston, Massachusetts.

Leonard Schlup

YOUNGER, THOMAS COLEMAN (15 January 1844–21 March 1916), outlaw. "Cole" Younger was born near Lee's Summit, Missouri, and attended local schools, where he became interested in history and theology. During the Civil War he joined the Confederate Army, though his father favored the Union. Younger rose to captain but, like some twentieth-century Vietnam War veterans, he had trouble adjusting to civilian life. He joined the James brothers, whose daring robberies of banks and trains gained them notoriety and romanticization. Their attempt to rob a bank in Northfield, Minnesota, on 7 September 1876 provoked a gun battle that killed three robbers and two customers. Police arrested Younger as he tried to escape, and in November a jury sentenced him to life imprisonment. In 1882 Confederate veterans began to campaign for his release, asserting that he had been a victim of the Civil War and was not a criminal by nature. In 1903 the Minnesota Board of Pardons finally released Younger. He spent his remaining years in a Wild West exhibition and doing odd jobs. He fell ill in 1915 and died near his birthplace.

Further Reading: Marley Brant, *The Outlaw Youngers: A Confederate Brotherhood*, 1992.

Christopher Cumo

ZAHM, JOHN AUGUSTINE (14 June 1851–10 November 1921), Roman Catholic author and educator. Born in New Lexington, Ohio, Zahm graduated from the University of Notre Dame in 1871 with a degree in philosophy and, four years later, was ordained a priest. From 1875 until 1892, he served as an administrator and professor of physics there. Interested in the relationship between science and Catholic beliefs, Zahm published *Scientific Theory and Catholic Doctrine* in 1896 and, that same year, *Evolution and Dogma*. He then lectured and toured the United States and Europe as a popular speaker. Although Pope Leo XIII awarded him an honorary doctorate, Zahm encountered criticism from some church quarters concerning his interpretations and views on evolution. Ultimately he submitted to the Vatican's decree in 1898–1899 prohibiting further circulation of *Evolution and Dogma*. Zahm established a graduate program at the Catholic University of America. His explorations of South America resulted in publications describing the region's culture and history. Zahm's endeavors to develop Notre Dame into a great university and his theological opinions provided significant interpretations for comprehending the role of religion in American higher education and society during the late nineteenth century. He died in Munich, Germany.

Further Reading: Ralph E. Weber, *Notre Dame's John Zahm*, 1961; Thomas T. McAvoy, *The Great Crisis in American Catholic History, 1895–1900*, 1957; John A. Zahm Papers, Division of Archives, University of Notre Dame, Notre Dame, Indiana.

Leonard Schlup

ZIEGFELD, FLORENZ (21 March 1867–22 July 1932), theatrical producer. Ziegfeld was born in Chicago into a musical family, and attended Chicago public schools. He entered show business by booking acts emphasizing beautiful women entertainers for Chicago's World's Columbia Exhibition in 1893. Over the next few years he established himself, producing a variety of light musical comedies that toured the nation. In 1896 he invited the French actress Anna Held to come to the United States, then featured her in a variety of shows designed to display her talents. In 1907 Ziegfeld staged the first of his annual reviews, called *Follies*. He renamed them *Ziegfeld's Follies* in 1911, and produced them until 1931. All were extravagant productions, with elaborate scenery and settings.

Inspired in part by the Parisian Folies Bergère, Ziegfeld's semi-nude tableaux tested the boundaries of contemporary propriety. Ziegfeld also produced stage musicals in cooperation with the outstanding composers of the early twentieth century, including Jerome Kern, Irving Berlin, and Victor Herbert. Late in life, Ziegfeld tried unsuccessfully to transfer his formula to Hollywood productions, but the industry had not yet developed the "movie musical" format. He died in Hollywood, California.

Further Reading: Richard Ziegfeld and Paulette Ziegfeld, *The Ziegfeld Touch: The Life and Times of Florenz Ziegfeld*, 1993; Randolph Carter, *The World of Flo Ziegfeld*, 1974; Michael Lasser, "The Glorifier: Florenz Ziegfeld and the Creation of the Modern American Showgirl," *American Scholar* 63 (1994): 441–448.

James M. Bergquist

ZOLLARS, ELY VAUGHAN (19 September 1847–10 February 1916), minister and educator. Born near Lower Salem, Ohio, Zollars farmed, taught school, and graduated from Bethany College in 1875. President of two small Kentucky colleges and pastor of a Springfield, Illinois, church in the 1870s and 1880s, he accepted the presidency of Hiram College in Ohio, serving from 1888 to 1902. He later became president of Texas Christian University and Oklahoma Christian (now Phillips) University. A strong believer in religious higher education during the Gilded Age and the Progressive Era, Zollars was an able administrator, a writer, and a member of the Disciples of Christ Church. He died in Warren, Ohio.

Further Reading: *Christian Standard*, 19 February, and 11 March 1916.

Leonard Schlup

ZOOS. Before 1890, the Philadelphia Zoo was America's only world-class institution of its kind. Several menageries, scattered around the country, housed animals in brick buildings. The 1890 creation of the U.S. National Zoological Park in Washington, D.C., changed the concept of the zoo in America. The National Zoo's first superintendent, William Temple Hornaday, grouped animals together on the basis of their geographic associations, and provided large, open pastures so they could roam freely. Subsequently constructed zoos imitated this design. Advocates hoped that zoos, in addition to educating the public about nature, would stimulate wildlife conservation by showcasing animals in danger of extinction. In an era of park building, urban reformers used zoos as instruments to inspire civic pride. Millions of Americans visited their local zoo every year. Nativists, such as Madison Grant of the New York Zoological Society, believed that focusing on species endangered in America would call attention to the alleged threat immigration posed to Anglo-American civilization. Zoos, always associated with wealth and power, seemed an ideal institution for imperialists hoping to prove that America was a world power.

Further Reading: Jeffrey Stott, "An American Idea of a Zoological Park: An Intellectual History," Ph.D. diss., University of California, 1981; Helen Horowitz, "Animals and Man in the New York Zoological Park," *New York History* 55 (1975): 426–455.

Gregory Dehler

Chronology

1868   William Davis obtained patent for a refrigerated railroad car

John Muir arrived in Yosemite Valley to sketch nature

Fourteenth Amendment added to the Constitution

Ulysses S. Grant received Republican presidential nomination

Horatio Seymour nominated by Democrats for president

Impeachment trial of President Andrew Johnson

Treaty signed with Navajos

Death of Kit Carson

Publication of *Little Women* by Louisa May Alcott

The *Overland Monthly* issued its first number

Christopher Latham Sholes constructed a typewriter

Decoration (Memorial) Day celebrated for the first time

John and Charles Deere incorporated their firm as Deere and Company

First issue of *The World Almanac*

Open-hearth process introduced into the American steel industry by Abram S. Hewitt

Ulysses S. Grant elected president of the United States

1869   Inauguration of Ulysses S. Grant as president

Judiciary Act amended to increase from seven to nine the number of Supreme Court justices

John Wesley Powell began exploring the Grand Canyon

Organization of the Colored National Labor Union

Union Pacific and Central Pacific transcontinental railroad complete and celebrated at Promontory Point, Utah

Supreme Court delivered *Texas* v. *White* opinion

Black Friday financial panic

Formation of the National Woman Suffrage Association

George Westinghouse obtained patent on the air brake

Prohibition party organized in Chicago

Wyoming Territory granted the first woman's suffrage in the United States

Henry J. Heinz established a food-packing company in Pennsylvania

First professional baseball team was the Cincinnati Red Stockings

Knights of Labor formed at Philadelphia

Ely S. Parker, a Native American, appointed to head Office of Indian Affairs

First caricature of Uncle Sam with chin whiskers appeared in *Harper's Weekly*

"Little Brown Jug" was a hit song

Massachusetts established the first state board of health in the United States

Arabella Mansfield gained admittance to the Iowa bar as the first woman lawyer in the United States

1870   Congress established U.S. Weather Bureau

John D. Rockefeller organized Standard Oil Company of Ohio

William Marcy Tweed ring broken in New York City

Hiram R. Revels became the first African-American to hold a seat in the U.S. Senate

Organization of the Great Atlantic and Pacific Tea Company

Congress created the Department of Justice

Death of Robert E. Lee

Armour and Company started operations

Completion of the first boardwalk in America at Atlantic City, New Jersey

Corcoran Art Galley, in Washington, D.C., incorporated by act of Congress

Scribner's Monthly founded

Adoption of the Fifteenth Amendment to the Constitution

Thomas Mundy Petersen heralded as first African American to vote after ratification of the Fifteenth Amendment

Thomas Nast first used the donkey, in a political cartoon in *Harper's Weekly*, as a symbol for the Democratic Party

Red Cloud's peace crusade to Washington

Senate rejected treaty to annex Dominican Republic

U.S. population: 38,558,371

1871   Charles A. Pillsbury received full title to a flour mill called Pillsbury and Company

Formation of a citizens commission to investigate Tammany Hall

Equal Rights party nominated Victoria C. Woodhull for president and Frederick Douglass for vice president in the election of 1872

Treaty of Washington signed with Great Britain

Chicago fire

Territorial government provided for the District of Columbia

Congress passed the Indian Appropriation Act

George William Curtis headed the first Civil Service Commission

First undergraduate daily newspaper in United States published at the University of Illinois

Andrew Smith Hallidie invented devices for making cable cars possible

Exhibition of *Whistler's Mother* (*Arrangement in Grey and Black*)

Henry James recorded his impressions on a trip to Niagara Falls

Polaris expedition

U.S. Supreme Court declared Legal Tender Act constitutional

Zoologist Addison E. Verrill was placed in charge of the operations of the U.S. Commission on Fish and Fisheries.

1872   Revelation of Crédit Mobilier stock scandals

Establishment of the Yellowstone National Park Reserve

Montgomery Ward and Company began in Chicago under Aaron Montgomery Ward

Liberal Republicans and Democrats nominated Horace Greeley for the presidency

Republican Party renominated Ulysses S. Grant for a second term

New York Catholic Charles O'Conor chosen by Straight-out Democrats for president

National Labor Reform Party selected David Davis as its presidential contender

Charlotte E. Ray became the first African-American woman attorney

Congress passed resolution setting the date for congressional elections on the Tuesday after the first Monday in November, effective in 1876

Charles Taze Russell organized the Jehovah's Witnesses

Edward Campbell Simmons of Saint Louis controlled the Simmons Hardware Company, the first mercantile corporation in the United States

Arbor Day commenced in Nebraska, primarily through the efforts of J. Sterling Morton

Reelection of Ulysses S. Grant as President of the United States

Yellowstone National Park established, making it the first and oldest national park in the world.

1873   Presidential inauguration of Ulysses S. Grant

Collapse of Jay Cooke and Company

Panic of 1873

Farmers' Alliance started with local meetings

Coinage Act demonetized silver

Mark Twain and Charles Dudley Warner published *The Gilded Age: A Tale of Today*

Organization of the Union of American Hebrew Congregations

Salary Grab Act

William Marcy Tweed convicted of fraud

Introduction of penny postcards in the United States

First issue of *Congressional Record*

Coors brewery founded in Denver

Epidemics of smallpox, yellow fever, and cholera in several southern cities

Congress passed legislation prohibiting the mailing of obscene literature

Dr. Edward Clarke's book, *Sex in Education*, challenged women's physical ability to withstand higher education

Known as the "Mother of Arizona," Josephine Brawley Hughes, a rugged pioneer, temperance advocate, and suffragist, secured appointment as the first woman public school teacher in Arizona and opened the first public school for girls in Tucson

1874 Joseph F. Glidden invented barbed wire

Formation of the Greenback Party

Mary Ewing Outerbridge laid out the first lawn tennis court in the United States, on Staten Island

A commission replaced territorial government in the District of Columbia

Establishment of the Woman's Christian Temperance Union in Cleveland

Democrats gained control of the House of Representatives in congressional elections

Thomas Nast's first cartoon featuring an elephant to symbolize the Republican Party appeared in *Harper's Weekly*

Erection of the Soldiers' and Sailors' Monument by Martin Milmore on Boston Common

Lewis Miller and John H. Vincent founded the Chautauqua movement

Andrew T. Still of Kansas developed osteopathy

Red River Indian War began

First public zoo in the United States opened in Philadelphia

First steel arch bridge, build by James Eads, to span Mississippi River dedicated at Saint Louis

President Grant appointed Morrison R. Waite as chief justice of the United States Supreme Court

1875 Specie Resumption Act approved by Congress

James A. Healy became the first African-American Roman Catholic bishop in the United States

Congress passed the Civil Rights Act

Signing of the Hawaiian Reciprocity Treaty

Revelations of Whiskey Ring scandals

Resignation of Orville E. Babcock as President Grant's private secretary

John McCloskey appointed first Catholic cardinal in the United States

Strike of the Molly Maguires

Dwight L. Moody began his revival meetings in the United States

Luther Burbank set up a plant nursery in California

Charles G. Waite introduced an unpadded baseball glove

Phineas T. Barnum inaugurated the three-ring circus

First Kentucky Derby ran at Churchill Downs

Death in office of Vice President Henry Wilson

The Society for the Prevention of Cruelty to Children selected Henry Bergh, who had incorporated the Society for the Prevention of Cruelty to Animals in 1866, as its first president

Death of Senator Andrew Johnson

Founding of the Theosophical Society of America in New York City by Henry Steel Olcott and Helena Petrovna Blavåtsky

Work began on the Yuma Territorial Prison, which later held some of the most notorious desperados of the Southwest

1876   Formation of the American Chemical Society

Centennial Exposition held in Philadelphia

Republican delegates nominated Rutherford B. Hayes of Ohio for president

Nomination of Samuel J. Tilden of New York by Democrats as the party's presidential contender

Alexander Graham Bell invented the telephone

Sioux Native Americans led by Sitting Bull slaughtered all of George A. Custer's 265-man Seventh Cavalry at the Battle of Little Big Horn in Montana

Repeal of the Southern Homestead Act of 1866

Professor Josiah Willard Gibbs published "On the Equilibrium of Heterogeneous Substances"

James Gordon Bennett brought polo to the United States

First fraternity house in the United States opened at Williams College in Massachusetts

Fred W. Thayer invented baseball catcher's mask

Greenback Party chose Peter Cooper as its presidential standard-bearer

Missouri Congressman Richard Parks Bland proposed a bill for free and unlimited coinage of silver

John W. Draper took the first photograph of the solar spectrum

Thomas A. Edison invented a mimeograph device

Felix Adler established the New York Society for Ethical Culture

Completion of Central Park in New York City

Melvil Dewey originated Dewey decimal classification system for arrangement of library books

Charles Sanders Peirce formulated the philosophy of pragmatism

Formation of the professional baseball National League

Establishment of the American Library Association in Philadelphia

Founding of Eli Lilly Company

Representative Henry W. Blair of New Hampshire introduced a prohibition amendment to the U.S. Constitution

Disputed presidential contest between Hayes and Tilden resulted in an electoral commission to determine outcome

Great Sioux War

House investigation resulted in resignation of Secretary of War William W. Belknap

1877   Compromise of 1877

Inauguration of Rutherford B. Hayes as president of the United States

Removal of the last federal troops from the South

End of Reconstruction

Surrender of Chief Joseph and the Nez Percé

First observance of Flag Day

Henry O. Flipper became the first African American to graduate from the U.S. Military Academy

Railroad strikes

Helen Magill was the first woman to earn a Ph.D. in the United States

Founding of the Society of American Artists

Supreme Court handed down *Munn* v. *Illinois* opinion

Treaty with the Sioux

Formation of the American Humane Association in Cleveland

Charles Elmer Hires produced and distributed root beer

Thomas A. Edison completed his phonograph

1878 Formation of the Greenback Labor Party

District of Columbia given a government of three commissioners appointed by the president

Establishment of the American Bar Association with James O. Broadhead as president

Congress passed the Bland-Allison Act over presidential veto

Enactment of Timber and Stone Act by Congress

Exodusters settled in Kansas

Yellow fever epidemic in South claimed 14,000 lives

Bannock War

Democrats gained political strength in congressional elections

First electric light company formed in New York City

Commercial treaty signed with Samoa

Chinese embassy officials received by President Hayes

First American manufacture of bicycles

Dismissal of Alexander Winchell, professor of geology at Vanderbilt University, for his scientific contradictions of biblical chronology

Edward Kemeys, foremost American sculptor of animals, exhibited *Bison and Wolves* in Paris

Celebrated robbery of $3 million from the Manhattan Savings Institution credited to George L. Leslie

First Easter egg roll at the White House

1879 Women attorneys gained the right to argue cases before the U.S. Supreme Court

Belva Ann Lockwood became the first woman admitted to practice before the Supreme Court of the United States

Thomas A. Edison perfected the first incandescent electric lamp

Resumption of specie payment

Carlisle Indian School founded in Pennsylvania by Richard Henry Pratt

James and John Ritty granted patent on cash register

First telephone installed in White House

Yellowstone National Park officially designated

Victorio War

Establishment of Radcliffe College as an adjunct to Harvard University

Mary Baker Eddy organized the Church of Christ, Scientist

Gilbert and Sullivan introduced to New York City with the U.S. opening of *H.M.S. Pinafore*

Geologist and mining engineer Clarence King appointed director of the U.S. Geological Survey within the Department of the Interior

Installation in Cleveland of first public electrical street lighting system in nation

Frank W. Woolworth began his venture in retailing

Henry James published *Daisy Miller*

Madison Square Garden in New York City opened to the public

Progress and Poverty, by Henry George, emerged as a landmark work in economics, concentrating on land value and a single tax

Osprey Affair at Sitka

1880 U.S. Supreme Court declared unconstitutional the exclusion of African Americans from jury duty

Greenback Labor Party offered James B. Weaver as its presidential nominee

Salvation Army made its debut in the United States

Republican Party delegates compromised on James A. Garfield as their presidential hopeful

Democrats chose Winfield S. Hancock to head the party's national ticket

Prohibition Party named Neal Dow for president

George Eastman patented a successful roll film for cameras

Kampfe Brothers devised a safety razor

Women constituted 80 percent of elementary schoolteachers nationwide

Sherwin-Williams manufactured house paint from standard formulas

Margaret Sidney (Harriett Lothrop) published *Five Little Peppers and How They Grew*

Samuel R. Lowery recognized as the first African-American lawyer to argue a case before the U.S. Supreme Court

James A. Garfield elected president of the United States

Charles Loring Brace, founder of the Children's Aid Society of New York, published *The Dangerous Classes of New York*

Galivants Ferry Stump biennial meeting in South Carolina began when local businessman John W. Holliday invited county Democratic candidates to speak from his store

Pioneer prospectors Richard Harris and Joseph Juneau accidentally found gold on the banks of the Gastineau Channel in Alaska

U.S. population: 50,189,209

1881 James A. Garfield inaugurated President of the United States

Richard Watson Gilder became editor of *The Century Illustrated Monthly*

Construction of first central electric power plant in the world in New York City

The Wharton School of Finance and Economy established within the University of Pennsylvania

Judge James J. Logan of California developed the loganberry

William K. Vanderbilt's mansion in New York City completed at a cost of $3 million

Helen Maria Fiske Hunt Jackson wrote *A Century of Dishonor*

Founding of an American branch of the Red Cross by Clara Barton

Charles Burleigh Purvis became the first African-American surgeon to head a hospital under civilian auspices, and the first African-American doctor to serve the president of the United States

Death of William H. "Billy the Kid" Bonney

Tuskegee Institute opened with Booker T. Washington as its president

Spotted Tail killed in Rosebud, South Dakota

Post Office Department discovery of fraudulent payments for mail services (Star Route frauds)

President Garfield assassinated by Charles J. Guiteau

Vice President Chester A. Arthur succeeded to the presidency of the United States

OK Corral gunfight occurred in Tombstone, Arizona Territory

1882 Jesse James killed

Chinese Exclusion Act

Charles J. Guiteau convicted and hanged in Washington for President Garfield's murder

Treaty of peace and commerce signed with Korea

Congress voted a pension for widows of presidents

Passage of Edmunds Act, designed to suppress polygamy in territories, especially Utah

Schuyler Skaats Wheeler developed an electric fan

Professor Granville Stanley Hall received a special lectureship in psychology and the money to establish a psychological laboratory

First appearance of inexpensive books known as Lovell's Library

Joseph Pulitzer began the *New York Morning Journal*

Michael J. McGivney founded the Knights of Columbus in New Haven, Connecticut

Knights of Labor sponsored the first Labor Day parade, in New York City

John Slocum founded the Indian Shaker Church

Formation of the American Forestry Association

Henry W. Seely patented an electric flatiron

Congress passed a River and Harbors Bill over President Arthur's veto

Congress authorized appointment by the president of a tariff commission, which recommended substantial tariff reductions

1883 Pendleton Act established civil service

Fire at the Newhall House hotel in Milwaukee, Wisconsin, killed seventy-one persons

Brooklyn Bridge opened

Standard time adopted

U.S. Supreme Court ruled Civil Rights Act of 1875 unconstitutional

Northern Pacific Railroad completed

Publication of Sarah Winnemucca's *Life Among the Piutes*, believed to be the first Native American woman's autobiography

Formation of the Southern Immigration Association

Mongrel Tariff Act passed by Congress

Founding of the Modern Language Association

Rebuilding of the U.S. Navy began with funds for the first steel vessels

American anarchists organized the International Working People's Association

Thomas C. Eakins painted *The Swimming Hole*

The high society costume ball thrown by the Vanderbilts gained notoriety as the nation's costliest party

Ex Parte Crow Dog ruling by the U.S. Supreme Court held that state and federal courts had no jurisdiction on Native American land

Sojourner Truth died in Michigan

African American Jan E. Matzeliger invented a machine that manufactured an entire shoe

First appearance of *Life* and *Ladies' Home Journal*

Benjamin F. Keith opened the first of the four hundred theatres that bore his name by 1914

Edwin L. Godkin was named editor of the *New York Evening Post*

Dorman B. Eaton named head of Civil Service Commission

Metropolitan Opera House opened in New York City

1884   Anti-Monopoly Party founded in Chicago with Benjamin F. Butler as its presidential candidate

Bureau of Labor created within Department of the Interior

Mississippi Industrial Institute and College chartered as nation's first state-supported women's college

William T. Sherman's succinct statement categorically removing himself from presidential politics

Supreme Court in *Elk* v. *Wilkins* declared that Native Americans were not citizens of the United States under the Fourteenth Amendment

Republicans nominated James G. Blaine for president of the United States

Prohibition Party named John P. St. John as its presidential contender

Democrats chose Grover Cleveland as their nominee for U.S. president

National Equal Rights Party selected Belva A. Lockwood for president

Reverend Samuel D. Burchard's "Rum, Romanism, and Rebellion" remark

Mugwumps opposed Republican presidential nomination of James G. Blaine

Establishment of territorial government in Alaska with the Organic Act

World's Industrial and Cotton Centennial Exposition at New Orleans

American Historical Association organized

The horse Buchanan, ridden by African-American jockey Isaac Murphy, won the Kentucky Derby

Indian Homestead Act

Samuel Sidney McClure established first newspaper syndicate

Hiram Stevens Maxim invented Maxim machine gun

Ottmar Mergenthaler patented the linotype automatic typesetting machine

Knights of Labor designated that Labor Day be celebrated annually on the first Monday in September

Moses Fleetwood Walker gained attention as first African-American major league baseball player

Publication of Helen Maria Fiske Hunt Jackson's best-seller *Ramona*, dubbed the "Indian *Uncle Tom's Cabin*"

Winslow Homer moved into a cottage studio in Maine

Grover Cleveland elected president of the United States

Architect William L. Jenney first used steel skeleton construction, inaugurating the skyscraper age

Birth of Eleanor Roosevelt

Birth of Harry S Truman

Riot in Cincinnati, Ohio

Publication of Mark Twain's *The Adventures of Huckleberry Finn*

First patent for a circular roller coaster awarded to Alanson Wood

Ottmar Mergenthaler obtained a patent for the first direct-casting linotype machine

Five legal hangings occurred in Cochise County, Territory of Arizona, on 28 March

Dr. Edward L. Trudeau opened the first tuberculosis hospital in the United States

1885   Inauguration of Grover Cleveland as president of the United States

Dedication of the Washington Monument

Death in office of Vice President Thomas A. Hendricks

Combine harvester invented

Daniel E. Salmon described *Salmonella* bacteria

Death of Ulysses S. Grant

Congress passed the Foran Act, an anti-contract labor law

Founding of Stanford University

Congress prohibited fencing of public lands in the West

U.S. Post Office Department instituted special delivery service

Popularity of ragtime accelerated with performances by musician/composer Scott Joplin in St. Louis

American Economic Association founded

Edward L. Trudeau opened the Adirondack Cottage Sanatorium in New York State

The life and writings of Protestant minister Josiah Strong marked the beginning of the Social Gospel movement in United States

Clothing fashion described as "moyen age"

1886   Haymarket tragedy in Chicago

Congress enacted the Presidential Succession Act

President Grover Cleveland married Frances Folsom at the White House

Bernhard E. Fernow named head of Division of Forestry, U.S. Department of Agriculture

Surrender of Geronimo

Dedication of Statue of Liberty

Death of Chester A. Arthur

Dwight L. Moody founded Bible Institute for Home and Foreign Missions

Henry M. Flagler bought a railroad to serve his hotel in St. Augustine, Florida

Augustus Toltan ordained as first African-American priest to minister to African-American Catholics

Richard W. Sears began selling watches by mail

Frances Hodgson Burnett published *Little Lord Fauntleroy*

Andover religious controversy

First Tournament of Roses held in Pasadena, California

Milwaukee labor riots, resulting in seven deaths, triggered passage (1887) of Wisconsin's first labor laws

First settlement house in United States established in New York City by Dr. Stanton Coit

American Federation of Labor organized in Columbus, Ohio, with Samuel Gompers as first president

May Day demonstrations

187 Native American reservations covered 181,000 square miles of land inhabited by 243,000 people

Death of Emily Dickinson

Anti-Chinese riots in Territory of Washington compelled Governor Watson Squire to declare martial law

Dr. John S. Pemberton sold the first Coca-Cola at Jacob's Pharmacy in Atlanta, Georgia

The Cherokee Telephone Company placed in operation the first line in Indian Territory (Oklahoma).

1887   Pearl Harbor leased to United States as a naval station

Congress passed the Dawes Severalty (or General Allotment) Act

President Cleveland signed the Hatch Act

Repeal of Tenure of Office Act

William Randolph Hearst took control of the *San Francisco Examiner*

Interstate Commerce Act

Augustus Saint-Gaudens completed standing statue of Abraham Lincoln in Chicago

Marine Biological Laboratory founded in Woods Hole, Massachusetts, due mainly to promotion by Spencer F. Baird

Electoral Count Act approved by Congress

President Cleveland vetoed Dependent Pension Bill

Cleveland's annual message to Congress devoted to the tariff issue

Congress enacted Edmunds-Tucker Act to limit Mormon power in Utah

First true golf club in the United States founded at Foxbury, Pennsylvania

American Trotting Association organized in Detroit, Michigan

Congress chartered Catholic University in Washington, D.C.

Founding of the American Protective Association

Theodore Roosevelt appealed for the formation of the Boone and Crockett Club

George Nellis undertook a transcontinental bicycle journey from Herkimer, New York, to San Francisco, California.

1888 Secret ballot (kangaroo voting) adopted for first time, in municipal elections in Louisville, Kentucky

National Equal Rights Party decided upon Belva Ann Lockwood for president

Republican adoption of political slogan "As Maine goes, so goes the nation"

British Ambassador Lord Sackville-West's pro-Cleveland letter galvanized Irish vote against the chief executive

John La Farge painted the *Ascension*

George Eastman introduced the Kodak camera

Congress established the Department of Labor, without cabinet rank

First electric automobile, designed by Philip W. Pratt, demonstrated in Boston

Industrial Reform Party nominated Albert E. Redstone of California for president

Blizzard of 1888

Publication of Edward Bellamy's *Looking Backward*

Massachusetts adopted Australian ballot

Appointment of Melville Weston Fuller as chief justice of the U.S. Supreme Court

Congress granted U.S. citizenship to Native American women married to white men

Republicans turned to Benjamin Harrison as their candidate for president

Democrats nominated Grover Cleveland for a second presidential term

First successful electric trolley system began operations in Richmond, Virginia

Benjamin Harrison elected president of the United States with fewer popular votes than Cleveland

Bayard-Chamberlain Treaty

Birth of Jim Thorpe

1889 Benjamin Harrison inaugurated as the nation's twenty-third president

Oklahoma land rush

Johnstown, Pennsylvania, flood

North Dakota, South Dakota, Montana, and Washington admitted to Union

Iron Tail became part of Buffalo Bill Cody's Wild West Show

Jane Addams opened Hull-House

Washington Inaugural Centennial

Pan-American Conference

Kansas the first state to pass a law regulating trusts

Electric lights installed in White House but Harrison refused to touch switches

Wovoka, a Paiute shaman from Nevada, taught new religious movement, known as the Ghost Dance, to transform Native American lives

Susan LaFlesche Picotte, first Native American woman to earn a medical degree, began practicing on Omaha reservation in Nebraska

First number of *Munsey's Weekly* published by Frank A. Munsey

General Federation of Women's Clubs founded

Safety bicycle first manufactured

Singer Manufacturing Company produced the first electric sewing machine in United States

Department of Agriculture elevated to cabinet status with Norman J. Colman as first secretary

Wall Street Journal began publication

American Academy of Political and Social Science organized

Tower Buildings constructed in New York City

Andrew Carnegie outlined systematic theory of philanthropy to adjust inequities in capitalism

Berlin Conference on Samoa

1890 Sherman Silver Purchase Act

Sherman Antitrust Act

McKinley Tariff

Creation of Pan American Union

George Francis Train broke Nellie Bly's around-the-world record

Oklahoma Territory created

Wyoming admitted to Union and recognized as first state to give women the vote

Wounded Knee Massacre

Establishment of the Weather Bureau

Mormon Church discontinued sanctioning polygamy

Mississippi restricted African-American suffrage by imposing literacy tests

Democrats capture control of House of Representatives in a landslide

Death of Sitting Bull

Erection of Louis H. Sullivan's Wainwright Building in St. Louis, Missouri

Blair Education Bill defeated in House of Representatives

First Army-Navy football game held

Kicking Bear and Short Bull introduced Ghost Dance religion to Sioux at Pine Ridge Reservation

Publication of *How the Other Half Lives* by Jacob A. Riis

William Henry Lewis and W. T. S. Jackson became the first recorded African-American players on a white college football team

Alfred Thayer Mahan published *The Influence of Sea Power upon History*

Author George Washington Cable published *The Negro Question*

Antietam National Battlefield established to commemorate the single bloodiest day of the American Civil War (23,110 casualties)

U.S. population: 62,979,766

African-American population: 7,488,676

1891 Eleven indicted Sicilian immigrants lynched in New Orleans, Louisiana

Congress created U.S. circuit courts of appeal

International Copyright Act passed by Congress

Edwin Booth's last performance in *Hamlet*

James Naismith devised the game of basketball

Henry O. Havemeyer started American Sugar Refining Company

George E. Hale invented the spectroheliograph to photograph the sun

Orello Cone, president of Buchtel College, published *Gospel Criticism and Historical Christianity*

First correspondence school in United States pioneered by Thomas Jefferson Foster

Congress enacted legislation providing for Native American tribes to lease tribal lands to outsiders

Creek novelist Sophia Alice Callahan published *Wynema, A Child of the Forest*

Defeat of Lodge Bill designed to prevent infringements on the African American's right to vote

Forest Reserve Act

People's Party met in Cincinnati, Ohio

Opening of Carnegie Hall in New York City

Mob in Valparaiso, Chile, killed two American sailors

First billion-dollar Congress

Sophia Alice Callahan wrote the first novel by a Native American woman

1892   Homestead Strike

Ellis Island opened as the new entry point and receiving station for immigrants

Populist Party chose James B. Weaver as its presidential standard-bearer

Republicans renominated President Benjamin Harrison for a second term

Democrats decided upon former President Grover Cleveland as their nominee for president

Socialist Labor Party named Simon Wing of Massachusetts for president

Massachusetts murder trial of Lisbeth A. "Lizzie" Borden

Thomas Nelson Page published *The Old South*

Formation of General Electric Company

Death of Walt Whitman

University of Chicago established with funds from John D. Rockefeller under first president William Rainey Harper

Popular song was "Daisy Bell"

American Fine Arts Society organized

Charles K. Harris composed hit song "After the Ball Is Over"

Dalton gang of robbers virtually eliminated at Coffeyville, Kansas

First home (Charnley House) probably designed by Frank Lloyd Wright in Chicago

American School of osteopathy established at Kirksville, Missouri

Charles and Frank Duryea built the first successful gasoline-powered automobile in United States

James J. Corbett knocked out John L. Sullivan to win world heavyweight boxing championship

George Miller Sternberg published *A Manual of Bacteriology*

Ward McAllister coined phrase "the 400" with reference to Gilded Age society's elite

Heresy trial of Charles A. Briggs

American Psychological Association was founded

George W. G. Ferris designed Ferris wheel

Cleveland defeated Harrison in presidential election, becoming only chief executive to serve two nonconsecutive terms

Democrats won control of House of Representatives and Senate

Weaver garnered twenty-two electoral votes

Bering Sea dispute

Carl Schurz assumed presidency of National Civil Service Reform League

The first graduate department of sociology in the nation was formed at the University of Chicago

Oberlin's football team under John W. Heisman presumably defeated the Michigan players in Ann Arbor by the controversial score of 24 to 22

Completion in Chicago of the James Charnley (Persky) House, the first modern house in America, designed by architects Frank Lloyd Wright and Louis H. Sullivan, who invented a new abstract form of American architectural ornament and design

1893   Inauguration of Grover Cleveland as president of the United States

Panic of 1893

World's Columbian Exposition in Chicago

Repeal of the Sherman Silver Purchase Act

Frederick Jackson Turner's address "The Significance of the Frontier in American History"

Louis Comfort Tiffany developed Favrile glass

Clandestine surgery performed on President Cleveland aboard a yacht

Death of Rutherford B. Hayes

Nancy Green became the first Aunt Jemima and the world's first living trademark

Overthrow of Queen Liliuokalani of Hawaii

United States recognized provisional government of Hawaii under Sanford B. Dole

Commissioner James H. Blount submitted report on Hawaiian revolution to President Cleveland

President Cleveland withdrew Hawaiian annexation treaty from Senate consideration

Congress enacted Diplomatic Appropriation Act

Colorado adopted woman's suffrage

Henry Ford assembled his first successful gasoline engine

Esther Cleveland was the first child of a president to be born in the White House

Illinois Governor John Peter Altgeld pardoned three remaining Haymarket prisoners

Whitcomb L. Judson patented the zipper

Dedication of Mormon Temple at Salt Lake City

Lillian D. Wald founded Livingston Street Settlement in New York City

Formation of National Bimetallic League

Ice hockey introduced to United States from Canada

Daniel Hale Williams, an African-American surgeon, performed world's first successful heart operation in Chicago

Samuel Sidney McClure founded *McClure's Magazine*

Stephen Crane wrote *Maggie: A Girl of the Streets*

William Cary Renfrow, a banker and oil businessman, became the first and only Democratic territorial governor of Oklahoma

Robert M. Turner in Columbus, Ohio, opened the Villa, an amusement center later renamed Olentangy Park

1894   Jacob S. Coxey's army marched from Ohio to Washington, D.C.

Pullman Strike

Carey Desert Land Act, dealing with irrigation, approved by Congress

Wilson-Gorman Tariff

Congress legislated a graduated income tax

Hawaii made a republic

J. P. Morgan organized Southern Railroad Company

President Cleveland vetoed Bland Bill, authorizing coinage of silver bullion

William Hope Harvey published *Coin's Financial School*

Publication of Henry Demarest Lloyd's *Wealth Against Commonwealth*

Democratic Silver Convention convened in Nebraska

Congress created Bureau of Immigration

Clarence Darrow came to national prominence as legal counsel for Eugene V. Debs, head of American Railway Union

Republicans won off-year congressional elections in a political tidal wave that began the process of political realignment in the nation

A congressional resolution made Labor Day a legal holiday

Economic depression and unemployment in the nation worsened

Charles Lawler wrote lyrics and music for "The Sidewalks of New York"

President Cleveland ordered federal troops to Chicago to restore order in Pullman strike

Governor John Peter Altgeld of Illinois protested Cleveland's action on constitutional grounds

Rudyard Kipling, living in Brattleboro, Vermont, published his work entitled *The Jungle Book*

Elwood Haynes successfully tested an automobile in Kokomo, Indiana

Disputed Alabama gubernatorial contest

1895   U.S. Supreme Court case of *United States* v. *E. C. Knight Company*

Death of Frederick Douglass

Revolt in Cuba

Venezuela boundary dispute

Printing Act consolidated laws governing the printing, funding, and distribution of government publications

U.S. Supreme Court rendered opinion in landmark case *Pollock* v. *Farmers Loan and Trust Company*

Katharine Lee Bates's poem "America the Beautiful" first appeared in print

Sears, Roebuck and Company started mail-order business

Ida B. Wells compiled first statistical pamphlet on lynching

Field and Stream magazine first issued

First meeting of the National Conference of Colored Women

Charles E. Duryea received first patent for a gasoline-driven automobile awarded to a U.S. inventor

Booker T. Washington delivered "Atlanta Compromise" speech

Cotton States International Exposition in Atlanta, Georgia

Federal gold purchase made by Treasury Department from banking houses of J. P. Morgan and Company and August Belmont and Company

William Allen White bought the Emporia, Kansas, *Gazette*

George B. Selden received patent for his gasoline-driven automobile

Stephen Crane published *The Red Badge of Courage*

The National Association of Manufacturers assembled for the first time in Cincinnati, Ohio

"The Yellow Kid" comic character, created by Richard F. Outcault, first appeared in the *New York World*

1896   Currency issue divided Democrats

Utah admitted as a state

William Jennings Bryan's "Cross of Gold" speech

Democratic Party selected William Jennings Bryan as its presidential standard-bearer on a free coinage platform

National Democratic Party (Gold Democrats) nominated John M. Palmer for president on a sound money platform

Populist Party endorsed William Jennings Bryan to head its national ticket

Republicans named William McKinley for president on a sound currency platform

McKinley's famous front porch campaign took place at his home in Canton, Ohio

John Philip Sousa composed "The Stars and Stripes Forever"

U.S. Supreme Court delivered "separate but equal" doctrine in *Plessy* v. *Ferguson*

Finley P. Dunne's creation "Mr. Dooley," fictional Irish saloonkeeper and philosopher, gained nationwide following for his political observations in 1896 campaign

William Allen White editorialized "What's the Matter with Kansas?"

X-ray treatment for breast cancer first carried out by Emil H. Grube

Model steam-powered airplane designed by Samuel P. Langley flew for one minute

Newspaper innovation "advice to the lovelorn" column debuted in the New Orleans *Picayune*, written by Elizabeth Meriwether Gilmer, who used the pen name Dorothy Dix

William Ashley "Billy" Sunday turned evangelist

St. Louis cyclone

Richard F. Outcault's comic strip "The Yellow Kid," in *New York World*, initiated a new form of American humor, art, and journalism

Rabbi Isaac Elchanan Theological Seminary founded, the first yeshiva in the United States

Prohibition Party offered Joshua Levering as its presidential nominee

Rural free postal delivery commenced

Edward A. MacDowell appointed head of new music department at Columbia University

William McKinley elected president of the United States

James B. Connolly won the first gold medal of the modern Olympic games

1897   Retiring President Grover Cleveland vetoed bill requiring literacy tests for immigrants

National Monetary Conference met at Indianapolis, Indiana

Formation of Social Democracy of America

William McKinley took oath of office as president of the United States

National Congress of Mothers founded

Coal miner's strike

Faculty of Kansas Agricultural College dismissed for failure to support Populism

New York City's Astoria Hotel, designed by Henry J. Hardenbergh, opened to public and connected to four-year-old Waldorf Hotel

Dedication of Yerkes Observatory in Wisconsin

Establishment of American Osteopathic Association

Bimetallic Monetary Commission failed to secure agreement on international bimetallism

Dingley Tariff

M. H. Cannon, of Utah, first female state senator in nation

Klondike Gold Rush

First Boston Marathon won by John J. McDermott

Conspicuous consumption flourished at excessively lavish New York City party hosted by the Bradley Martins, who then fled to England to escape widespread criticism and avoid further disapproval

Secretary of the Treasury Lyman J. Gage introduced the Banking Bill

Louis Francis Sockalexis became the first Native American initiated into professional baseball

1898   Explosion of the U.S.S. *Maine* in Havana harbor

De Lome Letter

Senator Redfield Proctor's impassioned and influential speech on Cuba

Spanish-American War

Spain's Caribbean fleet defeated at Santiago, Cuba

Commodore George Dewey destroyed Spanish naval force at Manila Bay

United States took possession of Philippines, Guam, and Puerto Rico

Teller Amendment

Theodore Roosevelt and Rough Riders attracted national attention

Annexation of Hawaii to the United States

Treaty of Paris negotiated between Spain and the United States

South Dakota voters approved initiative and referendum

Robert Penn was the only African-American seaman during Spanish-American War to receive the Naval Medal of Honor

Biltmore Forest School opened by Dr. Carl A. Schenck

Congress passed War Revenue Act

President McKinley visited Tuskegee Institute in Alabama

Theodore Roosevelt elected governor of New York

Henry McNeal Turner became the first prominent African-American churchman to declare that God is black

National Institute of Arts and Letters established by American Social Science Association

Congress voted to sanction the Erdman Arbitration Act sponsored by Representative Jacob Erdman of Pennsylvania

In *United States* v. *Wong Kim Ark*, the Supreme Court ruled that native-born Americans possessed citizenship without respect to race or color

Wilmington, North Carolina, racial massacre

Monetary Commission of the Indianapolis Convention issued its report

1899 Treaty of Paris ratified by Senate, by one vote

Secretary of State John Hay's Open Door in China

Philippine insurgents started unsuccessful guerrilla war against United States

American Samoa acquired by partition treaty

President McKinley appointed Schurman Commission members

John Dewey's *The School and Society* revolutionized American educational theory and practice

Death in office of Vice President Garret A. Hobart

President McKinley rode in a Stanley Steamer automobile in Canton, Ohio

Carry Nation started anti-saloon drive in Kansas

Death of evangelist Dwight L. Moody, founder of Moody Bible Institute

Popular social protest poem "The Man with the Hoe," by Edwin Markham, published in *San Francisco Examiner*

Charles W. Chesnutt, foremost African-American novelist of the time, published *The Conjure Woman*

Hague Conference on armaments and warfare held in the Netherlands

Thorstein Veblen published *The Theory of the Leisure Class*

Beginning of the Christian Commercial Men's Association of America, better known as the Gideons

Congress created the Isthmian Canal Commission

Organization of the Anti-Imperialist League

Edward H. Harriman's expedition to Alaska

First electric motor patrol (paddy) wagon in the world for police use began operations in Akron, Ohio

1900 Taft Commission directed to establish civil government in Philippine Islands

Death of railroad engineer John Luther "Casey" Jones

Foraker Act provided for setting up civil government in Puerto Rico

Formation of a union of actors known as the White Rats

First issue of *The Smart Set*, a literary monthly, published by William D. Mann

International Ladies' Garment Workers Union established

Wilbur and Orville Wright built their first full-scale glider

Hall of Fame founded in New York City

National Negro Business League formed in Boston

Congress passed act organizing the Territory of Hawaii

Boxer Rebellion

Herbert C. Hoover took part in defense of Tientsin (Tianjin) in Boxer Rebellion

Gold Standard Act

Galveston hurricane

First meeting of the Automobile Club of America and first automobile show held in New York City

Eight thousand automobiles registered in United States and ten miles of paved roads

First direct primary in United States occurred in Hennepin County, Minnesota

Lumberman Frederick Weyerhaeuser incorporated Weyerhaeuser Company

Theodore Dreiser published *Sister Carrie*

Illiteracy in United States reached a new low of 10.7 percent

Year's most popular song was "Good-Bye, Dolly Gray"

U.S. Bureau of the Census reported 8,833,994 African Americans, 237,196 Native Americans, and 66,809,196 Caucasians living in the country

Union Reform Party designated Seth Hockett Ellis of Ohio as its nominee for president

Republicans renominated William McKinley for a second term as chief executive

Democrats adopted an anti-imperialist stance in their platform and rubber-stamped the nomination of William Jennings Bryan

Populist Party delegates anointed William Jennings Bryan as their choice for president

Middle-of-the-Road (Anti-Fusionist) Populists nominated Wharton Barker for president and Ignatius Donnelly for vice president

Silver Republicans endorsed William Jennings Bryan as their candidate for president

Social Democratic Party offered Eugene V. Debs as its choice to head the presidential ticket

William McKinley easily reelected president of the United States

Riot in Akron, Ohio

New Orleans race riot

U.S. population: 76,212,168

1901 William McKinley inaugurated president of the United States

Platt Amendment

Ransom Eli Olds began mass production of Oldsmobile motor car

Socialist Party organized by merger of parties led by Eugene V. Debs and Morris Hillquit

National Union Catalog established

United States Steel became nation's first billion-dollar corporation

Yellow Fever Commission issued report at Pan American Medical Congress

Clarence E. Dutton retired after a lifetime as a major figure in earth sciences and western explorations

Margaret Haley was the first woman to address a public forum of the National Education Association

Death of Benjamin Harrison

Insular Cases decided by U.S. Supreme Court

Spindletop oil strike in Texas

Capture of Filipino rebel leader Emilio Aguinaldo

Booker T. Washington published *Up from Slavery: An Autobiography*

William M. Trotter founded the *Boston Guardian*, a black newspaper demanding full equality for African Americans

Pan-American Exposition at Buffalo

President McKinley assassinated by anarchist Leon Czolgosz

Vice President Theodore Roosevelt assumed the presidency of the United States

Hay-Pauncefote Treaty

Booker T. Washington dined with President Theodore Roosevelt at the White House

Philadelphia's City Hall opened with a bronze William Penn sculpture on the top of the clock tower designed by Alexander M. Calder, making it the tallest statue on any building in the world

Gilded Age ended as Progressive Era and twentieth century began

Appendices

Presidents of the United States

Andrew Johnson	(1865–1869)	Grover Cleveland	(1885–1889)
Ulysses S. Grant	(1869–1877)	Benjamin Harrison	(1889–1893)
Rutherford B. Hayes	(1877–1881)	Grover Cleveland	(1893–1897)
James A. Garfield	(1881–1881)	William McKinley	(1897–1901)
Chester A. Arthur	(1881–1885)	Theodore Roosevelt	(1901–1909)

Vice Presidents of the United States

Schuyler Colfax	(1869–1873)	Levi P. Morton	(1889–1893)
Henry Wilson	(1873–1875)	Adlai E. Stevenson	(1893–1897)
William A. Wheeler	(1877–1881)	Garret A. Hobart	(1897–1899)
Chester A. Arthur	(1881–1881)	Theodore Roosevelt	(1901–1901)
Thomas A. Hendricks	(1885–1885)		

Secretaries of State

Elihu B. Washburne	(1869–1869)	John W. Foster	(1892–1893)
Hamilton Fish	(1869–1877)	Walter Q. Gresham	(1893–1895)
William M. Evarts	(1877–1881)	Richard Olney	(1895–1897)
James G. Blaine	(1881–1881)	John Sherman	(1897–1898)
Frederick T. Frelinghuysen	(1881–1885)	William R. Day	(1898–1898)
Thomas F. Bayard	(1885–1889)	John Hay	(1898–1905)
James G. Blaine	(1889–1892)		

Secretaries of the Treasury

George S. Boutwell	(1869–1873)	Hugh McCulloch	(1884–1885)
William A. Richardson	(1873–1874)	Daniel Manning	(1885–1887)
Benjamin H. Bristow	(1874–1876)	Charles S. Fairchild	(1887–1889)
Lot M. Morrill	(1876–1877)	William Windom	(1889–1891)
John Sherman	(1877–1881)	Charles Foster	(1891–1893)
William Windom	(1881–1881)	John G. Carlisle	(1893–1897)
Charles J. Folger	(1881–1884)	Lyman J. Gage	(1897–1901)
Walter Q. Gresham	(1884–1884)		

Secretaries of War

John A. Rawlins	(1869–1869)	Robert T. Lincoln	(1881–1885)
William T. Sherman	(1869–1869)	William C. Endicott	(1885–1889)
William W. Belknap	(1869–1876)	Redfield Proctor	(1889–1891)
Alphonso Taft	(1876–1876)	Stephen B. Elkins	(1891–1893)
James D. Cameron	(1876–1877)	Daniel S. Lamont	(1893–1897)
George W. McCrary	(1877–1879)	Russell A. Alger	(1897–1899)
Alexander Ramsey	(1879–1881)	Elihu Root	(1899–1904)

Secretaries of the Navy

Adolph E. Borie	(1869–1869)	William E. Chandler	(1882–1885)
George M. Robeson	(1869–1877)	William C. Whitney	(1885–1889)
Richard W. Thompson	(1877–1881)	Benjamin F. Tracy	(1889–1893)
Nathan Goff, Jr.	(1881–1881)	Hilary A. Herbert	(1893–1897)
William H. Hunt	(1881–1882)	John D. Long	(1897–1902)

Postmasters General

John A. J. Creswell	(1869–1874)	Frank Hatton	(1884–1885)
James W. Marshall	(1874–1874)	William F. Vilas	(1885–1888)
Marshall Jewell	(1874–1876)	Donald M. Dickinson	(1888–1889)
James N. Tyner	(1876–1877)	John Wanamaker	(1889–1893)
David M. Key	(1877–1880)	Wilson S. Bissell	(1893–1895)
Horace Maynard	(1880–1881)	William L. Wilson	(1895–1897)
Thomas L. James	(1881–1882)	James A. Gary	(1897–1898)
Timothy O. Howe	(1882–1883)	Charles E. Smith	(1898–1901)
Walter Q. Gresham	(1883–1884)		

Attorneys General

Ebenezer R. Hoar	(1869–1870)	Augustus H. Garland	(1885–1889)
Amos T. Akerman	(1870–1871)	William H. H. Miller	(1889–1893)
George H. Williams	(1871–1875)	Richard Olney	(1893–1895)
Edwards Pierrepont	(1875–1876)	Judson Harmon	(1895–1897)
Alphonso Taft	(1876–1877)	Joseph McKenna	(1897–1898)
Charles Devens	(1877–1881)	John W. Griggs	(1898–1901)
Wayne MacVeagh	(1881–1881)	Philander C. Knox	(1901–1904)
Benjamin H. Brewster	(1882–1885)		

Secretaries of the Interior

Jacob D. Cox	(1869–1870)	William F. Vilas	(1888–1889)
Columbus Delano	(1870–1875)	John W. Noble	(1889–1893)
Zachariah Chandler	(1875–1877)	Hoke Smith	(1893–1896)
Carl Schurz	(1877–1881)	David R. Francis	(1896–1897)
Samuel J. Kirkwood	(1881–1882)	Cornelius N. Bliss	(1897–1898)
Henry M. Teller	(1882–1885)	Ethan A. Hitchcock	(1898–1907)
Lucius Q. C. Lamar	(1885–1888)		

Secretaries of Agriculture

Norman J. Colman   (1889–1889)

Jeremiah M. Rusk   (1889–1893)

J. Sterling Morton   (1893–1897)

James Wilson   (1897–1913)

Commissioners of Indian Affairs

Nathaniel G. Taylor   (1867–1869)

Ely S. Parker   (1869–1871)

Francis A. Walker   (1871–1873)

Edward P. Smith   (1873–1875)

John Q. Smith   (1875–1877)

Ezra A. Hayt   (1877–1880)

Roland E. Trowbridge   (1880–1881)

Hiram Price   (1881–1885)

John D. C. Atkins   (1885–1888)

John H. Oberly   (1888–1889)

Thomas J. Morgan   (1889–1893)

Daniel M. Browning   (1893–1897)

William A. Jones   (1897–1904)

Wives of the Presidents and Official White House Hostesses

Eliza McCardle Johnson

Martha Johnson Patterson (President Johnson's daughter)

Julia Boggs Dent Grant

Lucy Ware Webb Hayes

Lucretia Rudolph Garfield

Ellen Lewis Herndon Arthur

Mary Arthur McElroy (President Arthur's sister)

Rose Elizabeth Cleveland (President Cleveland's sister)

Frances Clara Folsom Cleveland

Caroline Lavinia Scott Harrison

Mary Scott Lord Dimmick Harrison

Ida Saxton McKinley

Alice Hathaway Lee Roosevelt

Edith Kermit Carow Roosevelt

Wives of the Vice Presidents

Ellen Clark Colfax

Nellie Wade Colfax

Harriet Malvina Howe Wilson

Mary King Wheeler

Ellen Lewis Herndon Arthur

Eliza Morgan Hendricks

Lucy Kimball Morton

Anna Livingston Street Morton

Letitia Barbour Green Stevenson

Jennie Tuttle Hobart

Alice Hathaway Lee Roosevelt

Edith Kermit Carow Roosevelt

District Governors of Alaska

John H. Kinkead	(1884–1885)
Alfred P. Swineford	(1885–1889)
Lyman E. Knapp	(1889–1893)
James Sheakley	(1893–1897)
John G. Brady	(1897–1906)

Hawaii's Royalty

Kamehameha V	(1863–1872)
Lunalilo	(1873–1874)
Kalakaua	(1874–1891)
Liliuokalani	(1891–1893)

Dates of U.S. Congresses

Fortieth Congress	(1867–1869)
Forty-first Congress	(1869–1871)
Forty-second Congress	(1871–1873)
Forty-third Congress	(1873–1875)
Forty-fourth Congress	(1875–1877)
Forty-fifth Congress	(1877–1879)
Forty-sixth Congress	(1879–1881)
Forty-seventh Congress	(1881–1883)
Forty-eighth Congress	(1883–1885)
Forty-ninth Congress	(1885–1887)
Fiftieth Congress	(1887–1889)
Fifty-first Congress	(1889–1891)
Fifty-second Congress	(1891–1893)
Fifty-third Congress	(1893–1895)
Fifty-fourth Congress	(1895–1897)
Fifty-fifth Congress	(1897–1899)
Fifty-sixth Congress	(1899–1901)

Speakers of the House of Representatives

Schuyler Colfax	(1863–1869)	John G. Carlisle	(1883–1889)
Theodore M. Pomeroy	(1869–1869)	Thomas B. Reed	(1889–1891)
James G. Blaine	(1869–1875)	Charles F. Crisp	(1891–1895)
Michael C. Kerr	(1875–1876)	Thomas B. Reed	(1895–1899)
Samuel J. Randall	(1876–1881)	David B. Henderson	(1899–1903)
Joseph W. Keifer	(1881–1883)		

Presidents Pro Tempore of the Senate

Fortieth Congress	Benjamin F. Wade	Forty-ninth Congress	John Sherman
Forty-first Congress	Henry B. Anthony		John J. Ingalls
Forty-second Congress	Henry B. Anthony	Fiftieth Congress	John J. Ingalls
Forty-third Congress	Matthew H. Carpenter	Fifty-first Congress	John J. Ingalls
	Henry B. Anthony		Charles F. Manderson
Forty-fourth Congress	Thomas W. Ferry	Fifty-second Congress	Charles F. Manderson
Forty-fifth Congress	Thomas W. Ferry	Fifty-third Congress	Charles F. Manderson
Forty-sixth Congress	Allen G. Thurman		Isham G. Harris
Forty-seventh Congress	Thomas F. Bayard		Matt W. Ransom
	David Davis	Fifty-fourth Congress	William P. Frye
	George F. Edmunds	Fifty-fifth Congress	William P. Frye
Forty-eighth Congress	George F. Edmunds	Fifty-sixth Congress	William P. Frye

Clerks of the House

Edward McPherson	(1863–1875)	Edward McPherson	(1889–1891)
George M. Adams	(1875–1881)	James Kerr	(1891–1895)
Edward McPherson	(1881–1883)	Alexander McDowell	(1895–1911)
John B. Clark, Jr.	(1883–1889)		

Secretaries of the Senate

John W. Forney	(1861–1868)	Anson G. McCook	(1883–1893)
George C. Gorham	(1868–1879)	William R. Cox	(1893–1900)
John C. Burch	(1879–1881)	Charles G. Bennett	(1900–1913)
Francis E. Shober	(1881–1883)		

Librarians of Congress

Ainsworth Rand Spofford	(1864–1897)	Herbert Putnam	(1899–1939)
John Russell Young	(1897–1899)		

Chief Justices of the U.S. Supreme Court

Salmon P. Chase	(1864–1873)	Melville W. Fuller	(1888–1910)
Morrison R. Waite	(1874–1888)		

Justices of the U.S. Supreme Court

Samuel Nelson	(1845–1872)	Stanley Matthews	(1881–1889)
Robert C. Grier	(1846–1870)	Horace Gray	(1881–1902)
Nathan Clifford	(1858–1881)	Samuel Blatchford	(1882–1893)
Noah H. Swayne	(1862–1881)	Lucius Q. C. Lamar	(1888–1893)
Samuel F. Miller	(1862–1890)	David J. Brewer	(1889–1910)
David Davis	(1862–1877)	Henry B. Brown	(1890–1906)
Stephen J. Field	(1863–1897)	George Shiras, Jr.	(1892–1903)
William Strong	(1870–1880)	Howell E. Jackson	(1893–1895)
Joseph P. Bradley	(1870–1892)	Edward D. White	(1894–1910)
Ward Hunt	(1872–1882)	Rufus W. Peckham	(1895–1909)
John M. Harlan	(1877–1911)	Joseph McKenna	(1898–1925)
William B. Woods	(1880–1887)		

American Historical Association
Presidential Addresses

1884	Andrew Dickson White	*On Studies in General History and the History of Civilization*
1885	Andrew Dickson White	*On the Influence of American Ideas upon the French Revolution*
1886	George Bancroft	*On Self-Government*
1887	Justin Winsor	*Manuscript Sources of American History: The Conspicuous Collections Extant*
1888	William F. Poole	*The Early Northwest*
1889	Charles K. Adams	*Recent Historical Work in the Colleges and Universities of Europe and America*
1890	John Jay	*The Demand for Education in American History*
1891	William Wirt Henry	*The Causes Which Produced the Virginia of the Revolutionary Period*
1892–1893	James Burrill Angell	*The Inadequate Recognition of Diplomatists by Historians*
1893–1894	Henry B. Adams	*The Tendency of History*
1895	George Frisbie Hoar	*Popular Discontent with Representative Government*
1896	Richard Salter Storrs	*Contributions Made to Our National Development by Plain Men*
1897	James Schouler	*A New Federal Convention*
1898	George Park Fisher	*The Function of the Historian as Judge of Historic Persons*
1899	James Ford Rhodes	*History*
1900	Edward Eggleston	*The New History*
1901	Charles F. Adams	*An Undeveloped Function*

Presidents of the National Education Association

1871	J. L. Pickard		1887	W. E. Sheldon
1872	E. E. White		1888	Aaron Gove
1873	B. G. Northrop		1889	Albert P. Marble
1874	S. H. White		1890	J. H. Canfield
1875	W. T. Harris		1891	W. R. Garrett
1876	W. F. Phelps		1892	E. H. Cook
1877	M. A. Newell		1893	Albert G. Lane
1878	no session		1894	Albert G. Lane
1879	John Hancock		1895	Nicholas M. Butler
1880	J. Ormond Wilson		1896	Newton C. Dougherty
1881	James H. Smart		1897	Charles R. Skinner
1882	G. J. Orr		1898	J. M. Greenwood
1883	E. T. Tappan		1899	E. Oram Lyte
1884	Thomas W. Bicknell		1900	Oscar T. Corson
1885	F. Louis Soldan		1901	James M. Green
1886	N. A. Calkins			

Territorial Delegates to Congress

Territory of Arizona (1867–1901)

Coles Bashford

Richard C. McCormick

Hiram S. Stevens

John G. Campbell

Granville H. Oury

Curtis C. Bean

Marcus A. Smith

Nathan O. Murphy

John F. Wilson

Territory of Colorado (1867–1877)

George M. Chilcott

Allen A. Bradford

Jerome B. Chaffee

Thomas M. Patterson

Territory of Dakota (1867–1889)

Walter A. Burleigh
Solomon L. Spink
Moses K. Armstrong
Jefferson P. Kidder
Granville G. Bennett

Richard F. Pettigrew
John B. Raymond
Oscar S. Gifford
George A. Mathews

District of Columbia (territorial form of government lasted from 1871 to 1874)

Norton P. Chipman

Territory of Hawaii (1900–1901)

Robert W. Wilcox

Territory of Idaho (1867–1890)

Edward D. Holbrook
Jacob K. Shafer
Samuel A. Merritt
John Hailey
Thomas W. Bennett

Stephen S. Fenn
George Ainslie
Theodore F. Singiser
Fred T. Dubois

Territory of Montana (1867–1889)

James M. Cavanaugh
William H. Clagett
Martin Maginnis

Joseph K. Toole
Thomas H. Carter

Territory of New Mexico (1867–1901)

Charles P. Clever
J. Francisco Chaves
José Manuel Gallegos
Stephen B. Elkins
Trinidad Romero
Mariano S. Otero

Tranquilino Luna
Francisco A. Manzanares
Antonio Joseph
Thomas B. Catron
Harvey B. Fergusson
Pedro Perea

Territory of Oklahoma (1890–1901)

David A. Harvey

Dennis T. Flynn

James Y. Callahan

Territory of Utah (1867–1896)

William H. Hooper

George Q. Cannon

John T. Caine

Joseph L. Rawlins

Frank J. Cannon

Territory of Washington (1867–1889)

Alvan Flanders

Selucius Garfielde

Obadiah B. McFadden

Orange Jacobs

Thomas H. Brents

Charles S. Voorhees

John B. Allen

Territory of Wyoming (1867–1890)

Stephen F. Nuckolls

William T. Jones

William R. Steele

William W. Corlett

Stephen W. Downey

Morton E. Post

Joseph M. Carey

American Diplomatic Officers

Ministers to Great Britain

Charles Francis Adams	(1861–1868)	James Russell Lowell	(1880–1885)
Reverdy Johnson	(1868–1869)	Edward J. Phelps	(1885–1889)
J. Lothrop Motley	(1869–1870)	Robert Todd Lincoln	(1889–1893)
Robert C. Schenk	(1871–1876)	Thomas F. Bayard	(1893–1897)
Edwards Pierrepont	(1876–1877)	John Hay	(1897–1898)
John Welsh	(1877–1879)	Henry White	(1898–1899)
William P. Hoppin	(1879–1880)	(chargé d'affaires)	
(chargé d'affaires)		Joseph H. Choate	(1899–1905)

Ministers to France

John A. Dix	(1866–1869)	Whitelaw Reid	(1889–1892)
Elihu B. Washburne	(1869–1877)	T. Jefferson Coolidge	(1892–1893)
Edward F. Noyes	(1877–1881)	James B. Eustis	(1893–1897)
Levi P. Morton	(1881–1885)	Horace Porter	(1897–1905)
Robert M. McLane	(1885–1889)		

Ministers to Germany

George Bancroft	(1867–1874)	H. S. Everett	(1881–1882)
Nicholas Fish (chargé d'affaires)	(1874–1874)	Aaron A. Sargent	(1882–1884)
		John A. Kasson	(1884–1885)
John C. B. Davis	(1874–1877)	George H. Pendleton	(1885–1889)
H. S. Everett	(1877–1878)	William W. Phelps	(1889–1893)
Bayard Taylor	(1878–1878)	Theodore Runyon	(1893–1896)
H. S. Everett	(1878–1879)	Edwin F. Uhl	(1896–1897)
Andrew Dickson White	(1879–1881)	Andrew Dickson White	(1897–1902)

Ministers to Italy

George P. Marsh	(1861–1882)	J. J. Van Alen	(1893–1893)
William W. Astor	(1882–1885)	Wayne MacVeagh	(1893–1897)
Johann B. Stallo	(1885–1889)	William F. Draper	(1897–1900)
Albert G. Porter	(1889–1891)	George Von L. Meyer	(1901–1905)
William Potter	(1892–1893)		

Ministers to Russia

Cassius M. Clay	(1863–1869)	William H. Hunt	(1882–1884)
A. G. Custin	(1869–1872)	Alphonso Taft	(1884–1885)
James L. Orr	(1872–1873)	George Van Ness Lothrop	(1885–1888)
Marshall Jewell	(1873–1874)	Lambert Tree	(1888)
Eugene Schuyler (chargé d'affaires)	(1874–1875)	G. W. Watts	(1889–1890)
		Charles E. Smith	(1890–1892)
George H. Boker	(1875–1878)	Andrew Dickson White	(1892–1894)
Edwin W. Stoughton	(1878–1879)	Clifton R. Breckinridge	(1894–1897)
Wickham Hoffman	(1879–1880)	Ethan A. Hitchcock	(1897–1899)
John Watson Foster	(1880–1881)	Charlemagne Tower	(1899–1902)
Wickham Hoffman	(1881–1882)		

Ministers to Spain

John P. Hale	(1865–1869)	Jabez L. M. Curry	(1885–1889)
Daniel E. Sickles	(1869–1873)	P. Belmont	(1889–1889)
Alvey A. Adee	(1873–1874)	Thomas W. Palmer	(1889–1890)
Caleb Cushing	(1874–1877)	E. Bush Grubb	(1890–1892)
James Russell Lowell	(1877–1881)	Archibald L. Snowden	(1892–1893)
Lucius Fairchild	(1881–1881)	Hannis Taylor	(1893–1897)
Hannibal Hamlin	(1881–1883)	Stewart L. Woodford	(1897–1898)
John Watson Foster	(1883–1885)	Bellamy Storer	(1899–1902)

Presidential Election Results

1868

Ulysses S. Grant (Republican)
    3,013,650 popular votes
    214 electoral votes

Horatio Seymour (Democrat)
    2,708,744 popular votes
    80 electoral votes

1872

Ulysses S. Grant (Republican)
    3,598,235 popular votes
    286 electoral votes

Horace Greeley (Democrat, Liberal
    Republican)
    2,834,761 popular votes

Because Greeley died three weeks after the election, the six states he had carried split their electoral votes among Thomas A. Hendricks, Benjamin G. Brown, Charles J. Jenkins, and David Davis (63 electoral votes)

1876

Rutherford B. Hayes (Republican)
    4,034,311 popular votes
    185 electoral votes

Samuel J. Tilden (Democrat)
    4,288,546 popular votes
    184 electoral votes

1880

James A. Garfield (Republican)
    4,446,158 popular votes
    214 electoral votes

Winfield S. Hancock (Democrat)
    4,444,260 popular votes
    155 electoral votes

James B. Weaver (Greenback)
    305,997 popular votes

1884

Grover Cleveland (Democrat)
    4,874,621 popular votes
    219 electoral votes

James G. Blaine (Republican)
    4,848,936 popular votes
    182 electoral votes

John P. St. John (Prohibition)
    147,482 popular votes

1888

Benjamin Harrison (Republican)
    5,443,892 popular votes
    233 electoral votes

Grover Cleveland (Democrat)
    5,534,488 popular votes
    168 electoral votes

1892

Grover Cleveland (Democrat)
   5,551,883 popular votes
   277 electoral votes

Benjamin Harrison (Republican)
   5,179,244 popular votes
   145 electoral votes

James B. Weaver (Populist)
   1,024,280 popular votes
   22 electoral votes

1896

William McKinley (Republican)
   7,108,480 popular votes
   271 electoral votes

William Jennings Bryan (Democrat, Populist)
   6,511,495 popular votes
   176 electoral votes

John M. Palmer (National Democrat)
   133,435 popular votes

1900

William McKinley (Republican)
   7,218,039 popular votes
   292 electoral votes

William Jennings Bryan (Democrat, Populist, Silver Republican)
   6,358,345 popular votes
   155 electoral votes

Wharton Barker (Middle-of-the-Road People's Party)
   50,373 popular votes

Selective General Bibliography

Beisner, Robert L. *From the Old Diplomacy to the New, 1865–1900.* 1974.

Calhoun, Charles W., ed. *The Gilded Age: Essays on the Origins of Modern America.* 1995.

Campbell, Charles S. *The Transformation of American Foreign Relations 1865–1900.* 1976.

Cashman, Sean Dennis. *America in the Gilded Age: From the Death of Lincoln to the Rise of Theodore Roosevelt.* Second edition. 1993.

Cherny, Robert W. *American Politics in the Gilded Age, 1868–1900.* 1997.

Degler, Carl N. *The Age of the Economic Revolution, 1876–1900.* 1967.

De Santis, Vincent P. *The Shaping of Modern America, 1877–1920.* Second edition. 1989.

Faulkner, Harold U. *Politics, Reform, and Expansion, 1890–1900.* 1963.

Fine, Sidney. *Laissez-Faire and the General Welfare State: A Study of Conflict in American Thought, 1865–1901.* 1956.

Fink, Leon, ed. *Major Problems in the Gilded Age and the Progressive Era.* 1993.

Garraty, John A. *The New Commonwealth, 1877–1890.* 1968.

Ginger, Ray. *Age of Excess: The United States from 1877–1914.* Reissue edition. 1989.

Hicks, John D. *The Populist Revolt: A History of the Farmers' Alliance and the People's Party.* 1931.

Kirkland, Edward C. *Industry Comes of Age: Business, Labor, and Public Policy, 1860–1897.* 1961.

McCloskey, Robert Green. *American Conservatism in the Age of Enterprise, 1865–1910.* 1951.

Morgan, H. Wayne. *From Hayes to McKinley: National Party Politics, 1877–1896.* 1969.

Morgan H. Wayne. *Unity and Culture: The United States, 1877–1900.* 1971.

Morgan, H. Wayne, ed. *The Gilded Age: A Reappraisal.* 1963.

Schlereth, Thomas J. *Victorian America: Transformations in Everyday Life, 1876–1915.* 1992.

Smith, Page. *The Rise of Industrial America: A People's History of the Post-Reconstruction Era.* 1990.

Summers, Mark W. *The Gilded Age: Or, the Hazard of New Functions.* 1997.

Twain, Mark, and Charles Dudley Warner. *The Gilded Age: A Tale of Today.* Reprint Edition. 1995.

Walker, Robert H. *Life in the Age of Enterprise, 1865–1900.* 1971.

White, Leonard D. *The Republican Era, 1869–1901: A Study in Administrative History.* 1958.

Wiebe, Robert H. *The Search for Order, 1877–1920.* 1967.

About the Contributors

Tunde Adeleke is associate professor of history and director of Africana studies at Loyola University, New Orleans. He is the author of *UnAfrican Americans: Nineteenth Century Black Nationalists and the Civilizing Mission.*

Thomas G. Alexander, Lemuel Hardison Redd, Jr., Professor of Western American History at Brigham Young University, is author of *Mormonism in Transition: A History of the Latter-day Saints, 1890–1930* (1986, 1996); *Things in Heaven and Earth: The Life and Times of Wilford Woodruff, a Mormon Prophet* (1991); and numerous other books and articles.

Robert J. Allison teaches American history at Suffolk University in Boston.

John B. Anderson, a former member of Congress (1961–1981), is currently professor of law at Nova Southeastern University Law School in Fort Lauderdale, Florida. He ran for president of the United States on an independent ticket in 1980.

Michael J. Anderson is associate professor of history and chair of the department of history and political science at Clarke College in Dubuque, Iowa. He has written several essays and reviews on the history of American politics.

Thomas H. Appleton, Jr. is professor of history at Eastern Kentucky University. He is coeditor of *A Mythic Land Apart: Reassessing Southerners and Their History* and *Negotiating Boundaries of Southern Womanhood: Dealing with the Powers That Be.*

Peter H. Argersinger is professor of history at Southern Illinois University. He is the author of several books, including *Populism and Politics; Structure, Process, and Party*; and *The Limits of Agrarian Radicalism.*

Jane M. Armstrong received her master's degree in American history from Indiana University at Bloomington. She is the historical writer for the U.S. Senate Historical Office, and writes essays and articles for Senate publications and reports.

Walter L. Arnstein is professor of history emeritus at the University of Illinois at Urbana-Champaign. He is the author or editor of six books, including *Britain Yesterday & Today: 1830 to the Present* (8th ed., 2001).

Richard L. Aynes is dean and professor of law at the University of Akron School of Law. He has written widely in legal and history journals on the Fourteenth Amendment and its author, John A. Bingham.

C. Edward Balog is provost and dean of faculty and professor of history at Aquinas College in Grand Rapids, Michigan. He has written and presented several papers in the area of American intellectual history.

Richard A. Bartlett is professor emeritus of history at Florida State University. He is author of *Great Surveys of the American West, The New Country*, and two histories of Yellowstone Park.

Abel A. Bartley is associate professor of African-American and urban history at the University of Akron. He is the author of numerous articles, as well as *Keeping the Faith: Race, Politics, and Social Development in Jacksonville, Florida, 1940–1970.*

James L. Baumgardner is professor of history at Carson-Newman College in Jefferson City, Tennessee. He is the author of a number of articles and book reviews that have appeared in various historical and political science journals.

Maurine H. Beasley is professor of journalism at the University of Maryland, College Park. She is the author of *Eleanor Roosevelt and the Media*, coeditor of the *Eleanor Roosevelt Encyclopedia*, and author of articles on journalism history.

Scott Bedio is assistant archivist in the Archives and Research Center of the Salvation Army, National Headquarters, Alexandria, Virginia.

Robert E. Bennett is professor of classics at Kenyon College. His current principal area of research is fourth-century (C.E.) Cappadocian fathers.

Richard Bensel is a professor of government at Cornell University and the author of three books: *The Political Economy of American Industrialization, 1877–1980* (Cambridge, 2000); *Yankee Leviathan: The Origins of Central State*

Authority in America, 1859–1877 (Cambridge, 1990); and *Sectionalism and American Political Development, 1880–1980* (Wisconsin, 1984). He is currently working on two book manuscripts, one on mid-nineteenth-century voting practices in the United States and the other on the 1896 Democratic National Convention.

Lloyd Benson is Walter Kenneth Mattison associate professor of history at Furman University in Greenville, South Carolina. He is author of several essays and articles.

James M. Bergquist is professor emeritus of history at Villanova University, and editor of the *Immigration and Ethnic History Newsletter.* His research and publications deal with immigration history in general, and specifically with German Americans.

Alexander M. Bielakowski, an assistant professor of history at the University of Findlay, Findlay, Ohio, specializes in American military history.

William C. Binning is professor of political science at Youngstown State University. He is the coauthor of *The Encyclopedia of American Parties, Campaigns and Elections* (1999).

Edward Scott Blakeman is a doctoral candidate at the University of Kentucky. In 1997, he won the fourteenth Otto A. Rothert Award for the best article published in volume 70 of *The Filson Club History Quarterly*, "A Night Comes to Berea College: The Day Law and the African-American Reaction."

Mary Warner Blanchard is an associate fellow and member of the advisory board at the Rutgers Center for Historical Analysis. She is the author of *Oscar Wilde's America: Counterculture in the Gilded Age* and has contributed articles to several historical journals.

David Blanke is assistant professor of history at Texas A&M–Corpus Christi. He is the author of *Sowing the American Dream: How Consumer Culture Took Root in the Rural Midwest* and *The 1910s.*

Mary Ann Blochowiak received her M.A. in history from the University of Central Oklahoma, Edmond. She is associate editor of *The Chronicles of Oklahoma*, Oklahoma Historical Society, Oklahoma City.

Jack S. Blocker, Jr., is professor of history at Huron University College, University of Western Ontario. He is the author of several books and articles on temperance reform in the Gilded Age.

Allan G. Bogue has published widely in the fields of American economic, western, and political history.

Jerome D. Bowers II, a social studies teacher at the Madeira School in McLean, Virginia, is author of numerous entries for similar volumes. He is completing his Ph.D. dissertation in history at Indiana University–Bloomington, "Avowing Ourselves Christians: Joseph Priestly, the Pennsylvania Unitarians, and the Development of American Unitarianism, 1765–1820."

Ed Bradley is an employee of Harpweek, Inc., a web company focusing on Gilded Age politics and culture. The main site can be reached at http://www.harpweek.com.

T. R. Brereton is assistant professor of history at the University of Louisville. He is the author of *Educating the Army: Arthur L. Wagner and Reform, 1875–1905* and "First Lessons in Modern War: Arthur L. Wagner, the Santiago Campaign, and U.S. Army Lesson-Learning," in *Journal of Military History.*

Ron Briley is assistant headmaster and a history teacher at Sandia Preparatory School in Albuquerque, and an adjunct professor of history at the University of New Mexico–Valencia campus. His works on popular culture have appeared in *The History Teacher, Literature/Film Quarterly, American West, Social Education, Film & History,* and *OAH Magazine of History.*

Simon J. Bronner is Distinguished Professor of Folklore and American Studies at the Pennsylvania State University, Harrisburg. He is the author of *Following Tradition: Folklore in the Discourse of American Culture* and eleven other books on American folklore and cultural history.

Steve Bullock completed his Ph.D. in history at the University of Nebraska at Lincoln, where he specialized in the history of sport, and is currently teaching at the University of Nebraska at Omaha. His first book, *Vital Connections: Baseball and the American Military during World War II,* is scheduled to be published by the University of Nebraska Press in 2003.

Jack Burrows is a college professor. He has written *John Ringo: The Gunfighter Who Never Was* and *Black Sun of the Miwok.*

Robert Caldwell is a Ph.D. candidate in historical theology at Trinity Evangelical Divinity School in Deerfield, Illinois.

Charles W. Calhoun is professor of history at East Carolina University in Greenville, North Carolina, and a past president of the Society for Historians of the Gilded Age and Progressive Era. His latest book is *The Gilded Age: Essays on the Origins of Modern America.*

Colton C. Campbell is assistant professor of political science at Florida International University. He is coeditor of *New Majority or Old Minority? The Impact of Republicans on Congress* and has contributed essays to several congressional journals and books.

Robert W. Cherny is professor of history at San Francisco State University. He is the author of *American Politics in the Gilded Age; A Righteous Cause: The Life of William Jennings Bryan,* and other works, and is coauthor, with William Issel, of *San Francisco, 1865–1932: Politics, Power, and Urban Development.*

Gene Clanton is professor emeritus of history at Washington State University. He is the author of *Kansas Populism: Ideas and Men,* and has written other books, reviews, essays, and articles on populism, progressivism, and the Gilded Age.

Richmond L. Clow is professor of Native American studies at the University of Montana. He is coauthor of *Tribal Government Today: Politics on Montana Indian Reservations*, and has contributed articles to several historical journals and books.

John D. Coats is assistant professor of history at Quincy University in Quincy, Illinois. His research centers on inter-American relations, with a special emphasis on the development of U.S. policy toward the countries of the Caribbean basin.

Marvin D. Cohen earned the D.D.S. degree from the Ohio State University and has his practice at Dental Health Services in Akron, Ohio. He is locally known for his varied interests in magic, business, golf, and Sherlock Holmes.

Ann Mauger Colbert, journalism coordinator at Indiana University–Purdue University at Fort Wayne has been a professional journalist and editor. In her academic career, she has concentrated on Gilded Age women in journalism and Midwest journalism history; in addition, she writes an award-winning newspaper column.

Peter Cole is assistant professor of history at Western Illinois University. His research focuses upon ethnicity, race, and labor, specifically on an interracial longshoremen's union in Philadelphia.

Paolo E. Coletta taught mostly history at various universities and at the U.S. Naval Academy for thirty-seven years until he retired in 1983. In his second career, as a Naval Reserve officer, he served for thirty years, until he retired in 1973 in the grade of captain.

Michael J. Connolly teaches at St. Anselm College and Franklin Pierce College in New Hampshire, and specializing in nineteenth-century New England and American Catholic history.

Martha A. Conrad, MSN, RN, CNS, teaches at the University of Akron and Ashland University in Ohio, and is associate fellow at Akron's Institute of Life Span Development and Gerontology. She has educated thousands of nurses, relating nursing theory, research, and practice to a variety of clinical settings.

Maurice Law Costello, a contributor to the *Encyclopedia of the American West,* is emeritus professor of English and comparative literature at San Jose City College. His areas of interest include the American West, maritime history, and African literature.

Bryan Craig received his M.A. in history from Kent State University in 1995 and was an interpreter and national park ranger at the James A. Garfield National Historic Site in Mentor, Ohio. He is presently pursuing a library career.

David O'Donald Cullen is professor of history at Collin County Community College in Plano, Texas. His research interests are labor and civil rights movements of the twentieth century, and film and television as agents of historical memory.

Christopher Cumo is the author of *A History of the Ohio Agricultural Experiment Station, 1882–1997*, and *Seeds of Change*. His articles have appeared in journals and magazines on history, education, science, and religion.

Nelson L. Dawson is a specialist in twentieth-century U.S. history. He has been editor of publications for the Filson Historical Society since 1975.

Gregory Dehler is a Ph.D. candidate at Lehigh University. His dissertation is titled "An American Crusader: William Temple Hornaday and Wildlife Conservation in America, 1840–1940."

Lisa De Palo is the local history librarian in the reference department at the Elizabeth. N.J., Public Library. She has contributed articles to library and information science journals, including "Historical Foundations of Public Library Service on Staten Island, New York," published in the Spring/Fall 1999 issue of *Current Studies in Librarianship*.

Vincent P. De Santis is generally regarded as the dean of Gilded Age historians, and is professor emeritus and former chair of the history department at the University of Notre Dame. His numerous publications include *Republicans Face the Southern Question: The New Departure Years, 1877–1897*.

Mario R. DiNunzio is professor of history at Providence College. He is the editor of *Theodore Roosevelt: An American Mind*, and author of *American Democracy and the Authoritarian Tradition of the West*, as well as essays in a number of history journals.

L. Mara Dodge teaches U.S. history at Westfield State College in Westfield, Massachusetts. She is currently working on a book based on her dissertation, " 'Her Life Has Been an Improper One': Women, Crime, and Prisons in Illinois, 1835–1933."

Justus D. Doenecke is professor of history at New College, the University of South Florida. His publications include *The Presidencies of James A. Garfield and Chester A. Arthur*.

Timothy Dean Draper is a Ph.D. candidate in American history at Northern Illinois University, working on a dissertation treating race, ethnicity, and community development in turn-of-the-century Rock Springs, Wyoming. He also teaches at colleges in the Chicago metropolitan area.

Anna Mae Duane, a Ph.D. candidate at Fordham University in New York, is currently working on a dissertation that examines how depictions of suffering children negotiate questions of race, religion, and citizenship in early American culture. She has published articles and book reviews exploring masochism, pedagogy, and childhood trauma.

Mark E. Ellis is serials librarian at Albany State University, Albany, Georgia. He loves history and is a book reviewer for *Library Journal*.

Linda Eikmeier Endersby received her Ph.D. in the history of technology, and currently works at Rutgers University with the Thomas A. Edison papers. She has published on the history of mathematics and computer science, world's fairs, and nineteenth-century technology.

Damon Eubank is associate professor of history at Campbellsville University in Kentucky. He has contributed several essays to historical journals and books.

William M. Ferraro is on the editorial staff of the Ulysses S. Grant Association, Southern Illinois University, Carbondale. His research and publications on the United States during the nineteenth century have centered on John and William Tecumseh Sherman.

Jack C. Fisher is a physician, historian, and author. He lives in La Jolla, California.

Michael S. Fitzgerald is associate professor of history at Pikeville College, Pikeville, Kentucky. He is currently working on a major study of Anglo-American and Spanish-American relations after the War of 1812, *The Arkon Deluge: American Diplomacy and Military Policy, 1815–1821*.

Patrick Foley graduated from Union College with a degree in political science, and is currently working in New York City.

Richard A. Fox is professor of anthropology at the University of South Dakota. He is the author of *Archaeology, History, and Custer's Last Battle: The Little Big Horn Reexamined*, which details results of his historical archaeology investigations at the Little Big Horn Battlefield.

Joseph A. Fry is professor of history at the University of Nevada, Las Vegas. He is the author of *Henry S. Sanford: Diplomacy and Business in Nineteenth-Century America* and *John*

Tyler Morgan and the Search for Southern Autonomy.

Norman E. Fry is professor of American history at Southeastern Community College in West Burlington, Iowa. He is the author of *Study Guide to the McGraw History Series* and of several television documentaries on American society and history.

Charlene G. Garfinkle received a Ph.D. in art history from the University of California at Santa Barbara in 1996. She has published articles in *Stained Glass* and *American Art*, a book review in *CAA Reviews*, and entries in *American National Biography*.

Ralph G. Giordano is a registered architect in New York State. He is also adjunct professor of history at the College of Staten Island and has contributed articles to several historical journals.

Joel K. Goldstein is a professor of law at Saint Louis University. He is the author of *The Modern American Vice Presidency* and a coauthor of *Understanding Constitutional Law* (2nd. ed.).

Norman A. Graebner is Randolph P. Compton Professor of History and Public Affairs emeritus at the University of Virginia. For forty years his writing and teaching focused on U.S. diplomatic history.

Donald E. Greco is an assistant professor of political science and director of the American studies program at Baylor University.

Casey Edward Greene is head of special collections at the Rosenberg Library in Galveston, Texas. He heads its Galveston and Texas History Center, which has a significant collection of 1900 storm documentation, and has contributed historical articles about Galveston to several journals.

Larry D. Griffin presently serves as professor of English and dean of Arts and Sciences at Dyersburg State Community College in Dyersburg, Tennessee. He has published poems, short stories, articles, and essays in numerous little magazines and journals.

Kurt Hackemer is assistant professor of history at the University of South Dakota. He has written several journal articles on American military and naval history.

Richard F. Hamm is associate professor of history and public policy at the University of Albany, State University of New York. He is author of *Shaping the Eighteenth Amendment*.

Jack L. Hammersmith is professor of history at West Virginia University. The author of *Spoilsmen in a "Flowery Fairyland": The Development of the U.S. Legation in Japan, 1859–1906*, he has also published numerous articles in scholarly journals.

James Harley is a Ph.D. candidate in theater history and criticism at the University of Texas at Austin. He has contributed book reviews and articles on theater to several journals in the field.

Richard Harmond, who earned his Ph.D. at Columbia University in 1966, has taught at St. John's University (Queens), New York, since 1957. His published works include *Long Island as America* (coauthor, 1977), *Technology in the Twentieth Century* (coeditor, 1983), and *Biographical Dictionary of American and Canadian Naturalists and Environmentalists* (coeditor, 1997).

Gillis J. Harp is professor of history at Grove City College in Pennsylvania. He is the author of *Positivist Republic: Auguste Comte and the Transformation of American Liberalism, 1865–1920* (1995), as well as articles in the *Journal of the History of Ideas, Church History*, and other scholarly journals.

Keith Harper is associate professor of church history at Southeastern Baptist Theological Seminary in North Carolina. He is the author of *The Quality of Mercy: Southern Baptists and*

Social Christianity, 1890–1920 and has contributed essays to historical journals and books.

Melba Porter Hay is division manager for research and publications at the Kentucky Historical Society. She was formerly editor of *The Papers of Henry Clay* at the University of Kentucky.

C. Robert Haywood is professor emeritus of history at Washburn University in Topeka, Kansas. He is author of seven books on the West, including *Trails South: Wagon-Road Economy in the Dodge City–Panhandle Region*, and has contributed many articles to professional journals.

John H. Hepp IV is Assistant Professor of History at Wilkes University in Wilkes-Barre, Pennsylvania. He writes regularly on the intersection of business, technology, and culture during the Gilded Age and Progressive Era.

Phillip T. Heyn recently graduated from Ohio Wesleyan University, where he majored in history and earned his comprehensive teacher certification in social studies. He plans to attend graduate school to study educational administration.

Ted Hinckley is emeritus professor of history at San Jose State University, and adjunct professor of history at Western Washington University in Bellingham. He has published three books on nineteenth-century Alaska as well as articles dealing with the Gilded Age.

Bernard Hirschhorn is a historian who has held the positions of chairman of the social studies department at the Fiorello H. LaGuardia High School in New York City and adjunct professor of history at the Bernard Baruch College of the City University of New York. He is the author of *Democracy Reformed: Richard Spencer Childs and His Fight for Better Government*, and has contributed articles, essays, and reviews to history journals and books.

Sheldon Hochheiser is corporate historian at AT&T. He is author of *Rohm and Haas: History of a Chemical Company*, and has written and lectured widely on the history of telecommunications and AT&T.

Adam Hodges is a doctoral candidate in history at the University of Illinois at Urbana-Champaign. He has presented papers on urban and labor history, and is currently writing a dissertation on class relations and urban change on the west coast during World War I.

Kristin Hoganson is assistant professor of history at the University of Illinois, Urbana-Champaign. She is the author of *Fighting for American Manhood: How Gender Politics Provoked the Spanish-American and Philippine-American Wars*, and is currently writing a book on globalization and U.S. domesticity between 1865 and 1920.

Peter C. Holloran, assistant professor of history at Worcester State College in Massachusetts, is secretary of the New England Historical Association, and the author of *Boston's Wayward Children: Social Services for Homeless Children, 1830–1930* (1994).

Carol Goss Hoover, doctor of ministry, is professor of history at Colorado Technical University's Sioux Falls, South Dakota, campus and Mount Marty College in Yankton, South Dakota, with specialization in Native American and Catholic intercultural histories.

Herbert T. Hoover received his Ph.D. from the University of New Mexico and is professor of history at the University of South Dakota. He is the author or coauthor of thirteen books, including *Sioux Country: A History of Indian-White Relations* (with Carol Goss Hoover, 2000) and *Wildlife on the Cheyenne River and Lower Brule Reservations* (1992).

Charles F. Howlett teaches advanced placement history at Amityville Memorial High School in New York and is adjunct professor of history at Adelphi University. He has published numerous books and articles, including *Troubled Philosopher: John Dewey and the*

Struggle for World Peace and *The American Peace Movement: References and Resources.*

Harvey Gresham Hudspeth is history program coordinator at Mississippi Valley State University. He is author of a number of articles on Supreme Court history.

M. Thomas Inge is Robert Emory Blackwell Professor of Humanities at Randolph-Macon College in Ashland, Virginia, where he teaches and writes about American literature and culture. He is the editor of the five-volume *Handbook of American Popular Culture* and author of *Comics as Culture*, among other works.

James D. Ivy received his Ph.D. in the history of American civilization at Harvard University. He is currently writing a book on early prohibition campaigns in Texas.

Berman E. Johnson has over two decades of service in higher education as a history professor, educational researcher, and administrator. His book is *The Dream Deferred: A Survey of Black America, 1840–1896,* and he currently serves as vice president of student services at DeKalb Technical Institute, Clarkston, GA.

Hutch Johnson is professor of history at Gordon College in Barnesville, Georgia, where he has taught for two decades.

Troy R. Johnson is associate professor of American Indian studies and U.S. history at California State University, Long Beach. He is the author, editor, or associate editor of eleven books and numerous scholarly journal articles, including *The Occupation of Alcatraz Island: Indian Self-Determination and the Rise of Indian Activism* and *American Indian Activism: Alcatraz to the Longest Walk.*

Lacey Jordan has served as a guest curator at the High Museum of Art and at the Michael C. Carlos Museum. She completed her dissertation, "John Singer Sargent's Images of Artists in an International Contest" at Emory University in 1999.

Richard Junger is associate professor of journalism at Western Michigan University. He is the author of *The Journalist as Reformer: Henry Demarest Lloyd and Wealth against Commonwealth*, and has contributed essays on communication and legal history to several journals.

Victoria Kalemaris, formerly a museum technician at Sagamore Hill National Historic Site, Oyster Bay, New York, is now pursuing a master's degree in library science.

William Kamman is professor of history and associate dean of the College of Arts and Sciences at the University of North Texas at Denton. He is author of *A Search for Stability: United States Diplomacy Toward Nicaragua, 1925–1933.*

Lawrence S. Kaplan received a Ph.D. from Yale in 1951. A University Professor of History emeritus at Kent State University, he is currently a professorial lecturer in history at Georgetown University.

Paul Keenan, a native of New Hampshire, earned a master's degree in leisure and recreational studies from Indiana University in 1984. Since then he has been a recreational director for the U.S. Air Force at bases in South Carolina, Germany, and Nevada, and currently works at the Wright Patterson Air Force Base in Dayton, Ohio.

James A. Kehl is professor emeritus of history at the University of Pittsburgh. He is the author of *Ill Feeling in the Era of Good Feeling, Boss Rule in the Gilded Age,* and *When Civilians Manned the Ships: Life in the Amphibious Fleet During World War II*. He also has contributed to numerous scholarly journals.

Christian B. Keller is a doctoral candidate in American history at the Pennsylvania State University. He is the author of several articles to be published in historical journals, including the *Proceedings of the American Philosophical Society* and the *Yearbook of German-American Studies.*

Mary L. Kelley is a doctoral candidate at Texas Christian University in Fort Worth. She has written a supplement for a major history text and contributed to several historical encyclopedias

Sam S. Kepfield received his bachelor's degree from Kansas State University in 1986, a law degree from the University of Nebraska in 1989, and an M.A. in history from Nebraska in 1994. He is currently a doctoral candidate in environmental history at the University of Oklahoma. He resides with his wife, Mindy, and daughter, Valerie, in Hutchinson, Kansas, where he practices law.

James C. Klotter is the state historian, and professor of history at Georgetown College in Kentucky. He is the author or editor of a dozen books, including *A New History of Kentucky* (1997).

Susan H. Koester is professor of communications and teaches a variety of speaking and writing courses at the University of Alaska Southeast, in Juneau. Her research has focused on developing curriculum for both communication anxiety reduction programs and combined speaking-writing courses, as well as exploring the lives and rhetoric of two of her favorite turn-of-the century trendsetters: Victoria Claflin Woodhull-Martin and Kate Chopin.

Robert S. La Forte is professor emeritus of history at the University of North Texas at Denton. He is the author of *Leaders of Reform: Progressive Republicans in Kansas, 1900–1916*, and has contributed essays to several historical journals and books.

Nancy Lair is a retired lecturer from the Indiana University School of Library and Information Science in Bloomington.

Jane F. Lancaster has a doctorate in history from Mississippi State University and has taught on the high school and college levels. The author of *Removal Aftershock: The Seminoles' Struggles to Survive in the West, 1836–1866*, she has contributed articles and reviews to history journals and books.

Derek R. Larson is currently assistant professor of history and director of the Environmental Studies Program at the College of St. Benedict in St. Joseph, Minnesota, and St. John's University in Collegeville, Minnesota. His teaching and research interests include the history of the American West and the rise of the modern environmental movement in the United States.

Robert W. Larson taught at the University of Northern Colorado at Greeley from 1960 until his retirement in 1990. His major publications include *New Mexico's Quest for Statehood, New Mexico Populism: A Study of Radical Protest in a Western Territory, Populism in the Mountain West, Shaping Educational Change: The First Century of the University of Northern Colorado at Greeley*, and *Red Cloud: Warrior-Statesman of the Lakota Sioux.*

Amanda Laugesen completed her Ph.D. dissertation, "Making Western Pasts: Historical Societies of Kansas, Wisconsin, and Oregon, 1870–1920," in 2000. She is currently working as a researcher and editor at the Australian National Dictionary Centre, Linnaeus College, Australian National University.

Dimitri D. Lazo is professor of history at Alverno College in Milwaukee, Wisconsin. He is the author of a number of articles on American foreign relations in the Gilded Age and Progressive Era.

Dorothy Garrett Lerda handles research inquiries in the editorial offices of the National Geographic Society, and she contributes factual information to the company's web site.

Connie L. Lester is assistant professor of history at Mississippi State University. She was the associate editor of the *Tennessee Encyclopedia of History and Culture.*

John F. Lyons is assistant professor of history at Joliet Junior College in Illinois.

Thomas S. Mach is an associate professor of history at Mount Vernon Nazarene College in Mount Vernon, Ohio. He is completing a political biography of George Hunt Pendleton and is author of a forthcoming article in *Ohio History* concerning the "Ohio Idea."

Charles W. Macune, Jr., is professor of history and department chair at California State University, Northridge. He is the author of *El Estado de Mexico y la Federacion Mexicana, 1823–1836* and *The Building of the Atlantic Railroad of Costa Rica, 1812–1891.*

Michael Magliari is professor of history at California State University, Chico. He is the author of several articles on California populism and the DeBernardi Labor Exchange movement of the 1890s.

Christopher D. Marinaro is library assistant at the Westchester County Historical Society in Elmsford, New York.

John F. Marszalek is William L. Giles distinguished professor of history at Mississippi State University. He is the author of *Sherman: A Soldier's Passion for Order*, as well as books and articles on nineteenth-century U.S. history.

Martin E. Marty is a former Lutheran pastor and professor of the history of modern Christianity in the Divinity School of the University of Chicago. He has written several books, was senior editor of *Christian Century*, and currently is Fairfax M. Cone distinguished service professor emeritus at the University of Chicago.

Valerie Sherer Mathes, City College of San Francisco, is the author of *Helen Hunt Jackson and Her Indian Reform Legacy, The Indian Reform Letters of Helen Hunt Jackson, 1879–1885*, and numerous scholarly articles.

Jessica Matthews has a master's degree in women's history from Sarah Lawrence College in Bronxville, New York. She specializes in women's cultural history.

Kevin Mattson is associate professor of American intellectual history at the Ohio University. He is author of *Creating a Democratic Public: The Struggle for Urban Participatory Democracy During the Progressive Era* (1998) and *Intellectuals in Action: The Origins of the New Left and Radical Liberalism, 1945–1970* (2002).

David Mayers holds a joint professorship in the history and political science departments at Boston University. Among his books is *The Ambassadors and America's Soviet Policy*, winner of the 1995 book prize of the American Academy of Diplomacy.

Archie P. McDonald is Regent's Professor of History at Stephen F. Austin State University in Nacogdoches, Texas, and director of the East Texas Historical Association.

Gerald W. McFarland is professor of history at the University of Massachusetts, Amherst. He is the author of three books: *Mugwumps, Morals and Politics, 1884–1920; A Scattered People, An American Family Moves West*, and *The "Counterfeit" Man: The True Story of the Boorn–Colvin Murder Case.*

John T. McGuire is a lecturer at the State University of New York at Oneonta. His revised dissertation focuses on women's political activism during the 1920s will be published by the State University of New York Press in 2004.

Linda O. McMurry is professor of history at North Carolina State University in Raleigh and the biographer of Ida B. Wells, George Washington Carver, and Monroe Nathan Work, as well as coauthor of a college-level American history textbook.

Samuel T. McSeveney has taught at Vanderbilt University since 1972. He is author of *The Politics of Depression: Political Behavior in the Northeast, 1893–1896* and of numerous articles and essays.

F. Suzanne Miller has been the curator/acting site manager for the James A. Garfield National Historical Site since May 1991.

Worth Robert Miller is professor of history at Southwest Missouri State University. He is the author of *Oklahoma Populism* (1987), "A Centennial Historiography of American Populism," *Kansas History* (1993): 54–69, and "The Lost World of Gilded Age Politics," *Journal of the Gilded Age and Progressive Era* (2002): 49–67.

Michael Montagne, R.Ph., Ph.D., is Rombult Distinguished Professor of Pharmacy at the Massachusetts College of Pharmacy in Boston. He has published on the history of drug use and pharmacy, and he is coauthor of *Searching for Magic Bullets: Orphan Drugs, Consumer Activism, and Pharmaceutical Development* (1994).

H. Wayne Morgan is George Lynn Cross Research Professor Emeritus at the University of Oklahoma.

Malcolm Muir, Jr., is professor of history at Austin Peay State University in Clarksville, Tennessee. He is the author of *Black Shoes and Blue Water: Surface Warfare in the United States Navy, 1945–1975* and other publications.

Marie Marmo Mullaney is professor of history and political science at Caldwell College in Caldwell, New Jersey. She is the author of two volumes in the series *Biographical Directory of the Governors of the United States*, and a contributor to numerous other books and historical journals.

Janet Butler Munch is associate professor and special collections librarian at Lehman College of the City University of New York (CUNY). Dr. Munch's research interests, beyond librarianship, include biography and New York regional history.

M. Susan Murnane practiced law for many years with the Department of Justice in Washington, D.C., the U.S. Attorney in Detroit, Michigan, and in private practice. A Ph.D. candidate in history at Case Western Reserve University in Cleveland, Ohio, she is currently completing her dissertation, "Law Economics, and Income Tax Reform in the 1920s."

Claus-M. Naske is professor of history at the University of Alaska and director of the University of Alaska Press. He is the author of ten books, including *Alaska: History of the 49th State*, and has contributed essays to several historical journals and books.

Stephen H. Norwood is associate professor of history at the University of Oklahoma. He is the author of *Labor's Flaming Youth: Telephone Operators and Work Militancy, 1878–1923*, which won the Herbert G. Gutman Award. He has contributed articles to many history journals, and has almost completed a book on the social history of strikebreaking and anti-unionism in the United States.

Kathleen Banks Nutter is reference archivist at the Sophia Smith Collection, Smith College. She is the author of *The Necessity of Organization: Mary Kenney O'Sullivan and Trade Unionism for Women, 1892–1912*, as well as of several articles.

Edwin Dale Odom received a Ph.D. in history from Tulane University in 1961. He taught in the department of history at the University of North Texas in Denton from 1961 until retirement in 1994, and now is professor emeritus at the University of North Texas.

S. Paul O'Hara is a doctoral student in American history at Indiana University–Bloomington. He specialized in urban industrialization and working-class ethnicity.

Martin T. Olliff is assistant archivist in the special collections and archives department of the Auburn University Libraries. He writes about the self-identification of chefs in nineteenth- and twentieth-century America.

Robert L. Osgood is assistant professor of educational foundations at Indiana University–Purdue University Indianapolis. In addition to articles in the *Indiana Magazine of History, Teachers College Record,* and *History of Education Quarterly,* he has written *"For Children Who Vary from the Normal Type": Special Education in Boston, 1838–1930,* published in 2000 by Gallaudet University Press.

Bruce Palmer is professor of history at the University of Houston, Clear Lake. He is the author of *"Man over Money": The Southern Populist Critique of American Capitalism,* and has contributed essays to several journals and books.

Stephen Paschen is senior archives associate and ad hoc graduate faculty at the University of Akron. He is the author of *Order in the Court: The Courts and the Practice of Law in Akron, Ohio 1787–1945* and *Molding a Legacy: A Centennial History of the Akron Porcelain & Plastics Company.*

Art Petersen, a professor of English at the University of Alaska in Juneau, edits historical books on gold rush figures in the north, including *Gold Fever* (1997) and *The Alaska Gold Rush Letters & Photographs of Leroy S. Townsend* (1999).

Allan Peskin is professor emeritus of history at Cleveland State University. He is the author of *Garfield* and numerous articles on Gilded Age politics, as well as *Winfield Scott and the Profession of Arms,* to be published in 2003.

Leslie Petteys is a professor of music at Marshall University in Huntington, West Virginia. In addition to her dissertation, "Julie Rive-King, American Pianist," Petteys, an active performer, has contributed articles to several dictionaries and musical journals.

Donald K. Pickens is professor of history at the University of North Texas in Denton. He is the author of *Eugenics and the Progressives,* as well as several other books, and has published numerous articles and entries on wide range of subjects in the history of ideology.

Michael Pierce is a doctoral student at Ohio State University. He is coauthor of *In the Workers' Interest: The History of the Ohio AFL-CIO, 1958–1998.*

Nicholas C. Polos is professor emeritus of history at the University of La Verne in La Verne, California. He has published eight books and seventy-two monographs in history and education. His latest two are *John Swett: A California Frontier Schoolmaster* and *Preserving the Western Spirit* (winner of four book awards, including the California Historical Society Gold Award on California History).

Kimberly K. Porter is assistant professor of history at the University of North Dakota. She focuses her attention on the late nineteenth- and early twentieth-century American experience.

Paul M. Pruitt, Jr., is a historian and librarian with an interest in the Bourbon, Populist, and Progressive eras. He is assistant law librarian at the Bounds Law Library, University of Alabama.

Jim Quinn is a feature writer and journalist for the *Akron Beacon Journal* in Ohio.

Brad F. Raley is a doctoral candidate at the University of Oklahoma. He is writing a dissertation on irrigation development in Colorado, "On the Banks of the Grand: Irrigation, Autonomy and Community Development in Colorado's Grand Valley, 1882–1920."

Joanne Reitano is professor of history at LaGuardia Community College of the City University of New York. She is author of *The Tariff Question in the Gilded Age: The Great Debate of 1888,* an article on working girls clubs, and several articles on community colleges.

Michael P. Riccards is president of Fitchburg State College in Massachusetts and the author of *The Ferocious Engine of Democracy*, a two-volume study of the American presidency.

R. Volney Riser is a Ph.D. candidate at the University of Alabama. He has published in the *Alabama Law Review*.

Barbara Ryan is assistant professor in the department of English and the program in African-American world studies at the University of Missouri–Kansas City.

James G. Ryan received a Ph.D. from the University of Notre Dame in 1981, served for many years as an adjunct in Philadelphia, and since 1996 has been associate professor of U.S. history at Texas A&M University at Galveston. Author of *Earl Browder: The Failure of American Communism* (1997), he is under contract to coedit the *Historical Dictionary of the 1940s* (M.E. Sharpe), and to write a monograph on Soviet espionage in North America (University of Wisconsin Press).

William W. Savage, Jr., is professor of history at the University of Oklahoma. He has published eleven books, including *The Cherokee Strip Live Stock Association, The Cowboy Hero*, and *Comic Books and America, 1945–1954*.

Leonard Schlup, an independent historian who earned a Ph.D. from the University of Illinois at Urbana-Champaign and the M.L.S. degree from Indiana University, has written over two hundred journal articles and as well as numerous essays for biographical encyclopedias. His book, *It Seems To Me: Selected Letters of Eleanor Roosevelt*, was published in 2001 by the University Press of Kentucky.

Kim P. Sebaly is associate professor of education at Kent State University. He specializes in the history of American education and education in British India.

Nina Silber is associate professor of history at Boston University. She has published *The Romance of Reunion: Northerners and the South, 1865–1900* (1993) and an edited collection of essays on gender and the Civil War, *Divided Homes* (1992).

Joel H. Silbey is President White Professor of History at Cornell University. He has written *The American Political Nation, 1838–1893* (1991) and other books and articles on nineteenth century politics.

Rita J. Simon is university professor in the School of Public Affairs and the College of Law at American University. She is author or editor of forty-one books, including *Immigrant Women* (2000), *In the Golden Pond: A Century of Russian and Soviet Immigration* (1997), *The Ambivalent Welcome: Media Coverage of American Immigration* (with Susan Alexander, 1993), *International Migration: The Female Experience* (with Caroline Brettell, 1986), and *New Lives: The Adjustment of Soviet Jewish Immigrants in the United States and Israel* (1985).

John J. Sloan III is associate professor of criminal justice and sociology at the University of Alabama at Birmingham. He is coauthor of *Campus Crime: Legal, Social, and Policy Perspectives*, and has contributed numerous essays to criminal justice and criminology journals and books.

Duane A. Smith is professor of history at Fort Lewis College in Durango, Colorado. He is the author of twenty-nine books.

John David Smith is Graduate Alumni Distinguished Professor of History at North Carolina State University in Raleigh. He has written or edited fourteen books, including *A Union Woman in Civil War Kentucky: The Diary of Frances Peter* (2000) and *When Did Southern Segregation Begin?* (2001).

David W. Southern is professor of history at Westminster College in Fulton, Missouri. He is the author of *Gunnar Myrdal and Black-White Relations* and *John LaFarge and the Limits of Catholic Interracialism, 1911–1963*.

Donald R. Stabile is professor of economics at St. Mary's College of Maryland. He is the author of six books, the latest of which is *The Origins of American Public Finance,* and numerous scholarly articles.

Shirley Stallings, M.A., an independent scholar, has contributed essays to several historical journals and books, and with M. Montagne has written *From Popular Entertainment to Medical Revelation: The History of Anesthesia in New England* (1994).

Harold K. Steen is a member of the environmental studies faculty at the University of North Carolina, Wilmington. He is author of *U.S. Forest Service: A History*, and has a general interest in public lands and the agencies that manage them.

Douglas Steeples is dean of the College of Liberal Arts and professor of history at Mercer University in Macon, Georgia. He has published numerous reviews and articles, and five books, including most recently *Treasure from the Painted Hills: A History of Calico, California, 1882–1907* and (with David O. Whitten) *Democracy in Desperation: A History of the Depression of 1893.*

Thomas E. Stephens, a graduate of the University of Kentucky, is associate editor in the Kentucky Historical Society's publications department.

Jon Sterngass is the husband of Karen Weltman and the father of Eli and Aaron Sterngass. His running route circles the site of Frank Leslie's old mansion, and he collects Currier & Ives prints of Saratoga Springs, New York.

Peter C. Stewart, a native of southern Rhode Island, obtained his Ph.D. in history at the University of Virginia in 1967. He taught history, including the history of sports, for twenty-eight years at Old Dominion University, published several articles and books on Virginia history, and now teaches on an adjunct basis in semi-retirement.

Kelly McMichael Stott is a Ph.D. candidate at the University of North Texas in Denton. She is currently completing her dissertation on gender and Confederate veterans organizations in Texas.

James Summerville's books include *The Carmack-Cooper Shooting: Tennessee Politics Turns Violent* (1994) and *With Kennedy and Other Stories* (1998). A resident of Nashville, he serves as a trustee of the Theodore Roosevelt Association.

Terri Pedersen Summey is assistant professor at Emporia State University in Kansas with the Division of Library Services and serves as an adjunct instructor with the School of Library and Information Management. She is a frequent presenter at conferences and has contributed articles to several library journals.

Robert M. Sutton, a former chair of the history department and director of the Illinois Historical Survey, is professor emeritus of history at the University of Illinois at Urbana-Champaign. He has published several articles relating to Illinois history.

Thomas C. Sutton is an assistant professor of political science at Baldwin-Wallace College in Berea, Ohio, where he teaches institutions of government, public policy, and law and the courts. His research interests include state courts and school funding and institutionalist theory.

Stephen Svonavec is a 1999 Ph.D. recipient from Texas A&M University and has taught at Texas A&M and Purdue. His research focuses on the role of Congress in determining military policy.

A. Jacqueline Swansinger is professor at State University of New York at Fredonia, where her work is primarily in economic/diplomatic history. She has contributed essays to *Journal of World History* and *New York History*.

James R. Sweeney is associate professor of history at Old Dominion University. He is the author of numerous essays published in historical journals and of the fiftieth anniversary history of Old Dominion University.

Joel A. Tarr is Richard S. Caliguiri Professor of History and Policy at Carnegie Mellon University, where he has been on the faculty since 1967.

Jennifer L. Tebbe is professor of American studies and political science at the Massachusetts College of Pharmacy and Health Sciences. She has contributed essays to journals and books on subjects related to health care history and public policy, and to mass media and popular culture.

Samuel J. Thomas is professor of history at Michigan State University. He is the author of "Maligning Poverty's Prophet: Puck, Henry George and the New York Mayoral Campaign of 1886," *Journal of American Culture* (Winter 1998), and has written essays for several other historical journals.

David Traxel teaches at the University of the Sciences in Philadelphia, and is the author of *1898: The Birth of the American Century.*

Hans L. Trefousse is Distinguished Professor Emeritus at Brooklyn College and the Graduate Center of the City University of New York. He is the author of biographies of Radical Republicans, Andrew Johnson, and works on Lincoln and the Civil War.

Michael Ayers Trotti, who received his doctorate from the University of North Carolina, Chapel Hill, is assistant professor at Ithaca College in New York. He is currently at work on a project investigating sensational crime in the late nineteenth and early twentieth centuries.

Emily Miller Troxell is librarian at the Missouri Historical Society. Several of her articles have appeared in *Gateway Heritage.*

Spencer C. Tucker holds the John Biggs '30 Chair of Military History at Virginia Military Institute. He has published nine books on naval and military subjects.

Frank P. Vazzano is professor of history at Walsh University in North Canton, Ohio. He has contributed articles on immigration and ethnicity, and on nineteenth- and twentieth-century American politics to a number of historical journals and books.

Santos C. Vega is an academic professional in the Hispanic Research Center, Arizona State University, Tempe. He has contributed numerous encyclopedia articles about Mexican Americans and Hispanic culture.

Michael W. Vogt is curator and historian with the Iowa Gold Star Military Museum, Camp Dodge, Iowa. He has written articles and curated exhibits on the American frontier, and on social and military history.

Wyn Wachhorst has taught American history and American studies at the University of California and San Jose State. He has published numerous articles and essays and two books: *Thomas Alva Edison: An American Myth* (1981), a History Book Club selection, and *The Dream of Spaceflight: Essays on the Near Edge of Infinity* (2000).

Louise Carroll Wade is professor emerita of history at the University of Oregon. She is author of *Graham Taylor, Pioneer for Social Justice* and *Chicago's Pride, the Stockyards, Packingtown, and Environs in the Nineteenth Century*, and is writing a biography of Mary E. McDowell.

Timothy Walch is director of the Herbert Hoover Library in West Branch, Iowa, and author of *Catholicism in America.*

Leonard Warren is American Cancer Society Research Professor at the Wistar Institute in Philadelphia. He has published numerous papers on the biochemistry of carbohydrates, glycoproteins, and cell membranes. He is presently engaged in writing the biographies of nineteenth-century scientists.

Robert P. Watson is associate professor of political science at the University of Hawaii, Hilo. He is author of *The Presidents' Wives: Reassessing the Office of the First Lady, First Ladies of the United States*, and other publications on the First Ladies and American politics.

Robert E. Weir is associate professor of liberal studies at Bay Path College in Logmeadow, Massachusetts. He is author of *Beyond Labor's Veil: The Culture of the Knights of Labor* (1996), the forthcoming *Knights Unhorsed: Internal Conflict Among Knights of Labor*, and numerous articles, reviews, and encyclopedia entries pertaining to Gilded Age labor, culture, and politics.

W. Thomas White is curator of manuscripts at the James J. Hill Library in Saint Paul, Minnesota. He has taught business and labor history at universities in the Minneapolis/St. Paul area and has contributed essays on those subjects to historical journals and anthologies.

David O. Whitten is professor of economics at Auburn University. He is the author (with Douglas Steeples) of *Democracy in Desperation: The Depression of 1893* (a Choice Outstanding Academic Title for 1999) and is writing (with Bess E. Whitten) *The Spirit of Giant Enterprise: Big Business Comes of Age, 1860–1914.*

Wayne A. Wiegand is professor in the School of Library and Information Studies at the University of Wisconsin-Madison. He is author of *Irrepressible Reformer: A Biography of Melvil Dewey, "An Active Instrument for Propaganda": The American Public Library During World War I*, and over sixty scholarly articles.

Ann Thomas Wilkins is assistant professor of classics at Duquesne University. She is the author of *Villain or Hero: Sallust's Characterization of Catiline* and articles on Roman topography and the classical tradition.

David G. Wilkins is professor and chair of the department of art at the University of Pittsburgh. He is coauthor of *Donatello* and *Art Past/Art Present*, and the author/editor of many other works.

Kevin B. Witherspoon is a doctoral candidate at Florida State University. He completed the master's program at the University of Maine, and has written a number of articles concerning U.S. social history.

Philip H. Young is director of Krannert Memorial Library at the University of Indianapolis and codirector of an archaeological excavation in Cyprus. He is the author of *Children's Fiction Series, A Bibliography 1850–1950*, and has contributed articles and chapters on librarianship and classical archaeology to several journals and books.

Xiaojian Zhao teaches Asian-American history at the University of California, Santa Barbara.

Guide to Contributors' Entries

Index

Boldfaced topics refer to major topics. Page numbers in boldface refer to major articles on the topic.

Citizenship, 66, 506–7, 534, 545, 547
Civic organizations, 91–92. *See also* Women's clubs
Civil Rights Act of 1866, 64, 173, 499
Civil Rights Act of 1875, 51–52, 58, 73, 92, 138, 263, 413, 443
Civil Rights Act of 1964, 444
Civil Rights Cases, 58, **92**, 138
Civil Service Commission, U.S., 46, 92, 105, 119, 148, 173, 203, 362, 426, 461
Civil Service reform, 23, **92–93**, 204, **361–62**
Civil Service Reform Act of 1883 (Pendleton Act), 23, 148, 203, 263, 292, **361–62**, 461, 511
Civil War: African-American troops, 129, 159, 275, 370, 419, 446, 492; *Alabama* claims from, **7–8**, 124, 154, 164, 198, 322, 498, 514; battles, 38, 68, 114, 120, 123, 160, 213, 267, 294, 382, 447–48; Butler in, 73; Confederate soldiers and officers, 8, 32, 34, 38, 61, 68, 76, 82, 99, 102, 116, 123, 160, 229, 254, 267, 277, 293, 318, 320, 340, 366, 379, 402, 408, 501, 540, 556; Custer in, 119–20; food provisions, 438; funding for, 85, 100, 202, 362; funeral practices during, 177; Grant in, 27, 68, 197, 356; and Great Britain, 36, 170, 190; Hancock in, 213; Lee's surrender at Appomattox, 356; medical care during, 9, 31, 40, 193, 223, 338–39; military transportation and communications during, 79; munitions during, 143, 310; Navy in, 293; paintings and illustrations of, 237–38, 329; Peace Democrats during, 362; photography of, 60; prisoners of war, 38, 164, 307; Sheridan in, 447–48; Sherman in, 409, 449; Union soldiers and officers, 10, 11, 22, 23, 24, 27, 35, 46, 56, 60, 63, 74, 85, 98, 104, 114, 115, 119–20, 136, 139, 159, 217, 223, 228, 231, 263, 294, 298, 311–12, 320, 341, 353, 382, 401, 446, 496, 503, 528
Clanton, Billy, 342
Clanton, Ike, 342
Clark, Champ, 141
Clark, Edward, 93
Clark, Jonas, 211
Clark, William, 377
Clark, William Andrews, 80, **93**

Clark, Sarah Orr, 109
Clarkson, James Sullivan, **93–94**
Clark University, 211, 367, 492
Clay, Henry, 395
Clayton-Bulwer Treaty (1850), 171, 174, 175, 222, 225, 252, 534
Clemens, Orion, 94
Clemens, Samuel Langhorne (Mark Twain), 19, 39, **94**, 168, 182, **187–88**, 220, 242, 276, 285, 364, 404, 430, 473, 503, 504, 514, 523
Clemson University, 228
Clendenin, Henry Wilson, **94**
Clergy, 1, 36, 48, 55, 59, 64, 70, 115–16, 186, 189, 203, 226, 253–54, 271, 279, 308, 324, 337, 346–47, 357, 396, 402, 408–9, 416, 446–47, 470, 476, 477, 480, 486, 490, 492, 503, 516, 531, 557–58. *See also* Evangelism; Rabbis; Religion
Cleveland, Cynthia, 482
Cleveland, Esther, 151
Cleveland, Frances Folsom, **94–95**, 96, 151
Cleveland, Grover, **95–96**; and anti-imperialism, 19, 75; cabinet of, 33, 53, 96, 150, 156, 181, 215, 274; currency policy, 27, 50, 83, 87, 95, 115, 124, 191, 216–17, 259, 268, 355, 417, 451; dismissal of government officials by, 417; electoral strategy of, in 1892, **96**; and fishing rights, 17; foreign policy, 171, 175, 344, 513; and forests, 171; as governor, 195, 232, 275, 295, 537; and Hawaii annexation, 52, 96, 170, 282, 471, 502; homes, 391; immigration policy, 164; Jacksonian ideology, 130; marriage, 94–95, 96, 151; and Mormonism, 321; Native American policy, 127, 166, 205; as New York governor, 167; presidential appointments, 46, 52, 60, 78, 88–89, 102, 114, 119, 133, 154, 174, 199, 215, 217, 253, 260–61, 274, 277, 292, 320, 322, 344, 360, 417, 454, 459, 464, 471, 477, 482, 487, 505, 515, 520; presidential elections, 49, 95, 96, 97, 131, 133, 154, 199, 218, 229, 266, 324, 326, 386–89, 418, 427, 615; presidential secretary for, 275; Presidential Succession Act, 391; and Pullman strike (1894), 11, 87, 95, 312, 399; and Franklin Roosevelt, 425; Secret Service

protection for, 442; social functions during presidency of, 151; and Statue of Liberty, 469; and Stetson, 470; surgery of, 37, **96–97**, 275; and tariffs, 194, 314–15, 324; vice president of, 229; and Whitman, 536
Clifford, Nathan, 385
Cline, Peter, 242
Clinton, Bill, 537
Clothing, 186, **286**, 475–76, 515, 521
CMIU. *See* Cigar Makers International Union (CMIU)
Coal Miners War, 68
Coal mining. *See* Mines and mining
Coast and Geodetic Survey, U.S., 360, 361
Cobb, Elizabeth, 521
Cobb, Rufus W., 303
Cocaine, 140–41
Cochrane, Elizabeth (Nellie Bly), **97**
Cockran, William Bourke, **97**
Cockrell, Francis Marion, **98**
Codman, Henry Sargent, 71
Cody, William Frederick (Buffalo Bill), 44, 71, **98**, 111, 205, 323, 453, 514
Coeur D'Alene, **98–99**, 470
Coffeen, Henry, **99**
Coinage Act of 1792, 41, 191
Coinage Act of 1873, **99**, 118, 263, 355
Coin's Financial School (Harvey), 221
Coke, Richard, **99–100**
Colby, William E., 451
Colcord, Roswell Keyes, **100**
Coleman, Patrick, 210
Colfax, Schuyler, **100**, 113, 384, 457
Colgate, James Boorman, **100**
Collector v. *Day*, **100–101**
College Entrance Examination Board, 74, 149
College of Wooster, 176
Colleges and universities, **101**; African-American students, 17, 101, 108, 109, 141, 202, 275, 313, 338, 419, 548; American university movement, 188–89, 216, 533; Catholic colleges, 548; curriculum, 17, 148, 220; for deaf students, 179; and M. Dewey, 132; doctorates awarded, 211, 534, 546, 548; entrance requirements, 74, 148–49; funding, 367, 369–70, 511; law schools, 1, 275, **278**; libraries at, 1; Morrill Land Grant Act, 321; presidents and other administrators, 1, 17, 70, 73–74, 108, 109, 119, 139, 148, 176, 188–89, 203, 216, 226,